Springer International Handbooks of Education

The Springer International Handbooks of Education series aims to provide easily accessible, practical, yet scholarly, sources of information about a broad range of topics and issues in education. Each Handbook follows the same pattern of examining in depth a field of educational theory, practice and applied scholarship, its scale and scope for its substantive contribution to our understanding of education and, in so doing, indicating the direction of future developments. The volumes in this series form a coherent whole due to an insistence on the synthesis of theory and good practice. The accessible style and the consistent illumination of theory by practice make the series very valuable to a broad spectrum of users. The volume editors represent the world's leading educationalists. Their task has been to identify the key areas in their field that are internationally generalizable and, in times of rapid change, of permanent interest to the scholar and practitioner.

More information about this series at http://www.springer.com/series/6189

Susen R. Smith
Editor

Handbook of Giftedness and Talent Development in the Asia-Pacific

Volume 1

With 71 Figures and 89 Tables

Editor
Susen R. Smith
GERRIC, School of Education
University of New South Wales
Sydney, NSW, Australia

ISSN 2197-1951 ISSN 2197-196X (electronic)
ISBN 978-981-13-3040-7 ISBN 978-981-13-3041-4 (eBook)
ISBN 978-981-13-3042-1 (print and electronic bundle)
https://doi.org/10.1007/978-981-13-3041-4

© Springer Nature Singapore Pte Ltd. 2021
This work is subject to copyright. All rights are reserved by the Publisher, whether the whole or part of the material is concerned, specifically the rights of translation, reprinting, reuse of illustrations, recitation, broadcasting, reproduction on microfilms or in any other physical way, and transmission or information storage and retrieval, electronic adaptation, computer software, or by similar or dissimilar methodology now known or hereafter developed.
The use of general descriptive names, registered names, trademarks, service marks, etc. in this publication does not imply, even in the absence of a specific statement, that such names are exempt from the relevant protective laws and regulations and therefore free for general use.
The publisher, the authors, and the editors are safe to assume that the advice and information in this book are believed to be true and accurate at the date of publication. Neither the publisher nor the authors or the editors give a warranty, expressed or implied, with respect to the material contained herein or for any errors or omissions that may have been made. The publisher remains neutral with regard to jurisdictional claims in published maps and institutional affiliations.

This Springer imprint is published by the registered company Springer Nature Singapore Pte Ltd.
The registered company address is: 152 Beach Road, #21-01/04 Gateway East, Singapore 189721, Singapore

This handbook is dedicated to my husband Raymond John Smith, my daughter Sheridan Hewson-Smith, and my grandsons Lawson and Zak, all of whom are the lights of my life. Your unwavering support, encouragement, joy of learning, creativity, exploration, exceptionality, and capacity to find love and laughter in the midst of unimaginable sadness nurture my soul every day. Thank you will never be enough, but love always will be!

Foreword

No one has ever accused Americans of being overly deferential to citizens of other countries or of being reluctant to place their country squarely in the centre of the universe. This is as true in the field of education as it is in many other arenas, even if international comparisons of educational achievement do not lend support to claims of American superiority.

However, one area in which we Yanks can claim a reasonable degree of primacy is the field of gifted education. Although many in this field cite the brilliant, if odious, Englishman Sir Frances Galton as the *fons et origo* of the construct of giftedness, that is a tenuous link (VanTassel-Baska, 2016). For gifted education, in a form we can recognise as such, was sprung upon the world sometime in the second decade of the twentieth century by Lewis M. Terman and other American educators and psychologists (Warne, 2019). Indeed, gifted education can rightly be considered an American export.

Thus, for many, if not most, educators in the USA, American gifted education is gifted education. One might even claim that gifted education is *as American as apple pie* (the first printed recipe for which, by the way, was produced by that great *American* poet Geoffrey Chaucer; Eschner, 2017). The idea that: (a) some students are gifted, although most are not; (b) gifted students require curricular and instructional modifications that other students do not; and (c) these modifications should occur in full-time or part-time segregated settings—all of these foundational axioms of our field sprang, like amber waves of grain, directly from American soil. And, since discourse in this field is still dominated by American educators (although volumes such as this one are making that less and less the case), in order to be considered gifted, students everywhere must pretty much conform to American conceptions of what constitutes giftedness (ignoring the fact that there is anything but a consensus in this country as to how to define the construct).

Moreover, the three foundational axioms cited above are usually regarded as universal, at least in the USA. That is, the prevailing belief is that gifted students are gifted students irrespective of where they live. Do a roundup of conceptions of giftedness and you will quickly realise that few of our ways of thinking about giftedness take sociocultural contexts into consideration.

I was disabused of this notion of universality and absolute American hegemony with respect to the discourse around gifted education when I was invited a number of years ago to participate in a conference in Seoul, South Korea, that focused on under-represented populations of gifted students. I was one of ten invited speakers, each of us hailing from a different country. As the conference unfolded and more of us spoke, it became quite clear to me that giftedness is anything but universal, that the construct is profoundly shaped by the various cultures in which it is created, and that there is no such thing as giftedness divorced from a specific context.

For example, it became clear that, whereas in the USA giftedness is typically, if not unanimously, regarded as something that one is blessed with by virtue of inborn and acquired characteristics and that gifted students are more or less passive recipients of, well, a gift, educators in some other countries regard it as something altogether different. In some cultures, for example, giftedness is not thought of as something with which some students are blessed, but rather as something that students can earn through hard work. In addition, there are countries and cultures in which the construct is meaningless; the culture has not seen a need to create the category of gifted students, for whatever reasons. And it was striking to learn from a Russian educator that, in that country, the construct of socio-economic status, which we regard as indispensable in discussions of under-represented groups of gifted students, was relatively unfamiliar since it was incoherent in the classless society that the Soviet Union purported to be.

All of which brings me to the volume at hand. Susen Smith has made a significant contribution to the field of gifted education by conceiving of, carefully editing, and contributing to the *Giftedness and Talented Development in the Asia-Pacific, Springer International Education Handbook*. This is a very ambitious project in at least two respects. First, Susen adopts an appropriately expansive view of what constitutes the "Asia-Pacific". As she writes, "The Asia-Pacific region is defined by countries being in or near the Pacific Ocean that encompass East Asia, South Asia, Southeast Asia, Oceania, and the Americas." This chunk of the world's geography comprises the majority of the people living on Earth and, more important, encompasses a diversity of cultures in which we can see the construct of giftedness play out in its various sociocultural contexts.

Second, as even a quick glance at the table of contents reveals, the range of topics included herein is impressive: Socialcultural conceptions and perceptions; Social and emotional needs and learning processes; Identifying and nurturing diversely gifted and talented students; Assessment, pedagogy, and curricula; Diverse dimensions of gifted education; and Educational contexts, transitions, and community engagement. These would be sufficient to provide the outline for a comprehensive course on gifted education or even the framework for a degree program in this field. The overlay of such an exhaustive array of areas of scholarship onto the book's vast geographical reach allows for the consideration of perennial issues within the field in contexts that, in some cases, to me at least, are novel and productive of new ideas and practices.

This is not a slim volume. Its heft may be sufficient to make even the most resolute Luddite long for a compact e-reader. Moreover, it is not necessarily a book that one would read in order from beginning to end, although that approach would yield many valuable insights. Rather, it is a source of ideas that one will want to keep handy, to dip into when one's thinking needs a jolt of fresh thinking.

Some books zoom into and out of our lives, quickly read (or not) and then consigned to a place on one's bookshelf, gathering dust over the years. Others become long-time companions, continuing to challenge our thinking and to broadening our knowledge. This book is one of the latter.

Teachers College, Columbia University James H. Borland
New York, NY, USA

References

Eschner, K. (2017). Apple pie is not all that American. *The Smithsonian*. Retrieved from https://www.smithsonianmag.com/smart-news/why-apple-pie-linked-america-180963157/

VanTassel-Baska, J. (2016). Sir Francis Galton: The Victorian polymath (1822–1911). *APAPsychNet*. Retrieved from https://psycnet.apa.org/record/2013-37318-002

Warne, R. T. (2019). An evaluation (and vindication?) of Lewis Terman: What the father of gifted education can teach the 21st century. *Gifted Child Quarterly, 63*, 3–21. https://doi.org/10.1177/0016986218799433

James H. Borland, PhD, is Professor of Education in the Department of Curriculum and Teaching at Teachers College, Columbia University, New York, NY, where he directs the graduate programs in the education of gifted students. The author of numerous books, book chapters, journal articles, and miscellanea, Borland is also editor of the Education and Psychology of the Gifted series of Teachers College Press. He was editor of the section on 'Teaching, Learning, and Human Development' of the American Educational Research Journal from 1993 to 1995 (with two Teachers College colleagues), and he has served on the editorial boards of the Gifted Child Quarterly, Roeper Review, and Journal of Secondary Gifted Education. He has won two Paper of the Year awards from the Gifted Child Quarterly (with Lisa Wright and with Lisa Wright and Rachel Schnur) and has twice won the Award for Excellence in Research from the Mensa Education and Research Foundation. He has lectured and consulted on the education of gifted students across the USA and abroad, undertakes staff development programs for teachers of the gifted; develops and evaluates programs for the gifted; and provides media consultancies and appearances.

Preface

Welcome to the first ever handbook on giftedness and talent development for the Asia-Pacific region! The Asia-Pacific region is defined by countries being in or near the Pacific Ocean that encompass East Asia, South Asia, Southeast Asia, Oceania, and the Americas. Experts in academia and practice in the field were invited to contribute and, ultimately, over 60 submissions derived from over a hundred authors from 18 nations: Australia, Canada, Chile, China/Taiwan/Hong Kong, Japan, South Korea, Malaysia, Mexico, New Zealand, Peru, Philippines, Singapore, Thailand, United Arab Emirates, the UK, and the USA. The handbook evolved from the inaugural *GERRIC Gifted Education Forum for Talent Enhancement* in Australia in 2015. It deals with critical issues for an important group of students; addresses a number of gaps in the current understandings of gifted education in the region; traverses substantial intellectual, empirical, and theoretical terrain; and draws on past and present research literature.

All invitees were requested to provide abstract submissions on a proposed chapter that incorporated an overview of the current research on their topic, their own research, and implications for future research and practice. These were double-blind peer reviewed in phase one. Phase two incorporated double-blind peer review of chapters, and phase three involved editing by the editor and section editors reviewing and preparing separate parts of the handbook. These peer-review processes ensured higher quality of chapters, especially as many came from authors whose native language was not English. The chapters derive from the authors' own research, wider recent research, theories, discourse, and practice and reflect the cultural, educational, linguistic, and ethnic diversity emanating from the Asia-Pacific and Pacific-rim nations.

The handbook represents a comprehensive overview of contemporary research and practice in the Asia-Pacific region that has not been highlighted elsewhere. While the list of authors reflects esteemed experts in the field, and many have already contributed significantly to other publications or handbooks in the past, the process also targeted emerging scholars who are not widely published in such handbooks, such as doctoral candidates or postdoctoral fellows or early career academics, but are nevertheless significant contributors to gifted education in their own countries.

Another aspect of the handbook is the focus on collaborative and multi-disciplinary partnerships. While individual submissions were accepted from contributors in various stages of their careers, contributions that involved inter-country partnerships and mentorships by senior academics of early career and postgraduate researchers were particularly encouraged. Hence, authors from other countries such as Britain, Germany, Sweden, Egypt, and UAE co-authored chapters. Additionally, the process promoted networking across universities, education sectors, gifted education associations, and disciplines to encourage a foundation for future collaborative projects. It is noteworthy that PhD candidates, Endeavour Fellowship scholarships, and University Postdoctoral grants for inter-country research also evolved from the handbook process.

The handbook differs from other handbooks or monographs in the gifted education field as it highlights contemporary sociocultural issues rather than adopt the traditional approach of focusing on conceptions, identification, curriculum, programs, and the like. Nevertheless, as the aforementioned foci are important, they are incorporated into one or more of the six parts of the handbook that emanated from the author guidelines combined with the collated chapter themes, though some chapters crossed more than one part: (1) Socialcultural Conceptions and Perceptions; (2) Social and Emotional Needs and learning Processes; (3) Identifying and Nurturing Diversely Gifted and Talented students; (4) Assessment, Pedagogy, and Curricula; (5) Diverse Dimensions of Gifted Education; and (6) Educational Contexts, Transitions, and Community Engagement.

Besides esteemed experts who have contributed to the handbook, many of the contributors have never collaborated on a project of this nature, and many are new to the field or are from other fields altogether. This author diversity ensured that a unique collation of contemporary research and practice on giftedness and talent development in the Asia-Pacific region was produced that is not highlighted in other handbooks in the field, nor across fields. While there are other international handbooks in gifted education, they often do not include many experts from the Asia-Pacific nations. For example, in recent times, new handbooks in gifted education have been published, such as the *SAGE Handbook of Gifted and Talented Education*, the *APA Handbook of Giftedness and Talent*, and the *Handbook of Giftedness in Children: Psychoeducational Theory, Research, and Best Practices*. However, they do not focus on the issues most prevalent in the Asia-Pacific region and usually only include one or two chapters from the Asian, Australasian, or South American part of the world, if any. In addition, new Australasian books have been published on gifted education recently, but they only tell part of the narrative of the Asia-Pacific regions and rim countries rather than a comprehensive overview from this diverse region. Taken together, I view this handbook as complementary to past and current publications; therefore, it is also of international importance. Indeed, this handbook builds on the prolific work emanating from other parts of the world, such as Britain, Europe, and the USA.

The chapters in the Asia-Pacific handbook extend current gifted education research on selected topics and include: sociocultural concepts of giftedness, talent development, differentiated pedagogy and curriculum, and life of extraordinary people. Some original foci include: seeking intuitive theories, Social-Emotional Learning (SEL), youth scholarship, wisdom, spirituality, ethics, popular culture, dynamic pedagogy, STEM/STEAM, mindfulness, career choices, transitions, and community partnerships. Coverage of topics also includes: innovations in technology, theoretical growth, critical arguments, and recommendations that may inform future research and practice. The handbook has a stronger focus on pedagogy that could assist researchers, academics/educators/specialists, postgraduate students, families, advocates, teachers/practitioners, and other stakeholders to support gifted students in practice.

Thank you to all involved in this project. This monumental task could not have been achieved without the collegiality shared amongst us. I was blessed to work with such a dedicated range of experts in the field, many of whom I eagerly reference in my research, and many of whom I am honoured to have met throughout my career. Initially, thank you to all the authors; your work is unique and exceptional and I am delighted to showcase it in this handbook. While not all invitees were able to provide a chapter, many did contribute to the advisory or review boards. Reviewers also came from additional Pacific-rim countries, such as, Brazil, Columbia, and Uruguay. Thank you especially to each of the section editors (in order from Part I to Part VI): Roger Moltzen, Rhoda Myra Garces-Bacsal, Sheyla Blumen, Maria Leonor Conejeros-Solar, James Watters, Seokhee Cho, and Selena Gallagher whose role involved editing and reviewing the chapters with me in the final stages to ensure acceptance of higher quality manuscripts. So, my sincere thanks are extended to everyone who contributed to the peer-review, editing, and writing process. I greatly appreciate your generosity of time and expertise which helped to ensure the quality that the handbook deserved.

The Springer production team also added to the quality of the chapters with their ongoing support and finalising of chapters. Thank you to the Editor Nick Melchior and Reference Editorial team's Audrey Wong-Hillmann, Sindhu Ramachandran, Mokshika Gaur, Madhivathani Madhi Maran, and Mary Antony in particular. Nick you were there right from the beginning and encouraged me when I almost gave up at the start. Your enthusiasm for the project reassured me to take the original project from a small volume to double its size for an international handbook. Thank you also to my virtual Springer colleagues, Audrey, Sindhu, Mokshika, and Madhi who provided almost weekly support over the last two plus years and, beyond everything else, helped me come to terms with the differences between Springer formatting and APA formatting! I appreciated our email and Skype interchanges which added that personal touch to an otherwise lonely endeavour. I also thank sincerely my mentors Margaret Ivanyi, my principal when I first started teaching all those years ago; Professor Andrew Martin and Professor Iva Strnadova from the UNSW, Australia; and Professor James Borland from Columbia University, USA, without whose guidance, genuine joy of learning, exceptional expertise, critical discourse, and encouragement this project would never have evolved.

Last, but by no means least, a heartfelt thank you to my husband Mr. Raymond Smith and daughter Sheridan, whose love, encouragement, proofing, technical expertise, referencing, understanding, and other immeasurable support during this very difficult transition was so invaluable. Thank you for giving up all those wonderful recreation moments and family memories to support me in this momentous endeavour.

Thank you to all who contributed in some way, if, in my error, I have failed to mention you. This was a first-time process for me as an editor-in-chief, so I'm sure I can be forgiven if my inexperience reflects in this inaugural handbook. Nonetheless, I do believe that the handbook content should inform pre-service education programs in gifted education, in-service professional learning programs, familial support, and future research and practice in this region of the world and beyond. Thank you all for your enthusiasm and commitment to this collaborative project and to gifted education in particular. I look forward to seeing this ambitious volume online for easier access and in print and also to see how it contributes to supporting you in your role as nurturers of talent development in children and youth in your part of the world.

January 2021

Susen R. Smith
Editor-in-Chief

Contents

Volume 1

1 Gifted Education in the Asia-Pacific: From the Past for the Future – An Introduction 1
Susen R. Smith

Part I Sociocultural Conceptions 21

2 Social and Cultural Conceptions and Perceptions: Part I Introduction 23
Roger Moltzen

3 Towards Exceptionality: The Current Status and Future Prospects of Australian Gifted Education 31
Shane N. Phillipson and Albert Ziegler

4 Implementing the DMGT's Constructs of Giftedness and Talent: What, Why, and How? 71
Françoys Gagné

5 Sociocultural Perspectives on the Talent Development Megamodel 101
Paula Olszewski-Kubilius, Rena F. Subotnik, Frank C. Worrell, Janna Wardman, Liang See Tan, and Seon-Young Lee

6 The Young Gifted Learner: What We Know and Implications for Early Educational Practice 129
Anne Grant and Anne-Marie Morrissey

7 Being of Like-Mind: Giftedness in the New Zealand Context 151
Tracy Riley

8 Learning from International Research Informs Academic Acceleration in Australasia: A Case for Consistent Policy 171
Ann Lupkowski-Shoplik, Susan G. Assouline, Cara Wienkes, and Ann Easter

9   Gifted, Talented, and High-Achieving Students and Their
    Gifted Education in Mexico 203
    Pedro Antonio Sánchez-Escobedo, Ana Karen Camelo-Lavadores,
    and Angel Alberto Valdés-Cuervo

10 Innovative Practices to Support High-Achieving Deprived
    Young Scholars in an Ethnic-Linguistic Diverse Latin
    American Country 223
    Sheyla Blumen

11 In Search of an Explanation for an Approach-Avoidance Pattern
    in East Asia: The Role of Cultural Values in Gifted Education ... 239
    David Yun Dai and Yong Zhao

12 Spirituality and Giftedness: Threading the Path of Identity 257
    Russell Walton and Wilma Vialle

Part II Social and Emotional Needs and Learning Processes 283

13 Social and Emotional Needs and Learning Processes: Part II
    Introduction 285
    Rhoda Myra Garces-Bacsal

14 Self-Regulated Learning for High-Ability and High-Achieving
    Students in Mixed-Ability Classrooms Throughout the
    Asia-Pacific 291
    Heidrun Stoeger, Daniel Patrick Balestrini, and Julia Steinbach

15 Fostering Resilience in 'At-Risk' Gifted and Talented
    Young People 319
    Nadine Ballam

16 Motivational Issues in Gifted Education: Understanding the
    Role of Students' Attribution and Control Beliefs, Self-Worth
    Protection and Growth Orientation 339
    Emma C. Burns and Andrew J. Martin

17 Overexcitability and Giftedness Research: Whose Constructs
    Are Being Investigated and How? 359
    Salvatore Sal Mendaglio

18 Put Them Together and See How They Learn! Ability Grouping
    and Acceleration Effects on the Self-Esteem of Academically
    Gifted High School Students 377
    Miraca U. M. Gross and Susen R. Smith

19 Gifted and Twice-Exceptional Children in the South of the World:
    Chilean Students' Experiences Within Regular Classrooms 405
    María Paz Gómez-Arízaga and María Leonor Conejeros-Solar

| 20 | Of Grit and Gumption, Sass and Verve: What Gifted Students Can Learn from Multicultural Picture Book Biographies | 431 |

Rhoda Myra Garces-Bacsal

Part III Identifying and Nurturing Diversely Gifted and Talented Students ... 455

| 21 | Identifying and Nurturing Diversely Gifted and Talented Students: Part III Introduction | 457 |

Sheyla Blumen and Maria Leonor Conejeros-Solar

| 22 | Identifying Underrepresented Gifted Students: A Developmental Process | 465 |

Pamela Peters, E. Jean Gubbins, Rashea Hamilton, D. Betsy McCoach, Del Siegle, and Jeb Puryear

| 23 | Identifying Gifted Learning in the Regular Classroom: Seeking Intuitive Theories | 487 |

John Munro

| 24 | Self-Nomination in the Identification Process of Gifted and Talented Students in Mexico | 509 |

María Alicia Zavala Berbena and Gabriela de la Torre García

| 25 | Place-Based Gifted Education in Rural Schools | 535 |

Carolyn M. Callahan and Amy Price Azano

| 26 | Gifted Girls with Autism Spectrum Disorders: Provisions and Priorities in Australian School Settings | 555 |

Aranzazu M. Blackburn and Geraldine Townend

| 27 | Teachers' Knowledge and Understandings of Twice Exceptionality Across Australia | 579 |

Catherine Wormald and Michelle Bannister-Tyrrell

| 28 | Underachievement and the Quest for Dignity: Contemporary Perspectives on a Timeless Issue | 607 |

James R. Delisle and Robert Arthur Schultz

| 29 | Exploring Diverse Perceptions of Wise Persons: Wisdom in Gifted Education | 631 |

Kyungbin Park and Eunhyang Kim

| 30 | The Lives and Achievements of Four Extraordinary Australians: A Master, a Maker, an Introspector, and an Influencer | 649 |

Carmel Diezmann

| 31 | The Development of Mana: Five Optimal Conditions for Gifted Māori Student Success | 671 |

Melinda Webber

32 Gifted and Talented Aboriginal Students in Australia 693
    Susanne Garvis, Sally Windsor, and Donna Pendergast

33 Supporting Australian Gifted Indigenous Students' Academic
    Potential in Rural Settings 709
    Geraldine Townend, Peta K. Hay, Jae Yup Jung, and Susen R. Smith

Volume 2

Part IV Assessment, Pedagogy, and Curriculum 727

34 Assessment, Pedagogy, and Curriculum: Part IV Introduction ... 729
    James Watters

35 How Do Teachers Meet the Academic Needs of High-Ability
    Students in Science? 737
    Jenny Horsley and Azra Moeed

36 Why Is It So? Interest and Curiosity in Supporting Students
    Gifted in Science 761
    James Watters

37 STEAM in Gifted Education in Korea 787
    Jiyoung Ryu, Youngju Lee, Youngmin Kim, Payal Goundar,
    Jihyun Lee, and Jae Yup Jung

38 Fostering and Developing Talent in Mentorship Programs:
    The Mentor's Perspectives 809
    Liang See Tan, Jing Yi Tan, and Terence Titus Chia

39 Nurturing Mathematical Talents of Young Mathematically
    Gifted English Language Learners 833
    Seokhee Cho, Marcella Mandracchia, and Jenny Yang

40 Online Learning for Mathematically Talented Students:
    A Perspective from Hong Kong 857
    Joyce J. Y. Fung, Mantak Yuen, and Allan H. K. Yuen

41 Engaging Gifted Students in Solving Real Problems Creatively:
    Implementing the Real Engagement in Active Problem-Solving
    (REAPS) Teaching/Learning Model in Australasian and Pacific
    Rim Contexts 885
    C. June Maker and Myra Wearne

42 Attuned Pedagogy: The Artistry of Differentiated Instruction
    from a Taiwanese Cultural Perspective 917
    Chin-hsieh Lu and Wei-Ren Chen

| 43 | Differentiation of Instruction for Gifted Learners: Collated Evaluative Studies of Teacher Classroom Practices 945
Joyce VanTassel-Baska, Gail Fischer Hubbard, and Janice I. Robbins |

Part V Diverse Dimensions of Gifted Education **981**

| 44 | Diverse Dimensions of Gifted Education: Part V Introduction ... 983
Seokhee Cho |

| 45 | A Counselling Framework for Meeting the Needs of Gifted Students in Malaysia 991
Abu Yazid Abu Bakar and Linda E. Brody |

| 46 | Bricolage and the Evolution of Giftedness and Talent in Taiwan 1011
Dale Albanese, Ming-Jen Yu, and Jing-Jyi Wu |

| 47 | Creativity Talent Development: Fostering Creativity in Schools 1045
Carly Lassig |

| 48 | Creative and Gifted Education in Korea: Using the CATs Model to Illustrate How Creativity Can Grow into Innovation 1071
Kyung Hee Kim and Jeongkyu Lee |

| 49 | Trends and Challenges of Creativity Development Among Selected Asian Countries and Regions: China, Hong Kong/Macau, Japan, Malaysia, and South Korea 1107
Bonnie Cramond, Kyung Hee Kim, T. W. Chiang, Takeo Higuchi, Takuya Iwata, Min Ma, and Ananda Kumar Palaniappan |

| 50 | Using the Idea-Marathon System (IMS) in University Education and Creativity Development 1135
Takeo Higuchi, Shozo Saegusa, and Daehyun Kim |

| 51 | Rural Adolescent Gifted Girls: Exploring the Impact of Popular Culture on Their Talent Development 1163
Denise Wood |

| 52 | A Model for Growing Teacher Talent Scouts: Decreasing Underrepresentation of Gifted Students 1193
Julie Dingle Swanson, Lara Walker Russell, and Lindsey Anderson |

Part VI Educational Contexts, Transitions, and Community Engagement **1213**

| 53 | Educational Contexts, Transitions and Community Engagement: Part VI Introduction 1215
Selena Gallagher |

54	More than Passion: The Role of the Gifted Education Coordinator in Australasian Schools 1221
	Lesley Henderson and Jane Jarvis

55	Leadership Development of Gifted Adolescents from a Korean Multicultural Lens 1245
	Seon-Young Lee, Yun-Kyoung Kim, and Eunjoo Boo

56	Rural Voices: Identifying the Perceptions, Practices, and Experiences of Gifted Pedagogy in Australian Rural and Regional Schools 1267
	Michelle Bannister-Tyrrell and Denise Wood

57	Homeschooling the Gifted: What Do We Know from the Australian, Chilean, and US Context? 1295
	María Leonor Conejeros-Solar and Susen R. Smith

58	Highly Able Students in International Schools 1325
	Selena Gallagher

59	The Predictors of the Decisions by Gifted Students to Pursue STEM Careers: The Case of Brazilian International Students in Australia 1343
	Jae Yup Jung, Tay T. R. Koo, Peta K. Hay, and Susen R. Smith

60	The Career Decisions of Gifted Students: An Asian-Pacific Perspective 1367
	Jae Yup Jung

61	Transitioning to Career: Talented Musicians' Identity Development 1385
	Jennifer Rowley

62	Teaching Gifted Education to Pre-service Teachers: Lessons Learned 1409
	Margaret Plunkett and Leonie Kronborg

63	Australian Teachers Who Made a Difference: Secondary Gifted Student Perceptions of Teaching and Teacher Effectiveness 1431
	Karen B. Rogers

Conclusion **1457**

64	Some Implications for the Future of Gifted Education in the Asia-Pacific 1459
	Susen R. Smith

Index 1481

About the Editor

Susen R. Smith
GERRIC, School of Education
University of New South Wales
Sydney, NSW, Australia

Dr. Susen Smith is a GERRIC Senior Research Fellow and Senior Lecturer in Gifted and Special Education at the School of Education, University of NSW, Australia, where she teaches in the Master in Gifted Education program and supervises PhD students. She has four decades of leadership, teaching, and research experience from pre-K to adult education. Her research and practice interests include: differentiating curriculum and pedagogy for diverse student needs in multi-disciplinary contexts, gifted underachievement and indigeneity, twice-exceptionalities, social-emotional learning, academic engagement, enrichment, education for sustainability, and community outreach programs. Susen is published internationally and is on the editorial boards of the *Gifted Child Quarterly, Roeper Review, International Journal for Talent Development and Creativity,* and the *Australasian Journal of Gifted Education*. She has been a visiting scholar to Columbia University, Imperial College London, CUNY, National Taipei University of Education, and the Hong Kong Institute of Education; has acquired many competitive research grants; is widely published; and keynoted at national and international conferences. She has been an academic adviser for educational departmental policies and programs for decades in addition to having on-going advisory board and association memberships. Susen chaired the inaugural national *GERRIC Gifted Futures Forum for Talent Enhancement* in Australia and has organised regional, national, and world conferences and many gifted education outreach enrichment programs across several universities in Australia and internationally, such as the *TalentEd* program and the *2eMPower* project. She created the *Model of Dynamic Differentiation* (MoDD) for supporting student diversity across the learning continuum, provides professional learning across Australia and internationally, and is Editor of the first ever *Handbook of Giftedness and Talent Development in the Asia-Pacific*, in the series *Springer International Handbooks of Education.* E-mail: susen.smith@unsw.edu.au

Section Editors

Part I: Sociocultural Conceptions

Professor Roger Moltzen Division of Education, The University of Waikato, Hamilton, New Zealand

Part II: Social and Emotional Needs and Learning Processes

Associate Professor Rhoda Myra Garces-Bacsal College of Education, Special Education Department, United Arab Emirates University, Al Ain, United Arab Emirates

Part III: Identifying and Nurturing Diversely Gifted and Talented Students

Professor Sheyla Blumen Department of Psychology, Pontificia Universidad Católica del Perú, Lima, Peru

Professor Maria Leonor Conejeros-Solar Escuela de Pedagogía, Pontificia Universidad Católica de Valparaíso, Viña del Mar, Chile

Part IV: Assessment, Pedagogy, and Curriculum

Associate Professor James Watters Faculty of Education, Queensland University of Technology, Brisbane, QLD, Australia

Part V: Diverse Dimensions of Gifted Education

Professor Seokhee Cho St. John's University, Queens, Queens, NY, USA

Part VI: Educational Contexts, Transitions, and Community Engagement

Dr. Selena Gallagher Cairo American College, Cairo, Egypt

International Advisory Board Members

Usanee Anuruthwong Bangkok, Thailand

Susan Assouline Iowa City, IA, USA

Sheyla Blumen Lima, Peru

Linda E. Brody Baltimore, MD, USA

Seokhee Cho Queens, NY, USA
ChungCheongbuk-Do, South Korea

Bonnie Cramond Athens, GA, USA

David Yun Dai Albany, NY, USA

James R. Delisle Kent, OH, USA

Françoys Gagné Montréal, QC, Canada

Miraca U. M. Gross Sydney, NSW, Australia

E. Jean Gubbins Storrs, CT, USA

Jae Yup Jared Jung Sydney, NSW, Australia

Leonie Kronborg Frankston, VIC, Australia

Chin-hsieh Lu Taipei, Taiwan

C. June Maker Tucson, AZ, USA

Andrew J. Martin Sydney, NSW, Australia

Roger Moltzen Hamilton, Waikato, New Zealand

John Munro East Melbourne, VIC, Australia

Kyungbin Park Seongnam-si, Gyeonggi-do, South Korea

Paula Olszewski-Kubilius Evanston, IL, USA

Susana Graciela Pérez Barrera Montevideo, Uruguay

María Paz Gómez-Arízaga Santiago, Chile
Shane N. Phillipson Frankston, VIC, Australia
Margaret Plunkett Churchill, VIC, Australia
Marion Porath Vancouver, BC, Canada
Tracey Riley Palmerston North, New Zealand
Karen B. Rogers Minneapolis, MN, USA
Jiyoung Ryu Daejeon, South Korea
Del Siegle Storrs, CT, USA
Jiannong Shi Beijing, China
Heidrun Stoeger Regensburg, Germany
Rena F. Subotnik Washington, DC, USA
Manabu Sumida Matsuyama City, Japan
Julie Dingle Swanson Charleston, SC, USA
Liang See Tan Singapore, Singapore
Joyce VanTassel-Baska Williamsburg, VA, USA
Wilma Vialle Wollongong, NSW, Australia
James Watters Brisbane, QLD, Australia
Frank C. Worrell Berkeley, CA, USA
Albert Ziegler Nuremberg, Germany

International Review Board Members

Abu Yazid Abu Bakar Bangi, Malaysia

Dale Albanese Taipei, Taiwan

Lindsey Anderson Charleston, SC, USA

Amy Price Azano Blacksburg, VA, USA

Daniel Patrick Balestrini Regensburg, Germany

Nadine Ballam Hamilton, Waikato, New Zealand

Michelle Bannister-Tyrrell Armidale, NSW, Australia

Aranzazu M. Blackburn Brisbane, QLD, Australia

Lindsey Blackmon Charleston, SC, USA

Carolyn M. Callahan Charlottesville, VA, USA

Rosemary Cathcart Rotorua, New Zealand

Laura Ceretta Moreira Curitiba, Peru

Serene Chan Hong Kong, China

Maria Leonor Conejeros-Solar Viña del Mar, Chile

Carmel Diezmann Brisbane, QLD, Australia

Joyce Joy Yan Fung Hong Kong, China

Rhoda Myra Garces-Bacsal Al Ain, United Arab Emirates Singapore, Singapore

Maria Caridad García-Cepero Bogotá, Colombia

Susanne Garvis Gothenburg, Sweden Queensland, Australia

Selena Gallagher Thailand and Cairo, Egypt

Anne Grant Melbourne, VIC, Australia
Peta K. Hay Sydney, NSW, Australia
Lesley Henderson Adelaide, SA, Australia
Mary Anne Heng Singapore, Singapore
Jenny Horsley Wellington, New Zealand
Jane Jarvis Adelaide, SA, Australia
Mohd Hasrul Kamarulzaman Bangi, Selangor, Malaysia
Eunhyang Kim Seongnam-si, Gyeonggi-do, South Korea
Kyung Hee Kim Williamsburg, VA, USA
Gail Fischer Hubbard Manassas, VA, USA
Youngmin Kim Daejeon, South Korea
Yun-kyoung Kim Seoul, South Korea
Sandra N. Kaplan Los Angeles, CA, USA
Lara Walker Kessler Charleston, SC, USA
Carly Lassig Brisbane, QLD, Australia
Jihyun Lee Sydney, NSW, Australia
Youngju Lee Daejeon, South Korea
Seon-Young Lee Seoul, South Korea
Jeongkyu Lee Seoul, South Korea
D. Betsy McCoach Storrs, CT, USA
Salvatore Sal Mendaglio Calgary, AB, Canada
Anne-Marie Morrissey Melbourne, VIC, Australia
Ben North Sydney, NSW, Australia
Donna Pendergast Brisbane, QLD, Australia
Denise Maria de Matos Pereira Curitiba, Peru
Pamela Peters Storrs, CT, USA
Jeb Puryear Hersham, UK and Storrs, CT, USA
Janice I. Robbins Williamsburg, VA, USA
Jennifer Rowley Sydney, NSW, Australia
Shozo Saegusa Okayama, Japan

Pedro Sanchez-Escobedo Mérida, Yucatán, Mexico

Robert A. Schultz Toledo, OH, USA

Julia Steinbach Regensburg, Germany

Theresa Thor Singapore, Singapore

Gabriela de la Torre García Mexico City, Mexico

Geraldine Townend Sydney, NSW, Australia

Russell Walton Wollongong, NSW, Australia

Janna Wardman Auckland, New Zealand

Melinda Webber Auckland, New Zealand

Wei-Ren Taipei, Taiwan

Denise Wood Bathurst, NSW, Australia

Catherine Wormald Wollongong, NSW, Australia

Jing-Jyi Wu Taipei, Taiwan

Mantak Yuen Hong Kong, China

Yong Zhao Beijing, China and Lawrence, KS, USA

Contributors

Dale Albanese Center for Creativity and Innovation Studies, National Chengchi University, Taipei, Taiwan

Lindsey Anderson Javits Project, College of Charleston, Charleston, SC, USA

Susan G. Assouline Belin-Blank Center, College of Education, University of Iowa, Iowa City, IA, USA

Amy Price Azano Virginia Tech, Blacksburg, VA, USA

Abu Yazid Abu Bakar Faculty of Education, Universiti Kebangsaan Malaysia, Bangi, Malaysia

Daniel Patrick Balestrini University of Regensburg, Regensburg, Germany

Nadine Ballam University of Waikato, Hamilton, New Zealand

Michelle Bannister-Tyrrell School of Education, University of New England, Armidale, NSW, Australia

Aranzazu M. Blackburn Brisbane, QLD, Australia

Sheyla Blumen Department of Psychology, Pontificia Universidad Católica del Perú, Lima, Peru

Eunjoo Boo Seoul National University, Seoul, South Korea

Linda E. Brody Johns Hopkins University Center for Talented Youth, Baltimore, MD, USA

Emma C. Burns School of Education, University of New South Wales, Sydney, NSW, Australia

Carolyn M. Callahan University of Virginia, Charlottesville, VA, USA

Ana Karen Camelo-Lavadores Universidad Autónoma de Yucatán, Mérida, Yucatán, México

Wei-Ren Chen Department of Special Education, National Chiayi University, Chiayi City, Taiwan

Terence Titus Chia Centre for Research in Pedagogy and Practice, Office of Education Research, National Institute of Education, Singapore, Singapore

T. W. Chiang Gaterac Limited, Sheung Wan, Hong Kong, China

Seokhee Cho St. John's University, New York, NY, USA

Maria Leonor Conejeros-Solar Escuela de Pedagogía, Pontificia Universidad Católica de Valparaíso, Viña del Mar, Chile

Bonnie Cramond The University of Georgia, Athens, GA, USA

David Yun Dai University at Albany, State University of New York, Albany, NY, USA

Gabriela de la Torre García PAUTA, Institute of Nuclear Sciences, Universidad Nacional Autónoma de México UNAM, Mexico City, México

James R. Delisle Kent State University, Kent, OH, USA

Carmel Diezmann Faculty of Education, Queensland University of Technology, Brisbane, QLD, Australia

Ann Easter Gifted Education Consultancy Services, Aotearoa, New Zealand

Joyce J. Y. Fung Center for Advancement in Inclusive and Special Education, Faculty of Education, University of Hong Kong, Hong Kong, China

Françoys Gagné Université du Québec à Montréal (UQAM), Montréal, QC, Canada

Selena Gallagher Cairo American College, Cairo, Egypt

Rhoda Myra Garces-Bacsal College of Education, Special Education Department, United Arab Emirates University, Al Ain, United Arab Emirates

Susanne Garvis University of Gothenburg, Gothenburg, Sweden

María Paz Gómez-Arízaga Universidad de Los Andes, Santiago, Chile

Payal Goundar UNSW, Sydney, NSW, Australia

Anne Grant Deakin University, Melbourne, VIC, Australia

Miraca U. M. Gross GERRIC, School of Education, University of New South Wales, Sydney, NSW, Australia

E. Jean Gubbins University of Connecticut, Storrs, CT, USA

Rashea Hamilton Washington Student Achievement Council, Olympia, WA, USA

Peta K. Hay GERRIC/School of Education, The University of New South Wales, Sydney, NSW, Australia

Lesley Henderson Flinders University, Adelaide, SA, Australia

Takeo Higuchi Idea-Marathon Institute (IMS Institute), Tokyo, Japan

Jenny Horsley Victoria University of Wellington, Wellington, New Zealand

Gail Fischer Hubbard Prince William County Public Schools, Manassas, VA, USA

Takuya Iwata The University of Georgia, Athens, GA, USA
NIC International College, Osaka, Japan

Jane Jarvis Flinders University, Adelaide, SA, Australia

Jae Yup Jung GERRIC/School of Education, The University of New South Wales, Sydney, NSW, Australia

Daehyun Kim Torrance Center for Creativity and Talent Development, University of Georgia, Athens, GA, USA

Eunhyang Kim Gachon University, Seongnam-si, Gyeonggi-do, South Korea

Kyung Hee Kim The College of William & Mary, Williamsburg, VA, USA

Youngmin Kim Korea Advanced Institute of Science and Technology, GIFTED, Daejeon, South Korea

Yun-Kyoung Kim Seoul National University, Seoul, South Korea

Tay T. R. Koo The University of New South Wales, Sydney, NSW, Australia

Leonie Kronborg Faculty of Education, Monash University, Clayton, VIC, Australia

Carly Lassig Queensland University of Technology, Brisbane, QLD, Australia

Jeongkyu Lee The Korea Foundation for the Advancement of Science, Seoul, South Korea

Jihyun Lee School of Education, The University of New South Wales, Sydney, NSW, Australia

Seon-Young Lee Seoul National University, Seoul, South Korea

Youngju Lee Korea Advanced Institute of Science and Technology, GIFTED, Daejeon, South Korea

Chin-hsieh Lu Department of Special Education, National Taipei University of Education, Taipei, Taiwan

Ann Lupkowski-Shoplik Belin-Blank Center, College of Education, University of Iowa, Iowa City, IA, USA

Min Ma Central University of Finance and Economics, Beijing, China

C. June Maker Department of Disability and Psychoeducational Studies, The University of Arizona, Tucson, AZ, USA

Marcella Mandracchia Adelphi University, New York, NY, USA

Andrew J. Martin School of Education, University of New South Wales, Sydney, NSW, Australia

D. Betsy McCoach University of Connecticut, Storrs, CT, USA

Salvatore Sal Mendaglio University of Calgary, Calgary, AB, Canada

Azra Moeed Victoria University of Wellington, Wellington, New Zealand

Roger Moltzen Division of Education, The University of Waikato, Hamilton, New Zealand

Anne-Marie Morrissey Deakin University, Melbourne, VIC, Australia

John Munro Faculty of Education and Arts, Australian Catholic University, East Melbourne, VIC, Australia

Paula Olszewski-Kubilius Center for Talent Development, School of Education and Social Policy, Northwestern University, Evanston, IL, USA

Ananda Kumar Palaniappan Tunku Abdul Rahman University College, Kuala Lumpur, Malaysia

Kyungbin Park Gachon University, Seongnam-si, Gyeonggi-do, South Korea

Donna Pendergast Griffith University, Brisbane, QLD, Australia

Pamela Peters University of Connecticut, Storrs, CT, USA

Shane N. Phillipson Faculty of Education, Peninsula Campus, Monash University, Frankston, VIC, Australia

Margaret Plunkett School of Education, Federation University, Churchill, VIC, Australia

Jeb Puryear ACS-Cobham International School, Hersham, UK

Tracy Riley Massey University, Palmerston North, New Zealand

Janice I. Robbins The College of William and Mary, Williamsburg, VA, USA

Karen B. Rogers University of St. Thomas, Minneapolis, MN, USA

Jennifer Rowley The University of Sydney, Sydney, NSW, Australia

Lara Walker Russell Javits Project, College of Charleston, Charleston, SC, USA

Jiyoung Ryu Korea Advanced Institute of Science and Technology, GIFTED, Daejeon, South Korea

Pedro Antonio Sánchez-Escobedo College of Education, Universidad Autónoma de Yucatán, Mérida, Yucatán, México

Shozo Saegusa Shujitsu University, Okayama, Japan

Robert Arthur Schultz University of Toledo, Toledo, OH, USA

Del Siegle University of Connecticut, Storrs, CT, USA

Susen R. Smith GERRIC, School of Education, The University of New South Wales, Sydney, NSW, Australia

Julia Steinbach University of Regensburg, Regensburg, Germany

Heidrun Stoeger University of Regensburg, Regensburg, Germany

Rena F. Subotnik American Psychological Association, Washington, DC, USA

Julie Dingle Swanson College of Charleston, Charleston, SC, USA

Liang See Tan Centre for Research in Pedagogy and Practice, Office of Education Research, National Institute of Education, Singapore, Singapore

Jing Yi Tan Centre for Research in Pedagogy and Practice, Office of Education Research, National Institute of Education, Singapore, Singapore

Geraldine Townend GERRIC/School of Education, The University of New South Wales, Sydney, NSW, Australia

Angel Alberto Valdés-Cuervo Instituto Tecnológico de Sonora, Ciudad Obregón, Sonora, México

Joyce VanTassel-Baska The College of William and Mary, Williamsburg, VA, USA

Wilma Vialle University of Wollongong, Wollongong, NSW, Australia

Russell Walton Learning Development, University of Wollongong, Wollongong, NSW, Australia

Janna Wardman University of Auckland, Auckland, New Zealand

James Watters Faculty of Education, Queensland University of Technology, Brisbane, QLD, Australia

Myra Wearne NSW Department of Education, North Sydney Demonstration School, Waverton, NSW, Australia

Melinda Webber Faculty of Education and Social Work, The University of Auckland, Auckland, New Zealand

Cara Wienkes Belin-Blank Center, College of Education, University of Iowa, Iowa City, IA, USA

Sally Windsor University of Gothenburg, Gothenburg, Sweden

Denise Wood Charles Sturt University, Bathurst, NSW, Australia

Catherine Wormald Faculty of Social Sciences, School of Education, University of Wollongong, Wollongong, NSW, Australia

Frank C. Worrell University of California Berkeley, Berkeley, CA, USA

Jing-Jyi Wu Center for Creativity and Innovation Studies, National Chengchi University, Taipei, Taiwan

Jenny Yang St. John's University, New York, NY, USA

Ming-Jen Yu Center for Creativity and Innovation Studies, National Chengchi University, Taipei, Taiwan

Allan H. K. Yuen Centre for Information Technology in Education (CITE), University of Hong Kong, Hong Kong, China

Faculty of Education, The University of Hong Kong, Hong Kong, China

Yew Chung College of Early Childhood Education, Hong Kong, China

Mantak Yuen Center for Advancement in Inclusive and Special Education, Faculty of Education, University of Hong Kong, Hong Kong, China

María Alicia Zavala Berbena Universidad De La Salle Bajío, León, México

Yong Zhao University of Kansas, Lawrence, KS, USA

Albert Ziegler University of Erlangen-Nuremberg, Nuremberg, Germany

Gifted Education in the Asia-Pacific: From the Past for the Future – An Introduction

Susen R. Smith

Contents

Introduction	2
Sociocultural Conceptions and Perceptions	5
Social and Emotional Needs and Learning Processes	7
Identifying and Nurturing Diversely Gifted and Talented Students	8
Assessment, Pedagogy, and Curricula	10
Diverse Dimensions of Gifted Education	13
Educational Contexts, Transitions, and Community Engagement	14
Conclusion	15
References	16

Abstract

In this chapter, a brief introduction to the handbook is provided. There are six sections in the handbook that include: (1) sociocultural conceptions and perceptions, (2) social and emotional needs and learning processes, (3) identifying and nurturing diversely gifted and talented students, (4) assessment, pedagogy and curricula, (5) diverse dimensions of gifted education and (6) educational contexts, transitions, and community engagement. An overview of selected concepts and issues raised in the sections of the handbook will be highlighted and discussed. This chapter is meant to be informative and is not an in-depth review, in fact, I have chosen key points that emanate from the most recent Asia-Pacific research literature, recent reviews in international handbooks, and books and from the chapters submitted to this handbook. Hence, the discussion is not meant to be exhaustive, though it is hoped that it will encourage further discourse and provide the background to your reading of the following sections. For more details of the

---

S. R. Smith (✉)
GERRIC, School of Education, University of New South Wales, Sydney, NSW, Australia
e-mail: Susen.smith@unsw.edu.au

© Crown 2021
S. R. Smith (ed.), *Handbook of Giftedness and Talent Development in the Asia-Pacific*,
Springer International Handbooks of Education,
https://doi.org/10.1007/978-981-13-3041-4_1

content of each of the chapters from Part I to Part VI, please refer to the introductions provided by the section editors at the beginning of each part of the handbook.

Keywords

Gifted and talented · Sociocultural conceptions · Social-emotional learning needs · Diversity · Assessment · Pedagogy · Curriculum · Varying educational contexts

The aims in this chapter are to:
1. Provide an overview of key issues and concepts raised in the handbook chapters.
2. Discuss some key issues relevant to the Asia-Pacific region in relation to the recent literature.
3. Introduce the six parts of the handbook.

Introduction

Four decades ago, I embarked on my career as a primary school teacher and my first class was grade one. Three years later, I found myself teaching grade five, and I was quite perturbed about the move as I did not feel experienced enough to cater for the mixed abilities that I encountered in class sizes of over thirty students! Even in grade one, the diversity in ability in students was starkly evident. For example, there were students who were still learning their alphabet, while there were others who were reading fluently and writing pages of creative narratives derived from their advanced abilities, vivid imaginations, and diverse experiences! I was an early career teacher, so I started to experiment with ways to cater for the individual needs of my students so achievement ensued, ways to keep them engaged and interested so creativity was enabled, and ways to maintain laughter and joy in learning! If anyone had told me back then the extent of the influence of these early teaching years on my career, I am not sure I would have believed them. Notably, I started teaching the same day that my child began kindergarten 40 years ago and several years later I learnt my child was gifted, which was the final impetus for initiating my gifted education journey.

I continued my postgraduate studies while teaching fulltime and took on varying educational leadership roles over the years, including being a gifted education coordinator and consultant. Twenty years later, in the context of academia, I became an academic in special education and gifted education for the second half of my career.

During my journey, I have learnt about the diversity of the gifted child, the advocacy of parents and guardians of gifted children, the dedication of teachers/educators/specialists, the commitment of academics in the field of gifted education, the generosity of gifted association members, the foresight of leaders, and the mentoring of volunteers in gifted education programs. Additionally, in the gifted education field there are the interculturality of issues, interdisciplinarity of concepts, broadness of the field, complexity of perceptions and conceptions, originality of the intellectual discourse, challenges of the research, innovation of the theorising, and misconceptions of societal attitudes. All of the aforementioned factors have been monumental in their influence, either as hindering or supporting gifted children and gifted education. We are all advocates for our children, but, in the gifted education field, there cannot be a more passionate and committed group of people around the world surely! It has been my trilogy of experiences as a parent, teacher, and academic that has led me to initiate this handbook. It is my honour to showcase the expertise and talent evident within the content of this tome.

There are many books and handbooks on gifted education. So, what makes this one different? A few reasons why this handbook is different to others in the field were enlightened in the preface. However, the main reason for its difference is that the large numbers of contributors are from countries where academics are rarely authors in international handbooks or books derived from international sources, or have publications scattered throughout several international journals. Fortunately, this diversity is reflected in the unique content in the chapters within and advocates for gifted children have many options to source resources to support gifted education. For example,

> About 60% of the states in the United States, plus Korea, Indonesia, Israel, Singapore, Australia and other countries, as well as Taiwan, China and Hong Kong, have passed special legislation and established relevant research institutions. Also, they make research and educational plans for supernormal children, funded especially to guarantee the implementation of research and education. (Shi & Li, 2018, p. 452)

There are also a number of journals in the Asia-Pacific region, for example, the *Australasian Journal of Gifted and Talented*, *APEX: New Zealand Journal of Gifted Education* and the *Talincrea*, Mexico in which readers can explore local issues and perspectives of giftedness and talent (e.g., Bicknell & Riley, 2013; Lassig, 2009). Overviews of gifted education in selected regions are found in a variety of sources (e.g., Alencar, Fleith, & Blumen, 2016; Dai, 2018; Kronborg, 2018; Kuo, 2018). For recent overviews of broader perspectives of Australian and New Zealand gifted education see the Jolly and Jarvis' (2018) book authored by Australian and New Zealand experts in the field and Ballam and Moltzen's (2017) book that collated Australasian doctoral studies. The editors and authors reiterated many practical strategies for supporting gifted students, targeted a number of key issues, and detailed some research and policies from that part of the world, but Australasia is only part of the wider Asia-Pacific and rim region and more research and practice need to be elaborated. For ease of reading, I will refer to Asia-Pacific nations as inclusive of Asia-Pacific rim nations.

Many countries around the world now have associations for high potential or gifted or talented students where advocates develop policies and practices to support children's talent development. For example, in Australia there is the *Australasian Association for the Education of the Gifted and Talented (AAEGT)*, in the USA is the *National Association for Gifted Children (NAGC)*, in Taiwan/China is the *Chinese*

Association of Gifted Education, in Thailand is the *Association for Developing Human Potentials and Giftedness*, in Chile there is the *High Intellectual Capabilities* association and then there is the *High Capabilities in Colombia* association, not to mention the various smaller associations in states and regions within these and other countries in the region. Beyond advocacy, these associations support networking, research, and practice in varying ways and hold regular seminars, forums, and conferences to spread the word about gifted students' educational, social, emotional, physical, and spiritual needs that bring diversity in culture, perspectives, values, and beliefs together at regular intervals.

The *Biennial World Council for Gifted and Talented Children (WCGTC) Conference* is the premier conference in gifted education that originated in London in 1975 (World Council for Gifted and Talented Children [WCGTC], 2019). Reflecting its diversity, the conference has been held in Australia, Canada, Czech Republic, Denmark, England, Germany, Hong Kong/China, Israel, Philippines, Spain, The Netherlands, Turkey, United Arab Emirates, and the USA. These conferences (along with numerous other fora) are opportunities to challenge advocates', educators', academics', administrators', psychologists', counsellors', parents', and gifted children's perspectives and find insightful suggestions to combat society's widespread misconceptions about gifted education. Not to mention, the benefits of networking and exploring innovative, relevant, and unique research and practice and debate controversial and provocative issues that trouble the field to this day. For example, in the Asia-Pacific context, the fifth WCGTC World Conference was hosted in Manila, Philippines in 1983. Though we only know its title: *Gifted and Talented Children, Youth, and Adults: Their Social Perspectives and Culture* and no other records of the event are available, the conference is thought to be the impetus for more structured research in gifted education in Australasia (Kronborg, 2018). By 1989, when the eighth WCGTC Conference was held in Sydney Australia, we are aware of a little more about the content where the main foci of presenters were on: identification, curriculum and programs for gifted students, creativity, special talents, gifted individuals with learning disabilities, social and emotional development, and policy and procedures. This conference also included two extra strands, which were considered important and contemporary at the time, that were: Information and Communication Technology in the twenty-first century and Music and the Arts (Urban & Matison, 2003, para. 2).

Still in the Asia-Pacific region, the 11th World WCGTC Conference was on *Maximising Potential: Lengthening and Strengthening our Stride* and was held in Hong Kong in 1995. A hard copy of the conference proceedings was published, but again, the details are not readily available (Chan, Li, & Spinks, 1997). The 15th WCGTC World conference titled *Gifted 2013: A Celebration Downunder* was held in Adelaide Australia in 2003, but beyond a web link to the list of keynotes, the content is unknown (World Council for Gifted and Talented Children [WCGTC], 2003). Then, once again, the world conference was held in Sydney Australia in 2017 and entitled *Global Perspectives in Gifted Education*. The same foci from the earlier Sydney (1989) world conference continued to dominate the 2017 conference program. However, this time, there appeared to be a wider focus on diversity: issues, conceptions of giftedness, gifted and/or talented students; ethnic, linguistic, cultural, spiritual perspectives; topics ranging from popular culture to online learning; and educational contexts. Today, these diverse research and practice foci are also reflected in the Asia-Pacific region and rim countries' education of gifted and talented students (Bicknell & Riley, 2013; Wu & Kuo, 2016).

In this chapter six foci will be elaborated from the perspectives of some Asia-Pacific nations' experts in gifted education: (1) sociocultural conceptions and perceptions, (2) social and emotional needs and learning processes, (3) identifying and nurturing diversely gifted and talented students, (4) assessment, pedagogy and curricula, (5) diverse dimensions of gifted education, and (6) educational contexts, transitions and community engagement. A brief overview of each of these parts of the handbook will now be provided.

Sociocultural Conceptions and Perceptions

First, in Part I of the handbook, the aim was to explore a variety of conceptions and perceptions from various sociocultural stances. Some topics, for example, include inhibiters and promoters of giftedness or talent development, gifted education, cross-cultural views and values, stereotypes, and unique cultural responses to giftedness, talent development, policy, and pedagogy. The authors present a variety of challenges from conceptions of giftedness to talent development, from early childhood to university contexts, from theoretical models to proposed practice and the ever-increasing need for further research on sociocultural specificities.

Varying ethno-linguistic responses from Asian, Australasian, Latin American, Canadian, and North American researchers are evident in this section. Part I begins with three diverse models represented. The three models are Gagné's *Differentiating Model of Giftedness and Talent* (DMGT), Ziegler's *Actioptope Model* and the *Talent Development Megamodel* that present three diversely different but overlapping conceptions of giftedness and talent, which reflect the diversity of perspectives in the field of how giftedness or high ability is conceived. Even after decades of debate, there is still no agreed definition or conception of *giftedness* and *talent* and both the terms are (often erroneously) used synonymously. Other terms are also used, such as *high potential, high ability, highly able, supernormal, accelerand, creative,* or *high achiever,* with a greater focus on achievers perceived as gifted than underachievers who are not viewed as gifted. Indeed, there are now dynamic and complex models showing conceptual interrelationships between key principles that suggest giftedness is a developmental process or that talent development should be the focus rather than giftedness (Gagné, 2013; Plucker & Callahan, 2014). Additionally, there are contextual, cultural, economic, ideological, political, philosophical, empirical, and other factors, such as misconceptions, stereotypes, egalitarianism, meritocracy, seeking excellence, or ensuring equity that influence perceptions and conceptions of gifted children, giftedness and talent, gifted education, and associated policy and practice (Frantz & Larsen McClarty, 2016; Shi & Li, 2018; Stoeger, 2009; Vista, 2015). The link between the models and their use in practice across several countries was a worthwhile reiteration in this section, more of which is needed for the gap between the theories expressed in these models to be applied usefully in practice.

Australia has a strong egalitarian approach to gifted education inspired by its colonial past, while many Asian countries (while still more diverse than homogenous), such as Singapore, Japan, or China, seem to embrace a meritocratic approach, based on their families' high expectations, pride in the pursuit of excellence, and value of achievement in education for future wealth and security (Chan, 2018; Frantz & Larsen McClarty, 2016). Here, I will refer you to Chan (2018) for an in-depth review of largely Asia-Pacific nations' sociocultural and pedagogical stance on educating supernormal or gifted students.

Addressing the *talent development* needs of the gifted using a sociocultural approach is one focus of this section. A range of programming options from cross-cultural views of learning for talent development within sociocultural contexts with like-minded peers is also reinforced. Sociocultural contexts for teaching and learning are widely supported in the research literature on acceleration and grouping gifted students together so relevant provisions for gifted students ensues, especially as most gifted students learn in heterogeneous, mixed-ability classes (e.g., Assouline, Colangelo, Van Tassel-Baska, & Lupkowski-Shoplik, 2015; Rogers, 2007).

In 2007 Phillipson and McCann edited the only book on giftedness and sociocultural conceptions from the Asia-Pacific (Phillipson & McCann, 2007), highlighting broad perspectives, key issues, research, and practice from several nations in the region. Since then, a book on Australasian perspectives generally has been published with a small focus on sociocultural issues, especially those related to Indigenous Australasians (Jolly & Jarvis, 2018). Likewise, a few journal articles on issues associated with specific sociocultural aspects of gifted education in the Asia-Pacific have been published in international journals, such as the *Gifted Child Quarterly, Gifted and Talented International, Journal for the Education of the Gifted*, or *Roeper Review* to name a few (e.g., Blumen, 2013; Dai & Chen, 2013). Additionally, a few chapters with a sociocultural focus from Asian-Pacific academics have found their way into international handbooks (e.g., Alencar, Fleith, & Arancibia, 2009; Blackburn & Smith, 2018; Kronborg, 2018; Phillipson et al., 2009).

What the authors in this section appear to reinforce are either/or views of giftedness and/or talent (Dai, 2018); creativity instead of testing; the need for more practice emanating from sound theoretical and researched models; diverse student individuality based on culture and context rather than gifted students as an homogenous group; and spirituality as a possible new domain to build upon current views of domains of giftedness and talent. Spirituality, creativity, and giftedness conjointly have only recently been explored in the Australasian context (e.g., Vialle, 2007) and in the South American context (e.g., Alencar, Braga, Prado, & Chagas-Ferreira, 2016). While the gifted education field has been dominated by Eurocentric and Americentric views, much of this has been useful in supporting gifted and talented students around the world. However, as knowledge about cultural processes and the dimensions underlying cultural differences accumulates, researchers can reevaluate the cultural validity of Western-based theories and practices, and the conditions under which these theories apply, and enhance the success and sustainability of the development of gifted education in Asian countries. (Chan, 2018, p. 72)

In respecting the diversity evident in all the cultures, a similar stance can be undertaken in other nations within the Asia-Pacific region.

Social and Emotional Needs and Learning Processes

Next, the topics aimed to be covered in Part II included: varying social/emotional constructs, influences, misconceptions, Social and Emotional Learning (SEL) frameworks and programs, and varying contexts and concepts, such as resiliency, self-regulation, motivation, over excitability, self-esteem, and sense of identity that may inform SEL and the well-being of gifted students.

The authors in this second section span the four corners of the Pacific Ocean and include expertise from collaborations from Europe in their midst. They illuminate several key factors that can contribute to lack of well-being, especially students with some added challenge, such as low-socio-economic circumstances, being 'at risk' of failure, having twice-exceptionalities, multi-cultural misunderstandings, or the educational context failing to match the student needs. Balancing these difficulties is one key aspect that was reinforced in this section. For example, the benefits of the positive professional relationship between gifted students and teachers as integral to positive well-being.

There are varying social and emotional learning needs of gifted students, depending on many variables, such as their *domain*, *level*, or *profile* of giftedness, personal characteristics, age, familial context, or educational experiences and the like (Gross, 2010; Smith, 2017). Social and emotional characteristics and needs of gifted students have been well researched for decades now (e.g., Gross, 2010; Jung & Gross, 2014). For example, there is the burgeoning debate on whether *overexcitabilities* are psychosocial constructs, or if gifted children can have overexcitabilities, or whether there is no relationship between overexcitabilities and gifted children's social and emotional development. While Dabrowski's Theory of Positive Disintegration (of which overexcitabilities are a part) did not originate with research on gifted children, it is a good example of exploring interdisciplinary research to support gifted education and gifted children, as today's debate is grounded in strong international research supporting Dabrowski's overexcitabilities in gifted children (e.g., see Mendaglio, 2012, 2021; Siu, 2010).

There are many aspects of social and emotional learning. For example, one characteristic often attributed to gifted students is perfectionism. Previously, perfectionism was viewed uni-dimensionally and dysfunctionally, with a focus on the negative influences of perfectionism. Today perfectionism is viewed multi-dimensionally and functionally, with the focus on using positive perfectionism to assist talent development (Chan, 2018). Furthermore, there are a number of SEL strategies that can be used to target specific SEL needs of gifted students, for example, nurturing personal goal setting and growth-orientated mindsets are SEL strategies to assist perfectionists to be more accepting of their mistakes and help them plan constructive future actions (Mofield, Parker Peters, & Chakraborti-Ghosh, 2016; Wardman, 2018).

It is well reiterated in the literature that the quality of teaching and learning in the educational context can impact the gifted student's social-emotional development. One example study from China indicated gifted students' motivations to learn were impacted negatively by inappropriate provisions, inclusive of the test-based approach to acceleration and teachers untrained in gifted education (Shi & Li, 2018). Conversely, in Australian research, profoundly gifted students' self-efficacy, self-esteem, and self-concept were viewed as improved with appropriately supported enrichment and acceleration practices and well-trained teachers in accepting learning environments (Gross, 2010).

Fortunately, we have progressed from the view that gifted students 'suffer' more social and emotional decline than their typical same age peers. While gifted children have similar or stronger psychosocial constructs as their same-age typical peers, it will be developmentally appropriate provisions that help maintain the gifted child's well-being (Lubinski, 2016). Teaching holistically to the students' readiness, strengths, and interests rather than focusing on their weaknesses has become the mantra in recent times to reduce social and emotional distress and support positive psychological development and healthy well-being aligned with academic achievement (Shi & Li, 2018; Smith, 2017). *Holistically* refers to the interrelationships between cognitive, social, emotional, physical, artistic, and spiritual development of the child (Shi & Li, 2018). Just like elsewhere in the world, the Asia-Pacific nations promote teacher professional learning in gifted education in order to better support gifted students holistically (e.g., Kronborg & Plunkett, 2013; Lassig, 2009; Shi & Li, 2018). Teacher Professional Learning (TPL) is reinforced throughout several sections in this handbook, but, unfortunately, TPL is often viewed as the panacea to many gifted education *ills*, though of course much more is needed to ensure the well-being of gifted students.

Identifying and Nurturing Diversely Gifted and Talented Students

The implications of diversity in giftedness are explored in Part III. For example, identification processes, underachievement, indigeneity, underrepresentation, disadvantage, gender, prodigies, twice/multi-exceptionalities, and the profoundly gifted are a few foci examined in this section. The chapters derive from a diverse range of authors, from Australia, Chile, Korea, Mexico, New Zealand, Peru and the USA; with an international contributor now based in Sweden.

Diversity has many definitions. In this context, diversity refers to the different *domains, profiles*, and *levels* of giftedness. Gagné's (2013) research suggests that there are several *domains* of giftedness: intellectual, creative, social, sensory, and psychomotor in his *Differentiating Model of Giftedness and Talent* (DMGT). In other models, *characteristics* of giftedness are elaborated, for example, *creativity* is viewed as a characteristic rather than a domain in Renzulli's (2016) *Three-ringed Conception of Giftedness* model. Gross's (2010) life work focused on profoundly gifted students and she reinforced the different *levels* of giftedness from mildly to profoundly gifted. Betts and Neihart's (1988) research indicated that there can also be different *profiles* of giftedness, depending on the classification of grouped characteristics, behaviours and needs, such as *being autonomous, being at risk* or *having twice-exceptionalities*. So, the one student can be *profoundly* (level), *creatively* (domain) gifted and be *twice exceptional* (profile). Other factors add to the diversity, such as cultural context, for example, indigeneity or English as Another Language (EAL), which may result in underrepresentation in gifted education programs or under-achievement. Underrepresentation may be due to a number of factors but is largely credited to lack of identification and culturally insensitive assessment, which are issues highlighted in this part of the handbook (Blackburn & Smith, 2018).

It seems that most researchers, educators, and policymakers in most Asian countries have emulated the American approach to gifted education with the move from the uni-dimensional approach to identification using IQ testing to a more multi-dimensional identification process (Dai, 2018). The main concerns appear to be around identifying complex student populations, such as those who are considered twice exceptional or from backgrounds that may disadvantage their access to gifted education programs, such as indigeneity, low socio-economic background, or being rurally isolated.

While educational, departmental, policy, and funding support for gifted education has waxed and waned in many countries over the last several decades, depending on too many variables to list, for example, attitudes, ideologies, or political influences, what appears to be on the increase is the focus on indigenous students in gifted education (Ballam & Moltzen, 2017; Jolly & Jarvis, 2018). However, Australian Aboriginals are often a disenfranchised group (Chaffey, 2009). Hence, another dimension of this section is racial-ethic identity in the context of Australasian indigeneity where familial and cultural factors play a large role in student engagement that can lead to motivation that enables achievement or talent development. Access to resources that enable culturally sensitive assessments, identification, and programming for all Indigenous students is required, but even more so for those who are recognised as future leaders (i.e., *gifted* in Indigenous terms).

The widening of the excellence gap has been more poignant in the last three decades with underrepresentation in gifted education programs by disadvantaged students even more prevalent today (e.g., Borland & Wright, 1994; Plucker & Peters, 2016). In this section, the authors reinforce contexts that contribute to this underrepresentation, such as low socio-economic status, poverty twinned with ethno-linguistics, indigeneity, and having twice exceptionality (2e) or underachievement. Fortunately, there has been the move from a deficit view of capacities towards the realisation of strengths and more socially just and culturally fair identification procedures. Such moves should enhance the opportunity for access to gifted education programs by disadvantaged populations, such as those with twice-exceptionalities (Plucker & Peters, 2016).

Indeed, today there has been a shift from an identification-based ideology of *identifying* gifts to *scaffolding and cultivating* gifts within dynamic ecological-, systems-based pedagogy that can reduce underachievement (Lo & Porath, 2017). Research-based identification strategies and the link with programming options relevant to different student populations are needed in practice and are also highlighted in this section. Using identification and learning process strategies within classroom practice, where most gifted students are educated, are key recommendations. Overall, Part III reiterates the need for multi-dimensional and inclusive identification processes and collaboration for successful programming to reduce underrepresentation and underachievement. The lack of access to resources for rurally isolated students and the disadvantage this engenders is a sad reminder, that even in the general classroom in a highly populated mid-city school, while being surrounded by people and resources, the gifted child is often isolated socially (Gross, 2010). The multi-faceted needs of underachievers have become a major issue within the field (Olszewski-Kubilius & Clarenbach, 2012). This section attempts to address some of these difficulties by recommending alternative resources, identification, programming, and provisional options to enhance student potential.

Issues of gender difference can impede or promote talent potential, but when you consider gender with twice-exceptionality, and then add rural isolation and other factors, the complexity of the diversity of giftedness, gifted education, and educational context are exacerbated many fold (Peters, Gentry, Whiting, & McBee, 2019). While there are now a number of publications on 2e, rurality, and gender to guide the practitioner, some interventions are usefully provided in Part III.

Based on an identification-based ideology, it has long been thought that identifying intelligence and eminence were the main goals in gifted education, as the wider myth was that every gifted child had the capacity to grow up to become eminent (Lo & Porath, 2017). While this has been criticised, as only some gifted children may achieve eminence in their adult years, striving for excellence and eminence can be viewed as the stimulus for a country's economic success (Chan, 2018). Nonetheless, it is highly relevant that eminent people with intercultural competence are case-studied in this section of the handbook.

In Asian cultures, it is believed that the collective of cognitive abilities, excellence, creativity, and spirituality stem from wisdom (Chan, 2018). This wisdom may derive from gifted children feeling more deeply, abstractly, ethically, morally, and sensitively than their same-age peers of typical ability. Finally, the concept of wise persons is explored in this section with the view that we should be cultivating wisdom in our students, specifically gifted students, whose characteristics may provide the foundation for the development of wisdom.

Assessment, Pedagogy, and Curricula

The chapters in Part IV were authored by Australian, Chinese/Hong Kong/Taiwanese, New Zealand, North American, Singaporean, and South Korean experts in the field. Many countries do not have a national curriculum, for example, Canada or the

USA. In recent years, national curricula have been developed or updated in many Asia-Pacific countries, for example, the *Australian Curriculum, Assessment and Reporting Authority* (Australian Curriculum Assessment and Reporting Authority [ACARA], 2016) in Australia, *The New Zealand Curriculum* and the *Te Marautanga o Aotearoa* (Ministry of Education, 2018), the *Chinese National Curriculum*, the *South Korea Standardised Curriculum* and the *Chilean National Curriculum* to acknowledge a few. While some government policies give some credence to gifted education, there are no national curricula or policies for gifted students specifically, though New Zealand and the USA have endeavoured to develop a more national approach to gifted education—the USA through their associations, development of national standards in programming, and federal laws acknowledging gifted students' needs (Alencar, Fleith, & Blumen, 2016; Henderson & Jarvis, 2016; Jolly & Jarvis, 2018; National Association for Gifted Children, NAGC, 2019). Gifted students are mentioned in many of these national curricula though, however briefly, and usually under the umbrella of students with diversity or special needs. How these national curricula are being translated into classroom practice for gifted students remains to be seen, but this section does provide some insights into this issue, beginning with reinforcing assessment, curriculum, and pedagogy as inseparable aspects of a gifted student's educational journey.

Innovative, interdisciplinary, or differentiated assessment, curriculum, and pedagogy are foci of this fourth section. For example, some topics covered include: teaching and learning models, strategies, metacognition, technology usage, enrichment programs, acceleration, mentoring, on-line learning, national standards, STEM/STEAM, authentic learning, and teacher traits and perspectives. Specifically, goal setting, feedback, enquiry learning, real world problem-solving, and creative thinking are also stressed in Part IV.

Assessment, pedagogy, and curricula are multi-dimensional interrelated processes and content within teaching and learning (Cao, Jung, & Lee, 2017). For gifted students, this 'interrelatedness' is even more crucial, as their individual learning needs or readiness usually warrant a faster pace, higher level curriculum with more complex content, and relevant challenge that can enhance students' interests, engagement, creativity, outcomes, and achievement (Gross, 2010). Hence, the evolvement of differentiated curriculum, assessment, and pedagogy to match individual gifted student's needs in many countries across the world, which has also been emulated in the Asia-Pacific nations (Chan, 2018). Flexibility in provision of content, teaching styles, and learning strategies also align with the complexity of the students' individual needs (Shi & Li, 2018). These days, the challenge is to nurture talent development within the general school context (Hertzog, 2017).

Pedagogy for gifted students usually can be classified as either enrichment (teaching & learning content beyond the usual grade level curriculum that offers depth and breadth) or acceleration (that involves progressing faster than same-age peers through the curriculum to higher grade content), within a variety of grouping contexts (e.g., in-class ability grouping, pull-out classes, special classes, selective schools). China and Japan favour accelerative provisions, but it appears that Australia, South Korea, and New Zealand strive for the balance of both enrichment and acceleration in their provisions and programs for gifted students, while Hong Kong, Indonesia, Malaysia, the Philippines, Singapore, Taiwan, Chile, Brazil, and Peru tip the scales towards enrichment rather than acceleration (Alencar et al., 2016; Blumen, 2013; Chan, 2018), which may be related to their focus on testing or their more traditional approach to schooling.

In countries, such as Australia, China, Japan, New Zealand, and South Korea, curriculum enrichment and acceleration options, special classes in primary schools, and special secondary schools for the gifted are more common (Dai, 2018). However, it is the interrelationship between these dynamic programming options, systems-based educational contexts, and with the quality of the teachers' teaching and the students' learning within these different grouping contexts that can nurture gifted students towards achieving to their talent potential (Chan, 2017; Smith, 2017). This section provides some programming options that reinforce this interrelationship, with some programs implemented across different countries.

The STEM or STEAM curricula seem to be increasingly valued in education today, especially for gifted students who are viewed as the future doctors or scientists who make the discoveries that could supposedly 'save humanity' medically or 'save the world' environmentally (Watters, 2020). In many Asian nations, the focus is on STEM subjects (Chan, 2018). It is noteworthy that the 'sciences' of STEM are being complemented by the 'arts' of STEAM. Such a balance can encourage educators to recognise the different domains of giftedness beyond the sciences, as well as the interrelatedness of the sciences and the arts during provisions. In this section, the authors reiterate the need to engage gifted students' interests and curiosity in challenging, autonomous, real-world problem-solving projects that reinforce the balance of STEAM in action.

Much discourse and research literature have focused on the teacher as being responsible for talent development; while this is only part of the case, teachers need to be supported in their endeavours to provide for gifted students (Hertzog, 2017). Online learning and mentoring come immediately to mind. The *Wings Project* in Beijing is an exemplar mentoring program that promotes a holistic, project-based approach that matches gifted students with a scientist mentor while emulating real life research and practice (Shi & Li, 2018). Part IV also provides an overview of the effective qualities of mentoring and reinforces its value for both enrichment and acceleration of gifted students. Effective school and pedagogical leadership are other supports for teachers; however, more still needs to be explored in this regard (Long, Barnett, & Rogers, 2015).

In the wider research literature, Dai (2018) also raised the issue of "how to harness technology for talent development" (p. 463), stressing that appropriate use of the internet can increase access to gifted education programs or relevant curricula and pedagogy, with representation or lack of as an issue also explored by authors in this handbook. Chen, Dai, and Zhou (2013) also support this view and provide a framework for using technology for greater access to educational options. Online programs with:

> enrichment strategies to maximize the creativity and potential of gifted learners are likely to continue and become more complex and sophisticated. Such online courses and resources

could help maximize the capacity to serve gifted students who might otherwise be unreachable because of geographical distance or socioeconomic disadvantages in many underdeveloped parts of Asian countries, such as China and India. New technology and computer software will certainly not only create new teaching modes and new learning opportunities transforming conventional gifted education, but also help build and support a network of experts for mentoring beyond national boundaries within and outside Asian countries. (Chan, 2018, pp. 82–83)

Diverse Dimensions of Gifted Education

Authors in Part V examine a variety of foci around diverse dimensions of gifted education, such as new or revised theories, models, frameworks or programs, critiques, perspectives, and the like. Gifted education is complex, socially and culturally specific, and is as diverse as general education in its implementation, resources, and infrastructure (Lo & Porath, 2017). This focus on diverse dimensions of gifted education provided authors the opportunity to explore innovative research and discourse on diverse trends and challenges. Authors from Australia, China/Hong Kong/Macau/Taiwan, Japan, Malaysia and South Korea example some specific dimensions in this section, such as: creativity, counselling, ethics, and popular culture.

The diversity of creativity seems to have emerged in different ways in gifted education as a: domain of giftedness, characteristic of a gifted person, learning goal, or skill needed in the twenty-first century, to such an extent, that the three terms *gifted, talented*, and *creative* are now viewed as separate conceptions or descriptors in gifted education (Dai, 2018). There is the increasing distinction between giftedness and creativity that is represented in different ways. However, varying representations are shown in journals, for example, there is the *International Journal for Talent Development and Creativity*, where 'gifted' is not considered in the title of the journal but the content of the articles use the terms *gifted* and *creative* and *talent*, both distinctly and synonymously. (IJTDC, 2013) and then there is the *Journal of Gifted Education and Creativity* which separates *gifted* and *creative*, but excludes talent in its title and, again, the conceptions and content are variable (JGEC, 2014).

There are many perspectives of creativity in gifted education, for example, the link between intelligence, giftedness, and creativity, that creativity can be culturally founded, and that creativity development can be a process from small c to big C (Lassig, 2021). In the twenty-first century, a nurturing, authentic learning educational environment with challenge, choice, collaboration, and autonomous learning is viewed as imperative ingredients supportive of creativity development across all curriculum areas. Such social-constructivist contexts, where students can express their choices within learning processes, can assist creative outputs (Lassig, 2021). However, competitive learning contexts and standardised testing can still overpower creativity in practice (Beghetto, 2005). How to identify creativity is an oft-voiced query with the return chorus usually to focus on domain specific assessments (Agnoli, Corazza, & Runco, 2016). The link with creativity development and other important areas, such as morals or ethics, is evident in the literature (Sternberg, 2013) and is reiterated in Part V as well. Dai (2018) also argued that the:

creativity economy of the 21st century demands a cultural transformation of education worldwide (the way we think about the means and ends of education), and gifted education should be a force to promote such a change. A long-term vision is needed by the educational leadership at multiple levels to make committed efforts to nurture talent and encourage personal creativity, and to engage in sustained infrastructure and capacity building for that purpose. Whether the 21st century will be truly a Century of Asia is contingent on this endeavor. (p. 476)

Educational Contexts, Transitions, and Community Engagement

Asian-Pacific rim authors were invited to discuss a variety of interrelated ecological- or systems-based foci in the last section of the handbook, from different educational contexts, to transitions across educational levels and contexts, to transitions to career opportunities and including the support of community partnerships.

Some *contextual* foci included: early entry, rural schooling, remote education, home-schooling, and international schooling. Quality educational contexts play a vital role in nurturing student talent. Often there is not the educational fit between traditional schools and the gifted child, so parents seek other options that are more relevant for their child. These options may include home-schooling or international schooling. There is little research on international schooling, so there is an avenue of exploration that is worthwhile, considering many of our gifted students are educated through the International Bachelaureate (Hertberg-Davis, Callahan, & Kyburg, 2006).

Then the *personnel* related to varying educational contexts can include: families, teachers, administrators, specialists, advocacy groups, paraprofessionals, school coordinators, counsellors, or mentors. In Part VI, pre-service teacher attitudes, characteristics of the effective teacher, the role of the gifted education coordinator, and teacher professional learning that may impact the educational journey of the gifted child are explored. There is much in the literature that assesses teacher attitudes and effectiveness and the impact on gifted student outcomes (e.g., Gómez-Arizaga, Conejeros-Solar, & Martin, 2016; Kronborg & Plunkett, 2013; Lassig, 2009). The collaboration between significant personnel is also reinforced in this section, for example, the collaboration between family, teachers, paraprofessionals, and specialist teachers, and the support of advocacy groups, counsellors, and mentors. There is a large body of research that supports the importance of constructive relationships between teachers and students (Gross, 2010; Smith, 2017). This interrelationship has evolved into including all significant others, such as parents, guardians, specialists, coaches, tutors, and the like (Shi & Li, 2018). These personnel have major influences over the gifted child's identity development and decisions regarding what subjects to take in school, what courses to study if they attend university, or the career decisions they may make that can influence their future professional and personal lives (Jung & Gross, 2014).

Additionally, *community-based provisions or partnerships* with organisations feature in this part of the handbook and examples may include: cross-institutional systems, associations, educational departments, competitions/awards, cross-system provisions, funding options, pre-service teacher education, workplace internships, and teacher effectiveness. Community engagement with parents, association members, academics, and varying educators can enable further enrichment of the gifted child's learning. For example, many enrichment programs (e.g., Tournament of Minds, Future Problem Solving) are run by volunteers, though there is now a bourgeoning industry of community enrichment programs where parents pay hundreds of dollars, pesos, won, or yuan for their child to attend (e.g., after school tutoring programs, G.A.T.E.W.A.Y.S., GERRIC Scientia Programs).

Finally, there are the *transitional* foci noted in this section, such as early entry, career choices, decision-making, leadership, and managerial aspects. Transitions between home and school, between school and higher school, between secondary school and university and between university and work or the community are common for all students, but are particularly relevant for gifted students, especially accelerands who progress through schooling at a faster rate (Gross, 2010). Such transitions can be tangled with concerns, so collaboration between all personnel involved, including the students themselves, is paramount (Te Kete Ipurangi, 2019).

Conclusion

In this chapter, the six parts of the handbook were reiterated along with the specification of some key issues and concepts discussed in each section, with links to some wider literature.

The authors ranged from highly respected international experts in the field to virtually unknown early career researchers and practitioners. The aim was to provide a forum for experts to showcase their careers' work as well as to nurture the professional career writings of future academics in the field. The authors presented their chapters with a combination of empirical research, theoretical analysis, and intellectual discourse. As a consequence, the authors presented complementary, diverse, and new perspectives of giftedness and talent, old or new ideologies, conflicting theories, or multi-dimensional models, original interdisciplinary knowledge and understandings of gifted education and assessment, socially-related gifted education contexts, cross-linguistic backgrounds and inter-cultural views, and examples of educational practices, policies, and research.

This chapter provides the pathway to the remainder of the handbook. Each chapter and part can be read independently of the others, while links between chapters and parts can be found by choosing to read chapters with a similar focus and the titles and abstracts of each chapter and the section editor's introductions should guide you on this approach to the handbook. Overall, you are encouraged to explore the content with view to stimulating future empirical research, encouraging further theoretical enquiry, inspiring ground-breaking discourse, and guiding innovative practice for gifted children for talent development, to build on the field's current successes. In the final chapter, a conclusion to the handbook is provided that reiterates the main implications highlighted in the chapters in the handbook.

References

Agnoli, S., Corazza, G. E., & Runco, M. A. (2016). Estimating creativity with a multiple-measurement approach within scientific and artistic domains. *Creativity Research Journal, 28*(2), 171–176. https://doi.org/10.1080/10400419.2016.1162475

Alencar, E. M. S., Braga, N. P., Prado, R. M., & Chagas-Ferreira, J. F. (2016). Spirituality and creativity of indigenous societies in Brazil and their legacy to Brazilian culture and creative giftedness. *Gifted Education International, 32*(3), 224–231. https://doi.org/10.1177/0261429415602581

Alencar, E. M. S., Fleith, D., & Arancibia, V. (2009). Gifted education and research on giftedness in South America. In L. V. Shavinina (Ed.), *International handbook on giftedness. Recent developments in gifted education in East Asia* (pp. 1491–1506). Dordrecht, Netherlands: Springer.

Alencar, E. M. S., Fleith, D., & Blumen, S. (2016). Trends in gifted education in South America: The Brazilian and Peruvian scenario. *Gifted and Talented International, 17*(1), 7–12. https://doi.org/10.1080/15332276.2002.11672980

Assouline, S. G., Colangelo, N., Van Tassel-Baska, J., & Lupkowski-Shoplik, A. (2015). *A nation empowered: Evidence trumps the excuses holding back America's brightest students*. University of Iowa, USA: Belin-Blank International Center for Gifted Education and Talent Development, College of Education. Retrieved from https://files.nwesd.org/website/Teaching_Learning/HiCap/2015-16%20meetings/NationEmpowered%20Vol1.pdf

Australian Curriculum Assessment and Reporting Authority (ACARA). (2016). *The Australian Curriculum, 8*(2). Retrieved from http://www.australiancurriculum.edu.au/

Ballam, N., & Moltzen, R. (2017). *Giftedness and talent: Australasian perspectives*. Singapore, Singapore: Springer. https://doi.org/10.1007/978-981-10-6701-3

Beghetto, R. A. (2005). Does assessment kill student creativity? *The Educational Forum, 69* (Spring 2005), 254–263. Retrieved from https://files.eric.ed.gov/fulltext/EJ683512.pdf

Betts, G., & Neihart, M. (1988). Profiles of the gifted and talented. *Gifted Child Quarterly, 32*(2), 248–253. https://doi.org/10.1177/001698628803200202

Bicknell, B., & Riley, T. (2013). Gifted and talented education in New Zealand schools: A decade later. *APEX: The New Zealand Journal of Gifted Education, 18*(1), 1–16. Retrieved from https://hdl.handle.net/10289/8872

Blackburn, A. M., & Smith, S. R. (2018). Capacities, challenges, and curriculum for Australian learners with exceptional potential for English-language learning. In B. Wallace, D. Sisk, & J. Senior (Eds.), *The SAGE handbook of gifted & talented education* (pp. 357–372). Los Angeles, CA: Sage.

Blumen, S. (2013). New trends in talent development in Peru. *Journal for the Education of the Gifted, 36*(3), 346–364. https://doi.org/10.1177/0162353213492925

Borland, J. H., & Wright, L. (1994). Identifying young, potentially gifted, economically disadvantaged students. *Gifted Child Quarterly, 38*(4), 164–171. https://doi.org/10.1177/001698629403800402

Cao, T. H., Jung, J. Y., & Lee, J. (2017). Assessment in gifted education: A review of the literature from 2005 to 2016. *Journal of Advanced Academics, 28*(3), 163–203. https://doi.org/10.1177/1932202X17714572

Chaffey, G. (2009). Gifted but underachieving: Australian indigenous children. In T. Balchin, B. Hymer, & D. J. Matthews (Eds.), *The Routledge international companion to gifted education* (pp. 106–114). London, England: Routledge.

Chan, J., Li, R., & Spinks, J. A. (1997). Maximizing potential: Lengthening and strengthening our stride. In *Proceedings of the 11th World conference on gifted and talented children*. Hong Kong: University of Hong Kong, Social Sciences Research Centre. Retrieved from http://hdl.handle.net/10722/120112

Chan, D. W. (2017). Gifted education in Asia. In S. I. Pfeiffer (Ed.), *APA handbook of giftedness and talent* (pp. 71–84). Washington, DC: American Psychological Association Press.

Chan, L. K. (2018). Parental influence on perfectionism among Chinese gifted children in Hong Kong. In B. Wallace, D. Sisk, & J. Senior (Eds.), *The SAGE handbook of gifted and talented education* (pp. 196–212). Los Angeles, CA: SAGE Publishing.

Chen, J., Dai, D. Y., & Zhou, Y. (2013). Enable, enhance, and transform: How technology use can improve gifted education. *Roeper Review, 35*(3), 166–176. https://doi.org/10.1080/02783193.2013.794892

Dai, D. Y. (2018). Gifted education in Asia: Vision & capacity. In B. Wallace, D. Sisk, & J. Senior (Eds.), *The SAGE handbook of gifted and talented education* (pp. 462–478). Los Angeles, CA: SAGE Publishing.

Dai, D. Y., & Chen, F. (2013). Three paradigms of gifted education: In search of conceptual clarity in research and practice. *Gifted Child Quarterly, 57*, 151–168. https://doi.org/10.1177/0016986213490020

Frantz, R. S., & Larsen McClarty, K. (2016). Gifted education's reflection of country-specific cultural, political, and economic features. *Gifted and Talented International, 31*(1), 46–58. https://doi.org/10.1080/15332276.2016.1220794

Gagné, F. (2013). The DMGT: Changes within, beneath, and beyond. *Talent Development and Excellence, 5*(1), 5–19. Retrieved from https://www.researchgate.net/publication/285946236_The_DMGT_Changes_Within_Beneath_and_Beyond

Gómez-Arizaga, M., Conejeros-Solar, M. L., & Martin, A. (2016). How good is good enough? A community-based assessment of teacher competencies for gifted students. *SAGE Open, 6*, 1–14. https://doi.org/10.1177/2158244016680687

Gross, M. U. M. (2010). *In her own write: A lifetime in gifted education*. Sydney, NSW: Gifted Education Research, Resource and Information Centre, UNSW.

Henderson, L., & Jarvis, J. (2016). The gifted dimension of the Australian professional standards for teachers: Implications for professional learning. *Australian Journal of Teacher Education, 41*(8), 60–83. Retrieved from https://files.eric.ed.gov/fulltext/EJ1118418.pdf

Hertburg-Davis, H., Callahan, C. M., & Kyburg, R. M. (2006). *Advanced placement and international baccalaureate programs: A "Fit" for gifted learners?* Retrieved from https://nrcgt.uconn.edu/wp-content/uploads/sites/953/2015/04/rm06222.pdf

Hertzog, N. B. (2017). Designing the learning context in school for talent development. *Gifted Child Quarterly, 61*(3), 219–238. https://doi.org/10.1177/0016986217705712

IJTDC. (2013). *International Journal for Talent Development and Creativity*. Retrieved from http://icieworld.net/newicie/images/ijtdcpdf/IJTDC-11-2013-Web.pdf

JGEC. (2014). *Journal of Gifted Education and Creativity*. Retrieved from https://dergipark.org.tr/en/pub/jgedc

Jolly, J. L., & Jarvis, J. M. (2018). *Exploring gifted education Australian and New Zealand perspectives*. New York, NY: Routledge.

Jung, J. Y., & Gross, M. U. M. (2014). Highly gifted students. In J. A. Plucker & C. M. Callahan (Eds.), *Critical issues and practices in gifted education: What the research says* (2nd ed., pp. 305–314). Waco, TX: Prufrock Press.

Kronborg, L. (2018). Gifted education in Australia and New Zealand. In S. I. Pfeiffer (Ed.), *APA handbook of giftedness and talent* (pp. 85–96). Washington, DC: American Psychological Association Press.

Kronborg, L., & Plunkett, M. (2013). Responding to professional learning: How effective teachers differentiate teaching and learning strategies to engage highly able adolescents. *Australasian Journal of Gifted Education, 22*(2), 52–63. Retrieved from https://www.researchgate.net/publication/288133787_Responding_to_professional_learning_How_effective_teachers_differentiate_teaching_and_learning_strategies_to_engage_highly_able_adolescents

Kuo, C.-C. (2018). Developments and issues of gifted education in Taiwan. In B. Wallace, D. Sisk, & J. Senior (Eds.), *The SAGE handbook of gifted and talented education* (pp. 479–491). Los Angeles, CA: SAGE Publishing.

Lassig, C. (2009). Teachers' attitudes towards the gifted: The importance of professional development and school culture. *Australasian Journal of Gifted Education, 18*(2), 32–42. Retrieved from https://eprints.qut.edu.au/32480/

Lassig, C. (2021). Creativity talent development: Fostering creativity in schools. In S. R. Smith (Ed.), *International handbook of giftedness and talent development in the Asia-Pacific*. Singapore, Singapore: Springer International Handbooks of Education.

Lo, C. O., & Porath, M. (2017). Paradigm shifts in gifted education: An examination vis-à-vis its historical situatedness and pedagogical sensibilities. *Gift Child Quarterly, 61*(4), 343–360. https://doi.org/10.1177/0016986217722840

Long, L. C., Barnett, K., & Rogers, K. B. (2015). Exploring the relationship between principal, policy, and gifted program scope and quality. *Journal for the Education of the Gifted, 38*(2), 118–140. https://doi.org/10.1177/0162353215578279

Lubinski, D. (2016). From Terman to today: A century of findings on intellectual precocity. *Review of Educational Research, 86*(4), 900–944. https://doi.org/10.3102/0034654316675476

Mendaglio, S. (2012). Overexcitabilities and giftedness research: A call for a paradigm shift. *Journal for the Education of the Gifted, 35*(3), 207–219. https://doi.org/10.1177/0162353212451704

Mendaglio, S. (2021). Overexcitability and giftedness research: Whose constructs are being investigated and how? In S. R. Smith (Ed.), *International handbook of giftedness and talent development in the Asia-Pacific*. Singapore, Singapore: Springer International Handbooks of Education.

Ministry of Education. (2018). *New Zealand curriculum*. Retrieved from https://parents.education.govt.nz/primary-school/learning-at-school/new-zealand-curriculum/#NZcurriculum

Mofield, E., Parker Peters, M., & Chakraborti-Ghosh, S. (2016). Perfectionism, coping, and underachievement in gifted adolescents: Avoidance vs. approach orientations. *Education Sciences, 6*(3), 1–22. Retrieved from https://pdfs.semanticscholar.org/7873/51e77dfa0729b02375ecc050aa545e605d82.pdf?_ga=2.114980418.411157145.1572723221-301769339.1572723221

National Association for Gifted Children. (2019). *National standards in gifted and talented education*. Retrieved from http://www.nagc.org/resources-publications/resources/national-standards-gifted-and-talented-education

Olszewski-Kubilius, P., & Clarenbach, J. (2012). *Unlocking emergent talent: Supporting high achievement of low-income, high-ability students*. Washington, DC: National Association for Gifted Children.

Peters, S., Gentry, M., Whiting, G. W., & McBee, M. T. (2019). Who gets served in gifted education? Demographic representation and a call for action. *Gifted Child Quarterly, 63*(4), 273–287. https://doi.org/10.1177/0016986219833738

Phillipson, S. N., & McCann, M. (2007). *Conceptions of giftedness: Socio-cultural perspectives*. New York, NY: Routledge.

Phillipson, S. N., Shi, J., Zhang, G., Tsai, D.-M., Quek, C.-G., Matsumura, N., & Cho, S. (2009). Recent developments in gifted education in East Asia. In L. V. Shavinina (Ed.), *International handbook on giftedness. Recent developments in gifted education in East Asia* (pp. 1427–1461). Dordrecht, Netherlands: Springer.

Plucker, J. A., & Callahan, C. M. (2014). Research on giftedness and gifted education: Status of the field and considerations for the future. *Exceptional Children, 80*(4), 390–406. Retrieved from https://www.researchgate.net/publication/268522910_Research_on_Giftedness_and_Gifted_Education_Status_of_the_Field_and_Considerations_for_the_Future

Plucker, J. A., & Peters, S. J. (2016). *Excellence gaps in education: Expanding opportunities for talented students*. Cambridge, MA, USA: Harvard Education Press.

Renzulli, J. S. (2016). The three-ring conception of giftedness: A developmental model for promoting creative productivity. In S. M. Reis (Ed.), *Reflections on gifted education: Critical works by Joseph S. Renzulli and colleagues* (pp. 55–90). Waco, TX, US: Prufrock Press.

Rogers, K. (2007). Lessons learned about educating the gifted and talented: A synthesis of the research on educational practice. *Gifted Child Quarterly, 51*(4), 382–396. https://doi.org/10.1177/0016986207306324

Shi, J., & Li, P. (2018). New century gifted education in mainland China. In B. Wallace, D. Sisk, & J. Senior (Eds.), *The SAGE handbook of gifted and talented education* (pp. 446–461). Los Angeles, CA: SAGE Publishing.

Siu, A. F. Y. (2010). Comparing overexcitabilities of gifted and non-gifted school children in Hong Kong: Does culture make a difference? *Asia Pacific Journal of Education, 30*(1), 71–83. Retrieved from https://positivedisintegration.com/Siu2010.pdf

Smith, S. R. (2017). Responding to the unique social and emotional learning needs of gifted Australian students. In E. Frydenberg, A. Martin, & R. Collie (Eds.), *Social and emotional learning in Australia and the Asia-Pacific: Perspectives, programmes, and approaches* (pp. 147–166). Singapore: Springer.

Sternberg, R. J. (2013). Creativity, ethics, & society. *International Journal for Talent Development and Creativity, 1*(1), 15–24. Retrieved from http://icieworld.net/newicie/images/ijtdcpdf/IJTDC-11-2013-Web.pdf

Stoeger, H. (2009). The history of giftedness research. In L. V. Shavinina (Ed.), *International handbook on giftedness. Recent developments in gifted education in East Asia* (pp. 17–38). Dordrecht, Netherlands: Springer.

Te Kete Ipurangi. (2019). *Gifted transitions – Me mahi tahi tātou hei oranga mō te katoa*. Author. Retrieved from https://gifted.tki.org.nz/responsive-practice/gifted-transitions/

Urban, S., & Matison, A. (2003). *Organising committee 15th world conference for gifted and talented children*, President and Vice President of the Gifted and Talented Children's Association of South Australia. Retrieved from http://www.gtcasa.asn.au/world-conference/index.html

Vialle, W. J. (2007). Spiritual intelligence: An important dimension of giftedness. In K. Tirri (Ed.), *Values and foundations in gifted education* (pp. 171–186). Bern, Switzerland: Peter Lang.

Vista, A. (2015). Equity in cross-cultural gifted screening from a Philippine perspective: A review of literature. *Gifted Education International, 31*(3), 232–243. https://doi.org/10.1177/0261429414526657

Wardman, J. (2018). Supporting the affective needs of gifted learners. In J. L. Jolly & J.M. Jarvis (Eds.), *Exploring gifted education Australian and New Zealand Perspectives* (pp. 66–81). London: Routledge. https://doi.org/10.4324/9781351227704

Watters, J. (2020). Why is it so? Interest and curiosity in supporting students gifted in science. In S. R. Smith (Ed.), *International handbook of giftedness and talent development in the Asia-Pacific*. Singapore: Springer International Handbooks of Education.

World Council for Gifted and Talented Children (WCGTC). (2003). *Gifted 2003: A celebration downunder*. Retrieved from http://www.gtcasa.asn.au/world-conference/index.html

World Council for Gifted and Talented Children (WCGTC). (2019). *Conference history*. Retrieved from https://world-gifted.org/about-wcgtc/history/world-conference-history/

Wu, W.-T., & Kuo, Y.-L. (2016). Gifted and talented education in Taiwan: A 40-year journey. In D. Y. Dai & C. C. Kuo (Eds.), *Gifted education in Asia: Problems and prospects* (pp. 33–50). Charlotte, NC: Information Age Publishing.

Part I

Sociocultural Conceptions

Social and Cultural Conceptions and Perceptions: Part I Introduction

Roger Moltzen

Contents

Introductions to the Individual Chapters 25
Conclusion 29
References 29

Abstract

The chapters in this section cover a diverse range of topics, loosely grouped within the category of social and cultural conceptions and perceptions. This range includes contrasting ways of conceptualising giftedness and talent, national and regional perspectives and practices, approaches to supporting the academic and social development of gifted and talented learners, and spirituality. The common thread that provides the rationale for the grouping of these chapters is the 'social' and 'cultural'.

Keywords

Gifted · Talent · Social · Cultural

More than 30 years ago, I entered academia following 20 years in the school system as a teacher and principal. During those early years as a teacher, I developed an interest in the education and development of gifted and talented children and young people. I built on that early interest and experience in my tertiary role and latterly extended my research focus to include gifted and talented adults. This has enabled

R. Moltzen (✉)
Division of Education, The University of Waikato, Hamilton, New Zealand
e-mail: roger.moltzen@waikato.ac.nz

me to view first-hand developments in this field over more than five decades, and while I think the area of giftedness and talent sometimes lags behind shifts socially and educationally, quite dramatic changes in thinking and practice have occurred across all aspects of the field during that period. At the forefront of these changes has been an increased awareness of the impact and implications of social and cultural dimensions on how giftedness and talent are conceptualised, how gifted and talented learners are identified, and how we respond to the academic, physical, psychological, social, emotional, cultural, spiritual, and other needs of this group (Moltzen, 2011a).

This continues to be a challenge, particularly to teachers and in schools. In this part of the handbook, interesting insights are offered into how researchers and practitioners are responding within and in response to different social and cultural contexts. There are examples of culturally responsive theorising and practice and clear evidence that the Eurocentric and Americentric dominance in gifted and talented education is largely a thing of the past. In countries like Australia and New Zealand, we have become very aware that traditional constructs and practices in gifted and talented education have marginalised and even excluded some cultural and social groups (see Bevan-Brown, 2011; Bishop, Berryman, & Wearmouth, 2014; Webber, 2011). A more recent commitment to honouring the traditions, views, and values of our indigenous peoples has led to increased social and cultural awareness more generally (Moltzen, 2011b; Vialle, 2011). This section adds to that expanded view, offering perspectives, not only from Australia and New Zealand, but also Mexico, Peru, Singapore, South Korea, and the region of East Asia.

Expanding social and cultural perceptions to create more equitable and inclusive practices cannot be considered an option, but rather acting on a basic human right. However, this is not easy, particularly for those charged with enacting these principles. Academics thrive on the cut and thrust of philosophical debate, dealing with ambiguity, and grappling with competing and conflicting ideas. It is pretty much grist for the intellectual mill. However, our teachers are looking for what this means for their classroom practice. That is not to suggest that teachers are not interested in the conceptual and avoid engaging with theoretical concepts and complex ideas. Quite the contrary, I have found from three decades of engaging with the teaching profession as an academic that the stereotype of teachers only wanting practice 'tips' is a myth. However, I believe it behoves those of us that enjoy the luxury of being able to focus in depth on a particular aspect of giftedness and talent to also consider the practice implications of our discoveries. I commend the authors of the chapters in this section for doing exactly this.

Even a very cursory glance of the gifted and talented literature reveals a wide range of often competing views across virtually every dimension of this field, starting with how the very notion/s of giftedness and talent are constructed (Kaufman & Sternberg, 2008; Phillipson & McCann, 2007). This marked lack of consensus is often viewed as an impediment to presenting a compelling rationale for dedicated educational provisions for this group of learners. On the other hand, there are many examples from around the world where this relative open-endedness has accommodated flexibility and innovation, particularly in response to differing social and cultural contexts and priorities (e.g., Chan, 2017; Freeman, 2011; Heuser, Wang, & Shahid, 2017; Kronborg, 2018; Neihart & Teo, 2013; New Zealand

Ministry of Education, 2012; Vialle, 2011). This section reflects a range of interpretations and approaches, but rather than creating confusion, the reader who takes the time to read with an open mind will find a level of complementarity that adds to the richness of this field.

Introductions to the Individual Chapters

In ▶ Chap. 3, "Towards Exceptionality: The Current Status and Future Prospects of Australian Gifted Education", Shane Phillipson and Albert Ziegler identify some of the challenges that they believe are currently facing gifted education in Australia. The authors provide an overview of the broader educational context in Australia and explain the country's approach to educational policy, governance, management, and funding. They then identify a number of challenges that the country faces, including "the relatively poor performance of Australian students in comparison with students from East Asia and other OECD countries" in the PISA testing. This is followed by a detailed review and evaluation of one federal and two state (Victoria and New South Wales) gifted education policies. There is a very informative outline of current research initiatives that add to our knowledge of what it is like to be gifted in Australia. The reader is then introduced to the *Actiotope Model of Giftedness,* developed by Ziegler to describe the development of exceptional achievement. The authors provide examples of how this model could be used to address some of the challenges identified earlier.

Next, Françoys Gagné's ▶ Chap. 4, "Implementing the DMGT's Constructs of Giftedness and Talent: What, Why, and How?" starts with a brief historical overview of the *Differentiating Model of Giftedness and Talent (DMGT)*. He notes the popularity of the model in Australia, where it is the preferred approach across most states and territories. However, despite its widespread popularity in Australia and beyond, the author laments the fact that the DMGT is selectively used and even the foundational notion of a distinction between giftedness and talent remains unused. What follows is a detailed explanation of the basic foundations of the DMGT, a demonstration of the operationalisation of the two constructs, an illustration of three specific uses of the differentiated constructs and a somewhat pessimistic look into the future impact of the model. In reading this chapter in its entirety and giving the ideas the careful consideration they deserve, one can very easily see how the DMGT has been so misused and misquoted over the past four decades. This information is not peripheral to understanding the DMGT; it is at the very core of it. Any person that professes to understand the model who has not understood these principles is doing its creator a disservice and potentially contributing to its misuse.

Third, Paula Olszewski-Kubilius, Rena Subotnik, Frank Worrell, Janna Wardman, and Liang See Tan collaborated to write ▶ Chap. 5, "Sociocultural Perspectives on the Talent Development Megamodel". The megamodel for talent development originated from a motivation to develop a definition of giftedness and framework for talent development based on psychological science. A strength of this model is its application to a broad range of talent domains and across the lifespan of talent development. The authors explain the key principles the model is based on, its relevance to domain-specific abilities and trajectories, and the critical role of psychosocial skills. The second part of this chapter focuses on the applicability of the megamodel in New Zealand, Singapore, and South Korea. The contributors to these countries' profiles explain how the model could be applied in their education system, but also note areas where the model is not a good fit. They emphasise the need to broaden the model to include sociocultural factors that influence talent development. This chapter concludes with a commitment from the developers to take these concerns and further develop the megamodel to enhance its usability as a tool for practice across different national contexts.

Anne Grant and Anne-Marie Morrissey both have extensive practice and research experience in early education, and their ▶ Chap. 6, "The Young Gifted Learner: What We Know and Implications for Early Educational Practice" examines current understandings about gifted young learners and the implications of this research for early years practice. They note the dearth of research historically into giftedness in early childhood, but point to a recent growth of research activity in Australia. Despite this, the authors point out that there are few resources available to early childhood teachers to guide the identification and the provision of appropriate learning opportunities for 'advanced learners'. They emphasise the importance of a sociocultural approach to understanding and responding to giftedness. This is followed by the tabling of some behaviours characteristic of advanced potential at this level, guidance on how to identify these behaviours and ways to respond to the learning and developmental needs of young gifted children. There is a sense from this chapter that the national frameworks given as examples (from Australia, New Zealand, and Singapore), while not specifically referring to those with advanced potential, reflect an inclusive and culturally responsive philosophy that encourages each child to be considered as an individual with a unique array of dispositions, qualities, and strengths. What these authors identify as missing is research and resources to assist teachers at this level to understand and respond to the specific needs of their advanced young children.

In her ▶ Chap. 7, "Being of Like-Mind: Giftedness in the New Zealand Context," Tracy Riley notes that while there is a widely held view that gifted and talented students benefit from being with like minds, there is little research investigating what it means to be like-minded or what these students see as the benefits and challenges of being together. This chapter is based on the author's research undertaken in New Zealand with students from the ages of 8–12 years. Consistent with the literature, the gifted students in this study reported that engaging with like minds gave them a sense of belonging, with potentially positive effects socially, emotionally, and academically. The author emphasises the importance of gifted and talented students being provided with opportunities to meet, engage, and learn with peers of like abilities and suggests a range of ways that this might be facilitated. She notes that this is even more critical in education systems like New Zealand, where almost all gifted students receive almost all their schooling in mixed ability classrooms alongside their same-age peers.

▶ Chapter 8, "Learning from International Research Informs Academic Acceleration in Australasia: A Case for Consistent Policy" by Susan Assouline, Ann Lupkowski-Shoplik, Cara Wienkes, and Ann Easter discusses acceleration for talent development as practised in Australasia and within the cultural values specific to Australia and New Zealand. This was a bold undertaking, as it is common knowledge that most of the literature on acceleration and its widespread support as an educational option for gifted students emanates from the United States. We know that cultural differences are often nuanced and not necessarily obvious to an outsider. The authors provide a historical overview comparing developments in gifted education in the United States with those in Australia and New Zealand. While there are clear differences, the chronology of key events is very similar. They then examine the research on acceleration across the three contexts and follow this with examples of accelerative practices, underscoring the fact that acceleration is not a singular educational provision, but has at least 20 distinct forms. The authors point to a lack of specific policies on acceleration across most states in the United States, all states and territories in Australia, and nationally in New Zealand. They maintain that acceleration policies are essential to the equalisation of opportunities and can help in translating the research findings on acceleration into universal practice.

Pedro Antonio Sánchez-Escobedo, Ana Karen Camelo-Lavadores, and Angel Alberto Valdés-Cuervo offer some unique insights and perspectives in their ▶ Chap. 9, "Gifted, Talented, and High-Achieving Students and Their Gifted Education in Mexico." Within the chapter they provide a brief overview of the country, its education system, and the history of gifted education in Mexico. They report on a range of initiatives starting from the 1980s, but conclude that it remains an undeserved area of education. The terms gifted, talented, and high-achieving student are often used interchangeably and this confusion amongst teachers acts as an impediment to the identification and support of students with exceptional abilities. There are descriptions of programs and provisions for talent development, high-achieving students, and gifted students. The authors report that as an emerging field, gifted education has received little attention in Mexico. However, there is a body of research emerging from within the country, but as is common in many countries, there is a need to improve the channels of communication between researchers and teachers. They point to the value of partnership approaches, where teachers and researchers work together.

Sheyla Blumen focuses on ethnic-linguistic diverse scholars in her ▶ Chap. 10, "Innovative Practices to Support High-Achieving Deprived Young Scholars in an Ethnic-Linguistic Diverse Latin American Country." She outlines the many challenges facing Latin-American countries, such as poverty, violence, a lack of basic services, corruption, a lack of safety, and weak democratic institutions, resulting in people with depressive symptoms and relatively low aspirations. Peru, the specific focus of this chapter, mirrors the above situation. The author reports that up until the beginning of this century, giftedness was seen as commensurate with general intelligence. However, in a country with such ethnic-linguistic diversity, where different worldviews will impact on how giftedness is conceived, a singular approach to giftedness is inappropriate. The author provides interesting examples of variations in how the construct is understood by different cultural groups. She reports on research initiatives in the country, a range of educational provisions, and makes recommendations for the future. Most notably, she underscores the importance of improving our understanding of talent development from the contexts of ethnic-linguistic diversity.

At the start of their ▶ Chap. 11, "In Search of an Explanation for an Approach-Avoidance Pattern in East Asia: The Role of Cultural Values in Gifted Education," David Yun Dai and Yong Zhao reference the high PISA performance of students from South East Asian countries, which has drawn the attention of educators and policymakers from countries outside the region, and who see the results as an example of academic excellence. However, as the authors note, concerns have been raised about whether such achievement is at the expense of innovation, entrepreneurship, and creativity. While noting that academic achievement is important for an innovation-driven economy, they argue that a valuing of self-expression and a risk-taking disposition are very important in sustaining innovation. In defining gifted education as any school provision towards academic excellence, they address the question of whether or not PISA success represents the success of gifted education. They conclude that high academic scores should not be viewed as representing success in gifted education, as it indicates a value orientation "inconsistent with the spirit of nurturing individuality, independent thinking, and personal creativity". The authors then identify some important implications of their findings for those with a role in gifted education.

In a relatively short time, we have moved from the question of whether or not spirituality has any relationship to giftedness to the question of what is that place and even if spirituality might be considered a domain of giftedness. Russell Walton's and Wilma Vialle's ▶ Chap. 12, "Spirituality and Giftedness: Threading the Path of Identity," examines the relationship between the two. They first discuss the concept of spirituality and its relationship to religion and question whether spirituality could be considered a specific intelligence. This is followed by a review of theoretical models and constructs of spirituality. Within the context of giftedness, the authors note that the gifted are typically characterised by higher levels of spirituality than their non-gifted counterparts. They also discuss the relationship between giftedness, spirituality, and ethical motivations and moral behaviour, noting that the gifted are often considered to have greater moral and ethical 'inclinations' than the non-gifted. There exist in many countries clear mandates for including spiritual development as a curriculum area, for both gifted and non-gifted, although the authors question the extent to which this is happening. They make a compelling argument for the inclusion of spirituality in provisions for the gifted, and the chapter points to numerous ways that this could be done. What remains is a need for further research to build on the foundation laid by these and other researchers.

Conclusion

This first part of the handbook reflects the breadth and diverse nature of interest and activities in gifted and talented education. It brings together research and perspectives from a range of contexts, demonstrating that to understand giftedness and talent, one must be first aware of and responsive to the social and cultural contexts of gifted and talented learners. This section contributes to a much more expansive view of gifted and talented learners and their education. The astute reader will identify many synergies between these chapters and realise that as we better understand and appreciate the social and cultural perceptions of giftedness and talent, the greater the likelihood our provisions, across all domains, will extend to areas where potential was formerly overlooked.

In his chapter Françoys Gagné expresses some disappointment at how his model has been interpreted and for this reason expresses pessimism about the future of the DMGT. This is a model that is arguably one of, if not the most 'popular' approach in the region and represents a lifetime of work. This illustrates the importance of policymakers, teacher educators, researchers, gifted and talented specialists and advisers, and others in leadership roles in this field making a commitment to understanding and working through the complex and competing ideas that are evident in this chapter and throughout this handbook. It also honours the work and effort writers, such as those represented in this chapter make to adding to our knowledge and to a future where gifted and talented students, whatever their culture or social circumstances, will receive education and support commensurate with their abilities, interests, and needs.

References

Bevan-Brown, J. M. (2011). Gifted and talented Māori learners. In R. Moltzen (Ed.), *Gifted and talented: New Zealand perspectives* (3rd ed., pp. 82–110). Auckland, New Zealand: Pearson.

Bishop, R., Berryman, M., & Wearmouth, J. (2014). *Te Kotahitanga: Towards effective education reform for indigenous and other minoritised students*. Wellington, New Zealand: NCER Press.

Chan, D. W. (2017). Gifted education in Asia. In S. I. Pfeiffer (Ed.), *APA handbook of giftedness and talent* (pp. 71–84). Washington, DC: American Psychological Association Press.

Freeman, J. (2011). *What the world does for the gifted and talented*. Paper presented at the Hungarian EU Presidential Conference on Talent Support, Budapest, Hungary, 7–9 April, 2011.

Heuser, B. L., Wang, K., & Shahid, S. (2017). Global dimensions of gifted and talented education: The influence of national perceptions on policies and practices. *Global Education Review, 4*(1), 4–21. Retrieved from https://www.academia.edu/32415619

Kaufman, S. B., & Sternberg, R. J. (2008). Conceptions of giftedness. In S. I. Pfeiffer (Ed.), *Handbook of giftedness in children: Psychoeducational theory, research, and best practices* (pp. 71–91). New York, NY: Springer Science + Business Media.

Kronborg, L. (2018). Gifted education in Australia and New Zealand. In S. I. Pfeiffer (Ed.), *APA handbook of giftedness and talent* (pp. 85–96). Washington, DC: American Psychological Association Press.

Moltzen, R. (2011a). Conceptualising of giftedness and talent. In R. Moltzen (Ed.), *Gifted and Talented: New Zealand Perspectives* (3rd ed., pp. 31–53). Auckland, New Zealand: Pearson.

Moltzen, R. (2011b). Historical perspectives. In R. Moltzen (Ed.), *Gifted and talented: New Zealand perspectives* (3rd ed., pp. 1–30). Auckland, New Zealand: Pearson.

Neihart, M., & Teo, C. T. (2013). Addressing the needs of the gifted in Singapore. *Journal for the Education of the Gifted, 36*(3), 290–306. https://doi.org/10.1177/0162353213494821

New Zealand Ministry of Education. (2012). *Gifted and talented students: Meeting their needs in New Zealand schools*. Retrieved from http://gifted.tki.org.nz/

Phillipson, S. N., & McCann, M. (2007). *Conceptions of giftedness: Socio-cultural perspectives*. New York: Routledge.

Vialle, W. (Ed.). (2011). *Giftedness from an indigenous perspective*. Retrieved from http://www.aaegt.net.au/

Webber, M. (2011). Gifted and proud: On being exceptional and Māori. In P. Whitinui (Ed.), *Kia tangi te tītī: Permission to speak. Wellington, New Zealand* (pp. 227–241). Wellington, New Zealand: NCER Press.

Roger Moltzen PhD, is an Emeritus Professor and former Dean of Education at the University of Waikato. A former teacher and principal, his career focus as an academic has been in the areas of inclusive education and talent development. His recent research has focused on the lives of eminent adults to better understand how talent develops across the lifespan. He is Patron of the New Zealand Association of Gifted Children and editor of Gifted and Talented: New Zealand Perspectives. In 2000 he chaired the Ministerial Working Party on Gifted Education and in 2005 he was awarded the Prime Minister's Supreme Award for Tertiary Teaching Excellence. He is a member of the Ako Aotearoa Academy of Tertiary Teaching Excellence.

Towards Exceptionality: The Current Status and Future Prospects of Australian Gifted Education

3

Shane N. Phillipson and Albert Ziegler

Contents

Introduction	32
Evaluating Gifted Education Policies	33
The Current Educational Context in Australia	36
Regulating Australian Education	37
Funding Education	38
Challenges Facing Australian Education	39
Being Gifted in Australia: Federal and State Policies	41
Policy Attributes	53
Being Gifted in Australia: Current Research Efforts	57
Towards Exceptionality in Australia's *General* Educational Environment	61
Conclusion: Our Crystal Ball of Broad Implications and Challenges	63
Cross-References	64
Appendix	64
References	65

Abstract

In this chapter some challenges currently facing gifted education in Australia will be identified, and we will outline what we believe are its future prospects. To better understand these challenges, however, it is important to place gifted education within a broader educational context, including a discussion of Australian gifted education policy and Australian research into gifted education. We argue that, at best, the relevance of gifted education is being undermined by what

---

S. N. Phillipson (✉)
Faculty of Education, Peninsula Campus, Monash University, Frankston, VIC, Australia
e-mail: shane.phillipson@monash.edu

A. Ziegler
University of Erlangen-Nuremberg, Nuremberg, Germany
e-mail: albert.ziegler@fau.de

© Springer Nature Singapore Pte Ltd. 2021
S. R. Smith (ed.), *Handbook of Giftedness and Talent Development in the Asia-Pacific*,
Springer International Handbooks of Education,
https://doi.org/10.1007/978-981-13-3041-4_2

can be described as a 'crowded classroom'. We conclude that in order to ensure that the needs of Australian students with the potential for exceptional achievement are met, gifted education must evolve in the way it defines giftedness and implements gifted education. This evolution must take advantage of the current regulatory environment, beginning with a National Policy that focuses on the development of exceptionality, supported by a systems-based model of talent development, that is, the actiotope model.

Keywords

Actiotope model · Australia · Evaluation · Gifted education · Policy

The aims in this chapter are to:
1. Review the Australian gifted education research.
2. Critique the current Australian definition of giftedness and talent.
3. Evaluate the Australian gifted education policies using research-based frameworks.
4. Reiterate the benefits of the actiotope model.
5. Provide some broad implications and challenges for future inclusive gifted education practice.

Introduction

In 1985, gifted education in Australia regained its momentum through the formation of the *Australian Association for the Education of the Gifted and Talented Students* (AAEGT; McCann, 2007; Plunkett & Kronborg, 2007). Since then, however, its perceived importance amongst policymakers has waxed and waned, reflecting changes in educational priorities at both State and Federal government jurisdictions.

In this chapter, the Australian policies for gifted education will be evaluated against VanTassel-Baska's (2009) and Phillipson et al.'s (2011) frameworks and a review of the Australian research into gifted education will be provided, with particular reference to Australia's commonly accepted definition of giftedness and talent. We begin with a brief outline of developments in gifted education since 2000. In the most comprehensive review of the Australian gifted educational landscape to date, McCann (2007) noted that policy statements in the 1980s were based largely on Gardner's (1983) multiple intelligences (MI) theory. At the time, submissions to the Australian National Senate Employment, Workplace Relations, Small Business and Education References Committee (2001) from the *Gifted Education Research and Resource Information Centre* (GERRIC) at the University of New South Wales included complaints that MI as a theory had a limited research base and that, as a consequence, it was 'disturbing' that it had influenced the (then) definitions of giftedness (cited in McCann, p. 424). As an alternative, GERRIC and others put forward Gagné's *Differentiated Model of Giftedness and Talent* (DMGT). Clearly, the educational community listened and the DMGT is now widely acknowledged as Australian educators' preferred definition of giftedness (Henderson, 2018; McCann; Merrotsy, 2017).

According to McCann (2007), the attractiveness of the DMGT is that it emphasised the "complex interplay of hereditary factors and the environment" (p. 426). Furthermore, the importance of the child's internal environment (e.g., personality and motivation) and external environment (e.g., family circumstances and educational opportunities) is recognised in the model in the development of gifts into talent. Underpinning the development of talent is the influence of chance in all aspects of the model.

Despite the widespread adoption of Gagné's DMGT in Australian policies, Merrotsy (2017) raised concerns regarding how well the model is understood by the same policymakers and groups. Moreover, he noted that defining the model is not the same as implementing the model (p. 37), where, for example, the methods used to identify gifted students are oftenly not based on the DMGT.

Similarly, Slater (2018) evaluated the gifted education policies in all eight Australian States and Territories, raising concerns regarding the processes used to identify gifted students. In particular, Slater was critical of their failure to use instruments that are "valid and reliable indicators of the gifted construct ... [founded] in peer-reviewed research ... [and] inclusive of minority groups ..." (p. 12). Furthermore, she argued that the methods do not always match the definition of giftedness outlined in their policy. Despite these concerns, Slater concluded that the Australian States of New South Wales (NSW) and South Australia (SA) lead the way in gifted education because of their insistence on using multiple criteria to identify gifted students. Finally, she suggested that a single Australian gifted education policy is key to ensuring consistency in the processes, as well as an important first step in ensuring the instruments are valid and reliable.

This chapter extends Slater's (2018) and Merrotsy's (2017) submissions by using the components and attributes of a high-quality gifted education policy (Phillipson, Phillipson, & Eyre, 2011; VanTassel-Baska, 2009) as our analytical framework. Because of limitations imposed by space, however, our analysis focuses on the States of NSW and Victoria and the Federal government policy documents. Nevertheless, an examination of the two States provides a contrast in terms of a mandated policy (NSW) versus a guideline-only approach (Victoria).

Evaluating Gifted Education Policies

Phillipson, Kaur, and Phillipson (2003) proposed that an effective national environment for gifted education depended on the existence of four components, including: (1) the presence of national gifted education policy; (2) effective implementation of this policy; (3) a relevant research agenda; and (4) the existence of strong advocacy groups (Fig. 1). Furthermore, Phillipson et al. argued that any gifted education policy should be placed within a broader educational context where the education of its gifted students serves both individual and national needs. Of course, each

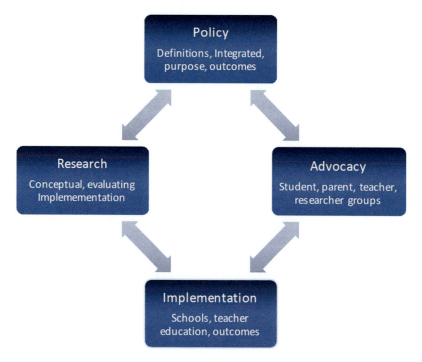

Fig. 1 The four components of an effective gifted education, including policy, advocacy, implementation and research. (Adapted from Phillipson et al., 2003)

component needs to interact with each other and with the key stakeholders, if gifted education is to be effective.

In broad terms, the evaluation of public policy is important because it provides a measure of its effectiveness (Bell & Stevenson, 2006). Policies are almost always designed to meet a social, health, or educational need, and what may be effective when originally implemented may become ineffective over time because of changing contexts. Despite being a 'common sense idea' (Berk & Rossi, 1999, p. 1), the evaluation of policies related to gifted education is rare (Gallagher, 2006; VanTassel-Baska, 2009). In our current evaluation of the States of NSW and Victoria and the Federal government policy documents, we rely on the seminal work of VanTassel-Baska and the Hong Kong example (Phillipson et al., 2011) to begin the process of evaluating Australia's gifted education policy.

In describing a systemic approach to gifted education, Ziegler and co-authors (Ziegler, Balestrini, & Stoeger, 2018; Ziegler & Phillipson, 2012; Ziegler & Stoeger, 2017) argued that the development of exceptionality is the outcome of a system working together, rather than a feature of an individual. In this system, a gifted education policy is one item within the system, alongside students, schools, teachers, and parents, amongst many others. As a consequence of a systems perspective, gifted education should focus on optimising the interactions between the components and not just optimising each individual component. Furthermore, the components need to be coordinated and integrated at the national level.

Specifically, we consider policy as providing the institutional framework to support the development of cultural, social, infrastructural, and didactic educational capitals which, in turn, support the objectives of gifted education. According to Ziegler et al. (2018), *cultural educational capital* refers to value systems and thinking patterns that support the objectives of gifted education, *social educational capital* refers to persons and institutions, and *infrastructural educational capital* refers to the material resources, such as buildings and equipment. Finally, *didactic educational capital* refers to the accumulated know-how, such as qualified teachers and curriculum resources.

Finally, we consider policy as important drivers and consumers of research. In terms of consumers of research, the policy can draw upon existing models of giftedness, identification, models of curriculum differentiation and service evaluation, for example. In terms of driving research, gifted education policy should outline areas where there is a distinct lack of knowledge, particularly when existing knowledge has focused on different contexts.

According to VanTassel-Baska (2009) and Phillipson et al. (2011), an effective gifted education policy has six components and five attributes (Fig. 2). Hence, the alignment of the policy with these components and attributes becomes one indicator of its effectiveness. The six components include: (1) an appropriate, comprehensive and defensible *identification regime*; (2) *program and service provisions*; (3) links with *broader educational policies*; (4) *appropriate preparation of personnel*; and (5) *program management* (VanTassel-Baska, 2009). The sixth is an overarching component which is termed as a *clearly articulated set of aims and objectives* (Phillipson et al., 2003). The details of each component are highlighted in Tables 2–25. The five attributes for judging the quality of a gifted education policy include its *clarity, comprehensiveness, connectedness, feasibility*, and a *basis in research* (Tables 26–30).

To the best of our knowledge, there have been no attempts to fully evaluate the effectiveness of the Australian gifted education environment. In our chapter, we initiate this evaluation by focusing on the policy itself and its interdependence on

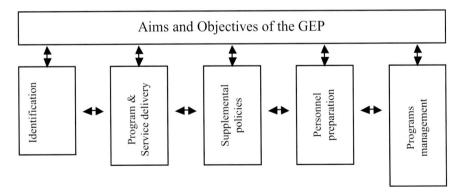

Fig. 2 The six components of a high quality policy for gifted education. (Adapted from VanTassel-Baska 2009, and Phillipson et al. 2011)

research. Because of space limitations in this chapter, we are not able to look in depth at whether or not implementation strategies or advocacy groups are effective in meeting their objectives. We do note, however, Henderson's (2018) anecdotal conclusion that the various advocacy groups are largely effective in meeting their objectives and, hence, contribute positively to the gifted education environment.

We also draw attention to the relatively large corpus of Australian research describing implementation strategies and the attitudes of participants within interventions (Luburic & Jolly, 2019). Relatively fewer research focuses on the nature of giftedness and identification issues. A closer examination of this and other research will also show that Gagné's DMGT is not always mentioned and when it is, the model is often mentioned only in passing. Despite its ubiquity as the preferred model of giftedness and talent in Australian education and policies, we conclude that as a model of giftedness, there is little evidence that the DMGT has made an impact in Australian research, casting doubt as to its utilitarian value.

To provide the reader with the appropriate background, we present a brief description of the demographic and policy context of the Australian educational environment.

The Current Educational Context in Australia

Australia has a current population of around 25,250,000 persons (Australian Bureau of Statistics, 2019b), living mainly in urban areas surrounding the capital cities of each of the seven States and Territories. In the 2016 census, Australians were outlined as being born in nearly 200 different countries, speak more than 300 languages, and adhere to 100 religions (Australian Bureau of Statistics, 2017). Furthermore, they identify with 300 different ancestries broadly grouped into 'Australian' (31% of total population), followed by Northeast Asia (6.2%), Southeast Asia (4%), Central Asia (2.9%), Oceania (2.4%), sub-Saharan Africa (1%), Southern and Eastern Europe (0.8%), North Africa and Middle East (0.3%), and Americas (0.1%; idcommunity, 2017).

As well as meeting the needs of a culturally diverse population, Australian schools are also expected to implement inclusive practices to ensure that no child is disadvantaged because of social and cultural background, gender, learning need, disability, or where they live. Such expectations reflect the Australian Federal government initiatives in curriculum development and teacher education. Supporting this diversity we describe an educational system that has seen significant changes since 2000, including the increasing regulation of Australian education, in ways that education is funded and the opening of Australian education to the international market.

Despite these changes, there continues to be debate within the Australian community on issues centred on the cost of education, falling educational standards, the purpose and quality of the primary and secondary curriculum, the quality of teachers, and the role of parents in the education of their children (Masters, 2016). Although gifted education is found in all Australian educational policies, there is a sense that the needs of gifted students are not always given the same priority as students with other needs. The challenges of gifted education within what can be described as a 'crowded classroom' (Masters) are significant.

Nevertheless, an Australian education is viewed internationally as highly desirable, and Australia is considered a sought-after place to pursue studies, with education and related activities valued in 2017 at AUD32.2B (Australian Bureau of Statistics, 2018), being the third largest export earner, behind iron ore and coal. This figure is expected to increase over the next 5–10 years (Deloitte Access Economics and EduWorld, 2015).

According to Catriona Jackson (cited in Universities Australia, 2018), the maintenance of a highly regulated education system is crucial to ensure continual growth of international enrolments. Indeed, the regulatory environment, with a focus on 'quality assurance' (Future Unlimited, n.d.), is being marketed internationally as one of a number of desirable features of a higher education in Australia.

Regulating Australian Education

The implementation of educational policy in Australia lies with the eight Australian States and Territories, including the Australian Capital Territory, NSW, South Australia, Northern Territory, Queensland, Tasmania, Victoria, and Western Australia (Lubric & Jolly, 2019). Within each jurisdiction are dedicated departments of education. In Victoria, for example, the *Department of Education and Training* (DET) oversees the management and implementation of government (or Public) school education, including early childhood, primary, and secondary education, and the registration of non-government schools. Teachers wanting to teach in Victorian government and nongovernment schools, such as those with religious affiliations and those designated as independent (or private) schools must be registered with the *Victorian Institute of Teaching* (VIT; 2019). The other Australian States and Territories have similar organisational structures and requirements.

The Australian Federal government has enacted the *Australian Curriculum Assessment and Reporting Authority* (ACARA; 2016) to develop and implement a national primary and secondary school curricula and the *Australian Institute for Teaching and School Leadership* (AITSL, 2017) to regulate national standards in initial teacher education (ITE) and school leadership. The responsibility for setting national standards in early childhood education lies with *Australian Children's Education & Care Quality Authority* (ACECQA; n.d.). Finally, the *Australian Skills Quality Authority* (ASQA; n.d.) is the national regulator for the sector related to vocational education and training.

The creation of these organisations appears to be the result of recent efforts to unify Australian education and to raise educational standards. ACARA's responsibilities include the implementation of national standardised testing of all students in numeracy and literacy (National Assessment Program—Literacy and Numeracy, 2016). In relation to gifted and talented students, ACARA states that "[they] are entitled to rigorous, relevant and engaging learning opportunities drawn from the Australian Curriculum and aligned with their individual learning needs, strengths, interests, and goals" (para. 1). It describes giftedness in terms of three different models: Gagné's (2008) DMGT,

Tannenbaum's (2003) Sea Star Model, and Renzulli's (1978) Three-Ring Model, conceding that there is no universally accepted definition of giftedness.

Overarching ACARA ACECQA, and ASQA is the *Australian Qualifications Framework* (AQF, n.d.), being responsible for regulating the learning outcomes of all schools, vocational education and training providers, and higher education institutions in order to ensure that there is consistency in terminology and standards. Finally, the *Tertiary Education Quality and Standards Agency* (TEQSA, 2017a) undertakes compliance and quality assessments of Australia's higher education sector. TEQSA (2017b) is also responsible for the quality of courses offered to students studying in Australia on student visas, including primary, secondary, and tertiary education, issuing *Commonwealth Register of Institutions and Courses for Overseas Students* (CRICOS) registration to providers of primary, secondary, and tertiary education. Furthermore, TEQSA (2017a) provides reviews of the AQF and the response by the higher education sector on issues relating to sexual assault and harassment.

In 2015, the *Teacher Education Advisory Group* (TEMAG; Australian Government Department of Education, 2017) released their findings on how the Federal government can support providers of initial teacher education. In response, the Federal Department of Education and Training implemented a range of reforms, including requiring all students wanting to enrol in initial teacher education programs to be assessed for their potential for teaching. Many Australian universities are using commercially produced selection tools based on judgements of hypothetical scenarios such as CASPer (n.d.) test for this purpose.

In addition, AITSL (2015) requires all graduating teachers to demonstrate levels of personal literacy and numeracy skills in the top 30% of the Australian adult population. Accordingly, graduating students must complete the *Literacy and Numeracy Test for Initial Teacher Education* (LANTITE) successfully. In Victoria, for example, the VIT does not grant teacher registration unless the applicant has successfully completed the LANTITE.

Students graduating from initial teacher education must meet the standards relating to AQF, AITSL, and the VIT (including the Federal government's standards of literacy and numeracy). In the face of these reforms, it is not surprising that commentators in the media as well as within education have noted that Australia is one of the most regulated countries in the world in terms of education (c.f., Masters, 2016).

Funding Education

Australian education is funded by governments, both State and Federal, the contributions from Australian households and contributions from international students. Recent figures from the Australian Bureau of Statistics (2019a) estimated that the total (Federal, State and Local government) expenditure on education in 2016–2017 was AU$91,271M, an increase of 20.3% from 2011 to 2012. Of this amount, 51.9% was spent on primary and secondary education, 36.2% on tertiary education (universities and TAFEs) and 6% on pre-school and other undefinable educational levels.

In 2011, the Australian Government released its review into school funding (Gonski et al., 2011). Known as the Gonski report, the review made note of the relatively poor performance of Australian students in international and national tests of academic achievement. The Gonski report recommended a fundamental change in the way that schools are funded, irrespective of where students live and whether or not they attend government, Catholic, or independent schools.

Although the costs related to the purchase of textbooks, private tutoring, and living costs are difficult to estimate, OECD (2019) estimates of private spending directly related to school fees, for example, show that in 2015 Australian households contributed 0.20% of GDP to early childhood education. This figure is exceeded only by 6 of the 35 OECD countries, including Iceland (0.23%), Israel (0.31%), Norway (0.27%), Portugal (0.22%), Slovenia (0.28%) and the UK (0.23%). On the other hand, Australian figures exceed that of Finland (0.13%) and Germany (0.17%), amongst others.

In terms of primary education, Australian spending of 0.23% of GDP is exceeded by Chile (0.27%), Mexico (0.26%) and Spain (0.22%; OECD, 2019). On the other hand, Australian figures far exceed those of Finland (0.01%), Germany (0.02%), the UK (0.18%), and the USA (0.12%). In terms of secondary education, Australian spending is exceeded only by New Zealand (0.53%). The Australian figures far exceed that of Finland (0.03%) by a factor of 16, the USA (0.16%) by a factor of 3, and Germany (0.27%) by a factor of 2. Finally, the OECD estimates are that Australian spending on tertiary education is exceeded only by Chile (1.31%), the UK (1.33%), and the USA (1.67%). The comparisons show that Australian figures far exceed that of Finland (0.06%), Germany (0.19%), and Japan (0.94%).

More broadly, a significant proportion of parents support their children's musical, dramatic, and dance interests through after-school providers. A survey of 2700 Australian students across Grades 5–12 showed that nearly 30% of students learned to sing or play instruments outside of their regular school (McPherson, Osborne, Barrett, Davidson, & Faulkner, 2015). The financial burden was cited as the main impediment to more students learning an instrument.

Although country comparisons need to be made cautiously, it is clear that parental and community perceptions of the cost of education in Australia are likely to be based on private spending patterns rather than through contributions from personal and other taxes. When households directly contribute to their child's education, costs such as school fees, uniforms, and associated items are uppermost in the minds of many Australian families. The direct costs of education are topics of intense media debate, particularly when government elections are imminent.

Challenges Facing Australian Education

It seems paradoxical that, in spite of international perceptions of the high quality of Australian education and the funding towards education, the results of international tests of academic achievement such as PISA and TIMMS continue to emphasise the relatively poor performance of Australian students in comparison with students from

East Asia and other OECD countries (cf. Gonski, 2018; Masters, 2016; Phillipson, Stoeger, & Ziegler, 2013; White, Graham, & Blaas, 2018). Within Australia, recent *National Assessment Program—Literacy and Numeracy* (NAPLAN) results have highlighted that the development of literacy and numeracy amongst Australian children differs from region to region and State to State. For example, the NAPLAN National Report showed that Year 9 students varied across six bands (Bands 5–10) of achievement. Overall, NAPLAN scores have shown that there have been declines at all levels of achievement (Masters, 2016).

Masters (2016) outlined the five major challenges facing Australian education. The first of the five challenges focused on equipping students to be ready for the twenty-first century, arguing that literacy in reading, mathematics, and science is fundamental to equipping students for this century. However, Masters noted that students also need to be taught skills that are valued by employers, including problem-solving and collaborative skills. Masters also described the classroom as 'crowded' (p. 8), with students learning many subjects superficially rather than learning fewer subjects in depth. Other research showed that many parents want schools to be involved in teaching their child about cyber safety, sexual education and social skills (Phillipson, S. N. & Phillipson, S., 2017). Phillipson and Phillipson also suggested that parents' views differ according to year level, with parents wanting their school's involvement in nonacademic areas to decrease as their child progresses from primary to secondary school. Hence, the focus on secondary schools should be on academic skills. There were also indicators of differences based on membership of a cultural and ethnic group. For example, parents identifying themselves as Indian feel that schools are the best place for sex education.

The second challenge refers to the disparities in student academic achievement in Australian schools, largely based on socio-economic lines. As Masters (2016) and others have noted, increased funding for some schools must be associated to changes in curriculum, teacher quality, and instructional amendments.

Masters' (2016) third challenge focused on reducing the 'long tail' of underachieving students who, year-on-year, fall further behind the expectations for each year level. Masters suggested that personalised teaching and learning, rather than a lock-step curriculum, would go a long way to addressing this challenge.

The fourth challenge that Masters (2016) addressed was that some children are not school ready and so are at risk of ongoing low achievement. As Masters pointed out, "Some children are at risk because of developmental delays or special learning needs … limited mastery of English … impoverished living circumstances … [or] multiple forms of disadvantage" (p. 18), indicating that some children may not be ready for the formal school environment. However, Masters argued that the problem lies not with the child but with their school because all children are ready to learn, irrespective of their background. Hence, the challenge is for teachers and schools to be flexible in their expectations for each child.

Masters' (2016) fifth challenge draws heavily on Hattie's (2011) argument that quality teachers make a significant difference to educational standards. As we have previously noted in this chapter, national standards are being introduced to ensure that candidates enter initial teacher education for the appropriate reasons and graduate with adequate levels of literacy and numeracy. Additionally, AITSL has issued national standards that all graduates must attain. Of relevance to this chapter are standards relating to the demonstration of:

- Knowledge of teaching strategies that are responsive to the learning strengths and needs of students from diverse linguistic, cultural, religious, and socio-economic backgrounds (1.3).
- Broad knowledge and understanding of the impact of culture, cultural identity, and linguistic background on the education of students from Aboriginal and Torres Strait Islander backgrounds (1.4).
- Knowledge and understanding of strategies for differentiating teaching to meet the specific learning needs of students across the full range of abilities (1.5).
- Understanding strategies for working effectively, sensitively, and confidentially with parents/carers (7.3).

Under the current regulatory environment, universities are not prescribed how these standards are reached, leading to the possibility that there is still variability in graduate teachers' capacity to meet these (and other) objectives.

Masters (2016) and Rickards (2016) proposed that raising the status of the teaching profession can help lift teaching standards. This can be achieved by raising the minimum educational standards of entry into all ITE courses, by increasing starting salaries for graduate teachers or restricting ITE graduates. The South Australian Government has introduced this latter requirement, with the Victorian government considering this option. Because these strategies will reduce university income from student fees (Rickards, 2016) and government costs for education, the likelihood that such strategies will be widely implemented is low.

Given that the focus of this chapter is the Australian policies for gifted education, we elaborate on one Federal and two State policies in the next section. To assist this elaboration, we use the framework outlined in VanTassel-Baska (2009) and Phillipson et al. (2011). We stress, however, that our assessment is based on the policies as published online rather than associated documents and the views of policymakers.

Being Gifted in Australia: Federal and State Policies

All departments of education in the eight Australian States and Territories, make reference to the needs of gifted and talented students (Henderson, 2018; Merrotsy, 2017; Slater, 2018). Although all State and Territory policies are independent from each other and the Federal government in terms of the development and implementation of educational policy, the Federal government provides funding incentives if the States and Territories adopt the National Curriculum as set out in ACARA (n.d.). Hence, it is not surprising if the States and Territories either adopt or incorporate the

National Curriculum into their own documents. In addition, AITSL requires all teachers to understand and implement State and Territory policies, including those related to gifted education.

Despite all eight States and Territories referring to the needs of gifted students, policies are mandated in only six, with Victoria and Queensland providing only guidelines (Merrotsy, 2017; Slater, 2018). Although Merrotsy, Slater, and others (e.g., Henderson, 2018) noted that Gagné's DMGT is commonly described as the underlying basis for gifted education in all States and Territories, there are discrepancies in a number of key areas, including who is responsible for the identification of gifted students (e.g., whole school vs principal vs teacher), the basis for identification (i.e., school-wide approach vs multiple criterion, amongst others) and the methods used to identify gifted students (i.e., responses to classroom activities vs self-nomination, teacher nomination, amongst several others).

In accordance with Slater's (2018) method, we used publicly available documents to evaluate the current NSW policy and the Victorian guideline against the six components and five attributes. Although we understand that supplementary unpublished documents may provide information that expands on key points of the policy and guideline, we focus only on these documents. The evaluation of the Federal government policy on gifted education focuses on three documents.

In the evaluation of the NSW government policy, our analysis focuses on the three documents that describe the current policy. We note that the new policy for gifted education is planned for implementation in 2021, and so we also refer to the future NSW policy. We also note the NSW Centre for Education Statistics and Evaluation (2019) have also released an accompanying review of the gifted education literature. Finally, the evaluation of the Victorian policy on gifted education focuses on one document. All documents are shown in the Appendix.

Our findings are presented component by component, beginning with an *Overall Statement of Aims and Objectives—Preamble*. To support our findings, we present a limited number of tables that provide a detailed comparison of each component.

1. **Overall Statement of Aims and Objectives: Preamble**
   Table 1 summarises each policy's preamble. As expected, the summary reveals remarkable differences in how the policies are presented, making it difficult to move from one jurisdiction to another. However, we suggest that these differences could be interpreted positively in that they are evident of a high degree of independence. The lack of reference to the ACARA policy could change over time, given the linking of State funding to the National curriculum.
2. **Overall Statement of Aims and Objectives: Clear Articulation of Aims and Objectives of Gifted Education**
   In Table 2 there is an outline of the aims and objectives of gifted education in each of the three jurisdictions. Although all policies focus on students, our findings demonstrate a lack of procedural consistency across the three

Table 1 Overall statement of aims and objectives: Preamble

Jurisdiction	Details
Federal government	Although all states and territories have agreed to embrace the Australian curriculum, ACARA cannot mandate which subjects are taught or how it is implemented. The Australian curriculum aims to support teachers in meeting needs of students, builds on a 3-dimensional process designed to meet the learning needs of all students, [and] refers to the relevant legislative, administrative, and organisational policies and processes required for teachers according to school stage.
NSW	The current NSW policy is described over three documents. However, the policy does not refer to ACARA. The document *Gifted and Talented Policy* sets out the broad aims and objectives and the roles and responsibilities of key personnel. The document *Policy and Implementation Strategies for the Education of Gifted and Talented Students* sets out the responsibilities of key personnel. The document *guidelines for the use of strategies to support gifted and talented students* provides information on acceleration, grouping, and counselling options. The 2021 policy refers to the responsibility of schools to support the talent development of students with high potential and those who are gifted. The document does not refer to ACARA. The review of the literature suggests that this is to ensure that gifted students meet their potential and highlights the research that suggests that gifted students do not always realise their potential.
Victoria	The Victoria Department of Education and Training (DET) doesn't appear to have a policy for gifted education. Nevertheless, the DET outlines its strategy for gifted education in *Aiming High: A strategy for gifted and talented children and young people (2014–2019) as a series of aims.* Despite the absence of the term 'early childhood', the focus of this document is on early childhood education. Furthermore, much of the document refers to what DET intends to achieve rather than outlining what schools are required to do. A detailed search of the Victorian DET website showed that Most, if not all, of the supplementary resources devoted to the identification of giftedness and/or talent focuses on early childhood education. Of these most are addressed to parents. Most of these resources are between one to two pages and cover the same format. For example, the publication *Teach gifted and talented students*[a] begins with the reasons why schools should meet the needs of gifted students. This is followed by some examples of school programs that have been adopted by some Victorian schools. There are then examples of individualised learning programs. The final two sections cover definitions and 'more information'. Under definitions, the terms 'gifted' and 'talent' are briefly described. The final section leads the reader to several other DET resources.

[a]https://www.education.vic.gov.au/school/teachers/learningneeds/Pages/gifted.aspx

jurisdictions. The current NSW policy is highly prescriptive, consistent with its purpose to ensure compliance. On the other hand, the Victorian policy provides schools with a high degree of autonomy, suggesting schools develop a school-based policy.

Table 2 Overall statement of aims and objectives: Clear articulation of aims and objectives of gifted education

Jurisdiction	Details
Federal government	Gifted and talented students are entitled to a rigorous, relevant, and engaging learning opportunities and aligned with their individual learning needs, strengths, interests, and goals. Teachers must differentiate teaching to meet learning needs across full range of abilities.
NSW	The objective of the policy is to identify and maximise learning outcomes of gifted and talented students in public schools. These outcomes include high achievement, originality, problem-solving, higher-order thinking skills, and creativity (*Policy and Implementation Strategies for the Education of Gifted and Talented Students*, p. 11). The *Senior Curriculum Policy Officer* (SCPO; gifted and talented) monitors the implementation of this policy and will report, as required, to the director, NSW curriculum, and learning innovation Centre. The SCPO works with regions and school communities (parents, principals, teachers, and counsellors). *Regions* are responsible the coordination of provision and the professional development of relevant personnel. *School communities* are responsible for the identification of students, the fostering of parent-school partnerships, the provision of a wide range of programs, and the monitoring and evaluating of programs. *Principals* are responsible for the implementation of the policy. *Teachers* are responsible for the identification, selection, and implementation of strategies. Finally, schools have a responsibility to develop their own gifted education policy. Furthermore, it is the responsibility of the school community to develop and evaluate gifted programs (*Policy and Implementation Strategies for the Education of Gifted and Talented Students*, p. 9). Although there is little information regarding how programs should be evaluated, school communities are encouraged to liaise with their regional and state officers. The NSW High Potential and Gifted Education Policy (2021) outlines the aims and objectives and the various responsibilities of key personnel. In a departure from the current policy, the 2021 policy emphasises the need for evidence to inform practice and decision-making.

Victoria	The 'vision' of the guideline is to:
	  a) Identify all 'gifted and talented students', irrespective of their language, cultural socio-economic circumstance, or where they live.
	  b) Provide them with a differentiated 'learning experience and acceleration and extension'.
	  c) Establish partnerships with parents/caregivers.
	  d) Support early childhood professionals with resources.
	  e) Build community understanding (p. 5).
	The objective is to ensure that 'gifted and talented learners' are intellectually challenged and their social and emotional development supported to reduce the potential for social emotional issues, such as boredom and depression, and to enhance societal benefits (p. 5).

Table 3 Identification: Operational definition(s) of giftedness that acknowledge both general and specific abilities

Jurisdiction	Details

Federal government	In *gifted and talented students*, three models are described, including:
	    Gagné's (2003, 2008) DMGT, where (a) students *distinctly above average* in intellectual, creative, social, and physical domains are gifted; (b) students *distinctly above average* in one or more areas of student performance are talented; and (c) schools are important if students are to develop their *gifts or high abilities* into *talents or high achievements*.
	    Tannenbaum's sea star model (2003) where (1) there is a distinction between *giftedness in a child being their potential to become an adult with a developed talent* (Para. 6); (2) producers *produce ideas or things* and performers who *interpret or re-create* these things or ideas; and (3) five factors influence the process, including cognitive, personality, and environment (Para. 6).
	    Renzulli's three-ring model where giftedness results from the development of a cluster of three clusters of human traits (above-average general ability, high levels of creativity, high levels of task commitment) and their application in a valuable area of human performance (Para. 8).

NSW	Giftedness is first defined as "potential distinctly beyond the average for the student's age and encompasses a broad range of abilities in the intellectual, creative, socio-emotional and physical domains. Talent denotes achievement distinctly beyond the average for a student's age as a result of application to training and practice" (*Gifted and Talented Policy,* Para. 3). The policy adopts Gagné's (2003) DMGT, where "gifted students are those whose potential is distinctly above average in one or more of the following domains of human ability: Intellectual, creative, social, and physical. On the other hand, talented students are those whose skills are distinctly above average in one or more areas of human performance" (*Policy and Implementation Strategies for the Education of Gifted and Talented Students*, p. 6). Although the two documents are part of the same policy, the two definitions are broadly similar but not identical. More broadly, the policy documents recognise that students may be underachievers. In a departure from the current policy, the 2021 policy refers to high potential, gifted, and highly gifted students. The accompanying literature review doesn't refer to the DMGT as the preferred model. Nevertheless, the review highlights Gagné's (2009) DMGT as providing the framework for understanding the "...internal and external drivers of talent development" (p. 5).
Victoria	The *Aiming High* document refers to Gagné's (2004) DMGT as the adopted definition. In contrast to Gagné's definition, the document extends 'giftedness' to the top 10–15%. No prevalence is offered for talent. The document warns that the identification of gifted and talented children may be problematic because expressions of giftedness may vary from culture to culture. Accordingly, the document suggests that the identification process "must be tailored to the individual" (*Aiming High*, p. 9). Although each child is unique, the document describes some characteristics that may aid the identification of intellectual giftedness, including learning at a faster pace, advanced speech, and language skills, amongst others. These skills are broadly in line with Gagné's (2004) suggestions (p. 122).

3. **Identification: Operational Definition(s) of Giftedness that Acknowledge both General and Specific Abilities**

   In Table 3 there is a description of the operational definition of giftedness. Consistent with previous observations, the policies include definitions that are based on Gagné's DMGT. Although the citations differ slightly, the version of the DMGT is similar. However, we note that the citations are no later than 2008 and we understand that the DMGT has undergone a number of refinements since that time. Despite ACARA describing two other models (i.e., Tannenbaum's Sea Star Model and Renzulli's Three-Ring Model), they have not been adopted by the two State policies.

4. **Identification: Multiple (at Least Three) Criteria Used to Identify each Category of Giftedness**

   Table 4 outlines the criteria used to identify gifted students. However, the link with operational definitions is not explicit. Gagné's DMGT refers to four domains of gifts, namely, *intellectual, creative, social*, and *physical*, and several areas of talent. It appears that only one of the policies specifies 'multiple' criteria for each of the domains and areas. For the Victorian policy, it is up to the school to identify and implement the methods used to identify giftedness and talent. Furthermore, Gagné also recognises levels within each domain of gift and areas of talent. Only the current NSW policy mentions the need to identify degrees of giftedness.

Table 4 Identification: Multiple (at least three) criteria used to identify each category of giftedness

Jurisdiction	Details
Federal government	No criteria are described.
NSW	The process should use 'multiple criteria' and from multiple sources to ensure that all domains of giftedness and areas of talent are identified (*Policy and Implementation Strategies for the Education of Gifted and Talented Students,* p. 8). Furthermore, in identification processes degrees of giftedness must be recognised (p. 8). The *NSW High Potential and Gifted Education Policy* (2021) refers to multiple means to identify students with high potential, gifted, and highly gifted students and the importance of identifying students from diverse backgrounds, including those with disability, cultural, and socio-economic backgrounds.
Victoria	In the document, it is acknowledged that because identification is complex, the methods are also complex. However, details of any methods are not provided. A detailed search of the Victorian DET website showed that most, if not all, of the supplementary resources devoted to the identification of giftedness and/or talent focus on early childhood education. Of these, most are addressed to parents.

5. **Identification: Instruments Sensitive to Underrepresented Groups of Students**
   Instruments are not described in the Federal government documents. On the other hand, in the three NSW documents, there is an outline of the need for school communities to develop identification strategies that are effective, equitable, and defensible, taking into account culture, socio-economic background, social-emotional issues, metacognitive skills, learning difficulties, conduct disorder, gender, and disability, amongst others. The 2021 policy includes detailed reference to underrepresented groups.

   Finally, a number of underrepresented groups, including Koori, English as an Additional Language (EAL) learners, cultures that define giftedness and talent differently, children with disabilities, and those children with a unique learning style are mentioned in the Victorian document. As previously mentioned, however, most of the resources in gifted education focus on early childhood. Finally, in both State policies, reference is made to the need to develop identification strategies that can identify underrepresented groups. These groups of students are at risk of not being identified.

6. **Identification: Equally Stringent Standards Applied to all Instruments Used to Identify Students**
   A range of identification methods are described, including: responses to classroom activities; nominations by teacher, peer, self or parents; off-level testing; standardised tests of creativity; IQ tests; observations; behavioural checklists; and academic grades which are recommended only in the current NSW policy. In all three policies, however, there is little mention of required minimum standards of validity or reliability in the instruments used to identify giftedness and/or talent.

   Because the details of instruments used by NSW and Victoria are missing, it is difficult to establish whether or not the instruments are assessed for their validity and reliability in the Australian context. However, the NSW High Potential and Gifted Education Policy (2021) and accompanying literature review insist on the use of instruments that have a strong basis in evidence, including 'validity and reliability', and the use of local norms to assist in identification (p. 14).

7. **Identification: Clear Specifications that Identification May Occur in all Categories of Giftedness Should be Cited**
   It is not specified in the Federal policy that identification should occur in all categories of giftedness. According to the current and future NSW policy, giftedness occurs in four domains (namely, *intellectual, creative, social, and physical*). In the current and updated NSW policies, the identification processes appear to focus on intellectual and creative, with little reference to the social-emotional or physical domains. The Victorian policy refers to each of the four domains of giftedness and 'one or more areas' of talent (p. 8), but there is no clear specification regarding the need to identify all categories of giftedness.

8. **Identification: A Systematic Process for Linking Identification Procedures to Programs and Services**
   There appears to be no link between identification and provision in either of the policy documents, other than the NSW reference to it being 'fundamental'. In

the NSW High Potential and Gifted Education Policy (2021), a clear link is made between identification and an assessment of the learning needs of each student.

9. **Identification: A Clearly Delineated Process for Equitable Decision-Making at Screening, Identification, Selection and Placement (Including Appeals Process)**
Both the current and future NSW policies describe the process in detail, but the only exception is any reference to an 'appeals process'.
10. **Program Delivery and Service: A Match between the Mechanisms Used to Identify Students and the Educational Programs and Services that Are Provided**
The need to match mechanisms used to identify students and the programs that they receive are mentioned in both the current and future NSW policies. In the current policy, teachers must select and implement 'a variety of teaching strategies' and 'consider the individual needs of... students' so as to include a range of gifted and talented students in their class. Again, however, no details are provided. In the NSW High Potential and Gifted Education Policy (2021), there are details on the merits of a number of implementation strategies.
11. **Program Delivery and Service: Contact Time for Gifted Programs Should be No Less than 150 Minutes per Week**
None of the three policies refer to minimum contact time, except the current NSW reference to 'daily basis'. On the other hand, acceleration and grouping imply more or less permanent contact time.
12. **Program Delivery and Service: Curriculum for each Subject Should be Modified beyond the Standard Curriculum to Include Acceleration, Complexity, Depth, Challenge, and Creativity and Should be Based on Appropriately Designed Curriculum for Gifted Students**
Table 5 outlines each policy's reference to curriculum modification. All three documents refer to acceleration, grouping, and curriculum modification. Although the current NSW policy does not provide curriculum models, several textbooks are listed to provide source materials that could be used. Of these, three showcase US models, with one from Australia. However, the Australian example predates the Gagné definition. The presumption is that teachers are free to choose a model from any of four textbooks.

As already mentioned, the NSW High Potential and Gifted Education Policy (2021) provides advice on how to implement a modified curriculum using many of the stated models. Moreover, the future policy stresses the importance in evaluating the outcomes of any differentiation.
13. **Program Delivery and Service: Instruction Should be Appropriately Diverse in Technique and Include an Emphasis on Problem-Solving, Critical Thinking, Creative Thinking, and Research Skills**
Recommendations regarding instructional approaches are described in Table 6. Reference to diverse instructional strategies is in both the Federal and NSW policy. On the other hand, a number of hypothetical exemplars as well as advice to early childhood teachers and parents are provided in the Victorian policy.

Table 5 Program delivery and service: Curriculum for each subject should be modified beyond the standard curriculum to include acceleration, complexity, depth, challenge and creativity and should be based on appropriately designed curriculum for gifted students

Jurisdiction	Details
Federal government	Content modification *should begin* by first considering what is their age-equivalent content. Content *may need* to be more complex, abstract. And varied and to organise differently. Breadth of content *may need* to be increased. Pace of teaching *may need* to be increased. Learning environment *may need* to be adjusted. Decisions on what is adjusted depends on the needs of the student, including their learning goals at that point of their learning.
NSW	Specific reference is made to differentiate the curriculum in order to cater for differences between gifted students and their age peers. A range of learning strategies are offered, including extension activities, enrichment, contract work, hypothesis testing, and individual research, amongst others. The NSW High Potential and Gifted Education Policy (2021) details a number of strategies to differentiate the curriculum.
Victoria	The document outlines what the DET intends to do to support school-based gifted education policies, including resources that 'may address' (*Aiming High*, p. 19) identification, extension and enrichment activities, acceleration, and ability grouping.

Table 6 Program delivery and service: Instruction should be appropriately diverse in technique and include an emphasis on problem-solving, critical thinking, creative thinking and research skills

Jurisdiction	Details
Federal government	Thinking processes *may be* adjusted to include higher-order thinking, problem-solving, critical and creative thinking, and individual choice. Product of student learning *may shift* from summarising content to transforming learning. Product of student learning *may include* the use of authentic tasks and address real problems. A number of examples of curriculum modification are provided.
NSW	Although the policy documents mention that "gifted students learn at faster rates, find, solve and act on problems more readily and manipulate abstract ideas and make connections" (p. 11), the development of these traits is not specifically mentioned. However, they are implied as components of instructional strategies. The NSW High Potential and Gifted Education Policy (2021) outlines the difficulties faced by teachers when implementing differentiation in a mixed-ability classroom. The policy also outlines the need for gifted students to be scaffolded. Although the policy includes diversity, there is little mention of the advised skills.
Victoria	No mention is made regarding diversity of instruction.

14. **Program Delivery and Service: Assessment Practices Should be Matched to the Curriculum Objectives, with off-Level Standardised Tests, Performance-Based Tasks and Portfolio Approaches Encouraged**

    Only the National and current and future NSW policies explicitly refer to the need to assess student outcomes and the effectiveness of programs and services. However, no details are provided as to the criteria used to determine effectiveness.

15. **Program Delivery and Service: Programs Should be Modified and Extended to Cater for at-Risk and Highly Gifted Student Populations**

    The response from each policy is summarised in Table 7. The importance of developing programs that meet the needs of at-risk student populations is recognised in all policies. Both the current and future NSW documents refer to different levels of giftedness. The current policy refers to the distinction between gifted and talented students, whereas the NSW High Potential and Gifted Education Policy (2021) refers to three levels of potential, including students with high potential, gifted, and highly gifted students.

16. **Program Delivery and Service: Options that Allow for the Accelerated Rate of Student Learning**

    Only the current and future NSW policies have reference to acceleration as an option.

17. **Program Delivery and Service: Provision for the Support of the Social-Emotional Development of Students**

    None of the three policies refer to the need to provide services and programs that develop students' social-emotional development. Although both the current and

Table 7 Program delivery and service: Programs should be modified and extended to cater for at-risk and highly gifted student populations

Jurisdiction	Details
Federal government	Gifted and talented students are not homogenous and, hence, may require different adjustments based on their individual learning needs, interests, strengths, and goals (*Who are gifted and talented students?* Para. 1) as well as students with those with specific learning disability (*Personalized learning* Para. 3 and students with a disability (1.6).
	Although the highly gifted are not specifically mentioned, ACARA does refer to the heterogeneity of gifted students. (*Who are gifted and talented students?* Para. 1).
	At-risk populations are mentioned in AITSL under *Physical, social and intellectual development and characteristics of students* (1.1) and *Students with diverse linguistic, cultural, religious and socio-economic backgrounds* (1.3). The needs of *Aboriginal and Torres Strait Islander students* are mentioned in 1.4.
NSW	Although the policy recognises that the gifted and talented are at risk of not being identified, there is no explicit requirement that programs should be modified to cater for at-risk students.
	However, the overall impression is that the policy must meet the needs of a diverse student group.
	The NSW High Potential and Gifted Education Policy (2021) requires that programs be designed to ensure that students 'at risk' are catered for.
Victoria	In responding to the needs of gifted and talented in the classroom, the document refers to supporting schools to be culturally inclusive, including "Koorie cultural elements . . . into programs" (*Aiming High*, p. 19).

future NSW policies mention social-emotional domains within potential and giftedness, the NSW literature review does not refer to the social-emotional development of gifted students.

18. **Program Delivery and Service: A Council to Oversee the Policy's Delivery**
Only the current NSW policy refers directly to a reference group to oversee the policy delivery. The current policy requires schools to develop a School Committee to oversee the development and implementation of a gifted education policy. At the State level, however, the responsibility for gifted education lies with the Senior Curriculum Policy Officer (Gifted and Talented), reporting directly to the Director-General, NSW Curriculum and Learning Innovation Centre. The policy also refers to the development of a reference group to monitor and oversee a structured evaluation of the policy (p. 13).

    In the NSW High Potential and Gifted Education Policy (2021), the directors of Early Learning, Primary, and Secondary Education are responsible for monitoring the implementation of the policy and for reviewing its effectiveness. According to the revised policy, the effectiveness is to be reviewed every three years.

    In Victoria, the policy refers to partnerships between DET and schools in the development of delivery. Furthermore, the DET undertakes to evaluate its policies and programs, but no details are provided.

19. **Supplemental Australian Educational Policies: A Clear Linkage between the Differentiation of the Curriculum, Instructional Practices, and Assessment for Gifted Students, and the Standards of the Broader Educational Reforms**
The responses in the three policies are outlined in Table 8. Although the National Curriculum is not referred to in the current NSW and Victoria policies, this is understandable given the mismatch between timeframes of their respective development. However, both the NSW and Victorian policies place gifted education within the broader reforms within each State.

20. **Supplemental Australian Educational Policies: Promotion of Such 'Hallmark' Secondary Programs**
Selective and/or special high schools as options for gifted students are mentioned in both the NSW and Victorian documents. The NSW High Potential and Gifted Education Policy (2021) and accompanying literature review do not specifically mention selective schools as options. When mentioned, selective schools are described in terms of their potential to offer services and/or delivery options.

21. **Supplemental Australian Educational Policies: Annual Monitoring of Student Data to Ensure that Gifted Students Are Reaching Desired Proficiency Levels in Areas Related to their Identification**
The closest any of the three policies mention the monitoring of student outcomes is NSW. However, their policy does not mention frequency. In the NSW High Potential and Gifted Education Policy (2021), for example, school Principals are required to assist teachers in developing learning goals of students across the

Table 8 Supplemental Australian educational policies: A clear linkage between the differentiation of the curriculum, instructional practices and assessment for gifted students and the standards of the broader educational reforms

Jurisdiction	Details
Federal government	ACARA makes clear the link between provision for gifted students and the broader educational context.
	The section *Personalized learning* draws on the age-related curriculum as the starting point for program differentiation.
	The section *General capabilities and cross-curriculum priorities* states that gifted and talented students need their general capabilities developed.
NSW	Although the current NSW policy does not refer to the National Curriculum, it is located with the broad framework of the NSW educational reforms, including its indigenous policy and anti-racism policy, amongst many others. On the other hand, the gifted education policy is dated no later than 2006, well before the implementation of several national reforms, such as the ACARA.
	Although the NSW 2021 policy and the accompanying literature review refer to the educational reforms in NSW, there is no mention of the national reforms.
Victoria	Although the document does not make clear the link between provision for gifted education and broader educational reforms, it does refer to the place of gifted education within Victorian education. For example, the aims of gifted education in early childhood are consistent with Victoria's select entry and specialist high schools, its early years' framework, and DET's commitment for increasing school-based autonomy (*Aiming High*, p. 12).

range of potential and to lead in the monitoring of procedures, programs, and practices that support gifted students.

22. **Supplemental Australian Educational Policies: Monitoring of Gifted Students' Participation in 'Hallmark' Secondary Programs, Such as International Baccalaureate (IB)**

    While no mention of the monitoring of students in hallmark programs is made in the Federal, NSW, nor Victorian documents, this may occur as part of the overall education policy of each State.

23. **Programs Management, Including:**
    (a) A minimum of 12 hours of coursework in gifted education.
    (b) Linkage of coursework to a university-based program and university network.
    (c) Frequent staff development opportunities regarding the needs of gifted persons engaged in gifted programs and all classroom teachers, counsellors, and administrators.
    (d) Program coordinators provided with 15 hours of courses in educational administration.

    Although the need for professional development is recognised in both the NSW and Victoria policies, it is not outlined how much is required. Instead they refer to professional development on an at-needs basis. Professional development options include working within the resources of the Education Department and with universities.

24. **Programs Management, Including:**
    (a) Federal and/or State jurisdictions require an annual plan from schools specifying how they plan to identify and serve gifted students.
    (b) Federal and/or State jurisdictions should undertake annual reviews of school plans.
    (c) The components of the plan should be specified by regulation.
    (d) Compliance of schools to the plan should be enforced by visits to schools every five years.
    (e) Funding to schools should be tied to the submission of their plans.

At the Federal level, there is no mention of its intention to review school plans for gifted education. Given that funding is provided to schools and/or State jurisdictions that adopt the National Curriculum, it is possible that these plans are reviewed before funding is provided. However, NSW requires schools to develop annual plans for review at regional and State levels. On the other hand, Victoria does not outline any compliance terms.

Policy Attributes

The following sections (Tables 9, 10, 11 and 12) outline our subjective interpretation of the attributes of each policy, beginning with *Clarity*. This is followed by *Comprehensiveness*, *Connectedness*, *Feasibility for implementation*, and *Basis in Research*.

1. **Clarity of a Quality Gifted Education Policy**
   The main impediment to clarity is in the definitions of giftedness (Table 9). As others (e.g., Merrotsy, 2017) have argued, definitions play an important role in the development of instruments used to identify giftedness and in the provision of programs and support. Thus, it appears that the role of the Gagné definition is a 'place-holder' in the two State documents. The reasons behind its adoption as the 'national' definition remain speculative. As we have mentioned earlier, the DMGT was adopted in Australian educational policies as a replacement of MI-based definitions.

2. **Comprehensiveness**
   The current NSW policy for gifted education covers almost all of the major components, except for details regarding the instruments being used (Table 10). Of greater concern is that there are no criteria regarding validity and reliability. The absence of almost all of the major components in the Victorian policy reflects its commitment to devolve responsibility to the schools. However, the Victorian policy could have provided a model for schools to follow. Such models may exist within departmental resources, but they are not publicly available.

Table 9 Clarity of a quality gifted education policy

Jurisdiction	Is the policy written in clear and unambiguous terms?	Does the policy allow for a common understanding and interpretation?
Federal government	Although the distinction between gifted and talented is attributed to Gagné's (2008) DMGT, the terms giftedness and talent do not refer to the top 10%. According to the ACARA definition, gifted students are those "whose potential is distinctly above average" (Para. 4), and talented students possess "skills ... distinctly above average" (Para. 5).	There are two main issues (and one minor issue) with the ACARA definition, leading to the potential for misunderstanding and interpretation of the definition.
		Gagné uses the term giftedness to refer to the possession and use of untrained natural abilities (gifts) to the level exceeding 90% of age peers.
		On the other hand, the ACARA policy refers to students 'distinctly above average'.
		Gagné's DMGT clearly distinguishes between giftedness and talent.
NSW	The current policy refers to Gagné's (2004) version of the DMGT. The terms giftedness (someone in possession of gifts) and talent (someone in possession of outstanding skills and knowledge) appear to be misused in the same way as in the ACARA definition.	Although both policies mention that there are many models of talent development, the current policy identifies the DMGT as the preferred definition.
	On the other hand, the NSW High Potential and Gifted Education Policy (2021) refers to students with high potential, and as gifted or highly gifted students. Although this nomenclature is clearly explained, it is only appears to be broadly consistent with Gagné's DMGT.	The NSW High Potential and Gifted Education Policy (2021) does not mention the DMGT. Although, the literature review highlights the DMGT but does not refer to it as the preferred definition.
Victoria	The document is written as a guideline and intentions. Given that the guideline is reaching its expiry date, it is not clear if it is the intention of DET to determine whether or not the objectives have been achieved.	The guidelines are generally well written. However, the terms giftedness and talent appear to be used interchangeably. A detailed reading of the original Gagné (2004) would clear up any misunderstanding.

3. **Connectedness**

   Neither the NSW nor the Victorian policies mention the National Curriculum nor the national reform agenda (Table 11). This is not surprising given the documents are dated before the national reforms were implemented. On the other hand, both States refer to the developments within their own State.

4. **Feasibility for Implementation**

   The current NSW and future policies excel in the description of who are the key stakeholders and what their responsibilities are. Given the Victorian commitment to devolve responsibility to the schools, the key stakeholders and their

Table 10 Comprehensiveness

Jurisdiction	Does the policy cover all major components?	Is each component sufficiently explained in order to be implemented?
Federal government	The ACARA policy omits almost all of the components related to the identification of gifted students. Furthermore, several of the features within the component 2 (program delivery and service) are absent, including reference to grouping, time, support for social-emotional development, and National Council.	As previously mentioned, Gagné's DMGT is inaccurate and confusing, leading to the distinct possibility that its implementation would be problematic.
NSW	The current and future policies cover almost all of the major components.	Information regarding the instruments, including their validity and reliability in the Australian context, is missing. It is possible, however, that this information exists at the state and/or regional levels.
		The literature review provides citations to a number of instruments, including those from the USA and in Australia.
Victoria	The document does not cover each component, including identification, program delivery, links with National Curriculum, personnel preparation, and program management. The document neglects to mention primary and secondary education.	Notes that the intention of DET is to support schools to develop their own policy for gifted and talented education.

responsibilities would be expected to be subject to negotiation. However, there doesn't appear to be any publicly available research that tests the implementation strategies of either the NSW nor Victorian policies.

5. **Basis in Research**

   There are two ways to view *Basis in Research*. The first is to determine whether the policy fully references the definitions and resources it needs to be successful. The second way is to compare the cited research against what we believe are the current contexts and development in research.

   Against the first criteria, all polices fully reference the Gagné's DMGT although there is a lack of consistency in these references. This is a minor point, and we might expect to see updates to the Gagné references in the next iteration of the three documents. We suggest that, like its predecessor, the DMGT has broad appeal to educators because it clearly delineates the difference between potential and achievement, leaving 'catalysts' such as personal motivation and schools, parents and teachers with the responsibility to transform giftedness into talent.

   Although Gagné's description is very detailed, it is unlikely that teachers, parents or policymakers have time to read original references or their many updates in their entirety. Hence, it is up to others to provide summaries of the

Table 11 Connectedness

Jurisdiction	Does the policy flow logically from one component to another?	Is the policy consistent with general education policies?
Federal government	Given the absence of several key features, it is difficult to agree that the policy flows across each component. Nevertheless, the policy is succinctly written and not overloaded with jargon.	The gifted education policy is written as a subset of the National Curriculum and between *Students with disability* and *Students where English is an additional language or dialect*. Hence, we perceive a high degree of consistency with the National Curriculum.
NSW	The current and future policies flow logically from one component to the other.	Although there is reference to general education in NSW, there is no mention of the wider curriculum reforms. This absence is surprising given that there was an attempt to update the *Gifted and Talented Policy* in 2016. Note, however, that the two supporting documents were published in 2004. At first glance, the literature review accompanying the NSW High Potential and Gifted Education Policy (2021) appears consistent with general education policies.
Victoria	The stated aim of the Victorian document is to support schools, not to outline policy. As a support, it flows from one section to another. As a policy document, however, it is unrealistic to expect logical flow.	Although there is reference to general education in Victoria, there is no mention of the wider curriculum reforms.

DMGT, leading to the possibility that continual retelling of the model leads to omissions and/or misunderstanding of key points.

Of greater significance is the lack of information regarding the validity and reliability of the instruments used to determine giftedness and talent. Although Gagné both clearly describes and justifies the inclusion of four types of gifts (*intellectual*, *creative*, *socio-affective*, and *sensorimotor*), Australian educators and parents do not normally have access to the instruments that can be used to determine whether or not any given child has one or more gifts at the required level of 10%. This is particularly important if instruments need to be sensitive to diverse student groups.

Fundamentally, the DMGT is a developmental model, describing how an individual acquires the necessary skills and knowledge that could, one day, place them in the top 10% of age-matched peers. In its latest iteration, the model describes the complex interactions occurring at different explanatory levels, including molecular (genetics), the individual (i.e., personality and goals), and environmental (including micro- and macroscopic perspectives; Gagné, 2013, 2018). To date, however, the power of the DMGT to describe the developmental process has never been put to the scientific test. This observation is surprising, given its importance in the Australian context for nearly 20 years.

Against the second criteria, we argue that the Australian policies are not consistent with new research in the field of gifted education. Given the relative age of the two State documents, this is not surprising. On the other hand, the National Policy's omission of recent research reflects negatively on the policy. The National Policy does cite a number of Australian descriptions of best practice, but again, these are quite dated. In a later section, we explore one avenue of research that we believe is particularly relevant to the Australian context.

In terms of a systems approach to gifted education, the three policies do not appear to be internally coordinated, integrated with each other, nor linked with the Federal policy. Using Ziegler et al.'s (2018) terminology, each policy consists of a proto-system where there are 'occasional productions of the desired outcome' (p. 23). Future research should focus on the outcomes of the policy to check whether or not the outcomes are consistent with its objectives. Our hypothesis, however, is it that the outcomes are indicative of a system that is less than optimal.

Given the importance of research in VanTassel-Baska's (2009) framework, we devote the next section to our evaluation of Australian giftedness research and its links with Australian policies for gifted education.

Being Gifted in Australia: Current Research Efforts

Luburic and Jolly (2019) reported their review of Australian gifted education research published in leading international journals in the field as well as the two Australian journals, including the *Australasian Journal of Gifted Education* (AJGE) and Talent*Ed*. Covering the years between 1983 and 2017, their purpose was to establish research trends so as to predict future directions. Their search of relevant articles using the key terms *gifted, education*, and *Australia* yielded a total of 200 articles: of these, 63% published in *AJGE* and Talent*Ed* with the remainder published principally in US journals. The most common themes in the published research included: interventions and giftedness (29%); attitudes of parents, teachers, and/or students towards giftedness and/or the other themes (26%); psychological and socioemotional constructs in relation to giftedness; gifted populations such as twice exceptional in relation to giftedness (10%); followed by teacher training (8%) and the nature of giftedness (8%); and identification issues (5%). The least studied was policy and its impact on gifted students (0.5%).

Our own search of the empirical research focused on the period between 1983 and 2019 using the criterion outlined in Luburic and Jolly (2019), but using the additional search term *Gagné* and/or *Differentiated Model of Gifted and talent* and/or *DMGT*. Our search extends the number of years available to Lubric and Jolly, but will likely reduce the number of published research because of the additional search terms. Of course, our search is restricted to education and would exclude research outside this field.

Our search yielded 15 articles (Table 12). Our summary of the articles focuses on the way that the DMGT is used rather than the findings of the research. We also use three codes to describe how the DMGT is used within each article.

Table 12 Articles published in the period 1983–2019 that meet of the search criteria of *gifted, education, Australia, Gagné,* and/or *DMGT*

References	How the DMGT was used in the article	Code
Heller (2001)	The author describes the DMGT as one of many multidimensional constructs of giftedness but does not focus on the Australian context.	A
Vialle, Heaven, Ciarrochi (2005)	The DMGT is mentioned in passing but not used as the conceptual basis of the research nor to explain the findings.	A
Vialle (2007)	The DMGT is described as an accepted model of giftedness but not used as the conceptual basis of the research nor to explain the findings.	A
Watters (2010)	The author mentions the DMGT in passing but not used as the conceptual basis of the research nor to explain the findings.	A
Vialle (2017)	Although the author describes the DMGT as important in the Australian context, it is not used as the conceptual basis of the research. In contrast, the actiotope model is used to guide the design and explain the findings. The author did point out that the findings are not inconsistent with the DMGT.	A
Wellisch (2017)	The author makes only passing reference to the DMGT.	A
Walsh & Jolly (2018)	The authors critically review the Australian gifted educational context.	A
Tomlinson (2010)	The study is a case study of one Australian gifted music student. The DMGT was used as the conceptual basis of giftedness.	B
Walton (2014)	The author mapped the DMGT against Gardner's theory of multiple intelligences.	C
Ronksley-Pavia (2015)	The author provides a comprehensive review of the DMGT and conceptions of disability before describing how they can be integrated.	C
Wellisch (2016)	The author argued against the DMGT as a useful model to identify underachieving gifted students.	C
Bannister-Tyrrell (2017)	Given the plethora of versions of the DMGT, the author argues which version is most useful for educators.	C
Merrotsy (2017)	The author debated the importance and understanding of the DMGT in Australian gifted education policies.	C
Henderson (2018)	The author continued the debate begun by Merrotsy (2017) regarding the importance and understanding of the DMGT in Australian gifted education policies.	C
Slater (2018)	The author argues for the importance of policy in the identification of gifted students.	C

The following codes were used to categorise each article:

Code A = The focus of the article is not on the DMGT, but makes a reference to the DMGT in terms of its status as the accepted model of giftedness and talent in Australia or in passing.

Code B = Uses the DMGT to either design the research or explain the findings.

Code C = The article either critiques or argues for the usefulness and extension of the DMGT in the Australian context.

Of the 15 articles, 7 (47%) made reference to the DMGT as the accepted model of giftedness and talent in Australia or made only passing reference to it. Of these, a number provided extended descriptions of the DMGT. Seven (47%) articles focused on the DMGT in terms of a critique of the model in the Australian context or attempted to extend the usefulness of the model to include multiple intelligences, conceptions of disability, and underachievement. One article (0.1%) used the DMGT as the conceptual basis of giftedness (Tomlinson, 2010). However, this research concerns an investigation of a single person and assumed that the DMGT was a useful model to explain the case.

Our analysis of the research literature is consistent with the findings in Luburic and Jolly (2019) that there has been no research to test the validity of the DMGT in the Australian context. When it is the focus of the article, the discussion focuses on extending the model to include aspects of disability or underachievement, or whether or not it is useful and/or its place in Australian policies.

Luburic and Jolly's (2019) survey showed that most of the research focused on *interventions* and *attitudes*. Of course, interventions play an important role in meeting the needs of gifted students; however, it appears that such research is not based on Gagné's DMGT. This absence is puzzling, considering that the DMGT plays an important role of Australian policy and, hence, should *either* form the basis of any identification procedures and/or explanations for why the intervention has been successful. In terms of research focusing on attitudes, the absence of the DMGT is also puzzling. Given that attitudes play an important role in the environment of gifted students, explanations of the impact of attitudes on the transformation process would be easily made.

Perhaps most puzzling of all is the absence of the DMGT in research that focuses on identification of giftedness and/or talent. Although constituting 5% of the 200 published research, we would expect around 10 articles that link identification with the DMGT. Of these a high proportion should either focus on the development of instruments that reflect the DMGT in the Australian context and/or use such instruments to identify those Australian students who demonstrate giftedness and/or talent.

Of course, we can only speculate on the reasons behind the absence of the DMGT in research describing interventions and identification. In speculating, we do not believe that it is simply that researchers are unaware of the DMGT. Given the importance of the DMGT in Australian policy and Gagné's efforts to justify the development of the DMGT in terms of other research, Australian researchers may simply believe that its validity has already been established, and, hence, it is unnecessary to establish its validity in the Australian context. Given the relatively small pool of researchers working within gifted education in Australia (Luburic & Jolly, 2019), perhaps the absence of such research reflects the lack of interest and/or expertise in validation research.

We do not intend this as a criticism of any one researcher or line of research, however we believe that there is a feature within the DMGT that renders it unattractive to education researchers. The model is a detailed synthesis of the best available research, drawing on a number of levels of interaction. Herein, however, lies its fundamental problem: not only does the DMGT draw on the molecular (i.e., genetics); it also focuses on physiology (i.e., psychomotor skills), personality (i.e., motivation; goal States), and social (i.e., schools and teacher), making it difficult to test the model scientifically. [At this point, we note that Gardner's multiple intelligences theory was similarly critcised by researchers working in the field of intelligence for cutting across too many explanatory levels (c.f. Anderson, 1992)].

Furthermore, we suggest that it is timely for researchers working in interventions to begin to describe effect sizes of the interventions. This omission is surprising given the current regulatory climate in Australia as well as the growing awareness and influence of John Hattie's (2011) work to establish the importance of any intervention. If Hattie's criteria were adopted in gifted education, an intervention needs to demonstrate an effect size of at least 0.4 if the change is deemed important.

Of course, our findings explain the lack of reference to relevant research in our analysis of the Australian policies for gifted education. In other words, the absence of key components in the policy is simply because such work is yet to be completed, either in Australia or elsewhere. Following this argument, it is interesting to note that Gagné's DMGT has not garnered much interest in the international community in terms of its ability to generate new educational research. [We do note the research in two recent studies that use the DMGT as the conceptual framework (Gulbin, Weissensteiner, Oldenziel, & Gagné, 2013; Portenga, 2019).] Certainly, if we apply the criteria outlined earlier when MI was displaced by the DMGT as the preferred model, then it may be time to consider alternatives to the DMGT as the basis of Australian policies related to gifted education.

One way to broaden the pool of researchers working in gifted education may be to broaden the relevance of gifted education within general education. As defined by Gagné, the DMGT focuses on 10% of the school population, with identification primarily based on intellectual gifts. Because the DMGT does not, by definition, refer to the other 90% of the school population, we believe that its usefulness as a model to explain 'talent' development for this larger group is limited.

The next section describes an alternative to the DMGT that we believe provides a seamless fit with the broad educational environment as well as meeting the needs of students with the potential for outstanding academic achievement. The model has an established research basis, including a clear description of the various factors that influence the development of academic achievement and instruments that have been tested for their validity and reliability. Rather than a standalone gifted education policy, we suggest that the model be established as the developmental model explaining all levels of academic achievement. Furthermore, we believe that the valuable lessons we have learned to date in Australian gifted education can be more widely applied to general education.

We also believe that the full integration of gifted education with general education is consistent with Australia's regulatory environment and is uniquely marketable.

Towards Exceptionality in Australia's *General* Educational Environment

The Actiotope Model of Giftedness was developed by Ziegler to describe the development of exceptional achievement (cf. Phillipson, Phillipson, & Francis, 2017; Phillipson, Phillipson, & Kewalramani, 2018; Ziegler, 2005; Ziegler & Baker, 2013; Ziegler, Chandler, Vialle, & Stoeger, 2017; Ziegler & Phillipson, 2012; Ziegler, Stoeger, & Balestrini, 2017). Specifically, the actiotope model describes the interactions between five elements of the educational environment (i.e., economic, culture, social, infrastructure, educational) and five elements of the learning resources (i.e., skills and knowledge, health, goal States, attention, application). It is a systems model where interactions between these elements change over time and in response to each other. Although one resource is not more important than another, academic achievement is the outcome of the elements working within the system, rather than any one element.

In broad terms, changes to the educational environment are required when the student's learning goals have been attained through the development of new skills and knowledge. Changes to the learning environment may include providing new resources such as equipment, more complex curriculum resources or appropriate social groups. Once the environment has met the new learning goals, the system has reached a state of equilibrium. Disrupting the system may require a further change in the environment and/or the learning needs of the student. Importantly, the five educational and five learning resources, termed capitals in the actiotope model, can be measured. Instruments have been developed to measure each of parent's and student's perceptions of the availability of these capitals. Furthermore, the factor structure of the instruments has been investigated and confirmed through empirical studies.

Currently, the actiotope model has been used in a variety of contexts, including Australian parents' perceptions of their child's environment (Phillipson et al., 2018), being based on instruments validated in the Australian context (Phillipson et al., 2017), and with children from China, Germany, and Turkey, again using instruments assessed for their validity and reliability in their respective contexts (Vladut, Liu, Leana-Tascilar, Vialle, & Ziegler, 2013; Vladut, Vialle, & Ziegler, 2015). Finally, the actiotope model has been used to explain gender differences amongst German students enrolling in STEM courses (Stoeger, Greindl, Kuhlman, & Balestrini, 2017).

Although intelligence is recognised in the actiotope model, it is not considered the most important predictor of academic achievement. Hence, the actiotope model does not require identification regimes based on intelligence; rather, the actiotope model looks at the educational and learning environment, asking the question: *Is the child's environment conducive to the academic achievement of the child?*

The actiotope model is also consistent with Australian educational policies that emphasise the important role played by parents in the educational achievement of their children. Research conducted within and beyond the field of gifted education have demonstrated the important role played by parents on the cognitive development of their children (cf. Phillipson, S., & Phillipson, S. N, 2012, 2017). Although the DMGT refers to parents as part of the child's environment, recent research based on the Actiotope Model of Giftedness has suggested *how* parents contribute to their child's development (Veas, Castejon, O'Reilly, & Ziegler, 2018; Ziegler & Baker, 2013; Ziegler, Chandler, et al., 2017; Ziegler et al., 2017; Ziegler, Vialle, & Wimmer, 2013). Of course, the actiotope model takes into account funding, infrastructure, the cultural environment, social environment, and the quality of educational resources such as teachers and curricula.

Finally, the actiotope model takes into account the importance of the child's mental and physical health, their learning goals, the development of skills and knowledge, the child's capacity to implement their skills and knowledge, and their capacity to attend to the task at hand. Although the DMGT describes a number of intrapersonal and environmental catalysts, the actiotope model clearly describes how these features interact with each and how they can be measured.

There are other reasons why integrating gifted education into general education will be an attractive proposition. In order to maintain Australia's appeal to international students and thereby ensure continual economic growth, we foresee that a 'gifted education' will be recognised as one important aspect of this marketability. We believe that in order for this to happen, however, gifted education will need to be redefined and reimagined, and implemented consistently across Australia. This is unlikely to happen in its current format, where gifted education is siloed alongside children with other special needs. As a feature of general education, it will be subject to the same rules of accountability, including the need to demonstrate impact.

To be meaningful and inclusive for all Australian families, we believe that definitions of giftedness will become increasingly sensitive to cultural and ethnic diversity. As a consequence of this increasing sensitivity, we suggest that gifted education will also become increasingly marketable to the wider school community.

In his latest report, Gonski et al. (2018) referred to the need to develop high performance schools. When the current technologies for gifted education are integrated into general education, a natural consequence is that schools become centres of high performance. A similar change can be seen with the development of a whole-school approach to 'performance development', developed by Professor Deborah Eyre. Professor Eyre's (2019) position as CEO of *High Performance Learning* (HPL) draws on her extensive experience as the former Director of the *National Academy for Gifted and Talented Youth* in the UK. Rather than focusing on gifted students, the framework of HPL assumes that all students can enhance their performance when schools work to adopt changes in curriculum (i.e., enquiry-based learning), pedagogical approach (i.e., practice and training, feedback and developing quality relationships with students), student mindsets, expertise development and engagement of parents. Of course, we believe that the outcomes of some students will be exceptional, we do not predetermine what the proportion might be. We consider many of these elements consistent with both Gagné's DMGT and the actiotope model.

Finally, integrating gifted education and the actiotope model will assist in overcoming a number of challenges facing Australian education (Masters, 2016). For example, teachers may face a less crowded classroom in needing to deal with a 'gifted' cohort of students. Schools and teachers will understand the relationship between each students' socio-economic and cultural context and academic achievement. Furthermore, the emphasis in the actiotope model on personalised trajectories meets Masters' requirements for a personalised education and need to understand students' school readiness. When integrated within the general educational system, the requirement to be specifically trained in gifted education is no longer necessary; rather, the emphasis in initial teacher education becomes an understanding of the interrelationships between the educational and learning environment in the development of academic and other achievement.

Conclusion: Our Crystal Ball of Broad Implications and Challenges

The impetus for change from general education will come from a number of areas. Looking to the future, we feel that the tensions within the community are likely to increase rather than decrease, especially when parents expect schools to teach life skills such as money management, job preparation, and domestic skills *as well as* technological subjects related to coding and Artificial Intelligence in order to prepare them for future jobs (Leahy & Selwyn, 2019). There are two possible outcomes.

First, the tensions will lead to increasing specialisms at both secondary and, eventually, primary school level. Responding to 'market' demands, parents will exercise their freedom of choice to send their children to schools they feel will best meet their children's needs. Thus, we will have secondary and primary schools specialising in either academic or nonacademic areas.

More likely, however, schools will turn to alternate instructional technologies to ensure that schools meet the needs of parents and their children in both academic and nonacademic areas. Furthermore, the outsourcing of nonacademic areas such as life skills would place less direct pressure on teachers. On the other hand, the instructional technologies around gifted education could provide the impetus for raising academic standards for all children, particularly given its focus on personalised learning, high expectations, and outcomes that are not predetermined. Of course, this change would have implications for a number of other broad challenges as outlined in Masters (2016) as well as current policies for gifted education.

As a consequence, a redistribution of funding means that other schools (mainly Independent and Catholic schools) may be pressured to rely on other sources to maintain current standards. Although parents are suggested as the means to make up the difference, alternate sources of income will need to be found. Given the attractiveness of Australian higher education for international students, we predict that secondary and primary schools negatively affected by funding changes will turn to the families of international higher education students as sources of income.

One way to distinguish between schools and to increase their attractiveness to international students could be a focus on the needs of parents wanting a school that promotes outstanding academic achievement. Given Australia's current reliance on

Asian international students, it would be natural for these schools to promote values that are consistent with the Confucian heritage cultures, such as high academic standards, hard work, and persistence (Phillipson, Ku, & Phillipson, 2013). Again, the instructional strategies developed within gifted education would be ideal for this purpose. As outlined earlier, however, this would also require changes at the policy level.

As we have explored, the instructional strategies already exist, not only for students with learning disabilities, but also for students with the potential for outstanding academic achievement.

In terms of a curriculum philosophy, it means that assessment is focused on monitoring individual student's progress against personal growth rather than against year-level standards. In other words, this recognises that learning development is unique for each student, taking into account changes in individual growth, motivations, and the learning environment. Developmental models that take into account different trajectories for each student and, at the same time, allow for exceptional achievement would need to be a feature of educational policies.

Cross-References

- ▶ Australian Teachers Who Made a Difference: Secondary Gifted Student Perceptions of Teaching and Teacher Effectiveness
- ▶ Gifted and Talented Aboriginal Students in Australia
- ▶ Gifted Education in the Asia-Pacific: From the Past for the Future – An Introduction
- ▶ Gifted Girls with Autism Spectrum Disorders: Provisions and Priorities in Australian School Settings
- ▶ Identifying Underrepresented Gifted Students: A Developmental Process
- ▶ Implementing the DMGT's Constructs of Giftedness and Talent: What, Why, and How?
- ▶ More than Passion: The Role of the Gifted Education Coordinator in Australasian Schools
- ▶ Rural Voices: Identifying the Perceptions, Practices, and Experiences of Gifted Pedagogy in Australian Rural and Regional Schools
- ▶ Social and Cultural Conceptions and Perceptions: Part I Introduction
- ▶ Some Implications for the Future of Gifted Education in the Asia-Pacific
- ▶ Supporting Australian Gifted Indigenous Students' Academic Potential in Rural Settings
- ▶ Teachers' Knowledge and Understandings of Twice Exceptionality Across Australia

Appendix

The policy documents used in the valuation are:

Australian Government
1. Australian Curriculum Assessment and Reporting Authority. (n.d.). *Australian curriculum, v8.3 F-10 curriculum*: *Student diversity: Gifted and talented*

students. Retrieved from https://www.australiancurriculum.edu.au/resources/student-diversity/gifted-and-talented-students/
2. Australian Curriculum Assessment and Reporting Authority. (n.d.). *Student Diversity*. Retrieved from https://www.australiancurriculum.edu.au/resources/student-diversity/
3. Australian Institute for Teaching and School Leadership. (2011). *Australian professional standards for teachers*. Melbourne, Vic: Education Services Australia. Retrieved from http://www.aitsl.edu.au/australianprofessional-standards-for- teachers/standards/list

New South Wales
1. State of New South Wales, Department of Education. (2006). *Gifted and Talented Policy*. Sydney, NSW: Author. Retrieved from https://education.nsw.gov.au/policy-library/policies/gifted-and-talented-policy. Last updated 2016.
2. State of New South Wales, Department of Education. (2004). *Policy and implementation strategies for the education of gifted and talented students*. NSW Department of Education and Training. https://education.nsw.gov.au/policy-library/policies/gifted-and-talented-policy
3. State of New South Wales, Department of Education. (2004). Guidelines for the use of strategies to support gifted and talented students. NSW Department of Education and Training. https://education.nsw.gov.au/policy-library/policies/gifted-and-talented-policy
4. State of New South Wales, Department of Education. (2019). High Potential and Gifted Education Policy. Sydney, NSW: Author. Retrieved from https://education.nsw.gov.au/teaching-and-learning/high-potential-and-gifted-students/high-potential-and-gifted-education-policy. Last updated 7 June 2019.
5. North, B., & Griffiths, K. (2019) *Revisiting Gifted Education*, Centre for Education Statistics and Evaluation, NSW Department of Education. Retrieved from https://www.cese.nsw.gov.au/publications-filter/revisiting-gifted-education

Victoria
1. State Government Victoria, Department of Education and Early Childhood Development. (2014). *Aiming high: A strategy for gifted and talented children and young people, 2014–2019*. Melbourne, VIC: Author.

References

ACARA. (n.d.). *Australian curriculum, v8.3 F-10 curriculum: Student diversity: Gifted and talented students*. Retrieved from https://www.australiancurriculum.edu.au/resources/student-diversity/gifted-and-talented-students/

Anderson, M. (1992). Intelligence and development: A cognitive theory. Great Britain: Blackwell Publishers

Australian Bureau of Statistics. (2017). *Census of population and housing: Reflecting Australia – Stories from the census, 2016 – Cultural diversity* (Table 5). Commonwealth of Australia.

Australian Bureau of Statistics. (2018). *International trade in services, by country, by state and by detailed services category, calendar year, 201. ABS* (ABS Catalogue no. 5368.0.55.004). Retrieved from http://www.abs.gov.au/AUSSTATS/abs@.nsf/DetailsPage/5368.0.55.0042015. Updated 23 May 2017.

Australian Bureau of Statistics. (2019a). *Government expenditure on education in Australia.* Canberra, ACT: Author. Retrieved from http://www.abs.gov.au/ausstats/abs@.nsf/mf/5518.0.55.001. Updated 26 April 2018.

Australian Bureau of Statistics. (2019b). *Population clock.* Canberra, ACT: Author. Retrieved from http://www.abs.gov.au/ausstats/abs%40.nsf/94713ad445ff1425ca25682000192af2/1647509ef7e25faaca2568a900154b63?OpenDocument. Updated 14 February 2019.

Australian Children's Education & Care Quality Authority. (n.d.). *Australian Children's Education & Care Quality Authority.* Retrieved from https://www.acecqa.gov.au

Australian Curriculum Assessment and Reporting Authority. (2016). *ACARA: Australian Curriculum Assessment and Reporting Authority.* Retrieved from https://www.acara.edu.au

Australian Government: Department of Education. (2017). *Teacher Education Ministerial Advisory Group.* Retrieved from https://www.education.gov.au/teacher-education-ministerial-advisory-group

Australian Institute for Teaching and School Leadership. (2015). *Accreditation of initial teacher education programs in Australia, standards and procedures.* Melbourne, VIC: Author.

Australian Institute for Teaching and School Leadership. (2017). *AITSL: Australian Institute for Teaching and School Leadership.* Retrieved from https://www.aitsl.edu.au

Australian National Senate Employment, Workplace Relations, Small Business and Education References Committee. (2001). *The education of gifted students.* Canberra, ACT: Commonwealth of Australia.

Australian Qualifications Framework. (n.d.). *Australian Qualifications Framework.* Retrieved from https://www.aqf.edu.au

Australian Skills Quality Authority. (n.d.). *Australian Skills Quality Authority.* Retrieved from https://www.asqa.gov.au

Bannister-Tyrrell, M. (2017). Gagné's DMGT 2.0: A possible model of unification and shared understandings. *Australasian Journal of Gifted Education, 26*(2), 43–50. https://doi.org/10.21505/ajge.2017.0015

Bell, L., & Stevenson, H. (2006). *Education policy: Process, themes and impact.* New York, NY: Routledge/Taylor and Francis Group.

Berk, R. A., & Rossi, P. H. (1999). *Thinking about program evaluation* (2nd ed.). Thousand Oaks, CA: Sage.

CASPer. (n.d.). *You are more than your grades.* CASPer is a commercially produced selection tool based on situational judgements of hypothetical scenarios. Retrieved from https://takecasper.com/about-casper/

Deloitte Access Economics and EduWorld. (2015). *Growth and opportunity in Australian international education: A report prepared for Austrade.* Melbourne, VIC: Author.

Eyre, D. (2019). *High performance learning. Eyre's high performance learning limited.* Retrieved from https://www.highperformancelearning.co.uk

Future Unlimited. (n.d.). *World class education.* Australian Government. Retrieved from https://www.studyinaustralia.gov.au/english/why-australia/world-class-education

Gagné, F. (2003). Transforming gifts into talents: The DMGT as a developmental theory. In N. Colangelo & G. A. Davis (Eds.), *Handbook of gifted education* (3rd ed., pp. 60–74). Boston, MA: Allyn & Bacon.

Gagné, F. (2004). Transforming gifts into talents: The DMGT as a developmental theory. *High Ability Studies, 15*(2), 119–147. https://doi.org/10.1080/1359813042000314682

Gagné, F. (2008). *Building gifts into talents: Overview of the DMGT.* Keynote address, 10th Asia-Pacific conference for giftedness. Asia-Pacific Federation of the World Council for Gifted and Talented Children, Singapore, 14–17 July.

Gagné, F. (2009). The Differentiated Model of Giftedness and Talent. In J. Renzulli, E. Gubbins, K. McMillen, R. Eckert, & C. Little (Eds.), Systems & models for developing programs for the gifted and talented (2nd ed., pp. 165–192). Mansfield Centre, CT: Creative Learning Press. https://doi.org/10.4135/9781412971959.n111

Gagné, F. (2013). The DMGT: Changes within, beneath, and beyond. *Talent Development and Excellence, 5*, 5–19.

Gagné, F. (2018). The DMGT/IMTD: Building talented outputs of gifted inputs. In C. M. Callahan & H. L. Hertberg-Davis (Eds.), *Fundamentals of gifted education: Considering multiple perspectives* (pp. 22–31). New York, NY: Routledge.

Gallagher, J. J. (2006). *Driving change in special education*. London, England: Paul H. Brookes.

Gardner, H. (1983). *Frames of mind: The theory of multiple intelligences*. New York, NY: Basic Books.

Gonski, D., Arcus, T., Boston, K., Gould, V., Johnson, W., O'Brien, L., Perry, L-A., & Roberts, M. (2018). *Through growth to achievement: The report of the review to achieve educational excellence in Australian schools*. Retrieved from Canberra https://docs.education.gov.au/system/files/doc/other/662684_tgta_accessible_final_0.pdf

Gonski, D., Boston, K., Greiner, K., Lawrence, C., Scales, B., & Tannock, P. (2011). *Review of funding for schooling – Final report*. Canberra, ACT: Australian Government. Retrieved from https://docs.education.gov.au/system/files/doc/other/review-of-funding-for-schooling-final-report-dec-2011.pdf

Gulbin, J., Weissensteiner, J., Oldenziel, K., & Gagné, F. (2013). Patterns of performance development in elite athletes. *European Journal of Sport Science, 13*(6), 605–614. https://doi.org/10.1080/17461391.2012.756542

Hattie, J. A. C. (2011). *Visible learning: A synthesis of over 800 meta-analyses relating to achievement*. London, England/New York, NY: Routledge.

Heller, K. A. (2001). Gifted education at the beginning of the third millennium. *Australasian Journal of Gifted Education, 10*(1), 48–61.

Henderson, L. C. (2018). Reflecting on the DMGT in the Australian context: Response to Merrotsy. *Australasian Journal of Gifted Education, 27*(1), 59–65. https://doi.org/10.21505/ajge.2018.0006

.idcommunity. (2017). *Australia ancestry*. .idcommunity. Retrieved from http://profile.id.com.au/australia/ancestry

Leahy, D., & Selwyn, N. (2019). *Public opinions on Australian schools and schooling*. Melbourne, VIC: Monash University. Retrieved from https://www.monash.edu/__data/assets/pdf_file/0005/1653548/Education-Futures-Research-Report-Public-Opinions.pdf

Luburic, I., & Jolly, J. L. (2019). An examination of the empirical literature: Gifted education in the Australian context. *Journal for the Education of the Gifted, 42*(1), 64–84.

Masters, G. N. (2016). *Five challenges in Australian school education. Policy insights issue 5*. Camberwell, VIC: ACER.

McCann, M. (2007). Such is life . . . in the land down under: Conceptions of giftedness in Australia. In S. N. Phillipson & M. McCann (Eds.), *Conceptions of giftedness: Socio-cultural perspectives* (pp. 413–458). Mahwah, NJ: Erlbaum.

McPherson, G. E., Osborne, M. S., Barrett, M. S., Davidson, J. W., & Faulkner, R. (2015). Motivation to study music in Australian schools: The impact of music learning, gender, and socio-economic status. *Research Studies in Music Education., 1*, 1–20. https://doi.org/10.1177/1321103X15600914

Merrotsy, P. (2017). Gagné's differentiated model of giftedness and talent in Australian education. *Australasian Journal of Gifted Education, 26*(2), 29–42.

National Assessment Program—Literacy and Numeracy. (2016). *NAP: National Assessment Program*. Retrieved from https://www.nap.edu.au

North, B., & Griffiths, K. (2019). *Revisiting gifted education*. Centre for Education Statistics and Evaluation, NSW Department of Education. Retrieved from https://www.cese.nsw.gov.au/publications-filter/revisiting-gifted-education

OECD. (2019). *Private spending on education (indicator)*. https://doi.org/10.1787/6e70bede-en. Accessed 14 Feb 2019.

Phillipson, S., Ku, K. Y. L., & Phillipson, S. N. (Eds.). (2013). *Constructing educational achievement: A socio-cultural perspective*. London, England/New York, NY: Routledge.

Phillipson, S., & Phillipson, S. N. (2012). Children's cognitive ability and their academic achievement: The mediation effects of parental expectations. *Asia Pacific Education Review, 13*, 495–508. https://doi.org/10.1007/s12564-011-9198-1

Phillipson, S., & Phillipson, S. N. (2017). Generalizability in the mediation effects of parental expectations on children's cognitive ability and self-concept. *Journal of Child and Family Studies, 26*(12), 3388–3400. https://doi.org/10.1007/s10826-017-0836-z

Phillipson, S., Phillipson, S. N., & Kewalramani, S. (2018). Cultural variability in the educational and learning capitals of Australian families and its relationship with children's numeracy outcomes. *Journal for the Education of the Gifted*, 1–21. https://doi.org/10.1177/0162353218799484. Online First.

Phillipson, S. N., Kaur, I., & Phillipson, S. (2003). A late developer-gifted education in Malaysia within a global context. *The Asia-Pacific Education Researcher, 12*(2), 135–175. Retrieved from https://ejournals.ph/article.php?id=3767

Phillipson, S. N., & Phillipson, S. (2017). *Australian parents speak: Perceptions of the quality of their educational environment*. Unpublished Report.

Phillipson, S. N., Phillipson, S., & Eyre, D. M. (2011). Being gifted in Hong Kong: An examination of the region's policy for gifted education. *Gifted Child Quarterly, 55*(4), 235–249. https://doi.org/10.1177/0016986211421959

Phillipson, S. N., Phillipson, S., & Francis, M. A. (2017). Validation of the family educational and learning capitals questionnaire in Australia. *Journal for the Education of the Gifted, 40*, 350. https://doi.org/10.1177/0162353217734373. Online First.

Phillipson, S. N., Stoeger, H., & Ziegler, A. (2013). *Exceptionality in East Asia: Explorations in the actiotope model of giftedness*. New York, NY: Routledge.

Plunkett, M., & Kronborg, L. (2007). Gifted education in Australia: A story of striving for balance. *Gifted Education International, 23*, 72–83. https://doi.org/10.1177/026142940702300109

Portenga, S. T. (2019). High-performance talent development in golf. In R. F. Subotnik, P. Olszewski-Kubilius, & F. C. Worrell (Eds.), *The psychology of high performance: Developing human potential into domain-specific talent* (pp. 23–58). Washington, DC: American Psychological Association.

Renzulli, J. S. (1978). What Makes Giftedness? Reexamining a Definition. Phi Delta Kappan, 60, 180–184.

Rickards, F. (2016). *What are the main challenges facing teacher education in Australia? The Conversation*. The Conversation Media Group Ltd. Retrieved from https://theconversation.com/what-are-the-main-challenges-facing-teacher-education-in-australia-63658

Ronksley-Pavia, M. (2015). A model of twice-exceptionality: Explaining and defining the apparent paradoxical combination of disability and giftedness in childhood. *Journal for the Education of the Gifted, 38*(3), 318–340. https://doi.org/10.1177/0162353215592499

Slater, E. (2018). The identification of gifted children in Australia: The importance of policy. *TalentEd, 30*, 1–16.

Stoeger, H., Greindl, T., Kuhlman, J., & Balestrini, D. P. (2017). The learning and educational capital of male and female students in STEM magnet schools and in extracurricular STEM programs: A study in high-achiever-track secondary schools in Germany. *Journal for the Education of the Gifted, 40*(4), 394–416. https://doi.org/10.1177/0162353217734374

Tannenbaum, A. J. (2003). Nature and nurture of giftedness. In N. Colangelo & G. A. Davis (Eds.), *Handbook of gifted education* (3rd ed., pp. 45–59). Boston, MA: Allyn and Bacon.

Tertiary Education Quality and Standards Agency. (2017a). *Australian Government: Tertiary Education Quality and Standards Agency*. Retrieved from https://www.teqsa.gov.au.

Tertiary Education Quality and Standards Agency. (2017b). *CRICOS registration*. Retrieved from https://www.teqsa.gov.au/cricos-registration

Tomlinson, M. M. (2010). Cassie: A gifted musician: Socio-cultural and educational perspectives related to the development of musical understanding in gifted adolescents.

Australian Journal of Music Education, 2, 87–102. Retrieved from https://files.eric.ed.gov/fulltext/EJ916793.pdf

Universities Australia. (2018). *Quality central to Australia's international education success story.* Universities Australia. Retrieved from https://www.universitiesaustralia.edu.au/Media-and-Events/media-releases/Quality-central-to-Australia-s-international-education-success-story#.XGYfly2B1Zi

VanTassel-Baska, J. (2009). United States policy development in gifted education: A patchwork quilt. In L. Shavinina (Ed.), *International handbook on giftedness* (pp. 1295–1312). Dordrecht, The Netherlands: Springer Science and Business Media.

Veas, A., Castejon, J.-L., O'Reilly, C., & Ziegler, A. (2018). Mediation analysis of the relationship between educational capital, learning capital, and underachievement among gifted secondary school students. *Journal for the Education of the Gifted, 41,* 2. https://doi.org/10.1177/0162353218799436

Vialle, W. (2007). Pink or Paris? Giftedness in popular culture. *Australasian Journal of Gifted Education, 16*(1), 5–11.

Vialle, W. (2017). Supporting giftedness in families: A resources perspective. *Journal for the Education of the Gifted, 40*(4), 372–393. https://doi.org/10.1177/0162353217734375

Vialle, W., Heaven, P. C. L., & Ciarrochi, J. (2005). The relationship between self-esteem and academic achievement in high ability students: Evidence from the Wollongong Youth Study. *Australasian Journal of Gifted Education, 14*(2), 39–45.

Victorian Institute of Teaching. (2019). *Registering as a teacher.* Retrieved from https://www.vit.vic.edu.au/registering-as-a-teacher

Vladut, A., Liu, Q., Leana-Tascilar, M. Z., Vialle, W., & Ziegler, A. (2013). A cross-cultural validation study of the Questionnaire of Educational and Learning Capital (QELC) in China, Germany and Turkey. *Psychological Test and Assessment Modeling, 55,* 462–478.

Vladut, A., Vialle, W., & Ziegler, A. (2015). Learning resources within the actiotope: A validation study of the QELC (questionnaire of educational and learning capital). *Psychological Test and Assessment Modeling, 57,* 40–56.

Walsh, R. L., & Jolly, J. L. (2018). Gifted Education in the Australian Context. Gifted Child Today, 41(2), 81–88. https://doi.org/10.1177/1076217517750702

Walton, R. (2014). Mapping MI to the DMGT: A theoretical framework. *Australasian Journal of Gifted Education, 23*(2), 37–44. Retrieved from https://pdfs.semanticscholar.org/48b8/60c564cd8773d73d01e3ed8a6072e3a863ad.pdf

Watters, J. (2010). Career decision making among gifted students: The mediation of teachers. *The Gifted Child Quarterly, 54*(3), 222–238. https://doi.org/10.1177/0016986210369255

Wellisch, M. (2016). Gagné's DMGT and underachievers: The need for an alternative inclusive gifted model. *Australasian Journal of Gifted Education, 25*(1), 18–30. https://doi.org/10.21505/ajge.2016.0003

Wellisch, M. (2017). Re-introduction of cognitive screening for all school children. *Australasian Journal of Gifted Education, 26*(1), 34–43.

White, S., Graham, L., & Blaas, S. (2018). Why do we know so little about the factors associated with gifted underachievement? A systematic literature review. Educational Research Review, 24, 55–66. https://doi.org/10.1016/j.edurev.2018.03.001

Ziegler, A. (2005). The actiotope model of giftedness. In R. J. Sternberg & J. E. Davidson (Eds.), *Conceptions of giftedness* (2nd ed., pp. 411–436). Cambridge, UK: Cambridge University Press.

Ziegler, A., & Baker, J. (2013). Talent development as adaptation: The role of educational and learning capital. In S. N. Phillipson, H. Stoeger, & A. Ziegler (Eds.), *Exceptionality in East Asia: Explorations in the actiotope model of giftedness* (pp. 18–39). New York, NY: Routledge.

Ziegler, A., Balestrini, D. P., & Stoeger, H. (2018). An international view of gifted education: Incorporating the macro-systemic perspective. In S. I. Pfeiffer (Ed.), *Handbook of giftedness in children* (2nd ed., pp. 15–28). Cham, The Netherlands: Springer. https://doi.org/10.1007/978-3-319-77004-8_2

Ziegler, A., Chandler, K., Vialle, W., & Stoeger, H. (2017). Exogenous and endogenous learning resources in the actiotope model of giftedness and its significance for gifted education. *Journal for the Education of the Gifted, 40,* 310–333. https://doi.org/10.1177/0162353217734376

Ziegler, A., & Phillipson, S. N. (2012). Towards a systemic theory of gifted education. *High Ability Studies, 23*, 3–30. https://doi.org/10.1080/13598139.2012.679085

Ziegler, A., & Stoeger, H. (2017). Systemic gifted education. A theoretical introduction. *Gifted Child Quarterly, 61*, 183–193. https://doi.org/10.1177/0016986217705713

Ziegler, A., Stoeger, H., & Balestrini, D. (2017). Systemic gifted education. In J. Riedl Cross, C. O'Reilly, & T. Cross (Eds.), *Providing for the special needs of students with gifts and talents* (pp. 15–55). Dublin, Ireland: Kazoo Independent Publishing.

Ziegler, A., Vialle, W., & Wimmer, B. (2013). The actiotope model of giftedness: A short introduction to some central theoretical assumptions. In S. Phillipson, H. Stoeger, & A. Ziegler (Eds.), *Exceptionality in East-Asia: Explorations in the actiotope model of giftedness* (pp. 1–17). New York, NY: Routledge.

Shane N. Phillipson, PhD, is an associate professor in the Faculty of Education at Monash University and previously at the Education University of Hong Kong. After working as a mathematics and science teacher, he obtained a PhD from Flinders University. He has been awarded a number of research grants, resulting in research publications in many international peer-reviewed journals, including *High Ability Studies* and *Educational Psychology,* and he is also a reviewer of research articles for these two journals. His edited books include *Learning Diversity in the Chinese Classroom: Contexts and Practice for Students With Special Needs (2007)* and *Conceptions of Giftedness: Socio-cultural Perspectives* (with M. McCann, 2007).

Albert Ziegler, PhD, is chair professor of educational psychology and research on excellence at the University of Erlangen-Nuremberg, Germany. He is the founding director of the Statewide Counselling and Research Centre for the Gifted. He has published approximately 300 books, chapters, and articles in the fields of talent development, excellence, educational psychology, and cognitive psychology. Presently, he serves as the secretary general of the *International Research Association for Talent Development and Excellence,* as vice president of the *European Council for High Ability,* as chairman of the *European Talent Support Network,* and as editor-in-chief of *High Ability Studies.*

Implementing the DMGT's Constructs of Giftedness and Talent: What, Why, and How?

4

Françoys Gagné

Contents

Introduction	73
Origins of the DMGT	73
The Australian Experience: Pluses and Minuses	74
Three Key Assumptions of the DMGT	76
Assumption 1: Potentialities and Achievements	77
Assumption 2: Differentiated Assessment	79
Assumption 3: Causal Relationship	81
How Many Intellectually Gifted (GI) Students Are Academically Talented (TA)?	82
Academic Talent Development	83
The Statistics of the GI Versus TA Differentiation	86
Some Practical Applications	91
Appropriate Labelling	91
Whom to Prioritise: The Gifted or the Talented?	92
Research Interpretations	93
Conclusions	95
Cross-References	96
References	96

Abstract

This chapter begins with a brief history of the *Differentiating Model of Giftedness and Talent* (DMGT). It focuses on its introduction to Australian educators, and its rapid spread to all its states, making it the most widely discussed talent development model in that country. However, recent analyses of policy and advocacy documents suggest that few of the model's constituent elements are implemented

---

F. Gagné (✉)
Université du Québec à Montréal (UQAM), Montréal, QC, Canada
e-mail: fysgagne@gmail.com

© Springer Nature Singapore Pte Ltd. 2021
S. R. Smith (ed.), *Handbook of Giftedness and Talent Development in the Asia-Pacific*,
Springer International Handbooks of Education,
https://doi.org/10.1007/978-981-13-3041-4_3

in policies or school practices, even its key differentiated constructs of giftedness and talent. Keeping in mind all potential users worldwide, I attempt to alleviate this problem in three ways. First, I discuss the three main assumptions behind the giftedness/talent differentiation (the *What*): (a) the commonly accepted distinction between aptitudes (gifts) and achievements (talents); (b) the relative ease of differentiated assessment; and (c) the role of aptitudes as building blocks of competencies (knowledge and skills). Second, I focus on the close relationship (the *Why*) between intellectual aptitudes, commonly measured as IQ scores, and academic achievements to assess the relative prevalence of intellectually gifted (GI) *and* academically talented (TA) students (conjunctive view) within the larger group of GI *or* TA students (disjunctive view). In spite of a strong ($r = 0.5$) average correlation between IQ scores and school grades, my analysis reveals that the conjunctive population of GI *and* TA students represents at best 20% of the disjunctive population (GI *or* TA); in other words, a large majority of these students are either 'gifted non-talented' or 'non-gifted talented'. Thirdly, I propose practical applications (the *How*) for this empirically confirmed differentiation, namely, how it affects: (a) the types of students most commonly identified as 'gifted' when both types of assessment tools are used; (b) the proper terminology to adopt depending on the aptitude-achievement profiles of students; and (c) the impact of differently selected 'gifted' samples on research analysis and interpretation. I conclude that the stranglehold that the 'gifted' label has on the field's terminology, unchanged since the initial appearance of the DMGT over three decades ago, will make it difficult for agents of change (academics and local professionals) to successfully implement the DMGT's conceptual views without very targeted initiatives.

Keywords

ACARA · Aptitudes · COGE · Competencies · DMGT · DMNA · Giftedness · IMTD · Intelligence · Prevalence · Talent · Talent development

The aims in this chapter are to:
1. Briefly recount the love story between the DMGT and Australian educators.
2. Identify major blockages to the dissemination of the DMGT's key constituent ideas.
3. Conceptually distinguish aptitudes from achievements and gifts from talents.
4. Operationally distinguish gifts and talents through specific assessment tools.
5. Demonstrate the limited overlap between the subpopulations of intellectually gifted (GI) students and of academically talented (TA) students.
6. Discuss differences between 'gifted non-talented' and 'non-gifted talented' students.
7. Propose some practical applications of this limited overlap in terms of terminology, identification, and research interpretation.

Introduction

When I entered the field of gifted education in the late 1970s, I soon discovered that it suffered from a serious case of conceptual and terminological chaos, a situation that brought to my mind the biblical 'Tower of Babel'.

Origins of the DMGT

Among the main symptoms were: (a) the lack of any consensual definition for its key concept of 'giftedness' and its related concept of talent; (b) the supremacy of the term 'gifted' in the designation of the field itself, its target populations, its dedicated professionals, most professional journals, and most enrichment programs; and (c) the almost total disregard for the label 'talent', except in the common expression 'the gifted and talented are…', an expression that suggested a practical synonymous relationship between the two labels (Gagné, 1985). Yet, at the same time, scholars and educational practitioners almost unanimously recognised that the ubiquitous term *giftedness* could designate two distinct types of human abilities: early emerging forms of *potential* giftedness, as opposed to fully developed forms of *achieved* giftedness. They would express that distinction through various pairs of labels, for instance, potential/realisation, aptitude/achievement or promise/fulfilment (Gagné, 1999, 2004); yet, these scholars kept using a single label, *giftedness*, to represent either of them, sometimes within the same sentence. These conceptual and terminological practices created an unnecessary confusion. As an example, consider the phenomenon of (gifted) underachievement; professionals commonly define it "as a discrepancy between expected performance (ability or potential) and actual performance (achievement)" (Siegle & McCoach, 2013, p. 377). According to the dual meaning given to the term giftedness, these underachievers would be at the same time gifted (high potential) and non-gifted (average or low achievement)—a clear oxymoron! Similarly, when advocates insist that all gifted children should be able to fulfil their high potential, they are requesting special educational services that will help the gifted become gifted!

It took me little time to find a way out of that confusion; simply associate the two key labels 'giftedness' and 'talent' to the concepts of potentialities and achievements, respectively. Thus, was born the *Differentiating Model of Giftedness and Talent* (DMGT, identified until recently as *Differentiated*), with its two well-known definitions. Not only did the DMGT terminologically differentiate potentialities from achievements, but it also used that differentiation as the foundation for a theory of talent development, in which, very crudely expressed, high aptitudes, the gifts, serve as building blocks in the progressive development of talents. I will introduce later in the chapter crucial nuances to that rudimentary definition. The editor of the journal in which the DMGT first appeared (Gagné, 1985) hailed that text as "the best discussion of giftedness and talent presented in the last decade" (Feldhusen, 1985, p. 99). A few professionals in the field concurred. For instance, Borland (1989) stated:

> Gagne's [sic] use of the terms *giftedness* and *talent* appears to be the least arbitrary and the most useful of those proposed thus far. The distinction between competence and performance is a real and meaningful one, and it allows for the building of a model that permits the operationalization of the concepts. (p. 23)

Unfortunately, these early laudatory comments did little to bring the DMGT to the forefront of theoretical models of talent development. To this day, even though almost every handbook in the field includes a chapter on the DMGT (e.g., Gagné, 2013b, 2017, 2018a, 2018b), it remains one perspective among many as these handbooks illustrate profusely.

The Australian Experience: Pluses and Minuses

If the DMGT has not achieved dominance in spite of its robust longevity, it has enjoyed special popularity in one corner of the world, Australia, and also, to a more modest extent, in New Zealand (Roger Moltzen, February 26, 2019, 'personal communication'). As evidence, the *Australian Curriculum, Assessment, and Reporting Authority* (ACARA), a somewhat recent creation (2008) of the *Council of Australian Governments* (COAG) Education Council, acknowledges that "in Australia today, Gagné's model provides the most generally accepted definition of both giftedness and talent" (ACARA, 2018, para. 3; see also Bannister-Tyrrell, 2017; Kronborg & Cornejo-Araya, 2018). Similarly, Merrotsy's (2017) brief overview of national and state "policy and related documents, as well as websites and grey literature" (p. 29) suggests that the DMGT's differentiating definitions of giftedness and talent, or at least the model's name and source, appear in a large diversity of educational sources.

How can we explain that geographically circumscribed popularity? No doubt that the strong endorsement given by a pioneer Australian scholar in gifted education, Professor Miraca U. M. Gross, founder of the *Gifted Education Research and Resource Centre* (GERRIC) at The University of New South Wales (UNSW), played a crucial role. Coincidentally, Professor Gross had been a PhD student at Purdue University when Professor Feldhusen received the manuscript that would launch the DMGT's international career. She witnessed—and shared—his excitement towards that essay, which explains her spontaneous promotion of the DMGT upon her return to Australia. Very soon after, she invited me to teach the first cohort (1991) of students enrolled in the *Certificate of Gifted Education* (COGE) program at GERRIC, UNSW, an invitation frequently repeated over the next decade and a half. Of course, one could argue—modestly—that the quality of the DMGT also contributed significantly to its popularity. My regular participation in the COGE program helped spread the DMGT's ideas within state and local school systems, and advocacy associations; and it sparked off numerous additional invitations to keynote throughout the country, further expanding the model's dissemination.

Unfortunately, ubiquity of mention does not necessarily ensure that local academics, educators and concerned parents will apply in their writings the DMGT's explicit conceptual, and terminological proposals. This is essentially what Merrotsy (2017) tried to ascertain through his analysis of the DMGT's mention in some Australian gifted education documents. He first summarised over a dozen key elements of the DMGT and then proposed to "explore the extent to which Gagné's DMGT has been embraced by those involved in various ways with the education and support of gifted and talented children and youth in Australia" (2017, p. 30). His analysis of local citations in the few Australian documents he examined led him to a harsh verdict:

> [These local documents] cite only part of Gagné's DMGT, or misrepresent it. In particular, most quote, or partially quote, only the definitions of "gifted" and of "talent", or the "definition of giftedness and talent [sic]", then either refer obliquely to other aspects of the DMGT, or do not touch on any other aspect of the model at all. And all too often the policy language related to the DMGT is mangled. (2017, p. 38)

Henderson (2018) soon published a strong response to Merrotsy's article. She described as follows the aims of her critique:

> [My text] addresses a perceived lack of academic rigour in Merrotsy's article, seeks to provide a more balanced insight into both the application of the DMGT and the Australian gifted associations, and calls for all scholars to maintain a respectful tone in their academic critiques. (p. 59)

I appreciated her defence of volunteer advocacy associations, whose academic knowledge may sometimes be limited, but who invest much energy in their promotion of the special needs of gifted (talented?) children and adolescents; I also appreciated her appeal to researchers and other professionals "to be respectful at all times, of our field, our colleagues, our work, and our impact" (p. 63). On the other hand, I did not find any clear rebuttal of Merrotsy's critique, namely, the very limited and often-biased implementation of the DMGT's key ideas, including its core differentiation of the giftedness and talent constructs. Just to give one example, the concept of talent remains as unused in today's Australian texts as I observed almost 40 years ago in the North American professional literature. In spite of decades of efforts on my part to promote a more balanced use of the concepts of giftedness and talent, the hegemony of the gifted label remains as strong. One point that neither author mentioned should be made clear. If Merrotsy's observations appear somewhat acute, it is just because of the DMGT's very broad dissemination throughout Australia. I am convinced that Australian educators have no endemic difficulty understanding the DMGT's ideas; from what I have observed over many years, most educators in other countries manifest similar problems, but these problems remain circumscribed simply because few people there have heard or read about the DMGT.

Why and how to concretely apply the DMGT's differentiated constructs is the key theme I will address in this text, and I will do it through three distinct sub-themes. First, I will reassert the basic foundations of the DMGT, not only as a differentiation of giftedness and talent but also by highlighting their causal relationship in the talent development process. Second, focusing on the field of education, I will demonstrate that the operationalisation of these two constructs within the DMGT framework reveals, surprisingly, limited overlap between the two groups and thus creates very distinct subpopulations, not only in terms of intellectual gifts and academic talents but also beyond these two basic subgroups. Third, I will illustrate three specific uses of the differentiated constructs: (a) in the labelling of different subgroups of gifted and/or talented students; (b) in the identification procedures and decisions; and (c) in the analysis of the differentiated characteristics of research participants in most comparative studies of 'gifted' and 'non-gifted' youth and adults. Finally, I will look—with limited hope—at future impacts.

Three Key Assumptions of the DMGT

"Optimise your talents!"—"Maximise your capacities!" —"Achieve your full potential!"

These slogans summarise rather correctly, if a bit simplistically, the core of the DMGT. They appear almost everywhere: in the media, in self-help books, in motivational videos and, indeed, in all fields related to personal growth or talent development. These slogans have also been given special attention in general education. Countless authorities around the world have chosen this 'dream' as the most fundamental mission for their national or regional educational systems, namely, to ensure that all students under their responsibility will maximally develop their aptitudes. In doing so, they are following the lead of the United Nations Organization in its *Convention on the Rights of the Child*. Article 29 states: "the education of the child shall be directed to ... the development of the child's personality, talents, and mental and physical abilities to their fullest potential" (United Nations, 1989). The basic goal of achieving one's full potential is based on three key assumptions. First, it assumes the existence of two types of human abilities, namely, human *potentialities* that are distinct from human *achievements*. Second, it assumes that these two types of abilities can be separately assessed and measured. Third, it assumes that they are related; human achievements have their source in potentialities that will influence both their type and their level. These three assumptions play a key role as foundations for both the DMGT's differentiation of the concepts 'giftedness' and 'talent' and its theory of talent development. Let us examine them more closely.

Assumption 1: Potentialities and Achievements

Human abilities manifest themselves along a continuum anchored by two poles: *natural abilities* (potentialities) and *systematically developed abilities* (achievements). This basic distinction explains my use of the term 'ability' as an umbrella concept that covers the whole range; thus, I differentiate myself from many scholars in the field of psychology who associate that label strictly with aptitudes (e.g., Carroll, 1993; Lohman, 1999; Lubinski & Dawis, 1992). For instance, Gentry and Tay (2017, Fig. 4.1, p. 74) directly oppose the concepts of ability and achievement. The DMGT follows instead a more popular usage by considering both potentialities and achievements as human abilities, namely, expressions of the 'power to do something (physical or mental)' (Webster, 1983, p. 4). Indeed, the vast majority of scholars and professionals in the field of gifted education have always recognised, often implicitly, that the ubiquitous term *giftedness* could designate these two distinct types of human abilities, that is, early emerging forms of *potential* 'giftedness', as opposed to fully developed forms of *achieved* 'giftedness'.

Potentialities appear in scientific and popular publications under many labels: aptitudes, capacities, (innate) abilities, natural abilities, innate, or natural talents and so forth. I will henceforth use the term 'aptitude' as my preferred label to refer to them. Many popular expressions acknowledge the existence of aptitudes, for instance, 'he/she is a born musician,' 'he/she is a natural athlete,' 'it's God's gift' or 'it's something you don't learn, either you have it or you don't!' Aptitudes appear 'innate' to the common eye not only because they develop more or less spontaneously during childhood and adolescence, but also because they all have well-recognised biological and genetic roots (Knopic, Neiderhiser, DeFries & Plomin, 2017). I created some years ago a special model, called the *Developmental Model for Natural Abilities (DMNA)*, to describe the distinct developmental processes that govern the growth of aptitudes (Gagné, 2013a). Aptitudes vary qualitatively. As shown at left in Figure 1, the DMGT proposes six distinct *domains* of natural abilities: four mental domains (cognitive, creative, social, perceptual) and two physical domains (muscular and motor control). Achievements also receive many labels: accomplishments, competencies, expertise, realisations, and the like. I will henceforth use the term 'competencies' to designate these systematically developed abilities, acknowledging that they manifest themselves both as knowledge and skills. Competencies imply a formal—structured or unstructured—learning process; they are commonly assessed through examinations and sanctioned by some form of accreditation or diploma. Competencies also vary qualitatively. As shown in Figure 1, the DMGT proposes nine distinct *fields* of competencies, six of which are based on Holland's RIASEC structure of occupationally oriented personality types (Anastasi & Urbina, 1997; Wikipedia: eponymous). The additional three ensure an almost exhaustive coverage of occupational fields.

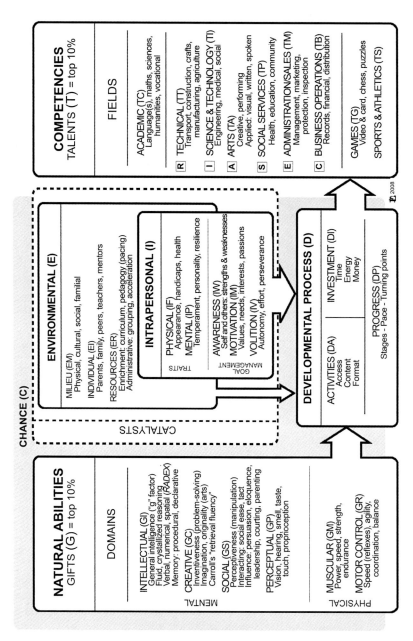

Fig. 1 Gagné's Differentiating Model of Giftedness and Talent (DMGT)

4 Implementing the DMGT's Constructs of Giftedness and Talent:...

Table 1 Differentiating characteristics of aptitude and competency measures adapted from Angoff (1988)

	Aptitude measures (natural abilities)	Competency measures (systematically developed abilities)
	Content	
A	More *general* content	More *specific* content
B	*Old formal* learning	*Recent* acquisitions
C	More widely *generalisable*	*Narrower* transfer to other situations
	Processes	
D	Major *genetic* underpinnings	Major *practice* component
E	*Slow* growth	*Rapid* growth
F	*Resistance* to stimulation	*Susceptibility* to stimulation
G	*Informal* learning	*Formal* learning
	Purpose	
H	*Prospective* use (predict future learning)	*Retrospective* use (assess amount learned)
I	Usable for *general population* evaluation	Limited to *systematically exposed individuals*
J	Usable before any formal learning	Assessment requires formal learning

Assumption 2: Differentiated Assessment

Even though we call aptitudes 'potentialities', assessing them implies the measurement of some type of performance. So, how can we distinguish aptitude measures from achievement measures if both rely on performances? The difference is not qualitative; there are no 'pure' measures of aptitudes on one side and pure measures of achievements on the other. As mentioned earlier, measures of human abilities range along a continuum defined at one end by spontaneously developed and biologically anchored natural abilities and at the other by abilities that individuals systematically develop through learning and training; the respective labels aptitudes, and competencies apply perfectly to these two anchoring points. Angoff (1988) proposed ten differentiating characteristics between aptitude and achievement measures; Table 1 shows my adapted version of his inventory. Angoff aptly worded all the descriptions as *quantitative* differences between types of instruments that simply lean in opposite directions with regard to each criterion. The disparities stand out strikingly if we compare well-known examples in each category, for instance, any—individually or group administered—test of general intelligence, as opposed to any comprehensive examination, or standardised achievement test in a school subject. The specificity (criterion A) and recency (B) of content differ markedly; the abilities assessed with the IQ test will apply to the learning of any subject, whereas the subject matters in a school curriculum focus on a clearly delimited set of competencies (knowledge and skills). Similarly, clear differences emerge as we continue down the list of pairs in Table 1; for instance, the abilities measured in an IQ test were acquired mostly through daily life experiences, most of the time without any formal learning (criterion G), and they aim to predict future learning much more than assess what has been mastered (H). Is there any hierarchy among these ten characteristics? The labels used in the DMGT ('natural' vs. 'systematically developed') point at Angoff's choice as the overarching differentiator, namely, the strength of genetic and biological input in the case of aptitudes as opposed to the capital role of learning and training in the case of competencies; the weight of their direct biological underpinnings makes measures of intellectual aptitudes—in fact *all* aptitudes—purer indices as opposed to measures of academic competencies.

Measures of aptitudes and competencies generate large individual differences that are usually distributed according to the well-known normal curve. It is of course at the top end of these curves that we will situate *outstanding* levels of aptitude or competency. In the DMGT, an outstanding level of aptitude in a particular domain is called *giftedness*, whereas an outstanding mastery of competencies in a particular field is called *talent*. But what does the label 'outstanding' mean concretely? How far above their peers do individuals need to perform to deserve the labels 'gifted' or 'talented'? I chose as minimum threshold of *prevalence* for both the gifted and talented populations, the 90th percentile (top 10%), a decision discussed in detail elsewhere (Gagné, 1998). But there are important individual differences even among the gifted and talented; accordingly, the DMGT proposes a MB (for Metric system-Based) hierarchy of four (previously five) levels: (a) the basic threshold of top 10%, (b) the top 1% labelled *highly*, (c) the top 1:1,000 labelled *exceptionally*, and (d) the top 1:10,000 labelled *extremely* or *profoundly*. The MB system applies to all domains of giftedness and all fields of talent. Note that even within the gifted or talented populations, extremely gifted/talented individuals make up a tiny subgroup (0.001 of the top 10%).

The above discussion of the first two assumptions explains the precise wording of the following DMGT definitions of giftedness and talent:

> **Giftedness (G)** designates the possession and use of biologically anchored and informally developed outstanding natural abilities or aptitudes (called gifts), in at least one ability domain, to a degree that places an individual at least among the top 10% of age peers.

> **Talent (T)** designates the outstanding mastery of systematically developed competencies (knowledge and skills) in at least one field of human activity to a degree that places an individual at least among the top 10% of 'learning peers', namely, those having accumulated a similar amount of learning time from either current or past training.

In summary, in order to respect the DMGT's precise terminological choices, keep in mind the following distinctions: (a) between two types of human abilities, *natural* abilities (aptitudes) and *systematically developed* abilities (competencies); (b) between *aptitudes* (all levels) and *gifts* (top 10%); (c) between *competencies* (all levels) and *talents* (top 10%); (d) between *domains* (aptitudes/gifts) and *fields* (competencies/talents); and (e) between average (or above average) and *outstanding* (top 10%).

Assumption 3: Causal Relationship

Achieving one's full potential, creating as many competencies as possible with our aptitudes, implies a direct causal relationship between the two types of abilities; human achievements have their origin in potentialities that will influence both their qualitative diversity and their quantitative level of expression. As repeatedly stated in the DMGT publications and presentations, it is because they are both abilities that aptitudes play that unique qualitative and quantitative role as building blocks for the competencies (knowledge and skills) that people decide to develop in a specific academic or occupational field. Qualitatively speaking, the DMGT figure illustrates a partial parallelism between the left-hand aptitude domains and the right-hand occupational fields. For instance, muscular aptitudes are the primary building blocks of sporting skills; high creative aptitudes will help differentiate those who excel in visual arts or music composing from those who do not; high social aptitudes will improve the competencies of people who work in constant interaction with other people (e.g., teachers, nurses, salespeople, politicians). And as we will see in the next section, intellectual aptitudes will be the key building blocks of all academic competencies people accumulate in the course of their education. Quantitatively speaking, high levels of a particular aptitude will accelerate most of the time the growth of related competencies. If there is one easily observable trademark characteristic of aptitudes, it is their impact on learning pace: individuals who are gifted in a particular domain will master much more easily and rapidly the competencies associated with that domain. This third assumption anchors the DMGT's definition of talent development.

> ***Talent development (TD or D)*** corresponds to the progressive transformation through a long-term learning process of biologically anchored, informally developed, and above-average natural abilities (some of them gifts) into outstanding (top 10%) systematically developed competencies (knowledge and skills), the talents, thanks to constant positive and negative modulating interactions with two large groups of catalysts, intrapersonal characteristics and environmental influences.

This detailed definition would require many pages to fully explain all the nuances it contains. Unfortunately, it is beyond the scope of this chapter to offer a detailed overview of the DMGT, of the more recent DMNA, and of their fusion into the *Integrative Model of Talent Development* (IMTD). Interested readers will find elsewhere (e.g., Gagné, 2013a, 2017; Gagné & McPherson, 2016) detailed descriptions of these intertwined models. Yet, because of their relevance for the rest of this chapter, I judged it important to highlight the following nuances:

1. The DMGT is a special case of a broader model of competence development that uses all levels of aptitudes in the explanation of all levels of achievements. Indeed, Figure 1 does illustrate that general model since gifts and talents appear as subscripts in the headings of the left (natural abilities) and right (competencies) components of the model.

2. As shown in Figure 1, gifts are just one of many causal factors contributing to the emergence of talents; the other three causal components (D, I and E in Fig. 1) also contain multiple significant causal sources, for instance, investment in time and energy (focus and concentration), intrinsic and/or extrinsic motivations, willpower and perseverance, clear talent development policies at the national and local levels, significant supportive—or non-supportive!—individuals (parents, teachers, mentors), appropriate resources (enriched curriculum, ability grouping, acceleration) and so forth. These other sources can compensate for below top 10% natural abilities (non-gifted individuals) in bringing out talents. This is why the above definition uses the expression 'above-average natural abilities' instead of 'outstanding aptitudes'. On the other hand, I believe that very few individuals with just average natural abilities can hope to reach talent-level (top 10%) competencies. This nuance will be at the heart of the next section's discussion.
3. The DMGT is both a model and a theory. As a *model*, it attempts to present the most exhaustive view of all causal influences that can affect the emergence of competencies, whatever the field examined. This is why the DMGT subdivides the five components into *subcomponents* (e.g., the six aptitude domains, or the three developmental dimensions) and then subdivides these subcomponents into *facets* or more specific subcategories within each subcomponent. This three-level structure makes possible the placement of any predictive study of human achievements in one of the 'slots' of this hierarchical model. As a *theory*, the DMGT not only proposes the building block role of aptitudes, but also a causal hierarchy of the four components; some overviews of the DMGT include a section devoted to that discussion, called 'What makes a difference' (e.g., Gagné & McPherson, 2016).

How Many Intellectually Gifted (GI) Students Are Academically Talented (TA)?

As discussed above, individual differences in aptitudes account only in part for individual differences in competencies. It follows logically that whatever the aptitude domain many gifted individuals will not reach talent-level competencies (think of underachievers); conversely, since the MB system of prevalence levels fixes at the top 10% the prevalence threshold for both the gifted and talented populations, many talented individuals will not be labelled gifted. So, addressing the second of our three sub-themes, the key question is: How many people share both labels, in other words are 'gifted *and* talented'? Recall that when I entered the field of gifted education 40 years ago, the expression 'gifted and talented' appeared somewhat regularly in chapters and articles; in fact, the term talent appeared almost nowhere else in these texts, apart from its occasional use in the undefined expression 'talent development' (Gagné, 1985, 2015). And if we put aside one educational policy paper (US Department of Education, 1993) in which the two concepts were clearly differentiated (in a direction opposite to that of the DMGT!), the expression 'gifted and talented' always conveyed a synonymous relationship, nothing more. In a nutshell, the presence of 'talented' added nothing significant to our understanding of that population. But what happens when scholars and professionals utilise it within the DMGT framework? Merrotsy (2017), concerned for proper language use, recommended to abandon it:

> The concept "gifted and talented", as noun or adjective, conflates the meaning of the two separate terms; the way this term and its related acronyms are used tends to become clichéd and confused, so that the concept loses any meaning that it might have had. (2017, p. 37)

For her part, Henderson (2018) disagreed with his position:

> [It] highlights an important issue, and one that is often misunderstood: that giftedness alone is no guarantee of successful achievement. Therefore, references to 'gifted and talented students' acknowledge this complexity and are inclusive of all students with high ability and a range of achievement profiles. … Used together, 'gifted and talented students' is a term that indicates the confluence of a range of profiles and developmental stages, rather than "conflates" the meaning of the two terms. (p. 60)

We will see below my own proposal with respect to that expression. Although introduced in the context of academic talent development, the debate over that conjunctive (G *and* T) expression applies to all aptitude domains and all fields of occupation. Indeed, we could discuss it with regard to physical aptitudes and sporting talents, creative aptitudes, and artistic talents, and so forth. For example, measures of creativity might not predict equally well competencies in fiction writing, music composition, or graphic arts. The same would apply for the relationship between some physical aptitudes and specific sports. To remain within the general thematic of this handbook, I chose to focus the discussion on Academic Talent Development (ATD) and the specific aptitudes that serve as the building blocks of that developmental process.

Academic Talent Development

Among the six natural ability domains, the intellectual domain appears uniquely associated with the emergence of outstanding academic achievements; decades of research have shown that no other aptitude domain, not even creativity, entertains a substantial causal relationship with academic achievement. Correlations between IQ scores and K–12 academic results commonly hover between 0.50 and 0.60; they decrease at the high school level, but still generally range between 0.40 and 0.50 (Jensen, 1998; Macintosh, 2011). This is why educators and parents spontaneously associate the 'gifted' label with high intelligence, usually measured through tests of cognitive (natural) abilities, the well-known—and controversial—IQ tests. But what is this intelligence that IQ tests measure?

About intelligence. Scholars have proposed so many definitions of intelligence and so many types of intelligences (e.g., Macintosh, 2011; Sternberg & Kaufman, 2011) that we should not be surprised that no unique definition has rallied a consensus. I personally favour the definition proposed by a group of 52 eminent cognitive psychologists in a position statement titled *Mainstream Science on Intelligence* (MSOI; see Gottfredson, 1997). It comprises 25 short statements, each of them focusing on a specific question, for instance, the definition and measurement of intelligence, individual and group differences, and the impact of intelligence in education, in the work place, and in daily life. In the first two statements, the authors describe what they mean by intelligence and how it is best measured.

1. Intelligence is a very general mental capability that, among other things, involves the ability to reason, plan, solve problems, think abstractly, comprehend complex ideas, learn quickly and learn from experience. It is not merely book learning, a narrow academic skill, or test-taking smarts. Rather, it reflects a broader and deeper capability for comprehending our surroundings—"catching on," "making sense" of things, or "figuring out" what to do.
2. Intelligence, so defined, can be measured, and intelligence tests measure it well. They are among the most accurate (in technical terms, reliable and valid) of all psychological tests and assessments. They do not measure creativity, character, personality, or other important differences among individuals, nor are they intended to. (Gottfredson, 1997, p. 13)

The first article defines the core of the intelligence construct; it focuses on the thinking and learning process more than its products (e.g., an extended vocabulary or broad general knowledge), although products do contribute to the assessment of intelligence. The second article is very important for two reasons. First, it defends IQ tests as the best available measure of that specific definition. This is very important in view of regular attempts by educators to 'diversify' definitions and measures of 'giftedness' away from 'constricting' IQ measures. For instance, Hertzog, Mun, DuRuz, and Holliday (2018) state (clearly pejoratively):

Throughout the greater part of the 20th century, giftedness was construed as high intelligence and intelligence was generally considered a unitary construct that could be assessed through IQ tests ... In the 1970s, theorists began to emphasize the multi-dimensional aspects of giftedness. (p. 302)

Of course, as defended in the DMGT, giftedness is multidimensional, but, as explained in the MSOI definition, *intellectual* giftedness (GI) can be construed as essentially unidimensional and its most relevant measure, the IQ score, as the best assessment tool for that unitary core, commonly called 'the g factor'. Second, it clarifies the conceptual limits these authors have set for the construct of intelligence; GI individuals *do not* necessarily possess high creativity, personal maturity, keen judgment, or exceptional wisdom; the absence of any of these 'frills' does not make them less intelligent or gifted. This is an important point to stress in view of the growing diversity of identification procedures (Hertzog et al., 2018), with the introduction of many instruments, especially checklists (e.g., Merrotsy, 2015) that assess characteristics outside intellectual aptitudes and academic achievement (e.g., creativity, personality, leadership, and so forth). In such cases, I seriously doubt that the DMGT-based gifted or talented labels would apply!

Assessing academic achievement. If we now turn to measures of academic achievement, all teacher-administered monthly or yearly exams and all standardised achievement tests belong to the achievement pole of the ability continuum mentioned early in this chapter. Similarly, examinations supervised by professional bodies at the end of a professional course of study (e.g., law, administration, medicine) clearly sample systematically acquired competencies. It is worth pointing out that many entrance examinations lean much more towards the aptitude pole than the achievement pole. Such is the case for the well-known American SAT and ACT college admission tests, although with respect to their contents, they have progressively moved towards the achievement pole over the past two decades (Lawrence, Rigol, Van Essen, & Jackson, 2003). As proof of their generality, even if both tests specifically target high school seniors who are applying to college-level institutions, the US *Talent Searches* have chosen them to measure the advancement of academically talented seventh and eighth grade students (Assouline, Lupkowski-Shoplik, & Colangelo, 2018).

This middle-of-the-road status applies also to the placement test that the New South Wales (NSW) Education Department administers to Year 6 students who wish to enter one of the 46 fully or partially selective high schools (NSW Education, 2018). The NSW selective school entry test contents include a general ability test, as well as a writing test that is graded more in terms of cognitive abilities (e.g., respect of topic, quality of thinking, organisation of ideas, and use of language) than specific academic acquisitions. Consequently, from the information given, the scores on that placement test appear to represent individual differences in intellectual aptitudes more so than differences in the mastery of the Year 6 curriculum. But there is a definite probability that students who register to pass this placement test are high academic achievers; more average students would certainly be aware of their low probability of success on that placement test, and thus would not even participate. We do not know either what is the correlation between the results on that placement test and the students' Year 6 academic results; logically, even considering the strong self-selection of the participants, there should be a substantial correlation between the two sets of measures, thus making the selected students well above average both intellectually and academically.

A variety of technical questions probably come to the readers' minds, like differences between different types of IQ tests (e.g., verbal, perceptual, numerical) or differences between teacher-administered exams as opposed to standardised achievement tests. Unfortunately, discussion of these technicalities is beyond the scope of this chapter; anyway, they would not modify the basic assessment differentiations proposed above.

The Statistics of the GI Versus TA Differentiation

We have seen that the DMGT's differentiation between gifts and talents implies logically that the intellectually gifted (GI) and academically talented (TA) populations overlap only partially. Consequently, some students are both GI and TA (the gifted *and* talented), whereas some GI students are not TA (mild or strong *underachievers*) and still others are TA but not GI (non-gifted achievers); of course, a majority of students will not belong to either the GI or TA subpopulations. How many belong to these various subgroups? Can we associate specific prevalence estimates to each of them? Bélanger and Gagné (2006) examined that question in depth; they identified four parameters that needed to receive numerical values in order to compute combined prevalence indices (as a percentage of a general population):

(a) The *average minimum threshold* that separates each marginal subgroup from the general population.
(b) The *number of abilities* or characteristics simultaneously considered, for instance, the DMGT's six giftedness domains or Renzulli's (2005) three components of giftedness (above-average abilities, creativity, task commitment).
(c) The *conjunctive* (Renzulli's A *and* B *and* C) or *disjunctive* (the DMGT's A *or* B *or* C) combination of these abilities.
(d) The *average correlation* between the various criteria.

Using four plausible values for three ('c' remained a dichotomy) of these four parameters, they constructed tables that identified relevant prevalence estimates for all combinations of these values. Let us see how their analysis applies to our situation, namely, a top 10% threshold, just two abilities (IQ and academic achievement), both conjunctive (GI *and* TA) and disjunctive (GI *or* TA) combinations and the research based 0.5 average correlation between the two abilities. Note that this approach assumes normal distributions for all variables.

Basic selection situation. Imagine that we start with a diversified school population of 1,000 students from multiple grade levels; we have for each of them valid measures of general intelligence (IQ) and academic achievement. First, we subdivide the student population into three subgroups for each measure: (a) the intellectually gifted (GI, top 10%, IQ $\geq$ 120) and the academically talented (TA, top 10%, $P_{90}+$); (b) the next 15%, corresponding to intellectually *bright* (BI) students with IQs between 110 and 119 and academic *high achievers* (HA, P_{75}–P_{89}); and (c) the remaining student population, the intellectually and academically average or below (lower 75%). The second subgroup of above average, but neither GI nor TA students serves as a buffer group of students with above-average aptitude and/or achievement; they will play an important role in the following analyses. As shown in Tables 2 and 3, this operation creates nine subpopulations of varying size; keep in mind that the bottom subgroups AI and AA cover a broad span of aptitudes (all IQs < 110) and achievements (all grades < P_{75}), which includes a significant

Table 2 Estimated distribution of a student population between nine subgroups according to their IQ and their academic achievement, when both measures have a 0.5 correlation. Population size = 1,000

Academic achievement	Intellectual aptitudes		
	AI = all others (75%) (IQ: < 110)	BI = next 15% (IQ: 110–119)	GI = top 10% (IQ: 120+)
TA = top 10% (P_{90+})	AI-TA 30	BI-TA = 40	GI-TA = 30
HA = next 15% (P_{75-89}) high achievers	AI-HA = 60	BI-HA = 50	GI-HA = 40
AA = all others (75%) (grades < P_{75})	AI-AA = 660	BI-AA = 60	GI-AA = 30

Note: There is a very small probability that we would find students from the bottom 25% in IQ (<90) within the high-achieving AI-TA and AI-HA subgroups

Table 3 Estimated distribution of a student population between nine subgroups according to their IQ and their academic achievement, when both measures have a 0.5 correlation. Distribution in a typical classroom (30 students)

Academic achievement	Intellectual aptitudes		
	AI = all others (75%) (IQ: < 110)	BI = next 15% (IQ: 110–119)	GI = top 10% (IQ: 120+)
TA = top 10% (P_{90+})	TA = 1	BI-TA 1	GI-TA 1
HA = next 15% (P_{75-89}) high achievers	HA = 2	BI-HA 2	GI-HA 1
AA = all others (75%) (grades < P_{75})	AA = 19	2	1

number (around 20%) of slightly *above-average* results, in terms of both intellectual aptitudes and academic performance.

I recommend a very careful reading of the following discussion of Table 2. That table illustrates the approximate composition of the nine subgroups; Bélanger's simulations mathematically ascertain only one value, that of the GI-TA subgroup; that certainly surprising overlap estimate of only 30% (3% of the total population) comes directly from Bélanger and Gagné's (2006) Table 3; this value for the *conjunctive* prevalence of GI *and* TA students results from our choice of just two abilities, a top 10% selection ratio *per ability* and an average 0.5 correlation between the two variables. Note the significant role of the correlation level: the GI-TA percentage can vary from 1% when $r = 0$ to 10% when $r = 1$. In fact, it is easy to compute the cell values when $r = 1$ (AI-AA = 75%; BI-HA = 15%; GI-TA = 10%; all other cells empty), and also when $r = 0$ (compute the product of the row by column percentages; GI-TA = 10% × 10% = 1%, BI-TA = 15% × 10% = 1.5%, GI-AA = 75% × 10% = 7.5%, etc.). I used these two 3 × 3 tables as extreme cases to estimate the cell values for $r = 0.5$, since the only known value was the 3% obtained from Bélanger and Gagné's (2006) computations. My main decision consisted in distributing the 7% leftover GI students between the two lower cells (GI-HA, GI-AA); I opted for a 4% and 3% distribution, considering that the AA cell could easily accommodate a third of that group since that bottom row included 75% of all students in the table, with a fair number of them having above-average academic results. To ensure equilibrium, I used that same 4/3 ratio for the two (non-GI) TA subgroups in the top row (BI-TA, AI-TA). All other percentages were adjusted accordingly. [*Note*. The author invites sceptical readers to draw the two anchoring 3 × 3 tables ($r = 0, r = 1$) and then use them to imagine the $r = 0.5$ table whose only mathematically ascertained value is the conjunctive 3% in the upper right corner. From there, try estimating the most logically probable distribution. It should not be very different from the one I propose in Table 2.]

With respect to the prevalence of gifted and/or talented students, we obtain three distinct populations: (a) the 30 (3%) 'gifted *and* talented' students (GI-TA), (b) the 70 (7%) 'gifted non-talented' students (GI-HA, GI-AA), and (c) the 70 (7%) 'non-gifted but academically talented' students (BI-TA, AI-TA). It ensues that only 18% (30/170) of the *disjunctive* group of GI *or* TA students belong to the *conjunctive* group of gifted *and* talented (GI-TA) students. In other words, more than 80% of all identified gifted *or* talented students *do not* belong to the select 'gifted *and* talented' subgroup! The subgroup of intellectually gifted (GI) students includes a large diversity of achievement levels. Table 2 shows an equal number of GI students in the two extreme achievement categories, a distribution that seems improbable at first glance. But keep in mind that the 30 gifted talented students represent 30% of the students in that top row, whereas the 30 gifted non-talented students represent only 4% (30/750) of the bottom row. Moreover, that large group of 'all others' includes above-average (P_{55}–P_{74}) achievements that reduce the apparent aptitude-achievement gap. Still, a fair number of, maybe 15–20%, students obtain just average and even below average academic results; we would call them appropriately 'gifted underachievers' or 'gifted non-talented' depending on the size of the aptitude-achievement gap. The fact that no one in our field—at least to my knowledge—has yet proposed a clear operational definition of the gifted underachiever construct, for example, in terms of a minimum aptitude/achievement gap, makes it difficult to estimate the size of that special population. For instance, Veas et al. (2018) mentioned a 40% range (from 10% to 50%) for published prevalence estimates. If we now focus on the left column of students, we note a significant percentage (30%) of intellectually average (IQ < 110) but academically talented students (AI-TA). The same reasoning proposed above for the 'gifted non-talented' students applies here. I have often heard teachers describe some of their students as high achievers but 'not truly gifted;' the BI-TA (bright talented) and especially the AI-TA (average talented) students could well be the targets of such comments. On the other hand, we would never say 'not truly talented' because, by definition, talent means confirmed academic achievement. Finally, keep in mind that the DMGT stresses the role of multiple sources (e.g., D, I, and E components) as causal factors of talent emergence, thus giving more plausibility to the BI-TA and AI-TA subgroups. Table 3 illustrates what a regular classroom of 30 students would look like in terms of student distribution between the nine cells. Notice again that out of five gifted *or* talented students, only one (3% of that group) belongs to the GI-TA subgroup, whereas four others (13%) can be disjunctively labelled gifted *or* talented.

Two additional plausible simulations. Let us now apply the Table 2 data to a typical selection procedure that will demonstrate even more emphatically the impact of the differentiated definitions of giftedness and talent; it is typical because it involves giving *equal priority* to aptitude and achievement measures, labelled 'traditional' by Brodersen, Brunner, and Missett (2018). If a 'gifted program' coordinator decides to create her top 10% special group of 'gifted' students by equally weighing these two criteria, which students will comprise that select group? Applying that weighing process, she will first select, of course, the 30 GI-TA students who excel both intellectually and academically. Then, she will favour the *gifted* students who obtain the highest achievement scores just below the top 10% threshold (the best GI-HA), as well as the *talented* students who obtain the highest IQ scores just below the top 10% IQ threshold (the best BI-TA). In other words, that group of 100 'gifted' students will be composed of the 30 GI-TA students, as well as the 70 brightest *and* highest achievers within the combined ($n = 80$) GI-HA and BI-TA groups. No students would be chosen from the slightly lower—neither gifted nor talented—subgroup of bright high-achieving (BI-HA) students. The fact that *all* chosen students in her top 10% group will be the best of the 'bright high achievers'—either GI (TA or HA) or TA (GI or BI)—helps us understand the spontaneous tendency of educators who combine measures of aptitude and achievement to consider the selected students 'gifted *and* talented', although fewer than a third of them (just 30%) really deserve the DMGT's twin labels. Again, Table 3 confirms at the classroom level these selection results based on the DMGT's threshold of top 10%; the three students composing the top 10% of identified 'gifted' group would be selected from the GI-TA, GI-HA, and BI-TA categories. As a last note, if we chose a more selective threshold, for instance, the top 5% (IQ $\geq$ 125, and $P_{95}+$), we would disjunctively identify only 50 GI and 50 TA students. According to Bélanger and Gagné's (2006) Table 3, only 12 of them would be gifted *and* talented (GI-TA) students, which means 14% (12/88) of the GI *or* TA groups and just 1.2% of the total population. Said differently, under that stricter selection ratio, the *conjunctive* gifted and talented students will represent just 14% (as opposed to 18% with a top 10% selection ratio) of the *disjunctive* gifted *or* talented subpopulation. Whichever way you look at it, any selection process will identify many times more gifted non-talented students or non-gifted talented students than the 'gifted *and* talented' students mentioned again and again in the professional literature.

Bélanger and Gagné (2006, Table 4) examined another common administrative situation, one in which the 'gifted program' coordinator is given a predetermined target percentage for the 'gifted' population that will receive special services (usually once-a-week pullout classes). What could be that target percentage? Callahan, Moon, and Ho (2017) surveyed over 1,500 school districts about their policies and practices concerning their 'gifted' population. They stated "the majority of district coordinators ... reported that between 1% and 10% of the students in their districts were identified as gifted" (p. 29). So, an average or a median of 5% would not be too far from reality. If that coordinator applies the same selection procedure as above, namely, equal priority to IQ and academic achievement data having a 0.5 correlation, what percentage (of top students of course) will she need to select *for each ability measure* so that the conjunctive subgroup attains that 5% predetermined target? 7%? 10%? Even more? Believe it or not, just to identify that select group of 5% of the brightest and highest achievers, she would need to put aside the top 13.5% on each measure, which means *22% of the total school population* (13.5% + 13.5%, minus the 5% overlap). Of course, if you look at 'prototypical' G & T students, those who stand out well above the thresholds of excellence, the selection is easy. But when you face a full selection process that includes students close to the selection thresholds, then the choices become much less evident!

In summary, this second section aimed to quantify the aptitude-achievement differentiation process. It required clear operational definitions for both the aptitude and achievement constructs. In continuity with the present handbook's educational focus, I chose to examine the relationship between academic talent, assessed through combined subject matter grades, and intellectual aptitudes, operationalised as IQ scores in continuity with the MSOI conceptual framework (Gottfredson, 1997), as well as common school district practices (at least in the USA). I then applied Bélanger's theoretical work (Bélanger & Gagné, 2006) to obtain both conjunctive and disjunctive prevalence estimates for subgroups of intellectually gifted (GI) and/or academically talented (TA) students within a typical school population. Three distinct simulations confirmed beyond any doubt the very limited overlap between the gifted and talented groups. Even though we could take advantage of an unusually high (0.5) correlation between the aptitude and achievement indices (compared to other domains and fields), only 30% of the GI students achieved talent level (top 10%) academic grades (and vice versa). Indeed, there were twice as many (70%) non-gifted talented students than gifted talented ones, as well as an equivalent percentage of gifted non-talented students.

In a nutshell, about 20% of the *disjunctive* population of gifted *or* talented students belonged to the *conjunctive* population of gifted *and* talented students, leaving 80% of identified students outside the conjunctive group. I must add that if program coordinators were to broaden their definition of 'giftedness' by merging

Table 4 DMGT-based suggested labels

Aptitude -> achievement	AI (average IQ) (lower 75%)	BI (bright) (next 15%)	GI (gifted) (top 10%)
TA (top 10%)	(Academically) talented	Bright talented	Gifted talented
HA (next 15%)	Acad. high achievers	Bright high achievers	Gifted high achievers
AA (lower 75%)	Acad. average Acad. competent	Bright competent Bright average	Gifted non-talented Gifted underachievers

Note: There is a very small probability that we would find students from the bottom 25% in IQ (<90) within the AI-TA and AI-HA subgroups. Also, the AI-AA labels do not apply to the lowest (25%?) achievers a variety of measures other than IQ, the correlation between that aggregate score and academic achievement would most probably decrease significantly, thus reducing the overlap between the 'GI' (whatever the conceptual meaning of that score) and TA subpopulations.

Some Practical Applications

One question remains: How should we practically implement this differentiated approach to giftedness and talent? The DMGT offers a diversity of practical applications, for scholars, educators, parents, and the students themselves. The following three applications represent those I consider more basic.

Appropriate Labelling

The key question is of course the proper semantic use of the giftedness and talent concepts. Table 4 proposes a series of distinct labels for each of the nine subpopulations created in the preceding section. Note that most expressions identify both the aptitude level (gifted, bright, average, or less) and the achievement level (talented, high achieving, average, or less). In any field of occupation, educators aim to develop competencies (knowledge and skills), and learners will be judged first and foremost by their level of mastery of these competencies, independent of their underlying level of relevant aptitudes. This is why I believe it is more appropriate to focus on achievements than aptitudes. Consequently, I chose to use the aptitude label as a qualifier of the achievement label, preferring to describe students, for instance, as 'gifted high-achieving' students instead of 'high-achieving gifted' students. For the same reason, I would substitute the common expression 'gifted and talented' with 'gifted talented', thus isolating a 'gifted' subgroup within the population of talented students. This is one way to acknowledge the important descriptive role of the 'talent' label. The labels in Table 4 are just suggestions; for instance, some local users might prefer to substitute the label 'superior' for 'high achieving'. The key point is to implement a terminology that respects: (a) the giftedness/talent differentiation, (b) the recognition of multiple domains and fields, and (c) the explicit recognition of the DMGT's MB system of prevalence levels or its equivalent.

When can we properly use the 'gifted' (G) label? All individuals professionally identified—not diagnosed, please!—through some relevant aptitude measure can receive the G label if their score reaches or exceeds the top 10% basic threshold defined in the MB system. Local administrators can adopt another minimum threshold as long as they identify it explicitly; keep in mind that a prevalence threshold is an essential constituent of any good operational definition (Gagné, 1998). When people do not have access to aptitude measures, they can look for indirect behavioural indices, especially the individual's *pace of progress* in a learning situation; as I have said repeatedly, ease and speed of learning constitute interesting—if not perfectly valid—indices of giftedness, whatever the domain is. Again, users should not forget to add: (a) the proper *qualitative* adverb specifying the aptitude domain (e.g., intellectually, creatively, socially) and (b) the proper *quantitative* adverb (e.g., highly, exceptionally, extremely) if the score justifies it. These precisions remind everyone that aptitudes vary both qualitatively and quantitatively. It is not necessary to include these precisions each time the label is used, only when it is first introduced. In the specific case of intellectual giftedness, I strongly recommend adopting the MSOI definition of intelligence (Gottfredson, 1997) and its most relevant measure, the IQ test. In the absence of psychometric data, educators can look for clear signs of *outstanding* (top 10%) reasoning processes with respect to age peers; Article 1 of the MSOI describes seven such observable processes. These indirect indices will be particularly important to detect potentially gifted non-talented students (GI underachievers). Equivalent criteria apply to the label 'intellectually bright', (BI) targeting the subgroup of 15% just below the gifted level. When we have any doubt about the exact threshold of exceptionality of a particular subgroup, we should use the lower, more inclusive label (e.g., BI instead of GI).

For its part, the label 'talented' applies to *outstanding* (top 10%) achievements, as long as there is stability over time; in the same way that 'one swallow does not a summer make', one outstanding achievement does not a talent make! Again, it is important to mention: (a) the proper field specification, usually as an addition (e.g., talented *in* science, *in* mechanical engineering, *in* photography, *in* swimming); and (b) the proper MB-based adverb (when necessary) to specify the level of talent above the basic threshold. The 'high-achieving' (HA) label follows the same rules of application as the BI label.

Whom to Prioritise: The Gifted or the Talented?

In their efforts to maximise the effectiveness and efficiency of their academically oriented talent development programs (e.g., special schools, honours classes), administrators seek to identify the most promising students, those best equipped to profit maximally from the program's more demanding curriculum. And since DMGT-inspired ATD programs must focus on academic excellence (Gagné, 2015), such programs should look for selection criteria that have consistent strong correlations with academic achievement. What are these criteria? Although I highlighted earlier the special strength of IQ scores as predictors of academic performance, research has shown that past or current academic achievement outperforms any other predictor of future achievement. For instance, Marques, Pais-Ribeiro, and Lopez (2011) found correlations above 0.90 between consecutive aggregated subject matter achievements in grades 6–8. For his part, Muijs (1997) observed an "extremely strong relationship [between] school achievement in wave 1 [Grade 4] with school achievement in wave 2 [Grade 5] ... a fact borne out by a Pearson correlation of 0.88 ($p < 0.001$) over time" (p. 272). I did not find published averages for these correlations based on large sets of achievement data. But, my educated guess would place that average around 0.85 ($r^2 = 0.72$); in other words, current achievement explains at least 70% of the variance in future achievement, with a progressive decrease in explanatory power as the time gap increases between pairs of measures. If we compare that value with the 0.5 ($r^2 = 0.25$) predictive power of IQ, we immediately realise the large difference in explained variance between these two 'predictors', almost three times as much for achievement measures. These differential results should surprise no one: correlations between successive indices of academic achievement measure that variable's *stability* over time, a form of *reliability* (Anastasi & Urbina, 1997). By contrast, all the other factors spread throughout the DMGT components (G, I, D, E) are distinct causal influences, and their correlations with academic achievement are indices of their predictive *validity*. And we expect of course much higher values in the case of reliability indices as opposed to validity indices. In short, because all achievement measures reflect in their individual differences the same complex sources of achievement, current academic achievement predicts future academic achievement much more effectively than any IQ test could do.

Practically speaking, what does that mean? Suppose that we have to choose between 'bright talented' and 'gifted high-achieving' students, which should we favour? Personally, I would not hesitate to give a definite advantage to students who have demonstrated that they possess strong enough personal qualities and environmental support to reach talent-level performances in spite of somewhat lower natural cognitive aptitudes. In the long run, these qualities, especially motivation and volition, should ensure enduring high performances. That conviction constitutes an additional argument to acknowledge talent over giftedness; it might also help focus the attention of school administrators on the specific educational needs of bright achieving students, who represent a much larger population than the commonly highlighted highly gifted or non-talented gifted (underachieving) students.

Research Interpretations

Hundreds of published studies have compared the personal characteristics or environments of 'gifted' youth and adults with those of more average people. How do the authors of these studies obtain their samples of 'gifted' individuals? In most cases, they take advantage of 'convenience' samples, samples usually composed of students who were selected by outside agencies to participate in a 'gifted program'. But the members of these samples may not really be 'gifted' students as the DMGT would define them, since a majority of them are usually identified with 'traditional' measures, namely, both IQ and achievement data. In other words, they are probably the same kind of special mixed group of best gifted *or* talented students I extracted from Table 2 as part of the second simulation. They do not constitute a representative sample of all GI students, because the procedure not only excludes the significant subgroup of gifted non-talented (GI-AA) students, the underachievers, but also the lowest achievers among the group of gifted high-achieving (GI-HA) students. That selection bias should lower to some extent measures of intrapersonal characteristics (e.g., personality, motivation, volition), as well as indices of environmental quality (e.g., supportive parents, family SES, classroom atmosphere). In other words, we should not be surprised that the bright high achievers (BI-HA+) typically selected for gifted programs will prove themselves, on average, somewhat more motivated, socially adept, or psychologically stable than both 'pure' GI students or average peers. This is indeed the more common conclusion of literature reviews of such studies, as exemplified by this quote:

> The major conclusions of the earlier publication appear to be alive and well: As a group, gifted young people are inherently no more socially or emotionally vulnerable than their age peers, and indeed, many appear even more robust, but they are immune to none of the ills that befall their peers. (Robinson & Reis, 2016, p. XIII)

I have mentioned once in a while in past Australian workshops—but never in print, I believe—that the common use of convenience samples in our field's research could engender an observable selection bias in the direction mentioned above. I found recently that others were also beginning to question the purity of these convenience samples. As a case in point, Francis, Hawes, and Abbott (2016) systematically reviewed studies that compared the psychopathological characteristics of 'gifted' versus average students; they concluded "that gifted children demonstrate superior socio-emotional adjustment and fewer behavioural difficulties than their typically developing peers" (p. 279), but they added among their methodological issues the following caveat:

> It is possible that the nature of the gifted program selection process results in members who are functioning well in school (academically, behaviourally, and socially), potentially leading to participant selection bias in studies that underestimates the prevalence of intellectually gifted children with behavioural or other difficulties. (Francis et al., 2016, p. 295)

In her chapter on perfectionism in 'gifted' children, Speirs Neumeister (2016) made a similar comment:

> The importance of operationalizing giftedness within the study of perfectionism is paramount. Many published studies on perfectionism within gifted education may be more appropriately named as studies of perfectionism within *high achieving* gifted students as the students are frequently taking honors classes at the middle and high school level or enrolled in an Honors College. Use of these samples is problematic because participation in these services requires one to be high achieving as well as high ability. [Researchers need to study also] those who are gifted and *not* participating in these services in spite of their availability. Inclusion of this group of "underachieving" gifted students may paint an entirely different picture of the incidence of perfectionism with [within?] the population and its correlates to adaptive and maladaptive outcomes. (Speirs Neumeister, 2016, pp. 33–34)

These quotes state perfectly the point I am trying to make: a proper use of the DMGT's differentiated perspective would make it easy to examine the respective roles of aptitude and achievement measures in the selection of research samples and thus improve the data analysis and interpretation process. Notice how this practical

Table 5 DMGT-inspired terminological proposals

Current label (CL)	Proposed label	Comment
Gifted education	Academic Talent Development (ATD) field	CL semantically incorrect. Proposal focuses on desirable goal to be pursued by the field.
NAGC	NADAT (National Association for the Development of Academic Talent)	Follows logically from above suggestion. It states clearly the desired educational goal.
Gifted *and* talented	Gifted talented	See Table 4.
Gifted *or* talented	Gifted high achieving, brighttalented, etc.	Use 'bright achieving' for broadest coverage. See Table 4 for details.
Gifted program	1. Enrichment (provision or service) 2. ATD (program or provision)	See Gagné (2015) for distinction between programs and provisions. Use proposal 1 for non-ATD services (e.g., pullout classes).
Gifted teachers	1. Enrichment specialists 2. ATD teachers	CL semantically incorrect and potentially insulting for colleagues! Use proposal 1 for non-ATD services (e.g., pullout classes).
Gifted learners	Gifted (or talented) learners	Use G when focusing on learning processes (ease/speed); use T when focusing on products (achievement).
Differentiation	1. Enrichment 2. ATD curriculum	Enrichment is THE specific type of differentiation for talented students. Use proposal 2 when applicable.
Gifted coordinator	1. Enrichment coordinator 2. ATD coordinator	CL semantically incorrect. Use proposal 2 when applicable.

use of the DMGT definitions parallels an earlier discussion on the analysis of achievement tests in terms of the degree of content leaning towards aptitude tests. Both analyses pursue the same goal, namely, assessing the relative importance of aptitudes and competencies in the identification of outstanding individuals.

Conclusions

I have tried in this chapter to: (a) clarify the conceptual and empirical foundations of differentiated definitions for the labels 'gifted' and 'talented'; (b) show their empirical distinctiveness; and (c) illustrate appropriate ways to apply this differentiation. Will that new effort achieve better results than all my former attempts spread over a 40-year career in this field? I must confess that I entertain serious doubts about it. Yet, a few well-targeted initiatives by a small group of Australian educators could possibly bring about one of those tipping points so well discussed by Gladwell (2002). And, once achieved, that tipping point might produce similar impacts elsewhere in Australasia and then in other countries outside that region. But could that be just one more utopian or quixotic dream on my part? Indeed, I cannot ignore the very realistic—pessimistic?—fact that I have not witnessed any significant evolution in conceptual views and terminological habits during the past 40 years. As I said at the beginning of this chapter, all the signs I observed when I entered the—mislabelled—field of gifted education (see Table 5 for a list of terminological counter-proposals), for instance, the hegemony of the 'gifted' label associated with the almost total exclusion of the label 'talent', appear as firmly rooted now as they were then. Although I pleaded repeatedly for significant changes to that conceptual and terminological Tower of Babel (Gagné, 1995, 2004, 2015), I have not yet observed any significant impact.

If academics and professionals accept and maintain without question our field's 'conceptual ruts', how can we expect those in the 'trenches', the teachers in the schools and the parents who keep alive advocacy associations, to go against the field's pundits who keep using that improper terminology in scholarly and policy publications? Sometimes I fear that the only practical solution resides in Max Planck's famous observation (see Wikiquotes, eponymous):

> A new scientific truth does not triumph by convincing its opponents and making them see the light, but rather because its opponents eventually die, and a new generation grows up that is familiar with it.

Cross-References

- ▶ Creativity Talent Development: Fostering Creativity in Schools
- ▶ Gifted Education in the Asia-Pacific: From the Past for the Future – An Introduction
- ▶ Identifying Gifted Learning in the Regular Classroom: Seeking Intuitive Theories
- ▶ Put Them Together and See How They Learn! Ability Grouping and Acceleration Effects on the Self-Esteem of Academically Gifted High School Students
- ▶ Social and Cultural Conceptions and Perceptions: Part I Introduction
- ▶ Some Implications for the Future of Gifted Education in the Asia-Pacific
- ▶ Supporting Australian Gifted Indigenous Students' Academic Potential in Rural Settings
- ▶ Teaching Gifted Education to Pre-service Teachers: Lessons Learned
- ▶ Towards Exceptionality: The Current Status and Future Prospects of Australian Gifted Education

References

ACARA. (2018). *See section on "Student diversity: Gifted and talented students' webpage."* Retrieved from https://www.australiancurriculum.edu.au/resources/student-diversity/gifted-and-talented-students

Anastasi, A., & Urbina, S. (1997). *Psychological testing* (7th ed.). Upper Saddle River, NJ: Prentice-Hall.

Angoff, W. H. (1988). The nature-nurture debate, aptitudes, and group differences. *American Psychologist, 41*, 713–720.

Assouline, S. G., Lupkowski-Shoplik, A., & Colangelo, N. (2018). Acceleration and the talent search model: Transforming the school culture. In S. Pfeiffer, M. Foley-Nicpon, & E. Shaunessy-Dedrick (Eds.), *APA handbook of giftedness and talent* (pp. 333–346). Washington, DC: American Psychological Association.

Bannister-Tyrrell, M. (2017). Gagné's DMGT 2.0: A possible model of unification and shared understandings. *The Australasian Journal of Gifted Education, 26*(2), 43–49. https://doi.org/10.21505/ajge.2017.0015

Bélanger, J., & Gagné, F. (2006). Estimating the size of the gifted/talented population from multiple identification criteria. *Journal for the Education of the Gifted, 30*, 131–163. https://doi.org/10.4219/jeg-2006-258

Borland, J. H. (1989). *Planning and implementing programs for the gifted*. New York, NY: Teachers College Press.

Brodersen, A. V., Brunner, M. M., & Missett, T. C. (2018). Traditional identification instruments. In C. M. Callahan & H. L. Hertberg-Davis (Eds.), *Fundamentals of gifted education: Considering multiple perspectives* (2nd ed., pp. 103–115). New York, NY: Routledge.

Callahan, C. M., Moon, T. R., & Oh, S. (2017). Describing the status of programs for the gifted: A call for action. *Journal for the Education of the Gifted, 40*, 20–49. https://doi.org/10.1177/0162353216686215

Carroll, J. B. (1993). *Human cognitive abilities: A survey of factor-analytic studies*. Cambridge, UK: Cambridge University Press.

Feldhusen, J. F. (1985). From the editor. *The Gifted Child Quarterly, 29*, 99.

Francis, R., Hawes, D. J., & Abbott, M. (2016). Intellectual giftedness and psychopathology in children and adolescents: A systematic literature review. *Exceptional Children, 82*, 279–302. https://doi.org/10.1177/0014402915598779

Gagné, F. (1985). Giftedness and talent: Reexamining a reexamination of the definitions. *The Gifted Child Quarterly, 29*, 103–112. https://doi.org/10.1177/001698628502900302

Gagné, F. (1995). From giftedness to talent: A developmental model and its impact on the language of the field. *Roeper Review, 18*, 103–111. https://doi.org/10.1080/02783199509553709

Gagné, F. (1998). A proposal for subcategories within the gifted or talented populations. *The Gifted Child Quarterly, 42*, 87–95. https://doi.org/10.1177/001698629804200203

Gagné, F. (1999). Is there any light at the end of the tunnel? *Journal for the Education of the Gifted, 22*, 191–234.

Gagné, F. (2004). An imperative, but, alas, improbable consensus! *Roeper Review, 27*, 12–14. https://doi.org/10.1080/02783190409554281

Gagné, F. (2013a). The DMGT: Changes within, beneath, and beyond. *Talent Development and Excellence, 5*, 5–19.

Gagné, F. (2013b). Yes, giftedness (aka "innate" talent) does exist! In S. B. Kaufman (Ed.), *The complexity of greatness: Beyond talent or practice* (pp. 191–221). Oxford, UK: Oxford University Press.

Gagné, F. (2015). Academic talent development programs: A best practices model. *Asia Pacific Education Review, 16*, 281–295. https://doi.org/10.1007/s12564-015-9366-9

Gagné, F. (2017). The integrative model of talent development (IMTD): From theory to educational applications. In J. A. Plucker, A. N. Rinn, & M. C. Makel (Eds.), *From giftedness to gifted education: Reflecting theory in practice* (pp. 149–182). Waco, TX: Prufrock Press.

Gagné, F. (2018a). Academic talent development: Theory and best practices. In S. I. Pfeiffer, E. Shaunessy-Dedrick, & M. Foley-Nicpon (Eds.), *APA Handbook of giftedness and talent* (pp. 163–183). Washington, DC: American Psychological Association.

Gagné, F. (2018b). Expertise development from an IMTD perspective. In D. Z. Hambrick, G. Campitelli, & B. N. Macnamara (Eds.), *The science of expertise: Behavioral, neural, and genetic approaches to complex skill* (pp. 307–327). New York, NY: Routledge.

Gagné, F., & McPherson, G. E. (2016). Analyzing musical prodigiousness using Gagné's integrative model of talent development. In G. E. McPherson (Ed.), *Musical prodigies: Interpretations from psychology, education, musicology and ethnomusicology* (pp. 3–114). Oxford, UK: Oxford University Press.

Gentry, M., & Tay, J. (2017). Using cluster grouping to improve student achievement, equity, and teacher practices. In J. A. Plucker, A. N. Rinn, & M. C. Makel (Eds.), *From giftedness to gifted education: Reflecting theory in practice* (pp. 65–90). Waco, TX: Prufrock Press.

Gladwell, M. (2002). *The tipping point: How little things can make big differences*. New York, NY: Back Bay Books.

Gottfredson, L. S. (1997). Mainstream science on intelligence: An editorial with 52 signatories, history, and bibliography. *Intelligence, 24*, 13–23. Retrieved from http://www1.udel.edu/educ/gottfredson/reprints/1997mainstream.pdf

Henderson, L. C. (2018). Reflecting on the DMGT in the Australian context: Response to Merrotsy. *Australasian Journal of Gifted Education, 27*(1), 59–64. https://doi.org/10.21505/ajge.2018.0006

Hertzog, N. B., Mun, R. U., DuRuz, B., & Holliday, A. A. (2018). Identification of strengths and talents in young children. In S. Pfeiffer, M. Foley-Nicpon, & E. Shaunessy-Dedrick (Eds.), *APA handbook of giftedness and talent* (pp. 301–316). Washington, DC: American Psychological Association.

Jensen, A. R. (1998). *The 'g' factor: The science of mental ability*. Westport, CT: Preager.

Knopic, V. S., Neiderhiser, J. M., DeFries, J. C., & Plomin, R. (2017). *Behavioral genetics* (7th ed.). New York, NY: Worth Publishers.

Kronborg, L., & Cornejo-Araya, C. A. (2018). Gifted educational provisions for gifted and highly able students in Victorian schools, Australia. *Universitas Psychologica, 17*(5), 1–14. https://doi.org/10.11144/Javeriana.upsy17-5.gepg

Lawrence, I. M., Rigol, G. W., Van Essen, T., & Jackson, C. A. (2003). *A historical perspective on the content of the SAT*. New York, NY: College Entrance Examination Board.

Lohman, D. F. (1999). Minding our p's and q's: On finding relationships between learning and intelligence. In P. L. Ackerman, P. C. Kyllonen, & R. D. Roberts (Eds.), *Learning and individual differences: Process, trait, and content determinants* (pp. 55–76). Washington, DC: American Psychological Association.

Lubinski, D., & Dawis, R. V. (1992). Aptitudes, skills, and proficiencies. In M. D. Dunnette & L. M. Hough (Eds.), *The handbook of industrial/organizational psychology* (2nd ed., pp. 1–59). Palo Alto, CA: Consulting Psychologists Press.

Macintosh, N. J. (2011). *IQ and human intelligence* (2nd ed.). Oxford, UK: Oxford University Press.

Marques, S. C., Pais-Ribeiro, J. L., & Lopez, S. J. (2011). The role of positive psychology constructs in predicting mental health and academic achievement in children and adolescents: A two-year longitudinal study. *Journal of Happiness Studies, 12*, 1049–1062. https://doi.org/10.1007/s10902-010-9244-4

Merrotsy, P. (2015). Supporting outstanding learners. In A. Ashman (Ed.), Education for inclusion and diversity (5th ed., pp. 233–262). Frenchs Forest, NSW: Pearson.

Merrotsy, P. (2017). Gagné's differentiated model of giftedness and talent in Australian education. *Australasian Journal of Gifted Education, 26*(2), 29–41.

Muijs, R. D. (1997). Predictors of academic achievement and academic self-concept: A longitudinal perspective. *British Journal of Educational Psychology, 67*, 263–277. https://doi.org/10.1111/j.2044-8279.1997.tb01243.x

NSW Education. (2018). https://education.nsw.gov.au/public-schools/selective-high-schools-and-opportunity-classes/year-7/the-test#Test1

Renzulli, J. S. (2005). The three-ring conception of giftedness: A developmental model for promoting creative productivity. In R. J. Sternberg & J. E. Davidson (Eds.), *Conceptions of giftedness* (2nd ed., pp. 246–279). New York, NY: Cambridge University Press.

Robinson, N. M., & Reis, S. (2016). Foreword. In M. Neihart, S. I. Pfeiffer, & T. L. Cross (Eds.), *The social and emotional development of gifted children* (2nd ed., pp. XIII–XXVI). Waco, TX: Prufrock.

Siegle, D., & McCoach, D. B. (2013). Underachieving gifted students. In C. M. Callahan & H. L. Hertberg-Davis (Eds.), *Fundamentals of gifted education: Considering multiple perspectives* (pp. 377–387). New York, NY: Routledge.

Speirs Neumeister, K. (2016). Perfectionism in gifted students. In M. Neihart, S. I. Pfeiffer, & T. L. Cross (Eds.), *The social and emotional development of gifted children* (2nd ed., pp. 29–39). Waco, TX: Prufrock.

Sternberg, R. J., & Kaufman, S. B. (Eds.). (2011). *The Cambridge handbook of intelligence*. New York, NY: Cambridge University Press.

U.S. Department of Education, Office of Educational Research and Improvement. (1993). *National excellence: A case for developing America's talent*. Washington, DC: U.S. Government Printing Office.

United Nations. (1989). Convention on the rights of the child. Retrieved from http://www.ohchr.org/EN/ProfessionalInterest/Pages/CRC.aspx

Veas, A., Castejon, J.-L., O'Reilly, C., & Ziegler, A. (2018). Mediation analysis of the relationship between educational capital, learning capital, and underachievement among gifted secondary school students. *Journal for the Education of the Gifted*, 1–17. https://doi.org/10.1177/0162353218799436

Webster, N. (1983). *Webster's new universal unabridged dictionary.* (J. L. McKetchnie, Ed.). (Deluxe 2nd edition). New York: Dorset & Baber.

Françoys Gagné, PhD. After earning his PhD in Psychology from l'Université de Montréal (1966), Professor Gagné spent most of his professional career in the Department of Psychology at l'Université du Québec à Montréal (UQAM). He devoted most of his research and teaching activities to the field of giftedness. He has gained international renown through his theory of talent development: the *Differentiating Model of Giftedness and Talent (DMGT)*. Professor Gagné has received many professional prizes, including the prestigious *Distinguished Scholar Award (1996)* from the National Association of Gifted Children (NAGC, USA). Officially retired since 2001, Dr. Gagné maintains regular publishing projects.

Sociocultural Perspectives on the Talent Development Megamodel

5

Paula Olszewski-Kubilius, Rena F. Subotnik, Frank C. Worrell, Janna Wardman, Liang See Tan, and Seon-Young Lee

Contents

Domain-Specific Abilities	103
Domain-Specific Trajectories	106
Psychosocial Skills	108
Opportunities Must Be Offered	110
Opportunities Must Also Be Taken	111
Eminence as the Outcome of Gifted Education	111
Commentary on the Applicability of the Megamodel in New Zealand	112
Commentary on the Applicability of the Megamodel in Singapore	116

P. Olszewski-Kubilius (✉)
Center for Talent Development, School of Education and Social Policy, Northwestern University, Evanston, IL, USA
e-mail: p-olszewski-kubilius@northwestern.edu

R. F. Subotnik
American Psychological Association, Washington, DC, USA
e-mail: rsubotnik@apa.org

F. C. Worrell
University of California Berkeley, Berkeley, CA, USA
e-mail: frankc@berkeley.edu

J. Wardman
University of Auckland, Auckland, New Zealand
e-mail: j.wardman@auckland.ac.nz

L. S. Tan
Centre for Research in Pedagogy and Practice, Office of Education Research, National Institute of Education, Singapore, Singapore
e-mail: liangsee.tan@nie.edu.sg

S.-Y. Lee
Seoul National University, Seoul, South Korea
e-mail: seonylee@snu.ac.kr

© Springer Nature Singapore Pte Ltd. 2021
S. R. Smith (ed.), *Handbook of Giftedness and Talent Development in the Asia-Pacific*, Springer International Handbooks of Education,
https://doi.org/10.1007/978-981-13-3041-4_4

Commentary on the Applicability of the Megamodel in South Korea	118
Conclusion	121
Cross-References	121
References	122

Abstract

In this chapter, the first three authors briefly present their megamodel of talent development, and the following three authors provide a commentary to discuss the model's applicability to three Asian-Pacific cultures and national school systems. The megamodel was developed to describe important components of talent development from its earliest appearance in childhood to eminent levels of achievement in adulthood across diverse domains, including sport, the performing arts and academic fields. The model emphasises that exceptional levels of abilities are important to high achievement, the nature of these abilities varies with the domain and domain-specific abilities are malleable. For all talent domains, giftedness begins with potential and with learning, coaching, practice, or study moves to competency, expertise and, in some cases, eminence. The megamodel also emphasises that domains have varying and unique trajectories that differ in terms of starting, peak, and end points, and these trajectories have implications for when talent can initially be identified and nurtured. Psychosocial skills, a critical component of talent development, include motivation, resiliency, and strategic risk-taking, which are also malleable and must be actively cultivated via appropriate classroom and education contexts, to enable students' progress to higher stages of talent development. Scholars from Singapore, South Korea, and New Zealand offer their perspectives on the usefulness of the megamodel's individual components and as a whole for their country's school systems, as well as how the model fits with cultural values and ideals.

Keywords

Talent development · Domains · Psychosocial skills · Culture and talent

The aims in this chapter are to:
1. Provide a comprehensive model of talent development across and among performance domains, domains of creative production, and national school systems.
2. Channel the focus of gifted education to supporting domain specific talent.
3. Promote the importance of integrating co-curricular opportunities with opportunities outside of school.
4. Ensure equitable exposure to psychosocial skills and insider knowledge to all children pursuing the development of their talents.
5. Emphasise the influence of culture and national policy on future manifestations of the megamodel.

A decade ago, the first three authors set out to delineate a definition of giftedness and framework for talent development that was based on psychological science (e.g., see Subotnik, Olszewski-Kubilius, & Worrell, 2011). The goal was to create a model that applied across varied domains of talent, trace the talent development process from early childhood through the life span, and include critical factors and components that research has shown to be involved in the fruition of talent. Critical to our thinking was the seminal work of Benjamin Bloom and his associates (1982, 1985a) who studied the progression of fields such as sports (e.g., tennis), music (e.g., piano), and neuroscience and concluded that there were common stages of talent development across disparate domains.

Bloom's (1985b) stages progressed from: (a) early romance and playful involvement with topics in the area; to (b) mastery of the knowledge, skills and value systems of a domain; to (c) unique creative contributions, with each stage requiring a different type of teacher and approach to training and instruction. Subotnik and Jarvin (2005) elaborated on Bloom's stage model with their study of music students at the Julliard, Curtis, and New England Conservatories. This study resulted in a model that specified that talent development begins with ability and moves with training, study, and practice to competency and expertise and, finally, to scholarly productivity and artistry. According to Subotnik and Jarvin, the levers for transitions to higher stages include appropriate opportunities and critical psychosocial skills that can vary by developmental level within a musical domain. These seminal studies, as well as research from education and psychology, resulted in the megamodel for talent development shown in Figure 3 of Subotnik et al. (2011, p. 34).

The megamodel proposes the following definition of giftedness:

> Giftedness is the manifestation of performance that is clearly at the upper end of the distribution in a talent domain even relative to other high functioning individuals in that domain. Further, giftedness can be viewed as developmental in that in the beginning stages, potential is the key variable, in later stages, achievement is the measure of giftedness, and in fully developed talents, eminence is the basis on which this label is granted. Psychosocial variables play an essential role in the manifestation of giftedness at every developmental stage. Both cognitive and psychosocial variables are malleable and need to be deliberately cultivated. (Subotnik et al., 2011, p. 7)

The psychological science literature suggested several features included in our model (see Table 1). We explicate each of these below.

Domain-Specific Abilities

The first factor suggested by the literature was the importance of domain-specific abilities. Although much of gifted education practice within schools in the United States revolves around measures of general cognitive ability, particularly IQ, gifted education in other countries and research within domains as disparate as sport, music, and academic areas points to the importance of recognising and acknowledging more specific abilities, particularly as individuals progress to higher stages of

Table 1 Elements of the megamodel of talent development

	Implications for practice
Domain-specific abilities.	• IQ tests and general ability tests are useful, especially with young children and with students who have had limited opportunities to learn (e.g., low-income students). • Domain-specific assessments need to be used no later than middle school, but a variety of assessments can be employed, depending upon the domain (e.g., tests, auditions and judgments by professionals and experts, portfolios). • Critical to match assessment to the domain of talent.
Domain-specific developmental trajectories.	• Students need different kinds of instruction/programming at different stages of talent development (e.g., exposure via enrichment to domains for younger children, development of skills and competency within domains for older children, opportunities to pursue special interests via independent projects for secondary students). • Articulated sequence of programs K–12 within major domains that enable students to move ahead at a faster pace and provide continuous skill development. • Early exposure to domains for all students via enrichment in early grades, especially for low-income students. • Earlier exposure to some fields, such as philosophy or engineering, typically not studied until college. • More varied program models for secondary students are needed (e.g., mentorships, research opportunities, apprenticeships). • Ways to capture late bloomers via enrichment or multiple entry points to talent development paths must be in place. • Focus on talent development needs to extend beyond grade 12 and outside of school into informal education. • All teachers need deeper content expertise; secondary teachers need multiple content area expertise.
Ability is malleable.	• Ongoing assessment so as to identify late bloomers and students whose talents emerge later due to poverty or lack of early opportunity. • Creation of multiple opportunities and multiple paths for students to enter gifted programs (e.g., testing and portfolios). • Intense frontloading of opportunities in early years for students from poverty, under-identified gifted students. • Preparatory programs to help students qualify for school gifted programs. • Reverse the typical process of 'identification, followed by programming' to offering opportunities for the development of abilities first, followed by assessment for placement—especially critical for students who have had fewer opportunities to learn due to poverty, etc.

(continued)

Table 1 (continued)

	Implications for practice
Psychosocial characteristics are essential and teachable.	• Must be actively and deliberately cultivated via programming, counselling and mentoring of students. • Parents assist with psychosocial skill development at home. • Develop a plan for what skills to focus on at different stages of talent development (e.g., attitudes towards effort and ability; attitudes towards competition, resiliency and coping skills; a scholar identity). • Understand what psychosocial skills are most important for particular domains of talent, e.g., performing arts versus academic domains.
Opportunity must be available and taken.	• Programming and educational opportunities should be available earlier for all children, especially low-income children. • Multiple types of opportunities for students at different stages of developed talent need to be available at every level of schooling in major domains (e.g., enrichment for students with emergent talent and motivation, acceleration for students with well-developed ability and high motivation). • Include children in programs with high motivation and achievement even if ability is somewhat lower.
Creative productivity in adulthood and eminence are the desired outcomes.	• Opportunities to engage in creative production must be available to students earlier. • Cultivation of attitudes and mindsets (e.g., openness, risk-taking) conducive to being a creative producer needs to be deliberate and a part of programming. • Emotional support for students choosing a path of creative productivity needs to be continuous. • Programming for students needs to go beyond high school and extend into the post-secondary years of education and development. • School personnel need to foster connections with domain experts along the school and career continuum.

talent development. Krutetskii (1976) identified mathematical cast of mind as an early basic ability of exceptional mathematical creativity, and voice teachers identified intonation, timbre, musicality, and ability to control pitch as important factors related to singing talent (Watts, Barnes-Burroughs, Andrianopoulos, & Carr, 2003).

Lubinski and colleagues' work in the Study of Mathematically Precocious Youth (e.g., Lubinski, Benbow, Webb, & Bleske-Rechek, 2006; Wai, Lubinski, & Benbow, 2005) indicated that specific mathematical and verbal reasoning abilities measured around age 13 have predictive value for important educational and occupational outcomes and that verbal versus quantitative tilt in abilities predicts differences in domains of accomplishment, with verbal tilt increasing the probability of accomplishments (degrees, publications) in the humanities and quantitative tilt increasing the probability of accomplishments (e.g., degrees, patents) in STEM fields (Park, Lubinski, & Benbow, 2007; Wai et al., 2005). Spatial skills have been found to be important to success in STEM domains, with different types of spatial and visual processing skills (e.g., mental rotation, spatial visualisation, mental manipulation) important in fields such as chemistry, physics, and art (Stieff, Hegarty, & Dixon, 2010), dentistry (Hegarty, Keehner, Khooshabeh, & Montello, 2009) and drawing (Kozbelt & Kanowitz, 2019). In the culinary field, talent potential can be indicated by dexterity and coordination in basic culinary operations, precision, and concentration (e.g., cutting vegetables efficiently, coordinating several items that are cooking, and mixing ingredients in exact proportions; Aron, Botella, & Lubart, 2019).

In addition to studies that support the importance and greater predictive validity of more specific abilities to adult achievement within domains, research also suggests that these abilities are more malleable than previously thought. For example, spatial skills can be improved with training and practice, and relatively late, such as in the first year of college so as to enable more female students to persist in engineering undergraduate programs (Uttal et al., 2013).

The educational and practical implications of focusing on more specific abilities include looking for and assessing individuals within those domains, particularly by adolescence. Identification of talent via a more specific set of skills and abilities is more traditional within fields such as the performing arts and sport. This practice is less evident in academic domains, even though there is strong support for specific abilities in some fields, and research shows that teachers are much better at identifying children with exceptional mathematical or verbal reasoning skills than high general cognitive ability or IQ (Pendarvis & Wood, 2009). In addition, a variety of assessments can be used to make judgments about potential based on more specific cognitive skills, including subject-specific tests, portfolios, and judgments of experts and professionals who work in the domain. The malleability of specific cognitive skills suggests that lack of some specific skills should not be considered an absolute obstacle to pursuit of a domain and that intervention programs can help individuals acquire needed specific skills. Scaffolding skill development in intervention programs are especially critical for children who come from poverty contexts and have had fewer opportunities to learn. For these children, enrichment opportunities to develop skills and display talent potential may be needed prior to formal identification.

Domain-Specific Trajectories

The psychological literature also indicates that domains of talent have different trajectories including when abilities and talent initially emerge, when production or achievement typically peaks and when involvement in the domain commonly ends (Olszewski-Kubilius, Subotnik, & Worrell, 2016). Subotnik et al. (2011) illustrated these varied trajectories in Figure 2 (p. 32) of their monograph. For example, talent in mathematics may be evident early in childhood, demonstrated by a child who mathematises his or her world via counting, creating, and noticing patterns or demonstrating the ability to think logically in spatial, numerical, and symbolic relationships (Leikin, 2019). Instruction in some musical fields can start early (e.g., violin) whereas in others, it starts later (e.g., voice). Trajectories in sport fields such as gymnastics and figure skating begin early, and careers end relatively early as well. Most athletes start golf training in high school, but can continue playing throughout adulthood (Portenga, 2019). Although there is some variation, in many academic fields, serious study starts in adolescence or later, but careers can continue until death (Simonton, 2019).

Knowing when trajectories in different domains begin and peak is important if our goal is to look for signs of emergent talent and put students on a path to develop them (Olszewski-Kubilius & Thomson, 2015). In some fields, late identification may preclude individuals from having the time and opportunity to develop to expert or elite levels of performance (Olszewski-Kubilius et al., 2016). Educators must also work, particularly in academic domains such as the social or behavioural sciences, to determine indicators and valid assessments of talent so as not to miss students with potential.

In some domains, milestones of the trajectory are much better known than in others. Research shows that serious interest in science fields is often apparent by middle school and can be nurtured through specialised STEM high schools, science clubs, and competitions (Almarode et al., 2014; Subotnik, Olszewski-Kubilius, & Worrell, 2014). In medicine, early interest is followed by science coursework in undergraduate school, medical school, internship and residency, fellowships in medical subspecialties for some, initial board certification, and finally, entry into clinical or academic practice (McWilliams, Holding, & Knotek, 2019). Early interest in technology may be followed by the pursuit of a career in software engineering and cutting-edge companies, such as Pixar and Google where employers look for programming experience beyond what can be obtained from formal courses, typically acquired through engagement in side projects. Mentoring and working with a team are essential components of further training and the development of skills to manage and lead future projects in this field (McWilliams et al., 2019).

Simonton (2019) identified key developmental benchmarks in the domain of psychology: (a) developing an enthusiasm for psychological science by the undergraduate years that may be sparked by early access to psychology courses in high school; (b) working with a distinguished mentor with whom a distinctive research program is first developed; (c) developing a fully independent research program, starting with the doctoral dissertation; (d) publishing frequently in high impact journals; (e) acquiring a ladder-track position at a research university; (f) being promoted through the ranks of professorship; and (g) earning progressively more important awards and honours (Simonton, 2019). In the culinary arts, the path to expertise and eminence includes culinary school followed by apprenticeships, initially to less well-known chefs, and ultimately to highly regarded, creative chefs. Mentoring and networking with other chefs increases tacit knowledge, the tricks of the trade and creativity (Aron et al., 2019).

Knowing the trajectories of different domains and particularly the milestones that typically must be traversed can be very helpful for all aspiring students. This kind of knowledge is especially important for individuals who do not have someone in their immediate environment who can guide them or share tacit knowledge about a long-term career path (Olszewski-Kubilius & Thomson, 2015; Worrell, 2015; Worrell & Young, 2011). Although teachers and coaches only deal with students for part of the talent development path, having and sharing a long-term vision can better ensure that students garner appropriate, talent development opportunities at the right time and take responsibility for their own development. Educators in schools need to be focused on developing talent development paths with articulated sequences of courses and opportunities that enable students to step onto talent development trajectories in their chosen domains (Worrell, Subotnik, & Olszewski-Kubilius, 2018).

Psychosocial Skills

The literature is quite clear that psychosocial skills and psychological strength are critical levers that enable individuals to move to higher stages of talent development, achievement and accomplishment (Olszewski-Kubilius, Subotnik, & Worrell, 2015). Psychological strength is needed to deal with pressure and stress, to rebound from perceived setbacks and critique, and to manage the tensions arising from working on substantial, complex, and ambiguous problems or generating creative products (Simonton, 2000; Subotnik & Jarvin, 2005). Performance fields such as sport have developed a number of techniques for coaching the development of psychosocial skills to enhance performance including goal setting, use of imagery, relaxation techniques, and self-talk (Burton & Raedeke, 2008; Hanton, Thomas, & Mellalieu, 2009; Kornspan, 2009; Lehman, Sloboda, & Woody, 2007; MacNamara & Collins, 2009; MacNamara, Holmes, & Collins, 2008; Weinberg & Comar, 1994; Williams & Krane, 2005).

Jarvin and Subotnik (2010) suggested that the type and relative importance of various psychosocial skills required at each stage of talent development differs and that one of the functions of a good teacher is to deliberately cultivate psychological skills and provide psychological strength training so that individuals can advance to the higher stages. For example, in the earliest stage, responsiveness to feedback and persistence and intrinsic motivation are important for gaining competency in the basic skills and foundational knowledge of a domain and should be promoted by all K–12 educators. As students develop their skills, knowledge of their own strengths and weaknesses as well as self-directed learning and goal setting are required for the hours of study and practice required to reach the level of expertise. When transitioning to the highest stages, individuals need strategic risk-taking, social skills, and charisma to generate independent creative work, resist entrenchment, and garner support for one's ideas.

Variations of these important psychosocial skills are evident in domains of talent beyond music. Portenga (2019) identified the ability of golfers to regulate and take responsibility for their own growth and development within the sport as critical to reaching higher levels of performance. Golfers progress in their ability to reflect on their performances in competitions and post-practice, set goals for improvement and development, utilise experts for feedback and guidance and network to gain tacit knowledge about the path of careers in competitive golf.

In the field of software engineering, McWilliams et al. (2019) identified self-motivation, willingness to engage in side projects to gain knowledge, and knowledge of strengths and weaknesses as important in moving from the novice to apprentice stage. The ability to prioritise, self-regulate, manage ambiguity, work autonomously, balance risk and rewards, and move from a mentee to mentor role is important in the next stage of talent development. Movement to the expert or master stage within software engineering involves developing leadership skills and managing people and complex projects.

In medicine, prospective medical students must be able to engage in self-promotion to demonstrate that they are strong candidates for highly competitive seats in medical schools (McWilliams et al., 2019). During medical school, students manage the tremendous work load via excellent time management skills and work-life balance skills. Internship requires having confidence in applying knowledge to clinical settings. During residency, individuals take on increasing responsibility for patient care, apply self-regulation and autonomous learning skills to enhance their knowledge when needed, shore up weaknesses, recognise their limitations, use experts judiciously, and supervise and train others including interns and medical students. As physicians begin either academic or clinical medical careers, they are expected to take on leadership positions (e.g., department chair) within their institutions, practices, or medical organisations and continue to train and supervise others (McWilliams et al., 2019). In the culinary field, important psychosocial skills include respect for the codes and hierarchy of the kitchen, the ability to work as a member of a team and having an aesthetic sensibility and a desire for artistic expression (Aron et al., 2019).

Research on the critical role of psychosocial skills and talent development suggests that these skills can be deliberately and actively cultivated within aspiring students by teachers, coaches, and parents and that this must start early (MacNamara, Button, & Collins, 2010a, 2010b; Subotnik & Jarvin, 2005). Lack of these skills is often what blocks further progress on a talent trajectory and alternatively, strong psychosocial skills can compensate for lower levels or underdevelopment of specific skills and abilities. Psychosocial skills, particularly growth mindsets, teachability, and persistence, are particularly important for children at the earlier stages of talent development and should be valued above actual performance when targeting underserved children for gifted education services (Olszewski-Kubilius et al., 2015). Educators and coaches can incorporate psychological skills training into their programs and lessons, often by providing emotional support and modelling as students take on increasing challenges within their domains of talent. All domains of talent involve some kind of performance for authentic audiences, whether it is dancing in front of an audience, giving an audition, delivering PowerPoint presentations in class, or competing in a science fair (Portenga, 2018). Reaching high levels of achievement in all domains involves consistent productivity and autonomous learning as well as the ability to cope with increased demands and challenges. Thus, all students can benefit from training in ways to enhance performance and productivity and reduce anxiety (Herbein et al., 2018).

Opportunities Must Be Offered

The fruition of talent potential into actual achievement requires nurturing in the form of appropriate opportunities. Some talent domains such as mathematics or psychology are developed primarily through schooling or formal education, whereas others, such as sports, are primarily developed via private lessons and outside of school programs. There are specialised high schools for the performing arts, and STEM academies, as well as acting and cooking schools (Almarode, Subotnik, & Lee, 2016). However, no talent area is developed completely within school. Outside of school enrichment opportunities, such as weekend or summer programs, are often the only venue in which talented students receive instruction at an appropriate pace and level alongside of peers with similar levels of ability and interest (Olszewski-Kubilius, Calvert, & Corwith, 2015; Olszewski-Kubilius, Subotnik, & Worrell, 2017).

Additionally, different talent areas require different kinds of programming and opportunities at different stages of development. For example, most athletics training can initially occur through school teams, club sports, or community programs, but movement to elite levels often requires private coaching. Individuals who progress in golf need access to a golf club (Portenga, 2019) for the hours of intense practice and play, and speed skaters eventually need access to an Olympic-sized ice rink for training. Mathematical talent is developed through the provision of interesting, complex, and challenging problems with multiple solutions (Leikin, 2019) that can occur within school or within outside-of-school opportunities, such as summer programs, mathematics circles or clubs and competitions.

Programming should match the developmental progression of talent (Olszewski-Kubilius & Calvert, 2016). That is, for young children, enrichment that enables students' exposure to different domains, to dabble playfully and to *fall in love* with a domain is most appropriate. These can be unstructured family activities or programs through schools or community organisations. As children develop and interest grows, programs should focus on developing fundamental skills and knowledge (Olszewski-Kubilius & Thomson, 2015). During this stage it may be difficult for children to maintain interest and motivation, and the use of extrinsic rewards coupled with strategies such as acceleration can help. As students progress and interests are solidified, it is important that programming engages and exposes them to the culture of the domain so that a domain identity can be formed. Values can be developed by way of authentic work in the domain, engagement with other students with similar interests and abilities, and interactions with professionals (Olszewski-Kubilius, Calvert et al., 2015; Olszewski-Kubilius et al., 2016).

Opportunities Must Also Be Taken

As critical as it is that appropriate opportunities are made accessible to children with interest and talent, these opportunities must be taken. Psychosocial skills, particularly motivation, resilience, and the ability to manage fears, anxiety, and moods, play an important role. Too often, children avoid challenging opportunities for growth out of fear of failure or rejection by peers, fixed mindsets or lack of understanding of how this opportunity may help them meet their goals (Olszewski-Kubilius, Subotnik et al., 2015; Olszewski-Kubilius et al., 2016).

Eminence as the Outcome of Gifted Education

Subotnik et al. (2011) proposed that creative, scholarly, and artistic contributions at an eminent level ought to be the outcome of gifted education. This was proposed as the long-term outcome, recognising that schools and other institutions typically deal with individuals for only a component of the talent development trajectory. However, given that talent development is a process that occurs over time, and requires particular inputs at different points, it is important that teachers and parents are aware of the trajectory, the particular experiences and opportunities within and outside of school that are most helpful in maintaining or developing commitment to the domain, and the psychosocial skills that must be developed in order for students to make further progress in their talent development (Olszewski-Kubilius, Subotnik, Worrell, & Thomson, 2018). Teachers and coaches who work with students at a particular developmental stage should see their job as preparing students with the knowledge and psychosocial skills to transition to the next stage (Worrell et al., 2018).

One of the implications of aspiring to creative scholarly and artistic contributions at an eminent level as the outcome of gifted education is that individuals involved in youth development must be knowledgeable about domain trajectories and provide opportunities at the appropriate time so that students can continue onto higher stages. The path to eminence in any field is peppered with short-term goals, such as performance on tests or in classes and competitions and other demonstrations of achievement, interest, and commitment (Worrell et al., 2018). Beyond the basics, each domain has special rigours and unique features that lead, directly or indirectly, to creative productivity. Not all individuals will desire nor have the necessary qualities or support to pursue a path towards eminence, and some may choose to put their talent to use in other ways, such as towards greater social justice, but if those working with students are conscious of what it takes, they can better guide students towards the level of achievement they desire (Subotnik & Rickoff, 2010).

Subotnik et al. (2011) proposed the megamodel with the hope that individual components as well as the model as a whole would be informative for school systems. The following three sections by scholars from New Zealand (Janna Wardman), Singapore (Liang See Tan), and South Korea (Seon Young Lee) describe insights about which components of the megamodel apply to their systems and how, and which, if any, may not. They also elaborate on future directions for talent development and the megamodel.

Commentary on the Applicability of the Megamodel in New Zealand

When the megamodel of talent development as described by Subotnik et al. (2011) was first published, it attracted global debate around the term, 'eminence'. Contrary to responses from some nations, New Zealanders have no difficulty with the concept of eminence; surprisingly, it is the term 'gifted' that makes some New Zealanders squirm, especially when it is linked to academic fields. The 'tall poppy' syndrome that aims to cut everyone down to the same size is prevalent in academic domains (Gross, 2004). In sport, music, and other domains, however, there is willingness in New Zealand to celebrate exceptional abilities and achievement—but seldom is the 'g' word used. Talent development is a more palatable term to New Zealanders.

As a nation of just 4.6 million, we have made an impact on the sporting stage in rugby (both men and women), sailing, golf, netball, softball, rowing, and canoeing– to name just a few sports where the current world leaders are New Zealanders (at time of writing this commentary). The practice of experts in various sporting fields recognising children with potential, and developing their talent through mentoring, coaching and a supportive club environment, is commonplace. From an early age, boys gifted in rugby are offered coaching and equipment to enable their foundational abilities to be developed at club level (see Fig. 1). Building resiliency to a high level is part of the program. As a result, the chance of a boy profoundly gifted in rugby from any socio-economic background in even a remote area of New Zealand, becoming an *All Black* is possible.

The national *All Black* rugby team also supports young talent in various ways. The family-oriented rugby clubs around New Zealand are testament to how foundational talent can be nurtured and given the opportunities to develop into eminence. Rugby scholarships are available from elementary through high school, and expert coaches often compete for the best players who then have a pathway forward through New Zealand Schools Rugby and the Junior All Blacks. The opportunities are not so widespread for girls gifted in rugby, but this is improving thanks to the success of *The Black Ferns* who are also World Champions. Before, readers exclaim, "Utopia! Let's all move to New Zealand with our talented children", a word of caution; it is another story with nationwide recognition and development of talents in *academic* domains.

Let us examine the situation through the educational sectors. In early childhood education (ECE), as the megamodel explains, it is the child's potential that is the focus. Early childhood teachers in New Zealand generally prefer the view that *all* young children have some sort of special abilities and that it is elitist or unfair to the rest if some children are identified as having potential exceptional abilities/talents. Difficulties have been identified as gifted children transition to elementary school, as the 'one size fits all' approach to the beginning of formal education does not suit those who are already two or more years ahead of same-aged peers in their foundational abilities (Grant, 2013).

Since 2005, it has been mandatory through the National Administration Guidelines, for all state schools in New Zealand to demonstrate to the Education Review Office (and others) how they are meeting the needs of their gifted and talented learners (Ministry of Education, 2012). There is, however, no targeted budget for this effort (Riley & Bicknell, 2013). In practice, the focus of elementary schools has tended to be to lift those at the tail end of the achievement spectrum (Wardman, 2018). Those children who exhibit exceptional abilities in specific domains either: (a) have their talents developed by individual teachers who have an interest in or knowledge of gifted education; (b) are encouraged in their talents by coaches and parents; (c) do not receive an opportunity to develop their talents and therefore do not reach their potential; or (d) are offered an opportunity, but for whatever reason, do not take it up. In New Zealand, the lack of recognition and development opportunity at crucial times for the learner is more likely to occur in those whose

Fig. 1 Building resilience New Zealand style

talents lie in the academic fields and whose parents do not have the financial or human capital wherewithal to take over the talent development of their child.

Having painted a rather negative picture, it is important to add that there are wonderful teachers and programs in schools around New Zealand where domain trajectories are nurtured (Wardman, 2009, 2015). Along the way, the students develop the psychosocial skills of risk-taking and resiliency and, most importantly, a growth mindset. An example of how this works can be seen on this YouTube clip of STEM projects in a state elementary school in suburban Auckland. Importantly, this clip–entitled 'Cockle Bay School STEM Integration Project'–is of mixed ability classes and therefore represents the talent development that is available in *some* schools for *all* students (https://www.youtube.com/watch?v=Q1ANbeNw1Iw).

The system of National Standards for elementary students has just been abandoned (National standards removed, 2017). This system had reported to the Ministry of Education the numbers of students who were annually meeting the expected standard of achievement in reading, writing, and mathematics, and the numbers for those above and below the standard. There was also a 'well-below standard' category, but there was no corresponding 'well-above standard' category, which again is an indication that those at the top end of the spectrum are not at the forefront of the Ministry of Education's agenda. Teachers have celebrated the elimination of this testing regime, saying it will provide time for more teaching. The megamodel highlights the importance of general ability as determined by cognitive measures and the role of domain-specific and off-level testing, but it is doubtful if these would be adopted in the New Zealand school system at present. Questions would be asked as to where the funding would come from to administer these tests. There is also a dearth in practitioner professional development regarding gifted education, so even if funding could be found to carry out a variety of assessments, providing staff with the necessary knowledge and time allocation to track individual students and develop talents would be a challenge (Riley & Bicknell, 2013).

There are only approximately 330 high schools in New Zealand, but some have rolls of over 3,000 students. Typically, the time allowance for the teacher coordinator of gifted and talented students amounts to no more than a few hours a week; therefore, realistically, there are limited opportunities for the many suggestions emanating from the megamodel (Wardman & Hattie, 2012). In high schools, standardised testing is carried out at entry (13 years). The results of these tests are used primarily as placement tools for broadband streaming, especially in mathematics. The tests utilised by New Zealand high schools tend to be based on achievement rather than aptitude, and therefore they may miss those who have not yet reached a point in their trajectory where their talent in a particular domain is recognised (Wardman & Hattie, 2018).

There tends to be a window of opportunity in New Zealand at age 13 to 14 where, if talents are not recognised or opportunities are not taken, then the window can close. That age is a time of immense change, and, in general, it is not a time when our young teenagers exhibit risk-taking and resiliency, unless it has already been fostered. The model recognises that individuals begin, peak, and end their trajectories at different ages in different domains. The opportunities to transform potential may not have eventuated—or perhaps, the individual did not recognise or take the opportunity when it arose. Underdeveloped psychosocial skills may mean that some, at a crucial point in their lives, did not have the confidence to be a risk-taker (Millward, Wardman, & Rubie-Davies, 2016). Therefore, it is possible that as young adults, students can become 'untalented'. The megamodel identifies that opportunities need to be cultivated in order to maximise potential. In some domains, it is currently a matter of chance whether students are at the right stage with the right people at the right time.

The megamodel explains that individual talent trajectories vary across individuals and domains (Subotnik et al., 2011, 2018); however, in New Zealand, the system is set up for a trajectory of five years of high school. It is now common for students to accelerate a full year in one or more subject areas (Wardman, 2018). However, this does not often result in early entry to university as students are usually required to stay on at school for a 5th year and to take extra subjects to fill a timetable. They can also dual enrol in tertiary education for some subjects, but relatively few actually have early enrolment in tertiary education (Wardman, 2018).

When coaching and mentoring students, educators need to take into account the values of diverse populations. The indigenous peoples of Aotearoa New Zealand are Māori and they are a collective culture. In order to avoid misunderstandings, it is vital to recognise the Māori perspective in terms of culture and identity (Webber, 2011). For example, creativity in the Western concept explores differences or originality, whereas in Māori culture, it is the combined notion of creativity, that is, kotahitanga (acting in unity) that is valued. At the core is the belief that gifts and talents belong to the group, not the individual. Thus, the outcomes of gifted performance should result in a benefit to society at large, a point noted by Subotnik et al. (2011). Only if those conditions are met can the collective culture celebrate the gifts (Macfarlane, 2006). In Māori culture, there are strong sanctions against boasting.

There are components of the megamodel that are already in place in our schooling system, but they are not available in every school for every student. New Zealanders, however, are pragmatic. We will strive for more funding; the identification and nurturing of the individual trajectory of our talented children in all domains is a goal. It may be that the answer for New Zealand is not so prescriptive. A different pathway, one that relies on identification procedures that are already in use and on people to mentor and coach, may be our recipe to success. Think of the New Zealand cyclors in the Americas Cup (https://www.stuff.co.nz/sport/other-sports/93016340/super-athletes-powering-the-americas-cup), an innovation in the sport of sailing and New Zealand won!

The author's wish is that researchers around the world extend the same generosity of spirit that is evident here in the invitations to comment on the megamodel, which was developed in the United States. We have much to learn from each other and collaborative evidence-based studies, based on the megamodel, would be informative. A warm welcome awaits you in New Zealand.

Commentary on the Applicability of the Megamodel in Singapore

This sociocultural perspective on the talent development megamodel (Subotnik et al., 2011) draws on Benjamin Bloom's (1985) stage paradigm and builds a model that is beyond domain-specific abilities and trajectories. The megamodel underscores not only individual differences, but also the interactions among the individual, significant others, and the contexts in which the potential talents are identified. Taking a sociocultural perspective highlights the intricateness and nuances in nurturing talents. My entry point into the discussion of the megamodel is drawn from two studies conducted in Singapore. Study 1 took place in the context of domain-specific talents (Ponnusamy, Tan, Rahamat, & Ibrahim, 2017; Tan, Lee, Ponnusamy, Koh, & Tan, 2016), and Study 2 involved a group of schools that focused on developing subject-specific talents (Tan, Koh, Lee, Ponnusamy, & Tan, 2017; Tan et al., 2016). The studies provide insights and nuanced understandings of the Singapore system in relation to the components of the megamodel.

The landscape of the Singapore education system has evolved from a focus on survival (1959–1978) and efficiency (1979–1996) to one that is ability-based and aspiration-driven (1997–2011), and since 2012, to one that is student-centric and values-driven (Heng, 2012a, 2012b). In the spirit of offering multiple pathways for students of different potentials and talents to develop, the system has become more flexible and diverse (Heng, 2012b). The year 2004 was a defining moment in the history of Singapore's education system whereby the system recognised the importance of domain-specific talents. A few new, pre-tertiary Specialised Independent Schools were established to cater to talents in mathematics and science, sports, and the performing arts (Ministry of Education, 2018). These schools were set-up to nurture innovators, sports achievers, and creative producers. The gifted education curricula and concomitant instruction were also extended to the next top 4% of primary school students in regular classrooms. More importantly, the implementation of an integrated program in selected secondary schools allowed university-bound students to skip the high-stake examination (O levels) typically taken at the end of year 4 and be enrolled in a 6-year seamless program (see Neihart & Tan, 2016). Although such schools cater to only about 10–12% of each secondary school cohort, the impact of these programs in developing researchers, innovators, and artistic producers of the future cannot be underestimated.

Researchers generally agree that the development of human potential, particularly for children who are from an underprivileged background, should begin in school. It is useful to know that domains—as mentioned in the megamodel—have varying and unique trajectories that differ in terms of starting points, peaks, and ending times. Schools need to have knowledge about these trajectories and understand their implications when identifying and nurturing talents. In Singapore, sports talents can be recruited from the *Annual National Primary School Track and Field Meet* and various sporting events, and mathematical and science talents can be identified by academic performance and competitions; however, talent development and education in the arts, such as dance, visual art, theatre, and music are rather basic and generic in Singapore primary schools. In Study 1 (Tan et al., 2016), informants shared that among the four major art forms, dance and music have early starting points and peaks, and Singapore misses the opportunities to identify and foster the growth of these talents.

It has been a challenge for the pre-tertiary independent schools to assess 12-year-olds for talent in any of the arts as these talents are totally underdeveloped in schools (Ministry of Information and the Arts, 2000). Talent development in these areas is very dependent on parents who have the will, means, resources, and networks to support their children's potential by providing opportunities leading to the appropriate trajectories. Additionally, such commitment from parents is usually hindered by the academic demands of school. Besides support from parents, the communities where the expertise in the arts resides must be willing to take on the responsibility to ignite the fire in children and youth. Hence, recognising the varying and unique trajectories of talent development implies that in any sociocultural context, the schools are not the sole agency in developing talents; families, schools, and communities play specific key roles as part of the talent development ecology.

In both studies, Tan et al. (2016, 2017) noted the variations of school programs in developing talents in the system by documenting multiple programs. Although these school-based programs can be the cradles for identifying and facilitating talent in numerous domains, the availability of resources in a school determine the type and number of programs to be promoted, as well as the number of students the program will serve. In Study 2, they noted that the decision to choose the type of talent development program is dependent on the culture of the school and the beliefs of educators. These factors have implications for how the school defines talent and who the talented students are. Students with talents that are beyond the scope of school curriculum face difficulties in advancing the development of their specific abilities and interests. In these situations, the schools need to allocate resources and adjust school routines to accommodate the learning needs of the students.

Moreover, schools need to build networks of knowledgeable teachers or other individuals who have the expertise to guide students. In Study 1, Tan et al. (2016) documented how these experts mentored psychosocial skills, including psychosocial motivation, resiliency, and strategic risk-taking, which are also malleable and must be actively cultivated via appropriate classroom and training contexts to enable students to progress to higher stages of talent development. "Advanced development occurs when opportunities for learning are available in the environment and are seized by the person" (Cross & Coleman, 2005, p. 53). Besides creating opportunities and conditions for exposure to talent domains, teachers are also the key counsellors to advise and motivate students to seize the opportunities in developing their potentials into talents.

Although the school is an agent to identify the potential of talented individuals, schools do not have all the necessary resources nor time with students to nurture the potential of talented individuals to the level of eminence aspired to by the megamodel; rather, schools can put students on the talent development pathway. In Study 1, analyses showed that schools can expose students to new ideas, teach them the language of disciplines in a specific domain, create opportunities to encourage problem finding and experimentation to develop artistic insights, and provide opportunities to perform with the artists (Tan & Ponnusamy, 2014a). All these efforts were supported by: (a) building a school campus in the arts belt; (b) providing artistic thinking and an immersive culture by recruiting teachers who are practising artists; and (c) implementing a fluid curriculum that adapts to the arts in education (Tan & Ponnusamy, 2014b).

In both studies, we also noted three roadblocks in the talent development pathway during the formative years: lack of definitive career opportunities; lack of an in-depth understanding of self that resulted in lack of confidence in one's performance; and lack of opportunity for international benchmarking. These three gaps explained participants' lack of commitment to developing their talents in the arts. Despite the enabling supports provided by the school, lack of commitment on the part of the students may lead them to veer from pursuing the arts professionally. The findings clearly showed how opportunities can be seized or missed and are very much dependent on knowledge about the benchmarks of talent development in that specific talent domain, readiness to take on challenges and the maturity to think about and embrace a future in the talent domain. All of these considerations speak to the important role of teachers, mentors, and parents in guiding young talented individuals. One of the teacher informants said, "Initially, not all of them came to school with being a professional artist in mind". One student informant reported that her teachers encouraged her and recommended conservatories to her. The teachers convinced her to take a chance and participate in the auditions. With the vote of confidence from her teachers, she auditioned in the United States and realised she was almost on par with other international music students.

Overall, the results of the two studies provide snapshots of the talents that are being developed in Singapore and how they are being developed. Notably, the avenues and opportunities to develop talent can be rather diffuse in the case of Singapore. Hence, the success of talented individuals is not necessarily seen as the result of gifted education. Better alignment and coherence at the system level is needed to bolster the ecology to nurture talented individuals in diverse domains. The enterprise of talent development needs to take into consideration not only individual needs, but also the complexities of the social, political, and economic needs of the country.

Commentary on the Applicability of the Megamodel in South Korea

Since its publication, the talent development megamodel (Subotnik et al., 2011) is one of the well-cited theoretical models of giftedness and talent. The model inspires many researchers and scholars in the field of gifted education because it addresses both the developmental nature of giftedness and talent and the potential for eminent outcomes. In particular, the megamodel suggests differentiated educational involvement according to domains and identifies eminence as the final outcome of gifted education. The developmental and educational perspectives of giftedness and talent development are likely to intrigue many researchers and educators in South Korea where gifted education has been developing quickly since its inception in the early 2000s. In the following paragraphs, the aspects of the megamodel that resonate with gifted educators in South Korea are addressed as well as support and suggestions for the model.

First, one of the merits of the megamodel is its comprehensive approach to the conception of giftedness and talent. As widely documented, gifted education has been loved and hated simultaneously due to its perceived elitist view on giftedness and the fact that services are provided exclusively for superior students. Since the end of the Korean War in 1953, education has been an issue of utmost importance to the Korean people as a promising avenue for advancement; through hard work and effort, education can result in the betterment of individuals and society. Although gifted education started with the strong support of the Korean government, a large number of Korean people believe that gifted education is only for the few students who are worthy of receiving national support due to their extraordinary giftedness, which is likely innate (Lee, 2013, 2015). This perception of giftedness often evokes deeply rooted and mixed feelings about gifted education. For Korean students, parents, and educators, the megamodel is encouraging because it suggests that giftedness is based not only on natural ability, but also on training and nurture following the developmental trajectories in domains.

Second, gifted education in South Korea began in the fields of *Science, Technology, Engineering, and Mathematics* (STEM) about two decades ago. Recently, there has been a growing interest in art, particularly for creative education, but the focus remains on STEM (Kim, Moon, Park, & Seo, 2016). More often, the goal of integrating art in education is to promote creativity in STEM through art activities, and gifted education endorses this 'convergence education' as one of its major tasks (Baek et al., 2011; Hong, 2017; Korea Foundation for the Advancement of Science and Creativity, 2014, 2016). The megamodel supports the domain-specific nature of giftedness and suggests differentiated educational services are commensurate with the needs of domains, while many Korean educators are apt to dismiss differentiation practices. The suggested model indicates that understanding the uniqueness and varying developmental paths of domain-specific talents ought to precede integrating different domains and designing convergence education for gifted students.

Third, under a special law for gifted education, there are eight high schools for the gifted in South Korea (see Kim et al., 2016, for a summary). Six of these are science schools, and the other two are science and art schools that aim to integrate science and art for *convergence* gifted education (Kim et al., 2016). Although students undoubtedly benefit from entering these selective schools, a major drawback is the fierce competition among Korean teenagers for admission to these schools for the gifted. Further, many believe that only students who are admitted to the schools for the gifted are truly gifted and should receive services provided for the gifted. Unfortunately, this misconception engenders another elitist view of gifted education. The talent development megamodel reminds Korean students, parents, and educators of the importance of opportunities that are appropriately designed and offered to gifted students according to the developmental stages of one's talent. Hence, besides the educational support from the gifted high schools, Korean students should be exposed to a variety of educational opportunities in and outside of their regular schools in order to identify their interest areas and develop their talents in the domains in which they show potential.

Fourth, the megamodel involves multiple contributors consisting of intrapersonal, psychosocial, and educational factors that facilitate one's talent development. The basic premise of the model is that domains and the contributing variables interactively affect each other in the process of talent development. Given that giftedness has traditionally been perceived as an inborn aptitude (Delisle, 2003; Gagné, 2005; Lee, 2013; Lee et al., 2017; Simonton, 2013) mainly related to innate intrapersonal traits or abilities, the inclusion of multiple variables as contributing factors not only expands the conception of giftedness, but also provides support for the developmental nature of giftedness. In this regard, the model would help Korean society to change their views of gifted students and gifted education in general.

In conclusion, the talent development megamodel should be endorsed as one of the central conceptual giftedness and talent development models in South Korea for the following reasons. Generally, Korean students are identified as gifted once they get admission to the gifted schools or similar types of gifted programs in science and mathematics. They benefit from the high quality educational services provided by the nationally accredited gifted schools and institutions. Consequently, 'gifted education fever' is widespread across the nation, which ignites overheated competitions among young children to be qualified for the gifted services, thereby resulting in students being identified as gifted as early as in their elementary school years. In fact, issues related to the early identification of giftedness and the subsequent selection of gifted students have always been two of the leading agendas for educators and policy-makers in South Korea (Lee, 2017, 2018), and thus, the idea of giftedness as a long-term talent development process with opportunities provided for and taken by the potential young child has been dismissed in gifted education policy in the nation. One of the strengths of the megamodel is its focus on the process of talent development. Thus, Korean gifted educators should pay more attention to providing students with quality educational services rather than finding young children to label them as gifted. The megamodel can serve as one basis for this reconceptualisation.

The developmental view of the megamodel starts with a stage where potential abilities appear as an indication of giftedness. Yet, the originators of this model were not hesitant to declare that eminence should be the ultimate outcome of gifted education although few people reach the highest level of performance and achievement. They pointed out that giftedness in the later stages should be manifested in actual accomplishments and that eminence is the ultimate form of fully realised talent. This author supports the model in addressing eminence as the final end of gifted education, although it is not always easy for even researchers and educators to acknowledge that education looks for eminence for its final goal. And this author thinks that it is courageous, but realistic and practical to include eminence in the model.

Last, I suggest that the megamodel consider sociocultural contributors beyond personal and educational factors for talent development. As talent development does not follow universal stages, but is rather based on individual differences, the addition of multicultural factors to the talent development process, such as values, beliefs, lifestyles, and social conventions in the Eastern world, would make the talent development model more applicable beyond Western societies. The integration of cultural values and social conventions will allow Korean educators and researchers to better understand the personal, social, and environmental factors that facilitate the process of talent development in the Korean society. If the current version focused on domains and the developmental factors in the domains, the future version may want to include the cultural context as one of the driving forces for talent development and propel the megamodel into a global talent development model.

Conclusion

In this chapter, the authors reviewed the major tenets of Subotnik et al.'s (2011, 2018) megamodel of talent development as well as commentaries about the megamodel in the context of New Zealand, Singapore, and South Korea. The commentaries by scholars of gifted education in these different national contexts raised some critical issues for the megamodel. All three commentaries noted where the tenets of the megamodel fit or did not fit in their current school system, from the very basic level of beliefs and values that underlie notions of giftedness (South Korea and Singapore) to issues regarding testing and implementation (New Zealand). All three respondents recognised the developmental focus of the megamodel as well as the value of a more domain-oriented view of giftedness, with the main benefit of identifying and nurturing more children with talent. All three respondents also acknowledged the importance of talent development opportunities within and outside of school.

However, the respondents unanimously lamented the relatively fractured approach to gifted education within their countries, noting specifically the challenge of fierce competition for too few spots in specialised schools (Singapore and South Korea), and the absence of similar talent development opportunities in areas beyond STEM such as the arts and humanities (Singapore), and a great deal of variability between schools in terms of gifted programming and services (Singapore and New Zealand). Additionally, all the respondents emphasised the importance of broadening the model to include sociocultural factors that influence talent development, including the socio-political context, values, and beliefs. These concerns challenge us to think more deeply about the utility of the megamodel and on how to assist educators in translating the megamodel for practice in different national contexts.

Cross-References

- ▶ Being of Like-Mind: Giftedness in the New Zealand Context
- ▶ Gifted Education in the Asia-Pacific: From the Past for the Future – An Introduction

- In Search of an Explanation for an Approach-Avoidance Pattern in East Asia: The Role of Cultural Values in Gifted Education
- Social and Cultural Conceptions and Perceptions: Part I Introduction
- Some Implications for the Future of Gifted Education in the Asia-Pacific
- STEAM in Gifted Education in Korea
- The Development of Mana: Five Optimal Conditions for Gifted Māori Student Success
- Trends and Challenges of Creativity Development Among Selected Asian Countries and Regions: China, Hong Kong/Macau, Japan, Malaysia, and South Korea

References

Almarode, J., Subotnik, R. F., & Lee, G. M. (2016). What works: Lessons from a research study of specialized science high school graduates. *Gifted Child Today, 39*, 185–190. https://doi.org/10.1177/1076217516662096

Almarode, J. T., Subotnik, R. F., Crowe, E., Tai, R. H., Lee, M. L., & Nowlin, F. (2014). Specialized high schools and talent search programs: Incubators for adolescents with high ability in STEM disciplines. *Journal of Advanced Academics, 25*, 301–331. https://doi.org/10.1177/1932202X14536566

Aron, L., Botella, M., & Lubart, T. (2019). Culinary arts: Talent and their development. In R. F. Subotnik, P. Olszewski-Kubilius, & F. C. Worrell (Eds.), *The psychology of high performance: Developing human potential into domain-specific talent* (pp. 345–359). Washington, DC: American Psychological Association.

Baek, Y., Park, H., Kim, Y., Noh, S., Park, J.-Y., Lee, J., … Han, H. (2011). STEAM education in Korea. *Journal of Learner-Centered Curriculum and Instruction, 11*(4), 149–171.

Bloom, B. S. (1982). The role of gifts and markers in the development of talent. *Exceptional Children, 48*, 510–522. https://doi.org/10.1177/001440298204800607

Bloom, B. J. (Ed.). (1985a). *Developing talent in young people*. New York, NY: Ballantine Books.

Bloom, B. J. (1985b). Generalizations about talent development. In B. J. Bloom (Ed.), *Developing talent in young people* (pp. 507–549). New York, NY: Ballantine.

Burton, D., & Raedeke, T. D. (2008). *Sports psychology for coaches*. Campaign, IL: Human Kinetics.

Cross, T. L., & Coleman, L. J. (2005). School-based conception of giftedness. In R. J. Sternberg & J. E. Davidson (Eds.), *Conceptions of giftedness* (2nd ed., pp. 52–63). New York, NY: Cambridge University Press.

Delisle, J. (2003). To be or to do: Is a gifted child born or developed? *Roeper Review, 26*, 12–13. https://doi.org/10.1080/02783190309554232

Gagné, F. (2005). From gifts to talents: The DMGT as a developmental model. In R. J. Sternberg & J. E. Davidson (Eds.), *Conceptions of giftedness* (2nd ed., pp. 98–119). New York, NY: Cambridge University Press.

Grant, A. (2013). Young gifted children transitioning into preschool and school: What matters? *Australasian Journal of Early Childhood, 38*(2), 23–31. https://doi.org/10.1177/183693911303800204

Gross, M. U. M. (2004). *Exceptionally gifted children*. London, England: Routledge.

Hanton, S., Thomas, O., & Mellalieu, S. D. (2009). Management of competitive stress in elite sport. In B. Brewer (Ed.), *International Olympic committee sport psychology handbook* (pp. 30–42). Hoboken, NJ: Wiley-Blackwell.

Hegarty, M., Keehner, M., Khooshabeh, P., & Montello, D. R. (2009). How spatial abilities enhance, and are enhanced by, dental education. *Learning and Individual Differences, 19*, 61–70. https://doi.org/10.1016/j.lindif.2008.04.006

Heng, S. K. (2012a, February). *Education for competitiveness and growth*. Paper presented at the Singapore Conference, Washington, DC. Retrieved from http://www.moe.gov.sg/media/speeches/2012/02/08/speech-by-mr-heng-swee-keat-at-the-singapore-conference-washington-dc-usa.php

Heng, S. K. (2012b, September). Keynote address by Mr. Heng Swee Keat, Minister for Education, at the Ministry of Education Work Plan Seminar, Ngee Ann Polytechnic Convention Centre. Retrieved from https://www.moe.gov.sg/news/speeches/keynote-address-by-mr-heng-swee-keat%2D%2Dminister-for-education%2D%2Dat-the-ministry-of-education-work-plan-seminar%2D%2Don-wednesday%2D%2D12-september-2012-at-920-am-at-ngee-ann-polytechnic-convention-centre

Herbein, E., Golle, J., Tibus, M., Schiefer, J., Trautwein, U., & Zettler, I. (2018). Fostering elementary school children's public speaking skills: A randomized controlled trial. *Learning and Instruction, 55*, 158–168. https://doi.org/10.1016/j.learninstruc.2017.10.008

Hong, O. (2017). STEAM education in Korea: Current policies and future direction. In Korea Foundation for the Advancement of Science and Creativity (Ed.), *Science and technology trends: Policy trajectories and initiatives in STEM education* (pp. 92–102). KOFAC: Seoul, South Korea.

Jarvin, L., & Subotnik, R. F. (2010). Wisdom from conservatory faculty: Insights on success in classical music performance. *Roeper Review, 32*, 78–87. https://doi.org/10.1080/02783191003587868

Kim, J., Moon, D., Park, K., & Seo, J. (2016). *An annual statistical report of gifted education*. Retrieved from https://ged.kedi.re.kr

Korea Foundation for the Advancement of Science and Creativity. (2014). *Development of evaluation tool for outcome of STEAM*. Seoul, South Korea: KOFAC.

Korea Foundation for the Advancement of Science and Creativity. (2016). *Introduction to STEAM education*. Seoul, South Korea: KOFAC.

Kornspan, A. S. (2009). *Fundamentals of sport and exercise psychology*. Champaign, IL: Human Kinetics.

Kozbelt, A., & Kanowitz, A. (2019). Talent and ability in drawing and visual arts. In R. F. Subotnik, P. Olszewski-Kubilius, & F. C. Worrell (Eds.), *The psychology of high performance: Developing human potential into domain-specific talent* (pp. 311–335). Washington, DC: American Psychological Association.

Krutetskii, V. A. (1976). *The psychology of mathematical abilities in school children*. Chicago, IL: University of Chicago Press.

Lee, S.-Y. (2013). Are the conceptions of giftedness and creativity homogeneous or heterogeneous in nature?: Based on analyses of their relationships. *The Journal of the Korean Society for the Gifted and Talented, 12*(1), 107–127.

Lee, S.-Y. (2015). Civic education as a means of talent dissemination for gifted students. *Asia Pacific Education Review, 16*, 307–316. https://doi.org/10.1007/s12564-015-9372-y

Lee, S.-Y. (2017). Redesigning gifted education: For what not for whom. In *Proceedings of the 2017 Korea Science Academy Forum on Gifted Education in Science*, Busan, South Korea, pp. 4–13.

Lee, S.-Y. (2018). Gifted education as an educational process of talent development for all. In *Proceedings of the 2018 Spring Conference of the Korean Society for Gifted Education*, Masan, South Korea, pp. 155–157.

Lee, S.-Y., Kim, S., Min, J., Lee, B., Park, J., Park, H., & Choe, S. (2017). Examining teachers' recommendation letters according to teachers' and students' genders using the text network analysis. *Asian Journal of Education, 18*, 629–660.

Lehman, A. C., Sloboda, J. A., & Woody, R. H. (2007). *Psychology for musicians: Understanding and acquiring the skills*. Oxford, UK: Oxford University Press.

Leikin, R. (2019). Developing mathematical talent in schoolchildren: Who, what, and how? In R. F. Subotnik, P. Olszewski-Kubilius, & F. C. Worrell (Eds.), *The psychology of high performance: Developing human potential into domain-specific talent* (pp. 173–192). Washington, DC: American Psychological Association.

Lubinski, D., Benbow, C. P., Webb, R. M., & Bleske-Rechek, A. (2006). Tracking exceptional human capital over two decades. *Psychological Science, 17*, 194–199. https://doi.org/10.1111/j.1467-9280.2006.01685.x

Macfarlane, A. H. (2006). Becoming educultural: Te whakawhitinga o ngā mātauranga—Interfacing the knowledge traditions. *Kairaranga, 7*(2), 41–43.

MacNamara, Á., Button, A., & Collins, D. (2010a). The role of psychological characteristics in facilitating the pathway to elite performance Part 1: Identifying mental skills and behaviors. *The Sport Psychologist, 24*, 52–73. https://doi.org/10.1123/tsp.24.1.52

MacNamara, Á., Button, A., & Collins, D. (2010b). The role of psychological characteristics in facilitating the pathway to elite performance Part 2: Examining environmental and stage-related differences in skills and behaviors. *The Sport Psychologist, 24*, 74–96. https://doi.org/10.1123/tsp.24.1.74

MacNamara, A., & Collins, D. (2009). More than the "X" factor! A longitudinal investigation of the psychological characteristics of developing excellence in musical development. *Music Education Research, 11*, 377–392. https://doi.org/10.1080/14613800903144270

MacNamara, A., Holmes, P., & Collins, D. (2008). Negotiating transitions in musical development: The role of psychological characteristics of developing excellence. *Psychology of Music, 36*, 335–352. https://doi.org/10.1177/0305735607086041

McWilliams, M. A., Holding, E. Z., & Knotek, S. E. (2019). Talent development in medicine and software engineering. In R. F. Subotnik, P. Olszewski-Kubilius, & F. C. Worrell (Eds.), *The psychology of high performance: Developing human potential into domain-specific talent*. Washington, DC: American Psychological Association.

Millward, P., Wardman, J., & Rubie-Davies, C. (2016). Becoming and being a talented undergraduate student. *Higher Education Research and Development, 35*, 1242–1255. https://doi.org/10.1080/07294360.2016.1144569

Ministry of Education. (2012). *Gifted and talented students: Meeting their needs in New Zealand schools*. Wellington, NZ: Learning Media.

Ministry of Education. (2018). *Nurturing students: Flexibility and diversity*. Retrieved from https://www.moe.gov.sg/education/education-system/nurturing-students

Ministry of Information and the Arts. (2000). *Renaissance City report: Culture and arts in Renaissance Singapore*. Retrieved from https://www.nac.gov.sg/dam/jcr:defaf681-9bbb-424d-8c77-879093140750

National standards removed. (2017, December). Retrieved from https://education.govt.nz/news/national-standards-removed/

Neihart, M., & Tan, L. S. (2016). Gifted education in Singapore. In D. Dai & C. K. Ching (Eds.), *A critical assessment of gifted education in Asia: Problems and prospects* (pp. 77–96). Bloomington, IL: Chinese American Educational Research and Development Association.

Olszewski-Kubilius, P., & Calvert, E. (2016). Implications of the talent development framework for curriculum design. In T. Kettler (Ed.), *Modern curriculum for gifted and advanced academic students* (pp. 37–54). Waco, TX: Prufrock.

Olszewski-Kubilius, P., Calvert, E., & Corwith, S. (2015). Serving rural gifted students through supplemental and out-of-school programming. In T. Stambaugh & S. Woods (Eds.), *Best practices for serving gifted students in rural settings* (pp. 239–256). Waco, TX: Prufrock Press.

Olszewski-Kubilius, P., Subotnik, R. F., & Worrell, F. C. (2015). Antecedent and concurrent psychosocial skills that support high levels of achievement within talent domains. *High Ability Studies, 26*, 195–210. https://doi.org/10.1080/13598139.2015.1095077

Olszewski-Kubilius, P., Subotnik, R. F., & Worrell, F. C. (2016). The role of domains in the conceptualization of talent. In D. Ambrose & R. J. Sternberg (Eds.), *Giftedness and talent in the 21st century* (pp. 81–100). Rotterdam, The Netherlands: Sense Publishers.

Olszewski-Kubilius, P., Subotnik, R. F., & Worrell, F. C. (2017). Talent development as a framework for the delivery of services to gifted children. In J. L. Roberts, T. F. Inman, & J. H. Robbins (Eds.), *Introduction to gifted education* (pp. 277–298). Waco, TX: Prufrock Press.

Olszewski-Kubilius, P., Subotnik, R. F., Worrell, F. C., & Thomson, D. (2018). Talent development as a framework for the delivery of services to gifted children. In J. L. Roberts, T. F. Inman, & J. Robins (Eds.), *Introduction to gifted education* (pp. 277–298). Waco TX: Prufrock Press.

Olszewski-Kubilius, P., & Thomson, D. (2015). Talent development as a framework for gifted education. *Gifted Child Today, 38*(1), 49–59.

Park, G., Lubinski, D., & Benbow, C. P. (2007). Contrasting intellectual patterns predict creativity in the arts and sciences: Tracking intellectually precocious youth over 25 years. *Psychological Science, 18*, 948–952. https://doi.org/10.1111/j.1467-9280.2007.02007.x

Pendarvis, E., & Wood, E. W. (2009). Eligibility of historically underrepresented students referred for gifted education in a rural school district: A case study. *Journal for the Education of the Gifted, 32*, 495–514. https://doi.org/10.1177/016235320903200403

Ponnusamy, L. D., Tan, L. S., Rahamat, S., & Ibrahim, N. A. M. (2017). Negotiating the complexity of curriculum integration: Metalanguages as levers that shape the innovation process. *International Journal of Innovation in Education, 4*, 126–146. https://doi.org/10.1504/IJIIE.2017.088098

Portenga, S. (2018). Performance skills for academic talent development: Integrating sport and performance psychology skills into the classroom. In P. Olszewski-Kubilius, R. F. Subotnik, & F. Worrell (Eds.), *Talent development as a framework for gifted education* (pp. 153–184). Waco, TX: Prufrock Press.

Portenga, S. (2019). High performance talent development in golf. In R. F. Subotnik, P. Olszewski-Kubilius, & F. C. Worrell (Eds.), *The psychology of high performance: Developing human potential into domain-specific talent* (pp. 23–51). Washington, DC: American Psychological Association.

Riley, T., & Bicknell, B. (2013). Gifted and talented education in New Zealand schools: A decade later. *APEX: The New Zealand Journal of Gifted Education, 18*(1), 1–16. Retrieved from www.giftedchildren.org.nz/apex

Simonton, D. K. (2000). Creative development as acquired expertise: Theoretical issues and an empirical test. *Developmental Review, 20*, 283–318. https://doi.org/10.1006/drev.1999.0504

Simonton, D. K. (2013). The genetics of giftedness. In K. H. Kim, J. C. Kaufman, J. Baer, & B. Sriraman (Eds.), *Creatively gifted students are not like other gifted students: Research, theory, and practice* (pp. 167–180). Rotterdam, The Netherlands: Sense Publishers.

Simonton, D. K. (2019). Talent development in the domain of academic psychology. In R. F. Subotnik, P. Olszewski-Kubilius, & F. C. Worrell (Eds.), *The psychology of high performance: Developing human potential into domain-specific talent* (pp. 201–218). Washington, DC: American Psychological Association.

Stieff, M., Hegarty, M., & Dixon, B. (2010). Alternative strategies for spatial reasoning with diagrams. *Diagrams, 2010*, 115–127. https://doi.org/10.1007/978-3-642-14600-8_13

Subotnik, R. F., & Jarvin, L. (2005). Beyond expertise: Conceptions of giftedness as great performance. In R. J. Sternberg & J. E. Davidson (Eds.), *Conceptions of giftedness* (2nd ed., pp. 343–357). New York, NY: Cambridge University Press.

Subotnik, R. F., Olszewski-Kubilius, P., & Worrell, F. C. (2011). Rethinking giftedness and gifted education: A proposed direction forward based on psychological science. *Psychological Science in the Public Interest, 12*, 3–54. https://doi.org/10.1177/1529100611418056

Subotnik R. F., Olszewski-Kubilius, P., & Worrell, F. C. (2014, August). The talent gap: The U.S. is neglecting its most promising science students. *Scientific American, 13*. Retrieved from http://www.scientific-american.com/article/the-u-s-neglects-its-best-science-students/

Subotnik, R. F., & Rickoff, R. (2010). Should eminence based on outstanding innovation be the goal of gifted education and talent development? Implications for policy and research. *Learning and Individual Differences, 20*, 358–364. https://doi.org/10.1016/j.lindif.2009.12.005

Tan, L. S., Koh, E. R., Lee, S. S., Ponnusamy, L. D., & Tan, K. C. K. (2017). The complexities in fostering critical thinking through school-based curriculum innovation: Research evidence from Singapore. *Asia Pacific Journal of Education, 37*, 517–534. https://doi.org/10.1080/02188791.2017.1389694

Tan, L. S., Lee, S. S., Ponnusamy, L. D., Koh, E. R., & Tan, C. K. K. (2016). Fostering creativity in the classroom for high ability students: Context does matter. *Education in Science, 6*(36), 1–17. https://doi.org/10.3390/educsci6040036

Tan, L. S., & Ponnusamy, L. D. (2014a). Adaptivity and creativity in the arts: The nexus and affordances. In D. Hung, K. Y. T. Lim, & S. S. Lee (Eds.), *Adaptivity as transformative disposition for learning in the 21st century* (pp. 177–208). Dordrecht, The Netherlands: Springer.

Tan, L. S., & Ponnusamy, L. D. (2014b). Weaving and anchoring the arts into curriculum: The evolving curriculum processes. In C. H. Lum (Ed.), *Contextualised practices on arts education: An international dialogue on Singapore arts education* (pp. 219–258). Dordrecht, The Netherlands: Springer.

Uttal, D. H., Meadow, N. G., Tipton, E., Hand, L. L., Alden, A. R., Warren, C., & Newcombe, N. S. (2013). The malleability of spatial skills: A meta-analysis of training studies. *Psychological Bulletin, 139*, 352–402. https://doi.org/10.1037/a0028446

Wai, J., Lubinski, D., & Benbow, C. P. (2005). Creativity and occupational accomplishments among intellectually precocious youths: An age 13 to age 33 longitudinal study. *Journal of Educational Psychology, 97*, 484–492. https://doi.org/10.1037/0022-0663.97.3.484

Wardman, J. (2009). Secondary teachers', student teachers' and education students' attitudes to full-year acceleration for gifted students. *Australasian Journal of Gifted Education, 18*(1), 25–36.

Wardman, J. (2015). Full-year acceleration at high school: Parents support the social and emotional challenges of their children. *Gifted and Talented International, 29*(2), 49–62.

Wardman, J. (2018). Full-year acceleration of gifted high school students: A 360° view. In N. Ballam & R. Moltzen (Eds.), *Giftedness and talent: Australasian perspectives* (pp. 227–251). Singapore, Singapore: Springer.

Wardman, J., & Hattie, J. (2012). Administrators' perceptions of full-year acceleration at high school. *Australasian Journal of Gifted Education, 21*(1), 32–41.

Wardman, J., & Hattie, J. (2018). What works better than the rest? The impact of various curricula provisions for gifted learners. In B. Wallace, D. Sisk, & J. Senior (Eds.), *The SAGE handbook of gifted and talented education* (pp. 321–334). London, England: SAGE Publications.

Watts, C., Barnes-Burroughs, K., Andrianopoulos, M., & Carr, M. (2003). Potential factors related to untrained singing talent: A survey of singing pedagogues. *Journal of Voice, 17*, 298–307. https://doi.org/10.1067/S0892-1997(03)00068-7

Webber, M. (2011). Look to the past; Stand tall in the present: The integral nature of positive racial-ethnic identity for the academic success of Māori students. In W. Vialle (Ed.), *Giftedness from an indigenous perspective* (pp. 100–110). Wollongong, NSW: Australian Association for the Education of the Gifted and Talented.

Weinberg, R. S., & Comar, W. (1994). The effectiveness of psychological interventions in competitive sport. *Sports Medicine, 18*, 406–418. https://doi.org/10.2165/00007256-199418060-00005

Williams, J. M., & Krane, V. (2005). Psychological characteristics of peak performance. In J. Williams (Ed.), *Applied sport psychology: Personal growth to peak performance* (5th ed., pp. 162–178). New York, NY: McGraw-Hill.

Worrell, F. C. (2015). Being gifted and adolescent: Issues and needs of diverse students. In F. A. Dixon & S. M. Moon (Eds.), *The handbook of secondary gifted education* (2nd ed., pp. 121–153). Waco, TX: Prufrock Press.

Worrell, F. C., Subotnik, R. F., & Olszewski-Kubilius, P. (2018). Talent development: A path towards eminence. In S. Pfeiffer, E. Shaunessy-Dedrick, & M. Foley-Nicpon (Eds.), *APA handbook of giftedness and talent* (pp. 247–258). Washington, DC: American Psychological Association. https://doi.org/10.1037/0000038-016

Worrell, F. C., & Young, A. E. (2011). Gifted children in urban settings. In T. L. Cross & J. R. Cross (Eds.), *Handbook for counselors serving students with gifts and talents: Development, relationships, school issues, and counseling needs/interventions* (pp. 137–151). Waco, TX: Prufrock Press.

Paula Olszewski-Kubilius is a director at the Center for Talent Development and a professor within the school of education at Northwestern University in Evanston, Ill. She has spent the last 35 years developing and implementing program models for gifted learners and doing research on talent development.

Rena F. Subotnik is the Director of the Center for Psychology in School and Education at the American Psychological Association. One of the Center's primary missions is to generate public awareness, advocacy, clinical applications, and cutting-edge research ideas that will enhance the achievement of children with special gifts and talents in all domains.

Frank C. Worrell is a professor at the University of California, Berkeley. His areas of expertise include talent development and cultural identities. Dr. Worrell is a Fellow of the Association for Psychological Science, the American Educational Research Association, and the American Psychological Association and a recipient of NAGC's Distinguished Scholar Award.

Janna Wardman is a lecturer at the University of Auckland, teaching and supervising on Gifted and on Initial Teaching Education programs. Janna is an experienced international presenter and adviser to parents and schools. A strong theoretical background, informed by research, supports her practical experience of 30 years in education.

Liang See Tan is a Senior Research Scientist at the Centre for Research in Pedagogy and Practice at the National Institute of Education, Nanyang Technological University, Singapore. She specialises in high ability studies, teacher leadership, and learning. She works closely with schools on differentiating curriculum and instruction and published in peer-reviewed journals.

Seon-Young Lee is a professor in the Department of Education at Seoul National University in South Korea. She is an executive editor of *Asia Pacific Education Review*, an editor of the *Journal of the Korean Society for the Gifted and Talented*, and an associate editor of *Gifted Child Quarterly*. Her research interests lie in talent development, gifted programs, creativity, and psychosocial and leadership development of gifted and creative populations. She received the Gifted Child Quarterly Paper of the Year Award for 2011.

6. The Young Gifted Learner: What We Know and Implications for Early Educational Practice

Anne Grant and Anne-Marie Morrissey

Contents

Introduction	130
Sociocultural Approaches to Gifted Education	132
Cultural Views of Giftedness	133
What Is Known About Young Advanced Learners?	135
Social-Emotional Development	137
Early Childhood Education	138
High-Quality Educational Responses to Young Gifted Children	139
Research Directions	144
Conclusion	144
Cross-References	145
References	146

Abstract

Research into giftedness in early childhood has been a neglected area in gifted education studies, there being until relatively recently only a handful of older studies carried out in the USA (Gottfried, Gottfried, Bathurst, & Guerin, 1994; Robinson, 1993; Roedell, 1986). Over the last two decades, in the Asia-Pacific area research into giftedness and gifted education in the early years has become an area of relative strength. Some major areas of investigation have been gifted development from infancy to early school years, transition of gifted children into formal education settings, response of early childhood teachers to young gifted children, gifted early readers, and educational planning and practice with young gifted children (Grant, 2005; Hodge & Kemp, 2006; Margrain, 2010; Morrissey,

A. Grant (✉) · A.-M. Morrissey
Deakin University, Melbourne, VIC, Australia
e-mail: anne.grant.education@gmail.com; morram@deakin.edu.au; anne-marie.morrissey@deakin.edu.au

© Springer Nature Singapore Pte Ltd. 2021
S. R. Smith (ed.), *Handbook of Giftedness and Talent Development in the Asia-Pacific*, Springer International Handbooks of Education,
https://doi.org/10.1007/978-981-13-3041-4_57

2007; Walsh, Bowes, & Sweller, 2017). However, the real value of a body of evidence-based information is in its application to educational practice to enable young gifted children to thrive in their educational program. While a reasonable body of evidence about early characteristics of giftedness is now available, there is less empirical detail about reliable educational practice. Nonetheless, these current findings about young gifted children can be applied to high-quality early educational practice with them, including across cultures. In this chapter, many research-based suggestions for effective practice will be provided, Towards the end, the implications for future research directions within the early childhood field are included.

Keywords

Young gifted children · Early childhood education · Planning from a sociocultural perspective · Gifted and culturally diverse

The aims in this chapter are to:
1. Draw attention to the slowness in the early childhood education field, in relation to other levels of education, to recognise young advanced (gifted) children in their educational programs and the children's need for extended and more complex learning.
2. Elaborate on a sociocultural approach to educational planning for young children, how it aligns with current early childhood education philosophy and can provide an inclusive way of offering challenging learning for all levels of ability.
3. Discuss the information available in gifted research literature about cultural differences in recognition of giftedness and the consequent need for teachers to work in partnership with their different cultural communities to support all young gifted children to realise the potential valued by their community.
4. Discuss the body of evidence now available to support early identification of advanced development (potential giftedness), why early identification is important, and the approaches that best support early identification.
5. Review the body of evidence about high-quality educational practice with young advanced children and describe how teachers can adjust a play-based curriculum to provide a stimulating learning environment for these children.

Introduction

Researchers in the Australasian region have carried out studies in a number of different areas of giftedness in the early childhood years, providing a small, but now increasing body of evidence-based understanding of the very young gifted learner. As a result, the literature can inform us about when such advanced development may start to become apparent, what behaviours may signal this, and how such development shapes learning, particularly as young children start to experience an educational program outside the family. This information is essential if early childhood educators are to be alert to the presence of gifted children in their programs and responsive to their learning needs.

It is well accepted that experiences in the early years of life significantly influence later well-being and achievements in education (Sylva, Melhuish, Sammons, Siraj-Blatchford, & Taggart, 2004). This is equally true for young gifted children. So, it is important that the educational programs they attend are a positive influence on their feelings of well-being and provide opportunities to develop their potential. To ensure the inclusion of young gifted children, teachers need to take two steps: one is to be able to identify such children and the second is to plan for their learning.

Identification of giftedness depends on the definition used as well as the aims of the program intended to support giftedness or talent development. Gifted studies researchers have provided several definitions of giftedness, frequently referred to in Australasian literature, that are intended to apply specifically to identifying giftedness in very young children (e.g., Harrison, 2003; Porter, 2005). The one we consider most useful for early childhood teachers because it refers to the nature of development in a young child as well as the aims of an early childhood program is Morrissey's (2012) definition:

> Giftedness in early childhood involves advanced development beyond age-typical expectations, and a potential for advanced learning and achievement in one or more areas. The level of advancement is significant enough to require specific planning for their education and care that accounts for the child's advanced capacities, so that they can experience wellbeing and achieve their full potential in all areas of their development. (p. 11)

This definition indicates, as does Gagné's conceptualisation of giftedness in his Expanded Model of Giftedness and Talent (2013), that giftedness in very young children is likely to be only beginning to appear or may be still latent, depending on a variety of influences both innate and external, for instance, the child's intrapersonal development and sociocultural environment. It is particularly relevant to the early childhood field to note that early signs of giftedness are most likely to be observable as a greater "ease and speed in how they advance through successive stages [of development]" (Gagné, 2013, p. 13), in comparison to other children going through the same developmental stages. Such advanced development can be in one or a number of areas and will not yet be identifiable as similar to an adult level of performance or skill; in other words, giftedness is not yet identifiable as a 'talent' (Gagné, 2013).

We prefer the descriptors 'advanced development' or 'advanced learner' and will use these as far as possible in this chapter. While they imply the same developmental characteristics as 'giftedness', we feel they are more accessible terms in supporting understanding of these very young children. However, when discussing the contributions of other writers, it can be more appropriate to use their descriptor *giftedness or the gifted child* (Harrison, 2016), but our intention is always to focus on those young children who have the potential to be gifted and develop talents.

There have been a number of reports and discussions in Australia and New Zealand about provision for gifted children in the early childhood sector (e.g., Delaune, 2018; Hodge 2015: Margrain & Farquar, 2012; Morrissey & Grant, 2017; Parliament of Victoria, 2012). In these publications difficulties have been noted for early childhood teachers in responding to young children with advanced ability, because of particular attitudes in the field about child development and the notion of giftedness. For instance, in the above reports, teachers were found to be confused about the meaning of 'giftedness' in a very young child, and even when they did identify some areas of advanced development, they did not know what educational response to make. In addition, the general early childhood literature provides very little in the way of information or guidance about advanced development, how to identify it, and the implications of identification for educational programming (e.g., Arthur, Beecher, Death, Dockett, & Farmer, 2017). In general, the early childhood field was considered in these reports as not responding adequately in meeting the learning needs of this group of children.

There is much scholarly writing on the nature of an effective educational program for older gifted children. Some authors have presented an extrapolation of the principles from such programs as a way of differentiating a program for very young gifted children (e.g., Porter, 2005). As well there are a few, relatively recent publications available based on actual early childhood practice with young gifted children (e.g., Grant, 2004; Harrison, 2016; Hertzog, 2008; Margrain, Murphy, & Dean, 2015). However, it should be noted that little evaluation has occurred, of either the extrapolation of principles of differentiation or the reports from early childhood programs focused on young gifted children (Walsh, Kemp, Hodge, & Bowes, 2012), to validate the findings reported. Accordingly, the early childhood field needs to recognise that this area of education is only at the beginning of building a body of knowledge about appropriate educational programming for these children. Educational planners should be confident about adapting such information to local or particular cultural needs.

What is known so far will be discussed in this chapter, specifically, current findings about the characteristics of young gifted children, how a sociocultural perspective can inform high-quality educational practice, and how a sociocultural framework enables the inclusion of differing cultural perceptions about giftedness. In addition, the implications of the current level of knowledge and understanding about young gifted children will be considered in regard to future research directions.

Sociocultural Approaches to Gifted Education

Lo and Porath (2017) in a meta-theoretical discussion on paradigm shifts within gifted education studies argue that the thinking in this field has moved towards investigating the sociocultural construction of giftedness. As such, the manifestation of giftedness and talent is viewed as the outcome of a dynamic interaction between the individual, the environment, and their sociocultural context. Consequently, the educational context, including the role of the teacher, becomes most important—requiring a context that will recognise and be inclusive of high ability—however it is conceptualised by a culture.

A sociocultural perspective of education views a child's learning and development as influenced within and by their social and cultural context: family, community, early childhood program, and classroom. In his concept of the *Zone of Proximal Development (ZPD)*, Vygotsky (1960/1981) argued that the ZPD represents what the child can do with the support of adults or expert peers and is where real learning and development occurs.

The usefulness of this viewpoint when considering the learning of young gifted children is discussed in the work of Kanevsky (1992) and Moss (1992). They propose that Vygotsky's concept of learning as a sociocultural phenomenon provides useful insights into the important social-interactional influences on the development of early giftedness and talent. Specifically, a sociocultural perspective places the emphasis on learning as 'potential' and on 'future learning' (rather than past achievement) and as such is a particularly relevant approach for teachers working with young gifted and talented children.

Many of these children, because of their young age, may not be demonstrating their advanced capabilities or full potential yet. Nonetheless, pedagogical strategies such as scaffolding and sustained shared thinking (see Sylva, et al., 2004) can 'invite' children, and in particular advanced learners, to show their level of ability (Hodge & Kemp, 2002). This thinking aligns with Lo and Porath's (2017) theorising that the focus needs to be on provision of "education that is gifted" instead of the previous focus on "education for the gifted" (p. 352).

Cultural Views of Giftedness

In early childhood education, contemporary understanding is that child development is modified by culture. Grounded in the sociocultural theories of Vygotsky, this understanding is expanded through Bronfenbrenner's (1979) model of contextual influences on development. Accordingly, perceptions of giftedness, that is, advanced development and the nature of support needed for it, will be subject to the ways of thinking and behaving important in a community's culture. Recognition of this is present in the work of prominent theorists in the gifted education field (Gagné, 2013; Sternberg, 2007; Ziegler, 2005). While there is no published work about cultural influences on development of giftedness in very young children, and how this may vary between cultural groups, scholarly theorising plus research with older children furnishes relevant information about how differences in beliefs, values, customs, and skills change perceptions of giftedness within some cultures (Vialle, 2011).

Insightful discussion by three authors illustrates how cultural perceptions of giftedness can vary from Western thinking and how teachers may find such families holding differing values and beliefs about giftedness. Nyugen (2011) explores conceptions of giftedness from an Eastern and Western perspective identifying ideologies in Eastern and Western culture that have resulted in different understandings and emphases in identifying and supporting giftedness. Simplistically, Western cultures have historically focused on inherited, individual expressions of giftedness, whereas Eastern thinking—Confucian-heritage cultures—has viewed giftedness as the outcome of "long standing endeavours" by the individual (p. 46).

However, as noted above, contemporary Western theorising about giftedness or high ability no longer holds a view of giftedness as simply inherited high ability, but as a phenomenon located within a social and cultural system. As such, environmental influences play an important role in the actualisation of giftedness (Gagné, 2013). Similarly, contemporary Eastern thinking as illustrated in government policies and educational planning indicates recognition of giftedness as a combination of inherited high ability plus effort and hard work (Nyugen, 2011).

Chandler (2011) discussed giftedness from an Australian Aboriginal perspective with the immediate qualification that there is no one Aboriginal culture, there are actually many. Each culture having its own language, which within sociocultural theory, is a significant influence on learning (Vygotsky, 1960/1981). Thus, individual Aboriginal cultures when identifying giftedness are likely to focus on different attributes and priorities. Nonetheless Chandler (2011, p. 3) states, if any generalisation about giftedness in Aboriginal culture is to be made, giftedness would be identified in an individual's ability to have deep "knowledge of ancestry, of [their] land and kin, and [in demonstration of] respect for community and elders". In such identification elders would look for a capacity to carry greater responsibility towards certain family groups, certain totems, certain knowledge, and the natural environment.

Webber's (2016) discussion of New Zealand Māori beliefs and values identifies particular Māori perspectives on the behaviours and skills to be nurtured as indicating giftedness—for instance, a different understanding of gifted leadership from that held by the mainstream non-Māori community. Māori communities may also vary from each other, in the values and emphases placed on different behaviours, customs, and skills. Bevan-Brown (2009) describes a number of straightforward steps to guide teachers towards inclusion of varying cultural perceptions of giftedness. While these were devised from investigation of Māori views of giftedness, they accord with the views expressed by other authors concerned about dominant cultural concepts of giftedness which fail to account for cultural diversity (see Vialle, 2011).

Educators are advised, not to presume they know, but to ask the community:

- In what areas are giftedness recognised?
- How is each area perceived and demonstrated?
- What priority is given to each area of giftedness?
- What are culturally appropriate and effective ways of identifying gifted students (Bevan-Brown, 2009)?
- How can programs and learning opportunities incorporate culturally valued knowledge and practices so gifted students "feel they belong and find their realities reflected" in their experience of educational provision (Webber, Riley, Sylva & Scobie-Jennings, 2018, p. 1)?

In order to answer these questions, teachers and educational planners need to recognise that much of the research currently available, including forms of assessment, are derived from mainstream Western educational perspectives. These can provide much background information, but nonetheless educational programs should reflect the values and beliefs about giftedness of the individual community.

What Is Known About Young Advanced Learners?

Australian and New Zealand researchers in this area have contributed significantly to the information provided by earlier researchers—most originating in the USA. Although the empirical base continues to be small, recent Australasian studies have contributed:

- Parent documentation of their children's early development (Harrison, 2005).
- A study of infants and very young gifted children in the context of dyadic activity with their mothers (Morrissey, 2011).
- Studies of young gifted children transitioning to school (Grant, 2013; Masters, 2015).
- How is giftedness recognised in the early years of school (Hodge & Kemp, 2006)?
- Gross's 20-year longitudinal case studies of exceptionally gifted children (2004).
- Documentation of early development of reading skills (Margrain, 2010).
- Use of picture books to stimulate higher-order thinking in young children (Walsh, Bowes, & Sweller, 2017).
- Australian teacher perceptions towards use of multiple assessment measures in identifying young gifted children (Slater & Howitt, 2018).
- New Zealand Infant and Toddler Teacher's perspectives on the use of the term 'giftedness' with such young children (Delaune, 2018).

These retrospective and case studies give evidence of gifted children showing some differential and characteristic development from birth and of educational responses to their learning needs.

Specifically, the information now available indicates that as infants and toddlers, gifted children are alert, responsive and interactive with their environment, seek novelty and stimulation from caregivers, and frequently show early language development (Gross, 2006; Harrison, 2005; Lewis & Michalson, 1985; Robinson, 2008). In the preschool years, these children are frequently described as showing advancement in abstract thinking, learning, attention, memory, home language/mother tongue, and intellectual motivation (Cukierkorn, Karnes, Manning, Houston, & Besnoy, 2007; Harrison, 2005; Perleth, Lehwald, & Browder, 1993; Porter, 2005; Robinson, 2008; Walsh et al., 2017).

Some challenging characteristics are also recognised in these children, for instance:

- A low threshold for boredom.
- Emotional intensity.
- Perfectionism.
- A sense of being different from other children.

- Difficulty or lack of interest in socialising with others of the same age (Farrent & Grant, 2005; Grant, 2004; Harrison, 2005, 2016; Porter, 2005).

The degree to which children with advanced development display these recognised characteristics in early childhood can often be linked to the later level of giftedness they demonstrate. For example, Gross' (2004) case study of exceptionally gifted children showed particularly high levels of such behaviours in their infant and preschool years.

There is limited empirical research on the early learning of young developmentally advanced children, but what is reported does support the findings from research in the broader field. A major contribution to knowledge was an empirical study, the Fullerton Longitudinal Study (Gottfried et al., 1994), a relatively larger-scale, longitudinal study that was prospective rather than retrospective. The findings in the Gottfried et al. study were that advanced intellectual development was evident from the first year of life and that these children were more motivated and sought higher levels of stimulation from their environment. Other findings in the study were that each gifted child demonstrated a unique developmental profile, with individual timing of peaks and plateaux in their learning. Their home backgrounds were more stimulating than those of age-typical children, with the gifted children eliciting and receiving higher levels of stimulation from their parents. The study's findings support the roles of genetics and environment, as it reported a bi-directional flow of interactions where young gifted children both influence and are influenced by their environment. For example, there is evidence that young gifted children seek higher levels of stimulation from the environment and that, in turn, their caregivers provide the higher levels of stimulation that the children seek (Gottfried & Gottfried, 2004; Gottfried et al., 1994).

Researchers in two studies have looked at very early development of gifted children in the context of dyadic activity with their mothers. Moss (1992) found that the mothers of the gifted children modelled more metacognitive strategies and proposed that they did this as a response to the more frequent higher-level verbalisations of their children. An Australian study by Morrissey (2011; Morrissey & Brown, 2009) found that the higher IQ children became independent in pretend play faster than the children in the average IQ group and that their mothers recognised this and allowed their child to take greater responsibility for such play earlier than the other mothers. Morrissey also found that mothers of the children in the higher IQ group introduced scaffolding of their children's metacognitive and analogical thinking earlier than mothers of children in the average IQ group (Morrissey, 2011).

There have as well been a handful of studies on specific aspects of advanced intellectual development in young children. They have been found to have effective early exploratory skills and higher levels of curiosity in early childhood than more typically developing children (Harrison, 2005; Lehwald, as cited in Perleth et al., 1993; Raine, Reynolds, Venables, & Mednick, 2002). Gottfried and Gottfried (2004) found higher levels of intellectual motivation in young gifted children, concluding that cognitive mastery motivation in infancy was an "early correlate and developmental precursor of future academic intrinsic motivation" (p. 126). Kanevsky (1992) found that advanced four to five year olds showed higher than usual metacognitive and executive functioning in variations of the Tower of Hanoi task. These children were more motivated and strategic in their thinking than their non-gifted peers. They also created and imposed higher-level goals for themselves.

Social-Emotional Development

Research on young gifted children's social and emotional development is even more limited than that on their intellectual development. However, there are anecdotal and case study findings suggesting young children with advanced intellectual development often also demonstrate particular social and emotional characteristics. These include:

- Emotional intensity in responding to events and experiences.
- Great sensitivity to others, animals, the environment.
- Perfectionism.
- Early concern with ethical and justice issues.
- A sense of being different from other children (Grant, 2013; Harrison, 2005).

Some scholars have also suggested that their emotional development can be *qualitatively different* and *asynchronous*—that is, their cognitive development is in advance of their development in other areas (Cukierkorn et al., 2007; Silverman, 2002). This developmental asynchrony can result in their advanced intellectual development exposing them to inner experiences and awareness that poses a challenge to their comparatively immature emotional development. Porter (2005) argues that the social and emotional characteristics described in the literature may be more evident in highly gifted children and notes the lack of solid evidence on early emotional development of these children.

In regard to social development, the research indicates that moderately gifted young children are generally socially well-adjusted (Neihart, Pfeiffer, & Cross, 2016), although the preschool period can be challenging as these children may struggle to find like-minded peers (Grant, 2004, 2013). The highly gifted young child can face more challenges in establishing positive social relationships with peers (Farrent & Grant, 2005).

In summary, although the evidence base is small, the research presents a consistent picture of the young developmentally advanced child. Their development is described as atypical and advanced from infancy. They seek stimulation from their environment and their caregivers, are curious, and intellectually motivated from a young age. They have been shown to demonstrate advanced intellectual development from the first year of life, and their parents appear to recognise and respond to this advancement. These findings indicate a dynamic, involving both genetics and environment, and in particular the crucial role of caregivers in supporting early gifted development. As Robinson (1993) notes, "Parents of gifted children are both contributors to their child's advancement and responders to their child's behaviour—a complex interplay of cause and effect that cannot ever really be sorted out" (p. 513).

It is worthwhile reiterating at this point that the research findings reported here are predominantly framed within a Western European perception of education and giftedness. As stated earlier in this chapter, there are no findings or discussion in the literature about understandings of giftedness in young children from other cultural perspectives. Therefore, the best that teachers can do for the present is to work from what is currently understood about this group of children. This situation underscores the need for there to be more investigation of other cultural perspectives of advanced development in very young children.

Early Childhood Education

Current understanding of high-quality educational practice with all young children is based on a perception that learning happens within a sociocultural context. As such the learning offered is a response to each child's strengths as well as learning needs and is inclusive of cultural and social diversity. See, for example, the curriculum guidelines in:

- Australia: *Early Years Learning Framework* [EYLF] (DEEWR, 2009).
- New Zealand: *Te Whariki* (Ministry of Education New Zealand, 2017).
- Singapore: *Nurturing Early Learners* [NEL] (Ministry of Education, Singapore, 2012).

While the content of the learning offered and the skills that are valued will be particular to each culture, nonetheless each of these documents present educational goals of nurturing the potential of each young child in all areas of their development—so that they become active and confident learners, self-confident and emotionally resilient, and conscious of their self as a part of as well as a contributor to their community.

High-quality pedagogical practice to implement such goals has been detailed in *The Effective Provision of Preschool Education* (EPPE) project (Sylva, et al., 2004), a major longitudinal study of young children's development, where the main principles determining high quality are:

- Teachers hold high expectations of children's learning.
- Intentional/instructive learning interactions occur between teacher and children focused on content that reflects knowledge valued by that community.
- Opportunities are facilitated for sustained shared thinking between children and between teachers and children.
- Support is provided to develop social skills, including learning to resolve conflict.

- Affirmation is provided of diversity in cultures, genders, abilities, or interests.
- There are warm, supportive relationships between staff and children, enabling emotional well-being and increasing maturity in children.

High-Quality Educational Responses to Young Gifted Children

In a very general sense, the main principles for high-quality practice in working with all children should also be satisfactory in providing for the learning needs of gifted children. However, the twin guiding principles of gifted education do need consideration within the framework of early childhood education:

- How to ensure effective identification.
- How to provide effective differentiation of the curriculum.

Walsh, Hodge, Bowes, and Kemp (2010) note that the early childhood field has been shy about reliable identification of advanced ability because amongst a number of reasons, there was a strongly held and widespread feeling that 'to label' young children was inappropriate. They also comment that effective differentiation has not been widely described, thus limiting professional awareness of high-quality practice with these children. Nonetheless, acknowledgement of the early years as formative in regard to later learning and achievement requires all involved in early education to ensure that early learning opportunities are high quality for all children.

Identification. Currently, it is accepted that identification of very young gifted children needs to be based on information about their level of development gathered from a variety of sources (Kettler, Oveross, & Salman, 2017; Porter, 2005). This can include sources such as parent and family anecdotes, teacher observations and documentation of children's work (if teachers have background knowledge of characteristics of giftedness), or forms of identification by other appropriate professionals who know the child. In some cultural groups, it is the elders who will have relevant information about identification. For instance, information should be sought from elders about the knowledge and attributes that indicate giftedness within their community, as well as characteristic perspectives on identifying gifted traits (e.g., Christie, 2011). Offering highly challenging learning experiences was also found by early childhood and primary early years teachers, participating in a professional development program, to enable identification of hitherto unidentified advanced learners (Morrissey & Grant, 2017).

Identification can also include formal approaches ranging from IQ assessment (for older preschool-aged children) to reliable assessment tools appropriate for young children (see Porter, [Assessing Developmental Advances] 2005). However, caution is advised in relying only on IQ or achievement tests as these are known to be unreliable for children under six years (Pfeiffer & Petscher, 2008). While high performance by a young child on such assessments would indicate advanced cognitive development, others with high potential may not be identified with these instruments due to issues of performance or variable developmental factors (Gottfried, Gottfried, & Guerin, 2009).

Traditional formal assessments developed within the western mainstream culture may identify gifted children from different cultures or low socio-economic groups, where these children show advanced ability in the intellectual areas used to assess the level of advanced capability. However, these traditional approaches can also be problematic if advanced ability is demonstrated in beliefs, values, customs, and skills particular to another culture or in a socio-economic group that is sufficiently different to the mainstream of a community (Ballam, 2011; Matthews & Farmer, 2017).

Where such diversity is likely, a number of scholars advocate alternative assessment approaches. Munro (2011) discusses the advantage of authentic tasks—testing the extent of students' knowledge and skills gained from their own culture—and their ability to apply this to relevant everyday problems. Also advocated is the use of dynamic assessment—current relevant learning is assessed, followed by provision for learning relevant knowledge and skills, followed by an appropriate form of assessment to gauge the extent of learning by the student (Chaffey, Bailey, & Vine, 2011).

Such assessment approaches can be readily used in early childhood contexts where the choice of learning content and strategies to promote learning should be suitable for the stage of development for the child. Then assessment—of an authentic task or dynamic learning approach—will aim to determine how well or how much the child/children had learnt from the particular topic offered. For instance, a rubric could be devised incorporating different levels of learning or skill directly linked to a learning opportunity. Topics can range from physical skills to social skills or understandings about numeracy, science, music, or any topic important within a particular culture.

'Differentiating' the early childhood program for young advanced learners. Adopting a sociocultural perspective provides a straightforward way to differentiate an early childhood program. Educational planning takes into consideration the whole learning environment of the class or group, that is, the intellectual, social, emotional, cultural, and physical learning relevant to the children. Consequently, the content of the program can be inclusive of the learning characteristics and needs of the individual child with advanced learning as well as those who will be more age-typical. Thus, the child with advanced ability will be seen as part of a group of learners experiencing a stimulating curriculum that includes learning challenges for all. For instance, a child with a characteristic of advanced development, such as advanced vocabulary and advanced expressive language, will be challenged by tasks that ask the child to employ these attributes in exploring the topic being offered by the teacher to the whole class or group (see information about other advanced characteristics described in earlier sections).

With this approach the advanced learners have opportunities to gain new learning through access to concepts and intellectual skills that are new to them, but they also, by being part of a learning group, gain important learning about making relationships and developing emotional independence and resilience. This sociocultural approach to early education is reflected in the following anecdote:

Charlie (4 years old) is already reading and writing but does not play with the other children at his early childhood centre. The class are interested in a house being built across the road from their centre and have started a project about its construction. Charlie has been encouraged by his teacher to use his skills to read information found on the internet about house building and he—sometimes with help from the teacher—also writes the information on the class documentation about the new house. Charlie is making new relationships with the other children as a result of the co-operative work on the project, there has been an increase in interest in learning to read amongst the other children, and Charlie's parents have commented that he is now much happier to come to pre-school each day.

Pedagogical approaches that support young gifted children. Mandated early childhood learning frameworks that guide practice across the Asia-Pacific region are grounded in play-based pedagogy (e.g., Australian, EYLF; New Zealand, Te Whariki; Singapore, NEL). While these frameworks do not specifically refer to the teaching of advanced learners, it is usually possible to account for gifted learning needs through expanded explication of their guiding principles. However, we have found from informal discussions with early childhood teachers that many appear to hold the view that young gifted learners are somehow 'beyond play' and require a program of structured academic learning. This view may be a factor in their apparent reluctance to engage with the subject of provision for young gifted children. Contrary to this perception, young gifted children can benefit from play-based programs.

The play of young gifted children has been found to be advanced, and they may engage in extended and sophisticated play activities (Cukierkorn et al., 2007; Margrain, Murphy, & Dean, 2015). Some may develop an early interest in 'games with rules' that are more typical of older children, such as chess or card games. Toddlers may demonstrate early pretend play as a reflection of advanced abstract thinking (Morrissey, 2011; Morrissey & Brown, 2009). Young gifted children may become leaders with their age peers in dramatic play or enjoy authentic projects (Hertzog, 2008; Margrain et al., 2015). Or, they may prefer to work alone on activities potentially engaging in these at a more advanced cognitive level and not wishing to be distracted by the need to be inclusive of other children at the same time (Grant, 2004; Wilson, 2015). This latter play preference should not be automatically interpreted as a lack of social maturity.

Appropriate pedagogical approaches range from child-directed free play to intentional teaching within a play activity and to inclusion of more structured approaches within play. The following anecdote illustrates how 'play' offered an opportunity for this advanced two years old to use her excellent memory skill and advanced learning ability:

Nivash (2 years old) was sitting at a table with several older girls and the teacher. On the table was a Russian doll puzzle pulled apart into separate pieces (four hollow dolls, from small to large, and each separated into two halves. The puzzle is to join the correct size halves and then place one inside the next size until they are all inside the largest doll). The teacher put the pieces in front of Nivash thinking she might enjoy simply exploring and manipulating them. Nivash picked some of the pieces up and looked at them, but then looked at the teacher as if to ask, "What do I do with these?" The teacher hesitated, thinking that the puzzle would be too difficult for a two-year-old, and not wanting her to experience failure with it. While she was thinking how to respond, Sophie (4-year-old), who was sitting opposite, picked up the pieces and put the puzzle together. Nivash watched her closely. Sophie said "See Nivash, that's how you do it", as she took the doll apart again and passed the pieces back. Nivash then quickly put it back together again without hesitation. Another teacher who was watching was amazed that Nivash had learnt just by watching Sophie.

Some authors (Margrain et al., 2015; Morrissey, 2012; Morrissey & Grant, 2013) have described appropriate strategies to be inclusive of all children:

- Support the strengths and interests of individual children, groups, and cultures; such as through long-term projects and use of community resources—people and material resources.
- Provide opportunities for children to initiate and direct their own learning activities, including organising the learning environment and resources.
- Become a co-learner and co-researcher with children, working with them to find resources, reading material for them, and discussing learning goals with them (teachers do not have to know 'everything') and ways of achieving those goals.
- Avoid putting a ceiling on expectations for children. As argued by Morelock and Morrison (1999), developmentally appropriate learning means offering learning at the child's advanced developmental level, not the developmental level that is age-typical.

Planning for content with challenge and high expectations. Morrissey (2012) advises educators to use the open and flexible nature of the early childhood approaches to include content or learning experiences that offer challenging ideas and language for those children who are capable of responding. This could be seen as a 'buffet' approach, where learning experiences can offer varying levels of challenge to provide for all ability levels, through a variety of forms of play. For example, a group of young children wanted to explore drumming following the visit of a child's father who was a drummer in a band. The teacher supported opportunities for all children to experiment with drumming patterns and for those children interested to challenge themselves by creating their own form of musical notation. They readily offered to 'write down' the drumming patterns of the other children.

Differentiated content can be added to everyday learning experiences when teachers:

- Engage in rich conversations with children.
- Give children the language they need, including advanced vocabulary and technical terms.
- Support young advanced learners in all areas of their development.
- Remember that young advanced learners will each have their own unique pathways of learning and development. They may sometimes leap ahead, or plateau, or even appear to go backwards.

Sometimes advanced abilities can be hidden or masked, as illustrated in the following anecdote:

> Max attended a three-year-old group. He was a very shy boy but appeared otherwise to be a typical three-year old. Fatima, his educator, was sitting with another group of children but was observing Max carefully because of some comments Max's mother had made about him showing advanced learning at home. Max was sitting at the play-dough table rolling and thumping the play-dough just like the other children. However, Fatima saw him suddenly jump up and go over to several other three-year-olds who were having difficulties with the computer game they were playing. "Look", said Max, pointing to the screen, "it says to move the cursor here and click, I'll show you". He quickly made several adjustments to what was on the screen and the other children were able to continue their game. Fatima reflected that if she had simply noted Max' level of play with the play-dough and not been watching him more closely following his mother's comments, she would not have realised he was potentially advanced in some areas. Fatima attempted later in the day to find out the extent of Max's reading ability, but he was reluctant to read for her. Fatima discussed this behaviour with Max's mother who confirmed that he was teaching himself to read and also that Max played computer games at home with his older brother. Max later told his mother that he wouldn't read for Fatima because, "children don't read at *kinder [preschool]*".

Walsh et al. (2017) discuss how challenge can be embedded into early childhood programs through use of strategic questions to prompt children's higher-order thinking. As implied in the title of their paper, *Why would you say goodnight to the moon?* this question does not ask for simple thinking, for names, or remembered parts of a story but instead aims to prompt creative thinking—*why would you say goodnight to the moon?* They also describe how other types of complex thinking can be prompted by use of questions based on higher-order thinking skills, for instance, *how is the moon like (or not like) the earth?*

Both the Reggio Emilia and the International Baccalaureate Primary Years (Early Years) programs have been cited as examples of satisfactory early learning programs for young gifted learners. Within these, play-based pedagogy is used to create classroom climates of challenge, intellectual inquiry, creative thinking, and metacognitive awareness (Barbour & Shaklee, 1998; Cukierkorn et al., 2007; Morrissey, Rouse, Doig, Chao, & Moss, 2014).

Transition. Transition for young gifted children from one learning environment to another can be stressful in ways different to the experience of more age-typical children (Grant, 2013). Transition experiences for all children—from home into an early learning setting and from that setting into school—require them to reorientate their sense of self (Pollard & Filer, 1999). Grant found the adaptation to a new sense of self required for a young gifted child was likely to involve significant shifts in their understanding of the new (school) learning approach and of changes in relationships with 'more knowledgeable others', and a need for the child to manage their heightened awareness of and sensitivity to personal and institutional expectations. Teachers and parents need to recognise these transition differences in a young gifted child and be ready with appropriate understanding and support.

Webber et al. (2018) drew their readers' attention to the psychological load imposed when children need to adapt their cultural sense of self, as well as their gifted sense of self, to a mainstream educational setting. The 'identity work' (p. 1) required for an individual child, especially if very young, in redefining the 'gifted self', the different 'cultural self', and possibly learning a different language can become so complex to manage alone it may lead to disengagement from the educational program. Thus, it is important for parents and educational professionals to be supportive and perceptive in enabling young gifted children to maintain a positive sense of their own capability and a positive sense of their own cultural background as they adjust to a new educational setting and engage with the learning program.

Research Directions

There is now a sufficient body of evidence about the early characteristics of advanced ability to allay any justifiable concern about early identification, and parents have been validated as reliable in identifying their own child's advanced development (Harrison, 2003; Koshy & Robinson, 2006; Morrissey, 2011; Sankar-DeLeeuw, 2004). However, a pressing research need is to validate suitable curriculum and pedagogical approaches. While a number of authors have reported on the delivery of early childhood programs for young gifted children (Grant, 2004; Margrain, et al., 2015; Wilson, 2015), we still need evaluation of such programs to know how efficacious such approaches are with a range of young gifted children. As noted earlier, the early childhood field, especially with the current emphasis on supporting diversity, needs to know how such program approaches work to support advanced development in children from different cultural groups and different socio-economic groups, and how different early childhood curriculum models work in supporting young advanced learners.

Initial feedback to Morrissey and Grant (2017) from teachers using a sociocultural perspective was enthusiasm about the approach of providing challenge to all the children they worked with, in contrast to the need to provide separate individual plans for gifted children. However, longer-term research is required into differentiated early childhood programs to provide more detail. How do we describe stimulating content as well as effective pedagogy for very young developmentally advanced children? How do adaptations to incorporate differing cultural values about giftedness shape an early childhood program? What does evaluation tell us about both short-term and long-term outcomes? In a 'nutshell', when thinking about very young children, we need more detail about an "education [program] that is gifted" (Lo & Porath, 2017) and how it can provide for all students.

Conclusion

The broader early childhood education field in Australia, New Zealand, and the Asia-Pacific region has been slow—compared to other levels of our formal education system—to acknowledge the presence and learning needs of young gifted children in their programs. The research discussed in this chapter clearly illustrates that behaviours indicating advanced development can be apparent at a very early age and are indicative of different learning needs. Combining this knowledge with the accepted awareness that early learning is formative underscores the necessity for early childhood practice to respond to the learning needs of young advanced learners.

Although there is still much to learn about early childhood best practice with young gifted children, the field now has sufficient knowledge to guide practice that will be supportive of the learning needs of these children. As we have argued, a sociocultural approach is an especially effective one, because by planning challenging learning for all levels of ability, teachers can be inclusive of young gifted children rather than needing to plan or think of them as separate to the mainstream. In addition, a sociocultural perspective supports awareness of diverse values and beliefs, including those about giftedness.

The titles of the national early childhood guidelines mentioned in this chapter present an optimistic goal for early childhood education: for all young children to develop their potential through *Belonging, Being, and Becoming* (DEEWR, 2009), *Nurturing Early Learners* (Ministry of Education, Singapore, 2012), and *Te Whariki* (weaving of a mat) as a metaphor for the learning journey of a young child. We now know that the different developmental pathways taken by gifted children starts early and that to help them also achieve the goals held for them by their community, we need to recognise them and ensure they are included in educational planning. As stated so cogently by Koshy and Robinson (2006), neglecting this need means "[t]here are losses for the children themselves ... and for society at large ... all children thrive best in [learning] environments that are a good fit for the level and pace of their development" (p. 117).

Cross-References

- ▶ Being of Like-Mind: Giftedness in the New Zealand Context
- ▶ Gifted Education in the Asia-Pacific: From the Past for the Future – An Introduction
- ▶ Gifted and Talented Aboriginal Students in Australia
- ▶ In Search of an Explanation for an Approach-Avoidance Pattern in East Asia: The Role of Cultural Values in Gifted Education
- ▶ Place-Based Gifted Education in Rural Schools
- ▶ Social and Cultural Conceptions and Perceptions: Part I Introduction
- ▶ Some Implications for the Future of Gifted Education in the Asia-Pacific
- ▶ Supporting Australian Gifted Indigenous Students' Academic Potential in Rural Settings
- ▶ The Development of Mana: Five Optimal Conditions for Gifted Māori Student Success
- ▶ Towards Exceptionality: The Current Status and Future Prospects of Australian Gifted Education

References

Arthur, L., Beecher, B., Death, E., Dockett, S., & Farmer, S. (2017). *Planning and programming in early childhood settings* (7th ed.). Southbank, VIC: Cengage Learning Australia.

Ballam, N. (2011). Talented and living on the wrong side of the tracks. In W. Vialle (Ed.), *Giftedness from an indigenous perspective* (pp. 123–139). Wollongong, NSW: Australian Association for the Education of the Gifted and Talented.

Barbour, N. E., & Shaklee, B. D. (1998). Gifted education meets Reggio Emilia: Visions for curriculum in gifted education for young children. *Gifted Child Quarterly, 42*(4), 229–237. https://doi.org/10.1177/001698629804200406

Bevan-Brown, J. M. (2009). Identifying and providing for gifted and talented Māori students. *APEX, 15*(4), 6–20. Retrieved online from http://www.giftedchildren.org.nz/apex/

Bronfenbrenner, U. (1979). *The ecology of human development: Experiments by nature and design*. Cambridge, MA: Harvard University Press.

Chaffey, G. W., Bailey, S. B., & Vine, K. W. (2011). Identifying high academic potential in Australian Aboriginal children using dynamic testing. In W. Vialle (Ed.), *Giftedness from an indigenous perspective* (pp. 77–94). Wollongong, NSW: Australian Association for the Education of the Gifted and Talented.

Chandler, P. (2011). Prodigy or problem child? Challenges with identifying Aboriginal giftedness. In W. Vialle (Ed.), *Giftedness from an indigenous perspective* (pp. 1–9). Wollongong, NSW: Australian Association for the Education of the Gifted and Talented.

Christie, M. (2011). Some Aboriginal perspectives on gifted and talented children and their schooling. In W. Vialle (Ed.), *Giftedness from an indigenous perspective* (pp. 77–94). Wollongong, NSW: Australian Association for the Education of the Gifted and Talented.

Cukierkorn, J. R., Karnes, F. A., Manning, S. J., Houston, H., & Besnoy, K. (2007). Serving the preschool gifted child: Programming and resources. *Roeper Review, 29*, 271–276. https://doi.org/10.1080/02783190709554422

Delaune, A. (2018). Tensions with the term 'gifted': New Zealand infant and toddlers teachers' perspectives on giftedness. *Australasian Journal of Gifted Education, 27*(2), 5–15. https://doi.org/10.21505/ajge.2018.0012

Department of Education, Employment, and Workplace Relations (DEEWR). (2009). *Belonging, being, and becoming: The early years learning framework for Australia*. Canberra, ACT: Commonwealth of Australia.

Farrent, S., & Grant, A. (2005). Some Australian findings about the socio-emotional development of gifted pre-schoolers. *Gifted Education International, 10*(2), 142–152. https://doi.org/10.1177/026142940501900208

Gagné, F. (2013). The DMGT: Changes within, beneath, and beyond. *Talent Development & Excellence, 5*(1), 5–19. Retrieved from https://www.researchgate.net/publication/285946236_The_DMGT_Changes_Within_Beneath_and_Beyond

Gottfried, A. E., & Gottfried, A. W. (2004). Toward the development of a conceptualization of gifted motivation. *Gifted Child Quarterly, 48*(2), 121–132. https://doi.org/10.1177/001698620404800205

Gottfried, A. W., Gottfried, A. E., Bathurst, K., & Guerin, D. W. (1994). *Gifted IQ. Early developmental aspects. The Fullerton Longitudinal Study*. New York, NY: Plenum Press.

Gottfried, A. W., Gottfried, A. E., & Guerin, D. W. (2009). Issues in early prediction and identification of intellectual giftedness. In F. D. Horowitz, R. F. Subotnik, & D. J. Matthews (Eds.), *The development of giftedness and talent across the lifespan* (pp. 43–56). Washington, DC: American Psychological Association.

Grant, A. (2004). Picasso, physics, and coping with perfectionism: Aspects of an early childhood curriculum for gifted preschoolers. *Journal of Australian Research in Early Childhood Education, 11*(2), 61–69.

Grant, A. (2013). Young gifted children transitioning into preschool and school: What matters? *Australasian Journal of Early Childhood, 38*(2), 23–30. https://doi.org/10.1177/183693911303800204

Gross, M. U. M. (2004). *Exceptionally gifted children* (2nd ed.). London, England: Routledge Falmer.

Gross, M. U. M. (2006). Exceptionally gifted children: Long-term outcomes of academic acceleration and non-acceleration. *Journal for the Education of the Gifted, 29*, 404–429. https://doi.org/10.4219/jeg-2006-247

Harrison, C. (2003). *Giftedness in early childhood* (3rd ed.). Sydney, NSW: Inscript Publishing.

Harrison, C. (2005). *Young gifted children: Their search for complexity and connection*. Exeter, NSW: Inscript Publishing.

Harrison, C. (2016). *Gifted and talented: Inclusion and exclusion*. Canberra, ACT: Early Childhood Australia.

Hertzog, N. B. (2008). *Early childhood gifted education*. Waco, TX: Prufrock Press.

Hodge, K. (2015). *Gifted children prior to school: What do their educators believe and do regarding their education?* Paper presented at the Biennial Conference of the World Council for the Gifted and Talented Odense, Denmark.

Hodge, K., & Kemp, C. (2002). The role of an invitational curriculum in the identification of giftedness in young children. *Roeper Review, 27*(1), 33–38. https://doi.org/10.1177/183693910202700107

Hodge, K., & Kemp, C. (2006). Recognition of giftedness in the early years of school: Perspectives of teachers, parents, and children. *Journal for the Education of the Gifted, 30*(2), 164–204. Retrieved from https://pdfs.semanticscholar.org/8f31/9c47d698fb9e6ce712ce44c0db5e4b7fd72b.pdf

Kanevsky, L. (1992). The learning game. In P. S. Klein & A. J. Tannenbaum (Eds.), *To be young and gifted* (pp. 204–244). Norwood, NJ: Ablex.

Kettler, T., Oveross, M. E., & Salman, R. C. (2017). Preschool gifted education: Perceived challenges associated with program development. *Gifted Child Quarterly, 61*(2), 117–132. https://doi.org/10.1177/0016986217690228

Koshy, V., & Robinson, N. M. (2006). Too long neglected: Gifted young children. *European Early Childhood Education Research Journal, 14*(2), 113–126. https://doi.org/10.1080/13502930285209951

Lewis, M., & Michalson, L. (1985). The gifted infant. In J. Freeman (Ed.), *The psychology of gifted children: Perspectives on development and education* (pp. 35–37). New York, NY: Wiley.

Lo, C. O., & Porath, M. (2017). Paradigm shifts in gifted education: An examination vis-a-vis its historical situatedness and pedagogical sensibilities. *Gifted Child Quarterly, 61*(4), 343–360. https://doi.org/10.1177/0016986217722840

Margrain, V. (2010). Parent-teacher partnerships for gifted early readers in New Zealand. *International Journal About Parents in Education, 4*(1), 39–48. Retrieved from www.ernape.net/ejournal/index.php/IJPE

Margrain, V., & Farquar, S. (2012). The education of gifted children in the early years: A first survey of views, teaching practices, resourcing and administration issues. *Apex, 17*(1), 1–13. Retrieved from https://www.childforum.com/images/stories/gifted_research_paper.pdf

Margrain, V., Murphy, C., & Dean, J. (Eds.). (2015). *Giftedness in the early years: Informing, learning, and teaching*. Wellington, New Zealand: NZCER Press.

Masters, N. (2015). *Put your seatbelt on, here we go! The transition to school for children identified as gifted*. (Unpublished doctoral thesis). Charles Sturt University, Wagga Wagga, NSW.

Matthews, M. S., & Farmer, J. (2017). Predicting academic achievement growth among low-income Mexican-American learners using dynamic and static assessments. *Australasian Journal of Gifted Education, 26*(1), 5–21. https://doi.org/10.21505/ajge.2017.0002

Ministry of Education, New Zealand. (2017). *Te Whariki – Early childhood curriculum*. Wellington, New Zealand: New Zealand Ministry of Education. Retrieved from https://education.govt.nz/assets/Documents/Early-Childhood/ELS-Te-Whariki-Early-Childhood-Curriculum-ENG-Web.pdf

Ministry of Education, Singapore. (2012). *Nurturing early learners: A curriculum framework for kindergartens in Singapore*. Singapore, Singapore: Ministry of Education.

Morelock, M. J., & Morrison, K. (1999). Differentiating 'developmentally appropriate': The multidimensional curriculum model for young gifted children. *Roeper Review, 22*, 185–191. https://doi.org/10.1080/02783199909553961

Morrissey, A.-M. (2007). *Relationships between early pretence, mother-child interactions, and later IQ: A longitudinal study of average to high ability children* (Unpublished PhD thesis). The University of Melbourne, Melbourne, VIC.

Morrissey, A.-M. (2011). Maternal scaffolding of analogy and metacognition in the early pretence of gifted children. *Exceptional Children, 77*, 351–366. https://doi.org/10.1177/001440291107700306

Morrissey, A.-M. (2012). *Young gifted children: A practical guide to understanding and supporting their needs*. Albert Park, VIC: Teaching Solutions.

Morrissey, A.-M., & Brown, P. M. (2009). Mother and toddler activity in the zone of proximal development for pretend play as a predictor of higher child IQ. *Gifted Child Quarterly, 53*, 106–120. https://doi.org/10.1177/0016986208330563

Morrissey, A.-M., & Grant, A. (2013). *Making a difference for young gifted and talented children*. Department of Education and Early Childhood Development, Melbourne, VIC. Retrieved from: https://www.education.vic.gov.au/childhood/professionals/learning/Pages/gtmakedifference.aspx

Morrissey, A.-M., & Grant, A. (2017). Making a difference: A report on educators learning to plan for young gifted children. *Australasian Journal of Gifted Education, 26*(2), 16–26. https://doi.org/10.21505/ajge.2017.0013

Morrissey, A. M., Rouse, L., Doig, B., Chao, E., & Moss, J. (2014). *Early years education in the Primary Years Programme: Implementation strategies and programme outcomes*. Bethesda, MD: International Baccalaureate Organisation.

Moss, E. (1992). Early interactions and metacognitive development of gifted preschoolers. In P. S. Klein & A. J. Tannenbaum (Eds.), *To be young and gifted*. Norwood, NJ: Ablex.

Munro, J. (2011). Identifying gifted knowledge and learning in indigenous cultures: Africa and Australia. In W. Vialle (Ed.), *Giftedness from an indigenous perspective* (pp. 24–35). Wollongong, NSW: Australian Association for the Education of the Gifted and Talented.

Neihart, M., Pfeiffer, S., & Cross, T. (Eds.). (2016). *The social and emotional development of gifted children* (2nd ed.). Waco, TX: Prufrock Press.

Nyugen, P. (2011). Eastern and Western perspectives of giftedness: Is there a difference? *Australasian Journal of Gifted Education, 20*(1), 46–51.

Parliament of Victoria. (2012). *Inquiry into the education of gifted and talented students* (Parliamentary paper of no. 108 session 2010–2012). Melbourne, VIC: Victorian Government Printer.

Perleth, C., Lehwald, G., & Browder, C. S. (1993). Indicators of high ability in young children. In K. A. Heller, F. J. Monks, & A. H. Passow (Eds.), *International handbook of research and development of giftedness and talent* (pp. 283–310). Oxford, UK: Pergamon Press.

Pfeiffer, S. I., & Petscher, Y. (2008). Identifying young gifted children using the gifted rating scales preschool/kindergarten form. *Gifted Child Quarterly, 52*(1), 19–29. https://doi.org/10.1177/0016986207311055

Pollard, A., & Filer, A. (1999). *The social world of pupil career*. London, England: Open University Press.

Porter, L. (2005). *Gifted young children: A guide for teachers and parents* (2nd ed.). Sydney, NSW: Allen & Unwin.

Raine, A., Reynolds, C., Venables, P. H., & Mednick, S. A. (2002). Stimulation seeking and intelligence: A prospective longitudinal study. *Journal of Personality and Social Psychology, 82*, 663–674. Retrieved from https://www.apa.org/pubs/journals/releases/psp-824663.pdf

Robinson, N. M. (1993). Identifying and nurturing gifted, very young children. In K. A. Heller, F. J. Monks, & A. H. Passow (Eds.), *International handbook of research and development of giftedness and talent*. Oxford, UK: Pergamon Press.

Robinson, N. M. (2008). Early childhood. In J. A. Plucker & C. M. Callahan (Eds.), *Critical issues and practices in gifted education: What the research says* (pp. 179–194). Tallahassee, Florida: Springer.

Roedell, W. C. (1986). Socioemotional vulnerabilities of young gifted children. In J. R. Whitmore (Ed.), *Intellectual giftedness in young children*. New York, NY: The Haworth Press.

Sankar-DeLeeuw, N. (2004). Case studies of gifted kindergarten children: Profiles of promise. *Roeper Review, 26*(4), 192–207. https://doi.org/10.1080/02783190409554270

Silverman, L. K. (2002). Asynchronous development. In M. Neihart, S. M. Reis, N. M. Robinson, & S. M. Moon (Eds.), *The social and emotional development of gifted children: What do we know?* (pp. 31–37). Waco, TX: Prufrock Press.

Slater, E., & Howitt, C. (2018). Teacher perceptions of a pilot process for identifying intellectually gifted 6- and 7- year-old children in the classroom. *Australasian Journal of Gifted Education, 27*(1), 5–19. https://doi.org/10.21505/ajge.2018.0002

Sternberg, R. J. (2007). Cultural concepts of giftedness. *Roeper Review, 29*(3), 160–165. https://doi.org/10.1080/02783190709554404

Sylva, K., Melhuish, E., Sammons, P., Siraj-Blatchford, I., & Taggart, B. (2004). *The effective provision of preschool education (EPPE) project*. Retrieved from www.desf.gov.uk

Vialle, W. (2011). *Giftedness from an indigenous perspective*. Wollongong, NSW: Australian Association for the Education of the Gifted and Talented.

Vygotsky, L. S. (1981). The genesis of higher mental functions. In J. V. Wertsch (Ed.), *The concept of activity in Soviet psychology* (pp. 144–188). Armonk, NY: M. E. Sharpe (original work published 1960).

Walsh, R. L., Bowes, J., & Sweller, N. (2017). "Why would you say goodnight to the moon?" The response of young intellectually gifted children to lower and higher order questions during storybook reading. *Journal for Education of the Gifted, 40*(3), 220–246. https://doi.org/10.1177/0162353217717032

Walsh, R. L., Hodge, K. A., Bowes, J. M., & Kemp, C. R. (2010). Same age, different page: Overcoming the barriers to catering for young gifted children in prior-to-school settings. *International Journal of Early Childhood, 42*, 43–58. https://doi.org/10.1007/s13158-010-0004-8

Walsh, R. L., Kemp, C., Hodge, K., & Bowes, J. M. (2012). Searching for evidence-based practice: A review of the research on educational interventions for intellectually gifted children in the early childhood years. *Journal for the Education of the Gifted, 35*, 103–128. https://doi.org/10.1177/0162353212440610

Webber, M. (2016). *In search of greatness: Gifted indigenous students and the power of positive racial-ethnic identities*. Paper presented at the Biennial Conference of the Australian Association for the Education of the Gifted and Talented, Sydney, NSW.

Webber, M., Riley, T., Sylva, K., & Scobie-Jennings, E. (2018). The Ruamano Project: Raising expectations, realising community aspirations and recognising gifted potential in Māori boys. *The Australian Journal of Indigenous Education*, 1–12. https://doi.org/10.1017/jie.2018.16

Wilson, H. E. (2015). Patterns of play behaviour and learning center choices between high ability and typical children. *Journal of Advanced Academics, 26*, 143–164. https://doi.org/10.1177/1932202X15577954

Ziegler, A. (2005). The Actiotope model of giftedness. In R. Sternberg & J. E. Davidson (Eds.), *Conceptions of giftedness* (2nd ed., pp. 437–447). Cambridge, UK: Cambridge University Press.

Anne Grant, PhD, has taught in the early childhood field for many years as well as at university level. She has worked with children who demonstrate a range of levels of ability, including those who are gifted. Her research interests have been in how parents manage family life with a gifted child and how they make an initial decision that their child might be gifted. A particular focus has been on how young gifted children make the adjustment required when transitioning into a new educational program. Her broad interests in early childhood education include—the nature of early learning needs in young gifted children and how early childhood programs can be structured to meet those needs. She is currently involved in writing on the educational needs of young gifted children, in provision of preservice teacher education, in consulting with several educational organisations on the learning needs of young gifted children and in professional development in gifted education.

Anne-Marie Morrissey, PhD, is Associate Professor in Early Childhood Education at Deakin University and has taught in initial teacher education courses for over 20 years. Prior to working in academia, Anne-Marie had extensive professional experience as an early childhood teacher and centre coordinator. She has a particular interest in early gifted development and education, including studying gifted development in the infant/toddler years and the role of maternal interactions in supporting that development. She has also had a leading role in a number of research and professional development projects including a major mentoring program for early childhood teachers, a project investigating program processes and outcomes in IB PYP Early Years program in Australia and Singapore, and professional learning in gifted education for early years educators.

Being of Like-Mind: Giftedness in the New Zealand Context

7

Tracy Riley

Contents

Introduction	152
Being Like-Minded and Gifted	153
A Mixed Methods Approach to Exploring Like-Minds	156
Understanding Like-Minds: Some Findings and Discussion	158
Relating to Like-Minds	160
Learning with Like-Minded Friends	161
Flexibly Grouped with Like-Minded Peers	163
Research and Practice: Implications and Future Directions	165
Conclusion	166
Cross-References	166
References	166

Abstract

Gifted and talented learners in New Zealand are identified by their special abilities and qualities, across a range of areas, often by classroom teachers who make an effort to serve their needs in regular classrooms. The opportunity for learning with other like-minded peers is most commonly facilitated in within-class ability groups or withdrawal or pull-out programs; as an example, the *New Zealand Centre for Gifted Education* (NZCGE) provides a one-day-a-week program, *MindPlus*, for intellectually and creatively gifted children. Gifted and talented students are said to benefit from learning with like-minds, but there is limited research investigating what it means to be like-minded or how like-minds perceive the benefits and challenges of learning together. A mixed methods study, using student surveys, individual interviews, and focus group discussions probed perceptions of like-mindedness, as a basis for students working with the

---

T. Riley (✉)
Massey University, Palmerston North, New Zealand
e-mail: T.L.Riley@massey.ac.nz

© Springer Nature Singapore Pte Ltd. 2021
S. R. Smith (ed.), *Handbook of Giftedness and Talent Development in the Asia-Pacific*,
Springer International Handbooks of Education,
https://doi.org/10.1007/978-981-13-3041-4_5

researcher to co-construct the implications for practice. Students most often referred to 'thinking' as the common denominator of like-mindedness, with their like-minded peers described as other gifted students, family members, and their specialist teachers. The perspectives of participants in this study support the important connections between how and what one thinks, in relation to their peers, particularly in contexts for learning. Engaging with like-minded peers afforded these gifted students not only opportunities for learning, but also a sense of belonging and the chance to learn more about managing self, relating to others, participating, and contributing. Implications for practice include the need for ability grouping for learning and socialisation.

Keywords

Like-minds · Belonging · Enrichment · Grouping · Friendship · Social-emotional

The aims in this chapter are to:
1. Explain like-mindedness from the perspective of a group of students identified as creatively or intellectually gifted.
2. Explore different like-minded relationships in different contexts and for different purposes.
3. Explain the academic and social-emotional challenges and benefits for gifted students who engage with like-minded peers.
4. Consider flexible grouping as one way of ensuring like-minded engagement in learning for gifted students.

Introduction

Gifted education policy, research, advocacy, and practice documents often make reference to like-minded learners and like-minded peers; relationships between the gifted are considered an advantage of educational provisions as they provide opportunities for enhanced social and emotional development. For example, in a recent article in *The Conversation,* Wormald (2017) claimed that grouping gifted students with like-minded peers of similar abilities and interests can provide emotional and social support. Similarly, Post (2017) asserted, "gifted children thrive when surrounded by like-minded peers, where they are challenged, can compete and collaborate with students of similar intellectual abilities, and where they do not feel compelled to mask their talents to fit in . . ." (para 5). Riley and White (2016) argued that engagement with learners of "similar, yet individually unique, abilities and qualities" (p. 213), is essential for the development gifted students' sense of belonging. Gemert and Bear (2018) urged parents to engage their gifted children in social situations with like-minded peers by finding a place (in this case, Mensa) where they can interact with others who share their personal interests.

It is not surprising, therefore, that one of the rationales for a continuum of provisions advocated by the New Zealand Ministry of Education (2012) is the opportunity to engage with like-minded peers. The Ministry's schoolwide strengths and needs indicator, designed to assist in developing gifted education provisions, includes a criterion under teacher practice that checks if gifted students are provided with "regular ongoing opportunities to interact with like-minded peers" (p. 106). The criterion develops beyond facilitating peer interactions, which is seen as progressing towards good practice, to assisting students in understanding their talents and abilities and then using those to enact social change. These indicators imply that self-development and social action opportunities follow on from engagement with like-minded peers.

But what do we mean by the term like-minded peer? There is a dearth of discourse offering any definition, and it is the intent of this author to explore what like-mindedness means to a group of children identified as gifted based on their intellectual and creative qualities and abilities. Using a mixed methods study of gifted children's perspectives as the backbone for the chapter, readers will be helped to understand like-mindedness in different contexts and the important benefits of engaging with others who think and feel in similar ways. Flexible grouping in a range of educational contexts needs to be further explored in both research and practice to ensure all children, including those with exceptional gifts and talents, have opportunities to engage with like-minds.

Being Like-Minded and Gifted

As the introduction explains, there is a limited amount of literature that explores what the term like-minded means, especially when referring to gifted like-minds. Levine and Cox (2005) described like-minded students as those who share perspectives and viewpoints. An alternative view relates more to group identity and connectedness, whereby individuals deemed like-minded are those who "are socially well connected and share interests" (Mondoni et al., 2014, p. 908). This second definition infers social connections with one another, as opposed to having social capital or a presence on social media. For the purposes of the research reported in this chapter, like-minded was defined as students who share similar learning characteristics and dispositions, those who learn, think, and feel in comparable ways.

However, this definition, with its focus on learning, thinking, and feeling, and the ones found in the literature are but a starting point. Further exploration of the perspectives of gifted students can illuminate and expand these limited—and perhaps inaccurate—researcher, practitioner, and parental notions of like-mindedness. Furthermore, it is important to acknowledge that each gifted person is unique and different, and these differences make defining giftedness, and more specifically gifted like-minds, even more complex.

How one defines giftedness acts in turn to determine the behaviours of those abilities and vice versa. In New Zealand, giftedness is defined liberally and inclusively, with acknowledgement of special abilities and qualities related to traditional academic subjects, leadership, creativity, culture, the arts, and physical skills. Common clusters of characteristics are often associated with giftedness in relation to learning, creative thinking, motivation, social leadership, and self-determination (New Zealand Ministry of Education, 2012). While these behaviours are often cited with regard to intellectual prowess, many can be applied across different types of giftedness, revealing themselves in different ways.

For example, the New Zealand Ministry of Education (2012) identified learning, motivational, leadership, and creative characteristics associated with giftedness. Based on the work of McAlpine and Reid (1996) who developed rating scales for the gifted, the Ministry indicates that gifted students often learn at a rapid pace, easily grasping underlying concepts and making connections between big ideas. Intellectual playfulness and risk-taking, a quirky sense of humour, innovative problem-solving, and challenging the norm are just a few of the markers of creatively gifted learners. Motivational characteristics of many gifted learners include a preference for working independently, with self-direction, personal goal setting, and persistence—especially in areas of strength that combine interests with abilities. Some gifted learners are natural leaders, especially amongst their intellectual peers, connecting and communicating well with others, taking responsibility, and activating plans. Being self-determined learners, some gifted students can become easily bored and frustrated, pushing the boundaries of authority and not playing by the rules (McAlpine & Reid, 1996; Ministry of Education, 2012). These behaviours can potentially affect like-minded peer relationships (Bate & Clark, 2013; Riley & White, 2016).

Nonetheless, like-minded peers are sought by gifted and talented learners, often facilitated by their parents and teachers, through different connections and relationships based on a sharing of common interests, preferences, or values (personal or cultural). These relationships may evolve through early childhood centre and school experiences, extra-curricular activities, community-based programs, or cultural opportunities, and these experiences may be online, face-to-face, or a blend of both. While peers are often thought of as those who are of a similar age or year level within early childhood education and school, like-minded peers may cut across ages and the traditional lock-step stages of schooling. For gifted learners, like-minded peers may include: classmates; teachers; family members, such as cousins, parents or grandparents; neighbours, mentors or others who share an interest or have similar goals and motivations (Chin & Harrington, 2009; Hertberg-Davis & Callahan, 2009; Riley & White, 2016). While some of these relationships have been explored by researchers, usually like-minded relationships are only studied as an aside to explorations of educational or community provisions that bring gifted learners together. There is limited research pertaining specifically to family members, or cultural mentors, as like-minded peers.

Having opportunities to spend time with like-minded others has been purported to be important to the well-being and academic advancement of gifted learners (New Zealand Education Review Office, 2008; New Zealand Ministry of Education, 2012). Specific to socio-affective needs, advantages for gifted students who spend time with like-minded others include:

- Increased opportunities for connectedness.
- Improved chances of being understood and accepted.
- Better prospects of forming high-quality friendships.
- More suitable occasions to practise socio-affective skills.
- Greater chances of 'feeling normal' (Adams-Byers, Whitsell, & Moon, 2004, p. 15).

This desire to feel normal resonates with the voices of gifted students who express "longing to belong" (Blackett, 2006, p. 15) and the desire to feel accepted and understood for who they are (Adams-Byers et al., 2004; Wood, 2010). Eckstein (2009) reported that gifted students are seeking peers who share common experiences of growing up gifted and who are responsive to personal and emotional needs (Chin & Harrington, 2009). Wanting to belong and feel normal is not necessarily uncommon or unusual for any child or young person to express, but for gifted students, there is a unique set of differences due to their special abilities and qualities.

For example, gifted learners' ways of thinking have been reported as presenting social challenges (Riley, 2015). "Being able to think metaphorically; reason logically, yet in the abstract; solve multiple problems in tandem; think paradoxically; and make logical connections, leads to different ways of communicating, feeling, and experiencing the world around us" (Riley, 2015, para 9). These different ways of being can also mean that the interests, motivations, and ways of learning for gifted students do not necessarily meet social norms and expectations of their same-age peers (or their parents and teachers). Pressures to conform may relate not only to age acceptability but also gender, culture, and academic norms (e.g., school subjects; Handel, Vialle, & Zeigler, 2013; Jung, Barnett, Gross, & McCormick, 2011, Lovett, 2011). Gross (1989) described gifted students as feeling pressure to choose between social acceptance and academic goals as a 'forced choice dilemma'.

Relating more directly to academic development, spending time with like-minded peers has been shown to afford opportunities for engaging in thinking and learning with others in complementary ways, thus increasing opportunities for challenge (Riley & White, 2016). Being with like-minds also provides a more acceptable context within which to ask questions (Adams-Byers et al., 2004), receive constructive criticism (Chin & Harrington, 2009; Handel et al., 2013), set germane mastery and performance goals, and strive for and celebrate success.

While the academic and socio-affective advantages for gifted students have been well documented, what is missing is an understanding of what is meant by like-mindedness, particularly from the perspectives of gifted students. Because being in a like-minded peer group may mean dislocation from age peers, classmates, community, or even family, not only socially, emotionally, creatively, or cognitively but also physically, it is important to understand the perspectives of gifted students, whose voices have not always been sought in research studies. Outlined in the next section of this chapter is a mixed methods study that enabled those voices to be heard.

A Mixed Methods Approach to Exploring Like-Minds

A sequential exploratory mixed methods study was designed to investigate and better understand the perceptions of like-mindedness, as explained by a group of students identified as intellectually and creatively gifted. A mixed methods study was determined the best approach to understanding like-mindedness from children's perspectives, as it could bring together the "sum of quantitative and qualitative" approaches which is "greater than either approach alone" (Creswell, 2009, p. 104). By its very definition, mixed methods research is a methodology aimed at collecting, analysing, and integrating data, often from different perspectives, in a single study that aims to create a better understanding of the research problem. A sequential exploratory design is a two-phase design, whereby the qualitative data is collected first, followed by a collection and analysis of quantitative data.

In the study reported in this chapter, the research developed following a pilot study (Riley et al., 2015) and began with interviews which were undertaken until data saturation was reached (Fusch & Ness, 2015). Based on the interviews, a survey was designed to test the veracity and explore the meanings of the interview findings. One of the challenges of a mixed methods approach is how to integrate the quantitative and qualitative findings (Fetters, Curry, & Creswell, 2013). For this study, given its aim of exploring gifted children's perceptions, it was determined that one way of integrating the data may be through engaging the gifted students in a participatory process. Therefore, focus group interviews were employed to provide the children an opportunity to help make sense of and assist with the integration of the quantitative and qualitative findings.

The first phase of the research involved interviews with 23 children, between the ages of 8 and 12, who were students in the New Zealand Centre for Gifted Education's MindPlus program. At the time the study was conducted, the identification process was multidimensional, involving subjective and objective data, with both group and individual assessment components and information gathering from multiple sources. The students were referred to the program by their teachers or parents, based on outstanding academic and/or creative potential or performance. Upon referral, potential students were invited to participate in a three hour entry selection workshop, with activities facilitated by specialist educators to identify characteristics and behaviours of giftedness that most suited the curriculum of the *MindPlus* program. This approach to identification makes explicit the too-often implicit interrelationship between how one defines, identifies, and provides for giftedness (New Zealand Ministry of Education, 2012).

The multimethod identification approach relied on observable characteristics of creativity and intellect that are linked to specific areas of the curriculum of MindPlus. Importantly, the entry process sought to identify children who would benefit from the program, its curriculum, and specialist teaching approaches (rather than those in search of a gifted label). The identification process was specifically designed to identify students' potential by collecting information on the child's intellectual, creative, and personal abilities and traits from home and school, as well as the children themselves.

The 23 students (13 boys and 9 girls) who were interviewed were specifically asked to describe what like-mindedness meant to them, who they considered their like-minded peers and what opportunities they had both in the MindPlus program and in their regular schooling to engage with like-minded peers. At the outset of the interview process, there was not a known number of students to be interviewed, as what was hoped for was rich (quality) and thick (quantity) data. After interviewing students in three different classrooms in two cities, it became clear that the questioning had reached the point of saturation. As Fusche and Ness (2015) explain, "If one has reached the point of no new data, one has also most likely reached the point of no new themes; therefore, one has reached data saturation" (p. 1409).

The key themes that arose from the interview process were used to develop an online survey of both closed and open-ended questions, which was completed by 130 gifted students from ages 8 to 12 engaged in MindPlus, across New Zealand. While all students in the program were invited to participate, the boys seemed particularly keen, making up approximately 73% of the overall responses to the survey. However, this high male response rate is not a representative sample of students in the program, which at the time had a more equal number of boys and girls. The survey probed the students' definitions and perceptions of like-mindedness, the opportunities they engage in, who they engage with as like-minded peers, and the benefits and challenges of learning with like-minds. The survey was administered electronically, using SurveyMonkey, following parental consent.

Following the survey, two focus groups of 8 and 10 senior students (ages 10–12), respectively, were given an opportunity to discuss the findings and to specifically comment on the characteristics of thinking—which had emerged as a central theme of defining like-mindedness. The focus groups were also asked to consider the implications of like-mindedness for teachers in all classrooms. The focus group students were given paper and pens to write notes or doodles as ideas came to them in the discussion. This focus group allowed "the voices of the targeted population in the research to inform the direction of the research" (Fetters et al., 2013, p. 2139) and, in this study, influence the integration of qualitative and quantitative results.

The data analysis was iterative and ongoing throughout the phases of the project and involved preparing, reviewing, analysing, and representing the results. The qualitative interview and survey data were analysed thematically, while the quantitative survey data were analysed using basic frequency analysis. An inductive, or bottoms up, approach (Braun & Clarke, 2006) to the qualitative analysis enabled themes to arise from the interviews and surveys, as opposed to being driven by an external theory or framework. This method of analysis also ensured that the children's voices drove the themes, and this was especially important given the lack of research investigating like-mindedness from the perspective of gifted students. Because the quantitative findings would be shared with the focus group students, it was determined that simple, descriptive statistics would adequately and appropriately describe what the survey data showed.

While only one study is reported in this chapter, its findings potentially have much wider implications for teachers, researchers, parents, and gifted students, as the study taps into a group of gifted students' experiences of engaging with like-minds.

Given the dearth of research investigating student experiences of like-mindedness from their perspectives, new grounds for research are explored in this chapter, but this is limited by way of comparable studies of like-mindedness in different settings. However, the MindPlus program is an enrichment program designed for students identified with creative and intellectual strengths, like many other enrichment and extension programs.

The results of the study are reported in the next section, alongside relevant literature that discusses or explains the findings. As the results will show, a common feature of like-mindedness amongst creative and intellectually able students is thinking—and how one thinks seems to influence engagement with peers.

Understanding Like-Minds: Some Findings and Discussion

When asked to describe what the term like-minded meant to them, the most common single term reported by students, in interviews and surveys, was 'thinking'. In fact, almost a quarter (23%) of the survey respondents used the phrase "people who think . . .", juxtapositioned alongside axioms such as 'like me', 'similar to me' or 'in the same way'. Approximately 17% of the survey respondents used the word 'similar' to describe their thinking, and the same number described their peers as thinking in 'the same way'. This similarity in thinking was further described as leading to understanding and enabling them to work well together. As one of the students wrote in his survey response, like-minded peers were "two people who think alike (I really enjoy talking with them because I very very rarely find someone who understands me)". As another student explained, "they get the things you get", and this similar style of thinking seemed to draw like-minds to one another.

This reciprocal interaction between like-minded learners fosters positive well-being and achievement (Wolf & Chessor, 2011). In turn, having shared motivation and energy to learn results in better work habits, higher levels of connectedness, and commitment to school (Barber & Woodford Wasson, 2014; Chin & Harrington, 2009; Hertberg-Davis & Callahan, 2008; Matthews & Kitchen, 2007; Neihart, 2007). Thinking similarly may enable some of these benefits for gifted learners, but there is a need for deeper investigations of the role thinking plays for like-minded learners, including differences.

In the survey responses, the students acknowledged differences in thinking. While they felt gifted like-minds thought in similar ways, they did not seem to think that this meant the gifted were a homogenous group of thinkers. As one of the students explained, like-minds are "people in the same or similar situations to me who see things in a similar way or at a similar level to the way I do, even though we may see different things or draw different conclusions" (Survey Respondent 47, 2015). In other words, gifted learners "think alike, but think differently" (Anonymous Student Brainstorming Web Comment, Focus Group 1, 2016), or as another student elaborated, "really differently" (Anonymous Student Brainstorming Web Comment, Focus Group 1, 2016).

The focus group discussions provided an opportunity to dig a bit deeper in to this notion of thinking as being central to like-mindedness. It was unclear from the interviews and surveys what the students meant by this peer connection through thinking, so the focus group students were asked to elaborate on what made 'gifted thinking' unique. The most common theme to arise from their discussion was the depth of their conceptual thinking. The students talked about 'seeing the big picture' and thinking 'big' as they sought to understand 'big issues'. They also described overthinking and a tendency to 'overcomplicate things' by 'thinking a lot'. The ability to think quickly, in detail, creatively, critically, and analytically was also described by the students in the focus groups. As one of the students doodled, alongside a hand drawn image of a very pointy head, he stated "we always want the why" and "we like to think about a lot of things at once" (Anonymous Student Brainstorming Web Comment, Focus Group 2, 2016).

These similarities in gifted students' approaches to thinking and learning and their tendency to explore with depth and complexity, as explained by the students, provide fertile ground for:

- Cultivating new learning and growth (Sanderson & Greenberger, 2010).
- Asking questions, sharing ideas, and achieving with acceptance, rather than rejection and ridicule (Adams-Byers et al., 2004).
- Engaging in high-level discussion and discourse (Netz, 2014).
- Working at an appropriate pace that is commensurate to their abilities (Burney, 2008).
- Feeling challenged and inspired by other like-minded peers (Sanderson & Greenberger, 2010).

Importantly, as gifted students grapple with ideas, concepts and knowledge, they begin to formulate their own thinking. Working with peers of similar abilities enables what Hughes (2010) labelled 'knowledge-related identity congruence' which has been shown to have an important role in engagement in learning. As Riley and White (2016) stated, "knowledge-related congruence can be negotiated as gifted students identify with ideas, concepts, and knowledge under construction" (p. 216).

The gifted like-minds in this study saw themselves as qualitatively different, as these survey responses to a question seeking a definition of like-mindedness highlight:

- It's not just a different way of looking at it, you've got a different way of understanding it.
- They could also match me in smartness because I am very smart.
- Like-minded peers means to me other people that have the same brain power as me.
- Pretend you are good at maths, then somebody comes to you that has the same interest: maths. It's like being a mirror image, not just in looks but in age, talent, or many other things.

The students, across all methods of data collection, freely described themselves as gifted and recognised their differences from peers. This self-understanding was a fundamental element of the curriculum for MindPlus, based on the premise that understanding giftedness and having the tools to work with it would be beneficial. The students in this study also seemed to know giftedness when they saw it and were drawn towards these relationships, as the next section explains.

Relating to Like-Minds

The interviews revealed like-minded relationships tended to be with others identified as gifted, often in their MindPlus classes. The students also identified their specialist teachers and family members as like-minded peers. This connection with their teachers and family, who may or may not have also been gifted, may reflect relationships with others who have empathy towards giftedness. These results were supported by survey respondents who were asked to identify their like-minded peers from a list of possibilities generated by the individual interviews. Perhaps not surprisingly, over 90% of the students identified like-minded peers in their specialist program, MindPlus, but this was contrasted by less than half (44%) who identified like-minded peers in their regular classrooms. This finding reflects the findings of an earlier study in New Zealand (Clark, 2009), which showed that 63% of students in a one-day-a-week program described having difficulty making friends in any learning setting, yet 98% had made friends in the program.

While over half (57%) of the students in this study indicated like-mindedness with their specialist teachers in MindPlus, only 28% said the same of their regular classroom teachers. Why did the students tend to see their specialist teachers as like-minded but their regular classroom teachers less so? This seems a critical point to further understand, for as Graffam (2006) concluded, "the relationships a teacher of gifted learners develops with her students are the keys to opening doors (and setting fires) to higher challenge, motivation, and personal investment on the parts of the students" (p. 130). A study conducted by Kesner (2005) showed that teachers of gifted students reported higher levels of closeness and dependency and lower levels of conflict, with their students than teachers of non-gifted students. Kesner (2005) speculated that "Gifted students, by virtue of their advanced intellectual capabilities may be even more dependent upon the teacher to provide for their specific academic needs" (p. 222). Croft (2003) believes that gifted students are profoundly affected by their interactions with all teachers, including those who are specialists, and the respondents' like-minded relationships with teachers support this notion.

Family as like-minds also featured strongly, with over half the students (56%) identifying like-mindedness with their parents, 39% with siblings, and 34% other (e.g., cousins, grandparents). Reichenberg and Landau (2009) acknowledged the positive educational and social development these familial relationships can help create. Like-minded families may have developed their own distinctive approaches to learning: home life may be enriched, with lots of intellectual stimulation; adult-like conversations, discussions, and debates; and intense periods of pursuing topics of interest. The students in this study shared stories of enjoying learning with family members who accepted them: "They are all family and they all have different feelings for me". The students described family members with similar interests (e.g., "We almost speak in unison".) and ways of learning (e.g., "My mum. She is also visual special". [sic]). The gifted students in this study readily identified like-minded peers in formal learning environments and at home.

However, less than a quarter of the students identified with like-minds through sports (14%); music, dance, or drama classes (13%); or church (12%). One of the perplexing results was the fact that only 11% of the students reported like-minded peers in school-based gifted programs, but this may be as much an indicator of provision and opportunity in school as any other factors. A few students identified 'other' like-minded peers, and these included members of a rock and mineral club, the school principal, coaches, and music teachers and, for one student, 'a computer guy'. Only one student wrote on the survey that he did not have any like-minded peers in any context.

Less than 5% of survey respondents indicated in their definitions of like-mindedness that these like-minds were peers of the same age. Yet, when asked specifically about the ages of their like-minded peers in a multiple-choice question, 20% of students stated that their like-minded peers were the same age. This is contrasted by the majority of students (64%) who indicated that their like-minded peers were younger, older, and/or of the same age. Only 16% of the participants to the survey indicated that their like-minded peers were only those older than them. This is an interesting finding in light of some gifted checklists indicating a preference for relationships with older peers; it is clear that gifted students relate to like-minds of all different ages. These connections seem to be context and relationship-specific, rather than more generalised. Many of these like-minded peer relationships develop into friendships, mediated by giftedness, as the next section explains.

Learning with Like-Minded Friends

Gross (2002) found that friendships for gifted children were not dictated so much by chronological age as by mental age and, furthermore that there was a relationship between levels of ability and conceptions of friendship. The intellectually gifted children in her study were more developmentally mature in their friendships than their same-age peers of average ability. Gross described "young gifted children whose accelerated conceptions of friendship are urging them to seek the sure shelter of a relationship of trust, fidelity, and authenticity, at ages when their age-peers are seeking playmates or casual conversation" (para. 21). It seems that the children in Gross' study were seeking like-minded peers as friends, as was the case for the students in this study.

In the interviews, the students talked about friendships in their descriptions of like-minded relationships. The survey showed that 90% of the students would describe their like-minded peers as their 'good friends'. As one of the girls wrote, "it's much easier to become BFFs if you are both like-minded peers!" (Survey

Respondent 35, 2015). However, the open-ended comments illustrated that not all like-minded peers are friends and not all friends are like-minded peers. There is also some context-setting of the relationships, and so as one of the students said, "I tend to associate more with older students in a learning environment, but sometimes they're not as open to that outside learning" (Survey Respondent 51, 2015). Another girl stated, "I like playing with all people, but I like working with smart people" (Survey Respondent 30, 2015). One-third of the students described their like-minded friends as people they enjoyed learning with and from. As one boy explained, "I like learning with my friends. When I have friends who are not as smart as me I like to teach them even though it drives them nuts" (Survey Respondent 100, 2015).

Like-minded friendships led to a question about learning with like-minds, both in and out of school, and specifically probing how these peers are like and different from the gifted students in the study. The students responded in interesting ways, mainly highlighting their similarities with those with whom they enjoy learning. As one of the girls wrote in the survey:

> They are crazy like me. They like doing silly things and they like learning new things and they never want to stop when we like what we are doing. They like pretending and making things up and imagining. They like my books and my games and my ideas. Some are not girls like me. Some are not my age. (Survey Respondent 53, 2015)

Their giftedness and its related behaviours seemed to be the lynchpin that created enjoyable learning with like-minded friends. The students' descriptions of traits they shared with those with whom they enjoyed learning included activities, like chess and gaming; advanced skills and knowledge, with specific mention of mathematics, writing and reading; and personality traits, like humour, passion, and kindness. The students also used words associated with giftedness, describing themselves and their preferred learning peers as smart, out of the ordinary, intelligent, creative or, as one student put it, "we stand out a bit" (Survey Respondent 26, 2015). One of the boys explained, "they are often intelligent and love to learn, talk, and debate about things" (Survey Respondent 85, 2015).

The gifted students in the survey could also see the differences between themselves and others with whom they enjoyed learning. The differences related to individual abilities and qualities, interests, age, and ways of thinking and learning. For example, a survey respondent explained that there was "a wide range of knowledge and interests represented, not all of them that interest me. But then sometimes, things I love don't interest them either" (Survey Respondent 51, 2015). As one of the boys wrote, "differences include: working things out differently, but to the same result; using different strategies, but both correct. I think in pictures, most people think in words" (Survey Respondent 9, 2015). A survey response mentioned age: "the people in my music group are like me in the way that we all get music ... we are all different in age though, people aged 9–25 can join" (Survey Respondent 45, 2015). The level of self-awareness provided an insight into giftedness that, coupled with acute observations of others, seemed to bring an understanding and acceptance to like-minded relationships.

Not surprisingly, this meant that the other students in MindPlus were considered their like-minded friends, though when probed in interviews, it became clear that many did not socialise with one another outside the one-day-a-week program. The students also had peers with whom they enjoyed learning who did not attend MindPlus. In the interviews and focus group discussions, several of the students elaborated that these peers also had a range of abilities, including giftedness. The students were able to manage and navigate these friendships across contexts and settings, as these statements from the survey explain:

> I enjoy learning with lots of my friends at MindPlus, and sometimes with my peers at school. My friends at school are different to me because they don't have the same learning ability as me. (Survey Respondent 94, 2015)

> My friends at school are like me because they are in the same groups and have the same interests, but they are different from me because they don't go to MindPlus and are not gifted. (Survey Respondent 35, 2015)

The students in this study had multiple opportunities to connect and reconnect with different like-minded peers in different contexts and with different motivations and outcomes. This study affirms earlier research that shows variance in the numbers and types of connections gifted students seek (Berlin, 2009; Kindermann, 2007; Olszewski-Kubilius, Lee, & Thompson, 2014). Furthermore, "seeking and engaging peers with similar processes of thinking reflects the development of knowledge-related identity, alongside seeking multiple peer groups, familial relationships, and friendships as part of social identity development ... a powerful combination for gifted learners" (Riley & White, 2016, p. 221). It is also important to acknowledge the difficulties and challenges some gifted students face in obtaining opportunities to be with suitably like-minded peers (Woods, 2010). Specific groups of gifted students may face significant challenges based on higher degrees of giftedness (Gross, 2002), multi-exceptionality (King, 2005), minority culture or other status (Jung et al., 2011) or misalignment, out of sync interests and abilities in relation to social norms and expectations (Chin & Harrington, 2009).

Flexibly Grouped with Like-Minded Peers

Engagement with like-minded peers was afforded for the students in this study through the MindPlus program, but their perceptions of like-mindedness demand us to explore other grouping patterns, which may prove valuable as they provide different experiences and outcomes for students. Riley et al. (2015, p. 31) concluded that:

> A flexible grouping approach can provide the challenge and differentiation in thinking and learning needed by gifted students (Harrison, 2005), while also offering opportunities to meet and connect with peers who simply think the same and have similar interests—like-minded peers.

The results from the interviews and survey were shared with the focus group students, and they were asked to translate these into implications for schools. They struggled to do this without reflecting upon their characteristics of giftedness, and the conversation centred on their differences and expressed desire for teachers who would acknowledge those. For example, their notes included comments like, "don't explain things twice" (Anonymous Student Brainstorming Web Comment, Focus Group 2, 2016) and "let us say our opinions" (Anonymous Student Brainstorming Web Comment, Focus Group 2, 2016) and "don't make us stop working at lunch" (Anonymous Student Brainstorming Web Comment, Focus Group 12, 2016).

When pushed, the students explained that they would prefer to be working with like-minded peers, kids like themselves, but, as with the pilot study, their enjoyment of different groupings was "context, activity, and membership specific" (Riley et al., 2015, p. 29). The mediating factor between having a like-minded peer (or peers) and being in a group that enabled this engagement seemed to be the characteristics associated with giftedness. For example, the students in the focus group linked their speed of thinking with the people they considered peers and the need to be in a group that allowed them to 'just do it'. Similarly, one girl explained that when asked in learning settings to be creative, she needed to be able to 'piggyback' off others who "think of other possibilities instead of the most obvious answers" (Focus Group 2, 2016).

These types of responses resounded with the survey responses to the question of the benefits of learning with like-minds. Again, the most common word students used to describe the learning benefits was 'think', but they also described understanding, friendships, and interests as developing in these like-minded learning opportunities. Interestingly, around a quarter of students could not list any disadvantages or problems related to learning with like-minded peers, but, again, when there were challenges, they seemed to stem from gifted characteristics identified by the students (e.g., over-excitability, strong opinions, diverse interests). Table 1 pulls together some of the qualitative and quantitative data from the study to display the primary mediating characteristic—thinking—in relation to context and peers. It shows the effect gifted characteristics potentially play on finding and connecting with like-minded peers in different contexts. Although the table only shows one characteristic and certainly lacks strong evidence to show any sort of causal effect, it displays the integration of data from across the study. The contrasts across the two contexts—admittedly at either extreme of any continuum of provision for gifted students—are nonetheless powerful indicators of the impact of grouping for learning with like-minds. Riley et al. (2015) concluded that flexible grouping was the most appropriate approach, rather than a one-group-fits-all approach.

Flexibly grouping gifted learners is not a new idea and basically means that students are grouped in different combinations for different reasons, within, between, and across learning contexts (Riley, 2011). Groups may be formal, informal, teacher-selected, or student-selected as determined by ability, interests, preferences, needs, and outcomes. With flexible grouping, students are not always in the same group all the time, which means that from an ability perspective, some groups may appear more homogenous or heterogeneous than others. An important point,

Table 1 Thinking as a mediating factor of like-minded engagement

Context	Characteristics	Like-minded peers
Specialist gifted provision	'People who think like me' (e.g., complex, big ideas).	Students (90%) Teachers (57%)
Regular classroom	'Think really differently' (e.g., quality and pace).	Students (44%) Teachers (28%)

particularly for gifted learners, is that "flexible grouping is about learning: grouping for learning" (Riley, 2011, p. xx).

Thus, flexible grouping enables students and teachers to "flow in and out of different working patterns throughout the day, week or term, within and across lessons, curriculum areas and activities" (Riley et al., 2015, p. 31). Dependent on learners, the groups may change. Flexible grouping is not in conflict with inclusive practices or calls for mixed ability groups, because, as the students reminded us throughout this study of like-minds, the gifted themselves are far from homogenous. They are as different in abilities, strengths, skills, knowledge, interests, and thinking, as any other group of individuals. Flexible grouping means that all learners get a chance to identify and engage with like-minded peers, including the gifted.

Research and Practice: Implications and Future Directions

The opportunity to engage with like-minded peers can be facilitated in schools and communities across a continuum of approaches. It is critical that gifted students have opportunities to meet, engage, and learn with other students of similar abilities and qualities, especially in New Zealand where there is a preference for all learners to be in mixed ability groupings in regular classrooms for the majority of their education. Being in like-minded learning groups requires teachers who are aware of the abilities and qualities of their gifted students and the relationship this has with their learning and grouping arrangements. This implies, as outlined above, that teachers provide opportunities for flexible grouping within and across educational settings. There is also a need for a stronger relationship between out of school or withdrawal programs, like MindPlus, and the regular classroom, school, and home environments, to facilitate ongoing like-minded friendships for gifted students. Given the like-minded relationships within families, teachers may have a role to play in supporting parents in thinking about how they engage with their gifted children and siblings, as well as understanding the home learning environment and connecting families with opportunities both in and out of school.

From a research perspective, this study of like-minds was limited to students who were part of one program. It is difficult to judge whether some of the findings are generalisable to gifted students in other contexts or how much of the student voice was influenced by the curriculum and program. There may be a 'curricular effect' coming into play in the results, as the students were all engaged with a curriculum that explored personal development, including concepts, characteristics, and theories of giftedness. The program also had a strong focus on thinking skills. Further research exploring these questions with other groups of gifted students would be beneficial. There is also limited empirical research exploring flexible grouping for gifted students. While flexible grouping is a recommended practice, research on the impact of moving in and out of different groups for different purposes on gifted learners' socially, emotionally, or academically is needed. Familial like-minded relationships, which foster learning outside of school for gifted children, need to be better understood.

Conclusion

As the literature shows and the student voices upheld, engaging with like-minded peers gives gifted students a sense of belonging which potentially has positive social, emotional, and academic impacts. The students in this study described like-mindedness as connections through thinking, and this thinking mediated opportunities for engagement with one another through different provisions. The stark contrast between the reported number of like-minded peers and teachers in their specialist program versus the regular school classroom is a reminder of the need for gifted children to learn with other gifted children and for *all* teachers to work to develop understandings of special abilities and qualities.

Cross-References

- ▶ Creativity Talent Development: Fostering Creativity in Schools
- ▶ Fostering and Developing Talent in Mentorship Programs: The Mentor's Perspectives
- ▶ Gifted Education in the Asia-Pacific: From the Past for the Future – An Introduction
- ▶ Put Them Together and See How They Learn! Ability Grouping and Acceleration Effects on the Self-Esteem of Academically Gifted High School Students
- ▶ Social and Cultural Conceptions and Perceptions: Part I Introduction
- ▶ Some Implications for the Future of Gifted Education in the Asia-Pacific
- ▶ The Development of Mana: Five Optimal Conditions for Gifted Māori Student Success

References

Adams-Byers, J., Whitsell, S. S., & Moon, S. (2004). Gifted students' perceptions of the academic and social/emotional effects of homogeneous and heterogeneous grouping. *Gifted Child Quarterly, 48*(1), 7–20. https://doi.org/10.1177/001698620404800102

Barber, C., & Woodford Wasson, J. (2014). A comparison of adolescents' friendship networks by advanced coursework participation status. *Gifted Child Quarterly, 59*(1), 23–37. https://doi.org/10.1177/0016986214559639

Bate, J., & Clark, D. (2013). Like minds learning well together. *Set: Research Information for Teachers, 1*, 49–57. https://doi.org/10.18296/set.0350

Berlin, J. E. (2009). It's all a matter of perspective: Student perceptions on the impact of being labeled gifted and talented. *Roeper Review 31*(4), 217–223. https://doi.org/10.1080/02783190903177580

Blackett, J. (2006). *Investigating best practice in guidance and counselling for gifted students in New Zealand schools*. Unpublished Masters dissertation, Massey University, Palmerston North, New Zealand.

Braun, V., & Clarke, V. (2006). Using thematic analysis in psychology. *Qualitative Research in Psychology, 3*, 77–101. https://doi.org/10.1191/1478088706qp063oa

Burney, V. (2008). Applications of social cognitive theory to gifted education. *Roeper Review, 30* (2), 130–139. https://doi.org/10.1080/02783190801955335

Chin, C., & Harrington, D. (2009). InnerSpark: A creative summer school and artistic community teenagers. *Gifted Child Today, 32*(1), 14–22. https://doi.org/10.4219/gct-2009-838

Clark, D. (2009). *Student voice: Perceptions of the Gifted Kids program alumni, 2000–2007*. Unpublished Master's thesis, Massey University, Palmerston North, New Zealand.

Croft, L.J. (2003). Teachers of the gifted: Gifted teachers. In N. Colangelo & G.A. Davis (Eds.), Handbook of Gifted Education (3rd ed.; pp. 558–571). Boston: Allyn and Bacon.

Eckstein, M. (2009). Enrichment 2.0: Gifted and talented education for the 21st century. *Gifted Child Today, 32*(1), 59–63. https://doi.org/10.4219/gct-2009-841

Fetters, M. D., Curry, L. A., & Creswell, J. W. (2013). *Achieving integration in mixed methods designs: Principles and practices*. Retrieved from https://www.ncbi.nlm.nih.gov/pmc/articles/PMC4097839/pdf/hesr0048-2134.pdf

Fusch, P. I., & Ness, L. R. (2015). Are we there yet? Data saturation in qualitative research. *The Qualitative Report, 20*(9), 1408–1416. Retrieved from http://tqr.nova.edu/wp-content/uploads/2015/09/fusch1.pdf

Gemert, L. V., & Bear, P. (2018). *Friendship 101*. Retrieved from https://www.us.mensa.org/learn/gifted-youth/insights-into-gifted-youth/making-friends/

Graffam, B. (2006). A case study of teachers of gifted learners: Moving from prescribed practice to described practitioners. *Gifted Child Quarterly, 50*(2), 119–131. https://doi.org/10.1177/001698620605000204

Gross, M. (1989). The pursuit of excellence or the search for intimacy? The forced-choice dilemma of gifted youth. *Roeper Review, 11*(4), 189–194. https://doi.org/10.1080/02783198909553207

Gross, M. U. M. (2002). "Play Partner" or "Sure Shelter": What gifted children look for in friendship. *The SENG Newsletter, 2*(2). Retrieved from http://sengifted.org/play-partner-or-sure-shelter-what-gifted-children-look-for-in-friendship/

Handel, M., Vialle, W., & Ziegler, A. (2013). Student perceptions of high-achieving classmates. *High Ability Studies, 24*(2), 99–114. https://doi.org/10.1080/13598139.2013.843139

Harrison, C. (2005). *Young gifted children: Their search for complexity and connection*. Exeter, Australia: Inscript.

Hertberg-Davis, H., & Callahan, C. (2008). A narrow escape: Gifted students' perceptions of advanced placement and International Baccalaureate programs. *Gifted Child Quarterly, 52*(3), 199–216. https://doi.org/10.1177/0016986208319705

Hertberg-Davis, H., & Callahan, C. (2009). A narrow escape: Gifted students' perceptions of Advanced Placement and International Baccalaureate programs. *Gifted Child Quarterly, 52*(3), 199–216. https://doi.org/10.1177/0016986208319705

Hughes, G. (2010). Identity and belonging in social learning groups: The importance of distinguishing social, operational and knowledge-related identity congruence. *British Educational Research Journal, 36*(1), 47–63. https://doi.org/10.1080/01411920902834167

Jung, J., Barnett, K., Gross, M., & McCormick, J. (2011). Levels of intellectual giftedness, culture, and the Forced-Choice Dilemma. *Roeper Review, 33*(3), 182–197. https://doi.org/10.1080/02783193.2011.580501

Kesner, J. E. (2005). Gifted children's relationships with teachers. *International Education Journal, 6*(2), 218–223. Retrieved from https://files.eric.ed.gov/fulltext/EJ854973.pdf

Kindermann, T. (2007). Effects of naturally existing peer groups on changes in academic engagement in a cohort of sixth graders. *Child Development, 78*(4), 1186–1203. https://doi.org/10.1111/j.1467-8624.2007.01060.x

King, E. W. (2005). Addressing the social and emotional needs of twice exceptional students. *Teaching Exceptional Children, 38*(1), 16–20. https://doi.org/10.1177/004005990503800103

Levine, M., & Cox, D. (2005). Teaching war and violence to the like-minded. *Peace Review, 17*, 247–259. https://doi.org/10.1080/14631370500332981

Lovett, P. (2011). Solutions for Jay and other underrepresented gifted minority students. *Gifted Child Today, 34*(1), 55–59. https://doi.org/10.1177/107621751103400115

Matthews, D., & Kitchen, J. (2007). School-within-a-school gifted programs. *Gifted Child Quarterly, 51*(3), 256–271. https://doi.org/10.1177/0016986207302720

McAlpine, D., & Reid, N. (1996). *Teaching observation scales for children with special abilities*. Wellington, New Zealand: NZCER.

Ministry of Education. (2012). *Gifted and talented students: Meeting their needs in New Zealand schools*. Retrieved from https://gifted.tki.org.nz/assets/Gifted-and-talented-students-meeting-their-needs-in-New-Zealand-Schools.pdf

Mondoni, N., Nagar, S., Shannigrahi, S., Gupta, R., Dey, K., Goyal, S., & Nanavati, A. (2014). Like-minded communities: Bringing familiarity and similarity together. *World Wide Web, 17*(5), 899–919. https://doi.org/10.1007/s11280-013-0261-1

Neihart, M. (2007). The socioaffective impact of acceleration and ability grouping. *Gifted Child Quarterly, 51*(4), 330–341. https://doi.org/10.1177/0016986207306319

Netz, H. (2014). Gifted conversations. *Gifted Child Quarterly, 58*(2), 149–163. https://doi.org/10.1177/0016986214523312

New Zealand Education Review Office. (2008). *Schools' provisions for gifted and talented students: Good Practice*. Wellington, New Zealand: Education Review Office.

New Zealand Ministry of Education. (2012). *Gifted and talented students: Meeting their needs in New Zealand schools*. Wellington, New Zealand: Published for the Ministry of Education by Learning Media.

Olszewski-Kubilius, P., Lee, S.-Y., & Thomson, D. (2014). Family environment and social development in gifted students. *Gifted Child Quarterly, 58*(3), 199–216. https://doi.org/10.1177/0016986214526430

Post, G. (2017). *Social emotional learning and the gifted child*. Retrieved from https://giftedchallenges.blogspot.co.nz/2017/09/social-emotional-learning-and-gifted.html

Reichenberg, A., & Landau, E. (2009). Families of gifted children. In L. V. Shavinina (Ed.), *International handbook on giftedness* (pp. 873–883). Dordrecht, Netherlands: Springer.

Riley, T. (2011). *Teaching gifted students in the inclusive classroom*. Waco, TX: Prufrock Press.

Riley, T. (2015). Thinking along the same lines. *SENGVine*, April. Retrieved from http://sengifted.org/archives/articles/thinking-along-the-same-lines. Accessed 1 Feb 2016.

Riley, T., Sampson, C., Wardman, J., & Walker, D. (2015). Connecting like-minded learners through flexible grouping. *SET, 1*, 25–33. https://doi.org/10.18296/set.0005

Riley, T., & White, V. (2016). Developing a sense of belonging through engagement with like-minded peers: A matter of equity. *New Zealand Journal of Educational Studies, 51*, 211–225. https://doi.org/10.1007/s40841-016-0065-9

Sanderson, E., & Greenberger, R. (2010). Evaluating online programs through a gifted lens. *Gifted Child Today, 34*(3), 42–53. https://doi.org/10.1177/107621751103400311

Wolf, N., & Chessor, D. (2011). The affective characteristics of gifted children: Can peer victimization make a difference? *Australasian Journal of Gifted Education, 20*(1), 38–52.

Wood, S. (2010). Best practices in counseling the gifted in schools: What's really happening? *Gifted Child Quarterly, 54*(1), 42–58. https://doi.org/10.1177/0016986209352681

Wormald, C. (2017). *Should gifted students go to a separate school?* Retrieved from https://theconversation.com/should-gifted-students-go-to-a-separate-school-71620

Tracy Riley, PhD, is associate professor and the Dean of Research and specialises in gifted and talented education at Massey University in Palmerston North, New Zealand. Tracy designed the Postgraduate Diploma in Specialist Teaching (Gifted and Talented) and supervises postgraduate research investigations. She is a Director on the Board of SENG: Supporting Emotional Needs of the Gifted and Secretary for the World Council for Gifted and Talented Children. Tracy is the 2017 recipient of the Te Manu Kotuku award given for her services to gifted education by giftEDnz: The Professional Association for Gifted Education (NZ).

Learning from International Research Informs Academic Acceleration in Australasia: A Case for Consistent Policy

8

Ann Lupkowski-Shoplik, Susan G. Assouline, Cara Wienkes, and Ann Easter

Contents

Introduction	173
American Gifted Education History in Relation to Australasian Gifted Education	174
Review of the Research	178
Applications of Accelerative Interventions	182
Talent Search Programs: An Extracurricular Application of Acceleration	182
Grade Acceleration	184
Early Entrance to College or University	186
Policy in Australasia	188
Acceleration Policies Are Essential to Equalisation of Opportunities	189
Implications and Future Directions	193
Conclusions	194
Cross-References	194
References	195

Abstract

Pressey's definition of academic acceleration, "progress through an educational program at rates faster or at ages younger than conventional" (Pressey, 1949, p. 2), although situated in an American context, has served the worldwide gifted education community for several decades. The simplicity of the definition belies the complexity of implementing the intervention in schools anywhere in the world. Furthermore, the robustness of the research supporting academic acceleration as an intervention that has strong positive effects across the academic, psychological, and social-emotional realms (Rogers, 2015) has not translated to

---

A. Lupkowski-Shoplik · S. G. Assouline (✉) · C. Wienkes
Belin-Blank Center, College of Education, University of Iowa, Iowa City, IA, USA
e-mail: ann-shoplik@uiowa.edu; susan-assouline@uiowa.edu; cara-wienkes@uiowa.edu

A. Easter
Gifted Education Consultancy Services, Aotearoa, New Zealand
e-mail: anneaster.gecs@gmail.com

© Springer Nature Singapore Pte Ltd. 2021
S. R. Smith (ed.), *Handbook of Giftedness and Talent Development in the Asia-Pacific*,
Springer International Handbooks of Education,
https://doi.org/10.1007/978-981-13-3041-4_6

full acceptance of the intervention. These paradoxes provided the impetus for Colangelo, Assouline, and Gross (2004a, 2004b) to produce the two-volume report *A Nation Deceived: How Schools Hold Back America's Brightest Students* Colangelo, (2015) and Assouline, Colangelo, VanTassel-Baska, and Lupkowski-Shoplik (2015) to update the Colangelo et al. publications with the two-volume publication *A Nation Empowered: How Evidence Trumps Beliefs Holding Back America's Brightest Students*. This chapter reviews some of the 20 types of acceleration as described by Southern and Jones (2015) and addresses the advantages for talent development when implementing acceleration as well as the consequences when withholding accelerative opportunities from students who are ready for a faster pace and greater depth of content. We discuss academic acceleration as practised in Australasia within the context of cultural values specific to Australia and New Zealand. We present three applications of acceleration and discuss implications for bridging the current divide between university-based research (Assouline et al., 2015) and school-based practice and policy.

Keywords

Academic acceleration · Intervention · Radical acceleration · Excellence · Equity

The aims in this chapter are to emphasise that:
1. Acceleration is the most effective, yet least used, intervention for students who are ready for curriculum presented at a faster pace and greater depth.
2. There are at least 20 types of acceleration (Southern & Jones, 2015), and the intensity of the types ranges from radical acceleration of two or more years (Gross, 2004, 2006; Jung, Young, & Gross, 2015) to curriculum compacting or various forms of grouping.
3. Some countries use one or more types (e.g., grouping such as that found in opportunity classes or radical acceleration, which is a grade skip of two or more years at the same time) more extensively than other types (e.g., early entrance to kindergarten).
4. Consistency among schools with respect to weighting the information pertinent to acceleration in a way that would be helpful for decision-making is limited. Therefore, we recommend a systematic process and objective tools such as the *Iowa Acceleration Scale* (*IAS*; Assouline, Colangelo, Lupkowski-Shoplik, Lipscomb, & Forstadt, 2009).
5. Limited exposure to pre-service training about acceleration or gifted education indicates that educators would benefit from additional professional development on those topics.
6. Adopting a relatively inclusive definition of giftedness, such as Australia has done through use of Gagné's (1995) *Differentiated Model of Giftedness and Talent* (DMGT), results in a broader talent pool of students. School districts

that use broad definitions may benefit from tailoring specific interventions to match the broad range of academic needs found in a talent pool of students.
7. Policy is the bridge between the robust research supporting the various accelerative options and the implementation of one or more of the options (VanTassel-Baska, 2015). Carefully crafted policies based on research encourage reluctant administrators and teachers to use acceleration as an intervention.

Introduction

The occasion for us to write about academic acceleration in general and within the two Australasian countries of Australia and New Zealand in particular represents an opportunity to synthesise commonalities among three similar, yet distinct, Western cultures as well as broaden our international educational horizons. Following a brief introduction to the intervention known as academic acceleration and its origins in the United States, we identify points of convergence and divergence intrinsic to different educational cultures.

Academic acceleration, defined by Pressey (1949) seven decades past, as an educational intervention based on progress through an educational program at ages younger or at rates faster than typical, remains as relevant in the twenty-first century as it was in the latter half of the twentieth century. Each of the 20 types of acceleration listed in Table 1 captures the essence of the definition. Some of the types of acceleration (e.g., early entrance to university or other grade-based strategies) represent a service delivery model. Indeed, grade-based strategies tend to shorten the number of years that a student spends in the K–12 system. Other types (e.g., subject acceleration) represent a curriculum model in that students receive high-level content or skills in advance of the typical age or grade for such instruction. Throughout the chapter we refer to the educational terms grade or grade level; grade is synonymous with the educational term 'year', in Australia and New Zealand. In the United States, elementary grades are commensurate with the Australian or New Zealand terminology of primary school. The US terms middle school and junior high are broadly similar to the early years of the Australian and New Zealand secondary school years.

With such straightforward terminology about acceleration as an educational intervention for gifted students, it would be logical to assume that its implementation is not only understood but also widespread. Although there has been substantial research conducted regarding the effectiveness of the intervention (Gross, 2009; Kulik, 2004; Lubinski, 2004; McClarty, 2015; Rogers, 2015; Steenbergen-Hu, Makel, & Olszewski-Kubilius, 2016; Wai, 2015), the implementation of academic acceleration in school settings in its many forms has not kept pace with the research evidence. Nor has it kept pace with the broader field of gifted education.

Colangelo, Assouline, and Gross (2004a) commented on the observation that Gold (1965) was one of the first to note that implementation of acceleration in schools lagged in comparison to the research support for the effectiveness of the intervention. Twenty-five years later, Borland (1989) also addressed the disparity

Table 1 The 20 types of acceleration

1. Early admission to kindergarten
2. Early admission to first grade
3. Grade skipping
4. Continuous progress
5. Self-paced instruction
6. Subject-matter acceleration/partial acceleration
7. Combined classes
8. Curriculum compacting
9. Telescoping curriculum
10. Mentoring
11. Extracurricular programs
12. Distance learning courses
13. Concurrent/dual enrolment
14. Advanced placement courses
15. International baccalaureate program
16. Accelerated/honour high school or residential high school on a college campus
17. Credit by examination
18. Early entrance into middle school, high school or college
19. Early graduation from high school or college
20. Acceleration in college

Table adapted from Southern and Jones (2015).

between the research on acceleration and the implementation of the intervention. A half-century of documentation of the relatively less-effective non-accelerative school-based interventions for bright students (Rogers, 2015) ushered in a zeitgeist relative to academic acceleration. Despite the research evidence and increased awareness, academic acceleration is still finding its place among educators *in schools*. Although, as will be addressed later in the chapter, acceleration *outside of the traditional school* setting proved to be an indisputably relevant intervention (Lubinski, 2004; Wai, 2015).

American Gifted Education History in Relation to Australasian Gifted Education

A brief review of the history of gifted education and academic acceleration in Australia reveals the extent to which activities in the United States influence educators outside of the United States. For example, Plunkett and Kronborg (2007) indicated that the 1972 release of the US Marland Report motivated, in part, the establishment of Australia's 1973 Schools Commission. Prior to the early 1970s, when then US Secretary of Education Sidney P. Marland (1972) produced the watershed report, *Education of the Gifted and Talented: Report to the Congress of the United States*, awareness of the needs of gifted students was left largely to the individual US states and local districts. The steady increase in awareness and services for gifted students in the United States, and, following, in Australia, seems largely due to the momentum that started with the Marland Report. Modest improvements in US gifted education notwithstanding, it was not until the beginning of the twenty-first century that there was greater awareness about academic acceleration as a relevant intervention for academically able students (Colangelo, Assouline, & Gross, 2004b) in the United States.

Jung and Worrell (2017) offer a comprehensive look at gifted education in Australia. On the one hand, Australian gifted education shares many similarities with the United States, including the chronology related to awareness of academic acceleration in Australia, which mirrors that in the United States. In 2002, the Australian Senate initiated 20 recommendations that emphasised the need for appropriate teacher education in identifying gifted students, providing additional opportunities for gifted students, and developing higher achievement targets (Jung & Worrell, 2017; Plunkett & Kronborg, 2007). On the other hand, there are important differences. In particular, with respect to gifted education, a definite distinction between the United States and Australia is the widespread adoption of Gagné's (1995, 2004) Differentiated Model of Giftedness and Talent (DMGT) across Australia (Jung & Worrell, 2017).

Every few years, the US *National Association for Gifted Children* publishes a comprehensive review of gifted education on a state-by-state basis. The most current report available, published in 2015 (National Association for Gifted Children and Council of State Directors of Programs for the Gifted, 2015), revealed that relatively few states (13 out of 42 responding states) had policy specifically permitting acceleration strategies. A review of the 37 US states that indicated a state definition for giftedness revealed that no state specifically used the DMGT model and the majority refer to intellectual giftedness as the main area of focus (Callahan, Moon, & Oh, 2017). A focus on intellectual giftedness seems to be a remnant from the 1972 Marland Report (Jolly & Robins, 2016). Jolly and Robins (2016, p. 140) also note that the Marland report states "... the gifted and talented will encompass a minimum of 3 to 5% of the school population", whereas the almost exclusive use of Gagné's (1995) DMGT in educational policies across Australia suggests that a wider net is cast to include 10–15% of students in this population. These differences offer another sharp contrast between the United States and Australia with respect to gifted education.

Gifted education in the United States is characterised by local control (VanTassel-Baska, 2015); in comparison, Australia provides a more flexible approach in terms of identifying and serving gifted students. That is, the *Melbourne Declaration of Education Goals for Young Australians* provides the policy framework for the recently developed Australian Curriculum (Australian Curriculum, Assessment, and Reporting Authority [ACARA]). The Australian Curriculum states "all students are entitled to rigorous, relevant and engaging learning opportunities that align with their individual learning needs, strengths, interests and goals" (ACARA, 2012, p. 20). The Australian Curriculum goes further to acknowledge that the:

learning needs of gifted and talented students may differ dramatically from those of other students, [and] not only are gifted and talented students likely to make progress towards these objectives at a faster pace…but they are also often capable of achieving at a level beyond their same-aged peers. (ACARA, 2012)

The National Assessment Program, a sector of ACARA, serves as a measure for government, schools, teachers, and the like, to determine if young Australians are meeting educational standards (ACARA, 2012). Although the assessment program promotes improvement in student achievement, the program does not specifically identify and set out to promote talent. Rather, the assessment information is useful to reduce performance gaps and provide tailored learning (National Assessment Program [NAP], n.d.). This logic aligns with Australia's traditionally adopted egalitarian values and previous literature discussing Australia's educators' priority of using educational resources for poorly performing students (Jung & Worrell, 2017). Understanding the nuances of ACARA offers a context for discussions related to interventions for gifted students, such as academic acceleration.

Educational policy for gifted education in Aotearoa New Zealand has also been influenced by international trends, albeit to a much lesser degree. Parkyn, a distinguished scholar in the field of educational research, first drew attention to the needs of gifted students in New Zealand more than 70 years ago. In his classic text, *Children of High Intelligence: A New Zealand Study*, Parkyn (1948) observed that "in the ordinary mixed-ability classes of the primary school the bright child often spends a large part of his school time waiting for the next question, the next turn, the next subject, the next task, and so on" (p. 145). He believed that some form of ability grouping, either within the regular classroom or on a wider scale throughout the school, was critical to ensure that 'bright' students remained challenged and motivated in their learning. Parkyn (1948) also proposed that, in order to improve the education of 'more intelligent' students, teachers needed to ascertain each child's level and rate of development and plan lessons accordingly, an idea that was considered novel at the time.

Nevertheless, until recently, little sustained interest or attention has been given to the needs of gifted students in New Zealand schools. While some improvements have been made over the last 20 years, Moltzen (2011) reported that these gains have often resulted from the efforts of just a handful of individuals and have been relatively short-lived. He suggested that one of the major factors that has constrained attempts to implement appropriate educational provisions for this group of learners is the notion of egalitarianism (see also Jarvis, Jolly, & Moltzen, 2018). From this perspective, the gifted are seen as 'innately advantaged', and, therefore, any form of special provision is regarded as 'elitist' (Moltzen, 2011). Other commentators have also noted that there is a general lack of awareness about the needs of gifted students in New Zealand, as reflected in the 'tall poppy syndrome' and associated myths and misconceptions about giftedness and talent (Bourne, 2009; Cathcart, 2017; Horsley, 2010; Riley, Bevan-Brown, Bicknell, Carroll-Lind, & Kearney, 2004; Riley & Bicknell, 2013; Tapper, 2017; Tapper & Riley, 2015; White & Riley, 2017).

Over the last 20 years, a number of initiatives have been introduced in an attempt to strengthen schools' capability to meet the needs of gifted students, including the following: appointment of a national *Gifted Education Advisory Group* in 1997; publication of a handbook for schools (Ministry of Education, 2000; updated 2012); development of supporting materials for gifted students on the Ministry of Education's portal website *Te Kete Ipurangi* (*TKI*) in 2000; establishment of a Ministerial Working Party on Gifted Education in 2001; publication of a set of national policy initiatives (Office of the Minister of Education, 2002); funding for gifted education advisory support to schools (2003–2009); establishment of a national coordination team and a contestable funding pool designed to encourage the development of innovative programs for gifted students (2003–2009); national research into schools' provision for gifted students (Riley et al., 2004); *Rising Tides* national gifted education conference sponsored by the Ministry of Education in 2006; and publication of a handbook for parents and whānau of gifted children (Bevan-Brown & Taylor, 2008).

Arguably, however, the most significant change was an amendment to the *National Administration Guidelines* (*NAGs*) in 2003, whereby gifted and talented students were specifically included as a group of learners with special educational needs (New Zealand Government, 2003, December 18). Since the beginning of 2005, it has been mandatory for all state and state-integrated schools in New Zealand to identify gifted students and to plan and implement appropriate programs to meet their needs. According to Moltzen (2011), these developments signalled an unprecedented level of commitment from the then labour-led government (1999–2008). However, like many other initiatives in the history of gifted education in New Zealand, the momentum generated by this support does not appear to have been sustained long term. New Zealand still does not have a national gifted education policy, advisory support to schools has largely been disestablished, and opportunities for specialist teacher training at the pre-service level are both minimal and optional (Riley & Rawlinson, 2005, 2006, 2008).

In New Zealand, the preferred approach to provision for gifted students is firmly centred on enrichment in the regular classroom (McDonough, 2004; Riley & Bicknell, 2013; Riley et al., 2004; Townsend, 2011). Although the Ministry of Education (2012) recommends that schools utilise a continuum of approaches to meet the needs of gifted learners, including both enrichment and acceleration, in practice very few students are accelerated in New Zealand. A comprehensive national survey of educational provision for gifted students found that acceleration by means of early entry to various levels of schooling was the least frequently cited form of school-based provision, with just 8.3% of schools mentioning that they utilised this approach (Riley et al., 2004). Furthermore, only 2.7% of schools in this study reported that acceleration was their preferred method for catering for gifted students. A follow-up study conducted a decade later found very similar results, with even fewer schools (1.8%) reporting that they provided opportunities for acceleration, such as early entry or dual enrolment (Riley & Bicknell, 2013).

More recently, there have been some encouraging signs that gifted education is, once again, back on the agenda. Currently, the government is undertaking a wide-ranging strategic review of the New Zealand education system as part of its 3-year education portfolio work program (Office of the Minister of Education, 2018). The accompanying cabinet paper outlines an aspirational vision for the future of education in New Zealand and notes that previous policy decisions, especially those aimed at ensuring public sector accountability and compliance, have been "rooted in a 20th century educational mindset" (p. 4). The paper also acknowledges that the New Zealand education system lacks personalisation and does not cater well for some groups of learners, including gifted students. This statement is significant because it publicly acknowledges that gifted students will not necessarily 'make it on their own' and succeed at school without appropriate educational support. However, despite this commitment, the only initiatives that are in place currently to support improved outcomes for gifted students are the development of *Gifted Aotearoa*, a Network of Expertise (Ministry of Education, 2018) and the maintenance of the *TKI Gifted and Talented Education Online* website (Ministry of Education, n.d.).

Review of the Research

Pressey's succinct definition of acceleration as an educational intervention allowing students to move through educational programs at younger ages or at rates faster than typical derives from a 1949 monograph; however, the relevance of Pressey's highly informative publication extends well beyond the provision of a definition of acceleration. Early in Pressey's discussion, he offers insight into the American higher-education culture in the late 1800s and early 1900s, citing the 1888 Presidential Address of Harvard President Eliot as an early indicator of looking for ways to "save time" (p. 5) for bright students who are ready to enter college early. Pressey posited that "the evidence was practically unanimous that younger entrants were most likely to graduate, had the best academic records, won the most honours and presented the fewest disciplinary difficulties" (1949, p. 7). Pressey's words ring true decades later, that is:

> The long-term studies reviewed here show that adults who had been accelerated in school achieved greater educational and occupational success and were satisfied with their choices and the impact of those choices in other areas of their lives. (Wai, 2015, p. 81)

Kulik (2004), along with Steenbergen-Hu et al. (2016), Wai (2015), Wai and Rogers (2004, 2015), offered indisputable evidence regarding the effectiveness of the various types of acceleration. Rogers' 2015 chapter is of particular relevance because she reports on the socialisation and psychological effects as well as on the academic effects. Assouline, Colangelo, VanTassel-Baska and Lupkowski-Shoplik (2015) derived four main points from Rogers' 2015 chapter that succinctly summarise the research findings:

- Extensive research has indicated that acceleration has positive effects on the academic as well as affective lives of students.
- The data indicate that the effects on the affective realm (social and emotional) are not as robust and straightforward as effects on the cognitive realm.
- Results of acceleration on psychological adjustment (i.e., feelings about self and measures of well-being are positive but small in terms of effects).
- While we can be confident of the positive cognitive and affective impact of acceleration on white [American] students, we do not have enough studies of diverse [and international] students to make the same claim regarding these students (p. 2).

Many of the findings about the benefits of acceleration over the last several decades have resulted from the work done by researchers associated with the *Study of Mathematically Precocious Youth* (SMPY), which Julian Stanley founded at Johns Hopkins University (e.g., Lubinski, 2004; Park, Lubinski, & Benbow, 2013; Wai, 2015). The SMPY work was the foundation for the creation of myriad accelerated extracurricular programs for middle school students across the US; fast-paced summer courses that have been the hallmark of SMPY's work with talented youth, and research results have demonstrated the students' readiness to learn advanced material at a fast pace and to retain that information. Swiatek (2007) summarised many of these findings, including both short- and long-term benefits. For example, students taking fast-paced (accelerated) courses in mathematics were more likely to take advanced mathematics courses in high school and college, accelerate their education, and enter college at a young age. Students demonstrated continued strong performance in mathematics, without gaps in their mathematical knowledge. Swiatek (2007) also pointed out that helping students learn material at a faster pace is beneficial to their sense of challenge and engagement in school; additionally, it may help prevent problems such as underachievement and increase students' motivation.

Gross (2006, 2009, also Jung & Gross, 2015) has made an important and unique contribution to the study of acceleration, particularly in an Australian context, with her longitudinal study of 60 Australian students with IQs of 160 higher. She observed the students and carefully measured their progress for over 20 years. Gross noted that all of the students in her study would have benefitted from some type of academic acceleration and recommended radical acceleration for a number of them. She discovered that over half of the students (33 of the 60) were not permitted to accelerate their education; instead, they remained with age-mates for the duration of their schooling. When comparing accelerated to non-accelerated students who were in the longitudinal study, important findings included the accelerated students reported higher degrees of life satisfaction, attended more prestigious universities, and reported more positive social relationships than the non-accelerated students.

One form of whole-grade acceleration, that is, early entrance to college (or university in the Australasian context), has been studied systematically with students who entered college early as part of a special program or simply entered college early on their own. Entering college or university at a young age and collapsing the years of the college/university program were fairly common in the earlier part of the twentieth century (Brody & Muratori, 2015), although that trend had reversed by the 1970s. By the later part of the twentieth century, however, a number of universities had established special programs for early entrants, as a way of supporting their social-emotional needs while recognising their academic needs (see the list of university-based early entrance programs provided in Brody & Muratori 2015). Research from these US programs has been quite positive; students have been successful academically throughout their college careers and into their broader careers. As a group, the accelerated students published their first papers at a younger age than similarly talented students and earned their degrees earlier (Park et al., 2013). Based on their examination of many pertinent research studies, Brody and Muratori (2015) suggest that the students who are best prepared to enter college early have developed strong study skills, have a strong content knowledge base, and are self-confident enough to interact with others in a new environment.

Outside of the United States, longitudinal studies in Australia reveal accelerated students achieved highly and became more independent and autonomous (Gross, 2006; Jung et al., 2015; Murphy, 1995). Gross and van Vliet (2005) reported students' high levels of satisfaction with both academic and socio-affective outcomes, and Jung et al. (2015) revealed that students expressed no regrets about their acceleration (i.e., early university/college entry). Overall, the accelerated students reported positive, intellectually stimulating, and socially satisfying experiences with beginning their university studies early (Jung et al., 2015).

Students who were radically accelerated have been the subject of research studies in Australia as well (e.g., Jung & Gross, 2015). Jung and Gross (2015) defined radical acceleration as resulting in a student graduating from high school at least three years earlier than usual. Radical acceleration may be most appropriate for *exceptionally* talented students, since a single grade skip or acceleration in one subject is unlikely to meet the students' needs. Radical accelerands have been extremely successful academically, as demonstrated by winning prestigious academic prizes and earning very high grades in school and university (Gross, 2006). Their social experiences have been generally positive and they have often chosen to use the time saved to pursue graduate degrees and challenging careers (Gross & Van Vliet, 2005; Jung et al., 2015). Jung et al. (2015) recommend that counsellors and psychologists should evaluate radical accelerands before accelerations and the students should be monitored regularly to enable detection of potential problems.

Dare, Smith, and Nowicki (2016) provided a unique perspective by examining parents' experiences with their children's grade-based acceleration in Australian schools. Parents offered many insightful comments that were consistent with other research, noting that their children were more engaged academically and experienced generally positive social and emotional outcomes. They also provided a negative picture of their children's experiences with school before acceleration; for example, one child went from being excited about school before beginning kindergarten to crying and resisting going to school just six weeks into the school year. Interestingly, some parents noted a strain on their own relationships with educators, family, and friends, because others judged them for permitting their child to accelerate in school. Another important point made by the parents in this study was that acceleration is not always a 'one and done' experience; that is, even if a student is skipped ahead a grade, he or she may find the new grade still isn't challenging enough and may require further challenges, possibly including additional whole-grade or subject acceleration.

Vialle, Ashton, Carlon, and Rankin (2001) conducted several research projects in New South Wales focusing on acceleration and found a general attitude of reluctance or even antagonism towards acceleration, in spite of the research supporting it. In general, educators who were supportive of acceleration had received some training, while those who opposed it had not. Lassig's (2009) study provided similar findings, in that untrained teachers assumed that gifted students who were accelerated would have difficulties with social adjustment. Parents in one research study (Dare et al., 2016) put into words what researchers have also noted, that "teachers need a lot of training to help this process [of acceleration] along" (p. 13). Untrained teachers may oppose acceleration and make the child's transition to the new grade difficult. Lassig (2009) hypothesised that educators do not prioritise acceleration or ability grouping because many Australian government education departments champion the concept of inclusion in the regular classroom for as many students as possible; since acceleration and ability grouping are not emphasised in gifted education professional development, educators are unsure how to implement them. However, forward progress is being made; Gross, Urquhart, Doyle, Juratowitch, and Matheson (2011) have found that Australian schools are gradually adopting the practice of acceleration.

In New Zealand, many educators have expressed reluctance to accelerate gifted students, often because of misguided concerns about the perceived negative social and emotional outcomes for this group of learners (e.g., Townsend & Patrick, 1993). In a large study examining New Zealand schools, Riley et al. (2004) found the majority (62%) preferred to combine acceleration plus enrichment and those who selected one option preferred enrichment, especially at the primary level. Interestingly, the schools in the study did not use a comprehensive or systematic approach for identifying students in need of acceleration. Instead, they approached decision-making on a case-by-case basis (Riley et al., 2004).

It has been suggested that New Zealand educators tend to take a more conservative approach towards acceleration because the positive findings in the research literature are not as widely known in this country. While subject acceleration is regarded as an effective means of providing for able secondary school students who excel in specific subject areas, many principals and teachers are generally unaware of the potential benefits that other forms of acceleration can provide for gifted students (Anthony, Rawlins, Riley, & Winsley, 2002; Macleod, 2004). Townsend (2011) argued that it is highly unlikely that this situation will change unless teachers know how to recognise the characteristics of gifted students and understand how to use appropriate educational strategies, such as enrichment and acceleration, to meet their special learning needs.

A survey of New Zealand teachers' attitudes towards acceleration, measured in a sample group of 152 experienced classroom practitioners and 140 teacher trainees, provides additional support for this view (Townsend & Patrick, 1993). In this study, the majority of teachers, including those who had prior experience in working with gifted students, were apprehensive about certain features of acceleration programs for young gifted children, especially with regard to the psychosocial outcomes. Furthermore, only 9% of New Zealand teachers, compared with 66% of teachers in a similar study conducted in the United States (Southern, Jones, & Fiscus, 1989), believed that retaining gifted children with their same-age peers might have possible negative consequences.

Other New Zealand research, conducted in an independent girls' school (Y1–Y13), reported similar findings (Watts, 2006). In this exploratory case study, teachers were surveyed about their attitudes to gifted students and aspects of their education using a questionnaire developed by Gagné and Gagnier (2004). The results showed that while teachers generally held positive views about the needs of gifted students, they did not support the use of acceleration and were opposed to having separate classes for this group of learners: "An interesting outcome from this survey is the contradiction between teachers' views that the gifted should be better provided for and their apparent lack of enthusiasm for some of the methods by which this can be achieved" (Watts, 2006, p. 14).

Interestingly, there is some evidence to suggest that teachers' beliefs about acceleration may be starting to change. In a more recent study that surveyed practising secondary teachers, tertiary education students, and student teachers, Wardman (2009) found strong support for full-year acceleration as an appropriate educational strategy for gifted learners. Despite the fact that 68% of teachers ($n = 264$) and 83% of students ($n = 191$) who responded to this survey stated that they had no direct experience of acceleration, in general the participants were very supportive of this practice.

Applications of Accelerative Interventions

The research is consistent and clear that academic acceleration works (Rogers, 2015). Yet, there is a divide between what researchers know and how practitioners implement the information. We will focus on three principal ways in which research findings about academic acceleration have been applied: (1) creating university-based Talent Search programs that provide extracurricular challenging opportunities to students (typically outside of the school day); (2) using research-based tools to make decisions about grade and subject acceleration; and (3) establishing opportunities for talented students to enter college early.

Talent Search Programs: An Extracurricular Application of Acceleration

Extracurricular programming, one of the 20 types of acceleration (Southern & Jones, 2015), is grounded in the Talent Search programs that were an outgrowth of the Talent Search Model. The model, developed in the 1970s by Dr. Julian C. Stanley at

Johns Hopkins University, applies Leta Hollingworth's concept of above-level testing (Stanley, 1990) on a large scale to students in grades 7 and 8 who demonstrated they were ready for challenges beyond their regular education programs. Stanley's process begins with students in the top 3–5% of their age group (as measured by a nationally normed grade-level standardised test) who are invited to take a much more challenging nationally normed test, the College Board's SAT, which was typically administered to college-bound 11th and 12th graders. In the initial step of the Talent Search Model, students' grade-level test scores clustered in the right tail of the bell curve. The students encountered the 'ceiling effect' because the test did not adequately measure their abilities. In the second step of the Talent Search Model, Stanley offered the students a much harder test, the SAT. The scores created a new bell curve representing a distribution of performance for high-achieving students; students' scores spanned the entire range of possible scores on the more difficult test.

As Stanley developed the process, he did not simply focus on testing and discovering highly able students. Rather, his goal was to develop these students' talents. Students scoring high on the SAT were invited to participate in summer programs and fast-paced weekend classes (Benbow & Stanley, 1983). The objective was to encourage the students to move ahead in academic subjects in a systematic fashion, so they were consistently challenged and able to demonstrate mastery of the material. Stanley and his team drew on their knowledge of research on acceleration and devised a model that allowed students to move ahead faster and at a more advanced level than they would typically encounter in the regular classroom. Students' scores on the above-level test provided objective information that helped researchers determine educational recommendations to ensure the appropriate level of challenge. Beyond the use for educational recommendations, earning high SAT scores when in junior high school—even many years later—was found to be predictive of excellent performance (Wai, 2015).

Over the years, Stanley's research teams thoroughly investigated the groups of talented students as part of the Study of Mathematically Precocious Youth (SMPY). The SMPY longitudinal research study continues today at Vanderbilt University. Findings of some of the major SMPY studies were summarised in Wai (2015) and include: academically talented students who were accelerated view the acceleration experience and its impact on their lives quite positively; grade-based acceleration had positive effects on long-term productivity in STEM fields (even 30 years after the intervention); and students who had higher doses of STEM educational acceleration and enrichment before college were more likely to have earned creative educational and occupational achievements more than 20 years later. These longitudinal studies demonstrate the power of identifying, via an above-level test, elementary and middle school students who are ready for challenges beyond those offered by the typical school curriculum.

Above-level testing is a process that can be applied with any standardised achievement or aptitude test (Assouline, Lupkowski-Shoplik, & Colangelo, 2018); results from above-level testing provide extremely useful information related to student's need for academic challenge or acceleration, especially in specific content areas such as mathematics. Although beyond the scope of this chapter, there is new evidence that this powerful model, applied traditionally outside of the regular school setting, has relevance in schools especially those that served under-represented students. Assouline, Ihrig, and Mahatmya (2017) determined that applying the process in schools effectively broadens the talent pool to include students who are often over-looked, thereby increasing opportunities for under-served gifted students.

Grade Acceleration

The *Iowa Acceleration Scale* (IAS; Assouline et al., 2009; Lupkowski-Shoplik, Assouline, & Colangelo, 2015) provides a systematic way for educators and families to gather appropriate information and make an informed decision about another form of acceleration, that is, whole-grade acceleration. Written for educational systems in the United States, the procedures used in the IAS can be generalised to students elsewhere. The main ideas are to: (1) gather objective information about the student's aptitudes, abilities, and achievements, via nationally standardised grade-level and above-level testing; (2) synthesise information and evaluate the student relative to school and academic factors, developmental factors, interpersonal skills as well as attitude and support from the student, school system, and parents; and (3) determine the student's likelihood for continued excellent performance in the next grade based upon the objective information. Rather than becoming sidetracked by conversations grounded in individual biases for or against acceleration, the IAS requires a team-based decision and is designed to facilitate team meetings that focus on the important factors that should be considered when making decisions about grade skipping. Gross et al. (2011) note that, although the IAS is highly recommended and is increasingly used in schools considering acceleration, Australian educators may be cautious about using it because they are unfamiliar with the specific test instruments listed in the IAS. Gross et al. recommended the development of a brief paper explaining how the IAS may be adapted for use in Australian schools. To our knowledge, no such paper is available. The review of the literature on assessment by Cao, Jung, and Lee (2017) may be a starting point.

To date, only a small number of studies have looked at the outcomes of academic acceleration for students in New Zealand schools. Martin (2006) followed the transition of three gifted girls, aged 9 and 10 years, who had been accelerated by one year. The research also sought the views of teachers and parents over a 6-month period as the girls adjusted to their new classes. In two cases, the school had initiated the acceleration process, while one student had been accelerated at the request of her parents. Martin (2006) reported that the participants in her study were all extremely positive about their experiences of acceleration. An interesting feature of this study is that participants were invited to document their experiences by compiling a portfolio of artifacts made up of items that held personal significance for each individual (Martin & Merrotsy, 2006). The researcher used the portfolios as a tool to facilitate ongoing dialogue with the participants and to encourage deeper reflection about their experiences (Martin, 2006).

In another small-scale study, Kirby and Townsend (2005) used conversational interviews to explore the personal perspectives of eight gifted children, aged from 11 to 13 years, about their school experiences. Four of the children had been accelerated in primary school, while the remainder had not. Overall, the participants expressed a very positive attitude towards acceleration, regardless of whether they had actually experienced it or not. The main reason given was that acceleration alleviated the boredom that these gifted students typically experienced at school by providing greater intellectual challenge and rigour. When asked about social and emotional issues associated with being gifted, participants also responded unanimously as a group. In particular, they mentioned feeling different from other children and said that they often felt misunderstood, both by peers and teachers. In their concluding remarks, Kirby and Townsend suggested that teachers need to adopt a mentoring role in order to facilitate the social inclusion of gifted students within the wider school culture and recommended that greater attention should be given to student voice.

An earlier study undertaken by Rawlins (2000) also highlighted the need for schools to consider the long-term implications of acceleration for individual students. This study utilised focus group interviews to explore the perceptions of gifted students from four different secondary schools who had been accelerated by one year in mathematics. Overall, participants viewed the process as beneficial to their learning and reported increased confidence and self-esteem as a result of their participation in these programs. Positive factors mentioned by students included greater challenge in their mathematics learning, early completion of secondary schooling, increased opportunity for higher examination results, and the option to broaden subject choices by completing secondary school mathematics sooner than expected. However, some participants also expressed concern that early entrance to university (i.e., by one year) might cause problems further down the track.

In a recent doctoral dissertation (Crawford, 2016) the effectiveness of acceleration at the secondary level was also demonstrated. In this mixed-methods study, Crawford investigated acceleration as an educational intervention for gifted girls who attended single-sex secondary schools (Y9–Y13). Responses to a national survey ($N = 40$) showed that almost all girls' schools, regardless of school size, decile rating or school type, reported that they provided acceleration in one or more forms. Both content- and grade-based accelerative options were offered to individual students, groups of students or whole classes. Most schools provided accelerative options in one or more subjects and one-third used grade skipping. Further evidence from three in-depth case study schools showed that flexible timetabling, adaptive school systems, and the inherent flexibility of NCEA for multilevel assessments were key factors in facilitating ongoing educational pathways through secondary school to university.

Additional support for the benefits of academic acceleration at the secondary level from the perspectives of students, their parents, and school administrators is provided by Wardman (2010). As part of a series of studies, 12 students who had participated in a planned program of full-year acceleration at high school were interviewed about their experiences seven years later, along with a control group of six equally able siblings who had not been accelerated. The findings indicated a high level of satisfaction with this program from the students, their parents, and school administrators, with the latter two groups crediting the mentoring/academic coaching of accelerated students as being a key factor in its success (Wardman, 2010). The majority of students went on to enter university at 16 years of age and appeared to be very successful in their academic studies, with no major long-term adverse social or emotional effects identified as a result of being accelerated.

Early Entrance to College or University

Considered the culminating accelerative experience, early entrance to college or university provides students the opportunity to seek additional academic challenges and gain a head start on their career paths. Such programs are ideal for highly capable students who have exhausted the curriculum at their local high schools and demonstrate social and emotional readiness to leave home a year or two younger than typical. Several US colleges or universities offer specialised programs for students who leave high school early (Brody & Muratori, 2015), and many early entrance programs offer a residential component, where young students are housed together and experience outside-of-class activities together, therefore removing (or lessening) some of the pressure on them to experience the university social scene before they are ready. Robinson and the Davidson Institute Team (2005a, 2005b) have produced guidebooks to help students and parents weigh important factors and make informed decisions about early entrance to college.

There are various models for implementing early entrance programs on university campuses. One form, as practised at the Gatton Academy on the campus of Western Kentucky University (https://www.wku.edu/academy/) or the Texas Academy of Mathematics and Science at the University of North Texas (tams.unt.edu), combines the last two years of high school with the first two years of college. Another state-university program model is that of the University of Washington Early Entrance Program (https://robinsoncenter.uw.edu/programs/eep/), which supports cohorts of very young students when they are on campus; however, this program is not a residential early entrance program. Finally, the Bucksbaum Academy at the University of Iowa (www.belinblank.org/academy) offers early entrance to qualified students who have completed the first two years of high school. They enter the university as full-time first-year honour students.

The use of early entrance to university programs is gradually increasing in Australia (Young, Rogers, Hoekman, van Vliet, & Long, 2015). Although as of 2015 the University of New South Wales was the only institution with a formal written policy for full-time early entrance, an additional 12 Australian universities were willing to offer full-time early enrolment on a case-by-case basis (Jung et al., 2015). Despite the increasing formalisation of early entrance to university programs, it is still relatively rare for students to enter university early in Australia. Concerns about the potential negative social consequences of acceleration plus the emphasis in Australian states on completing the state graduation tests to determine if a student is ready to enter a university are powerful factors that limit this practice (Young et al., 2015).

However, a few Australian studies have reported on students who entered universities early (e.g., Bailey, 1997; Gross, 2004; Young et al., 2015). Gross (2004) is well known for her work with a longitudinal study of highly gifted students who were radically accelerated (see Gross, 1992, 2006, 2009). As reported in Jung et al. (2015), radical acceleration is an intervention for the most highly gifted students and typically results in positive academic, social, career, and life outcomes for those students. Young et al. (2015) found that students who entered university early were generally pleased to have been accelerated and experienced a sense of relief at the additional academic challenge.

Very few studies have focused on the experiences of students who enter university early in New Zealand. Horsley (2013) investigated perceptions of students with experience in either dual enrolment at school and university or early enrolment at university. Participants ($N = 90$) were drawn from three New Zealand universities and included 40 students who had entered university early. The data for this mixed-methods study were gathered through an online survey ($n = 81$) and semi-structured telephone interviews ($n = 12$). The results indicated that dissatisfaction with school processes (e.g., subject choices, timetables) limited teacher subject content knowledge and poor student-teacher relationships were contributing factors in students' decisions to enter university early. In particular, participants reported feeling frustrated by the slow pace of instruction and the lack of academic rigour that they experienced at secondary school. Interestingly, despite the fact that some students had not demonstrated 'strong performance' in their NCEA exams prior to enrolling at university, Horsley reported that they had all been successful in their tertiary studies. These findings highlight the need for teachers to design curriculum that will motivate and challenge high-ability students to ensure that they remain engaged in their learning at school. As Horsley pointed out, the results of this exploratory study also suggest that many more students may be capable of achieving at an advanced level, if they have access to appropriate opportunities for acceleration.

In another study, Yeo (2016) explored issues of academic self-concept and belonging in a cohort of gifted adolescent males ($N = 30$) who had been placed together in a Year 13 accelerated class at a large, urban single-sex secondary school. As part of their academic program, the students were concurrently enrolled in first-year courses at a local university that had strong community links with the school. The participants were studying a wide range of subjects, with science and mathematics being the most popular choices: calculus (63.3%), physics (46.7%), and chemistry (40%). Although Yeo did not focus on the participants' experiences of attending university, the findings of this exploratory study suggest that academic acceleration and dual enrolment contributed positively to their overall sense of well-being at school. Consistent with the results of other studies (e.g., Gross, 2004; Merrotsy, 2002; Tapper, 2014; Young, 2010), Yeo (2016) also reported that participation in extracurricular sporting activities facilitated greater social acceptance by non-accelerated peers.

In a recent doctoral thesis (Easter, 2019), the lived experiences of accelerated students (N = 10) who entered university early in New Zealand were investigated. Consistent with the findings of overseas research, the young people in this exploratory study were very positive about their decision to enter university early. Many of the participants had endured years of boredom and frustration at school, as well as ongoing issues with bullying and social isolation. Although some students found the initial transition from secondary school to university difficult, the findings suggested that most of the challenges they faced were relatively minor and tended to be short-lived (c.f., Young, 2010). Ongoing support and encouragement from family/whānau and friends, as well as active involvement in extracurricular activities, were viewed by the young people in this study as critical enabling factors for positive adjustment. Overall, Easter concluded that accelerated students who gain early admission to university in New Zealand can be very successful, not only in terms of their academic achievement, but also in relation to their social and emotional development. With the benefit of hindsight, none of the participants regretted their decision to enter university early, and most could identify significant advantages, such as being awarded prestigious international scholarships and having more time for early career exploration. The findings also highlighted a need for parents/whānau and educators to be better informed about the potential benefits of academic acceleration and early admission to university as a legitimate pathway for high-ability students in New Zealand schools.

Policy in Australasia

No other intervention in gifted education offers research support as robust as the support for academic acceleration. "Because research on the effectiveness of acceleration is the bedrock for best practice in gifted education, it should play a major role in policy development and enactment of gifted education practices at state and local levels" (VanTassel-Baska, 2015, p. 43). Policy statements should define giftedness, detail the educational and developmental needs of the students and provide schools and education systems with responsibilities and steps for supporting giftedness (Danylchuk, 2010).

Similar to the United States, currently there is not a standardised, national approach to identifying giftedness in Australian schools, although a multiple criteria approach is recommended (Jung & Worrell, 2017). Multiple criteria include a variety of sources (e.g., intelligence tests, achievement tests, academic performance, and teacher, parent, peer and self-nominations; Jung & Worrell, 2017); however, there is little consistency in the weight given to various information sources (Jarvis & Henderson, 2012) or to the manner in which the information can be used for educational planning. Blackburn, Cornish, and Smith (2016) highlight that relying only on traditional identification procedures can often lead to invalid results or misidentification of giftedness for English Language Learner (ELL) Australian students.

All Australian states and territories have policies concerning the education of gifted and talented students, and some of the policies specify the use of academic acceleration (Young et al., 2015). However, policies vary considerably between education sectors, systems, and individual schools (Gross et al., 2011). There is still work to be done in terms of making policies about acceleration explicit and comprehensive (Young et al., 2015). If policies are not enforced consistently, students who are most vulnerable (i.e., those whose parents are not familiar with the process of advocacy) are at greatest risk of not receiving the intervention they most need (Plucker, 2018). This is a loss for individual students who may not fully develop their talents as well as for humanity that needs the talents of youth to be as developed as much as possible.

New Zealand does not have a national policy for the education of gifted and talented students or any official guidelines for academic acceleration. Responsibility for decision-making lies with individual schools, through their Boards of Trustees, and, as a result, there is widespread disparity between schools in terms of what they offer for gifted and talented students. The most recent national evaluation undertaken by the Education Review Office (ERO, 2008a, 2008b) in a representative sample of 315 schools across New Zealand found that only 17% of the schools reviewed had developed effective practices for their gifted students in all five key evaluative areas (i.e., school leadership, definition and identification, programs and provision, school self-review, and positive student outcomes). These findings are consistent with the results of a previous evaluative report conducted 10 years earlier, as well as the findings of large-scale national research commissioned by the Ministry of Education (Riley et al., 2004), and subsequent national studies of provision (Riley & Bicknell, 2013; N. Ballam, personal communication, September 4, 2018).

However, as discussed in the previous section, evidence from recent New Zealand research that has specifically investigated academic acceleration (e.g., Crawford, 2016; Easter, 2019; Horsley, 2013; Wardman, 2010; Yeo, 2016) appears to suggest that attitudes towards this form of educational intervention may be changing and signals cautious optimism for the future. It should also be noted that the *New Zealand Curriculum* (*NZC*) allows for variable progression through the broad-based achievement levels and encourages schools to tailor programs of study to meet individual student needs (Ministry of Education, 2007). Similarly, the structure of the *National Certificate of Educational Achievement* (*NCEA*), the main exit qualification for school leavers in New Zealand, is inherently flexible, and students may be enrolled concurrently in achievement standards at different levels of the qualifications framework (New Zealand Qualifications Authority, 2017).

Educators are the ones who implement accelerative processes, so how do educators, who typically regard themselves as practitioners, get involved in policy-making that informs such practice? The first step is to understand the relevance of research to effective educational practice (Plucker, 2018). The next step is to see the relevance of policy in their everyday practice and understand that decisions made by them, or for them, are typically the result of educational policies (Plucker, 2018). Although a thorough discussion of educational policy is beyond the scope of this chapter, the topics presented offer a sample of issues that are impacted by the presence, or lack, of policy related to academic acceleration and gifted education (Table 2).

Acceleration Policies Are Essential to Equalisation of Opportunities

In the United States, a few states have policies specifically addressing acceleration for gifted students (such as Ohio, Colorado, Illinois, and Minnesota); of significance, even educational leaders who do not have a background in gifted education or are unaware of the research on academic acceleration are required to apply the research supporting acceleration for gifted learners in their area. For example, all public school districts in Ohio must create acceleration policies, which the state department of education reviews. They are required to include an acceleration assessment process (typically the *Iowa Acceleration Scale*, Assouline et al., 2009), which includes a comprehensive academic assessment of the acceleration candidate, gathering information about the student's physical, social, and emotional development, and team meetings in which the various aspects of acceleration are discussed. A team that includes parents, educators, and administrators makes the final decision, based upon a review and discussion of the relevant data, about acceleration. Furthermore, we recommend that this team approach be included in written acceleration policies (Lupkowski-Shoplik et al., 2015).

The South Australian policy concerning gifted students compares favourably to the approach by the US state of Ohio. "The learning environment [for gifted students] needs to provide educational pathways and appropriately challenging enrichment, extension and *acceleration experiences*" (South Australia Department for Education and Child Development [DECD], 2016, p. 4). The policy acknowledges that gifted learners may benefit from early entry to school, for example, and provides items for parents, educators, and principals to consider. Recommendations include a full-scale IQ three or more standard deviations above the average, completion of the Gifted and Talented Checklist (which is included in the appendices of the policy itself) and parent and teacher nomination forms (DECD, 2016). According to the DECD (2016), the principal makes the final decision. This is in contrast to the team-based approach used with the *Iowa Acceleration Scale* (Assouline et al., 2009) in which a team of people (including parents, psychologist, current teacher, receiving teacher, gifted educator, and administrator) are recommended to participate in the discussion concerning acceleration.

The *Guidelines for the Use of Strategies to Support Gifted and Talented Students* produced by the New South Wales Department of Education and Training (2004) offers definitions of subject acceleration and 'year or stage acceleration' (known in the United States as grade skipping). It describes several types of acceleration and provides a list of school considerations for acceleration. The first recommendation is that a total school policy about acceleration is required, so school staff and families have a clear understanding about why and how acceleration occurs in school. The *Guidelines* state that school principals have the final responsibility for deciding if early entrance or any form of accelerated progression is appropriate for a student, but they also recommend that a team of professionals (including a trained psychologist, receiving teacher, and parents) contribute information for the decision. This policy is currently being updated.

In at least some of the states in Australia and New Zealand, policies about gifted students include a discussion about academic acceleration (Young et al., 2015). This point can be leveraged to craft more specific policies that emphasise procedure, that is, explaining how students who would benefit from acceleration can be identified as well as how acceleration can be implemented to challenge gifted students.

Table 2 Acceleration and gifted education within Australia

	Gifted and talented	Acceleration	Notes
New Zealand	The Ministry of Education publishes in 2012 document focusing on gifted and talented students and ways teachers can meet the demands (Kronborg, 2018).	Acceleration definition: vertical extension of the curriculum as opposed to horizontal extension (Wardman, 2015). More enrichment than acceleration (Wardman, 2015).	Utilises Gagné's DMGT Model (2004). Recommended schools develop and implement plans/procedures and classroom programs to support gifted students by using 'collaborative inquiry approach' (Kronborg, 2018).
Australia	1. Curriculum differentiation. 2. Ability grouping (opportunity classes). 3. Acceleration options. 4. Enrichment activities. 5. Independent learning. 6. Academic competitions. 7. Mentorships (Jung & Worrell, 2017). Utilises Gagné, Tannenbaum and Renzulli models of giftedness (Kronborg, 2018).	43 universities in Australia. Most universities accept gifted students as an acceleration option. 35 have no minimum age requirement. 33 participate in dual enrolment (Young, Rogers, & Ayres, 2007).	Innovative approaches but inconsistent implementation. Australian Curriculum: key goal is to promote equity and excellence (Kronborg, 2018). ACARA's educational policy emphasises flexibility: all state/territories have own organised departments of education that coordinate/fund education in government-organised schools.
South Australia	Revisions of gifted policy not substantial; policy never mandated in schools (Jarvis & Henderson, 2012).	Acceleration (grade skipping, subject acceleration) available in more than half of schools (Jarvis & Henderson, 2012). 3 specialised high schools provide accelerated academics (Kronborg, 2018). IGNITE program allows students to complete years 8–10 in 2 years (McCann, 2005).	Schooling for gifted students also provided by SA Catholic Education Office. Schools in independent sector develop own gifted policies/programs. Gifted students will be taught in mainstream classes in response to differentiated curriculum (Kronborg, 2018).
New South Wales	Opportunity classes: provide student challenge and guidance (75 primary schools; Kronborg, 2018).	Acceleration considered to be readily available (Jung & Worrell, 2017). 17 selective HS. 25 high schools with selective classes. Virtual stream for rural/remote locations.	Policy and implementation strategies for education for gifted and talented students began in 2004, the same year *A Nation Deceived: How Schools Hold Back America's*

(continued)

Table 2 (continued)

	Gifted and talented	Acceleration	Notes
		4 agriculture HS with selective placement. 75 primary schools with opportunity classes (Kronborg, 2018).	*Brightest Students* (Colangelo et al., 2004a, b) was published. Miraca Gross, one of the authors of *A Nation Deceived*, is professor emerita at the University of New South Wales.
Western Australia	School-based supplementary programs.	2 selective high schools. 17 selective academic secondary programs. Online selective academic program for rural areas. Primary Extension and Challenge (Kronborg, 2018).	Uses *Curriculum Framework* versus Iowa' Acceleration Scale (Assouline et al., 2009). SES and cultural considerations with resources, availability and selection (Kronborg, 2018).
Victoria	Aiming high (new strategy for gifted students)—as of 2017, not being implemented. Emphasis on early identification (Kronborg, 2018).	4 select-entry HS. 36 government secondary schools with select-entry accelerated programs. 2 senior schools (Kronborg, 2018). SEAL (Select Entry Accelerated Learning) in secondary schools (Plunkett & Kronborg, 2007).	Catholic Education Office advocates for gifted students in the Catholic sector, and independent school systems provide for highly able and gifted students (Kronborg, 2018).
Queensland	Prep to year 12 curriculum—specifies that teachers apply curriculum differentiation (Kronborg, 2018).	3 selective entry high schools (academics; Kronborg, 2018). Subject/grade acceleration considered to be appropriate option for gifted students (Jung & Worrell, 2017).	Provides general supporting info to teachers on identification, emphasis on multiple criteria (Kronborg, 2018).
Tasmania			Document for extended learning for gifted student procedures only addresses Personalised Learning Plan (PLP), which is collaboratively developed with student and family, and this procedure is also implemented in other states.

Implications and Future Directions

Academic acceleration in its many forms is well-supported by research, and there are several tools (e.g., the *Iowa Acceleration Scale*, Assouline et al., 2009; the Talent Search Model, Assouline & Lupkowski-Shoplik, 2012) that are effective in the decision-making process, yet the intervention remains underused in both general and gifted education settings. To a certain extent, this is because post-secondary institutions, where future teachers are prepared for the profession, tend not to recognise academic acceleration as either a service delivery model or a curriculum intervention. This is likely due to a variety of reasons (see Colangelo et al., 2004a, for an extensive discussion of the myths related to academic acceleration), including the fact that gifted education is not necessarily included in the general pre-service curriculum to which pre-service teachers are exposed (e.g., Kronborg, 2018). Similar issues were also uncovered in an exploratory qualitative case study of ten government secondary schools in NSW, Australia. Long, Barnett, and Rogers (2015) found that when schools had a documented gifted policy *and* the principal had previous training and/or a commitment towards giftedness, gifted programs were implemented more effectively and efficiently. Gross et al. (2011) set a hopeful tone; they reported that the ease of access via a free online pdf of *A Nation Deceived* (Colangelo et al., 2004a, 2004b) prompted many Australian educators to read the report and to 'try out' acceleration with one or more students. Gallagher, Smith, and Merrotsy (2011) found that teachers viewed subject acceleration more favourably than whole-grade acceleration, which may indicate another manner in which to introduce acceleration into a school or system. As a result of positive experiences with individual students, educators have been more likely to consider acceleration as one of the tools they have available to challenge other academically talented students (Gross et al., 2011). Gross et al. (2011) also found that access to continuing professional development programs that include some information about acceleration has encouraged more educators to view acceleration as something they may consider. Plunkett and Kronborg (2011) replicated that finding with pre-service teachers who changed their preconceived notions about acceleration as a result of training in gifted education. As Croft and Woods (2015) stated, "professional development in gifted education topics that include acceleration as an intervention is the glue that holds together appropriate opportunities for such students" (p. 96).

In New Zealand, teachers have limited access to specialist training in gifted education, both at the pre-service and in-service levels (Working Party on Gifted Education, 2001). Research commissioned by the Ministry of Education (Riley & Rawlinson, 2005) found that, while gifted education content was included by all six of the university-based initial teacher education (ITE) providers, there was considerable variation between institutions in terms of coverage, ranging from between two and five hours within compulsory inclusive education papers to optional full-semester specialised papers at both undergraduate and postgraduate levels. A national evaluation of schools' provision for gifted and talented students (ERO, 2008a) also highlighted the need for high-quality teacher professional development as a critical factor in building schools' capability to cater effectively for gifted learners. However, budget cuts to gifted education advisory support to schools in New Zealand since 2009 have significantly reduced opportunities for teachers to participate in school-based professional learning programs.

Conclusions

Academic acceleration, long recognised as a highly effective intervention, is undervalued and underused around the world. Two US-based publications (Colangelo et al., 2004a, 2004b) and the extensive update (Assouline, Colangelo, & VanTassel-Baska, 2015; Assouline et al., 2015) have significantly impacted the educational landscape with respect to academic acceleration. The research remains strong and unambiguous regarding the effectiveness of the intervention (see Colangelo et al., 2004b and Assouline et al., 2015 for a full discussion of the topic). Stanley's Talent Search Model (Assouline & Lupkowski-Shoplik, 2012; Assouline et al., 2018) offers a bastion of evidence in support of providing talented students with accelerated opportunities in specific content areas. The Iowa Acceleration Scale (Assouline et al., 2009) and evidence gathered by longitudinal studies on academic acceleration (e.g., Gross, 2006) provide specific information about making decisions about grade acceleration.

In this chapter, academic acceleration as practised in Australasia within the context of cultural values specific to Australia and New Zealand was discussed. It was found that adopting a relatively inclusive definition of giftedness, such as Australia has done through use of Gagné's (1995) Differentiated Model of Giftedness and Talent (DMGT), results in a broader talent pool of students. School districts that use broad definitions may benefit from tailoring specific interventions to match the broad range of academic needs found in a talent pool of students.

Both New Zealand and Australian educational policy for gifted education have been influenced by international trends, especially research in the United States. Policy is the bridge between the robust research supporting the various accelerative options and the implementation of one or more of the options (VanTassel-Baska, 2015). Carefully crafted policies based on research encourage reluctant administrators and teachers to use acceleration as an intervention. Policy, therefore, can help to translate the research into universal practice. Universal practice will ensure that the most vulnerable of students receive the intervention that will best meet their academic, psychological, and social-emotional needs.

Cross-References

- ▶ Australian Teachers Who Made a Difference: Secondary Gifted Student Perceptions of Teaching and Teacher Effectiveness
- ▶ Gifted Education in the Asia-Pacific: From the Past for the Future – An Introduction

▶ Gifted, Talented, and High-Achieving Students and Their Gifted Education in Mexico
▶ Innovative Practices to Support High-Achieving Deprived Young Scholars in an Ethnic-Linguistic Diverse Latin American Country
▶ Implementing the DMGT's Constructs of Giftedness and Talent: What, Why, and How?
▶ Put Them Together and See How They Learn! Ability Grouping and Acceleration Effects on the Self-Esteem of Academically Gifted High School Students
▶ Social and Cultural Conceptions and Perceptions: Part I Introduction
▶ Some Implications for the Future of Gifted Education in the Asia-Pacific
▶ The Development of Mana: Five Optimal Conditions for Gifted Māori Student Success

References

Anthony, G., Rawlins, P., Riley, T., & Winsley, J. (2002). Accelerated learning in New Zealand secondary school mathematics. *Australasian Journal of Gifted Education, 11*(2), 11–17.

Assouline, S. G., Colangelo, N., Lupkowski-Shoplik, A. E., Lipscomb, J., & Forstadt, L. (2009). *The Iowa Acceleration Scale Manual* (3rd ed.). Scottsdale, AZ: Great Potential Press.

Assouline, S. G., Colangelo, N., & VanTassel-Baska, J. (2015). *A nation empowered: Evidence trumps the excuses holding back America's brightest students* (Vol. 1). Iowa City, IA: The University of Iowa, The Connie Belin & Jacqueline N. Blank International Center for Gifted Education and Talent Development.

Assouline, S. G., Colangelo, N., VanTassel-Baska, J., & Lupkowski-Shoplik, A. (Eds.). (2015). *A nation empowered: Evidence trumps the excuses holding back America's brightest students* (Vol. 2). Iowa City, IA: The University of Iowa, The Connie Belin & Jacqueline N. Blank International Center for Gifted Education and Talent Development.

Assouline, S. G., Ihrig, L. M., & Mahatmya, D. (2017). Closing the excellence gap: Investigation of an expanded talent search model for student selection into an extracurricular STEM program in rural middle schools. *Gifted Child Quarterly*, 1–12. https://doi.org/10.1177/0016986217701833.

Assouline, S. G., & Lupkowski-Shoplik, A. (2012). The talent search model of gifted identification. *Journal of Psychoeducational Assessment, 30*(1), 45–59. https://doi.org/10.1177/0734282911433946

Assouline, S. G., Lupkowski-Shoplik, A. E., & Colangelo, N. (2018). Acceleration and the talent search model: Transforming the school culture. In S. Pfeiffer, M. Foley-Nicpon, & E. Shaunessy-Dedrick (Eds.), *APA handbook of giftedness and talent* (pp. 333–346). Washington, DC: American Psychological Association.

Australian Curriculum, Assessment, and Reporting Authority (ACARA). (2012). *The shape of the Australian curriculum, version 4.0*. Sydney: ACARA. Retrieved from http://www.australiancurriculum.edu.au

Bailey, S. (1997). 'Doing acceleration': Fast but not loose. In J. Chan, R. Li, & J. Spinks (Eds.), *Maximizing potential: Lengthening and strengthening our stride* (pp. 60–65). Hong Kong, China: The University of Hong Kong Social Sciences Research Centre.

Benbow, C. P., & Stanley, J. C. (1983). *Academic precocity: Aspects of its development* (No. 7). Baltimore, MD: Johns Hopkins University Press.

Bevan-Brown, J., & Taylor, S. (2008). *Nurturing gifted and talented children: A parent-teacher partnership*. Wellington, New Zealand: Ministry of Education.

Blackburn, A. M., Cornish, L., & Smith, S. R. (2016). Gifted English language learners: Global understandings and Australian perspectives. *Journal for the Education of the Gifted, 39*(4), 338–360. https://doi.org/10.1177/0162353216671834

Borland, J. H. (1989). *Planning and implementing programs for the gifted.* New York, NY: Teachers College Press.

Bourne, J. (2009). Gifted children left behind: Is New Zealand doing enough for our talented kids? *New Zealand Principals' Federation Magazine, 24*(2), 22.

Brody, L. E., & Muratori, M. (2015). Early entrance to college: Academic, social, and emotional considerations. In S. G. Assouline, N. Colangelo, J. VanTassel-Baska, & A. Lupkowski-Shoplik (Eds.), *A nation empowered: Evidence trumps the excuses holding back America's brightest students* (Vol. 2, pp. 153–167). Iowa City, IA: The University of Iowa, The Connie Belin & Jacqueline N. Blank International Center for Gifted Education and Talent Development.

Callahan, C. M., Moon, T. R., & Oh, S. (2017). Describing the status of programs for the gifted: A call to action. *Journal for the Education of the Gifted, 40*(1), 20–49. https://doi.org/10.1177/0162353216686215

Cao, T. H., Jung, J. Y., & Lee, J. (2017). Assessment in gifted education: A review of the literature from 2005 to 2016. *Journal of Advanced Academics, 28*(3), 163–203.

Cathcart, R. (2017). *Gifted education globally and in relation to Aotearoa-New Zealand. Report to the Ministry of Education.* Retrieved from http://www.giftedreach.org.nz/pdf/moe-report-gifted-education.pdf

Colangelo, N., Assouline, S., & Gross, M. U. M. (2004a). *A nation deceived: How schools hold back America's brightest students* (Vol. 1). Iowa City, IA: The University of Iowa, The Connie Belin & Jacqueline N. Blank International Center for Gifted Education and Talent Development.

Colangelo, N., Assouline, S., & Gross, M. U. M. (Eds.). (2004b). *A nation deceived: How schools hold back America's brightest students* (Vol. 2). Iowa City, IA: The University of Iowa, The Connie Belin & Jacqueline N. Blank International Center for Gifted Education and Talent Development.

Crawford, M. E. (2016). *Acceleration and gifted girls* (Doctoral thesis). Massey University, Palmerston North, New Zealand. Retrieved from http://mro.massey.ac.nz/handle/10179/9879

Croft, L. J., & Woods, S. (2015). Professional development for teachers and school counselors: Empowering a change in perception and practice of acceleration. In S. G. Assouline, N. Colangelo, J. VanTassel-Baska, & A. Lupkowski-Shoplik (Eds.), *A nation empowered: Evidence trumps the excuses holding back America's brightest students* (Vol. 2, pp. 87–98). Iowa City, IA: The University of Iowa, The Connie Belin & Jacqueline N. Blank International Center for Gifted Education and Talent Development.

Danylchuk, D. L. (2010). The importance of global awareness in an early entrance to university program. *Gifted Education International, 27*(1), 63–80. https://doi.org/10.1177/026142941002700111

Dare, L., Smith, S., & Nowicki, E. (2016). Parents' experiences with their children's grade-based acceleration: Struggles, successes, and subsequent needs. *Australasian Journal of Gifted Education, 25*(2), 6. https://doi.org/10.21505/ajge.2016.0012

Easter, A. M. D. (2019). *'Time on my side': Experiences of accelerated students who entered university early in Aotearoa New Zealand* (Doctoral thesis). University of Waikato, Hamilton, New Zealand. Retrieved from https://researchcommons.waikato.ac.nz/handle/10289/12362

Education Review Office. (2008a). *Schools' provision for gifted and talented students.* Wellington, New Zealand: Education Evaluation Reports. Retrieved from http://www.ero.govt.nz/National-Reports/Schools-Provision-for-Gifted-and-Talented-Students-June-2008

Education Review Office. (2008b). *Schools' provision for gifted and talented students: Good practice.* Wellington, New Zealand: Education Evaluation Reports. Retrieved from http://www.ero.govt.nz/National-Reports/Schools-Provision-for-Gifted-and-Talented-Students-Good-Practice-June-2008

Gagné, F. (1995). From giftedness to talent: A developmental model and its impact on the language of the field. *Roeper Review, 18*, 103–111. https://doi.org/10.1080/02783199509553709

Gagné, F. (2004). Transforming gifts into talents: The DMGT as a developmental theory. *High Ability Studies, 15*, 119–147. https://doi.org/10.1080/1359813042000314682

Gagné, F., & Gagnier, N. (2004). The socio-affective and academic impact of early entrance to school. *Roeper Review, 26*(3), 128–138. https://doi.org/10.1080/02783190409554258

Gallagher, S., Smith, S. R., & Merrotsy, P. (2011). Teachers' perceptions of the socioemotional development of intellectually gifted primary aged students and their attitudes towards ability grouping and acceleration. *Gifted and Talented International, 26*(1–2), 11–24. https://doi.org/10.1080/15332276.2011.11673585

Gold, M. I. (1965). *Education of the intellectually gifted*. Columbus, OH: Merrill Books.

Gross, M. U. M. (1992). The use of radical acceleration in cases of extreme intellectual precocity. *Gifted Child Quarterly, 36*, 91–99. Retrieved from https://www.davidsongifted.org/search-database/entry/a10099

Gross, M. U. M. (2004). *Exceptionally gifted children* (2nd ed.). London, England/New York, NY: Routledge Falmer.

Gross, M. U. M. (2006). Exceptionally gifted children: Long-term outcomes of academic acceleration and non-acceleration. *Journal for the Education of the Gifted, 29*(4), 404–429. Retrieved from https://files.eric.ed.gov/fulltext/EJ746290.pdf

Gross, M. U. M. (2009). Highly gifted young people: Development from childhood to adulthood. In L. V. Shavinina (Ed.), *International handbook on giftedness* (pp. 337–351). Dordrecht, Netherlands: Springer.

Gross, M. U. M., Urquhart, R., Doyle, J., Juratowitch, M., & Matheson, G. (2011). *Releasing the brakes for high-ability learners: Administrator, teacher, and parent attitudes and beliefs that block or assist the implementation of school policies on academic acceleration*. Sydney, NSW. Retrieved from https://education.arts.unsw.edu.au/media/EDUCFile/Releasing_the_Brakes_Overview_A4__Nov2011.pdf

Gross, M. U. M., & van Vliet, H. E. (2005). Radical acceleration and early entry to college: A review of the research. *Gifted Child Quarterly, 49*(2), 154–171. https://doi.org/10.1177/001698620504900205

Horsley, J. M. (2010, August 1). Gifts, talents and a roll of the dice. *New Zealand Education Review*. Retrieved from http://www.educationreview.co.nz/pages/section/article.php?s=Leadership+%26+PD&idArticle=19266

Horsley, J. M. (2013). Access and opportunity: Student perceptions of dual and early enrolment at university. *SET: Research Information for Teachers, 1*, 59–66.

Jarvis, J. M., & Henderson, L. (2012). Current practices in the education of gifted and advanced learners in South Australian schools. *Australasian Journal of Gifted Education, 21*(1), 5. https://doi.org/10.21505/ajge.2015.0018

Jarvis, J. M., Jolly, J. L., & Moltzen, R. (2018). Gifted education in Australia and New Zealand: Reflections and future directions. In J. L. Jolly & J. M. Jarvis (Eds.), *Exploring gifted education. Australian and New Zealand perspectives* (pp. 206–211). London, England: Routledge.

Jolly, J. L., & Robins, J. H. (2016). After the Marland Report: Four decades of progress? *Journal for the Education of the Gifted, 39*(2), 132–150. https://doi.org/10.1177/0162353216640937

Jung, J. Y., & Gross, M. U. M. (2015). Radical acceleration. In S. G. Assouline, N. Colangelo, J. VanTassel-Baska, & A. Lupkowski-Shoplik (Eds.), *A nation empowered: Evidence trumps the excuses holding back America's brightest students* (Vol. 2, pp. 199–208). Iowa City, IA: The University of Iowa, The Connie Belin & Jacqueline N. Blank International Center for Gifted Education and Talent Development.

Jung, J. Y., & Worrell, F. C. (2017). School psychological practice with gifted students. In M. Thielking & M. Terjesen (Eds.), *Handbook of Australian school psychology* (pp. 575–593). Zug, Switzerland: Springer International Publishing. https://doi.org/10.1007/978-3-319-45166-4_29

Jung, J. Y., Young, M., & Gross, M. U. (2015). Early college entrance in Australia. *Roeper Review, 37*(1), 19–28.

Kirby, A., & Townsend, M. A. R. (2005). Conversations with accelerated and non-accelerated gifted children. *APEX: The New Zealand Journal of Gifted Education, 14*(1). Retrieved from http://www.giftedchildren.org.nz/apex

Kronborg, L. (2018). Gifted education in Australia and New Zealand. In S. Pfeiffer, E. Shaunessey-Dedrick, & M. Foley-Nicpon (Eds.), *APA handbooks of giftedness and talent* (pp. 85–96). Washington, DC: American Psychological Association. https://doi.org/10.1037/0000038-006

Kulik, J. A. (2004). Meta-analytic studies of acceleration. In N. Colangelo, S. G. Assouline, & M. U. M. Gross (Eds.), *A nation deceived: How schools hold back America's brightest students* (Vol. 2, pp. 13–22). Iowa City, IA: The University of Iowa, The Connie Belin & Jacqueline N. Blank International Center for Gifted Education and Talent Development.

Lassig, C. J. (2009). Teachers' attitudes towards the gifted: The importance of professional development and school culture. *Australasian Journal of Gifted Education, 18*(2), 32–42. https://doi.org/10.21505/ajge.2015.0012

Long, L. C., Barnett, K., & Rogers, K. B. (2015). Exploring the relationship between principal, policy, and gifted program scope and quality. *Journal for the Education of the Gifted, 38*(2), 118–140. https://doi.org/10.1177/0162353215578279

Lubinski, D. (2004). Long-term effects of educational acceleration. In N. Colangelo, S. G. Assouline, & M. U. M. Gross (Eds.), *A nation deceived: How schools hold back America's brightest students* (Vol. 2, pp. 23–38). Iowa City, IA: The University of Iowa, The Connie Belin & Jacqueline N. Blank International Center for Gifted Education and Talent Development.

Lupkowski-Shoplik, A. E., Assouline, S. G., & Colangelo, N. (2015). Whole-grade acceleration: Grade-skipping and early entrance to kindergarten or first grade. In S. G. Assouline, N. Colangelo, J. VanTassel-Baska, & A. Lupkowski-Shoplik (Eds.), *A nation empowered: Evidence trumps the excuses holding back America's brightest students* (Vol. 2, pp. 53–73). Iowa City, IA: The University of Iowa, The Connie Belin & Jacqueline N. Blank International Center for Gifted Education and Talent Development.

Macleod, R. (2004). Educational provision: Secondary schools. In D. McAlpine & R. Moltzen (Eds.), *Gifted and talented: New Zealand perspectives* (2nd ed., pp. 239–262). Palmerston North, New Zealand: Kanuka Grove Press.

Marland, S. P., Jr. (1972). *Education of the gifted and talented: Report to the Congress of the United States by the U.S. Commissioner of Education and background papers submitted to the U.S. Office of Education* (2 Vols, Government Documents, Y4.L 11/2: G36). Washington, DC: U.S. Government Printing Office.

Martin, J. (2006). *Padfoot, Pup and Claire: Academic acceleration in Aotearoa* (Unpublished master's thesis). University of New England, Armidale, Australia.

Martin, J., & Merrotsy, P. (2006). Portfolio of artifacts: Promising data for qualitative research. *Australasian Journal of Gifted Education, 15*(1), 39–43.

McCann, M. (2005). Our greatest natural resource: Gifted education in Australia. *Gifted Education International, 19*(2), 90–106. https://doi.org/10.1177/026142940501900203

McClarty, K. L. (2015). Life in the fast lane: Effects of early grade acceleration on high school and college outcomes. *Gifted Child Quarterly, 59*(1), 3–13. https://doi.org/10.1177/0016986214559595

McDonough, E. (2004). Developing New Zealand's gifted educational policy. *Australasian Journal of Gifted Education, 13*(2), 35–40.

Merrotsy, P. (2002). *Appropriate curriculum for academically accelerated students: Listening to the case studies of gifted students* (Doctoral thesis). Northern Territory University, Darwin, Australia. Retrieved from http://espace.cdu.edu.au/view/cdu:6395

Ministry of Education. (2000). *Gifted and talented students: Meeting their needs in New Zealand schools*. Wellington, New Zealand: Learning Media.

Ministry of Education. (2007). *The New Zealand curriculum*. Wellington, New Zealand: Learning Media.

Ministry of Education. (2012). *Gifted and talented students: Meeting their needs in New Zealand schools*. Retrieved from http://gifted.tki.org.nz/

Ministry of Education. (2018). *Networks of expertise*. Retrieved from http://services.education.govt.nz/pld/networks/

Ministry of Education. (n.d.). *Te Kete Ipurangi: Gifted and talented education online* [website]. Retrieved from https://gifted.tki.org.nz

Moltzen, R. I. (2011). Historical perspectives. In R. Moltzen (Ed.), *Gifted and talented: New Zealand perspectives* (3rd ed., pp. 1–30). Auckland, New Zealand: Pearson.

Murphy, B. (1995). *Evaluation of a program of accelerated learning for gifted children at University High School, Melbourne, Australia*. (Unpublished doctoral dissertation). University of Melbourne, Melbourne, Australia.

National Assessment Program. (n.d.). *The National Assessment Program* [website]. Retrieved from http://www.nap.edu.au/home

National Association for Gifted Children & Council of State Directors of Programs for the Gifted. (2015). *State of the states in gifted education 2014–2015*. Washington, DC: Author.

New South Wales Department of Education and Training. (2004). *Guidelines for the use of strategies to support gifted and talented students*. Sydney, NSW: State of New South Wales Department of Education and Training. Retrieved from https://education.nsw.gov.au/policy-library/associated-documents/polgdl.pdf

New Zealand Government. (2003, December 18). *Departmental notice amending the National Administration Guidelines (2003-go8413)*. Wellington, New Zealand: New Zealand Gazette Office. Retrieved from https://gazette.govt.nz/notice/id/2003-go8413

New Zealand Qualifications Authority. (2017). *NCEA levels and certificates*. Retrieved from http://www.nzqa.govt.nz/qualifications-standards/qualifications/ncea/understanding-ncea/how-ncea-works/ncea-levels-and-certificates

Office of the Minister of Education. (2002). *Initiatives for gifted and talented learners*. Wellington, New Zealand: Ministry of Education.

Office of the Minister of Education. (2018). *Education portfolio work programme: Purpose, objectives and overview [Cabinet paper]*. Wellington, New Zealand: New Zealand Government. Retrieved from http://www.education.govt.nz/assets/Documents/Ministry/Information-releases/R-Education-Portfolio-Work-Programme-Purpose-Objectives-and-Overview.pdf

Park, G., Lubinski, D., & Benbow, C. P. (2013). When less is more: Effects of grade skipping on adult STEM productivity among mathematically precocious adolescents. *Journal of Educational Psychology, 105*(1), 176–198. https://doi.org/10.1037/a0029481

Parkyn, G. W. (1948). *Children of high intelligence, a New Zealand study*. Wellington, New Zealand: New Zealand Council for Educational Research.

Plucker, J. A. (2018). Policy and gifted education. In C. M. Callahan & H. L. Hertberg-Davis (Eds.), *Fundamentals of gifted education: Considering multiple perspectives* (2nd ed., pp. 504–514). New York, NY: Routledge.

Plunkett, M., & Kronborg, L. (2007). Gifted education in Australia: A story of striving for balance. *Gifted Education International, 23*(1), 72–83. https://doi.org/10.1177/026142940702300109

Plunkett, M., & Kronborg, L. (2011). Learning to be a teacher of the gifted: The importance of examining opinions and challenging misconceptions. *Gifted and Talented International, 26*(1–2), 31–46.

Pressey, S. L. (1949). *Educational acceleration: Appraisals and basic problems* (Bureau of Educational Research monographs, no. 31). Columbus, OH: Ohio State University Press.

Rawlins, P. (2000). *Acceleration in mathematics: Students' perspectives* (Master's thesis). Massey University, Palmerston North, New Zealand. Retrieved from http://mro.massey.ac.nz/handle/10179/6775

Riley, T., Bevan-Brown, J., Bicknell, B., Carroll-Lind, J., & Kearney, A. (2004). *The extent, nature and effectiveness of planned approaches in New Zealand schools for providing for gifted and talented students. Report to the Ministry of Education*. Palmerston North, New Zealand: Massey University. Retrieved from http://www.educationcounts.govt.nz/publications/schooling/5451

Riley, T., & Bicknell, B. (2013). Gifted and talented education in New Zealand schools: A decade later. *APEX: The New Zealand Journal of Gifted Education, 18*(1), Retrieved from http://www.giftedchildren.org.nz/apex

Riley, T., & Rawlinson, C. (2005). *An investigation of teacher education in gifted and talented education in New Zealand. Report to the Ministry of Education*. Palmerston North, New Zealand: Massey University.

Riley, T., & Rawlinson, C. (2006). Teacher education in gifted and talented education in New Zealand. In T. Riley & J. Bevan-Brown (Eds.), *Proceedings of the rising tides: Nurturing our gifted culture national gifted education conference* (pp. 80–85). Wellington, New Zealand, 3–5 August 2006. https://www.confer.co.nz/gnt/finalpapers1.pdf.

Riley, T., & Rawlinson, C. (2008). Gifted education in teacher education: Is it more than just a one-off lecture? In C. M. Rubie-Davies & C. Rawlinson (Eds.), *Challenging thinking about teaching and learning* (pp. 209–213). New York, NY: Nova Science Publishers.

Robinson, N. M. & the Davidson Institute Team. (2005a). *Considering the options: A guidebook for investigating early college entrance: Parent version*. Davidson Institute for Talent Development. Retrieved from http://print.ditd.org/young_scholars/Guidebooks/Davidson_Guidebook_EarlyCollege_Parents.pdf

Robinson, N. M. & the Davidson Institute Team. (2005b). *Considering the options: A guidebook for investigating early college entrance: Student version*. Davidson Institute for Talent Development. Retrieved from http://print.ditd.org/young_scholars/Guidebooks/Davidson_Guidebook_EarlyCollege_Students.pdf

Rogers, K. B. (2004). The academic effects of acceleration. In N. Colangelo, S. G. Assouline, & M. U. M. Gross (Eds.) *A Nation deceived: How schools hold back America's brightest students* (V. II., pp. 47–57). Iowa City, IA: The Connie Belin & Jacqueline N. Blank International Center for Gifted Education and Talent Development.

Rogers, K. B. (2015). The academic, socialization, and psychological effects of acceleration: Research synthesis. In S. G. Assouline, N. Colangelo, J. VanTassel-Baska, & A. Lupkowski-Shoplik (Eds.), *A nation empowered: Evidence trumps the excuses holding back America's brightest students* (Vol. 2, pp. 19–29). Iowa City, IA: The University of Iowa, The Connie Belin & Jacqueline N. Blank International Center for Gifted Education and Talent Development.

South Australia Department for Education and Child Development. (2016, June). *Policy: Gifted and talented children and students*. Retrieved from https://www.decd.sa.gov.au/sites/g/files/net691/f/gifted-talented-students-policy.pdf?v=1467090054

Southern, W. T., & Jones, E. D. (2015). Types of acceleration: Dimensions and issues. In S. G. Assouline, N. Colangelo, J. VanTassel-Baska, & A. Lupkowski-Shoplik (Eds.), *A nation empowered: Evidence trumps the excuses holding back America's brightest students* (Vol. 2, pp. 9–18). Iowa City, IA: The University of Iowa, The Connie Belin & Jacqueline N. Blank International Center for Gifted Education and Talent Development.

Southern, W. T., Jones, E. D., & Fiscus, E. D. (1989). Practitioner objections to the academic acceleration of gifted children. *Gifted Child Quarterly, 33*(1), 29–35. https://doi.org/10.1177/001698628903300105

Stanley, J. C. (1990). Leta Hollingworth's contributions to above-level testing of the gifted. *Roeper Review, 12*, 166–171.

Steenbergen-Hu, S., Makel, M. C., & Olszewski-Kubilius, P. (2016). What one hundred years of research says about the effects of ability grouping and acceleration on K–12 students' academic achievement. *Review of Educational Research, 86*(4), 849–899. https://doi.org/10.3102/0034654316675417

Swiatek, M. A. (2007). The talent search model: Past, present, and future. *Gifted Child Quarterly, 51*(4), 320–329. https://doi.org/10.1177/0016986207306318

Tapper, L. (2014). *'Being in the world of school'. A phenomenological exploration of experiences for gifted and talented adolescents* (Doctoral thesis). University of Canterbury, Christchurch, New Zealand. Retrieved from http://ir.canterbury.ac.nz/handle/10092/9057

Tapper, L. (2017, October 13). Where are the gifted learners in "inclusive education"? [Blog]. Retrieved from https://nzareblog.wordpress.com/2017/10/13/gifted-learners/

Tapper, L., & Riley, T. (2015). Turning rhetoric into reality. *Education Review: Sector Voices*, 34–35. Retrieved from https://issuu.com/apnedmedia/docs/edr-dec2015-e-edition

Townsend, M. A., & Patrick, H. (1993). Academic and psychosocial apprehensions of teachers and teacher trainees toward the educational acceleration of gifted children. *New Zealand Journal of Educational Studies, 28*(1), 29–41.

Townsend, M. (2011). The need to balance acceleration with enrichment in gifted education. In R. Moltzen (Ed.), *Gifted and Talented: New Zealand Perspectives* (3rd ed., pp. 252–275). Auckland, New Zealand: Pearson.

VanTassel-Baska, J. (2015). The role of acceleration in policy development in gifted education. In S. G. Assouline, N. Colangelo, J. VanTassel-Baska, & A. Lupkowski-Shoplik (Eds.), *A nation empowered: Evidence trumps the excuses holding back America's brightest students* (Vol. 2, pp. 43–51). Iowa City, IA: The University of Iowa, The Connie Belin & Jacqueline N. Blank International Center for Gifted Education and Talent Development.

Vialle, W., Ashton, T., Carlon, G., & Rankin, F. (2001). Acceleration: A coat of many colours. *Roeper Review, 24*(1), 14–19. https://doi.org/10.1080/02783190109554119

Wai, J. (2015). Long term effects of educational acceleration. In S. G. Assouline, N. Colangelo, J. VanTassel-Baska, & A. Lupkowski-Shoplik (Eds.), *A nation empowered: Evidence trumps the excuses holding back America's brightest students* (Vol. 2, pp. 73–83). Iowa City, IA: The University of Iowa, The Connie Belin & Jacqueline N. Blank International Center for Gifted Education and Talent Development.

Wardman, J. (2009). Secondary teachers', student teachers' and education students' attitudes to full year academic acceleration as a strategy for gifted students. *Australasian Journal of Gifted Education, 18*(1), 25–36.

Wardman, J. (2010). *Full-year acceleration of gifted high school students: The road not taken* (Unpublished doctoral thesis). University of Auckland, Auckland, New Zealand.

Wardman, J. (2015). To act or not to act? Academic acceleration worked in the past, so what's the current hold-up in NZ? *APEX: The New Zealand Journal of Gifted Education, 19*(1). Retrieved from http://www.giftedchildren.org.nz/apex.

Watts, G. (2006). Teacher attitudes to the acceleration of the gifted: A case study from New Zealand. *Gifted & Talented, 10*(1), 11–19. Retrieved from http://www.potentialplusuk.org/

White, V., & Riley, T. (2017). Advancing early childhood educators' access to professional learning in gifted and talented education. *New Zealand International Research in Early Childhood Education, 20*(2), 34.

Working Party on Gifted Education. (2001). *Report to the Minister of Education*. Wellington, New Zealand: Author.

Yeo, L. J. (2016). *Exploring the self-concept and sense of belonging of academically accelerated gifted male adolescents in a New Zealand context* (Master's thesis). Massey University, Manawatū, New Zealand. Retrieved from https://mro.massey.ac.nz/handle/10179/10416

Young, M., Rogers, K., Hoekman, K., van Vliet, H., & Long, L. C. (2015). Acceleration in Australia: Flexible pacing opens the way for early university admission. In S. G. Assouline, N. Colangelo, J. VanTassel-Baska, & A. Lupkowski-Shoplik (Eds.), *A nation empowered: Evidence trumps the excuses holding back America's brightest students* (Vol. 2, pp. 225–240). Iowa City, IA: The University of Iowa, The Connie Belin & Jacqueline N. Blank International Center for Gifted Education and Talent Development.

Young, M., Rogers, K. B., & Ayres, P. (2007). The state of early tertiary admission in Australia: 2000 to present. *Australasian Journal of Gifted Education, 16*(2), 15.

Young, M. O. (2010). *Admission to Australian universities for accelerated students: Issues of access, attitude and adjustment* (Doctoral thesis). University of New South Wales, Sydney, NSW. Retrieved from http://handle.unsw.edu.au/1959.4/45489

Ann Lupkowski-Shoplik, PhD, is the Administrator, Acceleration Institute and Research at the University of Iowa Belin-Blank Center. She founded and directed the Carnegie Mellon Institute for Talented Elementary Students (C-MITES) at Carnegie Mellon University for 22 years. She co-authored *Developing Math Talent: A Comprehensive Guide to Math Education for Gifted Students* and the *Iowa Acceleration Scale* and co-edited the 2015 publication on academic acceleration *A Nation Empowered: Evidence Trumps the Excuses Holding Back America's Brightest Students*.

Susan G. Assouline is the director of the Belin-Blank Center, holds the Myron and Jacqueline N. Blank Endowed Chair in Gifted Education and is a professor of school psychology. She is especially interested in identification of academic talent in elementary students. In 2015, she co-edited with Nicholas Colangelo, Joyce VanTassel-Baska and Ann Lupkowski-Shoplik the two-volume publication *A Nation Empowered: Evidence Trumps the Excuses Holding Back America's Brightest Students*. She is the 2016 recipient of the National Association for Gifted Children Distinguished Scholar award.

Cara Wienkes, B.A., is a doctoral candidate. in the University of Iowa's Counseling Psychology program and a graduate assistant at the University of Iowa Belin-Blank Center.

Ann Easter, PhD, is a consultant in gifted and talented education. Her doctoral research investigated the lived experiences of accelerated students who entered university early in Aotearoa New Zealand.

Gifted, Talented, and High-Achieving Students and Their Gifted Education in Mexico

9

Pedro Antonio Sánchez-Escobedo, Ana Karen Camelo-Lavadores, and Angel Alberto Valdés-Cuervo

Contents

Introduction	204
Overview of Mexico	204
History of Gifted Education in Mexico	205
Gifted, Talented, and High-Achieving Students	206
Programs and services in Mexico	209
Programs and Practices for Talent development	209
Programs for High-Achieving Students	210
Programs or Provisions for Gifted Students in Mexico	211
Research Implications and Future Directions	213
Conclusion	214
Cross-References	215
References	215

Abstract

This chapter describes the emergence and the historical development of gifted education in Mexico. A review and a critical analysis of actual educational policies related to identification and intervention processes in this field is presented. To better understand social perceptions of the gifted, we distinguish between the concepts of gifted, talented, and high-achieving students since these are often used interchangeably in Mexico. We analyse the relationship between

---

P. A. Sánchez-Escobedo (✉)
College of Education, Universidad Autónoma de Yucatán, Mérida, Yucatán, México
e-mail: psanchez@correo.uady.mx

A. K. Camelo-Lavadores
Universidad Autónoma de Yucatán, Mérida, Yucatán, México
e-mail: annykaren1@gmail.com

A. A. Valdés-Cuervo
Instituto Tecnológico de Sonora, Ciudad Obregón, Sonora, México
e-mail: angel.valdes@itson.edu.mx

© Springer Nature Singapore Pte Ltd. 2021
S. R. Smith (ed.), *Handbook of Giftedness and Talent Development in the Asia-Pacific*, Springer International Handbooks of Education,
https://doi.org/10.1007/978-981-13-3041-4_9

the social perception of these students and the services and programs available for them. Research in this field is summarised and reviewed. We argue that gifted education in Mexico should be separated from special education, and that investment in and implementation of programs and provisions for this elite group of students must be considered as a vehicle of economic development and national security.

Keywords

Mexico · Gifted · Talented · High-achieving students

The aims in this chapter are to:
1. Provide the context and an historical view of gifted education in Mexico.
2. Analyse the sociocultural perceptions and conceptualisation of gifted, talented, and high-achieving students in Mexico.
3. Review programs and services available to gifted students.
4. Establish the implications of research in future policy and services in this area.

Introduction

Many governments in developing countries have failed to recognise the strategic importance of servicing gifted and high-achieving students. Arguing economic delays and social vulnerability associated with poverty, governments seem to be more concerned with school failure and dropout rates (Secretary of Public Education [SEP], 2012). However, they do not realise that servicing gifted students may become an efficient strategy for social and economic development and thus a source of wealth and social advancement.

Heredia and Franco (2014) estimated that double the number of academically talented students in Mexico could lead to an increase in the gross domestic product (GDP) of 3.8 billion pesos by 2024, which represents more than 20% of the country's current GDP. Moreover, the literature reports that 44% of identified gifted students achieve a doctoral degree, compared to only 2% of the general population (Kell, Lubinski, & Benbow, 2013). Therefore, it seems to be socially accepted that gifted students make substantial contributions in their areas of knowledge such as publications of articles, patents, works of art, and the like (McClarty, 2015).

Overview of Mexico

Mexico, a country of nearly 120 million inhabitants and almost two million square kilometres, was the site of advanced Amerindian civilisations that came under Spanish rule for three centuries before achieving independence early in the nineteenth century. About 76% of the people live in urban areas and nearly 15% of the population has immigrated to the north. The official currency is the peso and the GNI per capita is US $9,040 (World Bank, 2017).

Schooling is compulsory for 12 years (National Institute of Statistic and Geography [INEGI], 2015), with an alarming dropout rate in high school that affects half of the teenagers between 15 and 18 years old (SEP, 2012). In Mexico, enrolment is particularly low in preschool (42%) and upper secondary schools (65%; National Institute of Educational Evaluation [INEE], 2016).

Indeed, only around 68% of students accessing the first grade will complete all nine years of basic education. Graduation rates in upper secondary are around 63% (INEGI, 2015) and only 32% of the population aged 18 and older in Mexico had accessed college level studies in 2015 (Mexican Senate, 2015). Public schools serve 90% of all students in the country at the basic education level and around 60% at college level (SEP, 2016). School governance is centralised at the national level with the SEP prescribing a compulsory universal curriculum and providing free textbooks in every corner of the country (Sánchez & Lisbona, 2018).

Mexico's public spending on education amounts to 6.2% of the country's gross domestic product (Center for Social Studies and Public Opinion [CESOP], 2015), about $28 billion dollars a year or almost a quarter of its government's programmable budget. The SEP and the teachers' union (SNTE) are the two main influencers in the educational policy area. International organisations, such as The World Bank and the Inter-American Development Bank also have a major and longstanding presence in Mexican education and their influence on policies and educational reform is significant considering their rather small contribution (350 million and 80 million USD, respectively) to the education budget: less than 5% (Inter-American Development Bank, 2013; World Bank, 2017).

Private foundations and parents still play a very limited role in educational policy and services. Policies and services for gifted, talented, and high-achieving students are scarce in a country with tremendous educational challenges.

History of Gifted Education in Mexico

As in many other countries, gifted education emerged as a distinctive branch within special education services under the assumption that both children with disabilities, as well as those with talents, presented specific special education needs. Thus, programs to develop giftedness and talent were mixed, administered by teachers with little training in gifted education, and a limited budget since attention and resources were focused mainly on services and materials for students with disabilities.

The first official program for the gifted was implemented early in 1980 as the model for servicing gifted students, best known as *Outstanding Skills and Abilities* (CAS). Student selection relied on nominations or recommendations from teachers and other education authorities who may not have accurate training to identify gifted students. Lack of teacher training in gifted education affects the quality of services because there is a prevalence of children without the potential to excel that consume resources of gifted programs. This first program focused on primary school students and was implemented only in 12 of the 32 federal states (SEP, 2006). It grouped students on a part-time basis to provide them with curricular enrichment. However, major flaws in screening students and follow-up assessment of program effectiveness soon caused disenchantment and discontinuation of programs.

The CAS program was cancelled in 1992 due to budget shortages and the introduction of a new educational model that emphasised educational integration as its central element (SEP, 2006). In 2002, the Mexican federal government invested, for the first time, in a research project specifically directed to yielding data to help understand available services for gifted children. Results indicated several problems. For instance, relative few gifted students were involved in gifted education programs. There was a lack of clear criteria and procedures for screening, and intervention was usually temporary and carried out by teachers without specific training in gifted education (Sánchez, Acle, De Agüero, Jacobo, & Rivera, 2003). In response, the federal government set up training programs for teachers to identify and provide proper attention to talented students. There was also a change in policy that discarded teachers' nominations from the screening of gifted students to a more systematic and structured assessment of the child, including standardised intelligence testing.

In 2007, the Senate amended the 41st article of the Mexican general law of education, recognising that gifted and talented students are valuable resources for the nation's progress, requiring the state to provide services for the full development of their potential. Lawmakers wanted to reduce the brain drain of talents towards the USA and Canada, and to promote the instalment of specific programs for gifted students across the country. A landmark in gifted education was achieved in 2010, when Mexican authorities published for the first time the guidelines for gifted acceleration (SEP, 2010). These guidelines resulted in educators taking relevant action to fight against prejudice and rejection of acceleration as an effective intervention for gifted students. Like gifted education policies in many other countries, in Mexico the discussion on services and financial support is marked by the explicit or implicit debate between the philosophical principles of Equality vs. Elitism (Brown & Wishney, 2017).

Nowadays, giftedness in Mexico is an underserved area in education that needs many transformations in policy and service to match the economic growth, competitiveness, and technological advancement of other countries (Sánchez, 2013).

Gifted, Talented, and High-Achieving Students

Perceptions of gifted students are mediated by several factors. Among those are the cultural contexts, belief systems, social perceptions, and the language used to refer to specific social groups. In the Spanish language, there are some difficulties in the ways we refer to gifted people. Various terms are often used interchangeably to label a gifted, talented, or high-achieving student. Likewise, the same term may be used to refer to various students' profiles.

In general, there is considerable semantic and conceptual confusion in Mexican-Spanish literature when discussing the gifted. From a sociocultural perspective, labelling is a key factor to understand the social and cultural perceptions of the talented and gifted in this country that result in misunderstandings in the way we identify and respond to these individuals. Furthermore, since labelling is at the bottom of attributions and expectations of these students, the analysis of the semantics used and the discourse to refer to the gifted is relevant to understand the social perceptions of these students (Berlin, 2009; Hertzog, 2003).

Terminology can illustrate some underlying assumptions of Mexican teachers regarding the origins and meaning of giftedness. Hence, in this section we address this terminology, we propose a few definitions, and we argue how best to use these terms in the school system for the purpose of screening, interventions, and classification. We attempt to characterise three major groups of students: talented, high-achievers, and gifted. Furthermore, we will elucidate the meaning and significance of each of these labels.

'Talent' is the first term we want to discuss as this refers to students who show specific abilities and strengths in performing a specific sport or a given art. Talent is rarely general and a particular student is almost always recognised in a specific field within sports (football, basketball, weight lifting, and the like) or in the arts (poetry, dance, music, and the like). Thus, in Mexico, we tend to divide talents into either physical, that is related to sports, or aesthetical, that is related to the arts (Hernández, 2003; Sánchez, Cantón, & Sevilla, 1997).

Talents are not usually nourished in Mexican schools. Students with physical potential are sent to highly specialised sports training centres, and they are expected to compete in national contests to select the best athletes for the Olympics and other related games. Unfortunately, educators in Mexican universities do not typically have a strategic interest in the field of sports, in contrast to the interest shown by academics in American universities (Groen & White, 2004). In the USA, college sports convey well-known financial, academic, and identity implications (Edmunds, 2014; Harper, 2009). For this, many athletes and students with physical potential in Mexico must choose between professional sports and college. In the same way, students with artistic potential are sent to special academies that specialise in diverse artistic domains and in many cases, they are encouraged to pursue a career in the artistic field such as acting, music, or dance (Palacios, 2006). They often come from families of artists and having parental support to pursue and develop an artistic talent is of great value. As in sports, in many cases students must delay or quit their artistic inclinations if they want to finish a college degree. Many scholars addressing the emerging field of gifted education and talent development would like to see both sports and arts embedded in the national education curriculum, as integral parts of the student's formation (e.g., Gutiérrez, 2004; Ibarrola, 2012). However, the investment needed seems to be against the national priority of assigning existing resources to decrease school failure rates in basic education and improve the number of students accessing and finishing high school (Official Journal of the Federation, 2013).

Our second term refers to 'high achievers'. These are students whose academic performance, efforts, and dedication distinguish them from average students (Valdés, Sánchez, & Valadez, 2015). These students score the highest grades and place themselves in the top 10% of the frequency distribution of grades. Effort, motivation, commitment, and hard work are usually associated with top grades (Bolling, Otte, Elsborg, Nielsen, & Bensen, 2018; Xu, 2018). High achievers are students who fit very well into the normal school system because they focus on mastery of the given curriculum at a very high level (DiFrancesca, Nietfeld, & Cao, 2016; Likupe & Mwale, 2016; Valadez et al., 2016). Additionally, Camelo-Lavadores (2018) demonstrated that high-achieving students have a positive social perception and that they are well accepted by their peers, particularly if they are women. Their success is attributed to effort and that they show higher academic self-efficacy.

Unfortunately, many teachers confuse gifted students with high achievers within the identification process. Past research (Deku, 2013; Machts, Kaiser, Schmidt, & Mollen, 2016; Neber, 2004) underlines that teacher nomination has a low reliability when trying to identify gifted students. Clearly, there are difficulties in recognising and accepting the epigenetic origin of giftedness, which is unrelated to the commitment and effort needed to be considered as a high achiever.

Finally, the most commonly confused term is 'gifted'. In the Spanish language, several terms are used to refer to gifted children. By using these terms without a clear sense of what sort of students need to be nominated, screening and services for students becomes confusing. Teachers, headmasters, and parents seem to have difficulties in distinguishing between high achievers, talented, and gifted students. Semantics in this context are very important. The label that applies in this context is to connote gifted student in the Spanish language in the traditional concept of academically gifted for the following reasons:

(a) It is biologically epigenetic in nature, which supports the students' high ability.
(b) Not every gifted student is a high achiever; some even are at risk of school failure due to boredom (gifted underachieving student).
(c) This label is helpful to distance teachers from perspectives of educational interventions based upon deficits or disability scenarios.
(d) The label 'academically gifted' implies specific educational interventions, for example acceleration or advanced placement.
(e) Clear criteria may be used to refer talented sportive and artistic students to services and support outside the school.
(f) The academically gifted label facilitates educational policy development focused to foster the skills of gifted students and protect these key intellectual assets for the country's economic and technological success.

In sum, the sociocultural perceptions of the gifted are important in setting clear-cut criteria for screening and planning of services for gifted students and to promote the social recognition of this rather small group of students. In Mexico, as Zacatelco (2005) broadly evidenced, the concept of giftedness remains unclear and training is needed both in research and in educational practice to distinguish between the concepts of talent and gift. "As some authors assert, giftedness may be as simple as the ability to solve real life problems in a creative manner" (Castro, Oyanadel, Paez, & Quintanilla, 2000 as cited in Sánchez, 2008, p. 88) or as complicated as an educational category with several abstruse inclusion criteria.

Terminology should help educators and parents to label gifted students in an unambiguous fashion. A gifted student has an inherited high ability in at least, but usually in more than one area of knowledge, and these abilities need to be nurtured and stimulated in the educational establishment. These high-ability students must have an IQ above 130 and demonstrate the ability to produce valuable outputs of an intellectual nature and be susceptible to becoming high achievers with the right motivation, challenge, and support (from differentiated enrichment or acceleration). Beyond intelligence, the term academically gifted must provide a framework to support understandings of giftedness and interventions for the gifted that fully develop the students' talent potential (Gagné, 2007; Reis & Morales-Taylor, 2010; Wong, 2002).

Programs and services in Mexico

According to the classification of students sketched in the previous section, this section will reiterate existing services and programs in three broad categories: (a) programs for talented students; (b) actions for high-achieving students; and (c) formal gifted education programs.

Programs and Practices for Talent development

In Mexico, two broad clusters of programs can be identified in this category. The first has to do with fostering and appraising athletic talents; the second regards art education and nurturing fine arts. Regarding sports, in early education physical activities are developed either for recreational purposes or for health concerns, considering that Mexico is the number one country in the world for child obesity. In high school, screening for students with physical qualities provides evidence of the emerging importance of college sports in Mexico (SEP, 2013). However, Mexico is still far from scouting, screening, fostering, and nurturing athletes for college as it is in the USA (Groen & White, 2004). Also, many Mexican adolescents with sporting abilities choose to quit school considering the financial advantages of practising professional sport in comparison with the financial expectations of completing a college degree. In Mexico, being able to speak English means that a person is usually paid more than having a college degree and not being able to speak English (Hernández, 2015).

Although federal and state governments have specific sports programs for high school and college students, based primarily in centres for athletic performance enhancement, these efforts have not proven to be as effective as initially planned (CESOP, 2012). Usually, these centres are full boarding schools, in which individual or small groups of students study under a tutor to complete and advance in high school or college along with the specific rigorous training in each sport. Strict daily training is complemented with curricular adaptations and special tests or the development of education projects that eventually are credited for the school year. However, there is a lack of systematic research and follow-up studies that may yield an objective balance of the benefits and risks of such intervention. There are also a number of undocumented vocational, emotional, and cognitive issues associated with this training that requires further investigation (Carrillo, 2012).

Likewise, arts receive little attention in the national curriculum. Children with artistic abilities are generally stimulated within their family contexts and supported by parents, many of whom are artists themselves (López-Aymes, Roger, & Durán, 2014). Artistic education and the cultivation of *fine arts* are usually related to extracurricular learning in private and public specialised academies alike (Lizcano & Sánchez, 2016). And, as with the sports, many students decide themselves to cultivate their artistic talent rather than completing a college degree. In contrast with the various centres for athletic performance enhancement, there are few artistic training programs in Mexico, with similar tutorial services, curriculum adaptations or recognised academic projects to guarantee grade completion and school advancement along with cultivating excellence in the arts (Yohary & Araujo, 2014).

It is clear from this brief analysis that the Mexican educational system must include arts and sports in the national curriculum and systematise the screening, referral, educational interventions, and monitoring of these students within the educational system. The mutually exclusive decision that many Mexican students confront—talent or degree—seems to be unfair and detrimental to the development of their full talent potential and the improvement of the country's talent wealth. Practices need to be implemented, such as pro-active talent searches in the communities and to state in the various official educational policy documents the need and importance of a balanced formation process in Mexican public schools that recognises activities related to the arts, physical education, and knowledge content in the official curriculum (Fajardo, 2003; Fernández, 2002).

Programs for High-Achieving Students

The most salient finding regarding programs for high-achieving students is the lack of them. Sánchez et al. (2003) have asserted that high achievers matter very little in classrooms where almost a third of the students are underachievers or have learning disabilities. Mexican teachers assume that high-achieving children need no extra attention and few attempts are directed to reinforce their effort and encourage higher goals in their educational lives (Camelo-Lavadores, Sánchez, & Pinto, 2017). There are a few programs that are based on enrichment activities that aim to foster scientific vocation, interest in college studies, and the establishment of long-term education goals towards graduate school (Zúñiga, 2013). Since they are often offered under the label gifted and talented students, these programs will be further depicted in the following section.

Several universities and colleges offer to their students some special curriculum adaptations with a higher difficulty level and extra-academic activities (Pozón, 2014). There are also many scholarships supporting these students, such as programs that apply exemption from tuition (Andraca, 2006). Moreover, there are several federal, state, and local organisations that promote scientific vocation through research and innovation activities for children and young students from elementary school to upper high school. One example is the *Early Development of Scientists* program that is held in the Yucatan to enhance students' scientific and technological knowledge (Secretariat for Research, Innovation and Higher Education Mexican [SIIES], 2017). Mexican educators need to promote policies with guidelines that promote more effective enrichment or acceleration practices for gifted students, as in many other countries, to incentivise high achievement, and value the students' commitment and achievement in the school context (Farkas, Duffet, & Loveless, 2008). Camelo-Lavadores (2018) reviewed research in Mexico that shows that high-achieving students have higher probabilities of vocational success, higher income, and finishing a college degree (ACT Solutions for College and Career Readiness, 2009). Thus, strategies such as honour charts, comprehensive grants for high achievers, and active recruitment of these students in elite public and private universities are needed (Chan, Frey, Gallos, & Torgler, 2014; Kool, Mainhard, Jaarsma, Brekelmans, & van Beukelen, 2016).

Programs or Provisions for Gifted Students in Mexico

Finally, let us review specific services and programs for gifted students in Mexico. In most cases, these services are provided to high-achieving, talented, or gifted students with no distinction between these three labelled groups of students. The lack of a comprehensive diagnosis based on psychometric and clinical evidence and the conceptual confusion regarding gifted students hinders the selection criteria for services and extra-curricular activities alike. Nonetheless, four major programs or provisions can be identified: enrichment activities, vocational orientation, competitions, and acceleration.

State governments, universities, and research centres organise several enrichment activities embedded in formal scientific formation programs. For example, many states organise a week for early training of scientists, under the tenet that future scientists can be identified early in middle school. These rather expensive programs have confusing selection criteria (i.e., either GPA or manifested interest in science), and they include several diverse activities such as experiments, field trips, and conferences. Indeed, these activities seem to be isolated in nature, they are costly, and few follow-up studies are carried out to assess their impact (Covarrubias & Marín, 2015). Hence, many gifted students are left behind, when their rightful place is taken by someone else (Armenta, 2008).

Beyond real training, there is an intention to foster vocations for scientific fields. Policies and provisions aim to foster interest and the pursuit of careers in Science, Technology, Engineering, and Mathematics (STEM) to increase the country's statute in innovations at the forefront (Estévez et al., 2018). Programs or provisions include scientific fairs, field trips, guest speakers, and role modelling through lectures by renowned scientists. Again, these actions are carried out with the general student population usually, and in our view, there is a lack of screening and inclusion criteria and a lack of evidence to judge the impact of these programs. Hence, there is a need for clear selection criteria and systematic assessment of potential candidates to existing programs.

Regarding competitions, several of them are organised yearly within the Mexican educational system to foster and nurture specific academic abilities. This is the case of the National Olympics in mathematics, the robotics games, spelling bee, and legal debate contests, just to give a few examples of well-publicised events (check, for instance: http://www.ommenlinea.org/).

These activities may be effective in identifying gifted high-achievers because they are based on their products or performance, and there is a meritocratic system involving external and objective judges. However, again, we could not identify follow-up studies or reports of objective evaluations of the effectiveness of these activities in our review. In fact, in our practice, we have heard many cases of lack of systematic recruitment of winners, follow-up of students, and long-lasting support that endures achievement in the long term. Hence, because of the above, we posit that policy for gifted and talent development in Mexico should establish clear long-term actions to transform the existing system of grants, based mostly in family income, towards a more comprehensive support system based on achievement and intellectual potential.

Regarding gifted students, scholars in the gifted education field around the world have fought against prejudice and resistance towards acceleration, despite the enormous amount of educational research arguing its benefits and low cost (e.g., see Assouline, Colangelo, & VanTassel-Baska, 2015; Colangelo, Assouline, & Gross, 2004). In Mexico, acceleration has been poorly implemented since 2012 when this intervention strategy was officially approved and guidelines for its implementation were published. Since then, efforts have been made to develop various intervention strategies in all 32 federal states. Problems, however, have impeded a true national policy to effectively serve these children (Carrillo, 2012). For example, we have observed that children with talents pertaining to art or sports usually do not get attention in the school system, and certainly programs and practices lack rigorous evaluations. In addition, services are lacking infrastructure, such as materials for testing, computer services and labs, and teachers who are either ill-trained in gifted education or new teachers replace them after they have completed training. Again, there is a need of educational research in the field that provides feedback to implement and improve intervention policy and practices (Valadez et al., 2015).

Intervention models in Mexico can be found in different texts (e.g., Granado, 2005; Zavala, 2006). However, these models are more theoretical than practical and more political in nature than technical. They usually emphasise the discourse rather than practices and techniques, and they all lack objective indicators of pertinence and efficiency (Yañez & Valdés, 2012). Indeed, one can conclude that services for the gifted in Mexico are just emerging and they need strong technical and logistical support.

Nonetheless, current intervention programs for gifted students in Mexico have made some improvements to the selection process. For many years, they were limited to 5th and 6th graders, except for various state or independent programs, such as the program of *Gifted Support in the State of Sinaloa* (ASES), which serves 270 gifted students at primary, secondary, and high school level throughout the north-western state of Sinaloa (López-Nevárez, 2015). Typically, once students complete sixth grade, services for gifted studies are terminated. A common complaint in servicing both gifted students and special education students is the lack of follow-up studies or the existence of indicators of program efficiency and the poor liability of personnel involved in existing services (Sánchez et al., 1997).

In sum, gifted education within Mexican educational policy has evolved without fully addressing practice. In general, the programs or provisions lack well-defined objectives or clear profiles of gifted and talented students, with little flexibility in intervention strategies, few assessment procedures, and scarce research on the subject (Valadez et al., 2015; Yañez & Valdés, 2012).

Finally, services for gifted students in Mexico should no longer be considered a branch of special education, and we lobby for changes in the programs and services for the gifted and talented. We have argued that gifted education should be an independent field of study, with its own theoretical and methodological endowment and that research results should be able to address the specific issues of these students. Gifted and talented students face educational challenges different to those in need of special education services. They do not need specialised personnel since they can be accelerated within the school, neither do they require expensive disability tools or assistive support. Gifted students instead need vocational guidance, financial support, and the opportunities to access higher education (Camelo-Lavadores, 2018). Furthermore, according to our view, gifted education in Mexico should be seen beyond the educational domain as a strategy for economic development and national security.

Research Implications and Future Directions

As an emerging field, little research has been formally carried out regarding gifted education in Mexico. In this section the authors will explore emerging trends in research in gifted education through a bibliometric and content analysis of the scientific production by screening for publications from 2013 to 2016. Forty-eight articles published in indexed journals related to the topic were found (e.g., Camelo-Lavadores et al., 2017; Chávez & Acle, 2018; Valdés, Sánchez, & Yáñez, 2013). Ninety percent were published in the Spanish language, and these studies were developed in only eight of the 32 Mexican states. Nearly half of the studies were carried out in basic education and mainly at elementary school level.

Research focused mostly on socio-affective aspects of gifted students (e.g., Cervantes, Valadez, Valdés, & Tánori, 2018; López-Ayme & Acuña, 2010; Valadez,

Borges, Ruvalcaba, Villegas, & Lorenzo, 2013), intervention strategies (e.g., Covarrubias & Marín, 2015; Nechar, Sánchez, & Valdés, 2016), and identification tools and processes (e.g., Valadez, Meda, & Zambrano, 2006; Valdés, Carlos, Vera, & Montoya, 2012; Zacatelco & Acle, 2009). There is a lack of research about teachers' competencies, views, and practice in gifted education that deserves immediate attention. Most of these studies had a quantitative approach (e.g., Cervantes et al., 2018; Sánchez, Park, Hollingworth, Misiunieve, & Ivanova, 2014; Valdés et al., 2013). Consistent with the emerging nature of this field, research interest of many studies was exploratory and descriptive with a correlational scope. A quarter of the studies were qualitative in nature, all with naturalistic approaches to better understand the situation of gifted students and their teachers (e.g., Martín, Medrano, & Sánchez, 2005; Sánchez, 2013; Sánchez et al., 2014; Valdés et al., 2015). Results usually argued for teacher training or the clarification of the concept of gifted, and only two studies were related to assessing the effects of acceleration of specific students (i.e., López-Nevárez, 2015; Sánchez & Medrano, 2010). In three studies, it was argued that Mexican teacher perception overvalues the child's academic potential as evidenced by testing of their abilities (e.g., Martín et al., 2005; Valdés, Vera, & Carlos, 2013).

In sum, research on gifted education in Mexico is emerging along with the implementation of services. It has obviously been affected by the lack of clarity in what Mexican educators view as gifted and the conceptual confusion between giftedness, talent development, and high achievement. There is the need for better communication between scholars in the field and practitioners who need to incorporate emerging knowledge into service in schools. Meanwhile, the views and perceptions of teachers, their accounts of educating gifted students, and partnerships with researchers seem to be valuable points to start investigating. On the other hand, teachers crave for knowledge, training, and guidance regarding gifted students' needs and challenges in their daily practice.

Conclusion

Mexico is a developing country with a huge educational system, threatened by high rates of dropout and school failure. The perception of gifted, talented, and high-achieving students within the context of Mexico has been discussed. The authors have argued that a definitional clarification of these three different types of students is needed before judging the pertinence of specific practices and services, as different programming and provisional options require different actions and policies. For instance, acceleration within the schools seems appropriate for academically gifted students, whereas activities in academies and specialised centres outside the school are needed for those with sports and artistic talents. High achievers deserve more attention to foster their academic excellence.

As an emerging field, gifted education needs to be separated from special education to have its own identity created. The future of gifted education in Mexico deserves government and institutional recognition that ensures that it will become an independent field of study with appropriate theoretical and methodological tools and procedures. To date, many gifted, talented, and high-achieving students remain invisible for teachers and educational authorities alike. Hence, gifted education needs to address the challenges of gifted students who may have the potential to have a tremendous impact in the country's future.

Cross-References

▶ Creativity Talent Development: Fostering Creativity in Schools
▶ Fostering and Developing Talent in Mentorship Programs: The Mentor's Perspectives
▶ Gifted and Twice-Exceptional Children in the South of the World: Chilean Students' Experiences Within Regular Classrooms
▶ Gifted Education in the Asia-Pacific: From the Past for the Future – An Introduction
▶ Identifying Gifted Learning in the Regular Classroom: Seeking Intuitive Theories
▶ Identifying Underrepresented Gifted Students: A Developmental Process
▶ Innovative Practices to Support High-Achieving Deprived Young Scholars in an Ethnic-Linguistic Diverse Latin American Country
▶ Put Them Together and See How They Learn! Ability Grouping and Acceleration Effects on the Self-Esteem of Academically Gifted High School Students
▶ Self-Nomination in the Identification Process of Gifted and Talented Students in Mexico
▶ Social and Cultural Conceptions and Perceptions: Part I Introduction
▶ Some Implications for the Future of Gifted Education in the Asia-Pacific

References

ACT Solutions for College and Career Readiness. (2009). *The path to career success: High school achievement, certainty of career choice, and college readiness makes a difference. Issues in college success*. Iowa City, IA: ACT.

Andraca, A. (2006). *Programas de becas estudiantiles. Experiencias latinoamericanas* [Student scholarship programs. Latin American experiences]. París, France: UNESCO.

Armenta, C. (2008). Educación incluyente para sobresalientes en las sociedades del conocimiento [Inclusive education for high achievers in the knowledge society]. *International Journal of Social Sciences & Humanities, 18*(1), 109–131. Retrieved from http://www.redalyc.org/pdf/654/65411190006.pdf

Assouline, S. G., Colangelo, N., & VanTassel-Baska, J. (2015). A nation empowered: Evidence trumps the excuses holding back America's brightest students. In *The Connie Belin & Jacqueline N. Blank International Center for Gifted Education and Talent Development*. Iowa City, IA: The University of Iowa.

Berlin, J. E. (2009). It's all a matter of perspective: Student perceptions on the being labeled gifted and talented. *Roeper Review, 31*, 217–223. https://doi.org/10.1080/02783190903177580

Bolling, M., Otte, C. R., Elsborg, P., Nielsen, G., & Bertsen, P. (2018). The association between education outside the classroom and students' school motivation. Result from a one school-year quasi-experiment. *International Journal of Educational Research, 89*, 22–35. https://doi.org/10.1016/j.ijer.2018.03.004

Brown, E., & Wishney, L. (2017). Equity and excellence: Political forces in the education of gifted Students in the United States and abroad. *Global Education Review, 4*, 22–33. Retrieved from https://files.eric.ed.gov/fulltext/EJ1137995.pdf

Camelo-Lavadores, A. K. (2018). *Percepción social del alumno con alto rendimiento académico* [Social perception of high achieving students] (Doctoral thesis). Doctorate in Social Sciences, Autonomous University of Yucatan, Mérida Yucatán México.

Camelo-Lavadores, A. K., Sánchez, P., & Pinto, J. (2017). Academic self-efficacy of high achieving student in Mexico. *Journal of Curriculum and Teaching, 6*, 84–89. https://doi.org/10.3430/jct.v6n2p84

Carrillo, P. (2012). *Apoyos educativos en los centros de alto rendimiento académico de Yucatán* [Educational support in the centers of high academic performance of Yucatan]. Unpublished master Thesis, Autonomous University of Yucatan, Yucatán, México.

Castro, P., Oyanadel, C., Paez, A., & Quintanilla, R. (2000). *Implicaciones de una educación especial para superdotados* [Implications of a special education for the gifted]. Retrieved from http://www.geocities.com/Athens/Thebes/1663/pablo1.htm

Center for Social Studies and Public Opinion. (2012). *Práctica deportiva en México* [Sports practice in Mexico]. Ciudad de México, México: CESOP.

Center for Social Studies and Public Opinion. (2015). *Evaluación del gasto educativo en México* [Evaluation of educational spending in Mexico]. Ciudad de México, México: CESOP.

Cervantes, D., Valadez, M., Valdés, A., & Tánori, J. (2018). Diferencias en autoeficacia académica, bienestar psicológico y motivación al logro en estudiantes universitarios con alto y bajo desempeño académico [Differences in academic self-efficacy, psychological well-being and achievement motivation in university students with high and low academic performance]. *Psicología desde el Caribe, 35*, 1–10. https://doi.org/10.14482/psdc.35.1.11154

Chan, H., Frey, B., Gallus, J., & Torgler, B. (2014). Academic honors and performance. *Labour Economics, 31*, 188–204. https://doi.org/10.1016/j.labeco.2014.05.005

Chávez, B. I., & Acle, G. (2018). Niños con altas capacidades: Análisis de las variables familiares implicadas en el desarrollo del potencial [Children with high capacities: Analysis of family variables involved in the development of potential]. *Electronic Journal of Research in Educational Psychology, 16*, 273–300. Retrieved from http://ojs.ual.es/ojs/index.php/EJREP/article/view/2094

Colangelo, N., Assouline, S., & Gross, M. (2004). *A nation deceived: How schools hold back America's brightest minds*. Iowa City, IA: The University of Iowa.

Covarrubias, P., & Marín, R. (2015). Evaluación de la propuesta de intervención para estudiantes sobresalientes: Caso Chihuahua, México [Evaluation of the proposed intervention for gifted: Case Chihuahua, Mexico]. *Actualidades Investigativas en Educación, 15*(3), 1–32. Retrieved from http://www.scielo.sa.cr/pdf/aie/v15n3/1409-4703-aie-15-03-00206.pdf

Deku, P. (2013). Teacher nomination of gifted and talented children: A study of basic and senior high schools in the Central Region of Ghana. *Journal of Education and Practice, 4*(18), 1–7. Retrieved from https://www.iiste.org/Journals/index.php/JEP/article/download/7815/7879

DiFrancesca, D., Nietfeld, J. L., & Cao, L. (2016). A comparison of high and low achieving students on self-regulated learning variables. *Learning and Individual Differences, 45*, 228–236. https://doi.org/10.1016/j.lindif.2015.11.010

Edmunds, M. (2014). The financial gap between athletic scholarships and athlete expenses. *Sport Management Undergraduate, 5*, 1–38. Retrieved from https://fisherpub.sjfc.edu/cgi/viewcontent.cgi?referer=https://www.google.com.mx/&httpsredir=1&article=1006&context=sport_undergrad

Estévez, E., Parra-Pérez, L., González, E., Valdés, A., Durand, J., Lloyd, M., & Martínez, J. (2018). Moving from international ranking to Mexican higher education's real progress: A critical perspective. *Cogent Education, 5*, 1–14. https://doi.org/10.1080/2331186X.2018.1507799

Fajardo, V. (2003). Situación y desafíos de la enseñanza del arte en América Latina y el Caribe. In UNESCO (Ed.), *Métodos contenidos y enseñanza de las artes en Latinoamérica y el Caribe* [Content methods and teaching of the arts in Latin America and the Caribbean] (pp. 9–14). París, France: UNESCO. Retrieved from http://unesdoc.unesco.org/images/0013/001333/133377s.pdf

Farkas, S., Duffett, A., & Loveless, T. (2008). *High-achieving students in the era of no child left behind*. Washington, DC: Thomas B. Fordham Institute.

Fernández, A. (2002). La educación artística y musical en México: incompleta, elitista y excluyente [Artistical and musical education in Mexico: incomplete, elitist and exclusive]. *Cuadernos Interamericanos de Investigación en Educación Musical, 2*, 87–100. Retrieved from http://www.revistas.unam.mx/index.php/cem/article/view/7322

Gagné, F. (2007). Ten commandments for academic talent development. *Gifted Child Quarterly, 51*, 93–118. https://doi.org/10.1177/0016986206296660

Granado, M. (2005). *El niño superdotado* [The gifted childen]. Madrid, Spain: Abecedario.

Groen, J. A., & White, M. J. (2004). In state versus out of state: The divergence of interest between public universities and state government. *Journal of Public Economics, 88*, 1793–1814. https://doi.org/10.1016/j.pubeco.2003.07.005

Gutiérrez, M. (2004). El valor del deporte en la educación integral del ser humano [The value of sport in the integral education of the human being]. *Revista de Educación*, (335), 105–126. Retrieved from http://www.revistaeducacion.mec.es/re335/re335_10.pdf

Harper, S. R. (2009). Race, interest convergence and transfer outcomes for black male student athletes. *New Directions for Community Colleges, 147*, 29–37. https://doi.org/10.1002/cc.375

Heredia, B., & Franco, E. (2014). *La brecha de Talento en México y sus costos económicos* [The talent gap in Mexico and its economic costs]. Ciudad de México, México: Centro de Investigación y Docencia Económicas.

Hernández, M. (2003). *La capacidad sobresaliente. Una necesidad educativa especial en todos los sujetos* [Outstanding ability A special educational need in all subjects]. Retrieved from http://quadernsdigitals.net/datos_web/articles/educar/numero11/capacidad.htm

Hernández, L. (2015). Hablar inglés mejora sueldo y abre puertas [Speaking English improves your salary]. The Excelsior, pp. A6. Retrieved from https://www.excelsior.com.mx/nacional/2015/03/05/1011730

Hertzog, N. (2003). Impact of gifted programs from the students' perspectives. *Gifted Child Quarterly, 47*, 131–143. https://doi.org/10.1177/001698620304700204

Ibarrola, M. (2012). Los grandes problemas del sistema educativo mexicano. *Perfiles Educativos, 34*, 16–28. Retrieved from http://www.scielo.org.mx/scielo.php?script=sci_arttext&pid=S0185-26982012000500003&lng=es&tlng=es.

Inter-American Development Bank. (2013). *IDB country strategy with Mexico*. Retrieved diciembre from http://idbdocs.iadb.org/wsdocs/getdocument.aspx?docnum=38281503

Kell, H. J., Lubinski, D., & Benbow, C. P. (2013). Who rises to the top? Early indicators. *Psychological Science, 24*, 648–659. https://doi.org/10.1177/0956797612457784

Kool, A., Mainhard, M., Jaarsma, A., Brekelmans, M., & van Beukelen, P. (2016). Academic success and early career outcomes: Can honors alumni be distinguished from non-honors alumni? *High Ability Studies, 27*, 179–192. https://doi.org/10.1080/13598139.2016.1238818

Likupe, G., & Mwale, M. (2016). The study of attributions of low achievers and high achievers about the perceived courses of their success and failure: The case of adolescent students in secondary school-Malawi. *Journal of Child and Adolescent Behavior, 4*, 2–4. https://doi.org/10.4172/2375-4494.1000312

Lizcano, P., & Sánchez, P. (2016). Personality traits and life experiences influencing highly creative people: Six life stories. *Journal of Special & Gifted Education, 3*(1), 93–108. Retrieved from https://www.researchgate.net/publication/307509621_Personality_traits_and_life_experiences_influencing_highly_creative_people_Six_life_stories

López-Aymes, G., & Acuna, S. R. (2010). Desarrollo emocional de estudiantes con altas capacidades [Emotional development of students with high capacities]. *Ideacción, 31*, 366–379.

López-Aymes, G., Roger, S., & Durán, G. G. (2014). Families of gifted children and counselling program: A descriptive study in Morelos, Mexico. *Journal of Curriculum and Teaching, 3*, 54–62. https://doi.org/10.5430/jct.v3n1p54

López-Nevárez, V. (2015). Programa apoyo a sobresalientes en el estado de Sinaloa: una atención oportuna al talento [Support program for outstanding students in the state of Sinaloa: Timely attention to talent]. *Ra Ximhai, 11*(3), 19–34. Retrieved from http://www.redalyc.org/html/461/46135409002/

Machts, N., Kaiser, J., Schmidt, F. T., & Muller, J. (2016). Accuracy of teachers' judgments of students' cognitive abilities: A meta-analysis. *Educational Research Review, 19*, 85–103. https://doi.org/10.1016/j.edurev.2016.06.003

Martín, S., Medrano, R., & Sánchez, P. (2005). Necesidades de capacitación de docentes y estudiantes de de educación primaria para la detección de niños con aptitudes y capacidades sobresalientes [Training needs of primary school teacher and students for the detection of children with oustanding aptitudes and capabilities]. *Educación y Ciencia, 9*(18), 55–66.

McClarty, K. (2015). Early to rise: the effects of acceleration on occupational prestige, earnings, and satisfaction. In S. Assouline, N. Colangelo, J. VanTassel-Baska, & A. Lupkowski-Shoplike (Eds.), *A nation empowered: Evidence trumps the excuses holding back America's brightest students* (pp. 171–180). Iowa City, IA: Belin-Blank Center.

Mexican Senate. (2015, julio 12). *Cobertura de educación superior en México inferior a la de otros países de América Latina: IBD* [Higher education coverage in Mexico lower than that of other Latin American countries: IBD]. Retrieved noviembre from http://comunicacion.senado.gob.mx/index.php/informacion/boletines/21714-2015-07-11-00-01-22.html

National Institute of Educational Evaluation (2016). *Panorama Educativo de México 2016. Indicadores del Sistema Educativo Nacional. Educación Básica y Media Superior* [Educational Panorama of Mexico 2016. Indicators of the National Educational System. Basic Education and High School]. Mexico: INEE.

National Institute of Statistic and Geography. (2015). *Encuesta Intercensal 2015* [Intercensal survey 2015]. Retrieved from http://www.beta.inegi.org.mx/proyectos/enchogares/especiales/intercensal/

Neber, H. (2004). Teacher identification of students for gifted programs: Nominations to a summer school for highly-gifted students. *Psychology Science, 46*(3), 348–362. Retrieved from http://psycnet.apa.org/record/2005-05211-005

Nechar, E., Sánchez, P., & Valdés, A. (2016). Desarrollo de un programa de orientación con padres de estudiantes sobresalientes [Development of an orientation program with parents of outstanding students]. In M. Valadez, G. López, M. Borges, J. Betancourt, & R. Zambrano (Eds.), *Programas de intervención para niños con altas capacidades y su evaluación* (pp. 119–126). Ciudad de México, México: Manual Moderno.

Official Journal of Federation. (2013). *Programa Sectorial de Educación 2013–2018* [Sectoral Education Program 2013–2018]. Ciudad de México, México: SEGOB. Retrieved from http://www.dof.gob.mx/nota_detalle.php?codigo=5326569&fecha=13/12/2013

Palacios, L. (2006). El valor del arte en el proceso educativo [The value of art in the educational process]. *Reencuentro*, (46), 1–21. Retrieved from http://www.redalyc.org/articulo.oa?id=34004607

Pozón, J. (2014). Los estudiantes universitarios ante las actividades extracurriculares. *Anduli Revista Andaluza de Ciencias Sociales*, (13), 137–150. https://doi.org/10.12795/anduli.2014.i13.08

Reis, S., & Morales-Taylor, M. (2010). From high potential to gifted performance: encouraging academically talented urban students. *Gifted Child Today, 33*, 28–38. https://doi.org/10.1177/107621751003300408

Sánchez, P. (2008). Methods and procedures in screening gifted Mayan students, *Gifted and Talented International, 23*(1), 87–96. Retrieved from http://www.templeton fellows.org/projects/docs/screening_gifted_mayans.pdf

Sánchez, P. (2013). Forewords. In P. Sánchez (Ed.), *Talent development around the world* (pp. 19–28). Mérida, Yucatán, México: Universidad Autónoma de Yucatán.

Sánchez, P., Acle, G., De Agüero, A., Jacobo, M., & Rivera. (2003). *Aprendizaje y desarrollo. Estados del conocimiento en educación* [Learning and development States of knowledge in education]. México: Consejo Mexicano de Investigación Educativa.

Sánchez, P., Cantón, M., & Sevilla, D. (1997). *Compendio de educación especial* [Special education compendium]. Ciudad de México, México: Manual Moderno.

Sánchez, P., & Lisbona, M. (2018). Education and Nationalism in Mexico. In *Nationalism and nationlaism movements: Global attitudes, emergin patterns and impact on immigration*. New York, NY: Nova Sciences.

Sánchez, P., & Medrano, R. (2010). Un test académico para la acreditación y el avance de la colocación (aceleración) de estudiantes sobresalientes en México [Academic test for the accreditacion and advanced location (acceleration) of gifted children in Mexico]. *Ideaccion, 31*, 1–8.

Sánchez, P., Park, K., Hollingworth, L., Misiunieve, J., & Ivanova, L. (2014). A cross-comparative international study on the concept of wisdom. *Gifted Education International, 30*, 228–236. https://doi.org/10.1177/0261429413486575

Secretariat for Research, Innovation and Higher Education Mexican. (2017). *Secretaría de Investigación, Innovación y Educación Superior* [Secretariat for Research, Innovation and Higher Education]. Retrieved from http://www.siies.yucatan.gob.mx/programas.php

Secretary of Public Education. (2006). *Propuesta de intervención: atención educativa a alumnos y alumnas con aptitudes sobresalientes* [Intervention proposal: educational attention to students with outstanding aptitudes]. Retrieved from http://www.educacionepecial.sep.gob.mx/pdf/aptitudes/intervencion/Propuesta_inter.pdf

Secretary of Public Education. (2010). *Lineamiento para la acreditación, promoción y certificación anticipada de alumnos con aptitudes sobresalientes en educación básica* [Guidelines for the accreditation, promotion and advance certification of students with outstanding skills in basic education]. Ciudad de México, México: SEP.

Secretary of Public Education. (2012). *Reporte de la Encuesta Nacional de Deserción en la Educación Media Superior* [Report of the National Survey of High School Dropout]. Mexico: SEP.

Secretary of Public Education. (2013). *Informe sectorial 1: Educación física y deporte en el sistema educativo. Deporte Universitario* [Sector report 1: Physical education and sport in the education system. University Sports]. Ciudad de México, México: SEP.

Secretary of Public Education. (2016). *Estadística del Sistema* [System statistics]. Ciudad de México, México: SEP.

Valadez, M., Borges, M., Ruvalcaba, N., Villegas, K., & Lorenzo, M. (2013). Inteligencia emocional y su relación con el género, desempeño académico y capacidad intelectual del alumnado universitario [Emotional intelligence and its relationship with gender, academic performance and intellectual abilities of undergraduates]. *Electronic Journal of Research in Educational Psychology, 11*(30), 395–412. Retrieved from http://www.redalyc.org/articulo.oa?id=293128 257005

Valadez, M., Meda, R., & Zambrano, R. (2006). Identificación de ninos sobresalientes que estudian en escuelas públicas [Identification of gifted children in public school]. *Revista de Educación y Desarrollo, 5*, 39–45. Retrieved from http://www.cucs.udg.mx/revistas/edu_desarrollo/anteriores/5/005_Valadez.pdf

Valadez, M., Valdés, A., Aguiñaga, L., Morales, J., Cervantes, D., & Zambrano, R. (2016). Diferencias en el locus de control y la motivación al logro en estudiantes de secundaria con altas habilidades intelectuales y promedio [Differences in locus of control and achievement motivation in high school students with high intellectual abilities and high average]. *Revista de Educación y Desarrollo, 37*, 33–38. Retrieved from http://www.cucs.udg.mx/revistas/edu_desarrollo/anteriores/37/37_Valadez.pdf

Valadez, M., Valdés, A., Galan, M., López, G., Wendlant, T., & Reyes, A. (2015). Analysis of the scientific productivity of Mexican researchers on the topic of gifted students. *British Journal of Education, 8*(4), 216–226. https://doi.org/10.9734/BJESBS/2015/16947

Valdés, A., Carlos, E., Vera, J., & Montoya, G. (2012). Propiedades psicométricas para medir relaciones familiares en adolescentes intelectualmente sobresalientes [Psychometric properties of an instrument to measure relationships family members in intellectually outstanding adolescents]. *Pensamiento Psicológico, 10*(1), 39–50.

Valdés, A., Sánchez, P., & Valadez, M. (2015). Gender differences in self-concept, locus of control, and goal orientation in Mexican high-achieving students. *Gifted and Talented International, 19* (1–2), 19–24. https://doi.org/10.1080/15332276.2015.1137451

Valdés, A., Sánchez, P., & Yáñez, A. (2013). Perfiles de estudiantes mexicanos con aptitudes intelectuales sobresalientes [Psychological profiles of Mexican gifted students]. *Acta Colombiana de Psicología, 16*(1), 25–33.

Valdés, A., Vera, J., & Carlos, E. (2013). Variables que diferencian a estudiantes de bachillerato con y sin aptitudes intelectuales sobresalientes [Variables that differentiate baccalaureate students with and without outstanding intellectual aptitudes]. *Revista Electrónica de Investigación Educativa, 15*(3). Retrieved from http://redie.uabc.mx/index.php/redie/article/view/562/841

Wong, K. (2002). Catering for the needs of gifted and talented students by defining an appropiate curriculum. *Hong Kong Teachers' Centre Journal, 1*, 166–171. Retrieved from https://www.edb.org.hk/hktc/download/journal/j1/2_1.2.pdf

World Bank. (2017). *Mexico School Based Management Project*. Retrieved from http://projects.worldbank.org/P147185?lang=en

Xu, J. (2018). Reciprocal effects on homework self-concept, interest, effort, and math achievement. *Contemporary Educational Psychology, 55*, 44–52. https://doi.org/10.1016/j.cedpsych.2018.09.002

Yañez, A., & Valdés, A. (2012). Políticas públicas y modelos para la identificación y atención de estudiantes intelectualmente sobresalientes en México. In A. Valdés & J. Vera (Eds.), *Estudiantes intelectualmente sobresalientes* [Intellectually outstanding students] (pp. 141–156). Ciudad de México, México: Pearson.

Yohary, A., & Araujo, C. (2014). Retos de la educación artística en el siglo XXI en México [Challenges in the artistic education in the XXI century in Mexico]. *Universita Ciencia. Revista Electrónica de Investigación de la Universidad de Xalapa, 3*(8), 59–69. Retrieved from https://ux.edu.mx/wp-content/uploads/Investiga/Revistas/Revista%2008/Revista%2008/06_Retos%20de%20la%20educ.%20art.pdf

Zacatelco, F. (2005). *Modelo para la identificación de niños sobresalientes en las escuelas de educación primaria* [Model for the identification of outstanding children in primary schools]. Ciudad de México, México: Universidad Autónoma de México.

Zacatelco, F., & Acle, G. (2009). Validación de un modelo de identificación de la capacidad sobresalientes en estudiantes de primarias [Validation of an outstanding capacity identification model in elementary students]. *Revista Mexicana de Investigación Psicológica, 1*(1), 41–53. Retrieved from http://www.revistamexicanadeinvestigacionenpsicologia.com/article/view/91/4

Zavala, M. (2006). Modelos teóricos de la superdotación, el talento y las aptitudes sobresalientes. In M. Valadez, J. Betancourt, & M. Zavala (Eds.), *Alumnos superdotados y Talentosos. Identificación, evaluación e intervención. Una perspectiva para docentes* (Gifted and talented students. Identification, evaluation, and intervention. A perspective from teacher) (pp. 25–35). Ciudad de México, México: Manual Moderno.

Zúñiga, M. (2013). Las vocaciones científicas y tecnológicas en los jóvenes con aptitudes sobresalientes y talentosos, la experiencia del Programa de Difusión y Divulgación de la Ciencia del Consejo de Ciencia y Tecnología del Estado de Hidalgo [The scientific and technological vocations in young people with outstanding and talented skills, the experience of the Science Dissemination and Dissemination Program of the Council of Science and Technology of the State of Hidalgo]. *Revista Iberoamericana para la Investigación y el Desarrollo Educativo* (10), 1–24. Retrieved from http://ride.org.mx/1-11/index.php/RIDESECUNDARIO/article/viewFile/492/483

Pedro Antonio Sánchez-Escobedo has carried out extensive research on intelligence in Mexico, and he is a pioneer of research in gifted education. Since 1992, he has belonged to the prestigious Mexican National System of Research.

Ana Karen Camelo-Lavadores is a doctoral student and research assistant. Her dissertation work focuses on high achieving students.

Angel Alberto Valdés-Cuervo is originally from Cuba. Dr Valdés is a full professor and recognised researcher at the Department of Education in ITSON. He has published several original research manuscripts. He has been member of the National System of Researchers of Mexico since 2013.

Innovative Practices to Support High-Achieving Deprived Young Scholars in an Ethnic-Linguistic Diverse Latin American Country

10

Sheyla Blumen

Contents

Introduction	224
The Highly Able in Peru	225
What Does the Research Suggest?	227
Provisions for the Highly Able in Peru	228
Colegios de Alto Rendimiento/COARs: Academies for the High Achievers	230
Issues that Need to Be Addressed	233
Conclusion: Future Directions for Research and Program Development	233
Cross-References	234
References	234

Abstract

The current status of ethnic-linguistic, diverse, and deprived young scholars in South American countries will be explored in this chapter. Even though there is a scarcity of resources for public education, several programs with public and private funding are among the best practices to promote talent development and excellence among youth and young scholars. The challenges of gifted education in Peru that underline the advocacy efforts towards the indigenous population facing socio-economic inequity will be presented from a developmental and cross-cultural approach. Implications for future research will be elaborated on, along with recommendations for practice that includes the reiteration of promising approaches to support the talent development of gifted students from low socioeconomic circumstances, who belong to ethnic-linguistic minority groups.

Keywords

High ability · Gifted children · Talent development · Indigenous gifted · Peru

S. Blumen (✉)
Department of Psychology, Pontificia Universidad Católica del Perú, Lima, Peru
e-mail: sblumen@pucp.pe; sblumen@mentefutura.org

The aims in this chapter are to:
1. Describe the challenges of gifted education in Latin America.
2. Analyse the case of Peru in regard to the scientific studies on poverty, cognition, and talent development based on a developmental and cross-cultural approach.
3. Discuss the impact of the 25 nationwide public boarding academies for high achievers that constitute an example of a promising attempt with results that will be worth monitoring in the near future.
4. Discuss the challenges for the indigenous young scholars in the future.

Introduction

Diversity in Latin American countries related to the ethnic-linguistic background and socio-economic levels may lead to high levels of polarisation among the societies. Significant differences, that are difficult to be aligned, seem to provoke irreconcilable perspectives among citizens of the same nation. Latin America constitutes a paradox, being the only region in the world in which democratic regimes involve 30.7% sectors of their populations living below the poverty line (Economic Commission for Latin America and the Caribbean [ECLAC], 2016), with an uneven economic distribution, involving high levels of corruption and showing the highest homicide rates in the world. This may constitute a dangerous combination for the stability of democratic institutions in the region.

The days in which Latin America had more middle class than poor people seem to be far away (Rigolini & Vakis, 2017). In 2010, the economic boom and the shrinkage of the income gap allowed 70 million people to come out of poverty. However, 20% of Latin Americans, so-called the chronic poor, never left poverty and are in need of the support of the weak social assistance services (Bertelsmann Stiftung Transformation Index [BTI], 2018; Chronic Poverty Research Centre [CPRC], 2012). Dreadfully, after more than a decade of poverty decline, since 2016, poverty levels are more pronounced in most of the Latin American countries (ECLAC, 2016). Low endowments, lack of basic services, corruption in all sectors of society, weak democratic institutions, and the lack of safety due to either natural hazards or international crime are all risk factors that lead those in poverty to live in survival conditions, exhibiting depressive symptoms with relatively low aspirations for their future (Blumen, 2016b; Blumen & Cornejo, 2006; Blumen et al., 2017; Sorokowska et al., 2017).

This situation becomes particularly dramatic in Peru, an ethnic-linguistic diverse country that managed to drop its poverty rate to 31.3% in 2010 and was successful in lowering inflation, improving macroeconomic stability, as well as reducing the external debt, with significant improvements in social and development indicators (World Bank, 2016). However, although reductions of inequality occurred, it is still high, exhibiting a GINI Index of 0.45 and showing 19.7% poverty contexts in the rural population. Low-income jobs, poor teaching skills, particularly in the rural areas, and the absence of benefits for basic health care lead poor people in rural areas to live under vulnerable conditions (World Bank, 2016). Moreover, the population growth and the overcrowding of the cities affect the social welfare system and the poverty rates (CPRC, 2012). However, successive Peruvian governments chose to support assistance-based models that reproduce the parameters of 'hard-core' poverty, instead of improving the quality of education and training teachers to develop autonomous and independent learners in its citizenry.

Among the many options international agencies, such as the CPRC (2012) and the World Bank (2016), suggested to exit poverty were as follows: (a) house and context improvements related to available opportunities; (b) the integration of early childhood needs into the social agenda, in order to stop malnutrition, poor stimulation, fragile health, absent parents, and the exposure to a violent environment, which limits a person's ability to develop towards their full potential; (c) labour income-promoting strategies, involving training and labour insertion programs; (d) equity between rural and urban families; (e) coordination among the social programs, involving clear goals for each of them; and (f) a policy design to include a social safety net system that involves strategies to address the mindset and low aspirations of the chronic poor. Therefore, these suggestions should be considered in any intervention program that aims to meet the needs of the population living under low socio-economic or poverty conditions.

The Highly Able in Peru

Peru, the third largest country in South America and the 20th largest country in the world, exhibits eight life zones or natural regions, from those at the sea level up to the *Janca* [white], that is, 15,000ft above sea level. A challenging geography involves the desert coast bordering the Pacific Ocean (11.6% of territory; 55% of its population), which meets the highlands located at the Andean Heights (28.1% of the territory; 32% of its population), and the Amazon rainforest (60% of the area; 13% of its population), which are all in close proximity (Instituto Nacional de Estadística e Informática [National Institute of Statistics and Informatics] [INEI], 2018; Pulgar Vidal, 1979). The coastal area is densely populated, while the Amazon jungle is scarcely inhabited.

Since its beginning as a modern republic in 1837, the Peruvian government has followed a central system style, where the Ministry of Education (Ministerio de Educación [Secretary of Education] [MINEDU], 2006; World Bank, 2016) formulates, implements, and supervises the national educational policy of the country. Schooling is compulsory from K to 11th grade, which marks the end of secondary education. The total expenditure for education in the past 30 years has been around 3% of the gross domestic product (GDP), among the lowest in the Latin American region (BTI, 2018). However, Peru achieved a higher degree of education coverage and gender equity compared to other countries of Latin America with significant heavy indigenous populations (BTI, 2018; World Bank, 2016). Nonetheless, education and training facilities vary in quality. By 2012, Peruvian education showed the following results: (a) the quality of education was still below international levels; (b) gender equity improved, but differences between socio-economic status groups remained; (c) decentralisation of the country needed to be promoted; and (d) the university system exhibited low quality, with few internationally accredited programs (BTI, 2018).

Until the beginning of this century, the conception of giftedness in Peru was associated with general intelligence (*g*) (Blumen, 2016a; MINEDU, 2006; Thorne & Blumen, 1996). However, if we consider giftedness as a social construct, there is no one-size-fits-all conception of giftedness (Sternberg, 2000, 2007). Following Bevan-Brown (2011). From a cultural perspective, the cultural beliefs, needs, values, concepts, attitudes, and language influence giftedness. And taking into consideration the high levels of ethnic-linguistic diversity of Peru, where three varieties of Quechua, the Aymara language, together with 64 vernacular languages coexist, it is expected that different worldviews will influence perceptions of giftedness (Phillipson & Phillipson, 2007).

Blumen and Cornejo (2006) outlined Western/native differences in the identification of culturally diverse gifted children. Peruvian natives from the Andes highlands showed more convergence with Māori beliefs of giftedness (Bevan-Brown, 2009), such as: (a) collective giftedness, referring to the notion that giftedness develops as a result of communal work (e.g., giftedness is perceived as belonging to the group rather than to individuals); (b) emphasis on the importance of interpersonal and intrapersonal domains, giving priority to sensitivity towards their people, as well as hospitality and humility, moral values, and strength of character; (c) service to their community and to others; (d) valuing intuition and spirituality; and (e) the development of leadership ability, that is understanding those who lead with their example.

However, the gifted natives of the Amazon rainforest (Blumen & Cornejo, 2006) tended to exhibit a giftedness view convergent to the four intellectual strengths that typify the Australian Aboriginal, as reported by Gibson and Vialle (2007): (a) linguistic intelligence, mainly oral language; (b) spatial intelligence, a survival ability needed in the Amazon jungle, particularly strengthened through parenting practices since early childhood; (c) interpersonal intelligence due to the egalitarian nature of the Amazon native society and the tribal style of the communal groups; and (d) naturalist/spiritual intelligence, as they have a strong connection between the 'Pachamama' (motherland in Quechua) and the individual (e.g., daily life is related to the way the individuals honour the land while living on it).

Talent development is considered a right for highly able girls and boys in Peru, and since the educational reforms of 1972, the law of special education supports programs to promote the creative, figural, and verbal performances inside the regular classrooms. During the 1970s, significant attention was given to provisions related to the visual and performing arts, under the auspices of the former Federal Republic of Germany (CONCYTEC [National Council of Science and Technology], 1992). In 1983, the official definition of the gifted individual, following the Supreme Decree DS 02-83ED, was related to "the special girl or boy who exhibits high abilities that significantly surpass the normal level of intellectual functioning and needs special programs in different modalities" (Ministerio de Educación [Secretary of Education] [MINEDU], 1983). Although focused on cognitive skills and academic achievement, the Supreme Decree promoted identification services and talent development provisions, as well as the foundations for teacher training programs.

By the beginning of this century, a political situation shook the Peruvian people, and during the reorganisation of the democratic republic, polarised debates emerged among the officials of education in relation to the concepts of ability and intelligence. Concepts related to inclusive education prevailed, without considering gifted children's needs as part of it. Later, in 2009, a meritocratic-based public policy was installed, and educational accommodations to foster academic talent among the high achievers coming from vulnerable conditions were established (Blumen, 2016a).

Moreover, initiatives coming from scientific settings (Alencar, 2008; Blumen, 2013a, 2013b; Crea Talentum, 2015; Kluwin, Gonsher, & Samuels, 1996; Pfeiffer & Thompson, 2013; Robinson, 2006) revealed that cognitive and conative factors with correlate variables such as access to opportunities and perseverance (Ambrose, 2016; Bandson & Precker, 2013; Ziegler, Vialle, & Wimmer, 2013) needed to be considered. Furthermore, the development of expertise (Sternberg & Davidson, 2005) involves training and interventions in domain-specific skills, as well as self-regulated thinking to achieve levels of expertise and outstanding performance in adulthood (Stoeger & Ziegler, 2016; Subotnik & Rickoff, 2010). Conventional models of talent tended to focus on personality traits (Ziegler et al., 2013). But there was a need of models that emphasise the dynamic interaction of the person with the environment in order to have a better understanding of the processes related to high achievement under poverty conditions. Furthermore, the lack of culturally fitted foundations for establishing provisions for talent development in Peru refrained the development of policies that were related to talent identification services in the community for more than a decade (Blumen, 2013b).

What Does the Research Suggest?

Since 1978, the type of research carried out in Peru has mainly been descriptive or comparative, and the relationships between variables, such as the demographics and socio-economic level, and creativity were examined. In the 1980s, various mediating and conditioning processes were incorporated into research and creativity was defined as a measurable cognitive function that may be developed through exercise and practice. At the beginning of the 1990s, research was focused on specific cognitive domains related to creative ability. Proposals and methodological suggestions were made regarding how creativity could be oriented and expressed in different ways, and more practical tendencies emerged in the scientific literature (Alencar, Blumen, & Castellanos, 2000; Blumen, 2016c).

Personality characteristics of intellectually talented youths coming from low-income households were described in a study using the Rorschach Psychodiagnostic Test (Blumen & Cornejo, 2006). Results revealed that intellectually talented youths exhibited the following personality characteristics: (a) tendency to approach situations from their personal reflections; (b) sophisticated emotional resources; (c) high levels of initiative and creativity; (d) tendency for perfectionism; (e) need to control situations; (f) unconventionality; (g) high levels of sensibility; (h) oppositeness; and (i) being insightful. They also exhibited characteristics expected in poverty contexts, such as cautiousness and low levels of self-confidence, high levels of stress and alertness towards the environment, as well as tendency towards having depression. Recommendations for interventions were given, as well as identifying the need to develop research approaches from a multidisciplinary approach.

In a cross-cultural study with 1794 participants from five countries, the motivational orientations of high-achieving students were studied as mediators of a positive perception of a high-achieving classmate (Oh et al., 2016). Results revealed that a learning goal orientation and a performance approach motivation predicted positive perceptions of a high-achieving classmate's intellectual ability in all participating countries, except in Peru. Further studies are needed in order to establish the factors that influence the perceptions of high-achieving students as a threat in Peru.

One of the most important research findings about gifted and talented children in Peru was the positive impact of teacher training programs in the development of creativity and talent among students in ability-grouping programs (Blumen, 2016b). The empirical data provided support for the following: (a) to lobby with officers of the Ministry of Education and policy-makers to improve the provisions available for the gifted and talented nationwide, particularly for the underserved populations; (b) to prepare the legal framework for launching the residential academy for the academically talented youth who live in poverty; (c) to expand in-service teacher training programs in gifted education; and (d) to include gifted education training in teacher preparation programs.

Provisions for the Highly Able in Peru

Modern provisions for the highly able in Peru emerged under the cooperation of the *Pontifical Católica University del Perú* (PUCP) and Radboud University (Wechsler, Blumen, & Bendelman, 2017). In May 1997, an experimental teacher workshop was launched as the first documented effort to train regular public-school teachers to meet the needs of gifted students in the regular classroom; it benefitted 100 teachers of 3000 children. It was sponsored by the Ministry of Education and the *German Technical Cooperation Agency* (GTZ) for education (Blumen, 2013b, 2016b). Positive outcomes of the workshop lead to its broader application on a national basis as a relevant course in the Peruvian teacher training programs.

In December 1997, Mönks, Ypenburg, and Blumen published the book *Nuestros niños son talentosos: Manual para padres y maestros* (Our children are gifted: A manual for parents and teachers) as the first advocacy effort towards the needs of the gifted. Between 1997 and 1998, several international academic and professional events were organised, committed to informing policy-makers, mental health workers, education officers, social workers, teachers, and parents about the needs of the highly able. Moreover, in December 1998, the *Mente Futura* Foundation, an associated European talent centre (European Talent Support Network [ETSN], 2016) that aims to promote the social-emotional well-being of the highly able native Peruvians, started operations. During 1998, a dynamic schedule related to the identification of and provision for the highly able in Lima City was organised, particularly focused on poor children attending public schools. Furthermore, in January 1999, the European Advanced Diploma in Educating the Gifted sponsored by the European Council for High Ability trained 40 teachers, 60% from public schools and 20% from rural schools. Later, many of those trained teachers were granted promotions and entered the public service (Blumen, 2001; Mönks, Ypenburg, & Blumen, 1997).

Talent development in school settings. By the end of the 1990s, inclusive policies which promoted the development of differentiated teaching in regular schools gained popularity in Peru. And following inclusive education models, teachers were trained in gifted education (Blumen, 2013b). Creative enrichment programs for the highly able children who attended public schools were launched in primary state-run schools (Blumen, 2013a), with ability grouping becoming a common enrichment provision for grades 1–5 (Blumen, 2001). Other resources, such as universities, research institutions, museums, and other professional organisations, became committed to the support of talent development as well (Blumen, 2013b, 2016b). Moreover, enrichment activities related to chess clubs, Model UN debates, drama, music classes, and mathematics- and science-related clubs were also available at mixed-funded and privately-funded schools (Alencar et al., 2000; Blumen, 2013a, 2013b). Furthermore, private schools and those who belonged to international communities offered the International Baccalaureate (IB) Diploma and Advanced Placement (AP) classes, as well as a variety of enrichment programs in science and technology. As many of the International Baccalaureate Organization/IBO schools belonged to foreign communities, the learning process usually considered the mastery of a second modern language, such as Chinese, English, French, German, Hebrew, Italian, or Japanese. Students also participated in the various talent search programs sponsored by universities, such as the Peruvian Mathematical Olympic competitions, science fairs, inventor's fairs, and mathematics competitions, among others. Also, they participated in international events, building up an important network among their international peers.

Additionally, for mathematically talented students, the use of talent search testing and associated provisions in secondary schools has grown rapidly over the past decade (Blumen, 2013b, 2016b). At the beginning of this century, counselling services were needed to support the youth members of the Peruvian Mathematical Olympic team who were exposed to intensive training for more than 10-hours per working day. They were trained using the philosophy that learning can improve intelligence (Bloom & Sosniak, 1981). Therefore, tailor-fitted counselling programs were developed, based on cognitive processing therapy (Schnurr, 2008), for the members of the Peruvian team, most of them coming from ethnic-linguistic poverty contexts (Blumen, 2016a). Improvement, as measured by the positions achieved at the *International Mathematical Olympiads* (IMO), showed that social-emotional support was important as a significant variable in any teamwork.

Taking into consideration the low quality of education provided in Peruvian state-run schools nationwide (BTI, 2018), as well as the lack of educational standards, acceleration strategies were the most cost-effective alternatives to provide challenges for the needs of the gifted and talented (Subotnik, Olszewski-Kubilius, & Worrell, 2011). However, academic acceleration is not a feasible alternative in the Peruvian school system anymore. Although the literature related to provisions for the highly able suggests that the highly able who are left among their age peers may lose their talent, and any barriers associated with age grouping within the educational system must be suppressed, in Peru the Law of General Education establishes chronological age as the criteria for grade placement in schools without exceptions (MINEDU, 2006).

Colegios de Alto Rendimiento/COARs: Academies for the High Achievers

García's second-term government (2006–2011) provided generously for academically talented students, launching a state-run residential academy for high achievers living in poverty. Following an 8th grade talent search, based on a multistep nationwide selection process, students at state-run schools were provided fellowships to attend a residential academy launched in 2010 to serve the talented youths coming from disadvantaged and poverty contexts (Blumen, 2013a, 2016a, 2016b; Gladwell, 2008). The name of the first residential academy placed outside Lima City was *Colegio Mayor Presidente de la República*. In the following administration, the name was changed to *Colegio de Alto Rendimiento/COAR* (Academy for High Achievers; Ministerio de Educación [Secretary of Education] [MINEDU], 2014). The first school was developed as a pilot study to foster academic talent in students coming from highly vulnerable conditions, either due to low-income households below the poverty line or due to the intersection of poverty and ethnic-linguistic background.

However, positive results lead to the expansion of the model to all Peruvian regions through three consecutive administrations. Humala's administration (2011–2016) expanded the number of COARs to 15 and Kuczynski's government (2016–2018) to 25 COARs (Ministerio de Educación [Secretary of Education] [MINEDU], 2016). Nowadays, the COARs are serving 6700 9th- to 11th-grade high-achieving, ethnic-linguistic, diverse students coming from low-income households below the poverty line in every Peruvian region. This initiative constitutes an example of a promising attempt with results that will be worth monitoring in the near future (Pronabec, 2018; Wechsler et al., 2017).

The COAR is based on the Peruvian General Education Law No. 28044 (MINEDU, 2006) and the *Proyecto Educativo Nacional al 2021* (National Educational Project towards 2021; 2007), which aim at nurturing citizens who are able to reach their personal goals through the principles of equity, inclusion, interculturality, and quality of education. Their mission is to provide nationwide high achievers in regular education with an international high standard educational service, which allows them to consolidate their personal, academic, artistic, and sportive competences (Ambrose, Sriraman, & Cross, 2016; Sternberg, 2016). Their vision is to become an academic, organisational, and management referent of an educational model that contributes to improving state-run public education as the foundation for national development to form a community of positive leaders able to promote local, regional, national, and global development (Sisk, 2016).

The COAR staff members are selected among professionals of education, psychology, social sciences, humanities, and pure sciences. To become part of the COAR, staff professionals follow a tailor-fitted training program in the COAR educational service model and need to become certified by the International Baccalaureate Organization as IBO teachers. English teachers also need international and Blended Learning certificates. The training program's study plan involves lectures for 60–hours per week, with compulsory subjects and elective workshops, such as robotics, oratory, dance, music, painting, and the like, as well as other after-school activities. Ten hours of English per week are needed to reach level B2 in mastering English as a second language (MINEDU, 2016).

Selected students in the 8th-grade talent search program enter COAR in the beginning of the 9th grade and are placed in the Learning Strengthening Program to consolidate previous learning. Particular attention is placed on adaptation skills to overcome the changes in family life from being in a residential setting. In 10th grade, students start the IB Diploma program, and special attention is placed on the consolidation of socio-emotional and leadership competencies. The 11th grade, which is the last year of regular schooling in Peru, is focused on the development of their personal life project to support their vocational orientation and planning for their future.

Moreover, in the COARs, there are an articulated number of programs and resources in order to guarantee the psycho-pedagogical conditions to smoothen the integral development of the students. A 24–hour service of psychologists provides monitoring through tutoring, vocational orientation, the promotion of intercultural democratic coexistence, residential monitoring, and social service, as well as participating in learning circles and after-school opportunities. Parents also assume their responsibilities of keeping a healthy family environment.

Talent development out of educational settings. The first public afterschool pedagogical accommodation for the gifted was started in 1989, based on the belief that IQ was the sufficient measure for the provision of services. However, it lacked solid scientific foundations and could not show significant evidence to the officers of Education. However, well-recognised talents in sports, such as soccer and surfing, have since reached high levels of value in modern Peruvian society. On the one hand, soccer is the most valued sport in Peru, and the availability of soccer fields for initiating children into this sport is possible all over the country—from the shantytowns in the urban areas to any small town in the highlands or in the rainforest—these contexts support the dream of many poor children to become international soccer stars. On the other hand, Peru has achieved a world championship in surfing and keeps high positions in the international rankings. The availability of the Pacific Ocean all along the coastal area and the emergence of many surfing academies for school-age children have facilitated surfing practice for years. Both in soccer and surfing, international Peruvian stars are available to children as role models (Blumen, 2013a, 2016a).

Musical talent is also highly valued in Peru. This value is facilitated by having world-recognised tenor Juan Diego Flores as the best representative in Peru (Blumen, 2013a, 2013b). He was supported by a group of Peruvian entrepreneurs to continue his studies abroad, and now he promotes musical talent within disadvantaged populations (Alencar & Blumen, 2002).

Mathematical talent is an area in which the Peruvian Olympic Mathematical team has significantly improved its position in the international rankings (International Mathematical Olympiad [IMO], 2017). Although there are also youth winners in physics and chemistry international competitions, mathematical, and science-related talents are not valued as much as sports or music in Peruvian modern society. This situation is also extended to chess, for example, in 2017, Julio Granda was awarded the Senior World Chess Championship in Italy, but this award was completely unnoticed by the Peruvian public. It seems that any talent related to mathematics, science, or chess is perceived as a type of talent inherent to the person. However, the talents in sports and arts are perceived as the result of motivation, perseverance, and training and related to the individual as part of a group or team (Rathunde & Csikszentmihalyi, 2012; Sternberg, 2005). Moreover, the communal configuration of the Andean society leads to praise of collective giftedness more than individual success, significantly affecting the reinforcement society provides to the people who exhibit an outstanding achievement in the sporting and the artistic areas.

Talent development in college education. Provisions for academically talented students in college (or university) studies are beginning to be considered in Peru, and different models of mentoring programs are being developed for high-achieving students attending college (Blumen, 2013b). From the cultural relational theory perspective, the literature suggests that the academic relationship established between college students and their mentors may constitute a creative and enrichment learning space for students, as well as a regenerative power for professors or mentors (Blumen, 2013b). Moreover, mentors seem to play an important role in the talent development process with college students, and high achievement is the result of the dynamic process, which involves the given mentoring opportunity (Erwin & Worrell, 2012).

Humala's government launched the *Beca 18 Program*—a fellowship covering all required expenses for poor intellectually talented youth to enable them to continue college studies in either Peruvian or international universities. Every year, 2000 fellowships by merit are available for the high achievers who are living in poverty or extreme poverty conditions to continue college education (Pronabec, 2017).

One of the leading initiatives for talent development in university or college education is the *Talent Seeds Program*, launched by the No. 1-ranked Bank of Peru, which chose to promote the talent development of high-achieving college students coming from an intersection of poverty and ethnic-linguistic diversity. Fifty students are selected every year through the 11th-grade talent search program, following a multi-method three-phase detection process involving integrity measures, as well as psychological risk indicators (Wechsler et al., 2017). From a pool of around 2000 senior high school students nationwide, only 50 students will become the beneficiaries. They are provided the means to cover the 5-year undergraduate studies, as well as related housing, transportation, and living expenses. The differential element with other fellowships is the tailor-fitted close counselling program, as well as the labour placement program. The Talent Seeds Program also involves psychoeducational monitoring, so-called tutoring, a variety of mentoring programs, team-group activities, as well as the participation in a socially responsible initiative. Positive results are emerging from the first alumni, who are ranked above the average of their class and are strongly encouraged to lead the development of their communities.

Issues that Need to Be Addressed

Unresolved issues concerning talent development in Peru are related to the need for: (a) a comprehensive paradigm to meet the needs of the highly able (Blumen, 2013a); (b) a legal framework to smoothe academic acceleration and early entrance to universities; (c) training in gifted education to be part of every teacher education program; (d) advocacy in the media to support the needs of the highly able (Blumen, 2013b); and (e) prescribed policies in terms of potential cost-effectiveness, based on research. Moreover, there is the need for a theoretical framework that considers ethnic-linguistic and poverty variables in the study of the highly able. It may incorporate biological, social, and individual variables in any identification process. Furthermore, there is the need to provide incentives to enterprises that foster domain-specific talents nationwide (Blumen, 2016b).

The following are the most difficult issues that need to be addressed: (a) any definition about talent development is likely to include environmental factors (Cummings & Blatherwick, 2017); (b) the importance of nutrition in school achievement and its relation to the development of basic cognitive processes; (c) the relevance of prior schooling and its relation to intelligence test performance (Blumen, 2013b, 2016a); and (d) theoretical foundations that support the identification process, with goals established around the pedagogical demands and the theoretical constructs that support an effective learning process (Blumen, 2013a, 2016a).

Conclusion: Future Directions for Research and Program Development

Peru has made progress in the field of high ability in the past few decades. However, there are still many recommendations to follow: (a) the promotion of comparative research about the beliefs and conceptions on the highly able between the different ethnic-linguistic groups is desirable; (b) it is imperative to study culture-fitted provisions for the talented students coming from ethnic-linguistic diverse societies to offer them advanced placement classes, through a self-selection process; (c) gifted education content should be included in the pedagogical formation of curricula; (d) acceleration should be permitted in the national educational policies of Peru; and (e) homeschooling programs for the gifted need to be developed to provide intervention programs in rural areas, where multigraded schools still prevailed.

Finally, it is of utmost importance to improve our understanding about talent development within ethnic-linguistic diversity contexts. Broader policies of talent development are needed, with the commitment of parents, teachers, and the students themselves, with the support of educational institutes, with the officials of education, in order to support talent development with sociocultural responsibility.

Cross-References

- ▶ Gifted and Talented Aboriginal Students in Australia
- ▶ Gifted Education in the Asia-Pacific: From the Past for the Future – An Introduction
- ▶ Homeschooling the Gifted: What Do We Know from the Australian, Chilean, and US Context?
- ▶ Learning from International Research Informs Academic Acceleration in Australasia: A Case for Consistent Policy
- ▶ Nurturing Mathematical Talents of Young Mathematically Gifted English Language Learners
- ▶ Social and Cultural Conceptions and Perceptions: Part I Introduction
- ▶ Some Implications for the Future of Gifted Education in the Asia-Pacific
- ▶ Supporting Australian Gifted Indigenous Students' Academic Potential in Rural Settings
- ▶ The Development of Mana: Five Optimal Conditions for Gifted Māori Student Success
- ▶ Transitioning to Career: Talented Musicians' Identity Development

References

Alencar, E. S. (2008). Dificultades socio-emocionales del alumno con altas habilidades [Social-emotional difficulties of the highly able student]. *Revista de Psicología de la PUCP, 26*, 43–62.

Alencar, E. S., & Blumen, S. (2002). Trends in gifted education in South America: The Brazilian and Peruvian scenario. *Gifted and Talented International, 17*, 7–12. https://doi.org/10.1080/15332276.2002.11672980

Alencar, E. S., Blumen, S., & Castellanos, D. (2000). Programs and practices for identifying and nurturing talent in Latin American countries. In K. A. Heller, F. J. Mönks, R. J. Sternberg, & R. F. Subotnik (Eds.), *International handbook of giftedness and talent* (2nd ed., pp. 817–828). Oxford, UK: Pergamon Press.

Ambrose, D. (2016). Twenty-first century contextual influences in the life trajectories of the gifted and talented. In D. Ambrose & R. J. Sternberg (Eds.), *Giftedness and talent in the 21st century* (pp. 15–42). Rotterdam, The Netherlands: Sense Publishers.

Ambrose, D., Sriraman, B., & Cross, T. L. (Eds.). (2016). *The Roeper school*. Rotterdam, The Netherlands: Sense Publishers.

Bandson, T. G., & Precker, F. (2013). Intelligence and creativity. Their relationship with special attention to reasoning ability and divergent thinking. Implications for giftedness research and education. In K. H. Kim, J. Baer, & B. Sriraman (Eds.), *Creative gifted students are not like other gifted students: Research, theory, and practice* (pp. 181–212). Rotterdam, The Netherlands: Sense Publishers.

Bertelsmann Stiftung's Transformation Index. (2018). BTI 2018. Retrieved from https://www.bti-project.org/en/home/

Bevan-Brown, J. (2009) Identifying and providing for gifted and talented Māori students. *Apex 15*(4), 6–20. Retrieved online from http://www.giftedchildren.org.nz/apex/.

Bevan-Brown, J. (2011). Indigenous conceptions of giftedness. In W. Vialle (Ed.), *Giftedness from an indigenous perspective* (pp. 10–23). Retrieved from http://trove.nla.gov.au/work/153628143?selectedversion=NBD47320153

Bloom, B. S., & Sosniak, L. A. (1981). Talent development vs. Schooling. *Educational Leadership, 39*, 86–94. Retrieved from http://www.ascd.org/ASCD/pdf/journals/ed_lead/el_198111_bloom.pdf

Blumen, S. (2001). *Enriqueciendo el talento en el aula de clases* [Talent enrichment in the schools]. In Documento Técnico No. 11. Lima, Perú: Ministry of Education/World Bank/MECEP.

Blumen, S. (2013a). Motivacao e desenvolvimento de talentos no Peru [Motivation and talent development in Peru]. In E. M. L. S. de Alencar & D. de Souza Fleith (Eds.), *Superdotados: Trajetorias de desenvolvimento e realizacoes* (pp. 193–206). Brasilia, Brazil: Juruá Editora Psicologia.

Blumen, S. (2013b). New trends in talent development in Peru. *Journal for the Education of the Gifted, 36*, 246–264. Retrieved from http://dx.doi.org/10.1177/0162353213492925

Blumen, S. (2016a). Gifted education programming: Serving the native Peruvian. In J. L. Davis & J. L. Moore III (Eds.), *Gifted children of color around the world: Diverse needs, exemplary practices, and directions for the future (Advances in race and ethnicity in education, volume 3)* (pp. 1–15). Bingley, UK: Emerald Group Publishing Limited. https://doi.org/10.1108/S2051-231720160000003001. ISBN: 978-1-78560-119-4. eISBN: 978-1-78560-118-7.

Blumen, S. (2016b). High achieving deprived young people facing the challenges of the 21st century. In D. Ambrose & R. Sternberg (Eds.), *Giftedness and talent in the 21st century adapting to the turbulence of globalization* (pp. 147–162). Rotterdam, The Netherlands: Sense Publishers. Retrieved from https://www.sensepublishers.com/media/2739-giftedness-and-talent-in-the-21st-century.pdf

Blumen, S. (2016c). New trends on intellectual assessment in Peru. *International Journal of School and Educational Psychology, 4*(4), 254–261. Retrieved from http://www.tandfonline.com/doi/full/10.1080/21683603.2016.1166744

Blumen, S., Bayona, H. A., Givoli, S., Pecker, G., & Fine, S. (2017). Validation study of a multi-method integrity test in a Peruvian sample. *Revista de Psicología/Journal of Psychology PUCP, 35*(1), 347–370. Retrieved from http://revistas.pucp.edu.pe/index.php/psicologia/article/view/16104/16525

Blumen, S., & Cornejo, M. (2006). Una mirada desde el Rorschach hacia l aniñez con talento intellectual end resign [A glance from Rorschach towards the intellectually talented children at risk]. *Revista de Psicología, 24*, 267–299.

Chronic Poverty Research Centre/CPRC. (2012). *What is chronic poverty? Findings from the Chronic Poverty Research Centre 2000–2011*. Retrieved from https://www.odi.org/publications/10485-what-chronic-poverty-findings-chronic-poverty-research-centre.

CONCYTEC [National Council of Science and Technology]. (1992). *Programa de detección y apoyo a niños superdotados* [Detection and attention program for the gifted]. Lima, Peru.

Crea Talentum. (2015). *Grupo Interdisciplinario de Investigación PUCP: Creatividad, Tecnología y Talento* [PUCP Interdisciplinary Research Group: Creativity, Technology & Talent]. An associated European Talent Point. Retrieved from http://puntoedu.pucp.edu.pe/impresos/puntoedu324.

Cummings, J. B., & Blatherwick, M. L. (2017). *Creative dimensions of teaching and learning in the 21st century*. Rotterdam, The Netherlands: Sense Publishers.

Economic Commission for Latin America and the Caribbean/ECLAC. (2016). *Social Panorama 2017*. Retrieved from https://www.cepal.org/en/pressreleases/poverty-increased-2016-latin-america-and-reached-307-population-percentage-seen

Erwin, J. O., & Worrell, F. C. (2012). Assessment practices and the underrepresentation of minority students in gifted and talented education. *Journal of Psychoeducational Assessment, 30*, 74–87. https://doi.org/10.1177/0734282911428197

European Talent Support Network/ETSN. (2016). *Associated European Talent Centers*. Retrieved from http://etsn.eu

Gibson, K., & Vialle, W. (2007). The Australian aboriginal view of giftedness. In S. N. Phillipson & M. McCann (Eds.), *Conceptions of giftedness. Socio-cultural perspectives* (pp. 169–196). Mahwah, NJ: Lawrence Erlbaum.

Gladwell, M. (2008). *Outliers: The story of success* (pp 307). New York: Little, Brown And Company.

Instituto Nacional de Estadística e Informática [National Institute of Statistics and Informatics]/INEI. (2018). *Population and living in Peru*. Retrieved from https://www.inei.gob.pe/estadisticas/indice-tematico/poblacion-y-vivienda/

International Mathematical Olympiad/IMO. (2017). 58th International Mathematical Olympiad. Retrieved from https://www.imo2017.org.br

Kluwin, T., Gonsher, W., & Samuels, J. (1996). The E.T. class: Education together! Team teaching and students with hearing impairments and students with normal hearing together. *Teaching Exceptional Children, 29*(1), 11–15. https://doi.org/10.1177/004005999602900104

MINEDU/Ministerio de Educación [Secretary of Education]. (1983). Ley general de educación [General Law of Education]. In *Reglamento de Educación Especial* [Norms for Special Education] (p. 16). Lima, Peru.

MINEDU/Ministerio de Educación [Secretary of Education]. (2006). *Reglamentación de la ley general de educación No. 28044* [Norms for the General Law of Education No. 28044]. Dirección Nacional de Educación Básica Especial [National Direction of Special Basic Education]. Lima, Peru: MINEDU/Dirección Nacional de Educación Básica Especial.

MINEDU/Ministerio de Educación [Secretary of Education]. (2014). *Colegio Mayor Secundario Presidente del Perú*. Retrieved from http://www.colegiomayor.edu.pe/admision2014.php

MINEDU/Ministerio de Educación [Secretary of Education]. (2016). Red COAR. Retrieved from http://www.minedu.gob.pe/coar/pdf/brochure-coar-2016.pdf

Mönks, F.J., Ypenburg, I., & Blumen, S. (1997). *Nuestros niños son talentosos. Manual para padres y maestros* [Our children are gifted. Manual for parents and teachers]. Lima, Peru: Fondo Editorial de la PUCP.

Oh, H., Badia-Martín, M. d. M., Blumen, S., Maakrun, J., Nguyena, Q. A.-T., Stack, N., ... Ziegler, A. (2016). Motivational orientations of high-achieving students as mediators of a positive perception of a high-achieving classmate: Results from a cross-national study. *Annals of Psychology, 32*(3), 695–701. https://doi.org/10.6018/analesps.32.3.259451

Pfeiffer, S. I., & Thompson, T. L. (2013). Creativity from a talent development perspective. How it can be cultivated in the schools. In K. H. Kim, J. Baer, & B. Sriraman (Eds.), *Creative gifted students are not like other gifted students: Research, theory, and practice* (pp. 231–256). Rotterdam, The Netherlands: Sense Publishers.

Phillipson, S. & Phillipson, S. N. (2007). Academic expectations, belief of ability, and involvement by parents as predictors of child achievement: A cross-cultural comparison. *Educational Psychology 27*(3), 329–34. https://doi.org/10.1080/01443410601104130

Pronabec (2017). Resolución Directoral Ejecutiva No. 16 [Director Executive Resolution No. 16]. Lima: MINEDU/VMGI-PRONABEC

Pronabec. (2018). Becas Pronabec/Beca 18. Retrieved from https://www.pronabec.gob.pe/2018_Beca18.php

Proyecto Educativo Nacional al 2021 [National Educational Poryecto towards 2021]. (2007). *La educación que queremos para el Perú*. Retrieved from http://www.minedu.gob.pe/DeInteres/xtras/PEN-2021.pdf

Pulgar Vidal, J. (1979). *Geografía del Perú; Las Ocho Regiones Naturales del Perú*. Edit. Universo S.A., Lima First Edition (his dissertation of 1940): Las ocho regiones naturales del Perú, *Boletín del Museo de Historia Natural* (pp. 145–161). Javier Prado, n° especial, Lima, Peru, 1941, 17.

Rathunde, K., & Csikszentmihalyi, M. (2012). The social context of middle school: Teachers, friends, and activities in Montessori and traditional school environments. In *Applications of flow in human development and education: The collected works of Mihaly Csikszentmihalyi* (pp. 189–213). https://doi.org/10.1007/978-94-017-9094-9

Rigolini, J. & Vakis, L. (2017, December 6). Four facts about poverty in Latin America you probably didn't know. *The blog at Huffington Post.* Retrieved from https://www.huffingtonpost.com/jamele-rigolini/four-facts-about-poverty-_b_6820048.html

Robinson, K. (2006, August 3). *Las escuelas matan la creatividad* [Schools kill creativity]. Keynote presented at the TED 2006 Conference, Long Beach, CA. Retrieved from http://www.youtube.com/watch?v=nPB-41q97zg

Schnurr, P. P. (2008). Treatments for PTSD: Understanding the evidence. *PTSD Research Quarterly, 19*(3). Retrieved from https://www.ptsd.va.gov/professional/newsletters/research-quarterly/V19N3.pdf

Sisk, D. A. (2016). Creativity and leadership development: Can they co-exist for transformational change in education? In D. Ambrose & R. J. Sternberg (Eds.), Creative intelligence in the 21st century (pp. 233–254). Rotterdam, The Netherlands: Sense Publishers.

Sorokowska, A., Sorokowski, P., Hilpert, P., Cantarero, K., Fracowiak, T., Ahmadi, K., ... Pierce, J. (2017). Preferred interpersonal distances: A global comparison. *Journal of Cross-Cultural Psychology, 48*(4), 577–592. Retrieved from http://journals.sagepub.com/doi/full/10.1177/0022022117698039

Sternberg, R. (2000). Giftedness as developing expertise. In K. A. Heller, F. J. Mönks, & R. Sternberg (Eds.), *International handbook for research on giftedness and talent* (2nd ed., pp. 55–66). London, England: Pergamon Press.

Sternberg, R. (2005). The WICS model of giftedness. In R. J. Sternberg & J. E. Davidson (Eds.), *Conceptions of giftedness* (2nd ed., pp. 327–342). New York, NY: Cambridge University Press.

Sternberg, R. J. (2007). Forward. In S. N. Phillipson & M. McCann (Eds.), *Conceptions of giftedness. Sociocultural perspectives* (pp. xv–xviii). Mahwah, NJ: Lawrence Erlbaum.

Sternberg, R. J. (2016). What's wrong and how to fix it: Balance of abilities matters more than levels. In D. Ambrose & R. J. Sternberg (Eds.), *Creative intelligence in the 21st century* (pp. 257–262). Rotterdam, The Netherlands: Sense Publishers.

Sternberg, R. J., & Davidson, J. E. (Eds.). (2005). *Conceptions of giftedness* (2nd ed., pp. 327–342). New York, NY: Cambridge University Press.

Stoeger, H., & Ziegler, A. (2016). Motivational orientations and cognitive abilities: An empirical investigation in primary school. *Gifted and Talented International, 20*(2), 7–18. https://doi.org/10.1080/15332276.2005.11673449

Subotnik, R. F., Olszewski-Kubilius, P., & Worrell, F. (2011). Rethinking giftedness and gifted education: A proposed direction forward based on psychological science. *Psychological Science in the Public Interest, 12*, 3–54. Retrieved from https://www.apa.org/ed/schools/gifted/rethinking-giftedness.pdf

Subotnik, R. F., & Rickoff, R. (2010). Should eminence based on outstanding innovation be the goal of gifted education and talent development? Implications for policy and research. *Learning and Individual Differences, 20*, 358–364. https://doi.org/10.1016/j.lindif.2009.12.005

Thorne, C., & Blumen, S. (1996, August). Age, schooling and the Raven scores. Paper presented at the *XIII International Conference of Applied Psychology*, Montreal.

Wechsler, S., Blumen, S., & Bendelman, K. (2017). Challenges on the identification and development of giftedness. In S. Pfeiffer (Ed.), *APA handbook of giftedness and talent* (pp. 97–112). Washington, DC: APA. ISBN: 1433826968.

World Bank. (2016). Peru: Poverty assessment and social policies and programs for the poor. Retrieved from http://web.worldbank.org/WBSITE/EXTERNAL/TOPICS/EXTPOVERTY/EXTPA/0,,contentMDK:20208438~isCURL:Y~menuPK:435735~pagePK:148956~piPK:216618~theSitePK:430367,00.html

Ziegler, A., Vialle, W., & Wimmer, B. (2013). The actiotope model of giftedness: A short introduction to some central theoretical assumptions. In S. N. Phillipson, H. Stoeger, & A. Ziegler (Eds.), *Exceptionality in East Asia* (pp. 1–17). London, England: Routledge.

Sheyla Blumen is full professor of psychology at the Pontificia Universidad Católica del Perú (PUCP), editor of *Revista de Psicologia PUCP*, and board member of the School of Graduate Studies. Instrumental in the design of public policies to provide special services to Peruvian highly able students, she developed the scientific proposal of the boarding academies for the highly able coming from poverty conditions in Peru. Also, she developed the psychoeducational model to monitor young scholars to prevent dropping out along college studies, which is now being transferred to the Peruvian public system. She is director of *Future Minds Talent Center*, chair of the 35th Inter-American Conference of Psychology, and is keynote and invited professor in North American, Latin American, and European universities.

In Search of an Explanation for an Approach-Avoidance Pattern in East Asia: The Role of Cultural Values in Gifted Education

11

David Yun Dai and Yong Zhao

Contents

Introduction	240
An Approach-Avoidance Phenomenon in Focus	241
Correlation Patterns Between Each International Measure	243
Profiles of East Asian and the Most Advanced Countries in Innovation	246
Asian Values Reflected in Educational Preferences	247
Why Values Matter for Gifted Education	249
Implications and Conclusion	251
Cross-References	253
References	253

Abstract

East Asian countries are touted as exemplary for high academic achievement. They ranked among the highest on the *Programme for International Scholastic Assessment* (PISA) performance. PISA is used to serve as an international benchmark of how a country fares in supporting high-ability students and high academic achievement (Finn and Wright 2015), but PISA performance has been consistently found to be negatively correlated with entrepreneurship (Zhao, 2012), suggesting that a high PISA score is associated with a low intent to engage in a more adventurous endeavour toward a career. To further understand the phenomenon, we used more recent data of PISA and *Global Entrepreneurship Monitor* (GEM), as well as two more global indices: *Global Innovation Index* (GII) and *Survival vs. Self-Expression*, a cultural value measure. The results suggest that high PISA

D. Y. Dai (✉)
University at Albany, State University of New York, Albany, NY, USA
e-mail: ydai@albany.edu

Y. Zhao
University of Kansas, Lawrence, KS, USA
e-mail: yongzhaoeducation@gmail.com

© Springer Nature Singapore Pte Ltd. 2021
S. R. Smith (ed.), *Handbook of Giftedness and Talent Development in the Asia-Pacific*,
Springer International Handbooks of Education,
https://doi.org/10.1007/978-981-13-3041-4_11

performance indicates a solid educational foundation for an innovation-driven economy. However, a PISA result is not, in and of itself, a good indicator of how innovative a nation is. Rather, cultural values significantly regulate how intellectual capital is channelled and used. We compare East Asian countries and the most advanced Western countries on PISA and cultural values. We further identify a set of values conducive to high academic achievement reflected in high PISA performance in these countries, such as prestige of academic accomplishments, work ethic, focus and discipline (self-control), and long-term perspectives. However, we also identify a set of values that impede a creative spirit: credentialism (education as a stepping stone to social success), achievement through conformity (following dominant social standards of success), and a preference for institutionalised pathways to success (avoiding nonconventional, high-risk endeavours). We analyse the psychosocial underpinnings of each of the three dimensions and argue that gifted education needs to embrace value systems that are conducive to nurturing what Renzulli calls 'creative productive giftedness' rather than merely 'schoolhouse giftedness'. We conclude that a gifted education aiming to produce a new generation of discoverers, innovative problem-solvers, and creative designers entails a change of culture.

Keywords

PISA · Credentialism · Cultural values · Intrinsic motivation · Creativity · Entrepreneurship · Innovation · Achievement · Productive creative giftedness

The aims in this chapter are to:
1. Highlight that although high PISA performance in East Asian countries indicates a solid educational foundation for an innovation-driven economy, it is not, in and of itself, a good indicator of how innovative a nation is.
2. Demonstrate that cultural values significantly regulate how intellectual capital is channelled and used.
3. Reiterate that a significant downside of East Asian values is a view of education as instrumental for social success rather than self-discovery and self-fulfilment.
4. Examine the benefits and deficits of outstanding academic performance of East Asian students as evidenced by the international comparison data which will be delineated.
5. Indicate that gifted education that seeks to produce a new generation of discoverers, innovative problem-solvers, and creative designers entails a change of culture.

Introduction

The *Programme for International Scholastic Assessment* (PISA) is a test developed by the *Organisation for Economic Co-operation and Development* (OECD) to assess secondary or middle school graduates' (aged 15) academic achievement in terms of mathematic reasoning, scientific reasoning, and reading. More than 72 countries and regions participated in this test in 2015 (OECD, 2018). High performance on the PISA, by students from East Asian countries, along with other international comparison data (e.g., *Trends in International Mathematics and Science Study* or TIMMS; see NCES, 2015), has recently drawn a great deal of attention from policymakers and school leaders worldwide (e.g., Benavot & Meyer, 2013; Carvalho & Costa, 2015). The fact that significantly larger portions of East Asian students excelled on these tests are touted as an education success, equivalent to what is expected of gifted education in terms of academic excellence (Finn & Wright, 2015; Phillipson, Ziegler, & Stoeger, 2013). In other words, we can equate standardised achievement as a benchmark of academic excellence, equally applicable to gifted education. On the other hand, concerns have been raised as to whether such high academic achievement is reached at the cost of individuality and creativity (Zhao & Meyer, 2013).

In this context, we aim to carefully evaluate the proposition that international comparisons of academic excellence as indicated by PISA can be used to benchmark education success and that success indicated by PISA for a nation or region is equivalent to the success of gifted education. For the purpose of this chapter, we broadly define gifted education as any school provision gearing toward high-level excellence in school, particularly in academic domains. We start with an observation of negative correlations between PISA performance variations across nations and a national index of entrepreneurship. Then we end with arguments that the outstanding showing of PISA by East Asian students is a mixed blessing and that the success of gifted education should be better indexed by enhanced creative productivity and achievement with authentic tasks than standardised tests.

An Approach-Avoidance Phenomenon in Focus

Zhao and Meyer (2013) identified negative correlations between PISA national averages and entrepreneurship indexes, namely, social values, perceived capabilities and levels of entrepreneurial activity. As shown in the following plots, a nation scoring high on PISA tends to have lower scores on entrepreneurship as indexed by perceived competence, social value, and early engagement in entrepreneurial activities. Although the more recent data (Fig. 1, the second plot) show a weaker correlation compared to the earlier data (the first plot), the patterns are consistent over time. What do these results mean exactly? Does it indicate a distinct approach-avoidance tendency—which is a conflict that occurs when making or avoiding a decision that has either positive or negative connotations—for example, in this context a preference for high achievement in academic success as compared to an avoidance tendency when it comes to pursuits of presumably more risky entrepreneurial activities?

Before we discuss the results of the findings in our research, a brief introduction to measurements we used and caveats related to these measurements are warranted. PISA reports are issued every three years by the OECD. The most recent PISA report was issued in 2016 on the 2015 assessment. In addition to mathematics, science, and

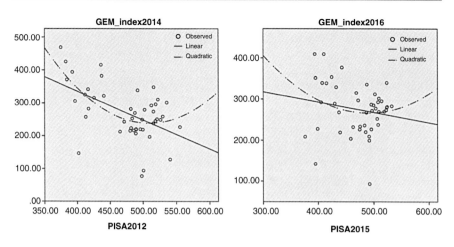

Fig. 1 Regression of Global Entrepreneurship Monitor (GEM) index on the national sum of three PISA subtests, showing a consistently negative relationship

reading performance, the 2015 assessment added a new test of *Collaborative Problem-Solving*, which aimed to assess students' ability to use knowledge and skills in solving practical problems. The *Global Entrepreneurship Monitor* (GEM, 2018) report is issued annually based on survey results from more than 70 countries and regions on a wide range of issues regarding opportunities for entrepreneurship and self-perceptions of competence and values.

To further clarify the high PISA/low entrepreneurship pattern, we expand our investigation beyond these two indices to include two more indices: The first is the *Global Innovation Index* (GII; Dutta, Lanvin, & Wunsch-Vincent, 2018), which provides rankings of 141 economies (as well as a wide range of innovation indicators) regarding levels of advances in an innovation-driven economy. The second is the *Survival vs. Self-Expression* (SSE) ratings that are issued by the *World Value Survey* (WVS) association (Haerpfer, 2018). The GII indicates how advanced a particular nation or region is in its technological and economic development, while the SSE indicates whether a nation (or culture) overall leans toward a 'survival' orientation or 'self-expression' orientation in its value systems. The survival orientation gives priorities to economic and physical security and success and shows a low level of social tolerance. The self-expression orientation gives priorities to political participation and environmental protection, that shows a high tolerance for diversity.

A distinct advantage of selecting these measurements is that they provide a common basis or scale for comparing nations or economies. International comparison data provide a macro-level perspective that cannot be obtained otherwise. However, precisely due to the nature of such large-scale comparisons, caveats are in order that these countries or economies are by no means homogeneous. First of all, aggregating information to make an international ranking is always a simplification exercise at the cost of nuances and within-nation (i.e., within-group) variance

(Carvalho & Costa, 2015). Second, context matters in determining what specific ratings exactly mean. For example, GEM categorises all economies into three development levels: the factor-driven economy is more agriculture-based, heavily relying on natural resources for subsistence; the efficiency-driven economy features more production-based activities with increased product quality; and, as development moves to the innovation-driven phase, business becomes more knowledge-intensive, and the service sector of an economy expands greatly. Thus, given different levels of economic development, entrepreneurship may mean different undertakings under different economic and technological conditions. By the same token, comparable aggregated PISA scores at the national level may reflect different educational and social-cultural contexts.

With this caution in mind, we first present a set of correlation and regression data that show interesting patterns and regularities regarding how national (or regional) average performance on the PISA is related to economic development and value systems. We then compare East Asian countries and regions with several top-ranked innovation-driven economies on the relevant measures to highlight important differences between the two groups.

Correlation Patterns Between Each International Measure

There is a strong positive correlation (rs = .80–.83; see Table 1 below) between PISA and the GII. Note that relationship may not be causal, in that a country can be strong or weak in both aspects of development, a third variable (e.g., national resources). It should also be noted that GII uses PISA scores as an input variable. Therefore, this correlation is partly a correlation with PISA itself. Nevertheless, it is

Table 1 Intercorrelations of PISA 2012, PISA 2015 and PISA 2015 Collaborative Problem-Solving (CPS), Global Innovation Index (2015) and Global Entrepreneurship Indices (GEM 2014, GEM 2016)

Variables	1	22 2	3	4	5	6
1. PISA 2012	–					
2. PISA 2015	.95**	–				
3. PISA 2015_CPS	.94**	.96**	–			
4. Global Innovation Index (GII)	.80**	.83**	.89**	–		
5. Survival vs. Self-Expression (SSE)	.34*	.43**	.42**	.61**	–	
6. GEM Index 2014	−.53**	−.50**	−.36*	−.40**	−.14	–
7. GEM Index 2016	−.26	−.18	−.13	−.13	.20	.90**

Note: Ns = 42–63
PISA 2012, PISA 2015 combined mathematics, science, and reading scores
PISA 2015_CPS = PISA 2015 Collaborative Problem-Solving
GEM Index = social value + perceived competence + intention/early engagement
** $p < .01$, * $p < .05$

safe to assume that a strong education foundation is important for any innovation-driven economy, which relies heavily on knowledge capital. We can further assume that national average PISA scores likely reflect a host of economic, social, and cultural factors, such as national policy and priorities, educational resources and infrastructure, and investment on the part of schools, teachers, parents, and students (see Benavot & Meyer, 2013). Beyond the normal range, extremely high PISA performance shown in some East Asian countries likely indicates a broad-based cultural phenomenon (Feniger & Lefstein, 2014). For example, Shanghai ranked first in the 2012 PISA; 55% of the participants belong to high-performing groups (Levels 5 and 6), compared to only 9% for the United States. Such a great showing of academic achievement, however, does not automatically make a country more 'innovative'. As the quadratic function of the relationship (see Fig. 2) suggests, beyond a threshold point, the positive correlation between the national average PISA and the innovation index diminishes; high innovation economies seemed to be clustered around the PISA score of 500, but not higher. This is further confirmed by calculating combined PISA scores of the top five GII countries (see Table 2).

Figure 3 below shows a distinct positive correlation between GII and Survival vs. Self-Expression (high innovation is related to high self-expression). It should be noted that if PISA reflects a country's overall resources and investment in education,

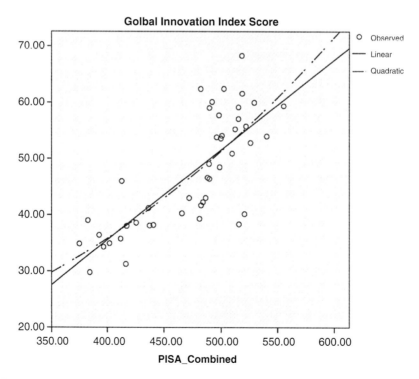

Fig. 2 Regression of Global Innovation Index on PISA-combined

Table 2 Comparison of East Asian and the most innovative countries on four indices

Economies	GII	SSE	PISA2015	GEM2016
Singapore	59.36	N/A	555.33	230
Hong Kong	57.23	.10	532.67	283
South Korea	56.23	−.60	542.67	269
Japan	53.97	.40	528.67	190
China (BSJG)	47.47	−1.00	514.33	295
Taiwan	N/A	−.60	523.67	280
Switzerland	68.30	1.49	506.33	252
United Kingdom	62.42	1.50	499.67	285
Sweden	62.40	2.30	495.67	286
Netherlands	61.58	1.45	508.00	292
United States	60.10	1.30	487.67	335
Finland	59.97	1.40	522.67	273
Australia	55.22	1.90	502.33	311

Note: for comparison purposes, Australia is listed along with the top-ranked countries in GII. GEM is calculated by summing up items indicating social values, perceived capabilities and intentions and levels of engagement of entrepreneurial activity

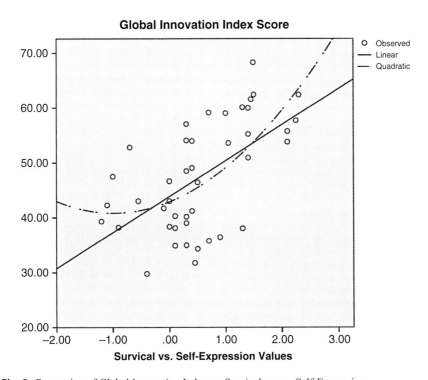

Fig. 3 Regression of Global Innovation Index on Survival versus Self-Expression

Survival vs. Self-Expression (SSE) represents an overall value orientation. Using Maslow's (1970) hierarchy of needs, those countries that value self-expression tend to value higher-level growth needs, whereas those leaning toward 'survival' tend to gear toward lower-level 'deficiency' needs and material and social success (i.e., the need to get ahead).

Again, we don't know whether such a correlation indicates a causal relationship between self-expression values vs. survival values and a nation's level of innovation as indicated by GII. For example, it may be that more innovation-driven economies tend to be those countries that hold more individualist and liberal values, hence the endorsement of self-expression more than mere survival. Alternatively, it may also be due to levels of economic and social advances; thus, people in developing countries are more likely to endorse the survival value of personal endeavour and are socially less tolerant, while people in developed countries are more likely to be concerned over long-term well-being, such as environmental protection. At any rate, for economic as well as cultural reasons, when people operate on a 'survival' mode, they are collectively more likely concerned with efficiency than innovation. As shown in Figure 2, cases of low-to-median self-expression scores are noticeable for some East Asian countries known for high PISA performance—for example, China, Taiwan, Hong Kong, Japan, and South Korea—further reinforcing the conjecture that low self-expression value and high survival value are behind the distinct approach-avoidance pattern found in East Asian countries discussed earlier (Figure 1). In the WVS mapping of values, many East Asian countries fall into the category of the broadly defined Confucian culture, with their value systems leaning toward survival rather than self-expression and secular rather than religious concerns. We can argue that as a country transitions from an efficiency-driven economy to an innovation-driven one, its value system also needs to change from a survival mode to a self-expression mode. However, given that any long-held cultural tradition has some inertia, a survival mode or way of life can become an obstacle to the development of an innovative spirit in its people as the approach-avoidance tendency indicated in Figure 1 seems to suggest.

Profiles of East Asian and the Most Advanced Countries in Innovation

As shown in Table 2, East Asian countries and regions ranked lower in innovation (GII) compared to the most advanced countries, and their rankings on GII are comparable to that for Australia. Together, they can be seen as second-tier, innovation-driven economies.

In addition, ratings of East Asian countries and regions on the value dimension of Survival vs. Self-Expression (SSE) are consistently lower (i.e., less self-expressive and more survival-oriented). Corresponding to the data in Table 2, in the upper-right quadrant of Figure 3, all top innovation-driven economies have GII values above 1, effectively excluding all East Asian countries and regions in Table 2, although their PISA performance is consistently higher than for those Western countries that ranked top on the GII. This contrast is paradoxical, given that both PISA and SSE are highly correlated with GII. This apparently bewildering pattern of results becomes more understandable when we consider distinct East-West differences in value orientations (see Table 2). A closer investigation of the PISA-GEM patterns indicates a sharp contrast between East Asian cultures (high PISA and low GEM) and Latin American cultures (low PISA and high GEM). While PISA clearly indicates a level of educational preparedness for an innovation-driven economy, it is the value of individualism (and consequently creativity) that provides an innovative edge to an economy (Runco, 2010). The value differences also partly explain, for instance, why Singapore and Japan ranked quite high on PISA, but scored quite low on GEM (see Table 2), a distinct example of the approach-avoidance pattern, which is of central interest to this chapter.

Summary

To sum up the findings of national indices of academic performance, value orientation and economic status, it seems that academic achievement is clearly important as part of the intellectual capital for an innovation-driven economy. However, the findings also suggest that valuing self-expression and willingness to take risks for that purpose can also be a very important underlying cultural value that helps sustain innovative endeavour. Although the pattern of intercorrelations of these national indices is complex, the data point to the importance of creating a culture of innovation conducive to the viability and sustainability of an innovation-driven economy. In the following section, we provide a more in-depth analysis of the underlying impetus for the East Asian countries' phenomenal PISA performance and explain why it does not provide a viable model of gifted education for other countries to follow. Our main argument is that gifted educators should be concerned with values as they determine what are deemed as desirable goals and outcomes for gifted education.

Asian Values Reflected in Educational Preferences

To fully unpack the complexities of the results presented in the previous section, it is necessary to dig deeper into a set of 'Asian values' behind the high PISA performance of East Asian students. What makes East Asian students so successful? A common explanation for the academic success of students in East Asian countries and regions is that these cultures show a strong preference on academic achievement as a pathway to social success (Cheng, 2011; Schleicher, 2018; Zhao, 2014; Zhao & Wang, 2018). Confucianism is clearly part of influences given its time-honoured tradition of encouraging the intellectually able to pursue careers in civil office (學而優則仕: 'Academic excellence is an essential credential for civil office'), which has been seen as the most honourable and prestigious occupation (Zhao, 2014, 2016). Another explanation is that Asian cultures value *long-term orientation*, defined as the tendency toward setting long-term goals, persistence and personal stability (see Minkov & Hofstede, 2012). However, a broader cultural perspective suggests that gravitating toward academic excellence as a pathway to social and personal success involves deeper value commitments reflected in the dimension of pursuing self-expression and self-cultivation (individualism) vs. securing social success as defined by societal norms (collectivism; Zhao, 2014).

Yu (1996) identified two contrasting patterns of achievement motivation, *Social-Oriented Achievement Motivation* (SOAM) and *Individual-Oriented Achievement Motivation* (IOAM); he characterised the former as a tendency to "reach an externally determined goal or standard of excellence in a socially approved way" [reflecting] "strong social instrumentality and weak functional autonomy" (pp. 234–235). The two motivation patterns differ on goals, behavioural patterns, outcome evaluation, consequentiality, and overall characteristics. Yu considered SOAM to be more dominant in Eastern cultures and IOAM as reflecting a Western individualistic orientation. This way of framing the East-West differences in achievement motivation slightly varies from the Survival vs. Self-Expression contrast, but consistent with the latter is its emphasis on whether the ultimate concerns are competition and social success or personally defined excellence and personal concerns that go beyond self-interest.

For the purpose of elucidating educational implications from the differences in achievement motivation patterns, we identify three distinct characteristics of East Asian values, which are: credentialism (Wu & Kuo, 2016); achievement through conformance rather than personal excellence (Yu, 1996; Zhao & Meyer, 2014); and non-risk-taking preference for institutionalised education.

The first characteristic is the enormous energy and time invested in building academic and other credentials to ensure social success, which is called credentialism (Wu & Kuo, 2016). Education itself does not mean much beyond a stepping stone to social and material success. The frenzy of academic competition in East Asia not only leads to academic burnout for many students but also does so at the cost of the individual's interest development, internal drive and desire for personal excellence (Cheng, 2011; Zhao, 2014, 2018).

The second characteristic is relying on prevailing social norms and standards in defining excellence and success, namely, achievement through conformance rather than pursuits of personal goals that help achieve personal excellence and autonomy, a point emphasised by Yu (1996) and Zhao and Meyer (2014). It is not that these norms and standards are wrong, rather, when they become fads, so to speak, individual interests and goals that do not align well with them are suppressed, to say the least. Moreover, education becomes a race against these norms and standards rather than engaging and inspiring students personally.

The third and last characteristic is a preference for institutionalised training and education, rather than ill-structured, uncertain, 'risky' tasks for which no clear path to success can be well defined nor secured. A distinct example besides academic pursuits is music training and education. Careers in classical music are vigorously pursued by East Asian parents, not because it is easy (think of the extremely competitive nature of places such as the Julliard School or Ivy League universities), but because it is highly institutionalised, with a finite repertoire and well-charted pathways to success, despite the entailment of enormous dedication and personal and family sacrifice (Sue & Okazaki, 1990).

These values reinforce and are reinforced by the educational institutions and practices in East Asian countries. Systems of high-stakes exams, for example, are the hallmark of East Asian education, dating back to Ancient times, but are still alive and well (Zhong & Wu, 2007). These systems exist because they are deemed necessary for granting credentials, sorting individual students according to predetermined norms, and ensuring compliance. These exams function as a gateway to progression in the education system and thus are closely aligned with a centralised and uniform definition of success codified in national curriculum and standards. The exam systems have been credited as a major contributor to the high academic performance of East Asian students (Schleicher, 2018; Tucker, 2011); but at the same time, they reinforce the idea that education is to help individuals achieve success as defined by external agencies, rather than the individual (Zhao, 2018).

Zhao and Meyer (2014) explored the approach-avoidance pattern of academic vs. entrepreneurial achievement motivation and concluded that the spirit of entrepreneurship will suffer under the collectivist pressure for conformity. We further argue that the above characteristics of achievement orientations undermine intrinsic motivation, personal creativity, and individual development, which would otherwise lead to a more personally gratifying career. This is what Zhao (2018) calls the side effects of education. That is, education values, practices, institutions, and policies—like medical products—can be effective resulting in both beneficial and harmful outcomes.

Why Values Matter for Gifted Education

In light of the potential side effects of education (Zhao, 2018), we need to consider the role of the East Asian values for gifted education. It seems apparent that East Asian education is capable of producing academic excellence, at least as measured by international assessments such as PISA and TIMSS (e.g., Phillipson et al., 2013). It is equally apparent that East Asian education under the influence of these values can potentially suppress qualities essential for entrepreneurship and innovation at the same time (i.e., side effects discussed earlier; see Zhao). If this holds true, policymakers and practitioners need to ask the tough question: Is the academic excellence worth the cost of entrepreneurship and innovation?

Renzulli (1986, 2005) distinguished between schoolhouse giftedness and creative productive giftedness; the former refers to excellence demonstrated in academic studies and basic skill development, and the latter refers to excellence demonstrated in creative problem-finding and solving in authentic contexts. We can argue that gifted education involves developing both aspects of giftedness. Indeed, in a way the high correlation between the PISA and the Global Innovation Index at the national level (see Fig. 2) alludes to connections between the two, as we mentioned earlier. However, we argue that creative productive giftedness, in the form of generating new and useful ideas and products that can potentially make a social impact, is more essential to gifted education in that one of the purposes of gifted education is to prepare youth for solving pressing problems in the world (Renzulli, 2005).

In light of the vision of gifted education proposed above, we argue that the East Asian values articulated in the previous section is not compatible with the spirit of gifted education. For one, evoking interest and passion should be part of the focus of gifted education; however, credentialism is the core value that downplays the importance of intrinsic motivation and makes education only the means to an extrinsic end and thus less personally meaningful (Yu, 1996). For another, gifted education is expected to encourage critical and creative thinking and cultivate one's distinct strengths and interests (VanTassel-Baska & Brown, 2007); however, going after common norms and standards of social success makes one's individuality secondary (e.g., preferring Survival over Self-Expression values), even undesirable. Finally, gifted education that is meant to promote creativity should encourage nonconventional careers and more adventurous endeavours, such as entrepreneurial activities, whereas East Asian values prefer convention to innovation (Yu, 1996). Studies (Yue, Bender, & Cheung, 2011; Yue & Rudowicz, 2002) show that college students in China are more likely than their German counterparts to name people in power as 'creative' and less likely to identify personal characteristics, such as artistic sensitivity and a sense of humour as associated with creativity. Such implicit conceptions of creativity further reveal the salience of a utilitarian orientation of Chinese culture (i.e., social status is more important than internal qualities) rather than an ultimate concern over self-actualisation (i.e., a mode of self-cultivation and expression of individuality).

It should be pointed out, while we view some East Asian values as impeding the cultivation of personal creativity, we by no means imply that they are unique to Asia or East Asia. For example, Young (2014) laments the fact that many college graduates in the United States aspire to finance, consulting, law, or medical careers out of a desire for financial gains, social status, and prestige, rather than from a genuine passion or fit for a particular domain. He points out the necessity of restoring a culture of achievement through cultivation of a personal interest in innovation rather than conventional financial and material success. We argue that the general trend toward pursuing lucrative careers is even more acute for developing countries, where people are working hard to overcome the hurdle of the 'middle-income trap'. Ironically, while a critical transition from an efficiency-driven economy to an innovation-driven one (GEM, 2018) entails gifted education gearing toward developing creative potential, the deeply entrenched values permeating their educational traditions tend to stand in the way of such a transition, as our data indicate. Therefore, taken altogether, education is more about survival, status, and prestige and less about personal passion and aspirations (Zhong & Wu, 2007).

In addition to values that underlie an innovative spirit in gifted education, there is another reason for cautioning against the overemphasis on schoolhouse giftedness or standardised tests such as PISA as an international benchmark for academic achievement and excellence. In an increasingly innovation-driven world, mastering the past does not necessarily translate readily to creating the future. What we consider talent in the past may not be as important today; what we consider precious talent may be replaced easily by Artificial Intelligence in the foreseeable future (Zhao, 2012). Gifted education has to be more mindful of preparing young generations of leaders and innovators, who are adaptive and lifelong learners, capable of dealing with an ever-changing world with many degrees of uncertainty, and who are maintaining an innovative spirit (Jeff Bezos or Sheryl Sandberg come to mind).

More specific to gifted education, we may think of two alternative prototypes of talent development: maker space and classical music training. Which one is a better model of gifted education for the future: *maker space*, that is, creating the unknown, or *classical training*, that is, mastering the well-known? Our response is that *maker space* represents a better way of thinking about a future-oriented gifted education in that the focus of our education is not just to master the things we already know (e.g., a classic repertoire researched for centuries), but explore things we don't know or have not yet mastered (Dai, 2016). We want to prepare the younger generations of individuals who know how to create a better future through innovation as well as preserve the precious past in this fast-changing world. Anecdotally, Asian students should not be merely 'good students', capable of absorbing lots of academic knowledge, but falling short of personal initiatives and pursuits of personal interests. Indeed, concerns about Asian students being 'passive' in school were expressed by the former principal of a famous science high school in New York City (personal communication). This school has a glorious history of having many alumni who became eminent leaders and innovators in scientific and technological fields (including several Nobel Laureates). Now that 70% of students in this school are Asian, can they still carry the legacy of creative edge if they are content with 'schoolhouse giftedness'?

To be sure, many East Asian American students actively participate in research and creative work, as evidenced by the results of *Intel Science Talent Search* (ISTS, now taken over by *Regeneron*) in the United States. In the past several years, a disproportionally large group of Asian students have been semi-finalists or finalists for this academic competition (https://student.societyforscience.org/regeneron-sts). These achievements are not confined to the United States, or to competitions, but have extended to special classes for the gifted and special schools for the gifted (e.g., Dai & Steenbergen-Hu, 2015). The question remains, however, as to whether they can have an equally good showing in technological innovation and entrepreneurship. Whatever the case, we argue that it takes a change of culture or values, not only in East Asia, but also across the world, to make gifted education more responsive to the increasingly innovation-driven world. In this regard, the approach-avoidance pattern that starts this conversation is only a tip of the iceberg that warrants further investigation, clarification, and understanding both in the research and in practice (see Dai & Kuo, 2016 for a broader assessment of gifted education in Asia).

Implications and Conclusion

In this chapter, we discussed the benefits and costs of outstanding academic performance of East Asian students as evidenced by the international comparison data. Our main argument is that the high academic scores should not be taken as equivalent to achievement due to gifted education, as it indicates a value and motivation orientation, that is inconsistent with the spirit of nurturing individuality, independent thinking, and personal creativity. There are many implications for gifted education practitioners in terms of how educators and administrators can develop and manage their programs and services with this caution in mind:

- As we discussed earlier, treating education as the means to an end of social success is often at the cost of appreciating the intrinsic value of education for self-actualisation. Gifted education in Asian and other countries runs the same risk, particularly when gaining a gifted status is like membership in an elite club coveted by many parents. We suggest that gifted education should take a more inclusive approach to involve those students who demonstrate their talent and the will to pursue their interests and cultivate their strengths. In other words, gifted education should operate like a talent incubator (inclusive and accessible), rather than an elite club (exclusive and confined to a few). The gifted-non-gifted bifurcation or categorical approach becomes problematic, as access is perceived as securing a ticket to social success rather than an opportunity to cultivate oneself.
- Historically, gifted education is characterised by two programming orientations: acceleration and enrichment. In the context of credentialism we discussed earlier, acceleration is clearly more appealing to Asian parents and students as faster always means better; the value of enrichment can be dubious from a utilitarian point of view, as exploratory activities often do not yield tangible advances and rewards as acceleration does and even look like a waste of time. Indeed, acceleration of curriculum is often initiated by East Asian parents so that their children can gain a competitive advantage over and get ahead of their peers. Although acceleration is still a viable option (see Dai & Steenbergen-Hu, 2015), gifted education in East Asia will be better off without such an 'ulterior' motivation for acceleration.
- When adopting a talent development approach (Dai, 2015), educators and parents should stress not just the instrumental utility value of specific education endeavours, but their potential for self-exploration and self-expression. This is particularly relevant when we try to raise career awareness to gifted students. Instead of following conventional pathways to success, nonconventional talent development should also be encouraged.
- In the spirit of creativity and innovation, gifted education should provide choices for students to explore their interests and individuality rather than dictate what they do. Students should be encouraged to take sensible risks and learn to deal with uncertainties and novelties as part of their endeavour, be it a scientific exploration or entrepreneurial venture. Choice often means self-initiation and self-direction, necessary qualities for sustained development of talent and creativity.

We live in a fast-changing world. How to educate our bright and talented minds to be more adaptive and innovative is the main challenge facing educators for the twenty-first century. However, credentialism, conformity to societal norms of success, and a preference for conventional or institutionalised pathways to success, which we identify in East Asian cultures, tend to hinder such development. We should be, therefore, fully aware of the role of cultural values, for better or for worse, in shaping one's motivation and life trajectory. These values may not be evident when international comparisons of academic performances are made, as in the case of PISA or TIMMS; nonetheless, they are important in gifted education. Although our argument is subject to further discussion and debate, we hope it serves as a cautionary note for equating standardised achievement as a benchmark of academic excellence, particularly for gifted education.

Cross-References

- Gifted Education in the Asia-Pacific: From the Past for the Future – An Introduction
- Innovative Practices to Support High-Achieving Deprived Young Scholars in an Ethnic-Linguistic Diverse Latin American Country
- Leadership Development of Gifted Adolescents from a Korean Multicultural Lens
- Learning from International Research Informs Academic Acceleration in Australasia: A Case for Consistent Policy
- Self-Regulated Learning for High-Ability and High-Achieving Students in Mixed-Ability Classrooms Throughout the Asia-Pacific
- Social and Cultural Conceptions and Perceptions: Part I Introduction
- Some Implications for the Future of Gifted Education in the Asia-Pacific
- Transitioning to Career: Talented Musicians' Identity Development

References

Benavot, A., & Meyer, H.-D. (Eds.). (2013). *PISA, power, and policy: The emergence of global educational governance*. Oxford, UK: Symposium Books.

Carvalho, L. M., & Costa, E. (2015). Seeing education with one's own eyes and through PISA lenses: Considerations of the reception of PISA in European countries. *Discourse: Studies in the Cultural Politics of Education, 36*, 638–646. https://doi.org/10.1080/01596306.2013.871449

Cheng, K.-M. (2011). Shanghai: How a big city in a developing country leaped to the head of the class. In M. S. Tucker (Ed.), *Surpassing Shanghai: An agenda for American education built on the world's leading systems* (pp. 21–50). Cambridge, MA: Harvard Education Press.

Dai, D. Y. (2015). A Jeffersonian vision of nurturing talent and creativity: Toward a more equitable and productive gifted education. *Asia Pacific Education Review, 16*, 269–279. https://doi.org/10.1007/s12564-015-9364-y

Dai, D. Y. (2016, July). *PISA, rocket boys, and looking for 1871, Chicago*. Keynote speech at the Biannual conference of the Asia-Pacific Federation on Giftedness, Macau, China.

Dai, D. Y., & Kuo, C. C. (2016). *Gifted education in Asia: Problems and prospects*. Charlotte, NC: Information Age Publishing.

Dai, D. Y., & Steenbergen-Hu, S. (2015). Special class for the gifted young: A 34-year experimentation with early college entrance programs in China. *Roeper Review, 37*, 9–18. https://doi.org/10.1080/02783193.2014.975882

Dutta, S., Lanvin, B., & Wunsch-Vincent, S. (Eds.). (2018). *Global Innovation Index (GII) report*. Retrieved from https://www.globalinnovationindex.org/Home

Feniger, Y., & Lefstein, A. (2014). How not to reason with PISA data: An ironic investigation. *Journal of Education Policy, 29*(6), 845–855. https://doi.org/10.1080/02680939.2014.892156

Finn, C. E., & Wright, B. L. (2015). *Failing our brightest kids: The global challenge of educating high-ability students*. Cambridge, MA: Harvard Education Press.

GEM. (2018). *Global Entrepreneurship Monitor annual report*. Retrieved from https://www.gemconsortium.org/report

Haerpfer, C. (2018). *World Values Survey (WVS)*. Retrieved from http://www.worldvaluessurvey.org/wvs.jsp

Maslow, A. H. (1970). *Motivation and personality*. New York: Harper & Row.

Minkov, M., & Hofstede, G. (2012). Hofstede's fifth dimension: New evidence from the World Values Survey. *Journal of Cross-Cultural Psychology, 43*, 3–14.

NCES. (2015). *TIMMS 2015 report*. Retrieved from https://nces.ed.gov/timss/

OECD. (2018). *PISA 2015 results*. Retrieved from http://www.oecd.org/pisa/

Phillipson, S. N., Ziegler, A., & Stoeger, H. (2013). *Exceptionality in East Asia: Explorations in the actiotope model of giftedness*. London, England: Routledge.

Renzulli, J. S. (1986). The three-ring conception of giftedness: A developmental model for creative productivity. In R. J. Sternberg & J. E. Davidson (Eds.), *Conceptions of giftedness* (pp. 53–92). Cambridge, England: Cambridge University Press.

Renzulli, R. S. (2005). The three-ring conception of giftedness: A developmental model for promoting creative productivity. In R. J. Sternberg & J. E. Davidson (Eds.), *Conceptions of giftedness* (2nd ed., pp. 98–119). Cambridge, England: Cambridge University Press.

Runco, M. (2010). Education based on a parsimonious theory of creativity. In R. A. Beghetto & J. C. Kaufman (Eds.), *Nurturing creativity in the classroom* (pp. 235–251). Cambridge, UK: Cambridge University Press.

Schleicher, A. (2018). *World class: How to build a 21st-century school system*. Paris: OECD.

Sue, S., & Okazaki, S. (1990). Asian-American educational achievements. *American Psychologist, 45*, 913–920. https://doi.org/10.1037/0003-066X.45.8.913

Tucker, M. (Ed.). (2011). *Surpassing Shanghai: An agenda for American Education built on the world's leading systems*. Boston: Harvard Education Press.

VanTassel-Baska, J., & Brown, E. (2007). Toward best practice: An analysis of the efficacy of curriculum models in gifted education. *Gifted Child Quarterly, 51*, 342–358. https://doi.org/10.1177/0016986207306323

Wu, W.-T., & Kuo, Y.-L. (2016). Gifted and talented education in Taiwan 1 40-year journey. In D. Y. Dai & C. C. Kuo (Eds.), *Gifted education in Asia: Problems and prospects* (pp. 33–50). Charlotte, NC: Information Age Publishing.

Young, A. (2014). *Smart people should build things: How to restore our culture of achievement, build a path for entrepreneurs, and create new jobs in America*. New York, NY: Harper Business.

Yu, A. B. (1996). Ultimate life concerns, self, and Chinese achievement motivation. In M. H. Bong (Ed.), *The handbook of Chinese psychology* (pp. 227–246). Hong Kong: Oxford University Press.

Yue, X. D., Bender, M., & Cheung, C.-K. (2011). Who are the best-known national and foreign creators: A comparative study among undergraduates in China and Germany. *Journal of Creative Behavior, 45*, 23–37. https://doi.org/10.1002/j.2162-6057.2011.tb01082.x

Yue, X., & Rudowicz, E. (2002). Perception of the most creative Chinese by undergraduates in Beijing, Guangzhou, Hong Kong, and Taipei. *Journal of Creative Behavior, 36*, 88–104. https://www.researchgate.net/publication/236596969_Perception_of_the_most_creative_Chinese_by_undergraduates_in_Beijing_Guangzhou_Hong_Kong_and_Taipei

Zhao, Y. (2012). *World class learners: Educating creative and entrepreneurial students*. Thousand Oaks, CA: Corwin.

Zhao, Y. (2014). *Who's afraid of the big bad dragon: Why China has the best (and worst) education system in the world*. San Francisco, CA: Jossey-Bass.

Zhao, Y. (2016). Who's afraid of PISA: The fallacy of international assessments of system performance. In A. Harris & M. S. Jones (Eds.), *Leading futures* (pp. 7–21). Thousand Oaks, CA: Sage.

Zhao, Y. (2018). *What works may hurt: Side effects in education*. New York, NY: Teachers College Press.

Zhao, Y., & Meyer, H.-D. (2013). High on PISA, low on entrepreneurship? What PISA does not measure. In A. Benavot & H.-D. Meyer (Eds.), *PISA, power, and policy: The emergence of global educational governance* (pp. 267–278). Oxford, UK: Symposium Books.

Zhao, Y., & Wang, Y. (2018). Guarding the past or inventing the future: Education reforms in East Asia. In Y. Zhao & B. Gearin (Eds.), *Imagining the future of global education: Dreams and nightmares* (pp. 143–159). New York, NY: Routledge.

Zhong, Q., & Wu, G. (Eds.). (2007). *Reflection on education in China (in Chinese)*. Shanghai, China: East China Normal University Press.

David Yun Dai is a Professor of Educational Psychology and Methodology at University at Albany, State University of New York, in 2001. Dr. Dai was a Fulbright scholar to China during 2008–2009 and to Germany during 2015–2016. He was the recipient of the Distinguished Scholar Award in 2017 conferred by the National Association for Gifted Children. He is internationally known for his work on gifted education, talent development and creativity. He currently serves on the editorial boards of *Gifted Child Quarterly*, *Journal for the Education of the Gifted*, *Roeper Review* and *Journal of Special Education* (Taiwan). His current theoretical and research interests include: (a) the psychology of talent development; (b) motivational and cognitive processes underlying creativity; and (c) foundational and policy studies in gifted education. His practical interests include formulating national and regional educational strategies and policies for promoting and nurturing talent and creativity at a macro level and fashioning pedagogical strategies for developing talent and creativity at a micro level.

Yong Zhao is a Foundation Distinguished Professor in the School of Education at the University of Kansas. His research interests include personalisation of education, education reforms and international assessments. He publishes widely on education. His recent books include *What Works Can Hurt: Side Effects in Education* (Teachers College Press, 2018), *Reach for Greatness: Personalisable Education for All Children* (Corwin, 2018) and *Counting What Counts: Reframing Education Outcomes* (Solution Tree, 2016).

Spirituality and Giftedness: Threading the Path of Identity

12

Russell Walton and Wilma Vialle

Contents

Introduction	258
Framing Spirituality	259
Theoretical Framework	260
Spiritual Identity in the Context of Giftedness	265
Giftedness and Spirituality	265
Ethical and Moral Considerations	266
Domain Specificity	267
Implications for Future Practice: Links with the Wider Community	269
Implications for Future Research	273
Conclusion	274
Cross-References	275
References	275

Abstract

A relationship between spirituality and giftedness has become an accepted part of gifted orthodoxy, and spirituality has even been suggested as a form of giftedness itself. This chapter, thus, adopts a structure of discussing spirituality in general and its characteristics before linking to giftedness itself. Initially the chapter sets out to present theories of spirituality, with particular attention to variances and their relationship to whether spirituality is considered as an

---

R. Walton (✉)
Learning Development, University of Wollongong, Wollongong, NSW, Australia
e-mail: Wordsmith.RW@bigpond.com

W. Vialle
University of Wollongong, Wollongong, NSW, Australia
e-mail: wvialle@uow.edu.au

© Springer Nature Singapore Pte Ltd. 2021
S. R. Smith (ed.), *Handbook of Giftedness and Talent Development in the Asia-Pacific*,
Springer International Handbooks of Education,
https://doi.org/10.1007/978-981-13-3041-4_12

'optional' component of existence or a fundamental component of who each of us are. This will include a discussion of the roles of religion and spirituality within the literature. Factors associated with spirituality will be discussed, including altruism, ethical behaviour, and social awareness, as well as their contributions to individual and collective development. A subsequent review of the literature will be presented to examine spirituality's contribution to giftedness. There is limited literature that addresses spirituality, as a whole, and its role in and contribution to giftedness. Therefore, the component factors of spirituality will form the bridge to link to related features of giftedness, with an emphasis on research-based contributions. The chapter will include an argument for the inclusion of spirituality at a curricular level, with the associated educational implications, as well as suggestions for future research and practice.

Keywords

Spirituality · Gifted · Domain · Connectedness · MSI · Socialisation · DMMI

The aims in this chapter are to:
1. Present spirituality as a function of the everyday, rather than being a purely aspirational concept.
2. Differentiate between intent and action in the process of spiritual development.
3. Identify potential causes for variation in male and female spirituality.
4. Link spirituality to instances of gifted educational practice.

Introduction

'Every castle has an enchanted hare' was the start of a tale Russell once studied for a storytelling performance. The hare can be viewed as a correlate for spirituality. In the tale, the purpose of each castle's hare was that of beacon, guide, and moral compass, while remaining out of reach until enlightenment was obtained. Attaining the hare is, thus, a transcendent aspirational concept; the associated journey is a path of development within a given social and cultural framework, just like spirituality. How spirituality is viewed and whether it is valued is very much dependent upon the social and cultural mores within which an individual has developed, whether at the level of the family or wider grouping. Given that those same influences can contribute to a perceived continuum of 'spiritualness', in order to address the role of spirituality in gifted education, a conceptualisation of what spirituality is will first be established. This will be followed by a discussion of the role of spirituality in giftedness, including educational implications.

Framing Spirituality

One of the more common aspects in historical discussions of spirituality is the role of religion, where the two terms have often been conflated (e.g., Radford, 2004). Fiona Gardner (2011) suggested that the consequent confusion is grounded in the move from collective concepts—where the role of religion was as a "shared and public experience" (p. 19)—to individual concepts, where religion can be an adjunct to spiritual development, but is not a requirement (see also, e.g., Hay & Nye, 2006; Heelas & Woodhead, 2005; Saucier & Skrzypińska, 2006). This should not be interpreted as a consensus view in modern society, where there remain both collective and individual views of spirituality and its relative association to religion. Two examples illustrate this point: citing Boyatzis (2005), Cervantes and Arczynski (2015) noted that "spirituality and religion are central dimensions of human development" (p. 246); by contrast, Sisk and Torrance (2001) noted spirituality's role in achieving "the highest realisation of human nature" (p. 7), but emphasised that it "is not about organised religion" (p. 12). The view taken in this chapter is in line with that of William James (1963) who, in the Gifford lectures of 1901, presented spirituality as a birth right of all humanity and thus independent of religion. For James, spiritual expression was the culmination of an individual's experiences and influences, with an emphasis on the transformative nature of the subjectivity of personal spiritual experience. See Walton (2015) for a fuller discussion of the respective roles of religion and spirituality, and Howard and Walton (2015) for the educational implications.

Even within that framework, however, spirituality often remains a contentious topic, whether it be related to what comprises spirituality, how spirituality functions or who is spiritual. Attempting to proffer a standardised agreement on the foundations of spirituality perspectives can, therefore, be fraught with peril. Palmer (2003) considered spirituality to be part of "the eternal human yearning to be connected with something larger than our own egos" (p. 377). While "in principle, the word 'spiritual' is a neutral term" (Sinetar, 2000, p. 18) in practice it is heavily loaded with both meaning and context, all of which are dependent upon individual and collective experience and values. Those influences position spirituality at the congruence of individual and societal expectations, with spiritual expression—including aspects of both light and dark (Lovelock & Adams, 2017)—being fundamental to every individual's balanced worldview and healthy emotional, psychological, and social existence (e.g., Büssing, Föller-Mancini, Gidley, & Heusser, 2010; Hay & Nye, 1996, 2006; Land, 2015; Moritz et al., 2006; Saucier & Skrzypińska, 2006), while being specifically indicated as having a protective influence on factors such as depression (Paine & Sandage, 2017; Talib & Abdollahi, 2017), sense of self (Mata-McMahon, 2016; Pandya, 2017), hopelessness and suicidal behaviour (Talib & Abdollahi, 2017). Researchers such as James and Miller (2017) also encourage taking spirituality into account for health interventions, while others identify spirituality's importance for adolescent psychological well-being (e.g., Kumar, 2015) and self-adjustment (e.g., Japar & Purwati, 2014). James, Fine, and Turner

(2012) considered spirituality to be a fundamental personal developmental 'asset'; in this role, spirituality is influential for overall quality of life (Panzini et al., 2017), resilience and values/moral development (Pandya, 2017), while Sagberg (2017) viewed spiritual development as "a matter of survival and flourishing as human beings" (p. 24). Spirituality is a key concept of importance for both Australian Aboriginals (Grieves, 2008, 2009; Taylor, 1999) and New Zealand Māori (Fraser, 2004b), while kahupō ('spiritual blindness') is a recognised indicator for suicide prevalence in Māori culture (Emery, Cookson-Cox, & Raerino, 2015). Ignoring the spiritual component of educational practice, thus, may work against student well-being.

A point relevant to this discussion should be made in regard to Howard Gardner's suggested addition of a spiritual/existential intelligence (SI) to his multiple intelligences (MI) theory (Gardner, 1993, 1999b, 2011). Whether or not spirituality should be considered as an 'intelligence' is beyond the scope of this chapter, so will not be addressed here—see, for example, the differing perspectives of Emmons (1999, 2000a, 2000b) and Gardner (1999a, 2000). There is no universal acceptance of MI theory, neither within the wider academic community nor the gifted community specifically. There is wider acceptance of Françoys Gagné's model that differentiates the conceptions of giftedness and talent (DMGT; e.g., Gagné, 2009, 2013), with near-universal inclusion of at least aspects of the model into Australian gifted education policies (Bannister-Tyrrell, 2017; Walton, 2015, 2017)—although there have been recent suggestions that there is a need to move beyond the DMGT, as well as questions over to what extent the DMGT is incorporated into practice, as opposed to policy (e.g., Henderson, 2018). Walton (2014, 2015, 2017) utilised the DMGT as a theoretical framework for his research by mapping MI theory onto the DMGT, with the resulting *Differentiated Model of Multiple Intelligences* (DMMI) illustrating how MI and the process of moving from giftedness to talent mirror each other, *including* the spiritual dimension (see Figs. 1 and 2). Spirituality is not explicit in the DMGT 2.0 as a separate domain, but would likely be listed as a mental domain rather than a physical one (although there would be physical components, suggesting holistic aspects). In the DMMI, however, spirituality is included as a later addition to MI theory. See Walton (2014, 2015) for a fuller comparison and discussion of the two models. However, whether the discussion is of 'spirituality' or 'spiritual intelligence' is of little importance, because they are referring to the same concept—how a person interacts with and within their world. This aspect is addressed throughout this chapter, utilising the term 'spirituality' (which should be read as inclusive of SI where that was the focus of the original author/s).

Theoretical Framework

Much of the modern research into spirituality draws on the frameworks proposed by Nye (1998) and, more specifically, Hay and Nye (1996, 2006). The categorisation of spiritual sensitivity into the three components of awareness-sensing, mystery-sensing, and value-sensing (Nye, 1998) led into the concept of 'relational consciousness' (Hay & Nye, 2006). To these three categories, Tirri, Nokelainen, and Ubani (2006, 2007) added 'community-sensing', as an acknowledgement of the importance of

12 Spirituality and Giftedness: Threading the Path of Identity

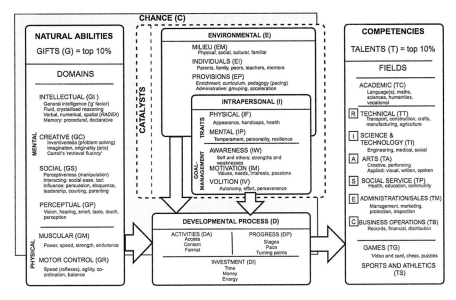

Fig. 1 Gagné's Differentiated Model of Giftedness and Talent (DMGT 2.0; Gagné, 2009, 2013)

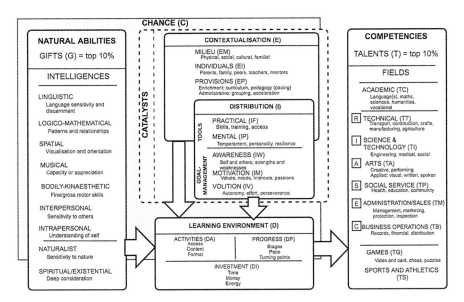

Fig. 2 Walton's Differentiated Model of Multiple Intelligences (DMMI; Walton, 2014, 2015, 2017). Adapted from Gagné's Differentiated Model of Giftedness and Talent (DMGT 2.0; Gagné, 2009, 2013)

social context in spirituality. The original three 'sensing' categories were used as a framework for Australian studies of children's spirituality undertaken by Vialle, Walton, and Woodcock (2008; see also Vialle, 2007) and Hyde (2008b), while also featuring in Nemme (2008). They also continue to contribute to international research in the field (e.g., Tirri et al., 2006, 2007; Tirri & Quinn, 2010).

Vialle et al. (2008) used the sensing categories as a starting point for focus groups with primary school students (both public schools and Catholic, Kindergarten, Year 2, Year 4, Year 6), centred around discussions on provided artefacts. From the responses, seven facets of spirituality were identified: (1) links to knowledge and personal experience; (2) importance and utility; (3) importance and aesthetics; (4) importance and uniqueness; (5) the nature of Nature; (6) circle of life; and (7) learned concepts.

Hyde's (2008a, 2008b) qualitative study also used Nye's (1998) sensing categories as a theoretical starting point. The participants were drawn from three Catholic primary schools, with the method utilising a combination of activities, discussion and writing. Four themes were identified: (1) felt sense; (2) integrating awareness; (3) weaving the threads of meaning; and (4) spiritual questing. While Hyde's themes appear more-closely tied to Nye's original sensing categories than do Vialle et al.'s (2008) themes, this has a likely basis in difference of qualitative approach. Hyde's research practice was deliberately constructed around active utilisation of the sensing categories whereas, despite using the same framework, Vialle et al.'s approach used the sensing categories as a starting point, with the themes emerging inductively. Despite this difference of approach, both Hyde's and Vialle et al.'s research studies identified commonalities in children's spirituality.

Moriarty (2011) developed a conceptual model of the dimensions of spirituality drawn from extant literature, including Hay and Nye (2006), but drawing heavily on Champagne (2003), as a framework for her research into young children's spirituality. The model components were: input, consciousness, relationality, identity, 'roadmap', and worldview. Following a series of interviews with 24 primary school students (aged 8–10), this model was then refined in light of the study results, with four core components: (1) consciousness, (2) relationality, (3) roadmap, and (4) identity. These components continued to be fed by input, as in Moriarty's first model. However, whereas previously 'identity' had been one component of a 'process' (p. 283) contributing to worldview, in the revised model identity arises *from* consciousness, relationality, and roadmap. Identity ('self') is thus positioned as a culmination of the preceding aspects and, in turn, contributing to future progression of spirituality and its expressed identity through lived experience. Moriarty's characterisation of the components of spirituality—and identity as "'signature' worldview" (p. 276), in particular—has close ties to Walton's (2015) model of spiritual identity (MSI; see Fig. 3). Moriarty (2011) framed identity as "*how* a person relates" (p. 275, original emphasis), with "reference to a defining community which provides a background reference for moral values, intuitions and relations" (p. 275).

Utilising a computer analogy, Walton's MSI explicitly grounds all spirituality in the context of the individual, whereby all experiences and influences are processed for internalisation—in a mirror of the store model of information processing for memory (e.g., Atkinson & Schiffrin, 1968). It is acknowledged that early models of information processing, such as the store model, have been superseded by models that better consider factors, such as the interaction of the model elements and the role of executive processes (Howard & Walton, 2015). The usage here is framed for those

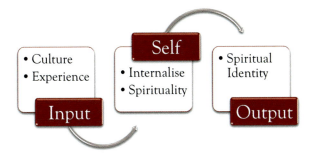

Fig. 3 Walton's (2015) model of spiritual identity (MSI)

unfamiliar with information-processing models and takes into account modern views of component interactivity. In the store model's simplest form there are three primary components: sensory register, working memory, and long-term memory. Everything the individual experiences, whether conscious or otherwise and in all its forms (e.g., visual, aural, tactile), is received by the sensory register where, if a perception of potential value is attached to the data, it is passed on to the working memory (if a perception of value is not attributed then the data are lost). There is still a huge amount of information passed into working memory, with only the data deemed to have further value to the individual being paid attention to, processed, and transferred to long-term memory, while the rest 'decays' (e.g., Sternberg & Sternberg, 2012). Given the vast amount of data taken in by the sensory register, this is necessarily an unconscious process, but is inherently grounded in the context of the individual and their pre-existing experiences. The 'potential value' that needs to be attached for processing in working memory can only realistically be judged in light of information that is already stored in long-term memory, whether that be through omission or amendment (e.g., Baddeley & Logie, 1999). The *input* of the MSI can, thus, be considered analogous to the sensory register because it, too, is a provider of information. At any given point in time, we are all a product of all the experiences we have had to that point. This is the case regardless of whether those experiences have been positive or negative, shallow or deep, light or dark, deeply personal, or inconsequential. What we experience as *input* is assessed against the pre-existing knowledge, concepts, attitudes, and so on that already exist in *self*. Memory is thus considered as fundamental to not only a personal understanding of spirituality, but also its expression (*output*). The *self*'s role as 'background reference' (as per Moriarty, 2011, above) informs what value is attached to the *input* information, as well as influencing how that information is dealt with in the working memory, with consequent impact upon long-term memory.

The internalisation process of assessing information against what is already considered known and working out what to do with the information is inherently personal, and one that should not be underestimated. Dependent on the individual's pre-existing accepted norms, whether that information confirms, contradicts, or complements still needs processing. This is not to say that new information automatically constitutes a change—history is littered with examples of individuals who have not accepted a change in their world, thus, choosing to ignore new information is a personal form of processing in itself. Nonetheless, how the information in *self* is processed influences who we *are* at any given point in time. The *self*, in the MSI, is presented as a snapshot of an individual's existence in a fluidly dynamic process of continuous development. Jean-Paul Sartre (1957) observed that "man is nothing else but what he makes of himself" (p. 15). The applicability of this to the MSI is that Sartre's 'himself' can be considered to be what comprises the *self*, regardless of sex/gender. Even then, while *self* can be viewed as fluid, it is also static, in that it is an internal definition and thus not expressive itself. Without expression the *self* lacks direction. *Output* is the face that is presented to the world—whereas *self* may be loaded with 'intent', it is *output* that is laden with 'action'. For varied reasons, aspects of the *self* may not be given free rein in society at whatever level, that is, they may be modified for acceptability. This renders *output* as the domain of choice, where decisions are made in regard to how the *self* should be acted upon. Ultimately, *output* is what we do in the world, within the bounds of *self* as internalised from *input*. All of which, of course, is suggested as a cyclical ongoing process that is fundamental to the expression of spirituality.

Many discussions of spirituality focus on the higher levels, such as transcendence—for example, some developmental theories also include transcendence. Most notable, perhaps, is Maslow's amended hierarchy of needs (e.g., Duchesne, McMaugh, Bochner, & Krause, 2013; Huitt, 2011). This model represents transcendence as the pinnacle of personal needs. It is notable, however, that Maslow did not include transcendence in his original model (Maslow, 1943), nor did he represent the 'needs' in the form of a pyramid (a representation he disagreed with; see McInerney & McInerney, 2010; Rowan, 1998).

The extant literature on spirituality also reiterates connections with a higher state of being, whether as the goal or as aspects of overall spirituality—in Moriarty's (2011) model, for example, these aspects are included under consciousness and relationality, respectively. Attainment of such concepts, however, is reliant on having a solid grounding in other aspects of life. People do not generally live their day-to-day lives as a search for transcendence, rather, while that may be an aspiration, their lives are concerned with existence and managing the world that is, right now, both imminent and pressing. This view is consolidated by de Souza, Bone, and Watson (2016), for whom "the spiritual dimension of life helps individuals create frameworks of meaning and provides individuals with a way of being in the world which influences their decisions and actions. It enables them to interpret their life experiences, which can help them to work through difficult and unhappy times, overcome challenges, and find purpose in being" (p. 346). The spirituality of the *now*, as represented through models such as Moriarty's (2011) and Walton's (2015, 2017), can, thus, form the foundation for higher states, while simultaneously being able to be directly influenced by the educational context.

Spiritual Identity in the Context of Giftedness

The concept of spiritual identity, the *now* of existence—evidenced through every person's everyday experiences and interactions—is equally applicable to gifted and non-gifted, being an inherent component of all human lives regardless of other differences. In specific relation to giftedness, there is a general acceptance that gifted individuals are characterised by higher levels of spirituality than non-gifted individuals (e.g., Lovecky, 1998; Roeper, 1995; Sisk, 2008). Despite this, there has been little research undertaken on the overall spirituality of students who are gifted in different domains (Walton, 2015, 2017, being the notable exception). There have, however, been significant contributions to moral and ethical aspects of spirituality. Indeed, a significant portion of the research in these areas for non-gifted has been undertaken by researchers with a giftedness background, such as Dorothy Sisk and Kirsi Tirri, although such research features less so in the Asia-Pacific region.

Giftedness and Spirituality

The intensity of the gifted experience has been recognised by numerous authors and researchers (e.g., Grant & Piechowski, 1999; Harrison, 2000; Lovecky, 1998; Piechowski, 2002, 2003, 2006), the characterisation of which Sisk (2008) described as "a unique way of perceiving their world and their relationship to it" (p. 24). The domains of giftedness appear to be imbued with a common thread of spirituality, regardless of cultural context (Ambrose, 2009), which Piechowski (2009) linked to higher levels of 'energy' in gifted children. The spiritual thus can be both a form of giftedness (e.g., Fraser, 2004a, 2004c; Kowalske, 2016) and a common denominator, with the potential for development. Anything that can be developed can be learnt, and if it can be learnt, then it can be taught. Sisk (2008) suggested access points for engaging gifted students' spirituality, in the process of classifying spiritual intelligence as SQ, characteristics of which include "connectedness, compassion, responsibility, balance, unity, and service" (Davis, Rimm, & Siegle, 2011, p. 274). Central to these characteristics are ethics and morals, which include altruistic factors. While many usages of 'ethics' and 'morals' are nearly interchangeable, the usage here is that ethics are governing factors that can influence morals, and thus moral behaviour. This approach is in line with Gibson and Landwehr-Brown (2010), building on Gibson, Rimmington, and Landwehr-Brown (2008), who made a distinction between ethics and morals, with ethics being based in a value system while morals is acting upon the value system. There is an inherent internalising spirituality factor in the process of ethics being applied to morals and associated behaviours—in the move from intent to action—which is evident as spiritual identity in Walton's MSI (2015, 2017) and in Wong's (2007) *Soul Care Project*.

Ethical and Moral Considerations

Two giants of giftedness—Annemarie Roeper and Leta Hollingworth—have been described by Silverman (2016) as proponents of ethical development for their pivotal role in gifted education. Ethical motivations are the basis of moral behaviour, which would suggest that if gifted individuals truly do have a tendency towards more ethical motivations than the non-gifted, then this should be paralleled by more moral behaviour. Yet this seemingly innocuous statement is countered by Sternberg's (2012) view that "many people identified as gifted through traditional means are nevertheless lacking in ethics" (p. 241). This somewhat depressing observation is aimed at gifted adults, but his reasoning is, nonetheless, applicable for all ages, because the lack of ethics occurs "in part because socialisation may not reward them for the development of ethical patterns of behaviour" (p. 241). So, the socialising input of feedback from ethical behaviours, whether personal or observed, is internalised in the framework of 'reward', with subsequent output behaviours modified accordingly. Any definition of what is ethical and/or moral behaviour is situated within its particular cultural context. Yet the ethics/morals of human interaction are surprisingly consistent across cultures, having a basis in honesty and fairness. Sternberg suggests that this can be encouraged through cultivation of wisdom or, at least, to value wisdom and its expression in wider society. His definition of wisdom has altruistic behaviours as a key component, as wisdom is fundamentally "directed toward the common good" (p. 248)—see Ricard (2015) for a detailed discussion of altruism.

The necessity of teaching children ethical rules and behaviour, perhaps even as a counterpoint to non-ethical/moral behaviours observed in the wider society, is positioned as important for inculcating wisdom in our future leaders (it should go without saying that not all leaders demonstrate wisdom). Abu Bakar, Ishak, and Abidin's (2014) research also linked gifted students' higher empathy to leadership capacity. From Sternberg's (2012) perspective, decision making through ethical reasoning is a process for all students, but especially for those who are gifted, with the observation of "can we afford to develop gifts [of all domains] without also developing their ethical utilisation?" (p. 249). Wisdom thus becomes a vehicle for altruism. O'Leary (2005) identified significantly higher strengths underlying altruistic motivations for gifted than non-gifted, while also observing that gifted females exhibited higher-level reasoning for altruism than gifted males.

The gifted are often considered to have more ethical/moral inclinations than non-gifted, with the gifted students in Tirri and Nokelainen's (2007) research rating their own ethical skills higher than did their non-gifted peers. The development of ethical sensitivity is stronger in gifted students, particularly the female gifted, which Tirri and Nokelainen (2007) attributed to the gifted students' "precocious intellectual growth" (p. 598). The possibility of different approaches within giftedness towards a task may also have a basis in differences of 'ways of knowing'. The research of Kohan-Mass (2016) examined years 5–6 gifted students' 'thinking styles', finding a tendency for boys to favour separate knowing (e.g., scepticism and analysis) and girls to favour connected knowing (e.g., empathy and co-operation)—following

Belenky, Clinchy, Godberger, and Tarule (1986). The gifted, however, have just as many variations of character as non-gifted, and being gifted itself does not necessitate a predetermination towards highly moral behaviour (Tirri, 2010).

Nonetheless, the expression of morality needs an outlet, a purpose. Concern for, and place in, the world is inherently linked to the need for social support to be happy and having the opportunity to give back to society (Johnstone, 2014). The twin factors of individual (personal happiness) and collective (giving back) are also evident in Miller's (2005, 2010) research with Māori gifted children, which led him to identify the two most identified characteristics of Māori gifted children as: (1) outstanding personal qualities and high moral values; and (2) service to others. Pramathevan and Garces-Bacsal's (2012) Singaporean investigation into altruistic factors in service learning for gifted female youth was formulated from their own observations of differences in how gifted youth approach service learning. They observed that being gifted, in itself, was not a predictor of passionate involvement, with clear distinctions between the gifted who met the school requirements, and no further, and those gifted who went 'above and beyond'. The latter group formed the population for Pramathevan and Garces-Bacsal's study, with indicators that a combination of personality, value system, social skills, and social factors were contributors to the displayed altruism. In other words, perhaps unsurprisingly, role modelling and life experience are fundamental to the development of altruism. Thus, there is a role for education in providing experiences for gifted students to better understand concepts of ethics and morality, as well as provision for opportunities to apply those concepts.

Domain Specificity

The literature does not generally differentiate between spirituality across the domains of giftedness. Finnish research with the academically gifted is suggestive of differences in gifted male and female spirituality, with gifted females more inclined to reflect on moral reasoning (Tirri & Pehkonen, 2002) and spend "more time pondering existential questions" (Tamminen, 1991, 1996, cited in Ubani, 2010, p. 3). For gifted boys there seems to be more of a focus on their relationship with nature as a "source of spirituality and mystery" (Ubani, 2010, p. 3). When giftedness is referred to across the literature, it is the academically gifted who are usually being referred to. This is no different with spirituality and giftedness, where spirituality of the academically gifted tends to be the focus. However, even when spirituality is related to other forms of giftedness, these tend to focus on a specific type of giftedness. The question remains as to whether comparisons can be made between how spirituality manifests in different forms of giftedness. In this regard, the quantitative research of Walton (2015, 2017) provides a rare glimpse.

Walton's participants were 352 students from years 11 and 12 across three New South Wales' high schools. The average age of participants was 16.43 years ($SD = 0.67$), of whom 54% were female. All of the participants were drawn from high schools with an identifiable gifted population in specific domains—academic, creative, or sport, as representatives of both the mental and physical domains in Gagné's (2009, 2013) DMGT 2.0 and the 'intelligences' of Walton's (2014, 2015, 2017) DMMI (see Figs. 1 and 2). The control group was drawn solely from the general entry students in the sport school. The students were asked to complete an adapted version of the *Integrated Spiritual Intelligence Scale* (ISIS; an 82-item self-report inventory), developed by Amram (2007) and Amram and Dryer (2008). The ISIS was adopted primarily because it offered both depth and breadth of statements; as no extant work could be located that made comparisons of spirituality between giftedness types, the baseline measure needed to consider the potential for variations in approach of the gifted in the different domains. The statements were grouped into five spirituality domains (Consciousness, Grace, Meaning, Transcendence, Truth) and 22 sub-scales. Minor changes to language were made, with the approval of the ISIS authors, in order to tailor ISIS to Australian adolescents, as the original ISIS was intended for American adults.

Independent-samples t-tests indicated no significant difference between the sport and control groups, except in a single sub-scale, so subsequent analyses treated these groups as a single control. Overall spirituality means (see Fig. 4) indicated that, consistent with research hypotheses, the creative group would score highest on spirituality, but the size of the difference between the creative group and the academic and control groups was unexpected. That was compounded when analysis was conducted on the interaction between sex and group (see Fig. 5). While the order of scores was the same for both male and female, the order of magnitude differed markedly. All of the male scores fell within a range that indicated no significant difference between any male groups, effectively rendering the males as a single homogenous group. By contrast, for the females there were significant differences between each group. The creative female group score was significantly above all other groups, the academic female group was only significantly different to the creative male group (and that to only a small degree), while the female control was

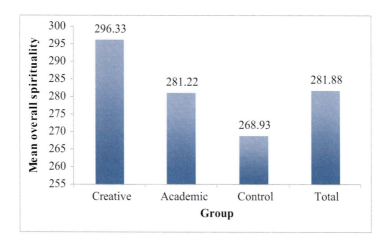

Fig. 4 Overall spirituality means for Group (Walton, 2015, 2017)

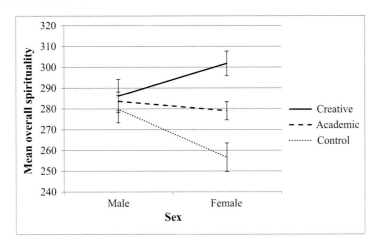

Fig. 5 Overall spirituality means for Sex and Group (Walton, 2015, 2017)

significantly below all other groups. The creative group also scored highest in four of the five spirituality domains. It was hypothesised that all gifted groups would rate higher in spirituality than the control, but this can only be said to apply to the creative group, and the female creative group specifically once sex was taken into account.

The disparity in scores cannot be explained with a single reason. Walton (2015, 2017) suggested a combination of inter-related reasons, including gender socialisation of roles and behaviours. This would include a relation to Kohan-Mass's (2016) research on thinking styles, cited earlier, whereby boys favoured separate knowing and girls favoured connected knowing, even from a young age. This variation of 'knowing' may manifest as a result of differences in parental conditioning of boys and girls (e.g., Blakemore, Berenbaum, & Liben, 2009; Bosacki, 2001; Hart, 2003; Tenenbaum & Leaper, 2003; Tenenbaum, Snow, Roach, & Kurland, 2005), rendering the difference in scores as the result of psychological rather than biological factors. In this context, it is worth noting that the creative group ($N = 83$) was 65% female, which is markedly more than the academic (52% female), sport (29% female), original control group (59% female), or combined control group (47%). Essentially, the higher spirituality of the creative females may have pulled up the scores of the creative males, contributing to the higher overall creative score.

Implications for Future Practice: Links with the Wider Community

Given the broad range of positive outcomes identified for spirituality, which are capable of enhancement through educational intervention, it is reasonable to expect that appropriate provision would be made in curricula. Spiritual development is already a right enshrined in various national and international rights-based documents (Sagberg, 2017). While spirituality is starting to be included in educational documents (e.g., DEEWR, 2009; Ministry of Health, 2017; NSW Department of Education and Communities [NSW DEC], 2015), it is questionable just how much is translated into concrete action. For example, attending to primary school students' spiritual development is mandated in the *Wellbeing Framework for Schools* (NSW DEC, 2015), where "all schools are *required* to have a planned approach to well-being in place that incorporates the elements [cognitive, emotional, social, physical, spiritual] of the Wellbeing Framework" (p. 7; emphasis added). Yet Russell's conversations with principals have indicated either ignorance of that requirement or a belief that no separate provision is needed as it is 'covered by scripture'. Setting aside the issues arising from the latter belief, these conversations support West's (2011) assertion that the educational environment does not cater for spirituality, while Natsis (2017) observed that spirituality is given limited educational attention, particularly in government schools.

The call for integration of spiritual perspectives into education has a storied history (e.g., Halford, 1993; Kessler, 2000; Montessori, 1989; Myers, Sweeney, & Witmer, 2000; Noddings, 2013; Palmer, 1999; Suhor, 1999), including by proponents of gifted education. At the centre of these calls is the concept of 'connectedness', whether that be to nature, people, or culture. All of the things we experience and all of our actions take place in the context of relationality, while that *now* context influences future contexts through internalising the effects. Early proponents of connectedness as central to spirituality in education include: Rachael Kessler's (2000) *Passages Program*, embedding spiritual questions into the adolescent curriculum; and Kieran Egan (2001), who advocated a new approach to education that captures and values the imagination and the spirit (Vialle et al., 2008). Also of note is Laurance Splitter's (2001) *Philosophy for Children* program, which sought to engage children in considering life's 'big questions', those "of belonging to something larger than oneself but not at the expense of one's sense of self" (p. 113).

Such questions can arise from a spontaneous occurrence and connection to real-life examples. When on Professional Experience (PEX)—a NSW teacher training requirement, where the trainee teacher acquires experience teaching a class under the supervision of a qualified teacher—with a Year 3 class, one of the female students (not classified as gifted, but one of a group of three students in that class who were considered by the school as such) brought Russell a bunch of flowers to class. The subsequent interaction was along the lines of: [Russell] 'Wow, thank you for these. That is really thoughtful'; [Student] smiles and starts to turn away; [Russell] 'Please thank your parents too, for growing them'; [Student] 'Oh, no, these are from a garden I pass on the way to school'; [Russell, after a pause] 'I appreciate them, really, but I am not sure that is OK. Would you mind if I asked the rest of the class what they think?'; [Student] 'Yes, let's [enthusiastically]'. The subsequent discussion was free flowing, engaged in by the whole class, ranged well beyond the flowers themselves and covered wide aspects of 'right' and 'wrong'. It was like a dam had burst. At the end of the discussion, an hour or so later, the student commented, 'That was cool', while positive feedback was received from other students and their parents throughout the PEX.

Connectedness also links the tangible to the intangible, prompting Joseph Campbell to observe that "myth makes a connection between our waking consciousness and the mystery of the universe" (Osbon, 1991, p. 56), that is, myth is a bridge linking lived experience and the divine. From Campbell's perspective, myth is a guidebook for reality, and for children myth acts as a primer for life, where all things have a spiritual relevance for interpreting (internalising). While the relevance of Campbell's insights should be plain, they are more exploratory than action based. Myth helps us understand our place in the world, but while myth provides guidance on connectedness, it does not predicate any given action, as it is the individual's role to internalise the meaning of myth and act upon it according to their own ethics.

Towards the end of summer, Russell was collecting pods from the almond tree in his front yard. While eyeing up which pods were ready, he noticed something odd about ten feet up. A closer look revealed it to be a bird's nest, but the unusually delicate structure and its size (no more than two inches across) meant that this was not a bird he was familiar with. Russell interpreted the scene according to his own insights, which included: the fragility of the tiny bird, for such a small nest, would belie the strength needed to build and survive in such a windy position; the nest itself, with its intricate and delicate weaving, was related to the Norns weaving the threads of fate. These two factors together were symbolic of how even the smallest living things have a right to that life, and to exist in synchrony with their surroundings, but also of how the tiniest things can inspire humans to both place their cares aside, in perspective, and to draw inspiration from those ostensibly weaker than themselves. These observations are a combination of cultural heritage, through myth, and life experience to inform the interpretation of the scene. Another viewing the exact same scene would likely interpret it differently; especially one with less of a sense of an innate connection to nature, but the scene itself does not change.

How action manifests in this instance can vary from individual to individual but can inform educational opportunities to enhance spirituality. These can be of a vicarious nature, taking advantage of unplanned opportunities as they arise. In a teaching situation, a photo of the nest, along with some of the pods and leaves from the almond tree, taken into class would provide a real-world scenario to be discussed. Aside from giving a recount of what Russell was doing and how he felt when discovering the nest, with consequent opportunity for students to input their own experiences, questions for students to research answers to may include: If the nest is only two inches across, what size range can the bird and its eggs, be? What types of birds are known to nest in almond trees? And what bird is it most likely to be? This can take place over an extended period, with further photos and a recording of bird sound. All of these possibilities give rise to opportunities for gifted students to add breadth and depth to the topic. The literature consistently supports connections with nature as being important to students' spiritual selves (e.g., Hyde, 2008a, 2008b; Jirásek, Veselsky, & Poslt, 2017; Kilcup, 2016; Schein, 2014; Suzuki, 2004; Vialle et al., 2008), including for gifted students (e.g., Kowalske, 2016; Lovecky, 1998; Sisk, 2008). In practice, this can take multiple forms, for example: 'wild places' excursions, school gardens, or in-school projects such as those based on the birds' nest example above. The option(s) chosen would often depend on practicality, but the key is to help students internalise the experiences in their own way.

Watson (2017) put forward four interconnected values for professional practice, including education, in relation to spirituality: (1) a broad working usage of spirituality that is inclusive; (2) recognition of human rights and the human voice of all, whether adult or child, to be listened and responded to; (3) "spirituality is a positive challenge to consumerism, marketisation and performativity" (p. 11); and (4) teaching of spiritual practice but without imposition of external world views. In most modern societies these values need to be considered within the context of multiculturalism, that is, the non-homogeneous nature of society. Mata-McMahon (2016) presented a complementary process that is inherently interactive and moves beyond multicultural considerations: "A pluricultural perspective to children's spirituality will allow scholars and researchers to approach spirituality, not from the typical understanding of multiculturalism, yet from a position of endless possibilities once different cultures are present within a group of children, or within the environment surrounding a particular child" (p. 149). Even then—whether multicultural, pluricultural or otherwise—any approach is beholden to the model lens adopted by the relevant governing body that it is viewed through.

Vialle et al. (2008) noted that "to rely on current models of cognitive, moral, and emotional development may not be adequate" (p. 148), yet such constrained models continue to be the norm. One such example is *Cognitive Load Theory* (CLT), which is solely focused on cognitive factors in task performance. CLT has its premise in the principle that every learning task places a 'load' on working memory (the part of memory where incoming information is evaluated and processed for potential retention in long-term memory), where capacity is limited (Pascual-Leone & Johnson, 2005, 2011; Sternberg & Sternberg, 2012). Adjustments to the task load, therefore, affect the impact on working memory and, thus, the likelihood of the task information being processed into long-term memory (Sweller, van Merriënboer, & Paas, 1998). Three types of cognitive load have been proposed: intrinsic (the inherent difficulty of the learning task); extraneous (how the task is designed and/or presented); and germane (related to 'learning-relevant processes'; Howard & Walton, 2015, p. 108). The intrinsic load of a task cannot be changed, although ensuring tasks are appropriate for the level of each learner can reduce this load. Extraneous load, however, is both manipulable and relevant, offering distinct opportunities to reduce the load on learners' working memory and, thus, the likelihood of task-relevant information being retained in long-term memory for later application (Sweller et al., 1998). The role, and even existence, of germane load is debated, as is its relation to intrinsic load (e.g., de Jong, 2010; Kalyuga, 2011), so will not be discussed further here. While the design and presentation of a task fall within the purview of learning instruction, the capacity for the learner to be able to complete a task successfully is dependent upon a non-learning-specific factor, that being the externalities that the learner brings to the task on any given day. Although the variable effects can be seen within the learning environment, these effects are influenced by external origins, most notably related to the home environment and familial/social relationships. Indeed, it is the contention here that spirituality is key to the externalities of cognitive load.

CLT tests measure performance at a given point in time, but performance on any task can vary day to day, or hour by hour, dependent upon circumstances being experienced. This is neither because of the task constraints nor the intrinsic/extraneous load, but results results from variations in what mindset the individual brings to the task, whether positive or negative, at the time the testing is performed. A difference in the internalised position of the student thus affects their performance on the task being tested. As an extension, paying attention to students' spiritual development can improve their mindset and contribute to lessening the deleterious effects of influences beyond the school. There may, thus, be potential for academic performance to be enhanced through spiritual development.

Spirituality cannot be separated into 'subject areas' because it does not fit within any border or concept. As an integral component of *everything* an individual thinks and does there is spiritual relevance across all subject areas. An educational environment that takes into account the student as a whole needs to (re)assess the value placed on the spiritual, by moving beyond rote iteration of standardised learning.

> Perhaps most important, as teachers, we can honour our students' search for what *they* believe gives meaning and integrity to their lives, and how they can connect to what is most precious for them. In the search itself, in loving the questions, in the deep yearning they let themselves feel, young people can discover what is essential in their own lives and in life itself, and what allows them to bring their own gifts to the world. (Kessler, 2000, p. 171; original emphasis)

Implications for Future Research

Walton's (2015, 2017) research into the spirituality of different gifted domains provided a baseline for further research in the area. This is partly due to the questions it raises, primarily through age, type of research, and instrument. While the research provides a snapshot of gifted spirituality, it is through a small window. The research was restricted to just two years at the end of high school, in the transition window from childhood to adulthood, but cannot provide an indication of whether that pattern is stable or is influenced by age. For example, would the patterns identified also be evident in Year 7 or Year 9? It was noted earlier that spirituality is a process of continuous development and a fluid dynamic, therefore, would a progressive increase, or decrease be evident across age ranges? Research with a sequential feature (i.e., covering a wider range of years) may contribute to understanding such factors.

Given the limited research database existing for spirituality and giftedness, a focus on research that is generalisable is encouraged. In this regard, it is suggested that further research to examine such factors as those mentioned above should, where possible and practical, follow Walton's quantitative approach. It is noted that this position differs markedly from such as that of Davis et al. (2016), who call for an increased role for qualitative research in regard to relational spirituality and psychology. However, there appears to be a greater depth of extant quantitative research in regard to spirituality within the psychology literature than there is within gifted literature. Qualitative approaches can always add value and, in this respect, mixed methods are encouraged—a position echoed by Davis et al. (2016). If following the quantitative route, attention should be given to the instrument(s) used. The ISIS used by Walton was chosen in order to capture a large range of responses, to see where the differences existed between gifted domains. Now that these differences have been initially identified there are two obvious options: (1) repeat the study with a larger/different population profile, to see if the results are replicated; or (2) whether stand-alone or in conjunction with ISIS, conduct comparable studies that utilise differing spirituality instruments, to compare instrument results.

Also worthy of consideration, given the distinct sex-based differences in responses, is whether to draw populations from single-sex or co-educational schools. All of the schools in Walton's research were co-educational and this should be considered when comparing results. It is potentially the case that the school environment may influence the depth of spirituality exhibited, in light of differences in the ways of thinking between boys and girls as already described. There is also the potential impact on career choices, as identified by Tirri and Ubani (2004). The question of whether similar patterns would be evident in different nations and/or cultures can only be addressed within those nations/cultures, so this is also an avenue for further research. Understanding more about spirituality and culture is particularly important given the Australasian context, a geographic area that includes a significant number of indigenous minorities, as well as growing migrant and refugee populations in countries like Australia and New Zealand. Research into family influences on contemporary child and adolescent spirituality would inform all of the above and may be inclusive of any differences between parent/carer styles of parenting of gifted and non-gifted.

Conclusion

The concept of spirituality as central to all human existence is not without its detractors but is, nonetheless, the most common position of modern academic authors and researchers. Viewing spirituality through the lens of Walton's (2015, 2017) MSI positions spirituality firmly within everyday existence, both through how spirituality can vary and evolve on a day-to-day basis and recognising a delineation between an individual's spirituality and subsequent expression through interactions in the world. It is the 'how' of our relationships, with the actions of spiritual identity not just an expression of internal spirituality, but also a key factor in relationships *with* the individual; of perceptions as well as deeds.

The intensity of the gifted experience extends into spirituality, with suggestions of spirituality being a separate domain of giftedness. Given the limited research base for spirituality and giftedness, this needs to be considered in the context of the components of spirituality, where the data is richer. Ethical and moral developments, inclusive of altruism, have been identified as being stronger in gifted students than non-gifted. In these fields, variation has been identified in regard to male and female gifted and their ways of thinking. This is particularly evident through Walton's research into differences between the spirituality of different domains of giftedness, where clear distinctions between male and female responses were identified. This was complicated by how the gifted domains manifested their spirituality by sex, with the males being effectively indistinguishable by domain and the females exhibiting significant differences.

Providing opportunities for the development of both the theoretical and practical natures of spiritual aspects is suggested. At the heart of such practice is respect, at all levels, in line with Watson (2017). The positive psychological aspects thus inculcated can provide an antidote to the desensitising characteristics of modern society. Children, and humanity in general, should understand themselves as being more than the material world within which they are immersed (Sagberg, 2017). In the process, gifted students' leadership and academic skills may be enhanced, while also providing opportunities for students to consider their own place and role in the world. Taking hold of the hare does not need to be a lonely quest, for each of us exists within wider frameworks. Education's role is to provide the tools to make the search purposeful; in this process, searching for the hare becomes a shared experience through daily existence. The fruits of that quest, the transcendent, are, by extension, also shared, with collective benefit prized above individual benefit.

Cross-References

- ▶ Exploring Diverse Perceptions of Wise Persons: Wisdom in Gifted Education
- ▶ Gifted Education in the Asia-Pacific: From the Past for the Future – An Introduction
- ▶ Implementing the DMGT's Constructs of Giftedness and Talent: What, Why, and How?
- ▶ In Search of an Explanation for an Approach-Avoidance Pattern in East Asia: The Role of Cultural Values in Gifted Education
- ▶ Social and Cultural Conceptions and Perceptions: Part I Introduction
- ▶ Some Implications for the Future of Gifted Education in the Asia-Pacific
- ▶ The Career Decisions of Gifted Students: An Asian-Pacific Perspective

References

Abu Bakar, A. Y., Ishak, N. M., & Abidin, M. H. Z. (2014). The relationship between domains of empathy and leadership skills among gifted and talented students. *Procedia, 116*, 765–768. https://doi.org/10.1016/j.sbspro.2014.01.294

Ambrose, D. (2009). Morality and high ability: Navigating a landscape of altruism and malevolence. In D. Ambrose & T. Cross (Eds.), *Morality, ethics, and gifted minds* (pp. 49–71). Dordrecht, Netherlands: Springer.

Amram, Y. (2007). *The seven dimensions of spiritual intelligence: An ecumenical, grounded theory.* Paper presented at the 115th Annual Conference of the American Psychological Association, San Francisco, CA.

Amram, Y., & Dryer, D. C. (2008). *The Integrated Spiritual Intelligence Scale (ISIS): Development and preliminary validation*. Paper presented at the 116th Annual Conference of the American Psychological Association, Boston, MA.

Atkinson, R. C., & Schiffrin, R. M. (1968). Human memory: A proposed system and its control processes. In K. Wartenbee & J. T. Spence (Eds.), *Psychology of learning & motivation* (Vol. 2, pp. 89–195). New York, NY: Elsevier.

Baddeley, A. D., & Logie, R. H. (1999). The multiple-component model. In A. Miyake & P. Shah (Eds.), *Models of working memory: Mechanisms of active maintenance and executive control* (pp. 28–61). New York, NY: Cambridge University Press.

Bannister-Tyrrell, M. (2017). Gagné's DMGT 2.0: A possible model of unification and shared understandings. *Australasian Journal of Gifted Education, 26*(2), 43–50. https://doi.org/10.21505/ajge.2017.0015

Belenky, M. F., Clinchy, B. M., Goldberger, N. R., & Tarule, J. M. (1986). *Women's ways of knowing: The development of self, voice, and mind*. New York, NY: Basic Books.

Blakemore, J. E. O., Berenbaum, S. A., & Liben, L. S. (2009). *Gender development*. New York, NY: Psychology Press.

Bosacki, S. L. (2001). Spirituality, gendered subjectivities, and education in preadolescents: Canadian preadolescents' reflections on gender-roles and their sense of self. *International Journal of Children's Spirituality, 6*(2), 207–221. https://doi.org/10.1080/13644360120068709

Boyatzis, C. J. (2005). Religious and spiritual development in childhood. In R. F. Paloutzian & C. L. Park (Eds.), *Handbook of the psychology of religion and spirituality* (pp. 123–143). New York, NY: Guilford Press.

Büssing, A., Föller-Mancini, A., Gidley, J., & Heusser, P. (2010). Aspects of spirituality in adolescents. *International Journal of Children's Spirituality, 15*(1), 25–44. https://doi.org/10.1080/13644360903565524

Cervantes, J. M., & Arczynski, A. V. (2015). Children's spirituality: Conceptual understanding of developmental transformation. *Spirituality in Clinical Practice, 2*(4), 245–255. https://doi.org/10.1037/scp0000037

Champagne, E. (2003). Being a child: A spiritual child. *International Journal of Children's Spirituality, 8*(1), 43–53. https://doi.org/10.1080/13644360304639

Davis, E. B., Cuthbert, A. D., Hays, L. W., Aten, J. D., Van Tongeren, D. R., Hook, J. N., . . . Boan, D. (2016). Using qualitative and mixed methods to study relational spirituality. *Psychology of Religion and Spirituality, 8*(2), 92–98. https://doi.org/10.1037/rel0000046

Davis, G. A., Rimm, S. B., & Siegle, D. (2011). *Education of the gifted and talented* (6th ed.). Boston, MA: Pearson.

de Jong, T. (2010). Cognitive load theory, educational research, and instructional design: Some food for thought. *Instructional Science, 38*, 105–134. https://doi.org/10.1007/s11251-009-9110-0

de Souza, M., Bone, J., & Watson, J. (2016). *Spirituality across disciplines: Research and practice*. New York, NY: Springer.

Department of Education, Employment and Workplace Relations (DEEWR). (2009). *Belonging, being & becoming: The Early Years Learning Framework for Australia*. Canberra, ACT: Commonwealth of Australia.

Duchesne, S., McMaugh, A., Bochner, S., & Krause, K.-L. (2013). *Educational psychology for learning and teaching* (4th ed.). South Melbourne, VIC: Cengage Learning Australia.

Egan, K. (2001). *Spirituality, education and the moral life*. Paper delivered at AERA conference, Seattle, WA.

Emery, T., Cookson-Cox, C., & Raerino, N. (2015). Te waiata a hinetitama: Hearing the heartsong. *AlterNative, 11*(3), 225–239. https://doi.org/10.1177/117718011501100302

Emmons, R. A. (1999). *The psychology of ultimate concerns: Motivation and spirituality in personality*. New York, NY: Guilford Press.

Emmons, R. A. (2000a). Is spirituality an intelligence? Motivation, cognition, and the psychology of ultimate concern. *International Journal for the Psychology of Religion, 10*(1), 3–26. https://doi.org/10.1207/S15327582IJPR1001_2

Emmons, R. A. (2000b). Spirituality and intelligence: Problems and prospects. *International Journal for the Psychology of Religion, 10*(1), 57–64. https://doi.org/10.1207/S15327582IJPR1001_6

Fraser, D. (2004a). The giftedness that dare not speak its name ... Some educational implications for spiritual giftedness. *Gifted Education International, 18*(3), 255–265. https://doi.org/10.1177/026142940401800304

Fraser, D. (2004b). Secular schools, spirituality and Māori values. *Journal of Moral Education, 33*(1), 87–95. https://doi.org/10.1080/0305724042000199996

Fraser, D. (2004c). Some educational implications for spiritual giftedness. *Gifted Education International, 18*, 255–265. https://doi.org/10.1177/026142940401800304

Gagné, F. (2009). Building gifts into talents: Detailed overview of the DMGT 2.0. In B. MacFarlane & T. Stambaugh (Eds.), *Leading change in gifted education: The festschrift of Dr Joyce VanTassel-Baska*. Waco, TX: Prufrock Press.

Gagné, F. (2013). The DMGT: Changes within, beneath, and beyond. *Talent Development & Excellence, 5*(1), 5–19. https://www.researchgate.net/publication/285946236_The_DMGT_Changes_Within_Beneath_and_Beyond

Gardner, F. (2011). *Critical spirituality: A holistic approach to contemporary practice*. Farnham, UK: Ashgate.

Gardner, H. (1993). *Frames of mind: The theory of multiple intelligences* (10th anniversary ed.). New York, NY: Basic Books.

Gardner, H. (1999a). Are there additional intelligences? The case for naturalist, spiritual, and existential intelligences. In J. Kane (Ed.), *Education, information and transformation* (pp. 111–131). Upper Saddle River, NJ: Prentice-Hall.

Gardner, H. (1999b). *Intelligence reframed: Multiple intelligences for the 21st century*. New York, NY: Basic Books.

Gardner, H. (2000). A case against spiritual intelligence. *International Journal for the Psychology of Religion, 10*(1), 27–34. https://doi.org/10.1207/S15327582IJPR1001_3

Gardner, H. (2011). Multiple intelligences: The first thirty years (30th anniversary introduction to *Frames of mind*). Retrieved from http://multipleintelligencesoasis.org/resources/

Gibson, K., & Landwehr-Brown, M. (2010). *Global learning: Collaborations for developing ethics, morality and global citizenship in gifted students*. Paper presented at the 11th Asia Pacific Conference on Giftedness, Sydney, NSW.

Gibson, K. L., Rimmington, G. M., & Landwehr-Brown, M. (2008). Developing global awareness and responsible world citizenship with global learning. *Roeper Review, 30*(1), 11–23. https://doi.org/10.1080/02783190701836270

Grant, B., & Piechowski, M. M. (1999). Theories and the good: Toward child-centered gifted education. *Gifted Child Quarterly, 43*(1), 4–12. https://doi.org/10.1177/001698629904300102

Grieves, V. (2008). Aboriginal spirituality: A baseline for indigenous knowledges development in Australia. *Canadian Journal of Native Studies, 28*(2), 363–398. Retrieved from http://www3.brandonu.ca/cjns/28.2/07Grieves.pdf

Grieves, V. (2009). *Aboriginal spirituality: Aboriginal philosophy. The basis of Aboriginal social and emotional wellbeing* (Discussion Paper Series no. 9). Darwin, NT: Cooperative Research Centre for Aboriginal Health.

Halford, G. S. (1993). *Children's understanding: The development of mental models*. Hillsdale, NJ: Lawrence Erlbaum.

Harrison, C. (2000). Out of the mouths of babes: Spiritual awareness and the young gifted child. *Advanced Development, 9*, 31–43.

Hart, T. (2003). *The secret spiritual world of children*. Makawao, HI: Inner Ocean.

Hay, D., & Nye, R. (1996). Investigating children's spirituality: The need for a fruitful hypothesis. *International Journal of Children's Spirituality, 1*(1), 6–16. https://doi.org/10.1080/1364436960010103

Hay, D., & Nye, R. (2006). *The spirit of the child* (Rev. ed.). London, England: Jessica Kingsley.

Heelas, P., & Woodhead, L., with Seel, B., Szerszynski, B., & Tusting, K. (2005). *The spiritual revolution: Why religion is giving way to spirituality*. Malden, MA: Blackwell.

Henderson, L. C. (2018). Reflecting on the DMGT in the Australian context: Response to Merrotsy. *Australasian Journal of Gifted Education, 27*(1), 59–65. https://doi.org/10.21505/ajge.2018.0006

Howard, S., & Walton, R. (2015). *Educational psychology: Foundations of learning and development*. Macksville, NSW: David Barlow.

Huitt, W. (2011). *Motivation to learn: An overview*. Educational Psychology Interactive. Valdosta, GA: Valdosta State University. Retrieved from http://www.edpsycinteractive.org/topics/motivation/motivate.html

Hyde, B. (2008a). *Children and spirituality: Searching for meaning and connectedness*. London, England: Jessica Kingsley.

Hyde, B. (2008b). The identification of four characteristics of children's spirituality in Australian Catholic primary schools. *International Journal of Children's Spirituality, 13*(2), 117–127. https://doi.org/10.1080/13644360801965925

James, A., Fine, M., & Turner, L. (2012). An empirical examination of youths' perceptions of spirituality as an internal developmental asset during adolescence. *Applied Developmental Science, 16*, 181–194. https://doi.org/10.1080/10888691.2012.722891

James, A. G., & Miller, B. (2017). Revisiting Mahoney's 'My body is a temple…' study: Spirituality as a mediator of the religion–health interaction among adolescents. *International Journal of Children's Spirituality, 22*(2), 134–153.

James, W. (1963). *The varieties of religious experience: A study in human nature. Gifford lectures on natural religion, Edinburgh, 1901–1902*. New York, NY: University Books.

Japar, M., & Purwati. (2014). Religiousity, spirituality, and adolescents' self-adjustment. *International Education Studies, 7*(10), 66–73. https://doi.org/10.5539/ies.v7n10p66

Jirásek, I., Veselsky, P., & Poslt, J. (2017). Winter outdoor trekking: Spiritual aspects of environmental education. *Environmental Education Research, 23*(1), 1–22. https://doi.org/10.1080/13504622.2016.1149553

Johnstone, C. (2014). Creating a cultural shift in happiness. *Positive News, 80*, 18. Retrieved from http://positivenews.org.uk/ (homepage)

Kalyuga, S. (2011). Cognitive load theory: How many types of load does it really need? *Educational Psychology Review, 23*(1), 1–19. https://doi.org/10.1007/s10648-010-9150-7

Kessler, R. (2000). *The soul of education: Helping students find connection, compassion, and character at school*. Alexandria, VA: Association for Supervision and Curriculum Development.

Kilcup, C. (2016). Secret wisdom: Spiritual intelligence in adolescents. *Gifted Education International, 32*(3), 242–257. https://doi.org/10.1177/0261429415602587

Kohan-Mass, J. (2016). Understanding gender differences in thinking styles of gifted children. *Roeper Review, 38*(3), 185–198. https://doi.org/10.1080/02783193.2016.1183737

Kowalske, K. (2016). Portrait of Olivia: A case study of a spiritually gifted student. *Gifted Education International, 32*(3), 258–270. https://doi.org/10.1177/0261429415602586

Kumar, M. V. (2015). Adolescence psychological well-being in relation to spirituality and pro-social behaviour. *Indian Journal of Positive Psychology, 6*(4), 361–366.

Land, H. (2015). *Spirituality, religion, and faith in psychotherapy: Evidence-based expressive methods for mind, brain, and body*. Chicago, IL: Lyceum Books.

Lovecky, D. V. (1998). Spiritual sensitivity in gifted children. *Roeper Review, 20*(3), 178–183. https://doi.org/10.1080/02783199809553887

Lovelock, P., & Adams, K. (2017). From darkness to light: Children speak of divine encounter. *International Journal of Children's Spirituality, 22*(1), 36–48. https://doi.org/10.1080/1364436X.2016.1268098

Maslow, A. H. (1943). A theory of human motivation. *Psychological Review, 50*, 370–396. https://psychclassics.yorku.ca/Maslow/motivation.htm

Mata-McMahon, J. (2016). Reviewing the research in children's spirituality (2005–2015): Proposing a pluricultural approach. *International Journal of Children's Spirituality, 21*(2), 140–152. https://doi.org/10.1080/1364436X.2016.1186611

McInerney, D. M., & McInerney, V. (2010). *Educational psychology: Constructing learning* (5th ed.). Englewood Cliffs, NJ: Prentice Hall.

Miller, G. (2005). Exploring perceptions of giftedness in the Cook Islands Māori community. *International Education Journal, 6*(2), 240–246. Retrieved from https://files.eric.ed.gov/fulltext/EJ854976.pdf

Miller, G. (2010). *Gifted and talented Māori and Pacifika students: Issues in their identification and programme provision*. Paper presented at the 11th Asia Pacific Conference on Giftedness, Sydney, NSW.

Ministry of Health, New Zealand. (2017). *Sit less, move more, sleep well: Active play guidelines for under-fives*. Wellington, NZ: Ministry of Health.

Montessori, M. (1989). *The child, society and the world: Unpublished speeches and writings*. Oxford, UK: Clio Press.

Moriarty, M. W. (2011). A conceptualization of children's spirituality arising out of recent research. *International Journal of Children's Spirituality, 16*(3), 271–285. https://doi.org/10.1080/1364436X.2011.617730

Moritz, S., Quan, H., Rickhi, B., Liu, M., Angen, M., Vintila, R., . . . Toews, J. (2006). A home study-based spirituality education program decreases emotional distress and increases quality of life: A randomized, controlled trial. *Alternative Therapies in Health and Medicine, 12*(6), 26–35.

Myers, J. E., Sweeney, T. J., & Witmer, J. M. (2000). The Wheel of Wellness counseling for wellness: A holistic model for treatment planning. *Journal of Counseling and Development, 78*(3), 251–266. https://doi.org/10.1002/j.1556-6676.2000.tb01906.x

Natsis, E. (2017). A qualitative study of the interdisciplinary approaches to adolescent spirituality in Australian government schools. *International Journal of Children's Spirituality, 22*(1), 72–83. https://doi.org/10.1080/1364436X.2016.1266997

Nemme, K. (2008). *Nurturing the inner lives of children: An exploration of children's spirituality in three educational settings*. Unpublished doctoral thesis. School of Education, University of Wollongong, Australia.

Noddings, N. (2013). *Caring: A relational approach to ethics & moral education* (2nd ed.). Berkeley, CA: University of California Press.

NSW Department of Education and Communities (NSW DEC). (2015). *The wellbeing framework for schools*. Sydney, NSW: Author.

Nye, R. (1998). *Psychological perspectives on children's spirituality*. Doctoral thesis, University of Nottingham, Nottingham. Retrieved from http://etheses.nottingham.ac.uk/1177/

O'Leary, K. (2005). *Development of personal strengths and moral reasoning in gifted adolescents*. Unpublished doctoral thesis, School of Education, University of New South Wales, Australia.

Osbon, D. K. (Ed.). (1991). *Reflections on the art of living: A Joseph Campbell companion*. New York, NY: HarperCollins.

Paine, D. R., & Sandage, S. J. (2017). Religious involvement and depression: The mediating effect of relational spirituality. *Journal of Religious Health, 56*, 269–283. https://doi.org/10.1007/s10943-016-0282-z

Palmer, P. J. (1999). Evoking the spirit in public education. *Educational Leadership, 56*(4), 6–11.

Palmer, P. J. (2003). Teaching with heart and soul: Reflections on spirituality in teacher education. *Journal of Teacher Education, 54*(5), 376–385. https://doi.org/10.1177/0022487103257359

Pandya, S. P. (2017). Teachers' views on spirituality for adolescents in high schools across countries. *Pastoral Care in Education, 35*(2), 88–110. https://doi.org/10.1080/02643944.2017.1290132

Panzini, R. G., Mosqueiro, B. P., Zimpel, R. R., Bandeira, D. R., Rocha, N. S., & Fleck, M. P. (2017). Quality-of-life and spirituality. *International Review of Psychiatry, 29*(3), 263–282. https://doi.org/10.1080/09540261.2017.1285553

Pascual-Leone, J., & Johnson, J. (2005). A dialectical constructivist view of developmental intelligence. In O. Wilhelm & R. W. Engle (Eds.), *Handbook of understanding and measuring intelligence* (pp. 177–201). London, England: SAGE.

Pascual-Leone, J., & Johnson, J. (2011). A developmental theory of mental attention: Its applications to measurement and task analysis. In P. Barrouillet & V. Gaillard (Eds.), *Cognitive development and working memory: From neo-Piagetian to cognitive approaches* (pp. 13–46). New York, NY: Psychology Press.

Piechowski, M. M. (2002). Experiencing in a higher key: Dabrowski's theory of and for the gifted. *Gifted Education Communicator, 33*(1), 28–36. Retrieved from http://www.positivedisintegration.com/Piechowski,%20M.%20M.%20(2002a).pdf

Piechowski, M. M. (2003). Emotional and spiritual giftedness. In N. Colangelo, & G. A. Davis (Eds.), *Handbook of gifted education* (3rd ed.) (pp. 403–416). Boston, MA: Allyn & Bacon.

Piechowski, M. M. (2006). *"Mellow out," they say. If I only could. Intensities and sensitivities of the young and bright*. Madison, WI: Yunasa Books.

Piechowski, M. M. (2009). The inner world of the young and bright. In D. Ambrose & T. Cross (Eds.), *Morality, ethics, and gifted minds* (pp. 177–194). Dordrecht, Netherlands: Springer.

Pramathevan, G. S., & Garces-Bacsal, R. M. (2012). Factors influencing altruism in the context of overseas learning experiences among gifted adolescent girls in Singapore. *Roeper Review, 34*(3), 145–157. https://doi.org/10.1080/02783193.2012.686421

Radford, M. (2004). The subject of spirituality. In D. Hayes (Ed.), *The RoutledgeFalmer guide to key debates in education* (pp. 87–90). London: RoutledgeFalmer.

Ricard, M. (2015). *Altruism: The power of compassion to change yourself and the world* (C. Mandell, & S. Gordon, Trans.). London, England: Atlantic Books.

Roeper, A. M. (1995). *Selected writings and speeches*. Minneapolis, MN: Free Spirit.

Rowan, J. (1998). Maslow amended. *Journal of Humanistic Psychology, 38*(1), 81–92. https://doi.org/10.1177/00221678980381008

Sagberg, S. (2017). Taking a children's rights perspective on children's spirituality. *International Journal of Children's Spirituality, 22*(1), 24–35. https://doi.org/10.1080/1364436X.2016.1276050

Sartre, J.-P. (1957). *Existentialism and human emotions*. New York, NY: Philosophical Library.

Saucier, G., & Skrzypińska, K. (2006). Spiritual but not religious? Evidence for two independent dispositions. *Journal of Personality, 74*(5), 1257–1292. https://doi.org/10.1111/j.1467-6494.2006.00409.x

Schein, D. (2014). Nature's role in children's spiritual development. *Children, Youth and Environments, 24*(2), 78–101. https://doi.org/10.7721/chilyoutenvi.24.2.0078

Silverman, L. K. (2016). A garden of ethics. *Roeper Review, 38*(4), 228–235. https://doi.org/10.1080/02783193.2016.1220856

Sinetar, M. (2000). *Spiritual intelligence: What we can learn from the early awakening child*. Maryknoll, NY: Orbis.

Sisk, D. (2008). Engaging the spiritual intelligence of gifted students to build global awareness in the classroom. *Roeper Review, 30*(1), 24–30. https://doi.org/10.1080/02783190701836296

Sisk, D. A., & Torrance, E. P. (2001). *Spiritual intelligence: Developing higher consciousness*. Buffalo, NY: Creative Education Foundation.

Splitter, L. (2001). Listen to them think: Reflections on inquiry, philosophy, and dialogue. In M. Robertson & R. Gerber (Eds.), *Children's ways of knowing: Learning through experience*. Camberwell, VIC: ACER Press.

Sternberg, R. J. (2012). Giftedness and ethics. *Gifted Education International, 28*(3), 241–251. https://doi.org/10.1177/0261429411435050

Sternberg, R. J., & Sternberg, K. (2012). *Cognitive psychology* (6th ed.). Belmont, CA: Wadsworth.

Suhor, C. (1999). Spirituality: Letting it grow in the classroom. *Educational Leadership, 56*(4), 12–16.

Suzuki, D. (2004). *The David Suzuki reader: A lifetime of ideas from a leading activist and thinker*. Vancouver, BC: Greystone Books.

Sweller, J., van Merriënboer, J. J. G., & Paas, F. (1998). Cognitive architecture and instructional design. *Educational Psychology Review, 10*, 251–296. https://doi.org/10.1023/A:1022193728205

Talib, M. A., & Abdollahi, A. (2017). Spirituality moderates hopelessness, depression, and suicidal behavior among Malaysian adolescents. *Journal of Religious and Health, 56*, 784–795. https://doi.org/10.1007/s10943-015-0133-3

Tamminen, K. (1991). Religious development in childhood and youth. *Annales academiae scientarium Fenniae*. Ser. B/259. Helsinki: Federation of Finnish Scientific Societies.

Tamminen, K. (1996). Gender differences in religiosity in children and adolescents. In L. J. Francis, W. K. Kay & W. S. Campbell (Eds.), *Research in religious education* (pp. 163–188). Leominster: Gracewing.

Taylor, S. (1999). Indigenous cultures and identities. In D. Meadmore, B. Burnett, & P. O'Brien (Eds.), *Understanding education: Contexts and agendas for the new millennium* (pp. 41–47). Frenchs Forest, NSW: Prentice Hall.

Tenenbaum, H. R., & Leaper, C. (2003). Parent–child conversations about science: The socialization of gender inequities? *Developmental Psychology, 39*(1), 34–47. Retrieved from https://pdfs.semanticscholar.org/2b28/494836ef140ddf21e09ed33d03edede3809b.pdf

Tenenbaum, H. R., Snow, C. E., Roach, K. A., & Kurland, B. (2005). Talking and reading science: Longitudinal data on sex differences in mother–child conversations in low-income families. *Journal of Applied Developmental Psychology, 26*(1), 1–19. https://doi.org/10.1016/j.appdev.2004.10.004

Tirri, K. (2010). Combining excellence and ethics: Implications for moral education for the gifted. *Roeper Review, 33*(1), 59–64. https://doi.org/10.1080/02783193.2011.530207

Tirri, K., & Nokelainen, P. (2007). Comparison of academically average and gifted students' self-rated ethical sensitivity. *Educational Research and Evaluation, 13*(6), 587–601. https://doi.org/10.1080/13803610701786053

Tirri, K., Nokelainen, P., & Ubani, M. (2006). Conceptual definition and empirical validation of the spiritual sensitivity scale. *Journal of Empirical Theology, 19*(1), 37–62. https://doi.org/10.1163/157092506776901870

Tirri, K., Nokelainen, P., & Ubani, M. (2007). Do gifted students have spiritual intelligence? In K. Tirri (Ed.), *Values and foundations in gifted education* (pp. 187–202). Bern, Switzerland: Peter Lang.

Tirri, K., & Pehkonen, L. (2002). The moral reasoning and scientific argumentation of gifted adolescents. *Journal of Secondary Gifted Education, 13*(3), 120–129. https://doi.org/10.4219/jsge-2002-374

Tirri, K., & Quinn, B. (2010). Exploring the role of religion and spirituality in the development of purpose: Case studies of purposeful youth. *British Journal of Religious Education, 32*(3), 201–214. https://doi.org/10.1080/01416200.2010.498607

Tirri, K., & Ubani, M. (2004). How do gifted girls perceive the meaning of life? *Gifted Education International, 19*(3), 266–274. https://doi.org/10.1177/026142940501900310

Ubani, M. (2010). Science and spirituality: An empirical study of Finnish academically gifted boys. *Religious Education Journal of Australia, 26*(1), 3–8.

Vialle, W. (2007). Spiritual intelligence: An important dimension of giftedness. In K. Tirri (Ed.), *Values and foundations in gifted education* (pp. 171–186). Bern, Switzerland: Peter Lang.

Vialle, W., Walton, R., & Woodcock, S. (2008). Children's spirituality: An essential element in thinking and learning in new times. In P. Kell, W. Vialle, D. M. Konza & G. Vogl (Eds.), *Learning and the learner: Exploring learning for new times* (pp. 143–160). Wollongong, NSW: Faculty of Education, University of Wollongong. Research Online. Retrieved from http://ro.uow.edu.au/edupapers/42

Walton, R. (2014). Mapping MI to the DMGT: A theoretical framework. *Australasian Journal of Gifted Education, 23*(2), 37–44. https://www.academia.edu/38879394/Mapping_MI_to_the_DMGT_A_theoretical_framework

Walton, R. (2015). *Precursor, indicator or mirage: What relationship exists between spirituality and type of giftedness?* Unpublished doctoral thesis, School of Education, University of Wollongong, Australia.

Walton, R. (2017). Spirituality and giftedness type: A tale of adolescent variance. In N. Ballam & R. Moltzen (Eds.), *Giftedness and talent: Australasian perspectives* (pp. 201–226). Singapore: Springer.

Watson, J. (2017). Every child still matters: Interdisciplinary approaches to the spirituality of the child. *International Journal of Children's Spirituality, 22*(1), 4–13. https://doi.org/10.1080/1364436X.2016.1234434

West, C. (2011). The confluence of education and children's spirituality in New South Wales. *Journal of Student Engagement: Education matters, 1*(1), 11–20. Retrieved from http://ro.uow.edu.au/jseem/vol1/iss1/3

Wong, S. S. M. (2007). A differentiated gifted program to nurture spiritual intelligence. *Gifted Education International, 23*, 63–71. https://doi.org/10.1177/026142940702300108

Russell Walton completed his PhD thesis on the relationship of spirituality to different types of giftedness in adolescents (specifically, creative, academic and sporting giftedness). This was in conjunction with teaching at the University of Wollongong, primarily in the areas of educational psychology and giftedness. He was founding editor of the Journal of Student Engagement: Education Matters (http://ro.uow.edu.au/jseem/), which was a platform for university students to develop talent progression in academia, both through their writing and development of ideas. His research interests are in spirituality in education and student engagement. In 2014 he received an Outstanding Contribution to Teaching and Learning award at UOW. Wordsmith.RW@bigpond.com

Wilma Vialle is a Professor in Educational Psychology at the University of Wollongong, Australia. Her research interests are predominantly in the nature of intelligence and creativity, with a particular focus on giftedness. She is the chief editor of the journal *Talent Development and Excellence* and is on the editorial board of several international journals. Wilma is also on the Executive Board of the *International Research Association for Talent Development and Excellence* (IRATDE). In 2006 she was awarded the Eminent Australian award by the *Australian Association for the Education of the Gifted and Talented* (AAEGT) for her contributions to gifted education. wvialle@uow.edu.au

Part II

Social and Emotional Needs and Learning Processes

Social and Emotional Needs and Learning Processes: Part II Introduction

Rhoda Myra Garces-Bacsal

Contents

Introduction to the Individual Chapters 286
Conclusion 289
References 289

Abstract

There has been an increasing interest and research focus over the past years on meeting the social and emotional needs of diverse learners, including high ability or gifted and talented children (Freeman, 2018). Social and Emotional Learning (SEL) has been linked to an overall improvement in academic performance, lower levels of emotional distress, and an increase in prosocial behaviour among students (Mahoney, Durlak, & Weissberg, 2018; Zins, Weissberg, Wang, & Walberg, 2004). The chapters in Part II roughly address the broad topics mentioned above as they deal with: (a) motivation, growth mindset, and self-regulated learning training leading to academic performance and achievement; (b) overexcitabilities which heighten one's physiological experience of the world, thereby increasing one's vulnerabilities to emotional distress; (c) the impact of ability grouping and acceleration to a gifted students' self-esteem and well-being; (d) experiences of twice exceptional students in regular classrooms; (e) the intersectional experiences of risk and resilience among gifted young people who are socio-economically disadvantaged and who belong to ethnic minorities and indigenous communities; (f) how explicitly teaching SEL and coping skills can help inhibit inappropriate behaviours; and (g) how the introduction of

---

R. M. Garces-Bacsal (✉)
College of Education, Special Education Department, United Arab Emirates University, Al Ain, United Arab Emirates
e-mail: myra.garcesbacsal@gmail.com; myrabacsal@uaeu.ac.ae

multicultural literature can help develop prosocial behaviours among gifted students.

> **Keywords**
>
> Social and Emotional Learning (SEL) · Motivation · Growth mindset · Self-regulated learning · Academic performance · Achievement · Overexcitabilities

It is worth mentioning that among most researchers and practitioners, *Social and Emotional Learning* (SEL) for high ability learners is not always perceived as an end in itself. Rather, it is often employed as a useful method or strategy to motivate high ability learners to succeed academically, develop social-emotional needs, actualise their potentials, and prevent underachievement (Freeman, 2018; Smith, 2017).

In the research literature, it is well reiterated that gifted or talented students are no more or no less socially emotionally adept than their same-age typical peers (Freeman, 2018). However, the neuroscientific links between the brain's emotional components and the neurocortical components that support cognition or thinking establish the strong link between emotions and learning. Hence, the explicit teaching of SEL becomes crucial given how academic learning and growth can be significantly impaired if the gifted student feels emotionally detached or socially isolated (Smith, 2017). While a few of the chapters in this section explore in detail how addressing the social and emotional needs of the gifted could help improve their academic performance, there is also an exploration of how meeting the intellectual needs of gifted students through acceleration or ability grouping could likewise contribute to gifted students' self-esteem and help them feel less invisible and more connected to their peers and teachers. The chapters also range from exploring the general foundations of social and emotional learning to a more specific sociocultural grounding on double minorities, foregrounding the significance of taking into account the unique cultural realities of various subgroups among the gifted, which is echoed in the wider research literature (Balestrini & Stoeger, 2018). It is hoped that the chapters can serve to highlight even further the heterogeneity and diversity of what is often perceived as an homogenous population.

Introduction to the Individual Chapters

The seven chapters in Part II derive from the research and practice of 11 authors from five countries around the Asia-Pacific rim region and beyond, Australia, Canada, Chile, Germany, and Singapore. The foci of the chapters range from SEL needs and characteristics, such as motivation, overexcitabilities, self-esteem, resilience and well-being, to SEL learning strategies, such as using growth mindset, goal-setting, pro-social and coping skills and self-regulated learning, to teaching strategies for SEL, such as scaffolding learning, ability grouping and acceleration, with at risk populations, such as the socio-economically disadvantaged, ethnic minorities, indigenous students, and students with twice-exceptionality.

▶ Chapter 16, "Motivational Issues in Gifted Education: Understanding the Role of Students' Attribution and Control Beliefs, Self-Worth Protection and Growth Orientation" is Emma Burns' and Andrew Martin's chapter. They explore the specifics on what motivates students to go beyond what they believe they are capable of, impacting academic development and outcomes. The authors discuss personal best goal setting and how it is linked to the Achievement Orientation Model, motivating gifted students to push themselves further. In the chapter, Burns and Martin also include helpful strategies for teachers, parents, and practitioners on how to support gifted students using a growth mindset which emphasises effort more than innate intelligence or abilities. This includes developing personally relevant goals and optimal challenge to facilitate *flow* experiences to sustain students' motivation and engagement.

This impact of SEL on gifted students' learning can further be seen in the chapter by Heidrun Stoeger, Daniel Patrick Balestrini, and Julia Steinbach, ▶ Chap. 14, "Self-Regulated Learning for High-Ability and High-Achieving Students in Mixed-Ability Classrooms Throughout the Asia-Pacific". The authors provide a very clear handle on how gifted learners can benefit greatly from being taught self-regulated learning, especially in light of how developing expertise now becomes an even more complex endeavour with the greater emphasis on lifelong professional learning. The studies cited likewise debunk the implicit assumptions about highly able learners not needing any kind of scaffolded instruction on learning strategies. The seven-step cycle of self-regulated learning known as the Ziegler-Stoeger model provides clarity for primary school students to self-regulate their learning to be more goal-directed, strategic, and reflective. Guidelines to adapting the training units in line with the Ziegler-Stoeger model have likewise been provided. However, the authors are also quick to point out that "cultural differences exist and are meaningful for understanding the cultural specificity of educational behaviours and outcomes".

The ways through which educational interventions, as evidenced through ability and grouping and acceleration, can possibly impact the self-esteem of academically gifted high school students are explored by Miraca Gross and Susen Smith in their ▶ Chap. 18, "Put Them Together and See How They Learn! Ability Grouping and Acceleration Effects on the Self-Esteem of Academically Gifted High School Students". Their chapter began with a deeply personal and moving account of Miraca's experience as a young gifted child. This narrative of Miraca's is further reflected in their research findings which suggested that students in comprehensive schools with mixed-ability settings and those who belong in a school catering exclusively to gifted students experienced a drop in their self-esteem, whereas students who experienced a blend of ability grouping and acceleration whereby their Years 7 and 8 are collapsed into a single year, only endured a modest diminution in their self-esteem, with their scores starting off high and remaining high. This is an interesting finding, especially in light of the expressed concerns of school teachers who claim that such a combination of acceleration and ability grouping may be too much for the students, an unfounded assumption as revealed by the students' self-esteem scores especially when compared to the first two groups of students who only experienced either just acceleration or only ability grouping. Their research alludes to how life-changing a supportive educational environment can be for an exceptional student who feels disenfranchised and invisible, much like how Miraca felt in her elementary years.

On the other hand, in María Paz Gómez-Arízaga and Maria Leonor Conejeros-Solar's ▶ Chap. 15, "Fostering Resilience in 'At-Risk' Gifted and Talented Young People", they examined the experiences of gifted students who are twice exceptional (both gifted/ADHD and gifted/ASD) and are enrolled in regular classrooms in Chile. The authors explore twice exceptionality from within a conceptual framework that includes two components of the classroom climate, inclusive of peer relationships and relationships with teachers. Findings from two qualitative research studies indicated that the gifted/ASD group had greater difficulties in finding peers they can connect with as compared to gifted/ADHD students; however, both groups still reported bullying episodes from peers. Both groups also value teachers who are 'strict but nice' and are able to establish boundaries and manage student behaviours.

This focus on the gifted child's inner life and qualitative experience is evidenced even more in Sal Mendaglio's ▶ Chap. 17, "Overexcitability and Giftedness Research: Whose Constructs Are Being Investigated and How?" He describes overexcitabilities to be a "heritable property of the central nervous system which is not evenly distributed across a population" from the perspective of the *Theory of Positive Disintegration*. Mendaglio rightfully cautions and critiques that the concept of OEs is now being widely researched in Asian-Pacific, European, Middle Eastern, and South American countries, but OEs are still perceived to be a construct separate to the TPD or are mistakenly perceived to be uniformly positive, and that gifted children are erroneously expected to possess all five forms of OE. If the OEs are to be understood and contextualised from within the Dabrowskian paradigm, scholars and practitioners would then be able to witness a progression of one's life from one that is more focused on the self to one that is more altruistic and autonomous, through a process of positive disintegration which is characterised by an inner conflict resulting in a disruption of one's self. This can ultimately be resolved into a reinvented being with new mental structures, or can also result in negative outcomes leading to psychoses or suicide if one belongs to a 'toxic social environment'. Hence, in this chapter, there is now a shift from just looking at SEL as an instrumental factor in one's cognitive-academic performance to highlighting the social and emotional functioning and well-being of the gifted student, as noteworthy on its own.

While Mendaglio focused primarily on the gifted *individual* who may (or may not) possess OEs and its implications on leading either an egocentric or altruistic existence, Nadine Ballam highlighted the intersectionality of identity, ethnicity, socio-economic status, and how such marginalisation may impact 'at-risk' gifted students in her chapter ▶ 15, "Fostering Resilience in 'At-Risk' Gifted and Talented Young People". One surprising finding from Ballam's study was that participants largely reported that their giftedness impacted more detrimentally on their sense of identity than their socio-economic circumstances did. This was because they believed their giftedness was the essence of who they were, whereas there was the potential for them to change their personal circumstances as they got older. While Ballam's findings do not negate the difficulties gifted young people from impoverished backgrounds can face, it is a point of difference between the influence of ethnicity (which cannot be changed) and socio-economic status (which has the potential to be changed) for 'at-risk' gifted young people.

This focus on culture and ethnicity leads us to the chapter in which Rhoda Myra Garces-Bacsal demonstrates the power of multicultural PictureBook Biographies (PBB) and how teachers can guide gifted and talented learners to use these narratives for social and emotional learning. The chapter is imaginatively titled: ▶ Chap. 20, "Of Grit and Gumption, Sass and Verve: What Gifted Students Can Learn from Multicultural Picture Book Biographies". The multicultural PBBs demonstrate the various pathways through which eminent individuals coming from different ethnicities ultimately succeed in their respective fields or disciplines. The stories not only humanise these internationally recognised experts, they also demonstrate the many challenges and tribulations that eminent individuals can face by virtue of their race, gender, ethnicity, socio-economic status, and identity. The chapter ends with recommended teaching strategies and activities in using the diverse multicultural picturebook biographies introduced from within a critical multicultural analysis framework to surface silenced voices and encourage gifted students to read from a social justice perspective.

Conclusion

Overall, the chapters reveal the multiple ways through which SEL is understood and explicated from within the gifted education academic community: from an instrumental strategy that can be used to engage students to improve their academic performance; to one that helps develop an inner resilience and a capacity to go beyond one's personal achievement; and to leading a more humane, purposeful, and meaningful existence that is of service to others.

As the educational landscape evolves in response to the growing diversity of students in today's classrooms, there is an urgent need for educators to move beyond just providing differentiated and challenging content to the highly able learner (Balestrini & Stoeger, 2018). The challenge now is how to provide more culturally responsive pedagogies that are meaningful and relevant, and provide spaces for representation, identification, and opportunities for the gifted student to not just intellectually engage with a subject matter, but to also be emotionally invested in it, and examine their enriched and accelerated content and processes from critical, psychosocial, and multicultural lenses.

References

Balestrini, D. P., & Stoeger, H. (2018). Substantiating a special cultural emphasis on learning and education in East Asia. *High Ability Studies, 29*, 79–106. https://doi.org/10.1080/13598139.2017.1423281.

Freeman, J. (2018). The emotional development of the gifted and talented. In B. Wallace, D. A. Sisk, & J. Senior (Eds.), *The SAGE handbook of gifted and talented education* (pp. 169–183). New York, NY: SAGE. https://doi.org/10.4135/9781526463074.n16.

Mahoney, J. L., Durlak, J. A., & Weissberg, R. P. (2018). An update on social and emotional learning outcome research. *Phi Delta Kappan* 100(4), 18–23. https://doi.org/10.1177/0031721718815668.

Smith, S. R. (2017). Responding to the unique social and emotional learning needs of gifted Australian students. In E. Frydenberg, A. Martin, & R. Collie (Eds.), *Social and emotional learning in Australia and the Asia-Pacific: Perspectives, programmes, and approaches* (pp. 147–166). Singapore: Springer.

Zins, J. E., Weissberg, R. P., Wang, M. C., & Walberg, H.J. (2004). *Building academic success on social and emotional learning: What does research say?* New York: Teachers College Press.

Rhoda Myra Garces-Bacsal, PhD, is Filipino and based in the middle east. She is currently serving as the Associate Professor with the Special Education Department at the United Arab Emirates University. Prior to moving to UAE, she served as the Programme Leader of the Masters of Education Program in High Ability Studies at the National Institute of Education, Nanyang Technological University Singapore where she also served as the Coordinator of the Diploma in Special Education and the Professional Development Leader and Pedagogical Development and Innovation Leader of Early Childhood and Special Needs Education Academic Group. She served as the Chair of the Programme Committee of the Asian Children's Writers and Illustrators Conference for the Asian Festival of Children's Content held annually in Singapore for nine years. Myra shares her passion for reading and book hunting in her website gatheringbooks.org

Self-Regulated Learning for High-Ability and High-Achieving Students in Mixed-Ability Classrooms Throughout the Asia-Pacific

14

Heidrun Stoeger, Daniel Patrick Balestrini, and Julia Steinbach

Contents

Introduction	292
Gifted Learners and Self-Regulated Learning Strategies	293
Giving All Learners a Good Chance to Develop Self-Regulated Learning Strategies: Teaching Self-Regulated Learning to Mixed-Ability Groups in Primary School	294
The Theory Behind Our SRL Training Units	296
Our Approach to Training Students of All Abilities in SRL in Mixed-Ability Classrooms	298
How Our Training Units Unfold	301
What the Data Say About Our Training Units	304
Applying Our Western SRL Approach in Non-Western Educational Contexts	307
Collectivistic East-Asian Learning and Education and Individualistic Western SRL: Two Theoretical Perspectives	308
Some Cross-Cultural Findings on SRL Usage in East-Asian Cultures	310
Concluding Remarks	312
Cross-References	312
References	313

Abstract

After defining Self-Regulated Learning (SRL) and explaining its overall importance, we discuss why cognitive and metacognitive learning strategies for SRL are important for gifted learners. We then describe how SRL can be taught to all students—including gifted students—in mixed-ability groups in primary school and introduce a series of SRL training units developed over the past 15 years. We provide extensive coverage of the guidelines according to which our training units were designed, thereby offering readers a toolbox of sorts for adapting

---

H. Stoeger (✉) · D. P. Balestrini · J. Steinbach
University of Regensburg, Regensburg, Germany
e-mail: heidrun.stoeger@ur.de; daniel-patrick.balestrini@ur.de; julia.steinbach@ur.de

© Springer Nature Singapore Pte Ltd. 2021
S. R. Smith (ed.), *Handbook of Giftedness and Talent Development in the Asia-Pacific*,
Springer International Handbooks of Education,
https://doi.org/10.1007/978-981-13-3041-4_13

existing training units to their own needs. We conclude this discussion with a description of the effectiveness research carried out for our training units. Finally, we briefly consider the adaptability of our SRL approach for non-Western cultures by discussing the example of East-Asian versus Western cultural orientations and earlier cross-cultural SRL research.

> **Keywords**
>
> Self-regulated learning · Asian education · Talent development · Gifted education · Teacher training

The aims in this chapter are to:
1. Define and explain the importance of self-regulated learning (SRL).
2. Explain the importance of SRL for gifted/high-ability and high-achieving learners.
3. Introduce an approach to training SRL in mixed-ability primary school classrooms.
4. Describe the findings of effectiveness research for the approach to SRL.
5. Consider the adaptability of the SRL approach for non-Western cultures in the Asia-Pacific.

Introduction

Any discussion of self-regulated learning must begin by specifying precisely what the authors understand as self-regulated learning. This is not a formality but a necessity. Over the decades, researchers and instructional designers have advanced numerous definitions of self-regulated learning (Boekaerts, Pintrich, & Zeidner, 2000). A widespread and, in our view, effective definition for researchers and practitioners alike is provided by Pintrich (2000a), on which we base our remarks. Pintrich (2000a) defines Self-Regulated Learning (SRL) as "an active, constructive process whereby learners set goals for their learning and then monitor, regulate, and control their cognition, motivation, and behavior, guided and constrained by their goals and contextual features in the environment" (p. 453). SRL in this sense is both highly effective and increasingly important—but as a complex skills set rather than a simple technique, as SRL is an educational affordance that requires a substantial initial investment in skill acquisition.

Research has shown that learners who self-regulate their learning are more effective learners. Self-regulated learners report higher overall levels of motivation and more propitious motivational characteristics (e.g., McInerney, Cheng, Mok, & Lam, 2012; Pintrich, 2000b); they display more positive emotions while learning (Ahmed, van der Werf, Kuyper, & Minnaert, 2013); and their learning outcomes are superior in comparison to those of non-self-regulating learners (McInerney et al., 2012;

Nota, Soresi, & Zimmerman, 2004). The advantages of SRL start in formal educational contexts and extend into the world of professional work (Fontana, Milligan, Littlejohn, & Margaryan, 2015).

Three factors explain why SRL is becoming an increasingly important skill around the world. First, dramatic increases in information (Hilbert, 2014) and the technological complexity of recent decades have fundamentally altered the nature of developing expertise in many domains. As developing expertise becomes more complex, so the need for a more strategic approach to learning becomes greater. Second, the rate at which adults change jobs is increasing (Brown, 2001), which is necessitating an ever-greater focus on lifelong professional learning. Third, ever more professions are seeing a shift away from repetitive tasks towards complex, less well-defined types of work for which continuous learning is absolutely necessary. This is because increasing numbers of well-defined cognitive tasks are being automated and creating new, less well-defined complex tasks for humans (van der Zande, Teigland, Sharyar, & Teigland, 2018). The need for sophisticated approaches to learning has thus never been greater.

Gifted Learners and Self-Regulated Learning Strategies

The majority of studies of the differential effects of SRL have focused on its effectiveness for low-achieving students and students with learning disabilities (for an overview, see Sontag & Stoeger, 2015). This focus is both unsurprising and surprising. The focus is unsurprising in light of Western implicit theories of giftedness. Implicit theories of giftedness indicate that giftedness is associated with seemingly effortless learning behaviour that occurs without recourse to effortful study or practice (Stone, 2002). It is in keeping with this lay view that researchers were less attentive to the use of SRL among advanced learners; SRL skills were perceived more strongly as remedial learning techniques (Sontag & Stoeger, 2015; Stoeger & Sontag, 2012).

The focus is at the same time surprising in light of expertise research and changing scientific conceptions of giftedness. Since the early 1990s, expertise research has investigated the development of high levels of competency in given performance domains as a function of effective practice routines (Ericsson, Hoffman, Kozbelt, & Williams, 2018), known as *deliberate practice*. Deliberate practice is defined as highly focused, goal-appropriate practice of relevant skills that is carried out at gradually increasing levels of difficulty (Ericsson, Krampe, & Tesch-Römer, 1993). There has been a widespread consideration of the deliberate practice framework and a gradual shift within giftedness conceptions away from traits towards actions (e.g., Subotnik, Olszewski-Kubilius, & Worrell, 2011) and the coevolutionary circumstances that facilitate the development of ever more potent action repertoires (e.g., Ziegler & Stoeger, 2017). These shifts have altered how researchers and practitioners view the development of high levels of achievement. The highest levels of achievement displayed by individuals of all ability profiles are dependent on effective practice routines and substantial investments of time and effort. From this perspective, specialised educational guidance is essential. The long-term development of expertise through deliberate practice requires highly skilled, ongoing didactic support (Degner & Gruber, 2011). At the same time, however, the necessarily long periods of sustained effort required to achieve domain-specific expertise mean that phases of practice and studying will also take place without ongoing external monitoring. For the phases of deliberate practice that require an individual to work on his or her own, SRL is crucial for successful practice routines and, finally, the development of high and highest levels of achievement (Nandagopal & Ericsson, 2012).

Frequently, however, the importance of SRL for developing high-level skills goes unnoticed. When gifted learners find themselves in classroom learning contexts that are not suitably challenging, they may thus—understandably—not display an interest in SRL. When learning goals are set too low, SRL may indeed be unnecessary (Ablard & Lipschultz, 1998; Stoeger, Steinbach, Obergriesser, & Matthes, 2014). A mismatch between their competencies and the class learning goals deprives gifted learners of an appropriate context for practising their learning skills. From the misguided lay assumption that gifted individuals do not need learning skills, teachers and parents might—mistakenly—also conclude that a lack of an opportunity to practise learning skills is not a problem for gifted students since they will, going forward, not need learning skills.

Once the deliberate practice framework and contemporary conceptions of giftedness are taken into account, however, it becomes clear in such a case that gifted children *are* being deprived of an important opportunity to develop a learning skill that will be essential for their pursuit of the highest levels of achievement in the future. Research has shown that highly intelligent and high-achieving fourth graders profited as much as students of average intelligence and achievement from a seven-week course of training in the use of SRL that offered suitable levels of difficulty for all participants (Sontag & Stoeger, 2015). In line with this finding, gifted learners who were self-regulating their learning reported more positive emotions and fewer negative emotions than gifted learners who were learning impulsively (Obergriesser & Stoeger, 2016).

Giving All Learners a Good Chance to Develop Self-Regulated Learning Strategies: Teaching Self-Regulated Learning to Mixed-Ability Groups in Primary School

The theoretical perspective and empirical findings described in the previous section leave no doubt about the importance of giving learners of all ability and achievement levels the opportunity to become proficient in the use of SRL. As research has shown that the effective use of learning strategies requires prolonged periods of regular training in their use (Dignath & Büttner, 2008), instruction should begin already during primary school and be integrated into authentic learning activities. Authentic learning activities require learning content and tasks that are suitably challenging and interesting for students' respective ability levels. When these requirements are met, academically gifted students and those of average academic abilities can profit equally from SRL training, as we will show in detail below.

Before we describe a concrete approach to teaching SRL in primary school, we briefly note two principles that should be kept in mind when assessing the appropriateness of SRL instruction for mixed-ability primary school classrooms, the principle of *proceduralisation* and the principle of *contingency*. Students will only begin to regularly self-regulate their learning once they have learned not only about SRL as a concept, but how to use SRL to work on authentic learning activities. This presents a substantial challenge, however, because SRL is not a simple idea or technique, but rather a complex set of skills. Students must proceduralise the SRL skills set by, first, breaking it up into its component steps and practising each of these steps carefully and repeatedly (i.e., as individual component procedures) and then, second, reintegrating the steps back into one skills set. Only after such a meticulous process of proceduralisation can students begin to correctly and effectively employ SRL on their own in new learning contexts.

Effective proceduralisation of SRL also depends on meaningful opportunities to practise its use. When learning content for an SRL intervention has been appropriately chosen and is affording students of varying ability levels meaningful chances to practise the learning skill, then—and only then—will students begin to realise, through experience, that improving their learning behaviour leads to higher achievements. The ability-aligned, authentic training context will allow students to understand how their improved learning outcomes are *contingent* on (i.e., causally linked to) their use of SRL. Teachers can help students recognise this contingency by, for example, regularly drawing their attention to the connection between strategy use and achievement as they practise SRL (Dignath & Büttner, 2008; Hattie & Timperley, 2007).

Our research group has designed SRL instructional units for primary school that fulfil the aforementioned criteria. The units are for mixed-ability classrooms, built around teaching SRL as a complex skills set in need of systematic proceduralisation, and designed to regularly remind students of the contingency between effective SRL use and improved learning outcomes. The units rely on a *normative model of SRL*—which we will describe below—and systematically introduce students to metacognitive learning strategies (e.g., self-assessment, goal setting, monitoring) and cognitive learning strategies (e.g., ecological strategies, text reduction strategies) as they work on specially selected learning content (e.g., mathematics exercises, scientific texts). Students' classroom teachers implement the units during regular classroom instruction. The units also include authentic, curriculum-aligned homework activities that feed back into the in-class SRL instruction. In designing our interventions, we made it a priority that both gifted students and their peers of average abilities profit equally. The units were developed for fourth graders of different ability levels in the same classrooms. They are also appropriate for younger students in gifted programs. We will now go into more detail about our SRL training units. We start by describing our theoretical approach and then explain how the units are structured and share some findings from our evaluation studies about the units' effectiveness for different groups of learners.

The Theory Behind Our SRL Training Units

We based our training units on the model of SRL developed by Barry J. Zimmerman (1986, 2000) in the 1980s and 1990s at the City University of New York. Throughout this chapter, we will refer to the *Zimmerman model* in reference to Zimmerman's descriptions of his model of SRL (1986, 2000) as found in the two aforementioned publications. The Zimmerman model provides a theoretical framework based on social cognitive theory and is a good choice for our training units. Meta-analyses have shown that self-regulation training is most effective when it is based on social cognitive theory (Dignath & Büttner, 2008; Dignath, Buettner, & Langfeldt, 2008).

The Zimmerman model distinguishes cognitive, metacognitive, and motivational aspects of SRL and structures the sequence of SRL-related events into a *forethought phase*, a *performance or volitional control phase*, and a *self-reflection phase* of SRL. The forethought phase includes the prerequisite processes that precede students' actions and learning efforts. The performance or volitional control phase captures the processes that are important during learning and influence the learner's focus and behaviour. The self-reflection phase starts after students have completed their learning activities and consists of learners' self-evaluations of the outcomes of their learning.

The Zimmerman model provides insight into the overall design of highly effective SRL in light of a careful review of the theory and findings of social cognitive theory. As such, it serves as a useful guide for designing SRL units and researching their effectiveness. One fundamental insight of designing training units for students on the basis of theoretical models is that it is important that the target audience be made aware of the theoretical framework on which a training unit is based (Salomon & Perkins, 1989; Weinstein, Husman, & Dierking, 2000). In the case of the Zimmerman model, fulfilling this criterion of effective instructional design presents a special challenge. Each of the phases of the Zimmerman model consists of numerous components that cannot be easily explained to primary school learners within a training unit (Zimmerman, 1990). To surmount this challenge, we developed a normative model of SRL, the *seven-step cycle of self-regulated learning* (Ziegler & Stoeger, 2005)—which we will refer to as the *Ziegler–Stoeger model*. It includes cognitive and metacognitive aspects of the Zimmerman model that are known to be particularly important for teaching primary school students to self-regulate their learning (Dignath & Büttner, 2008; Dignath et al., 2008). In the Ziegler–Stoeger model, motivational aspects described within the Zimmerman model are emphasised less as motivation appears to be a less salient issue for primary students than for secondary students (Dignath & Büttner, 2008).

Figure 1 shows readers how the Ziegler–Stoeger model operationalises the three phases of the Zimmerman model for young learners. The Ziegler–Stoeger model

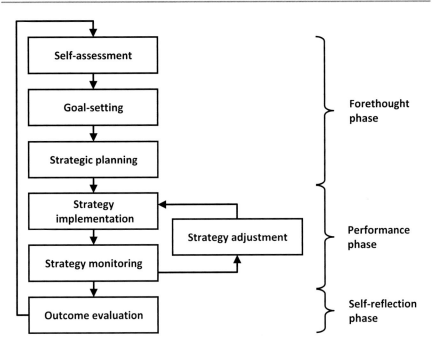

Fig. 1 Seven-step normative model of self-regulated learning by Ziegler and Stoeger (2005) and its relationship to the three phases of Zimmerman's model (1986, 2000)

represents the Zimmerman forethought phase with three steps: *self-assessment*, *goal setting*, and *strategic planning*. Then, three subsequent steps—*strategy implementation*, *strategy monitoring*, and *strategy adjustment*—capture selected aspects from the performance or volitional control phase of the Zimmerman model. These three steps constitute an internal cycle within the Ziegler–Stoeger model. By practising these three steps repeatedly, students have an opportunity to discover that a learning strategy is not a sort of simple virtual tool that one learns to use immediately and effortlessly, but rather a complex procedure that must be mastered through practice before effective use becomes possible. In other words, the internal cycle of strategy implementation, strategy monitoring, and strategy adjustment in the Ziegler–Stoeger model will help primary school students to understand—through experience—that strategy use needs to be developed through constant monitoring and adjustments. The steps can be applied to various (cognitive) learning strategies (e.g., ecological strategies, organisational strategies or rehearsal strategies; for an overview, see Weinstein & Mayer, 1986).

After the internal cycle (i.e., strategy implementation, strategy monitoring, and strategy adjustment), the Ziegler–Stoeger model then foresees a phase of outcome evaluation. This relates to the third phase, *self-reflection*, in the Zimmerman model. Learners assess whether the application of the previous steps in the model has helped them to achieve their individual learning goals. The outcome evaluation leads learners back to the beginning of the Ziegler–Stoeger model, to *self-assessment*, and thereby influences how students approach future learning activities.

Our Approach to Training Students of All Abilities in SRL in Mixed-Ability Classrooms

Over the last 15 years, our research group has developed and evaluated training units based on the Ziegler–Stoeger model of SRL (Pronold-Günthner et al., 2014; Schilcher et al., 2013; Stoeger & Ziegler, 2004, 2008b; Ziegler & Stoeger, 2005; Ziegler, Stoeger, & Vialle, 2013). We chose to develop and evaluate our SRL training units with mathematics and reading comprehension on account of the crucial importance of these two areas of learning for primary school instruction around the world. The mathematics-based SRL training unit has been tested and employed in German-speaking schools and also adapted for use in English-speaking classrooms (Ziegler et al., 2013); the reading comprehension-based SRL training units have been tested and employed in German-speaking classrooms.

In light of extensive scientific evaluations of the units carried out in authentic classroom contexts with randomised control groups, we know that the units are effective and work, as intended, in line with our educational intentions and the perspective of the Ziegler–Stoeger model (e.g., Stoeger, Fleischmann, & Obergriesser, 2015; Stoeger, Sontag, & Ziegler, 2014; Stoeger & Ziegler, 2008a; Sontag & Stoeger, 2015). However, SRL training according to the Ziegler–Stoeger model is not only applicable in the two curricular areas mentioned. The units can—and, we hope, will—be adapted by educationalists in different cultures and contexts in line with local curricular conventions for a variety of school subjects.

In creating our training units in line with the Ziegler–Stoeger model, we followed a number of design guidelines that reflect existing knowledge about effective training in educational settings (Stoeger & Ziegler, 2011). We will describe these guidelines extensively here, because those who wish to implement or adapt our training units should carefully consider these guidelines. For all of these guidelines, we know from existing research that they are generally important for instructional design. Moreover, the evaluations of our training units also suggest that our selection of guidelines is appropriate for the ends of our self-regulated training units (e.g., Stoeger, Steinbach, et al., 2014; Stoeger & Ziegler, 2008a). We now describe each guideline in turn.

Guideline 1: Pedagogical introduction of the normative model of SRL

Research shows that interventions are more successful and facilitate the transfer of newly learned skills to other contexts and domains when they make participants aware of the theoretical framework on which the intervention is predicated (e.g., Weinstein et al., 2000). For this reason, in our training units—which we refer to in some publications as modules—the normative model of SRL (described above) is introduced in an age-group-appropriate manner. All seven steps are introduced and applied to different day-to-day and learning activities.

Guideline 2: Authentic learning content
For the effective inculcation of learning strategies, learning-strategy instruction needs to be integrated into authentic instruction with specific learning content (e.g., Dignath & Büttner, 2008; Hattie, Biggs, & Purdie, 1996). Our training units heed this guideline by introducing the cognitive and metacognitive strategies described in the Ziegler–Stoeger model in combination with specific curricular content from primary school mathematics and reading comprehension instruction in separate training units.

Guideline 3: Systematic introduction of learning strategies
Not only the selection of learning content, but also the introduction of specific learning strategies must be highly specific and selective to be effective (Stoeger, Sontag, et al., 2014). In fulfilment of this guideline, our units direct students' attention to one specific type of learning strategy at a time. Students implement, monitor, and adapt one specific type of learning strategy as they work on specific learning content. For example, in our mathematics-based SRL training unit, students are systematically introduced to a series of *ecological learning strategies*. Hence, they work on strategies such as avoiding distractions, organising their desks, and managing their time usage during homework. In our reading comprehension-based SRL training, students work on text reduction strategies such as drawing mind maps, underlining main ideas and writing summaries. In each unit, one type of learning strategy is introduced and practised in a highly structured fashion.

Guideline 4: Adequate practice time to allow for proceduralisation
Students also need ample opportunities and time to practise these learning strategies. Teachers and instructional designers often overlook this aspect, although learning-strategy research leaves no doubt that short-term learning strategy interventions will not achieve desired goals (Alexander, Graham, & Harris, 1998; Dignath & Büttner, 2008; Pressley, Graham, & Harris, 2006). The aforementioned principle of proceduralisation can only be heeded when students can practise a learning skill regularly and for an extended period. Our training units prescribe a *minimum* of six weeks of daily training. The training is carefully designed to lead the students through extended cycles of systematically practising individual cognitive and metacognitive learning strategies. Only then will the students have a chance to proceduralise (Renkl, Mandl, & Gruber, 1996) the new knowledge about SRL and learning strategies. Barring such an extended practice routine, any new knowledge to which students are exposed will likely remain declarative knowledge. Students may, for a time, have a somewhat better understanding of SRL, but they will not be able to effectively use this knowledge to its intended ends when they need it.

Guideline 5: Deep integration into the existing learning routine
In addition to ensuring that students have an adequate amount of time to practise, teachers and instructional designers must also make sure that the SRL training unit is

integrated organically into students' overall learning routines. Scheduling five hours for SRL training on six consecutive Fridays, for example, would, from a purely quantitative standpoint, come close to fulfilling our recommendation for the minimum amount of instructional time required to train SRL with students. However, the scheduling would not be advisable. Students in most countries invest substantial portions of their *daily* routines in attending classes or working on schoolwork outside of school, at home or in tutoring centres (for overviews, see Bray & Kobakhidze, 2014; Verma & Larson, 2003). The systematic practice of learning strategies should be embedded as evenly as possible throughout the overall learning routine and within different learning settings (Ramdass & Zimmerman, 2011). Our SRL units, therefore, prescribe the daily integration of SRL practice into both in-class work and homework. Only then will students have a good chance to learn, through experience, that the SRL skills they are practising are broadly applicable to their learning activities in all manner of settings.

Guideline 6: Salience of contingencies between learning behaviours and learning outcomes

As briefly described above, the principle of contingency (i.e., cause and effect) is of particular importance for effective training in the use of learning strategies. Students need to be able to recognise that better learning behaviour actually leads to improvements in performance. While this may seem trivial, it is not so when students are working on the proceduralisation of a complex suite of interrelated learning strategies, which is the case for SRL training. To help primary school students make explicit connections between their own learning behaviour and performance on a given task, students fill out learning journals in order to systematically monitor their learning behaviour and track their daily performance when working on specific kinds of daily tasks. The daily tasks in our training units are of comparable length and difficulty. By holding these task-related factors constant, our SRL units create a learning situation in which teachers will be better able to guide their students towards self-reflection about how their own learning behaviours (i.e., their application of the selected learning strategies) are driving their learning outcomes. Were the daily tasks of varying length and difficulty, it is likely that students would be more prone to perceive their outcomes on learning tasks as being largely or even solely a result of the nature of the daily task.

Guideline 7: Challenging learning content for mixed-ability groups

As indicated in Guideline 6, SRL training will only be effective when individual students are able to perceive a clear contingency between the training-enhanced learning behaviour and their learning outcomes. This will only be possible if a learner is working on SRL with learning content that is sufficiently challenging. When a learner is capable of solving or completing a learning activity with little or no cognitive exertion, she or he may not need to use SRL (Ablard & Lipschultz, 1998; Stoeger, Steinbach, et al., 2014). Making sure that all learners will have adequately challenging learning material within the SRL training unit and still adhering to Guideline 6 (i.e., ensuring that daily assignments within the training unit are consistently difficult for the sake of illustrating the contingency of learning behaviours and learning outcomes) may strike some readers as paradoxical at first. Both guidelines can be fulfilled simultaneously, however. It is possible to create a series of daily learning tasks that are: (a) consistent in their overall level of difficulty from day to day and (b) expansive enough in their breadth of material on each day to offer an appropriate challenge to all learners.

We achieved the integration of Guidelines 6 and 7 in our SRL training units by constructing daily learning activities that each consist of a series of gradually more complex tasks. Our mathematics-based SRL units, for example, present daily learning activities that each consist of ten problems. Our units ask each learner to specify from one day to the next the number of problems she or he expects to be able to complete correctly within the allotted time. The variety in difficulty level is great enough to ensure that even the most advanced primary school students would find the entire daily learning activity to contain challenging elements. Less advanced students are assured that it is fine if they are not able to solve all problems. Rather, their attention is drawn to their own performance improvements over the duration of the intervention.

Guideline 8: Thorough preparatory training of teachers
Research on the effectiveness of SRL has described a worrisome pattern. Teacher-led in-class SRL training measures appear to be less effective than researcher-led in-class SRL training measures (Dignath et al., 2008). This circumstance likely reflects a lack of training on the part of the teachers in the theoretical underpinnings and implementation of the SRL units they are implementing. We therefore developed extensive training seminars that teachers must complete before implementing our SRL units in their classrooms. The teachers who implement our interventions first participate in a two-day to three-day preparatory professional development seminar on all relevant theoretical and practical aspects of our SRL training units. Over the course of two or three eight-hour days, the teachers learn about the concept of SRL, the Ziegler–Stoeger model, the day-to-day implementation of the intervention units, and the instructional materials. Once the teachers start implementing the SRL training, our units also prescribe additional follow-up meetings for teachers with SRL experts that take place while the teachers are implementing the training units in their classrooms. Moreover, we recommend that researchers or master teachers who have extensive experience with the SRL training units also maintain regular informal contact with teachers who are implementing an SRL training unit for the first time to ensure that teachers' concerns are addressed quickly as they arise during training implementation. Our experience has been that a variety of questions will arise that will differ from teacher to teacher and classroom to classroom in some cases.

How Our Training Units Unfold

Our goal for this section is to describe, step-by-step, how our SRL training units work in light of the Ziegler–Stoeger model and the eight guidelines just introduced.

Each SRL training unit requires seven (ideally contiguous) weeks to implement. Unit implementation takes place on a daily basis during regular class time and homework. The seven weeks consist of two *informational weeks* and five *learning cycle weeks*. During the informational weeks, students learn about SRL and the individual learning strategies described above. During the learning cycle weeks, students then put these ideas into action with their own learning—they start to proceduralise the knowledge imparted during the informational weeks. They do so by working on the learning content while following, step-by-step, the Ziegler–Stoeger model. The units and various materials guide them in doing this both during class time and homework.

The Informational Weeks

During the informational weeks, students work with their teachers for about 45 to 60 minutes per day during class time on the concepts of the SRL training unit. Teachers start by presenting the SRL cycle at the heart of the training units to their students. A series of lessons then guides teachers and students through an exploration and application of each cycle step. The informational weeks work with student-centred everyday examples designed to help students contextualise what they are learning in familiar terms. For example, the training units discuss common skills such as caring for a pet, practising a certain athletics skill or studying for a test in order to illustrate how the SRL skills being imparted can be implemented in various learning contexts.

These examples were selected for primary school students in Central European and European Heritage Australian cultural contexts; adaptation of the training units to other cultural contexts should consider whether these everyday examples are germane for the respective target audience and, if not, find suitable analogous examples.

After applying the seven steps of the Ziegler–Stoeger cycle to various learning contexts, particular attention is given to explaining the relationships between each cycle's step and introducing the individual learning strategies planned for each training unit. The mathematics-focused SRL unit introduces ecological learning strategies (e.g., avoiding distractions, organising a workspace, and time management). The reading comprehension-focused unit introduces three text reduction strategies: underlining and copying main ideas verbatim, drawing mind maps, and writing summaries. The training units provide various learning materials for use during the informational weeks (Stoeger & Ziegler, 2004, 2008b; Ziegler & Stoeger, 2005; Ziegler et al., 2013).

The Learning Cycle Weeks

After students have worked on understanding the concepts behind the skills described in the seven-step cycle of SRL (during the two informational weeks), they then move on to the learning cycle weeks. Here, they begin to transform their new declarative SRL knowledge into skills—proceduralising their knowledge, as described above—through practice with specific content and with the help of various learning materials. During the learning cycle weeks, teachers will need to allocate about 40 minutes of instructional time on Tuesdays, Wednesdays and Thursdays as well as about 60 minutes on Mondays and Fridays. The days of the school week are specified for a Monday–Friday school week. The days should be adjusted accordingly in school systems that start school weeks on other days of the week.

The learning cycle weeks create a framework in which students repeatedly and mindfully practise all steps of the learning cycle. Using the tasks supplied in the training units, the students self-assess, set goals, plan strategically, implement their strategy, monitor their strategy implementation, adjust the strategy, and evaluate their learning outcomes. Implementation and proceduralisation of all strategies are supported by an assortment of materials (e.g., learning journals, daily worksheets).

Students self-assess their strengths and weaknesses with respect to learning tasks and learning behaviour. To facilitate their learning task self-assessment, students receive daily worksheets. In the mathematics-based SRL unit, each worksheet consists of ten mathematics problems. In the reading comprehension-based SRL unit, each worksheet presents one text on a topic from the grade 4 science curriculum that contains ten main ideas, which students work to identify. As described above, the similarity in length and difficulty level of the worksheets makes self-assessment easier and ensures that students will be able to draw connections between their own learning behaviour and their own achievement. Before the students start to work on their daily worksheets at home, they complete guided self-assessments. In the mathematics unit, they indicate for each of the ten tasks whether they think they will solve the problem correctly. In the reading comprehension unit, they indicate how many of the ten main ideas they expect to be able to find. After students have worked on the worksheets at home, they discuss their solutions in class and compare their self-assessments with their actual results.

Students self-assess their learning behaviour by keeping learning journals. In the mathematics-based SRL unit, the learning journals help students recognise their strengths and weaknesses in doing homework by focusing their attention on ecological strategy use. Students systematically record when they learn, how many breaks they take and whether they experience any distractions during homework, among other things. In the reading comprehension-based SRL unit, students maintain records about their strengths and weaknesses in their use of text reduction strategies.

Students set a specific outcome goal for themselves at the beginning of every learning cycle week based on their self-assessments. For example, in the mathematics-based SRL unit, students specify how many mathematics exercises they aim to solve every day. The students are encouraged to set goals for themselves that are challenging but achievable. They record their goals in their learning journals, and they choose strategies in order to achieve their goals (strategic planning). To do this, they use the learning strategies introduced during the informational weeks.

Teachers review the students' learning journal entries. The units provide guidance for teachers on how to systematically and constructively discuss students' self-assessments, goal setting, and strategic planning in light of: (a) students' performance in their worksheets and (b) the information students record in their learning journals.

As the focus of the learning cycle weeks is on proceduralisation, students work on the unit-specific learning tasks described above during homework on a daily basis. During homework, they apply the learning strategies they chose during their strategic planning (i.e., during the strategy implementation phase) and use their learning journals to monitor and reflect on their strategy use (i.e., during the strategy monitoring phase). The learning journal also helps the students to focus their attention on whether and how they can adapt their learning strategies from day to day (i.e., during the strategy adjustment phase) should their strategy monitoring imply nonoptimal implementation of the chosen learning strategies.

At the end of each learning cycle week, the learning journal facilitates a process of outcome evaluation. We designed our learning journals in line with scientific guidelines about how learning journals can be used to help students improve their effectiveness in using learning strategies (Hübner, Nückles, & Renkl, 2010). The journal's structure—which makes use of colourful infographics that students fill out about their own daily learning progress—allows students to systematically and retrospectively evaluate the quality of their self-assessment, goal setting, learning behaviour (i.e., strategic planning, strategy implementation, strategy monitoring and strategy adjustments), and achievement each week. Students think about how well each of the SRL steps worked for them and how well their individual learning steps fit together and thereby construct a coherent picture of their self-regulatory efforts. This reflection on the week helps students to make adequate adaptations to steps of the SRL cycle that did not work well and to know when to maintain their chosen learning approach in areas where it proved effective. The weekly reflection also helps students to improve their self-assessments and the other steps of the SRL cycle when they start their learning process in the following week.

To sum up, in each of the learning cycle weeks, students work through all steps of the SRL cycle and evaluate the effectiveness of their learning behaviour. To help students recognise the usefulness of the metacognitive and cognitive strategies they have been practising (Schunk & Rice, 1987), connections between learning behaviour and learning outcomes are stressed systematically and consistently at all times throughout the course of the unit. To this end, the learning journals not only reflect students' learning behaviour, but also register their achievement in the daily training task. Students should see, in the mathematics-based SRL unit, for instance, that on days on which they recorded better learning behaviour, they also solved more mathematics exercises. In the reading comprehension-based unit, data recorded in students' journals show students' links between better learning behaviours and greater numbers of correctly identified main ideas. Finally, readers must not forget that all of the steps described here are dependent on the ongoing involvement and support of students' teachers (as described above). Teachers' use of the instructional units facilitates their training of students in SRL. However, the training itself is certainly not autodidactic.

What the Data Say About Our Training Units

Since 2005, we have evaluated our training units in studies that collectively involved 1,934 elementary school students of mixed abilities (Sontag & Stoeger, 2015; Stoeger, Sontag, et al., 2014; Stoeger & Ziegler, 2005, 2006, 2008a, 2010). Table 1 provides an overview of the studies' respective hallmarks. In addition to the actual

Table 1 Studies of the overall and differential effectiveness of both SRL training units

Unit	Study	Participants	Design	Measures	Key findings
Math	Stoeger & Ziegler, 2005	36 high-IQ gifted students from 25 heterogeneous fourth-grade classrooms with randomized assignment of classrooms to treatment and control conditions.	Pretest–posttest.	Self-efficacy; willingness to exert effort; helplessness; mathematics aspiration; mathematics performance; ability level.	Training suitable for reducing the underachievement of gifted students.
Math	Stoeger & Ziegler, 2006	393 students from 20 heterogeneous fourth-grade classrooms with randomized assignment of classrooms to treatment and control conditions.	Pretest–posttest.	Motivational orientations; success expectancy; ability self-concept; time management and learning self-assessment; mathematics performance.	Improvements on time management, learning self-assessment and mathematics performance.
Math (revised)	Stoeger & Ziegler, 2008a	219 students from 17 heterogeneous fourth-grade classrooms with randomized assignment of classrooms to treatment and control conditions.	Pretest–posttest.	Time management and learning self-assessment; self-efficacy; helplessness; willingness to exert effort; motivational orientations; mathematics interest; mathematics performance.	Revised unit effective, also in light performance development modelled via growth curve analyses.
Math (revised)	Stoeger & Ziegler, 2010	201 students from 16 heterogeneous fourth-grade classrooms with randomized assignment to treatment and control conditions.	Pretest–posttest.	Homework behaviour; learning self-assessment; self-efficacy; mathematics interest; willingness to exert effort; learning goal orientation; helplessness; mathematics	Propitious training effects for all ability groups for avoiding distractions, homework organization, learning self-reflection, self-efficacy, mathematics interest, effort willingness,

(continued)

Table 1 (continued)

Unit	Study	Participants	Design	Measures	Key findings
				performance; ability level.	learning goal orientation.
Reading	Stoeger, Sontag et al., 2014	763 students from 33 heterogeneous fourth-grade classrooms with semi-randomized assignment of 2 treatment conditions and 1 control condition.	Pretest–posttest–follow-up.	Family immigration background; preference for SRL; reading comprehension; finding main ideas.	Propitious training effects for preference for SRL and identifying main ideas for all students; propitious training effects for reading comprehension for students without an immigration background.
Reading	Sontag & Stoeger, 2015	322 students of varying ability and achievement levels with treatment and control conditions.	Pretest–posttest–follow-up.	Ability level; school achievement; preference for SRL; finding main ideas.	Propitious training effects for all groups of learners.

studies, we refer interested readers to an extensive summary of the studies carried out by our group (Stoeger et al., 2015).

The overall impression of our findings from these quasi-experimental control group longitudinal studies is that our mathematics-embedded and reading comprehension-embedded SRL training units are effective for improving students' skills in SRL and in the respective subject. Moreover, our studies show that the training units are effective for students of differing ability and achievement levels, which we suggest as a key takeaway from our SRL training research for readers of this handbook. SRL training is necessary also for highly able and high-achieving students; and SRL skill acquisition is achievable for all students within heterogeneous classrooms. Perhaps the greatest impediment to training elementary students of all achievement and ability levels to self-regulate their learning lies in the unchecked—and scientifically untenable—implicit assumptions about the most able students either not needing learning strategies or not needing instruction in their use (Stoeger & Sontag, 2012).

In our view, one key area of unfinished empirical evaluation is the cultural robustness of our training units. To date, all evaluations of our SRL training units have, to the best of our knowledge, taken place in Germany in German. While we have published our findings extensively in English, evaluations of the training materials in other cultures and languages are nevertheless needed. This desideratum is the focus of the next, and final, section of our chapter.

Applying Our Western SRL Approach in Non-Western Educational Contexts

The approach to training SRL described thus far in this chapter reflects a line of research conducted in the United States and Europe. The units that our research group has developed were designed and implemented for students in Germany. More recently, our mathematics-based SRL training was translated for students in Australia (Ziegler et al., 2013). While we are optimistic—but due to a lack of studies not yet certain—that our training units should prove similarly effective in various Western education systems, we cannot currently say with any degree of confidence whether our SRL training units will prove effective in non-Western educational systems. We do suspect that they may prove adaptable to and beneficial for learners in non-Western education systems, as we will explain on theoretical and empirical grounds in this section.

The Asia-Pacific presents, we argue, the ideal proving ground for considering the application of our Western approach to SRL in non-Western educational contexts. As the table of contents and the introduction to this handbook make clear, the Asia-Pacific—East Asia, South Asia, Southeast Asia, Oceania, Russia, and the Americas—encompasses a remarkable segment of the world's population. The space (see Fig. 2) accounts for about 63% of the world's population. We arrived at this figure as follows: we combined current population estimates for all nations in or on the Pacific Ocean according to http://worldpopulationreview.com. This population amounted to 4,837,329,085. We then divided this figure by the current estimate for overall world population from the same source—7,632,819,325—to arrive at our figure of 63%.

Moreover, the Asia-Pacific reflects vast cultural diversity. Between the European Heritage cultures of the Americas and Oceania, on the one hand, and the Confucian cultures of East Asia, on the other, lies a spectrum of ecologically derived cultural orientations that evince marked differences (Chang et al., 2011; Nisbett, 2005).

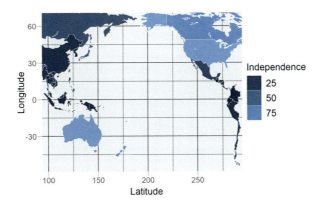

Fig. 2 Levels of self-reported independence throughout the Asia-Pacific

Members of these cultures differ—to cite just one example—in their endorsement of individualism (Hofstede, 2001). The range of scores for self-reported individualism within the Asia-Pacific is substantial. Self-report scores on individualism for Asia-Pacific countries range from a high of 91 out of 100 for the United States to a low of 6 for Guatemala (Compare Countries, 2018; Hofstede, 2001), with some of the lowest individualism scores among non-Western industrialised countries to be found in East Asia. Figure 2 plots these scores for all Asia-Pacific countries, with lighter colours indicating higher levels of individualism (e.g., the United States) and darker colours indicating lower levels of individualism (e.g., China). In the dataset provided by the Hofstede Insights website (Compare Countries, 2018), values were missing for some countries. In the case of the following countries, available data from neighboring countries (those in parentheses) were used: North Korea (South Korea), Brunei (Indonesia), Cambodia (Vietnam), East Timor (Indonesia), Laos (Vietnam), Myanmar (Thailand), Papua New Guinea (Indonesia), Nicaragua (Honduras) and Columbia (Panama).

Collectivistic East-Asian Learning and Education and Individualistic Western SRL: Two Theoretical Perspectives

Our Western SRL units were designed within a cultural framework that is highly individualistic. Consideration of the effectiveness of our SRL units within collectivistic cultures such as those found in East Asia, for example, is intriguing in light of two seemingly contradictory circumstances. At a broad cultural level, pro-learning, pro-effort East-Asian cultural orientations should be quite amenable to the approach to SRL we have presented. At the same time, however, at the level of educational institutions and learning practices, a stronger reliance in East Asia on socially oriented learning and on external direction during learning would seem to obviate the necessity for SRL. In an effort to shed light on paths for future research, we will describe each of these two circumstances in more detail. Finally, we will provide a brief summary of extant cross-cultural SRL research.

On the one hand, cultural orientations favouring learning and education and work and effort should *encourage* the uptake of SRL as defined in our training units. Stronger cultural orientations towards learning and education and towards the application of work and effort have been noted for collectivist East-Asian cultures in comparison to Western cultures (Balestrini, 2018; Balestrini & Stoeger, 2018). The observation appears to reflect ecological circumstances. It is plausible, from the standpoint of culture–ecology coevolution, that the special emphases on learning and education and work and effort observed in East-Asian cultures are historically linked with the high levels of collectivism in these regions of the world (Balestrini & Stoeger, 2018; Chang et al., 2011; Fincher, Thornhill, Murray, & Schaller, 2008). As this chapter has borne out, the training and use of SRL are both quite effortful. Internalising SRL requires persistent effort on the part of both educators and learners. Once mastered, SRL makes learners' learning more effective, but not because they learn to work less but, rather, because habitually self-regulating learners will typically learn and study more overall, due to: (a) their increased effectiveness and (b) the sheer lack of an upper bound for those whose learning is directed towards highest levels of achievement (e.g., high-ability and high-achieving students). In suitably complex domains, learners who set their sights high will never run out of material to learn and skills to master. Cultural orientations that emphasise the importance of learning and effort—such as those found in East Asia—thus provide an excellent motivational basis for teaching, practising, and using SRL.

On the other hand, the greater extent of social orientation and teacher directedness of formal learning activities in East Asia may rather *discourage* the uptake of SRL in East Asia. Decades of research have described systematic East–West differences in the extent to which formal educational learning is more socially oriented and more teacher-directed in East-Asian classrooms in comparison to the West. Whole-group instruction is more common in East Asia (for an overview, see Wang & Lin, 2005), as are larger class sizes (Chan & Rao, 2010; Jin & Cortazzi, 1998). There is also some evidence that learning tasks situated in a group context elicit more propitious motivational states among East-Asian Heritage, but not Western students (Iyengar & Lepper, 1999). Outside of school, students in East Asia are also likely to experience higher levels of external direction on their learning. Extensive anecdotal evidence suggests a historically greater reliance on professional tutoring in East Asia (Bray & Kobakhidze, 2014; Mori & Baker, 2010). While we stress in this context that much of the earlier evaluation of these differences by Western researchers has been misguided and indicative of a myopic Western view upon a complex cross-cultural question (for an overview, see Rao & Chan, 2010), there appears to be somewhat of a consensus that cultural differences exist and are meaningful for understanding the cultural specificity of educational behaviours and outcomes (Ho & Hau, 2010; Leung, 2001).

Why, one might ask, should a child in an East-Asian education system invest precious learning time resources in the mastering of SRL, a skills set for which he or she would have little recourse in an educational system that steers him or her towards learning as part of a group and provides him or her with high levels of external guidance during learning activities both in and outside of school? The most likely answer is that SRL would be discouraged in this case. Such a context could potentially undermine the *use case* of the approach to SRL we described in this chapter, for which phases of learning without recourse to expert guidance (or indeed any external guidance) are expected.

Yet, such an interpretation is only a partial explanation. More nuanced interpretations of East-Asian learning practices (e.g., Ho & Hau, 2010; Leung, 2001) have made clear—as a corrective for Western observers in particular—that the prominence of coaching and mastery learning in East-Asian classrooms does *not* mean that East-Asian students lack traditions of individual agency in learning. East-Asian learning traditions *do* recognise individual agency (Li, 2010). The relationship between external and internal direction in learning is, however, typically different than in Western contexts (Ho & Hau, 2008; Leung, 2001; Li, 2010). These observers of East-Asian education recognise the importance of helping learners to move beyond directed knowledge reproduction by cultivating self-reflection in learning.

They justify this need in light of the increased pace of knowledge accumulation and workplace change. Hence, SRL will likely be crucial in this context in East Asia, too. The technological change-induced necessity that individuals learn ever more on their own throughout their life spans applies for all industrialised cultures in East and West.

Our SRL units aim to prepare learners to become habitual self-regulators in the long run, while focusing on the externally regulated training of the skill itself for the short and medium term. Herein lies a reason why our approach to SRL in particular may turn out to prove easily adaptable to East-Asian contexts. Our SRL approach uses the power of effective external regulation to systematically, gradually guide learners towards more individually regulated learning. This training process takes time. Our seven-week training timeframe is an absolute minimum value for achieving even modest initial progress in the direction of effective self-regulation. The development of habitual SRL skills that a learner can apply on the spot as needed in a variety of domains is clearly a long-term goal that will require years of guidance and practice. In other words, there is considerable scope in our SRL approach for aligning its (already substantial) external-guidance component in accordance with East-Asian cultural orientations, learning traditions, and educational settings (e.g., intensive after-school core curriculum-focused tutoring).

Nevertheless, the specifics of such adaptations to the endemic learning traditions of East-Asian education systems and cultures have yet to be clarified. It is possible, for example, that the greater focus on external direction and social learning in primary and secondary education may mean that SRL training units will be introduced in later grades or even in tertiary education. Here, basic research is needed upon which theories and hypotheses can be articulated.

Some Cross-Cultural Findings on SRL Usage in East-Asian Cultures

In concluding this discussion, we summarise what researchers have reported about SRL in the context of East–West cross-cultural research. Due to the overall paucity of comparative research in this area, the findings cannot yet be integrated into a cogent theory of how Western approaches to SRL can be effectively adapted to the circumstances and needs of non-Western education systems in the Asia-Pacific. Current findings are worth summarising, however, as they can provide an impetus for such a research program in the future. Evidence of both similarities and differences between East-Asian and Western cultures are to be found in the literature. We briefly highlight both.

Cross-cultural research indicates substantial overlap in SRL strategy use in East-Asian and Western cultures. An interview format vignette-based comparison of Japanese and Australian students (Purdie, Hattie, & Douglas, 1996) with a reliable interrater coding process ($\kappa = 0.82$) revealed remarkably similar responses across a 24-category characterisation of SRL strategies (adapted from the Zimmerman model) for Japanese and Australian respondents. Additional studies have corroborated and expanded this finding by describing an association between constructivist beliefs about learning—i.e., understandings of "learning outcomes that indicate greater complexity of cognitive processing" (Purdie et al., 1996, p. 88)—and overall endorsement of the use of a broad range of SRL strategies in Western (Australia) and East-Asian (Japan and Hong Kong) cultures (Law, Chan, & Sachs, 2008; Purdie et al., 1996). All three findings suggest that SRL is likely—as we cautiously postulated above—a culturally robust technique that has a place in the education systems of cultures that differ in their approaches to learning and education.

At the same time, research has noted ways in which learners of different cultural backgrounds utilise different aspects of the SRL skills set. Purdie et al. (1996) reported a greater emphasis placed on memorisation strategies by Japanese and Japanese Heritage study participants in comparison to Australian study participants. This finding may reflect a more widespread understanding among educators and learners in East Asia about the utility of memorisation as a higher-level component skill within self-regulatory learning activities (Law et al., 2008; Purdie et al., 1996). Connections have also been described between the cultural importance of collective identity for self-construal—high in Japan and low in the United States or Australia, for example—and the utilisation of various self-regulation strategies (Chong, 2007; Law et al., 2008; Purdie et al., 1996). For example, Chong (2007) noted a positive association between fear of failure and academic self-regulation in a study of 1,304 Singaporean seventh graders that would have been unexpected according to Western theories of the relationship between fear of failure and self-efficacy beliefs.

On the interactions of culture, SRL utilisation and ability level research findings are even more scant. In a cross-cultural comparison of 315 high-ability students' SRL utilisation in grades 10–12 in New York City, Munich, and Beijing, the high-ability Chinese students endorsed the usage of SRL strategies less than their high-ability US peers (Tang & Neber, 2008). The finding appears to be in line with the general observation made for education systems in low-independence (i.e., more collectivistic) societies that they have traditionally afforded their learners less scope for individualised learning (Chang et al., 2011; Dai, 2016; Ho & Hau, 2010).

More recently, however, an interview study of English proficient, second-generation Chinese Heritage students in the United States described a positive interaction effect between the Confucian Heritage love of learning (Li, 2002) and students' overall endorsement and utilisation of SRL strategies (Bempechat, Li, & Ronfard, 2018). While the findings reported by Tang and Neber (2008) and Bempechat et al. (2018) cannot be directly compared, they appear to point in different directions. The earlier finding suggested less endorsement of SRL among Chinese high-ability students than among a US comparison group; the more recent study, however, suggests that a Confucian Heritage emphasis on learning may be positively associated with students' willingness to regulate their own learning. The seeming heterogeneity of the findings likely reflects various factors. Chinese students and Chinese Heritage students in the United States represent related, but fundamentally different student populations. Moreover, the heterogeneity may also reflect the two theoretical perspectives we outlined above, describing how East-Asian cultural orientations (i.e., emphases on learning and education and work and effort) may encourage

SRL uptake, while educational and learning practices found in East Asia may provide less scope for adopting SRL. More theorising and empirical investigation are needed.

Concluding Remarks

With our chapter, we introduced our readers to SRL and explained how teachers can train their students' SRL skills in mixed-ability fourth-grade classrooms such that all profit from the training. We explained why this is worth the effort—because all students need to be capable of self-regulating their learning, both for their careers in formal education and throughout their professional lives thereafter. That this applies to gifted students, too, needs to be stressed in particular, as their learning of SRL skills is frequently discounted, as we noted. As also explained in our introductory remarks, learning skills are crucial for potential maximisation in the twenty-first century. Furthermore, we described from the standpoint of learning research why just learning about SRL does not mean that learners will automatically be able to apply the skills set. We provided readers with additional background on this crucial point by introducing the concept of the *proceduralisation* of skills.

We then introduced a series of subject matter-specific training units for SRL that our research group has developed and tested over the course of 15 years. We encourage readers interested in helping gifted students to improve their self-regulatory skills to review and adapt our work to their specific educational needs in the Asia-Pacific. When doing this, we note that the interactions between culture and learning and education exist, but are only poorly understood. In the case of the training and utilisation of SRL, cross-cultural research findings are still extremely limited. Thus, we would also encourage practitioners and researchers to cooperate on careful, research-based implementation of SRL units in cross-cultural and multicultural settings so as to learn more about how the multifarious cognitive, metacognitive, and motivational components of SRL can be effectively trained in heterogeneous classrooms that bring together students who differ both culturally and with regard to their abilities and achievements.

Cross-References

- ▶ Bricolage and the Evolution of Giftedness and Talent in Taiwan
- ▶ Fostering Resilience in 'At-Risk' Gifted and Talented Young People
- ▶ Gifted Education in the Asia-Pacific: From the Past for the Future – An Introduction
- ▶ In Search of an Explanation for an Approach-Avoidance Pattern in East Asia: The Role of Cultural Values in Gifted Education
- ▶ Motivational Issues in Gifted Education: Understanding the Role of Students' Attribution and Control Beliefs, Self-Worth Protection and Growth Orientation
- ▶ Social and Emotional Needs and Learning Processes: Part II Introduction
- ▶ Some Implications for the Future of Gifted Education in the Asia-Pacific

References

Ablard, K. E., & Lipschultz, R. E. (1998). Self-regulated learning in high-achieving students: Relations to advanced reasoning, achievement goals, and gender. *Journal of Educational Psychology, 90*, 94–101. https://doi.org/10.1037/0022-0663.90.1.94

Ahmed, W., van der Werf, G., Kuyper, H., & Minnaert, A. (2013). Emotions, self-regulated learning, and achievement in mathematics: A growth curve analysis. *Journal of Educational Psychology, 105*, 150–161. https://doi.org/10.1037/a0030160

Alexander, P. A., Graham, S., & Harris, K. (1998). A perspective on strategy research: Progress and prospects. *Educational Psychology Review, 10*, 129–154. https://doi.org/10.1023/A:1022185502996

Balestrini, D. P. (2018). *Substantiating cultural orientations supportive of high academic achievement: A comparison of cultural products in East Asia and the United States*. Dissertation, University of Regensburg.

Balestrini, D. P., & Stoeger, H. (2018). Substantiating a special cultural emphasis on learning and education in East Asia. *High Ability Studies, 29*, 79–106. https://doi.org/10.1080/13598139.2017.1423281

Bempechat, J., Li, J., & Ronfard, S. (2018). Relations among cultural learning beliefs, self-regulated learning, and academic achievement for low-income Chinese American adolescents. *Child Development, 89*, 851–861. https://doi.org/10.1111/cdev.12702

Boekaerts, M., Pintrich, P. R., & Zeidner, M. (Eds.). (2000). *Handbook of self-regulation*. San Diego, CA: Academic.

Bray, M., & Kobakhidze, M. N. (2014). The global spread of shadow education. In D. B. Napier (Ed.), *Qualities of education in a globalised world* (pp. 185–200). Rotterdam, Netherlands: Sense Publishers.

Brown, P. (2001). Skill formation in the twenty-first century. In P. Brown, A. Green, & H. Lauder (Eds.), *High skills: Globalization, competitiveness and skill formation* (pp. 1–55). Oxford, UK: Oxford University Press.

Chan, C. K. K., & Rao, N (Eds.). (2010). Preface. In C. K. K. Chan & N. Rao (Eds.), *Revisiting the Chinese learner: Changing contexts, changing education* (Vol. 25, pp. xvii–xix). Hong Kong, China: Comparative Education Research Centre.

Chang, L., Mak, M. C. K., Li, T., Wu, B. P., Chen, B. B., & Lu, H. J. (2011). Cultural adaptations to environmental variability: An evolutionary account of east–west differences. *Educational Psychology Review, 23*, 99–129. https://doi.org/10.1007/s10648-010-9149-0

Chong, W. H. (2007). The role of personal agency beliefs in academic self-regulation: An Asian perspective. *School Psychology International, 28*, 63–76. https://doi.org/10.1177/0143034307075681

Compare Countries. (2018). Data retrieved from https://www.hofstede-insights.com/product/compare-countries/

Dai, D. (2016). Looking back to the future: Toward a new era of gifted education. In D. Y. Dai & C. C. Kuo (Eds.), *Gifted education in Asia: Problems and prospects* (pp. 295–319). Charlotte, NC: Information Age Publishing.

Degner, S., & Gruber, H. (2011). Persons in the shadow: How guidance works in the acquisition of expertise. In B. Weber, E. Marsal, & T. Dobashi (Eds.), *The politics of empathy: New interdisciplinary perspectives on an ancient phenomenon* (pp. 103–116). Münster, Germany: Lit.

Dignath, C., Buettner, G., & Langfeldt, H.-P. (2008). How can primary school students learn self-regulated learning strategies most effectively? A meta-analysis on self-regulation training programmes. *Educational Research Review, 3*, 101–129. https://doi.org/10.1016/j.edurev.2008.02.003

Dignath, C., & Büttner, G. (2008). Components of fostering self-regulated learning among students: A meta-analysis on intervention studies at primary and secondary school level. *Metacognition and Learning, 3*, 231–264. https://doi.org/10.1007/s11409-008-9029-x

Ericsson, K., Hoffman, R., Kozbelt, A., & Williams, A. (Eds.). (2018). *The Cambridge handbook of expertise and expert performance*. Cambridge, UK: Cambridge University Press. https://doi.org/10.1017/9781316480748

Ericsson, K. A., Krampe, R. T., & Tesch-Römer, C. (1993). The role of deliberate practice in the acquisition of expert performance. *Psychological Review, 100*, 363–406. https://doi.org/10.1037/0033-295x.100.3.363

Fincher, C. L., Thornhill, R., Murray, D. R., & Schaller, M. (2008). Pathogen prevalence predicts human cross-cultural variability in individualism/collectivism. *Journal of Personality and Social Psychology, 275*(1649), 1279–1285. https://doi.org/10.1098/rspb.2008.0094

Fontana, R. P., Milligan, C., Littlejohn, A., & Margaryan, A. (2015). Measuring self-regulated learning in the workplace. *International Journal of Training and Development, 19*, 32–52. https://doi.org/10.1111/ijtd.12046

Hattie, J., Biggs, J., & Purdie, N. (1996). Effects of learning skills interventions on student learning: A meta-analysis. *Review of Educational Research, 66*, 99–136. https://doi.org/10.3102/00346543066002099

Hattie, J., & Timperley, H. (2007). The power of feedback. *Review of Educational Research, 77*, 81–112. https://doi.org/10.3102/003465430298487

Hilbert, M. (2014). How much of the global information and communication explosion is driven by more, and how much by better technology? *Journal of the Association for Information Science and Technology, 65*, 856–861. https://doi.org/10.1002/asi.23031

Ho, I. T., & Hau, K.-T. (2008). Academic achievement in the Chinese context: The role of goals, strategies, and effort. *International Journal of Psychology, 43*, 892–897. https://doi.org/10.1080/00207590701836323

Ho, I. T., & Hau, K.-T. (2010). Consequences of the Confucian culture: High achievement but negative psychological attributes? *Learning and Individual Differences, 20*, 571–573. https://doi.org/10.1016/j.lindif.2010.08.006

Hofstede, G. (2001). *Culture's consequences: Comparing values, behaviors, institutions, and organizations across nations* (2nd ed.). Thousand Oaks, CA: Sage.

Hübner, S., Nückles, M., & Renkl, A. (2010). Writing learning journals: Instructional support to overcome learning-strategy deficits. *Learning and Instruction, 20*, 18–29. https://doi.org/10.1016/j.learninstruc.2008.12.001

Iyengar, S. S., & Lepper, M. R. (1999). Rethinking the value of choice: A cultural perspective on intrinsic motivation. *Journal of Personality and Social Psychology, 76*, 349–366. https://doi.org/10.1037/0022-3514.76.3.349

Jin, L., & Cortazzi, M. (1998). Dimensions of dialogue: Large classes in China. *International Journal of Educational Research, 29*, 739–761. https://doi.org/10.1016/S0883-0355(98)00061-5

Law, Y., Chan, C. K. K., & Sachs, J. (2008). Beliefs about learning, self-regulated strategies and text comprehension among Chinese children. *British Journal of Educational Psychology, 78*, 51–73. https://doi.org/10.1348/000709907X179812

Leung, F. K. S. (2001). In search of an east Asian identity in mathematics education. *Educational Studies in Mathematics, 47*, 35–51. https://doi.org/10.1023/A:1017936429620

Li, J. (2002). A cultural model of learning: Chinese "heart and mind for wanting to learn". *Journal of Cross-Cultural Psychology, 33*, 248–269. https://doi.org/10.1177/0022022102033003003

Li, J. (2010). Learning to self-perfect: Chinese beliefs about learning. In C. K. K. Chan & N. Rao (Eds). *Revisiting the Chinese learner: Changing contexts, changing education* (Vol. 25, pp. 35–69). Hong Kong, China: Comparative Education Research Centre.

McInerney, D. M., Cheng, R. W., Mok, M. M. C., & Lam, A. K. H. (2012). Academic self-concept and learning strategies: Direction of effect on student academic achievement. *Journal of Advanced Academics, 23*, 248–269. https://doi.org/10.1177/1932202X12451020

Mori, I., & Baker, D. (2010). The origin of universal shadow education: What the supplemental education phenomenon tells us about the postmodern institution of education. *Asia Pacific Education Review, 11*, 36–48. https://doi.org/10.1007/s12564-009-9057-5

Nandagopal, K., & Ericsson, K. A. (2012). An expert performance approach to the study of individual differences in self-regulated learning activities in upper-level college students. *Learning and Individual Differences, 22*, 597–609. https://doi.org/10.1016/j.lindif.2011.11.018

Nisbett, R. E. (2005). *The geography of thought: How Asians and westerners think differently, and why.* London, England: Nicholas Brealey.

Nota, L., Soresi, S., & Zimmerman, B. J. (2004). Self-regulation and academic achievement and resilience: A longitudinal study. *International Journal of Educational Research, 41,* 198–215. https://doi.org/10.1016/j.ijer.2005.07.001

Obergriesser, S., & Stoeger, H. (2016). The influence of emotions and learning preferences on learning strategy use before transition into high-achiever track secondary school. *High Ability Studies, 27*(1), 5–38. https://doi.org/10.1080/13598139.2015.1100980

Pintrich, P. R. (2000a). The role of goal orientation in self-regulated learning. In M. Boekaerts, P. R. Pintrich, & M. Zeidner (Eds.), *Handbook of self-regulation* (pp. 451–502). San Diego, CA: Academic.

Pintrich, P. R. (2000b). Multiple goals, multiple pathways: The role of goal orientation in learning and achievement. *Journal of Educational Psychology, 92,* 544–555. https://doi.org/10.1037/0022-0663.92.3.544

Pressley, M., Graham, S., & Harris, K. (2006). The state of educational intervention research as viewed through the lens of literacy intervention. *British Journal of Educational Psychology, 76,* 1–19. https://doi.org/10.1348/000709905X66035

Pronold-Günthner, F., Winkler-Theiß, V., Schilcher, A., Pissarek, M., Sontag, C., Steinbach, J., … Lichtinger, U. (2014). *Burg Adlerstein: Lesetraining: Lehrerband zum Lesetraining* (Castle Adlerstein: Reading training: Teacher's guide). Braunschweig, Germany: Westermann.

Purdie, N., Hattie, J., & Douglas, G. (1996). Student conceptions of learning and their use of self-regulated learning strategies: A cross-cultural comparison. *Journal of Educational Psychology, 88,* 87–100. https://doi.org/10.1037/0022-0663.88.1.87

Ramdass, D., & Zimmerman, B. (2011). Developing self-regulation skills: The important role of homework. *Journal of Advanced Academics, 22,* 194–218. https://doi.org/10.1177/1932202X1102202202

Rao, N., & Chan, C. K. K. (2010). Moving beyond the paradoxes: Understanding Chinese learners and their teachers. In C. K. K. Chan & N. Rao (Eds.), *Evisiting the Chinese learner: Changing contexts, changing education* (Vol. 25, pp. 3–32). Hong Kong, China: Comparative Education Research Centre.

Renkl, A., Mandl, H., & Gruber, H. (1996). Inert knowledge: Analyses and remedies. *Educational Psychologist, 31,* 115–121. https://doi.org/10.1207/s15326985ep3102_3

Salomon, G., & Perkins, P. N. (1989). Rocky roads to transfer: Rethinking mechanism of a neglected phenomenon. *Educational Psychologist, 24,* 113–142. https://doi.org/10.1207/s15326985ep2402_1

Schilcher, A., Stoeger, H., Pissarek, M., Sontag, C., Pronold-Günthner, F., & Steinbach, J. (2013). *Burg Adlerstein: Lesetraining: Arbeitsheft* (Castle Adlerstein: Reading training: Workbook). Braunschweig, Germany: Westermann.

Schunk, D. H., & Rice, J. M. (1987). Enhancing comprehension skill and self-efficacy with strategy value information. *Journal of Reading Behavior, 19,* 285–302. https://doi.org/10.1080/10862968709547605

Sontag, C., & Stoeger, H. (2015). Can highly intelligent and high-achieving students benefit from training in self-regulated learning in a regular classroom context? *Learning and Individual Differences, 41,* 43–53. https://doi.org/10.1016/j.lindif.2015.07.008

Stoeger, H., Fleischmann, S., & Obergriesser, B. (2015). Self-regulated learning (SRL) and the gifted learner in primary school: The theoretical basis of and empirical findings on a research program dedicated to ensuring that all students learn to regulate their own learning. *Asia Pacific Education Review, 16,* 257–267. https://doi.org/10.1007/s12564-015-9376-7

Stoeger, H., & Sontag, C. (2012). How gifted students learn: A literature review. In A. Ziegler, C. Fischer, H. Stoeger, & M. Reutlinger (Eds.), *Gifted education as a lifelong challenge: Essays in honour of Franz J. Mönks* (pp. 315–336). Münster, Germany: LIT.

Stoeger, H., Sontag, C., & Ziegler, A. (2014). Impact of a teacher-led intervention on preference for self-regulated learning, finding main ideas in expository texts, and reading comprehension. *Journal of Educational Psychology, 106,* 799–814. https://doi.org/10.1037/a0036035

Stoeger, H., Steinbach, J., Obergriesser, S., & Matthes, B. (2014). What is more important for fourth-grade primary-school students for transforming their potential into achievement: The individual or the environmental box in multidimensional conceptions of giftedness? *High Ability Studies, 25*, 5–21. https://doi.org/10.1080/13598139.2014.914381

Stoeger, H., & Ziegler, A. (2004). Selbstreguliertes Lernen im Mathematikunterricht: Ein Trainingsprogramm für GymnasiastInnen der 6. Und 7. Jahrgangsstufe (self-regulated learning during mathematics instruction: A training program for high-achiever-track pupils in grades 6 and 7). In C. A. von Gleichenstein (Ed.), *Schulpsychologie als Brücke zwischen Familie und Schule [CD]*. Bonn, Germany: Deutscher Psychologen-Verband.

Stoeger, H., & Ziegler, A. (2005). Evaluation of an elementary classroom self-regulated learning program for gifted mathematics underachievers. *International Education Journal, 6*, 261–271. Retrieved from https://ehlt.flinders.edu.au/education/iej/articles/V6n2/Stoeger/paper.pdf

Stoeger, H., & Ziegler, A. (2006). On the influence of motivational orientations on a training to enhance self-regulated learning skills. *Georgian Electronic Scientific Journal: Education Science and Psychology, 9*, 13–27.

Stoeger, H., & Ziegler, A. (2008a). Evaluation of a classroom based training to improve self-regulation in time management tasks during homework activities with fourth graders. *Metacognition and Learning, 3*, 207–230. https://doi.org/10.1007/s11409-008-9027-z

Stoeger, H., & Ziegler, A. (2008b). *Trainingshandbuch selbstreguliertes Lernen II: Grundlegende Textverständnisstrategien für Schüler der 4. bis 8. Jahrgangsstufe* (Self-regulated learning training handbook II: Basic reading-skills strategies for pupils in grades 4–8). Lengerich, Germany: Pabst.

Stoeger, H., & Ziegler, A. (2010). Do pupils with differing cognitive abilities benefit similarly from a self-regulated learning training program? *Gifted Education International, 26*, 110–123. https://doi.org/10.1177/026142941002600113

Stoeger, H., & Ziegler, A. (2011). Self-regulatory training through elementary-school students' homework completion. In B. J. Zimmerman & D. H. Schunk (Eds.), *Handbook of self-regulation of learning and performance* (pp. 87–101). New York, NY: Routledge.

Stone, K. M. (2002). A cross-cultural comparison of the perceived traits of gifted behavior. *Gifted and Talented International, 17*, 61–75. https://doi.org/10.1080/15332276.2002.11672990

Subotnik, R. F., Olszewski-Kubilius, P., & Worrell, F. C. (2011). Rethinking giftedness and gifted education: A proposed direction forward based on psychological science. *Psychological Science, 12*, 3–54. https://doi.org/10.1177/1529100611418056

Tang, M., & Neber, H. (2008). Motivation and self-regulated science learning in high-achieving students: Differences related to nation, gender, and grade-level. *High Ability Studies, 19*, 103–116. https://doi.org/10.1080/13598130802503959

van der Zande, J., Teigland, K., Sharyar, S., & Teigland, R. (2018). The substitution of labor: From technological feasibility to other factors influencing job automation. Innovative Internet Report 5. Stockholm, Sweden: Center for Strategy and Competitiveness, Stockholm School of Economics Institute for Research.

Verma, S., & Larson, R. (Eds.) (2003). Examining adolescent leisure time across cultures: Developmental opportunities and risks [special issue]. New Directions for Child and Adolescent Development, 99.

Wang, J., & Lin, E. (2005). Comparative studies on U.S. and Chinese mathematics learning and the implications for standards-based mathematics teaching reform. *Educational Researcher, 34*(5), 3–13. https://doi.org/10.3102/0013189X034005003

Weinstein, C. E., Husman, J., & Dierking, D. R. (2000). Self-regulation interventions with a focus on learning strategies. In M. Boekaerts, P. R. Pintrich, & M. Zeidner (Eds.), *Handbook of self-regulation* (pp. 727–747). San Diego, CA: Academic.

Weinstein, C. E., & Mayer, R. E. (1986). The teaching of learning strategies. In M. C. Wittrock (Ed.), *Handbook of research on teaching* (3rd ed., pp. 315–327). New York, NY: Macmillan.

Ziegler, A., & Stoeger, H. (2005). *Trainingshandbuch selbstreguliertes Lernen I: Lernökologische Strategien für Schüler der 4. Jahrgangsstufe zur Verbesserung mathematischer Kompetenzen* (Self-regulated learning training handbook I: Study-ecology strategies for pupils in grade four for improving their mathematics competencies). Lengerich, Germany: Pabst.

Ziegler, A., & Stoeger, H. (2017). Systemic gifted education: A theoretical introduction. *Gifted Child Quarterly, 61*, 183–193. https://doi.org/10.1177/0016986217705713

Ziegler, A., Stoeger, H., & Vialle, W. (2013). *Learning how to learn through homework: A six-week training program for children in the middle primary years with sample mathematics content*. Victoria, Australia: Hawker Brownlow.

Zimmerman, B. J. (1986). Becoming a self-regulated learner: Which are the key subprocesses? *Contemporary Educational Psychology, 16*, 307–313. https://doi.org/10.1016/0361-476X(86)90027-5

Zimmerman, B. J. (1990). Self-regulating academic learning and achievement: The emergence of a social cognitive perspective. *Educational Psychological Review, 2*, 173–201. https://doi.org/10.1007/BF01322178

Zimmerman, B. J. (2000). Attaining self-regulation: A social cognitive perspective. In M. Boekaerts, P. R. Pintrich, & M. Zeidner (Eds.), *Handbook of self-regulation* (pp. 13–39). San Diego, CA: Academic.

Heidrun Stoeger, PhD, is chair professor for School Research, School Development, and Evaluation at the University of Regensburg, Germany. She is currently serving as the vice president of the International Research Association for Talent Development and Excellence (IRATDE). She has published about 200 books, chapters and articles in the fields of talent development, educational psychology and education. She has served as editor in chief of the journal *High Ability Studies* and is a member of the editorial board of the German-language *Journal of Talent Development*. Her main interests in the field of talent development and excellence are teacher training, the Actiotope Model of Giftedness, educational and learning capital and learning and motivational training programs.

Daniel Patrick Balestrini, PhD, is lecturer at the Chair for School Research, School Development, and Evaluation at the University of Regensburg and coordinator of an international research project in extracurricular education.

Julia Steinbach, PhD, is lecturer at the Chair for School Research, School Development, and Evaluation at the University of Regensburg and coordinator of an international research project in extracurricular education.

Fostering Resilience in 'At-Risk' Gifted and Talented Young People

15

Nadine Ballam

Contents

Introduction	320
Giftedness, Resilience, and the Significance of Context	321
Giftedness and Talent in the Australasia-Pacific	321
The Resilience Framework	322
The Significance of Context	323
Fostering Resilience	324
Identity and Resilience	325
Relationships and Resilience	327
Implications and Concluding Thoughts	329
Cross-References	331
References	331

Abstract

Despite efforts around the world to advocate for gifted and talented young people, there are common groups that remain underrepresented in gifted and talented education programs. Two such groups are young people from Indigenous or minority ethnicities and young people living in poverty. These groups are consistently labelled as 'disadvantaged', 'at-risk' or 'vulnerable' and likely represent a large proportion of gifted underachievers. Australasia-Pacific nations have felt the impact of global human rights concerns, despite their relatively isolated location, and this has resulted in increasingly multicultural societies and a rise in issues such as child poverty. These changes are additional to some of the unique collective and individual sociocultural issues that nations in this corner of the globe experience. The focus in this chapter is on gifted young people from Indigenous and minority ethnicities and from low socio-economic circumstances.

N. Ballam (✉)
University of Waikato, Hamilton, New Zealand
e-mail: nadine.ballam@waikato.ac.nz

© Springer Nature Singapore Pte Ltd. 2021
S. R. Smith (ed.), *Handbook of Giftedness and Talent Development in the Asia-Pacific*,
Springer International Handbooks of Education,
https://doi.org/10.1007/978-981-13-3041-4_14

A range of international and Australasia-Pacific research indicates that a strong sense of identity and caring and supportive relationships are two essential factors for promoting resilience. Some insight into how resilience might be fostered in gifted young people, in particular those from Indigenous and minority ethnicities and from low socio-economic circumstances, will be provided in this chapter.

Keywords

Giftedness · Risk · Resilience · Identity · Relationships

The aims in this chapter are to:
1. Contextualise giftedness and resilience in Australasia-Pacific settings.
2. Explore two key elements associated with resilience: identity and relationships.
3. Offer insights into how educators and other professionals might reflect on their own practices with gifted young people from high-risk environments.

Introduction

Around the world, gifted and talented young people from Indigenous and minority ethnicities and those who live in poverty are two groups commonly reported to be 'disadvantaged', 'at-risk' or 'vulnerable' (Chaffey, 2009; Ministry of Education, 2012; Plucker, Giancola, Healey, Arndt, & Wang, 2015). The reasons for this are many, but of great concern is that these young people likely represent a large proportion of gifted underachievers. Despite its relatively isolated location, the Australasia-Pacific region has followed global trends, becoming increasingly multicultural and experiencing rising rates of poverty, particularly amongst children and young people (Duncanson et al., 2017; Social Policy Research Centre, 2016; St John & So, 2018; United Nations Development Programme, 2014). If these trends continue, increasing numbers of gifted and talented young people throughout the Australasia-Pacific region will experience challenges associated with marginalisation and limited access to resources, the outcome of which could well include unrealised fulfilment of potential at both personal and societal levels (Moltzen, 2011).

There is increasing recognition in the field of giftedness and talent of the unique context and sub-contexts that make up the Australasia-Pacific region. Unlike much of the rest of the world, nations in this region are relatively isolated islands, ranging in population from approximately 24,860,000 in Australia to 1,300 in Tokelau (World Population Review, 2018). Each nation has its own history, traditions, culture, and values, and yet these elements also unite the Australasia-Pacific region in unique ways. Australian, New Zealand, and Pacific governments support each other in various capacities, and there is vast movement of people between the nations that make up this part of the world (Department of Labour, 2012; Fraenkel, 2018).

All of these characteristics combine to make providing for gifted and talented young people a complex endeavour.

Giftedness, Resilience, and the Significance of Context

Giftedness and Talent in the Australasia-Pacific

The field of giftedness and talent in the Australasia-Pacific region is 'young' in comparison to other parts of the world, and ideas about giftedness in this context have traditionally been influenced by the United States, the United Kingdom, and, more recently, Europe and Asia (Moltzen, Jolly, & Jarvis, 2018). Consequently, approaches to gifted education across the Australasia-Pacific (particularly in Australia and New Zealand) are underpinned by various international models of giftedness and talent. In Australia, although states and territories have their own policies regarding gifted education, Gagné's *Differentiated Model of Giftedness and Talent* (DMGT; Gagné, 1985, 2003, 2009, 2015) has been widely adopted (Jung & Hay, 2018). The first and recently implemented nationwide Australian curriculum (Australian Curriculum, Assessment, and Reporting Authority, 2015) has also emphasised the theories of Tannenbaum (2003) and Renzulli (1986). New Zealand has also traditionally emphasised Gagné's ideas, but Renzulli's (1978, 2003) three-ring concept of giftedness and Gardner's (1993, 2011) theory of multiple intelligences are featured prominently in the Ministry of Education's (2012) guidelines for conceptualising giftedness and talent. Official documentation related to gifted education in other Australasia-Pacific nation contexts is sparse.

There is a growing body of literature related to culturally responsive approaches to identification of and provisions for Indigenous gifted learners in Australia (Chaffey, 2002, 2011; Chaffey, Bailey, & Vine, 2003, 2011; Christie, 2011; Garvis, 2006; Gibson & Vialle, 2007) and New Zealand (Bevan-Brown, 2011, 2012; Miller, 2011, 2015, 2017; Webber, 2011a, 2015, 2017). Research and literature about Pasifika gifted learners—Pacific Islanders, Melanesian, Micronesian, or Polynesian cultures—are limited, with most related to these learners' educational experiences in the New Zealand context (Faaea-Semeatu, 2011, 2015; Miller, 2011, 2015, 2017). Information about Pasifika gifted learners in Pacific nations or in Australia is less available. Likewise, research related specifically to gifted young people who are migrants, refugees, or from other ethnic minority groups is difficult to find, although there is acknowledgement of their underrepresentation in gifted and talented education programs in Australia and New Zealand.

Literature and research related specifically to gifted and talented learners living in poverty in the Australasia-Pacific region is also limited. Ballam (2013, 2017) investigated the lived experiences of gifted and talented young people from low socio-economic backgrounds in New Zealand, in one of few studies from this region to focus specifically on poverty and giftedness. Several studies focused on Indigenous populations or minority ethnicities emphasise the overrepresentation of these groups in poverty statistics (Chaffey, 2002, 2011; Miller, 2015, 2017), but do not have a primary focus on poverty itself.

Amongst the issues associated with the identification of 'at-risk' gifted and talented young people are perceptions of disadvantage and low educational expectations. Differences that are sometimes observed in children from Indigenous and minority ethnicities or low socio-economic backgrounds may be interpreted as deficits, and, consequently, these learners are labelled 'at-risk'. This label can perpetuate views that these young people are dysfunctional, resulting in a focus on their shortcomings and weaknesses rather than strengths (Seeley, 2003). Deficit or stereotypical thinking diminishes the ability and willingness of some educators to recognise the potential in their learners (Alton-Lee, 2003) and impedes access to gifted and talented education programs for 'at-risk' learners (Ford & Whiting, 2008).

Clark (2013) suggests that views and beliefs about what constitutes giftedness or talent can be restrictive. The way that communities conceptualise giftedness influences who is given opportunities to succeed and who will have greater and lesser opportunities to contribute. Nations and communities in the Australasia-Pacific region differ in the ways that they 'define' (and consequently cater for) giftedness and talent. Adding to this, ethnic and cultural groups evaluate their own members and members of other ethnicities or cultures in terms of their own conceptions of giftedness (Sternberg, 2007). What one cultural group values as intelligence, giftedness, or talent may not be valued as highly, if at all, in another. This is especially relevant in the Australasia-Pacific region, where movement of ethnic and cultural groups between nations in this area of the world is widespread.

The Resilience Framework

Understandings about risk and resilience have developed over time from a deficit view of negative life experiences and adjustment (Luthar, 2006) to a contemporary notion of resilience as a process through which individuals draw on resources to positively adapt in the face of adversity (Masten & Powell, 2003; Rutter, 2000; Yates, Egeland, & Sroufe, 2003). The resilience framework is complex and multifaceted; however, in general terms, resilience is developed as a process of interaction between risk and protective factors. Risk factors encompass elements that are more likely to drive an individual towards less productive outcomes, while protective factors are more likely to move the individual towards adaptive outcomes (Masten, 2002). While each factor on its own can impact an individual, it is the complex underlying processes of interaction between these factors that build resilience.

One important point that highlights the complexity of ideas about resilience is that cultural, social, developmental, political, and historical contexts influence how resilience is defined and conceptualised (Masten & Obradovic, 2006; Ungar, 2008). The ways that people perceive and respond to risk also differ amongst individuals and communities (Harvey & Delfabbro, 2004). Ungar (2008) cautions that much of the resilience literature focuses on western understandings of 'healthy' functioning and that we have not yet adequately explored what resilience means to non-western populations, marginalised groups, or Indigenous communities.

With this caution in mind, the resilience framework provides a useful lens through which to consider fostering resilience in 'at-risk' gifted and talented young people in the Australasia-Pacific region. Resilience literature commonly identifies high intellectual capacity or giftedness as a major protective factor (Bland & Sowa, 1994; Masten & Coatsworth, 1998; Werner, 2000). Poverty is consistently cited as a significant risk factor (Gallagher, 2008; Pianta & Walsh, 1998; Pungello, Kupersmidt, Burchinal, & Patterson, 1996; Schoon, 2006), and Indigenous and ethnic minority groups across the Australasia-Pacific region are overrepresented in poverty statistics (Easton, 2013). Both giftedness and poverty also have cumulative impacts; for example, there may be additional advantages that come with giftedness, such as confidence and increased self-esteem, and poverty may generate further risks, including heightened levels of stress and lack of access to adequate health care or other resources.

This perspective does not fully capture the complexity of notions of resilience, however. Racz, McMahon, and Luthar (2011) caution against making assumptions about various populations and the likelihood of risk or protective conditions. For example, while poverty is seen to be a significant risk, these authors outline that studies of affluent children indicate that high socio-economic status can pose just as many difficulties. Additionally, studies indicate that giftedness does not always serve as a protective factor and can sometimes present as a risk (Ballam, 2013; Lopez & Sotillo, 2009; Luthar, 1991; Morales, 2010; Pfeiffer & Stocking, 2000). This can result in gifted young people who are already 'at-risk' becoming 'twice vulnerable' (or in some cases, 'multi-vulnerable'). Mueller (2009) points out that potential characteristics of giftedness (e.g., perfectionism and oversensitivity, amongst others) may lead to young people being at risk for psychosocial adjustment issues. This is also highlighted by other authors. For example, in their revised profiles of the gifted and talented, Neihart and Betts (2010) identify categories of gifted young people who are very much 'at-risk', although as yet, there is no updated peer-reviewed publication to support these types of giftedness beyond their 1988 seminal work (Betts & Neihart, 1988). Pfeiffer and Stocking (2000) outline five specific risk factors that relate specifically to academically gifted children. These are asynchronous or uneven development, unrealistic expectations of significant others, parental over-involvement, a mismatch between their capabilities and the instructional environment, and social and emotional issues resulting from challenges with peers. In essence, 'risk' is relatively and subjectively understood, and people's perceptions and experiences of risk can be vastly different.

The Significance of Context

One reason why constructs such as giftedness, talent, risk, and resilience are so difficult to define and conceptualise is because context matters. These phenomena are socially and culturally constructed, and, consequently, careful attention must be paid to the contexts within which each play out (Ungar, 2008). Writers in the area of giftedness (e.g., Gagné, 2003; Renzulli, 2003; Tannenbaum, 2003) have argued that key ingredients for the realisation of exceptional potential lie within the individual and their environments and the interactions that occur between both. Understanding developmental changes requires not just the recognition of an individual's giftedness but also the consideration of environmental conditions, such as interventions, resources and support systems that are crucial to the development of gifts and talents (Barab & Plucker, 2002; Feldman, 2003). In the same way, resilience is considered to be fluid rather than a 'fixed' characteristic, or a process rather than a trait, and an individual's resilience can alter in different contexts and as their circumstances change (Gilligan, 2001). Consequently, it is not simply ethnicity, culture, or socio-economic status that determines levels of achievement; instead, the complex combination of other aspects of the home, school, and wider environments and the unique personal attributes of the gifted individual is what ultimately influences the development of gifts and talents.

An important consideration for 'at-risk' gifted and talented young people in the Australasia-Pacific, which further complicates the notion of risk, is the rate of movement between countries in this region. The latest census data for Australia and New Zealand indicate that the number of people identifying with one or more Pasifika ethnicities is growing in both countries (Ravulo, 2015; Stats NZ, 2018). One-sixth of Māori are now living in Australia, with one in three of these people Australian-born (Haami, 2018). While less Australian and New Zealand citizens migrate to islands that make up Pacific nations, there has traditionally always been movement between Australia and New Zealand. This movement between nations has significant implications for gifted and talented young people as, while they may be considered gifted in one location where their gifts and talents are valued, those same abilities may not be recognised or valued when they move to another context. For 'at-risk' gifted young people, this situation can add more complexity to the development of gifts and talents or resilience; for example, the move from one's native country might mean they become an ethnic minority in another or experience significant changes in socio-economic status.

Fostering Resilience

Across the Australasia-Pacific region, the message that more needs to be done to recognise, identify, and cater for gifted young people from Indigenous and minority ethnicities and low socioeconomic backgrounds has been explicitly communicated over a number of years (Biddulph, Biddulph, & Biddulph, 2003; Chandler, 2011; Jarvis, Jolly, & Moltzen, 2018; Riley, 2004; Versteynen, 2001). Work by and with Indigenous populations in Australia and New Zealand has brought more recognition and understanding of diverse conceptions of giftedness (e.g., Bevan-Brown, 2011, 2012; Chaffey, 2002, 2011; Christie, 2011; Miller, 2011, 2015, 2017; Webber, 2011a, 2015, 2017). Gifts and talents that are valued amongst Aboriginal, Māori, and Pasifika populations are being identified and ways of working with gifted

Indigenous young people proposed. Reminders that gifts and talents exist in all social, cultural, and socio-economic groups are widespread (Ministry of Education, 2012), and messages about equity and inclusion are rife (Ministerial Council on Education, Employment, Training and Youth Affairs [MCEETYA], 2008; Ministry of Education, 2007, 2015). However, the increasingly glaring issue that gifted young people from Indigenous and minority ethnicities and low socio-economic backgrounds remain underrepresented in gifted and talented education programs has not yet been adequately addressed, and difficult questions need to be asked as to why this is still occurring.

A strong sense of identity and supportive relationships are two elements that are extensively reported as being essential for promoting resilience (Masten & Coatsworth, 1998; Masten & Obradovic, 2006), and this is consistent with research with 'at-risk' gifted and talented young people. The following sections will explore these elements.

Identity and Resilience

Aspects of identity feature prominently in resilience literature and research. Protective elements include self-efficacy, self-confidence, and high self-esteem as well as aspects such as faith, optimism, and strong familial, cultural, and societal systems (Masten & Coatsworth, 1998; Masten & Obradovic, 2006). Masten and colleagues contend that resilience is dependent on the functional presence of these elements in people's lives. A sense of identity is developed as individuals interact with and within their social and cultural environments (Erikson, 1968; Haney, 2007; Reay, 2010; Wetherell, 2009). The way in which individuals define, perceive, and position themselves socially and culturally contributes to the consolidation of personal identity. A sense of identity is also influenced by the way in which individuals are defined, perceived, and positioned by others, and the development of a strong sense of identity is likely to increase a positive sense of well-being (Schwartz, Zamboanga, Weisskirch, & Wang, 2010).

Alongside personal identity, the development of the 'gifted self' also occurs in relation to and with others. The nature of gifted identity is dependent on how acceptable the gifted individual perceives him or herself to be in the eyes of significant others (Greenspon, 1998) and how valued his or her abilities are (Neihart, 1998). Mueller (2009) points out that characteristics of giftedness are generally viewed in two ways: first, that these put young people at risk for poor psychological adjustment and, second, that resources that come with giftedness are an advantage or a protective factor. There are mixed reports in research about the ways in which high abilities influence the sense of identity of gifted and talented individuals. While some studies of gifted individuals indicate that high self-esteem, positive self-concept and a strong belief in self might be characteristic of those who achieve to high levels (e.g., Borland, Schnur, & Wright, 2000; Morales, 2010; Reis, Colbert, & Hébert, 2005), there is also indication of the opposite. Amongst the 'eight great gripes' of gifted children in Galbraith's (1985) research, for example, was reference to the unrealistic expectations of others, feelings of being 'different', and social isolation. Other potentially detrimental impacts on self-concept for gifted individuals include uneven development (Morelock, 1992), unhealthy perfectionism (Rimm, Siegle, & Davis, 2017) and heightened sensitivity (Piechowski, 2003).

Reflecting on aspects of identity is crucial in relation to the 'at-risk' gifted young people who are the focus of this discussion, and it is evident that the environments these young people interact with, both immediate and distal, are significant. Indigenous and minority ethnicity populations tend to be socially and culturally stereotyped, both in their immediate contexts and in wider society, and Webber (2008, 2011b) asserts that these stereotypes are often used to justify beliefs that Indigenous peoples and those from ethnic minorities are less deserving of opportunities. However, this view that young people from Indigenous or minority ethnicity backgrounds behave in particular ways, hold particular beliefs and values, or are deserving of particular resources or not, cuts across the grain of the very argument that is often put forward about gifted young people, that they are not a homogenous group, but unique, and should be treated first and foremost as individuals. Nakata (2011) aptly points out that Indigenous young people are diverse and "not a homogenous lump of humanity" (p. 3). As Bevan-Brown (2011) stresses, Indigenous young people differ from one another in terms of their human characteristics and also the degree to which they identify with and adhere to cultural beliefs, values, and practices. To perceive and consequently work with specific groups of young people in such a way that their uniqueness is clouded by judgments and evaluations of 'their particular type' limits not only their capacity to develop a strong sense of identity, but also the capacity to demonstrate resilience in the development and demonstration of their gifts.

Gifted young people from low socio-economic backgrounds also face unique challenges in terms of the development of a strong sense of identity and of gifts and talents. In her research with gifted young people from low socio-economic backgrounds, Ballam (2013, 2017) found that their sense of identity was dependent on how they viewed themselves and their perceptions of how others evaluated them in light of both their high abilities and socio-economic circumstances. One surprising finding from Ballam's study was that participants largely reported that their giftedness impacted more detrimentally on their sense of identity than their socio-economic circumstances did. This was because they believed their giftedness was the essence of who they were, whereas there was the potential for them to change their personal circumstances as they got older. While Ballam's finding does not negate the difficulties gifted young people from impoverished backgrounds can face, it is a point of difference between the influence of ethnicity (which cannot be changed) and socioeconomic status (which has the potential to be changed) for 'at-risk' gifted young people.

Phrases such as 'culturally responsive', 'culturally appropriate', and 'culturally safe', amongst others, are commonplace in educational circles throughout the Australasia-Pacific. However, without truly understanding the notion of 'intercultural space' (Nakata, 2011, p. 2), efforts to provide for diverse gifted young people can be tokenistic. Nakata's notion of the 'cultural interface', or the contested space between Indigenous and non-Indigenous knowledge systems, ways of being and ways of doing, offers the potential for "recognition of all the disruptions, discontinuities, continuities, and convergences of knowledge' and 'appreciation of the complexities that exist there" (p. 5). Consideration of this notion in light of the many social and cultural groups gifted young people are part of is essential, again, with the underpinning understanding that every young person is unique.

Resilience in 'at-risk' gifted young people is enhanced when they are supported to draw on the essence of who they are—their unique characteristics, beliefs, values, and social and cultural identities. In her research with gifted young people in New Zealand secondary schools, Webber (2017) found that those with strong positive racial-ethnic identities were more 'culturally flexible' or able to more easily navigate their way through and across multiple cultural contexts. This identity then enabled them to focus more on what they could achieve than who they 'needed to be'. An implication of this recognition of identity for those working with 'at-risk' gifted young people is the need to first be strong in their own identities, so as to grow their capacity to embrace diverse, unfamiliar, and sometimes uncomfortable ways of knowing, being and doing. Gifted young people from Indigenous and minority ethnicities or low socio-economic backgrounds should never have to compromise their sense of identity for a sense of belonging or to facilitate their success (Webber, 2017).

Relationships and Resilience

It would come as no surprise to those familiar with studies of resilient individuals that relationships are ascribed as playing a critical role in the successes of young people. Resilience research reports that relationships with supportive adults, such as parents, caregivers, teachers, and mentors, appear to be most significant (Masten, 2001, 2014; Masten & Coatsworth, 1998; Rutter, 1987). Further to this, Ungar (2013) proposed that the greater the adversity young people face, the more they benefit from protective elements such as empowering relationships with adults who care about their success. According to Ungar, it is the *quality* of these relationships that makes the difference; young people will engage best with adults who "offer themselves as resources in ways that young people value" (p. 333). In light of this, the onus for developing resilience in children and young people lies not only with the young people themselves, but with all who interact with them.

One of the biggest risks for 'at-risk' young people is the stereotypical ideas and attitudes about and towards them. The widespread reporting of statistics indicating poor outcomes in a range of areas, including education, means that young people who are Indigenous, of ethnic minority, or from low socio-economic backgrounds can be subjected to low expectations (Ellis, Bianchi, Griskevicius, & Frankenhuis, 2017; Webber, McKinley, & Hattie, 2013; Yunkaporta & McGinty, 2009). Consequently, gifts and talents are sometimes overshadowed by deficit perspectives of potential or ability amongst these groups (Turner, Rubie-Davies, & Webber, 2015). These deficit attitudes might also extend to home environments and parental support, with generalised assumptions made about how interested or not parents and caregivers are in their children's educational or other successes. However, many studies of 'at-risk' gifted young people (e.g., Ballam, 2013; Bloom, 1985; Macfarlane, Webber, Cookson-Cox, & McRae, 2014; Miller, 2015; Shumow, 1997; Van Tassel-Baska, 1989) have shown that, despite the limited assets or advantages available to them, their parents generally valued education and achievement. Parents also tended to expose their children to a range of environments and activities, which compensated for a lack of financial or other resources and gave them a broad perspective of options available to them.

In the same way that supportive and positive relationships with parents can influence the development of gifts and talents in 'at-risk' gifted young people, home relationships that appear to be less supportive can also play a crucial role. For example, one participant in Ballam's (2013) research with gifted young people from low socio-economic backgrounds described a turbulent relationship with her father, who was often not present and, when he was around, was usually emotionally unavailable. For this young woman, the less adequate characteristics of her relationship with her father became a strong source of her drive to develop her gifts and talents in the hope of 'breaking the cycle' of poverty in the family and becoming a better role model for her siblings. Another participant in this study described his parents as 'distant' and 'inconsistent' but recognised the love his mother had for him and his father's strong work ethic. While he lamented that they were unable to provide him with the material resources he needed to develop his gifts and talents, he perceived their modelling of these qualities to be fundamental to his growth. This familial modelling indicates clearly that relationships have the capacity to surpass limitations, such as a lack of resources and other disadvantages.

For 'at-risk' gifted young people from more challenging and chaotic home environments, other significant adults (such as educators and coaches) inadvertently become key role models and mentors who can offer something more than what these individuals might see modelled in their home contexts. As indicated earlier in this section, it is the quality of these relationships that counts (Ungar, 2013). Consequently, rather than these significant adults simply being 'encouraging' or 'available', these relationships require focused thought and strategy to really influence the capacity of 'at-risk' gifted young people to develop resilience. Beyond encouragement and support, studies of 'at-risk' gifted young people have shown that an important aspect of their relationships with other significant adults is that they are often catalysts for further opportunities (Ballam, 2013). For example, these significant adults might empower 'at-risk' gifted young people to more easily navigate contexts that are typically Eurowestern or middle or higher class. They might also facilitate access to a range of wider enrichment activities or networks with others in the gifted young person's areas of ability.

Miller (2015, 2017) emphasises another crucial element associated with the teacher-student relationship identified by the Māori and Pasifika young men in his research. These boys talked about having a sense of belonging or "a place to stand" (Miller, 2017, p. 142), where mutual respect and mentoring enabled them to develop their gifts and talents. This sense of belonging resonates with Webber's (2011a) findings, that is, providing an environment where young people can genuinely strengthen their racial-ethnic identities contributes to achievement and success. Gibson and Vialle (2007), writing about Australian Aboriginal young people's views of giftedness, also indicated that the realisation of their gifted potential appeared to be dependent on a strong sense of cultural identity. For those working and interacting with these young indigenous people, getting to know them in a genuine and validating way is critical.

Implications and Concluding Thoughts

The importance of a strong sense of identity and authentically supportive relationships for developing the gifts and talents of 'at-risk' young people has been outlined prolifically throughout gifted and resilience research and literature, as evidenced in earlier sections of this chapter. Without negating the contributions of countless devoted people in these fields, it can be easy to fall into a trap of simply restating implications that have been proposed previously and, consequently, missing what 'could be'. It is time to challenge existing dominant notions around what a strong sense of identity might mean for 'at-risk' gifted young people. It is also time to rethink the quality of relationships we have with these young people and the implicit messages we send, sometimes without realising, regarding what is valued and by whom. Our understanding of both giftedness and resilience needs to be socially and culturally embedded, with a firm willingness to 'blur the lines' to see, as much as we are able, beyond our individual perspectives and through other lenses.

Throughout this chapter, the term 'at-risk' has been used to represent young people who are commonly perceived or labelled as 'disadvantaged' and 'vulnerable'. While this has served a purpose in the context of this chapter, it also highlights one crucial implication for future practice with 'at-risk' gifted and talented young people: that deficit ways of looking at and talking about these young people need to stop. We are well versed at looking for the impacts on the development of 'at-risk' young people under the well-intentioned 'guise' of a strengths-based approach—or being able to put interventions in place to 'fix' them or their situations to facilitate 'better' outcomes. However, implicit in this approach are value judgments about desirable behaviours, knowledge, and belief systems and outcomes, often based on dominant ideas of how people should be, think or do.

Ellis et al. (2017) present a perspective that moves beyond a strengths-based approach to what these authors call an *adaptation-based approach*. While their work has been undertaken in the broader field of resilience research, this has some crucial implications for those working with 'at-risk' gifted young people. Ellis et al. explain that an adaptation-based approach to resilience "recognizes, utilizes, and values the skills and abilities that develop in response to high-risk environments" (p. 566), a term they use instead of 'at-risk' or 'disadvantaged'. This approach acknowledges that all individuals have strengths, regardless of background, experience, or social and cultural standing—and regardless of dominant perceptions of 'acceptable' ways of being, knowing, and doing. It embraces the notion that individuals are unique, and this uniqueness has been shaped by the many diverse experiences each individual has had—and that this should be celebrated. This high-risk environment approach resonates with and adds to notions already put forth by writers and researchers in the field of giftedness and talent in the Australasia-Pacific region (see earlier references to the works by Ballam, Bevan-Brown, Chaffey, Faaea-Semeatu, Garvis, Gibson, & Vialle, Miller, & Webber), who have advocated for acknowledging, embracing, and celebrating diverse social, cultural and racial-ethnic conceptions of giftedness. In essence, according to Ellis et al., this adaptation-based approach shifts the question from "What's wrong with and how can we help these kids?" to "What's right with these kids?" (p. 561) and what's wrong with the various learning environments that influence their developmental potential?

'At-risk' gifted and talented young people could well remain unrecognised as long as we insist on identifying and cultivating only those whose gifts and talents are valued by dominant, advantaged social, and cultural groups or who reflect dominant group identity and ideology. Sternberg (2007) claims that when cultural context is taken into consideration the recognition and support for talented individuals is improved. In their work related to the adaptation-based approach outlined here, Ellis et al. (2017) drew on Sternberg's (1999, 2014) theory of successful intelligence, which suggests that context is fundamental to success. In Sternberg's words, "Successful intelligence is one's ability to choose and successfully work toward the attainment of one's goals in life, within one's cultural context or contexts" (2014, p. 209). 'At-risk' gifted and talented young people develop social and cognitive skills from their various contexts that allow them to think and behave in ways that may be unique from those in lower-risk environments. These skills, regardless of how 'wrong', 'broken' or 'inappropriate' they might look from more dominant perspectives, are strengths that should be leveraged and worked with to promote outcomes that meet these young people's needs and desires.

There is no 'recipe' for adopting an adaptation-based approach to identifying and working with 'at-risk' gifted and talented young people throughout the many, increasingly varied environments they interact with in Australasia-Pacific nations. As suggested earlier, our work with young people needs to be uniquely tailored to both person and context. It should also take into consideration the view through our own 'lenses', not because these must change, but because if we cannot see the 'lines' around our own beliefs, values, and understandings, then we are unable to see beyond these. Consequently, working with 'at-risk' gifted and talented young people should first involve thorough reflection on our own conceptions of constructs, such as giftedness, talent, risk, and resilience, both individually and collectively, in our communities of practice. What do *we* actually believe giftedness and talent to be? What do *we* perceive to be 'risks' in young people's lives? And what is resilience? What do *we* expect a resilient young person might look like? These questions should then be revisited with the person and context in mind. What does *this person* value as gifts and talents? How might those qualities and abilities manifest in *this context*? And how do my ideas of what might present as 'risk' in this person's life align with *their own* perceptions and experiences of risk? What might I expect resilience in *this* young person in *this* context to look like? While these questions are simply a starting point, it is likely that authentic reflection will facilitate a broadening of lenses and recognition of biases or dominant ideas and provide insight into how individuals and groups in specific contexts might be more effectively catered for.

Cross-References

- ▶ Being of Like-Mind: Giftedness in the New Zealand Context
- ▶ Gifted and Talented Aboriginal Students in Australia
- ▶ Gifted Education in the Asia-Pacific: From the Past for the Future – An Introduction
- ▶ Implementing the DMGT's Constructs of Giftedness and Talent: What, Why, and How?
- ▶ Self-Regulated Learning for High-Ability and High-Achieving Students in Mixed-Ability Classrooms Throughout the Asia-Pacific
- ▶ Social and Emotional Needs and Learning Processes: Part II Introduction
- ▶ Some Implications for the Future of Gifted Education in the Asia-Pacific
- ▶ Supporting Australian Gifted Indigenous Students' Academic Potential in Rural Settings
- ▶ The Development of Mana: Five Optimal Conditions for Gifted Māori Student Success

References

Alton-Lee, A. (2003). *Quality teaching for diverse students in schooling: Best evidence synthesis*. Wellington, New Zealand: Ministry of Education.
Australian Curriculum, Assessment and Reporting Authority. [ACARA]. (2015). *Australian Curriculum*. Retrieved from https://www.acara.edu.au/curriculum
Ballam, N. (2013). *Defying the odds: Gifted and talented young people from low socioeconomic backgrounds*. Doctoral thesis. University of Waikato, Hamilton, New Zealand. Retrieved from https://hdl.handle.net/10289/8424
Ballam, N. (2017). Risk and resilience in gifted young people from low socio-economic backgrounds. In N. Ballam & R. Moltzen (Eds.), *Giftedness and talent: Australasian perspectives* (pp. 7–31). Singapore, Singapore: Springer Nature.
Barab, S. A., & Plucker, J. A. (2002). Smart people or smart contexts? Cognition, ability, and talent development in an age of situated approaches to knowing and learning. *Educational Psychologist, 37*(3), 165–182. https://doi.org/10.1207/S15326985EP3703_3
Betts, G. T., & Neihart, M. (1988). Profiles of the gifted and talented. *Gifted Child Quarterly, 32*(2), 248–253. https://doi.org/10.1177/001698628803200202
Bevan-Brown, J. (2011). Gifted and talented Māori learners. In R. Moltzen (Ed.), *Gifted and talented: New Zealand perspectives* (3rd ed., pp. 82–110). Auckland, New Zealand: Pearson.
Bevan-Brown, J. (2012). Digging deeper, flying higher. *APEX: The New Zealand Journal of Gifted Education, 17*(1). Retrieved from www.giftedchildren.org.nz/apex
Biddulph, F., Biddulph, J., & Biddulph, C. (2003). *The complexity of community and family influences on children's achievement in New Zealand: Best evidence synthesis*. Wellington, New Zealand: Ministry of Education.
Bland, L. C., & Sowa, C. J. (1994). An overview of resilience in gifted children. *Roeper Review, 17*(2), 77–80. https://doi.org/10.1080/02783199409553629

Bloom, B. S. (Ed.). (1985). *Developing talent in young people*. New York, NY: Ballantine Books.

Borland, J. H., Schnur, R., & Wright, L. (2000). Economically disadvantaged students in a school for the academically gifted: A postpositivist inquiry into individual and family adjustment. *Gifted Child Quarterly, 44*(1), 13–32. https://doi.org/10.1177/001698620004400103

Chaffey, G. (2002). *Identifying Australian Aboriginal children with high academic potential using dynamic testing*. Unpublished PhD thesis, University of New England, Australia.

Chaffey, G. (2009). Gifted but underachieving: Australian indigenous children. In T. Balchin, B. Hymer, & D. J. Matthews (Eds.), *The Routledge international companion to gifted education* (pp. 106–114). London, England: Routledge.

Chaffey, G., Bailey, S., & Vine, K. (2003). Identifying high academic potential in Australian aboriginal children using dynamic testing. *Australasian Journal of Gifted Education, 12*(1), 42–55.

Chaffey, G. W. (2011). Is gifted education a necessary ingredient in creating a level playing field for indigenous children in education? In W. Vialle (Ed.), *Giftedness from an indigenous perspective* (pp. 96–99). Wollongong, NSW: Australian Association for the Education of the Gifted and Talented.

Chaffey, G. W., Bailey, S. B., & Vine, K. W. (2011). Identifying high academic potential in Australian aboriginal children using dynamic testing In W. Vialle (Ed.), Giftedness from an indigenous perspective (pp. 77–95). Wollongong, NSW: Australian Association for the Education of the Gifted and Talented.

Chandler, P. (2011). Prodigy or problem child? Challenges with identifying aboriginal giftedness. In W. Vialle (Ed.), *Giftedness from an indigenous perspective* (pp. 1–9). Wollongong, NSW: Australian Association for the Education of the Gifted and Talented.

Christie, M. (2011). Some aboriginal perspectives on gifted and talented children and their schooling. In W. Vialle (Ed.), *Giftedness from an indigenous perspective* (pp. 36–42). Wollongong, NSW: Australian Association for the Education of the Gifted and Talented.

Clark, B. (2013). *Growing up gifted* (8th ed.). Upper Saddle River, NJ: Pearson.

Department of Labour. (2012). *Population movement in the Pacific: A perspective on future prospects*. Wellington, New Zealand: Crown Copyright.

Duncanson, M., Oben, G., Wicken, A., Morris, S., McGee, M., & Simpson, J. (2017). *Child poverty monitor: Technical report*. Dunedin, New Zealand: New Zealand Child and Youth Epidemiology Service.

Easton, B. (2013). *Ethnicity, gender, socioeconomic status and educational achievement: An exploration*. Wellington, New Zealand: Post-Primary Teachers' Association.

Ellis, B. J., Bianchi, J., Griskevicius, V., & Frankenhuis, W. E. (2017). Beyond risk and protective factors: An adaptation-based approach to resilience. *Perspectives on Psychological Science, 12*(4), 561–587.

Erikson, E. H. (1968). *Identity: Youth and crisis*. New York, NY: Norton.

Faaea-Semeatu, T. (2011). Celebrating gifted indigenous roots: Gifted and talented pacific island (pasifika) students. In W. Vialle (Ed.), *Giftedness from an indigenous perspective* (pp. 116–122). Wollongong, NSW: Australian Association for the Education of the Gifted and Talented.

Faaea-Semeatu, T. (2015). Pasifika transformers: More than meets the eye. *SET, 1*, 34–41. https://doi.org/10.18296/set.0006

Feldman, D. H. (2003). A developmental, evolutionary perspective on giftedness. In J. H. Borland (Ed.), *Rethinking gifted education* (pp. 9–33). New York, NY: Teachers College Press.

Ford, D. Y., & Whiting, G. W. (2008). Recruiting and retaining underrepresented gifted students. In S. I. Pfeiffer (Ed.), *Handbook of giftedness in children: Psycho-educational theory, research, and best practices* (pp. 293–308). New York, NY: Springer Science & Business Media, LLC.

Fraenkel, J. (2018). *Pacific Islands and New Zealand*. Retrieved from http://www.TeAra.govt.nz/en/pacific-islands-and-new-zealand/print

Gagné, F. (1985). Giftedness and talent: Reexamining a re-examination of the definitions. *Gifted Child Quarterly, 29*(3), 103–112. https://doi.org/10.1177/001698628502900302

Gagné, F. (2003). Transforming gifts into talents: The DMGT as a developmental theory. In N. Colangelo & G. A. Davis (Eds.), *Handbook of gifted education* (3rd ed., pp. 60–74). Boston, MA: Pearson Education.

Gagné, F. (2009). Debating giftedness: Pronat vs. Antinat. In L. V. Shavinina (Ed.), *International handbook on giftedness. Part one* (pp. 155–198). Dordrecht, Netherlands: Springer.

Gagné, F. (2015). Academic talent development programs: A best practices model. *Asia Pacific Education Review, 16*(2), 281–295. https://doi.org/10.1007/s12564-015-9366-9

Galbraith, J. (1985). The eight great gripes of gifted kids: Responding to special needs. *Roeper Review, 8*(1), 15–18. https://doi.org/10.1080/02783198509552920

Gallagher, J. J. (2008). Psychology, psychologists, and gifted students. In S. I. Pfeiffer (Ed.), *Handbook of giftedness in children: Psycho-educational theory, research, and best practices* (pp. 1–11). New York, NY: Springer Science & Business Media, LLC.

Gardner, H. (1993). *Frames of mind: The theory of multiple intelligences*. New York, NY: Basic Books.

Gardner, H. (2011). *Frames of mind: The theory of multiple intelligences*. New York, NY: Basic Books.

Garvis, S. (2006). Optimising the learning of gifted aboriginal students. *International Journal of Pedagogies and Learning, 2*(3), 42–51. https://doi.org/10.5172/ijpl.2.3.42

Gibson, K., & Vialle, W. (2007). The Australian aboriginal view of giftedness. In S. N. Philipson & M. McCann (Eds.), *Conceptions of giftedness: Socio-cultural perspectives* (pp. 169–196). Mahwah, NJ: Lawrence Erlbaum Associates.

Gilligan, R. (2001). *Promoting resilience: A resource guide on working with children in the care system*. London, England: British Agencies for Adoption and Fostering.

Greenspon, T. S. (1998). The gifted self: Its role in development and emotional health. *Roeper Review, 20*(3), 162–167. https://doi.org/10.1080/02783199809553884

Haami, B. (2018). *Urban Māori: The second great migration*. Auckland, New Zealand: Oratia Books.

Haney, T. J. (2007). "Broken windows" and self-esteem: Subjective understandings of neighbourhood poverty and disorder. *Social Science Research, 36*, 968–994. https://doi.org/10.1016/j.ssresearch.2006.07.003

Harvey, J., & Delfabbro, P. H. (2004). Psychological resilience in disadvantaged youth: A critical overview. *Australian Psychologist, 39*, 3–13. https://doi.org/10.1080/00050060410001660281

Jarvis, J. M., Jolly, J. L., & Moltzen, R. (2018). Gifted education in Australia and New Zealand: Reflections and future directions. In J. L. Jolly & J. M. Jarvis (Eds.), *Exploring gifted education: Australian and New Zealand perspectives* (pp. 206–211). New York, NY: Routledge.

Jung, J. Y., & Hay, P. (2018). Identification of gifted and twice-exceptional students. In J. L. Jolly & J. M. Jarvis (Eds.), *Exploring gifted education: Australian and New Zealand perspectives* (pp. 12–31). New York, NY: Routledge.

Lopez, V., & Sotillo, M. (2009). Giftedness and social adjustment: Evidence supporting the resilience approach in Spanish–speaking children and adolescents. *High Ability Studies, 20*(1), 39–53.

Luthar, S. (1991). Vulnerability and resilience: A study of high-risk adolescents. *Child Development, 62*, 600–616. https://doi.org/10.1111/j.1467-8624.1991.tb01555.x

Luthar, S. S. (2006). Resilience in development: A synthesis of research across five decades. In D. Cicchetti & D. J. Cohen (Eds.), *Developmental psychopathology, volume three: Risk, disorder, and adaptation* (2nd ed., pp. 739–795). New York, NY: Wiley.

Macfarlane, A., Webber, M., Cookson-Cox, C., & McRae, H. (2014). *Ka Awatea: An iwi case study of Māori students' success*. Christchurch, New Zealand: Te Rū Rangahau. University of Canterbury.

Masten, A. S. (2001). Ordinary magic: Resilience processes in development. *American Psychologist, 56*(3), 227–238. https://doi.org/10.1037/0003-066X.56.3.227

Masten, A. S. (2002). *Ordinary magic: A resilience framework for policy, practice, and prevention*. Paper presented at the Conference on Risk and Resilience: Protective Mechanisms and School-Based Prevention Programmes, 25–27 October, 2002, Cambridge, MA.

Masten, A. S. (2014). *Ordinary magic: Resilience in development*. New York, NY: Guilford.

Masten, A. S., & Coatsworth, J. D. (1998). The development of competence in favorable and unfavorable environments: Lessons from research on successful children. *American Psychologist, 53*, 205–220.

Masten, A. S., & Obradovic, J. (2006). Competence and resilience in development. *Annals of the New York Academy of Sciences, 1094*, 13–27. Retrieved from https://insidestories.nl/wp-content/uploads/2015/06/Resilience.pdf

Masten, A. S., & Powell, J. L. (2003). A resilience framework for research, policy, and practice. In S. S. Luthar (Ed.), *Resilience and vulnerability: Adaptation in the context of childhood adversities* (pp. 1–25). Cambridge, UK: Cambridge University Press.

Miller, G. (2011). Gifted and talented Māori and Pasifika students: Issues in their identification and program and pastoral care provision. In W. Vialle (Ed.), *Giftedness from an indigenous perspective* (pp. 111–115). Wollongong, NSW: Australian Association for the Education of the Gifted and Talented.

Miller, G. (2017). Academic success amongst a cohort of gifted and talented Māori and Pasifika secondary school boys: Elements that have contributed to their achievement. In N. Ballam & R. Moltzen (Eds.), *Giftedness and talent: Australasian perspectives* (pp. 129–154). Singapore, Singapore: Springer Nature.

Miller, G. O. (2015). *Academic success amongst a cohort of gifted and talented Māori and Pasifika secondary school boys: Elements that have contributed to their achievement* (Thesis, Doctor of Philosophy (PhD)). University of Waikato, Hamilton, New Zealand. Retrieved from https://hdl.handle.net/10289/9779

Ministerial Council on Education, Employment, Training and Youth Affairs [MCEETYA]. (2008). *Melbourne declaration on education goals for young Australians*. Retrieved from www.mceetya.edu.au/mceecdya/melbourne_declaration,25979.html

Ministry of Education. (2007). *The New Zealand curriculum*. Wellington, New Zealand: Learning Media.

Ministry of Education. (2012). *Gifted and talented students: Meeting their needs in New Zealand schools*. Wellington, New Zealand: Learning Media. Retrieved from http://gifted.tki.org.nz/For-schools-and-teachers

Ministry of Education. (2015). *Four year plan 2015–2019: Better education for New Zealand*. Wellington, New Zealand: Author.

Moltzen, R. (2011). Underachievement. In R. Moltzen (Ed.), *Gifted and talented: New Zealand perspectives* (3rd ed., pp. 404–433). Auckland, New Zealand: Pearson Education.

Moltzen, R., Jolly, J. L., & Jarvis, J. M. (2018). Framing gifted education in Australia and New Zealand. In J. L. Jolly & J. M. Jarvis (Eds.), *Exploring gifted education: Australian and New Zealand perspectives* (pp. 5–11). New York, NY: Routledge.

Morales, E. E. (2010). Linking strengths: Identifying and exploring protective factor clusters in academically resilient low-socioeconomic urban students of colour. *Roeper Review, 32*, 164–175.

Morelock, M. J. (1992). Giftedness: The view from within. *Understanding Our Gifted, 4*(3), 11–15. Retrieved from http://www.davidsongifted.org/search-database/entry/a10172

Mueller, C. E. (2009). Protective factors as barriers to depression in gifted and nongifted adolescents. *Gifted Child Quarterly, 53*(1), 3–14. https://doi.org/10.1177/0016986208326552

Nakata, M. (2011). Pathways for indigenous education in the Australian curriculum framework. *The Australian Journal of Indigenous Education, 40*, 1–8. https://doi.org/10.1375/ajie.40.1

Neihart, M. (1998). Creativity, the arts, and madness. *Roeper Review, 21*(1), 47–50. Retrieved from https://www.davidsongifted.org/search-database/entry/a10187

Neihart, M., & Betts, G. (2010). *Revised profiles of the gifted and talented.* Retrieved from http://www.ingeniosus.net/archives/dr-george-betts-and-dr-maureen-neihart-share-revised-profiles-of-gifted

Pfeiffer, S. I., & Stocking, V. B. (2000). Vulnerabilities of academically gifted students. *Special Services in the Schools, 16*(1/2), 83–93. https://doi.org/10.1300/J008v16n01_06

Pianta, R. C., & Walsh, D. J. (1998). Applying the construct of resilience in schools: Cautions from a developmental systems perspective. *School Psychology Review, 27*, 407–417.

Piechowski, M. M. (2003). Emotional and spiritual giftedness. In N. Colangelo & G. A. Davis (Eds.), *Handbook of gifted education* (3rd ed., pp. 403–416). Boston, MA: Allyn & Bacon.

Plucker, J., Giancola, J., Healey, G., Arndt, D., & Wang, C. (2015). *Equal talents, unequal opportunities: A report card on state support for academically talented low-income students.* Lansdowne, VA: Jack Kent Cooke Foundation. Retrieved from http://www.jkcf.org/news/research/

Pungello, E. P., Kupersmidt, J. B., Burchinal, M. R., & Patterson, C. J. (1996). Environmental risk factors and children's achievement from middle childhood to early adolescence. *Developmental Psychology, 32*(4), 775–767.

Racz, S. J., McMahon, R. J., & Luthar, S. S. (2011). Risky behaviour in affluent youth: Examining the co-occurrence and consequences of multiple problem behaviours. *Journal of Child and Family Studies, 20*, 120–128. https://doi.org/10.1007/s10826-010-9385-4

Ravulo, J. (2015). *Pacific communities in Australia.* Sydney, Australia: University of Western Sydney.

Reay, D. (2010). Identity making in schools and classrooms. In M. Wetherell & C. T. Mohanty (Eds.), *The SAGE handbook of identities* (pp. 277–294). Thousand Oaks, CA: Sage.

Reis, S. M., Colbert, R. D., & Hébert, T. P. (2005). Understanding resilience in diverse, talented students in an urban high school. *Roeper Review, 27*(2), 110–120. https://doi.org/10.1080/02783190509554299

Renzulli, J. (2003). The three-ring conception of giftedness: Its implications for understanding the nature of innovation. In L. V. Shavinina (Ed.), *The international handbook on innovation.* Oxford, UK: Elsevier Science.

Renzulli, J. S. (1978). What makes giftedness? Re-examining a definition. *PhiDelta Kappan, 60*, 180–184.

Renzulli, J. S. (1986). The three-ring conception of giftedness: A developmental model for creative productivity. In R. J. Sternberg & J. E. Davidson (Eds.), *Conceptions of giftedness* (pp. 51–92). New York, NY: Cambridge University Press.

Riley, T. (2004). Looking ahead: Research to inform practice in the education of gifted and talented students in New Zealand. *The New Zealand Journal of Gifted Education, 14*(1). Retrieved from http://www.giftedchildren.org.nz/apex/v14no1art01.php

Rimm, S. B., Siegle, D., & Davis, G. A. (2017). *Education of the gifted and talented* (7th ed.). Upper Saddle River, USA: Pearson.

Rutter, M. (1987). Psychosocial resilience and protective mechanisms. *American Journal of Orthopsychiatry, 57*, 316–331. https://doi.org/10.1111/j.1939-0025.1987.tb03541.x

Rutter, M. (2000). Resilience reconsidered: Conceptual considerations, empirical findings, and policy implications. In J. P. Shonkoff & S. J. Meisels (Eds.), *Handbook of early childhood intervention* (pp. 651–682). Cambridge, UK: Cambridge University Press.

Schoon, I. (2006). *Risk and resilience: Adaptations in changing times.* Cambridge, UK: Cambridge University Press.

Schwartz, S. J., Zamboanga, B. L., Weisskirch, R. S., & Wang, S. C. (2010). The relationships of personal and cultural identity to adaptive and maladaptive psychosocial functioning in emerging adults. *The Journal of Social Psychology, 150*(1), 1–33. https://doi.org/10.1080/00224540903366784

Seeley, K. (2003). High risk gifted learners. In N. Colangelo & G. A. Davis (Eds.), *Handbook of gifted education* (3rd ed., pp. 444–451). Boston, MA: Allyn & Bacon.

Shumow, L. (1997). Daily experiences and adjustment of gifted low-income urban children at home and school. *Roeper Review, 20*(1), 35–38. https://doi.org/10.1080/02783199709553848

Social Policy Research Centre. (2016). *Poverty in Australia*. Strawberry Hills, NSW: Australian Council of Social Service.

St John, S., & So, Y. (2018). *Will children get the help they need? An analysis of effectiveness of policies for children in the worst poverty in 2018*. Auckland, New Zealand: Child Poverty Action Group.

Stats NZ. (2018). *Ethnic populations projected to grow across New Zealand*. Retrieved from https://www.stats.govt.nz/news/ethnic-populations-projected-to-grow-across-new-zealand

Sternberg, R. J. (1999). Intelligence as developing expertise. *Contemporary Educational Psychology, 24*, 359–375. https://doi.org/10.1006/ceps.1998.0998

Sternberg, R. J. (2007). Culture, instruction, and assessment. *Comparative Education, 43*(1), 5–22. https://www.jstor.org/stable/29727813

Sternberg, R. J. (2014). The development of adaptive competence: Why cultural psychology is necessary and not just nice. *Developmental Review, 34*, 208–224. https://doi.org/10.1016/j.dr.2014.05.004

Tannenbaum, A. J. (2003). Nature and nurture of giftedness. In N. Colangelo & G. A. Davis (Eds.), *Handbook of gifted education* (3rd ed., pp. 45–59). Boston, MA: Pearson Education.

Turner, H., Rubie–Davies, C. M., & Webber, M. (2015). Teacher expectations, ethnicity and the achievement gap. *New Zealand Journal of Educational Studies, 50*(1), 55–69. https://doi.org/10.1007/s40841-015-0004-1

Ungar, M. (2008). Resilience across cultures. *British Journal of Social Work, 38*, 218–235. https://doi.org/10.1093/bjsw/bcl343

Ungar, M. (2013). Resilience, trauma, context, and culture. *Trauma, Violence and Abuse, 14*(3), 255–266. https://doi.org/10.1177/1524838013487805

United Nations Development Programme. (2014). *The state of human development in the Pacific: A report on vulnerability and exclusion in a time of rapid change*. Suva, Fiji: UNDP Pacific Centre.

Van Tassel-Baska, J. (1989). The role of the family in the success of the disadvantaged gifted learners. *Journal for the Education of the Gifted, 1*, 22–36. https://doi.org/10.1177/016235328901300103

Versteynen, L. (2001). Issues in the social and emotional adjustment of gifted children: What does the literature say. *APEX: The New Zealand Journal of Gifted Education, 13*(1). Retrieved from http://www.giftedchildren.org.nz/apex/v13no1art04.php

Webber, M. (2008). *Walking the space between: Identity and Māori/Pakeha*. Wellington, New Zealand: NZCER Press.

Webber, M. (2011a). *Identity matters: Racial-ethnic representations among adolescents attending multi-ethnic high schools*. Unpublished PhD thesis, Auckland, NZ: University of Auckland.

Webber, M. (2011b). Look to the past; stand tall in the present: The integral nature of positive racial-ethnic identity for the academic success of Māori students. In W. Vialle (Ed.), *Giftedness from an indigenous perspective* (pp. 100–110). Wollongong, NSW: Australian Association for the Education of the Gifted and Talented.

Webber, M. (2015). Racial-ethnic identity, resilience and responsiveness. In C. M. Rubie-Davies, J. M. Stephens, & P. Watson (Eds.), *Routledge international handbook of social psychology of the classroom* (pp. 102–110). New York, NY: Routledge.

Webber, M. (2017). The role of racial-ethnic identity to the educational engagement of culturally diverse gifted New Zealand adolescents. In N. Ballam & R. Moltzen (Eds.), *Giftedness and talent: Australasian perspectives* (pp. 253–275). Singapore, Singapore: Springer Nature.

Webber, M., McKinley, E., & Hattie, J. (2013). The importance of race and ethnicity: An exploration of New Zealand Pākehā, Māori, Samoan and Chinese adolescent identity. *New Zealand Journal of Psychology, 42*(2), 17–28.

Werner, E. E. (2000). Protective factors and individual resilience. In J. P. Shonkoff & S. J. Meisels (Eds.), *Handbook of early childhood intervention* (2nd ed., pp. 115–132). New York, NY: Cambridge University Press.

Wetherell, M. (2009). *Identity in the 21st century: New trends in changing times.* London, England: Palgrave Macmillan.

World Population Review. (2018). *2018 World population by country (live).* Retrieved from http://worldpopulationreview.com

Yates, T. M., Egeland, B., & Sroufe, A. (2003). Rethinking resilience: A developmental process perspective. In S. S. Luthar (Ed.), *Resilience and vulnerability: Adaptation in the context of childhood adversities* (pp. 243–266). Cambridge, UK: Cambridge University Press.

Yunkaporta, T., & McGinty, S. (2009). Reclaiming aboriginal knowledge at the cultural interface. *The Australian Educational Researcher, 36*(2), 55–72.

Nadine Ballam, PhD, is a Senior Lecturer in the Faculty of Education at the University of Waikato in New Zealand. Her research interests include giftedness and talent, risk and resilience and sociocultural aspects of human development, and her PhD research focused on gifted young people from low socio-economic backgrounds. Nadine is on the board of *giftEDnz*: the professional association for gifted education in New Zealand. She is also an Associate Editor for the *Australasian Journal of Gifted Education.*

Motivational Issues in Gifted Education: Understanding the Role of Students' Attribution and Control Beliefs, Self-Worth Protection and Growth Orientation

16

Emma C. Burns and Andrew J. Martin

Contents

Introduction	340
Theories of Giftedness and Motivation	341
Key Motivational Issues for Gifted Students	342
Attribution and Control Beliefs	342
Self-worth Protection	343
Implications for Talent Development	346
Summary of Key Motivational Issues	347
Growth Orientation and Gifted Students	347
Growth Goal Setting	348
Growth Mindset	349
How to Support Gifted Students' Growth Orientation and Talent Development	349
Summary of Growth Orientation	351
Implications for Future Research	351
Conclusion	352
Cross-References	352
References	353

Abstract

In this chapter the role of motivation in gifted education will be discussed. Although theories of giftedness have often included motivation as an important component of giftedness (Clinkenbeard, 2012), most research on motivation in giftedness has sought to establish the motivational characteristics of gifted students (Albaili, 2003). As a result, less is known about how different motivational factors impact gifted students' academic development and outcomes. Thus, building on arguments by Martin (2002, 2017) and recent research in gifted education, the present chapter examines key motivational issues that are

E. C. Burns (✉) · A. J. Martin
School of Education, University of New South Wales, Sydney, NSW, Australia
e-mail: emma.burns@unsw.edu.au; andrew.martin@unsw.edu.au

especially relevant for gifted students. First, we discuss attribution, control beliefs and self-worth protection. These are well-established areas of motivation that affect gifted students' motivation and learning. Herein we examine the implications of these factors for talent development and how to support gifted students in their use of adaptive rather than maladaptive motivational strategies. Next, we discuss recent developments within motivational research, namely, an increased focus on growth orientation and how such an orientation may benefit gifted students. Specifically, we discuss the role of growth goal setting (Burns et al., 2018a, 2018b; Martin, 2006) and growth mindset (Dweck, 2012). Following from this we provide practical strategies for teachers, practitioners, and parents to promote growth orientation among gifted students and describe how these strategies may support gifted students' talent development. Lastly, we discuss implications for future research regarding motivation and giftedness. Taken together, this chapter provides a substantial review of how different motivational factors may impact gifted students' learning and discusses new developments and strategies in motivational research that may be effective for gifted students.

Keywords

Gifted students · Giftedness · Motivation · Attribution beliefs · Control beliefs · Self-worth · Personal best goal setting · Growth mindset

The aims in this chapter are to:
1. Establish the importance of motivation within theories of giftedness and gifted education.
2. Discuss key motivational issues relevant to gifted students.
3. Address how to support gifted students' talent development as related to these motivational issues.
4. Discuss the relevance of growth orientation (a recent development in motivational research) to gifted education.
5. Examine the benefits of growth orientation for gifted students.
6. Discuss how to practically promote growth orientation among gifted students.
7. Address implications of growth orientation for talent development.
8. Present avenues for future research in gifted education.

Introduction

Motivation is considered an essential element of learning for all students (Martin, 2002, 2007). However, for specific groups of students, it is important to consider how different aspects of motivation may play an especially distinct role in their academic and skill development. Gifted students comprise one such group (Clinkenbeard, 2012; Gagné, 2004; Martin, 2002). Underachievement among gifted students is an issue of considerable concern, and many researchers suggest that improving current understanding of motivation among gifted students, both achievers and underachievers, may be one way to redress this (Reis & McCoach, 2000; Siegle & McCoach, 2005a). However, whereas a significant body of work has demonstrated that there are motivational differences between gifted and non-gifted students, as well as between gifted achievers and gifted underachievers (e.g., Albaili, 2003; D. W. Chan, 2010b; L. K. S. Chan, 1996; Dai, 2001; Lüftenegger et al., 2015; McCoach & Siegle, 2003; Vallerand, Gagné, Senecal, & Pelletier, 1994), less is known about *how* different motivational factors impact gifted students. It is important to understand the key motivational processes implicated in gifted students' academic development so as to appropriately support their optimal academic performance, socio-emotional well-being and talent development. One additional focus in our discussion (beyond the 'classic' motivation factors such as attributions, etc.) relates to growth orientation, which has recently been demonstrated to be effective for gifted students (D.W. Chan, 2012). As such, the present chapter: (a) reviews and summarises the research regarding key motivational issues for gifted students; (b) examines the role of growth orientation within gifted education; (c) discusses the implications of this research for improving and sustaining gifted students' motivation and their talent development; and (d) provides directions for future research.

Theories of Giftedness and Motivation

Motivation has long been considered a key component to understanding giftedness and is included in most seminal theories of giftedness (Clinkenbeard, 1996, 2012). Renzulli (1978), Gagné (1985, 2004, 2010), Ziegler and Phillipson (2012) and Subotnik, Olszewski-Kubilius and Worrell (2011), in their respective models of giftedness, each frame motivation as central to nurturing giftedness. In particular, Gagné's *Differentiated Model of Giftedness and Talent* (DMGT) highlights the critical role motivation plays in the development of giftedness. The DMGT establishes the formal relationship between giftedness and talent, such that giftedness, which is defined as untrained or natural ability, if appropriately supported, can transform into talent, which is defined as a systematically developed set of masterful skills (Gagné, 2004). Thus, for giftedness to flourish, its development must be properly nurtured. Gagné (2004, 2010) proposes that this support comes from a variety of catalysts: intrapersonal, environmental, talent development influences, and chance. Here the DMGT articulates motivation as a key intrapersonal catalyst, such that motivation is crucial to the development of giftedness and helping gifted students reach their potential. Moreover, Clinkenbeard (1996, 2012) argues that it is important to address gifted students' motivation in order to reduce the gap between their current performance and their potential. Taken together, it is clear that understanding the role of motivation for gifted students may not only provide insight about how giftedness develops, but how giftedness can be sustained and strengthened across a child's schooling.

Key Motivational Issues for Gifted Students

Previous research has detailed how gifted students, especially gifted achievers, are motivationally different from non-gifted students and gifted underachievers (e.g., L. K. S, Chan, 1996; Dai, 2001; Lüftenegger et al., 2015; McCoach & Siegle, 2003; Vallerand et al., 1994). For example, Lüftenegger et al. (2015) found that gifted achievers scored significantly higher than gifted underachievers on multiple dimensions of motivation (e.g., self-efficacy, interest; see also Albaili, 2003). Additionally, D. W. Chan (2010a) found that gifted students were more likely to report higher levels of perfectionism than non-gifted students. While these findings provide insight about the motivational characteristics of gifted students, it is important to consider the broader motivational issues that stand to benefit gifted students most. Drawing from Martin's (2002, 2017) arguments and relevant research in gifted education, the following motivational issues have been identified as especially pertinent to gifted students: (a) attribution and control beliefs and (b) self-worth protection.

Attribution and Control Beliefs

Attribution theory (Weiner, 1985) argues that what students perceive to be the causes of their successes and failures are likely to impact their motivation. Students differ in these perceptions in that some are more likely to attribute success or failure to internal causes (e.g., effort, ability), whereas others are more likely to attribute outcomes to external causes (e.g., luck, task difficulty). How students view the causes of their outcomes has a significant impact on their perceptions of control and their motivation for future school work (Martin, 2002; Weiner, 1985). Control beliefs refer to the extent to which students feel they can exert influence over their outcomes (Skinner, 1996). In this way, students who perceive the causes of their successes and failures as internal are more likely to have a higher sense of control; the opposite is true for those who perceive external causes. Similarly, students' perceptions of control have been found to predict their engagement and achievement (Skinner, 1996). Taken together, these attribution and control beliefs are important motivational factors for students.

Previous research has examined the attribution and control profiles of gifted students (Rinn, Boazman, Jackson, & Barrio, 2014; Siegle, Rubenstein, Pollard, & Romey, 2010). Generally, gifted students are more likely to report a higher sense of control and to attribute success and failure to internal factors (Assouline, Colangelo, Ihrig, & Forstadt, 2006; L. K. S. Chan 1996; Rinn et al., 2014). However, important differences arise when comparing gifted achievers and gifted underachievers. Gifted achievers are more likely to attribute success to their ability and effort and their failure to lack of effort (Assouline et al., 2006; L. K. S. Chan 1996; Lau & Chan, 2001; Vlahovic-Stetic, Vidovic, & Arambasic, 1999). Gifted underachievers on the other hand are more likely to report a lower sense of control (Rimm, 1995), and while they are also more likely to attribute success to their effort and ability (Lau & Chan, 2001; Vlahovic-Stetic et al., 1999), they are more likely to attribute their failure to external unstable factors, such as task difficulty (Lau & Chan, 2001). Because gifted achievers are more likely than gifted underachievers to perceive themselves as competent, it may be that gifted achievers are better able to attribute both success and failure to effort (or lack thereof) rather than external uncontrollable sources (Rinn et al., 2014).

Importantly, these differences in attribution and control beliefs have also been found to impact gifted students' academic outcomes (Tirri & Nokelainen, 2011). Indeed, in an investigation of literacy, Lau and Chan (2001) found that gifted students' personal sense of control significantly predicted knowledge and use of reading strategies, such that a lower sense of personal control negatively predicted knowledge and use of reading strategies. Similarly, Rinn et al. (2014) found that lower control was significantly associated with higher academic dishonesty for different groups of high-ability students. Taken together, these findings indicate that attribution and control beliefs have a significant impact on gifted students' (especially gifted underachievers') academic experiences and outcomes.

Self-worth Protection

How students conceptualise themselves in relation to school and academics has also been shown to significantly impact their motivation (Preckel et al., 2017). This is especially true if students feel their self-worth (i.e., feelings regarding personal value and worth) is contingent upon their academic success (Covington, 1992). For gifted students, this may be an acute problem (Kroesbergen, van Hooijdonk, Van Viersen, Middel-Lalleman, & Reijnders, 2016). Because a defining feature of giftedness is above average ability (Gagné, 2004; Renzulli, 1978), gifted students' sense of identity and self-worth may be more closely tied to their academic ability (Dai, 2000). Indeed, gifted students, as compared to non-gifted students, generally report lower perceived academic self-worth (Kroesbergen et al., 2016). As a result, gifted students may be more likely to engage in self-worth protection (Dai, 2000), which often manifests as: (a) fear of failure, (b) fear of success (e.g., 'imposter syndrome'), and (c) perfectionism. Each of these protective mechanisms has been found to impact gifted students' academic functioning; as such, it is important to more closely examine their motivational role.

Fear of failure. Fear of failure can be a particular challenge for gifted students, as failure presents a direct threat to their gifted status (i.e., whether or not students are labelled as gifted) and self-worth (Martin, 2002; Snyder, Malin, Dent, & Linnenbrink-Garcia, 2014). As a result, students may use maladaptive strategies to simultaneously avoid failure and protect their self-worth (Covington, 1992). Two of the most common failure-avoidant strategies are self-handicapping and defensive pessimism. Self-handicapping refers to the employment of self-sabotaging strategies that provide a plausible excuse for poor performance (Martin, Marsh, & Debus, 2003). For example, students may choose to undertake an activity other than studying in order to have a reason (i.e., lack of effort) for poor performance.

Defensive pessimism refers to the setting of unrealistically low expectations for performance (Martin et al., 2003). Defensive pessimists do this to reduce their chances of failure against this low standard and to avoid disappointment in the event of poor performance. Both self-handicapping and defensive pessimism have been shown to have a negative impact on academic functioning and well-being (Martin et al., 2003).

Previous research has demonstrated that gifted students employ failure-avoidant strategies when they feel their gifted status is under threat (Snyder et al., 2014). Indeed, previous research has shown that self-handicapping (Snyder et al., 2014) and defensive pessimism (Davis & Rimm, 1998; Rimm, Siegle, & Davis, 2018) are commonly used by gifted students in these situations. Furthermore, Dai (2000) found that the use of failure-avoidant strategies undermined gifted students' persistence on challenging tasks. Taken together, this suggests that fear of failure is a maladaptive motivational process that often occurs when gifted students want to protect their gifted status and which can negatively impact their academic functioning.

Fear of success and imposter syndrome. Fear of success reflects a stress of being labelled as different and potentially having to choose between academic success and acceptance by peers (i.e., forced-choice dilemma; Gross, 1989; Jung, Barnett, Gross, & McCormick, 2011). Additionally, fear of success reflects a belief that failure is an inevitable consequence of success, such that once success is achieved, the only place to go is down or to be potentially outperformed by another (Martin, 2002). A cognate concept to this latter form of fear of success is the 'imposter syndrome', which reflects a fear of inadequacy and a fear that success may incur scrutiny that exposes one's feared lack of ability (Fried-Buchalter, 1992). Fear of success, especially as it relates to peer acceptance and the imposter syndrome, are problems particularly pervasive among gifted students (Cross, Coleman, & Terhaar-Yonkers, 2014; Dai, 2001; Jung et al., 2011; Košir, Horvat, Aram, & Jurinec, 2016; Wright & Leroux, 1997).

Regarding fear of success, many gifted students report stress regarding peer relationships and being labelled as different (Coleman & Cross, 2014; Cross et al., 2014). Indeed, the forced-choice dilemma, which refers to the choice academically gifted students feel they must make between pursuing academic excellence and peer acceptance, is a consistent challenge for gifted students (for summary, see Jung et al., 2011). Similarly, some gifted students perceive their gifted status as a 'social handicap' that interferes with social acceptance from peers (Coleman & Cross, 2014). As a result, gifted students may use different self-management strategies that minimise the visibility of their giftedness (Coleman & Cross, 2014). For example, Cross et al. (2014) found that across a variety of social scenarios, the most common self-management strategy was to downplay their intelligence or expertise (i.e., placate) to others (for a cross-cultural perspective on self-management strategies, see Cross, O'Reilly, Kim, Mammadov, & Cross, 2015). This suggests that many gifted students feel a certain degree of pressure to mask their giftedness for fear of peer judgement or rejection.

The imposter syndrome has been identified as a common issue during academic transitions to high-ability contexts, such as moving into a gifted classroom or transitioning to university (Mendaglio, 2013; Wright & Leroux, 1997; Zeidner & Schleyer, 1998). During these transitions, gifted students often go from being one of a few to one of many high-performing students. When in the company of students with equal or greater ability, students can begin to doubt their ability and giftedness, which can cause anxiety (Preckel et al., 2017; Zeidner & Schleyer, 1998). Taken together, fear of success is associated with negative motivational outcomes for gifted students, such as perceived strain on peer relationships and increased anxiety.

Perfectionism. Perfectionism is one of the most studied motivational areas in gifted education (Parker, 2000). Perfectionism refers to the pursuit of and adherence to unrealistically high standards and is associated with feelings of conditional self-acceptance (Tan & Chun, 2014). Theories and research on perfectionism have identified that there are adaptive and maladaptive forms of perfectionism (D. W. Chan, 2010b; Parker, 2000; Schuler, 2000; Tan & Chun, 2014). Adaptive perfectionism (also referred to as healthy or normal perfectionism) is characterised by deliberate and conscientious efforts to pursue excellence, constructive responses to mistakes and realistic performance boundaries (D. W. Chan, 2012; Schuler, 2000). Maladaptive perfectionism (also referred to as unhealthy or neurotic perfectionism) is characterised by neurotic and obsessive behaviour in the pursuit of excellence, a disproportionate focus on mistakes and unrealistically high-performance boundaries (D. W. Chan, 2012; Schuler, 2000). Adaptive perfectionism is considered beneficial to performance and is associated with task enjoyment, whereas maladaptive perfectionism is considered detrimental to performance and well-being and is associated with decreased self-esteem (Schuler, 2000).

Recently, particular attention has been paid to the profiles of perfectionism that exist among gifted students (D. W. Chan, 2010a, 2010b, 2012; Dixon, Lapsley, & Hanchon, 2004; Schuler, 2000). D. W. Chan (2010a, 2010b, 2012) found that there were three major forms of perfectionism among gifted students: healthy, unhealthy, and non-perfectionism; Dixon et al. (2004) and Schuler (2000) also reported similar profiles. Across all five studies, the majority of gifted students consistently reported adaptive perfectionism profiles and to a slightly lesser extent, non-perfectionism profiles. Additionally, those who endorsed adaptive perfectionism also endorsed more adaptive motivational strategies, whereas those who endorsed maladaptive perfectionism were more likely to use avoidant motivational strategies (Neumeister & Finch, 2006; Neumeister, Fletcher, & Burney, 2015). This suggests that adaptive perfectionism may be motivationally beneficial for gifted students. However, it should also be noted that perfectionism, both adaptive and maladaptive, impacts students' emotional regulation (Dixon et al., 2004; Tan & Chun, 2014). For example, although adaptive perfectionism is associated with more positive academic emotions than maladaptive perfectionism, perfectionism in general is associated with increased anxiety (Tan & Chun, 2014). Taken together, this suggests that while there may be academic yields to promoting adaptive perfectionism among gifted students, attention should be paid to how perfectionism more generally differentially impacts students' motivation and emotional functioning.

Implications for Talent Development

According to the DMGT, giftedness transforms into masterful talent when giftedness is properly supported. Without this support, students may be less able to hone their skills and aptitudes and thus be unable to reach their potential (Gagné, 2004, 2010). Given that the DMGT highlights motivation as a critical catalyst of talent development, it is important to consider the ways in which attribution and control beliefs and self-worth protection may impact talent development. These considerations may be particularly important for gifted underachievers.

Attribution and control beliefs relate to how students perceive the causes of their successes and failures. As discussed above, researchers have found that gifted achievers and gifted underachievers differ in their perceptions of what causes their failure; gifted achievers are more likely to attribute failure to internal (i.e., controllable) causes, whereas gifted underachievers are more likely to attribute failure to external (i.e., uncontrollable) causes (Assouline et al., 2006; Lau & Chan, 2001). Importantly, previous research has established that attribution beliefs that focus on internal and controllable factors are more adaptive; this has implications for talent development, especially for gifted underachievers. Students who attribute failure to external and uncontrollable sources may be less likely to see mistakes or failure as important diagnostic information that can inform future learning (Schmitz & Skinner, 1993). As such, by more often attributing failure to external causes, gifted underachievers may be missing vital opportunities to identify areas where they can improve. Thus, to support gifted students (both achievers and underachievers), teachers, practitioners and parents may consider encouraging students to focus on factors that they can control and that can support their learning, such as skill development (Martin, 2002; Siegle & McCoach, 2005a). Similarly, teachers, practitioners, and parents may consider emphasising that effort and the learning process are just as (or more) important than the actual outcome (Clinkenbeard, 1996, 2012; Martin, 2002).

Self-worth protection commonly manifests as fear of failure, fear of success (including the imposter syndrome), and perfectionism. As discussed above, gifted students are likely to engage in self-worth protection across a variety of academic and social scenarios (Cross et al., 2014; Snyder et al., 2014). The use of self-worth protection, which is often considered maladaptive, may hinder talent development among gifted students. Regarding fear of failure, gifted students who use failure-avoidant strategies are less likely to persist on challenging tasks (Dai, 2000). As a result, because optimal challenge is required for skill and talent improvement (Locke & Latham, 2002), the continued use of failure-avoidant strategies may lead to stunted talent development. To address this, teachers, practitioners, and parents may consider discussing with gifted students that their self-worth is not predicated on their achievement or gifted status (Covington, 1992). Similarly, it may be important for teachers to emphasise the importance of challenge over achievement (Martin, 2002; Meece, Anderman, & Anderman, 2006).

In terms of fear of success, previous research has demonstrated that some gifted students feel a social stigma is ascribed to their giftedness, and this stigma reflects a perceived lack of social acceptance from peers (Cross et al., 2014; Jung et al., 2011). Social support is also a key catalyst within the DMGT (Gagné, 2004, 2010), which suggests that gifted students who feel social pressure to downplay their giftedness or choose between social acceptance and excellence may be experiencing suboptimal social support from their peers. As a result, their talent development may be hindered. It is thus important for teachers, practitioners, and parents to consider how to promote peer support for and acceptance of gifted students. For example, teachers may focus on developing classroom climates that support inclusivity of diverse skills (Hertzog, 2017). Similarly, teachers, practitioners, and parents may consider how to improve gifted students' resilience to feelings of social pressure (Kosir et al., 2016). This can be done, in part, by teachers, practitioners, and parents demonstrating positive support for talent development and by encouraging gifted students to explore their giftedness (Lerner, 2005; Smith, 2017).

Lastly, regarding perfectionism, past work has demonstrated that the majority of gifted students demonstrate adaptive perfectionism profiles (e.g., D. W. Chan, 2012). This in and of itself may be supportive of talent development such that adaptive perfectionism reflects a positive motivational attitude. However, as noted above, perfectionism is also associated with increased anxiety, which may negatively impact talent development (Tan & Chun, 2014). As such, it is important to consider how to support gifted students' healthy socio-emotional development alongside their talent development (for an in-depth review of socio-emotional learning for intellectually gifted students, see Smith, 2017).

Summary of Key Motivational Issues

Attribution and control beliefs and self-worth protection have been identified as key motivational issues relevant to gifted students. This discussion has summarised research identifying how gifted students perform on these motivational dimensions. The discussion has also articulated the implications of attribution and control beliefs and self-worth protection for talent development. The next part of the discussion turns to an emerging area of motivational research that is relevant for gifted education and talent development: growth orientation.

Growth Orientation and Gifted Students

Thus far this chapter has discussed well-established motivational considerations within gifted education. However, it is also important to consider emerging developments within motivational research and how these may be relevant to gifted education. One area of recent interest concerns growth orientation, namely, growth goal setting (Burns, Martin, & Collie, 2018a, 2018b; Martin, 2006) and growth mindset (Dweck, 2012). This is a burgeoning area within gifted research; thus, recent empirical work and relevant research in related areas (e.g., flow and implicit beliefs) provide a framework for understanding how growth orientation supports gifted students' motivation.

Growth Goal Setting

Growth goal setting refers to the use of goals that focus on self-improvement and personal excellence (Travers, Morisano, & Locke, 2015). Growth goal setting is most often investigated via personal best (PB) goal setting (Burns et al., 2018a). Thus, this section focuses on how PB goal setting, as one effective form of growth goal setting, may help gifted students. PB goal setting refers to the use of optimally challenging self-referenced goals that encourage students to strive to outperform past personal performances or efforts (Martin, 2006). While no research has yet examined the effectiveness of PB goal setting among gifted students, empirical links can be hypothesised by drawing on recent literature around the Achievement Orientation Model (AOM; Siegle & McCoach, 2005b). The AOM posits that gifted students' motivation, and ultimately their achievement, is regulated by positive self-efficacy, goal valuation and environmental perceptions (Siegle & McCoach, 2005b; Siegle, McCoach, & Roberts, 2017). Put another way, gifted students with higher self-efficacy, who set personally meaningful goals and who have positive perceptions of their environment are more likely to stay motivated in school (Siegle et al., 2017). In a review of interventions based on the AOM, Rubenstein, Siegle, Reis, McCoach, and Burton (2012) found that goal valuation was the most effective component of the AOM for improving gifted student motivation and achievement. This suggests that encouraging gifted students to utilise personally meaningful goals helps to maintain their motivation. As can be seen, goal valuation, as articulated under the AOM, aligns with the core components of PB goal setting, namely, the use of personally relevant and meaningful goals (Burns et al., 2018a). Moreover, because PB goal setting also focuses on personal challenge, PB goal setting may help sustain gifted student motivation and achievement over time.

PB goal setting has been shown to positively predict a variety of adaptive motivational strategies (e.g., planning, persistence, task management; Burns et al., 2018b). PB goal setting has also been shown to significantly predict flow (Liem, Ginns, Martin, Stone & Herrett, 2012), which is considered a critical element of gifted education. Flow refers to the optimal subjective task experience that arises when a student's ability matches the perceived challenge of the task (Csikszentmihalyi, 1990; Liem et al., 2012). Flow is associated with increased engagement (e.g., becoming absorbed in the task) and task enjoyment (Liem et al., 2012). Because most gifted students remain in general education classrooms where they may not be sufficiently challenged by the learning material, flow has been identified as a desirable way of promoting motivation and engagement and reducing underachievement for gifted students (Rea, 2001; Reis & McCoach, 2000; Siegle & McCoach, 2005a). However, increased challenge is not enough to induce flow for gifted students; personal relevance is also important (Siegle & McCoach, 2005a). Given that personal relevance and optimal difficulty are two defining features of PB goal setting and that PB goal setting has been found to predict flow over time, PB goal setting may be a particularly effective strategy for promoting flow in gifted students (Martin, 2017).

Growth Mindset

Growth mindset, which was born out of research into implicit theories of intelligence, refers to the extent to which a student believes intelligence is either fixed or malleable (Dweck, 2012). Students who have a growth mindset believe that intelligence can be developed over time through effort and are less likely to emphasise the importance of ability (Dweck, 2012). Growth mindset has been shown to be related to a variety of adaptive outcomes (Dweck, 2012). However, there has been considerable debate about how gifted status may impact growth mindsets (Snyder, Barger, Wormington, Schwartz-Bloom, & Linnenbrink-Garcia, 2013); recent research has provided important insight about this.

By and large, findings suggest that gifted students are more likely to endorse growth mindsets (D.W. Chan, 2012; Esparza, Shumow, & Schmidt, 2014; Makel, Snyder, Thomas, Malone, & Putallaz, 2015). Additionally, growth mindsets in gifted students were positively associated with happiness, life satisfaction, and adaptive perfectionism (D. W. Chan, 2012), as well as positive motivational strategies (Park, Callahan, & Ryoo, 2016). However, this work has also identified an important caveat that may impact gifted students' motivation. Specifically, Makel et al. (2015) and Snyder et al. (2014) identified that students' view of intelligence, although related, differed from their views of giftedness. Although students were more likely to have a growth mindset regarding intelligence, they were more likely to report a fixed view of gifted status (i.e., giftedness cannot be changed; Makel et al., 2015). Moreover, students who believed giftedness to be fixed were more likely to use maladaptive motivational strategies (Snyder et al., 2014). This suggests that while gifted students report growth mindsets about intelligence, the potential motivational benefits of this may be undermined by their fixed views about giftedness. This may be especially true when gifted students feel their gifted status is threatened and are more likely to use self-worth protection strategies (see above for discussion). Taken together, this suggests that promoting growth mindsets of intelligence may improve gifted students' academic and personal well-being and that these benefits may be amplified by also promoting a growth view of giftedness.

How to Support Gifted Students' Growth Orientation and Talent Development

Previous gifted research has identified that promoting personally relevant goals and optimal challenge (i.e., flow) and growth views of intelligence are important for sustaining gifted students' motivation (Clinkenbeard, 2012; Esparza et al., 2014; Siegle & McCoach, 2005a). Thus, it is important to consider practical strategies that increase students' growth orientation. Notably, Martin (2014) identified that PB goal setting is an effective strategy for promoting growth mindsets and reducing fixed mindsets over time. PB goal setting reflects a practical daily strategy that is potentially easier to implement than a mindset intervention. Additionally, the effectiveness of growth mindset interventions has received mixed evidence (Broda et al., 2018; Rienzo, Rolfe, & Wilkinson, 2015). As such, here we discuss important considerations for promoting PB goal setting among gifted students. Moreover, because improved motivation is an important component of talent development, according to the DMGT (Gagné, 2004, 2010), it is important to discuss how gifted motivation, via PB goal setting, may in turn foster talent development.

Martin (2006; see also Burns et al., 2018b; Locke & Latham, 2002) has identified several important considerations for how to effectively encourage PB goal setting in the classroom. First, it is important that students be able to effectively identify their level of optimal difficulty (Martin, 2006). Often students set goals that are not the right level of challenge, such that they are too hard or too easy, which can undermine their motivation (Locke & Latham, 2002; Polivy & Herman, 2002). For gifted students, this may be a particularly important consideration. Although research has demonstrated that gifted students tend to report adaptive perfectionism (D. W. Chan, 2010b), it is still important to ensure that gifted students are selecting optimally difficult goals for themselves and not pursuing impractically high standards. In terms of talent development, the use of optimally challenging goals, such as PB goals, may help gifted students better hone their abilities and aptitudes (Rubenstein et al., 2012).

Second, in order for students to effectively pursue their PB goals, it is important to build skills related to goal pursuit (Locke & Latham, 2002). Skill development among gifted students has also been identified as an important component of strengthening goal valuation and improving growth mindset, such that it helps gifted students engage and reduces the link between innate ability and performance (Martin, 2002; Rubenstein et al., 2012). Similarly, skill development, as it relates to goal pursuit and gifted ability, is considered fundamental to talent development (Gagné, 2004, 2010). Thus, it is important for teachers, practitioners, and parents to provide scaffolded activities for gifted students that promote skill development (Smith, 2017) and demonstrate effective skills, such as time management and affective regulation (Rubenstein et al., 2012), that may support both PB goal setting and talent development.

Third, specific and constructive feedback has been identified as an important part of the PB goal setting process (Burns et al., 2018b; Locke & Latham, 2002). Feedback (either during the learning process or after assessments) that focuses on specific areas for individual improvement and growth supports PB goal attainment (Martin, 2013). Such feedback, especially during the learning process, may be particularly helpful for gifted students. Given that gifted students may see mistakes as detrimental to their self-worth, providing growth-oriented feedback may help them see the value in mistakes and reduce their inclination towards failure-avoidant strategies (Clinkenbeard, 1996; Martin, 2002). As discussed above, reducing gifted students' use of self-worth protection strategies is similarly important for talent development.

Fourth, it is important for students to track their progress towards their PB goals (Burns et al., 2018b; Travers et al., 2015). While Martin (2006) identifies potential difficulties in tracking progress, given that assignments are rarely the same, Travers et al. (2015) suggest that diary keeping is an effective method for tracking progress across a variety of assignments. Similarly, Siegle, and McCoach (2005a) identify that tracking progress and growth as it relates to talent development may be particularly effective for gifted underachievers. As such, tracking PB goal progress may help gifted students, especially gifted underachievers, remain motivated and committed to achieving their PB goals and continuing to develop their talent.

Finally, it is important to consider the role of social support, especially from teachers, in growth goal setting. Indeed, Burns et al. (2018a) found that teacher support predicted significant gains in PB goal setting. Similarly, positive social support, such as that from teachers, practitioners, and parents is integral to gifted students' talent development. Taken together, this suggests that it is important for teachers, practitioners, and parents to create environments that are socially supportive of and conducive to PB goal setting (Burns et al., 2018a; Collie, Martin, Papworth, & Ginns, 2016). In the classroom, teachers can do this by showing interest in students' PB goal setting and by emphasising the importance of effort and personal progress, rather than inter-student competition (Burns et al., 2018a, 2018b). Given that gifted students have been shown to be influenced constructively by messages about growth (Snyder et al., 2014), creating a growth-oriented classroom may help students set PB goals as well as develop growth mindsets (Martin, 2014).

Summary of Growth Orientation

Growth goal setting and growth mindsets are two recent developments within motivational research that may support gifted students' motivation. Both growth goal setting and growth mindsets focus on personal improvement and are associated with a variety of adaptive outcomes (Martin, 2014). For gifted students, growth orientation is posited to improve and sustain gifted students' motivation by providing them with personally relevant and optimally challenging goals and by helping them understand the importance of effort in working towards these goals. Given that growth goal setting has also been found to be predictive of growth mindset, teachers, practitioners, and parents may consider using strategies, such as those discussed above, to promote PB goal setting among their gifted students to help them reconceptualise their beliefs about their ability and academic potential.

Implications for Future Research

As discussed above, there is a significant body of work detailing the motivational differences between gifted and non-gifted students and between gifted achievers and gifted underachievers (for a summary, also see Lüftenegger et al., 2015 and Albaili,

2003). Although our chapter has discussed the motivational issues shown to impact gifted students' academic functioning, more work is needed to better understand the unique impact of these motivational factors on gifted students' academic and personal well-being outcomes (Kroesbergen et al., 2016). For example, future work may consider examining the role of gifted students' motivational beliefs and strategies on their academic behaviours, performance, and personal well-being. In this way, researchers can begin to disentangle the effects of different motivational beliefs and strategies, as well as assess those which may be the most salient for gifted students (Clinkenbeard, 2012). Given that growth orientation may be helpful for gifted students, future work may also focus on examining the role of growth goal setting and growth mindset in gifted students' outcomes (D.W. Chan, 2012). Similarly, future work may consider examining the antecedents of gifted students' motivation, such as the role of personal relationships and classroom climate, each of which are salient predictors of motivation in 'general' populations (Burns et al., 2018a; Collie et al., 2016). By examining both the predictors and outcomes of gifted students' motivation, researchers can develop a broader understanding of how to support gifted students throughout school—and beyond.

Conclusion

Motivation is a critical component of student learning (Martin, 2002, 2007). Motivation is also considered a critical catalyst of talent development for gifted students (Gagné, 2004, 2010). Most work in gifted research has addressed the motivational profiles of gifted students, with less work focusing on which motivational factors benefit gifted students and how these factors do so. However, some key motivational issues for gifted students have been identified: attribution and control beliefs and self-worth protection. Similarly, recent motivational research about growth orientation has shown promise for gifted students. As such, this chapter discussed how attribution and control beliefs, self-worth protection and growth orientation impact gifted students' motivation and academic and socio-emotional outcomes. Similarly, implications of these motivational dimensions for talent development were discussed. Growth orientation (i.e., growth goal setting, growth mindset) has been identified as especially relevant for helping gifted students reach their potential. As such, future work may consider more closely examining the benefits of such approaches in gifted education, as well as more clearly articulating the role and consequences of these different motivational factors in gifted students' development.

Cross-References

- ▶ Fostering Resilience in 'At-Risk' Gifted and Talented Young People
- ▶ Gifted Education in the Asia-Pacific: From the Past for the Future – An Introduction

- Put Them Together and See How They Learn! Ability Grouping and Acceleration Effects on the Self-Esteem of Academically Gifted High School Students
- Self-Regulated Learning for High-Ability and High-Achieving Students in Mixed-Ability Classrooms Throughout the Asia-Pacific
- Social and Emotional Needs and Learning Processes: Part II Introduction
- Sociocultural Perspectives on the Talent Development Megamodel
- Some Implications for the Future of Gifted Education in the Asia-Pacific
- Underachievement and the Quest for Dignity: Contemporary Perspectives on a Timeless Issue

Acknowledgments This research was funded by the Australian Research Council (Grant #DP140104294).

References

Albaili, M. A. (2003). Motivational goal orientations of intellectually gifted achieving and underachieving students in the United Arab Emirates. *Social Behavior and Personality, 31*, 107–120. https://doi.org/10.2224/sbp.2003.31.2.107

Assouline, S. G., Colangelo, N., Ihrig, D., & Forstadt, L. (2006). Attributional choices for academic success and failure by intellectually gifted students. *Gifted Child Quarterly, 50*, 283–294. https://doi.org/10.1177/001698620605000402

Broda, M., Yun, J., Schneider, B., Yeager, D. S., Walton, G. M., & Diemer, M. (2018). Reducing inequality in academic success for incoming college students: A randomized trial of growth mindset and belonging interventions. *Journal of Research on Educational Effectiveness, 11*, 317–338. https://doi.org/10.1080/19345747.2018.1429037

Burns, E. C., Martin, A. J., & Collie, R. J. (2018a). Adaptability, personal best (PB) goal setting, and gains in students' academic outcomes: A longitudinal examination from a social cognitive perspective. *Contemporary Educational Psychology, 53*, 57–72. https://doi.org/10.1016/j.cedpsych.2018.02.001

Burns, E. C., Martin, A. J., & Collie, R. J. (2018b). Understanding the role of personal best (PB) goal setting in students' declining engagement: A latent growth model. *Journal of Educational Psychology, 111*, 557–572. https://doi.org/10.1037/edu0000291

Chan, D. W. (2010a). Healthy and unhealthy perfectionists among academically gifted Chinese students in Hong Kong: Do different classification schemes make a difference? *Roeper Review, 32*, 88–97. https://doi.org/10.1080/02783191003587876

Chan, D. W. (2010b). Perfectionism among Chinese gifted and nongifted students in Hong Kong: The use of the revised almost perfect scale. *Journal for the Education of the Gifted, 34*, 68–98. https://doi.org/10.1177/016235321003400104

Chan, D. W. (2012). Life satisfaction, happiness, and the growth mindset of healthy and unhealthy perfectionists among Hong Kong Chinese gifted students. *Roeper Review, 34*, 224–233. https://doi.org/10.1080/02783193.2012.715333

Chan, L. K. S. (1996). Motivational orientations and metacognitive abilities of intellectually gifted students. *Gifted Child Quarterly, 40*, 184–193. https://doi.org/10.1177/001698629604000403

Clinkenbeard, P. R. (1996). Research on motivation and the gifted: Implications for identification, programming, and evaluation. *Gifted Child Quarterly, 40*, 220–221. https://doi.org/10.1177/001698629604000407

Clinkenbeard, P. R. (2012). Motivation and gifted students: Implications of theory and research. *Psychology in the Schools, 49*, 622–630. https://doi.org/10.1002/pits.21628

Coleman, L. J., & Cross, T. L. (2014). Is being gifted a social handicap? *Journal for the Education of the Gifted, 37*, 5–17. https://doi.org/10.1177/0162353214521486

Collie, R. J., Martin, A. J., Papworth, B., & Ginns, P. (2016). Students' interpersonal relationships, personal best (PB) goals, and academic engagement. *Learning and Individual Differences, 45*, 65–76. https://doi.org/10.1016/j.lindif.2015.12.002

Covington, M. V. (1992). *Making the grade: A self-worth perspective on motivation and school reform*. Cambridge, UK: Cambridge University Press.

Cross, J. R., O'Reilly, C., Kim, M., Mammadov, S., & Cross, T. L. (2015). Social coping and self-concept among young gifted students in Ireland and the United States: A cross-cultural study. *High Ability Studies, 26*, 39–61. https://doi-org.libproxy.nie.edu.sg/10.1080/13598139.2015.1031881

Cross, T. L., Coleman, L. J., & Terhaar-Yonkers, M. (2014). The social cognition of gifted adolescents in schools: Managing the stigma of giftedness. *Journal for the Education of the Gifted, 37*, 30–39. https://doi.org/10.1177/0162353214521492

Csikszentmihalyi, M. (1990). *Flow: The psychology of optimal experience*. New York, NY: Harper and Row.

Dai, D. Y. (2000). To be or not to be (challenged), that is the question: Task and ego orientations among high-ability, high achieving adolescents. *The Journal of Experimental Education, 68*, 311–330. https://doi.org/10.1080/00220970009600641

Dai, D. Y. (2001). A comparison of gender differences in academic self-concept and motivation between high-ability and average Chinese adolescents. *The Journal of Secondary Gifted Education, 13*, 22–32. https://doi.org/10.4219/jsge-2001-361

Davis, G. A., & Rimm, S. B. (1998). *Education of the gifted and talented*. Sydney: Allyn & Bacon.

Dixon, F. A., Lapsley, D. K., & Hanchon, T. A. (2004). An empirical typology of perfectionism in gifted adolescents. *Gifted Child Quarterly, 48*, 95–106. https://doi.org/10.1177/001698620404800203

Dweck, C. S. (2012). Mindsets and human nature. *American Psychologist, 67*, 614–622. https://doi.org/10.1037/a0029783

Esparza, J., Shumow, L., & Schmidt, J. A. (2014). Growth mindset of gifted seventh grade students in science. *NCSSSMST Journal, 19*, 6–13. Retrieved from https://files.eric.ed.gov/fulltext/EJ1045824.pdf

Fried-Buchalter, S. (1992). Fear of success, fear of failure, and the impostor phenomenon: A factor analytic approach to convergent and discriminant validity. *Journal of Personality Assessment, 58*, 368–379. https://doi.org/10.1207/s15327752jpa5802_13

Gagné, F. (1985). Giftedness and talent: Reexamining a reexamination of the definitions. *Gifted Child Quarterly, 29*, 103–112. https://doi.org/10.1177/001698628502900302

Gagné, F. (2004). Transforming gifts into talents: The DMGT as a developmental theory. *High Ability Studies, 15*, 119–147. https://doi.org/10.1080/1359813042000314682

Gagné, F. (2010). Motivation within the DGMT 2.0 framework. *High Ability Studies, 21*, 81–99. https://doi.org/10.1080/13598139.2010.525341

Gross, M. U. M. (1989). The pursuit of excellence or the search for intimacy? The forced-choice dilemma of gifted youth. *Roeper Review, 11*, 189–194. https://doi.org/10.1080/02783198909553207

Hertzog, N. B. (2017). Designing the learning context in school for talent development. *Gifted Child Quarterly, 61*, 219–228. https://doi.org/10.1177/0016986217705712

Jung, J. Y., Barnett, K., Gross, M. U. M., & McCormick, J. (2011). Levels of intellectual giftedness, culture, and the forced-choice dilemma. *Roeper Review, 33*, 182–197. https://doi.org/10.1080/02783193.2011.580501

Košir, K., Horvat, M., Aram, U., & Jurinec, N. (2016). Is being gifted always an advantage? Peer relations and self-concept of gifted students. *High Ability Studies, 27*, 129–148. https://doi.org/10.1080/13598139.2015.1108186

Kroesbergen, E. H., van Hooijdonk, M., Van Viersen, S., Middel-Lalleman, M. M. N., & Reijnders, J. J. W. (2016). The psychological well-being of early identified gifted children. *Gifted Child Quarterly, 60*, 16–30. https://doi.org/10.1177/0016986215609113

Lau, K., & Chan, D. W. (2001). Motivational characteristics of under-achievers in Hong Kong. *Educational Psychology, 21*, 417–430. https://doi.org/10.1080/01443410120090803

Lerner, R. (2005). *Promoting positive youth development: Theoretical and empirical bases.* Washington, DC: National Research Council/Institute of Medicine.

Liem, G. A. D., Ginns, P., Martin, A. J., Stone, B., & Herrett, M. (2012). Personal best goals and academic and social functioning: A longitudinal perspective. *Learning and Instruction, 22*, 222–230. https://doi.org/10.1016/j.learninstruc.2011.11.003

Locke, E. A., & Latham, G. P. (2002). Building a practically useful theory of goal setting and task motivation: A 35–year odyssey. *American Psychologist, 57*, 705–717. https://doi.org/10.1037//0003-066X.57.9.705

Lüftenegger, M., Kollmayer, M., Bergsmann, E., Jöstl, G., Spiel, C., & Schober, B. (2015). Mathematically gifted students and high achievement: The role of motivation and classroom structure. *High Ability Studies, 26*, 227–243. https://doi.org/10.1080/13598139.2015.1095075

Makel, M. C., Snyder, K. E., Thomas, C., Malone, P. S., & Putallaz, M. (2015). Gifted students' implicit beliefs about intelligence and giftedness. *Gifted Child Quarterly, 59*, 203–212. https://doi.org/10.1177/0016986215599057

Martin, A. J. (2002). Motivating the gifted and talented: Lessons from research and practice. *The Australasian Journal of Gifted Education, 24*, 52–60. https://doi.org/10.21505/ajge.2015.0016

Martin, A. J. (2006). Personal bests (PBs): A proposed multidimensional model and empirical analysis. *British Journal of Educational Psychology, 76*, 803–825. https://doi.org/10.1348/000709905X55389

Martin, A. J. (2007). Examining a multidimensional model of student motivation and engagement using a construct validation approach. *The British Journal of Educational Psychology, 77*, 413–440. https://doi.org/10.1348/000709906X118036

Martin, A. J. (2013). Improving the achievement, motivation, and engagement of students with ADHD: The role of personal best goals and other growth-based approaches. *Australian Journal of Guidance and Counselling, 23*, 143–155. https://doi.org/10.1017/jgc.2013.4

Martin, A. J. (2014). Implicit theories about intelligence and growth (personal best) goals: Exploring reciprocal relationships. *British Journal of Educational Psychology, 85*, 207–223. https://doi.org/10.1111/bjep.12038

Martin, A. J. (2017). *How to motivate and engage students who are gifted.* Midland, WA: Australian Mensa Inc.

Martin, A. J., Marsh, H. W., & Debus, R. L. (2003). Self-handicapping and defensive pessimism: A model of self-protection from a longitudinal perspective. *Contemporary Educational Psychology, 28*, 1–36. https://doi.org/10.1016/S0361-476X(02)00008-5

McCoach, D. B., & Siegle, D. (2003). Factors that differentiate underachieving gifted students from high-achieving gifted students. *Gifted Child Quarterly, 47*, 144–154. https://doi.org/10.1177/001698620304700205

Meece, J. L., Anderman, E. M., & Anderman, L. H. (2006). Classroom goal structure, student motivation, and academic achievement. *Annual Review of Psychology, 57*, 487–503. https://doi.org/10.1146/annurev.psych.56.091103.070258

Mendaglio, S. (2013). Gifted students' transition to university. *Gifted Educational International, 29*, 3–12. https://doi.org/10.1177/0261429412440646

Neumeister, K. L. S., & Finch, H. (2006). Perfectionism in high-ability students: Relational precursors and influences on achievement motivation. *Gifted Child Quarterly, 50*, 238–251. https://doi.org/10.1177/001698620605000304

Neumeister, K. L. S., Fletcher, K. L., & Burney, V. H. (2015). Perfectionism and achievement motivation in high-ability students: An examination of the 2 × 2 model of perfectionism. *Journal for the Education of the Gifted, 38*, 215–232. https://doi.org/10.1177/0162353215592502

Park, S., Callahan, C. M., & Ryoo, J. H. (2016). Assessing gifted students' beliefs about intelligence with a psychometrically defensible scale. *Journal for the Education of the Gifted, 39*, 288–314. https://doi.org/10.1177/0162353216671835

Parker, W. D. (2000). Healthy perfectionism in the gifted. *The Journal of Secondary Gifted Education, 11*, 173–182. https://doi.org/10.4219/jsge-2000-632

Polivy, J., & Herman, C. P. (2002). If at first you don't succeed: False hopes of self-change. *American Psychologist, 57*, 677–689. https://doi.org/10.1037//0003-066X.57.9.677

Preckel, F., Schmidt, I., Stumpf, E., Motschenbacher, M., Vogl, K., & Schneider, W. (2017). A test of the reciprocal-effects model of academic achievement and academic self-concept in regular classes and special classes for the gifted. *Gifted Child Quarterly, 61*, 103–116. https://doi.org/10.1177/0016986216687824

Rea, D. (2001). Maximizing the motivated mind for emergent giftedness. *Roeper Review, 23*, 157–164. https://doi.org/10.1080/02783190109554088

Reis, S. M., & McCoach, D. B. (2000). The underachievement of gifted students: What do we know and where do we go? *Gifted Child Quarterly, 44*, 152–170. https://doi.org/10.1177/001698620004400302

Renzulli, J. S. (1978). What makes giftedness? Reexamining a definition. *Phi Delta Kappan, 60*, 180–184, 261.

Rienzo, C., Rolfe, H., & Wilkinson, D. (2015). *Changing mindsets: Evaluation Report and executive summary*. London, England: Education Endowment Foundation.

Rimm, S. B. (1995). *Why bright kids get poor grades and what you can do about it*. New York, NY: Crown.

Rimm, S. B., Siegle, D., & Davis, G. A. (2018). *Education of the gifted and talented* (7th ed.). Upper Saddle River, NJ: Pearson.

Rinn, A. N., Boazman, J., Jackson, A., & Barrio, B. (2014). Locus of control, academic self-concept, and academic dishonesty among high ability college students. *Journal of the Scholarship of Teaching and Learning, 14*, 88–114. https://doi.org/10.14434/v14i4.12770

Rubenstein, L. D., Siegle, D., Reis, S. M., McCoach, D. B., & Burton, M. G. (2012). A complex quest: The development and research of underachievement interventions for gifted students. *Psychology in the Schools, 49*, 678–694. https://doi.org/10.1002/pits.21620

Schmitz, B., & Skinner, E. (1993). Perceived control, effort, and academic performance: Interindividual, intraindividual, and multivariate time-series analyses. *Journal of Personality and Social Psychology, 64*, 1010–1028. https://doi.org/10.1037//0022-3514.64.6.1010

Schuler, P. A. (2000). Perfectionism and the gifted adolescent. *Journal of Secondary Gifted Education, 12*, 183–196. https://doi.org/10.4219/jsge-2000-629

Siegle, D., & McCoach, D. B. (2005a). Making a difference: Motivating gifted students who are not achieving. *Teaching Exceptional Children, 38*, 22–27. https://doi.org/10.1177/004005990503800104

Siegle, D., & McCoach, D. B. (2005b). *Motivating gifted students*. Waco, TX: Prufrock Press.

Siegle, D., McCoach, D. B., & Roberts, A. (2017). Why I believe I achieve determines whether I achieve. *High Ability Studies, 28*, 59–72. https://doi.org/10.1177/0016986209355975

Siegle, D., Rubenstein, L. D., Pollard, E., & Romey, E. (2010). Exploring the relationship of college freshmen honors students' effort and ability attribution, interest, and implicit theory of intelligence with perceived ability. *Gifted Child Quarterly, 54*, 92–101. https://doi.org/10.1080/13598139.2017.1302873

Skinner, E. A. (1996). Personality processes and individual differences: A guide to constructs of control. *Journal of Personality, 71*, 549–570. https://doi.org/10.1037//0022-3514.71.3.549

Smith, S. R. (2017). Responding to the unique social and emotional learning needs of gifted Australian students. In E. Frydenberg, A. J. Martin, & R. J. Collie (Eds.), *Social and emotional learning in Australia and the Asia-Pacific* (pp. 147–166). Singapore, Singapore: Springer.

Snyder, K. E., Barger, M. M., Wormington, S. V., Schwartz-Bloom, R., & Linnenbrink-Garcia, L. (2013). Identification as gifted and implicit beliefs about intelligence: An examination of potential moderators. *Journal of Advanced Academics, 24*, 242–258. https://doi.org/10.1177/1932202X13507971

Snyder, K. E., Malin, J. L., Dent, A. L., & Linnenbrink-Garcia, L. (2014). The message matters: The role of implicit beliefs about giftedness and failure experiences in academic self-handicapping. *Journal of Educational Psychology, 106*, 230–241. https://doi.org/10.1037/a0034553

Subotnik, R. F., Olszewski-Kubilius, P., & Worrell, F. C. (2011). Rethinking giftedness and gifted education: A proposed direction forward based on psychological science. *Psychological Science in the Public Interest, 12*, 3–54. https://doi.org/10.1177/1529100611418056

Tan, L. S., & Chun, K. Y. N. (2014). Perfectionism and academic emotions of gifted adolescent girls. *The Asia-Pacific Education Researcher, 23*, 389–401. https://doi.org/10.1007/s40299-013-0114-9

Tirri, K., & Nokelainen, P. (2011). The influence of self-perception of abilities and attribution styles on academic choices: Implications for gifted education. *Roeper Review, 33*, 26–32. https://doi.org/10.1080/02783193.2011.530204

Travers, C. J., Morisano, D., & Locke, E. A. (2015). Self-reflection, growth goals, and academic outcomes: A qualitative study. *British Journal of Educational Psychology, 85*, 224–241. https://doi.org/10.1111/bjep.12059

Vallerand, R. J., Gagné, F., Senecal, C., & Pelletier, L. G. (1994). A comparison of the school intrinsic motivation and perceived competence of gifted and regular students. *Gifted Child Quarterly, 38*, 172–175. https://doi.org/10.1177/001698629403800403

Vlahovic-Stetic, V., Vidovic, V., & Arambasic, L. (1999). Motivational characteristics in mathematical achievement: A study of gifted high-achieving, gifted underachieving and non-gifted pupils. *High Ability Studies, 10*, 37–49. https://doi.org/10.1080/1359813990100104

Weiner, B. (1985). An attributional theory of achievement motivation and emotion. *Psychological Review, 92*, 548–573. https://doi.org/10.1037/0033-295X.92.4.548

Wright, P. B., & Leroux, J. A. (1997). The self-concept of gifted adolescents in a congregated program. *Gifted Child Quarterly, 41*, 83–94. https://doi.org/10.1177/001698629704100304

Zeidner, M., & Schleyer, E. J. (1998). The big-fish-little-pond effect for academic self-concept, test anxiety, and school grades in gifted children. *Contemporary Educational Psychology, 24*, 305–329. https://doi.org/10.1006/ceps.1998.0985

Ziegler, A., & Phillipson, S. N. (2012). Towards a systemic theory of gifted education. *High Ability Studies, 23*, 3–30. https://doi.org/10.1080/13598139.2012.679085

Emma C. Burns, B.A., PhD, is a Postdoctoral Research Officer in Educational Psychology at the University of New South Wales, Australia. Her research focuses on student motivational attitudes and self-beliefs, goal setting, social relationships, engagement and growth approaches to education. Through her research, Emma aims to promote positive classroom environments for students, as well as develop best practices that foster adaptive attitudes and behaviours in students to help them succeed.

Andrew J. Martin, BA (Hons), MEd (Hons), PhD, is a Scientia Professor of Educational Psychology and Co-Chair of the Educational Psychology Research Group in the School of Education at the University of New South Wales, Australia. He specialises in motivation, engagement, achievement, and quantitative research methods. He is also an Honorary Research Fellow in the Department of Education at the University of Oxford, Honorary Professor in the School of Education and Social Work at the University of Sydney, Fellow of the American Psychological Association, Fellow of the American Educational Research Association, and Fellow of the Academy of the Social Sciences in Australia.

Overexcitability and Giftedness Research: Whose Constructs Are Being Investigated and How?

17

Salvatore Sal Mendaglio

Contents

Overexcitability and Giftedness Research: Whose Constructs Are Being Investigated?	360
OE and Intellectual Giftedness Research	361
OE Questionnaires	361
Brief Overview of the Usage of the OE Questionnaire in Some Asia-Pacific Nations	363
OE and Intelligence in the Theory of Positive Disintegration	366
Overexcitabilities	366
OE in Context	368
Conclusion	371
Application of OE in Practice	371
Research Implications when Using OE	373
Cross-References	374
References	374

Abstract

Interest in overexcitability (OE) in the field of gifted education has increased significantly since the 1980s. Research on its relationship to giftedness, once the sole province of a few American scholars, has expanded globally. It has captured the imagination of researchers in South American, Middle Eastern, European, and Asian-Pacific countries. OE is an integral part of a complex, coherent Theory of Positive Disintegration proposed by Kazimierz Dabrowski. With its growing popularity among researchers, there are indications that Dabrowski's depiction of OE is increasingly disregarded. Reviews of research suggest that the assumptions made and methods used are not necessarily consistent with Dabrowskian OE. As a result, it is difficult to interpret research findings investigating the relationship of OE and giftedness.

S. S. Mendaglio (✉)
University of Calgary, Calgary, AB, Canada
e-mail: mendagli@ucalgary.ca

Keywords

Overexcitabilities · Giftedness · Positive disintegration

The aims in this chapter are to:
1. Reinforce that the field of gifted education has embraced Dabrowski's complex Theory of Positive Disintegration. While it consists of numerous interconnected constructs, only one construct, overexcitability (OE), is the focus of empirical research both in North America and the Asia Pacific.
2. Review the research that suggests that the design and methodology used by researchers globally is inconsistent with Dabrowski's representation of the construct of overexcitability. Dabrowski's definitions and a synopsis of his theory are used to argue that existing research is not, in actuality, investigating overexcitability as depicted by the theorist.
3. Provide suggestions for theoretically consistent uses of overexcitability by educators and counsellors of gifted students.
4. Present some implications for future research using OE.

Overexcitability and Giftedness Research: Whose Constructs Are Being Investigated?

What began as the fascination of a handful of American proponents and researchers in the 1980s, overexcitability (OE) has risen to prominence in the field of gifted education (Bailey, 2011). The global popularity of OE is manifested in publications by researchers from numerous countries outside the USA: Turkey, Spain, Germany, France, Venezuela and, more recently, Malaysia, Taiwan, Hong Kong, Korea, New Zealand and Australia. Presentations at national and international conferences, popular literature, and countless websites make OE in its five forms—sensual, psychomotor, imaginational, intellectual, and emotional—accessible to educators, practitioners, and parents of gifted children. With the intense attention OE receives, novices can be forgiven if they conclude that OE is a theory unto itself, rather than one component of a comprehensive, complex theory; namely, the *Theory of Positive Disintegration* (TPD; Dabrowski, 1967, 1970, 1972). Scholars investigating OE in gifted education often show a similarity to individuals who are new to the construct. Though researchers typically include reference to TPD in their reports, noting that OE is part of TPD, their assumptions and methodology create the impression that they share neophytes' perception of the construct.

In my reviews of the literature, I have criticised the research on both conceptual and methodological grounds. In my most recent commentary on OE research (Mendaglio, 2012), I called for a paradigmatic shift in research. I observed that recent research investigating OE and intellectual giftedness, including that by a number of Asian-Pacific investigators, continues to use the old pattern (e.g., see Alias, Rahman, Majid, & Yassin, 2013). Researchers state that OE is part of TPD, then approach it as an atheoretical construct separate from the TPD (Tillier, 2009; Vuyk, Kerr, & Krieshok, 2016). After presenting a critique of current research, I discuss OE in the context of Dabrowski's TPD.

OE and Intellectual Giftedness Research

The established pattern of exploring the relationship between OE and giftedness is to conduct studies that investigate differences between gifted and non-gifted samples or explore profiles of OE among gifted samples. Use of the *Overexcitability Questionnaire Two* (OEQII), which has all but replaced the *Overexcitability Questionnaire* (OEQ), is part of the research methodology. The descriptions of the two questionnaires immediately explain why OEQII has supplanted the original version.

OE Questionnaires

The OEQ (Lysy & Piechowski, 1983) is designed to assess the five overexcitabilities. It consists of a 21-item open-ended self-report questionnaire with no space or time limits. The OEQ may be completed in groups or individually with the researcher either present or absent. The questions are intended to facilitate individuals' self-analyses and reflections. Responses are scored by trained raters who make judgements regarding the absence, or the presence and intensity, of an overexcitability in a participant's written answers. Questions were originally intended to identify a particular OE, but later the procedure was amended to examine each response for indications of any one of the five OEs. Sample items include: "Do you ever feel incredibly happy? Describe your feelings. When do you feel the most energy and what do you do with it? What do you like to concentrate on most? If you ask yourself 'who am I' what is the answer? When you read a book, what attracts your attention the most?" (see Piechowski & Miller, 1995 for the entire list of questions). Indices of reliability and validity of the OEQ are reported as respectable with test-retest reliability of 0.65, 3–6 weeks apart, for a group of adults. Construct validity was established by studies using practising artists who scored significantly high on emotional, imaginational, and intellectual OEs (see Silverman, 2008). While the OEQ yields rich material regarding OE, it is complicated and time-consuming to use in research. Piirto and Fraas (2012) illustrate this point: "The OEQ is cumbersome to score and analyze. Just scoring and entering the data for [our] small study took months" (p. 29).

The OEQII (Falk, Lind, Miller, Piechowski, & Silverman, 1999) is an adaptation of the original OEQ. The OEQII is a 50-item Likert-type self-report questionnaire also designed to measure the five overexcitabilities. Participants respond to the items using a 5-point scale ranging from one (not at all like me) to five (very much like me). Each OE is assessed by ten items. Sample items for each OE include: When I have a lot of energy, I want to do something really physical (psychomotor). Viewing art is a totally absorbing experience (sensual). Theories get my mind going (intellectual). Things that I picture in my mind are so vivid that they seem real to me (imaginational); and, I can be so happy that I can laugh and cry at the same time (emotional). For each OE, total scores are calculated. The higher the score, the greater the presence of the OE. Using normative sample data, Falk et al. (1999) reported high Cronbach alphas for each set of the OE items: psychomotor (0.86), sensual (0.89), imaginational (0.89), intellectual (0.89), and emotional (0.84).

While the OEQ sparked the investigation of OE and giftedness, it is the OEQII that is responsible for a dramatic increase in OE research productivity over the years. As can be seen in the descriptions of the two questionnaires, they are both easy to administer, but that is where the similarity ends. With the OEQII's easily accessible scores, data entry and analyses are readily conducted. The OEQII not only facilitates data analysis, but also has a particular advantage to researchers. Similar to investigating other constructs using Likert-type scales, researchers need not concern themselves with the conceptual basis of the construct. All that is required in the current research approach is minimal mention of TPD and review of previous empirical findings. Using the OEQII does not require researchers to have any actual knowledge of Dabrowski's conception of the construct they investigate. Therein lies the problem. An understanding of the nature of OE, as an integral part of TPD, is essential. In my view, the use of the OEQII is conceptually problematic. From a TPD perspective, OE is a heritable property of the central nervous system which is not evenly distributed across a population. Accordingly, some individuals inherit no OE, others inherit one or more and, finally, the rare individual inherits all five forms. Using Likert-type scales to assess OE suggests most if not all individuals have some level of OE (Mendaglio, 2012).

The OEQII has been criticised by others on psychometric grounds. Warne (2011) conducted a *Reliability Generalisation* (RG) of the measure: "RG is a specific type of meta-analysis in which reliability coefficients are meta-analyzed instead of effect sizes" (p. 674). Warne's extensive analyses of the reliability of scores in 16 studies provided a great deal of information to guide future researchers in designing their studies with the OEQII. However, it was one of his concluding remarks regarding limitations of his study that is relevant to my discussion of the measure:

> Finally, although this study constitutes the most thorough examination of the reliability of OEQII scores, it provides little—if any—information about the validity of the OEQII score interpretations. It has never been clear what exactly the OEQII measures and evidence of any sort of validity has been meager (Miller et al., 2009) or unfavorable for the OEQII (Warne, 2011). Further psychometric studies on the instrument should be conducted before the instrument gains widespread acceptance. (Warne, 2011, p. 688)

Winkler and Voight (2016) also meta-analysed the scores of 12 studies to investigate the relationship between giftedness and OE. They reported medium and small effect sizes for the five forms of OE, suggesting some support for relating OE and giftedness. However, they note that a number of considerations complicate the interpretations of results. For one thing, there is the dispute regarding psychometric and theoretical merits: "If the OEQII were a psychometrically flawed instrument as some have claimed (Warne, 2011), then this would make this meta-analysis at least partially invalid" (p. 251). Winkler and Voight conclude that the findings, given the controversy over the OEQII, should not be taken as support for the relationship between OE and giftedness. One suggestion they make is that it may be used by practitioners with individual gifted students and patients.

These meta-analyses support the conceptual reviews by Mendaglio and Tillier (2006) of studies from the 1980s to the early 2000s. The 14 studies reviewed generally lent partial support for the association of OE and giftedness. Greater support was found in studies that used adult participants. The greatest support was found in a few studies that used creativity as a criterion for giftedness, particularly when the participants were practising artists. While there was consensus on assessing the OE variable, the OEQ, this was not the case with assessing the giftedness variable. The samples of gifted individuals included elementary school children who had been assessed, counsellors and graduate students, practising artists, students in gifted programs, and children who scored high on tests of creativity.

In more recent studies concerned with comparing gifted and non-gifted and exploring gifted individuals' OE profiles, there is a greater agreement among researchers regarding the method of assessing both constructs (Mendaglio, 2012). The OEQII replaces the OEQ. Giftedness is determined by the use of intelligence, estimated directly or indirectly. In rare instances, researchers identify their gifted participants by administering a test of intelligence. More commonly, researchers use the criterion of enrollment in a school for the gifted or that of attendance at a summer camp for gifted youth. In the latter method, intelligence is assumed since it is the major criterion used for selecting gifted students. Technically, researchers are investigating the relationship between OE and intellectual giftedness.

Mendaglio and Tillier (2006) and Mendaglio (2012) identified theoretical issues that led to their questioning the validity of the studies. They noted researchers' disregard of Dabrowski's conception of OE and its boundedness to his TPD. Researchers mistakenly represented OE as a positive construct with no negative aspects, assumed that giftedness necessarily means possession of all five forms of OE, and implied that OE and intelligence are correlated, since giftedness is often assessed in terms of intelligence. In some cases, the belief in the relationship between giftedness and OE is such that researchers expect that OE should predict giftedness. These misconceptions appear in many articles published over the years and they persist today. Not surprisingly, they have been exported to Asia-Pacific investigators.

Brief Overview of the Usage of the OE Questionnaire in Some Asia-Pacific Nations

Interest in researching OEs took about 40 years to extend from America to Asian-Pacific countries, such as Australia (e.g., Harper, Cornish, Smith, &

Merrotsy, 2017), Hong Kong, China (e.g., Siu, 2010), Korea (e.g., Yoon & Moon, 2009), Taiwan (e.g., Chang & Kuo, 2009), and Malaysia (e.g., Alias et al., 2013) to name a few. It is not surprising that the design of studies is similar to the American approach in their underlying assumptions and data collection methods. To illustrate, I first briefly describe a sample of publications, followed by discussion of one study in depth to elaborate on my perspective regarding the current research approach to OE. Yoon and Moon (2009), using a Korean translation of OEQII, examined gender differences in OE scores within a large sample of gifted and non-gifted Korean students. They reported that the gifted sample scored higher than the nongifted on all OEs, with intellectual OE scores discriminating the most between gifted and nongifted participants. Findings included gender differences. Yoon and Moon concluded that the best predictor of giftedness is the intellectual OE, with the best predictor of giftedness among girls being imaginational OE.

Siu (2010) claimed to be the first to introduce Dabrowski's theory and overexcitabilities into the Chinese literature and use the OEQ for Hong Kong students. Siu explicitly stated that the purpose of the study was to find alternate, non-IQ methods of identifying gifted students. Similar to Yoon and Moon, Siu used a translation of the OEQII to examine group and gender differences among gifted and non-gifted Chinese school children in Hong Kong. Gifted children's scores were higher than non-gifted on all OEs. Interestingly, both gifted and non-gifted female students scored significantly higher on emotional OE than males. Further, gifted females scored significantly higher on sensual OE than gifted males. He and Wong (2014) were also interested in gender differences, including whether there was greater variability with respect to the five OEs. Using a Chinese translation of the OEQII, they surveyed a large number of adolescent students. The male pattern of scores indicated greater variability on the sensual, imaginational, and intellectual OE than females. Males scored significantly higher on psychomotor; females scored significantly higher on emotional.

He, Wong, and Chan (2017) investigated the prediction of creativity among Hong Kong students using overexcitabilities. The Chinese translation of OEQII and a measure of creativity were administered to a large sample of Hong Kong adolescent students. The sample consisted of students with a wide range of academic abilities. Results indicated significant, but low correlations among the five OEs and creativity. The most significant predictor of creativity was imaginational. The studies described above demonstrate similar concerns identified by Mendaglio and Tillier (2006).

In order to illustrate my perspective, I discuss a Malaysian study specifically. Alias, Rahman, and colleagues (2013) investigated the OE profiles of gifted Malaysian students using a Malay translation of the OEQII. The sample consisted of 335 students, aged 10–15 attending a summer camp specifically for gifted students. In the rationale for the study, the researchers clearly acknowledge that OE is part of Dabrowski's theory. They also express the belief that OE can be used by teachers to identify gifted students' strengths. Examples are provided for each form of OE. The following lengthy quotation is necessary to convey how the forms of OE are generally presented as exclusively positive in nature, contrary to OE in TPD (discussed in detail later in this chapter):

> ...overexcitabilities can be used to identify the gifted students' potentials based on their domains of Overexcitabilities. For example, gifted students who show the following characteristics have potentials in the respective fields: i) psychomotor overexcitability would bring out potential in the field of sports or extreme and challenging sports; ii) sensual overexcitability with high sensitivity to taste buds reflects the potential in the field of culinary arts; iii) imagination overexcitability shows potential in the field of performing or visual arts or creatively produce outstanding inventions; iv) intellectual overexcitability is essential in developing potentials academic fields such as science and technology; and finally v) emotional overexcitability would bring out the sensitivity towards potentially in the of social activities that concerns with the wellbeing of the human civilisation.
>
> Therefore, overexcitabilities should be accepted as part of the gifted students' personalities that should be understood, stimulated and also supported to ensure a healthy development of their potentials (Daniels & Meckstroth, 2009), rather than being labelled and punished as behavioural or problematic problems. (Alias et al., 2013, p. 121)

Initially, the researchers presumed that all gifted students possess OEs, which can be used to identify their potentials. On the first half of this point, assuming that all gifted students have OEs is problematic when contrasted with TPD, which indicates that some individuals are bereft of OE. Later in interpreting their findings, the authors created four profiles, one of which seemed to contradict this position. Of interest is Profile 4 in which 88 students had low scores on all forms of OE. Citing Piirto (2010), the authors interpreted the low scores as indicating an absence of OE. To their credit, in so doing, they illustrated the Dabrowskian perspective that not everyone, gifted or not, has OE. With respect to the second half of the presumption, Dabrowski's interest in OE was in its relationship to human development, not the actualisation of specific potentials. Citing other scholars, the authors claim that "Dabrowski had stated that an individual who possesses more than one overexcitability characteristic is a gifted and talented individual" (p. 122). This illustrates one of a number of common misconceptions about OE and intelligence. An implication of this erroneous statement is that OE can be used to identify giftedness. In a broader sense, because researchers' beliefs about OE influence their interpretation of their findings, it is essential that all scholars become familiar with all aspects of TPD.

Generally, studies investigating the relationship between giftedness and OE and profiles of OE among gifted students have some commonalities. Their results indicate various levels of correlation among one or more OE, as measured by the OEQII, and giftedness as measured by intelligence scores. Similarly, OE profiles of gifted students vary from those having high scores on all forms of OE to those having low scores. The studies generally represent assumptions that are inconsistent with Dabrowski's theorising. Lastly, their use of the OEQII has rendered findings that may be interesting, but which cannot be interpreted as testing TPD constructs.

OE and Intelligence in the Theory of Positive Disintegration

Overexcitabilities

Dabrowski (1972) defined OE as heightened physiological experience of sensory stimuli caused by increased sensitivity of neurons. OE is depicted as a "higher than average responsiveness to stimuli, manifested either by sensual, psychomotor, emotional (affective), imaginational, or intellectual excitability, or the combination thereof" (Dabrowski, 1972, p. 303). Dabrowski initially used *psychic overexcitability* to emphasise that the five forms represent the magnification and enhancement of cognitive processes. While many descriptions appear in original sources of TPD, the description provided in a posthumously published book (Dabrowski, 1996) captures the essence of the five forms. Given the variations appearing in the literature, it is important to review Dabrowski's original conceptualisation.

Sensual overexcitability is a function of a heightened experiencing of sensory pleasure. It manifests itself as need for comfort, luxury, aesthetics, fashions, superficial relations with others, frequent changes of lovers, etc. As with the psychomotor form it also may, but, need not be, a manifestation of a transfer of emotional tension to sensual forms of expression of which the most common examples are overeating and excessive sexual stimulation. In children, sensual overexcitability manifests itself as a need for cuddling, kissing, clinging to mother's body, early heightened interest in sexual matters, showing off and need to be with others all the time.

Psychomotor overexcitability is a function of an excess of energy and manifests itself, for example, in rapid talk, restlessness, violent games, sports, pressure for action or delinquent behaviour. It may either be a 'pure' manifestation of the excess of energy, or it may result from the transfer of emotional tension to psychomotor forms of expression such as those mentioned above.

Imaginational overexcitability in its 'pure' form manifests itself through association of images and impressions, inventiveness, use of image and metaphor in verbal expression, as well as strong and sharp visualisation. In its 'impure' form, emotional tension is transferred to dreams, nightmares, mixing of truth and fiction, fears of the unknown, etc. Imaginational overexcitability leads to an intense living in the world of fantasy, predilection for fairy and magic tales, poetic creations or invention of fantastic stories.

Intellectual overexcitability in contrast to the first three does not distinctly manifest the transfer of emotional tension to intellectual activity under specific forms. This does not mean that intellectual and emotional processes of high intensity do not occur together. They do, but they do not appear to take on such distinct forms. Intellectual overexcitability is manifested as a drive to ask probing questions, avidity for knowledge, theoretical thinking, reverence for logic, preoccupation with theoretical problems, etc.

Emotional overexcitability is a function of experiencing emotional relationships. The relationships can manifest themselves as strong attachment to persons, living things or places. From the developmental point of view presented here, intensity of feelings and display of emotions alone are not developmentally significant unless the experiential aspect of relationship is present. This distinction is very important. For example, when a child is refused candy he may throw a temper tantrum just to show his anger. Or, he may go away sad thinking he is not loved (Boldface in original; Dabrowski, 1996, pp. 72–73).

In TPD, not all forms of OE are inherently beneficial. Dabrowski specifically identified sensual and psychomotor as lower forms of OE (Dabrowski, 1972). Sensual is manifested in a cycle of intense sensual hunger leading to preoccupation with satisfaction of drives. Psychomotor is manifested in a need for novelty, restlessness, hyperactivity, and impulsivity. The higher forms—imaginational, intellectual and emotional—serve to attenuate the lower forms. The naturally occurring manifestations are sublimated into higher forms of expression and serve to energise the individuals' quest for higher functioning.

It is important to note that individuals may inherit no OE, one or more forms, or all forms. These various combinations have implications for development or lack of development. It is important to remember that development has a unique meaning in this theory. Simply stated, it refers to a nonlinear progression from a civilised animal-like existence to a highly aware, autonomous, altruistic, values-driven living. All five forms are required for individuals to be on that journey. A lack of OE suggests that individuals may lead a good life being solid citizens but with little awareness or autonomy, living under the influence of biology and society. Dabrowski was clear about the negative outcomes associated with the presence of only the lower forms: "When enhanced psychomotor and sensual overexcitability is combined with strong ambition, tendency to showing off and lying, it constitutes a nucleus of psychopathy with some neuropathic components" (1972, p. 11). (This statement is worth recalling when research findings claim to indicate that psychomotor assessment is the best form to differentiate gifted from non-gifted individuals.)

Intelligence. TPD's lexicon is replete with unique terminology (overexcitability, dynamisms; see Harper et al., 2017 for definitions), unexpected juxtapositions (positive disintegration, negative adjustment), and reframing of common terms (development, personality). *Intelligence* is an exception. In his clinical work, writing and research, Dabrowski retained the mainstream conception of the term. This is manifested in his use of Wechsler scales to assess intelligence in his patients and research participants (Dabrowski, 1967). In his discussions, he refers to below average, average, above average, or high level of intelligence. However, Dabrowski reframed the role of intelligence in development in general. According to Mendaglio (2014), Dabrowski relegated intelligence to a subservient role in daily functioning. Intelligence, regardless of level, is simply a tool that individuals use to achieve aims and goals. What an individual does with his or her intelligence depends on the type of development involved. In what Dabrowski described as biological development, intelligence is in the service of individuals' gratification of instincts, drives, and needs. In the extreme negative version of biological development, *one-sided development*, intelligence is directed by sociopathic and, at times, criminal aims and goals. In contrast, in autonomous development, intelligence serves higher aims and values, such as altruism and authenticity.

Thus, it is not the level of intelligence that is critical; it is how it is used by individuals. Intelligence, including high level—that is, giftedness—may be used for good or evil purposes, depending on the individual's level of development. Interestingly, Dabrowski attributes average intelligence to both one-sided and autonomous development. Giftedness, as defined in research on OE, cannot be used to differentiate between one-sided development (associated with, for example, coldness, cruelty, and lust for power) and autonomous development (associated with empathy, altruism, and personal responsibility). Therefore, it can be concluded that above average intelligence is a necessary, but not sufficient condition for autonomous development (Mendaglio & Pyryt, 2004). Of the two constructs, it is not intelligence that determines type of development, but rather OE, which is the expression of a larger factor in TPD developmental potential and will be discussed later in this chapter.

Dabrowski did not use giftedness as part of his theory, though he included significant commentary on intelligence. In fact, in TPD, there is a relationship between OE and intelligence. However, the relationship between these two constructs is not a positive correlation in which the higher the intelligence the more OE. The role Dabrowski attributes to intelligence is what makes the relationship complicated. Moreover, at first glance, it may seem appropriate to view intelligence as similar to intellectual OE. However, Dabrowski cautioned against this association because the intellectual form of OE, as described above, includes several factors which differ from simple cognitive ability. Unless researchers understand the Dabrowskian perspective on OE and intelligence, they cannot claim that they are investigating OE as a construct of TPD. In my reviews of research investigating OE and giftedness (Mendaglio, 2012, 2014), I have concluded that, in essence, OE is treated as if it were atheoretical, that it has meaning in and of itself. However, like virtually all of the Dabrowskian constructs, OE is qualitatively different from mainstream psychological constructs, and must be understood and investigated with respect to the theory in which it originated.

OE in Context

It is acknowledged here that parts of this section appeared in German in Preckel, Schneider, and Holling (2010). Permission to publish it here has been granted.

In his conception of OE, Dabrowski (1967, 1970) noted that individuals vary in their inheritance of overexcitability: some inherit none, other individuals, one or two or more, and some inherit all five forms. As noted earlier, OE is essential for development. OE creates inner conflict, which Dabrowski postulated was essential for his conception of human development (Dabrowski, 1972). It is important to note again, however, that not all forms of OE are of equal importance for development. Individuals who inherit only psychomotor and sensual forms, according to Dabrowski, may become successful in life but they will be motivated by self-interest, with little genuine concern for others; that is, they limit development to the lowest level (Dabrowski, 1996). Dabrowski stipulated that the emotional, intellectual, and imaginational forms are required for development (Dabrowski, 1972). Unlike common psychological perspectives, in Dabrowski's usage, development is not equivalent to the progression of life span stages, from infancy to old age; nor is it equated with Piagetian cognitive development (Piaget & Inhelder, 1969). It does have a superficial similarity to Kohlberg (1970) because both Kohlberg and Dabrowski were interested in moral development. However, unlike Kohlberg, Dabrowski focused on moral *behaviour* not moral reasoning. OE is fundamental to individuals' attainment of the highest level of human functioning characterised by moral-ethical living.

Although OE is a prerequisite for advanced development, how development occurs is a complex process which Dabrowski explained by numerous interrelated concepts (Dabrowski, 1973). Dabrowski's presentation of his theory is replete with idiosyncratic use of language (see Mendaglio, 2008a). To present a synopsis of the theory of positive disintegration, I have taken the liberty of replacing some original terminology with my own terms. Specifically, I use my terminology to represent in general Dabrowski's view of development. Based on my knowledge of the theory, I have elected to discuss Dabrowskian development as a progression from living an egocentric-robotic life to living an altruistic-autonomous one.

In an egocentric-robotic life, individuals use their resources—intelligence, skills, and talents—for the gratification of biological needs and drives such as self-preservation, self-promotion, and sexuality, which are expressions of Dabrowski's (1964) *primary integration*. The more common of two subtypes of the egocentric-robotic approach to living are the individuals who gratify biological urges and needs by complying with societal prescriptions. Such individuals, often motivated by social approval, may become very successful in societal terms but lack development from a Dabrowskian sense. A less common subtype of the egocentric-robotic are the individuals who become very successful in gratifying their biological urges by disregarding societal norms and by using other people for their own purposes. These two subtypes represent a lack of development because, for Dabrowski, such individuals are self-serving, which is most obvious in the second, antisocial subtype. Though not as apparent, the egocentrism is also active in the socialised subtype: when such individuals, for example, make a financial contribution to a charitable organisation, they do so because it is socially appropriate, not because they have thoughtfully considered the organisation's cause and concluded that it was the right thing to do. Their contribution is seen as altruistic; however, their rationale is egocentric. The three subtypes represent a lack of development which Dabrowski defines as "the movement toward higher and higher levels of personality functions in the direction of the personality ideal" (Dabrowski, 1964, p. 112). Further, Dabrowski proposes that the approaches to life described above as three subtypes represent the absence of mental health (Dabrowski, 1964).

In an altruistic-autonomous life, individuals use their resources in the process of development. The more common of the two subtypes of the altruistic-autonomous are the individuals who are successful in breaking the bonds of biology and society, through the process of positive disintegration (Dabrowski, 1967), placing such individuals on a developmental trajectory. Unfortunately, the bonds are extremely difficult to break requiring a great deal of mental energy. The energy required generally comes from experiences of developmental milestones, such as puberty, or environmental crises such as the death of a loved one (Mendaglio, 2008b). Natural milestones and environmental events trigger a disruption in the established mental organisation (how individuals construe their world and themselves) that individuals use to guide their day-to-day behaviour. Such disruptions result in individuals' becoming aware of how their lives have been focused on gratifying their urges and conforming to societal expectations, while rarely reflecting on oneself and the world. Growing awareness creates inner conflict where none existed previously. The inner conflict stems from their growing awareness of the discrepancy between the ways the world and themselves are and the way the world and they ought to be (Dabrowski, 1973). For example, intense emotions are created by the growing awareness of poverty, war, and disease in the world and world leaders' apparent disinterest in dealing with these issues. Similarly, emotions such as disappointment, anger, and anxiety arise from a growing dissatisfaction with oneself as one becomes aware of the way he or she should behave and how she or he actually behaves. While unseen by others, such individuals spend their lives in an ebb and flow of intense negative emotions as they experience themselves succeeding and failing in their battles over their biological urges and the need for social approval. Individuals in this subtype experience recurring inner conflicts with periods of calm throughout life, which Dabrowski (1972) termed psychoneurotics. The second and rare subtype consists of individuals who achieve the ultimate goal of behaving in an altruistic and autonomous way; they are living what Dabrowski termed their *personality ideal* (Dabrowski, 1967). Such individuals no longer experience inner conflict of the type described above because their daily behaviours are consistent with their ideals—they are their brothers' and sisters' keepers and not bound by societal norms but by their reflective moral approach to life. These individuals are exemplars of the phrase 'truly human' (Dabrowski, 1967). Both subtypes represent development because, for Dabrowski, human development is equated with a transcendence of one's biology and socialisation; in the first subtype, the transcendence is partial; in the second, it is complete.

That maturational and environmental events trigger development in some individuals and not others is not a chance occurrence; advanced development is possible only in individuals who possess more than the psychomotor and sensual forms of OE (Dabrowski, 1996). In rare cases when individuals possess high levels of all five forms of OE, the interaction among the forms themselves (without the need for environmental contribution) provide energy and internal psychic conflict that are necessary for advanced human development (Dabrowski, 1972). Through inner conflict and the negative emotions associated with it, particularly the experiencing of dissatisfaction with self, lower-level mental structures are destroyed—disintegrated—and replaced by new mental structures. When the outcome contributes to development, the process is termed *positive disintegration*, the phrase

Dabrowski chose to name his theory. Disintegration, however, may be negative as well. Persistent, intense emotions associated with OE-generated internal conflict and the presence of a toxic social environment may result in negative outcomes such as suicide and psychoses (Dabrowski, 1970). OE is an essential element in the process of development, but OE is the expression of a larger hereditary factor in the Theory of Positive Disintegration, that is, developmental potential.

Dabrowski (1972) defined developmental potential as the "constitutional endowment, which determines the character and the extent of mental growth possible for a given individual" (p. 293). There are four components of developmental potential: OE, special abilities, talents, and autonomous forces. Special abilities and talents include, for example, mathematical ability and musical talent. Autonomous forces, termed *dynamisms* in TPD, drive development. Dynamisms seem to be triggered by overexcitable individuals' interaction with their social environments. At the early stages of development, these forces serve to disintegrate the lower mental structures, and in later stages, autonomous forces direct individual course of development. For example, dissatisfaction with oneself is one such *disintegrating* autonomous force. In more advanced development, autopsychotherapy, a *developmental* autonomous inner force, enables individuals to become their own therapists by analysing and treating their own psychological issues (for a detailed account, see Mendaglio, 2008b). OE serves to create inner conflict; the disintegrating forces do the actual work of disintegration. Dabrowski assessed the level of developmental potential by the presence or absence of its four components and their relative strengths. Researchers have focused almost exclusively on OE as a measure of developmental potential, ignoring its complexity.

The synopsis of Dabrowski's theory discussed above presents only what I consider critical to the question of whether the focus of research on OEs, independent of the many other concepts and principles comprising TPD, is appropriate or likely to contribute value to the field of gifted education.

Conclusion

Application of OE in Practice

Educators and counsellors search for information to guide their work with gifted students. Of increasing concern is social-emotional functioning of these students not simply their cognitive-academic performance. Dabrowski's theory has grown in popularity among practitioners because scholars in gifted education have interpreted it as explaining the non-cognitive aspects of giftedness despite the fact that Dabrowski himself termed TPD as his theory of personality. Additionally:

> OEs separated from TPD become a problem, as in TPD OEs interact with dynamisms to achieve personality or advanced development (Pyryt, 2008) and should not serve merely as descriptive constructs. However, in gifted education OEs are presented mostly out of the context of TPD as if they were stable personality traits, thereby creating inconsistencies in the application of the original theory. (Vuyk et al., 2016, p. 60)

Hence, applying Dabrowski's theory to gifted students has meant using OE to reframe students' behaviours. Some common recommended applications of OE misrepresent the meaning of OE, creating a disservice to professionals eager to find means of assisting gifted students. Misrepresentation of OE is most commonly apparent in the application of psychomotor and emotional overexcitabilities. Psychomotor is used to reframe Attention Deficit Hyperactivity Disorder (ADHD). When discussing dual exceptionality of gifted and ADHD, there is a tendency to reframe it as gifted and psychomotor OE. However, a close reading of symptoms of ADHD and Dabrowski's psychomotor suggests that psychomotor and ADHD overlap. With respect to emotional OE, any intense emotional expression reframed as emotional OE is inconsistent with it in the TPD.

When applying OE, practitioners, first, should be aware of its meaning in TPD, and second, they should uncover the rationale for students' behaviour. The key is to understand why students are behaving the way they do. As indicated in the description of emotional OE presented earlier, a child may cry for a myriad of reasons some of which may indicate emotional OE; other reasons may be manipulative. Implicit in using OE is the requirement that we have more than a superficial knowledge of the student. We cannot accurately identify students' motivation underlying their behaviours without a relationship with them.

Adults' responding to children's expressions of OE should ensure that their responses reflect Dabrowski's conception of OE. As can be seen from the OE descriptions presented earlier in this chapter, sensual and psychomotor include some manifestations that are clearly negative in nature, requiring differentiated responses. Sensual OE is a heightened experiencing of sensory pleasure. A child's need for cuddling with mother suggests that an accepting response is appropriate. However, manifestation of overeating tends to require a response aimed at correcting the behaviour. Psychomotor OE is a function of excessive energy. Manifestations tend to be negative ranging from rapid speech to delinquent behaviours. The negative manifestations of excessive energy are transformed when the higher forms of OE are present. However, unless that occurs, parents' responses should be aimed at eliminating the negative behaviours.

Imaginational, intellectual, and emotional are the higher forms of OE; their manifestations are generally positive in nature, though they may challenge parents and teachers. Imaginational OE, as the name implies, is a function of imagination and fantasy. When children exhibit inventiveness, use of metaphors or sharp visualisations, parents should admire their children's creativity. More challenging manifestions are imaginary playmates and nightmares. These manifestations tend to worry parents. They need to transcend their own anxiety in order to respond effectively. In both cases, parents should avoid denying children's realities. With nightmares, children also need reassurance from parents. Intellectual OE is a function of enthusiasm for learning coupled with theoretical thinking. A manifestation that may challenge parents and teachers is asking probing questions. Adults may misinterpret expressions of curiosity as questioning or challenging their authority. Such misinterpretations lead to defensiveness in parents and teachers, with inappropriate, at times, punitive responses. The challenge posed by the feature of asking probing questions is that adults have to decipher the motivation underlying the questions. Young children asking why they should go to bed and questioning parents' reasoning are not manifestations that need to be nurtured. In a different vein, parents should not feel that they must be able to answer any question that children's OE generates. Rather, parents should encourage children to engage in independent research. Emotional OE is a function of experiencing emotional relationships—not simply being intensely emotional. Emotions are experienced and expressed in the context of relationships. A strong attachment to people and living things is a context in which manifestations of emotions occur. Experiencing a connection with other people's suffering creates intense emotions such as sadness. The challenge for parents is to inhibit the natural inclination to use logical explanations to reduce children's negative emotions, such as sadness in response to another person's plight. Such parental responses, though well-intentioned attempts to alleviate children's distress, in actuality, serve to deny children's emotions. Children need ackowledgement and acceptance when expressing emotions produced by emotional OE.

Research Implications when Using OE

While there are opposing views to overexcitabilities in the gifted education literature, opponents appear to be showcasing their own theories and recommendations for pragmatic services for gifted students as alternatives to OE, rather than advancing the benefits of OE within the TPD (e.g., see Vuyk et al., 2016). Nonetheless, there is a push for more empirical research associated with giftedness and overexcitabilities that recognises OE within the larger and more complex TPD (e.g., see Harper et al., 2017). Viewing giftedness through a Dabrowskian lens may provide new opportunities for designing more meaningful empirical research (e.g., Pyryt, 2008). There is little doubt that TPD has the potential to contribute significantly to our understanding of giftedness; the challenge is how we can take full advantage of Dabrowski's creation.

Overexcitability is a compelling component of TPD but we cannot treat its five forms as discrete variables, nor should we assume that OE correlates with intellectual giftedness. However, if researchers wish to continue an exclusive focus on OE, I suggest we reconceptualise the five forms as factors, not variables. In operationalising OE, a step closer to the Dabrowskian view is to emulate the Five Factor Model (FFM) of personality. The FFM consists of factors and facets, neuroticisim, extroversion, openness, agreeableness, and conscientiousness, which are each composed of several facets (Mendaglio, 2008c). For example, agreeableness includes facets such as trust, altruism, compliance, and modesty. A measure of OE reflecting the factor-facet approach, using Dabrowski's manifestations of each form, is a closer quantitative approximation of OE than the available questionnaires.

A better approach would be to study the five forms in the broader component of TPD, in which it is located. As we know, OE is one part of developmental potential, which also includes special abilities and talents, as well as dynamisms.

Research exploring all components of developmental potential should yield more meaningful results than simply tables of scores revealing various profiles of specific forms. Taking into account the degree to which OE is accompanied by special abilities and talents would likely support Dabrowski's firm contention that a high level of intelligence alone represents a prerequisite for OE, not a guarantee. Decidedly operationalising developmental potential is more difficult than creating a Likert-type measure. Whether investigating OE as isolated concepts or in the broader context of developmental potential, I recommend the use of qualitative methodology. Engaging participants in conversations and using Dabrowski's formulations to interpret the data would more likely enhance our understanding of the relationship between OE and giftedness. Qualitative methodology has an additional benefit: it would not have an "*a priori* belief that gifted persons were more overexcitable than nongifted persons" (Winkler & Voight, 2016, p. 252), which appears to underline the current OEQ questionnaires.

OE is a complex construct that is an integral part of the theory of positive disintegration. It cannot be investigated as an independent construct. The current approach to research is not reflective of or informed by Dabrowski's theory. OE is inextricably bound to developmental potential, which is integral to human development. Researchers interested in studying Dabrowski's OE ought to accept that it cannot be assessed by exclusively using questionnaires of any kind, especially not those composed of Likert-type scales. Simply acknowledging that OE is part of TPD is not sufficient; TPD, in its fullness, must permeate researchers' assumptions and methodology. Until researchers design their studies of OE and giftedness with Dabrowski's TPD in mind, the question remains: Whose constructs are being investigated?

Cross-References

- A Counselling Framework for Meeting the Needs of Gifted Students in Malaysia
- Exploring Diverse Perceptions of Wise Persons: Wisdom in Gifted Education
- Fostering Resilience in 'At-Risk' Gifted and Talented Young People
- Gifted Education in the Asia-Pacific: From the Past for the Future – An Introduction
- Motivational Issues in Gifted Education: Understanding the Role of Students' Attribution and Control Beliefs, Self-Worth Protection and Growth Orientation
- Self-Regulated Learning for High-Ability and High-Achieving Students in Mixed-Ability Classrooms Throughout the Asia-Pacific
- Social and Emotional Needs and Learning Processes: Part II Introduction
- Some Implications for the Future of Gifted Education in the Asia-Pacific

References

Alias, A., Rahman, S., Majid, R. A., & Yassin, S. F. M. (2013). Dabrowski's Overexcitabilities profile among gifted students. *Asian Social Science, 9*(16), 120–125. https://doi.org/10.5539/ass.v9n16p120

Bailey, C. L. (2011). An examination of the relationships between ego development, Dabrowski's theory of positive disintegration, and the behavioral characteristics of gifted adolescents. *The Gifted Child Quarterly, 55*, 208–222. https://doi.org/10.1177/0016986211412180

Chang, J. J., & Kuo, C. C. (2009). Overexcitabilities of gifted and talented students and its related researches in Taiwan. *Asia-Pacific Journal of Gifted and Talented Education, 1*(1), 41–74. Retrieved from https://www.academia.edu/3485140/Overexcitabilities_of_Gifted_and_Talented_Students_and

Dabrowski, K. (1964). *Positive disintegration*. Boston, MA: Little Brown.

Dabrowski, K. (1967). *Personality-shaping through positive disintegration*. Boston, MA: Little Brown.

Dabrowski, K. (1970). *Mental growth through positive disintegration*. London, England: Gryf.

Dabrowski, K. (1972). *Psychoneurosis is not an illness*. London, England: Gryf.

Dabrowski, K. (1973). *The dynamics of concepts*. London, England: Gryf.

Dabrowski, K. (1996). *Multilevelness of emotional and instinctive functions. Part 1: Theory and description of levels of behavior*. Lublin, Poland: Towarzystwo Naukowe Katolickiego Uniwersytetu Lubelskiego.

Daniels, S. & Meckstroth, E. (2009). Nurturing the sensitivity, intensity, and developmental potential of young gifted children. In Daniels, S. & Piechowski, M. (Eds.), Living with intensity: Understanding the sensitivity, excitability, and emotional development of gifted children, adolescents and adults. (pp. 33–56). Scottsdale, AZ: Great Potential Press.

Falk, R. R., Lind, S., Miller, N. B., Piechowski, M. M., & Silverman, L. K. (1999). *The overexcitability questionnaire–two (OEQII): Manual, scoring system, and questionnaire*. Denver, CO: Institute for the Study of Advanced Development.

Harper, A., Cornish, L., Smith, S., & Merrotsy, P. (2017). Through the Dąbrowski Lens: A fresh examination of the Theory of Positive Disintegration. *Roeper Review, 39*(1), 37–43. https://doi.org/10.1080/02783193.2016.1247395

He, W., & Wong, W. (2014). Greater male variability in overexcitabilities: Domain-specific patterns. *Personality and Individual Differences, 66*, 27–32. https://doi.org/10.1016/j.paid.2014.03.002

He, W., Wong, W., & Chan, M. (2017). Overexcitabilities as important psychological attributes of creativity: A Dabrowskian perspective. *Thinking Skills and Creativity, 25*, 27–35. https://doi.org/10.1016/j.tsc.2017.06.006

Kohlberg, L. (1970). Moral stages and moralization: The cognitive-developmental approach to socialization. In T. Kickona (Ed.), *Moral development and behaviour: Theory, research and social issues* (pp. 31–43). New York, NY: Holt, Rinehart & Winston.

Lysy, K. Z., & Piechowski, M. M. (1983). Personal growth: An empirical study using Jungian and Dabrowskian measures. *Genetic Psychology Monographs, 108*, 267–320.

Mendaglio, S. (Ed.). (2008a). *Dabrowski's theory of positive disintegration*. Scottsdale, AZ: Great Potential Press.

Mendaglio, S. (2008b). Dabrowski's theory of positive disintegration: A personality theory for the 21st century. In S. Mendaglio (Ed.), *Dabrowski's theory of positive disintegration* (pp. 13–40). Scottsdale, AZ: Great Potential Press.

Mendaglio, S. (2008c). The theory of positive disintegration (TPD) and other approaches to personality. In S. Mendaglio (Ed.), *Dabrowski's theory of positive disintegration* (pp. 227–248). Scottsdale, AZ: Great Potential Press.

Mendaglio, S. (2012). Overexcitabilities and giftedness research: A call for a paradigm shift. *Journal for the Education of the Gifted, 35*(3), 207–219. https://doi.org/10.1177/0162353212451704

Mendaglio, S., (2014). Dabrowski on intelligence: Dethroning a venerable construct. *International Journal for Talent Development and Creativity, 2*(1), 15–21.

Mendaglio, S., & Pyryt, M. C. (2004). The role of intelligence in Dabrowski's theory of positive disintegration. In W. Tillier (Ed.). *Developmental potential: From theory to practice: Educational and therapeutic perspectives*. Proceedings from the sixth international congress of the Institute for Positive Disintegration in Human Development. Calgary, AB.

Mendaglio, S., & Tillier, W. (2006). Dabrowski's theory of positive disintegration and giftedness: Overexcitabilities research findings. *Journal for the Education of the Gifted, 30*, 68–87.

Miller, N. B., Falk, R. F., & Huang, Y. (2009). Gender identity and the overexcitability profiles of gifted college students. *Roeper Review, 31*, 161–169. https://doi.org/10.1080/02783190902993920

Piaget, J., & Inhelder, B. (1969). *The psychology of the child*. New York, NY: Basic Books.

Piechowski, M. M., & Miller, N. B. (1995). Assessing developmental potential in gifted children: A comparison of methods. *Roeper Review, 17*, 176–180. https://doi.org/10.1080/02783199509553654

Piirto, J. (2010). 21 years with the Dabrowski Theory: An Autoethnography. *Advanced Development Journal, 12*, 68–90. Retrieved from https://www.positivedisintegration.com/Piirto2010.pdf

Piirto, J., & Fraas, J. (2012). A mixed-methods comparison of vocational and identified-gifted high school students on the Overexcitability Questionnaire. *Journal for the Education of the Gifted, 35*(1), 3–34. https://doi.org/10.1177/0162353211433792

Preckel, F., Schneider, W., & Holling, H. (Eds.). (2010). *Diagnostic von hodchbegabung*. Gottingen, Germany: Hogrefe. [Mendaglio, S. *Overexcitabilities* and Dabrowskis Theorie der Positiven Desintegration, pp. 169–196.].

Pyryt, M. (2008). The Dabrowskian lens: Implications for understanding gifted individuals. In S. Mendaglio (Ed.), *Dabrowski's theory of positive disintegration* (pp. 175–182). Tucson, AZ: Great Potential Press.

Silverman, L. K. (2008). The theory of positive disintegration in the field of gifted education. In S. Mendaglio (Ed.), *Dąbrowski's theory of positive disintegration* (pp. 157–173). Scottsdale, AZ: Great Potential.

Siu, A. F. Y. (2010). Comparing overexcitabilities of gifted and non-gifted school children in Hong Kong: Does culture make a difference? *Asia Pacific Journal of Education, 30*(1), 71–83.

Tillier, W. (2009). Dabrowski without the theory of positive disintegration just isn't Dabrowski. *Roeper Review, 31*, 123–126. https://doi.org/10.1080/02783190902737699

Vuyk, M. A., Kerr, B. A., & Krieshok, T. S. (2016). From overexcitabilities to openness: Informing gifted education with psychological science. *Gifted and Talented International, 31*(1), 59–71. https://doi.org/10.1080/15332276.2016.1220796

Warne, R. T. (2011). A reliability generalization of the Overexcitability Questionnaire-Two. *Journal of Advanced Academics, 22*, 671–692. https://doi.org/10.1177/1932202X11424881

Winkler, D., & Voight, A. (2016). Giftedness and overexcitability: Investigating the relationship using meta-analysis. *The Gifted Child Quarterly, 60*(4), 243–257. https://doi.org/10.1177/0016986216657588

Yoon, Y. H., & Moon, J. H. (2009). A comparison of the overexcitabilities: In gifted and non-gifted Korean primary-school children. *Journal of Gifted/Talented Education, 19*(3), 585–602. Retrieved from http://society.kisti.re.kr/sv/SV_svpsbs03V.do?method=download&cn1=JAKO200914035213357

Salvatore Sal Mendaglio, PhD, holds the position of professor, Graduate Programs in Education, Werklund School of Education and University of Calgary, Canada. In his long career with the University of Calgary, he has contributed to the preparation of psychologists and taught courses in gifted education. His area of interest is the psychology of giftedness and the theory of positive disintegration. In addition to publications on his topics, he regularly provides public lectures to parents and workshops for educators. As a registered psychologist, he has counselled gifted youth and their families for over 35 years.

Put Them Together and See How They Learn! Ability Grouping and Acceleration Effects on the Self-Esteem of Academically Gifted High School Students

18

Miraca U. M. Gross and Susen R. Smith

Contents

Miraca's Personal Vignette	378
Introduction	380
Overview of Acceleration, Ability Grouping, and Self-Esteem	381
Ability Grouping for Acceleration	383
Effects of Acceleration on Gifted Students	385
Self-Esteem: Task-Involvement and Ego-Involvement	386
Assessing Self-Esteem of Gifted Students and Non-gifted Students: An Exemplar Study	387
Instrumentation	387
Motivational Orientation	388
Participants: Year 7 Selective High School Students	388
Effects of Ability Grouping and Acceleration on the Self-Esteem of Academically Gifted High School Students	389
Self-Esteem: Selective School Accelerated Class Cohort	391
Implications for Research and Practice	393
Conclusion	396
Cross-References	397
References	397

Abstract

Case studies have long been used to research and illuminate the lives of gifted students. One example is the longitudinal study of profoundly gifted students by the first author elaborating the impact of acceleration, non-acceleration, and ability grouping on gifted students academically, socially, and emotionally. In this chapter an overview of ability grouping and acceleration for academically gifted high school students in Australia in relation to their self-esteem will be reiterated. Specifically, a study will be discussed that examined the effects of three

---

M. U. M. Gross · S. R. Smith (✉)
GERRIC, School of Education, University of New South Wales, Sydney, NSW, Australia
e-mail: m.gross@unsw.edu.au; susen.smith@unsw.edu.au

© Crown 2021
S. R. Smith (ed.), *Handbook of Giftedness and Talent Development in the Asia-Pacific*,
Springer International Handbooks of Education,
https://doi.org/10.1007/978-981-13-3041-4_17

interventions: (1) ability grouping; (2) acceleration; and (3) acceleration used concurrently with ability grouping, on the self-esteem of academically gifted high school students. Self-esteem was assessed on three occasions during the school year with three groups of academically gifted Australian students undertaking their first year of secondary school (Year 7): (a) students in comprehensive schools (mixed-ability settings); (b) students in selective high schools (full-time ability grouping in schools serving only gifted students); and (c) students in selective high schools who were also collapsing Years 7 and 8 into a single year—a blend of ability grouping and acceleration. Students in the first two groups experienced a diminution (but not a serious drop) in self-esteem, probably associated with the drop-in status from being the most senior students in a (relatively) small primary school to being one of the youngest students in a school that could be several times larger. By contrast, students in the third group, which was not only experiencing the shift from primary to secondary school status but also telescoping the first two high school years into one, experienced only a modest dip in self-esteem. Their scores started off high and remained high. Some teachers in the schools employing the blend of acceleration and grouping expressed their concern that the use of two treatments rather than one might be 'a bridge too far'. It does not seem to have been. Rather it seems to be an effective mode of blending two interventions whose effectiveness for supporting gifted students' self-esteem is already acknowledged. Implications for research and practice that links with current research will be elaborated.

Keywords

Academically gifted high school students · Ability grouping · Acceleration · Self-esteem · Task-orientation

The aims in this chapter are to:
1. Narrate a vignette to illustrate academically gifted student school experiences.
2. Provide a review of the advantages of ability grouping and acceleration for gifted high school students in Australia.
3. Explore the relationship between ability grouping, acceleration, and self-esteem for academically gifted students.
4. Example a concurrent study on acceleration with ability grouping and self-esteem.
5. Elaborate some implications for research and practice for enhancing self-esteem when accelerating and/or ability grouping academically gifted students.

Miraca's Personal Vignette

I was born and brought up in Scotland and entered school three months before my fifth birthday which was pretty normal in my country at that time. Our teacher, Miss Kay read us a story to settle us down on that first morning. She was a magical reader;

the story sprang to life and I fell in love with her right there and then! Somehow she found out that I, too, could read and she put me on an individualised reading program... rather as she did later, with James (Wee Jamie) who was developmentally delayed. Wee Jamie and I felt we were special to Miss Kay and we knew that she didn't mind us being different... Jamie in his way and me in my way.

By the end of the school year I was reading Enid Blyton's *Secret Seven* books. By the end of the year Wee Jamie was reading. He cried with happiness and I cried too with happiness *for* him. We were good friends. Well, nobody else in our class liked us very much. (What may have been some of the reasons?)

At the end of the year, like all our classmates, Wee Jamie and I had to move up to the next grade. Our new teacher, Miss Charter, tut-tutted at me, told me I shouldn't be reading books that were 'much too old' for me and put me back on what she informed my mother (in my presence) were 'age-appropriate' books. This was the first time I heard that term. I heard it many times in the following few years. Everyone at school wanted me to *be* 'age-appropriate'... in what I read, in how I spoke, and in how I behaved... but no-one could explain clearly what 'it' *was* that they wanted me to be; only what it *wasn't*.

Something that *was* new to us that year, however, was the school's prize award structure at the end-of-year prize-giving ceremony. The top three students in each class won prizes. The next six were awarded 'certificates of merit'. I came second in my class and therefore, to my delight, won a prize.

The day after the prize-giving (the last day of term), I was beaten up for the first time. Sheila, the girl who came first and Bob, the boy who came third, weren't beaten up. I couldn't work out *why*. Why me but not Bob or Sheila? Then it dawned on me. Sheila, who came first in the academic prize list, had also won all the races for our grade level at the previous week's sports day! Bob, who came second in the main race, just behind Sheila, was also rewarded then and there by his father... who also provided candies for the rest of the class! Me? I came last in every race, fell on my backside in the last one and was cuddled by Miss Kay who gently told me that I jumped high in my mind and my imagination and that it didn't matter a *great* deal that I didn't jump high in my body.

Sheila was the playground leader among the girls. She was (obviously!) a fast runner, incredibly skilled at rope skipping and owned a dog called Bruce after the Scottish patriot hero, King Robert the Bruce. Bob had a cousin who was a national football hero and he was already being coached every weekend by his famous cousin (or so he told us). And he had a pony, no less! A pony! Me? I had two left feet, no famous family, and a goldfish called Susie. I just simply wasn't 'politically correct winner' material. So I felt it would be a lot safer and a lot less fuss if I simply didn't *win* anything anymore... or if I just aimed at getting a certificate of merit... or, at the very least, if I confined myself to winning a prize that wasn't much valued by the other students.

So I aimed at coming 4th–6th in the class which would gain me a certificate of merit and would hopefully protect me from being beaten up... but also getting *some* sort of prize to keep my much-loved mother happy. What prize did I choose to aim for? The *Burns* Prize: a prize for reciting the poetry of Scotland's national poet, Robert Burns.

Certainly, kids who won the Burns Prize were regarded, by the other kids, as *utter nerds*, but as I was regarded as a nerd in any case, I decided I had nothing to lose if I won the darned thing ... and it would keep my mother quiet! (Also, and most importantly, I genuinely adored Burns' poetry!)

And would you believe it, my strategy worked! *Nobody* in the school seemed to mind me winning the Burns Prize (although some of the parents were vocal in their belief that my mother 'coached' me in recitation skills! ... Indeed, I won it that year and every year thereafter. There was no fuss made about that; the 'fuss' didn't start until 7th grade—or final year of elementary school in the Scottish education system at that time—when schools entered 7th grade students for a nationwide competition *built around* the poetry of Burns. And, oh boy, did the Heavens open! I won first prize for Scotland!

The school was ecstatic and held a special assembly to which all the local dignitaries were invited. My name was mentioned—but *very* briefly—and I wasn't even brought up on to the stage! Rather, the focus was placed firmly on how well *the school* fostered individual abilities.

I was revolted by the whole setup. I may have been only 11 but I knew hypocrisy when I saw it. Intellectually gifted children are in general, quite skilled in the higher-level reasoning skills of analysis, synthesis and evaluation (Chichekian & Shore, 2014). If a school is placing its gifted students at the service of the school rather than seeing itself as also being of service to the students, the gifted students *are* likely to realise this earlier than the others, and to resent it more. They may be placed in a forced-choice dilemma (Gross, 1989) in which they have to choose between intimacy (affection and *peer* acceptance) and achievement (success and *teacher* approval). *This is a critical lesson for schools to learn.*

Everyone is influenced to some degree by their school experience so let me briefly share a little more of mine. At the end of seven deeply unhappy primary and elementary school years, I gained a place in a Selective High School—a state school for academically gifted students—where I found enormous intellectual satisfaction, friends who shared my passion for learning and teachers who showed, and were happy to show it, a passion for teaching. The work was inspiring and I loved every day of it. I didn't top my class but I soared in my spirit. I found there were things I could do that I had never *dreamed* I could do.

In the first week, I met three girls who became lifelong friends. Elspeth, Janet, Dorothy ... and *me*—first author. We called ourselves 'the quartet' because there were four of us and because we harmonised so well. In the middle of the year, Myra, a new girl joined us. She was *so* shy and scared. The four of us looked at each other, opened our arms to her and we became a quintet. Happiness makes you generous because you can look outside yourself.

Introduction

Gross (1993, 1997, 2006b, 2010) has used comparative case studies in her longitudinal research project that examined the academic, social, and emotional lives of 60 profoundly gifted students. Such cases provide vivid narratives of gifted students as they progress through school and help to inform future practice. Many profoundly gifted students in Gross' (2006b) study were provided with differentiation in the form of acceleration within varying ability grouped contexts. In recent times, extant research has used vignettes or personal narratives to reiterate the educational lives of accelerands that illuminate the many stories of gifted students around the world (e.g., Assouline, Colangelo, VanTassel-Baska, & Lupkowski-Shoplik, 2015; Gross, 2015; Young, Rogers, Hoekman, van Vliet, & Chan, 2015). These narratives are mirrored by the poignant vignette above, which alludes to the influence of acceleration and like-ability grouping for cognitively advanced students on their educational and social-emotional growth. These children's narratives are supported by extensive research elaborating the well-known fact that acceleration is the most research-supported strategy and effective programming option for gifted students (Assouline et al., 2015; Southern & Jones, 2015).

The primary focus in this chapter is to provide a perspective based on the compelling personal narrative of the main author, followed by theoretical foundations, and an exemplar of an empirical study. Additionally, there is an exploration of the wider research on ability grouping, acceleration, and self-esteem of gifted students in the Australian context. Research and practice implications will be gleaned to help guide future self-esteem development, acceleration, and ability grouping for academically gifted students.

Overview of Acceleration, Ability Grouping, and Self-Esteem

Joyce VanTassel-Baska, a leading American scholar in gifted education, described acceleration and grouping as "the lightning rod issues that test the level of acceptance that gifted programs enjoy in a school district" (1992, p. 69). She further pointed out that, "the greater the commitment to serving gifted students, the greater the acceptance of advancing and grouping them appropriately" (1992, p. 69).

Acceleration may provide the educational environment for talent development to ensue (Gross, 2016), as acceleration enables a gifted learner to work at their own educational pace through a more advanced curriculum, but usually at a higher level than their own age peers and with older peers with whom they are more cognitively and emotionally aligned (Gross, 2015). Types of acceleration may include grade skipping, curriculum compacting, dual enrolment, or content acceleration, all of which can address the individual learning needs and social-emotional development of the academically gifted student (Gross, 2016; Lupkowsi-Shoplik, Assouline, & Colangelo, 2015; Steenbergen-Hu, Makel, & Olszewski-Kubilius, 2016). Acceleration for gifted students is strongly supported in the research literature as an effective teaching technique, is cost effective, easier to implement than most gifted education provisions and provides the contextual opportunity for students to be grouped with like-minded peers at similar developmental levels (Assouline et al., 2015; Neihart & Yeo, 2018; Rogers, 2015; Southern & Jones, 2015).

Such grouping for acceleration nurtures academic achievement which is reliant on the match between the teaching and learning environment with the students' individual abilities and needs (Makel, Lee, Olszewski-Kubilius, & Putallz, 2012;

Rogers, 2007). Ability grouping provides the instructional context within which like-ability students can be taught and can learn together (Vogl & Preckel, 2014). Ability grouping also has a strong research base as both a context and a strategy to support academic achievement (Rogers, 2007; Steenbergen-Hu et al., 2016). However, in Australia, ability grouping in the form of accelerands being grouped together is limited in the early years of schooling when it is thought to be most beneficial and it is applied more from middle primary onwards in special classes or pullout classes (Gross, 2006b). There are also strong foundations in the research literature, for the benefits of ability grouping for supporting both academic and social-emotional growth (Rogers, 2007).

Combining acceleration and ability grouping for self-esteem development is also founded on a firm research base (Gross, 2015; Rogers, 2007). *Self-esteem* in this context is the gifted child's opinion of their own self-worth and having confidence in their own ability. Self-esteem can be positively or negatively orientated towards self and there are different types of self-esteem, for example, social self-esteem, however, the focus here is on *academic* self-esteem. Academic self-esteem is the gifted student's view of their academic education, ability, and achievement and self-esteem underlies individual well-being (Gross, 2010).

The integration of acceleration with ability grouping enables the link to developmentally relevant curriculum and pedagogy so gifted students can learn at their level of academic capacity (Gross, 2016). However, such a combination also produces social-emotional benefits as well. For example, "it is in the early years of school that we should be identifying exceptionally and profoundly gifted children and developing programs of [both] acceleration and grouping to provide a more effective response to their accelerated intellectual and emotional development" (Gross, 2006b, p. 426), so students do not have to compromise their intellectual and emotional growth for peer acceptance (Gross, 2010).

The *Australian Curriculum and Reporting Authority* (ACARA) and most Australian gifted educational and association policies use Gagné's (2013) *Differentiating* (previously Differentiated) *Model of Gifted and Talent* (DMGT) conception of giftedness and talent. According to Gagné, in his DMGT academically gifted students are more advanced intellectually, in the top 10% cognitively, and show earlier readiness for learning, that is, learn more abstractly, quickly, and conceptually than their chronologically similar peers. Such characteristics of the intellectually gifted child engender them as perfect candidates for accelerated teaching and learning. The most influential report on acceleration is *A Nation Deceived* (Colangelo, Assouline, & Gross, 2004). Combined with its follow-up report, *A Nation Empowered* (Assouline et al., 2015), they impart detailed definitions and information on the characteristics of gifted students and research that emphatically supports acceleration and ability grouping.

While prospective accelerands gravitate naturally to older, developmentally similar peers for friendships, social connection, and same-interest intellectual stimulation, acceleration opportunities also link like-ability peers within a variety of grouping contexts that enable access to developmentally appropriate learning for advanced learners (Gross, 2009, 2010). Such grouping may also include cluster grouping within classes or special classes or special schools, such as selective schools (see Southern & Jones, 2015; Steenbergen-Hu et al., 2016 for detailed definitions and examples of ability grouping and acceleration).

Selective schooling is one form of ability grouping that has been available in Australia for nearly three decades (Gross, 2004c). Selective high schools are government schools that provide full-time ability grouping and also provide ability grouping within this context for academically gifted students across most Australian states (Kronborg & Cornejo-Araya, 2018; North & Griffiths, 2019). However, the existence of such special schools for gifted students is overshadowed by controversial perspectives. These perspectives derive from wider societal views that are focused on egalitarian and inclusive practices and where selective schools are viewed as exclusive and elitist. Outcomes of government reviews (e.g., Senate Reference Committee, 2001) and independent enquiries (e.g., Vinson, 2002) perpetuate these views by insisting that gifted students should stay in general comprehensive high schools to retain social, societal, and economic cohesiveness and inclusiveness. The prevailing view is that removing gifted students from local comprehensive public schools disadvantages other students who may be deprived of the leadership, role modelling, and tutorship of gifted students and that gifted students' social-emotional well-being may be inhibited in selective school contexts (Assouline et al., 2015; Smith, 2017). Very little consideration is given to the benefits of like-ability grouping for the well-being and achievement of academically advanced students (Gross, 2004c). In a recent review of the admission process for selective schools by the New South Wales Department of Education (NSW DET, 2018), it is stated that educators in selective schools need to:

> encourage and support high achievement for academically gifted students, [by] creating a specialist school environment for advanced academic study. Families and community groups report that selective schools provide social and emotional benefits to gifted students, who have opportunities to flourish by learning alongside like-minded peers in a supportive environment that accepts and celebrates high ability. (NSW DET, 2018, para. 4)

Indeed, a study by Long, Barnett, and Rogers (2015) found that teachers in selective high schools were more likely to differentiate the curriculum or accelerate academically gifted students, than teachers in comprehensive high schools. While initial dips in self-esteem of intellectually gifted students when starting at a selective school setting have been found in some studies, possibly due to the additional challenge and no longer being the 'big fish in the small pond', it has also been shown that familiarisation with ability grouping in selective schools plateaus and increases gifted students' self-esteem over time (Gross, 2001, 2002, 2004c).

Ability Grouping for Acceleration

Nearly three decades ago, two major syntheses of research conducted by American scholars Karen Rogers (1991) and James Kulik (1992) established two facts very strongly: (1) ability grouping of gifted and talented students results in enhanced academic achievement; and (2) full-time ability grouping of gifted and talented students produces *powerful* academic gains. Recent second-order meta-analyses supports these facts and goes one step further:

> ...the conversation needs to evolve beyond whether such interventions can ever work. There is not an absence of evidence, nor is there evidence of absence of benefit. The preponderance of existing evidence accumulated over the past century suggests that academic acceleration and most forms of ability grouping like cross-grade subject grouping and special grouping for gifted students can greatly improve K–12 students' academic achievement. (Steenbergen-Hu et al., 2016, p. 893)

Grouping gifted students with like-ability peers can allow them to progress at their own pace because they are no longer restrained by having to work at a pace substantially below their *natural* rate (Gross, 2010). Furthermore, grouping gifted students with like-ability peers allows teachers to use methods and tools of instruction that are geared to these students' levels of ability and achievement (Jung & Gross, 2015). These two facts have been known to the research and teaching community in education for nearly 30 years (Assouline et al., 2015; Colangelo et al., 2004; Rogers, 1991; Steenbergen-Hu et al., 2016). Certainly Elspeth, Janet, Dorothy, Myra, and Miraca noticed and were deeply gladdened by the quality of the teaching and the intellectual challenge provided by the work they were given in the selective high school.

A third practical advantage of ability grouping is that it provides a realistic range of competition that challenges and stimulates students (Preckel, Goetz, & Frenzel, 2010). The value of realistic and friendly competition in students who are gifted in sports, athletics, and music is recognised by society at large; academically gifted students should likewise have the opportunity to engage in realistic and friendly competition which does not require them to 'dumb down' to conceal their ability for peer acceptance (Gross, 2006b).

Ability grouping also raises gifted students' levels of social and general self-esteem (Gross, 2001). At primary school, Miraca was an unwilling 'soloist' and very lonely. In the fulltime grouping structure of the selective high school she was accepted and indeed liked and the knowledge that she was acceptable and likeable changed the way she felt about herself profoundly.

Academic underachievement is still a significant issue in gifted education with some researchers theorising up to 40% of gifted students may be in this category (Figg, Rogers, McCormick, & Low, 2012; White, Graham, & Blaas, 2018). Gifted underachievers are thought to achieve well below their potential capacity for academic performance (Cross & Cross, 2017). "Indeed, requiring a child to stay with age-peers when he or she is more than ready to move on and up to the work of the next grade is imposing underachievement on the child through the imposition of unnecessary and tedious curriculum review" (Gross, 2015, p. 12). Lack of academic motivation is also said to contribute to underachievement (Chan, 1996). Ability grouping with a differentiated curriculum can lead to a significant drop in deliberate underachievement and increased peer acceptance (Gross, 2015). Also, gifted students may even, for the first time, have to put in more effort and strive for success!

And lastly, ability grouping is a huge gift to the teacher; it makes teaching both easier and more effective by reducing the range of achievement found in any class (Gross, 1999). If educators recognise the following three fundamental principles of effective learning and effective teaching, then this question must be asked: If it is true that: (1) learning is a developmental and sequential process; (2) that there are striking differences in developmental rates among individuals of the same age; and (3) that effective teaching must be grounded where the learner currently is, then how can we justify an educational system that ignores competence and achievement and utilises chronological age as the primary, or only, factor in student placement (Gross, 1999)?

Acceleration in its many forms allows gifted students who are academically swift learners, and who are also socially and emotionally mature for their age, to pass through primary or secondary school in fewer years than is customary (Assouline et al., 2015; Southern & Jones, 2015). Some selective high schools in Sydney allow highly gifted students to telescope Years 7 and 8 into a single year—which is a synthesis of ability grouping and acceleration. Associated with such acceleration and ability grouping, there always seems to be societal mutterings about what effect this might have on these students' self-esteem but, in fact, according to Gross's (1993, 1997, 2006b) previous findings, the gifted students blossomed and thrived on it.

Effects of Acceleration on Gifted Students

Southern, Jones and Fiscus (1989) identified four major concerns that teachers held regarding the possibly maladaptive effects of acceleration on gifted students. They would:

(a) Lose their academic advantage in later school years.
(b) Experience difficulties in social and emotional development.
(c) Lack the physical and emotional maturity to work with older children.
(d) Become arrogant and elitist.

By contrast, longitudinal studies of accelerated gifted students show that they experience both short-term and long-term satisfaction with their acceleration (Gross, 2006b, 2015). These students report enhanced achievement motivation (Chan, 1996; Dai, Moon, & Feldhusen, 1998; McCoach, Yu, Gottfried, & Gottfried, 2017; Nicholls, 1983), increased friendship choices (Assouline et al., 2015; Gross, 2009), and greater enjoyment of school and learning (Colangelo et al., 2004; Gross, 2004a, 2004b; VanTassel-Baska, 1986).

However, in the authors' experience, the Australian teachers' unions have always been wary of special provisions for gifted students (also see the report commissioned by the Teachers' Federation; Vinson, 2002). The following sentiments are echoes from the past where the New South Wales (NSW) Teachers Federation raised the spectra of *social class divisiveness* by describing academically gifted students seeking early entry into university as:

the talented child brigade who have been pushing their middle-class wheelbarrow all the way to the University ... The sons and daughters of middle-class yuppies trying to steel (sic) more and more privileges under pretensions to greater abilities bestowed on them not by their class position but by God himself. (Poulos, 1990, p. 8)

Sadly, views such as these are still purported in the research literature with the gifted referred to as '*so-called* gifted and talented' students, under the guise of the need for inclusion, equity, and excellence influenced by global socio-economic needs, with elitism partially attributed to identification processes mainly focused on IQ measures (e.g., see Rasmussen & Lingard, 2018, p. 877). Such views are at the expense of the recognition of giftedness in students and their need for differentiation through acceleration and ability grouping for their personal well-being and to achieve excellence as a way to overcome large degrees of underachievement in academically gifted students (Gross, 2010; Kronborg & Cornejo-Araya, 2018; White et al., 2018).

Self-Esteem: Task-Involvement and Ego-Involvement

The authors considered whether shifts in self-esteem were also related to students' motivational orientation towards what Nicholls (1983) called task-involvement or ego-involvement. Task-involvement and ego-involvement are elements of intrinsic and extrinsic motivation, respectively. In ego-involvement, learning is a means to the end of looking smart and attention is focused on the self. On the other hand, in task-involvement learning is more inherently valuable, meaningful, and satisfying and attention is focused on the task and strategies to manage it rather than on the self. Feldhusen (1985) proposed that gifted students are generally characterised by a high degree of task-involvement. In a previous study by Gross (1997), reported elsewhere, gifted students were more motivationally orientated through task-involvement than self- or ego-involvement than their same-age typical ability peers. This is supported by a study by Chan (1996), who reported similar results.

Further, Gross (2006b) reported that accelerands' academic self-esteem was nurtured more likely through their seeking and mastering learning challenges, rather than wanting to surpass their peers through ego-orientated goal-seeking (i.e., "become a very visibly big fish in a little pond", 2006b, pp. 422–423). Indeed,

> substantial acceleration allows exceptionally gifted children to realize, often for the first time, the full extent of their abilities and therefore what they can *realistically* expect of themselves. Their moderate levels of self-esteem reflect a realization of how far they still have to go if they are to become all that they can be. (Gross, 2006b, p. 423)

During the authors' years of teaching gifted students in primary schools, high task-involvement was observed. Gross (1997) further hypothesised through her study that students in selective high schools (SHS) would, on average, present as significantly more task-involved than students in comprehensive high schools. Hence, the authors further hypothesised that students who *were* oriented towards ego-involvement would be more likely to focus on a comparison of their academic performance against that of their new classmates. Thus, they would be likely to have *lower academic self-esteem* in the SHS environment than students who were oriented towards task-involvement and who would focus on the intellectual challenge offered by the new environment rather than on comparisons against classmates.

Assessing Self-Esteem of Gifted Students and Non-gifted Students: An Exemplar Study

The example case study provided here imparts some findings from a larger longitudinal study reported elsewhere (e.g., Gross, 1993, 1997, 2004b, 2006b, 2009, 2010) where less than half of the profoundly gifted participants were accelerated. However, the case study outcomes reiterated that every accelerand benefitted from accelerative practices, were able to form long-term friendships and were academically and professionally successful (Gross, 2006b, 2010). In Gross' (2006b) longitudinal study, every student who was accelerated, benefitted from acceleration:

> In every case, these young people have experienced positive short-term and long-term academic and socio-affective outcomes. The pressure to underachieve for peer acceptance lessened significantly or disappeared after the first acceleration. (Gross, 2006b, p. 415)

The major concerns of educators were for the self-esteem of the accelerands, which inhibited radical or further acceleration for some of the participants in Gross' (2006b, 2007a) study. In fact, the non-accelerands in Gross' (2007c) study reported more social and emotional disconnections with peers and academic disengagement due to educational misplacement and the pedagogical mismatch with their learning needs. This coincides with findings in other research (e.g., Dare, Smith, & Nowicki, 2016; Gross & Van Vliet, 2005).

Instrumentation

In this example study, Gross (1993, 1997, 2006b, 2015) used the *Coopersmith Self-esteem Inventory* (Coopersmith, 1981) to measure four different aspects of self-esteem:

- *General*: Feelings about oneself as a manager of one's own life.
- *Academic*: Feelings about oneself as a learner.
- *Social*: Feelings about oneself as a member of the peer culture.
- *Home/family*: Feelings about oneself as a family member.

This test also generates a global score, but this should only be reported when one is also reporting subscale scores. It also includes a lie-scale that functions as an index of defensiveness or test-wiseness.

Gross assessed students on the *Coopersmith SEI* on three separate occasions during the students' Year 7 (their first year in secondary school). These occasions were: (a) in the first three days of Year 7; (b) six weeks later; and (c) six months later. See Gross (1993, 1997, 2006b) for the detailed data collection process.

Motivational Orientation

Gagné (2013) cites motivation as one catalyst to support talent development. Motivation orientation is viewed as the desire to learn, usually through orientations such as willingness for task mastery and seeking goal development that are linked with attitudes about self and context (Chan, 1996; Gross, 1995). Pilot studies for this exemplar project, which allowed preliminary versions of the *I Feel This Way (IFTW)* instrument to be developed and trialled, were conducted earlier in NSW state schools and reported to the Selective High Schools Principals' Conference (see the first author for a copy of the instruments used in this example study). Following successful trials, *I Feel This Way* was employed to assess motivational orientation towards task-involvement or ego-involvement.

Students completed the 28-item self-report *I Feel This Way* questionnaire on the first day of testing. The questionnaire items were scored on a 5-point Likert scale giving a possible range of total scores of 28–140. Respondents were asked to check the degree to which each of the statements reflected the way they felt, ranging from 'I never or hardly ever feel this way' to 'I always or almost always feel this way'.

Participants: Year 7 Selective High School Students

Subjects of the study comprised the entire cohort of Year 7 students from nine co-educational and single-sex Selective High Schools (n = 1462) and a comparison group of Year 7 students from co-educational and single-sex Comprehensive High Schools (n = 514) in NSW, Australia. For two reasons, no test of ability or achievement was given to the comparison group. First, the Selective High Schools Test was unavailable, being a restricted instrument and in addition, the off-level components of its achievement measures would almost certainly be too difficult for many of the comparison group. Second, standard achievement tests designed for their age-peers would have generated a ceiling effect for many students in selective high schools. However, the assumption was made that the comparison group contained something close to the full spread of ability normally found in an Australian Comprehensive High School.

Bouddhi High School (pseudonym), one of the nine SHS in this study, employed several forms of acceleration with students who were highly gifted in several academic areas. For example, one of the Bouddhi Year 7 classes was a self-contained gifted class which was telescoping Year 7 and 8 into a single year; a synthesis of ability grouping and acceleration. This selective accelerated class (n = 30) formed the third group in the study.

The Coopersmith SEI was administered on three occasions to the selective group (n = 1462), selective accelerated group (n = 30), and comparison group (n = 514), that is, in the: (1) first week of February (the first week of the Australian school year), (2) mid-March, and (3) August. *I Feel This Way* was administered to all three groups at the February testing.

Students who were absent on any of the three testing days or who had an SEI lie-scale score greater than 5 (out of a possible 8) on any of the three occasions were omitted from the analysis leaving an *n* of 1066 for the selective group and 291 for the comparison group. Attrition was significantly greater in the comparison group than in the SHS group. The selective accelerated class remained at n = 30.

Effects of Ability Grouping and Acceleration on the Self-Esteem of Academically Gifted High School Students

What was found regarding motivational orientation? As Feldhusen (1985) had proposed and as this study had hypothesised, significant differences in motivational orientation were indeed found between students in comprehensive and selective high schools with SHS students being *very* considerably more task-involved than age-peers in regular or comprehensive schooling $F(1, 1355) = 31.48$, $p < 0.0001$.

Students in selective high schools seem to be more likely to be powered by 'learning goals'—'the desire to increase one's competence, to understand or master something new' (Elliot & Dweck, 1988) rather than 'performance goals'—the desire to seek out external favourable judgment of their abilities or avoid unfavourable judgment.

Certainly, Selective High School students are competitive—competition is very much a part of Australian culture—but in general they are oriented to competing against themselves, wanting to improve their own understanding and mastery, rather than competing against their classmates (Chan, 1996; Gross, 1997).

Interesting patterns appeared when self-esteem shifts over the course of the year were compared on three occasions between comprehensive and selective high schools. Social, home/parents, general, and total self-esteem rose significantly in both groups while academic self-esteem showed a significant decrease for selective students. However, *even with this decrease*, the social, general, academic, and total self-esteem of selective high-school students was significantly higher on all three testings than that of their age-peers in mixed-ability comprehensive high schools.

When you think of it, this isn't surprising. Students entering Bouddhi's accelerated class (within the selective school) knew first that they were entering an extremely challenging environment and second that at the end of the year they would be compared not only with their age-peers, but also with the Year 8 students with whom they would be joining in Year 9 (Table 1).

Teachers in high schools traditionally spend the first few weeks of Year 7 in revision to find out what their students already know in their subject area—after all, the students come from a wide range of 'feeder' primary schools. The *significant* academic self-esteem shift occurred in subsequent months when the introduction of

Table 1 Self-esteem subscale and total scores for Selective and Comprehensive High School students in February, March and August

	Selective school			Comprehensive school			F. between	F. within	F. interaction
	Feb	March	August	Feb	March	August			
Social	12.23	12.73	12.70	11.68	12.30	12.47	3.94 ($p < 0.05$)	22.60 ($p < 0.001$)	1.27 ($p < 0.283$)
Home/parents	12.42	12.58	12.37	11.64	12.16	12.36	2.52 ($p < 0.114$)	6.96 ($p < 0.002$)	6.61 ($p < 0.002$)
Academic	11.95	11.88	11.14	10.81	11.41	10.99	9.40 ($p < 0.003$)	14.48 ($p < 0.001$)	10.97 ($p < 0.001$)
General	38.85	40.23	40.17	34.74	37.08	37.76	33.02 ($p < 0.001$)	47.93 ($p < 0.001$)	6.37 ($p < 0.003$)
Total	75.45	77.42	76.38	68.87	72.95	73.59	20.59 ($p < 0.001$)	33.16 ($p < 0.001$)	10.45 ($p < 0.001$)

new, more challenging, material required the students to *work* at what they were doing! For the gifted students this may have been a new and disturbing experience, where they had not been previously challenged academically!

A similar decrease in academic self-esteem appeared in the comparison group but the pattern was different—an initial rise from February to March followed by a sharp decline March–August which parallels the March–August SHS decline. Perhaps this arose from 'culture shock' as the new, harder work was introduced after the first few weeks of revision of Year 6 work. Comparison group students may have been misled into thinking that Year 7 work would be easier than they had expected. From Gross's (1997) previous findings, she did not believe the decrease in academic self-esteem in selective high school students was derived from an ego-involved comparison of themselves against other gifted students. However, Gross (2006b) does believe that these *task-involved* students were experiencing, for the first time, the need to match themselves against academically rigorous work that requires them to *strive* to succeed.

The SHS students between March and August were coming to realise the full extent of their abilities and therefore what they could expect of themselves. The decline in academic self-esteem reflected their realisation, for the first time, of the gap between their high achievement and their even higher potential. For many, it also reflects an acceptance of how far they still have to go if they are to become all they can be.

Self-Esteem: Selective School Accelerated Class Cohort

A particularly interesting finding of this study was that the gifted students in the accelerated class at a Selective High School, which is telescoping 7th and 8th grade into one year, displayed significantly higher self-esteem on all subscales of the SEI, and on the total score, than students in comprehensive high schools, and also displayed significantly higher social, general, home/parents, and total self-esteem than SHS students not experiencing this form of intervention in selective schools (Table 2).

Furthermore, this special acceleration class, which is experiencing the 'optimal environment' created by marrying differentiated teaching (i.e., strategies and processes) with a challenging and broad curriculum (i.e., learning content with depth and breadth) to fulltime ability grouping (i.e., educational environment) and thoughtfully planned and monitored acceleration (i.e., faster pace, density), is the only group of children in the study which did *not* display a significant decrease in academic self-esteem over the course of the year! If the drop in academic self-esteem were a function of the 'Big Fish Little Pond Effect' (Gross 2006a), surely the Bouddhi accelerated cohort, who were compacting two years' study into one and preparing to enter Grade 9 the following year with students a year older than themselves, would have experienced an even greater decline than SHS students who were not so accelerated. Yet, the opposite occurred: the decline in academic self-esteem was considerably less for the accelerated class cohort than for the other SHS students (0.21 as against 0.83)! This is a very powerful finding.

Table 2 Self-esteem subscales and total scores for Selective High School accelerated and non-accelerated students in February, March and August

	Accelerated Students			Non-accelerated Students			F. between	F. within	F. interaction
	Feb	March	August	Feb	March	August			
Social	13.58	14.42	14.21	12.20	12.70	12.67	4.40 ($p < 0.037$)	1.96 ($p < 0.142$)	0.11 ($p < 0.893$)
Home/parents	15.16	15.05	14.74	12.37	12.54	12.33	8.43 ($p < 0.005$)	0.30 ($p < 0.741$)	0.14 ($p < 0.867$)
Academic	12.53	12.63	12.32	11.94	11.86	11.11	1.59 ($p < 0.208$)	1.32 ($p < 0.268$)	0.36 ($p < 0.701$)
General	43.79	44.53	45.58	38.76	40.15	40.07	6.60 ($p < 0.010$)	1.85 ($p < 0.159$)	0.24 ($p < 0.769$)
Total	85.05	86.63	86.84	75.27	77.25	76.19	7.86 ($p < 0.006$)	0.83 ($p < 0.439$)	0.10 ($p < 0.904$)

These highly gifted, strongly task-involved students experienced a high level of academic challenge from almost their first week in the Selective High School. Their teachers—who were trained in gifted education—spent very little time reviewing 6th grade work; the whole premise of this class was that they would be ready for 8th grade work half way through the year. They knew that, in order to cover two years' work in one year, they would have to work hard, and they had received objective affirmation, both through their scores on the Selective High Schools' entry test and through selection for the accelerated class that they were capable of doing this. They were working with, and supported by, other task-involved, keenly motivated students who were undertaking the same program. They experienced success in a challenging, fast-paced learning environment and they received well-merited praise and affectionate, supportive guidance not only from their teachers but from each other—because it is in precisely this type of ability grouped setting that peer modelling can work and, indeed, works superbly. Indeed, teachers at Bouddhi had commented to the first author about the 'cohort effect' of peer bonding and mutual encouragement that appeared in this accelerated class. They like each other, they are similar in their abilities and interests, they are not ego-competitive, and they have a common goal. No wonder their academic self-esteem stayed high! Miraca's quintet certainly experienced such peer bonding, modelling, like-interests, and task-orientation.

Implications for Research and Practice

Miraca used her own childhood experiences as a foundation for her career in gifted education. Part of her far-sighted approach included longitudinal comparative case studies of profoundly gifted students that replicated, affirmed, and extended her educational experiences and her friends' (the quintet's), that were illustrated in the earlier vignette. Such cases have informed both Australian research and international research for decades (Assouline et al., 2015; Colangelo et al., 2004). Overall, in the exemplar study and in Gross' previous research (Gross, 2015), accelerands reported that they were supportive of acceleration and ability grouping practices, while gifted non-accelerands expressed that their social-emotional growth was impaired due to not being accelerated.

Today, in Australia a few researchers have investigated perspectives of acceleration and ability grouping practices, for example:

- Parents and gifted children's views of grade-based acceleration (Dare et al., 2016; Dare, Nowecki, & Smith, 2019);
- Radical acceleration (Jung & Gross, 2015).

It appears that no Australian researchers have explored acceleration and ability grouping combined and with constructs, such as self-esteem, though social-emotional needs have been examined more generally. For example:

- Teachers' and parents' attitudes towards ability grouping and acceleration and social-emotional development (Gallagher & Smith, 2013; Gallagher, Smith, & Merrotsy, 2011);

Additionally, research in selective schools with a variety of foci has included, for example:

- Teacher competencies in selective schools (Kronborg & Plunkett, 2012);
- Effectiveness of combining enrichment with acceleration (Kaman & Kronborg, 2012);
- Teachers and Principals in selective schools were more likely than in comprehensive schools to provide or partake in professional learning and implement gifted education policies (Long et al., 2015);
- The effects of academic pressure on gifted students in high-stakes exam contexts (North, Smith, & Gross, 2015).

Australian research is also emerging on gifted students in universities, for example:

- Decision-making and career choices (Jung & Young, 2019);
- Early entry to college (Jung, Young, & Gross, 2015).

Leveraging the momentum of the newly revised Australian policies and the new selective entry processes in NSW with corresponding research can support the ongoing use of research-based accelerative teaching strategies and models. The findings from the example study in this chapter suggested that acceleration in the form of advanced classes with two grade years telescoped into one year may advantage the self-esteem of committed academically gifted students who seek task-orientated challenges. Nonetheless, the study exampled here had limitations, such that it was too small and belated to generalise to today's context, but it does provide an incentive to replicate this study. While the Australian research on acceleration and ability grouping mirrors the international findings (e.g., Assouline et al., 2015; Gross, Urquhart, Doyle, Juratowitch, & Matheson, 2011), none of the above studies have been replicated in Australia or they are replications of studies undertaken internationally—mainly the USA. Hence, these studies warrant replication here in Australia, and perhaps more widely within the Asia-Pacific regions, also across selective schools in different states of Australia or comparatively with New Zealand or in China, South Korea, or Vietnam, where special schools for the gifted are evident, and across special classes in different Australian states to explore what can be learnt from the diverse practices implemented in diverse cultural, or regional, or rural contexts. These may enlighten our practice regarding supporting gifted non-accelerands or gifted underachievers, especially as the telescoped acceleration class can be replicated in practice in any comprehensive school or selective schools generally.

The pervasive view from both educators and society that acceleration and ability grouping are harmful for social and emotional development has been refuted by the research, but more is still needed that matches the specific constructs (i.e., self-esteem) contextually and strategically (Dare et al., 2016; Neihart, 2007; Neihart & Yeo, 2018). For example, non–accelerands felt their social-emotional development was impeded by lack of acceleration and ability grouping in Gross' longitudinal study (1993, 1997, 2006b, 2010, 2015). More longitudinal studies across different gifted populations in different types of selective schools may inform future practice to reduce underachievement, that supports both the academic achievement as well as the self-esteem of diversely academically gifted students.

Most researchers and advocates argue for more teacher training on acceleration and ability grouping for either the academic achievement or the social-emotional development of intellectually gifted students (e.g., Dare et al., 2016; Gross et al., 2011; Lassig, 2009; Missett, Brunner, Callahan, Moon, & Price Azano, 2014; North & Griffiths, 2019; Rimlinger, 2018). While lack of training can inhibit acceleration and ability grouping for gifted students (Kronborg & Cornejo-Araya, 2018), pre-service teachers can hold more positive views of acceleration and ability grouping following preservice training (Plunkett & Kronborg, 2011).

Indeed, educators who have been accelerated as students or who have implemented acceleration for gifted students are more attitudinally supportive of acceleration and ability grouping (Gross, 2006b). It would be beneficial, therefore, for students if more narratives of their cases were elaborated through staff professional learning, or even incorporated into personal/social/emotional development programs for gifted students, so students themselves can see that others feel similar and they can learn from others' experiences and feel supported by them.

Even though accelerands support acceleration practices (mainly grade skipping and subject acceleration), reviews of Australian attitudes towards accelerative practices found that acceleration is reliant on parent or teacher perspectives, decision-making, and leadership within individual schools and educational systems (Gross et al., 2011; Long et al., 2015). As a consequence, ability-grouping and acceleration are implemented unsystematically. Both accelerands and non-accelerands who need acceleration should be taught how to self-advocate for their own needs, to be able to voice if both their academic and social-emotional needs are being addressed or not (Smith, 2017). This student 'voice' can be in the form of published narratives of their own educational experiences in books that can be used for in-class strategies, such as bibliotherapy targeting self-esteem issues, or in research cases like those exampled in this chapter, or in pathways to academia in the field where they can advocate through research like Miraca did.

Fortunately, there are several Australian associations for gifted students and parents of gifted students (e.g., Australian Association for the Education of the Gifted and Talented AAEGT; Gifted NSW; and Gifted and Talented Children's Association of South Australia, GTCASA). Association members support and advocate for acceleration and ability grouping and for a more holistic approach to educating gifted students (e.g., Rimlinger, 2018; Smith, 2017). Members also serve as willing conduits for researchers to access participants when researching accelerative practices (e.g., Dare et al., 2016).

However, in the research literature it is also recommended that differentiation for academically gifted students incorporating both acceleration and ability grouping should be enhanced by enrichment (Gross, 2015; Kaman & Kronborg, 2012; Long et al., 2015; VanTassel-Baska & Brown, 2009). Additionally, a recent Australian review of the literature imparted that:

> purposeful talent development programs, incorporating evidence-based effective practices and explicit teaching, are needed to optimise the achievement and talent development of gifted learners (Stoeger, Hopp, & Ziegler, 2017). Strategies such as academic acceleration, purposeful gifted student programs, enrichment and extension are needed to extend and challenge students with high academic potential (Steenbergen-Hu et al., 2016; Subotnik, Olszeski-Kubilius, & Worrell, 2011). We especially need to work towards closing excellence gaps in achievement for gifted students from disadvantaged groups, who may rely more heavily on schools to provide programs for talent development. (North & Griffiths, 2019, p. 19)

These disadvantaged groups can include indigenous, underachievers, gifted English language learners, those with twice exceptionality, or in disadvantaged socio-economic, cultural, rural, or remote contexts (Blackburn & Smith, 2018; Gross, 2007b; Kronborg & Cornejo-Araya, 2018). Australian Senate reports (Senate Reference Committee, 2001; Senate Select Committee, 1988) and policies on gifted education recommend the use of ability grouping and acceleration (with curriculum and instructional differentiation) as options to support academically gifted students, especially the disadvantaged. For example, the revised New South Wales Department of Education (NSW DET, 2019) High Potential and Gifted Education Policy:

> promotes engagement and challenge for every student, regardless of background, in every school across intellectual, creative, social-emotional and physical domains. It supports every student to achieve their educational potential, through talent development opportunities and differentiated teaching and learning practices to ensure that their specific learning and well-being needs are met. (para. 1)

However, acceleration and ability grouping must also be well-planned, regularly monitored and evaluated, and empathetically implemented so a relevant and challenging curriculum meets the students' developmental needs (Gross, 2008a, 2008b; Masters, 2015).

Conclusion

In this chapter, issues associated with ability grouping and acceleration effects on academically gifted students' self-esteem were elaborated. The effects of ability grouping and acceleration on gifted students' self-esteem are still controversial today. While previous studies have suggested that the self-esteem of academically gifted students reduces once they enter selective schools and they are no longer the 'big fish in the little pond', the small study reiterated here suggests that—taking into consideration the influences of the school schedule—selective schools in general and accelerated classes within selective schools specifically may help to increase self-esteem. The students in the example case study, where the challenge of two grade's content was covered in one year, were found to be task-motivated, rather than ego-orientated and their self-esteem was higher and more consistent than those who attended selective schools with single grade progression or comprehensive high schools.

A strong perspective based on a compelling personal story followed by some theoretical foundations and an example empirical study were provided within this chapter. In primary school, Miraca's poetry was nurtured by her parents rather than her teachers. It was not until she attended a selective high school with teachers who were trained in gifted education that she found a friendship group and the joy in the challenge of task orientation in her educational experience. "Possibly the greatest gift we can give to a gifted child is a teacher who recognizes the gift, who is not threatened by it, but rather rejoices in it and works with joy to foster it" (Gross, 2006b, p. 418).

Poet Robert Browning (1855) threw out an intellectual, emotional, and spiritual challenge: "Ah, but a man's [and woman's] reach should exceed his [or her] grasp or what's a heaven for?" Costa and Kallick (2009) responded by describing school as "a home for the mind" (p. 149), gently reminding us that school is no home for the mind unless it is also a home for the loving and questing spirit.

Cross-References

- Being of Like-Mind: Giftedness in the New Zealand Context
- Fostering Resilience in 'At-Risk' Gifted and Talented Young People
- Gifted Education in the Asia-Pacific: From the Past for the Future – An Introduction
- Highly Able Students in International Schools
- Implementing the DMGT's Constructs of Giftedness and Talent: What, Why, and How?
- Motivational Issues in Gifted Education: Understanding the Role of Students' Attribution and Control Beliefs, Self-Worth Protection and Growth Orientation
- Self-Regulated Learning for High-Ability and High-Achieving Students in Mixed-Ability Classrooms Throughout the Asia-Pacific
- Social and Emotional Needs and Learning Processes: Part II Introduction
- Some Implications for the Future of Gifted Education in the Asia-Pacific

References

Assouline, S. G., Colangelo, N., VanTassel-Baska, J., & Lupkowski-Shoplik, A. (Eds.). (2015). *A nation empowered: Evidence trumps the excuses holding back America's brightest students.*

John Templeton Foundation: Connie Belin and Jacqueline N. Iowa City, IA: Blank International Center for Gifted Education and Talent Development, The University of Iowa.

Blackburn, A. M., & Smith, S. R. (2018). Capacities, challenges, and curriculum for Australian learners with exceptional potential for English-language learning. In B. Wallace, D. Sisk, & J. Senior (Eds.), *SAGE handbook of gifted and talented education* (pp. 357–372). Los Angeles, CA: SAGE.

Browning, R. (1855). Andrea del Sarto in men and women poetry collection. Retrieved from https://www.poetryfoundation.org/poems/43745/andrea-del-sarto

Chan, L. K. S. (1996). Motivational orientations and metacognitive abilities of intellectually gifted students. *Gifted Child Quarterly, 40*(4), 184–193. https://doi.org/10.1177/001698629604000403

Chichekian, T., & Shore, B. M. (2014). Cognitive characteristics of the gifted reconceptualized in the context of inquiry learning and teaching. In N. Colangelo, S. G. Assouline, & M. U. M. Gross (Eds.), *A nation deceived: How schools hold back America's brightest students* (pp. 117–129). Iowa City, IA: John Templeton Foundation: Belin-Blank Center for Gifted and Talented Education, The University of Iowa.

Colangelo, N., Assouline, S. G., & Gross, M. U. M. (2004). A nation deceived: How schools hold back America's brightest students. In *Iowa City, IA: John Templeton Foundation: Belin-Blank Center for Gifted and Talented Education*. Iowa City, IA: The University of.

Coopersmith, S. (1981). *Self-esteem inventories: Manual*. Palo Alto, CA: Consulting Psychologists Press.

Costa, A. L., & Kallick, B. (2009). *Habits of mind across the curriculum: Practical and creative strategies for teachers*. Alexandria, VA: ASCD.

Cross, T., & Cross, J. (2017). Maximizing potential: A school-based conception of psychosocial development. *High Ability Studies, 28*(1), 43–58. https://doi.org/10.1080/13598139.2017.1292896

Dai, D. Y., Moon, S. M., & Feldhusen, J. F. (1998). Achievement motivation and gifted students: A social cognitive perspective. *Educational Psychologist, 33*(2–3), 45–63. https://doi.org/10.1080/00461520.1998.9653290

Dare, L., Nowecki, E. A., & Smith, S. R. (2019). On deciding to accelerate: High-ability students identify key considerations. *Gifted Child Quarterly, 63*(3), 159–171. https://doi.org/10.1177/0016986219828073

Dare, L., Smith, S. R., & Nowecki, E. (2016). Parents' experiences with their children's grade-based acceleration: Struggles, successes, and subsequent needs. *Australasian Journal of Gifted Education, 25*(2), 6–21. Retrieved from https://pdfs.semanticscholar.org/6436/8ea616d3ee58715e477d7dd1c565b6076799.pdf

Elliot, E. S., & Dweck, C. S. (1988). Goals: An approach to motivation and achievement. *Journal of Personality and Social Psychology, 54*(1), 5–12. https://doi.org/10.1037/0022-3514.54.1.5

Feldhusen, J. F. (Ed.). (1985). *Toward excellence in gifted education*. Denver, CO: Love.

Figg, S. D., Rogers, K. B., McCormick, J., & Low, R. (2012). Differentiating low performance of the gifted learner: Achieving, underachieving, and selective consuming students. *Journal of Advanced Academics, 23*(1), 53–71. Retrieved from https://doi.org/10.1177/1932202X11430000

Gagné, F. (2013). The DMGT: Changes within, beneath, and beyond. *Talent Development and Excellence, 5*(1), 5–19. Retrieved from https://www.researchgate.net/publication/285946236_The_DMGT_Changes_Within_Beneath_and_Beyond

Gallagher, S., & Smith, S. R. (2013). Acceleration for talent development: Parents' and teachers' perspectives on supporting the social and emotional needs of gifted children. *International Journal for Talent Development and Creativity (IJTDC), 1*(2), 97–112.

Gallagher, S., Smith, S. R., & Merrotsy, P. (2011). Teachers' perceptions of the socioemotional development of intellectually gifted primary aged students and their attitudes towards ability grouping and acceleration. *Gifted and Talented International, 26*(1–2), 11–24. https://doi.org/10.1080/15332276.2011.11673585

Gross, M. (1995). *Relationships between self-esteem and motivational orientation among gifted students in full-time programs*. Paper presented at The Henry B. and Jocelyn Wallace National Research Symposium on Talent Development, University of Iowa.

Gross, M. U. M. (1989). The pursuit of excellence or the search for intimacy? The forced-choice dilemma of gifted youth. *Roeper Review, 11*(4), 189–194. https://doi.org/10.1080/02783198909553207

Gross, M. U. M. (1993). *Exceptionally gifted children*. London, England: Routledge.

Gross, M. U. M. (1997). How ability grouping turns big fish into little fish or does it? Of optical illusions and optimal environments. *Australasian Journal of Gifted Education, 6*(2), 18–30.

Gross, M. U. M. (1999). Inequity in equity: The paradox of gifted education in Australia. *Australian Journal of Education, 43*(1), 87–103. https://doi.org/10.1177/000494419904300107

Gross, M. U. M. (2001). Ability grouping, self-esteem and the gifted: A study of optical illusions and optimal environments. Keynote presentation. In N. Colangelo & S. Assouline (Eds.), *Talent development 1V: Proceedings of the 4th Biennial Henry B. and Jocelyn Wallace National Research Symposium on Talent Development* (pp. 59–88). Scottsdale, AZ: Gifted Potential Press.

Gross, M. U. M. (2002). How ability grouping turns big fish into little fish—Or does it? Of optical illusions and optimal environments. In W. Vialle & J. Geake (Eds.), *The gifted enigma* (pp. 131–163). Sydney, NSW: Hawker Brownlow Education.

Gross, M. U. M. (2004a). Benefits of gifted acceleration. *Directions in Education, 13*(18), 2.

Gross, M. U. M. (2004b). *Exceptionally gifted children* (2nd ed.). London, England: RoutledgeFalmer.

Gross, M. U. M. (2004c). Selective high schools: A mainstream alternative. *Understanding Our Gifted, 16*(3), 25–27.

Gross, M. U. M. (2006a). Big fish in little ponds? Motivation, self-esteem, and ability grouping. *Understanding Our Gifted, 18*(2), 22–23.

Gross, M. U. M. (2006b). Exceptionally gifted children: Long-term outcomes of academic acceleration and non-acceleration. *Journal for the Education of the Gifted, 29*(4), 404–429. https://doi.org/10.4219/jeg-2006-247

Gross, M. U. M. (2007a). A longitudinal study of radical acceleration with exceptionally and profoundly gifted children. In K. Kay, D. Robson, & J. F. Brennan (Eds.), *High IQ kids* (pp. 212–243). Minneapolis, MN: Free Spirit Publishing.

Gross, M. U. M. (2007b). Strangers in a strange land: Gifted indigenous children. *Understanding Our Gifted, 20*(1), 26–27.

Gross, M. U. M. (2007c). When not "risking" acceleration is just too great a risk. *Understanding Our Gifted, 19*(3), 24–25.

Gross, M. U. M. (2008a). Musings: "Hasten slowly": Thoughtfully planned acceleration. *Understanding Our Gifted, 20*(2), 6–8.

Gross, M. U. M. (2008b). Highly gifted children and adolescents. In C. M. Callahan & J. A. Plucker (Eds.), *Critical issues and practices in gifted education: What the research says* (pp. 241–251). Waco, TX: Prufrock Press.

Gross, M. U. M. (2009). How do intellectually gifted children perceive friendship? *Understanding Our Gifted, 21*(4), 23–25.

Gross, M. U. M. (2010). *Miraca Gross in her own write: A lifetime in gifted education*. Sydney, NSW: GERRIC, UNSW.

Gross, M. U. M. (2015). Characteristics of able, gifted, highly gifted, exceptionally gifted, and profoundly gifted learners. In H. E. Viderger & C. R. Harris (Eds.), *Applied practice for educators of gifted and able learners* (pp. 3–24). Rotterdam, Netherlands: Sense Publishers.

Gross, M. U. M. (2016). *What is acceleration and why would we accelerate a child through school? An Australian Mensa initiative*. Australian Mensa Inc. Retrieved from https://www.mensa.org.au/giftedchildren/amii

Gross, M. U. M., Urquhart, R., Doyle, J., Juratowitch, M., & Matheson, G. (2011). *Releasing the brakes for high ability learners: Administer, teacher and parent attitudes and beliefs that block* or assist the implementation of school policies on academic acceleration. Sydney, NSW: Gifted Education Research, Resource and Information Centre (GERRIC), University of New South Wales. Retrieved from https://education.arts.unsw.edu.au/media/EDUCFile/Releasing_the_Brakes_Overview_A4__Nov2011.pdf

Gross, M. U. M., & Van Vliet, H. E. (2005). Why radical acceleration works and when to use it. *Understanding Our Gifted, 17*(2), 22–25.

Jung, J. Y., & Gross, M. U. M. (2015). Radical acceleration. In S. G. Assouline, N. Colangelo, J. VanTassel-Baska, & A. Lupkowski-Shoplik (Eds.), *A nation empowered: Evidence trumps the excuses holding back America's brightest students* (Vol. 2, pp. 199–208). Iowa City, IA: The Connie Belin and Jacqueline N. Blank International Center for Gifted Education and Talent Development, University of Iowa.

Jung, J. Y., & Young, M. (2019). The occupational/career decision-making processes of intellectually gifted adolescents from economically disadvantaged backgrounds: A mixed methods perspective. *Gifted Child Quarterly, 63*, 36–57. https://doi.org/10.1177/0016986218804575

Jung, J. Y., Young, M., & Gross, M. U. M. (2015). Early collage entrance in Australia. *Roeper Review, 37*(1), 19–28. https://doi.org/10.1080/02783193.2014.976323

Kaman, Y., & Kronborg, L. (2012). Perceptions of learning at a select entry accelerated high school for high ability students. *Australasian Journal of Gifted Education, 21*(2), 47–61. Retrieved from https://www.researchgate.net/publication/288096967_Perceptions_of_learning_at_a_select_entry_accelerated_high_school_for_high_ability_students

Kronborg, L., & Cornejo-Araya, C. A. (2018). Gifted educational provisions for gifted and highly able students in Victorian schools, Australia. *Universitas Psychologica, 17*(5), 1–14. https://doi.org/10.11144/Javeriana.upsy17–5.gepg

Kronborg, L., & Plunkett, M. (2012). Examining teacher attitudes and perceptions of teacher competencies required in a new selective high school. *Australasian Journal of Gifted Education, 21*, 33–47. Retrieved from https://search.informit.com.au/documentSummary;dn=098906367453401;res=IELAPA

Kulik, J. A. (1992). *An analysis of the research on ability grouping: Historical and contemporary perspectives.* Storrs, CT: National Research Center on the Gifted and Talented.

Lassig, C. J. (2009). Teachers' attitudes towards the gifted: The importance of professional development and school culture. *Australasian Journal of Gifted Education, 18*(2), 32–42.

Long, L. C., Barnett, K., & Rogers, K. B. (2015). Exploring the relationship between principal, policy, & gifted program scope and quality. *Journal for the Education of the Gifted, 38*, 118–140. https://doi.org/10.1177/0162353215578279

Lupkowsi-Shoplik, A., Assouline, S., & Colangelo, N. (2015). Whole-grade acceleration: Grade skipping and early entrance to kindergarten or first grade. In S. Assouline, N. Colangelo, J. VanTassel-Baska, & A. Lupkowski-Shoplik (Eds.), *A nation empowered: Evidence trumps the excuses holding back America's brightest students* (pp. 53–72). Iowa City, IA: The Connie Belin & Jacqueline N. Blank International Centre for Gifted Education and Talent Development.

Makel, M., Lee, S., Olszewski-Kubilius, P., & Putallaz, M. (2012). Changing the pond, not the fish: Following high ability students across different educational environments. *Journal of Educational Psychology, 104*(3), 778–792. https://doi.org/10.1037/a0027558

Masters, G. (2015). *Challenging our most able students.* Retrieved from https://www.teachermagazine.com.au/geoff-masters/article/challengingour-most-able-students

McCoach, D., Yu, H., Gottfried, A., & Gottfried, A. (2017). Developing talents: A longitudinal examination of intellectual ability and academic achievement. *High Ability Studies, 28*(1), 7–28. https://doi.org/10.1080/13598139.2017.1298996

Missett, T. C., Brunner, M. M., Callahan, C. M., Moon, T. R., & Price Azano, A. (2014). Exploring teacher beliefs and use of acceleration, ability grouping, and formative assessment. *Journal for the Education of the Gifted, 37*(3), 245–268. https://doi.org/10.1177/0162353214541326

Neihart, M. (2007). The socioaffective impact of acceleration and ability grouping: Recommendation for best practice. *Gifted Child Quarterly, 51*, 330–341. https://doi.org/10.1177/0016986207306319

Neihart, M., & Yeo, L. S. (2018). Psychological issues unique to the gifted student. In S. Pfeiffer (Ed.), *APA handbook of giftedness and talent* (pp. 497–510). Washington, DC: American Psychological Association.

New South Wales Department of Education (NSW DET). (2018). *Review of selective education access: Findings and action plan.* Retrieved from https://education.nsw.gov.au/about-us/strategies-and-reports/our-reports-and-reviews/review-of-selective-education-access/Review-of-Selective-Education-Access.pdf

New South Wales Department of Education (NSW DET). (2019). *High potential and gifted education policy.* NSW Government. Retrieved from https://education.nsw.gov.au/teaching-and-learning/high-potential-and-gifted-students/high-potential-and-gifted-education-policy

Nicholls, J. G. (1983). Conceptions of ability and achievement motivation: A theory and its implications for education. In S. G. Paris, G. M. Olson, & H. W. Stevenson (Eds.), *Learning and motivation in the classroom* (pp. 211–237). Hillsdale, NJ: Erlbaum.

North, B., & Griffiths, K. (2019). *Revisiting gifted education.* Centre for Education Statistics and Evaluation Centre for Education Statistics and Evaluation, NSW Department of Education. Retrieved from https://www.cese.nsw.gov.au/publications-filter/revisiting-gifted-education

North, B., Smith, S. R., & Gross, M. U. M. (2015). *Under pressure: The effects of academic pressure on gifted students in high-stakes assessment contexts.* Paper presented at the Educating Gifted and Talented Children: Turning Research into Practice, 21st World Council for Gifted and Talented Children Conference, Odense, Denmark.

Plucker, J. A., & Peters, S. J. (2016). *Excellence gaps in education: Expanding opportunities for talented students.* Cambridge, MA: Harvard Education Publishing Group.

Plunkett, M., & Kronborg, L. (2011). Learning to be a teacher of the gifted: The importance of examining opinions and challenging misconceptions. *Gifted and Talented International, 26*(1–2), 31–46. https://doi.org/10.1080/15332276.2011.11673587

Poulos, J. (1990). Academic board goes to the movies. *Education, 71*(14), 8.

Preckel, F., Goetz, T., & Frenzel, A. (2010). Ability grouping of gifted students: Effects on academic self-concept and boredom. *British Journal of Educational Psychology, 80*, 451–472. https://doi.org/10.1348/000709909X480716

Rasmussen, A., & Lingard, B. (2018). Excellence in education policies: Catering to the needs of gifted and talented or those of self-interest? *European Educational Research Journal, 17*(6), 877–897. https://doi.org/10.1177/1474904118771466

Rimlinger, N. (2018). *Let's work together to advance the acceptance and needs of the gifted children in Australia.* Retrieved from http://www.aaegt.net.au/wp-content/uploads/Gifted-Awareness-Week-2018.pdf

Rogers, K. B. (1991). *The relationship of grouping practices to the education of the gifted.* Storrs, CT: National Research Center on the Gifted and Talented.

Rogers, K. B. (2007). Lessons learned about educating the gifted and talented: A synthesis of the research on educational practice. *Gifted Child Quarterly, 51*(4), 382–396. https://doi.org/10.1177/0016986207306324. Retrieved from http://aea11gt.pbworks.com/f/LessonsLrnd-Rogers.pdf

Rogers, K. B. (2015). Academic effects research synthesis. In S. Assouline, N. Colangelo, J. VanTassel-Baska, & A. Lupkowski-Shoplik (Eds.), *A nation empowered: Evidence trumps the excuses holding back America's brightest students* (pp. 19–30). Iowa City, IA: The Connie Belin & Jacqueline N. Blank International Centre for Gifted Education and Talent Development.

Senate Reference Committee (Employment, Workplace Relations, Small Business and Education). (2001). *The education of gifted children.* Canberra, ACT: Commonwealth of Australia. Retrieved from https://trove.nla.gov.au/work/31974215

Senate Select Committee. (1988). *The education of gifted and talented children.* Canberra, ACT: Australian Government Publishing Service.

Smith, S. R. (2017). Responding to the unique social and emotional learning needs of gifted Australian students. In E. Frydenberg, A. Martin, & R. Collie (Eds.), *Social and emotional learning in Australia and the Asia-Pacific: Perspectives, programs, and approaches* (pp. 147–166). Singapore: Springer.

Southern, W. T., & Jones, E. D. (2015). Types of acceleration: Dimensions and issues. In S. G. Assouline, N. Colangelo, J. VanTassel-Baska, & A. Lupkowski-Shoplik (Eds.), *A nation empowered* (Vol. 2, pp. 9–18). Iowa City, IA: Connie Belin and Jacqueline N. Blank International Center for Gifted Education and Talent Development.

Southern, W. T., Jones, E. D., & Fiscus, E. D. (1989). Practitioner objections to the academic acceleration of gifted children. *Gifted Child Quarterly, 3*(1), 29–35. https://doi.org/10.1177/001698628903300105

Steenbergen-Hu, S., Makel, M. C., & Olszewski-Kubilius, P. (2016). What one hundred years of research says about the effects of ability grouping and acceleration on K–12 students' academic achievement: Findings of two second-order meta-analyses. *Review of Educational Research, 86*(4), 849–899. https://doi.org/10.3102/0034654316675417

Stoeger, H., Hopp, M., & Ziegler, A. (2017). Online mentoring as an extracurricular measure to encourage talented girls in STEM (science, technology, engineering, and mathematics): An empirical study of one-on-one versus group mentoring. *Gifted Child Quarterly, 61*, 239–249. https://doi.org/10.1177/0016986217702215

Subotnik, R. F., Olszewski-Kubilius, P., & Worrell, F. C. (2011). Rethinking giftedness and gifted education: A proposed direction forward based on psychological science. *Psychological Science in the Public Interest, 12*(1), 3–54. https://doi.org/10.1177/1529100611418056

VanTassel-Baska, J. (1986). Acceleration. In C. J. Maker (Ed.), *Critical issues in gifted education* (pp. 179–196). Rockville, MD: Aspen Publications.

VanTassel-Baska, J. (1992). Educational decision making on acceleration and grouping. *Gifted Child Quarterly, 36*(2), 68–72. https://doi.org/10.1177/001698629203600203

VanTassel-Baska, J., & Brown, E. F. (2009). An analysis of gifted education curriculum models. In F. A. Karnes & S. M. Bean (Eds.), *Methods and materials for teaching the gifted* (pp. 75–106). Waco, TX: Prufrock Press.

Vinson, T. (2002). *Inquiry into the provision of public education in NSW: Report of the "Vinson inquiry"*. Annandale, NSW/Darlinghurst, NSW: New South Wales Teachers' Federation/Pluto Press. Retrieved from https://trove.nla.gov.au/version/19872236

Vogl, K., & Preckel, F. (2014). Full-time ability grouping of gifted students: Impacts on social self-concept and school-related attitudes. *Gifted Child Quarterly, 58*(1), 51–68. https://doi.org/10.1177/0016986213513795

White, S., Graham, L., & Blaas, S. (2018). Why do we know so little about the factors associated with gifted underachievement? A systematic literature review. *Educational Research Review, 24*, 55–66. https://doi.org/10.1016/j.edurev.2018.03.001

Young, M., Rogers, K., Hoekman, K., van Vliet, H., & Chan, L. C. (2015). Acceleration in Australia: Flexible pacing opens the way for early university admission. In S. Assouline, N. Colangelo, J. VanTassel-Baska, & A. Lupkowski-Shoplik (Eds.), *A nation empowered: Evidence trumps the excuses holding back America's brightest students* (pp. 225–240). Iowa City, IA: The Connie Belin & Jacqueline N. Blank International Centre for Gifted Education and Talent Development. Retrieved from https://files.nwesd.org/website/Teaching_Learning/HiCap/2015-16%20meetings/NationEmpowered%20Vol1.pdf

Miraca U. M. Gross is Emeritus Professor of Gifted Education in UNSW's School of Education and inaugural Director of the *Gifted Education Research and Resource Centre* (GERRIC). She is recognised nationally and internationally as a leading authority on the education of gifted and talented students. Miraca's research focuses on issues of equity for gifted students, ability grouping, acceleration, socio-affective development and the highly gifted. She has won several international research awards including, in 1987, the *Hollingworth Award for Excellence in Research in Gifted Education* and, in both 1988 and 1990, the Mensa International Education and Research Foundation Awards for Excellence. In 2008, this Foundation further honoured her with their *Lifetime Achievement Award*. Professor Gross received the 1995 UNSW Vice-Chancellor's Award for Excellence in Teaching, the 1997 inaugural *Australian Award for University Teaching in Education*, the 2003

Australian College of Educators Sir Harold Wyndham Medal for outstanding services to Australian education and was recognised in the 2008 Queen's Birthday Honours List with Membership in the Order of Australia.

Susen R. Smith, PhD, is GERRIC Senior Research Fellow and Senior Lecturer in Gifted and Special Education at the School of Education, University of NSW, Australia. She has extensive experience as a teacher, curriculum consultant and educational leader from early childhood to tertiary education and adult education. She has been an invited visiting scholar to Columbia University, City University New York, the Hong Kong Institute of Education, National Taipei University of Education, Taiwan, and Imperial College London. Her specific research interests include ecological systems theory underpinning dynamically differentiated curriculum and pedagogy models and matrices for students with giftedness, indigeneity, underachievement, and multi-exceptionalities. She is published in international journals and has keynoted at national and international conferences, she chaired the inaugural *GERRIC Gifted Futures Forum*, and is the inaugural editor of the first Asia-Pacific handbook on giftedness and talent development.

Gifted and Twice-Exceptional Children in the South of the World: Chilean Students' Experiences Within Regular Classrooms

19

María Paz Gómez-Arízaga and María Leonor Conejeros-Solar

Contents

Introduction	406
The Case of Chile	408
Status of Gifted Education	408
Theoretical Approach to Gifted Education in Chile	408
Chilean Research in Gifted Education	409
Gifted Students in the Regular Classroom: Conceptual Framework	410
Classroom Climate	410
Relationship with Peers	411
Relationship with Teachers	412
Gifted Students' Classroom Experiences: Evidence from Two Studies	413
Relationships with Peers	414
Relationship with Teachers	417
Discussion and Conclusions	420
Gifted and Twice-Exceptional Students and Their Relationships with Peers in the Classroom Context	420
Gifted and Twice-Exceptional Students and Their Academic and Socio-emotional Experiences with Their Teachers	421
Implications for Research and Future Directions	422
Implications for Practice and Future Directions	422
Conclusion	424
Cross-References	425
References	425

M. P. Gómez-Arízaga (✉)
Universidad de Los Andes, Santiago, Chile
e-mail: mpgomez@uandes.cl

M. L. Conejeros-Solar
Escuela de Pedagogía, Pontificia Universidad Católica de Valparaíso, Viña del Mar, Chile
e-mail: leonor.conejeros@pucv.cl

© Springer Nature Singapore Pte Ltd. 2021
S. R. Smith (ed.), *Handbook of Giftedness and Talent Development in the Asia-Pacific*,
Springer International Handbooks of Education,
https://doi.org/10.1007/978-981-13-3041-4_8

Abstract

In a country like Chile, in which provisions for gifted students are scarce and extracurricular, little is known about what happens with gifted students within their schools. This chapter presents a theoretical and research-based exploration on the experiences of gifted and twice-exceptional (2e) students in regular classrooms. With a focus on the interactions between peers and teachers, the construct of classroom climate and the complex interactions and relationships that emerge from this context will be examined. First, we present a context for the Chilean educational system. Second, we review the research on classroom climate and socio-emotional adjustment of gifted and twice-exceptional students. Third, we present two case studies conducted in Chile with gifted and 2e students that explored the complexities of students' classroom climate experiences. The quality of these experiences is mediated by gifted students' characteristics and by the focus set by teachers on their strengths or difficulties. They need an undisturbed and comprehensive environment to successfully progress through the curriculum. Practical recommendations are provided on how to support gifted students to face the complexities of the classroom climate.

Keywords

Gifted and talented students · Twice-exceptional · Classroom climate · Peers · Teachers

The aims in this chapter are to:
1. Provide a contextual overview on the situation of gifted education in Chile.
2. Offer a research-based and theoretical discussion about classroom climate and its relationship to gifted and twice-exceptional students' experiences and engagement within the regular classroom.
3. Analyse two studies conducted in Chile with gifted and twice-exceptional students and provide evidence about classroom climate factors that are critical in this context.
4. Delve into the socio-emotional aspects of students' experiences with classroom climate.
5. Include implications and future directions for both practitioners and researchers.

Introduction

In Chile, considerable efforts have been made over the past decade to serve gifted students through enrichment programs that operate outside regular classrooms. However, the number of students being served roughly approaches 1% of the total gifted population in the country (Conejeros-Solar, Sandoval-Rodriguez, & Gomez-

Arizaga, 2018). With almost no special programs implemented at the school level, thousands of students who are gifted must survive daily in their regular classrooms and face a social/psychological classroom climate that can be welcoming or in conflict with the characteristics displayed by gifted individuals.

Different results have been reported regarding gifted students' socio-emotional traits and behaviours within regular classrooms, with some authors leaning toward an adequate social adjustment (França-Freitas, Del Prette, & del Prette, 2014), whereas others reported isolation and/or exclusion from peers (Gross, 2006; Ogurlu, 2015). A major reason that has been investigated for these feelings of isolation is students' perceptions of being different from their same age peers (Dare & Nowicki, 2015; Yssel, Prater, & Smith, 2010).

To add complexity to the regular classroom scenario, the role of the teacher is crucial to positively promote giftedness or by contrast, may exacerbate the feelings of isolation a gifted student can experience. Results of studies regarding teachers' attitudes have found that not all teachers hold positive attitudes toward giftedness (Lassig, 2015; McCoach & Siegle, 2007) and that there are cultural differences among countries. For example, a study conducted by Shayshon, Gal, Tesler, and Ko (2014) focused on the teachers of mathematically talented students from the United States, Israel, and South Korea. They found that all the teachers showed positive attitudes toward working with gifted students within mainstream classrooms; however, South Korean teachers were more prone than their colleagues from Western countries to assign higher importance to the work with disadvantaged groups than nurturing the needs of gifted students.

Underlying teacher behaviours and/or attitudes toward gifted students stem from previous training and knowledge about giftedness and their own conceptions about this topic. Researchers have found that teachers', stereotypes of the gifted can lead to erroneous expectations (Baudson & Preckel, 2016) and, at the same time, these expectations can affect classroom climate and peer relationships (Rubie-Davies, 2010). Moreover, when a difficulty or disability is added to the equation, that is, when teachers are faced with twice-exceptional (2e) students—that is, students in which there is a co-occurrence of giftedness and a disability—they tend to overlook their potential and attend more to their weaknesses (Rinn & Nelson, 2008; Townend & Pendergast, 2015), which can lead to student invisibility within the classroom and a lack of adequate services for their particular characteristics (Conejeros-Solar, Gómez-Arizaga, Sandoval-Rodríguez, & Cáceres-Serrano, 2018). Teachers overlooking 2e potential may be due to misunderstandings of twice exceptionality that may result in students "who remain under-identified and, consequently, underserved" (Assouline, Foley- Nicpon, & Huber, 2006, p. 18). The problem is whether gifted and twice-exceptional students can adjust and/or integrate to this complex scenario in the regular classroom. Integration can lead to a successful experience due to students feeling highly engaged to the school community (Godor & Szymanski, 2017). However, researchers have found that the school experience can be radically different for these students, especially the relationship that gifted students may have with their peers (Peterson, Duncan, & Canady, 2009; Wang & Neihart, 2015). In the case of twice-exceptional students, difficulties with social skills and heightened sensitivities can leave them vulnerable to peer bullying (Danielian & Nilles, 2015).

In this chapter, we will focus on exploring the experiences of Chilean gifted and twice-exceptional students within the classroom climate. Through the results of two qualitative studies, we will focus on students' peer and teacher relationships, to explore how these interactions can affect and shape students' learning and socio-emotional well-being in the school context and how they cope with the complexities of the classroom climate. Implications for practitioners and future directions are also discussed.

The Case of Chile

Status of Gifted Education

The Chilean educational system is currently divided into three types of schools: public, voucher (charter), and private. These schools have been defined as highly segregated and homogenous in terms of Socio-Economic Status (SES), meaning that they tend to concentrate students from a similar SES (Ortiz, 2015). Regarding academic achievement, a similar pattern can be found, with public schools having lower scores on standardised national and international assessments (Mizala & Torche, 2012).

Given this scenario of inequity, the first extracurricular, university-based enrichment program for gifted students in the country was created in 2001, mainly to serve students from public schools who do not have opportunities to potentiate their giftedness (Conejeros, Cáceres, & Riveros, 2012). Currently, there are seven of these programs in the country. Students must be in grades 5 (elementary) or 9 (secondary) to enter and go through different stages of identification to become a participant. This educational provision does not serve twice-exceptional students, as they are not specifically identified within programs, and in the Chilean case, they have more probabilities to be identified in schools by their disability rather than their high ability (Gómez-Arízaga, Conejeros-Solar, Sandoval, & Armijo, 2016).

Despite all the efforts that have been made to date to establish adequate programming for gifted students in Chile, there are no services provided for this population at the school level, just a few private initiatives. There is no existing legislation that can guarantee sustained services for these students, leaving them adrift from enriched and complex educational opportunities. This is not different from what happens in some countries in the Asia-Pacific region, where the lack of a coherent and holistic approach to giftedness influences the type and quality of the services for the gifted population. Jarvis and Henderson (2014) assert this situation, "On a large scale, though, Australia joins other countries in being unable to boast a truly coordinated, system-wide, sustainable approach based on a shared vision" (p. 6).

Theoretical Approach to Gifted Education in Chile

In Chile, the most widely used theoretical model for understanding and providing educational opportunities for gifted students is Gagné's *Integrated Model of Talent*

Development, or IMTD (Gagné, 2015), as is the case of other countries in the Pacific region, such as Australia (Bannister-Tyrrell, 2017; Lassig, 2015). However, because no systematic interventions can be found at the school level, this model was adopted exclusively for university-based enrichment programs, with the goal of providing high quality educational opportunities for gifted students who come from low socio-economic backgrounds. The goal of these programs is, therefore, to offer educational provisions to underserved Chilean students who do not have extracurricular enrichment opportunities in their immediate contexts or schools. Gagné's model is coherent with its overall perspective of talent development from giftedness potential and because of the idea that an enrichment program can become a critical environmental catalyst in the process of talent development (Dever, 2016).

Chilean Research in Gifted Education

Even though giftedness is a research topic that is still very young and under development in Chile, several investigations have been conducted regarding environmental factors that are critical for talent development. Regarding schools, teachers appear to have been either the participants or the focus in most of the investigations. Research conducted by Cabrera-Murcia and Udaquiola (2016), for example, addressed the perceptions of Chilean primary teachers about giftedness. They found that teachers can recognise the characteristics of gifted students at cognitive and socio-emotional levels and hold views that are not stereotypical. The challenges they perceived, however, were the lack of strategies to work with this population. It is important to acknowledge that Chilean teachers do not receive special preparation to address the needs of gifted students in the classroom. Furthermore, researchers have claimed that they hardly receive any training to work with children with different needs and to face the diversity that exists in the classroom (Infante, 2010; Rufinelli, 2013; San Martín, Villalobos, Muñoz, & Wyman, 2017).

Regarding professional development, the only existing option is a diploma provided by one of the university-based enrichment programs. Conjointly to this diploma, the same program created an internship for teachers from regular classrooms to attend courses offered for gifted students. Garcia and Arancibia (2007) found that this experience helped teachers with knowledge and strategies for addressing the needs of regular students at their schools. Similarly, Cabrera-Murcia (2011) studied the impact of this internship experience and found that the strategies acquired by teachers can effectively transfer to the regular classroom and benefit gifted students' learning.

Another set of Chilean studies has been conducted regarding the ideal characteristics of teachers who work with gifted students. Conejeros-Solar, Gómez-Arizaga, and Donoso-Osorio (2013) explored this issue from the perspective of gifted students. They found that the best learning scenarios happened with teachers with whom students have a social and emotional connection, and those who are flexible, can move at a faster pace, and integrate theory into practice. Similarly, Gómez-Arizaga, Conejeros-Solar, and Martin (2016) investigated the critical competencies of an effective teacher of the gifted, considering the views of a learning community.

They found that for the teachers in the program, one of the essential elements was the mastering of content knowledge in a theoretical, interdisciplinary, and practical way. For the students, even though they recognised the importance of instructional strategies, socio-emotional characteristics were also deemed important by them, especially empathy, closeness, and passion. In this way, students feel that they can relate to a teacher who is actively engaged both with his or her teaching and with them as individuals. Moreover, students tended to make comparisons between teachers from the enrichment programs versus teachers from their regular classrooms, stating that the latter are less flexible and unmotivated due to the rigidity of the national curriculum. This situation is complicated due to the high possibility of seeing their classroom teachers in a negative manner and the resulting lack of learning motivation that these views can promote in gifted students (Conejeros-Solar et al., 2013).

Gifted Students in the Regular Classroom: Conceptual Framework

The conceptual framework in this context is inclusive of the classroom climate and experiences, relationships with peers and relationships with teachers.

Classroom Climate

The concept of *classroom climate* has multiple definitions in the existing literature. For this chapter, we incorporated this term—that is, classroom climate—to understand students' unique perceptions of the different elements that make up their classroom experience (Rowe, Kim, Baker, Kamphaus, & Horne, 2010), and the ways through which they envision the quality of the classroom environment. Particularly, we focused on two elements that can be critical in this context: the relationships students have established with their classroom peers and the connections and interactions with their teachers, two aspects that can have important impacts on academic and social outcomes (Wentzel, Battle, Russell, & Looney, 2010).

In the Chilean context, a classroom climate-related study that was developed with teachers and students showed that this relationship constitutes a recursive process of interactions where the action of the student and the teacher unfolds according to a series of norms, behavioural habits, rituals, and social practices existing in the context of the classroom. When teachers and students accept these, the type of climate tends to stabilise. Classroom climate and pedagogical practices influence each other determining the limits and possibilities of knowledge development (Ascorra, Arias, & Graff, 2003). Chilean research, in which classroom videos of 51,329 school teachers were analysed, found that classroom climate had a powerful influence on students' academic achievements and that an important aspect of it was classroom management by the teacher (Gazmuri, Manzi, & Paredes, 2015).

Relationship with Peers

Relationships that are established with peers are perhaps the most critical ones during students' lifespans, with a particular focus in the period of adolescence, in which profound bonds can be created that are relevant for students' psychosocial and educational development (Veiga, García, Reeve, Wentzel, & García, 2015). Gifted students' social adjustment and the connections they have with peers has been a matter of debate among researchers in the field, with some claiming that no differences exist in social adjustment between gifted and non-gifted students (Jenaabadi, Marziyeh, & Dadkan, 2015); whereas others acknowledge the existence of negative experiences with peers, bullying being the most commonly reported issue (Peterson, 2015). The prevalence of bullying for the 2e population, however, remains unknown (Foley-Nicpon & Assouline, 2015).

Setting potential problems with peer interactions aside, what usually occurs is that at early ages, gifted students can encounter and perceive differences between them and their peers, realising that there is a mismatch regarding interests and attitudes (Lee, Olszewski-Kubilius, & Thomson, 2012).

Twice-exceptional (2e) students are another group within the gifted population that face issues of social integration and adjustment in regular classrooms. This group of students can present with many challenges, as their strengths are often disregarded and they are often labelled by their disabilities (Reis, Baum, & Burke, 2014). Also, they can possess unique socio-emotional needs, as they usually struggle with low self-concept, perfectionism, and perceptions of themselves and their achievement that are unrealistic (Barber & Mueller, 2011).

Relationships with peers can vary within the population of twice-exceptional students. Foley-Nicpon, Rickels, Assouline, and Richards (2012), in a study comparing gifted students with and without a diagnosis of Attention Deficit Hyperactivity Disorder (ADHD), found that both groups had very similar profiles regarding interpersonal relationships, self-reliance, and social stress. These findings suggest similarities in social characteristics between both groups that are more closely related to giftedness than profiles with only an ADHD diagnosis. However, the same study found lower self-esteem and lower overall happiness in the gifted/ADHD group, highlighting the need for interventions (e.g., counselling) that is focused on satisfaction for these students.

For gifted students with a diagnosis of Autism Spectrum Disorder (ASD), social relationships and emotional expression can be difficult, because of the characteristics of the ASD that are still present in this duality (Rubenstein, Schelling, Wilczynski, & Hooks, 2015). In a qualitative study conducted in New Zealand, Ng, Hill, and Rawlinson (2016) found that one recurrent complaint of gifted/ASD students was the interaction with classroom peers, particularly regarding noise and distraction. The highly increased or severely decreased reactivity to sensory aspects of the surroundings, such as the constant noise made by classroom peers, had negative consequences for gifted/ASD students' learning (Assouline, Foley-Nicpon, & Fosenburg, 2013). Taking these problems into consideration, the interventions that had been suggested for the gifted/ASD population are related to student-focused services in which talents are nurtured and strengths amplified (Baum, Schader, & Hébert, 2014). These interventions include gifted programs to address both academic and social-emotional characteristics (Foley-Nicpon & Assouline, 2015).

Peer relationships of 2e students can also include negative experiences, such as bullying episodes. These episodes can have a greater impact on 2e students because they do not always have the abilities required to face the negative consequences of peer aggression. For example, Franklin-Rohr (2012) stated that twice-exceptional learners may not have the appropriate communication skills to address bullies at their schools. Also, 2e students have reported feelings of being outsiders, because of the many issues they face with peers like bullying, exclusion from games, and name calling (Ronksley-Pavia & Townend, 2017).

In a case study with 2e students conducted in Chile, Gómez-Arizaga, Conejeros-Solar, Sandoval, and Armijo (2016) found that 2e students had a small and close group of friends who were valued for their honesty, respect, and a sense of humour. However, both gifted/ADHD and gifted/ASD students reported having trouble with classroom peers who not only were seen as obstacles for an optimal learning process, but also gifted/ASD students had experienced physical and psychological bullying episodes in the past.

Relationship with Teachers

As with peers, the relationships that students establish with their teachers can be critical for their engagement (Furrer, Skinner, & Pitzer, 2014), participation, and interest in class and school activities. For gifted students, this relationship is also related to the views and conceptions of giftedness a teacher holds, because negative beliefs can be detrimental for this bond and can even foster a classroom climate that does not welcome the characteristics of gifted students (Baudson & Preckel, 2016). Negative stereotypes, associations, and affect toward giftedness can include believing that gifted students 'use' their high abilities for poor social behaviour, such as being insensitive and disrespectful (Geake & Gross, 2008), a view that was more negatively associated to gifted boys according to Preckel, Baudson, Krolak-Schwerdt, and Glock (2015). However, there are also positive experiences reported regarding teacher-student relationships and climate, such as the results reported by Tucker, Dixon, and Griddine (2010), in which gifted students reported feelings of being accepted, nurtured, and valued at the classroom and school levels. Other studies point to the competencies teachers need to have when interacting with students in the regular classroom. Samardzija and Peterson (2015), for example, found that students valued teachers who were able to adequately manage behaviours in the classroom that promoted self-regulation instead of constantly scolding them. Students also valued teacher traits, such as patience, ethics, and being calm and respectful.

The experiences of 2e students with their teachers appear to be critical for a successful school experience and to develop a sense of belonging to the school context (Townend & Pendergast, 2015). Relationships with teachers can have a negative impact where educators focus excessively on the difficulties rather than 2e students' strengths and exhibit a lack of understanding about the manifestation of dual exceptionalities (Ronksley-Pavia & Townend, 2017).

Townend and Pendergast (2015) found that most of the 2e students in their study were very sensitive and aware of the connection they had with their teachers, which helped them to feel valued and had an impact on their academic achievement. One gifted/ASD participant of their sample, however, did not achieve that connectedness, feeling isolated from his school. Ronksley-Pavia and Townend (2017) also reported bullying from teachers, which included verbal aggression and ridiculing students in front of the other students. The authors also reported an aggressive teaching style regarding classroom management, which particularly affected gifted/ASD students because of their sensitivity to noise.

As for the gifted/ADHD group, it has been found that teachers, even when acknowledging the coexistence of giftedness and a disability, remain sceptical about the co-occurrence of giftedness and ADHD (Schultz, 2012), which can translate into a negative disposition by the teacher when interacting with this group. However, some researchers have found that teachers of students who are gifted/ADHD can be supportive and provide help and guidance when needed (Wang & Neihart, 2015).

In the Chilean study with 2e students previously described, students also reported their relationships with teachers, with different connotations. Whereas the group of gifted/ADHD students cared and valued their teachers, some gifted/ASD students felt negatively about them, especially because teachers displayed negative attitudes and made 2e students feel uncomfortable (Gómez-Arizaga, Conejeros-Solar, Sandoval, & Armijo, 2016).

From the aforementioned studies, it can be inferred that both groups, gifted/ADHD and gifted/ASD, need a strong relationship with their teachers in which positive feedback can influence the way they feel about themselves and their schools (Coleman & Gallagher, 2015). A positive relationship with a teacher can foster good academic experiences, work on students' strengths and make the student feel less inadequate regarding his or her cognitive functioning deficits. For this purpose, Baum et al., (2014), proposed a strength-based model, where teachers are supportive, understanding, open, flexible, and have empathy with the students and work with them based on their strengths.

Gifted Students' Classroom Experiences: Evidence from Two Studies

In this section, we provide evidence of two studies conducted in Chile that were part of two different research projects. Study one was a two-year qualitative longitudinal study in which the main goal was to conduct an in-depth exploration of the experiences of *gifted-only students in regular classrooms*. In this study, 12 gifted students (ages 12–16) participated in different data collection activities, including in-depth interviews. The project had three foci of analyses: teaching and learning experiences, teachers' socio-emotional traits, and students' experiences within the climate of the regular classroom. Results of the classroom climate are reported here (For further information refer to Gomez-Arizaga & Truffello, 2018; Gómez-Arízaga, 2016; Gómez-Arizaga, Hébert, Castillo, & Valdivia, 2017).

Study two was a three-year project aimed at *characterising twice-exceptional (2e) students* for the first time in the country. The project was focused on two types of 2e: Giftedness with Autism Spectrum Disorder (ASD) and Giftedness with Attention Deficit Hyperactivity Disorder (ADHD). The study comprised several phases of testing with different instruments (i.e., cognitive, social-emotional) and interviews with parents, students, teachers, and peers (For more information see Conejeros-Solar, Sandoval-Rodriguez, & Gomez-Arizaga, 2018 and Gómez-Arizaga, Conejeros-Solar, Sandoval, & Armijo, 2016). Here we report the second phase of the project, in which 20 students, ages between 9 and 15 years old, were interviewed, with emphasis on the experience of being a 2e student immersed in the complexities of the classroom.

Regarding methods and analyses, both studies followed very similar qualitative techniques for student interviews, creating protocols that were easy to understand and that also allowed students to speak freely about their thoughts, feelings, and opinions. The analyses were framed in a grounded theory approach (Strauss & Corbin, 1998). In this way, data were collected and analysed as a systematic and ongoing process (Engward, 2013). This process informed further data collection procedures, allowing the researchers to orient future interviews to saturate the data. Triangulation techniques were conducted to ensure the credibility of the data analysis process: (a) participant checks before starting each new interview, in which emerging findings were discussed; and (b) investigator triangulation between investigators and research assistants. Hereunder, we present the results of both studies, divided into two components of the classroom climate: relationships with peers and ties created with teachers.

Relationships with Peers

Study 1: Exploring the experiences of gifted students and their peers in regular classrooms. For almost all the students in the study, meaningful experiences were reported with close friends, which were relevant and allowed an adequate social adjustment to the school environment. This is closely related to the developmental stage that they were undergoing (adolescence), in which the search for a positive interaction and acceptance is no exception in the case of gifted students, as stated by an elementary gifted student: "I have real friends…they don't tell anything…I have a friend who is my same age, he is very unconditional. He always supports me" (Thomas, Individual Interview, June 10th, 2016). Loyalty and trust are traits that were valued with intensity by students in the sample, as it was sharing common characteristics with their friends, as a secondary student mentions: "I found a friend who is silent as I am, and she goes from one topic to another. She loses track of time, as I do. So we stay together" (Veronica, Individual Interview, July 21st, 2016).

However, even when an adequate social adjustment exists between gifted students and their close friends, when it comes to peers that are part of the larger group (classmates), some experiences of bullying were reported that are more visible in male students who are younger (12–13 years old). In one case, one of the students had a long history of bullying at the school level. In another case, the bullying experience was among gifted students, a sort of 'gifted popular vs. gifted unpopular' type of rivalry and conflict that ended with the participating student moving to a new school.

Another set of unpleasant experiences for gifted students in the regular classroom was related to an academic/cognitive imbalance between them and their peers. In this case, the asynchronous development of the gifted student became more evident, because classmates did not match with the students' characteristics. In this context, the classmate was perceived as an obstacle, because of displaying less interest in learning and behaviours that are detrimental for gifted students' quick progress through content knowledge. A secondary student who attends an artistic high school described this situation as the frustration of not being able to 'ask more' from her classmates, especially when working in groups:

> because I couldn't make my classmate, because most of the work was done in groups, to play something more complex. Because if I did that they would say: "that's too difficult. Let's do this, that's easier". And for me this was a no, I don't like easy things. I've never liked easy things. (Mary, Individual Interview, June 22nd, 2016)

Therefore, a discrepancy was noticed between the importance of making significant bonds with true friends, especially at a critical developmental age versus a genuine interest in learning that is restricted by peer interruptions and behaviours that do not favour the display of gifted characteristics. An elementary student narrated this situation stating how hard learning can be in the context of the regular classroom: "I don't know, I have many differences with my classmates, because I take things, learning, very seriously. It is hard to learn new things, because they talk a lot. I try not to do the same" (Sebastian, Individual Interview, August 24th, 2016).

Study 2: Describing the relationships between twice-exceptional (2e) and their peers at the school level. For 2e students, relationships with their peers were complex and central to their school experience. The need to have friends and not be invisible to others emerged as an inner and profound wish both for ADHD and ASD students in the sample. For the gifted/ADHD group, fewer obstacles were found in the socialisation process; however, for gifted/ASD students it was found to be more difficult. The gifted/ADHD group reported having more friends: "Yes, I like it, I have a lot of friends…, yes! It's cool" (Ingrid, Middle School, Individual Interview, June 28th, 2016). Whereas for the gifted/ASD student socialisation was a less free-flowing process:

> It's just that basically it's hard to become friends with my classmates … almost all of them are different persons, is just that I don't know how to explain it, they are like…, that I don't find a reason to talk to them … is just that I don't find like… a way. (Lauren, Elementary, Individual Interview, July 18th, 2016)

Even though the need for friendship and closeness was salient in both groups—with different nuances—a different relationship occurs when facing classroom peers. It is important to state that Chilean classrooms have between 25 and 45 students, and they spend most of the day together in the same physical space. Hence, this was a critical aspect for gifted/ADHD and gifted/ASD students. Both groups tended to perceive negatively their group of classroom peers, noticing that they exclude them, they do not accept those who are different, and do not understand their needs and characteristics, such as a gifted/ASD student indicates: "Not very, accepted, I feel somehow excluded by my class, nobody wants me to get close, nobody asks me to come, I know that nobody wants to get close but I think that if they don't want me to be near them, okay!" (Michael, Middle School, Individual Interview, June 7th, 2016).

Another element that generated a feeling of lack of understanding by classroom peers refers to the interests and capacities of the 2e student, like this gifted/ADHD student expresses:

> I knew things they didn't know, then too and I felt kind of weird, I knew things they didn't know, I saw things they didn't see! Then I knew more about things and..., there, I was at school.... I didn't feel that different, actually that didn't interest me, but yes, it was weird, it was weird because like, they talked about other things I didn't talk about, I also knew other things and was used to talk about, like, bigger things. (James, Elementary, Individual Interview, June 13th, 2016)

Similarly to Study 1, there was also a negative view amongst both groups of 2e students about the academic conduct of classmates that was understood as a lack of interest and collaboration. Students could not understand why their classmates do not pay attention, do not focus, do not do homework and do not write. Students were bothered because their classmates did not make an effort in the school environment, which finally led toward a preference for individual work, refusing to work with classmates that do not do anything and leave them to take responsibility for all the work, as one of the gifted/ASD students expressed: "Since sometimes I finish first, I end up doing the work ... It doesn't work for me, no, I don't like that..." (David, Middle School, Individual Interview, November 18th, 2016). Students also preferred to work alone because of the distraction the classmates generate when they spend time talking and do not focus on the assignment.

Therefore, classmates are perceived as loud people, feisty, rude, and, with little interest in learning, a situation that causes difficulties and bothers the 2e students who want to learn and pay attention, like this gifted/ASD states:

> I like to be in school, but just what I don't like are my classmates that are always fighting and are very loud..., what I don't like is that the noise is so loud... They scream loudly!... An emotion appears every time the noise gets louder if the noise increases to the max, my fury arrives...and they make me really angry! (Michael, Middle School, Individual Interview, June 7th, 2016).
>
> This idea is reinforced by this gifted/ADHD student: "Yes, or they stick to their phones and then I have to try to pay attention. Also, I don't know, if they understand something

those people because noise pollution is very serious..." (Karlos, Secondary, Individual Interview, July 8th, 2016).

Also like in Study 1, both groups of 2e students reported bullying episodes at school that impacted their social interactions with peers and reinforced the negative view they had of them, like this gifted/ASD states: "Because they just ..., they just want to irritate me ..., they just want to bother me and they do it together, not one ..., but many!" (Michael, Middle School, Individual Interview, June 7th, 2016). Some students had their own 'methods' to deal with bullying, which allowed students to maintain control over a threatening and painful situation, such as peer abuse. This gifted/ADHD student explains his coping strategy:

> I have a technique, you know? When they start making fun of me, I am, my mom says I'm very smart about this, but, I keep making a fool of myself on that subject so that I'm laughing with them, and not that at the fact that they're laughing at me ... that's like my logic, laughing with them and that they do not laugh at me, ... it's like, making jokes with them, I laugh at what they tell me, so they're not making fun of me. (Tom, Elementary, Individual Interview, July 13th, 2016)

Like study 1, some students reported having close friends, some of which supported them in difficult situations and from whom help is received when needed. The relationship of mutual help—both academic and socio-emotional—seems to be a central aspect of the friendship relationship as this gifted/ASD states: "We used to play together ... They usually help me, we used to help each other when we are in trouble ..." (Daniel, Middle School, Individual Interview, November 18th, 2016). For the 2e students, friends were also individuals with whom they could share mutual interests as it is expressed by a gifted/ADHD student: "No, is that I generally hang out with people that are like me ... that we can understand each other and, are alike in the sense that we understand each other, help each other, hum.. all that, like the good we have, and some failures as well" (Aldo, Middle School, Individual Interview, June 29th, 2016).

Relationship with Teachers

Study 1: Experiences of gifted students and their teachers in regular classrooms. In the context of the classroom climate, the teacher appears as a crucial figure, as an individual who fosters meaningful learning experiences only if, before learning occurs, he or she can avoid student disruptions by firmly maintaining authority. Students in this study highly valued rules and order because these aspects allowed both the teacher and the student to be on constant progression toward learning outcomes. In this context, the concept of the teacher as a 'strict peer' emerged, which was more prevalent in secondary students. In this sense, teachers are considered peers, because students need teachers to be approachable as this secondary student mentions: "I like the relationship I have with my teachers, because we are like friends" (Sergio, Individual Interview, July 11th, 2016) and at the same time a person who can promote order and organisation for an optimal learning process, as put by one of the secondary girls, "she was strict, but she was cool. It's like opposites on the same person. I like this because with this style I can always learn" (Sara, Individual Interview, June 16th, 2016). For many secondary students, this was the way to keep learning within the chaos of the regular classroom: "I mean, relaxed and strict at the same time. It's weird...because he likes so much what he does that he wants to be heard. And for me it's a very comfortable way of learning. I can't learn otherwise. Someone who is strict but relaxed. Knows when to stop things that are not helping us learn" (Mary, Individual Interview, August 10th, 2016).

On the other side, negative experiences—although not an everyday event—were reported by students with teachers in the regular classroom. These narratives were related to the teacher expressly ignoring gifted students or publicly insulting them in front of the class because of their characteristics. An elementary student described recurrent 'ignoring' episodes by a Language Arts teacher:

> when I raised my hand to answer she ignored me. She asked someone else. And after everybody answered she would come back to me. Sometimes she said: "someone wants to read?" I would raise my hand and she would say "no, not you". (Kenneth, Individual Interview, July 23rd, 2016)

Other stories of the teacher ignoring a gifted student were the ones narrated by another elementary student: "...she always looks at me in a weird way. Once I didn't go to school and a classmate told me she said: For me, Andrea doesn´t exist in my classroom" (Andrea, Individual Interview, August 9th, 2016).

Other forms of teacher rejection were related to not being able to address the needs of gifted students. A secondary student reported an experience of being neglected in front of the whole class by a History teacher for her 'special needs': "He said that I needed special attention. That he wasn't prepared to teach someone like me" (Mary, Individual Interview, August 10th, 2016). In some cases, teachers opted to exclude the gifted student as this secondary student states: "there is a Science teacher who always kicks me out of the classroom, he says I'm the devil's advocate" (Daisy, Individual Interview, June 28th, 2016).

Study 2: Academic, social, and affective characteristics of the relationship between teachers and 2e students. For both groups of 2e students, it was important to have a teacher who offered support and was sensitive to their needs, showing interest and concern for them and making them feel secure in the classroom context. This support referred to clarifying doubts and resolving academic difficulties, besides emotional support in situations of emotional distress. This gifted/ADHD student addressed the academic support provided by his teacher: "Well, sometimes teacher Elena helps me with the assignments" (Aldo, Middle School, Individual Interview, June 29th, 2016). In certain occasions, teacher support was focused on 'the difference', which was not very well appreciated by students as this gifted/ADHD states:

> What, it makes me take, my head teacher makes me take special education tests and somehow, it irritates me and bothers me a lot that they make me take special education tests and that they treat me specially..., I like to be treated like the rest. (Tom, Elementary, Individual Interview, July 13th, 2016)

Twice-exceptional students in this study recognised having good relationships with their teachers. Teachers were described as fun, warm, understanding, and likable persons with whom you could talk and establish cordial relationships. Students also recognised that they had different types of teachers, which reflected a critical view of their work. For example, the teacher who tries to challenge students cognitively but fails despite her intentions, because she cannot focus in any student in particular, as stated by this gifted/ASD student:

> hummm, I don't feel it's a school, that challenges you, there are some teachers that do it, they try to help their students get better, make you a better student...but no, it's not possible because of the same fact that there are so many students in here, that they can't focus on anyone in specific or things like that. (Martin, Secondary, Individual Interview, June 16th, 2016)

Students also referred to other types of teachers, such as the 'fast' teacher (the one they cannot keep up with); the 'unpleasant' (who does not know the needs of the 2e student and is not receptive to students' demands); the 'reader'; the 'serious' teacher; and the 'nice' one. The 'nice teacher' is the most valued by the students as these two gifted/ADHD students state:

> I like the teacher a lot and besides doing a bunch of fun stuff, I like her and I like knowing things, learning things about history that no, that I didn't know . . . if I could I would tell the teacher 'teacher I want to stay here' and at least she gives me a homework that, that I can research, I don't care if it's 10, 20 pages, I don't care I still do them!" (Aldo, Elementary, Individual Interview, June 29th, 2016);

> . . . I need to be learning new things, repeatedly, because if not I get bored and I start to make a mess, so!" (James, Elementary, Individual Interview, June 13th, 2016).

In general, students indicated that they did not like when teachers were rigid or too inflexible, did not understand or see them, sat down doing nothing, did boring classes and when their teaching was slow. A gifted/ADHD student expresses this:

> No, I like how they teach me, even though some are like more..., relaxed! They are like 'we have to do this and if you don't do it like that is very bad'. . . . more than rigidness, is that, how do you say it? big fans of their ideas, like 'we are going to this and if it's not done like everything is going to go wrong' but in general, I like the education. (Ingrid, Middle School, Individual Interview, June 28th, 2016)

For most students in both 2e groups, school was seen as a boring place in which they have unpleasant feelings because of having to 'write too much', disgust for the classes that are not of the student's interest and for classes that are repetitive and not challenging, in addition to teachers—who in certain occasions—treat them as if the students do not understand, reminding them about their difficulties. Despite the feeling of school being useless and boring, students tried to pay attention because their interest and desire for learning came first, as this gifted/ASD states:

> I would like to learn more. I: To be more challenged? M: Mhum. I: . . . do you get bored sometimes during classes? M: Yes. I: Does that happen often or not? M: Yes, but I still pay attention. I: Do you

pay attention during the whole class? S: hum (Michael, Middle School, Individual Interview, June 7th, 2016); and this gifted/ADHD: Yes, I like learning, it's like fun, because... Like "woohoo" I'm learning (Ingrid, Middle School, Individual Interview, June 28th, 2016).

A particular aspect that emerged from the stories of the 2e students with ADHD is the difficulty of being in the classroom, because of the effort they must make to adapt to the working dynamics, since it requires them to 'focus', 'pay attention', 'being quiet', and 'not moving'. This scenario demanded students to look for strategies to manage the anxiety that was generated by the inability to control the lack of attention and worry is expressed by these two students: "No, more like exercises, too long, a lot of accumulated exercises even if they are too easy, if I see a paper with a lot of accumulated exercises, I begin to lose control..., I get a little nervous" (James, Elementary Student, Individual Interview, June 13th, 2016).

> Like I'm lost, the teachers tell me ... you are all the time on the moon and I don't know, a friend asked 'what's that?' I explain to him that is being lost, not paying attention, like, looking at the flies ... No, I don't even realise it..., like that, sometimes I begin to draw and I'm just gone ..... (Ingrid, Middle School, Individual Interview, June 28th, 2016)

Discussion and Conclusions

The results from both studies briefly illustrated in this chapter shed light on critical aspects that emerged from gifted-only and 2e students regarding their social and academic experiences with peers and teachers.

Gifted and Twice-Exceptional Students and Their Relationships with Peers in the Classroom Context

For all groups, there is a need to find a connection with a 'true' friend, in which values such as mutual trust and loyalty are considered a common ground for a solid friendship. This close group of friends can even act as a haven to face complex scenarios at the school level.

Proneness toward friendship, however, is not necessarily a guarantee of social competence, as differences between students were found. This may reflect the variability in results found by the researchers about the social adjustment of gifted students. Gifted-only and gifted/ADHD students reported friendship as being a straightforward process, the latter being consistent with previous research on gifted students with ADHD (Foley-Nicpon et al., 2012). The gifted/ASD group, however, had more difficulties in approaching and finding true peers with whom they could connect both at intellectual and social levels.

Both groups of students reported bullying episodes as negative experiences with peers, which is consistent with findings by Peterson (2015) and Ronksley-Pavia and

Townend (2017). Twice-exceptional students, especially the gifted/ASD group, felt at the periphery of school daily events, such as recess, and also perceived a lack of understanding and acceptance from their classmates. Social isolation can also be considered as a type of aggression that impacts students' lives.

One salient aspect in both the gifted-only and the 2e students was the interaction with classroom peers, which are viewed as an obstacle for learning. However, nuances were found regarding the nature and impact of this relationship. For all students, their academic skills and the seriousness attributed to the learning process is what separates them from classroom peers. These findings are similar to those reported by Lee et al. (2012), regarding a mismatch of interests between gifted students and their peers. For the 2e group, however, classroom peers not only were perceived as uninterested in learning but also as detractors of their efforts to overcome their difficulties. This aspect was more salient for the gifted/ASD group, causing emotional distress in students when facing sensory disruptions, such as constant noise. These findings relate to what authors in the field have found regarding obstacles to learning in gifted/ASD students (Assouline et al., 2013; Foley-Nicpon & Assouline, 2015).

Gifted and Twice-Exceptional Students and Their Academic and Socio-emotional Experiences with Their Teachers

As with peers, the role of the teacher in this study was critical in helping students become more engaged with school and their learning, and even to bring back gifted and 2e students from a peripheral role that they may have assumed because of their characteristics. Being close, warm, and empathetic were traits that were highly valued in both groups, which is consistent with findings at both the international level and the Chilean context (Conejeros-Solar et al., 2013; Tucker et al., 2010).

Particularly for the gifted-only study, the teacher profile that emerges is 'strict but nice', meaning that he or she can set boundaries and manage students' behaviour in an orderly manner, so students can learn effectively. These findings relate to Samardzija and Peterson's (2015) study, in which students valued a teacher's capacity to promote self-regulation. *Niceness* appeared for the gifted/ADHD group as well, but the connotation is different, because it relates to a teacher who is understanding and sufficiently flexible to adapt and adjust according to their students' needs, which is in line with the findings of Wang and Neihart (2015) with a group of gifted/ADHD students.

Regarding negative experiences, the most salient results had commonalities and differences between the gifted-only and the 2e group. In study one, students reported aggressive behaviours from teachers that ranged between deliberately ignoring them to making it clear in front of the class that they cannot deal with their unique characteristics. These teacher bullying behaviours have not been widely studied in the gifted population, though some research has been conducted for the 2e population in the Asia-Pacific region (Ronksley-Pavia & Townend, 2017). For the 2e group, negative experiences with teachers were that some of them would point out their differences in the form of 'support', but instead of helping, it was detrimental for students as they do want to be treated like everybody else. This focus on difficulties is consistent with the findings of Ronksley-Pavia and Townend (2017).

Also, the 2e group appeared to be more sensitive to teacher traits and characteristics, providing information about different classroom scenarios that they liked and disliked in relation to their teachers' behaviours, which is related to what was found by Townend and Pendergast (2015) about 2e students' awareness of the teacher-student relationship, and the sensitivity and connectedness they had with their teachers. An interesting result is that even if 2e students find school boring and frustrating, they do engage with learning, since for them learning is and must remain a priority. Also, if a teacher is flexible and challenging, this perceived student monotony can be inhibited.

Implications for Research and Future Directions

An important body of research exists on giftedness related to characteristics, identification, curriculum, and strategies, amongst others (Hodges, Tay, Maeda, & Gentry, 2018; Smith, 2017; VanTassel-Baska & Stambaugh, 2006). However, there is still a need to capture the everyday experiences and lives of gifted students in both academic and non-academic contexts. In the words of Coleman, Micko, and Cross (2015), "students' perspectives told through their voices need to be heard" (p. 2).

Qualitative methods have shown to be relevant to achieve depth and to capture details and nuances of students' lives. However, besides interviews, which are the most widely used method, researchers can use other qualitative techniques that have not been explored in the field, such as the use of photo elicitation and ethnography. Through the use of these techniques, which provide an immersion within the lived experiences of students and their context, one can deepen the exploration of some aspects that were salient in both studies, such as the following:

(a) Exploring teacher aggressive behaviours (sometimes disguised as 'punishment').
(b) Going in depth into the social relationships and dynamics with classroom peers.
(c) Knowing the type and quality of teacher support provided to 2e students and possible interventions to improve this relevant aspect of the student-teacher relationship.

Implications for Practice and Future Directions

Lack of teacher preparation to meet the needs of gifted and 2e learners is an aspect that urgently must be addressed in the Chilean context as stated by Conejeros et al. (2012). Strategies to cope with the unique characteristics of this diverse population of gifted and 2e students is a major challenge for teachers that teacher preparation programs will need to face in the near future, especially because of the national efforts toward more inclusive classroom practices.

A more rigorous effort needs to be undertaken, not only by the seven universities that are already developing enrichment programs, but also by the

Chilean educational system to offer talent-developing opportunities for the gifted and 2e learners, such as appropriate educational provisions (e.g., enrichment, acceleration, ability grouping, and the like, that are relevant to their individual needs); creating a differentiated learning environment that considers students' abilities, interests, and characteristics; and establishing regulations and policies about identification, curriculum, and instructional methods for working with this population (Assouline, Colangelo, & VanTassel-Baska, 2015; Castellano & Frazier, 2010; Olszewski-Kubilius, 2013; Renzulli & Reis, 2014; Tomlinson, 2014).

The existing Chilean enrichment programs may be relevant options for 2e students, as previous research has found a positive impact of academic programs on this population (Foley-Nicpon & Assouline, 2015; Baum et al., 2014). It is crucial that these programs offer some entry options or quotas for this group, because 2e students do not always match the profiles of traditional candidates that enter these programs (Beckmann & Minnaert, 2018; Silverman, 2013). These programs, at the moment, are the only formal option 2e students have for nurturing their potential in the Chilean educational system. The current legislation, educational supports, and opportunities are focused on identification services and interventions provided at the school level and aimed at 2e students' disabilities. High abilities are therefore invisible within this scenario (Gómez-Arizaga, Conejeros-Solar, Sandoval, & Armijo, 2016).

Teacher preparation needs to address teachers' beliefs and attitudes toward giftedness due to the aggressive behaviours found in Study one. Knowledgeable and sensitive teachers with a focus on students' strengths rather than difficulties are urgently needed to challenge and nurture this group of students. Also, a strength-based model (Baum et al., 2014) can be a strong framework for teacher training due to the characteristics that this model promotes in a teacher, such as: empathy, supportiveness, understanding, openness, and flexibility.

There is a scarcity of professionals and parent associations that can advocate for this population of children and adolescents in Chile. Therefore, the civil society needs to become empowered, organise, and advocate for the rights of these children, with a sustainable and shared vision that can facilitate the development of public policies.

Regarding the social and emotional development of gifted and 2e students, psychologists with preparation that includes developing understandings of the traits of this population are needed. They can offer possibilities of counselling regarding interpersonal aspects such as life satisfaction—especially for gifted/ADHD students—and social relationships with both groups, as proposed by Foley-Nicpon et al. (2012).

From an inclusive perspective, progress needs to be made in accepting students' differences, because both classmates and teachers generally do not recognise the characteristics of these groups, which increases the feeling of not fitting in by the gifted and/or 2e student. In this sense, pedagogical practices are critical to the generation of positive classroom climates (Gazmuri et al., 2015). Within a positive scenario, the gifted and 2e student will feel comfortable and have meaning in their school experience.

As expected, and given the characteristics of the group under study, gifted students' adjustment to the classroom climate is not easy and straightforward. Instead of choosing sides in the discussion about social adjustment in gifted students, we propose to address the topic in two levels: on one side, the micro level, in which meaningful relationships are indeed created by gifted and twice-exceptional students with a few friends who are close, loyal, and provide mutual support in times of need. Something similar occurs with a few teachers who are empathetic to their characteristics. On the other side, it is the macro level in which challenges and difficulties can be found, due to factors such as classmates' non-compliance to the social norms of the classroom and the indifference and lack of interest in learning perceived by gifted students in their peers.

Another relevant aspect in the macro level is that despite the fact that classes are perceived as boring, repetitive, and not challenging, students' interest in learning remains and is shown by focusing on and adhering to the norms of the classroom, even if they are not motivated or able to acquire new knowledge. This is particularly difficult and overwhelming for 2e students, because for some of them it can be hard to remain focused, which does not always lead to optimal results.

Conclusion

From the results of the two studies shown in this chapter, it can be inferred that for inclusion to be achieved in Chile—particularly at the school level—it is critical to generate awareness of the presence of gifted and 2e students, and to address their particular needs within the regular classroom. Stronger and more determined steps are therefore required to break the status quo and to successfully serve the gifted population, considering the existent diversity within this group.

It is important to acknowledge that students in the gifted-only and twice-exceptional samples in this chapter did not expect special treatment to make them feel superior or inferior from their classmates. From what was gathered and analysed in both studies, they aspire to be recognised, visualised, and to have the opportunity to learn and develop in a space that accepts and embraces their diversity. Nevertheless, they have to coexist daily within an environment that can be hostile, chaotic, and not welcoming or supportive of their characteristics. This then, is an overarching message to both teachers and peers of students with twice-exceptionalities: that diversity can come in many forms, and that from a social justice perspective, there is a need to show respect for others, regardless of differences. This can be achieved by forming meaningful and constructive peer and teacher relationships with gifted and 2e students and developing understandings of the unique characteristics of these unique students.

Cross-References

▶ Gifted Education in the Asia-Pacific: From the Past for the Future – An Introduction
▶ Gifted Girls with Autism Spectrum Disorders: Provisions and Priorities in Australian School Settings
▶ Gifted, Talented, and High-Achieving Students and Their Gifted Education in Mexico
▶ Homeschooling the Gifted: What Do We Know from the Australian, Chilean, and US Context?
▶ Innovative Practices to Support High-Achieving Deprived Young Scholars in an Ethnic-Linguistic Diverse Latin American Country
▶ Social and Emotional Needs and Learning Processes: Part II Introduction
▶ Some Implications for the Future of Gifted Education in the Asia-Pacific
▶ Teachers' Knowledge and Understandings of Twice Exceptionality Across Australia

Acknowledgments We gratefully acknowledge the Conicyt National Commission for Scientific and Technological Research for the grants Fondecyt Iniciación project 11140480 and Fondecyt Regular project 1151030.

References

Ascorra, P., Arias, H., & Graff, C. (2003). La escuela como contexto de contención social y afectiva. *Revista Enfoques Educacionales, 5*(1), 117–135. Retrieved from http://www.facso.uchile.cl/publicaciones/enfoques/07/Ascorra_Arias_Graff_EscuelaContencionSocialAfectiva.pdf

Assouline, S. G., Foley Nicpon, M., & Huber, D. H. (2006). The impact of vulnerabilities and strengths on the academic experiences of twice-exceptional students: A message to school counselors. *Professional School Counseling, 10*(1), 14–25. https://doi.org/10.1177/2156759X0601001S03

Assouline, S., Foley-Nicpon, M., & Fosenburg, S. (2013). *The paradox of twice-exceptionality, packet of information for professionals* (2nd ed.). Iowa City, IA: University of Iowa, Belin Blank International Center for Gifted Education and Talent Development.

Assouline, S. G., Colangelo, N., & VanTassel-Baska, J. (2015). *A nation empowered: Evidence trumps the excuses holding back America's brightest students* (Vol. I). Iowa City, IA: University of Iowa, Connie Belin & Jacqueline N. Blank International Center for Gifted Education and Talent Development.

Bannister-Tyrrell, M. (2017). Gagné's DMGT 2.0: A possible model of unification and shared understandings. *The Australasian Journal of Gifted Education, 26*(2), 43–50. https://doi.org/10.21505/ajge.2017.0015

Barber, C., & Mueller, C. T. (2011). Social and self-perceptions of adolescents identified as gifted, learning disabled, and twice-exceptional. *Roeper Review, 33*(2), 109–120. https://doi.org/10.1080/02783193.2011.554158

Baudson, T. G., & Preckel, F. (2016). Teachers' conceptions of gifted and average-ability students on achievement-relevant dimensions. *The Gifted Child Quarterly, 60*(3), 212–225. https://doi.org/10.1177/0016986216647115

Baum, S. M., Schader, R. M., & Hébert, T. P. (2014). Through a different lens. *The Gifted Child Quarterly, 58*(4), 311–327. https://doi.org/10.1177/0016986214547632

Beckmann, E., & Minnaert, A. (2018). Non-cognitive characteristics of gifted students with learning disabilities: An in-depth systematic review. *Frontiers in Psychology, 9*(504), 1–20. https://doi.org/10.3389/fpsyg.2018.00504

Cabrera-Murcia, E. P. (2011). Entretejiendo los aprendizajes: desde el programa de perfeccionamiento de la pasantía PENTA UC a la práctica pedagógica. *Magis. Revista Internacional de Investigación en Educación, 4*(7), 105–120. Retrieved from http://www.redalyc.org/pdf/2810/281021741006.pdf

Cabrera-Murcia, E. P., & Udaquiola, C. (2016). What do teachers think about children academically talented? An approach to middle school teachers conceptions in Chile. *Universitas Psychologica, 15*(2), 121–134. https://doi.org/10.11144/Javeriana.upsy15-2.ppnt

Castellano, J. A., & Frazier, A. D. (2010). *Special populations in gifted education: Understanding our most able students from diverse backgrounds*. Waco, TX: National Association for Gifted Children/Prufrock Press.

Coleman, L. J., Micko, K. J., & Cross, T. L. (2015). Twenty-five years of research on the lived experience of being gifted in school: Capturing the students' voices. *Journal for the Education of the Gifted, 38*(4), 358–376. https://doi.org/10.1177/0162353215607322

Coleman, M. R., & Gallagher, S. (2015). Meeting the needs of students with 2e. It takes a team. *Gifted Child Today, 38*(4), 252–254. https://doi.org/10.1177/1076217515597274

Conejeros, M. L., Cáceres, P., & Riveros, A. (2012). Educación de talentos académicos en Chile: Una década de aprendizajes e investigación. In E. J. Catalán (Ed.), *Investigación orientada al cambio en psicología educacional* (pp. 39–74). La Serena, Chile: Editorial Universidad de La Serena. ISBN: 978-956-7393-72-5.

Conejeros-Solar, M. L., Gómez-Arizaga, M. P., & Donoso-Osorio, E. (2013). Perfil docente para alumnos/as con altas capacidades. *Magis, Revista Internacional de Investigación en Educación, 5*(11), 393–411. Retrieved from http://www.redalyc.org/pdf/2810/281028437007.pdf

Conejeros-Solar, M. L., Gómez-Arizaga, M. P., Sandoval-Rodríguez, K., & Cáceres-Serrano, P. (2018). Aportes a la comprensión de la doble excepcionalidad: Alta capacidad con trastorno por déficit de atención y alta capacidad con trastorno del espectro autista. *Revista Educación, 42*(2), 645–676. https://doi.org/10.15517/revedu.v42i2.25430

Conejeros-Solar, M. L., Sandoval-Rodriguez, K., & Gomez-Arizaga, M. P. (2018). Chile: The challenges of identification. *Variations 2e, 1,* 10–12. Retrieved from https://www.2enews.com/category/magazine/

Danielian, J., & Nilles, K. (2015). *The exceptionality of being twice-exceptional. Connecting for high potential*. Washington, DC: National Association for Gifted Children.

Dare, L., & Nowicki, E. A. (2015). Twice-exceptionality: Parents' perspectives on 2e identification. *Roeper Review, 37*(4), 208–218. https://doi.org/10.1080/02783193.2015.1077911

Dever, W. (2016). The impact of teacher–student relationships on the development of talent: Connections with Gagné's DMGT 2.0. *Journal of Student Engagement: Education Matters, 6*(1), 2–12. Retrieved from https://ro.uow.edu.au/jseem/vol6/iss1/2/

Engward, H. (2013). Understanding grounded theory. *Nursing Standard, 28*(7), 37–41. https://doi.org/10.7748/ns2013.10.28.7.37.e7806

Foley-Nicpon, M., & Assouline, S. G. (2015). Counseling considerations for the twice exceptional client. *Journal of Counseling & Development, 93*(2), 202–211. https://doi.org/10.1002/j.1556-6676.2015.00196.x

Foley-Nicpon, M., Rickels, H., Assouline, S. G., & Richards, A. (2012). Self-esteem and self-concept examination among gifted students with ADHD. *Journal for the Education of the Gifted, 35*(3), 220–240. https://doi.org/10.1177/0162353212451735

França-Freitas, M. L. P. D., Del Prette, A., & Del Prette, Z. A. P. (2014). Social skills of gifted and talented children. *Estudos de Psicologia, 19*(4), 288–295. https://doi.org/10.1590/S1413-294X2014000400006

Franklin-Rohr, C. (2012). Bullying and the twice-exceptional student. *Understanding Our Gifted, 24*(3), 19–20. Retrieved from https://eric.ed.gov/?id=EJ984378

Furrer, C., Skinner, E., & Pitzer, J. (2014). The influence of teacher and peer relationships on students' classroom engagement and everyday motivational resilience. In D. Shernoff & J. Bempechat (Eds.), *Engaging youth in schools: Evidence-based models to guide future innovations* (pp. 101–123). New York, NY: Columbia University, Teachers College Record. ISSN-0161-4681.

Gagné, F. (2015). De los genes al talento: la perspectiva DMGT/CMTD. *Revista de Educación, 368*, 12–39. https://doi.org/10.4438/1988-592X-RE-2015-368-289

García, C., & Arancibia, V. (2007). Pasantías PENTA UC: Una propuesta innovadora de desarrollo profesional docente. *Psykhe, 16*(1), 135–147. https://doi.org/10.4067/S0718-22282007000100011

Gazmuri, C., Manzi, J., & Paredes, R. D. (2015). Disciplina, clima y desempeño escolar en Chile. *Revista CEPAL, 115*, 116–128. Retrieved from https://repositorio.cepal.org/bitstream/handle/11362/37833/1/REV115ManziParedes_es.pdf

Geake, J. G., & Gross, M. U. M. (2008). Teachers' negative affect toward academically gifted students: An evolutionary psychological study. *The Gifted Child Quarterly, 52*(3), 217–231. https://doi.org/10.1177/0016986208319704

Godor, B. P., & Szymanski, A. (2017). Sense of belonging or feeling marginalized? Using PISA 2012 to assess the state of academically gifted students within the EU. *High Ability Studies, 28*(2), 181–197. https://doi.org/10.1080/13598139.2017.1319343

Gómez-Arizaga, M. (2016, April). *The complexities of gifted students' inner lives. The social realm*. Paper presented at the American Educational Research Association (AERA), Washington, DC. Retrieved from http://www.aera.net/repository:

Gómez-Arizaga, M., Conejeros-Solar, M. L., & Martin, A. (2016). How good is good enough? A community-based assessment of teacher competencies for gifted students. *SAGE Open, 6*, 1–14. https://doi.org/10.1177/2158244016680687

Gómez-Arizaga, M., Conejeros-Solar, M. L., Sandoval, K., & Armijo, S. (2016). Doble excepcionalidad: Análisis exploratorio de experiencias y autoimagen en estudiantes chilenos. *Revista de Psicología, 34*(1), 5–37. https://doi.org/10.18800/psico.201601.001

Gómez-Arizaga, M., Hébert, T., Castillo, H., & Valdivia, M. (2017). *Tales from within: What are gifted students´ experiences with teaching and learning in regular classrooms?* (Manuscript in preparation).

Gómez-Arizaga, M., & Truffello, A. (2018). *Estudio exploratorio sobre las percepciones parentales respecto a la experiencia académica y social de sus hijos con altas capacidades* (Paper submitted for publication).

Gross, M. U. M. (2006). Exceptionally gifted children: Long-term outcomes of academic acceleration and nonacceleration. *Journal for the Education of the Gifted, 29*(4), 404–429. Retrieved from https://files.eric.ed.gov/fulltext/EJ746290.pdf

Hodges, J., Tay, J., Maeda, Y., & Gentry, M. (2018). A meta-analysis of gifted and talented identification practices. *The Gifted Child Quarterly, 62*(2), 147–174. https://doi.org/10.1177/0016986217752107

Infante, M. (2010). Desafíos a la formación docente: Inclusión educativa. *Estudios pedagógicos, 36*(1), 287–297. https://doi.org/10.4067/S0718-07052010000100016

Jarvis, J., & Henderson, L. (2014). Defining a coordinated approach to gifted education. *The Australasian Journal of Gifted Education, 23*(1), 5–14. Retrieved from https://www.researchgate.net/publication/307928828_Defining_a_coordinated_approach_to_gifted_education

Jenaabadi, H., Marziyeh, A., & Dadkan, A. (2015). Comparing emotional creativity and social adjustment of gifted and normal students. *Advances in Applied Sociology, 5*, 111–118. https://doi.org/10.4236/aasoci.2015.53010

Lassig, C. (2015). Teachers' attitudes towards the gifted: The importance of professional development and school culture. *The Australasian Journal of Gifted Education, 24*(2), 6–16. Retrieved from https://eprints.qut.edu.au/32480/1/32480.pdf

Lee, S. Y., Olszewski-Kubilius, P., & Thomson, D. (2012). The social competence of highly gifted math and science adolescents. *Asia Pacific Education Review, 13*(2), 185–197. https://doi.org/10.1007/s12564-012-9209-x

McCoach, D. B., & Siegle, D. (2007). What predicts teachers' attitudes toward the gifted? *The Gifted Child Quarterly, 51*(3), 246–254. https://doi.org/10.1177/0016986207302719

Mizala, A., & Torche, F. (2012). Bringing the schools back in: The stratification of educational achievement in the Chilean voucher system. *International Journal of Educational Development, 32*, 132–144. https://doi.org/10.1016/j.ijedudev.2010.09.004

Ng, S. J., Hill, M. F., & Rawlinson, C. (2016). Hidden in plain sight. *The Gifted Child Quarterly, 60*(4), 296–311. https://doi.org/10.1177/0016986216656257

Ogurlu, U. (2015). Ostracism among gifted adolescents: A preliminary study in Turkey. *Educational Process: International Journal, 4*(1–2), 18–30. https://doi.org/10.12973/edupij.2015.412.2

Olszewski-Kubilius, P. (2013). Setting the record straight on ability grouping. *Education Week*. Retrieved from http://www.edweek.org/tm/articles/2013/05/20/fp_olszewski.html

Ortiz, I. (2015). Escuelas inclusivas en el contexto de segregación social del sistema escolar chileno. *Calidad en la Educación, 42*, 93–122. Retrieved from https://scielo.conicyt.cl/pdf/caledu/n42/art04.pdf

Peterson, J., Duncan, N., & Canady, K. (2009). A longitudinal study of negative life events, stress, and school experiences of gifted youth. *The Gifted Child Quarterly, 53*(1), 34–49. https://doi.org/10.1177/0016986208326553

Peterson, J. S. (2015). School counselors and gifted kids: Respecting both cognitive and affective. *Journal of Counseling & Development, 93*(2), 153–162. https://doi.org/10.1002/j.1556-6676.2015.00191.x

Preckel, F., Baudson, T. G., Krolak-Schwerdt, S., & Glock, S. (2015). Gifted and maladjusted? Implicit attitudes and automatic associations related to gifted children. *American Educational Research Journal, 52*(6), 1160–1184. https://doi.org/10.3102/0002831215596413

Reis, S. M., Baum, S. M., & Burke, E. (2014). An operational definition of twice-exceptional learners: Implications and applications. *The Gifted Child Quarterly, 58*(3), 217–230. https://doi.org/10.1177/0016986214534976

Renzulli, J. S., & Reis, S. M. (2014). *The schoolwide enrichment model: A how-to guide for talent development* (3rd ed.). Waco, TX: Prufrock Press.

Rinn, A. N., & Nelson, J. M. (2008). Preservice teachers' perceptions of behaviors characteristic of ADHD and giftedness. *Roeper Review, 31*(1), 18–26. https://doi.org/10.1080/02783190802527349

Ronksley-Pavia, M., & Townend, G. (2017). Listening and responding to twice exceptional students: Voices from within. *TalentEd, 29*, 32–57. Retrieved from http://www.talented.org.au/listening-and-responding-to-twice-exceptional-students-voices-from-within/

Rowe, E., Kim, S., Baker, J. A., Kamphaus, R. W., & Horne, A. M. (2010). Student personal perception of classroom climate: Exploratory and confirmatory factor analyses. *Educational and Psychological Measurement, 70*(5), 858–879. https://doi.org/10.1177/0013164410378085

Rubenstein, L. D., Schelling, N., Wilczynski, S. M., & Hooks, E. N. (2015). Lived experiences of parents of gifted students with autism spectrum disorder: The struggle to find appropriate educational experiences. *The Gifted Child Quarterly, 59*(4), 283–298. https://doi.org/10.1177/0016986215592193

Rubie-Davies, C. M. (2010). Teacher expectations and perceptions of student attributes: Is there a relationship? *British Journal of Educational Psychology, 80*(1), 121–135. https://doi.org/10.1348/000709909X466334

Rufinelli, A. (2013). La calidad de la formación inicial docente en Chile: La perspectiva de los profesores principiantes. *Calidad en la educación, (39)*, 117–154. https://doi.org/10.4067/s0718-45652013000200005

Samardzija, N., & Peterson, J. S. (2015). Learning and classroom preferences of gifted eighth graders: A qualitative study. *Journal for the Education of the Gifted, 38*(3), 233–256. https://doi.org/10.1177/0162353215592498

San Martín, C., Villalobos, C., Muñoz, C., & Wyman, I. (2017). Formación inicial docente para la educación inclusiva. Análisis de tres programas chilenos de pedagogía en educación básica que incorporan la perspectiva de la educación inclusiva. *Calidad de la Educación, 46*, 20–52. Retrieved from https://scielo.conicyt.cl/pdf/caledu/n46/0718-4565-caledu-46-00020.pdf

Schultz, S. (2012). Twice-exceptional students enrolled in advanced placement classes. *The Gifted Child Quarterly, 56*, 119–133. https://doi.org/10.1177/0016986212444605

Shayshon, B., Gal, H., Tesler, B., & Ko, E. (2014). Teaching mathematically talented students: A cross–cultural study about their teachers' views. *Educational Studies in Mathematics, 87*(3), 409–438. https://doi.org/10.1007/S10649-014-9568-9

Silverman, L. K. (2013). *Giftedness 101*. New York, NY: Springer.

Smith, S. (2017). Responding to the unique social and emotional learning needs of gifted Australian students. In E. Frydenberg, A. J. Martin, & R. J. Collie (Eds.), *Social and emotional learning in Australia and the Asia-Pacific perspectives, programs and approaches* (pp. 147–166). Singapore: Springer Nature.

Strauss, A., & Corbin, J. (1998). *Basics of qualitative research. Techniques and procedures for developing grounded theory*. Thousand Oaks, CA: Sage.

Tomlinson, C. A. (2014). *The differentiated classroom: Responding to the needs of all learners* (2nd ed.). Alexandria, VA: ASCD.

Townend, G., & Pendergast, D. (2015). Student voice: What can we learn from twice-exceptional students about the teacher's role in enhancing or inhibiting academic self-concept. *Australasian Journal of Gifted Education, 24*(1), 37–51. Retrieved from https://core.ac.uk/download/pdf/143899736.pdf

Tucker, C., Dixon, A., & Griddine, K. S. (2010). Academically successful African American male urban high school students' experiences of mattering to others at school. *Professional School Counseling, 14*(2), 135–145. Retrieved from https://eric.ed.gov/?id=EJ952179

VanTassel-Baska, J., & Stambaugh, T. (2006). *Comprehensive curriculum for gifted learners* (3rd ed.). Boston, MA: Pearson Education.

Veiga, F., García, F., Reeve, J., Wentzel, K., & García, Ó. (2015). When adolescents with high self-concept lose their engagement in school. *Revista de Psicodidáctica, 20*(2), 305–320. https://doi.org/10.1387/RevPsicodidact.12671

Wang, C. W., & Neihart, M. (2015). Academic self-concept and academic self-efficacy: Self-beliefs enable academic achievement of twice-exceptional students. *Roeper Review, 37*, 63–73. https://doi.org/10.1080/02783193.2015.1008660

Wentzel, K. R., Battle, A., Russell, S. L., & Looney, L. B. (2010). Social supports from teachers and peers as predictors of academic and social motivation. *Contemporary Educational Psychology, 35*(3), 193–202. Retrieved from https://eric.ed.gov/?id=EJ890839

Yssel, N., Prater, M., & Smith, D. (2010). How can such a smart kid not get it? Finding the right fit for twice-exceptional students in our schools. *Gifted Child Today, 33*(1), 54–61. https://doi.org/10.1177/107621751003300113

Maria Paz Gomez-Arizaga is a Psychologist who obtained her PhD in Special Education from the University of Arizona. She currently works as an associate professor at the College of Education, Universidad de los Andes, Chile. She has participated in research projects related to the school experiences of secondary gifted students and twice-exceptional learners. Her main research interests and publications are related to traditionally underserved gifted students and their perceptions and experiences as learners in regular classrooms.

Maria Leonor Conejeros-Solar, PhD, is full Professor, Psychologist, Doctor in Education at the School of Pedagogy of the Pontificia Universidad Católica de Valparaíso. Among her duties, she has served as the Director of the Academically Talented Education Program BETA in the same University. Her main research interests are: academically talented students from underprivileged socio-economic backgrounds; gifted college students; provisions and socio-emotional issues of gifted and twice-exceptional students; and gifted homeschooling. She has published several articles and book chapters.

Of Grit and Gumption, Sass and Verve: What Gifted Students Can Learn from Multicultural Picture Book Biographies

20

Rhoda Myra Garces-Bacsal

Contents

Introduction	432
Multicultural Gifted Education, SEL, and Use of PBB	434
Critical Multicultural Analysis Framework Mapped Across SEL and Teaching Strategies and Activities	437
Recommended Multicultural PBB Text-Sets for the Gifted and Talented	438
Implications and Future Directions	449
Conclusion	449
Cross-References	450
References	450

Abstract

The significant role *Picture Book Biographies* (PBBs) play when it comes to providing readers with a deeper understanding of 'global connections and cultural diversity' is evident in the research (Morgan, 2009). This becomes even more important among gifted and talented readers who can use multicultural PBBs to know more intimately the life narratives of men and women who have achieved expertise and prominence in their respective fields and domains. Multicultural titles, in particular, would allow readers to see themselves as part of humanity and provide a window to other societies and lifestyles that may be unfamiliar to them. The use of biographies that focus on diverse populations allows students to see everyone as having equally high potential and helps develop an appreciation of alternative pathways to talent development and expertise. Based on a research project that looks into building a database of multicultural picture books for social and emotional learning, text-sets of PBBs by award-winning authors and artists

---

R. M. Garces-Bacsal (✉)
College of Education, Special Education Department, United Arab Emirates University, Al Ain, United Arab Emirates
e-mail: rhoda.bacsal@nie.edu.sg

© Springer Nature Singapore Pte Ltd. 2021
S. R. Smith (ed.), *Handbook of Giftedness and Talent Development in the Asia-Pacific*, Springer International Handbooks of Education,
https://doi.org/10.1007/978-981-13-3041-4_18

have been compiled, representing different types of giftedness including artistic, literary, musical, athletic, leadership, and intellectual skills. This would be linked to cognitive traits of the gifted and talented, social and emotional issues experienced by the gifted, and social and emotional traits of gifted learners and the highly creative. The PBBs of resilient individuals who demonstrate sass and verve and grit and gumption despite misfortune and adversity will likewise be shared and discussed. Through these inspired and well-crafted biographies, it is hoped that teachers can scaffold gifted readers' understandings of and identification with, diverse people from around the world and come to realise how the road to excellence can prove to be an arduous, but meaningful journey.

Keywords

Gifted students · High-ability learners · Picture book biographies · Multicultural children's literature · Social and emotional learning

The aims in this chapter are to:
1. Highlight the use of biographies in teaching the gifted.
2. Establish the link between multicultural gifted education, *Social and Emotional Learning* (SEL) and the use of *Picture Book Biographies* (PBB).
3. Discuss the criteria in the selection of multicultural PBB for gifted students.
4. Use the critical multicultural analysis framework to prompt affective engagement in reading the books, as well as provide teaching strategies and activities that can be used in the classroom.
5. Provide recommended text-sets grouped across key cognitive, social, and emotional traits of, and issues faced by, the gifted and highly creative.

Introduction

The examination of the biographies or the lives of highly able individuals in gifted education is not new (Bloom, 1985; Csikszentmihalyi, 1997; Ericsson, Charness, Feltovich, & Hoffman, 2006; Galton, 1892; Goertzel, Goertzel, Goertzel, & Hansen, 2004; Robinson & Jolly, 2013; Terman, 1925). In Robinson and Jolly's (2013) book, *Illuminating Lives*, a group of researchers documented the lives of pioneers in gifted education. Their purpose is to encourage more scholars to do biographical research, as it is "a thrilling pursuit as well as a scholarly investigation" (Robinson & Jolly, 2013, p. 4).

The use of biographies among the gifted can be traced from the 1920s when Leta Hollingworth, founder of the Speyer School for highly gifted children in New York, infused biographical studies as part of the standard curriculum (Hollingworth, 1926). Hildreth (1966) explained its value by showing how the reading of biographies can serve as a source of inspiration for gifted students, as they also identify with personalities who have achieved something of significance through their intelligence, hard work, and capacity to overcome obstacles. In fact, an intervention known as bibliotherapy was found to be useful to address mathematics anxiety among high-ability students (Furner, 2017) and address the affective needs of bright boys such as image management, self-inflicted pressure, and gender role conflict (Hebert, 1991) and help nurture the social and emotional development of gifted teenagers through young adult literature (Hebert & Kent, 2000). Bibliotherapy is also found to be useful when the gifted feel over-burdened by parental expectations or ridiculed by peers for independent thinking (Schlichter & Burke, 1994) and has been used with gifted students as early as 1956 who use it to solve their problems such as school boredom, being misunderstood by teachers, or peer rejection (Weingarten, 1956). It is defined as the use of reading to help the gifted "understand themselves and cope with problems by providing literature relevant to their personal situations and developmental needs at appropriate times" (Hebert & Kent, 2000, p. 168). A distinction is made between clinical bibliotherapy, which involves the use of psychotherapeutic methods by skilled practitioners for individuals experiencing serious emotional difficulties, and developmental bibliotherapy that is used to help students proactively in their emotional health and development, with the latter used by educators and gifted practitioners (Hebert & Kent, 2000). As noted by Smith (2017, p. 153), "through facilitated dialogue, bibliotherapy allows gifted students to connect their own personal concerns with those emulated by literary characters".

Apart from using biographies in scholarly investigations, researchers (Hebert, Long, & Speirs Neumeister, 2001) have also found the use of biographies to be particularly germane in counselling gifted young women and helpful in addressing their social and emotional issues and concerns. This is because gifted students are often prodigious readers and their affective concerns have been found to be effectively addressed through guided reading as it appeals to their love of literature and biographies in particular (Ford, Tyson, Howard, & Harris, 2000; Hebert et al., 2001).

Much has also been written (Duckworth, 2016; Duckworth, Peterson, Matthews, & Kelly, 2007) about the significance of non-cognitive traits in accounting for an individual's eventual success, with one trait being consistent across various domains: grit. Duckworth (2016) defined grit as perseverance and passion for long-term goals that were found to be positively correlated to African American college students' academic success at predominantly white institutions (Strayhorn, 2014). Grit was also found to play a critical role along with disciplinary climates in predicting low-SES students' high achievement in mathematics and science (Haigen & Hao, 2017). However, it is beyond the scope of this chapter to look into the considerable debate about the inadequacy of grit in explaining eventual success and eminence (see also Credé, Tynan, & Harms, 2017; Delisle, 2016). It is the author's contention that there are multidimensional and multiplicative (Simonton, 2001) interactions between one's innate gifts or talents, personality, and one's environment. This chapter is meant to provide researchers and practitioners with a preliminary database of multicultural *Picture Book Biographies* (PBB) of individuals across different fields and domains coming from varied cultural backgrounds who have achieved success and eminence in their fields through grit and gumption, sass and verve.

Multicultural Gifted Education, SEL, and Use of PBB

The heterogeneity and diversity in student demographics in today's classroom is becoming more the norm rather than the exception (Chong & Cheah, 2010). This has led researchers Montero and Robertson (2006) to claim that in many urban settings, the culturally homogenous classroom "is already extinct" (p. 27). In Singapore, for example, there can be as many as 39 different nationalities seen in a popular primary school (Forss, 2007), along with growing diversity in ability levels, socio-economic status, religion, linguistic, and cultural backgrounds (Khum, 2013). This has led countries such as Australia, for example, to adapt the *Early Years Learning Framework* (EYLF; Department of Education, Employment and Workplace Relations for the Council of Australian Governments [DEEWR], 2009) to support educators in providing effective learning environments across five basic principles, one of which has to do with *respect for diversity*, which is at the heart of multicultural education (Buchori & Dobinson, 2015). The changing educational landscape towards multiculturalism and diversity has also made the call for culturally responsive teaching even more salient. Culturally responsive teaching is defined by Gay (2000) as the use of frames of reference, cultural knowledge, and even performance styles of students who are ethnically diverse so that learning encounters are more relevant, engaging, and effective for them. This is evident from the search for and use of materials that provide representations to diverse populations in positive ways and efforts to ensure that educational access is provided to students and teachers to deepen awareness of the existence of such resources (Fears-Floyd & Hebert, 2010).

Gifted education programs, specifically, have been found wanting when it comes to the infusion of multiculturalism throughout its curricula (Ford, Moore, & Harmon, 2005). This becomes an issue especially since there are gifted students who are double minorities by virtue of their being gifted and of a different race or ethnicity or of low-income status, making them even more vulnerable as they navigate their own cultural norms and meet the expectations required of them within a larger school context (Stambaugh & Ford, 2015). In fact, Nguyen (2012, p. 15) noted that, "many seasoned teachers who have been teaching in demographically diverse communities have little knowledge of the heritage backgrounds and cultural practices of the students under their tutelage". This has led scholars such as Ford et al. (2005) to claim that gifted students of colour (and those from the dominant culture as well) are being short-changed and are essentially underrepresented in their educational experience. Research has also indicated that gifted students perceive their school curriculum as boring and irrelevant when it was not multicultural, and students who are not engaged in the curriculum tend to underachieve even though they have the potential to do well academically (Ford, 2011). Conversely, the more that gifted students of colour are reflected in the curricula, the more engaged they are in their learning and the more appreciative they are of course content that promotes self-affirmation and self-empowerment (Ford et al., 2005).

Nguyen (2012) noted that one of the specific ways through which multicultural education can be facilitated is by making use of the "plethora of multicultural literature" (p. 15) that is out there for teachers to use. The use of multicultural literature to address both the curricular and social and emotional needs of gifted learners has been documented and has been shown to not just benefit gifted students of colour, but also help those from the majority culture to be more understanding and open-minded about other cultural perspectives and ways of being (Ford et al., 2000; Pedersen & Kitano, 2006). Ford et al. (2000) stated that multicultural picture books have the potential to go beyond just the touristy (or contributions) approach to multicultural education, to one that is transformational as noted by Banks (2009) because "it has the power to serve as a catalyst for social action, for helping students to appreciate their similarities and their differences, and for increasing students' cultural awareness and sensitivity" (p. 236). All these competencies of self-awareness and management, empathy, perspective taking, conflict management and social justice are part of the competencies that make up the *Social and Emotional Learning* (SEL) framework.

The Collaborative for Academic, Social and Emotional Learning or CASEL (2013) defines SEL as the ability to acquire and apply the knowledge, attitudes, and skills to recognise and regulate emotions, set and achieve positive goals, feel and demonstrate compassion and empathy, establish and maintain positive relationships with others, and make responsible decisions. Research studies have established how multicultural books, in particular, can powerfully influence a child's capacity to understand and imagine other people's thoughts and feelings (Nikolajeva, 2013), help develop empathy among children (Bal & Veltkamp, 2013), promote recognition and appreciation of social diversity (Hymel, Schonert-Reichl, & Miller, 2006), and can serve as subtle but effective tools to discuss social and emotional issues (Harper, 2016). Sharing high-quality picture books has also been found to enhance children's sensitivity to other people's feelings, help foster moral development (Harper & Trostle-Brand, 2010), and provide the foundational framework to build empathy, appreciation of diversity, and reinforce conflict resolution skills among young children (Harper, 2016). Gopalakrishnan (2011, p. 34) further stated:

> ...there is an urgent need for multicultural children's literature to permeate the curriculum in schools, for genuine accounts that address many issues from an insider's point of view, to give children a way to validate their feelings and experiences; to create understanding, empathy, and tolerance; to break debilitating stereotypes; to give equal voice and representation.

Picture Book Biographies (PBB) and the gifted. Researchers have focused on multicultural PBB because they are found to inspire children and are often preferred over the traditional textbooks used in schools (Ellis, 2007). The compound word picturebook is also used to highlight the polysemic nature of the stories that indicate the seamless interaction between word and image, allowing for multiple interpretations by the reader (Ghosh, 2015). Hence, the visual narrative adds another layer to the understanding of the textual narrative, elevating the picture book to a veritable art form. Maurice Sendak (as cited in Salisbury & Styles, 2012) described it as a juxtaposition of picture and word, a counterpoint whereby words are left out, but the picture relays the narrative, or pictures are left out, but the word displays the narrative. Multicultural picture books, in particular, have been described as mirrors and windows (Sims Bishop, 2003), allowing readers to see their experiences reflected back to them, or providing them spaces to access realities and fields of experience that may be unfamiliar yet also demonstrate distinct universal resonances that readers can identify with.

Morgan (2009) contended, "culturally authentic biographies that represent the perspectives of cultural minorities are plentiful today and less likely to contain racial bias" (p. 221). In fact, Polette (2009) compiled an annotated bibliography of gifted biographies for gifted readers across a variety of fields and disciplines, which she calls "gifted meeting gifted through biography" (p. ix). She stated that through these narratives, gifted students would be able to fully appreciate the humanity, nobility of character, and even some of the challenging and troubling traits of unconventional eminent, individuals that society may not necessarily understand.

Research has documented the benefits of using PBB among gifted children of African American (Fears-Floyd & Hébert, 2010) and Hispanic (Abellán-Pagnani & Hébert, 2013) descent, enabling educators to respond more sensitively to address their social and emotional needs and concerns. This would include being bilingual, bicultural, finding a sense of belonging in school, as well as developing an ethnic identity and pride (Abellán-Pagnani & Hébert, 2013), which may not necessarily fit into cultural and societal expectations of what it means, to be gifted. Fears-Floyd and Hébert (2010) showed how the use of biographies that highlight diverse populations' benefits not just the highly able students but all learners in the classroom, providing them the opportunity to not just regard themselves, but one another as having equally high potential. The PBBs, in particular, are deemed to be particularly beneficial in teachers' efforts to provide appropriate enrichment (Abellán-Pagnani & Hébert, 2013; Fears-Floyd & Hébert, 2010), as picture book biographies serve to inspire and motivate young, gifted, and culturally diverse children, enabling them to draw parallels to their lives and recognise their capacity to actualise their potential.

Criteria in selecting PBBs for the gifted. The selection of quality multicultural literature follows the same basic criteria which apply to selecting quality children's literature in general, whereby the literary elements of plot, point of view, setting, theme, and characterisation are all interwoven to create a credible and realistic story that is, told in a compelling manner, allowing readers to make meaningful connections from the story (Harper & Trostle-Brand, 2010). While multicultural children's literature has traditionally been defined as stories about people of colour (Sims Bishop, 2003), the researcher has expanded the definition to include outstanding books that meet the standards of good literature noted above, as well as titles that represent lifestyle and cultural beliefs (be it gender and identity, ability, socioeconomic status, body image, language, political beliefs, ethnicity) of as many individuals as possible (Lukens, Smith, & Coffel, 2013).

Authenticity is also one of the key criterion, such that the books are able to portray cultural experiences in a realistic yet sensitive manner, with celebration of dialect and colloquial expressions in dialogues, as well as portray illustrations that capture historical events in an accurate and effective manner (Fears-Floyd & Hebert, 2010). Polette (2009) listed a few key questions to consider in selecting well-written PBBs, such as whether the dialogue, if present, is supported by research or whether it is invented and whether the events presented lead up to and illuminate the achievements of the main character who is presented as a person with both faults and accomplishments and strengths and weaknesses.

Ash and Barthelmess (2011) further described a good PBB as using "sophisticated imagery to complement the narrative with a sense of the time and place of the subject's life" (p. 41). While it is acknowledged that a comprehensive exploration of a person's life narrative is not possible in a 32- or 48-paged PBB, the 'ingenious' ones (Ash & Barthelmess, 2011, p. 42) are able to convey the essentials by providing excerpts of both struggles and accomplishments, reinforced by rigorously researched words and imagery that resonate with the reader. The presence of a comprehensive back matter is helpful; this can include photographs, a historical timeline, glossary, bibliography for further reading and notes about the author's and illustrator's own research (Ash & Barthelmess, 2011).

Critical Multicultural Analysis Framework Mapped Across SEL and Teaching Strategies and Activities

The critical multicultural analysis framework introduced by Botelho and Rudman (2009) acknowledges that the roots of multicultural children's literature are grounded in the historical silence of underrepresented groups. Hence, the discussion of the books brings into the forefront an understanding of the complexities of power relations. Additionally, there is the focus on the process of analysis, rather than simply looking at the presence or absence of characters that are people of colour in the narrative. It also provides a space for the reader to question and challenge the text, enrich the reader's historical, cultural, and socio-political imagination, as well as get readers to reimagine social worlds depictured in the book. Botelho and Rudman (2009) also warned teachers to be cautious of 'fictive unity' (p. 102), such that all Asians or Latinos or Mexicans are lumped together, without a finer appreciation of the diversity not just between but also within cultures. Teachers are asked to encourage young readers to engage in the text more closely by getting them to rewrite, revise, and even expand the book based on their social contexts or cultural background and realities. By adopting a critical multicultural stance, the gifted student would be able to ask themselves pertinent questions such as whose voices are silenced or heard in the narrative, reflect on world views or behaviours that are presented as normal in the text, examine how the story can be challenged further, or how else the story could have been written if presented by an author or an illustrator who may be writing a story from either inside or outside their own culture (Botelho & Rudman, 2009; Gopalakrishnan, 2011). This type of close reading is said to promote a greater affective engagement since teachers are no longer the keepers of textual meaning as they provide spaces for children to connect texts to their life experiences. Through this framework, the reader is encouraged to insert themselves into the narrative, examine its point of view, analyse positions of power, and even question and redefine the ending if they wish to (Botelho & Rudman, 2009). A set of key critical response questions adapted from Rycik and Irvin (2005) and Gopalakrishnan's key guide questions for educators, as well as the researcher's own original discussion questions, have been mapped across the five SEL domains as found in Table 1.

Teachers are encouraged to consider using extension activities, such as an open-minded portrait, which serves as an emotion book that focuses on the main character of the story (Harper & Trostle-Brand, 2010). In this strategy, the character is hand-drawn or illustrated by the gifted student in the front page of their emotion book, with the following pages used to demonstrate the character's feelings and thoughts at certain junctures in the narrative. This type of strategy has been found to be especially useful for children who are already highly proficient in reading and writing as it allows children to do perspective-taking, identify with characters, and analyse other people's perspectives (Harper & Trostle-Brand, 2010).

Fears-Floyd and Hébert (2010) mentioned that it is important for teachers to consider activities that incorporate art. An example provided is that teachers can select illustrations from the PBB and ask students to examine the art, describe what they see, and analyse the visual narrative in the story (in terms of colours, lines, textures, artistic style, medium used, typography, overall layout, and design of the narrative). Moreover, students may be asked to interview each other and share stories about their lives, while the teacher supports students as they write the biographies of their selected partners and create the art to illustrate their PBB. The final biographies can be put on display in the classroom or the school library to be enjoyed by others. Virtual field trips are likewise recommended if PBBs about eminent visual artists, musicians and other high creatives are shared or paired film viewing for PBBs of scientists and mathematicians, athletes, peacemakers, social activists and environmentalists (Polette, 2009; Fears-Floyd & Hebert, 2010).

Smith (2017) has also cited the importance of using creative forms of self-expression, such as dance or drama performance, or coming up with other artistic productions to explore the gifted students' emotions and other people's emotions. In Furner's (2017) research on using bibliotherapy in a mathematics classroom to address the anxieties experienced by highly able learners, he clarified that simply reading good books is not enough. There has to be opportunities for discussions, role-playing, creative problem-solving, relaxation with music, and even journal writing, a strategy supported by other researchers (Cross, 2005). Smith (2017) stated that the discussions engendered by bibliotherapy have to be facilitated with the use of strategies, such as Socratic dialogue, to probe deeper into an analysis of key social and emotional issues and values. Furner (2017) also recommended for teachers to consider working with the school counsellor once a month, providing more avenues for students to articulate their issues and anxieties more openly in a non-threatening environment.

Recommended Multicultural PBB Text-Sets for the Gifted and Talented

The recommended text-set is part of a much larger research project that examined the reading lives of teachers, educators, and students who were attending courses at a teacher-training institute in Singapore and the creation of a multicultural picture

Table 1 Adapted from Rycik and Irvin's (2005) critical response questions and Gopalakrishnan's (2011) reflection questions for the teacher and a few additional discussion questions mapped across the SEL framework

Self-awareness	Self-management	Social awareness	Relationship management	Responsible decision-making
Adapted from Rycik and Irvin (2005, p. 156): **What was the context for reading?** If the book was assigned, how did that affect your reading? If you chose it, what made you pick this rather than something else? Did the time and place where you typically read the book make reading easier or harder? More enjoyable, or less? **How did you 'read' yourself?** What are your characteristics that you think influenced your reaction to this work? How much do you think your responses were influenced by your own ethnic background, age, gender, experiences or values? Do you think the experience of reading this work has changed you in any way? **What were your feelings while reading?**	**How did you read the characters in the story?** How would you describe the character's ability to manage or take control of their emotions? Describe how the characters were able to achieve their goals in the end. What did it take for them to reach their dreams? What are your own goals and dreams? What do you think it would take to achieve them?	**How is your social awareness enriched through the story?** Who among the characters do you sympathise/empathise with? Describe their traits and characteristics. Draw parallels/differences between the characters' lives and your own. How similar and how different are the concerns, issues, struggles that you are facing? If you were to take the perspective of (mention a character in the story), would you behave differently or similarly? Adapted from Knickerbocker and Rycik: **How did you 'read' the author?** What do you know about the author's life and work? What can you guess about this author's knowledge, values and experiences?	**How did you read the main characters' relationship with others in the story?** Describe the main characters' relationship with his/her family, friends and community. How did the main character in the story ask for or receive help from others around him? If you were a character in this story, how would you have responded to this situation? Would you have helped or ask for help? How did the main character resolve their conflict with others in the story? What would you have done similarly or differently given the same situation?	Adapted from Gopalakrishnan's (2011, p. 13) reflection questions for the teacher but adapted for use with students: What real-life issues does this PBB relate to? What real-life event has happened, will possibly happen or is happening that can be connected to this PBB? If I were working or living within this real-life context, event or issue, how would I deal with it? What historical references can I draw and learn from what has happened before? What can I do to change and learn from the event, problem or issue? How can I connect this story to my current situation to make it better? What steps (however small or large) can I take to make a change?

(continued)

Table 1 (continued)

Self-awareness	Self-management	Social awareness	Relationship management	Responsible decision-making
Did reading this work bring back memories of experiences in your own life? What aspects of the work did you most/least enjoy, made you feel confused or frustrated?		How do you think the work was influenced by the author's ethnic background or by whether the author is male or female, rich or poor, young or old? What effect do you think the author intended to have on readers of this work? Do you think the author had someone like you in mind as the audience, or someone with different knowledge, values and experiences than yours? **What is your interpretation of this work?** How was this work like or unlike other things you have read? What will you remember most from this work? What particular parts of the work do you think are most important for understanding it? What do you think is the significance of this work?		How will my actions affect others now, later and in the future?

book database (with over 900 titles) that maps out themes across the five SEL domains. The research team has sought out recommendations from the National Library Board of Singapore and visited the Woodlands Regional Library, which houses the Asian Children's Literature Collection of over 15,000 titles. International school librarians in Singapore were likewise consulted, and visits to international school libraries in Singapore (Tanglin Trust School, Canadian International School, Singapore American School, United World College Southeast Asia) have been conducted. The researcher also served as an International Research Fellow for two months in 2016 and six weeks in 2017 at the International Youth Library in Munich, which is reputed to have the largest international children's collection in the world. The researcher, however, has limited this chapter to a listing of only 30 multicultural PBBs across a variety of disciplines, with the predominant themes mapped across the five SEL competencies, as well as highlighting the cognitive and social-emotional traits and concerns of the gifted and highly creative children.

Overlaps can clearly be discerned across the five SEL competencies and giftedness traits. Seeing how these competencies and traits are interconnected, the researcher used peer debriefing with the research team members (an applied sociolinguist and a special needs teacher educator) to identify the predominant themes in the PBBs. This was done in a continual and iterative process in a shared Google spreadsheet, similar to what is found in Table 2, based on recommendations provided by educators and librarians, whereby the picture book titles are arranged across the five SEL competencies. With international research consultants from the Philippines (a theoretical linguist) and New Zealand (a senior lecturer of children's literature and teacher educator), a consensus was reached among the research team members. From the existing database, the author has selected titles that fit into themes as found in the gifted education literature, such as *cognitive traits of the gifted and talented, social and emotional issues experienced by the gifted,* and those that highlight the *social and emotional traits of gifted learners and highly creative children.* A few highlights and excerpts from some of the books are shared below.

PBBs that highlight cognitive traits of the gifted and talented. Gifted and talented individuals' cognitive traits have been described, such as having avid curiosity, keen powers of observation, a drive to document their knowledge, and a leaning towards scholastic life, logical thinking, and a thirst for knowledge and reading books (Rimm, Siegle, & Davis, 2018). Avid curiosity about one's environment and nature is clearly evident in Patrick McDonnell's *Me... Jane.* Told in distilled but effective language, there are only two to five lines in each page-spread alongside the muted, pastel art. Yet its authenticity is felt in its carefully chosen phrases and the miscellany-scrapbook style of the book, with a few drawings made by Goodall and photographs interspersed in the pages. The depiction of the young Jane Goodall also highlights the quiet determination of a pioneer who grew up in impoverished conditions, at a time when girls were not encouraged to pursue fields in science requiring overseas travels. This can be paired with *Summer Birds: The Butterflies of Maria Merian* that also highlights Maria's affinity with the environment and nature's creatures. Maria Merian studied the whole life cycle of the summer birds and documented what she learned in her vibrant paintings back in

Table 2 PBB mapped across SEL and traits of the gifted and high creatives

Book title and name of author and illustrator.	SEL competencies (SA: self-awareness, SM: Self-Management, SocA: Social Awareness, RM: Relationship Management, RDM: Responsible Decision-Making).					Cognitive traits of G & T (thirst for knowledge, logical thinking and advanced interests, unremitting focus, tenacity and single-mindedness; scholastic life; avid curiosity; keen powers of observation; documentation; intellectual persistence).	Socio-affective traits of G & T and high creatives (personal adjustment and remaining true to one's self; resilience; intrinsic motivation and persistence; grit and gumption; tolerance for ambiguity; superior humour; commitment to serving others; moral courage).	Socio-affective issues and concerns (dual-exceptionality; depression; feelings of stress; social rejection; apathy; boredom; overcoming social rejection, prejudice, social injustice and discrimination).
	SA	SM	SocA	RM	RDM			
(1) The Boy Who Loved Math: The improbable Life of Paul Erdos by Deborah Heiligman and LeUyen Pham.								
(2) Su Dongpo by Demi.								
(3) Summer Birds: The Butterflies of Maria Merian by Margarita Engle and Julie Paschkis.								
(4) Of Numbers And Stars: The Story of Hypatia by D. Anne Love and Pamela Paparone.								
(5) Me… Jane by Patrick McDonnell.								
(6) The Amazing Discoveries of Ibn Sina by Fatima Sharafeddine and Intelaq Mohammed Ali.								

(continued)

Table 2 (continued)

(7) Tomas and the Library Lady by Pat Mora and Raul Colon.							
(8) Fifty Cents and a Dream: Young Booker T. Washington by Jabari Asim and Bryan Collier.							
(9) Pablo Neruda: Poet Of The People by Monica Brown and Julie Paschkis.							
(10) My Name is Gabriela: The Life of Gabriela Mistral / Me Llamo Gabriela: La Vida De Gabriela Mistral by Monica Brown and John Parra.							
(11) The Mangrove Tree: Planting Trees to Feed Families by Susan L. Roth and Cindy Trumbore.							
(12) Wangari Maathai: The Woman Who Planted Millions Of Trees by Franck Prévot and Aurelia Fronty.							

(continued)

Table 2 (continued)

(13) Twenty-two Cents: Muhammad Yunus And The Village Bank by Paula Yoo and Jamel Akib.								
(14) Sojourner Truth's Step Stomp Stride by Andrea Davis Pinkney and Brian Pinkney.								
(15) The Boy On Fairfield Street: How Ted Geisel Grew Up To Become Dr. Seuss by Kathleen Krull, Lou Fancher and Steve Johnson.								
(16) Emmanuel's Dream: The True Story of Emmanuel Ofosu Yeboah by Laurie Ann Thompson and Sean Qualls.								Dual-exceptionality
(17) Wilma Unlimited: How Wilma Rudolph Became The World's Fastest Woman by Kathleen Krull and David Díaz.								Dual-exceptionality
(18) A Boy And A Jaguar by Alan Rabinowitz and CaTia Chen.								Dual-exceptionality

(continued)

Table 2 (continued)

(19) The Noisy Paint Box: The Colors and Sounds of Kandinsky's Abstract Art by Barb Rosenstock and Mary Grandpré.							Dual-exceptionality
(20) Sixteen Years in Sixteen Seconds: The Sammy Lee Story by Paula Yoo and Dom Lee.							
(21) The Peasant Prince by Li Cunxin and Anne Spudvilas.							
(22) Drum Dream Girl by Margarita Engle and Rafael Lopez.							
(23) Little Melba And Her Big Trombone by Katheryn Russell-Brown and Frank Morrison.							
(24) Voice of Freedom: Fannie Lou Hamer by Carole Boston Weatherford and Ekua Holmes.							
(25) Red Bird Sings: The Story of Zitkala-Sa: Native American Author, Musician and Activist by Gina Capaldi and Q. L. Pearce.							

(continued)

Table 2 (continued)

(26) Ada's Violin: The Story of the Recycled Orchestra in Paraguay by Susan Hood and Sally Wern Comport.							
(26) Step Right Up: How Doc and Jim Key Taught The World About Kindness by Donna Janell Bowman and Daniel Minter.							
(27) My Name Is Amrita: Born To Be An Artist by Anjali Raghbeer.							
(28) A Splash of Red: The Life And Art of Horace Pippin by Jennifer Fisher Bryant and Melissa Sweet.							
(29) Be Water, My Friend: The Early Years of Bruce Lee by Ken Mochizuki and Dom Lee.							
(30) The Little Refugee: The Inspiring True Story of Australia's Happiest Refugee by Anh Do, Suzanne Do and Bruce Whatley.							

the Middle Ages when people believed that insects were evil and born from mud in a process called spontaneous generation. In *Of Numbers and Stars,* the reader gets to know another brilliant woman thinker who lived in the fourth century in Alexandria Egypt—a name that may not be as famous as Aristotle, Socrates, or Galileo, but a highly respected and eminent mathematician and scholar nonetheless. Hypatia was fortunate to have a professor for a father who was very progressive in his thinking and was determined to teach her, unlike most of his contemporaries who believed that a woman's role is confined to being a homemaker.

In Demi's *Su Dongpo,* readers get to know about a Chinese genius who lived between 1036 and 1101. In the author's foreword, he was described to be "a statesman, philosopher, poet, painter, engineer, architect, and humanitarian who approached everything with joy and grace". Another scholar with multipotentiality is Persian philosopher, poet, scientist, and physician, described by the author to be a polymath and a 'Genius of the Islamic Golden Age', Ibn Sina. The book is written in the first person, as author Fatima Sharafeddine envisions how Ibn Sina would most likely share his own life story.

PBBs that highlight social and emotional issues of the gifted and talented. Some of the social-emotional issues and problems commonly faced by the gifted and talented are feelings of social rejection and frustration towards an indifferent school with teachers who may misunderstand them and classmates who find them too strange (Rimm et al., 2018). In *The Boy on Fairfield Street*, Ted Geisel who eventually grew up to become Dr. Seuss was frequently scolded by his teacher for breaking so many rules in art: "the creatures he drew had ears nine feet long, his horses had wings, his animals looked like plants, and his plants looked like animals". He was also made fun of in school by classmates who would tease him because, on top of what was perceived as his oddities, he was also culturally different (he came from Germany). He experienced having classmates chase him and beat him up when they were on the playground.

This capacity to overcome racism, sexism, prejudice, and discrimination and the valuing of deliberate practice, intrinsic motivation, persistence, and tenacity are also traits of the gifted (Rimm et al., 2018). These 'grit and gumption' traits can be seen in the stories of *The Peasant Prince, Drum Dream Girl, Sixteen Years in Sixteen Seconds, Sojourner's Truth,* and *Little Melba and Her Big Trombone*, to cite a few. In *Sixteen Years in Sixteen Seconds,* Olympic champion diver, Sammy Lee, pursued his dream despite the fact that his father wanted him to become a medical doctor and the fact that people of colour were only permitted to use the public pool once a week. He eventually won gold medals in diving in two consecutive Olympic Games (in 1948 and 1952), notwithstanding the many difficulties he had to endure to actualise his dream. Grit and gumption can likewise be seen in the stories of fearless girls and women who had sass and verve in their stride as seen in *Sojourner's Truth*, who spoke for justice and women's rights despite being born into slavery, and the drum-dream courage of Cuban-African-Chinese Millo Castro Zaldarriaga, who dared defy social conventions by being the first girl to play the drums. In *Little Melba*, Melba Doretta Liston had to contend with jealous male colleagues from her own band who called her names and regarded her as largely invisible; she also had to perform amid a stoic, unresponsive, and predominantly white crowd who perceived her as naturally inferior because of the colour of her skin.

There are also PBBs that deal with twice-exceptionality as seen in *Emmanuel's Dream, Wilma Unlimited, A Boy and a Jaguar*, and *The Noisy Paint Box*. *Wilma Unlimited* tells the story of Wilma Rudolph who was stricken with polio at age 5. For a time, everyone thought that Wilma would not be able to walk again, and she had to wear a heavy steel brace on her leg. Wilma eventually went on to win three gold medals at a single Olympics event. This can be paired with *Emmanuel's Dream*, which tells the story of Emmanuel Ofosu Yeboah who bicycled nearly 400 miles across Ghana with only one leg, significantly altering how his country treats people with disabilities. In *A Boy and A Jaguar*, a young boy who felt a sense of brokenness because of his stuttering, eventually found his voice to speak for the voiceless as an adult, advocating for the protection of endangered species. In *The Noisy Paint Box*, the reader would get to know a rare condition called synaesthesia as Vasily Kandinsky heard colours and integrated it into his bold, ground-breaking, abstract art.

PBBs that highlight social-emotional traits of highly able and highly creative learners. Social-emotional traits of high ability learners include high moral thinking and empathy, as well as standing up for one's beliefs, interests and passions (Rimm et al., 2018). This can be seen in *Tomas and the Library Lady,* an inspiring snapshot in the life of Tomas Rivera, born in Crystal City, Texas, in 1935, who eventually became a professor, a university administrator, and a national education leader. While his parents looked for iron to sell in the town dump and his brother looked for toys, Tomas would look for books. He would put the books in the sun to bake away the smell, indicating his thirst for knowledge, grit, and determination to pursue his interests despite his impoverished circumstances. In *Fifty Cents and a Dream,* the reader witnesses the will to provide for people who are disadvantaged by building schools or places of knowledge where all are welcome through Booker T. Washington's vision. Themes of art and activism also abound in *Poet of the People* whereby Pablo Neruda used verse to represent the voice of the common people and their struggles. This would be a relevant book to pair with *My Name Is Gabriela Mistral*, which features the first Latin American to win the Nobel Prize in Literature. Gabriela worked as a teacher's aide without getting a formal degree in education and started when she was 15 to help support her family. Pablo Neruda was one of her students.

In *Red Bird Sings,* the reader gets to know Zitkala-a, born Gertrude Simmons Bonnin, a Native American woman at the turn of the nineteenth century. Zitkala-a was a writer, editor, musician, teacher, and political activist at a time when basic education was uncommon among Native Americans. Another musician is featured in *Harlem's Little Blackbird,* which tells the story of Florence Mills, born to parents who were former slaves. She used her talent as a performer to stand up for her rights and speak out against injustice. Her story is an example of remarkable moral courage and the importance of doing the right thing, no matter how difficult.

This sense of purpose and determination to do what needs to be done for the good of society can also be seen in *The Mangrove Tree* which features the PBB of Japanese-American cell biologist, Dr. Gordon Sato, who fought famine in Eritrea, a country in Eastern Africa, through the Manzanar Project meant to remind people to fight injustice with hope. The story is told through the deceptively simple but stunning collage artwork of Susan Roth. The life story narrative of Wangari Maathai, recipient of the Nobel Peace Prize in 2004, can be the foundation of an entire teaching unit for highly able learners. While the researcher has only included one PBB here, there are several more PBBs of Wangari Maathai that can comprise a text-set (including *Mama Miti* by Donna Jo Napoli and Kadir Nelson, *Planting the Trees of Kenya* by Claire A. Nivola, *Wangari's Trees of Peace* by Jeanette Winter and *Seeds of Change: Planting A Path to Peace* by Jen Cullerton Johnson and Sonia Lynn Sadler). Teachers can engage highly able learners in drawing parallels across the five PBBs and discuss the Green Belt Movement, an organisation that was founded by Wangari Maathai. A critical multicultural analysis of the books may also include examining not just the individual action of Wangari Maathai, but the collective and collaborative effort required to bring about social change, as well as the roots of the environmental issues and problems faced by the people of Kenya, bringing into the forefront the social and economic infrastructure that enabled this kind of reality and issues to exist in the first place.

Implications and Future Directions

While the above section provides some recommendations for future practice, there is much potential for enriched and deeply affecting discussions through the use of multicultural PBBs among highly able learners, if used by capable educators who are willing to go outside of the traditional, stipulated text-sets that they are accustomed to using. The opportunities for the development of gifted learners' cross-cultural understanding, while also tapping into social and emotional learning themes, provide spaces for engaged reflection and meaningful learning. These PBBs may likewise be paired with longer middle-grade biographies or graphic novel memoirs, which feature the same eminent individuals.

Research projects that may be linked to social justice themes may also be considered, especially as teachers can leverage on these inspiring stories to develop grassroots-driven projects, passion-projects, or initiatives for the community.

Conclusion

The significance of using biographies, particularly picture book biographies in teaching social and emotional learning to the gifted and talented was reiterated in this chapter. Criteria were provided for educators to assist with selecting multicultural picture books for the gifted to ensure greater representation and diversity in the resources used in the classroom. Suggestions by way of teaching strategies and activities have been shared for practitioners.

The critical multicultural analysis framework has been introduced to facilitate a more immersive experience and greater affective engagement among young readers as they read deeply moving stories based on the lives of eminent individuals, that would prompt them to reflect on who they are and their place in the world.

In summary, Polette (2009, p. xi) described a highly effective PBB in this manner:

> A good biography is not one-way communication. It is a catalyst to facilitate the reader's own unfolding thoughts. Reading is only incidentally visual or aural; the print has no power in itself. It is the power of the reader's deep personal intuition, knowledge, and understanding that activates the message... A single carefully researched, well-written biography can teach more than a lifetime of mediocre fiction. Such a biography plays upon the finest feelings and impels the reader to respond. (Polette, 2009, p. xi)

Through inspiring biographies, teachers can scaffold gifted readers' identification with diverse people and their understandings that the road to excellence can prove to be an arduous, but meaningful and rewarding journey. It behoves us as educators to ensure that such powerful books are made more accessible to our gifted students to encourage deeper reflection, global awareness, and social and emotional learning through authentic and compelling visual narratives.

Cross-References

▶ A Counselling Framework for Meeting the Needs of Gifted Students in Malaysia
▶ Exploring Diverse Perceptions of Wise Persons: Wisdom in Gifted Education
▶ Fostering Resilience in 'At-Risk' Gifted and Talented Young People
▶ Gifted Education in the Asia-Pacific: From the Past for the Future – An Introduction
▶ Gifted and Twice-exceptional Children in the South of the World: Chilean Students' Experiences within Regular Classrooms
▶ Put Them Together and See How They Learn! Ability Grouping and Acceleration Effects on the Self-Esteem of Academically Gifted High School Students
▶ Social and Emotional Needs and Learning Processes: Part II Introduction
▶ Some Implications for the Future of Gifted Education in the Asia-Pacific
▶ Spirituality and Giftedness: Threading the Path of Identity
▶ The Lives and Achievements of Four Extraordinary Australians: A Master, a Maker, an Introspector, and an Influencer

References

Abellán-Pagnani, L., & Hébert, T. (2013). Using picture books to guide and inspire young gifted Hispanic students. *Gifted Child Today, 36*(1), 47–56. https://doi.org/10.1177/1076217512459735

Ash, V., & Barthelmess, T. (2011). What makes a good picture book biography? *The Horn Book Magazine, 87*(2), 40–45.

Bal, P. M., & Veltkamp, M. (2013). How does fiction reading influence empathy? An experimental investigation on the role of emotional transportation. *PLoS One, 8*(1), 1–12. https://doi.org/10.1371/journal.pone.0055341

Banks, J. A. (2009). *Teaching strategies for ethnic studies*. Upper Saddle River, NJ: Pearson.
Bloom, B. (1985). *Developing talent in young people*. New York, NY: Ballantine Books.
Botelho, M. J., & Rudman, M. K. (2009). *Critical multicultural analysis of children's literature: Mirrors, windows, and doors*. New York, NY: Routledge.
Buchori, S., & Dobinson, T. (2015). Diversity in teaching and learning: Practitioners' perspectives in a multicultural early childhood setting in Australia. *Australasian Journal of Early Childhood, 40*(1), 71–79.
Chong, S. N. Y., & Cheah, H. M. (2010). Demographic trends: Impact on schools. *New Horizons in Education, 58*(1), 1–15. Retrieved from https://files.eric.ed.gov/fulltext/EJ893709.pdf
Collaborative for Academic, Social, and Emotional Learning. (2013). *CASEL schoolkit: A guide for implementing schoolwide academic, social, and emotional learning*. Chicago, IL: Author.
Credé, M., Tynan, M. C., & Harms, P. D. (2017). Much ado about grit: A meta-analytic synthesis of the grit literature. *Journal of Personality and Social Psychology, 113*(3), 492–511. https://doi.org/10.1037/pspp0000102
Cross, T. L. (2005). *The social and emotional lives of gifted kids: Understanding and guiding their development*. Waco, TX: Prufrock Press.
Csikszentmihalyi, M. (1997). *Creativity: Flow and the psychology of discovery and invention*. New York, NY: Harper Perennial.
Delisle, J. R. (2016). I'm tired of 'grit. *Education Week, 35*(20), 20–21.
Department of Education, Employment and Workplace Relations for the Council of Australian Governments [DEEWR]. (2009). *Belonging, being and becoming: The early years learning framework for Australia*. Canberra: Commonwealth of Australia.
Duckworth, A. L. (2016). *Grit: The power of passion and perseverance*. New York, NY: Scribner/Simon and Schuster.
Duckworth, A. L., Peterson, C., Matthews, M. D., & Kelly, D. R. (2007). Grit: Perseverance and passion for long-term goals. *Journal of Personality and Social Psychology, 92*(6), 1087–1101. https://doi.org/10.1037/0022-3514.92.6.1087
Ellis, A. K. (2007). *Teaching and learning elementary social studies*. Upper Saddle River, NJ: Pearson.
Ericsson, K. A., Charness, N., Feltovich, P. J., & Hoffman, R. R. (2006). *The Cambridge handbook of expertise and expert performance*. New York, NY: Cambridge University Press. https://doi.org/10.1017/CBO9780511816796
Fears-Floyd, E., & Hebert, T. (2010). Using picture book biographies to nurture the talents of young gifted African American students. *Gifted Child Today, 32*(2), 38–46. https://doi.org/10.1177/107621751003300211
Ford, D. Y. (2011). *Multicultural gifted education* (2nd ed.). Waco, TX: Prufrock Press.
Ford, D. Y., Moore, J. L., & Harmon, D. A. (2005). Integrating multicultural and gifted education: A curricular framework. *Theory Into Practice, 44*(2), 125–137. Rtrieved from https://www.jstor.org/stable/3497031
Ford, D. Y., Tyson, C. A., Howard, T. C., & Harris, J. J. (2000). Multicultural literature and gifted black students: Promoting self-understanding, awareness, and pride. *Roeper Review, 22*(4), 235–240. https://doi.org/10.1080/02783190009554045
Forss, P. (2007, 28 August). Queues form at Tanjong Katong Primary ahead of registration. *The Straits Times*. Singapore.
Furner, J. M. (2017). Helping all students become Einstein's using bibliotherapy when teaching mathematics to prepare students for a STEM world. *Pedagogical Research, 2*(1), 1–11.
Galton, F. (1892). *Hereditary genius: An inquiry into its laws and consequences*. London, England: Macmillan.
Gay, G. (2000). *Culturally responsive teaching: Theory, research, and practice*. New York, NY: Teachers College Press.
Ghosh, K. (2015). Who's afraid of the big bad wolf? Children's responses to the portrayal of wolves in picturebooks. In J. Evans (Ed.), *Challenging and controversial picturebooks* (pp. 201–224). New York, NY: Routledge.

Goertzel, M. G., Goertzel, V., Goertzel, T. G., & Hansen, A. M. W. (2004). *Cradles of eminence: Childhoods of more than 700 famous men and women*. Scottsdale, AZ: Great Potential Press.

Gopalakrishnan, A. (2011). *Multicultural children's literature: A critical issues approach*. California, USA: Sage.

Haigen, H., & Hao, Z. (2017). High achievers from low socioeconomic backgrounds: The critical role of disciplinary climate and grit. *Mid-western Educational Researcher, 29*(2), 93–116.

Harper, L. J. (2016). Using picture books to promote social-emotional literacy. *Young Children, 71*(3), 80–86.

Harper, L. J., & Trostle-Brand, S. (2010). More alike than different: Promoting respect through multicultural books and literacy strategies. *Childhood Education, 86*(4), 224–233.

Hebert, T. P. (1991). Meeting the affective needs of bright boys through bibliotherapy. *Roeper Review, 13*(4), 207–212.

Hebert, T. P., & Kent, R. (2000). Nurturing social and emotional development in gifted teenagers through young adult literature. *Roeper Review, 22*(3), 167–171.

Hebert, T. P., Long, L. A., & Speirs Neumeister, K. L. (2001). Using biography to counsel gifted young women. *Journal of Secondary Gifted Education, 12*(2), 62–79. https://doi.org/10.4219/jsge-2000-645

Hildreth, G. H. (1966). *Introduction to the gifted*. New York, NY: McGraw-Hill.

Hollingworth, L. S. (1926). *Gifted children: Their nature and nurture*. New York, NY: Macmillan.

Hymel, S., Schonert-Reichl, K. A., & Miller, L. D. (2006). Reading, riting, rithmetic and relationships: Considering the social side of education. *Exceptionality Education Canada, 16*(2/3), 1–44.

Khum, K. C. O. (2013). Student teachers' perceptions about multicultural education in Singapore. International Assembly at the National Council for Social Studies Conference, St. Louis, Missouri, USA, 22–24 November 2013. Retrieved from https://repository.nie.edu.sg/bitstream/10497/14620/1/International Assembly_National Council for Social Studies Conference-2013_a.pdf

Lukens, R. J., Smith, J. J., & Coffel, C. M. (2013). *A critical handbook of children's literature*. Boston, MA: Pearson Education.

Montero, M. K., & Robertson, J. M. (2006). 'Teachers can't teach what they don't know': Teaching teachers about international and global children's literature to facilitate culturally responsive pedagogy. *Journal of Children's Literature, 32*(2), 27–35.

Morgan, H. (2009). Picture book biographies for young children: A way to teach multiple perspectives. *Early Childhood Education Journal, 37*(3), 219–227. https://doi.org/10.1007/s10643-009-0339-7

Nguyen, H. T. (2012). Culturally and linguistically diverse students with giftedness: How teachers and parents can support their academic and social needs. *Multicultural Education, 19*(2), 10–17.

Nikolajeva, M. (2013). Picturebooks and emotional literacy. *The Reading Teacher, 67*(4), 249–254. https://doi.org/10.1002/TRTR.1229

Pedersen, K. S., & Kitano, M. K. (2006). Designing a multicultural literature unit for gifted learners. *Gifted Child Today, 29*(2), 38–49. Retrieved from https://files.eric.ed.gov/fulltext/EJ746300.pdf

Polette, N. (2009). *Gifted biographies, gifted readers! Higher order thinking with picture book biographies*. California, USA: Libraries Unlimited.

Rimm, S. B., Siegle, D., & Davis, G. A. (2018). *Education of the gifted and talented* (7th ed.). New Jersey, USA: Pearson.

Robinson, A., & Jolly, J. L. (2013). *A century of contributions to gifted education: Illuminating lives*. New York, NY: Routledge/Taylor & Francis Group.

Rycik, J. A., & Irvin, J. L. (2005). *Teaching reading in the middle grades: Understanding and supporting literacy development*. Boston, USA: Allyn & Bacon.

Salisbury, M., & Styles, M. (2012). *Children's picturebooks: The art of visual storytelling*. London, England: Laurence King Publishing Ltd.

Schlichter, C. L., & Burke, M. (1994). Using books to nurture the social and emotional development of gifted students. *Roeper Review, 16*(4), 280–283. https://doi.org/10.1080/02783199409553598

Simonton, D. K. (2001). Talent development as multidimensional, multiplicative, and dynamic process. *Current Directions in Psychological Science, 10*(2), 39–43. https://doi.org/10.1111/1467-8721.00110

Sims Bishop, R. (2003). Reframing the debate about cultural authenticity. In D. L. Fox & K. G. Short (Eds.), *Stories matter: The complexity of cultural authenticity in children's literature* (pp. 25–40). Illinois, USA: National Council of Teachers of English.

Smith, S. (2017). Responding to the unique social and emotional learning needs of gifted Australian students. In E. Frydenberg, A. J. Martin, & R. J. Collie (Eds.), *Social and emotional learning in Australia and the Asia-Pacific* (pp. 147–166). Singapore, Singapore: Springer Nature.

Stambaugh, T., & Ford, D. Y. (2015). Microaggressions, multiculturalism, and gifted individuals who are black, Hispanic, or low income. *Journal of Counseling and Development, 93*, 192–201.

Strayhorn, T. L. (2014). What role does grit play in the academic success of black male collegians at predominantly white institutions? *Journal of African American Studies, 18*(1), 1–10. https://doi.org/10.1007/s12111-012-9243-0

Terman, L. (1925). *Genetic studies of genius: Vol. 1. Mental and physical traits of a thousand gifted children*. Stanford, CA: Stanford University Press.

Weingarten, S. (1956). Reading can help the gifted adolescent. *The Reading Teacher, 26*, 598–601.

Rhoda Myra Garces-Bacsal, PhD, is Filipino and based in the middle east. She is currently serving as the Associate Professor with the Special Education Department at the United Arab Emirates University. Prior to moving to UAE, she served as the Programme Leader of the Masters of Education Program in High Ability Studies at the *National Institute of Education*, Nanyang Technological University Singapore where she also served as the Coordinator of the Diploma in Special Education and the Professional Development Leader and Pedagogical Development and Innovation Leader of Early Childhood and Special Needs Education Academic Group. She served as the Chair of the Programme Committee of the Asian Children's Writers and Illustrators Conference for the Asian Festival of Children's Content held annually in Singapore for 9 years. Myra shares her passion for reading and book hunting in her website gatheringbooks.org

Part III

Identifying and Nurturing Diversely Gifted and Talented Students

21. Identifying and Nurturing Diversely Gifted and Talented Students: Part III Introduction

Sheyla Blumen and Maria Leonor Conejeros-Solar

Contents

Introduction to the Individual Chapters 459
Conclusion 462
References 463

Abstract

Gifted students and youth belong to diversely different student populations, with diversely different backgrounds, living and being educated within diversely different contexts. Such diversity is even more pronounced within diversely cultural regions of the world, such as the Asia-Pacific. One challenge of these accumulated diversities of gifted students may include underrepresentation in gifted education programs that contribute to the excellence gap. Additional challenges of identification and intervention programs for underrepresented gifted and talented children in some Asia-Pacific Rim countries are discussed in the 12 chapters in Part III, with authors from seven different countries: from South Korea to Sweden, involving Australia, New Zealand, the USA, Mexico, and the UK. The aim of the authors in this part of the handbook is to address some existing gaps in the current understanding of gifted students in the Asia-Pacific region, with the emphasis on those underrepresented gifted children and youth who are still beyond the limits of our understanding.

S. Blumen (✉)
Department of Psychology, Pontificia Universidad Católica del Perú, Lima, Peru
e-mail: sblumen@pucp.pe; sblumen@mentefutura.org

M. L. Conejeros-Solar
Escuela de Pedagogía, Pontificia Universidad Católica de Valparaíso, Viña del Mar, Chile
e-mail: leonor.conejeros@pucv.cl

© Springer Nature Singapore Pte Ltd. 2021
S. R. Smith (ed.), *Handbook of Giftedness and Talent Development in the Asia-Pacific*,
Springer International Handbooks of Education,
https://doi.org/10.1007/978-981-13-3041-4_77

Keywords

Diversely gifted · Underrepresentation · Identification · Intervention programs

Surely the aim of all education is to nurture the holistic needs of all children. This aim is even more crucial when considering the needs of disadvantaged students and considering influential factors such as culture, socio-economic status, ethnolinguistic factors, special educational needs, or indigeneity, that may underlay excellence gaps. Underrepresented gifted students may be only a small proportion of a larger group of disadvantaged students, but underrepresentation means that many diversely gifted students are not represented in current gifted education programs. Some limitations that may enhance some gifted students' hidden status from access to gifted programs involve the following conditions: (a) belonging to low-income families; (b) living in poverty in ethnic-linguistic diverse collectives; as well as (c) exhibiting a less studied particular condition of giftedness, such as twice exceptionality (2e) or underachievement.

Belonging to families with low income is associated with the low representation of these students in high achievement quartiles (Plucker, Hardesty, & Burroughs, 2013; Robinson, Adelson, Kidd, & Cunningham, 2018) and, consequently, lack of identification of talent, even though high-achieving but low-income students can have similar possibilities of attending college as those students with high income and low achievement (Bailey & Dynarski, 2011). These school achievement and readiness gaps start early in life (Morgan, Farkas, Hillemeier, & Maczuga, 2016) so the importance of quality early education for gifted students is crucial (Renzulli & Brandon, 2017).

Early and accurate identification is a prelude to access to relevant education and additional gifted education programs, such as enrichment courses or acceleration classes (Plucker & Peters, 2016). Underrepresented students need a more comprehensive and diverse identification process that could offer real opportunities of recognition especially when belonging to ethnic-linguistic diverse collectives living in poverty. Renzulli and Brandon (2017) express that this underrepresentation could place "the field of gifted education in danger of program eliminations or cutbacks" (p. 72), because there is an inability to give reasonable solutions to the problem of disadvantage resulting in underrepresentation.

The ineffectiveness of the identification process has been a persistent problem in the recognition of these students in the diversity pool, but to find more accurate and culturally sensitive measures has been a challenge and should be a primary agenda in program or school selection (Naglieri & Ford, 2003). This is especially relevant for twice-exceptional students, because they tend to be under-identified due to masking effects between gifts and disabilities, so they have the risk of not expressing their exceptional abilities (Peters, Gentry, Whiting, & McBee, 2019). In the case of underachievers, a deficit orientation way of thinking in which this failure is attributed to inner deficiencies is also a limitation of a comprehensive identification process (Ford, Grantham, & Whiting, 2008; Payne, 2011).

Accurate identification and nurturance of student needs are required to ensure a diversely gifted student's potential has the opportunity to develop into talent (Plucker & Peters, 2016). Additionally, identifying and nurturing diversely gifted students are ethical and moral imperatives that need to be addressed urgently in the gifted field. We cannot only remain in the verification stage or the search for explanations zone of this problem. We need concrete actions that allow underrepresented students access to development opportunities within a framework of social justice (Plucker & Peters, 2016). The content of this section goes partway towards achieving this end from the perspective of the Asia-Pacific realm.

Introduction to the Individual Chapters

In the 12 chapters in Part III, authors from seven different countries provide a comprehensive overview of the challenges of identifying and nurturing the potential of underrepresented gifted and talented children in some Asia-Pacific Rim countries.

The first three chapters directly address the concerns about the fairness of the selection processes that aim to identify diversely gifted children and youth for diversely gifted provisions. In ▶ Chapter 22, "Identifying Underrepresented Gifted Students: A Developmental Process", Pamela Peters, Jean Gubbins, Rashea Hamilton, Betsy McCoach, Del Siegle, and Jeb Puryear address the issues related to the identification of so-called underrepresented gifted students. They state that the underrepresentation might be due to different factors: the lack of mastery of the hierarchical language of the country, belonging to indigenous groups, racial and ethnic minorities, and because of a disability condition. They show research-based evidence about the importance of a developmental process that involves pre-identification strategies and preparation programs for the gifted identification process, in order to mitigate the fairness gap. Also, they discuss the types of programs featuring best practices that have been implemented.

In ▶ Chapter 23, "Identifying Gifted Learning in the Regular Classroom: Seeking Intuitive Theories", John Munro links a contemporary model of gifted knowing and learning with identification procedures that can be implemented in the regular classroom. He describes two types of tasks that teachers can use as part of their regular teaching to provide gifted students with the opportunity to display their qualitatively different understanding, concept mapping, and scenario problem-solving, following Fischer's Dynamic Skill Theory (Fischer 2008).

Then, María Alicia Zavala Berbena's and Gabriela de la Torre García' ▶ Chapter 24, "Self-Nomination in the Identification Process of Gifted and Talented Students in Mexico", is focused on self-nomination, a particular strategy for the identification of the gifted. First, different types of self-nomination measures are analysed and categorised, as part of a multidimensional and inclusive approach for the identification of gifted and talented students. And second, the convergent validity of the 'Self-Nomination Inventory for Gifted and Talented Adolescents in Mexico' is presented. Initial results reveal the usefulness of the psychometric measure.

Recommendations for future research and intervention practices in educational settings are provided.

▶ Chapter 25, "Place-Based gifted Education in Rural Schools", starts the discussion about intervention programs for special populations among gifted students. The fourth chapter is authored by Carolyn Callahan and Amy Price Azano who focus on economically disadvantaged students, stating that the achievement and opportunity gaps between low-income students and their more economically advantaged peers present serious challenges for gifted education worldwide. Moreover, for rural gifted students, excellence gaps may be even more pronounced, since opportunities to maximise potential for gifted students in rural environments are scarce. Major issues in rural gifted education are addressed both internationally and specifically in the Australasia/Pacific Rim nations, which are related to fewer specialists in gifted education, limited resources, fewer program options, and fewer research opportunities and field trips. Moreover, a review of strategies to minimise these challenges is presented, including an alternative process for identifying gifted students in rural schools and the presentation of the CLEAR curriculum model. Modification of the empirically validated CLEAR curriculum model is illustrated by the integration of place-based pedagogy drawn from geographically and culturally relevant elements of the Australian, New Zealand, and Pacific region. The CLEAR modification provides an exemplar for engaging and challenging rural students in gifted programs. Findings from the study of the model and, perhaps, more importantly, lessons learned and more global takeaways for the field conclude the chapter.

▶ Chapter 26, "Gifted Girls with Autism Spectrum Disorders: Provisions and Priorities in Australian School Settings", authored by Aranzazu Blackburn and Geraldine Townend, calls attention towards an under-researched and underserved population: gifted girls with *Autism Spectrum Disorders* (ASD) in Australian school settings. They present evidence about the unique needs of twice-exceptional (2e) girls with ASD, synthesising existing literature in the field of ASD with respect to girls with ASD and students with twice exceptionality. Moreover, existing strategies and provisions for 2e girls with Autism Spectrum Disorder are examined, and some educational goals are identified. Recommendations involve best practices and implications for future research in light of their potential to establish the intervention proposals for this population.

Next, in ▶ Chapter 27, "Teachers' Knowledge and Understandings of Twice Exceptionality Across Australia", Catherine Wormald and Michelle Bannister-Tyrrell outline the findings from the first Australia-wide study about teacher perceptions of twice exceptionality across all Australian school sectors. The outcome of this study showed that many teachers were unaware about the meaning of the term 'twice-exceptional' students and that the focus is often on the student's disability rather than their high cognitive ability. The findings revealed the limitations of the understanding of the needs of twice-exceptional students, their uniqueness, as well as about the proper interventions for gifted students who have any disability.

In ▶ Chapter 28, "Underachievement and the Quest for Dignity: Contemporary Perspectives on a Timeless Issue", James Delisle and Robert Schultz discuss the gifted underachiever, a topic that has been studied for decades, yet there is no consensus about its aetiology or successful treatment. Underachievement is discussed as a complex phenomenon that involves curriculum, instruction, and cognition as well as the lack of autonomy the underachieving students perceive, having diminished control over his/her learning processes. Based on the scholarly research, a theory-based approach is considered, with specific suggestions for addressing the individual and multi-faceted needs of underachieving students, in order to guide these students to develop a strong sense of self and a desire to succeed academically while preserving their personal integrity and dignity.

▶ Chapter 29, "Exploring Diverse Perceptions of Wise Persons: Wisdom in Gifted Education", is written by Kyungbin Park and Eunhyang Kim from Korea who explore the conceptions of wise persons as a significant factor to be included in gifted programs. In the chapter, different definitions of wisdom are examined, along with contemporary studies and measures of wisdom in order to examine the concept of a wise person. Results of a Korean empirical study about concrete descriptors of a wise person following Asian values are discussed, reporting differences by age and gender. Recommendations involve conceptions of wisdom and wise persons, as well as the implications of the study.

▶ Chapter 30, "The Lives and Achievements of Four Extraordinary Australians: A Master, a Maker, an Introspector, and an Influencer", involves case studies on four types of eminent Australians based on Gardner's (1997) notion of an exemplary creator. In this chapter, Carmel Diezmann used a bibliographic approach to study the lives of four eminent Australians, representatives of these roles, a master, a maker, an introspector, and an influencer, with the aim to study the societal contributions of these gifted individuals and the implications for education. Results suggested that the creator's childhood involved the following facilitating factors: (a) created environments to foster their interests; (b) provided role models for their work; (c) inspired a director for their career; or (d) provided the foundations for intercultural competence. Moreover, the four of them actively pursued specialised knowledge, at the forefront of knowledge in their discipline and exhibited resiliency. Implications for gifted education are related to: (a) the democratic condition of potential exemplary creators; (b) the need of long-term effort and support beyond school requirements; (c) the need to promote resilience across the lifespan; and (d) that education may provide opportunities to develop any of these roles within individuals, as creators can take any of the noted roles.

The three final chapters in this section are related to indigenous gifted students in Australia and New Zealand. Melinda Webber from New Zealand discusses optimal conditions for the success of Māori gifted students, establishing the role of cultural factors on the affective and psychosocial drivers of success, in ▶ Chapter 31, "The Development of Mana: Five Optimal Conditions for Gifted Māori Student Success". The author focuses on the role of self-perceptions about the value of the ethnic identity and family support of Māori gifted students for motivation and academic engagement. Webber suggests that educators need to focus on the development of students' connectedness to their racial-ethnic identity and their sense of pride, status, and esteem.

In ▶ Chapter 32, "Gifted and Talented Aboriginal Students in Australia", Susanne Garvis, Sally Windsor, and Donna Pendergast argue that Australian Aboriginals are the most educationally disadvantaged group in the Australian education system. They provide an overview of Australian research and public policies and practices by states and territories nationwide. The authors suggest that suitable provisions for inclusion of gifted aboriginal students must be considered in collective action contexts, which integrate critical thinking and cultural values in decision-making based on a whole-system view of knowledge. They conclude that collective practices in local contexts should be considered as part of the provisions for gifted and talented Australian Aboriginal students and suggest five steps forwards for policy-makers to support gifted programs for Aboriginal students.

The last chapter of this section is ▶ Chapter 33, "Supporting Australian Gifted Indigenous Students' Academic Potential in Rural Settings", by Geraldine Townend, Peta Hay, Jae Yup Jung, and Susen Smith, who provide evidence-based research about the need to support gifted Aboriginal students' academic potential. The authors also highlight some potential problems and best practices in the identification of gifted indigenous students in rural settings, as well as some promising educational programming options for them. Culturally sensitive recommendations for rural educators to support Australian indigenous gifted students are also suggested.

Conclusion

Throughout Part III, we hope to have contributed to filling some of the gaps in current understandings of diversely gifted and talented students of the Asia-Pacific region, for those who remain underrepresented in gifted programs due to the limited understandings about the best ways to uncover their talents. We, as psychologists and educators, can think 'outside of the box' in order to establish dynamic strategies for identifying the still underserved gifted and talented students living in the Asia-Pacific region. Pre-identification strategies and preparation programs for the diversely gifted identification process, testing in their native language, and self-nomination strategies are some identification strategies that can mitigate the fairness gap. Moreover, intervention programs for the diversely gifted should consider the local cultural values, such as the collectivistic perspective, the configuration of the wise person from the cultural context, and teacher training on gifted special populations, such as twice exceptionality or underachievement. There is still a long path to walk in order to alleviate excellence gaps experienced by underachievers and the underrepresented, and providing culturally fair gifted programs for increased representation in gifted education programs is one step in the right direction for equitable provisions. The content of this section indicates that there are many colleagues around the Asia-Pacific Rim who are committed to working towards this goal.

References

Bailey, M., & Dynarski, S. (2011). Gains and gaps: Changing inequality in U.S. College Entry and Completion. National Bureau of Economic Research. Downloaded from http://www.nber.org/papers/w17633

Fischer, K. W. (2008). Dynamic cycles of cognitive and brain development: Measuring growth in mind, brain, and education. In A. M. Battro, K. W. Fischer, & P. Léna (Eds.), The educated brain, (pp. 127–150), Cambridge, U.K.: Cambridge University Press

Ford, D. Y., Grantham, T. C., & Whiting, G. W. (2008). Culturally and linguistically diverse students in gifted education: Recruitment and retention issues. *Exceptional Children, 74*(3), 289–306. Retrieved from https://www.researchgate.net/profile/Donna_Ford5/publication/268744447_Culturally_and_Linguistically_Diverse_Students_in_Gifted_Education_Recruitment_and_Retention_Issues/links/5aafdd940f7e9b4897c0ce5b/Culturally-and-Linguistically-Diverse-Students-in-Gifted-Education-Recruitment-and-Retention-Issues.pdf

Morgan, P. L., Farkas, G., Hillemeier, M. M., & Maczuga, S. (2016). Science achievement gaps begin very early, persist, and are largely explained by modifiable factors. *Educational Researcher, 45*, 18–35. https://doi.org/10.3102/0013189X16633182

Naglieri, J., & Ford, D. (2003). Addressing underrepresentation of gifted minority children using the Naglieri Nonverbal Ability Test (NNAT). *Gifted Child Quarterly, 47*(7), 155–160. Retrieved from https://lesacreduprintemps19.files.wordpress.com/2012/11/addressing-underrepresentation-of-gifted-minority-children-using-the-naglieri-nonverbal-ability-test.pdf

Payne, A. (2011). *Equitable access for underrepresented students in gifted education*. Center for Equity and Excellence in Education. The George Washington University. Retrieved from https://files.eric.ed.gov/fulltext/ED539772.pdf

Peters, S., Gentry, M., Whiting, G. W., & McBee, M. T. (2019). Who gets served in gifted education? Demographic representation and a call for action. *Gifted Child Quarterly, 63*(4), 273–287. https://doi.org/10.1177/0016986219833738

Plucker, J. A., Hardesty, J., & Burroughs, N. (2013). *Talent on the sidelines: Excellence gaps and America's persistent talent underclass*. Storrs: Center for Education Policy Analysis, Neag School of Education, University of Connecticut. Retrieved from https://www.researchgate.net/publication/304046990_Talent_on_the_sidelines_Excellence_gaps_and_America's_persistent_talent_underclass

Plucker, J. A., & Peters, S. J. (2016). *Excellence gaps in education: Expanding opportunities for talented students*. Cambridge, MA: Harvard Education Press.

Renzulli, J. S., & Brandon, L. E. (2017). Common sense about the under-representation issue: A school-wide approach to increase participation of diverse students in programs that develop talents and gifted behaviours in young people. *International Journal for Talent Development and Creativity, 5*(2), 71–94. Retrieved from: https://lpilearning.org/wp-content/uploads/Common-Sense-About-the-Under-Representation-Issue.pdf

Robinson, A., Adelson, J. L., Kidd, K. A., & Cunningham, C. M. (2018). A talent for tinkering: Developing talents in children from low-income households through engineering curriculum. *Gifted Child Quarterly, 62*(1), 130–144. https://doi.org/10.1177/0016986217738049

Sheyla Blumen is full professor of psychology at the Pontificia Universidad Católica del Perú (PUCP), editor of *Revista de Psicologia* PUCP, and board member of the School of Graduate Studies. Instrumental in the design of public policies to provide special services to Peruvian highly able students, she developed the scientific proposal of the boarding academies for the highly able coming from poverty conditions in Peru. Also, she developed the psychoeducational model to monitor young scholars to prevent dropping out along college studies, which is now being transferred to the Peruvian public system. She is director of Future Minds Talent Center, chair of the 35th Inter-American Conference of Psychology, and is keynote and invited professor in North American, Latin American, and European universities.

María Leonor Conejeros-Solar is full Professor, Psychologist, Doctor in Education at the School of Pedagogy of the Pontificia Universidad Católica de Valparaíso. Among her duties, she has served as the Director of the Academically Talented Education Program BETA in the same University. Her main research interests are: academically talented students from underprivileged socioeconomic backgrounds; gifted college students; provisions and socioemotional issues of gifted and twice-exceptional students; and gifted homeschooling. She has published several articles and book chapters.

22
Identifying Underrepresented Gifted Students: A Developmental Process

Pamela Peters, E. Jean Gubbins, Rashea Hamilton, D. Betsy McCoach, Del Siegle, and Jeb Puryear

Contents

Introduction	466
Current Definitions of Giftedness	467
Overview of Identification Systems	469
Identification Issues: Disproportionate Representation	470
Research Spotlight on Three States	471
Pre-identification Strategies and Preparation Programs	474
Research and/or Practice: Implications and Future Directions	476
Structured Elements of Pre-identification Strategies and Preparation Programs	478
Identification, Programming, Professional Development, and a Culture of Awareness	480
Conclusion	481
Cross-References	482
References	482

Abstract

Gifted education programs across the globe struggle with the disproportionate representation of underserved populations. These groups include majority language learners, indigenous people, racial and ethnic minorities, and gifted students with disabilities. This underrepresentation leads to missed talent and

P. Peters · E. J. Gubbins (✉) · D. B. McCoach · D. Siegle
University of Connecticut, Storrs, CT, USA
e-mail: pamela.peters@uconn.edu; ejean.gubbins@uconn.edu; betsy.mccoach@uconn.edu; del.siegle@uconn.edu

R. Hamilton
Washington Student Achievement Council, Olympia, WA, USA
e-mail: rashea.hamilton@gmail.com

J. Puryear
ACS-Cobham International School, Hersham, UK
e-mail: jebpuryear16@gmail.com

© Springer Nature Singapore Pte Ltd. 2021
S. R. Smith (ed.), *Handbook of Giftedness and Talent Development in the Asia-Pacific*, Springer International Handbooks of Education,
https://doi.org/10.1007/978-981-13-3041-4_21

opportunity and lends support to claims of elitism in gifted programs. Research, however, has demonstrated that pre-identification strategies and preparation programs might help to mitigate these problems. These programs are typically designed to prepare students for the identification process as well as for the advanced academic work that follows. This chapter provides an overview of recent research, including reports currently in preparation by the National Center for Research on Gifted Education, as well as information on types of programs that have been implemented featuring best practices.

Keywords

Gifted students · Identification · Underserved populations · Pre-identification strategies · Preparation programs

The aims in this chapter are to:
1. Present current definitions of giftedness.
2. Provide an overview of identification systems.
3. Address identification issues, including disproportionate representation.
4. Share current findings from a research study of identification in three states.
5. Describe pre-identification strategies and preparation programs.
6. Highlight research and/or practice: Implications and future directions.

Introduction

Students with high potential live in both advantaged and disadvantaged communities. Wyner, Bridgeland, and Dilulio (2009) used the phrase 'achievement trap' to highlight the status of 3.4 million children in the United States who do not live in economically advantaged homes, over one million of whom qualify for free and reduced-price (FRPL) lunch. Many of these students possess high potential for academic achievement. According to the Wyner et al. study, students caught in the achievement trap do not achieve academically at the same levels as their peers with similar potential, drop out of high school at higher rates and may not pursue postsecondary opportunities. Students from low-income families, as well as those who are African-American, Latino, or Native American, are underrepresented in gifted and talented programs in the United States (Ford 2014; Siegle et al., 2016; Yoon & Gentry 2009). Similar patterns are found outside of the United States as well. Aboriginal children in Australia (Harslett 1996) and Māori children in New Zealand (Bevan-Brown 1999) are also underrepresented in gifted programs. Plucker, Burroughs, and Song (2010) described this situation as the excellence gap: the differences in high-level achievement between white students and those from other racial/ethnic groups as well as the differences between students from low- and high-income backgrounds. Plucker et al. referred to the Wyner et al. study and stated it "illustrates the immediate and long-term dangers posed by festering excellence gaps" (p. 30).

Ford (2014) posited that the disproportionate identification of students who are African-American, Latino, or Native American is caused by social inequality, deficit thinking, and colour-blindness, arguing that the underrepresentation of minority students is a form of segregation. Indeed, in the case of McFadden v. Board of Education for Illinois School District–46 (2013), the court ruled that by having separate gifted programs for Hispanic students, the school district was breaking the law.

This form of 'identification segregation' is a global problem. Bevan-Brown (2011) analysed indigenous conceptions of giftedness from Māori, Navajo (Diné), and Australian Aboriginal perspectives and suggested that the underrepresentation of gifted minority students is related to identification practices influenced by low teacher expectations, low teacher referral, lack of cultural sensitivity and narrow conceptions of giftedness. Bevan-Brown (1999) and Scobie-Jennings (2013) focused solely on identification issues related to Māori students and contended that the barrier to culturally responsive identification is the lack of teacher expertise and knowledge about the characteristics and behaviours of students from indigenous groups.

To combat these trends related to the underrepresentation of gifted students from culturally, linguistically, and economically diverse communities and students with disabilities, it is important to focus on stages of talent development among students with obvious, emergent and latent talents and abilities (Gubbins, 2005; Worrell & Erwin, 2011) as well as to use culturally appropriate assessment (Ford, 2014).

Current Definitions of Giftedness

The identification of gifted students in the United States is the subject of ongoing debate. Is identification an endpoint or a developmental process that occurs over time? Is it a matter of confirming the preexistence of manifest abilities or an approach that emphasises nurturing latent or emergent talents? The United States does not have a consistent conception of giftedness that guides an identification team's decision-making procedures. Due to legislative initiatives, federal definitions morphed over time from the initial Marland (1971) Report to Congress to the *Every Student Succeeds Act* (ESSA, 2015). Marland's (1971) first definition emphasised categorical (singular or combinatory) identification by professionally qualified individuals who select students with demonstrated or potential achievement, who therefore require differentiated programs and/or services:

> Gifted and talented children are those identified by professionally qualified persons who, by virtue of outstanding abilities, are capable of high performance. These are children who require differentiated educational programs and/or services beyond those normally provided by the regular school program in order to realise their contribution to society.

Children capable of high performance include those with demonstrated achievement and/or potential in any of the following areas, singly or in combination:

- General intellectual ability,
- Specific academic ability,
- Creative or productive thinking,
- Leadership ability,
- Visual and performing arts, or
- Psychomotor ability. (pp. 20–21)

In 1978, Congress revised the earlier Marland definition and deleted any reference to psychomotor ability. Currently, the federal definition under the ESSA (2015) addresses the importance of identifying students, children, or youth with documented achievement capability in one or more areas or fields that need services to develop abilities:

> Gifted and talented, when used with respect to students, children, or youth, means students, children, or youth who give evidence of high achievement capability in areas such as intellectual, creative, artistic, or leadership capacity, or in specific academic fields, and who need services or activities not ordinarily provided by the school in order to fully develop those capabilities. (ESSA, 2015, Title 1V Part F, SEC. 4644)

While the federal definition of giftedness provides guidance to states and local school districts, there is no federal law in the United States that requires identification of nor services for gifted students. Without a consistent definition of giftedness, each state determines its own definition and corresponding identification system. Survey results from the *National Association for Gifted Children* (NAGC) and the *Council of State Directors of Programs for the Gifted* (CSDPG, 2015) indicated that of the 37 responding states' definitions, the foci were intellectually gifted ($n = 34$), academically gifted ($n = 24$), performing/visual arts ($n = 21$), creatively gifted ($n = 21$), and/or specific academic areas ($n = 20$). Few states included populations such as "low SES [socio-economic] ($n = 9$), ESL/ELL [English as a second language, English language learners], culturally or ethnically diverse ($n = 8$), gifted with a disability ($n = 6$), or geographically isolated/rural ($n = 3$)" (NAGC & CSDPG, 2015, p. 27). These results highlight the categorical approach to identification, as opposed to nurturing talents and abilities of students who live in challenging environments.

Unlike the United States' decentralisation of specific educational policies related to identifying and serving gifted and talented students, Australia adopted Gagné's (2008) *Differentiated Model of Giftedness and Talent* (DMGT) with particular attention to nomenclature (Wellisch, 2016):

> GIFTEDNESS designates the possession and use of outstanding natural abilities, called aptitudes, in at least one ability domain, to a degree that places an individual at least among the top 10% of age peers.
> "TALENT designates the outstanding mastery of systematically developed abilities, called competencies (knowledge and skills), in at least one field of human activity to a degree that

places an individual at least among the top 10% of age peers who are or have been active in that field. (Gagné, 2008, para. 7)"

Other scholars and psychologists offered definitions of giftedness. Roeper (1982) defined giftedness as "a greater awareness, a greater sensitivity, and a greater ability to understand and to transform perceptions into intellectual and emotional experiences" (p. 21). She emphasised connections between the intellect and emotions. The focus on sensitivity and intensity was explored further by the Columbus Group (1991, cited in Morelock 1992) when they offered a development perspective:

> Giftedness is Asynchronous Development in which advanced cognitive abilities and heightened intensity combine to create inner experiences and awareness that are qualitatively different from the norm. This asynchrony increases with higher intellectual capacity. The uniqueness of the gifted renders them particularly vulnerable and requires modifications in parenting, teaching, and counseling in order for them to develop optimally. (para. 10)

Despite the varying conceptions of giftedness, it is essential that definitions be codified, intentional and reflective of the culturally, linguistically and economically diverse populations in schools. As Gallagher (1975) stated:

> ... failure to help the gifted child is a societal tragedy, the extent of which is difficult to measure but which is surely great. How can we measure the sonata unwritten, the curative drug undiscovered, the absence of political insight? They are the difference between what we are and what we could be as a society. (p. 9)

Overview of Identification Systems

Typical identification systems have multiple phases. The first step is often deciding which students should be evaluated for gifted education programs. The multistage process continues with nomination—using formal or informal data collection through rating scales or naming of top students in one or more content areas followed by identification—reviewing existing data sources, and, perhaps, a request for further testing with an individual achievement or intelligence test. Placement is the final stage when professionally qualified individuals review all data sources and determine the students' status as meeting/not meeting the qualifications or scheduling further assessment procedures (Gubbins et al., 2018).

This framework is utilised differently and at various grade levels across the United States. According to Hamilton (2017) and the National Center for Research on Gifted Education (NCRGE, 2017), 1% of district survey respondents ($n = 300$) from three states with identification and programming mandates were identified as gifted and talented students in kindergarten, 3.33% in grade 1, 28.67% in grade 2, 51.67% in grade 3, 12.33% in grade 4, 1.33% in grade 5, and none of the higher-grade levels (1.67%). Some districts chose to screen all students at a particular grade level, commonly referred to as a universal screening. Districts in these three states also used a variety of measures as a screening tool. District survey respondents could select as many assessment options as appropriate. In the absence of a single, research-based approach to identification, it is important to note the ways that the varied procedures affect students with high potential, particularly those from economically disadvantaged homes and those who have been traditionally under-identified.

Research-based identification systems reflect current thinking about how best to design and implement procedures sensitive to acknowledging demonstrated achievement and uncovering potential achievement. According to the NAGC and CSDPG (2015) survey, 33 states specified their identification indicators, with 19 using multiple criteria models with a minimum of two types of data: achievement ($n = 13$), IQ scores ($n = 13$) and nominations/referrals ($n = 12$). Fewer states chose state assessments ($n = 9$), performance/portfolios ($n = 8$) or behaviours/characteristics ($n = 7$). These data sources may be employed in different sequences.

Identification Issues: Disproportionate Representation

Peters and Engerrand (2016) noted that African-American, Hispanic, Native Americans, English learners, twice-exceptional students (i.e., identification as gifted and special education status), and students from low-income families are underrepresented among identified, gifted and talented populations. Gubbins et al. (2018) stated that underrepresented is a term used to:

> describe the students' proportional representation by race/ethnicity, EL status, gender, free and reduced-price lunch status, or twice-exceptionality (identification as gifted and special education status) in gifted programs compared to the proportions in the general student population at the national, district or state levels. (p. 1)

Peters and Engerrand (2016) asserted that the:

> current level of economic, racial, and ethnic inequality is a problem not only for political and advocacy reasons but also because students from these subgroups represent the fastest-growing segments of the K–12 population and many of their talents are going overlooked and underdeveloped..... (p. 159)

The NAGC and CSDPG (2015) attempted to collect demographic survey data (race/ethnicity, English learners, twice-exceptional students, and low socio-economic status) on identified gifted and talented students; typical responses included 'data not collected' and 'data not available'. If states and districts are not collecting demographic data on proportionate representation of gifted students that mirror their local populations, then there is no recognition that a problem exists.

One available national data source about representation of identified gifted students by race/ethnicity is from the U.S. Department of Education Office for Civil Rights (2014):

> White and Asian-American students make up 70% of the students enrolled in gifted and talented education programs, compared to 55% of [W]hite and Asian-American enrolment in

schools offering gifted and talented programs. Latino and [B]lack students represent 26% of the students enrolled in gifted and talented programs, compared to 40% of Latino and Black student enrolment in schools offering gifted and talented programs. (p. 3)

The disproportionate representation of students enrolled in gifted and talented programs by disability and English learner status also is evident in the United States. According to the U.S. Department of Education Office for Civil Rights (2014), 7.3% of the gifted and talented students are without disabilities, 1.4% with disabilities, 7.0% non-English learners, and 2.0% English learners. Identification systems that led to the results cannot be determined. However, the availability of these public data by and across states should prompt conversations: Who are our gifted students?

Research Spotlight on Three States

One approach to addressing disproportionate representation includes universal screening as a purposeful approach to evaluate students' gifts and talents. Card and Giuliano's research study (2015) of the effects of universal screening concluded:

With no change in the minimum standards for gifted status the screening program led to a 180% increase in the gifted rate among all disadvantaged students, with a 130% increase for Hispanic students and an 80% increase for [B]lack students. (p. 20)

The following quotation emphasises the importance of casting a wider net when identification systems are implemented: "Outstanding talents are present in children and youth from all cultural groups, across all economic strata, and in all areas of human endeavor" (U.S. Department of Education, 1993, p. 3).

Data from the NCRGE district survey (2016) indicated that districts ($n = 301$) incorporated one or more of the following assessment tools for their universal screening procedure: group cognitive tests ($n = 81$), nonverbal cognitive tests ($n = 26$), achievement tests ($n = 54$), and teacher rating scales ($n = 185$). Of the respondents from reporting districts, 30.76% modified the identification process for students from underserved populations and 69.33% did not. Underserved is a term used to:

reference individuals or groups that have not had opportunities to learn at high levels or to be exposed to content, concepts, or skills to prepare them for challenging work. The lack of opportunities may be related to living in challenging economic communities or the inability to have access to multiple resources to promote learning. (Gubbins et al., 2018, p. 1)

According to the NCRGE district survey (2016) respondents, districts either always assessed English learners in their native language (16.44%), for common languages (19.8%), specific requests from parents or teachers (30.54%), or not at all (33.22%).

The NCRGE district survey (2016) respondents were asked if they modified the identification process for students from underserved populations and 69.33%

Table 1 Modification of identification options for underserved populations

Variable	No	Yes	Total
Evaluate English learners in native language	56	35	91
Use nonverbal assessment	25	66	91
Use a more flexible approach about qualifying scores	36	55	91
Use a talent pool approach	53	38	91
Give underserved students extra consideration	57	34	91
Use different weighting of identification data	66	25	91
Other	75	16	91
Total	368	269	637

selected 'yes', while 30.67% selected 'no'. Of those district respondents selecting 'yes', Table 1 documents the modification options.

For the respondents who chose 'other' in reference to modification of identification options for underserved populations, responses included referring students to individual testing when there is a discrepancy between group scores and classroom observations, using a portfolio process, focusing on local norms and conducting a case study of students' talents and abilities.

Districts' use of intentional and flexible strategies represents positive signs that educators attend to identification strategies. However, these findings are not universal nor do they represent identification systems across the United States or elsewhere for that matter. For example, identification processes are used in many nations, such as Canada (e.g., Chaffey, Halliwell, & McCluskey, 2006; Chaffey, McCluskey, & Halliwell, 2005), Australia (e.g., Cooper, 2005; Garvis, 2006), New Zealand (e.g., Bevan-Brown, 1999), Taiwan (e.g., Wu, 2000), and Thailand (e.g., Anuruthwong, 2017). However, there is no consistency in using these procedures for identifying gifted students generally nor for identifying underrepresented gifted students across these nations, nor within these nations neither (Chaffey, Bailey, & Vine, 2003). Gentry, Hu, and Thomas (2008) and Mun et al. (2016) contend that traditional screening tools and strategies often fail to reveal the talents and abilities of students from culturally, linguistically, and economically diverse backgrounds.

While the underrepresentation of students who are English learners, come from low-income households, and/or are members of certain racial groups, has been well documented, research suggests that these students also tend to exhibit lower academic achievement than their peers (Hamilton et al., 2018). Thus, it is possible that these traditionally underserved populations are underrepresented because of their lower achievement. Research from McCoach et al. (2016), however, suggests that these populations are underrepresented despite equivalent prior achievement.

Using data from three states that have state-level mandates to identify and serve gifted students, McCoach et al. (2016) examined the degree to which traditionally underserved students were under-identified as gifted. They conducted a series of three-level (student, school, district) logistic regression models, where students' identification status at grade 5 was the outcome variable. These analyses enabled researchers to predict directly the probability that a student would be identified as gifted, after controlling for student-, school-, and district-level predictors.

The models included student-level covariates such as underrepresented minority status, FRPL, and English learner status as well as students' grade 3 mathematics and reading achievement test scores. McCoach et al. (2016) also included several school- and district-level covariates: the percentage of students who were identified as gifted, the percentage of students who received FRPL, as well as school and district mean mathematics and reading scores. They tested same level interactions among variables and included these in the final model. Continuous variables were group mean centered at levels 1 and 2 and grand mean centered at level-3. They dummy coded dichotomous variables at level 1.

Across all three states, African-American, Latino, and Native American students were between 0.5 and 0.67 times less likely to be identified as gifted, even after controlling for student achievement, FRPL status, and school and district variables (State 1: OR = 0.67; State 2: OR = 0.5; State 3: OR = 0.67).

In two of the three states, non-FRPL students were between 1.5 and 2 times more likely to be identified as gifted, after controlling for student achievement, underserved status and school and district demographics (State 1: OR = 0.67; State 2: OR = 0.5). In State 3, FRPL was not a significant predictor of gifted identification after controlling for student, school and district covariates. However, State 3 utilised a selection process that results in achievement scores being less predictive of gifted status than the other two states. State 3 offers an alternative pathway, which includes flexible test scores for students who qualify for FRPL or who are English learners.

It is important to note that the aforementioned findings apply to students who are members of only *one* underrepresented group (low-income *or* racial/ethnic minority). However, Figs. 1, 2, and 3 demonstrate how being members of both groups influence students' probability of being identified. Across all three states, being both FRPL-eligible and belonging to a racial/ethnic minority were found to negatively affect a student's likelihood for identification, albeit to a lesser extent in State 3.

Unlike race/ethnicity and FRPL status, proficiency in English is less of a clear predictor of gifted status. After controlling for achievement, race/ethnicity and FRPL status, as well as school and district demographics, in one state, it positively predicted gifted identification; in another state, it negatively predicted identification status, and in another state, it did not predict identification (State 1: $\gamma 300 = -0.05$, $p = 0.36$; State 2: $\gamma 300 = 0.25$, $p = 0.07$; State 3: $\gamma 300 = -0.29$, $p = 0.04$).

McCoach et al.'s (2016) findings suggest that traditionally underserved students are less likely to be identified as gifted, even when their achievement is on par with their peers. These results support previous studies that indicate the existence of excellence gaps or differences between subgroups of students performing at the highest levels of achievement (Plucker et al., 2010). McCoach et al.'s research, however, also suggests an even more disturbing trend: economically disadvantaged, English learners, and historically underprivileged minorities who score at the highest levels of achievement are still less likely to be identified for gifted programs than their reference peers, a phenomenon they call the 'identification gap'. These findings may help to explain why the proportion of underserved high-achieving students decreases as they progress through school. When these high-achieving students do not have appropriate opportunities to thrive and to develop their abilities, they are

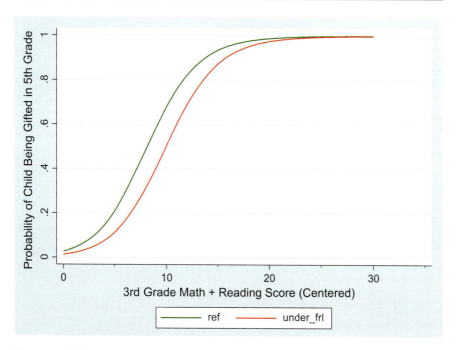

Fig. 1 Probability of being identified as gifted after controlling for achievement in State 1

unable to keep pace with their more advantaged peers. One possible approach to providing opportunities for latent and emergent talents and gifts to develop is the creation of pre-identification strategies and preparation programs.

Pre-identification Strategies and Preparation Programs

Pre-identification strategies and preparation programs offer exposure and curricular extensions to students who may not have had similar opportunities to learn at the highest levels because of "the variability in the quality of education students receive once in K–12 schools is further exacerbated by the wide variation in their preschool, informal education experiences" (Peters & Engerrand, 2016, p. 161). These learning and achievement traps also extend to the lack of exposure to rich vocabulary and sophisticated language patterns. Hart and Risley (2003) determined that "In four years, an average child in a professional family would accumulate experience with almost 45 million words, an average child in a working-class family 26 million words, and an average child in a welfare family 13 million words" (p. 9).

The NCRGE district survey (2016) included a series of questions related to pre-identification strategies and preparation programs. Pre-identification strategies include selecting students for emergent talent experiences. Teachers used informal and formal data in their search for talent potentials. These pre-identified students

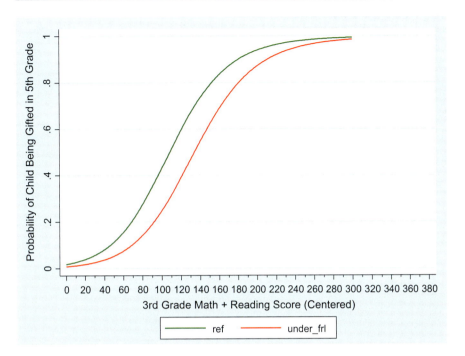

Fig. 2 Probability of being identified as gifted after controlling for achievement in State 2

participate in preparation programs to extend and enhance current knowledge and academic skills to promote the development of talents that will provide a potential pathway to full participation in the district's identification system in the future.

Of the NCRGE district survey respondents from three states, 92 districts (30.67%) offered special activities for potentially gifted elementary students from underrepresented populations to prepare them to be identified for the gifted program in later grades, while 208 districts (69.33%) did not provide similar opportunities. These programs were designed for students from low-income families, African-Americans, Hispanics, Native Americans, English learners, and twice-exceptional students. Of the districts offering preparation programs, 45 implemented them during the school day within general education classrooms, 58 held them during the school day and in special classes outside of general education classrooms, and 35 occurred outside of the regular school day (e.g., before school, after school, during summer). In these districts, various types of evidence were used to determine which students should be involved in special enrichment and extension activities as part of preparation programs. Data sources included the following: teacher nomination/referrals ($n = 70$), standardised tests ($n = 46$), observation tools or checklists ($n = 44$), and performance-based assessments ($n = 42$; NCRGE district survey, 2016).

Respondents from 92 districts with preparation programs were asked to indicate the degree to which specific activities were the focus based on the following scale

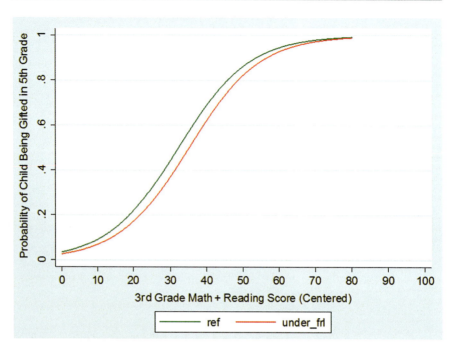

Fig. 3 Probability of being identified as gifted after controlling for achievement in State 3

Table 2 Focus of preparation programs

	Mean	SD
Reading/English language arts	42.63	33.48
Mathematics	48.01	31.10
Visual and/or performing arts	17.18	24.09
Process skills	58.43	34.63
General enrichment	44.79	35.55
Above grade-level content	42.84	35.50
Support services for students	20.94	30.72

(0 = Not a focus, 100 = Complete focus). Table 2 illustrates the varied foci of preparation programs with the highest being process skills (mean 58.43, *SD* 34.61) and mathematics (mean 48.01, *SD* 31.10).

Research and/or Practice: Implications and Future Directions

The difficulty in identifying subgroups of students for gifted programming is not a new phenomenon (Lee, Olszewski-Kubilius, & Peternel, 2009). Gifted education researchers and individual school districts have developed varied approaches in an attempt to mitigate this problem. Project GOTCHA (*Galaxies of Thinking and*

Creative Heights of Achievements) was developed in the Broward County Public Schools, located in Fort Lauderdale, FL in the 1980s. Using multiple criteria such as informal observation, parent and peer nomination forms, Renzulli behaviour rating scales, the Torrance Tests of Creative Thinking and more, GOTCHA focused on increasing the participation of English learners by identifying students in three stages: nomination, identification, and placement. Students in Broward County could be placed in full inclusion or pull-out programs.

Some districts have focused on preparing underrepresented students for gifted programs or advanced academic work. Project EXCITE, a partnership between the Evanston, IL schools and the Center for Talent Development (CTD) at Northwestern University, was created with the goal of raising the achievement of gifted minority students so that they might qualify for and succeed in advanced programs and acceleration in high school mathematics and science programs (Olszewski-Kubilius, 2006). Project partners used strategies focused on role models, parent support, teacher expectations, and enrichment opportunities. Students were eligible for the program beginning in grade 3. In a review of 14 program participants who had been in Project EXCITE for 6 years, Lee et al. (2009) found positive results, including academic outcomes, with 12 of the 14 students enrolled in accelerated mathematics courses and an increase in the number of students who exceeded standards on standardised testing from 3 in grade 3 to 10 in grade 8.

The Young Scholars Model, based in Fairfax, VA, is another example of districts preparing underrepresented students. Teachers work with groups of advanced young students who are clustered together. They provide advanced academic work in the classroom as well as in summer and/or after-school programs that provide additional opportunities for advanced material and enrichment (Horn, 2015). Students are chosen for this program using a number of assessments including nonverbal ability tests, achievement tests, portfolios, performance assessments, and observations/conversations with the student, the teacher, family, or other parties. Program staff particularly focus on young students with high ability who lack access, affirmation and/or advocacy (Lohman, 2005). Research on the Young Scholars Model is ongoing.

Project SPARK (*Supporting and Promoting Advanced Readiness in Kids*) is a current research project funded by the U.S. Department of Education under the Jacob K. Javits Gifted and Talented Education Act first authorised by Congress in 1988, focusing on identifying and serving students from culturally, linguistically, and economically diverse communities and students with disabilities. Project SPARK is testing a scaled-up version of the *Young Scholars Model*. Researchers at the University of Connecticut are attempting to bring the Young Scholars Model to a state that has neither a mandate nor funding for gifted education programming, but does require districts to identify gifted students. They are: providing professional development; modelling classroom lessons; conducting parallel identification of students (identifying students separately from the typical process at each district, which is happening concurrently); and providing summer intervention programs to students identified by the district and research staff. Project SPARK researchers hope that traditionally underserved students will develop readiness for advanced academic experiences and the knowledge and skills required for identification as they approach their districts' formal gifted program identification process (Little, Adelson, Kearney, Cash, & O'Brien, 2018). A second goal of the program is to improve teachers' understanding of the unique needs of gifted students from low-income families or underrepresented minority groups. Underrepresented groups include students from indigenous populations.

Cooper (2005) described a program in Western Australia to unmask potentials among Aboriginal students. The program titled *Moorditj Kulungar* ('bright children') included students ages 10–16 years old and focused on increasing self-esteem and content knowledge, improving attitudes towards learning and promoting aspirational educational goals. Aboriginal role models and school and community members served as mentors during the two-term program. Program content was "student-centered, abstract, and offered variety and constant challenge" (Cooper, 2005, p. 120). The program illuminated characteristics of Noongar gifted and talented students from Western Australia:

- The ability to freely explore their environment with peers and elders (to foster independence and cultural identity);
- To be very active and verbal;
- To have a laugh (many had a good sense of humour);
- To use symbols and numbers effectively in problem-solving activities in a global style;
- Demonstrated a good memory and creative abilities;
- Evidence of proficiency in non-verbal as well as verbal communication;
- Demonstrated physical prowess in well developed rhythm and movement; and,
- A strong preference for group activities, especially in verbal contexts. (Cooper, 2005, p. 120)

As researchers are creating and evaluating models for programs that prepare students for gifted identification and academic rigour, individual districts and schools are developing programs with these same goals. Researchers from the NCRGE (2016) found that some of these programs were developing organically, within individual schools or districts. As part of the NCRGE study, research teams visited 13 schools in State 1 that specifically promoted the potential of historically underrepresented students in grades K–3. Research teams conducted focus group interviews with general education teachers, parents of gifted students, and gifted students themselves as well as individual interviews with administrators, gifted specialists, and school counsellors. While program details varied, most included similar structural elements.

Structured Elements of Pre-identification Strategies and Preparation Programs

Many of the pre-identification strategies and preparation programs in the NCRGE study had three structural elements: push-in services, whereby gifted specialists work with students and general education teachers; pull-out services, whereby the gifted specialists work with small groups of students in another setting; and specific interventions with individuals or small groups of students that have not yet qualified for formal services. First, they began by having gifted specialists provide push-in services to all kindergarten and often grade 1 classrooms. Teachers would team-teach lessons with the general education teacher, typically focusing on creativity or critical thinking skills. During a focus group, one member of a school identification committee described these lessons:

> They had some really deep discussions and it was challenging for them like you would watch a lesson and they might spend you know, the entire 40 minutes trying to put a shape and sorting the shape and why does your piece not match where you used it. Let's say, you're not right. Let's think about it, pull back out, think some more, come back and so they were really in-depth lessons that got the kids really having to think about their thinking. And explaining their thinking and putting in a whole sentence and using the proper/language that they're [going to] hear in the upper grades, you know. I mean I can think when they called them to the carpet, it wasn't come sit on the edge of the carpet. It was sit on the perimeter. (Identification Committee member, A-1)

These push-in lessons would serve multiple purposes. All children would be exposed to this deeper level curriculum, providing all students with a basic level of gifted services. By team teaching with the general education teacher, gifted specialists were also using the lesson as an opportunity for coaching these teachers on gifted identification. As part of the lesson debriefing, they would often discuss the children's responses to the curriculum, facilitating the additional goal of looking for students who may benefit from additional services prior to the gifted identification testing that occurred in grade 3.

The second structural element, pull-out services, involved working with students who had been selected for preparation programs. Prior to universal screening, these students would be pulled out of the classrooms to work with the gifted specialist. Many of the schools used *Primary Education Thinking Skills* (PETS) or a similar curriculum that focused on higher-level thinking. Students were exposed to new concepts and challenging curriculum, and teachers were able to monitor their progress. One gifted specialist commented:

> Those who really stood out, whether it was convergent thinking, divergent thinking, whatever the lesson was about, or the lessons were geared towards. And so, we could, we could keep an eye on those children as they progressed to each grade.... Because I think you *develop* [italics added] the potential. (Gifted specialist, A-2)

Selection for these programs was flexible. Teachers could add students or adjust the composition of the groups as needed, with the goal of ensuring that all students who could benefit from preparation programs would receive them. This flexibility sometimes stimulated conversations with general education teachers, creating opportunities for informal professional development.

The third structural element, included in many of the programs the NCRGE research team visited, was ongoing services and retesting for students who were not identified at the time of the universal screening. Schools opted to include these students in the pull-out or accelerated programming, realising that some students just missed the cut-off score on the universal screener and knowing that additional data supported their inclusion in this programming. As one general education teacher commented, "Even if... [the students] missed it on something else but really are so close you know they won't label them, but they'll ... still group them with those higher-level students to maybe get them to that point" (General education teacher, D-1).

In addition to these structural elements, three broader themes emerged from the data: alignment, professional development, and culture of awareness.

Identification, Programming, Professional Development, and a Culture of Awareness

As the NCRGE researchers (2016) analysed the data, it became clear that the majority of schools visited in State 1 and a few of those visited in State 2 incorporated pre-identification strategies and preparation programs, while none were reported in State 3. For the purposes of this analysis, researchers focused on the schools with pre-identification programs in State 1. Three themes emerged from analysis of the data from the schools visited in State 1. The first was the alignment between the pre-identification strategies and the identification process. These programs should be viewed as part of the identification process, both in terms of curriculum and data collection. The most common curriculum utilised was the Primary Education Thinking Skills, which focuses on developing higher-level thinking skills such as divergent thinking, visual/spatial thinking, and evaluation. These skills build students' readiness for the universal screening process.

Much of the data collection in these programs happens informally; however some teachers mentioned keeping lists of students whom they believe could be identified based on their experiences in the pre-identification program. School staff were also aware of the need for equity in the identification process. One gifted specialist explained:

> Maybe [a child] doesn't have an engineering forte in the beginning because he never built even with Legos or something because his parents couldn't afford them. But after the experience, I come in and then they're like yeah, you know then we're going keep them in there. You got to do the exposure kind of thing and see what happens. (Gifted specialist, C-2)

The second theme was professional development. While many schools planned professional development components as part of their programs, in most cases it also happened serendipitously. Conversations about whether or not a child should be referred to the preparation program turned into teaching opportunities. Gifted specialists used these moments to discuss the characteristics of giftedness or how giftedness might present in different students:

> Okay, and usually like this year there is a male here; he is very hyper I would say, but he is loveable; he is a Kindergarten student and last year we had him for Pre-K. Now this student here, because he is so hyper, well the last time he got in trouble a lot, and therefore—even one of my teachers said, "I don't think I should recommend this student to you." I said, "No, go ahead and recommend him"; I said, "I can handle students who have hyper problems; that just means that they have more information that they want to share." She said, "Are you sure?" I said, "Yes ma'am, please give him to me." (Gifted specialist, G-1)

General education teachers and the gifted specialist would debrief after push-in lessons, leading to conversations about extending curriculum or infusing critical thinking skills. One district gifted program coordinator explained:

> We've done a lot with critical thinking through games, critical thinking through ... innovative and creative projects and pieces like that, discovery, curiosity, thinking skills, those are the different things, once we hit that fourth and fifth grade we're talking more content pieces, so we're looking more of the metacognition at K-3 what do they know, ... do they know how to learn, do they know they know how to learn, and how they move on from there. Okay, so that training is different in that is that we look at giftedness not content based, not accelerated, reading strategies, or accelerated math strategies, but how we're thinking and how we're thinking about our thinking. (District gifted program coordinator, I-1)

Finally, an overall culture of awareness was evident at many of these schools. Stakeholders were aware of the need for gifted services. Principals, general education teachers, and staff were aware of the gifted program and played an active role in the identification process, thinking about the characteristics of giftedness while interacting with students. Parents were offered information and sometimes coaching to help them understand the process and how to help their children. One gifted specialist explained that she would:

> pull parents in and talk to them about okay when they go in third grade this is what we need to be looking for and these are opportunities over the summer, these are things that you can be doing with them to help keep them moving and keep that ball rolling. (Gifted specialist, G-2)

Conclusion

Members of educated learning communities within and across continents in our culturally, linguistically, and economically diverse world must acknowledge that:

> in an age of increasing global competitiveness, it is somewhat harrowing to imagine a future in which the largest, fastest-growing segments of the K–12 student population have almost no students performing at advanced levels academically. (Plucker, Hardesty, & Burroughs, 2013, p. 29)

Researchers and practitioners have the responsibility to ensure that they do not leave emergent and latent "talent on the sidelines" (Plucker et al., 2013) of our educational systems. It is the responsibility of the field of gifted education and talent development to find ways to ratchet up early learning experiences and grade-level opportunities for all students, including students who have been historically underrepresented in gifted and talented programs. It is critical to find ways to create and implement pre-identification strategies and preparation programs that promote the hidden or masked talents and abilities of students who have been underserved as they have been caught up in the "achievement trap" (Wyner et al., 2009).

Cross-References

- ▶ Gifted Education in the Asia-Pacific: From the Past for the Future – An Introduction
- ▶ Highly Able Students in International Schools
- ▶ Identifying and Nurturing Diversely Gifted and Talented Students: Part III Introduction
- ▶ Identifying Gifted Learning in the Regular Classroom: Seeking Intuitive Theories
- ▶ Innovative Practices to Support High-Achieving Deprived Young Scholars in an Ethnic-Linguistic Diverse Latin American Country
- ▶ Rural Voices: Identifying the Perceptions, Practices, and Experiences of Gifted Pedagogy in Australian Rural and Regional Schools
- ▶ Self-Nomination in the Identification Process of Gifted and Talented Students in Mexico
- ▶ Some Implications for the Future of Gifted Education in the Asia-Pacific

Acknowledgments This research from the National Center for Research on Gifted Education (NCRGE; http://ncrge.uconn.edu) was funded by the Institute of Education Sciences, U.S. Department of Education PR/Award No. R305C140018.

References

Anuruthwong, U. (2017). Education for the gifted/talented in Thailand. *Cogent Education, 4*, 1332825. Retrieved from https://www.tandfonline.com/doi/pdf/10.1080/2331186X.2017.1332825?needAccess=true

Bevan-Brown, J. (1999). Special abilities: A Māori perspective. Implications for catering for gifted children from minority cultures. *Gifted Education International, 14*, 86–96. https://doi.org/10.1177/026142949901400110

Bevan-Brown, J. (2011). *Indigenous conceptions of giftedness*. Retrieved from http://www.aaegt.net.au/DEEWR%20Books/02%20Indig.pdf

Card, D., & Giuliano, L. (2015). *Can universal screening increase the representation of low income and minority students in gifted education?* (NBER working paper 21519). Cambridge, MA: National Bureau of Economic Research.

Chaffey, G. W., Bailey, S. B., & Vine, K. W. (2003). Identifying high academic potential in Australian Aboriginal children using dynamic testing. *The Australasian Journal of Gifted Education, 12*(1), 42–55. Retrieved from http://www.aaegt.net.au/DEEWR%20Books/06%20Indig.pdf

Chaffey, G. W., Halliwell, G., & McCluskey, K. W. (2006). Identifying high academic potential in Canadian Aboriginal primary school children. *Gifted Education International, 21*, 61–70. https://doi.org/10.1080/15332276.2006.11673476

Chaffey, G. W., McCluskey, K. W., & Halliwell, G. (2005). Using Coolabah Dynamic Assessment to identify Canadian Aboriginal children with high potential: A cross-cultural comparison. *Gifted and Talented International, 20*, 50–59. https://doi.org/10.1080/15332276.2005.11673453

Cooper, S. (2005). Gifted indigenous programs: Unmasking potential in minority cultures. *Gifted Education International, 19*, 114–125. https://doi.org/10.1177/026142940501900205

Every Student Succeeds Act. (2015). *Title IV, Part F, Section 4644: Supporting high-ability students,* Public Law 114–95. Retrieved from http://www.ncea.org/NCEA/Lead/Public_Policy/Every_Student_Succeeds_Act__ESSA__.aspx

Ford, D. Y. (2014). Segregation and the underrepresentation of Blacks and Hispanics in gifted education: Social inequality and deficit paradigms. *Roeper Review, 36*, 143–154. https://doi.org/10.1080/02783193.2014.919563

Gagné, F. (2008). *Building gifts into talents: Overview of the DMGT.* Retrieved from http://www.templetonfellows.org/program/francoysgagne.pdf

Gallagher, J. J. (1975). *Teaching the gifted child* (2nd ed.). Boston, MA: Allyn & Bacon.

Garvis, S. (2006). Optimising the learning of gifted aboriginal students. *International Journal of Pedagogies & Learning, 2*(3), 42–51. Retrieved from https://core.ac.uk/download/pdf/11039772.pdf

Gentry, M., Hu, S., & Thomas, A. T. (2008). Ethnically diverse students. In J. A. Plucker & C. M. Callahan (Eds.), *Critical issues and practices in gifted education* (pp. 195–212). Waco, TX: Prufrock Press.

Gubbins, E. J. (2005, Winter). NRC/GT offers a snapshot of intelligence. *The National Research Center on the Gifted and Talented Newsletter.* Retrieved from https://nrcgt.uconn.edu/newsletters/winter051/

Gubbins, E. J., Siegle, D., Hamilton, R., O'Rourke, P., Puryear, J., Peters, P., ... McCoach, D. B. (2018). *Exploratory study on the identification of English learners in gifted and talented programs.* Storrs, CT: University of Connecticut, National Center for Research on Gifted Education.

Hamilton, R. (2017). *National Center for Research on Gifted Education (NCRGE): District survey data.* Storrs: University of Connecticut, National Center for Research on Gifted Education.

Hamilton, R., McCoach, D. B., Tutwiler, M. S., Siegle, D., Gubbins, E. J., Callahan, C. M., ... Mun, R. U. (2018). Disentangling the roles of institutional and individual poverty in the identification of gifted students. *Gifted Child Quarterly, 62*, 6–24. https://doi.org/10.1177/0016986217738053

Harslett, M. (1996). The concept of giftedness from an Aboriginal cultural perspective. *Gifted Education International, 11*, 100–106. https://doi.org/10.1177/026142949601100207

Hart, B., & Risley, T. R. (2003). The early catastrophe: The 30 million gap by age 3. *American Educator, 27*(1), 4–9.

Horn, C. V. (2015). Young scholars: A talent development model for finding and nurturing potential in underserved populations. *Gifted Child Today, 38*, 19–31. https://doi.org/10.1177/1076217514556532

Lee, S. Y., Olszewski-Kubilius, P., & Peternel, G. (2009). Follow-up with students after 6 years of participation in Project EXCITE. *Gifted Child Quarterly, 53*, 137–156. https://doi.org/10.1177/0016986208330562

Little, C. A., Adelson, J. L., Kearney, K. L., Cash, K., & O'Brien, R. (2018). Early opportunities to strengthen academic readiness: Effects of summer learning on mathematics achievement. *Gifted Child Quarterly, 62*, 83–95. https://doi.org/10.1177/0016986217738052

Lohman, D. F. (2005). An aptitude perspective on talent: Implications for identification of academically gifted minority students. *Journal for the Education of the Gifted, 28*, 333–360. https://doi.org/10.1177/001698620504900203

Marland, S. P., Jr. (1971). *Education of the gifted and talented, Volume 1. Report to the Congress of the United States by the U. S. Commissioner of Education.* Washington, DC: U. S. Government Printing Office.

McCoach, D. B., Siegle, D., Callahan, C., Gubbins, E. J., Hamilton, R., & Tutwiler, M. S. (2016, April). *The identification gap: When just as good isn't good enough.* Poster session presented at annual meeting of American Educational Research Association, Washington, DC.

McFadden v. *Board of Education for Illinois School District U–46*, 5 C 0760. (2013). Retrieved from http://www.maldef.org/assets/pdf/U-46%5FTrial%5FDecision.pdf

Morelock, M. J. (1992). Giftedness: The view from within. *Understanding Our Gifted, 4*(3), 1, 11–15.

Mun, R. U., Dulong Langley, S., Ware, S., Gubbins, E. J., Siegle, D., Callahan, C. M., . . . Hamilton, R. (2016, December). *Effective practices for identifying and serving English learners in gifted education: A systematic review of literature.* Storrs: University of Connecticut, National Center for Research on Gifted Education.

National Association for Gifted Children and the Council of State Directors of Programs for the Gifted. (2015). *2014–2015 State of the states in gifted education: Policy and practice data.* Washington, DC: National Association for Gifted Children.

National Center for Research on Gifted Education. (2016). *NCRGE district survey.* Storrs: University of Connecticut, Author.

Olszewski-Kubilius, P. (2006). Addressing the achievement gap between minority and nonminority children: Increasing access and achievement through Project EXCITE. *Gifted Child Today, 29*(2), 28–37.

Peters, S. J., & Engerrand, K. G. (2016). Equity and excellence: Proactive efforts in the identification of underrepresented students for gifted and talented services. *Gifted Child Quarterly, 60*, 159–171. https://doi.org/10.1177/0016986216643165

Plucker, J. A., Burroughs, N., & Song, R. (2010). *Mind the (other) gap: The growing excellence gap in K–12 education.* Bloomington: Indiana University, Center for Evaluation & Education Policy.

Plucker, J., Hardesty, J., & Burroughs, N. (2013). *Talent on the sidelines: Excellence gaps and America's persistent talent underclass.* Storrs: University of Connecticut, Center for Education Policy Analysis. Retrieved from http://webdev.education.uconn.edu/static/sites/cepa/AG/excellence2013/Excellence-Gap-10-18-13_JP_LK.pdf

Roeper, A. (1982). How the gifted cope with their emotions. *Roeper Review, 5*, 21–23. https://doi.org/10.1080/02783198209552672

Scobie-Jennings, E. (2013). An investigation into the identification of Māori gifted and talented students in mainstream school. *APEX: The New Zealand Journal of Gifted Education, 18*(1). Retrieved from https://www.giftedchildren.org.nz/wp-content/uploads/2014/10/Scobie-Jennings.pdf

Siegle, D., Gubbins, E. J., O'Rourke, P., Dulong Langley, S., Mun, R. U., Luria, S. R., . . . Plucker, J. A. (2016). Barriers to underserved students' participation in gifted programs and possible solutions. *Journal for the Education of the Gifted, 39*, 1–29. https://doi.org/10.1177/0162353216640930

United States Department of Education. (1993). *National excellence: A case for developing American's talent.* Washington, DC: Author.

United States Department of Education Office for Civil Rights. (2014, March). *Civil rights data collection: Data snapshot (college and career readiness).* Retrieved from https://www2.ed.gov/about/offices/list/ocr/docs/crdc-college-and-career-readiness-snapshot.pdf

Wellisch, M. (2016). Gagné's DMGT and underachievers: The need for an alternative inclusive gifted model. *The Australasian Journal of Gifted Education, 25*(1), 18–30. https://doi.org/10.21505/ajge.2016.0003

Worrell, F. C., & Erwin, J. O. (2011). Best practices in identifying students for gifted and talented education programs. *Journal of Applied School Psychology, 27*, 319–340. https://doi.org/10.1080/15377903.2011.615817

Wu, W.-T. (2000). Talent identification and development in Taiwan. *Roeper Review, 22*, 131–134. https://doi.org/10.1080/02783190009554017

Wyner, J. S., Bridgeland, J. M., & DiIulio, J. J., Jr. (2009). *Achievement trap: How America is failing millions of high-achieving students from lower-income families* (Rev. ed.). Lansdowne, VA: Jack Kent Cooke Foundation and Civic Enterprises. Retrieved from http://www.jkcf.org/news-knowledge/research-reports/

Yoon, S. Y., & Gentry, M. (2009). Racial and ethnic representation in gifted programs: Current status of and implications for gifted Asian American students. *Gifted Child Quarterly, 53*, 121–136. https://doi.org/10.1177/0016986208330564

Pam Peters is a graduate student at the University of Connecticut pursuing a doctoral degree in Educational Psychology. She is also a Research Assistant with both the Renzulli Center for Creativity, Giftedness, and Talent Development and the National Center for Research on Gifted Education. Her research interests centre on issues of equity, including identification and excellence gaps, imposter syndrome in first-generation college students, and the development of parent/school partnerships to enhance gifted programming. Pam has spoken locally and nationally on parent partnership development and has consulted with school districts on both coasts of the United States.

E. Jean Gubbins, PhD, is Professor in the Department of Educational Psychology, University of Connecticut. Through grants from the U.S. Department of Education for The National Research Center on the Gifted and Talented, Dr. Gubbins implemented research studies on curricular strategies and practices. Currently, she is Associate Director for the National Center for Research on Gifted Education, focusing on exemplary practices in identification and programming for gifted and talented students from underrepresented groups. Her new federally funded grant entitled Thinking Like Mathematicians: Challenging All Grade 3 Students involves developing a pre-differentiated and enriched grade 3 unit on algebraic thinking, multiplication and division.

Rashea Hamilton, PhD, was formerly a Research Scientist for the National Center for Research on Gifted Education. Currently, she is the Assistant Director of Research for the Washington Student Achievement Council. Her work focuses on issues addressing access and equity across the educational pipeline, and she has over 10 years of research experience related to at-risk populations. Her primary areas of expertise include social inequality, parental engagement, and quantitative methodology.

D. Betsy McCoach, PhD, is Professor in the Measurement, Evaluation, and Assessment program at the University of Connecticut, has extensive experience in structural equation modelling, longitudinal data analysis, hierarchical linear modelling, instrument design, and factor analysis. She is the lead Quantitative Research Methodologist for the National Center for Research on Gifted Education.

Del Siegle, PhD, is Director of the National Center for Research on Gifted Education at the University of Connecticut, where he serves as Associate Dean for Research and Faculty Development in the Neag School of Education. He is a past president of the National Association for Gifted Children, past president of the Montana Association of Gifted and Talented Education, past chair of the Research on Giftedness, Creativity and Talent SIG of the American Educational Research Association and a former Editor of *Gifted Child Quarterly* and the *Journal of Advanced Academics*.

Jeb Puryear, PhD, is a former Research Associate at the National Center for Research on Gifted Education. He has over 15 years of experience as a Classroom Educator—primarily teaching and leading in advanced academics settings—and currently works as the Highly Able Coordinator for ACS-Cobham International School in the United Kingdom. His research interests include paradigms in gifted education and their influence on stakeholder actions; the interactions and overlaps of giftedness and creativity research; underrepresentation and excellence gaps based on rurality, socio-economic status and race/ethnicity; and the practical applications of STEM research to gifted education.

Identifying Gifted Learning in the Regular Classroom: Seeking Intuitive Theories

23

John Munro

Contents

Introduction	488
Gifted Thinking and Learning that Leads to Talented Interpretations and Outcomes	489
Tasks to Identify a Gifted Learning Capacity in the Classroom	493
Summary: The Use of Concept Mapping to Identify Gifted Learning in the Classroom	497
Scenario Problem-Solving	498
Implications for Practice	502
Summary: The Use of SPST to Identify Gifted Learning in the Classroom	502
Procedures for Combining Data from Multiple Tasks to Make Empirically Valid Decisions	503
Implications for Research and Future Directions	503
Conclusion	504
Cross-References	505
References	505

Abstract

Identifying instances of gifted thinking in the regular classroom is a continuing challenge for many educators. This chapter links a contemporary model of gifted knowing and learning with identification procedures that are readily implemented in the regular classroom. One way in which students' learning capacity is displayed in the classroom is through the interpretations or understandings they generate of the teaching. Thinking characteristics of gifted learners include the spontaneous use of high-level fluid analogistic, inferential, analytic, synthetic, and metacognitive strategies. These lead to interpretations that have the characteristics of 'intuitive theories'. These interpretations differ in their quality from those formed by students who are not gifted. This chapter describes two types of

J. Munro (✉)
Faculty of Education and Arts, Australian Catholic University, East Melbourne, VIC, Australia
e-mail: jkmunro@unimelb.edu.au

© Springer Nature Singapore Pte Ltd. 2021
S. R. Smith (ed.), *Handbook of Giftedness and Talent Development in the Asia-Pacific*,
Springer International Handbooks of Education,
https://doi.org/10.1007/978-981-13-3041-4_22

tasks that teachers can use as part of their regular teaching to provide gifted students with the opportunity to display their qualitatively different understanding, concept mapping, and scenario problem-solving. For each task context, summaries will be provided of recent original research studies that show that the task distinguishes between gifted and regular learning students and the characteristics of students gifted in multiple domains. How understanding classification frameworks, such as those provided by Fischer's (2008)) *Dynamic Skill Theory*, can be used to analyse and evaluate the understanding generated by students who are gifted in various domains will be explored. The methodology will be included for administering each type of task, the procedures used to interpret outcomes, and the implications for formative assessment and the differentiation of pedagogy and curriculum.

Keywords

Identifying gifted knowing and learning · Regular classroom · Intuitive theories · Concept mapping · Scenario problem-solving

The aims in this chapter are to describe:
1. The characteristics of gifted knowing in the regular classroom.
2. The characteristic of the 'intuitive theories' gifted learners form about teaching.
3. Two types of tasks that teachers can use as part of their regular teaching to identify gifted understanding, concept mapping and scenario problem-solving.
4. How each task distinguishes between gifted and regular learning students.
5. The methodology for administering each type of task, the procedures used to interpret outcomes, and the implications for formative assessment.

Introduction

Identifying instances of gifted thinking in the regular classroom is a continuing challenge for many educators (Reis & Renzulli, 2010). Educators generally lack the relevant professional knowledge for identifying gifted thinking capacities (VanTassel-Baska & Stambaugh, 2005). A consequence of this is the lack of appropriate differentiation of curriculum and teaching for some students (e.g., Hertberg-Davis, 2009; Reis & Renzulli, 2010).

A contemporary model of gifted knowing and learning with identification procedures that are readily implemented in the regular classroom will be provided in this chapter. The identification procedures have been shown to distinguish between gifted and regular learning students. These procedures can assist teachers to 'recognise' instances of a gifted learning capacity.

The differentiated models of giftedness and talent (e.g., DMGT, Gagné, 2010; Munich Model of Giftedness, Heller, Perleth, & Lim, 2005; The Actiotope Model,

Ziegler & Vialle, 2017) provide an approach that describes how giftedness is mapped into talented performance. This developmental approach distinguishes between giftedness as the natural ability or aptitude to learn at a high level and talent as the outstanding skills that are developed from these aptitudes. Talented outcomes are more likely in the presence of appropriate noncognitive or personality characteristics (the 'intrapersonal' moderators or catalysts) and environmental conditions, including informal and/or formal teaching.

One way in which students' learning capacity is displayed in the classroom is through the interpretations or understanding they generate of the teaching they experience. Students' interpretations are formed by integrating their ability to learn with their noncognitive or personality characteristics. This author proposes modifying the differentiated models to include an explicit specification of a student's interpretation of the teaching as an 'intermediate knowing phase' that mediates between the natural ability and the talented outcome.

Evidence of gifted learning in the regular classroom is displayed in a student's responses to the teaching. Gifted learners interpret classroom teaching differently from their peers (Munro, 2013a, 2015b). Their ways of learning and thinking lead to qualitatively different understanding of the teaching information. In particular they generate interpretations that have the characteristics of intuitive theories (Ericsson, Roring, & Nandagopa, 2007; Kaufman, 2007; Sastre-Riba, 2011; Shavinina, 2007). A summary of the recommended modification to the differentiated models is shown in Figure 1.

Analysis and evaluation of students' interpretations of the teaching assist teachers to identify a gifted learning capacity. The intuitive theory that comprises this understanding should lead to talented outcomes. Teachers' evaluation or formative assessment of the gifted students' learning capacity can inform follow-up planning and implementation of differentiation of the pedagogy and curriculum. Scaffolding gifted students to make explicit their intuitive theory increases the likelihood that they will form talented outcomes from it.

The following sections examine the thinking that leads to the generation of the intuitive theories, the characteristics of this understanding, and a protocol for evaluating gifted students' understanding to detect them.

Gifted Thinking and Learning that Leads to Talented Interpretations and Outcomes

Gifted learners use spontaneously a range of thinking and learning strategies that allow them to 'extend' the teaching information in various ways. They are more likely to show the following learning characteristics when engaging with teaching information. Gifted learners:

- Use more complex thinking strategies, such as inference more flexibly and selectively, spontaneously, and independently and shift between strategies more efficiently for complex problems (Carr, Alexander, & Schwanenflugel, 1996).

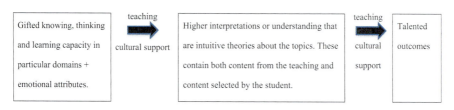

Fig. 1 Summary of the recommended modification to the differentiated models of giftedness and talent

- Link ideas in novel lateral, unexpected ways, make fluid analogies between topics that seem unrelated, cross 'topic boundaries', use 'far transfer' thinking, and draw in a wider range of ideas into a broader understanding (Geake, 2008).
- Chunk information more efficiently, think in larger jumps, keep track of several ideas or multiple aspects of a topic at once, and can think in several directions about it (Kornmann, Zettler, Kammerer, Gerjets, & Trautwein, 2015).
- Ask spontaneously complex questions about ideas and solve problems in unusual or novel ways (Maker, 2006; Maker, Zimmerman, Gomez-Arizaga, Pease, & Burke, 2015).
- Use imagination or fantasy and show 'intellectual playfulness' (Smith & Mathur, 2009).
- Synthesise the outcomes, organise and use their conceptual networks in a 'big ideas' way, and form subjective patterns and personal rules about the information (Rizza, McIntosh, & McCunn, 2001).
- Have the affective infrastructure necessary to self-scaffold independently the pursuit of knowledge when given the opportunity; show focused, intense interest in a topic; are self-motivated to think and learn about the topic; and maintain focus and persist with difficult tasks (Gagné, 2009; Subotnik, Olszewski-Kubilius, & Worrell, 2011).
- Manage, monitor, and direct their thinking and learning activity more ably while self-regulating and using metacognition more spontaneously and efficiently than their regular peers (Carr, Alexander, & Schwanenflugel, 1996).
- Plan how they will learn by setting learning goals (Fox, Dinsmore, & Alexander, 2010).
- Review progress.
- Learn new strategies more easily, operate as 'intuitive philosophers', and form their personal theory of intelligence (Hsueh, 1997).

In common with their peers in other regions, gifted students in the Asia-Pacific region use these learning characteristics to form the higher-level interpretations and understanding characteristics of gifted learners and to apply them more broadly (Phillipson et al., 2009). Classroom tasks intended to identify gifted learning need to detect evidence of these learning characteristics.

Multiple gifted learning profiles lead to talented interpretations. Students can be gifted in multiple ways; they differ in the domain of their gifted learning capacity.

These have been categorised in various ways. Used in this chapter are the three main types of gifted learning profiles noted by Sternberg and colleagues (Sternberg et al., 2007): the academic, creative, and practical types. The three profiles generate intuitive theories that differ in their characteristics. Each is described briefly here.

Academically gifted students learn efficiently what they are taught at school and use this knowledge at a high level. They are the 'school-house gifted' (Renzulli, 2012), 'consumers of knowledge' (Tannenbaum, 1987), 'analytically intelligent' (Sternberg, 2005), or 'academic activists' (Callahan & Miller, 2005). Their gifted learning capacity is shown in their achievement test scores and their ability to learn from the teaching (Renzulli, 2012). Frequently, these students are gifted verbally.

Others learn ideas that were not taught. They make links with ideas that were not mentioned in the teaching and broaden it. Their thinking leads to creative interpretations and outcomes that teachers often find unexpected and perplexing. They are described as creatively gifted (Renzulli, 2012; Sternberg, 2005) or 'producers of knowledge' (Tannenbaum, 1987).

Some show practical and innovative giftedness that are associated with applying and implementing what they know in novel ways (Shavinina, 2013). Their thinking leads to original productions and ways of solving problems, the 'problem-solving innovators' (Callahan & Miller, 2005). They include the students who are gifted in information technology and its applications.

Some gifted students have co-occurring learning issues that mask their gifted learning capacity, the 'twice exceptional' or 'dual exceptional' learners (Neihart & Betts, 2010; Munro 2002, 2005, 2010). The co-occurring issues can be emotional, social, or cognitive and often lead to academic underachievement, social and behavioural problems, and a disengagement from regular classroom participation. Some may show 'asynchronous development'—that is, advanced development in some areas and immature development or underachievement in others in comparison to their same-age peers. Some in the early-middle secondary years become alienated from regular schools (Beghetto & Kaufman, 2014).

In all cases, the multiple ways of being gifted allow students to form intuitive theories of the teaching. However, the qualities of their interpretations and the climate under which they learn best differ. Many teachers recognise the academically gifted and neglect the other gifted learning profiles. Teachers and schools need identification tools that take account of the multiple ways of being gifted and implement classroom cultures that support each (Munro, 2017).

The various ways of being gifted and their implications for teaching are described in depth in Munro (2013b, 2013c). Leaders and teachers can identify the various categories of giftedness by asking questions about students' high-level outcomes provided in Munro (2015b, 2017).

Talented interpretations of the teaching. The gifted ways of learning within the multiple ways of knowing, in turn, lead to qualitatively different understanding of the teaching information; as noted, students generate interpretations that have the characteristics of intuitive theories. Characteristics of their interpretations of the teaching information (Munro, 2013a, 2014a, 2014b, 2015b, 2017) include the following:

(a) They have more inferred concepts, often gained through fluid analogistic reasoning.
(b) The concepts are organised into statements that express more semantically complex relationships or 'propositions'.
(c) The propositions are organised around one or more inferred main or big ideas. The students are more likely to impose hierarchies on their propositions. They do this subjectively.
(d) The interpretations have the properties of an intuitive theory that can be tested by the learner. They may include propositions that are logically inaccurate.
(e) The students are subjectively 'problem-solution' directed; they are motivated intrinsically to 'know more' and to reduce uncertainty about the issue.
(f) An intuitive theory at any time is speculative; students are motivated intrinsically to test, evaluate, and modify it.
(g) The interpretations can be analysed in their complexity using semantic analysis procedures that compare and categorise the propositions and match them with the teaching information.

It is this type of understanding, generated in response to teaching information that teachers can use to identify instances of gifted learning. When teachers can recognise these outcomes in students' responses to their teaching, they can differentiate instruction formatively and scaffold higher-level outcomes. Over the past decade, we have researched how gifted students interpret the teaching provided quite differently from their regular peers.

Intuitive theories have ideas not mentioned in the teaching and a level of connectedness and organisation generated by the students. Regular achievement tasks such as tests that assess how well knowledge has been acquired are not suitable for assessing this type of understanding. Open-ended tasks and associated assessment that provide students the opportunity to communicate the breadth and depth of their understanding are more appropriate. The following section examines procedures for evaluating students' outcomes.

Procedures for describing the quality of a student's learning outcomes. The quality of a student's learning outcomes in the classroom is indicated in its cognitive or semantic complexity. Taxonomies for describing this are the *Structure of the Observed Learning Outcomes* (SOLO; Biggs & Collis, 1982) and the *Dynamic Skill Theory* (DST; Fischer, 2008). Each provides a means for evaluating a student's outcomes in terms of the complexity of the ideas they have learnt. They refer to the number of separate ideas in an outcome and the links between them. These taxonomies have been tested empirically. A greater level of complexity in the SOLO taxonomy predicts higher academic outcomes (e.g., Chan, Tsui, Chan, & Hong, 2002).

These taxonomies can be applied in a different way to identify gifted students' learning capacity. Rather than identifying what students understand as a result of teaching, they can be used to analyse and evaluate the quality of the inferences and syntheses in students' responses to the teaching. In other words, they can be used to examine the extent to which some students extend and elaborate the teaching information and form intuitive theories about it. Tools based on the taxonomies can help to assess the:

(a) Number of ideas that make up the student's interpretation (i.e., the fluency of the intuitive theory).
(b) Organisation of the constituent concepts.
(c) Semantic relationships that link the ideas taught with those that are inferred subjectively by the students.
(d) Hierarchical organisation of the constituent concepts.
(e) Inference of 'big' ideas or theme of the intuitive theory.

The two taxonomies differ in the types of relationships or propositions they identify and therefore the inferences and syntheses they would identify in students' intuitive theories. The types of inferences and syntheses students make about the teaching information and the closest relationships identified by each of the taxonomies are shown in Table 1.

The DST offers a more differentiated framework for describing students' intuitive theories. This framework is used to analyse and evaluate a student's interpretations and outcomes in terms of the complexity of the ideas.

Tasks to Identify a Gifted Learning Capacity in the Classroom

In this chapter, a description is provided of the use of two types of tasks that teachers can use as part of their regular teaching to provide gifted students with the opportunity to display their qualitatively different understanding of the teaching, that is, concept mapping and scenario problem-solving. For each task context, it will summarise recent research that shows that the task distinguishes between gifted and regular learning students and the characteristics of students gifted in multiple domains.

Concept mapping. Concept mapping techniques have been used extensively to assess the quality of an individual's understanding of a topic and the quality of the semantic links or relationships a student perceives between a set of ideas (Cañas & Novak, 2010). The map organises the concepts in terms of their generality, with the most general concepts located above the intermediate concepts and the most specific or detailed concepts below them. Each proposition is represented by two or more concepts linked by lines or arrows.

The map for any topic may show at least one hierarchy of concepts. As well, it may show links between hierarchies. These 'cross-links' (Cañas & Novak 2010) may indicate thinking creatively about the topic.

The research examining the use of concept mapping to identify gifted learning capacity. Concept mapping provides a tool for investigating students' intuitive theories about a set of concepts and for identifying instances of gifted thinking and learning. The features of a concept map that match each type of cognitive complexity

Table 1 The types of inferential and synthesis relationships identified by the SOLO and DST taxonomies

The type of relationship in the understanding: the student.	SOLO	DST
Infers a single pattern with ideas not stated in teaching information.	Uni-structural	Single representation
Infers two or more patterns that are not link them.	Multi-structural	Representational mappings
Infers two or more patterns and synthesises them into a single general idea. They link facts and theory and action and purpose and can apply the concept to familiar problems or work situations.	Relational	Representational system
Transfers/applies the single general abstract idea across a range of contexts or topics to form more abstract concepts.		System of representational systems
Infers links between two or more general ideas into two or more linked 'big ideas' and shows evidence of transfer and abstraction to multiple areas.	Extended abstract	Abstract mappings
Comprehends and links several abstractions into a complex relationship. They identify what all of the abstractions share and generalise about this.		Abstract systems
Synthesises a principle that integrates the abstract systems. They identify what the abstract systems share.		Single principles

specified in Table 1 are shown in Table 2. Each student's concept map was scored in terms of the frequency with which each feature was displayed.

Students' intuitive theories about the content can be inferred at various points in the teaching: prior to, during, and after the teaching. In one study (Munro, 2014a; Santoro, 2016), groups of fifth graders were provided with sets of 15 concepts from a topic, prior to being taught topics in history and science. They drew a concept map that showed how the concepts might be linked in the content they would learn. They had earlier been taught to draw concept maps for sets of propositions they generated about familiar topics, such as 'pets'.

As well, each student's fluid and crystallised reasoning ability were assessed using the *Raven's Standard Progressive Matrices-Plus* (RSPM+; Raven, Raven, & Court, 1998) and the *Mill Hill Vocabulary Scale* (MHV, Raven, Court, & Raven, 1994). Students were categorised as 'gifted' if they achieved scores in the top 10th percentile range on each of the tests (Gagné, 2009). Four groups of students were identified: a globally gifted group who scored above the 89th percentile on both the MHV and RSPM+ (n = 10); a nonverbally gifted group who scored above the 89th percentile only on the RSPM+ (n = 18); a verbally gifted group who scored above the 89th percentile only on the MHV (n = 19); and a not gifted group, who scored below the 90th percentile on both the MHV and RSPM+ (n = 49).

The concept maps were scored in terms of: their display of features consistent with intuitive theory generation shown in Table 2; the number and complexity of propositions generated about each topic; the number of 'big ideas' inferred; the number of hierarchies formed; and the number of cross-links made between hierarchies.

Table 2 The features of a concept map that match each type of cognitive complexity specified in the DSP

The student's inferred response shows evidence of	Matching feature in a concept map
A single representation: a single pattern not stated in teaching information.	One inferred semantic proposition.
Representational mappings: two or more patterns that are not linked.	Two or more inferred semantic propositions.
A representational system: two or more patterns are synthesised into a general idea.	The inferred semantic propositions are organised into a hierarchy.
A system of representational systems: the general idea is applied across a range of contexts/topics to form more abstract concepts.	Two or more hierarchies are inferred and generated.
Abstract mappings and systems: two or more general ideas are linked into a more abstract idea.	Cross-links are shown between two or more hierarchies.
Single principles: a principle that integrates the abstract systems is synthesised.	A 'big idea' across two or more hierarchies is inferred.

The maps were generated under the condition of independent, self-directed thinking. The links students generated were a consequence of their spontaneous thinking about each set of concepts. The trends in mean frequency for each characteristic across the four student categories for the set of science concepts are shown in Figure 2.

The outcomes show that the trend from not gifted to gifted in one domain to globally gifted as per the general ability measures is associated with an increasingly cognitive complex concept map of the intuitive theory for the set of concepts. The outcomes for the categories were compared using one-way ANOVA procedures. The trends for the four characteristics were significant and are consistent with the claim that the gifted students show an enhanced capacity to form a cognitively more complex and sophisticated intuitive theory about the set of concepts in each case. Their concept maps showed:

(a) A higher number of propositions about each topic than their not gifted peers and a higher number of more complex propositions ($p < 0.01$). Their maps showed that these students were more likely to form more complex relationships or propositions about the concepts. They maintained a semantic thread across a network of concepts.
(b) A higher ability to infer the 'big ideas' and to use these as semantic organisers for the remaining concepts ($p < 0.01$). Their concepts were highly related to the main idea.
(c) A higher number of hierarchies and an enhanced ability to organise concepts hierarchically ($p < 0.01$). Their maps suggested they can organise ideas selectively, both in hierarchies and linear chains.
(d) An increased tendency to make fluid analogies and far transfer; this was displayed in the higher number of cross-links ($p < 0.01$). They were more likely to infer cross-links between networks of ideas.

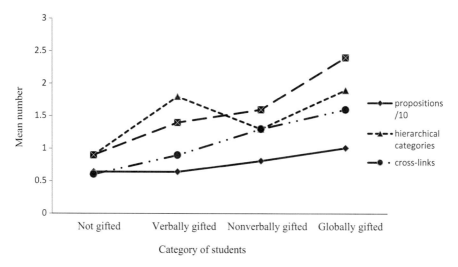

Fig. 2 The trends in mean number of each characteristic across the four student categories for the set of science concepts

The trends also showed differences between the various categories of gifted learners. The verbally gifted students identified more hierarchies than their nonverbally gifted peers ($p < 0.01$). This is not surprising; verbally gifted students have an advanced ability to comprehend and generate texts, whether they be written, spoken, behavioural, or visual (Munro, 2014a). The nonverbally gifted students, on the other hand, were more likely to make cross-links ($p < 0.01$). As noted earlier, this is associated with using analogistic thinking, leading to divergent and creative outcomes. The globally gifted cohort generally achieved at a higher level than the other categories.

The predictive validity of concept maps was examined using linear regression procedures. The two characteristics of concept maps that predicted verbal reasoning ability were the number and complexity of propositions ($\beta = 0.31, p < 0.001$) and the number of hierarchies ($\beta = 0.27, p <.001$). Neither the number of cross-links nor the number of big ideas had a significant impact. Nonverbal reasoning ability, on the other hand, was predicted by the number and complexity of propositions ($\beta = 0.39, p <.001$) and the number of big ideas ($\beta = 0.28, p <.001$); these accounted for approximately 30% of the variance. These findings suggest that while the verbally gifted students inferred and organised relationships using hierarchical thinking, the nonverbally gifted students inferred and synthesised big ideas.

An 'overall mapping complexity' score was calculated for each student by converting their raw scores on each characteristic to z-scores and then adding them. The correlation (Pearson's) between these scores and the standard reasoning ability scores were 0.54∗∗ and 0.49∗∗ for the RPM+ and MHV, respectively. These correlations were significant at the 0.001 level of significance and suggest a shared variance between the reasoning ability scores and the overall mapping complexity score of between 25 and 30%.

Table 3 The distinctive features of the concept maps of each category of giftedness

Feature	Verbal giftedness	Nonverbal giftedness	Global giftedness
Domain valid propositions	✓	✓	✓
Hierarchical categories	✓		✓
Cross-links		✓	✓
Big ideas		✓	✓

Taken together, these data show the extent to which a student's gifted learning capacity is indicated in the quality and complexity of the student's concept mapping of their intuitive theory about a topic they will learn.

Implications for practice. These data support the use of concept mapping as a formative assessment procedure for identifying instances of gifted learning and the quality of the intuitive theories students form. As an assessment procedure, concept mapping has several advantages:

- It is embedded in the topics teachers will teach or have taught. It provides a tool for assessing the quality of students' interpretation and understanding of topics that are on their curriculum. In a regular classroom context, it provides teachers with a means for identifying how gifted and regular students differ in the quality of their thinking.
- It is an easy procedure for teachers to use. Once a student cohort has been taught to use concept mapping, the procedure can be applied to any curriculum domain or topic the students will use. The research project described here used online concept mapping tools provided by the *Institute for Human and Machine Cognition* (IHMC, 2017) at https://cmap.ihmc.us. These tools include templates for constructing concept maps and for evaluating them.
- It helps teachers identify what the gifted learners know in an open-ended yet controlled way. Many frequently used assessment tasks assess how well students have learnt a topic. They do not provide students with the opportunity to share all that they know and believe about it. Concept mapping does offer this opportunity. Students are encouraged to share all that they know about the topic, that is, their intuitive theories about it.
- It provides an assessment context that permits teachers to 'recognise' instances of gifted learning and to form reasonable expectations of students. It was noted earlier that verbal giftedness is usually identified more easily by teachers than nonverbal giftedness. Concept mapping allowed nonverbal giftedness to be observed. The distinctive features of the concept maps of each category of giftedness are shown in Table 3.

Summary: The Use of Concept Mapping to Identify Gifted Learning in the Classroom

Concept mapping gives teachers a direct insight into a student's gifted architecture and supports the 'intuitive theory' model of gifted learning. Its focus on the quality of students' knowledge and understanding provides an alternative to the use of intelligence measures for identification.

Possible future developments of concept mapping procedures with gifted students may examine:

- Procedures for including and scoring the outcomes of inferential and 'possibilistic' thinking on the concepts.
- Multimodal concept maps to assist multiple gifted learning profiles.
- Improved online scoring procedures that match how gifted students learn.
- Collecting data about how a student knows longitudinally over several concept maps.

Scenario Problem-Solving

A challenge that teachers continue to face is the accurate identification of gifted students, particularly those who are gifted nonverbally. The identification tools preference those who are verbally gifted. Students who are creatively or practically gifted have innovative or lateral interpretations of the teaching that are less likely to be identified by conventional assessment tasks.

An identification format that increasingly has been shown to be effective across gifted cohorts is open-ended problem-solving (VanTassel-Baska, Feng, & Evans, 2007). One type of open-ended task is the 'diffuse social' or 'scenario' problem (Hedlund, Wilt, Nebel, Ashford, & Sternberg, 2006). Individuals are presented with a real-world scenario that has an embedded problem. They identify the problem and recommend a solution. An example of a scenario problem is: *iPods are bad for your hearing. Listening to your iPod at full volume can be like having a chainsaw near your ears. The loud noise they generate make many people deaf. Many people don't know how bad it would be to lose their hearing.*

These problems have the following characteristics. First, they are ill-defined, and the challenge needs to be identified. Second, they lack a single solution and may require the solver to deal with changing situations. Third, they may have time constraints and competing demands. Fourth, the problem or its solution may interact with other issues in the context; some solutions may not fit with broader goals and values in the context. Fifth, the information needed to solve them may not be obvious or readily available. Of the six types of hierarchical problems investigated by Maker and Schiever (2005), they are most like the most complex at types V and VI.

The scenario problem-solving task derives from Sternberg's WICS model of gifted knowledge and successful intelligence (Sternberg, 2010) and is proposed to permit the identification of the creativity and wisdom aspects of the WICS model. It assesses wisdom in terms of an awareness of how knowledge can be used to solve problems that achieve a 'common good'.

Scenario problem-solving provides the opportunity for individuals: to display the types of gifted thinking mentioned earlier; to use both convergent and divergent or inferential thinking strategies, such as fluid analogistic thinking (Geake, 2008) spontaneously and selectively in a balanced way; to think evaluatively and analytically; to synthesise their inferences into intuitive interpretations; and to show the personality attributes of tolerance of ambiguity and task-focused motivation.

The research examining the use of scenario problem-solving to identify gifted learning capacity. An exploratory investigation of the efficacy of scenario problem-solving for the identification of gifted primary school students (Munro, 2015a) showed that the gifted students achieved higher problem-solving scores than their not gifted peers. Those gifted globally achieved the highest scores. As well, their solutions showed evidence of more elaborated and differentiated conceptual knowledge and a higher level of inferential, divergent thinking. They are consistent with the gifted students forming intuitive theories about the scenario. This section reports the main aspects of this study.

The study involved 357 third to sixth graders, who offered a solution to scenario problems typified by the iPod example mentioned earlier. As well, their nonverbal and verbal reasoning ability were assessed using the *Raven's Progressive Matrices: Standard Form* (RPM; Raven et al., 1998) and the *Mill Hill Vocabulary Scales* (MHV; Raven et al., 1994), respectively.

The study used the stages models of creativity (Cropley & Urban, 2000) to develop a protocol for describing a student's solution outcomes. It proposed that a solution be analysed in terms of the following aspects: the main problem identified by the student and the recommended solution, the actions for achieving the solution, additional information and assistance needed to solve the problem, how possible obstacles and difficulties in implementing the solution may be overcome, and the effect of the solution on individuals and communities and how to monitor its effectiveness.

Each student's problem-solving activity was monitored for evidence of the student's ability to:

- Interpret and understand the problem and prioritise the information.
- Infer a plausible solution, evaluate it reflectively from various perspectives and modify it.
- Construct viable goal paths that may involve taking sensible risks.
- Use creative problem-solving and divergent thinking skills, and 'run with' ambiguous ideas or perspectives.
- Use the knowledge of others and recognise the importance of leadership in solving the problem.
- Show a positive self-efficacy for solving the problem and continue to pursue a problem when they encounter barriers and obstacles.
- Identify how possible solutions interact and generate multiple cultural positions on the issue.
- Identify possible obstacles and limitations and suggest ways of resolving issues that impede the solution.

This set of problem-solving strategies provides a set of criteria for evaluating a student's solution attempts.

To control variation in existing knowledge of a scenario, participants watched a five-minute video of the scenario, for example, swimming on the Great Barrier Reef or people listening to iPods. To control variation in knowledge of how to solve scenario problems, participants were taught how to solve three practice problems and received feedback.

Participants solved the problem by responding to the following set of probes. Each probe assessed one aspect of the model of problem-solving described earlier. The probes were written in the left-hand column of a *Scenario Problem Response Sheet*. Participants wrote their response in the space provided on the right-hand side of each probe. Each probe and the question(s) or direction to cue it were:

1. The problem: Write down what you think the problem is in your own words.
2. The solution: What is the solution to the problem? What would the situation look like after the problem is solved?
3. The actions needed to solve the problem: What would you need to do to solve the problem? List as many things as you can think of. Show the order in which you would do them.
4. The information/assistance you would need to solve problem: What additional information and help would you need to solve the problem?
5. Possible obstacles and difficulties in implementing the solution: What things might make it harder to solve the problem? What difficulties might you face? List as many as you can.
6. The ways of overcoming the obstacles and difficulties: What can you do to overcome these difficulties?
7. The people likely to be affected by your problem-solving activity: Who might be affected by your problem-solving activity? List all of the groups who may be affected. What effect would your actions have on them?
8. How the solution may affect the community: How would you get these people to support your solution and 'go with it'?
9. How to monitor the effectiveness of the solution: What can you do to help you see if your solution was working?
10. A solution in an integrated, coherent way.

A scoring protocol that reflected the types of propositions described in Table 1 was developed as follows. A student's response to each of the probes 1–9 was assessed in terms of its semantic complexity on two dimensions: the number of relevant ideas (or 'fluency') and the complexity of the thinking that led to it (i.e., literal versus inferential). Each probe was allocated a score in the range 0–6 using the criteria shown in Table 4.

A problem-solving score was calculated by adding the scores on the set of probes. The mean total problem-solving score for each student group at each year level is shown in Figure 3.

The data showed that each category of gifted learner at each grade level achieved a higher problem-solving score than their not gifted peers. The students who were gifted both verbally and nonverbally achieved a higher score than either the non-verbally or verbally gifted categories at each grade level ($p < 0.01$). The verbally

Table 4 The criteria used to score a student's response to each of the probes

		Fluency	
Cognitive complexity		1 idea	1+ ideas
	Literal	Literal interpretation of the problem using *single* piece of information (1 mark).	Literal interpretation of the problem using *multiple* pieces of information (2 marks).
	Low inferential	Plausible inferential interpretation of problem that comprises one inferred idea that extends *specific events* mentioned in the text (3 marks).	Plausible inferential interpretation of problem that comprise two or more inferred idea that extend *specific events* mentioned in text (4 marks).
	High inferential	Plausible inferential interpretation of the problem that comprises one inferred idea made within topics that were *not explicitly* mentioned (5 marks).	Plausible inferential interpretation of the problem that comprise two or more inferred ideas made within topics that were *not explicitly* mentioned (6 marks).

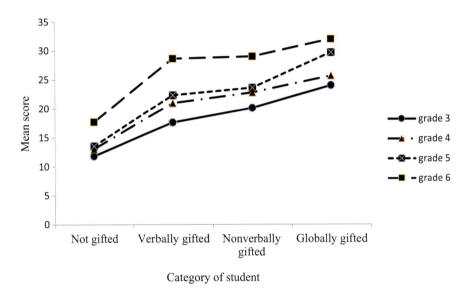

Fig. 3 The mean total problem-solving score for each student group at each year level

gifted category differed from the nonverbally gifted category only for grade 3 ($p < 0.05$).

The solutions of the gifted groups at each grade level included more relevant ideas and more inferential over literal responses than their not gifted peers. The solutions of the not gifted students usually comprised concepts mentioned in the scenarios, while their gifted peers included a larger number of concepts not mentioned in the scenario descriptions ($p < 0.01$). Their solutions suggested a greater likelihood of inference. They also suggested a higher probability of analogistic thinking. This observation supports Geake's (2008) cognitive model of giftedness.

The efficacy of SPST as a possible identification tool for gifted students' was examined using a procedure similar to that used by Sarouphim (2001) to evaluate the concurrent validity of the DISCOVER problem-solving protocol for identifying gifted students. SPST problem-solving ability was strongly associated with both verbal and nonverbal reasoning ability; the pooled correlations across the four grade levels (Spearman, two-tailed) were 0.69 ($p < 0.01$) and 0.63 ($p < 0.01$) for the SPM and the MHV, respectively. These correlations are in a similar range to those reported by Sarouphim (2001) for DISCOVER nonverbal tasks solved by primary students. They suggest the SPST may be a valid classroom assessment tool for identifying gifted students' learning in both fluid and crystallised ability.

Implications for Practice

Teachers can plan and implement SPSTs using the procedures described earlier. Problems can be constructed for most subject areas, for example, music, art, technology and engineering, information technology, sport, drama and theatre, or architecture. They can be presented in a range of formats that account for the multiple categories of giftedness, for example, in written, spoken, pictorial, and action forms, and combinations of these. Solutions can be presented in a range of expressive formats, for example, in spoken, pictorial, enactive, and multimodal modes, to match individual gifted student's learning profiles, for example, those who are twice exceptional, those from minority cultures, those disengaged and those who are economically disadvantaged. They can be aligned with the cultures to which students belong and draw on problem contexts from these cultures.

The SPSTs are frequently more likely to elicit positive emotional engagement from gifted students than more conventional assessment tools. They afford students the opportunity to share their unique thinking with others, to see that their unique interpretations and intuitive theories are relevant and valued and that these can lead to talented outcomes.

Summary: The Use of SPST to Identify Gifted Learning in the Classroom

Sternberg (2010) proposed that gifted students differ from their not gifted peers in their problem-solving ability. The research findings reported here support this prediction for using SPST to identify these students. They show that Maker's (2006) finding that problem-solving ability correlates with traditional identification measures can be extended to include SPSTs.

Gifted students differed from their not gifted peers in the quality and characteristics of their response to each aspect of SPST. Their responses showed evidence of more elaborated knowledge and more complex, inferential reasoning.

Procedures for Combining Data from Multiple Tasks to Make Empirically Valid Decisions

A key issue for teachers using multiple assessment tasks for identification is how to combine validly with the data. One protocol schools can use is to convert raw scores on all tasks used to z-scores and to combine these. VanTassel-Baska et al. (2007) recommend a set of procedures for combining data on traditional aptitude, achievement, and in-class performance tasks and criteria for interpreting them.

They showed that this type of decision-making identifies multiple types of giftedness, including students from underrepresented groups, such as gifted underachievers, and those from low-income and minority culture groups. This set of criteria can be extended to include assessment of productions and practical achievements and the learner's approach to learning.

Implications for Research and Future Directions

Teachers have access to a range of classroom-based tools that can be used to identify a gifted learning capacity in any of the academic, creative, and practical learning domains. However, they are frequently unskilled in the use and interpretation of these tools for this purpose (VanTassel-Baska & Stambaugh, 2005) and in establishing their validity for gifted identification. This leads to the preferential identification of some categories of giftedness and under-identification of others, including giftedness in minority cultures, twice exceptional students, gifted students with co-occurring psychological issues, and gifted students who are disengaged from formal education.

The evaluation of two types of gifted identification task contexts described here is exploratory. It is recognised that the numbers of students in the various categories are low and restrict the claims for concurrent validity reported for the two tasks. As well, the requirement that solutions be written restricts the generalisability of the findings. Future research will examine outcomes expressed in multiple formats.

Any identification tool needs to have predictive validity. The studies reported here used linear regression to provide tentative estimates of the predictive power of the two tools. Future studies may extend the analysis of predictive validity.

The studies exampled here are part of a broader research agenda that aims, in the future, to identify a range of validated tools teachers can use to identify gifted students' learning capacity in its multiple forms in classrooms. Their focus is on assessment in classroom learning activities and on using the assessment tools to enhance teachers' formative assessment of gifted students' learning outcomes.

Performance indicative of a gifted learning capacity was identified on the two tasks using dimensions of semantic complexity based on the DST. The calibration of these dimensions is likely to be refined in future research. A more finely graduated scale for measuring students' responses to each probe in the SPST context, for example, would enhance the accuracy of the identification tool.

The outcomes assessed here present a challenge. The tasks are intended to assess the outcomes of gifted learning and thinking. The assessment of inference, divergent, evaluative, analytic, and synthetic thinking is frequently in terms of what is plausible and reasonable, rather than in terms of whether responses are correct and match what was taught explicitly. To be efficacious, identification procedures for giftedness need to respond to this challenge.

The extent to which the SPST tasks assess Sternberg's (2010) wisdom aspect of the WICS model was not examined directly in this study. Responses to probes five to eight provide a partial estimate of this, in that they assess an awareness of how knowledge can be used to solve problems that achieve a 'common good'. It is expected that this aspect will be examined in future research.

Conclusion

The need for teachers to have the professional knowledge, skills, and tools needed to identify instances of gifted learning in its multiple forms by evaluating the learning outcomes of students in the classroom has been highlighted in this chapter. This contrasts with the perspective of a gifted learning capacity defined and identified only in terms of intelligence and achievement (Renzulli, 2012).

An alternative definition has been referenced in this chapter—that a gifted learning capacity in the classroom is indicated in the interpretations and understanding formed by students in their interactions with the teaching. The two assessment tools described here—concept mapping and SPST contexts—are referenced in classroom practice and can be readily designed, used and interpreted by teachers.

The efficacy of these tools and their validity have been explored as possible candidates for inclusion in a school's set of protocols for identifying gifted learners. The tools were selected because of their capacity to show evidence of a more elaborated and differentiated conceptual knowledge and a higher level of inferential, divergent thinking, and the ability to think analogistically and to form intuitive theories about the teaching information.

The data reported suggests the efficacy of these types of tools as valid identifiers of gifted learning, particularly for those students who may otherwise not be identified as gifted. Performance in both the concept mapping and SPST contexts discriminated between the gifted and not gifted students and between those students who were gifted globally and those who are gifted in a single domain.

These tools can be used across the multiple domains and modified to match the learning profiles of particular cohorts. They have implications for formative assessment and the differentiation of pedagogy and curriculum.

The focus of this handbook is on gifted education in the Asia-Pacific region. Gifted identification in East Asia is largely through the use of intelligence and cognitive tests (Phillipson et al., 2009). Several studies draw attention to the limitations of these measures for this purpose. VanTassel-Baska et al. (2007) showed how the use of performance tasks identified instances of gifted learning among students from Pacific cultures who would not have been identified using the more traditional intelligence and cognitive tests. Chaffey, Bailey, and Vine (2015) showed the efficacy of dynamic assessment procedures in identifying high academic potential in Australian Aboriginal children. Miller (2005) recommends the culturally relevant open-ended tasks to identify gifted learners in the Cook Islands. The types of classroom-based tasks described in this chapter offer valid alternatives to identification in the Asia-Pacific region.

Cross-References

- Creativity Talent Development: Fostering Creativity in Schools
- Engaging Gifted Students in Solving Real Problems Creatively: Implementing the Real Engagement in Active Problem-Solving (REAPS) Teaching/Learning Model in Australasian and Pacific Rim Contexts
- Exploring Diverse Perceptions of Wise Persons: Wisdom in Gifted Education
- Gifted Education in the Asia-Pacific: From the Past for the Future – An Introduction
- Identifying and Nurturing Diversely Gifted and Talented Students: Part III Introduction
- Identifying Underrepresented Gifted Students: A Developmental Process
- Some Implications for the Future of Gifted Education in the Asia-Pacific

References

Beghetto, R. A., & Kaufman, J. C. (2014). Classroom contexts for creativity. *High Ability Studies, 25*(1), 53–69. https://doi.org/10.1080/13598139.2014.905247

Biggs, J. B., & Collis, K. F. (1982). *Evaluating the quality of learning: The SOLO Taxonomy.* New York: Academic Press.

Callahan, C. M., & Miller, E. M. (2005). A child-responsive model of giftedness. In R. Sternberg & J. E. Davidson (Eds.), *Conceptions of giftedness* (2nd ed., pp. 38–51). West Nyack, NY: Cambridge University Press.

Cañas, A. J., & Novak, J. D. (2010). The theory underlying concept maps and how to construct and use them. *Práxis Educativa, 5*(1), 9–29. https://doaj.org/toc/1809-4309

Carr, M., Alexander, J., & Schwanenflugel, P. (1996). Where gifted children do and do not excel on metacognitive tasks. *Roeper Review, 18*(3), 212–217. https://doi.org/10.1080/02783199609553740

Chaffey, G. W., Bailey, S. B., & Vine, K. W. (2015). Identifying high academic potential in Australian Aboriginal children using dynamic testing. *Australasian Journal of Gifted Education, 24*(2), 24. Retrieved from http://www.aaegt.net.au/DEEWR%20Books/06%20Indig.pdf

Chan, C. C., Tsui, M. S., Chan, M. Y., & Hong, J. H. (2002). Applying the structure of the observed learning outcomes (SOLO) taxonomy on student's learning outcomes: An empirical study. *Assessment & Evaluation in Higher Education, 27*(6), 511–527. https://doi.org/10.1080/0260293022000020282

Cropley, A. J., & Urban, K. K. (2000). Programs and strategies for nurturing creativity. In K. A. Heller, F. J. Monks, R. J. Sternberg, & R. F. Subotnik (Eds.), *International handbook of research and development of giftedness and talent* (pp. 207–231). Oxford, UK: Pergamon.

Ericsson, K. A., Roring, R. W., & Nandagopa, K. (2007). Giftedness and evidence for reproducibly superior performance: An account based on the expert performance framework. *High Ability Studies, 18*(1), 3–56. https://doi.org/10.1080/13598130701350593

Fischer, K. W. (2008). Dynamic cycles of cognitive and brain development: Measuring growth in mind, brain, and education. In A. M. Battro, K. W. Fischer, & P. Léna (Eds.), *The educated brain* (pp. 127–150). Cambridge, UK: Cambridge University Press.

Fox, E., Dinsmore, D. L., & Alexander, P. A. (2010). Reading competence, interest, and reading goals in three gifted young adolescent readers. *High Ability Studies, 21*(2), 165–178. https://doi.org/10.1080/13598139.2010.525340

Gagné, F. (2009). The differentiated model of giftedness and talent (DMGT). In J. S. Renzulli, E. J. Gubbins, K. McMillen, R. D. Eckert, & C. A. Little (Eds.), *Systems and models for developing programs for the gifted and talented* (2nd ed., pp. 165–192). Mansfield Center, CT: Creative Learning Press.

Gagné, F. (2010). Motivation within the DMGT 2.0 framework. *High Ability Studies, 21*(2), 81–99.

Geake, J. G. (2008). High abilities at fluid analogising: A cognitive neuroscience construct of giftedness. *Roeper Review, 30*(3), 187–186. https://doi.org/10.1080/02783190802201796

Hedlund, J., Wilt, J. M., Nebel, K. L., Ashford, S. J., & Sternberg, R. J. (2006). Assessing practical intelligence in business school admissions: A supplement to the graduate management admissions test. *Learning and Individual Differences, 16*(2), 101–127. https://doi.org/10.1016/j.lindif.2005.07.005

Heller, K. A., Perleth, C., & Lim, T. K. (2005). The Munich model of giftedness designed to identify and promote gifted students. In R. J. Sternberg & J. E. Davidson (Eds.), *Conceptions of giftedness* (2nd ed., pp. 147–170). West Nyack, NY: Cambridge University Press.

Hertberg-Davis, H. (2009). Myth 7: Differentiation in the regular classroom is equivalent to gifted programs and is sufficient: Classroom teachers have the time, the skill, and the will to differentiate adequately. *Gifted Child Quarterly, 53*, 251–253. https://doi.org/10.1177/0016986209346927

Hsueh, W-C. (1997). *A cross-cultural comparison of gifted children's theories of intelligence, goal orientation and responses to challenge*. Unpublished PhD dissertation, Purdue University, Indiana (AAT 9808458).

Institute for Human & Machine Cognition. (2017). *Cmap*. Retrieved from https://cmap.ihmc.us

Kaufman, S. B. (2007). Investigating the role of domain general mechanisms in the acquisition of domain specific expertise. *High Ability Studies, 18*(1), 71–73. https://doi.org/10.1080/13598130701350767

Kornmann, J., Zettler, I., Kammerer, Y., Gerjets, P., & Trautwein, U. (2015). What characterizes children nominated as gifted by teachers? A closer consideration of working memory and intelligence. *High Ability Studies, 26*(1), 75–92. https://doi.org/10.1080/13598139.2015.1033513

Maker, C. J. (2006). *The DISCOVER Project: Improving assessment and curriculum for diverse gifted learners*. The National Research Center on the Gifted and Talented. Storrs, CT: University of Connecticut. Retrieved from http://www.eric.ed.gov/contentdelivery/servlet/ERICServlet?accno=ED505483

Maker, C. J., & Schiever, S. W. (2005). *Teaching models in education of the gifted* (3rd ed.). Austin, TX: Pro-Ed.

Maker, C. J., Zimmerman, R., Gomez-Arizaga, M., Pease, R., & Burke, E. (2015). Developing real-life problem solving: Integrating the DISCOVER problem matrix, problem based learning, and thinking actively in a social context. In H. Vidergor & R. Harris (Eds.), *Applied practice for educators of gifted and able learners* (pp. 131–168). Rotterdam, Netherlands: Sense Publishers.

Miller, G. (2005). Exploring perceptions of giftedness in the Cook Islands Māori community. *International Education Journal, 6*(2), 240–246.

Munro, J. (2002). Understanding and identifying gifted learning disabled students. *Australian Journal of Learning Disabilities, 7*(2), 20–30. https://doi.org/10.1080/19404150209546696

Munro, J. (2005). The learning characteristics of gifted literacy disabled students. *Gifted Education International, 19*, 154–173. https://doi.org/10.1177/026142940501900209

Munro, J. (2010). Gifted students who have academic learning difficulties: Analytic sequential processing problems? In W. Vialle (Ed.), *Giftedness from an indigenous perspective* (pp. 10–21). Wollongong, NSW: AAEGT Ltd.

Munro, J. (2013a). *Gifted students as expert$^+$: A teaching friendly model of gifted knowing and understanding* (Seminar Series No. 225). Jolimont, VIC: Centre for Strategic Education.

Munro, J. (2013b). *Teaching gifted student: A knowledge-based framework* (Occasional Paper No. 227). Jolimont, VIC: Centre for Strategic Education. Retrieved from http://gifted.dbbcso.org/uploads/1/2/3/4/12344194/john_munro_cse_seminar_paper_227_teach_gift.pdf

Munro, J. (2013c). High-ability learning and brain processes: How neuroscience can help us to understand how gifted and talented students learn and the implications for teaching. In G. Masters. (Ed.), *How the brain learns: What lessons are there? ACER Research Conference, Melbourne Convention Centre, 4–6 August 2013* (pp. 103–110). Retrieved from http://research.acer.edu.au/cgi/viewcontent.cgi?article=1163&context=research_conference

Munro, J. K. (2014a). *Mapping gifted understanding: A prelude to effective differentiated pedagogy.* Paper presented at the 28th International Congress of Applied Psychology, France from July 8th to 13th, 2014.

Munro, J. (2014b). *Gifted knowing & thinking: Research tells us what it looks like.* The Melbourne Graduate School of Education's 2014 Deans Lecture Series.. Retrieved from https://www.youtube.com/watch?v=6yRjHOA3T3A

Munro, J. K. (2015a). Scenario problem solving: A measure of the quality of gifted students' thinking. *Australasian Journal of Gifted Education, 24*(1), 23–29. ISSN: 1323-9686. [cited 14 Jan 18]. Retrieved from https://search-informit-com-au.ezp.lib.unimelb.edu.au/documentSummary;dn=433369775938947;res=IELHSS

Munro, J. (2015b). *Leading education for gifted and talented students.* Bastow Institute of Educational Leadership. Victoria, Australia.

Munro, J. (2017). Catering for the gifted: How inclusive is your school? *Australian Education Leader, 39*(1), 12–16. Retrieved from http://search.informit.com.au.ezp.lib.unimelb.edu.au/documentSummary;dn=774682856790859;res=IELHS

Neihart, M., & Betts, G. (2010). Revised profiles of the gifted and talented. Downloaded from https://sciencetalenter.dk/sites/default/files/revised_profiles_of_the_gifted_and_talented_-_neihart_and_betts.pdf

Phillipson, N. S., Shi, J., Zhang, G., Tsai, D. M., Quek, C. G., Matsumura, N., & Cho, S. (2009). Recent developments in gifted education in East Asia. In L. Shavinina (Ed.), *International handbook on giftedness* (pp. 1427–1461). Dordrecht: Springer.

Raven, J., Raven, J. C., & Court, J. H. (1998). *Manual for Raven's progressive matrices and vocabulary scales. Section 5: The Mill Hill vocabulary scale.* San Antonio, TX: Harcourt Assessment.

Raven, J. C., Court, J. H., & Raven, J. (1994). *Mill hill vocabulary scale,* 1994 edition. Oxford, UK: Oxford Psychologists Press.

Reis, S. M., & Renzulli, J. S. (2010). Is there still a need for gifted education? An examination of current research. *Learning and Individual Differences, 20*(4), 308–317. https://doi.org/10.1016/j.lindif.2009.10.012

Renzulli, J. S. (2012). Reexamining the role of gifted education and talent development for the 21st century: A four-part theoretical approach. *Gifted Child Quarterly, 56*(3), 150–159. https://doi.org/10.1177/0016986212444901

Rizza, M. G., McIntosh, D. E., & McCunn, A. (2001). Profile analysis of the Woodcock-Johnson III tests of cognitive abilities with gifted students. *Psychology in the Schools, 38*(5), 447–455. https://doi.org/10.1002/pits.1033

Santoro, G. F. (2016). *Gifted knowledge: What does it look like?* Unpublished doctoral dissertation. The University of Melbourne, Parkville, VIC. Retrieved from https://minerva-access.unimelb.edu.au/bitstream/handle/11343/92243/SANTORO%20GIUSEPPE%20PhD%20Thesis%20FInal.pdf?sequence=1

Sarouphim, K. M. (2001). DISCOVER: Concurrent validity, gender differences, and identification of minority students. *Gifted Child Quarterly, 45*(1), 130–138. https://doi.org/10.1177/001698629904300403

Sastre-Riba, S. (2011). Metacognitive functioning in gifted children. *Revista de Neurologia, 52* (Suppl 1), pS11–pS18.

Shavinina, L. V. (2007). On the advancement of the expert performance approach via a deep understanding of giftedness. *High Ability Studies, 18*(1), 79–82. https://doi.org/10.1080/13598130701350882

Shavinina, L. V. (2013). *The Routledge international handbook of innovation education*. Hoboken: Taylor and Francis.

Smith, M., & Mathur, R. (2009). Children's imagination and fantasy: Implications for development, education, and classroom activities. *Research in the Schools, 16*(1), 52.

Sternberg, R. J. (2005). The WICS model of giftedness. In R. J. Sternberg & J. E. Davidson (Eds.), *Conceptions of giftedness* (2nd ed., pp. 327–342). West Nyack, NY: Cambridge University.

Sternberg, R. J. (2010). WICS: A new model for school psychology. *School Psychology International, 31*, 599–616. https://doi.org/10.1177/0143034310386534

Sternberg, R. J., Grigorenko, E. L., Hart, L., Jarvin, L., Kwiatkowski, J., Newman, T., & Stepanossova, O. (2007). *Transitions in the development of giftedness*. New Haven: Yale University.

Subotnik, R. F., Olszewski-Kubilius, P., & Worrell, F. C. (2011). Rethinking giftedness and gifted education. A proposed direction forward based on psychological science. *Psychological Science in the Public Interest, 12*(1), 3–54. https://doi.org/10.1177/0016986212456079

Tannenbaum, A. J. (1987). *Gifted children: Psychological and educational perspectives*. New York: Macmillan

VanTassel-Baska, J., Feng, A. X., & Evans, B. L. (2007). Patterns of identification and performance among gifted students identified through performance tasks: A three-year analysis. *Gifted Child Quarterly, 51*(3), 218–231. http://dx.doi.org.ezp.lib.unimelb.edu.au/10.1177/0016986207302717

VanTassel-Baska, J., & Stambaugh, T. (2005). Challenges and possibilities for serving gifted learners in the regular classroom. *Theory Into Practice, 44*(3), 211–217. https://doi.org/10.1207/s15430421tip4403_5

Ziegler, A., & Vialle, W. (2017). Using the Actiotope Model of Giftedness to bridge the gap between experiences and practice. In J. A. Plucker, A. N. Rinn, & M. C. Makel (Eds.), *From giftedness to gifted education: Reflecting theory in practice* (pp. 203–225). Waco, TX: Prufrock Press.

John Munro, PhD, is Professor of Educational Psychology and Exceptional Learning in the Faculty of Arts and Education, Australian Catholic University, and a Principal Fellow at the University of Melbourne. He is a qualified primary and secondary teacher and a psychologist. His teaching and research are in literacy and mathematics learning difficulties, gifted education, creativity, instructional leadership and learning internationally. He developed the VELS English Curriculum and the creative and critical thinking competencies in the Australian Curriculum. He provides professional learning and consultancy to school improvement projects in Australia and internationally. These include the Aga Khan Academies and the International Baccalaureate.

Self-Nomination in the Identification Process of Gifted and Talented Students in Mexico

24

María Alicia Zavala Berbena and Gabriela de la Torre García

Contents

Introduction	510
Identification of Gifted Students	511
A Multidimensional and Inclusive Approach to Identification	512
Self-Nomination as a Complimentary Strategy for Gifted and Talented Identification	515
Development and Pilot Study of a Self-Nomination Inventory for Mexican Gifted and Talented Adolescents	520
Pilot Study of the Nomination Instrument	521
Limitations of the Nomination Instrumentation	525
Implications for Research and Practice	527
Conclusion	528
Cross-References	529
References	529

Abstract

In the Asia-Pacific Rim countries, it seems that self-nomination is a common practice when identifying gifted and talented students. Several authors are in favour of this practice, arguing that it is important that students have an active role in their educational process. Self-nomination may also contribute to the necessity of having new tools that broaden the screening process, showing strengths and weaknesses of gifted students beyond unidimensional intelligence tests. Although self-nomination have been used since the 1970s, to date there is little research on

M. A. Zavala Berbena (✉)
Universidad De La Salle Bajío, León, México
e-mail: alicia_zavala2@yahoo.com.mx

G. de la Torre García
PAUTA, Institute of Nuclear Sciences, Universidad Nacional Autónoma de México UNAM, Mexico City, México
e-mail: gabriela_de_la_torre@hotmail.com; gabriela.delatorre@pauta.org.mx

© Springer Nature Singapore Pte Ltd. 2021
S. R. Smith (ed.), *Handbook of Giftedness and Talent Development in the Asia-Pacific*,
Springer International Handbooks of Education,
https://doi.org/10.1007/978-981-13-3041-4_24

its efficacy and no clear methodology on how it can be implemented. In this chapter, self-nomination is analysed as part of a multidimensional and inclusive approach to the identification of diversely gifted and talented students. In addition, different types of self-nomination are analysed and categorised, such as interviews, questionnaires, autobiographies, self-evaluation scales and products. The aim is to distinguish the instruments and determine how to implement them within an identification process in order to make better use of them. Likewise, an overview is presented of specialised literature on advantages and disadvantages of self-nominations. The goal of this exercise is to understand the benefit of their use and their limitations. It also presents a Mexican experience of developing and validating an inventory for self-nomination of adolescents. This instrument is based on students' self-perceptions of performance in seven areas. The specific purpose of the trial was to evaluate the psychometric properties of the *Self Nomination Inventory for Gifted and Talented Adolescents* in a Mexican adolescent sample, so full results of the participant self-perceptions are not reported. However, in order to move forward with the inventory's convergent validation, a comparison was made between the results from the self-nominated students and their teachers' nominations. Some findings were indicated, that is, 55.4% of the students were confirmed by their teachers in their respective areas of talent, with the athletic and artistic areas being superior at close to 60%. The initial results suggested that the self-nomination inventory may be a useful instrument to support the identification process of diversely gifted and talented student participants in the screening phase of this Mexican study. Finally, recommendations for research and an effective application of self-nomination strategies in educational practices are provided.

Keywords

Self-nomination · Identification · Gifted · Talented · Adolescents

The aims in this chapter are to present:
1. Self-nomination as part of a multidimensional and inclusive identification process of gifted and talented students.
2. The concept of nomination as an action.
3. The instruments and procedures of self-reference that are used for the purpose of self-nomination.
4. The development of a pilot study of a self-nomination inventory for Mexican gifted and talented adolescents.
5. Research and practical implications when using self-nomination.

Introduction

Currently, identification of giftedness and talent of children and adolescents are still a controversial issue among experts in the field of gifted education (Acar, Sen, & Cayirdag, 2016). Some specialists are in favour of nomination strategies for identification (Davis & Rimm, 1998; Larroder & Ogawa, 2015; Renzulli, 1988; Rodríguez, Rabassa, Salas, & Pardo, 2017), while others do not consider it very useful (Fiske & Taylor, 1999; Gagné, Bégin, & Talbot, 1993; Hewston et al., 2005; Ionica-Ona, 2013). Nonetheless, nominations are a widely used process involving different nomination instruments that are part of varying identification processes in Asia-Pacific Rim countries (e.g., Merrick & Targett, 2004 in Australia; Massé & Gagné, 1996 in Canada; Acar et al., 2016 in the United States of America; Larroder & Ogawa, 2015 in the Philippines; Nagai, Nomura, Nagata, Ohgi, & Iwasa, 2014 in Japan; and the Secretaría de Educación Pública, 2006 in Mexico).

When leading an identification process, the first question that arises is: Who should be identified as gifted or talented? The identification process depends on what giftedness and talent mean. Therefore, giftedness and talent is a concept that needs to be clarified. In this chapter the *Differentiated Model of Giftedness and Talent* (DMGT; Gagné, 1999) will be considered, as stated:

> The term giftedness designates the possession and use of untrained and spontaneously expressed natural abilities (called aptitude of gifts), in at least one ability domain, to a degree that places on individual at least among the top 10% of his or her age peers. (Gagné, 1999, p. 230)

The next question is: What should be identified? It is a complex issue in which many variables arise that take the form of questions such as: How many features compose giftedness? What can be assessed? Are these features from giftedness or from talent or from the personality of the student? It is also important to clarify if stable or unstable features are examined; if, given the dynamic and diverse nature of giftedness, it is possible to have a generic identification; or if identification should be undertaken according to the evolutionary stage of the student?

In relation to the purpose of the evaluation, it can be useful to question *the reason for selecting* the identification procedures that are needed to determine whether identifying the student leads to an educational intention. Identification systems should be linked to an educational program or provisions, such as enrichment activities, acceleration, and grouping, or maybe considering other educational intentions, such as taking advanced classes, counselling, or others. An isolated identification test or procedure has no purpose if there is not a specific answer to the needs of the gifted children or adolescents (Frasier & Passow, 1994; Richert, 2003).

Identification of Gifted Students

While there are many singular tools used to help identify gifted students around the world (e.g., Chan, 2001; Gilliam & Jerman, 2015; Renzulli et al., 2010), the research literature generally supports a multidimensional and inclusive approach to the identification of gifted and talented students (George, 2001; Warburton, 2010; Zavala, 2004). This multidimensional and inclusive process will now be discussed.

A Multidimensional and Inclusive Approach to Identification

A multidimensional and inclusive approach to identification is a complex process that involves analyses of different aspects of a phenomenon, such as knowledge, abilities, and interests of students, valued as a multistep process, and one that requires different techniques, procedures, and stakeholders over time to accurately assess the student's individual needs (Warburton, 2010). This multidimensional and inclusive approach to identification implies that identification through an intellectual quotient and creativity is not enough. There are other important characteristics of the students, such as the social and emotional factors that should be considered (e.g., George, 2001; Hewston et al., 2005; Mee, 2002; Pfeiffer, 2002). Multidimensional and inclusive approaches are the reasons why psychoeducational assessment adds relevant and pertinent recommendations to the educative process. Assessing abilities, interests, values, and curricular competences of the students among other aspects such as the scholarly and family context are considered within the process (Mee, 2002). These identification processes that allow specialists to address interests and necessities of the students should be included (Brown et al., 2005).

In relation to the next question—How to identify gifted and talented students?—specialists have pronounced in favour of a group of techniques and instruments that are applied in different stages, which are part of an ongoing and open assessment process covering different parts of the school year (Warburton, 2010). Likewise, the identification process should be sensitive to the context and changes in students' needs (Frasier & Passow, 1994; Maker, 1996; Richert, 2003). Mixed systems with multiple criteria are the most used when identifying gifted and talented students as presented in the *National Association for Gifted Children* report (2015). Generally, these identification systems have three phases: (a) the exploratory detection phase, (b) the psychoeducational assessment phase, and (c) the permanent detection phase.

(a) **Exploratory detection phase**. This phase is the beginning of the complex process of evaluation that involves using assessment instruments and techniques for the purpose of identifying the gifted profile of the candidates (Zavala, 2004). The goal of this phase is to select viable candidates for a later, deeper analyses. Sometimes the exploratory phase is done with informal instruments, which are applied collectively and are more cost- and time-effective (George, 2001; McBee, Peters, & Miller, 2016; Zavala, 2004). This is the case of assessment scales for parents, teachers, peers, and gifted students, which are applied to support nominations and self-nominations. In this stage, performance and intelligence collective tests are also used (George, 2001; Zavala, 2004).

(b) **Psychoeducational assessment phase.** This is an intermediate phase of an evaluation, which consists of applying psychological and educative instruments and techniques to analyse the characteristics of the candidates with a gifted profile, in order to make decisions about their selection for an educative program targeted for gifted students, and that consider their specific needs (Zavala, 2004). This is a heterogeneous phase in which the goal is to determine students' characteristics and needs. It is a stage in which intelligence tests and tests on other specific areas are used. Interviews and product analysis are also used, such as artistic productions, essays, or experimental prototypes. The specialist in the area sometimes works alone or, in some cases, uses selection committees (George, 2001; Zavala, 2004).

(c) **Permanent detection phase.** This is an advanced stage of evaluation that takes into consideration observation instruments and techniques in order to obtain dynamic information of students' achievement in a particular educative program. In this phase new students are considered and through observation may start the first stage of this identification system (Zavala, 2004). This phase involves a student's follow-up, relative to his or her inclusion in a gifted program. In some models, it is an identification through practice, as proposed by McCoach, Kehle, Bray, and Siegle (2001). Occasionally, this phase includes its own identification process (Fig. 1).

Additionally, identification systems are characterised by using a *diversity of instruments and assessment procedures* (George, 2001; Warburton, 2010). There

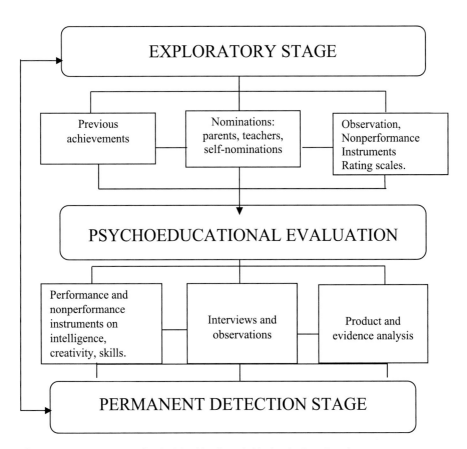

Fig. 1 Assessment system for the identification of gifted and talented students

are basically two groups of recognised instruments: performance, in which the student directly answers to the test, and nonperformance, in which the student is evaluated based on evidence or conduct (Acar et al., 2016). In the first group, there are intelligence, creativity, ability, and academic achievement standardised tests (George, 2001; Zavala, 2004). These are characterised by the obtained score, which indicates students' knowledge and abilities compared to normative groups. The second group includes instruments that collect data about the achievement of the students in an indirect way, through value judgments, such as opinions, autobiographies, observations, and anecdotal evidence (Brown et al., 2005; Gilliam, & Jerman, 2015; Jarosewich, Pfeiffer, & Morris, 2002; Pfeiffer & Jarosewich, 2003). Nevertheless, some of these instruments, such as teacher rating scales, teacher and parent nominations, self-ratings, and peer-ratings have been developed through qualitative techniques, psychometric techniques, and objective parameters (Acar et al., 2016).

One of the techniques and problems of identification practices is the absence of adequate criteria to apply them. In some cases, identification instruments tend to limit diversely gifted students' selection, by not being able to show all their capacities or by the way they are applied (Frasier & Passow, 1994; Richer, 2003). Sometimes, there is an improper use of identification instruments, and assessment categories are confused. For example, intelligence and achievement tests are used indistinctly. Multiple information from complex instruments are combined in a statistically incorrect manner, arriving at global scores that make no sense (Tourón, Peralta, & Repáraz, 1998). Likewise, it has been shown that, for years, such criteria have caused an underrepresentation of minority and vulnerable groups (Richert, 2003). Therefore, it is necessary to have solidly based, consistent theoretical foundations and principles to achieve a technically adequate, fair, and useful identification process to address the needs of the gifted, as Pfeiffer (2002) and Merrick and Targett (2004) asserted.

Pfeiffer (2002) proposed that it is imperative that the following principles are used to improve the identification process: (a) educators and psychologists gain familiarity with gifted children and their families; (b) recognition of the multiple manifestations of giftedness; (c) recognition of the developmental nature of talent development; (d) intervention is linked to identification; and (e) identification requires multiple measures.

Merrick and Targett (2004, p. 6) proposed the following principles: (a) using tools and strategies that are prescribed by, or in harmony with, the definitions of giftedness and talent adopted by your school; (b) using multiple criteria, so that you may identify as many of your gifted students as possible; (c) using a variety and balance of both subjective and objective measures; and (d) ensuring the tools and strategies are reliable and valid. Both researchers' proposals are formulated with the purpose of improving identification processes based on theoretical principles and well-founded concepts, and they are both important to the development of techniques and instruments.

It is important to mention that gifted and talented student identification is a complex procedure that requires a solid conceptual base and educational principles to collect information from different sources and stakeholders, making relevant use of effective instruments and procedures (Brown et al., 2005). In this context, self-nomination is a procedure that enriches identification practices and supports the complexity of the identification procedure (George, 2001; Zavala, 2004). It should be applied in the first phase of the gifted and talented students' identification procedure (Fig. 1). The self-nomination process should report that the students themselves are willing to show their desire to have an opportunity (e.g., a scholarship or a contest) or to be part of a program or a differentiated educational experience.

Self-Nomination as a Complimentary Strategy for Gifted and Talented Identification

There is a prevalent confusion in the theory and practice of gifted and talented identification: the concept of nomination and nomination forms is used only under the term nomination, so the term 'nomination' can wrongly be perceived both as an action and as an instrument. As an action, it refers to the act and effect of nominating or, in other words, presenting a student as a person to be considered for a specific purpose based on his or her preselected quality, by means of which the student is nominated. On the other hand, as an instrument, it refers to the procedures that support the nomination (McBee et al., 2016). It is important to make this distinction in order to have clarity as to the process and development, selection, application, and interpretation of the self-nomination.

Self-reference instruments are assessment instruments in which the person gives information and judgements about themselves (Dodorico, 2008; Fernández-Ballesteros, 2011). The following tools can be found among the instruments and procedures of self-reference used for the purpose of self-nomination: (a) self-nomination questionnaires (Merrick & Targett, 2004; Secretaría de Educación Pública, 2006), (b) autobiographies (Nichols, 2004), (c) self-rating scales (McBee et al., 2016; Tirri & Nokelainen, 2007); and (d) evidence and product-based self-nomination (Maker, 1996; Reis & Renzulli, 1991).

Self-nomination questionnaires. These are instruments with direct questions about abilities or self-perceived potential. It is a focused action that is carried out by means of a written or oral questionnaire (Merrick & Targett, 2004; Secretaría de Educación Pública, 2006). The following are examples of questions or statements used for this purpose:

- What potential, expertise and strength do you think you possess that makes you a special person?
- What is your best expertise? How much time per week do you spend on this expertise? What satisfaction can you get from it? What difficulties have you encountered? How do you handle them?
- What special things have you done? How long did you work on it or them?
- What things do you do well?
- Describe a project, product, or performance that you have created in which you excelled.
- What are your personal strengths or weaknesses?
- Explain the reasons for nominating yourself for the gifted and talented program.

Autobiographies. The purpose of an autobiography is to focus verbal or written questions on specific areas of personal history. It is used to contextualise information obtained from the application of a set of instruments, so it is a complementary instrument (Nichols, 2004). The following are among the most used questions:

- What is an event in your life when you considered yourself special?
- Which is your earliest memory?
- How do you describe your infancy in general?
- Which have been your greatest moments of joy?
- Which have been your greatest moments of sadness?
- What experience marked your life?
- Which has been your greatest success?
- Which has been your greatest failure?

Self-rating scales. These are all the tests in which students value their characteristics in relation to specific abilities, such as intellectual and learning abilities, motivation, or creativity. In some school districts in the United States, a self-nomination form is applied, in which the student is asked to indicate the areas in which he or she considers himself or herself to have special abilities or talents (McBee et al., 2016; Tirri & Nokelainen, 2007). The format contains eight areas: (a) general intellectual ability, (b) writing, (c) reading, (d) mathematics, (e) science, (f) social studies, (g) art, and (h) music. In order to help the student identify themselves within these areas, each of them is accompanied by items that characterise the skills related to selected subjects or areas; for example, for the general intellectual ability, two items or statements are "I usually answer questions quickly" and "school work is easy for me". These areas are related to a service program.

They also use validated and standardised instruments for self-nomination purposes. In Table 1, some of these instruments are presented.

Evidence and product-based self-nominations. Generally, in self-nomination, evidence is presented, such as academic merit certificates, personal achievement reports and products (essays, artistic works, scientific prototypes, or other creative products). These self-nominations are evaluated by committees that analyse the information and compare it to other sources of information (Maker, 1996; Reis & Renzulli, 1991). In this strategy, evaluation of creative products has been a highly polemic issue (Balchin, 2007; Hocevar & Bachelor, 1989; Holland, 1959). For this reason, some specialists, such as Treffinger, Young, Selby, and Shepardson (2002), have developed a theoretical and technical framework to evaluate, select, and use instruments for creative product assessment.

Self-nomination is a strategy that has been incorporated within gifted and talented identification procedures. Nevertheless, there are still controversies about some aspects of their usage, such as the ones described below:

1. *Students' ability to make a correct self-nomination.* Some authors consider that children and youngsters do not have an adequate knowledge of themselves, frequently students seek to show a positive self-image to adults, and

Table 1 Self-rating scales for the gifted and talented

Instrument	Objective	Description	Validation participants	Evidence for reliability, validity and structure
Perceived competence scale for children (Harter, 1982).	To value a child's sense of competence across different domains: cognitive, social and physical.	The child is asked to decide which kind of kid he is most like, the ones on the right or the ones on the left. Once having made this decision, the child decides whether the description on that side is sort of true or really true (1–4) of him.	133 9–12-year-old children from California, with replications with 2,271 middle school students in Connecticut, California, New York and Colorado.	Subscale reliability was assessed by employing coefficient alpha; the values were 0.76, 0.78, 0.83 and 0.73 for the cognitive, social, physical and general subscales, respectively.
24-item Chinese Student Multiple Intelligences Profile SMIP-24 (Chan, 2001).	A self-report measure that focuses on gifted students' activities or preferences that reflect their self-perceived multiple abilities or intelligences.	The SMIP-24 is a 24-item checklist of characteristics and behaviours constructed to reflect students' self-perceptions of their abilities in terms of Gardner's (1999) Multiple Intelligences. In completing SMIP-24, respondents were requested to rate themselves on the 24 items using a five-point scale ranging from 1 (least descriptive) to 5 (most descriptive).	192 grade 7 to grade 12 secondary students (73 boys and 118 girls, n 5 191, [one did not report gender and age]) aged 12–18 (M 5 13.87, SD 5 1.45, n 5 191), nominated by their schools to join the gifted program at the Chinese University of Hong Kong.	The original SMIP had seven scales that assessed the seven (except naturalist) intelligences of students. Moderate internal consistency (Cronbach's $\alpha = 0.64$–0.76) and significant correlations with external measures such as nonverbal reasoning (Raven, Raven, & Court, 1998) and leadership scores (Roets, 1997).
Auto-nomination inventory for identifying talent in the technical field *Inventarul de Autonominalizare a Talentului în*	To evaluate the expression of the superior endowment in different areas of technical field, as the excellence, demonstrated by	IATDT is structured according to three dimensions of the technical talent (expertise in using technology, interest and	210 students of the Technical University "Gh Asachi" from Iasi.	The alpha Cronbach index was 0.904 for the three dimensions: the size of the alpha Cronbach index for passion was 0.8588, for

(continued)

Table 1 (continued)

Instrument	Objective	Description	Validation participants	Evidence for reliability, validity and structure
Domeniul Tehnic (IATDT; Ionica-Ona, 2013).	an outstanding performance in this field or as a potential of excellence demonstrated by the results in various forms of evaluation.	initiative in using technology, and creative integration of technology) derived during the process of documentation and investigation of the teachers' view about the talent in the technical field.		the size of the technical expertise was 0.8585 and for creativity was 0.7181.
Revised Screening Scales for the Evaluation of Multiple Intelligences (Hernández-Torrano, Ferrándiz, Ferrando, Prieto, & Fernández, 2014).	To value the biopsychological potential to process information that can be activated in a cultural setting to solve problems or create products that are of value in a culture (Gardner, 1993).	Three rating scales include 28 items in which informants (teachers, parents and students) express their agreement about the characteristics and behaviours of the students on a 4-point scale ranging from 1 (never) to 4 (always), in terms of Gardner Multiple Intelligence theory.	566 secondary school students (46.5% girls) nominated as high-ability students by their teachers in the Region of Murcia (Spain).	Cronbach's alpha coefficients for students' MI scores were acceptable for naturalistic and musical intelligence ($\alpha = 0.66$, $\alpha = 0.73$, respectively), but low for the other intelligences ($\alpha < 0.50$).
Children's Perceived Competence Scale (CPCS; Nagai et al., 2014).	The CPCS is a questionnaire designed to measure children's self-perceived competence across. three domains of cognitive(C), social (S), physical (P) and the fourth domain of general	Based on Harter's Perceived Competence Scale for Children (Harter, 1982). They regard the domain of general self-worth as akin to self-esteem. All four domains consist of 10 items, each measured	768 Japanese children of elementary school grades 1 (6–7 years) through 6. (11–12 years) at 4 public schools in a classroom setting.	The CPCS subscale reliability was assessed using Cronbach's alpha in the range 0.75–0.87. CPCS was constructed based on PCSC, which itself has been confirmed as reliable and valid by Harter (1982), and the contents

(continued)

Table 1 (continued)

Instrument	Objective	Description	Validation participants	Evidence for reliability, validity and structure
	self-worth (G).	on a 4-point scale (1–4).		of the two questionnaires are very similar. The reliability of CPCS has been confirmed, but its validity has not (Nagai et al., 2014).
Sumida checklist on giftedness in science, Filipino validation (Larroder & Ogawa, 2015).	This instrument is used specifically with regard to science giftedness, considering which is a personal construct mediated by experience, language and culture. The aim is to be able to use these differences in science giftedness scores to help a variety of schools to address areas of science giftedness that need attention.	The checklist consists of 24 items that measure attitudes, thinking, skills and knowledge/ understanding specific to science. The revised instrument has twelve factors including scientific awareness, rational observation, experimentation, application, visualisation, initiative and quantification, disinterest in learning, engrossment in learning, integrated learning and acquiring of skills.	For the validation in the Philippines: 71 students (19.2%) were from a school catering to those with high aptitude in science and mathematics and the remaining 294 students (37.3%) were from a school with various special programs and with a special science curriculum.	Factor loading values ranged from 0.43 to 0.69. The instrument was highly reliable and valid for Filipino students (0.954 Cronbach's alpha). Alpha values ranged from 0.952 to 0.954 in all items. The Filipino checklist on science giftedness was highly valid and reliable in measuring the science giftedness (Larroder & Ogawa, 2015).

others do not really know about their true abilities and capacities (Fiske & Taylor, 1999). On the other hand, those who are in favour of self-nomination hold that it is a strategy that can be applied, especially with adolescents, who, unlike children, have more knowledge of their abilities (Renzulli, 1988; Rodríguez et al., 2017).

2. *Self-nomination instruments' validity and reliability.* Ionica-Ona (2013) observed that measurement instruments for the purpose of self-nomination that were available in professional practices had low validity and reliability levels. Even though it is true that these types of instruments are considered indulgent and less structured, in recent years tools have been developed for self-assessment with solid psychometric fundamentals and foundations (Table 1).
3. *Self-nomination efficiency.* The instrument's efficiency relates to the level it contributes to the proposed objective (Kimberlin & Winterstein, 2008). In this case, it refers us to the capacity and procedures for an adequate identification using self-nomination instruments. The literature reports the high frequency of false positives in self-nomination procedures (Gagné et al., 1993). Nevertheless, those who advocate in favour of self-nomination consider that it is a complementary strategy to other identification tools and that it is best used earlier in the identification process, supported by instruments that aid students to make more adequate assessments of their abilities (Acar et al., 2016). In addition, the adequate use of self-nomination avoids evaluation bias, such as low nomination of females or low achievement students, which are present in other instruments such as classmates' or teachers' nominations (Larroder & Ogawa, 2015).

Consequently, it can be said that self-nomination is a strategy that must be used carefully, mainly with adolescents and youngsters, and that, if used, may be improved with instruments that have validity and reliability. Due to the diversity of students and context, it is important to have a clear objective when a self-nomination instrument is selected, because with these instruments we are aiming for a wide pool to include the largest quantity of potentially gifted and talented students. In this way, self-nominated students in the first stage can be validated or not in the latter phases of the identification process.

Development and Pilot Study of a Self-Nomination Inventory for Mexican Gifted and Talented Adolescents

Educational enrolment in Mexico is close to seven million students from 12 to 15 years of age in middle school (Secretaría de Educación Pública, 2017). Special education coverage is about 14% in middle school, making it difficult to identify gifted and talented students at this level, especially in the exploratory detection phase. Their teachers—due to the few hours they spend with each group—see students for only a limited time, and there is insufficient service coverage. Teacher and parent nominations can be biased towards high achievers and not gifted students due to misconceptions of giftedness and talent and attitudinal factors (Maker, 1996). Hence, self-nominations are distinguished for covering information gaps that generally teachers, parents, and specialists cannot see (Secretaría de Educación Pública, 2006).

Under these conditions, students' self-nomination can help to direct the effort of special education services for gifted students, so an *Inventory for Gifted and Talented Adolescent Self-nomination* was developed (see Table 2). It is based on the middle school official curriculum courses (Secretaría de Educación Pública, 2006). For the design of this instrument, items were selected to be: (a) coherent with the conception of giftedness and with the specific expressions of intelligence, related to intellectual, social-emotional, and athletic aptitudes (Gagné, 1999); (b) standardised for performance in a positive way related to teenage scholarly behavior; and (c) validated by special education experts and, in particular, for the artistic and physical items, experts from the *National Institute of Fine Arts* and the *National Sports Commission*.

The purpose of the inventory is to obtain a students' assessment perspective of his or her abilities or interests, and students assess themselves relative to their classmates. The areas students assess are: (a) intellectual aptitude in language and communication, (b) intellectual aptitude in mathematics, (c) intellectual aptitude in the natural sciences, (d) intellectual aptitude in the social sciences, (e) socio-emotional aptitude, (f) artistic aptitude, and (g) physical aptitude in athletics. Originally, before analyses, each scale was composed of ten items, and the five-option Likert scale was retained to rate closed answer responses in which students compared their abilities to those of their classmates.

Pilot Study of the Nomination Instrument

The instrument trial was undertaken with a total sample of 4,499 students from grades 9–11 in public middle schools from all around México. From this sample, 51% were male and 49% were female; the mean age was 13.2 (SD = 0.993). Following the methodology of McCoach, Gable, and Madura (2013), two random samples were selected from the general sample of participants, the first sample with $n = 2250$ and the second with $n = 2249$ participants.

In the first sample, an EFA (exploratory factor analysis) was done after the appropriateness of this technique was reviewed using the Kaiser-Meyer-Olkin index and Bartlett's sphericity coefficient. The results are KMO = 0.973 and Bartlett's $\chi^2_{(1830)} = 59583.155; p < 0.001$ were excellent according to Hair, Hult, Ringle, and Sarstedt (2014). Afterward, the EFA technique was applied using the extraction principal component analysis and the Varimax Normalization Rotation Method with Kaiser, resulting in seven factors that explain 50.792% of the variance.

Based on the procedure of Ferrando and Anguiano-Carrasco (2010), the items that had better results in more than one factor or had low factorial results (less than 0.4) were promptly eliminated. In this way, seven factors forming the following areas were kept (see Table 3): mathematics (10 items), athletics (10 items), socio-emotional (10 items), artistic (10 items), natural sciences (8 items), social sciences (7 items), and language (6 items). The other factors were eliminated because, upon an evaluation of their theoretical content, that content was not considered important. After this procedure 61 items were left.

Table 2 Inventory for Gifted and Talented Adolescent Self-nomination

1. Intellectual aptitude: language and communication						
No.	Statements	Answering choices				
	Compared to my classmates, I …	Not at all	A little	Rather	Much	Very much
1	I can tell stories	1	2	3	4	5
3	It is easy for me to write texts such as letters, tales or poetry	1	2	3	4	5
4	I have an extensive vocabulary	1	2	3	4	5
5	I easily use new words I learn	1	2	3	4	5
6	I deduce the meaning of a new word based on the context in which it is used	1	2	3	4	5
10	I can say a definition in my own words	1	2	3	4	5
2. Intellectual aptitude: mathematics						
No.	Statements	Answering choices				
	Compared to my classmates, I …	Not at all	A little	Rather	Much	Very much
1	I find it easy to remember numbers, formulae and symbols	1	2	3	4	5
2	I make rapid mental calculations	1	2	3	4	5
3	I use logic to solve mathematical problems	1	2	3	4	5
4	I can solve harder problems than those that are in the mathematics textbook	1	2	3	4	5
5	I identify the formula I need to use to solve a mathematical problem	1	2	3	4	5
6	I can skip steps to solve a mathematical problem	1	2	3	4	5
7	When it is about solving a mathematical problem, I'm capable of finding easier ways to solve it than those the teacher explains	1	2	3	4	5
8	I can tell if the answer to a mathematical problem is correct	1	2	3	4	5
9	I'm capable of solving a mathematical problem using a different procedure than the one shown in the mathematics textbook	1	2	3	4	5
10	I'm capable of inventing games that apply mathematics	1	2	3	4	5
3. Intellectual aptitude: natural sciences						
No.	Statements	Answering choices				
	Compared to my classmates, I …	Not at all	A little	Rather	Much	Very much
2	I am passionate about chemistry, biology or physics	1	2	3	4	5
3	I like to have objects, plants or animal collections	1	2	3	4	5
4	When I make experiments, I know how to use the labware	1	2	3	4	5
5	I carry out experiments outside school from self-interest	1	2	3	4	5

(continued)

Table 2 (continued)

6	I can know with anticipation the results of a school experiment	1	2	3	4	5
7	I can explain the reasons why an experiment fails	1	2	3	4	5
9	I like to collect experimentation data, for example, when combining substance to obtain new mixtures	1	2	3	4	5
10	I can imagine new ideas to solve everyday problems through science	1	2	3	4	5

4. Intellectual aptitude: social sciences

No.	Statements	Answering choices				
	Compared to my classmates, I ...	Not at all	A little	Rather	Much	Very much
1	I would like to understand the causes that originate social problems	1	2	3	4	5
2	I am passionate about geography and/or history	1	2	3	4	5
3	I have read biographies of important personalities on my own	1	2	3	4	5
4	I can correctly read maps and blueprints	1	2	3	4	5
5	I have researched information about great civilisations mysteries	1	2	3	4	5
6	I know recent news about Mexico and the world	1	2	3	4	5
7	I can explain the reasons why an economic crisis occurs	1	2	3	4	5

5. Social emotional aptitude

No.	Statements	Answering choices				
	Compared to my classmates, I ...	Not at all	A little	Rather	Much	Very much
1	I have the ability to make friends	1	2	3	4	5
2	I make decisions in my group	1	2	3	4	5
3	I can solve problems among friends and colleagues	1	2	3	4	5
4	I find it easy to understand how others feel	1	2	3	4	5
5	I help my colleagues and friends when they are in trouble	1	2	3	4	5
6	I am capable of convincing others to pursue a goal	1	2	3	4	5
7	My colleagues and friends ask me for advice when they have a problem	1	2	3	4	5
8	I treat others with respect in spite of differences	1	2	3	4	5
9	I can correct others without making them feel bad	1	2	3	4	5
10	I can find several original ways to cheer up a colleague who is sad	1	2	3	4	5

(continued)

Table 2 (continued)

6. Artistic/creative aptitude						
No.	Statements	Answering choices				
	Compared to my classmates, I …	Not at all	A little	Rather	Much	Very much
1	I enjoy art in its different manifestations, for example, music, dance, drama or visual arts	1	2	3	4	5
2	I am interested in going to artistic places where they present plays, expositions or concerts	1	2	3	4	5
3	I appreciate different artistic manifestations and products of other times or cultures	1	2	3	4	5
4	I can comprehend ideas and feelings in the artistic productions I see, read, listen or participate	1	2	3	4	5
5	I would like to devote my free time to learn an artistic discipline	1	2	3	4	5
6	I can express my joyful feelings through colours, musical rhythms, gestures, forms, movements or dances	1	2	3	4	5
7	I know some techniques that help me improve in my favourite artistic discipline	1	2	3	4	5
8	I have read material related to the artistic discipline I'm interested in	1	2	3	4	5
9	I'm creative: I can invent ways to dance, create music and use my body with different gestures and voices	1	2	3	4	5
10	I enjoy making modifications to existing artistic productions to give them my personal touch	1	2	3	4	5
7.- Physical aptitude: Athletic						
No.	Statements	Answering choices				
	Compared to my classmates, I …	Not at all	A little	Rather	Much	Very much
1	I enjoy practising one or more sports	1	2	3	4	5
2	In relation to physical activities, I enjoy overcoming obstacles and challenging myself	1	2	3	4	5
3	I have the ability to make coordinated movements	1	2	3	4	5
4	I have good postural control; for example, when I stumble, I don't lose my balance, or when I run, I can spin without stopping	1	2	3	4	5
5	I have good orientation; I can place myself well in a given space	1	2	3	4	5
6	I am capable of doing physical exercises for a long time without feeling tired	1	2	3	4	5

(continued)

Table 2 (continued)

7	During a game, I can anticipate my opponents' movements, for example, where a ball will be thrown	1	2	3	4	5
8	In physical activities, I am capable of saving my energy so I don't exceed myself	1	2	3	4	5
9	I am persistent when I practice a sport or a physical activity	1	2	3	4	5
10	When I practice a sport, I have a personal style that distinguishes me	1	2	3	4	5

Note: This is the latest version of the instrument, so some items have been removed following factorial analyses

To measure the confidence of the internal consistency among the factors of the inventory, Cronbach's (1951) alpha coefficient was used. Each factor presented the following results: language = 0.733, mathematics = 0.901, natural sciences = 0.828, social sciences = 0.814, socio-emotional = 0.878, artistic = 0.890 and athletics = 0.909.

Later, using the data from the second sample, a CFA (Confirmatory Factorial Analysis) was done with the seven selected dimensions. We obtained a theoretically sustained model with an adequate adjustment, obtaining the following adjustment indexes: chi-squared test ($\chi2_{(1759)}$ = 6152.479; $p < 0.001$), comparative fit index (CFI = 0.925), Tucker-Lewis index (TLI = 0.922) and, finally, the approximation index of the square root of the mean square error (RMSEA = 0.033). These results were adequate (Bollen, 1989; Jöreskog & Sörbom, 1981; Muthén & Muthén, 1998–2007; Rigdon, 1996).

Similarly, the Cronbach's alpha scores were reported for each of the latent variables, obtaining the following results: language = 0.725, mathematics = 0.897, natural sciences = 0.811, social sciences = 0.844, socio-emotional = 0.878, artistic = 0.887 and athletic = 0.907, which were considered satisfactory (Cronbach, 1951; Hair et al., 2014). The latest version of the instrument is presented in Table 2.

In addition, in order to move forward with the inventory's convergent validation, a comparison was made between the results from the self-nominated students and their teachers' nominations. A total of 2,229 self-nominated students from the abovementioned sample were evaluated by their teachers, considering the same characteristics of the inventory. The results showed that 55.4% of the students were confirmed by their teachers in their respective areas of talent, the athletic and artistic areas being superior at close to 60%.

Limitations of the Nomination Instrumentation

The purpose of the trial was to evaluate the psychometric properties of the *Self-Nomination Inventory for Gifted and Talented Adolescents* in a Mexican adolescent sample. In the first study, as a result of exploratory analysis, seven factors were found that had been established as the components of the instrument design. The variance

Table 3 Rotated component matrix of Self-Nomination Inventory for Gifted and Talented Adolescents[a]

	Component						
Item	Athletic	Mathematics	Artistic	Socio-emotional	Natural sciences	Social sciences	Language
AT2	0.766						
AT6	0.734						
AT1	0.731						
AT7	0.727						
AT8	0.701						
AT9	0.701						
AT10	0.700						
AT3	0.685						
AT4	0.626						
AT5	0.575						
MA4		0.742					
MA5		0.723					
MA2		0.705					
MA9		0.703					
MA6		0.699					
MA1		0.696					
MA3		0.688					
MA7		0.659					
MA8		0.627					
M10		0.408					
AR5			0.695				
AR10			0.654				
AR2			0.652				
AR9			0.648				
AR7			0.633				
AR8			0.631				
AR6			0.605				
AR3			0.601				
AR1			0.598				
AR4			0.597				
SA8				0.724			
SA6				0.698			
SA10				0.671			
SA7				0.657			
SA4				0.654			
SA5				0.642			
SA3				0.567			
SA1				0.545			
SA2				0.504			
SA9				0.475			
NS5					0.663		
NS9					0.620		
NS2					0.589		
NS3					0.584		
NS10					0.566		
NS6					0.533		
NS7					0.523		
NS4					0.510		

(continued)

Table 3 (continued)

	Component						
Item	Athletic	Mathematics	Artistic	Socio-emotional	Natural sciences	Social sciences	Language
SS2						0.721	
SS3						0.656	
SS5						0.583	
SS6						0.555	
SS4						0.484	
SS7						0.449	
SS1						0.448	
LA4							0.630
LA5							0.614
LA6							0.516
LA10							0.472
LA1							0.438
LA3							0.438

Note: Extraction method: Principal component analysis
Rotation method: Varimax with Kaiser Normalization
[a]Rotation converged in six iterations

explained percentages had satisfactory results; nevertheless, it barely covers the minimum requirements for this type of analysis in the social sciences (Hair et al., 2014). Considering that, EFA is limited to hypothesising the number of factors, and it does not require a previous specification of the theoretical model in which the instrument is based on. It is considered a weak approximation to the instrument's validity. As a result, it was required to complement this analysis with a second study, but first the items with less factorial loadings were eliminated (Ferrando & Anguiano-Carrasco, 2010).

The second study, through the CFA, showed evidence in favour of the seven factors in the structure of the instrument, with an adequate adjustment index with the results previously reported. Additionally, through this second analysis, the appropriate factorial loadings were kept ≥ 0.438; they established high relations to the measured variables. An aspect to improve in the instrument is to seek equilibrium between the scales, which can result in it being less practical when applied and graded.

According to the reported results, the instruments' internal consistency of each of the factors was adequate (Cronbach, 1951; Hair et al., 2014). The lowest index of reliability ($\alpha = 0.733$) was found in the language and communication factor, for which this dimension should be strengthened in future studies, incrementing the number of adequate and pertinent items. These initial results suggest that the self-nomination inventory may be a useful instrument to support the identification process of gifted and talented student participants in the screening phase of this study.

Implications for Research and Practice

It was suggested in this chapter and two-phase study that self-nominations are valuable procedures to include in an identification process to help identify gifted and talented students. Despite the widespread usage of self-nominations, there is not a clear methodology for applying them. Frequently, nominations are implemented with instruments that have no methodological consistency, which result in a low efficacy. For this reason, it is important to analyse the instruments' characteristics and to evaluate their validity and reliability.

Additionally, there are few studies that show the effectiveness of self-nominations and many of the constructs needing investigation, such as the role of self-esteem, self-efficacy, and the motivation of the self-nominees. Thus, the need to establish future research lines that blend the analyses of the variables that influence these constructs is necessary.

In practice, self-nominations are based on the idea that students are more or less conscious of their abilities and that they are willing to recognise and report them, but this is not necessarily true. Therefore, its range and limitations must be kept in mind when using self-nomination in order to successfully include it in an identification process.

Finally, to optimise the use of the self-nomination strategy, it is important to consider the following advice to:

- Apply this strategy with populations older than 12 years, as they are more conscious of their abilities and can differentiate their strengths and weaknesses with more certainty.
- Identify which type of instrument is required for self-nomination and to select adequate instruments to have more impartiality, whether qualitative or quantitative.
- Help students define objective parameters of comparison in order to realise self-descriptions that avoid overvaluation.
- Search for evidence that supports self-nomination, especially creative products that should be contextualised to the students' means and opportunities.
- Be aware of the possibility that some students may not nominate themselves because of low self-esteem or low academic performance, so, it is important to consider other evidence and carry out interviews.
- Use complementary strategies, such as other instruments or information sources such as parents, teachers, and classmates to avoid possible student bias due to inadequate perceptions.

Conclusion

In this chapter, self-nomination has been understood as part of a multidimensional identification process, in which gifted and talented students are detected at the later phases using varied instruments and personnel. This type of identification is more complete and inclusive. It is also known as an action in which the students propose themselves to be considered and selected with specific educational purposes in mind.

In order to consider self-nomination as a part of an identification process, it must be used with other psychometric instruments. Self-nomination is an instrument that gives important information, but should be complemented with other instruments such as the ones described in this chapter. In between these instruments, standardised tests must be considered because they are constructed with psychometrical procedures that have been proven to be reliable and valid which helps improve the self-nomination quality.

An exemplar *Self-Nomination Inventory for Gifted and Talented Adolescents* tool was assessed using a Mexican sample, with some preliminary comparisons made between the results of the students' self-nominations and their teachers' nominations. Initial assessment and findings suggested that the self-nomination inventory may be a useful tool to support the identification process of the gifted and talented student participants in this study.

The above implications for research and practice were derived from a combination of the initial findings from the exemplar study reiterated in this chapter and the review of the literature, that is, mostly research from within the Asia-Pacific Rim countries. It is important to take them into account, because they are specific to the diverse cultural and regional context and may contribute to attaining better results in diversely gifted and talented students' identification processes within Asia-Pacific countries.

Few recent studies on self-nomination process with diversely gifted students were found in the literature, and this chapter highlights the need for future research studies in this direction. Future research with this focus may help educators to understand the variables that influence this type of identification instrument, such as students' perceptions of their own self-esteem and self-efficacy. Studies in which the motivations of the students to self-nominate or, on the contrary, the reasons why they reject self-nomination would be efficacious. Also, it would be useful to undertake studies that lead to diminishing the limitations of the identification process and to establish the conditions for the various types of nominations to be more efficient and inclusive in the Asia-Pacific context.

Cross-References

▶ Gifted Education in the Asia-Pacific: From the Past for the Future – An Introduction
▶ Gifted, Talented, and High-Achieving Students and Their Gifted Education in Mexico
▶ Identifying and Nurturing Diversely Gifted and Talented Students: Part III Introduction
▶ Identifying Gifted Learning in the Regular Classroom: Seeking Intuitive Theories
▶ Identifying Underrepresented Gifted Students: A Developmental Process
▶ Innovative Practices to Support High-Achieving Deprived Young Scholars in an Ethnic-Linguistic Diverse Latin American Country
▶ Some Implications for the Future of Gifted Education in the Asia-Pacific

References

Acar, S., Sen, S., & Cayirdag, N. (2016). Consistency of the performance and nonperformance methods in gifted identification. A multilevel meta-analytic review. *The Gifted Child Quarterly, 60*(2), 81–101. https://doi.org/10.1177/0016986216634438

Balchin, T. (2007). Identifications of the gifted: The efficacy of teacher nominations in British schools. *The Journal of the National Association for Gifted Children, 11*(1), 5–17.

Bollen, K. A. (1989). *Structural equations with latent variables*. New York, NY: Wiley.
Brown, S. W., Renzulli, J. S., Gubbins, E. J., Siegle, D., Zhand, W., & Chen, C. (2005). Assumptions underlying the identification of gifted and talented students. *The Gifted Child Quarterly, 49*(1), 68–79. https://doi.org/10.1177/001698620504900107
Chan, D. W. (2001). Assessing giftedness of Chinese secondary students in Hong Kong: A multiple intelligences perspective. *High Ability Studies, 12*, 215–234. https://doi.org/10.1080/13598130120084348
Cronbach, L. J. (1951). Coefficient alpha and the internal structure of tests. *Psychometrika, 16*(3), 297–334. https://doi.org/10.1007/BF02310555
Davis, G. A., & Rimm, S. B. (1998). *Education of the gifted and talented* (4th ed.). Needham Heights, MA: Allyn and Bacon.
Dodorico, J. (2008). Measuring personality constructs: The advantages and disadvantages of self-reports, informant reports and behavioural assessments. *Enquire, 1*(1), 75–94. Retrieved from https://www.nottingham.ac.uk/sociology/documents/enquire/volume-1-issue-1-dodorico-mcdonald.pdf
Fernández-Ballesteros, R. (2011). *Evaluación psicológica: conceptos, métodos y estudio de casos* (2nd ed.). Madrid, España: Pirámide.
Ferrando, P. J., & Anguiano-Carrasco, C. (2010). El análisis factorial como técnica de investigación en Psicología. *Papeles del Psicólogo, 31*(1), 18–33. Retrieved from http://www.papelesdelpsicologo.es/pdf/1793.pdf
Fiske, S. T., & Taylor, S. E. (1999). *Social cognition* (2nd ed.). New York, NY: McGraw Hill.
Frasier, M. M., & Passow, A. H. (1994). *Toward a new paradigm for identifying talent potential* (Research monograph series). Storrs, CT: The National Research Center on the Gifted and Talented.
Gagné, F. (1999). Gagné's Differentiated Model of Giftedness and Talent (DMGT). *Journal for the Education of the Gifted, 22*(2), 230–234. https://doi.org/10.1177/016235329902200209
Gagné, F., Bégin, J., & Talbot, L. (1993). How well do peers agree among themselves when nominating the gifted or talented? *The Gifted Child Quarterly, 37*(1), 39–45. https://doi.org/10.1177/001698629303700106
Gardner, H. (1993). *Frames of mind. The theory of multiple intelligences*. Nueva York, NY: Basic Books.
Gardner, H. (1999). *Intelligence reframed: Multiple intelligences for the 21st century*. Nueva York, NY: Basic Books.
George, D. (2001). *Gifted education identification and provision*. London, England: Bell & Bain Ltd., Glasgow.
Gilliam, J. E., & Jerman, O. (2015). *Gifted and talented evaluation scales: Examiner's manual* (2nd ed.). Austin, TX: Pro-Ed.
Hair, J., Hult, G., Ringle, C., & Sarstedt, M. (2014). *A primer on partial least squares structural equation modeling (PLS SEM)*. Thousand Oaks, CA: Sage.
Harter, S. (1982). The perceived competence scale for children. *Child Development, 53*(1), 87–97. https://doi.org/10.2307/1129640
Hernández-Torrano, D., Ferrándiz, C., Ferrando, M., Prieto, L., & Fernández, M. C. (2014). The theory of multiple intelligences in the identificación of high ability students. *Anales de Psicología, 30*(1), 192–200. https://doi.org/10.6018/analesps.30.1.148271
Hewston, R., Campbell, R. J., Eyre, D., Muijis, R. D., Neelands, J. G. A., & Robinson, W. (2005). A baseline review of the literature on effective pedagogies for gifted and talented students. Retrieved from https://giftedphoenix.files.wordpress.com/2012/11/nagty-occasional-paper-12-developing-expertise-school-based-case-studies-july-2006.pdf
Hocevar, C., & Bachelor, P. (1989). A taxonomy and critique of measurements used in the study of creativity. In J. A. Glover, R. R. Ronning, & C. R. Reynolds (Eds.), *Handbook of creativity* (pp. 53–75). New York, NY: Plenum Press.

Holland, J. L. (1959). Some limitations of teacher ratings as predictors of creativity. *Journal of Educational Psychology, 50*(5), 219–223. https://doi.org/10.1037/h0040598

Ionica-Ona, A. (2013). Identification of students with talent in the technical domains. *Studia Universitatis Babes-Bolyai, Psychologia-Paedagogia, 58*(1), 83–91.

Jarosewich, T., Pfeiffer, S. I., & Morris, J. (2002). Identifying gifted students using teacher rating scales: A review of existing instruments. *Journal of Psychoeducational Assessment, 20*, 322–336. https://doi.org/10.1177/073428290202000401

Jöreskog, K., & Sörbom, D. (1981). *LISREL: Analysis of linear structural relationships by maximum likelihood and least squares methods*. Chicago, IL: National Educational Resources.

Kimberlin, C. l., & Winterstein, A. G. (2008). Validity and reliability of measurement instruments used in research. *American Journal of Health-System Pharmacy, 65*(1), 2276–2284. https://doi.org/10.2146/ajhp070364

Larroder, A., & Ogawa, M. (2015). The development of a self-evaluation checklist for measuring Filipino students' science giftedness. *Asia-Pacific Science Education, 1*(5). https://doi.org/10.1186/s41029-015-0002-0

Maker, J. (1996). Identification of gifted minority students: A national problem, needed changes and a promising solution. *The Gifted Child Quarterly, 40*(1), 41–50. https://doi.org/10.1177/001698629604000106

Massé, L., & Gagné, F. (1996). Should self-nominations be allowed in peer nomination forms? *The Gifted Child Quarterly, 40*(1), 24–30. https://doi.org/10.1177/001698629604000104

McBee, M. T., Peters, S. J., & Miller, E. M. (2016). The impact of the nomination stage on gifted program identification: A comprehensive psychometric analysis. *The Gifted Child Quarterly, 60*(4), 258–278. https://doi.org/10.1177/0016986216656256

McCoach, B., Kehle, T. J., Bray, M. A., & Siegle, D. (2001). Best practices in the identification of gifted students with learning disabilities. *Psychology in the Schools, 38*(5), 403–411. Retrieved from: http://citeseerx.ist.psu.edu/viewdoc/download?doi=10.1.1.535.1598&rep=rep1&type=pdf

McCoach, D., Gable, R., & Madura, J. (2013). *Instrument development in the affective domain: School and corporate applications*. New York, NY: Springer.

Mee, S. (2002). Psychoeducational assessment. In M. Horne (Ed.), *Keys to effective LD teaching practice* (pp. 24–36). Knoxville, TN: The University of Tennessee, Knoxville Center for Literacy Studies.

Merrick, C., & Targett, R. (2004). Module two: The identification of gifted students. In DEST & GERRIC (Eds.), *Professional development package for teachers: Gifted education professional development package*. Sydney, NSW: DEST (Department of Education, Science and Training) & GERRIC. Retrieved from http://foi.deewr.gov.au

Muthén, B., & Muthén, L. (1998–2007). *Mplus version 5.0 statistical analysis with latent variables: User's guide* (4th ed.). Los Angeles, CA: Muthen & Muthen.

Nagai, Y., Nomura, K., Nagata, M., Ohgi, S., & Iwasa, M. (2014). Children's perceived competence scale reference values in Japan. *Journal of Child Health Care, 19*(4), 532–541. https://doi.org/10.1177/1367493513519295

National Association for Gifted Children (NAGC) & the Council of State Directors of Programs for the Gifted (CSDPG). (2015). *State of the states in gifted education: National policy and practice data 2014–2015*. Washington, DC: National Association for Gifted Children. Retrieved from http://www.nagc.org/sites/default/files/key%20reports/2014-2015%20State%20of%20the%20States%20%28final%29.pdf

Nichols, L. (2004). Giving students a voice: Learning through autobiography. *Thought & Action, 19*(2), 37–50. Retrieved from https://www.nea.org/assets/img/PubThoughtAndAction/TAA_04Win_04.pdf

Pfeiffer, S. I. (2002). Identifying gifted and talented students. *Journal of Applied School Psychology, 19*(1), 31–50. https://doi.org/10.1300/J008v19n01_03

Pfeiffer, S. I., & Jarosewich, T. (2003). *Gifted rating scales*. San Antonio, TX: Harcourt Assessment.

Raven, J., Raven, J. C., & Court, J. H. (1998). *Manual for Raven's progressive matrices and vocabulary scales. Section 1: General overview*. Oxford, England/San Antonio, TX: Oxford Psychologists Press/The Psychological Corporation.

Reis, S. M., & Renzulli, J. S. (1991). The assessment of creative products in programs for gifted and talented students. *The Gifted Child Quarterly, 35*(3), 128–134. https://doi.org/10.1177/001698629103500304

Renzulli, J. S. (1988). The multiple menu model for developing differentiated curriculum for the gifted and talented. *The Gifted Child Quarterly, 32*(3), 298–309. https://doi.org/10.1177/001698628803200302

Renzulli, J., Smith, L. H., White, A. J., Callahan, C. M., Hartman, R. K., Westberg, K. L., ..., Sytsma, R. E. (2010). *Scale for rating the behavioral characteristics of superior students. Technical and administration manual* (3rd ed.). Waco, TX: Prufrock Press.

Richert, E. S. (2003). Excellence with justice in identificaction and programming. In N. Colangelo & G. A. Davis (Eds.), *Handbook of gifted education* (3rd ed., pp. 146–158). Boston: Allyn and Bacon.

Rigdon, E. E. (1996). CFI versus RMSEA: A comparison of two fit indexes for structural equation modeling. *Structural Equation Modeling, 3*(4), 369–379. https://doi.org/10.1080/10705519609540052

Rodríguez, R., Rabassa, G., Salas, R., & Pardo, A. (2017). *Protocolo de identificación y evaluación del alumnado de altas capacidades. El reto de dar respuesta a las necesidades educativas de este alumnado*. Madrid, España: Santillana.

Roets, L. F. (1997). *Leadership: Skills training programs for ages 8–18* (8th ed.). Des Moines, IA: Leadership.

Secretaría de Educación Pública. (2006). *Propuesta de intervención educativa a alumnos y alumnas con aptitudes sobresalientes*. México, México: SEP.

Secretaría de Educación Pública. (2017). Datos de la Subsecretaría del Sistema de Planeación, Evaluación y Coordinación de la SEP. Retrieved from: http://spec.sep.gob.mx/web/?page_id=28

Tirri, K., & Nokelainen, P. (2007). Comparison of academically average and gifted students' self-rated ethical sensitivity. *Educational Research and Evaluation, 13*(6), 587–601. https://doi.org/10.1080/13803610701786053

Tourón, J., Peralta, F., & Repáraz, C. (1998). *La superdotación intelectual: modelos identificación y estrategias educativas*. Pamplona, España: Eunsa.

Treffinger, D. J., Young, J. C., Selby, E. C., & Shepardson, C. (2002). *Assessing creativity: A guide for educators*. Sarasota, FL: The National Research Center on the Gifted and Talented.

Warburton, E. C. (2010). From talent identification to multidimensional assessment: Toward new models of evaluation in dance education. *Research in Dance Education, 3*(2), 103–121. https://doi.org/10.1080/1464789022000050480

Zavala, M. A. (2004). Desarrollo y validación de un sistema para la detección de alumnos con aptitudes sobresalientes-superdotados. *Revista Educación y Desarrollo, 3*, 13–20.

María Alicia Zavala Berbena has a PhD in Education through the Universidad Autónoma de Aguascalientes; she concluded postgraduated studies in the Universidad Autónoma de México (UNAM). She is currently a professor from the Psychology Department of the Universidad de Guanajuato (México). Her professional interest field includes the education of the students that have intellectual outstanding capabilities and the study of the emotional intelligence. Also, she took part as a national consultant for the development of the Intervention's Proposal for the Educational Attention to Students with Outstanding Aptitudes in México. She was secretary of the Ibero-American Federation of the *World Council for Gifted and Talented Children*.

Gabriela de la Torre García has a PhD in Scholar Psychology and Development through the Universidad Complutense de Madrid. She is interested in family education of the gifted and in public policies. She directs the program 'Adopt a Talent' from the Institute of Nuclear Sciences of the Universidad Nacional Autónoma de México (UNAM). She was in charge for the parents of the 'Programa Estrella', Madrid, Spain. From 2007 to 2013, she was responsible for the gifted and talented education department of the National Ministry of Education (SEP). She is an active member of the *European Council for High Abilities* (ECHA), the *Spanish Society for Giftedness* (SEES) and the *World Council for Gifted and Talented Children*.

Place-Based Gifted Education in Rural Schools

25

Carolyn M. Callahan and Amy Price Azano

Contents

Place-Based Gifted Education in Rural Schools	536
Theoretical Framework	537
Major Issues in Rural Gifted Education Internationally	538
Understanding the Challenges Faced Globally in Identifying and Serving Gifted Students in Rural Schools	540
Definition	540
Instrument and Rater Bias	541
Opportunity to Learn	542
The Ways Giftedness May Manifest in Rural Populations	542
Minimising Challenges	543
An Application of the Principles Noted Above	544
Supporting Teachers	545
Using Place in the Gifted Curriculum	546
Model for Integrating Place-Based Concepts into High-Level Curriculum	546
Addressing Stereotype Threat and Growth Mindset for Rural Gifted Learners	548
Conclusion	549
Cross-References	550
References	550

Abstract

Across the global landscape, the achievement and opportunity gaps between low-income students and their more economically advantaged peers present serious

---

C. M. Callahan (✉)
University of Virginia, Charlottesville, VA, USA
e-mail: cmc@virginia.edu

A. P. Azano
Virginia Tech, Blacksburg, VA, USA
e-mail: azano@vt.edu

© Springer Nature Singapore Pte Ltd. 2021
S. R. Smith (ed.), *Handbook of Giftedness and Talent Development in the Asia-Pacific*,
Springer International Handbooks of Education,
https://doi.org/10.1007/978-981-13-3041-4_25

challenges for gifted education. Further, for rural students, these excellence gaps may be even more pronounced, and opportunities to maximise potential for gifted students in rural environments are even rarer. Drawing from prior curriculum work, *What Works in Gifted Education* (Callahan, Moon, Oh, Azano, & Hailey, 2015), and ongoing work in a five-year project focusing on promoting gifted education in rural schools, the initial focus of the chapter is on the major issues in rural gifted education internationally and specifically in the Australasia/Pacific Rim nations. These issues include fewer specialists in gifted education, limited resources, fewer program options, fewer research opportunities and field trips (Alston & Kent, 2003; Burney & Cross, 2006; Hébert & Beardsley, 2001; Riley & Bicknell, 2013). The description of issues is followed by a review of strategies to minimise these challenges. These strategies include an alternative process for identifying gifted students in rural schools and presentation of the CLEAR curriculum model. Modification of the empirically validated CLEAR curriculum model is illustrated by the integration of place-based pedagogy drawn from geographically and culturally relevant elements of the Australian, New Zealand, and Pacific region. The modification provides an exemplar for engaging and challenging rural students in gifted programs. Findings from the study of the model and, perhaps, more importantly, lessons learned and more global takeaways for the field conclude the chapter.

Keywords

Place-based education · Rural education · Rural gifted students · Low-income gifted students · Identification of gifted students · High-level curriculum

The aims in this chapter are to:
1. Provide an understanding of the challenges in identifying and serving gifted students in high-poverty rural schools.
2. Describe the challenges of rural education in the context of the USA, Australia, New Zealand, and other Pacific Rim nations.
3. Provide guidance for identifying gifted students in high-poverty rural areas.
4. Explicate the power of place-based education.
5. Provide a model of integration of place-based concepts and growth mindset into high-level curriculum for gifted students.

Place-Based Gifted Education in Rural Schools

For too long, rural education has been coded in deficit ideologies and has been characterised by 'problem' language in discussions of the context for rural schooling (Biddle & Azano, 2016). Rural education scholars, also routinely considered rural *advocates*, argue that asset and strength-based scholarship in rural schools can refocus efforts away from deficit views that aim to 'fix' rural 'problems' to advancing community or place-based efforts to capitalise on the inherent worth and value of rural places. For the purpose of understanding rural gifted education as an issue of educational equity for gifted students, one must first grapple with definitions of both giftedness and rurality and also consider the impacts of poverty. While scholars, including Renzulli (1976), Sternberg (1984), and Gagné (2018), have argued for expanded constructions of giftedness, less is known about how giftedness is valued, cultivated, and honoured in a given place or how these definitions can be applied or adapted in a variety of contexts. Further, the acceptance of these definitions in the scholarly literature and the development of clear criteria for identification of students with gifts and talents (e.g., Australian Association for the Education of the Gifted and Talented; National Association for Gifted Children, NAGT, 2010) have not been widely translated into concomitant processes and procedures at the local school level (Brodersen, 2016; Callahan, Moon, & Oh, 2017; Jarvis & Henderson, 2012). Even with differentiated or varied definitions a school may use for a gifted education program, arbitrary 'cut-off' scores on a given instrument or on matrices that combine test scores can still restrict the degree to which students who do not fall into the categories of the more affluent dominant culture and environment may be overlooked with talent potential unrealised.

In particular, rural students may be particularly at risk for under-identification by the application of historically accepted criteria for gifted on traditional gifted assessments. Traditional assessments may not be nuanced enough to capture concepts of giftedness of rural or culturally diverse gifted students, leading to underrepresentation (Bevan-Brown, 2011). What of the gifts in rural learners that do not manifest in traditional academic lessons or school-honoured ways? To conceptualise rural gifts in ways that honour the place in which those gifts are honed, it is important to understand the complexities and varied ways of rural life and how place identities are shaped in rural spaces. Australia's Aboriginal students represent one example of an underrepresented population resulting from a 'mismatch' of beliefs about giftedness and the home knowledge valued in a given culture (Thraves & Bannister-Tyrrell, 2017). By using assessment measures that honour cultural or community-based understandings of giftedness, educators can "identify and value the funds of knowledge these students bring with them to our classrooms" (p. 19). Further, the ways in which talents are nurtured once discovered must be examined in light of the rural environment.

Theoretical Framework

Framing this work is a theoretical lens shaped by critical pedagogies of place (Gruenewald, 2003), emancipatory and politicised literacies (Freire, 2000; Freire & Macedo, 1987), and nuanced understandings of rural communities (e.g., Carr & Kefalas, 2009; Corbett, 2007). Freire posed a radical understanding of literacy inextricably tied to culture and forever political. This politicised notion of literacy as a mechanism of freedom or democracy underlies our work in rural gifted education. We argue that critical literacy informs place identities and rural constructions of giftedness—that understanding the recursive nature of reading the word and the world (and understanding how the world *reads* a place) is key for understanding how gifts are honoured or nurtured in rural places. Gruenewald (2003) furthers this understanding by firmly rooting critical pedagogy to a place—that to challenge dominant power structures, for example, is to do so in a highly contextualised environment. Finally, we consider if and how rural schools as rural *institutions* inadvertently (or explicitly) teach students to leave their rural communities. Corbett's (2007) work provides a strong rationale for thinking of place not only as a theory of change for identifying or serving gifted students, but also for putting place at the heart of gifted curricula for rural learners.

The focus in this chapter will be on providing an understanding of the challenges related to gifted education in rural schools and, particularly, in identifying and serving gifted students in high-poverty rural schools. The first task will be to describe the challenges of rural education and to provide guidance for using community assets and understandings to identify students for gifted services by calling out the power of place to expand thinking about ways giftedness manifests. Second, appropriate curriculum for rural gifted students will be described as an extension of a research-validated curriculum model (Callahan, Moon, Oh, Azano, & Hailey, 2015) that explicates place-based pedagogy and provides a paradigm for integration of place-based concepts, growth mindset, and strategies for countering stereotype threat into high-level curriculum for rural gifted students.

Major Issues in Rural Gifted Education Internationally

The context in which education for rural gifted students is to be delivered is heavily impacted by issues that face all educational endeavours in rural schools. For example, rural schools in the USA and Australia struggle to access professional development overall, with only 27% of rural teachers having access to professional development in their schools compared to 40% in cities and suburbs (e.g., Jarzabkowski, 2003; Stambaugh & Wood, 2016). Staffing rural schools with qualified teachers is a pervasive challenge in the literature in rural education, particularly in isolated rural areas. Jarzabkowski (2003), for example, notes that in remote areas of Australia, the teaching staff are primarily young, relatively inexperienced teachers. Similarly, Stambaugh and Wood (2016) indicate that in the USA, rural schools are more likely to be staffed by first-year teachers or teachers teaching outside their subject area. In addition to these long-standing challenges, professional isolation (Fry & Anderson, 2011), difficulty in accessing resources because of geographic isolation, and underfunding (Brown, 2006; Alston & Kent, 2013; O'Callahan, 2015) further complicate opportunities for gifted education programs.

It is easy to see how these general issues have particular and exaggerated influence on gifted education in rural settings (Azano, Callahan, Brodersen, & Caughey, 2017). For example, as in the USA and other western nations (c.f., National Association for Gifted Children [NAGC] and Council of State

Directors of Gifted Programs [CSDGP], 2013), pre-service teachers in most Pacific Rim nations receive very little background in gifted education and teachers finishing their teacher preparation programs do not feel adequately prepared to deal with gifted students or students with special needs (Forlin & Chambers, 2011). Further preparation of specialists in gifted education is seldom provided in pre-service teacher training in countries in Pacific Rim nations, for example, in Australia (Fraser-Seeto, Howard, & Woodcock, 2013; Gindy, 2016), Japan (Basister & Kawai, 2018), or New Zealand (Riley & Bicknell, 2013).

With so few teachers prepared in gifted education to teach gifted students, the recruitment of these teachers to teach in isolated areas in a field where he or she may be the only teacher in a local school or across a multitude of schools is even more difficult than the recruitment of teachers for general education classrooms (Stambaugh & Wood, 2016). Further, the lack of financial resources to support professional development overall and the geographic isolation of gifted teachers result in limited accessibility to professional development (Jarzabkowski, 2003). The availability of online professional development is limited when access to reliable internet services is not available. When certification programs and/or professional development for educators *is* provided, the turnover in rural school staff that seek to move to more suburban or urban areas often makes the impact short-term. The lack of resources in schools exacerbates delivery of appropriate curricular options because the demand for teacher access to books, films, and other resources not part of the curriculum offered for the general education classroom is left unmet (Jarzabkowski, 2003). While the Internet has alleviated some of these issues, spotty and limited internet accessibility—particularly in remote rural settings (Federal Communications Commission, 2016; Thomas, Wilson, & Park, 2018)—makes this solution less viable than it may appear on its face.

One of the unique issues facing rural schools with limited resources is the small number of students identified as gifted. Most theory and policy statements place the numbers of expected gifted students between 5% and 10% of the population (Belanger & Gagné, 2006). And in many Asian countries, the identified percentage of students is considered to be even lower. For example, in China, the percentage of the gifted children is estimated to be between 1% and 3% of the total population of children and in Taiwan the ratio of gifted children is estimated to be between 3% and 5% (Ibata-Arens, 2012). The 'yield' therefore of gifted students in a given rural school or school district may present issues with the opportunity to offer a wide array of service delivery options and, thus, leave acceleration or differentiation within the general classroom (ideally, with clustering of students; Gentry, 2018) as the only viable options for offering services to gifted students. Because of the limited preparation of teachers to teach gifted students, offering the option of differentiation calls for the development of curriculum that teachers who are relatively inexperienced and with limited preparation are comfortable and capable of teaching—this is a research-based option to be presented in this chapter.

Finally, rural educators, including those who are teaching gifted students, are often limited by curricular parameters laid down by government agencies. While the process of establishing standards to ensure equity in outcomes for all students has value, the interpretations may limit the engagement of students because of the remoteness of meaning for students. A student interviewed by Grucho (1995; cited in Haas and Nachtigal; 1998) captured the essence of this issue eloquently:

> Among my science courses I took two full years of biology, but I never learned that the beautiful meadow at the bottom of my family's pasture was a remnant virgin prairie. We did not spend, so far as I can remember, a single hour on the prairies the landscape in which we were immersed in two years of biological study. I took history courses for years, but I never learned that one of the founders of my town and for decades the leading banker ... was also the author of the first comprehensive treatise on Minnesota's prairie botany. (pp. 1–2)

Understanding the Challenges Faced Globally in Identifying and Serving Gifted Students in Rural Schools

The identification of gifted students in rural areas requires consideration of four elements:

1. The definition of giftedness adopted by a nation, a state, and/or a local education agency.
2. Possible bias in instruments used in the identification of gifted students.
3. Level of opportunity to learn of the students in the school.
4. Ways the traits of giftedness may manifest in rural settings or among majority and minority groups within those settings (Callahan, 2018; Lohman, 2013).

Definition

The first challenge that faces schools seeking to identify rural students, especially those in high-poverty areas, rests in the multiplicity of definitions endorsed by the governments of various nations and subdivisions (states, territories, and the like) within those nations. Determining the ways in which formal, and perhaps bureaucratically approved, definitions can be applied within a rural setting is the first step in the identification process. The identification process cannot proceed with integrity until the school unit determines to whom gifted services should be provided.

A corollary issue reflects the influence of the values and views of giftedness held by particular subgroups on definitions of giftedness within the governmental geographic divisions (states, cities, school district boundaries). See, for example, the analyses of Thraves and Bannister-Tyrrell (2017) of the views on giftedness of the Australian Aboriginal people. They conclude that the wide diversity of beliefs about giftedness across just these groups has major implications for localised definitions and concomitant identification strategies. To successfully identify gifted students from indigenous groups and address the differences in learning rates and degree of depth and complexity of learning that should be provided to gifted indigenous students requires consultation with elders, parents, and the students themselves. Further, because many of these minority groups across nations are found in urban, suburban, *and* rural communities, the ways the characteristics of giftedness are manifest in the varying environments must be considered for adequate identification processes to be devised. For the purposes of this chapter, the processes to ensure fair and adequate identification which mines the ways giftedness may be manifest in rural environments will be the focus, with special attention given to students living in poverty and an underlying caution to take into account the minority issues that may impact any or all of these processes.

While individual nations, states, or local education agencies may have differing definitions, many share the inclusion of general intellectual ability and specific academic abilities. For the purposes of this chapter, a focus on these domains of giftedness will provide the framework for consideration of the underlying issues that often result in the under-identification of students who live in rural areas, live in poverty, and/or are members of groups who are historically underrepresented in gifted programs.

Instrument and Rater Bias

Scholars have identified factors that may inhibit performance of gifted students on instruments. Moreover, several factors in the way data from assessment tools are interpreted may result in under-identification of students who are poor and/or who live in rural environments (e.g., Brodersen, Brunner, & Missett, 2018; Matthews & Peters, 2018; Worrell, 2018). These factors often relate to both the characteristics of instruments used historically in the screening and identification process (particularly standardised tests and teacher rating scales) and the ways in which the scores from those instruments are considered in the decision-making process. Relative to the instruments themselves, one of these factors has been labelled *cultural bias* in test items, and much has been written about the bias (charges and counter-charges) in intelligence tests—both verbal and nonverbal—and will not be reiterated here (see Brodersen et al., 2018; Matthews & Peters, 2018; and Worrell, 2018). The most defensible conclusion would be that the judicious use of traditional tests of cognitive abilities as universal screening devices and standardised achievement tests is warranted when used *in conjunction with other measures* and in accord with a definition of gifted that matches the construct measured by the test. Endorsement of the use of universal screening is based on empirical evidence that low-income and minority student representation is likely to be increased when universal screening is part of the identification process (Card & Giuliano, 2015).

One reason universal screening adds to the pool of underrepresented students identified to receive services in gifted programs, lies in the inappropriate reliance on nominations from teachers or parents to initiate the process of identification. The potential parent and teacher bias in ratings of students as part of the screening and identification process has been widely documented in the USA and internationally. Biases reflecting lack of knowledge about gifted students as well as misconceptions and misunderstandings influence the ratings of students by teachers and the interpretation of item meanings by school administrators untrained in gifted education (Geake & Gross, 2008; Siegle & Powell, 2004).

As with scores on standardised tests, scores on teacher rating scales may reflect differentials according to minority status, school environment, or poverty. The disadvantage of referral is that nominations are thought to be biased when teachers do not recognise talents equally among all students and may overlook gifted and talented students who do not fit traditional archetypes of giftedness (Siegle & Powell, 2004). For example, on the HOPE scales, Peters and Gentry (2010) found that:

> mean scores for students from low-income families on both scales were lower than their non-low income peers, providing evidence that instruments need to be normed on the specific groups for which their use is intended. (p. 140)

Opportunity to Learn

The second factor has been labelled *opportunity to learn* by Lohman (2013). Opportunity to learn reflects the ways in which students have had exposure to the ideas, the concepts, and the skills of disciplines and ways of thinking that are reflected in the expected learning behaviours in schools and on the assessments that are used to assess the outcomes of instruction. The student in a rural school may be affected by the opportunity to learn in two distinct ways. First, in rural schools, poverty in the community as reflected in schools may influence the degree to which resources are available to teach the curriculum effectively (Howley, Rhodes, & Beall, 2009).

Second, the degree to which teachers are prepared is often a shortcoming in rural high-poverty schools (high turnover with teachers seeking to leave rural settings may result in many novice, inexperienced teachers in the classrooms). Finally, the students' opportunities to engage in experiences that would provide many of the prerequisite learning expected in a curriculum may be lacking. Minority groups that characterise some rural schools in some countries may not have had the same exposure to the dominant culture's language or cultural reference points. These influences of opportunity to learn have been noted particularly in relation to aptitude and achievement test performance. For example, recent statistical evidence identifies a gap in national and international academic test results between rural and urban students, and this trend "looks likely to continue into the future" (Thomson, De Bortoli, & Buckley, 2013, p. 5). These gaps may be attributed to the opportunity to learn and suggest a need to interpret test scores for students in rural schools relative to students' opportunity to learn.

The Ways Giftedness May Manifest in Rural Populations

Even rating scales with considerable reliability and validity evidence for the general population or across nations may include items that lead teachers to focus on only a limited interpretation of how the students may exhibit those behaviours, considering only behaviours as exhibited in classroom-based activities. For example, problem-solving abilities may manifest in the ways a child deals with extraordinary home responsibilities, or advanced verbal ability may be reflected in elaborated versions of local folklore or the ability to code switch from dialect to standard language patterns.

Minimising Challenges

The first step in addressing the challenges noted above is to ensure the use of multiple data points in the identification of gifted students. To that end one should collect data from both test and non-test sources (e.g., Australian Association for the Education of the Gifted and Talented; NAGC, 2010). Thus, a mix of scores from standardised measures of cognitive ability and/or standardised tests ideally would be considered in conjunction with teacher ratings, portfolio assessments, and/or performance assessments in determining which students would benefit from the advanced instruction and learning opportunities of gifted services. The appropriateness of any instrument rests on its validity as an indicator of talent for the area of giftedness to be assessed and for predicting success in the services and curriculum to be offered (Callahan, Renzulli, Delcourt, & Hertberg-Davis, 2018). Hence, educators would use a different set of assessments to assess talent in language arts than to assess mathematical talent, and these instruments would be distinctly different from those used to assess talents in the arts.

The recent data on the impact of universal screening would support use of a standardised test of cognitive ability as a critical step when assessing ability in general intellectual domains or specific academic areas (Card & Giuliano, 2015). The data on teacher rating scales suggest that the use of teacher rating scales can be another valuable source of data if teachers are provided training in the use of the instruments within the context of the schools and community in which the students live and learn (Peters & Gentry, 2010). In the case of rural schools, it is critical that the language of the instrument and the training provided to teachers include full access to examples of the ways in which giftedness may manifest in the student population.

However, universal screening, the use of multiple assessment tools, and the training of teachers in the appropriate ways of assessing students will not suffice to ensure that students from underrepresented populations, such as rural students, gain equal access to gifted education opportunities. Of equal importance is the appropriate interpretation and decision-making based on the scores obtained from universal screening, teacher rating scales, and portfolio assessments. Lohman (2013) recommended using local norms and scholars, such as Peters and Gentry (2010) recommend using group-specific local norms:

It is clear from the results discussed earlier that using group-specific norms for low income students will locate those students who have demonstrated high achievement (when compared with their peers), but who also often go unnoticed. (p. 140)

An Application of the Principles Noted Above

In the federally funded grant in the USA, *Promoting PLACE in Rural Schools* (Project PLACE), the investigators applied the principles outlined above in a place-conscious identification process to provide greater opportunities for rural students missed by traditional assessment measures. In this work, we intentionally recruited 'high-poverty' rural school districts, that is, districts with at least 50% or more students receiving federally funded meal assistance (although many of the school districts had 80% of students receiving this aid and one district received 100% aid for their students). We did not, however, have socio-economic status data on individual students participating in the grant. Therefore, we refer to the districts as 'high poverty' not students. After recruiting high-poverty rural districts and randomly assigning districts to either treatment or control groups, the investigators worked with district administrators to increase the number of students identified for gifted education. School personnel first applied their existing identification process to the pool of second-grade students in their districts. These identification procedures were largely based on screening using either an IQ test or a teacher nomination, application of national norms, and use of matrices for final decision-making. Upon completing district-level identification processes, the district administrators provided us with a list of rising third graders they had identified for gifted education services.

The identification of a second group of students to receive gifted services was based on data from two place-conscious assessment instruments: the *Cognitive Abilities Test-Verbal Battery Level 9* (CogAT-V; Lohman, 2013) and three subscales (motivation, creativity, and reading) of the *Scales for Rating the Behavioral Characteristics of Superior Students* (SRBCSS; Renzulli, et al., 2013). The instruments were selected based on the alignment of the *CogAT-V* test validity information with offering gifted services in the area of language arts and the congruence of the scales measuring higher levels of motivation, creativity, and reading engagement with the goals of the units in the *CLEAR* language arts curriculum. All second-grade students completed the CogAT-V assessment (universal screening), and all second-grade teachers participated in rural-specific, professional development training sessions designed to increase the validity and reliability of ratings prior to completing the ratings *of all students* in their classroom on the SRBCSS. Training included an overview of the characteristics of students gifted in language arts, videos from popular films that provided examples of how various characteristics represented in the scales may be exhibited, specifically in rural gifted students, and discussions of examples from the participating teachers' classrooms.

Data from the CogAT-V and SRBCSS were then presented to district personnel in spreadsheets that showed student scores based on national norms, the local norms for that district and classroom and district norms on the teacher rating scales (to counter issues of potential leniency and strictness in ratings by an individual teacher). The investigators highlighted patterns of performance by relatively high performers on a variety of combinations of test scores (those above 90th percentile on CogAT-V and more than two standard deviations above the mean on two or more rating scales, above the 75th percentile on CogAT-V and more than two standard deviations above the mean on three of the rating scales and additional combinations of scores representing high levels of performance on one or more measures). Additional students were identified at each site based on the values of the school district and arguments that can be made for potential benefit from the advanced curriculum. The focus was on examining the profile of each student to identify additional students to receive gifted services who may have been overlooked or 'missed' by the district. Note that neither cut-off scores nor matrices were used in the process as they are likely to mask the individual characteristics of students and are not psychometrically defensible (Moon, 2018). The process yielded additional students in each school district (in one case increasing the number of identified students from 1 to 40; in another the number of identified students went from 0 to 15). In every district the proportional representation of students from low Socio-Economic Status (SES) families increased significantly. The process was successful in identifying students with specific language arts aptitude as assessed by the CogAT combined with the specific reading, motivation, and creativity characteristics of the SRBCSS—school processes most often relied on the assessment of general intelligence and/or spatial ability and relied on national norms in their decision-making. Peters and Gentry (2012) provide a more complex process of considering student scores, but one aligned with the process above.

Supporting Teachers

After increasing the number of students identified for gifted services, project investigators then wanted to ensure that the proper supports were in place for teachers in the treatment group who may or may not have had any training in gifted education. In a prior study, we learned that rural teachers felt a great deal of professional isolation as it related to delivering gifted curricula (Azano, Callahan, Missett, & Brunner, 2014). Moreover, the gifted teachers in Project PLACE often work across multiple schools within a district and may confront a variety of challenges, such as resistance from general education teachers when students leave their classrooms for gifted services. Finally, many rural districts lack gifted education personnel, and, thus, general education teachers implement the curriculum.

To address these concerns, investigators sought ways to provide sustainable professional development and effective curricula. Our primary means for supporting teachers is by thoroughly orienting teachers to underlying principles prior to introducing them to the curriculum, but also by building the curriculum in ways teachers can implement instruction just by following the curriculum guidelines. This ensures that teachers understand and can readily identify foundational aspects in the unit (i.e., differentiation, depth, complexity, enrichment). As part of the grant, investigators work with administrators and school personnel to foster a sense of community for the teacher (Azano et al., 2014). The goal was to create a professional cadre, answer questions, listen to challenges, and brainstorm solutions. To this end, school districts seeking to further work in gifted education may consider how to facilitate support for teachers, either through web-based relationships or possibly with partnerships at regional universities.

Provision of an effective curriculum as documented by an RCT experiment (Callahan et al., 2015) also supports teachers. This curriculum guided teachers' efforts with rural students. Often teachers would ask if a poem or short story may be too difficult or express concerns over advanced vocabulary or literacy concepts. Use of an evidence-based curriculum model provided assurance to teachers to 'trust the lessons'. As a result, many teachers reported that the curriculum itself served as a form of professional development (e.g., teaching concepts related to differentiation by including not only a formative assessment, but suggestions for next day plans based on students' responses).

Using Place in the Gifted Curriculum

Another core component of this work is using place-based pedagogy within the gifted curriculum. Place-based education has its roots in ecological, environmental, or outdoor education; however, the use of place may be reflected in other disciplines and types of instruction. Application of place in the curriculum relies on consideration of multiple dimensions of place (Ardoin, 2006) conceptualised and contextualised by politics, sociocultural constructions of place, as well as the biophysical sphere of place. In essence, place may be the geographic 'container' in which students live and learn, but community members can experience place in varied, individualised ways. Even rural communities in the same geographic area represent unique diversity, assets, and challenges. As such, place-based pedagogy utilises a student's geographic context and the social construction of that particular place as instructional opportunities in the classroom.

Model for Integrating Place-Based Concepts into High-Level Curriculum

To characterise place in participating treatment districts, the empirically validated curriculum was revised to incorporate the various dimensions of culture, geography, events, industry, and the like of the school division (Callahan et al., 2015). Versions of the curriculum were developed to reflect one set of schools located in a rural farming area of the US state, a second version was developed for an area of the state characterised by coastal fishing and the poultry industry, and a third version was developed to reflect the place of a mountainous mining region. To best reflect the regions, data were collected by distributing a survey to all teachers in treatment districts asking questions about rural life in that particular district (Callahan et al., 2015). For example, questions focused on ascertaining major industries (i.e., agriculture, tourism, and the like); feelings of connectedness to nearby communities; local places, folklore and events with which most students would be familiar; and, perhaps more importantly, community factors that support and hinder student achievement. Responses provided insight into ways in which *rurality* and *place* were conceptualised within the particular school communities in which the curriculum is offered and guided insertion of examples, modifications in choices of literary inserts and products that would allow students to make personal connections to the curriculum through community-specific reflections (Callahan et al., 2015). While 'place' was a general concept used throughout the language arts units, these suggestions for suitable, place-based substitutions as they applied to specific regions freed teachers from needing to identify such references in the units, but also provided the working knowledge of how to develop place-based units themselves in the future. For example, as students studied a canonical poem, such as William Carlos Williams' 'The Red Wheelbarrow' (to learn about language arts concepts, such as abstract and concrete nouns, imagery, and rhythm), all teachers were introduced to the place concepts in the poem—like the fact that the poet is from New York and that New York, beyond the bright lights of New York City, is mostly rural. Using a wheelbarrow is a common image in rural places—even ones that seem far away. Teachers urged students to think about their own experiences with wheelbarrows. In a subsequent lesson, students are given the opportunity to think about what they rely on in their rural community, and examples, such as a rolling pin, tractor, and fishing pole, are provided.

However, beyond these examples and based on the surveys, each district received their own, place-specific suggestions. For a district located deep in Appalachia, a poem such as 'The Hills are Calling Me' (Muckenfuss, 1985) is suggested as a substitution, whereas in a coastal community, poems such as 'The Sandpiper' (Thaxton, 1896) and 'Sea Fever' (Masefield, 1902) were used. Additionally, throughout the units where teachers were encouraged to use specific community features, the survey responses guided suggestions—a renowned flea market and fiddler's convention in one area and wild ponies in another. Examples of Australian and New Zealand pieces that may be substituted can come from Internet sites such as https://www.poetrylibrary.edu.au/poets/catalano-gary/remembering-the-rural-life-0054002 or http://nzetc.victoria.ac.nz/iiml/bestnzpoems/BNZP10/t1-front1-d2.html.

These suggestions exemplify important takeaways for incorporating place into a high-level curriculum. The first is to appreciate the diversity of rural places. A 'rural curriculum' may include generalisations about rurality or a sense of community or creating space for conversations about rural places. However, more nuanced understandings of place (or to drive at critical pedagogies of place) must be community-driven and not imposed by curriculum developers or investigators. The survey from our work represents a comprehensive effort to drive at these diverse and unique understandings of place in participating school districts (Callahan et al., 2015). In other contexts, curricular choices would be different. For example, whereas we chose poems about 'the hills' to reflect the foothills of Appalachia and another poem about cows to be culturally responsive to an agricultural region, 'nature' poems in other places would reflect that specific geographical region, such as poetry by Oodgeroo Noonuccal (Kath Walker) or bush ballads by Banjo Paterson for an Australian context or Hone Tuwhare's poetry for a New Zealand one or to reflect Māori culture. Another takeaway is for school personnel to establish goals for incorporating place. Will place be used to increase relevance and engagement, to reduce stereotype threat, to promote a growth mindset, to serve as a scaffold to more abstract or global concepts or to value place in and of itself? Understanding these goals may serve to make strategic choices about curricula and by its very nature address larger issues related to rural sustainability. Place is a worthy endeavour for all students—perhaps even more so for those in rural areas.

Addressing Stereotype Threat and Growth Mindset for Rural Gifted Learners

In addition to place, two very important concepts to consider when developing programs and curriculum for rural gifted students are stereotype threat (Aronson & Steele, 2005) and mindset (Dweck, 2003). These constructs have been used to explain underachievement and failure to reach full potential. Aronson and Inzlicht (2004) define stereotype threat as the anxiety aroused when people are asked to demonstrate competency in an area where a group they identify with is stereotyped as lacking ability. Stereotype threat has been demonstrated to exist across multiple populations (e.g., middle-school minority students, white male university engineering students, females taking mathematics tests class, and African American students at highly regarded colleges; Aronson, Fried, & Good, 2002; Aronson & Inzlicht, 2004; Aronson, Lustina, et al., 1999; Aronson, Steele, Salinas, & Lustina, 1998; Steele & Aronson, 1995). Even identification as a 'Southerner' in the USA has been identified as a factor inhibiting student performance (Clark, Eno, & Guadagno, 2011). The broad network of settings in which the phenomenon has been observed suggests a need for consideration of the possible effects on rural students in any country and for minorities such as Māori, Aboriginal peoples of Australia, or the Russian Ainu or other minorities in remote areas of Pacific Rim countries. The combination of stereotypes of minority status and rural may provide added strength to the effects of stereotype threat.

Stereotype threat is important as an inhibitor of performance directly, but it is also important in its relationship to mindset. According to Dweck (2003), mindsets come in two forms: incremental and entity. Belief in an incremental mindset reflects acceptance of the tenet that everyone can become smarter by working to improve his or her intellectual potential. Because believers in incremental mindset are likely to blame a lack of effort for failure, they tend to pursue learning goals (work towards increasing competence) and work harder when faced with difficult learning tasks. However, students with an entity mindset believe that intelligence is fixed and use their performance to gauge their level of intelligence, thus making them more likely to pursue performance goals and tasks in which success is easily achieved (Dweck, 2003). Stereotype threat is associated with holding an entity mindset (Callahan, 2012) and pursuing performance goals (Aronson, Fried, & Good, 2002) leading students to avoid challenges, dismiss tasks on which they fail, and avoid them in the future, and attribute failure to lack of trying (Ablard, 2002). Teacher praise may influence student alignment with certain achievement goals. Mueller and Dweck (1998) found that teacher praise of fifth-grade students' intelligence influenced their preference for performance goals, while praise for hard work and effort led them to pursue learning goals. These findings make it vital that educators consider the impact of stereotypes about rural students and minority students in planning for optimum realisation of potential in gifted students.

Fortunately, researchers have demonstrated that simple interventions such as reading about struggles of famous individuals (Hong & Lin-Siegler, 2012; Lin-Siegler, Ahn, Chen, Fang, & Luna-Lucero, 2016) and reading articles supporting an incremental mindset (Ehrlinger, Mitchum, & Dweck, 2016; Schroder, Moran, Donnellan, & Moser, 2014) can be effective in altering students' mindsets and promoting a growth mindset (Blackwell, Trzesniewski, & Dweck, 2007; Boehm, 2012). Ziegler and Stoeger (2010) identified a combined fixed and growth mindset as characteristic of adaptive gifted adolescents. Similarly, Aronson and his colleagues developed strategies effective in reducing the effects of stereotype threat (Alter, Aronson, Darley, Rodriguez, & Ruble, 2010; Aronson, Fried & Good, 2002; Good, Aronson, Inzlicht, 2003). In Project PLACE, mindset and stereotype threat interventions are integrated. In each unit, specific directions are provided to teachers on language to use to encourage the development of a growth mindset (encouragement and persistence through challenging tasks) and two webquests—one offered each year of the program—to teach students about the brain and growth (neurogenesis) in potential by assuming a growth mindset and rejecting stereotypes of rural and minority status. Videos illustrating brain recovery and growth set the stage for challenges to reflect on personal examples of growth (Azano, Callahan, Brodersen, & Caughey, 2017).

Conclusion

While rural schools may struggle with limited resources for professional development and staffing in gifted education, there are opportunities for rural schools to increase the effectiveness of instructional opportunities for students with high potential. As illustrated in this chapter, searching for potential rather than being saddled with limitation may serve to find asset-based resources relative to gifted education in rural schools. Broadened identification measures, local norms on traditional assessments, place-specific teacher training for assessments, consulting with schools on place, and modifying curricula to reflect that place are all ways to leverage emancipatory literacies and create more opportunities to learn.

Challenges do exist in rural communities but so do the many gifts of its members. Exploring and celebrating rural gifts, as they are conceptualised by a given community, are a way to honour the diverse ways of knowing in rural communities. The examples provided from Project PLACE are indeed place specific to our participating districts and in no way represent the only way for moving forward with this work. Rather, we encourage researchers and practitioners to situate their work in the communities they intend to support, to question how instruments may be biased, to ask about opportunities to learn and funds of knowledge in students and to consider place as an academic construct for meeting the needs of diverse, rural students.

Cross-References

- A Model for Growing Teacher Talent Scouts: Decreasing Underrepresentation of Gifted Students
- Gifted and Talented Aboriginal Students in Australia
- Gifted Education in the Asia-Pacific: From the Past for the Future – An Introduction
- Identifying and Nurturing Diversely Gifted and Talented Students: Part III Introduction
- Identifying Gifted Learning in the Regular Classroom: Seeking Intuitive Theories
- Identifying Underrepresented Gifted Students: A Developmental Process
- Motivational Issues in Gifted Education: Understanding the Role of Students' Attribution and Control Beliefs, Self-Worth Protection and Growth Orientation
- Rural Adolescent Gifted Girls: Exploring the Impact of Popular Culture on Their Talent Development
- Rural Voices: Identifying the Perceptions, Practices, and Experiences of Gifted Pedagogy in Australian Rural and Regional Schools
- Self-Nomination in the Identification Process of Gifted and Talented Students in Mexico
- Some Implications for the Future of Gifted Education in the Asia-Pacific
- Supporting Australian Gifted Indigenous Students' Academic Potential in Rural Settings

Acknowledgments The research reported here was supported by the US Department of Education, under the Jacob K. Javits Gifted and Talented Students Education program, through Grant S206A140034-17.

References

Ablard, K. E. (2002). Achievement goals and implicit theories of intelligence among academically talented students. *Journal for the Education of the Gifted, 25*, 215–232. https://doi.org/10.1177/016235320202500302

Alston, M. M., & Kent, J. (2013). Educational access for Australia's rural young people: A case of social exclusion. *Australian Journal of Gifted Education, 47*. https://doi.org/10.1177/0004944103047001026

Alter, A. L., Aronson, J., Darley, J. M., Rodriguez, C., & Ruble, D. N. (2010). Rising to the threat: Reducing stereotype threat by reframing the threat as a challenge. *Journal of Experimental Social Psychology, 46*, 166–171. https://doi.org/10.1016/j.jesp.2009.09.014

Ardoin, N. M. (2006). Toward an interdisciplinary understanding of place: Lessons for environmental education. *Canadian Journal of Environmental Education, 11*(1), 112–126. Retrieved from https://cjee.lakeheadu.ca/article/view/508/410

Aronson, J., Fried, C. B., & Good, C. (2002). Reducing the effects of stereotype threat on African American college students by shaping theories of intelligence. *Journal of Experimental Social Psychology, 38*, 113–125. https://doi.org/10.1006/jesp.2001.1491

Aronson, J., & Inzlicht, M. (2004). The ups and downs of attributional ambiguity: Stereotype vulnerability and the academic self-knowledge of African American college students. *Psychological Science, 15*, 829–836. https://doi.org/10.1111/j.0956-7976.2004.00763.x

Aronson, J., Lustina, M. J., Good, C., Keough, K., Steele, C. M., & Brown, J. (1999). When White men can't do math: Necessary and sufficient factors in stereotype threat. *Journal of Experimental Social Psychology, 35*, 29–46. https://doi.org/10.1006/jesp.1998.1371

Aronson, J., & Steele, C. M. (2005). Stereotypes and the fragility of human competence, motivation, and self-concept. In C. Dweck & E. Elliot (Eds.), *Handbook of competence & motivation* (pp. 436–456). New York, NY: Guilford.

Aronson, J., Steele, C. M., Salinas, M. F., & Lustina, M. J. (1998). The effect of stereotype threat on the standardized test performance of college students. In E. Aronson (Ed.), *Readings about the social animal* (8th ed., pp. 415–430). New York, NY: Freeman.

Azano, A. P., Callahan, C. M., Brodersen, A. V., & Caughey, M. (2017). Responding to the challenges of gifted education in rural communities. *Global Education Review, 4*(1), 62–77. Retrieved from https://files.eric.ed.gov/fulltext/EJ1137998.pdf

Azano, A. P., Callahan, C. M., Missett, T. C., & Brunner, M. (2014). Understanding the experiences of gifted education teachers and fidelity of implementation in rural schools. *Journal of Advanced Education, 25*, 88–100. https://doi.org/10.1177/1932202X14524405

Basister, M. P., & Kawai, N. (2018). Japan's educational practices for mathematically gifted students. *International Journal of Inclusive Education, 6*(2), 1–11. https://doi.org/10.1080/13603116.2017.1420252

Belanger, J., & Gagné, F. (2006). Estimating the size of the gifted/talented population from multiple identification criteria. *Journal for the Education of the Gifted, 30*(2), 131–163. https://doi.org/10.4219/jeg-2006-258

Bevan-Brown, J. (2011). Indigenous conceptions of giftedness. In W. Vialle (Ed.), *Giftedness from an Indigenous perspective* (pp.10–23). Australian Association for the Education of the Gifted and Talented. Retrieved from http://www.aaegt.net.au/DEEWR%20Books/02%20Indig.pdf

Biddle, C., & Azano, A. P. (2016). Constructing and reconstructing the "rural school problem": A century of rurality and rural education research. *Review of Research in Education, 40*, 298–325. https://doi.org/10.3102/0091732X16667700

Blackwell, L. S., Trzesniewski, K. H., & Dweck, C. S. (2007). Implicit theories of intelligence predict achievement across an adolescent transition: A longitudinal study and an intervention. *Child Development, 78*, 246–263. https://doi.org/10.1111/j.1467-8624.2007.00995.x

Boehm, K. (2012). *Mindsets and Brainology: Self-theories of intelligence and an interventions.* Retrieved from https://www.scribd.com/document/123417774/Mindsets-and-Brainology-Self-Theories-of-Intelligence-and-an-Intervention

Brodersen, A. V. (2016). *Exploring alignment in gifted education program policies and practices* (Doctoral dissertation). Retrieved from https://doi.org/10.18130/V31P3N

Brodersen, A. V., Brunner, M. M., & Missett, T. C. (2018). Traditional identification instruments. In C. M. Callahan & H. L. Hertberg-Davis (Eds.), *Fundamentals of gifted education* (2nd ed., pp. 103–115). New York, NY: Routledge.

Brown, P. H. (2006). Parental education and investment in children's human capital in rural china. *Gansu Survey of Children and Families Papers.* 8. http://repository.upenn.edu/gansu_papers/8

Burney, V. H., & Cross, T. L. (2006). Impoverished students with academic promise in rural settings: 10 lessons from Project Aspire. *Gifted Child Today, 29*(2), 14–21. https://doi.org/10.4219/gct-2006-200

Callahan, C. M. (2012). In closing. In R. F. Subotnik, A. Robinson, C. M. Callahan, & E. J. Gubbins (Eds.), *Malleable minds: Translating insights from psychology and neuroscience to gifted education* (pp. 267–269). Storrs, CT: National Research Center on the Gifted and Talented.

Callahan, C. M. (2018). Identification. In C. M. Callahan & H. L. Hertberg-Davis (Eds.), *Fundamentals of gifted education: Considering multiple perspectives* (pp. 94–102). New York, NY: Routledge.

Callahan, C. M., Moon, T. R., & Oh, S. (2017). Describing the status of programs for the gifted: A call for action. *Journal for the Education of the Gifted, 40*, 20–49. https://doi.org/10.1177/0162353216686215

Callahan, C. M., Moon, T. R., Oh, S., Azano, A. P., & Hailey, E. P. (2015). What works in gifted education: Documenting the effects of an integrated curricular/instructional model for gifted students. *American Educational Research Journal, 52*, 137–167. https://doi.org/10.3102/0002831214549448

Callahan, C. M., Renzulli, J. S., Delcourt, M. A. B., & Hertberg-Davis, H. L. (2018). Considerations for the identification of gifted and talented students. In C. M. Callahan & H. L. Hertberg-Davis (Eds.), *Fundamentals of gifted education* (2nd ed., pp. 85–93). New York, NY: Routledge.

Card, D., & Giuliano, L. (2015). *Can universal screening increase the representation of low income and minority students in gifted education?* NBER working paper no. 21519. Retrieved from http://www.nber.org/papers/w21519

Carr, P., & Kefalas, M. (2009). *Hollowing out the middle: The rural brain drain and what it means for America*. Boston, MA: Beacon Press.

Clark, J. K., Eno, C. A., & Guadagno, R. E. (2011). Southern discomfort: The effects of stereotype threat on the intellectual performance of US southerners. *Self and Identity, 10*, 248–262. https://doi.org/10.1080/15298861003771080

Corbett, M. (2007). *Learning to leave: The irony of schooling in a coastal community*. Black Point, NS: Fernwood Publishing.

Dweck, C. S. (2003). Beliefs that make smart people dumb. In R. J. Sternberg (Ed.), *Why smart people can be so stupid* (pp. 24–41). New Haven, CT: Yale University Press.

Ehrlinger, J., Mitchum, A. L., & Dweck, C. S. (2016). Understanding overconfidence: Theories of intelligence, preferential attention, and distorted self-assessment. *Journal of Experimental Social Psychology, 63*, 94–100. https://doi.org/10.1016/j.jesp.2015.11.001

Federal Communications Commission. (2016, January 29). *2016 broadband progress report*. Washington, DC: Federal Communication Commission, Federal Government, USA. Retrieved from https://www.fcc.gov/reports-research/reports/broadband-progress-reports/2016-broadband-progress-report

Forlin, C., & Chambers, D. (2011). Teacher preparation for inclusive education: Increasing knowledge but raising concerns. *Asia-Pacific Journal of Teacher Education, 39*(1), 17–32. https://doi.org/10.1080/1359866X.2010.540850

Fraser-Seeto, K., Howard, S. J., & Woodcock, S. (2013). Preparation for teaching gifted students: An updated investigation into university offerings in New South Wales. *Australasian Journal of Gifted Education, 22*(2), 45–51. Retrieved from http://citeseerx.ist.psu.edu/viewdoc/download?doi=10.1.1.905.465&rep=rep1&type=pdf

Freire, P. (2000). *The pedagogy of the oppressed* (30th anniv. ed.; M.B. Ramos, Trans.). New York, NY: Continuum.

Freire, P., & Macedo, D. (1987). *Literacy: Reading the word and the world*. South Hadley, MA: Bergin & Garvey.

Fry, S. W., & Anderson, H. (2011). Career changers as first-year teachers in rural schools. *Journal of Research in Rural Education, 26*(12), 1–15. Retrieved from http://jrre.psu.edu/articles/26-12.pdf

Gagné, F. (2018). The DMGT/IMTD: Building talented outputs out of gifted inputs. In C. M. Callahan & H. L. Hertberg-Davis (Eds.), *Fundamentals of gifted education* (2nd ed., pp. 55–70). New York, NY: Routledge.

Geake, J. G., & Gross, M. U. M. (2008). Teachers' negative affect toward academically gifted students: An evolutionary psychological study. *Gifted Child Quarterly, 52*, 217–231. https://doi.org/10.1177/0016986208319704

Gentry, M. (2018). Cluster grouping. In C. M. Callahan & H. L. Hertberg-Davis (Eds.), *Fundamentals of gifted education* (2nd ed., pp. 214–224). New York, NY: Routledge.

Gindy, M. (2016). Gifted awareness week: Australia. http://www.aaegt.net.au/wp-content/uploads/Gifted-Awareness-Week-Australia-2016-Media-Release.pdf

Good, C., Aronson, J., & Inzlicht, M. (2003). Improving adolescents' standardized test performance: An intervention to reduce the effects of stereotype threat. *Applied Developmental Psychology, 24*, 645–662. https://doi.org/10.1016/j.appdev.2003.09.002

Gruenewald, D. A. (2003). The best of both worlds: A critical pedagogy of place. *Educational Researcher, 32*(4), 3–12. https://doi.org/10.3102/0013189X032004003

Haas, T., & Nachtigal, P. (1998). *Place value: An educator's guide to good literature on rural lifeways, environments, and purposes of education*. Charleston, WV: ERIC Clearinghouse on Rural Education and Small Schools. ERIC ED 420 461.

Hébert, T. P., & Beardsley, T. M. (2001). Jermaine: A critical case study of a gifted black child living in rural poverty. *Gifted Child Quarterly, 45*, 85–102. https://doi.org/10.1177/001698620104500203

Hong, H.-Y., & Lin-Siegler, X. (2012). How learning about scientists' struggles influences students' interest and learning in physics. *Journal of Educational Psychology, 104*, 469–484. https://doi.org/10.1037/a0026224

Howley, A., Rhodes, M., & Beall, J. (2009). Challenges facing rural schools: Implications for gifted students. *Journal for the Education of the Gifted, 32*(4), 515–536. https://doi.org/10.1177/016235320903200404

Ibata-Arens, K. C. (2012). Race to the future: Innovations in gifted and enrichment education in Asia, and implications for the United States. *Administrative Sciences, 2*, 1–25. https://doi.org/10.3390/admsci2010001

Jarvis, J. M., & Henderson, L. C. (2012). Current practices in the education of gifted and advanced learners in South Australian schools. *Australasian Journal of Gifted Education, 21*, 5–22.

Jarzabkowski, L. (2003). Teacher collegiality in a remote Australian school. *Journal of Research in Rural Education, 18*, 139–144. Retrieved from http://jrre.vmhost.psu.edu/wp-content/uploads/2014/02/18-3_3.pdf

Lin-Siegler, X., Ahn, J., Chen, J., Fang, F.-F. A., & Luna-Lucero, M. (2016). Even Einstein struggled: Effects of learning about great scientists' struggles on high school students' motivation to learn science. *Journal of Educational Psychology, 108*, 314–328. https://doi.org/10.1037/edu0000092

Lohman, D. (2013). Identifying gifted students: Nontraditional uses of traditional measures. In C. M. Callahan & H. H. l. Hertberg-Davis (Eds.), *Fundamentals of gifted education: Considering multiple perspectives* (pp. 112–127). New York, NY: Routledge.

Masefield, J. (1902). Sea fever. *Salt-water ballads*. London, England: Grant Richards. Retrieved from https://www.poetryfoundation.org/poems/54932/sea-fever-56d235e0d871e

Matthews, M. S., & Peters, S. J. (2018). Methods to increase the identification rate of students from traditionally underrepresented populations for gifted services. In S. I. Pfeiffer (Ed.), *APA handbook of giftedness and talent* (pp. 317–331). Washington, DC: American Psychological Association. https://doi.org/10.1037/0000038-021

Moon, T. R. (2018). Uses and misuses of matrices in identifying gifted students: Considerations for better practice. In C. M. Callahan & H. L. Hertberg-Davis (Eds.), *Fundamentals of gifted education* (2nd ed., pp. 116–124). New York, NY: Routledge.

Muckenfuss, L. T. (1985). The hills are calling me. *The Mountain Laurel: The Journal of Mountain Life*. Retrieved from http://www.mtnlaurel.com/poetry/845-the-hills-are-calling-me.html

Mueller, C. M., & Dweck, C. S. (1998). Praise for intelligence can undermine children's motivation and performance. *Journal of Personality and Social Psychology, 75*, 33–52. https://doi.org/10.1037/0022-3514.75.1.33

National Association for Gifted Children. (2010). *Pre-k–Grade 12 gifted programming standards*. Washington, DC: Author.

National Association for Gifted Children & Council of State Directors of Programs for the Gifted. (2013). *2012–2013 State of the states in gifted education*. Washington, DC: Author.

O'Callahan, J. (2015, August). Rural NZ schools: the forgotten group. *Stuff*. Retrieved from http://www.stuff.co.nz/national/education/71312397/Rural-NZ-schools-the-forgotten-group

Peters, S. J., & Gentry, M. (2010). Multigroup construct validity evidence of the *HOPE Scale*: Instrumentation to identify low-income elementary students for gifted programs. *Gifted Child Quarterly, 54*, 298–313. https://doi.org/10.1177/0016986210378332

Renzulli, J. S. (1976). What makes giftedness: Re-examining a definition. *Phi Delta Kapan, 60*, 180–184, 261.

Renzulli, J. S., Smith, L. White, A., Callahan, C., Hartman, R., Westberg, K., . . . Systma, R. (2013). *Scales for rating the behavioral characteristics of superior students*. Waco, TX: Prufrock Press.

Riley, T., & Bicknell, B. (2013). Gifted and talented education in New Zealand Schools: A Decade Later. *APEX: The New Zealand Journal of Gifted Education, 18*(1), 1–16. Retrieved from www.giftedchildren.org.nz/apex

Schroder, H. S., Moran, T. P., Donnellan, M. B., & Moser, J. S. (2014). Mindset induction effects on *cognitive* control: A neurobehavioral investigation. *Biological Psychology, 103*, 27–37. https://doi.org/10.1016/j.biopsycho.2014.08.004

Siegle, D., & Powell, T. (2004). Exploring teacher biases when nominating students for gifted programs. *Gifted Child Quarterly, 48*, 21–29. https://doi.org/10.1177/001698620404800103

Stambaugh, T., & Wood, S. M. (2016, April). Serving gifted students in rural setting: NAGC Webinar. Retrieved from http://www.nagc.org/sites/default/files/WebinarPowerPoints/Serving%20Gifted%20Students%20in%20Rural%20Settings.pdf

Steele, C. M., & Aronson, J. (1995). Stereotype threat and the intellectual test performance of African Americans. *Journal of Personality and Social Psychology, 69*, 797–811.

Sternberg, R. J. (1984). Toward a triarchic theory of human intelligence. *Behavioral and Brain Sciences, 7*, 269–316. https://doi.org/10.1017/S0140525X00044629

Thaxton, C. (1872). The sandpiper. In S. O. Jewett (Ed.) *The Poems of Celia Thaxton* (1896). Boston, MA: Houghton, Mifflin and Company. Retrieved from https://www.litscape.com/author/Celia_Thaxter/The_Sandpiper.html

Thomas, J., Wilson, C. K., & Park, S. (2018, March 29). Australia's digital divide is not going away. *The Conversation.* Retrieved from http://theconversation.com/australias-digital-divide-is-not-going-away-91834

Thomson, S., De Bortoli, L., & Buckley, S. (2013). *PISA 2012: How Australia measures up: The PISA 2012 assessment of students' mathematical, scientific and reading literacy.* ACER: Camberwell, Victoria. Retrieved from http://www.acer.edu.au/ozpisa/reports

Thraves, G., & Bannister-Tyrrell, M. (2017). Australian Aboriginal peoples and giftedness: A diverse issue in need of a diverse response. *TalentEd, 29*, 18–31.

Worrell, F. C. (2018). Identifying gifted learners: Utilizing nonverbal assessment. In C. M. Callahan & H. L. Hertberg-Davis (Eds.), *Fundamentals of gifted education* (2nd ed., pp. 125–134). New York, NY: Routledge.

Ziegler, A., & Stoeger, H. (2010). Research on a modified framework of implicit personality theories. *Learning and Individual Differences, 20*, 318–326. https://doi.org/10.1016/j.lindif.2010.01.007

Carolyn M. Callahan, PhD, is Commonwealth Professor of Education at the University of Virginia, where for more than 20 years she has been the principal investigator on projects of the *National Research Center on the Gifted and Talented* (NRC/GT), is currently the Co-PI for the National Center for Research in Gifted Education and has been coprincipal investigator on six Javits grants including a current grant focusing on rural gifted students. Dr. Callahan has published over 200 articles and 50 book chapters on topics in gifted education with one of those publications considered the definitive book on evaluation. She is the co-editor of *Critical Issues in Gifted Education.*

Amy Price Azano, PhD, is Associate Professor of Adolescent Literacy in the School of Education at Virginia Tech, concentrates her scholarship on rural literacies, place-based pedagogy, and the literacy needs of special populations. She is the coprincipal investigator of Promoting PLACE (Place, Literacy, Achievement, Community and Engagement) in Rural Schools, a US Department of Education grant focusing on gifted education programs in high-poverty rural communities. Dr. Azano has published book chapters and articles in national and international peer-reviewed journals, co-authored a curriculum series for gifted, and has served as a keynote speaker on rural topics in the USA and abroad.

Gifted Girls with Autism Spectrum Disorders: Provisions and Priorities in Australian School Settings

26

Aranzazu M. Blackburn and Geraldine Townend

Contents

Introduction	556
Girls with ASD: A Brief Overview	557
Twice Exceptionality	558
Typical Education Goals for Gifted Girls with ASD and Strategies to Meet These Goals	559
Communicative Domain	559
Social Domain	561
Emotional Well-Being Domain	562
Academic Domain	564
Physical Domain	565
Teaching and Other Recommended Interventions	567
Implications for Future Research	568
Conclusion	569
Cross-References	569
References	569

Abstract

Gifted girls with *Autism Spectrum Disorder* (ASD) are an under-researched and underserved population. When measured against the generalised research around ASD, predominantly sampled from male populations, a body of knowledge is emerging about the unique needs of twice-exceptional (2e) girls with ASD. Synthesising existing literature in the field of ASD, in particular with respect to girls with ASD and students with twice exceptionality, some educational goals are

---

A. M. Blackburn (✉)
Brisbane, QLD, Australia
e-mail: black_ba@bigpond.com

G. Townend
GERRIC/School of Education, The University of New South Wales, Sydney, NSW, Australia
e-mail: g.townend@griffith.edu.au

© Springer Nature Singapore Pte Ltd. 2021
S. R. Smith (ed.), *Handbook of Giftedness and Talent Development in the Asia-Pacific*,
Springer International Handbooks of Education,
https://doi.org/10.1007/978-981-13-3041-4_26

identified. Existing strategies and practices for 2e girls with ASD are examined. Recommended practices and implications for future research are discussed in light of their potential to shape the intervention landscape for this population of students.

Keywords

Gifted and talented students · Twice exceptional · Autism Spectrum Disorder · Girls · Educational interventions

The aims in this chapter are to:
1. Present and synthesise literature around twice-exceptional girls with ASD.
2. Review recommended strategies and practices for this population of students.
3. Recommend practices to support educational interventions
4. Provide some implications for future research.

Introduction

Educational and research communities are increasing their interest in girls with *Autism Spectrum Disorders* (ASD) and their characteristics as the focus to date has been on boys with ASD (Halladay et al., 2015). A frequently stated 4:1 ratio in gender difference around prevalence of ASD has been found from multiple studies (e.g., Werling & Geschwind, 2013), and the male preponderance is not unique to ASD, as studies have reliably documented prevalence of developmental conditions in males compared to females (e.g., Pinborough-Zimmerman et al., 2007). A lower identified prevalence in gifted girls is further augmented by the internationally inconsistent identification of ability, particularly gifted ability, in school-aged children (Townend, Pendergast, & Garvis, 2014). This is not helped by the many definitions of giftedness and the associated stigmas (Ronksley-Pavia, 2015).

Gifted girls with ASD are identified as having twice exceptionality; that is, they are gifted students with a disability that affects their learning (Townend & Brown, 2016). The growing body of scholarship around gifted girls with ASD and twice exceptionality has the potential to deliver benefits, including a greater understanding of the educational needs of girls with ASD across the learning continuum (e.g., Assouline, Foley-Nicpon, & Dockery, 2012; Foley-Nicpon, Allmon, Sieck, & Stinson, 2011). These emerging understandings not only provide increased opportunities for the implementation of research-into-practice processes, but also place current and frequently used strategies under review for their effectiveness and efficiency.

In educational settings, teachers collaborate with parents, caregivers, specialists, clinicians and, importantly, the student themselves to examine the specific educational needs of students with ASD and to negotiate accommodations and adjustments to derive equitable access to the curriculum. Typical educational goals for girls with ASD and twice-exceptional girls will be presented, and teaching strategies and approaches as well as other recommended interventions will be discussed. The effectiveness of strategies used more commonly in educational settings to meet the challenges these students face will be reviewed in terms of empirically-based research. Recommendations for future research based on gaps in the literature and emerging fields will be made.

Girls with ASD: A Brief Overview

Autism Spectrum Disorder (ASD) is a collective term that is used to describe a group of neurodevelopmental disorders where an individual may display a persistent deficit in social communication and social interaction in multiple situations, as well as restricted, repetitive patterns of behaviour and interests, originally manifested in the early developmental period and causing significant impairment in social, occupational, or other important areas of functioning. It may or may not accompany an intellectual or language disability or be associated with a known medical or genetic condition or environmental factor (American Psychiatric Association, 2013).

A growing body of research is emerging that considers gender differences across issues related to presentation, identification, diagnosis, and service provisions for individuals with ASD (e.g., Kreiser & White, 2015; Lai, Lombardo, Auyeung, Chakrabarti, & Baron-Cohen, 2015; Shefcyk, 2015). Critically, girls are often identified later than boys, delaying support at crucial developmental stages. These delays in identification are attributed generally to the moderation of disability symptoms by girls, with their behaviours presenting in a less obvious manner that are less overt and atypical (Baldwin & Costley, 2016). Diagnostic criteria such as difficulties with social communication and social interactions (American Psychiatric Association, 2013), for example, may not appear to be met, as girls with ASD often seem to have mature language skills and appear socially integrated. This ability of girls with ASD to imitate peers and adults to fit in often breaks down in adolescence as the social milieu becomes more complex to navigate (Hsaio, Tseng, Huang, & Gau, 2013).

Girls with ASD tend to display behaviours, particularly in adolescence and into adulthood, that require specialised and focused support. Girls with ASD can more commonly be identified with behavioural or psychiatric disorders such as anxiety (Solomon, Miller, Taylor, Hinshaw, & Carter, 2012), depression (Nolen-Hoeksema & Girgus, 1994; Sharpley, Bitsika, Andronicos, & Agnew, 2016), sleep problems (Baker, Richdale, Short, & Gradisar, 2013), eating disorders (Stewart, McEwen, Konstantellou, Eisler, & Simic, 2017), obsessive-compulsive disorder (OCD; Lewin, Wood, Gunderson, Murphy, & Storch, 2011), and opposition defiance disorder (ODD; Dickerson Mayes et al., 2012). These comorbidities often become the specific focus of therapy and support; however, full consideration of the broader needs of the individual with ASD should be examined further (Ehrenreich-May et al., 2014).

Twice Exceptionality

In this context, students with twice exceptionality (2e) are those students who have been identified as gifted (having advanced aptitudes or abilities or a potential for these) and whose giftedness develops in relation to a disability that affects their learning (Assouline, Foley-Nicpon, & Whiteman, 2010; Assouline & Whiteman, 2011; Townend & Brown, 2016). Researchers at the *National Association for Gifted Children* (NAGC) normalised the term twice exceptionality (https://www.nagc.org/resources-publications/resources-parents/twice-exceptional-students), and it has become a common term in the last decade internationally. Students who have twice exceptionality can present as a dual paradox for education systems, both in terms of having giftedness and disability simultaneously and in terms of the lamentable lack of nurturing of a potential resource on both an individual and a national level (Townend & Brown, 2016). Not only have educators struggled to understand the diverse nature of gifted children, but they do more so with twice exceptionality (Ronksley-Pavia, 2015). The paradox of two or more exceptionalities in schools is due primarily to a focus on behavioural issues, lack of community knowledge, and challenges with identification (Rowan & Townend, 2016; Vail, 1989).

Research with 2e students with ASD has been undertaken (Assouline et al., 2012), including girls specifically (Assouline, Foley-Nicpon, & Doobay, 2009), and individual program plans have been recommended that incorporate "strategies for enrichment of gifts and talents, strategies for remediation of and compensation for deficits, and strategies for enhancing personal development" (Lupart & Toy, 2009, p. 511). Provisions for 2e students with ASD also include emotional support, external scaffolding, and advocacy (Lupart & Toy, 2009; Ronksley-Pavia & Townend, 2016), as emotional and behavioural issues may arise as a result of the interactions between positive and negative characteristics. A dependent pattern of behaviour may also emerge because of too much focus on the disability and a neglect of the intellectual ability (Peterson & Ray, 2006). In order to alleviate these difficulties, practical recommendations have been offered. For example, Maker (1986) and others (Foley-Nicpon, Assouline & Colangelo, 2013; Townend & Pendergast, 2015) recommend using curriculum and social-emotional scaffolding to meet the needs of 2e students with ASD.

Assouline et al. (2012) have suggested that 2e students, including those with ASD, often have their giftedness overlooked. Though generally performing at grade level, these students are often underserved in terms of their giftedness and therefore underachieve (Burger-Veltmeijer, Minnaert, & Van Houten-Van den Bosch, 2011; Ronksley-Pavia, 2015; Townend & Brown, 2016). Aspects of ASD may impede students from performing to their full cognitive potential (Assouline et al., 2012). In fact, 2e students are more likely to be labelled and treated for a disorder than for their giftedness (Moon, 2002; Townend & Pendergast, 2015). Underidentification may be due to a lack of teacher knowledge regarding achievement as well as inadequate assessments or depressed IQ scores, so a broad and diverse approach to identification has been recommended (Foley-Nicpon & Assouline, 2015). Suggestions for better identification of 2e students include tracking individual ability and achievement over time (Nielsen, 2002) and identification of declining performance over time despite superior ability (McCoach, Kehle, Bray,

& Siegle, 2001). The implementation of a *Response To Intervention* (RTI) model, a multi-tiered, systematic, and coordinated approach that relies on early identification and intervention with evaluation of strategies for effectiveness, has also been endorsed (Crepeau-Hobson & Bianco, 2011).

Typical Education Goals for Gifted Girls with ASD and Strategies to Meet These Goals

The dearth of literature exploring the educational landscape specifically for gifted girls with ASD has left researchers, educators, and parents with the task of collating evidence from bodies of work regarding 2e girls as well as girls with ASD. A comprehensive summary undertaken by Foley-Nicpon et al. (2011) of 20 years' worth of empirical research about gifted students with coexisting disabilities, including ASD, has suggested that extrapolating from the research in different fields can drive future research, support the development of accommodation plans for 2e students, as well as develop intervention strategies to "target specific strength and growth areas" (p. 3). To this end, existing literature on typical education goals for 2e girls and girls with ASD will be reviewed, and research specific to gifted girls with ASD will be discussed.

In Australia, the *Melbourne Declaration on Educational Goals for Young Australians* (Ministerial Council on Education, Employment, Training and Youth Affairs [MCEETYA], 2008) has provided a vision that aims for both equity and excellence for all students, including those with a disability and those displaying gifts and talents. Educators in educational institutions of all kinds, from early childhood settings to primary and middle/secondary schools and higher education providers, are expected to aspire to these goals. For 2e girls with ASD, this means provisions for access to a high-quality education through "personalised learning that aims to fulfil the diverse capabilities of each young Australian" (p. 7).

Due to the nature of ASD, and in line with both diagnostic criteria and increasing research in the field, specific yet frequently overlapping domains have been identified where 2e girls with ASD may encounter their most significant challenges (e.g., Foley-Nicpon & Assouline, 2015). These domains may provide educators with a framework that support planning for the typical needs of these students while also allowing for an individualised approach to teaching and learning that is domain-specific. Five domains that have been identified include the communicative domain, the social domain, the emotional well-being domain, the academic domain, and the physical domain. Challenges faced by 2e girls and girls with ASD and twice exceptionality within each domain will be examined, typical educational goals will be briefly discussed, and support strategies will be recommended.

Communicative Domain

Persistent difficulties in social communication and social interaction in multiple situations are key criteria for an ASD diagnosis (American Psychiatric Association, 2013). Referred to as *theory of mind* by Premack and Woodruff (1978) in their seminal work, the ability to understand and predict the behaviour of others is considered vital to the development of social and emotional competencies such as the formation of friendships, understanding the emotions of others, and taking another's perspective. These skills are also considered as paramount for future academic success (Raver & Knitzer, 2002) as well as mental health, and well-being (Baker, Lang, & O'Reilly, 2009). For girls with ASD, these core deficits are often displayed as difficulties in understanding and labelling emotions (Baron-Cohen, Golan, & Ashwin, 2009), including learning the language of emotions (Lartseva, Dijkstra, & Buitelaar, 2015), which can lead to communicative challenges in social situations.

Typical goals for younger girls with ASD to support communication and learning needs include direct teaching of interpersonal communicative skills, such as turn-taking, pausing, tone, gestural use and conversation cues, as well as creating non-threatening opportunities to practise, and develop these skills with accommodating peers (Attwood, 2017). Additional goals include learning the language of emotions through direct teaching of vocabulary and visual associations, exposure and practice of social interaction skills when communicating with different people in different contexts and increasing knowledge of the use of various linguistic features of the English language, such as metaphors (Conallen & Reed, 2016; Lartseva et al., 2015). For adolescent girls, the need for specific skills to navigate the use of language in the social world increases in importance, and the ability to express their emotions in a positive and healthy way is critical to overall health and well-being (Baker et al., 2009).

As communication challenges are a hallmark of most students with ASD, identifying effective strategies is paramount to their academic and social success. Brunner and Seung (2009) conducted a literature review into the efficacy of communication-based treatments for ASD, their conclusions supporting Goldstein's (2002) findings of considerable evidence for the effectiveness of strategies involving applied behavioural analysis and naturalistic behavioural strategies. Critics of these methods have cited inadequate generalisation, a lack of motivation, and prompt dependency as detractors to their success (Simpson, 2001). Emerging research on practices such as peer-mediated intervention, use of visual supports and self-monitoring techniques also identified these as effective (Odom et al., 2003).

While none of these reviews specifically focused on girls with ASD, parents, teachers, and professionals rely on findings such as these to make informed choices when selecting strategies. Strategies more commonly accessed to address the communication needs of girls with ASD rely on functional communication training (Battaglia, 2017) and milieu teaching, creating opportunities to put skills into practice in authentic situations for the key areas of need. In terms of assisting girls with ASD to improve their understanding of the language of emotions, resources such as CAT-kit (*Cognitive Affective Training*; Attwood, 2017) have successfully been used by psychologists to deliver affective education to assist individuals with ASD to identify and measure emotional intensities and find alternative ways to express emotions. In terms of communicating with adults and peers, keeping statements and instructions simple and not assuming they have been understood are helpful (Faherty, 2000). Finally, assistance for understanding metaphors and figures of speech has also been endorsed (Auger, 2013; Stuart-Hamilton, 2004).

For 2e girls with ASD, there is little direct research with regard to their communicative skills and challenges. More broadly, Klin et al. (2007) measured 187 male high-functioning students with ASD at 1.5 to 2 standard deviations below the mean on the communicative aspects of adaptive functioning scales, and a single study on a gifted boy with ASD focused on his metalinguistic abilities rather than on his generalised communication skills and reinforced the need to assess "the meta-level of the verbal competencies of gifted children with ASD" (Melogno, Pinot, & Levi, 2015, p. 113). This scarcity of information along gender lines and the discrepancies between findings across domains significantly limit recommendations, prompting the call for further research.

Social Domain

Within the social domain, girls with ASD exhibit difficulties that increase over time as the peer group gains in influence in adolescence and beyond (Kopp & Gillberg, 2011). Girls with ASD have reported social interactions as challenging for them (Dean et al., 2014), particularly during adolescence where new demands for social adaptation arise (Hsaio, et al., 2013); similar findings impact on both 2e students (Shea & Mesibov, 2013) and gifted girls (Price, Wardman, Bruce, & Millward, 2016; Silverman, 2000). In a case study comparing a gifted girl with ASD and a gifted girl with no ASD diagnosis, Assouline et al. (2009) found a significant divergence in their social and adaptive behaviours, suggesting the importance of understanding and supporting such needs for overall enhanced well-being. Crucial to success in this domain are several factors, most notably the desire to make real friends, belong to a group, and navigate participation in the peer group, including managing bullying and exclusion (Hsaio et al., 2013). Aspects of the communicative domain that overlap include understanding the use of language in social interactions, in particular understanding facial expressions and interpreting tone of voice (e.g., when sarcasm is being used).

Typical social goals for 2e girls with ASD include the development of a better understanding of the covert rules of friendships. Seeking support for such development can be thwarted due to the masking of social difficulties. The success or failure of any intervention strategy is often veiled due to a lack of research-based evidence (Tierney, Burns, & Kilbey, 2016). Often, not until the emergence of secondary mental health issues, are attempts made by clinicians and support staff to look for social difficulties behind the mask. Masking is not assessed in diagnostic procedures yet is a well-documented strategy used by both gifted girls (Rudasill, Foust, & Callahan, 2007; Silverman, 2007) and 2e girls with ASD, particularly in adolescence, often leading to delays in diagnosis, clinical attention and intervention services (Mandy et al., 2012).

Programs that teach social skills, rules of friendship and conflict resolution skills have been recommended to support girls with ASD to navigate the social milieu;

however, very few studies have investigated the nature and extent of social support available for individuals with ASD (Symes & Humphrey, 2010) and even less with a focus on girls with ASD. Similarly, very few investigations of exclusion and bullying of students with ASD exist (Wainscot, Naylor, Sutcliffe, Tantam, & Williams, 2008). This lack of research makes identification of effective strategies for 2e girls with ASD highly challenging.

Students with ASD who experience social intimidation, bullying, and exclusion, which occur more frequently in adolescence (Humphrey & Symes, 2010), often benefit from the whole-school anti-bullying approaches and programs. Reinforcement from protective strategies such as peer support groups and safe spaces (Shochet et al., 2016) also assists to promote tolerance at school (Watkins, Zimmermann, & Poling, 2014), though these do not necessarily equate to 'real' friendships. In fact, little research-based evidence exists on the success or otherwise of intervention strategies targeting the covert rules of friendship (Tierney et al., 2016), though the *Social Tools and Rules for Teens* (START) Program allows for both the delivery of "a traditional didactic social cognition curriculum with experiential learning opportunities" (Vernon, Miller, Ko, Barrett, & McGarry, 2018, p. 1). The immersive aspect of the program has been found to provide students with both enjoyment and therapeutic benefits, though no data specific to girls with ASD was generated (Vernon et al., 2018).

Despite its perceived effectiveness by many, Attwood (1998) has suggested that teaching social skills in clinics does not always transfer to other contexts and can lead to an increase in teasing (Abele & Grenier, 2005). Similarly, the effectiveness of school-based social skills training programs for students with ASD has been found to be minimal, with little generalisation across participants and settings (Bellini, Peters, Benner, & Hopf, 2007). More recently, the efficacy of the well-regarded *Secret Agent Society* (SAS) program (Social Skills Training Institute, 2017) has been explored, with meaningful gains in social-emotional functioning and generalisation to the home environment that has challenged previous findings (Beaumont, Rotolone, & Sofronoff, 2015).

Research also suggests that students with ASD participate in leisure activities with less frequency and with less variety of environments and peers than neurotypical students (Rodger & Umaibalan, 2011). Studies have also found that the more solitary activities provide the most enjoyment for students with ASD compared to social activities (Eversole et al., 2016). With an increased interest in social relationships emerging in adolescence (Shea & Mesibov, 2013), participation in social and recreational activities has been endorsed (Orsmond, Krauss, & Seltzer, 2004) though not well-evaluated (Potvin, Snider, Prelock, Kehayia, & Wood-Dauphinee, 2013), particularly for 2e girls or girls with ASD.

Emotional Well-Being Domain

The emotional well-being of girls with ASD is an area fraught with needs that are more frequently manifesting at clinical levels in childhood, with a tendency to increase significantly in adolescence and lasting into adulthood (Tierney et al.,

2016). The literature regarding the social skills of gifted individuals and their associated well-being underscores a variation in difficulties depending on the level of giftedness of the individual (Neihart, 1999). The emotional well-being of 2e girls with ASD, then, is an area with many challenges. Self-esteem, for example, is frequently eroded due to perfectionism and executive functioning challenges (Foley-Nicpon et al., 2011). Social intimidation due to poor interpersonal social skills also contributes to reducing the self-esteem of girls with 2e and ASD (Tierney et al., 2016).

For girls with ASD, a range of comorbid conditions are consistently identified as affecting their emotional well-being. These include perfectionism, anxiety (Reaven et al., 2009), and depression (Solomon et al., 2012), as well as other significant disorders including OCD, ODD, and eating and sleeping disorders (Jamison & Schuttler, 2017). School refusal is identified as a well-used strategy by girls with ASD who are not coping with the complexity of the school environment, and withdrawal from interactions with family members and support systems can also occur. These behaviours require specific and targeted interventions, often outside of the scope and expertise of the school. For gifted girls, on the other hand, there is still no consensus that they are more at risk than their neurotypical peers for a significant number of comorbidities, such as eating and sleeping disorders (Cross, Cassady, Dixon, & Adams, 2008; Neihart, 1999), suggesting giftedness may act as a protective factor.

Typical emotional well-being goals for 2e girls with ASD within schools include identifying antecedents and triggers of behaviours associated with the above-listed comorbid disorders from the broader educational context and explicitly managing these antecedents and triggers within the school setting in order to reduce the incidence of disorders developing (Foley-Nicpon & Assouline, 2015). Tracking and monitoring the emotional well-being of all students is paramount practice for issues to be dealt with in a timely manner and to ensure referrals to appropriate out-of-school professionals occur promptly as needed. As many comorbidities require specialised intervention, sensitive management is required by school staff, who often do not have the professional expertise to deal with such complex presentations (Lai et al., 2011). The collaborative interface between professionals and school personnel can assist in the development and implementation of management plans based on the phase of treatment or intervention, supported by resources available based on building strengths and addressing the weaknesses of 2e girls with ASD (Mendaglo & Peterson, 2006). The identification of both protective and risk factors, psychopharmacological interventions, and ongoing cognitive behaviour therapy, and associated approaches has shown success in reducing symptoms from psychiatric comorbidities (Kreslins, Robertson, & Melville, 2015; Reaven et al., 2009) and promoting mental health, well-being, and adaptive functioning in students with ASD (Francis, 2005).

Frequently, issues impacting the emotional well-being of girls with ASD manifest within the school setting, and it is in this authentic setting that strategies can be applied and evaluated. Furthermore, 2e students with ASD who show academic decline and school refusal—outcomes that are often linked with perfectionism, anxiety, and depression—benefit from support through regular meetings with school counsellors or pastoral care teachers to develop better adaptive and coping strategies that are endorsed (Auger, 2013), though research on the effectiveness of such an approach for 2e students is limited (Foley-Nicpon & Assouline, 2015). Further effective strategies include the identification of personal strengths and talents, particularly beneficial for 2e students (Baum, Schader, & Hébert, 2014) as well as self-monitoring (Henderson, et al., 2015). Both school-wide pastoral care approaches that promote early intervention to develop resilience (Gerard, 2018; Shochet et al., 2016) and programs to develop a positive self-concept (Jamison & Schuttler, 2017) have also been found to be efficacious.

Academic Domain

Academic success and self-determination as a learner with a disability are impacted by all aspects of school life (Solberg, Howard, Gresham, & Carter, 2012). For girls with ASD, difficulties with achieving academic success is not uncommon, particularly as challenges from other domains impact achievement. This problem is more pronounced for 2e girls with ASD who may not be demonstrating their full potential in the school setting (Foley-Nicpon et al., 2011).

Research on learning issues in girls with ASD has identified areas of concern to include aspects of literacy such as reading comprehension, spelling, and word decoding (Åsberg, Kopp, Berg-Kelly, & Gillberg, 2010). Despite word decoding and vocabulary training being used as key intervention strategies, reading comprehension skills still need to be monitored and supported. As individuals with ASD often display specialised and restricted interests, focusing reading comprehension on texts of high interest topics has been advised (Åsberg et al., 2010).

Girls with ASD have also been found to have life-long difficulties in producing narratives (Eigsti, de Marchena, Schuh, & Kelley, 2011; Kauschke, van der Beek, & Kamp-Becker, 2016). These difficulties have been ascribed not only to the theory of mind deficits, but also to executive functioning deficits in working memory, inhibition and goal maintenance that impact on planning and response inhibition (Gillam, Hartzheim, Studenka, Simonsmeier, & Gillam, 2015), and similar deficits have also been identified in 2e students with ASD (Assouline et al., 2012). Similarly, weak central coherence theory, which describes how students with ASD have a tendency towards giving attention to specific details at the expense of integrating information into holistic representations, has been found to contribute to difficulties in organising information into coherent stories (Loukousa & Moilanen, 2009). Systematic teaching strategies that focus on providing organisational scaffolds to teach specific language structures that serve to clarify the causal relationships between events have been found to be successful in 2e students with ASD (Gillam et al., 2015).

Brown and Coomes (2016) suggest that support for students with ASD in the academic domain is beginning to move:

> away from a deficit driven, medical model of disability towards concepts of social construction and social justice. Many of the best practices … include promoting equity, valuing neurodiversity, empowering the student, and promoting universal design. (p. 477)

The focus on functional limitations viewed as aspects of diversity rather than disability is now yielding more evidence of effective practices for students with ASD, though evidence specifically focused on girls with ASD is lacking in this area.

Bolic Baric, Hellberg, Kjellberg, and Hemmingsson (2016) identified the success of strategies such as differentiated teaching methods that focused on: individual learning preferences; modified assignments based on individual preferences; individualised schedules for assignments that supported planning and organisation of tasks; use of technology to support handwriting difficulties; and choice of content and form of learning based on individual interests, when available, as important supports for individuals with ASD. The authors have suggested that "academic support, for example, differentiated teaching methods, needs to be combined with social and emotional support, such as trusting relationships with teachers, in order for the support to be effective in the learning situation" (Bolic Baric et al., 2016, p. 191).

More specific research on individual strategies and approaches to support academic learning goals for students with ASD has endorsed a number of successful practices, including honouring a preference for predictability, order and consistency by structuring the classroom with routines, and displaying schedules to reduce anxiety over change (Adreon & Stella, 2001; Dahle & Gargiulo, 2004); providing visual supports, as these have been found to reduce the time between the instruction given and the commencement of the task, particularly for students with executive functioning difficulties (Dettmer, Simpson, Myles, & Ganz, 2000). Also, making provisions for each individual's learning preferences, cognitive abilities, strengths, and weaknesses (Baum et al., 2014), as well as accommodations for learning, such as, personalised homework, clear frameworks and explicit task and assessment guides (e.g., rubrics, word length parameters, subheadings), and additional time for assessments and exams are considered effective strategies for effective learning for ASD students (Attwood, 1998).

An emphasis on viewing 2e students as "gifted first and disabled second" (Nielsen, 2002, p. 105) promotes a focus on student strengths while addressing difficulties. Access to services such as academic enrichment and acceleration programs has been a mainstay of gifted education programming for decades (Nielsen, 2002) and has been particularly recommended for 2e students (Assouline et al., 2012), as often their giftedness is overlooked or masked by their disability (Foley-Nicpon et al., 2011), though behavioural and socialisation issues will need to be addressed consistently, even in these settings (Assouline & Whiteman, 2011). Further investigations for different ASD populations are warranted.

Physical Domain

Research indicates that 2e girls with ASD may have greater fine motor, balance, and coordination challenges than their neurotypical peers (Kopp, Beckung, & Gillberg, 2010). These difficulties affect their participation and success in multiple activities, from handwriting development in the early years to participation in team sports in later years, further impacting the potential to develop social skills among their peers (Memari, Ghaheri, Ziaee, Kordi, Hafizi, & Moshayedi, 2013). They may also experience sensory overload from difficulties processing their environment, affecting their participation in group work and their ability to concentrate during learning engagements, and creating further stress that impacts on their emotional well-being.

Typical physical/sensory goals for girls with ASD focus on the implementation of special provisions tailored to individual needs (Fox, 2014). With regard to fine motor, balance, and coordination issues, intervention and support in the early years eventually make way for accommodations and adjustments as individuals develop and acquire new skills or plateau in their development. Individual exercise programs have been recommended and found to be successful (Fox, 2014), while integration of physical education as part of health and fitness rather than a traditional sport class to reduce anxiety over physical performance has also produced improved results for girls with ASD (Safran, 2002). Interface with professionals, such as occupational therapists and physiotherapists, can also add value to school motor developmental programs, if put in place from the early years.

Additional goals for girls with ASD with sensory challenges include a consideration of and modifications to the learning environment to ensure individual sensory needs are identified and targeted. Such modifications are suggested by the authors that may also have a positive influence supporting 2e girls with ASD. Accommodations to lighting, temperature and noise levels are typical adjustments that initially are teacher-directed. Self-removal, breathing, music, stress balls, and fidgets are all examples of proven strategies (Angeli & Whitehorn, 2004). Teacher awareness and ongoing management of indicators or triggers of sensory aversions, seeking behaviours and overload are key to assisting students with ASD to function in the school setting (Klintwall et al., 2011). A progression to the implementation of self-advocacy and self-regulation strategies over time has been recommended also (Lewis, Marcus, Pate, & Dunn, 2002).

Clinicians have a significant role to play in the development and maintenance of motor skills and sensory responses of students with ASD (Fuentes, Mostofsky, & Bastian, 2009). Of the preferred evidence-based approaches of occupational therapy practitioners, the sensory integration and perceptual-motor approaches have been comprehensively reviewed and have yielded positive results in improving tactile function and decreasing sensory defensiveness, though small sample sizes have hampered generalisability (May-Benson & Koomar, 2010). The more successful interventions are those that have a degree of mindfulness of how they affect the social competence and socialisation of the individual (Koenig & Rudney, 2010). Therefore, peer understanding of individual needs and support is also recommended (Odom et al., 2003). Unfortunately, most therapeutic approaches still suffer from a lack of sufficient empirical evidence (Ashburner, Rodger, Ziviani, & Hinder, 2014).

Teaching and Other Recommended Interventions

As knowledge about and interest in ASD increases, a growing number of books are published each year offering information, tips, strategies, and practicalities for students with ASD that are usually aimed at parents and teachers. A range of books with a focus on girls with ASD is emerging, ranging from personal stories (e.g., Fleischmann & Fleischmann, 2012), books for young girls with ASD (e.g., Bulhak-Paterson, 2015) and for adolescent girls with ASD (e.g., Simone, 2010) to books offering practical solutions for parents and professionals (e.g., Lyons, 2010; Nichols, Moravcik, & Pulver Tetenbaum, 2009; Riley-Hall, 2012).

Though there is no definitive publication to date for schools that comprehensively reviews the efficacy of different strategies to support the needs of girls with ASD, there is sufficient interest in the field from academics, school systems, teachers, parents, and various gifted and ASD communities themselves to strive for some consensus on the success or otherwise of different types of support available. Examples of efforts to formalise such processes include the Government of South Australia's Ministerial Advisory Committee Students with Disabilities 2006 review of investigations into how schools in the state were meeting the needs of students with Asperger's syndrome (AS). Though not specifically focused on girls across the broader ASD spectrum, the findings serve to put quality educational practices in the spotlight, particularly as the then-current students and graduates with AS who were key stakeholders were consulted to augment the literature in the field (Ministerial Advisory Committee: Students with Disabilities, Government of South Australia, 2006). Similarly, in the United States, the *National Autism Center* sets about "addressing the need for evidence-based practice standards and providing guidelines for how to make choices about interventions" (2017a, p. 1). The results of the 2009 and 2015 phases identified a range of established, emerging, and unestablished treatments and called for more research into treatments, with a suggested focus on age groups and diagnostic populations (National Autism Center, 2017b). Empirical support for behaviourally based interventions also increased over the two phases (National Autism Center, 2017c).

Formal research across various disciplines, ministerial inquiries, national and international conferences on giftedness and ASD, the work of advocacy and support groups, and—most importantly—the input from individuals with ASD have all contributed to an increase in knowledge about how girls with ASD differ from boys and how their educational goals should best be met. As well as the domain-specific strategies listed above, overarching strategies to support the needs of these learners have been developed that encompass the overall approach needed to support girls with ASD, including 2e girls.

As noted, personalised learning plans have been recommended for individuals requiring additional support to access the curriculum. For girls with ASD, this continues to be a priority, as their presentation and functioning vary across different settings, and is often dependent on maturity and skill development, and deficits can remain well-masked (Bargiela, Steward, & Mandy, 2016; Lai et al., 2011). This is even more important for 2e girls, who often have their giftedness overlooked and underserved due to the prioritisation of their difficulties stemming from ASD (Foley-Nicpon et al., 2011). Knowledge of each student's learning profile, including cognitive strengths and challenges, is crucial to the development of realistic individual learning goals.

With a greater understanding by professionals and parents, opportunities have arisen for girls with ASD to increasingly become more active participants in the development and modification of their own individual coping strategies (Schulze, 2016). While this approach in no way negates the need for ongoing adult support and intervention, taking responsibility for one's own learning, including knowing how and when to enact special provisions and accommodations (e.g., self-removal to a quiet space when sensory overload is occurring), can lead to greater self-determination and success at school and in life (Schulze, 2016). Ultimately, there is no greater overarching strategy for girls with ASD and 2e girls than to provide a situation-specific and flexible approach to their educational needs.

Implications for Future Research

While interest in ASD as neurodiversity rather than disability is growing, there is still much research that needs to be undertaken in order to meet the needs of all students with ASD and in particular girls who are a significantly under-researched and underserved population. Similarly, very little is known about 2e girls with ASD and how to meet their learning needs (Assouline & Whiteman, 2011) due to the significant conceptual barrier that exists between the two fields of giftedness and ASD (Rubenstein, Pierson, Wilczynski, & Connolly, 2013). Foley-Nicpon et al. (2011), for example, have recommended not only the development of a research agenda for all 2e students, but have also suggested the continuation of the examination of each diagnosis or exceptionality individually and include an investigation of gender differences.

Many strategies that are implemented with 2e girls with ASD require further inquiry and examination as to their suitability across all domains (Assouline et al., 2012). Lack of empirical evidence for the use of certain practices, little specificity of focus on 2e girls with ASD, and delays in the research-into-practice process can leave students underserved and challenged further. The call for replicability of research—particularly in the Asia-Pacific region—to allow for wider generalisation of findings, however, sits in tension with the often highly individualised lived experiences and needs of unique individuals. Indeed, case study methodology is recommended, due to the relative rarity of the phenomenon (Assouline et al., 2009). In the community of researchers, there is a valid place for, as Davidson (2007) has recommended, the valorising of autistic women's autobiographical narratives to allow them to become "active agents who can at least partially shape the direction of future research" (p. 673). Insights into their individual worlds can serve to both identify meaning behind individual experiences and highlight the strategies 2e girls with ASD need to acquire over their developmental years and beyond.

Conclusion

While no two gifted girls with ASD present with the same profile, examination of the literature has identified patterns of behaviour across several domains representative of the challenges shared by these students (Foley-Nicpon et al., 2011). This information is critical for determining typical educational goals and responding to learning needs by selecting the best provisions to allow these students access to the curriculum. These provisions can be considered as appropriate when supported by empirically based research that evaluates existing teaching and learning strategies as well as identifies desired and unintended outcomes. Emerging interventions may also gain credibility when trials are scrutinised and evaluated.

Increased research on girls with ASD, including 2e girls, is constantly shaping the intervention landscape that leads to a re-examination of strategies for 'best fit' for this population of students. In this chapter, as an exploration of the provisions and priorities for girls with ASD and 2e girls in Australian school settings, we have determined areas of success and more importantly identified areas where generalisations are still being made where the research has not specifically targeted girls. As boys with ASD present significantly different to girls with ASD, the need for more research on intervention strategies for girls with twice exceptionality inclusive of ASD cannot be emphasised enough.

Cross-References

▶ Fostering Resilience in 'At-Risk' Gifted and Talented Young People
▶ Gifted and Twice-Exceptional Children in the South of the World: Chilean Students' Experiences Within Regular Classrooms
▶ Gifted Education in the Asia-Pacific: From the Past for the Future – An Introduction
▶ Identifying and Nurturing Diversely Gifted and Talented Students: Part III Introduction
▶ Rural Adolescent Gifted Girls: Exploring the Impact of Popular Culture on Their Talent Development
▶ Some Implications for the Future of Gifted Education in the Asia-Pacific
▶ Teachers' Knowledge and Understandings of Twice Exceptionality Across Australia

References

Abele, E., & Grenier, D. (2005). The language of social communication: Running pragmatics groups in schools and clinical settings. In L. J. Baker & L. A. Welkowitz (Eds.), *Asperger Syndrome: Intervening in schools, clinics, and communities* (pp. 217–241). New Jersey, NJ: Lawrence Erlbaum & Associates.

Adreon, D., & Stella, J. (2001). Transition to middle and high school: Increasing the success of students with Asperger Syndrome. *Intervention in School and Clinic, 36*(5), 266–272. https://doi.org/10.1177/105345120103600502

American Psychiatric Association. (2013). *Diagnostic and statistical manual of mental disorders* (5th ed.). Washington, DC: Author.

Angeli, S., & Whitehorn, K. (2004). *Making sense of the seven senses*. Adelaide, SA: Autism SA.

Åsberg, J., Kopp, S., Berg-Kelly, K., & Gillberg, C. (2010). Reading comprehension, word decoding and spelling in girls with autism spectrum disorders (ASD) or attention-deficit/hyperactivity disorder (AD/HD): performance and predictors. *International Journal of Language and Communication Disorders, 45*(1), 61–71. https://doi.org/10.3109/13682820902745438

Ashburner, J. K., Rodger, S. A., Ziviani, J. M., & Hinder, E. A. (2014). Optimizing participation of children with autism spectrum disorder experiencing sensory challenges: A clinical reasoning framework. *Canadian Journal of Occupational Therapy, 81*(1), 29–38. https://doi.org/10.1177/0008417413520440

Assouline, S. G., Foley-Nicpon, M., & Dockery, L. (2012). Predicting the academic achievement of gifted students with autism spectrum disorder. *Journal of Autism and Developmental Disorders, 42*(9), 1781–1789. https://doi.org/10.1007/s10803-011-1403-x

Assouline, S. G., Foley-Nicpon, M., & Doobay, A. (2009). Profoundly gifted girls and autism spectrum disorder: A psychometric case study comparison. *The Gifted Child Quarterly, 53*(2), 89–105. https://doi.org/10.1177/0016986208330565

Assouline, S. G., Foley-Nicpon, M., & Whiteman, C. (2010). Cognitive and Psychosocial characteristics of gifted students with written language disability. *The Gifted Child Quarterly, 20*(10), 14. https://doi.org/10.1177/0016986209355974

Assouline, S. G., & Whiteman, C. S. (2011). Twice exceptionality: Implications for school psychologists in the Post-IDEA 2004 era. *Journal of Applied School Psychology, 24*(4), 380–402. https://doi.org/10.1080/15377903.2011.616576

Attwood, T. (1998). *Asperger Syndrome: A guide for parents and professionals*. London, UK: Jessica Kingsley Publishers.

Attwood, T. (2017). The CAT-kit. Retrieved 7 Nov 2017 from http://www.tonyattwood.com.au/the-cat-kit

Auger, R. W. (2013). Autism spectrum disorders: A research review for school counsellors. *Professional School Counseling, 16*(4), 256–268. https://doi.org/10.5330/PSC.n.2013-16.256

Baker, E., Richdale, A., Short, M., & Gradisar, M. (2013). An investigation of sleep patterns in adolescents with high-functioning autism spectrum disorder compared with typically developing adolescents. *Developmental Neurorehabilitation, 16*(3), 155–165. https://doi.org/10.3109/175118423.2013.765518

Baker, S. D., Lang, R., & O'Reilly, M. (2009). Review of video modeling with students with emotional and behavioral disorders. *Education and Treatment of Children, 32*(3), 403–420.

Baldwin, S., & Costley, D. (2016). The experiences and needs of female adults with high-functioning autism spectrum disorder. *Autism, 20*(4), 483–495. https://doi.org/10.1177/1362361315590805

Bargiela, S., Steward, R., & Mandy, W. (2016). The experiences of late-diagnosed women with autism spectrum conditions: An investigation of the female autism phenotype. *Journal of Autism and Developmental Disorders, 46*(10), 3281–3294. https://doi.org/10.1007/s10803-016-2872-8

Baron-Cohen, S., Golan, O., & Ashwin, E. (2009). Can emotion recognition be taught to children with autism spectrum conditions? *Philosophical Transactions of the Royal Society, B: Biological Sciences, 364*(1535), 3567–3574. https://doi.org/10.1098/rstb.2009.0191

Battaglia, D. (2017). Functional communication training in children with autism spectrum disorder. *Young Exceptional Children, 20*(1), 30–40. https://doi.org/10.1177/1096250615576809

Baum, S. M., Schader, R. M., & Hébert, T. P. (2014). Through a different lens: Reflecting on a strength-based, talent-focused approach for twice exceptional learners. *The Gifted Child Quarterly, 58*(4), 311–327. https://doi.org/10.1177/0016986214547632

Beaumont, R., Rotolone, C., & Sofronoff, K. (2015). The Secret Agent Society social skills program for children with high-functioning autism spectrum disorders: A comparison of two school variants. *Psychology in the Schools, 52*(4), 390–402. https://doi.org/10.1002/pits.21831

Bellini, S., Peters, J., Benner, L., & Hopf, A. (2007). A meta-analysis of school-based social skills interventions for children with autism spectrum disorders. *Remedial and Special Education, 28*(3), 153–162. https://doi.org/10.1177/07419325070280030401

Bolic Baric, V., Hellberg, K., Kjellberg, A., & Hemmingsson, H. (2016). Support for learning goes beyond academic support: Vices of students with Asperger's Disorder and Attention Deficit Hyperactivity Disorder. *The International Journal of Research and Practice, 20*(2), 183–195. https://doi.org/10.1177/1362361315574582

Brown, K. R., & Coomes, M. D. (2016). A spectrum of support: Current and best practices for students with autism spectrum disorder (ASD) at community colleges. *Community College Journal of Research and Practice, 40*(6), 465–479. https://doi.org/10.1080/10668926.2015.1067171

Brunner, D. L., & Seung, H. K. (2009). Evaluation of the efficacy of communication-based treatments for autism spectrum disorders. *Communication Disorders Quarterly, 31*(1), 15–41. https://doi.org/10.1177/1525740108324097

Bulhak-Paterson, D. (2015). *I am an Aspie girl*. London, UK: Jessica Kingsley Publishers.

Burger-Veltmeijer, A. E. J., Minnaert, A. E. M. G., & Van Houten-Van den Bosch, E. J. (2011). The co-occurrence of intellectual giftedness and autism spectrum disorders. *Educational Research Review, 6*(1), 67–88. https://doi.org/10.1016/j.edurev.2010.10.001

Conallen, K., & Reed, P. (2016). A teaching procedure to help children with autistic spectrum disorder to label emotions. *Research in Autism Spectrum Disorders, 23*, 63–72. https://doi.org/10.1016/j.rasd.2015.11.006

Crepeau-Hobson, F., & Bianco, M. (2011). Identification of gifted students with learning disabilities in a response-to-intervention era. *Psychology in the Schools, 48*(2), 102–109. https://doi.org/10.1002/pits.20528

Cross, T. L., Cassady, J. C., Dixon, F. A., & Adams, C. M. (2008). The psychology of gifted adolescents as measured by the MMPI-A. *The Gifted Child Quarterly, 52*(4), 326–339. https://doi.org/10.1177/0016986208321810

Dahle, K. B., & Gargiulo, R. M. (2004). Understanding Asperger disorder: A primer for early childhood educators. *Early Childhood Education Journal, 32*(3), 199–203. https://doi.org/10.1023/B:ECEJ.0000048973.89175.a3

Davidson, J. (2007). 'In a world of her own...': Re-presenting alienation and emotion in the lives and writings of women with autism. *Gender, Place and Culture, 14*(6), 659–677. https://doi.org/10.1080/0966360701659135

Dean, M., Kasari, C., Shih, W., Frankel, F., Whitney, R., Landa, R., ... Harwood, R. (2014). The peer relationships of girls with ASD at school: Comparison to boys and girls with and without ASD. *The Journal of Child Psychology and Psychiatry, 55*(11), 1218–1225. https://doi.org/10.1111/jcpp.12242

Dettmer, S., Simpson, R. L., Myles, B. S., & Ganz, J. B. (2000). The use of visual supports to facilitate transitions of students with autism. *Focus on Autism and Other Developmental Disabilities, 15*(3), 163–169. https://doi.org/10.1177/108835760001500307

Dickerson Mayes, S., Calhoun, S. L., Aggarwal, R., Baker, C., Mathapati, S., Anderson, R., & Petersen, C. (2012). Explosive, oppositional, and aggressive behavior in children with autism compared to other clinical disorders and typical children. *Research in Autism Spectrum Disorders, 6*(1), 1–10. https://doi.org/10.1016/j.rasd.2011.08.001

Ehrenreich-May, J., Storch, E. A., Queen, A. H., Hernandez Rodriguez, J., Ghilain, C. S., Alessandri, M, ... Wood, J. J. (2014). An open trial of cognitive-behavioral therapy for anxiety disorders in adolescents with autism spectrum disorders. *Focus on Autism and Other Developmental Disabilities, 29*(3), 145–155. https://doi.org/10.1177/1088357614533381

Eigsti, I.-M., de Marchena, A. B., Schuh, J. M., & Kelley, E. (2011). Language acquisition in autism spectrum disorders: A developmental review. *Research in Autism Spectrum Disorders, 5*(2), 681–691. https://doi.org/10.1016/j.rasd.2010.09.001

Eversole, M., Collins, D. M., Karmarkar, A., Colton, L., Phillips Quinn, J., Karsbaek, R., …Hilton, C. L. (2016). Leisure activity enjoyment of children with autism spectrum disorders. *Journal of Autism and Developmental Disorders, 46*(1), 10–20. https://doi.org/10.1007/s10803-015-2529-z

Faherty, C. (2000). *Asperger… what does it mean to me? Structured ideas for home and school*. Arlington, TX: Future Horizons.

Fleischmann, A., & Fleischmann, C. (2012). *Carly's voice: Breaking through autism*. New York, NY: Touchstone.

Foley-Nicpon, M., Allmon, A., Sieck, B., & Stinson, R. D. (2011). Empirical investigation of twice exceptionality: Where have we been and where are we going? *The Gifted Child Quarterly, 55*(1), 3–17. https://doi.org/10.1177/0016986210382575

Foley-Nicpon, M., & Assouline, S. G. (2015). Counseling considerations for the twice exceptional client. *Journal of Counseling & Development, 93*(2), 202–211. https://doi.org/10.1002/j.1556-6676.2015.00196.x

Foley-Nicpon, M., Assouline, S. G., & Colangelo, N. (2013). Twice exceptional learners: Who needs to know what? *The Gifted Child Quarterly, 57*(3), 169–180. https://doi.org/10.1177/0016986213490021

Fox, L. C. (2014). *Physical activity and adolescent girls with ASD: Effects of an individualized exercise program on cognitive, social, and physical-health indicators* (Unpublished doctoral dissertation). University of North Carolina, Chapel Hill, USA. Retrieved from https://cdr.lib.unc.edu/indexablecontent/uuid:38f63ab4-b106-43f6-8639-2c8590d286ac

Francis, K. (2005). Autism interventions: A critical update. *Developmental Medicine and Child Neurology, 47*(7), 493–499. https://doi.org/10.1111/j.1469-8749.2005.tb01178.x

Fuentes, C. T., Mostofsky, S. H., & Bastian, A. J. (2009). Children with autism show specific handwriting impairments. *Neurology, 73*(19), 1532–1537. https://doi.org/10.1212/WNL.0b013e3181c0d48c

Gerard, P. (2018). Evidence that low self-worth could be linked to anger and aggression in children with ASD. https://doi.org/10.17863/CAM.34882

Gillam, S. L., Hartzheim, D., Studenka, B., Simonsmeier, V., & Gillam, R. (2015). Narrative intervention for children with autism spectrum disorder (ASD). *Journal of Speech, Language, and Hearing Research, 58*, 920–933. https://doi.org/10.1044/2015_JSLHR-L-14-0295

Goldstein, H. (2002). Communication intervention for children with autism: A review of treatment efficacy. *Journal of Autism and Developmental Disorders, 32*(5), 373–396. https://doi.org/10.1023/A:1020589821992

Halladay, A. K., Bishop, S., Constantino, J. N., Daniels, A. M., Koenig, K., Palmer, K., … Taylor, J. L. (2015). Sex and gender differences in autism spectrum disorder: Summarizing evidence gaps and identifying emerging areas of priority. *Molecular Autism, 6*(1), 36–40. https://doi.org/10.1186/s13229-015-0019-y

Henderson, H. A., Ono, K. E., McMahon, C. M., Schwartz, C. B., Usher, L. V., & Mundy, P. C. (2015). The costs and benefit of self-monitoring for higher functioning children and adolescents with autism. *Journal of Autism and Developmental Disorders, 45*(2), 548–559. https://doi.org/10.1007/s10803-013-1968-7

Hsaio, M.-N., Tseng, W.-L., Huang, H.-Y., & Gau, S. S.-F. (2013). Effects of autistic traits on social and school adjustment in children and adolescents: The moderating roles of age and gender. *Research in Developmental Disabilities, 34*(1), 254–265. https://doi.org/10.1016/j.ridd.2012.08.001

Humphrey, N., & Symes, W. (2010). Perceptions of social support and experience of bullying among pupils with autistic spectrum disorders in mainstream secondary schools. *European Journal of Special Needs Education, 25*(1), 77–91. https://doi.org/10.1080/08856250903450855

Jamison, T. R., & Schuttler, J. O. (2017). Overview and preliminary evidence for a social skills and self-care curriculum for adolescent females with autism: The Girls Night Out model. *Journal of Autism and Developmental Disorders, 47*(1), 110–125. https://doi.org/10.1007/s10803-016-2939-6

Kauschke, C., van der Beek, B., & Kamp-Becker, I. (2016). Narratives of girls and boys with autism spectrum disorders: Gender differences in narrative competence and internal state language. *Journal of Autism and Developmental Disorders, 46*(3), 840–852. https://doi.org/10.1007/s10803-015-2620-5

Klin, A., Saulnier, C., Sparrow, S., Cicchetti, D., Volkmar, F., & Lord, C. (2007). Social and communication abilities and disabilities in higher functioning individuals with autism spectrum disorders: Vineland and the ADOS. *Journal of Autism and Developmental Disorders, 37*(4), 748–759. https://doi.org/10.1007/s10803-006-0229-4

Klintwall, L., Holm, A., Eriksson, M., Carlsson, L. H., Olsson, M. B., Hedvall, A., ... Fernell, E. (2011). Sensory abnormalities in autism: A brief report. *Research in Developmental Disabilities, 32*(2), 795–800. https://doi.org/10.1016/j.ridd.2010.10.021

Koenig, K. P., & Rudney, S. G. (2010). Performance challenges for children and adolescents with difficulty processing and integrating sensory information: A systematic review. *American Journal of Occupational Therapy, 64*(3), 430–442. https://doi.org/10.5014/ajot.2010.09073

Kopp, S., Beckung, E., & Gillberg, C. (2010). Developmental coordination disorder and other motor control problems in girls with autism spectrum disorder and/or attention-deficit/hyperactivity disorder. *Research in Developmental Disabilities, 31*(2). https://doi.org/10.1016/j.ridd.2009.09.017

Kopp, S., & Gillberg, C. (2011). The Autism Spectrum Screening Questionnaire (ASSQ)-Revised Extended Version (ASSQ-REV): An instrument for better capturing the autism phenome type in girls? A preliminary study involving 191 clinical cases and community controls. *Research in Developmental Disabilities, 32*(6), 2875–2888. https://doi.org/10.1016/j.ridd.2011.05.017

Kreiser, N. L., & White, S. W. (2015). ASD traits and co-occurring psychopathology: The moderating role of gender. *Journal of Autism and Developmental Disorders, 45*(12), 3932–3938. https://doi.org/10.1007/s10803-015-2580-9

Kreslins, A., Robertson, A. E., & Melville, C. (2015). The effectiveness of psychosocial interventions for anxiety in children and adolescents with autism spectrum disorder: A systematic review and meta-analysis. *Child and Adolescent Psychiatry and Mental Health, 9*(22), 1–12. https://doi.org/10.1186/s13034-015-0054-7

Lai, M.-C., Lombardo, M. V., Auyeung, B., Chakrabarti, B., & Baron-Cohen, S. (2015). Sex/gender differences in autism: Setting the scene for future research. *Journal of the American Academy of Child & Adolescent Psychiatry, 54*(1), 11–24. https://doi.org/10.1016/j.jaac.2014.10.003

Lai, M.-C., Lombardo, M. V., Pasco, G., Ruigrok, A. N. V., Wheelwright, S. J., Sadek, S. A., ...Baron-Cohen, S. (2011). A behavioral comparison of male and female adults with high functioning autism spectrum conditions. *PLoS One, 6*(6), e20835. https://doi.org/10.1371/journal.pone.0020835

Lartseva, A., Dijkstra, T., & Buitelaar, J. K. (2015). Emotional language processing in autism spectrum disorders: A systematic review. *Frontiers in Human Neuroscience, 8*, 1–24. https://doi.org/10.3389/fnhum.2014.00991

Lewin, A., Wood, J., Gunderson, S., Murphy, T., & Storch, E. (2011). Phenomenology of comorbid autism spectrum and obsessive-compulsive disorders among children. *Journal of Developmental and Physical Disabilities, 23*(6), 543–553. https://doi.org/10.1007/s10882-011-9247-z

Lewis, B. A., Marcus, B. H., Pate, R. R., & Dunn, A. L. (2002). Psychosocial mediators of physical activity behavior among adults and children. *American Journal of Preventive Medicine, 23*(2, Supplement 1), 26–35. https://doi.org/10.1016/S0749-3979(02)00471-3

Loukousa, S., & Moilanen, I. (2009). Pragmatic inference abilities in individuals with Asperger syndrome or high-functioning autism. A review. *Research in Autism Spectrum Disorders, 3*(4), 890–904. https://doi.org/10.1016/j.rasd.2009.05.002

Lupart, J. L., & Toy, R. E. (2009). Twice exceptional: Multiple pathways to success. In L. V. Shavinina (Ed.), *International handbook on giftedness* (pp. 507–525). New York, NY: Springer.

Lyons, T. (2010). *1,001 tips for the parents of autistic girls: Everything you need to know about diagnosis, doctors, schools, taxes, vacations, babysitters, treatment, food, and more*. New York, NY: Skyhorse Publishing.

Maker, C. J. (1986). Developing scope and sequence in curriculum. *The Gifted Child Quarterly, 30*(4), 151–158. https://doi.org/10.1177/001698628603000402

Mandy, W., Chilvers, R., Chowdhury, U., Salter, G., Seigal, A., & Skuse, D. (2012). Sex differences in autism spectrum disorder: Evidence from a large sample of children and adolescents. *Journal of Autism and Developmental Disorders, 42*(7), 1304–1313. https://doi.org/10.1007/s10803-011-1356-0

May-Benson, T., & Koomar, J. A. (2010). Systematic review of the research evidence examining the effectiveness of interventions using a sensory integrative approach for children. *American Journal of Occupational Therapy, 64*(3), 403–414. https://doi.org/10.5014/ajot2010.09071

McCoach, D. B., Kehle, T. J., Bray, M. A., & Siegle, D. (2001). Best practices in the identification of gifted students with learning disabilities. *Psychology in the Schools, 38*(5), 403–411. https://doi.org/10.1002/pits.1029

Melogno, S., Pinot, M. A., & Levi, G. (2015). Profile of the linguistic and metalinguistic abilities of a gifted child with autism spectrum disorder: A case study. *Child Language Teaching and Therapy, 31*(1), 113–126. https://doi.org/10.1177/0265659014530414

Memari, A. H., Gaheri, B., Ziaee, V., Kordi, R., Hafizi, S., & Moshayedi, P. (2013). Physical activity in children and adolescents with autism assessed by triaxial accelerometry. *Pediatric Obesity, 8*(2), 150–158. https://doi.org/10.1111/j.2047-6310.2012.00101.x

Mendaglo, S., & Peterson, J. S. (2006). *Models of counseling gifted children, adolescents, and young adults*. Waco, TX: Prufrock Press.

Ministerial Advisory Committee: Students with Disabilities, Government of South Australia. (2006). *Quality educational practices for students with Asperger syndrome*. Adelaide, SA: Author. Retrieved from https://www.decd.sa.gov.au/sites/g/files/net691/f/educational-practices-students-aspergers.pdf

Ministerial Council on Education, Employment, Training and Youth Affairs (MCEETYA). (2008). *Melbourne declaration on educational goals for young Australians*. Melbourne, VIC: Author. Retrieved from http://www.mceecdya.edu.au/verve/_resources/National_Declaration_on_the_Educational_Goals_for_Young_Australians.pdf

Moon, S. M. (2002). Gifted children with attention-deficit/hyperactivity disorder. In M. Neihart, S. Reis, N. Robinson, & S. Moon (Eds.), *The social and emotional development of gifted children: What do we know?* (pp. 193–201). Waco, TX: Prufrock Press.

National Autism Center. (2017a). National standards project. Retrieved from http://www.nationalautismcenter.org/national-standards-project/

National Autism Center. (2017b). Significant findings, Phase 1 of the project. Retrieved from http://www.nationalautismcenter.org/national-standards-project/history/significant-findings/

National Autism Center. (2017c). Significant findings, Phase 2. Retrieved from http://www.nationalautismcenter.org/national-standards-project/phase-2/significant-findings/

Neihart, M. (1999). The impact of giftedness on psychological well-being: What does the empirical literature say? *Roeper Review, 22*(1), 10–17. https://doi.org/10.1080/02783199909553991

Nichols, S., Moravcik, G. M., & Pulver Tetenbaum, S. (2009). *Girls growing up on the Autism Spectrum: What parents and professionals should know about the pre-teen and teenage years*. London, UK: Jessica Kingsley Publishers.

Nielsen, M. E. (2002). Gifted students with learning disabilities: Recommendations for identification and programming. *Exceptionality, 10*(2), 93–111. https://doi.org/10.1207/S15627035EX1002_4

Nolen-Hoeksema, S., & Girgus, J. S. (1994). The emergence of gender differences in depression during adolescence. *Psychological Bulletin, 115*(3), 424–443. https://doi.org/10.1037/0033-2909.115.3.424

Odom, S., Brown, W., Frey, T., Karasu, N., Smith-Canter, L., & Strain, P. (2003). Evidence-based practices for young children with autism: Contributions for single-subject design research. *Focus on Autism & Other Developmental Disabilities, 18*(3), 166–175. https://doi.org/10.1177/10883576030180030401

Orsmond, G. I., Krauss, M. W., & Seltzer, M. M. (2004). Peer relationships and social and recreational activities among adolescents and adults with autism. *Journal of Autism and Developmental Disabilities, 34*(3), 245–256. https://doi.org/10.1023/B:JADD.0000029547.96610.df

Peterson, J. S., & Ray, K. E. (2006). Bullying among the gifted: The subjective experience. *The Gifted Child Quarterly, 50*(3), 252–269. https://doi.org/10.1177/001698620605000305

Pinborough-Zimmerman, J., Satterfield, R., Miller, J., Bilder, D., Hossain, S., & McMahon, W. (2007). Communication disorders: Prevalence and comorbid intellectual disability, autism, and Emotional/Behavioral disorders. *American Journal of Speech-Language Pathology, 16*(4), 359–367. https://doi.org/10.1044/1058-0360(2007/039)

Potvin, M.-C., Snider, L., Prelock, P., Kehayia, E., & Wood-Dauphinee, S. (2013). Recreational participation of children with high functioning autism. *Journal of Autism and Developmental Disorders, 43*(2), 445–457. https://doi.org/10.1007/s10803-012-1589-6

Premack, D., & Woodruff, G. (1978). Does the chimpanzee have a theory of mind. *Behavioral and Brain Sciences, 1*(4), 515–526. https://doi.org/10.1017/S0140525X00076512

Price, E., Wardman, J., Bruce, T., & Millward, P. (2016). The juggling act: A phenomenological study of gifted and talented girls' experiences with Facebook. *Roeper Review, 38*(3), 162–174. https://doi.org/10.1080/02783193.2016.1183738

Raver, C. C., & Knitzer, J. (2002). *Ready to enter: What research tells policymakers about strategies to promote social and emotional readiness among three and four year olds*. New York, NY: National Center for Children in Poverty.

Reaven, J. A., Blakeley-Smith, A., Nicols, S., Dasari, M., Flanigan, E., & Hepburn, S. (2009). Cognitive-behavioral group treatment for anxiety symptoms in children with high functioning autism spectrum disorders: A pilot study. *Focus on Autism and other Developmental Disabilities, 24*(1), 27–37. https://doi.org/10.1177/1088357608327666

Riley-Hall, E. (2012). *Parenting girls on the Autism Spectrum: Overcoming the challenges and celebrating the gifts*. London, UK: Jessica Kingsley Publishers.

Rodger, S., & Umaibalan, V. (2011). The routines and rituals of families of typically developing children compared with families of children with autism spectrum disorder: An exploratory study. *British Journal of Occupational Therapy, 74*(1), 20–26. https://doi.org/10.4276/030802211X12947686093567

Ronksley-Pavia, M. (2015). A model of twice exceptionality: Explaining and defining the apparent paradoxical combination of disability and giftedness in childhood. *Journal for the Education of the Gifted, 38*(3), 318–340. https://doi.org/10.1177/0162353215592499

Ronksley-Pavia, M., & Townend, G. (2016). Student voice: Listening and responding to the experiences of twice exceptional students. *TalentEd, 62*, 4–18.

Rowan, L., & Townend, G. (2016). Early career teachers' beliefs about their preparedness to teach: Implications for the professional development of teachers working with gifted and twice exceptional students. *Cogent Education, 3*(1), 1–25. https://doi.org/10.1080/2331186X.2016.1242458

Rubenstein, L. D., Pierson, E. E., Wilczynski, S. M., & Connolly, S. C. (2013). Fitting the high ability program to the needs of individuals with autism spectrum disorders. *Psychology in the Schools, 50*(9), 910–922. https://doi.org/10.1002/pits.21719

Rudasill, K. M., Foust, R. C., & Callahan, C. M. (2007). The social coping questionnaire: An examination of its structure with an American sample of gifted adolescents. *Journal for the Education of the Gifted, 30*(3), 353–371. https://doi.org/10.1177/016235320703000304

Safran, J. S. (2002). Supporting students with Asperger syndrome in general education. *Teaching Exceptional Children, 34*(5), 60–66. https://doi.org/10.1177/004005990203400510

Schulze, M. M. (2016). Self-management strategies to support students with ASD. *Teaching Exceptional Children, 48*(5), 225–231. https://doi.org/10.1177/0040059916640759

Sharpley, C. F., Bitsika, V., Andronicos, N. M., & Agnew, L. L. (2016). Further evidence of HPA-axis dysregulation and its correlation with depression in autism spectrum disorders: Data from girls. *Physiology & Behavior, 167*, 110–117. https://doi.org/10.1016/j.physbeh.2016.09.003

Shea, V., & Mesibov, G. B. (2013). Adolescents and adults with autism. In F. R. Volkmar, R. Paul, A. Klin, & D. Cohen (Eds.), *Handbook of autism and pervasive developmental disorders* (Vol. 1, 3rd ed., pp. 288–311). New York, NY: Wiley.

Shefcyk, A. (2015). Count us in: Addressing gender disparities in autism research. *Autism, 19*(2), 131–132. https://doi.org/10.1177/1362361314566585

Shochet, I. M., Saggers, B. R., Carrington, S. B., Orr, J. A., Wurfl, A. M., Duncan, B. M., & Smith, C. L. (2016). The cooperative research centre for living with autism (CRC) conceptual model to promote mental health for adolescents with ASD. *Clinical Child and Family Psychology Review, 19*(2), 94–116. https://doi.org/10.1007/s10567-016-0203-4

Silverman, L. K. (2000). Social development, leadership and gender issues. In L. K. Silverman (Ed.), *Counseling the gifted and talented* (2nd ed., pp. 291–327). Denver, CO: Love.

Silverman, L. K. (2007). Asynchrony: A new definition of giftedness. *Duke Gifted Letter, 7*(2). Retrieved from http://tip-dev.oit.duke.edu/node/839

Simone, R. (2010). *Aspergirls: Empowering females with Asperger syndrome*. London, UK: Jessica Kingsley Publishers.

Simpson, R. L. (2001). ABA and students with autism spectrum disorders: Issues and considerations for effective practice. *Focus on Autism & Other Developmental Disabilities, 16*(2), 68–71. https://doi.org/10.1177/108835760101600202

Social Skills Training Institute. (2017). *Secret agent society: Solving the mystery of social encounters*. Retrieved from https://www.sst-institute.net/

Solberg, V. S., Howard, K., Gresham, S., & Carter, E. (2012). Quality learning experiences, self-determination, and academic success: A path analytic study among youth with disabilities. *Career Development and Transition for Exceptional Individuals, 35*(2), 85–96. https://doi.org/10.1177/0885728812439887

Solomon, M., Miller, M., Taylor, S. L., Hinshaw, S. P., & Carter, C. S. (2012). Autism symptoms and internalyzing psychopathology in girls and boys with autism spectrum disorders. *Journal of Autism and Developmental Disorders, 42*(1), 48–59. https://doi.org/10.1007/s10803-011-1215-z

Stewart, C. S., McEwen, F. S., Konstantellou, A., Eisler, I., & Simic, M. (2017). Impact of ASD traits on treatment outcomes on eating disorders in girls. *European Eating Disorders Review, 25*(2), 123–128. https://doi.org/10.1002/erv.2497

Stuart-Hamilton, I. (2004). *An Asperger dictionary of everyday expressions*. London, UK: Jessica Kingsley Publishers.

Symes, W., & Humphrey, N. (2010). Peer-group indicators of social inclusion among pupils with autistic spectrum disorders (ASD) in mainstream secondary schools: A comparative study. *School Psychology International, 31*(5), 478–494. https://doi.org/10.1177/0143034310382496

Tierney, S., Burns, J., & Kilbey, E. (2016). Looking behind the mask: Social coping strategies of girls on the autistic spectrum. *Research in Autism Spectrum Disorders, 23*, 73–83. https://doi.org/10.1016/j.rasd.2015.11.013

Townend, G., & Brown, R. (2016). Exploring a sociocultural approach to understanding academic self-concept in twice exceptional students. *International Journal of Educational Research, 80*, 15–24. https://doi.org/10.1016/j.ijer.2016.07.006

Townend, G., & Pendergast, D. (2015). Student voice: What can we learn from twice exceptional students about the teacher's role in enhancing or inhibiting academic self-concept. *Australasian Journal of Gifted Education, 24*(1), 37–51. Retrieved from https://core.ac.uk/download/pdf/143899736.pdf

Townend, G., Pendergast, D., & Garvis, S. (2014). Academic self-concept in twice exceptional students: What the literature tells us. *TalentEd, 28*(1/2), 75–89.

Vail, P. L. (1989). *Smart kids with school problems: Things to know and ways to help*. New York, NY: Plume.

Vernon, T. W., Miller, A. R., Ko, J. A., Barrett, A. C., & McGarry, E. S. (2018). A randomized controlled trial of the Social Tools and Rules for Teens (START) program: An immersive socialization intervention for adolescents with autism spectrum disorder. *Journal of Autism and Developmental Disorders, 48*(3), 1–13. https://doi.org/10.1007/s10803-017-3380-1

Wainscot, J. J., Naylor, P., Sutcliffe, P., Tantam, D., & Williams, J. (2008). Relationships with peers and use of the school environment of mainstream secondary school pupils with Asperger syndrome (High-functioning autism): A case control study. *International Journal of Psychology and Psychological Therapy, 8*(1), 25–38. Retrieved from https://www.ijpsy.com/volumen8/num1/181/relationships-with-peers-and-use-of-the-EN.pdf

Watkins, E. E., Zimmermann, Z. J., & Poling, A. (2014). The gender of participants in published research involving people with autism spectrum disorders. *Research in Autism Spectrum Disorders, 8*(2), 143–146. https://doi.org/10.1016/j.rasd.2013.10.010

Werling, D. M., & Geschwind, D. H. (2013). Sex differences in autism spectrum disorders. *Current Opinion in Neurology, 26*(2), 146–153. https://doi.org/10.1097/WCO.0b013e32835ee548

Aranzazu M. Blackburn, PhD, has been an educator for more than 20 years in Australia, undertaking diverse roles such as English as a second language (ESL) teacher, Spanish teacher, deputy principal, curriculum coordinator, and learning support coordinator. She attained her PhD from the University of New England, Australia. Her research focuses on diverse gifted and talented learners in the secondary years, particularly gifted English language learners and girls on the autism spectrum.

Geraldine Townend, PhD, a research fellow and lecturer at GERRIC, UNSW, Australia, seeks to extend understanding of giftedness, twice exceptionality and underachievement and to empower students and their educators to achieve the best educational outcomes. She researches and publishes within the sociocultural paradigm. Her research has focused on the link between students' academic self-concept and their educational outcomes, particularly the importance of social comparison theory, and she is interested in the importance of the interaction between teachers and students. Geraldine also provides schools, families, and national media (Australia) with support around school-based strategies to enable optimal educational outcomes within the inclusive classroom.

Teachers' Knowledge and Understandings of Twice Exceptionality Across Australia

27

Catherine Wormald and Michelle Bannister-Tyrrell

Contents

Introduction	580
Literature Review	581
Specific Learning Disabilities	582
Attention Deficit/Hyperactivity Disorder (ADHD)	582
Physical Disabilities	583
Autism Spectrum Disorder (ASD)	583
Dyslexia Spectrum Difficulties	584
Speech and Language Disorders	585
Identification of Students Who Are Twice Exceptional	585
The Australian Study: Methodology	586
The Research Questions That Informed This Australian Study	587
Implementing the Australian Twice Exceptional Needs Assessment Survey (ATENAS)	587
Data Analysis of the Australian Study	589
Some Findings of This Seminal Study on Twice Exceptionality	589
Limitations of This Study	593
Discussion: Twice Exceptionality in Australia	594
Link Between Some Findings and Implications for Future Research and Practice	597
Conclusion	599
Cross-References	599
Appendix A: Australian Twice Exceptional Needs Survey (Foley Nicpon et al., 2013)	599
References	602

C. Wormald
Faculty of Social Sciences, School of Education, University of Wollongong, Wollongong, NSW, Australia
e-mail: cwormald@uow.edu.au

M. Bannister-Tyrrell (✉)
School of Education, University of New England, Armidale, NSW, Australia
e-mail: mbannist@une.edu.au

© Springer Nature Singapore Pte Ltd. 2021
S. R. Smith (ed.), *Handbook of Giftedness and Talent Development in the Asia-Pacific*, Springer International Handbooks of Education,
https://doi.org/10.1007/978-981-13-3041-4_27

Abstract

This chapter outlines findings from the first Australia-wide study examining teacher knowledge and understandings of twice exceptionality across all school sectors. The study included public schools (government schools), Catholic, and independent schools (usually with religious affiliations). The outcome of this study indicated that many teachers were unaware of the term 'twice-exceptional' students. Students who are twice exceptional are those with high cognitive ability and a learning disability or disabilities. In class, the focus is often on students' disabilities rather than their high cognitive abilities. While the method in this study emulated a United States of America (USA) study, with appropriate modifications so as to be applicable to the Australian context, the findings proved insightful for the researchers involved in this study. The findings suggested that across Australia there is limited understanding of students who are twice exceptional. In order for this population of students with high cognitive ability and disabilities to have their educational needs met, there needs to be greater teacher knowledge and understanding of their unique characteristics, with a focus on the student's giftedness as well as any disability.

Keywords

Twice exceptional · Inclusive education · Gifted education · Learning difficulties/disabilities

The aims in this chapter are to:
1. Identify Australian teachers' knowledge and understandings of students who are classified as twice exceptional.
2. Examine the attitudes of Australian teachers with regard to understanding that students can have high cognitive ability and also disabilities, and highlight the many issues raised by teachers participating in the study.

Introduction

A student who is twice exceptional (also known as 2e) can demonstrate characteristics of students with giftedness as well as students who have a disability. As a consequence, students with twice exceptionality can have a high cognitive ability as well as learning disabilities that can undermine and disguise their high cognitive ability. It is the apparent contradiction between the high cognitive capacity and the disability that can confuse teachers and may mean that these students are not identified nor have their needs met in the classroom. Additionally, with the lack of consensus of a definition of giftedness and separate definitions for learning disabilities, the researchers developed a definition that incorporates both giftedness and disability.

The current research on students who are twice exceptional has been conducted mainly in the United States of America (USA). Hence, the research discussed in this chapter was based on a study conducted in the USA by Foley Nicpon, Assouline, and Colangelo (2013) to determine the knowledge and understanding of Australian classroom teachers in relation to their professional obligation to students who are twice exceptional. Minimal research has been undertaken in Australasia with the focus on 2e, and this study was the first of its kind conducted nationally in Australia.

Literature Review

There is often a misconception about students who may be considered gifted with many educators "having stereotypical views" of these students (Woodcock, Dixon, & Tanner, 2013, p. 194). The student who is twice exceptional is one who has high cognitive ability coupled with one or more learning disabilities. These students can be a challenge for teachers and their learning disability can often mask their exceptional abilities (Baum, Owen, & Dixon, 1991). According to the Australian Disability Clearinghouse on Education and Training (n.d.), there are marked differences between a learning difficulty and a learning disability. Foley Nicpon, Allmon, Sieck, and Stinson (2011) stated, that "gifted students can have a coexisting disability" (p. 13).

It is important to understand the difference between a learning difficulty and a learning disability. In Australia, the National Health and Medical Research Council (n.d.) estimates 10–16% of the population have learning difficulties, and that 2–4% of the population has learning disabilities. In line with the Australian National Health and Medical Research Council, the Australian Discrimination Act (1991, 2017), and the Australian Standards for Education, learning disabilities are viewed as a subset of learning difficulties (Australian Capital Territory Education and Training, n.d.). The Australian Disability Clearing House on Education and Training (n.d.) makes the distinction that learning difficulties respond to educational interventions and a learning disability is life long and pervasive and does not respond readily to intervention. Within the Australian context, in order to develop an appropriate and relevant definition of students who are twice exceptional for this study, the researchers combined the content from the Disabilities Discrimination Act (1992), the Disabilities Standards for Education (2005) and Gagné's (2008) *Differentiated Model of Giftedness and Talent*. The authors therefore propose the following definition of students who are twice exceptional:

> Learners who are twice exceptional are students with natural abilities in the intellectual, creative, social, perceptual and physical domains, while exhibiting evidence of one or more disabilities as defined by the Disability Discrimination Act (1992) and the Disability Standards for Education (2005) including, but not limited to, specific learning disabilities, speech and language disorders, emotional/behavioural disorders, physical disabilities, autism spectrum, and ADD/HD.

These students are often considered a dichotomy with high cognitive function coupled with a disability, such as any of those listed above. It is unclear how many students who are twice exceptional there may currently be within Australia. According to Baum, Schader, and Owen (2017), the United States Department of Education states, "there are approximately 360,000 twice-exceptional students in America's schools" (p. 11). In a USA study by Rogers (2011), she found that 14% of a group of 504 students in gifted programs were twice exceptional. These students were identified as gifted with the exceptionality of Attention Deficit Disorder/Attention Deficit Hyperactivity Disorder (ADD/ADHD), Emotional Behavioural Disorder (EBD), Autism Spectrum Disorder (ASD), or a Specific Learning Disability (SLD).

According to the Australian Disability Clearinghouse on Education and Training (n.d.), "a Specific Learning Disability (SLD) is the result of a neurological disorder which causes the learner to receive and process some information inaccurately. SLD can have a significant impact on learning" (para. 1). No information is currently available other than anecdotal evidence of the percentage of students who are twice exceptional within Australia. The next section will discuss some of the disabilities that gifted students may demonstrate.

Specific Learning Disabilities

According to the *Specific Learning Difficulties Association* (SPELD) Foundation (SPELD Victoria, 2019):

> Specific learning disabilities are not intellectual impairments. Students with intellectual impairments are generally assessed as having reduced cognitive capacity, which has a global impact on learning and daily functioning... Students with a specific learning disability have significant difficulty in one academic area while coping well, or even excelling, in other areas of academic, sporting or artistic achievement" (para. 1–2).

There are many reasons why a child or adult may struggle to learn. In Australia, the generic term 'Learning Difficulties' refers to the 20–25% of students who exhibit problems acquiring academic skills as a consequence of a range of causes.

Attention Deficit/Hyperactivity Disorder (ADHD)

Antshel, Faraone, Stallone, Nave, Kaufmann, Doyle, Fried, Seidman, and Biederman (2007) note that ADHD is a "chronic, heterogeneous neurobehavioural disorder with multifactorial inheritance affecting approximately 5–10% of children worldwide" (p. 687). These authors also state that the symptoms often lead to serious social, interpersonal and academic impairments. ADHD can often coexist with "disruptive behaviour, mood and anxiety disorders, learning disabilities and executive function deficits... Prefrontal cortex, basal ganglia and cerebella anomalies are the most frequently reported neuroanatomical findings in the extant ADHD literature" (p. 678). While much anecdotal evidence was collected by researchers in the first empirical study by Antshel et al. (2007), they found that it was possible for students with a high IQ to also have ADHD:

> (These students) repeated grades more often, needed more academic supports, had a poorer performance on the WISC-III Block Design, had more co-morbid psychopathology, and were rated by parents as having more functional impairments across a number of domains... Our data indicating that children with a high IQ and ADHD show a pattern of familial, cognitive, psychiatric, behavioural and functional features consistent with the diagnosis of ADHD documented in children of average IQ support the study hypothesis that the diagnosis of ADHD is valid among high IQ children. (p. 692)

This study ascertained that ADHD does impact on school performance for high IQ students, with Antshel et al. (2007) acknowledging that the disability rather than high intelligence often becomes the focus, meaning that individuals who are twice exceptional may not be identified until later in their adult lives.

Physical Disabilities

A physical disability is "a condition that interferes with a child's ability to use his or her body" (Kirk, Gallagher, & Anastasiow, 2000, p. 485). There are an extensive range of physical disabilities that can affect a student's performance, from fine motor difficulties to quadriplegia and can include visual or hearing impairment, cerebral palsy, and limb deficiencies. Many parents who became aware of the current study were keen that physical disabilities formed part of the twice exceptionality framework/definition used within this study.

Autism Spectrum Disorder (ASD)

Assouline, Foley Nicpon, Colangelo, and O'Brien (2008) state that "giftedness and ASD are not mutually exclusive" (p. 9) and students with ASD "have a developmental disorder that results in severe social, communication, and/or behavioural impairments" (pp. 8–9). They argue that students with ASD are often overlooked for gifted programs and that this needs to change. Moreover, according to Assouline et al. (2008):

> The gifted student who is also diagnosed with one of the autism spectrum disorders (ASD) has many behaviours, skills and characteristics that are paradoxical in nature. In other words, there are aspects of these areas that are extraordinarily well developed—especially academically—yet, within the same broad area, there are other aspects that, relative to the academic strength, are significantly weak and may create a situation where the regular classroom setting may not be optimal for learning. Accommodations can be used to ensure that the student's learning experience is commensurate with his or her ability. (p. 6)

According to Montgomery (2015), there can be a triad of impairments for these students:

- *Social interaction*: Difficulty with social relationships, for example, appearing aloof and indifferent to other people, or failure to follow social rules.
- *Social communication*: Difficulty with verbal and nonverbal communication, for example, not really understanding the meaning of gestures, facial expressions, or tone of voice.
- *Imagination:* Difficulty in the development of play and imagination, for example, having a limited range of imaginative activities, possibly copied and pursued rigidly and repeatedly; literal comprehension. (p. 76)

Assouline et al. (2008) provide a number of recommendations for teachers and parents to assist with cognitive processing speed and multitasking, written language, writing and fine motor coordination, gross motor skills, enhancing social skills, language, and communication difficulties, and behavioural characteristics.

Dyslexia Spectrum Difficulties

Dyslexia is a learning difficulty in the literacy area according to Montgomery (2015), and while it is common today for most individuals with dyslexia to learn to read, they may still have ongoing issues with spelling. Gifted students can certainly have dyslexia, although some do learn to overcome associated issues using their high visual memories, and sometimes are not recognised until eight years of age (Montgomery, 2015). Montgomery highlights a number of other disabilities that are linked with reading difficulties:

Dysorthographia: This learning disability relates to severe spelling difficulties that can continue into the adult years; however, there is usually no problem with reading. It can often appear to be a disconnect between the letters written and the sounds made. There also appears to be a disconnect between understanding and writing grammatical information.

Dysgraphia: This disability mainly affects handwriting and the ability to write down thoughts. According to the Dyslexia-SPELD Foundation (2014a) website, "Dysgraphia is a neurological disorder that generally appears when children are first learning to write. Experts are not sure what causes it, but early treatment can help prevent or reduce problems" (Para. 3).

Dyspraxia: This affects coordination of fine motor activities and the planning and completion of tasks. According to the SPELD Foundation (Dyslexia-SPELD Foundation 2014b) website, "it is associated with problems of perception, language and thought" (Para 10). There are two different types of dyspraxia identified on the SPELD (Dyslexia-SPELD Foundation 2014b) webpage including verbal dyspraxia and motor dyspraxia (Dyslexia-SPELD Foundation, 2014b).

Dyscalculia: This is a learning difficulty that affects mathematical ability. According to Montgomery (2015), it can affect issues such as mental arithmetic and reciting of times tables.

Speech and Language Disorders

Students who have speech and language disorders may experience difficulty with written as well as spoken language. If the student's difficulty is with written language they may have trouble with physically writing, spelling, and organising ideas. If the difficulty is with spoken language, they may experience problems with listening and speaking. Woodcock, Dixon, and Tanner (2013) highlight the following speech and language disorders:

- Speech-based impairments that affect regular speech.
- Language-based impairments that affect students' capacity to learn words, construct sentences, build vocabulary or understand words and sentences.
- Expressive language disorder: Students will understand what is being said to them but will have difficulty expressing themselves verbally.
- Receptive language disorder: Students hear what is being said but have difficulty processing it.
- Aphasia, resulting from damage to the language part of the brain, which affects production or comprehension of speech and the ability to read or write.
- Verbal dyspraxia which affects the production of speech.
- Semantic/pragmatic disorders which result in difficulty interpreting and understanding what is being said and understanding how to use appropriate speech.

Auditory Processing Disorder (APD) is described by the British Society of Audiology (2011) as being "characterised by poor perception of both speech and non-speech sounds" (p. 6). They also note that APD originates from impaired neural function and can impact on everyday life through a reduced ability to listen and therefore respond to sounds appropriately. All of these disabilities can coexist with giftedness and thus make identification a challenging process. Not only does the student's giftedness have to be identified, but also the disability or disabilities and an understanding of the impact of these on the students' learning.

Identification of Students Who Are Twice Exceptional

According to Reis, Baum, and Burke (2014):

> to be identified as twice exceptional requires comprehensive assessment in both the areas of giftedness and disabilities, as one does not preclude the other. Identification, when possible, should be conducted by professionals from both disciplines and, when at all possible, by those with knowledge about twice exceptionality in order to address the impact of co-incidence/comorbidity of both areas on diagnostic assessments and eligibility requirements for services. (pp. 222–223)

What this ultimately requires from educators is to ensure that psychologists assess both the disability *and* the giftedness in these students. Rather than simply trying to *fix* the disability, it is important that there is recognition of the advanced cognitive ability and that it is catered for to avoid intense frustration in the student. The issue for parents is to find a psychologist who has experience with students who are twice exceptional (Reis et al., 2014).

Additionally, as recommended by Wormald (2009) in her research, it was important that all relevant professionals were involved to ensure an accurate identification of twice exceptionality can be made. This was also supported by Rogers' (2011) suggestion that "there is a need for the identification team to identify precisely ... [and] the identification team needs to be trained in using an identification protocol" (p. 60). Rogers (2011) suggested the following strategies for improving the accuracy of identification:

- Utilise a tiered system of identification.
- Incorporate WISC IV, which is valuable in providing data on the potential of twice-exceptional students.
- Do not look far from the family tree.
- Look for students who are twice-exceptional students in self-contained gifted classes as well as in mixed-ability classes.
- May need to look harder for eligible girls.
- The school nurse or person in charge of sick bay may be one of the best identifiers.
- Parents need to be helped to understand the importance of early identification. (pp. 59–60).

As previously stated, the current study was based on research undertaken in the USA by Foley Nicpon et al. (2013), which sought to understand the knowledge and awareness that teachers and other educational professionals had in relation to students who are twice exceptional. An online Twice-Exceptional Needs Assessment was developed for this study and consisted of items related to twice exceptionality, gifted and special education (See 'Appendix A; *Australian Twice Exceptional Needs Survey*, 2018', developed from Foley Nicpon et al., 2013).

The Australian Study: Methodology

Unlike the long history of twice exceptionality studies in the USA, this research formed the first national study examining the understandings of teachers working in departmental (government schools), independent (usually with religious affiliations), and Catholic education schools across Australia. The researchers were keen to investigate what teachers knew about students who are twice exceptional, whether there was recognition of these students and whether programs were in place for them. Prior Australian research had focused mainly on small case studies (Carrington, Papinczak, & Templeton, 2003; Dixon & Norris, 2011; Dixon & Tanner, 2013; Munro, 2009; Ronksley-Pavia, 2016; Townend & Pendergast, 2015) with Wormald's (2009) study being the only one to focus on the perspectives of both the families of these students, as well as the teachers. Research on twice exceptionality in Australia is limited, compared to quantitative research that has been undertaken in the USA.

While the Australian case study research has provided valuable insights into the construct of twice exceptionality and particularly the challenges faced by these students and their families, it has not provided information on the extent of the knowledge and awareness of teachers regarding students who are twice exceptional (Carrington et al., 2003; Dixon & Tanner, 2013; Townend & Pendergast, 2015). Thus, the current study sought to gain knowledge at the national level in relation to current teacher understandings about twice exceptionality within the school system. Additionally, the study sought to investigate the type of information teachers wanted with respect to these students, which would inform future directions for professional learning about students who are twice exceptional.

The Research Questions That Informed This Australian Study

1. What is the level of understanding about students who are twice exceptional among Australian educators?
2. Does training in gifted education enhance understandings about students who are twice exceptional?
3. What beliefs do educational professionals have with respect to the educational requirements of these students?

This study was a joint project between the University of Wollongong and the University of New England and was conducted nationally. Quantitative methodology was used in the form of an online survey, as currently there is a lack of national data about this population of students. The majority of current research in Australia in the field of twice exceptionality is qualitative and consists mainly of case studies (e.g., Carrington, Papinczak, & Templeton, 2013; Dixon & Tanner, 2013; Townend & Pendergast, 2015).

Implementing the Australian Twice Exceptional Needs Assessment Survey (ATENAS)

The current study attempted to replicate a study undertaken in the USA by Foley Nicpon et al. (2013). The instrument used in the original study, the *Twice Exceptional Needs Survey,* was adapted to make it applicable to the Australian context. The American research was undertaken in response to the *Individuals with Disabilities Education Act* (IDEA) of 2004. This act described six principles, which focus on students' rights and the responsibility of schools to students with disabilities. These principles supported the implementation of a *Response To Intervention* (RTI) model for meeting the needs of students with disabilities. This meant that a component of the original survey focused on the knowledge that teachers had about RtI. This aspect of the survey was not relevant to the Australian context and was therefore not included as part of the survey used in this study. Additionally, the USA had specialist schools for students who are gifted with learning disabilities, which Australia does not. Hence, terminology was changed, for example, in relation to role descriptions and roles within schools, which are different in Australia. The design of the survey was influenced by the work of Gable and Wolf (1993) and Strachota, Conceicao, and Schmidt (2006) and in consultation with an expert in survey design and learning disabilities (Bailey, 2004). The number of items in this survey was kept purposefully low (as opposed to the more common large item-based surveys) to encourage time-poor educators to take part in this survey. With this in mind, it was necessary to carefully design each item to ensure they reflected and supported the research questions. The adapted survey instrument was titled the *Australian Twice Exceptional Needs Assessment Survey* (ATENAS; The full survey can be found in Appendix A).

The survey consisted of a range of items requiring different response formats, including scale responses, short answer, and extended written responses. For instance, items 3, 4 and 5 required a response using a six-point Likert scale. Items 6 and 7 also required participants to rank items in importance in relation to areas that may be difficult for students who are twice exceptional, and the type of information teachers needed in relation to these students. Additional demographic information was also requested: grade taught, qualifications, additional study in the field of gifted education or learning disabilities and responsibilities for gifted or special education. Finally, teachers were asked to provide any information they felt was worth sharing in relation to students who are twice exceptional and what other information they would like to know about these students. Teachers were able to comment on each item in the survey and provide additional information if they wished.

The original USA study used Survey Monkey to administer the survey instrument, while the Australian version used the online platform Qualtrics, which provided more online tools for analysis. The survey was aimed at professional personnel working in schools including teachers, executive staff, and school counsellors. Parents were not invited to be part of this research as the aim was to understand teachers' knowledge about students who are twice exceptional.

Ethics approval was granted by both universities, which were involved in the study. In addition, approval was sought from all State and Territory Education Departments and one Catholic Education Diocese using the National Research Application. For all other Catholic dioceses and independent schools, individual applications were required to be submitted. This involved a total of 30 research applications being completed and submitted. In addition, in order to have the survey completed by independent schools, each school needed to be approached individually. Despite approval to conduct the research being given by all State and Territory Departments of Education and Catholic Dioceses Education Offices, there was no assistance provided to the researchers in distributing the information about the study and an invitation to participate. Instead the researchers had to contact schools individually in order to notify them about the study and invite their teachers to participate. This meant over 7000 emails were sent to individual schools across

Australia, with the exception of three Catholic dioceses that did not provide permission to send the surveys to their schools. The emails included a letter to principals outlining the study, a copy of the survey and a participant information sheet providing the link to the survey. Consent was implied through completion of the survey.

In the current study, an interesting aspect related to the response rates. While more than 614 participants opened and read the survey, some sections received much lower levels of response including between 26 and 145 responses to some questions. This poor response rate, combined with many of the responses that came through and were analysed, suggests to the authors that much is unknown across Australia about students who are twice exceptional. These issues will be further explored in the 'Discussion' section of this chapter. One disappointing aspect was that not all participants completed the entire survey, with the range of questions answered falling between a low of 26 to a high of 243. (The researchers recognise that this is a very low response rate and a limitation of the study).

Data Analysis of the Australian Study

Adopting a *raw data grid*, the researchers used an excel spreadsheet to add all the raw data (Mutch, 2013), which transferred all the data collected from the surveys into the first page of an excel spreadsheet. Each researcher then manually examined the raw data grid for emergent themes. While NVivo completes a similar process, the themes can become unmanageable with multiple themes being selected by the process.

The second stage involved coding and transferring the survey responses into the first page of the excel spreadsheet. The researchers then separately analysed the thematic themes from the transcriptions. The level of inter-rater agreement between the researchers was calculated at 96% (Whitebread et al., 2009). As lecturers in gifted education with many years of teaching experience between them, this level of inter-rater reliability between the researchers was to be expected. The final 4% were discussed between the researchers and absolute agreement was achieved (Whitebread et al., 2009). Even though the results as a whole cannot be generalised across Australia, they did support the earlier Australian findings of Wormald (2009).

Some Findings of This Seminal Study on Twice Exceptionality

Overall, the majority of responses came from teachers in NSW and state and territory Departments of Education with primary school teachers the main respondents and only a small number of secondary teachers participating. Overwhelmingly, the participants were female which is indicative of the gender representation in primary schools in Australia. Information was gathered about participants' roles in schools and the number of years they had been teaching. This information is provided in Tables 1 and 2. As can be seen from Table 2, the greatest percentage of teachers had been teaching for a substantial period of time. The majority of participants had Bachelors' degrees (41%) and 48% of participants had undertaken postgraduate study. This included Masters by coursework or research as well as graduate diplomas.

Participants were asked whether the school they were in had any special provision for gifted students and students with learning disabilities. In addition, they were asked what these provisions were. Some of the provisions for gifted students included:

- Challenge classes;
- Accelerated programs;
- "Piecemeal responses to policy";
- Withdrawal groups;
- Qualitatively differentiated learning.

For students with a learning disability, the provisions included:

- A teacher's aide;
- Technology support;
- Withdrawal from the classroom either as a small group or individually;
- Individual Learning Programs (ILP);
- Learning support teachers.

One of the aims of the study was to understand what teachers' understandings of twice exceptionality are, and in order to achieve this, an item in the survey asked participants what familiarity they had of students who are gifted with either ADHD, ASD, behavioural disorders, diagnosed learning difficulties, or diagnosed emotional disorders. Participants were asked to rank their familiarity from not familiar to extremely familiar. The results are provided in Table 3. Teachers noted that they were most familiar with gifted students who were on the Autism Spectrum (26.67%) and who had ADHD (21.33%), with 25% indicating that they had no experience

Table 1 Participant information

School classification	Percentage of participants (%)
Classroom teacher	*40*
School executive (principal, deputy or assistant deputy)	*16*
Subject coordinator	*13*
Administrator with a teaching load (e.g., teaching principal)	*0*
Support teacher	*13*
School counsellor/psychologist	*0*
Other	*13*

Other included: Two teacher librarians; previous coordinator; second in charge of faculty

Table 2 Number of years teaching

Number of years teaching	Percentage of participants (%)
1–9	18
10–19	22
20–29	30
30–39	24
40–49	5
50–59	0.3

Table 3 Q3 How familiar are you with the following categories of twice exceptionality?

	Not familiar (%)	(%)	(%)	(%)	(%)	Extremely familiar (%)
Gifted students diagnosed with attention deficit/hyperactivity disorder (ADD/ADHD)	25	15.79	29.41	11.76	18.60	21.33
Gifted students with diagnosed Autism Spectrum Disorder (ASD)	25	15.79	5.88	11.76	25.58	26.67
Gifted students with diagnosed behaviour disorders	25	21.05	23.53	23.53	20.93	13.33
Gifted students with diagnosed learning difficulties	0	26.32	11.75	35.29	18.60	16.67
Gifted students with diagnosed emotional disorders	25	21.05	29.41	17.65	16.28	20.00

Note: The researchers gave no indication of what each of these categories meant, leaving it up to the participants to determine their own level of experience

with gifted students who have ADHD, ASD behavioural disorders, or emotional disorders.

Item 4 asked participants to rank their level of experience working with gifted students who had been identified with ADHD, ASD, behavioural, and emotional disorder and learning difficulties. Teachers indicated that they had most experience working with students who are gifted with ADHD (34.62%) and ASD (34.62%) and only a small number noting that they had no experience working with students who are gifted with the various learning disabilities (0–7%).

A number of items provided an opportunity for participants to make additional comments if they wished. This provided the researchers with data that was coded into themes. Some of the themes that emerged from extra information provided in response to item five about teachers' confidence in meeting the needs and assessing students who are twice exceptional were:

- School counsellors deal with educational assessments in schools—although some respondents found this process extremely slow, or assessments completed by school executive and staff suggested that they do not understand the outcome of these assessments.

- No time and no resources to address these issues.
- Some training in schools, but overall, very little in other schools;
- Barriers existed in schools as a result of required consultation processes.
- Little understanding of students who are twice exceptional in schools—some participants did not know that students who are twice exceptional existed.

In Australian schools, it is the school counsellor or psychologist who is responsible for diagnosing learning disabilities. If a student has not been identified as having a learning disability and the teacher has concerns, it is their responsibility to refer the student for assessment. This study sought to understand what demonstrated behaviours teachers would consider warranted a referral to the school counsellor or psychologist. The most common behaviour that teachers considered in this situation was if the student had social difficulties with their peers (61.54%). The category of 'other' (42.86%) enlisted a number of suggestions which are discussed later in this chapter.

In order to support students with disabilities or learning difficulties, schools are required to provide support and interventions. While the researchers are aware of the interventions that are required by law in Australia, they were interested in this study to find out whether these interventions and supports were different for students who not only have a disability but are also gifted. Participants indicated that the following programs were implemented in schools:

- Assistive technology;
- Tutoring;
- Enrichment/enrichment classes;
- Learning support;
- Monitoring/mentoring;
- Challenge activities;
- Training for staff;
- Assistance with aide;
- Differentiation;
- Individual plans;
- Social skills classes;
- Inclusive classrooms.

These programs and interventions were strategies that would be used for students who have learning disabilities or difficulties and therefore were not specific to students who were also gifted with a learning disability.

Realising that it was possible that teachers had other information that they would like to share about students who are twice exceptional that had not been covered in other sections of the survey an opportunity was presented for participants to provide this. Themes to emerge from this section included:

- Specialist teachers and relevant professionals are needed to deliver professional learning and support in schools, including identifying.

- Students who are twice exceptional are noticed as a result of behavioural issues or challenging behaviours.
- It is important to work with families.
- Issues such as dyslexia should not be on Negotiated Education Plans.
- Provide programs that cater specifically for students who are twice exceptional.
- Cultural issues often underdiagnosed.
- More training is required for school counsellors.

Finally, participants were asked whether there was any relevant information about students who are twice exceptional that they would like to know. This section was important to the researchers as it not only provided information about possible recommendations that could be made to schools as a result of this study, but it also provided some direction for further study of this special population of students. The suggestions made, particularly with respect to learning more about students who are twice exceptional, was supported by Wormald (2009) who found that teachers were keen to learn more if they were provided with support, time, and training from those who had professional expertise in this field. Some of the themes to come out of this section were:

- Teachers wish to know more about these students.
- How can differentiation assist these students?
- What is best practice for these students?
- How to identify them.

Limitations of This Study

If this study were to be replicated by researchers, they should ensure that each question was answered before participants were able to move to the next question. This can ensure that a larger representation of participants would complete the survey. As the level of response was low, this meant it was not possible to generalise the results across Australia despite this being the first study of its kind that studied students who are twice exceptional from an Australian perspective.

The understanding and definition of terms such as extensive experience, twice exceptional, behavioural, and emotional disorders, ASD and ADHD were not provided, rather, it was left up to the teachers to apply their own understanding of these terms. Unless the participant has been trained in special education, they may have been confused about the difference between a disability and a learning difficulty. Additionally, participants were not provided with a definition of students who are twice exceptional; again, this was left up to the teachers to make that determination. Confusion was also demonstrated about teachers' understanding of the difference between performances on class assessments as compared to class work.

While every effort was made to include only teachers working in Australian schools, the researchers had no way of knowing if all participants fell into this category as school principals were the gatekeepers of the survey. Some participants may have participated as they had an interest in the field of twice exceptionality or some experience. Additionally, some participants were also parents of students who are twice exceptional and therefore responded to items both as a teacher and a parent. The researchers tried to overcome these limitations by noting in the participant information that the survey was open to all teachers whether they had knowledge of, or experience with students who are twice exceptional, gifted, or have learning disabilities. Finally, the return rate was poor and very disappointing despite the number of direct email invitations sent to individual schools. In order to increase the response rate, the researchers in future would target groups of schools in each state and territory and different systems of education rather than sending the information to all schools. This would make the process more manageable and allow for the opportunity to follow-up with schools and encourage participation.

Discussion: Twice Exceptionality in Australia

Students who are twice exceptional are a fact of life for schools in Australia, but what do teachers know about them, the identification of these students and how to meet their educational needs? This Australian national study sought to understand teachers' knowledge of students who are twice exceptional. The teachers who participated in this study were mainly from the NSW Department of Education schools with more primary than secondary teachers completing the survey. Participants' level of teaching experience was variable with the largest group (30.2%), having 20–29 years' experience. Analysis determined that there was significant correlation between the number of years teaching and the level of confidence and experience that teachers had in their familiarity with the various manifestations of twice exceptionality. This group of teachers also rated highly their experience with the various types of twice exceptionality and their ability to identify and meet their educational needs. Just over a third of teachers had bachelor's degrees with only a minority (20.5%) having postgraduate qualifications at the MEd level. Previous research has noted that teachers who have postgraduate qualifications and/or training in gifted education are better able to meet the needs of students who are gifted (Fraser-Seeto, 2013, McEwin, 2003; Plunkett & Kronborg, 2007; Rowley, 2012; Vialle, 2017).

It was pleasing to note that the teachers who answered item three had some familiarity with students who are gifted with learning disabilities, although only 16.7% reported they were extremely familiar with this group of students. It was interesting that participants demonstrated familiarity with gifted students with ASD (26.7%) more so than students who are gifted with ADD/HD (21.3%), behavioural or emotional disorders (20.0%), or a specific learning disability (16.7%). This is in direct contrast to the research undertaken by Foley Nicpon et al. (2013) who found that participant teachers in the USA were most familiar with students who are gifted with ADD/HD. Individual case studies in Australia have been undertaken (Carrington, Papinczak, & Templeton, 2013; Dixon & Tanner, 2013) that have researched students who are gifted with ASD/ADHD or a behavioural disorder, but no studies to date have been undertaken in Australia that may provide an answer for why there is such a difference between teachers in the USA and Australia with respect to students who are gifted with ADD/HD (Dixon & Tanner, 2013; Holmes & Sutherland, 2010; Munro, 2002).

When asked about their experience working with students who are gifted with ADD/HD, ASD, behavioural disorders, learning difficulties, and emotional disorders, teachers were ambivalent with most responses around the 'some' to 'moderate' level of experience. The majority of teachers (30.8%) who responded to this item noted that they had moderate levels of experience working with students who are gifted with learning disabilities and less experience with the other sub groups of students who are twice exceptional. This was in contrast to the fact that only 16.7% stated that they had experience working with students who are gifted with learning disabilities.

Despite specialists, such as school counsellors being the ones to diagnose a learning disability, 38.4% of respondents to this question indicated that they were reasonably confident conducting assessments themselves to identify students who are twice exceptional followed by meeting the general educational needs of students who are twice exceptional (31.6%). However, teachers demonstrated some reluctance to initiate external assessment of students who are twice exceptional. This is concerning as teachers have demonstrated poor familiarity of students who are twice exceptional yet are suggesting that they can assess these students and do not refer them to the experts for identification! Themes that arose as a result of participants being asked if they would like to add anything to this section were: school counsellors undertook assessment but it was a slow process and classroom teachers often did not understand the reports; that there was no time and resources provided to address assessing and meeting twice-exceptional students' needs; some schools received training but others did not; and there was little or no understanding of twice-exceptional students.

Participants were also asked to rank in order the factors that they considered important when referring twice-exceptional students for evaluation. Behavioural issues were ranked first, followed by parental concerns with performance on class, and standardised tests being the least important. This is an interesting outcome considering the importance placed on standardised testing in Australia, which is used in some schools to identify students for gifted programs.

Students who are twice exceptional will experience difficulties in many areas and will need support in order to develop strategies to deal with their challenges (Nielsen, 2002; Willard-Holt, Weber, Morrison, & Horgan, 2013). Teachers were asked to rank what they believed would be the primary area of difficulty for twice-exceptional students. Social difficulties with peers was ranked the highest followed by other issues. Participants noted that some of the other issues experienced by twice-exceptional students that they considered important were:

- Feelings of anxiety and frustrations;
- Emotional well-being of students particularly when they cannot understand why they perform so badly sometimes;
- Making sense of their challenges when setting goals;
- Social/emotional issues;
- Behaviour;
- Clarity of tasks and assessment differentiation.

High school students in particular seem to be confused about their abilities and often withdraw or shut down, and students not able to effectively communicate their needs.

Research (Foley Nicpon et al., 2011; Rogers, 2011) supports these teachers' concerns about issues which are relevant to twice-exceptional students. Providing twice-exceptional students with an appropriate educational program by trained teachers will address many of these issues (Baum, Schader, & Hébert, 2014; Willard-Holt et al., 2013).

This Australian study sought to understand what teachers knew about students who are twice exceptional and to this end a number of free response questions were included asking teachers: *What interventions were implemented in their school for twice-exceptional students? What other information would they like to share?* and *Is there any other information about twice-exceptional students that you would like to know?* A number of themes arose as a result of these items. With respect to interventions implemented in schools, it was heartening to see that the most common intervention was enrichment or extension classes. It was disappointing though that learning support did not rank highly as these students need the assistance of the special needs team in order to develop strategies for their disability. Some understanding of the needs of these students and the requirements needed for them to reach their potential were demonstrated through the themes that emerged from the item. Other information teachers wanted to share are as follows:

- Specialist teachers are needed in schools.
- Twice-exceptional students are noticed because of behavioural issues.
- Issues such as dyslexia should not be on an Individual Education Plan (IEP).
- School does not cater for twice-exceptional students.
- Cultural issues often underdiagnosed.
- More training is required for school counsellors.

Participants provided in some detail the information they would like about these students. Teachers are keen to learn more about these students and how they can differentiate activities and assessment for students who are twice exceptional. This finding supports Wormald's (2009) research, which noted that teachers were willing to learn more about students with twice exceptionalities and just wanted the opportunity and support to be able to do so. This finding is important as it demonstrates that teachers are willing and want to help these students reach their potential.

Link Between Some Findings and Implications for Future Research and Practice

While educators trained in gifted education have a high level of confidence with regard to providing appropriate provisions for gifted students with learning disabilities, many comments have been received with respect to hearing the term twice exceptional for the first time in their teaching careers, including executive staff and principals. Comments supporting this notion include:

> Until this survey I didn't know that these diagnosed categories existed. I have worked with students who I suspected fell into these types of categories but I didn't realise they actually had a name. (A6.1, 2016)

Teachers need to be provided with professional learning and training on the characteristics these students may demonstrate. A process for identifying students who are twice exceptional that includes the teachers of the gifted as well as the special needs teacher needs to be implemented in schools.

A number of respondents provided additional information about in-school interventions that were provided for these students. This information demonstrated that there was appropriate understanding of the interventions that can support these students to achieve their potential within the classroom. Interventions implemented included using technology, such as Dyslexie font, SpeakIt apps and Voice to Text. The employment of teachers' aides in the classroom, specialist teachers and relevant external professionals, such as speech and occupational therapists were also supportive structures that were in place in some schools.

Teachers who participated in the study recognised that students who are twice exceptional exist in schools and are an under-identified group who are not having their educational needs met. As one teacher noted:

> Schools are not catering well for these students. We need more flexible arrangements where students can study online. More flexible classrooms, not standard classrooms with one teacher and many lessons a day. (M6.1, 2016)

Another stated:

> I think in general we need to raise awareness of these students and also build the capacity of staff in order to better support these children at school. We as educators should be providing for these students. The current system is not inclusive or supportive of their need. (S7.8, 2017)

A positive comment that progress has been made for these students was noted by a teacher who stated:

> There is much better understanding of the needs and abilities of these students than there was 10–15 years ago and a lot more cooperation between teachers, parents, students, and outside professionals. (C8.8, 2016)

Many comments have been received from participants with regards to teachers believing that their schools do not provide any specialist training for teachers to be able to meet the needs of their students who are twice exceptional. A number of respondents lamented the fact that there was no specific training available on twice exceptionality either at the undergraduate or postgraduate level. This is changing with the University of Wollongong introducing the first ever subject at postgraduate level in twice exceptionality. Wormald (2009) also found in her research that teachers were willing, but the professional learning was not available. One comment from this study reflecting this view stated:

> I think that there is insufficient information available to university students preparing for teaching—this was certainly absent from my degree and undergraduate studies. I also think that there is insufficient training and professional development opportunities for teachers who work with students who are twice exceptional students. This is especially true of teachers in selective high schools as there is little information and training out there for teaching a whole cohort of gifted students, with a substantial portion of students who are twice-exceptional. (J7.4, 2016)

A study that sought to understand how many students in Australia identified as gifted or with learning disabilities may also fit the profile of twice exceptionality would provide support for the implementation of professional learning for teachers. This lack of training means that teachers do not have the knowledge to identify and meet these students' educational needs and that those who do have some understanding of students who are twice exceptional may struggle to convince their colleagues. The argument for training in gifted education in general is ongoing and was raised as a recommendation at both Senate inquiries conducted in Australia (Commonwealth of Australia, 1988, 2001). A comment from this study supporting this observation stated from one participant:

> How do you explain to your colleagues your concerns and then see that a child can have a high IQ but be very challenged in the classroom when it comes to showing their skills or knowledge. (J8.5, 2016)

This current study demonstrates that overall, many teachers are aware of these students; however, they lack the training to identify and provide for these students in order that they can achieve their potential. Future directions for research would be to identify how many students in Australia are possibly twice exceptional. This can be undertaken by researching specialist gifted education classes or streams and specialist schools as well as looking at programs for students with learning disabilities. Additionally, Australian research needs to be undertaken to identify the programs that are required in order for students who are twice exceptional to be able to reach their full potential. This includes identification, teacher training and awareness-raising. In order to gain further understanding of interventions and programs that have seen students who are twice exceptional achieve their potential, a study that considers the students' and parents' perspective of a successful program would be relevant and important for the future of these students.

Conclusion

This study was an important first step in determining the needs of twice-exceptional students across Australia, that is those students who are gifted with an additional learning, emotional, physical, or behavioural disability. Beyond case studies, this was the first large-scale national study of its kind investigating the knowledge, understandings, and practices of schools within Australia with regard to students who are twice exceptional. Overall, teacher participants were quite positive and requested more information on students who are twice exceptional, despite many reporting a lack of awareness of the terminology.

Importantly, this study provided educators with suggestions for professional learning and supporting students who are twice exceptional and apprised researchers with important information about what teachers believe to be some of the issues that face students who are twice exceptional in Australia. There now needs to be follow-up research on what works in schools for students who are twice exceptional and what does not, so that these students may be assisted to reach their full potential.

Cross-References

▶ Gifted and Twice-Exceptional Children in the South of the World: Chilean Students' Experiences Within Regular Classrooms
▶ Gifted Education in the Asia-Pacific: From the Past for the Future – An Introduction
▶ Gifted Girls with Autism Spectrum Disorders: Provisions and Priorities in Australian School Settings
▶ Identifying and Nurturing Diversely Gifted and Talented Students: Part III Introduction
▶ Rural Voices: Identifying the Perceptions, Practices, and Experiences of Gifted Pedagogy in Australian Rural and Regional Schools
▶ Some Implications for the Future of Gifted Education in the Asia-Pacific
▶ Towards Exceptionality: The Current Status and Future Prospects of Australian Gifted Education

Appendix A: Australian Twice Exceptional Needs Survey (Foley Nicpon et al., 2013)

Q1. Does your school have any form of special provision for gifted and talented students?
   If "yes," please describe below.
Q2. Does your school have any form of special provision for students with a specific learning difficulty?
   If "yes," please describe below.

Q3.

How familiar are you with the following categories of twice-exceptionality?

	Not familiar	.	.	.	.	Extremely familiar
Gifted students diagnosed with Attention Deficit / Hyperactivity Disorder (ADD / ADHD)	○	○	○	○	○	○
Gifted students with diagnosed Autism Spectrum Disorder (ASD)	○	○	○	○	○	○
Gifted students with diagnosed behavioural disorders	○	○	○	○	○	○
Gifted students with diagnosed learning difficulties	○	○	○	○	○	○
Gifted students with diagnosed emotional disorders	○	○	○	○	○	○

Q4

How would you describe your experience working with the following groups of students?

	No experience	Minimal experience	Some experience	Moderate experience	Substantial experience	Extensive experience
Gifted students diagnosed with Attention Deficit / Hyperactivity Disorder (ADD / ADHD)	○	○	○	○	○	○
Gifted students with diagnosed Autism Spectrum Disorder (ASD)	○	○	○	○	○	○
Gifted students with diagnosed behavioural disorders	○	○	○	○	○	○
Gifted students with diagnosed learning difficulties	○	○	○	○	○	○
Gifted students with diagnosed emotional disorders	○	○	○	○	○	○

Q5

How confident are you with the following?

	Not confident	.	.	.	.	Extremely confident
Conducting assessment to identify twice-exceptional students	○	○	○	○	○	○
Initiating external assessment of a twice-exceptional student	○	○	○	○	○	○
Meeting general educational needs of twice-exceptional students	○	○	○	○	○	○
Meeting the social and emotional needs of twice-exceptional students	○	○	○	○	○	○
Providing appropriate curriculum differentiation for twice-exceptional students	○	○	○	○	○	○

If you would like to make an additional comment about question 5, please do so here.

Q6

Rank in order from 1 to 7 the following factors you think should be considered as essential knowledge for referring a twice-exceptional student to a school counsellor for assessment.
Let 1 be the most important and 7 be the least important.

☐ Behaviour issues in the classroom
☐ Parental concerns
☐ Peer relationships
☐ Performance on class tests
☐ Performance on class work
☐ Performance on IQ assessment
☐ Performance on standardised tests (e.g. NAPLAN)

Q7

Rank in order what you believe to be the primary area of difficulty that you observe for twice-exceptional students at school?
Let 1 be the most important and 3 or 4 be the least important.

- [ ] Academic difficulties
- [ ] Social difficulties with peers
- [ ] Social difficulties with adults
- [ ] Other - explain briefly below

Q8 In your school, what in-school interventions (e.g., assistive technology, tutoring, enrichment classes) have been implemented for students who are twice exceptional?

References

Antshel, K. M., Faraone, S. V., Stallone, K., Nave, A., Kaufmann, F. A., Doyle, A., ... Biederman, J. (2007). Is attention deficit hyperactivity disorder a valid diagnosis in the presence of high IQ? Results from the MGH longitudinal family studies of ADHD. *Journal of Child Psychology and Psychiatry, 48*(7), 687–694.

Assouline, S. G., Foley Nicpon, M., Colangelo, N., & O'Brien, M. (2008). The paradox of giftedness and autism: Packet of information for professionals: Revised. Belin & Blank international center for gifted education and talent development at the University of Iowa College of Education. Retrieved from https://www2.education.uiowa.edu/belinblank/clinic/pdfs/pif.pdf

Australian Capital Territory Government Education and Training. (n.d.). *Learning difficulties: The difference between a learning difficulty and a learning disability.* Retrieved from https://www.education.act.gov.au/__data/.../Learning-Difficulties-Factsheet-1.pdf

Australian Curriculum Assessment and Reporting Authority. (2015). *Australian curriculum, v8.3 F-10 curriculum. Student diversity: Gifted and talented students.* Retrieved from http://www.australiancurriculum.edu.au/studentdiversity/gifted-and-talented-students

Australian Disability Clearinghouse on Education and Training. (n.d.). Retrieved from http://www.adcet.edu.au/inclusive-teaching/specific-disabilities/specific-learning-disability/

Australian Discrimination Act. (1991, 2017). Retrieved from https://www.legislation.act.gov.au/a/1991-81/current/pdf/1991-81.pdf

Baum, S., Schader, R. and Owen. S. V. (2017). To be gifted and learning disabled: Strength based strategies for helping twice-exceptional students with LD, ADHD. USA: Prufrock Press.

Bailey, J. (2004). The validation of a scale to measure school principals' attitudes toward the inclusion of students with disabilities in regular schools. *Australian Psychologist, 39*(1), 7–87.

Baum, S., Owen, S. V., & Dixon, J. (1991). *To be gifted and learning disabled: From identification to practical strategies.* Melbourne, VIC: Hawker Brownlow Education.

Baum, S. M., Schader, R. M., & Hébert, T. P. (2014). Through a different lens: Reflecting on a strengths-based, talent-focused approach for twice exceptional learners. *Gifted Child Quarterly, 58*(4), 311–327. https://doi.org/10.1177/0016986214547632

British Society of Audiology. (2011). *Practice guidance: An overview of current management of auditory processing disorder (APD).* Retrieved from https://www.thebsa.org.uk/wp-content/uploads/2011/04/Current-APD-Management-2.pdf

Carrington, S., Papinczak, T., & Templeton, E. (2003). A phenomenological study: The social world of five adolescents who have Asperger's syndrome. *Australian Journal of Learning Disabilities, 8*(3), 15–25. https://doi.org/10.1080/19404150309546734

Commonwealth of Australia. (1988). Senate select committee report on the education of gifted and talented children. Retrieved from http://pandora.nla.gov.au/pan/25300/20020605-0000/www.aph.gov.au/senate/committee/EET_CTTE/gifted/GT%20Report%201988.pdf

Commonwealth of Australia. (2001). Senate employment workplace relations, small business and education references committee report on the education of the gifted child.

Disability Discrimination Act. (1992). Retrieved from https://www.legislation.gov.au/Series/C2004A04426

Disability Standards for Education. (2005). Retrieved from https://www.education.gov.au/disability-standards-education-2005

Dixon, R., & Norris, N. (2011). Twice exceptional gifted students with Asperger's syndrome. *The Australasian Journal of Gifted Education, 30*(2), 34–45.

Dixon, R., & Tanner, K. (2013). The experience of transitioning two adolescents with Asperger's syndrome in academically focused high schools. *Australasian Journal of Special Education, 37*(1), 28–48.

Dyslexia-SPELD Foundation. (2014a). Literacy and clinical services. Retrieved from https://dsf.net.au/what-is-dysgraphia/

Dyslexia-SPELD Foundation. (2014b). Literacy and clinical services. Retrieved from https://dsf.net.au/what-are-learning-disabilities/

Foley Nicpon, M., Allmon, A., Sieck, B., & Stinson, R. D. (2011). Empirical investigation of twice exceptionality: Where have we been and where are we going? *Gifted Child Quarterly, 55*(1), 3–17.

Foley Nicpon, M., Assouline, S., & Colangelo, N. (2013). Twice-exceptional learners: Who needs to know what? *Gifted Child Quarterly, 57*(3), 169–180. https://doi.org/10.1177/0016986213490021

Fraser-Seeto, K. (2013). Pre-service teacher training in gifted and talented education: An Australian perspective. *Journal of Student Engagement: Education Matters, 3*(1), 29–38. Retrieved from https://ro.uow.edu.au/cgi/viewcontent.cgi?article=1026&context=jseem

Gable, R. K., & Wolf, M. B. (1993). *Instrument development in the affective domain: Measuring attitudes and values in corporate and school settings* (2nd ed.). Boston, MA: Kluwer Academic Publishers.

Gagné, F. (2008). *Building gifts into talents: Overview of the DMGT*. Asia Pacific conference for giftedness. 10th conference, Asia-Pacific federation of the world council for gifted and talented children, Singapore. Retrieved from http://www.templetonfellows.org/program/FrancoysGagne.pdf

Holmes, B., & Sutherland, L. (2010). Mathematics: I just know it. Do you? The gifted student with Asperger's. In C. Wormald & W. Vialle (Eds.), *Dual exceptionality* (pp. 95–105). Wollongong, Australia: University of Wollongong Printery.

Individual with Disabilities Education Act. (2004). Retrieved from https://sites.ed.gov/idea

Kirk, S. A., Gallagher, J. J., & Anastasiow, N. J. (2000). *Educating exceptional children* (9th ed.). Boston, MA: Houghton Mifflin.

McEwin, A. (2003). Educational malpractice: More than an academic exercise for public school gifted students. *Australia & New Zealand Journal of Law & Education, 8*(1), 3–16. Retrieved from http://www.austlii.edu.au/au/journals/ANZJlLawEdu/2003/2.pdf

Montgomery, D. (2015). *Teaching gifted children with special educational needs: Supporting dual and multiple exceptionality*. New York, NY: Routledge.

Munro, J. (2002). Understanding and identifying gifted learning disabled students. *Australian Journal of Learning Disabilities, 7*(2), 20–31.

Munro, J. (2009). Gifted learning disabled students. *Australian Journal of Learning Disabilities, 7*(2), 12–30.

Mutch, C. (2013). *Doing educational research: A practitioner's guide to getting started* (2nd ed.). Wellington: New Zealand Council for Educational Research (NZCER Press).

National Health and Medical Research Council. (n.d.). Retrieved from https://www.australia.gov.au/directories/australia/nhrmc

Nielsen, M. E. (2002). Gifted students with learning disabilities: Recommendations for identification and programming. *Exceptionality, 10*, 93–111. https://doi.org/10.1207/S15327035EX1002_4

Plunkett, M., & Kronborg, L. (2007). Gifted education in Australia: A story of striving for balance. *Gifted Education International, 23*(1), 72–83. https://doi.org/10.1177/026142940702300109

Reis, S. M., Baum, S. M., & Burke, E. (2014). An operational definition of twice-exceptional learners: Implications and applications. *Gifted Child Quarterly, 58*, 217–230. https://doi.org/10.1177/0016986214534976

Rogers, K. B. (2011). Thinking smart about twice exceptional learners: Steps to find them and strategies for catering to them appropriately. In C. Wormald & W. Vialle (Eds.), *Dual exceptionality* (pp. 57–70). Wollongong, Australia: University of Wollongong Printery.

Ronksley-Pavia, M. (2016). The lived experience of twice exceptional children: Narrative perceptions of disability and giftedness. Unpublished Doctoral Thesis. Griffith University. Retrieved from https://www120.secure.griffith.edu.au/rch/file/39f8c43e-669a-4488-8d4f-ea4204f009de/1/Ronksley-Pavia_2016_01Thesis.pdf

Rowley, J. (2012). Professional development needs of teachers to identify and cater for gifted students. *Australasian Journal of Gifted Education, 21*(2), 75–80.

SPELD Victoria (2019). Retrieved from http://www.speldvic.org.au/information-for-teachers/

Strachota, E. M., Conceicao, S. C. O., & Schmidt, S. W. (2006). An instrument development model for online surveys in human resources development and adult education. *New Horizons in Adult Education and Human Resource Development, 20*(2), 24–37. https://doi.org/10.1002/nha3.10249

Townend, G., & Pendergast, D. (2015). Student voice: What can we learn from twice-exceptional students about the teacher's role in enhancing or inhibiting academic self-concept. *Australasian Journal of Gifted Education, 42*(1), 37–51. Retrieved from https://core.ac.uk/download/pdf/143899736.pdf

Vialle, W. (2017). Supporting giftedness in families: A resources perspective. *Journal for the Education of the Gifted, 40*(4), 372–393. https://doi.org/10.1177/0162353217734375

Whitebread, D., Coltman, P., Pino Pasternak, D., Sangster, C., Grau, V., Bingham, S., ... Demetriou, D. (2009). The development of two observational tools for assessing metacognition & self-regulated learning in young children. *Metacognition and Learning, 4*, 63–85. https://doi.org/10.1007/s11409-008-9033-1

Willard-Holt, C., Weber, J., Morrison, K. L., & Horgan, J. (2013). Twice exceptional learners' perspective on effective learning strategies. *Gifted Child Quarterly, 57*(4), 247–262. https://doi.org/10.1177/0016986213501076

Woodcock, S., Dixon, R., & Tanner, K. (2013). *Teaching in inclusive school environments*. Macksville, NSW: David Barlow Publishing.

Wormald, C. (2009). *An enigma: Barriers to identification of gifted students with a learning disability*. Doctoral Thesis. University of Wollongong, Wollongong, New South Wales, Australia. Retrieved from http://ro.uow.edu.au/cgi/viewcontent.cgi?article=4076&context=theses

Catherine Wormald, PhD, began her career as a secondary mathematics teacher and taught across all education systems. She coordinates and teaches in gifted and special needs education at undergraduate and postgraduate level at the University of Wollongong. Catherine has worked for the NSW and ACT Departments of Education, and Sydney Catholic Schools providing advice, reviewing policy, and providing professional learning for teachers. She is a past president of state and national gifted associations. She regularly presents at international, national, and state conferences. Catherine's research focus is on students who are twice exceptional, students with special needs, gifted education, and underachievement.

Michelle Bannister-Tyrrell, PhD, was a senior lecturer and the Director of Program Impact and Innovation at the University of New England. After teaching in schools for more than three decades as both a primary and secondary English teacher, her research now includes under-identified gifted students, such as rural, Indigenous, low socio-economic, and twice-exceptional students. Michelle regularly presents her research at international, national, and state conferences. Her thesis was awarded the 2015 John Geake Outstanding Thesis Award presented by AAEGT, and in 2014, Michelle won the Beth Southwell Research Award for outstanding thesis from the NSW Institute for Educational Research.

Underachievement and the Quest for Dignity: Contemporary Perspectives on a Timeless Issue

28

James R. Delisle and Robert Arthur Schultz

Contents

Introduction	608
Research on Underachievement: A Brief History	609
The Cupertino Project	610
From Then to Now	611
Bronfenbrenner's Ecological Theory of Human Development	612
Dabrowski's Theory of Positive Disintegration (TPD)	613
The Theoretical Foundation ... Distilled	614
Region-Specific Research on Underachieving Gifted Learners in the Asia-Pacific	615
Research on Underachievement: A Contemporary Overview	616
High-Scoring Studies	618
The 2007–2017 Literature Base: In Repose	620
Research into Practice: Reversing Underachievement While Respecting Student Dignity—Strategies for Educators and Counsellors	620
Conclusion	623
Cross-References	624
Analytic chart of article data set (2007–2017)	625
References	626

Abstract

Since the 1930s, the topic of underachievement has been studied by educators and psychologists with hopes of finding a 'cure' for this condition. Dozens of books and hundreds of research studies have been completed, yet there continues to be no consensus on the aetiology or successful treatment of gifted students who

---

J. R. Delisle (✉)
Kent State University, Kent, OH, USA
e-mail: jim.delisle@yahoo.com

R. A. Schultz (✉)
University of Toledo, Toledo, OH, USA
e-mail: robert.schultz@utoledo.edu

© Springer Nature Singapore Pte Ltd. 2021
S. R. Smith (ed.), *Handbook of Giftedness and Talent Development in the Asia-Pacific*,
Springer International Handbooks of Education,
https://doi.org/10.1007/978-981-13-3041-4_28

perform far below their measured academic aptitude. In this chapter, we explore underachievement as the complex phenomenon that is involving not just curriculum, instruction and cognition but also the lack of autonomy the underachieving student feels in having diminished control over his/her education. Following an overview of the scholarly research on underachievement, a theory-based approach based on current and historic psychological efforts to best understand and address concerns of underachieving students will be addressed. The chapter concludes with specific suggestions for addressing the individual and multifaceted needs of underachieving students, with the ultimate goal of guiding these students to develop a strong sense of self and a desire to succeed academically while preserving their personal integrity and dignity.

Keywords

Underachievers · Underachievement · Selective learners · Non-producers · Gifted · Talented.

The aims in this chapter are to:
1. Review the extant and historical research on the topic of academic underachievement of gifted students.
2. Provide a theory-based, critical analysis of research conducted between 2007 and present to put into clearer focus the topic of underachievement.
3. Accentuate the need to consider the distinction between those children who underachieve due to psychological and emotional factors and those who perform poorly on purpose, due to dissatisfaction with academic offerings.
4. Highlight specific studies conducted on underachieving students that blend together theory, research, and legitimate practice.
5. Suggest specific strategies that educators, counsellors, and parents could use in addressing the topic of underachievement in ways that preserve student respect and dignity.

Introduction

We have to wonder if, way back in the Pleistocene Era, a disgruntled Neanderthal mum or dad groused about their teenager who didn't bring home a sufficient number of carcasses for the evening meal. Our guess is 'yes', that even 130,000 years ago, underachievement was an issue that afflicted adolescents and flummoxed the adults around them.

Despite decades of theorising and researching, *underachievement* is too complex to define simply, and there are still no universal conceptions of giftedness nor underachievement (Reis & McCoach, 2000; Tsai & Fu, 2016). Indeed, underachievement is a word that conjures up universally negative attributes: lazy, bored, uninterested, unfocused, or frustrating, for example. And even though this condition has been probed and studied by educators and psychologists for several generations, underachievement continues to be as problematic as it is enigmatic—a complex, confusing phenomenon that seems to defy a ready resolution.

Why is the issue of capable students performing poorly in school so hard to 'fix'? What are the dynamics that cause intelligent students to turn their backs on high achievement and, instead, wallow in the trough of academic mediocrity? How is it that a countless number of both quantitative and qualitative research studies have not been able to offer definitive, long-term solutions to this perplexing dilemma?

These are not easy questions to answer. However, after having studied and researched this issue for decades ourselves, we believe the answers to remedying underachievement lie in a few mostly unexamined places. In this chapter, we will highlight those places that hold the most promise for addressing the issue of academic underachievement so that both the students who are labelled as underachievers and the adults in their lives who care about them maintain that most essential of human needs: the preservation of personal dignity.

Research on Underachievement: A Brief History

Although Pleistocene Era parents may have worried about their underachieving progeny, the real focus on underachievement didn't occur until centuries later, when educators and psychologists began to examine why it was that so many capable students did not perform up to academic expectations. One of the first research meta-analyses to explore this disconnect between abilities and school performance was conducted in 1961, by Raph and Tannenbaum, who looked at more than 90 empirical studies of underachievement conducted during the previous 30 years. Their frustrating conclusion was that there was no one unified explanation of why underachievement occurred. Asbury (1974) and Ziv (1977) came to the same conclusion in their own analyses: there were no psychosocial factors associated consistently with underachievement.

Paul Plowman, a gifted coordinator of some note from California, postulated that the most extreme underachievement occurs in rural areas, for the following reasons:

> A gifted child in a rural or low-density populated area may be (1) isolated from intellectual stimulation and from learning resources; (2) unsophisticated: uninformed, lacking in social and learning skills, and provincial; and (3) deprived: culturally and educationally. (1971, pp. 56–57)

Another study by Pringle (1970), in a book with the oddly named title, *Able misfits: A study of educational and behaviour difficulties of 103 very intelligent children (IQs 120–200)*, concluded that gifted underachievers were not identified initially due to low school performance, but rather because they were 'problem children' (Pringle actually called them *juvenile, delinquents*).

Undergirding this confusion on the genesis of underachievement is the wide range of opinions on how prevalent this phenomenon is. Strang (1960) postulated that 15% of the school-age population underachieves, while Hildreth (1966) ups the ante to 50%. And, just for good measure, Fine (1967) takes a more existential view of underachievement, proclaiming that:

> ... we are almost all of us underachievers...We are not living in a time or in a society that demands total performance... Almost all of us are specialists and are not expected to perform to the maximum of our abilities in more than a few limited areas. (pp. 233–234)

So, there you have it: a complete non-consensus on the prevalence of underachievement among gifted children. Given this rampant confusion on how underachievement is identified and how many gifted students are afflicted with it, you might imagine that methods of 'fixing' it are equally as diverse. And you'd be right. Then, along came a single researcher who did more to inform us of both the prevalence of underachievement and its remediation than any other individual before or since. Her name is Joanne Rand Whitmore.

The Cupertino Project

Joanne Whitmore was a primary school teacher in the 1960s–1970s in California's affluent Cupertino Union Elementary District (CUED), home to many Stanford University professors. Whitmore began to take note of many young, intelligent children who were excluded from her school's gifted program because their academic performance was weak. Instead, many of these youngsters were placed in either heterogeneously grouped classes, where boredom reigned for these intelligent children, or in special education programs, if their classroom behaviours were especially disruptive. At some point, CUED school administrators noticed this situation and decided to initiate the *Cupertino Program for Highly Gifted Underachievers*, an experimental program that "established self-contained classes for students who evidenced the need of an intensive program of social and emotional rehabilitation as well as academic remediation" (Whitmore, 1980, p. 206). Whitmore was chosen to be one of this program's teachers.

In documenting what these children needed, intellectually, emotionally, and socially, Whitmore determined that the following conditions would undergird her classroom:

- *Children needed to decrease invidious comparisons with high achievers*, whose academic achievements made these underperforming children feel inadequate.
- *Children needed to develop self-acceptance through acceptance of others with similar problems*, as this recognition that the underachieving child was not alone was instrumental in ameliorating feelings of frustration and worthlessness.
- *Children needed to enjoy rewarding intellectual stimulation and a curriculum centred on their strengths and past success*, instead of focusing on what children could not do or academic deficiencies that might be present.

- *Children needed to acquire a sense of genuine success*, which was accomplished through independent research, scientific experimentation, and creative productivity in the arts.
- *Children needed to develop social skills and the potential for leadership* by using the two most prominent attributes of gifted children: perceptiveness and sensitivity to their advantage, with classmates who had similar strengths.

A total of 29 students participated in this multi-year experimental program, and for her doctoral dissertation, Whitmore conducted formal follow-up studies of her students in 1972 and 1975, with a less-formal follow-up each year from 1976 to 1978. The result was a book, *Giftedness, Conflict, and Underachievement* (Whitmore, 1980), which presents a full review of the curriculum offered to these students, a thorough quantitative analysis of her data as well as case studies of four of her students.

As must be obvious after reading this section, research on gifted underachievers often results in imprecise conclusions and overly generalised recommendations for achieving student success. Whitmore's work stands alone in providing both evidence of the complexity of the underachievement phenomenon and methods of addressing it constructively in a classroom setting. Not every child in Whitmore's classroom achieved academic and personal success, although most did, yet her attempts to address this issue in a way that respected both her students' minds and their individual dignity remain the sine qua non of research on underachievement.

To be sure, other 'experts' and researchers (e.g., Betts & Neihart, 1988; Cavilla, 2017; Kim, 2008; Preckel & Brunner, 2015) have continued to study underachievement in ensuing decades, yet none has ever matched the efforts of Whitmore's experiment in CUSD.

From Then to Now

The above section of the chapter explored what we believe are the best contributions to the historical record associated with underachievement of the gifted. We would be remiss, however, in focusing your gaze upon these oft-ignored resources without providing context and a pathway for understanding the construct of underachievement of the gifted (UAG) as it currently is and how it might be explored in the future.

We believe this requires collectively broadening our focus to enable a more holistic means of examining the phenomenon. Indeed, a broadening of foundational focus is required away from the field of developmental psychology to move readers beyond the scholarly gaze of UAG depicted by descriptive accounts to an interpretive perspective.

Our goal is to provide a way of thinking about UAG guided by theory rather than anecdotal accounts based on loose connections to what individuals believe and define underachievement to be. Think of our approach as map building with theory acting as a compass, providing direction for our journey, but unable to delineate the fine-grain detail of the local terrain—yet.

Bronfenbrenner's Ecological Theory of Human Development

> ...much of contemporary developmental psychology is *the science of the strange behavior of children in strange situations with strange adults for the briefest possible periods of time.* (Bronfenbrenner, 1977, p. 513)

Our journey begins squarely within the metaphor of the terrain, where the murkiness of human beings piles dimensions of complex interactions at our feet. In our travels working with individuals bearing the label of gifted underachiever, we have yet to encounter any person who sets out to strive to achieve this goal—well, that would be rather ironic, achieving at underachievement?

Rather, we find individuals impacted by a label attached to them based on assumptions, beliefs and biases, leaving our participants confused and emotionally distraught. Most have no idea how or why others attached a label to them. And, all have become reactive to the label since it follows them, as one of our participants stated, "like a black cloud I can't seem to shake" (C. Jesper, October 24, 2017, personal communication).

We believe awareness about the impact of the label is an important consideration. And, much of this awareness can only be gained through exposure to, and exploration of, the complex milieu that makes up the participants' environments. "Social status and structure are of course interdependent, but attention must be given to both of these variables if the process of social development is to be properly understood" (Bronfenbrenner, 1943, p. 363).

Bronfenbrenner provided contextual clues about how social scientists might address these complexes, but not altogether clear lived experiences. He posited a mesosystems approach (1979, 1986b), whereby settings and contexts are recognised as components affecting development and tendencies/behaviours displayed by individuals. Due to the many layers (mesosystems) impacting individuals, pathways to development seem very convoluted and individualised.

As Bronfenbrenner's understanding developed and refined, he posited a chronosystem approach (1986a) where changes over time are determined by an individual's experiences within the environments in which they live. This is built from the mesosystems approach to one where longitudinal efforts documenting and describing interactive effects provided contextual clues as to how any individual developed based on their circumstances.

As an example of the mesosystem-chronosystem approach, consider the way artisans manipulate growing bamboo shoots into living sculptures. A market booth containing a litany of elegant spirals or other geometric shapes composed of interwoven bamboo shoots might catch your attention. It is apparent that these aesthetically pleasing arrangements took many hours of manipulation by the artisan (the chronosystem), constantly imposing force upon the growing shoots to steer the course of growth and development (the mesosystem). The marvel of the designs and results provides results of effort over long periods of time. Likewise, consider the ancient art of bonsai. At its core, the spiritual and physical interact to provide a miniature representation of life in the form of the bonsai sculpture; and the steady sense of slowing down provides the bonsai artist a sense of developing peace in the process of the endeavour. Again, complex interactions (meso-) over time (chrono-) provide the systemic context for the complete process.

Bronfenbrenner's *Ecological Theory of Development* (Bronfenbrenner & Crouter, 1983), where complexity is recognised, described, and explored over time—rather than controlled for—is the first component of our theoretical foundation.

Dabrowski's Theory of Positive Disintegration (TPD)

Developmental theory is often based on ontogenetic progression. One stage leads naturally to the next as the individual grows. Dabrowski's theory, in contrast, is not an age-based progression of development. However, levels of development frame it out. Distinctive stages are noted as transfer points as an individual obtains readiness and awareness and moves from one psychic level to another, rather than upon reaching age thresholds.

Conflict is an essential precept of the entire theory, triggering the beginning of the developmental process. Usually this conflict is externally imposed by others' assumptions, perceptions, and expectations based on their experience, not necessarily considering the lived experience of the target for their projections—the individual bearing the burden of the label associated with the expectations (Tillier, 1998):

> Human development seems to be impossible without the collision between some elements of the inner and outer milieus. The localization of conflicts in the inner milieu according to level is very important. Conflicts are subject to psychic transformation. In this way conflicts of both kinds can be sublimated and moved to a higher level. (Dabrowski, Kawczak, & Piechowski, 1970, p. 83)

As the individual moves from one developmental level to another, the conflict causes an emotional upheaval or crescendo that disintegrates the sense of self (Dabrowski, 1967; Dabrowski & Piechowski, 1977a, 1977b). As the process of reintegration occurs, self-concept changes and self-awareness takes firmer hold within the individual. Indeed, moving through the stages of development means an individual is becoming more internally guided and driven; thus the sense of *positive* disintegration is an outcome of developmental growth (Dabrowski & Piechowski, 1977a):

> The very concept of disintegration points out the drama of human existence; it is impossible to live as man all the time in the state of blessed harmony and self-complacency; we are human inasmuch as we experience disharmony and dissatisfaction, inherent in the process of disintegration. (Dabrowski et al., 1970, p. 122)

As an individual grows within the TPD, emotional and personality development are taking place. Each new stage presents the individual with a disintegration and reintegration experience—bolstering internal drive for development rather than mere reaction to externally imposed conflict (Dabrowski, 1964). This is the blossoming of the inner psyche or self, which ultimately channels adults to a sense of the workings of the world and how they fit within it.

It is this developing self that guides our exploration into underachievement. We prefer to categorise performance from the label bearer's perspective as either non-production or selective learning—the inner drive to have some semblance of control for one's actions in context. This is in opposition to the externally imposed label of underachiever, which can have a myriad of meanings fully dependent upon beliefs and assumptions with total disregard to the lived experience of the individual being labelled.

The Theoretical Foundation ... Distilled

In concert, Bronfenbrenner's ecological theory of human development and Dabrowski's Theory of Positive Disintegration allow us to uniquely explore the contemporary literature (i.e., published over the last decade, 2007–2017) associated with underachievement of the gifted, based on our theoretical foundation. Descriptor themes are italicised in the following bulleted list. These themes were used as focal points for examining the literature in our data set. We looked for:

- Authors who noted *coherence* between nature and nurture and the internal and external milieus working sometimes harmoniously and other times in direct opposition to self-development in their work with underachievers.
- *Researcher bias* in addressing underachievement from an 'imposed upon' basis by external assumptions, biases and/or beliefs devoid of recognition that the individual bearing the label is an individual with a complex set of lived experiences that impact their tendencies/behaviours.
- Recognition that the target of the work—the underachiever—is a complex and developing individual immersed in a complex environmental and mental state of self-development over time (*awareness of self*) that impacts his/her actions.

Distilling all of the above into a more straightforward narrative statement, positive disintegration is a process of resolving conflicts between ideals and values (what ought to be) and existing reality of life circumstance (what is). Psychic development involves the dynamic interplay between environmental factors and the developing self. Psychic movement from primarily reacting to environmental impositions to internal drive and self-awareness of choice requires multi-level integration (Dabrowski, 1976). This multi-level integration involves building meta-cognitive awareness that one can do more than react to the environment (Psychic Integration Level 1). Indeed, one is driven to play by the rules (Psychic Integration Level 2), but, over time and through conflict, realises you must fight for principles (Psychic Integration Level 3) to become an individual (M. M. Piechowski, November 1998, personal communication).

This state of becoming through multi-level integration is our compass. We use this compass as an awareness indicator and marker to judge the level of finesse (refined scholarly and/or theoretical awareness) existing in the current UAG literature base as we attempt to make sense of the complex terrain associated with underachievement.

Region-Specific Research on Underachieving Gifted Learners in the Asia-Pacific

In the past two decades, quantitative and qualitative research studies have been done across the Asia-Pacific focused on the topic of underachievement among gifted students. One of the larger studies involved complex quantitative analysis of 477 achieving and 118 underachieving gifted students in grades 7–9 (Phillips, 2017). The study was designed to investigate distinctions that might exist between these two groups of students in relation to their attitudes towards school and teachers, their motivation to achieve academically, and their personal acceptance of themselves as being gifted. Phillips was surprised to find that there were no statistically significant differences between the groups in relation to their attitudes towards school. However, there were three statistically significant factors that did distinguish between these groups of students: their motivation to achieve academically; their social self-efficacy (i.e., how much control they thought they had over their own achievement); and their willingness to accept (achieving students) or deny (underachieving students) their own giftedness.

In an earlier, related study (Dixon, Craven, & Martin, 2006), the researchers investigated whether several affective characteristics could distinguish between the 41 achieving and seven underachieving gifted students they examined. Addressing the factors of academic self-concept, self-expectations for future achievement, and locus of control, it was learned that while self-expectations for future achievement could not distinguish between these groups of students, the other two factors showed statistically significant differences.

In a meta-analysis of 771 studies on underachievement published between 2005 and 2014 (Banerjee, 2016), designed to determine which factors most contributed to underachievement in science and mathematics in economically disadvantaged students in British Commonwealth countries, the most frequently cited factors were a lack of positive learning environments coupled with weak support for academics from adults in the students' lives. Recommendations for addressing these issues ranged from increasing parent involvement in their children's education, early intervention with young gifted children who are not performing at levels commensurate with their abilities, a focus on self-concept education in addition to academic instruction, teacher education on the characteristics and learning patterns of underachievers, and involvement by underachievers in extracurricular activities related to school.

In a qualitative investigation of indigenous Māori and Pasifika underachievers, (New Zealand Principals' Federation, n.d.), it was noted that the lack of expected levels of achievement could be attributed to poverty, behavioural issues in classrooms, and (perhaps controversially) inherent differences in intellectual capacity. It was recommended that a closer link between the indigenous children's heritage and culture be established so that students would 'buy in' to the educational offerings they were receiving.

In a wide-ranging study (Phillipson et al., 2009) of how achievement and gifted education in particular are perceived in different East Asian nations—Singapore, China, South Korea, and others—the researchers concluded that, despite individual distinctions between nations, these factors were common: misperceptions that giftedness did not exist unless manifested in high academic achievement; misperceptions about the role of gifted education services within schools; a singular focus on pervasive testing which tended to exclude highly capable children whose test scores were high but classroom performance was low; and a lack of cohesive curriculum development for educating gifted students.

Finally, in a case study conducted on two underachieving gifted students who received specific instruction in creative writing in a withdrawal ('pull out') program at their schools (Bennett-Rappell & Northcote, 2016), the researchers suggest that to optimise achievement for underachievers, the following conditions would be beneficial: one-on-one instruction; a focus on the student-teacher relationship, not just academic instruction; a curriculum that was differentiated in both content and teaching methods; and an eclectic approach to dealing with underachieving students, as the label of 'underachievement' includes students who may not perform academically for a variety of personal, interpersonal, and school-related issues.

A primary finding from many of the studies cited above, as well as others not regionally specific, is that underachieving students are more than just a 'sum of their grades'. A strong, deliberate focus on self-concept and self-efficacy, combined with a student-teacher relationship that is more democratic than authoritarian, will likely see outcomes that are positive for the future development of these underachieving students' minds.

Research on Underachievement: A Contemporary Overview

We focused on the literature base for the last decade (2007–2017) as our definition of contemporary. A keyword search was used to accumulate a broad data set. A list was developed of databases and keywords used for the initial search. We also searched the archives of journals specific to the field of gifted education: *Gifted Child Quarterly*, *Roeper Review*, *Journal for the Education of the Gifted*, *Gifted Education International*, *Gifted and Talented International* and *High Ability Studies* (see Table 1). There were 3902 peer-reviewed journal articles compiled from this initial search. We searched the regional literature in Australasia for additional peer-reviewed work that was not represented in our original target journal list. Two additional studies were added to the data set (i.e., Banerjee, 2016; Bennett-Rappell & Northcote, 2016).

Keywords were then cross-listed to zero in on the literature from the period that included the constructs of gifted/talented and underachievement. The cross-listed data set included 109 articles that were then downloaded and read to look specifically for the theme of underachievement of the gifted (UAG) as a construct emphasised within the piece. We also explored pieces that were closely aligned with gifted individuals and achievement. This winnowed our data down to 41 peer-reviewed journal articles. This was the final data set used for our work in this chapter (see Appendix A).

Table 1 List of databases, journals and keywords used for initial literature search

Databases	Keywords
PsycINFO	Underachievers
PsycARTICLES	Underachievement
Academic search complete	Selective learners
Psychology and behavioral sciences collection	Non-producers
	Gifted
Field-specific journals	Talented
Gifted child quarterly	Gifted and talented
Roeper review	GT
Journal for the education of the gifted	Underachievement in education of gifted students
Gifted education international	Underachievement in education
Gifted and talented international	Underachieving students
High ability studies	Underachieving learners

For comparative purposes we scored each article using a Likert-type rating (see Fig. 1), along with narrative notes regarding the reader's overall perspective about the piece based on our theoretical foundation points. We do not claim validity or reliability for our cursory analysis—other than contextual face validity based on our joint development of the criteria and theoretical foundation.

We found out that of the total articles (n = 41), an emphasis upon discussing or exploring variables or instruments in order to measure underachievement (n = 15; e.g., Phillipson & Ka-on Tse, 2007; Snyder & Adelson, 2017) and treatments and interventions to resolve underachieving tendencies and behaviours (n = 9; e.g., Bennett-Rappell & Northcote, 2016; Berger, 2013; Morisano & Shore, 2010) accounted for 59% of the data set. This did not surprise us, as the core approach used by many scholars conducting research is to find a construct (or variable) and attempt to control, or otherwise measure, it so as to statistically represent the construct to a wider audience and, oh, to publish or perish as the old saw goes. There is nothing inherently wrong with this approach. However, it does perpetuate the philosophical perspective that to know something is to break it down to its most simplistic parts, study them, make statistically significant statements about them, and then infer generalisable understanding. Historically, this approach has not worked—and is likely not to add any appreciable understanding about UAG in all its complex splendour.

We did find an abundance of articles promoting theory and theory development (n = 19; e.g., Stojnov, Dzinivic, & Pavlovic, 2008; Ziegler, Ziegler, & Stoeger, 2012), often tied to some measure or intervention strategy. These articles are built from the existing literature base, perpetuating the same approaches, but in a slightly different format (using different measurement approaches), or seeking to integrate different theoretical approaches and discussing hoped-for studies associated with these approaches.

Based on the intended audience for this handbook, we are adding an annotated summary (see Appendix A) of studies—several of which were not peer-reviewed publications—to the chapter. Our goal is for readers to explore 'local' resources

Coherence nature-nurture   internal-external

    Unexplored   Evident

      0   1   2   3

Bias of researcher

    Not Evident   Evident

      3   2   1   0

Developing Self awareness

    Unexplored   Evident

      0   1   2   3

Narrative Statement: Total   ◯

Fig. 1 Theoretical Foundation Scoring Sheet

as well as to compare them to broadly conceived literature associated with UAG. We encourage you to get involved and contribute to the knowledge base.

High-Scoring Studies

It was much more difficult to find pieces that scored high on our criteria scale (an 8 or 9 using our Likert tool) based on the theoretical foundation. We were searching for works that followed a complex milieu or interrelational research philosophical approach—where constant comparison and reconceptualisation of truth claims are occurring as the work is conducted (Schultz, 2002). Happily, there were a few (n = 4; Gibbons, Pelchar, & Cochran, 2012; Hebert & Schreiber, 2010; Ritchotte & Graefe, 2017; Snyder & Linnenbrink-Garcia, 2013).

In their article, Hebert and Schreiber (2010) speak specifically to Schultz's (2002) challenge to stop trying to fix underachievers and, rather, focus on working with those bearing the label to better understand their lived experience and the impact the label has upon them. Hebert and Schreiber present case studies of two gifted underachievers and develop pathways to understanding these students' perspectives using their lived experiences as foundation and develop nuanced understanding about selective achievers:

> …we define selective achievers as intrinsically motivated individuals whose performance matches ability only in specific areas that satisfy their interests and personal goal orientations. (Hebert & Schreiber, 2010, p. 572)

The article is an elegant work of qualitative case study design—which scored an eight on our scale.

Gibbons et al. (2012) explored the impacts of gifted students coming from families with low-education backgrounds. In this study, the coherence factor and developing self were key factors that came through the narrative. Although the focus of the work is not UAG, the impact noted within the work is tied to complexities in lived experiences that do impact students' abilities to achieve:

> When considering gifted students from low-education backgrounds, it is vital to remember the cultural and structural factors that affect them as well... Educators can view their students within their cultural framework, leading to less blaming of parents and more understanding of the larger societal factors influencing achievement levels. (Gibbons et al., 2012, p. 120)

The article weaves between a sociological understanding of the circumstances associated with low education in families and an anthropological case study conversation sharing the stories of a mother and daughter working through the process of understanding one another and the context of achievement. The article also scored an eight on our scale.

Snyder and Linnenbrink-Garcia (2013) present a theoretically based discussion promoting a developmental, person-centred approach to studying motivation associated with underachieving gifted individuals. The article is dynamic in the thoroughness and support built for this approach. The authors also show great alacrity in stitching together very disparate unidimensional psychological approaches into a quilt that broadly addresses a myriad of complexities associated with motivational pathways:

> [O]ur model may help to redirect prevention and interventions from a focus on single variables across individuals ... toward addressing the shape and type of interrelated networks of beliefs. (Snyder & Linnenbrink-Garcia, 2013, p. 224)

Even with the process-product structural approach that grounds this work (Schultz, 2002), the promotion of complex interactions and interrelated events that impact motivation pathways and triggers earned a score of eight on our scale.

Ritchotte and Graefe (2017) present an article honouring the lived experience of individuals who ultimately dropped out of school for myriad reasons. The topical structure of the article had little to do with underachievement directly, but so many circumstances noted throughout the manuscript spoke volumes to situations (both internal and external) faced by individuals that impact their ability or choice to achieve:

> The phenomenon of high-potential students discontinuing their K–12 education is complex ... For the majority of participants, learning stopped before ever reaching high school, a prime example of the process of "falling out." They recalled feeling unchallenged by their classes at an early age, and this, coupled with "the progression of less and less support" in school, resulted in overall disillusionment with an educational system that was not meeting their needs. (Ritchotte & Graefe, 2017, p. 286)

The authors provide a strong descriptive account based on 14 participants' perspectives and lived experiences post-dropping out. These accounts are then used to support an interpretive ethnographic account that draws the reader back from the setting to consider broader perspectives associated with a rationale for why individuals make choices based on their lived experiences.

The work is qualitative in nature, but also quite thought-provoking when the broader interpretive overview is presented. This article earned our highest marks (a full score of nine) on our scale.

The 2007–2017 Literature Base: In Repose

Our worry was that our review of the most recent scholarly literature associated with underachievement of the gifted would leave us feeling that nothing substantive had changed from the last time an overview was presented noting 15 definitions of underachievement in the peer-reviewed scholarly literature (Dowdall & Colangelo, 1982). We did not find anyone focusing on contrasting definitions nor about comparing independent and dependent variables and effect sizes.

What we did find are subtle shifts in the approaches being taken to explore this construct. Yes, there remain many pieces content with measurement and testing interventions to alleviate underachievement in school settings (e.g., Obergriesser & Stoeger, 2015; Paunesku et al., 2015; Rubenstein, Siegle, Reis, McCoach, & Burton, 2012). However, evidence also exists supporting the notion that both theory and empirical work are diverging away from process-product measurement towards more qualitative and interpretive research designs that bring awareness to the complex lived experiences of individuals bearing myriad labels—both self- and externally assigned (e.g., Gibbons et al., 2012; Hebert & Schreiber, 2010).

It heartens us that an argument presented in an earlier context is coming to fruition. "Something more than measurable academic or cognitive outcomes must be addressed to understand adequately the complex needs of underachieving gifted learners in the classroom" (Schultz, 2002, pp. 204–205). Even though only 10% (n = 4) of the data set approached close alignment with our theoretical foundation, there is movement towards recognising and honouring the complex lived experiences of gifted individuals whom are often labelled by others without having any say in the matter.

Research into Practice: Reversing Underachievement While Respecting Student Dignity—Strategies for Educators and Counsellors

All the theories in the world will not help the adult trying to understand and aid the underachieving student if they are not partnered with practical ideas. However, as our review of more recent research on UAG shows clearly, 'practical' must be blended with 'respectful' if the results are to have the greatest likelihood of long-term, positive impacts on underachieving students. For example, putting a student on a contract where she/he agrees to attain particular academic and behavioural benchmarks in exchange for gaining driving or computer access privileges may be *practical*, but it lacks the element of respect; it does not take into account the student's primary reasons for underachieving in the first place. If the 'irrelevant' curriculum (from the student's perspective) remains in place, or homework that the student considers purposeless must still be completed in full, then the contract is written from the vantage of the adult trying to modify student behaviour without taking into account the student's underlying reasons for academic discontent. Lacking this element of respect, the contract is sure to fail, and the student will continue to stagnate or even regress in academic performance.

In attempting to find the right balance between academic expectations and student input for achieving them, let us return to a study previewed in the previous section of this article, the one authored by Ritchotte and Graefe (2017). To review, the authors examined the lives of 14 gifted students who dropped out of high school. This exploratory study was conducted to determine if any common elements existed among these 14 case studies. Using the qualitative research technique of a semi-structured interview, both researchers interacted with each participant separately, analysing their findings individually before comparing notes to reach consensus on themes and subthemes. Elaborate follow-up procedures with each of the 14 participants were conducted, to be certain that the researchers' interpretations were accurate representations of the students' words and ideas.

Ritchotte and Graefe (2017) determined six themes, with underlying subthemes, that were common to more than 90% of this population of gifted dropouts, including (p. 280):

- *Need for educational support* (100%), as epitomised in one student who stated "I kind of got upset at the educational system for not noticing who I was".
- *Social influences* (93%), as students felt isolated from and/or ostracised through peer interactions.
- *Outlets* (93%), in which students felt a lack of positive ways to cope with their school and social situations, instead choosing harmful alternatives.
- *An alternate path* (100%), in which participants viewed dropping out of school as an appropriate solution to an academic situation that was not meeting their needs.
- *Reflecting on the path* (100%), in which each dropout interpreted their leaving school as a catalyst for better ways to achieve their personal goals.

What these researchers did was something done too infrequently with underachieving students: they listened to them and then asked and recorded their opinions in a nonjudgemental manner. To be sure, dropping out of high school is not a goal that any educator wants to encourage in students, yet when that reality presents itself, the best thing adults can do is to then find alternate paths for these capable students to take.

Several authors have offered specific guidance for adults wishing to address the issue of underachievement directly with gifted students identified as low achievers. For example, Peterson (1993, 2008) promotes the use of open-ended group discussions between teachers and/or counsellors and their underachieving students to address directly the issues they are confronting. Peterson writes that:

> underachievers are the product of complex, interactive environments. It is unrealistic to hope or assume that a single discussion group session will have a significant impact on them. However, ongoing emphasis on self-awareness, family relationships, and emotions often provokes positive change. A supportive group, with a supportive leader, can make a difference over the long term. (1993, p. 57)

To get the discussion of underachievement going, Peterson suggested asking questions like these (1993, p. 59):

- Where in your life are you letting your intelligence show?
- Who in your life believes you are an intelligent person?
- What is the most comfortable part of school for you? The most uncomfortable?
- What are your feelings about being labelled as an 'underachiever'?
- What would happen if you started achieving in school?
- When you underachieve, who gives you attention?
- What would help you feel better about yourself and your life?

Douglas (2018), a proponent of encouraging gifted children, including underachievers, to take more personal responsibility for their school experiences, believes they are most successful when they advocate for their own learning through self-advocacy, defined as "the process of recognising and meeting the needs specific to one's learning ability without compromising the dignity of oneself or others" (Brinckerhoff, 1994, p. 229). Teaching students how to self-advocate involves the following four steps:

1. *Understanding their rights and responsibilities* so that they advocate from a base of strength, knowledge, and self-interest.
2. *Assessing and reflecting on their learning profile*, as students investigate their strengths and learning preferences that they find most enjoyable and effective.
3. *Matching personal attributes to options*, in which students are introduced to possible learning opportunities they might not be aware of that are open to them (e.g., independent study, online learning, mentorships, accelerated classes or grade skipping).
4. *Connecting with advocates who can support your goals*, a teacher or counsellor who is willing to partner with you in order to help you achieve your goals.

Underachieving students often believe that education is done *to* them and not *with* them. By introducing them to the steps of self-advocacy, and helping them to implement plans for change, academic success will be more likely to occur.

Delisle (2018) distinguishes between students who underachieve due to poor self-concept and a genuine disbelief in their own high abilities and those students who do poorly on purpose because they find much of school irrelevant, labelling these students as 'selective consumers'. He proposes six general strategies for getting to 'A' for these selective consumers, including:

1. *Autonomy*, in which students are introduced to psychological constructs that may help them to better understand themselves and their behaviours, including *locus of control*, *risk-taking* vs. *risk-making*, and *self-image* vs. *self-esteem*.
2. *Access*, including independent out-of-school activities of personal interest and importance to the student and meshing them with school-based goals and assignments.
3. *Advocacy*, which, similar to the Douglas' examples mentioned above, teaches students how to approach educators in a respectful, professional, and results-oriented manner in order to make educational experiences more relevant and purposeful.
4. *Alternatives*, which include creative and innovative approaches to showing mastery in subject areas that the school requires for course completion or graduation.
5. *Aspirations*, where students are introduced to actual people and fictional characters who have taken charge of their own learning and succeeded in unique ways.
6. *Approachable educators*, including locating and developing a relationship with those teachers or counsellors with whom a student connects at a personal level and, together, trying to make school both a successful and relevant experience.

There is little more ennobling for students than to realise that an adult they respect believes that they are more competent, kinder, creative, or aspirational than they, themselves, believe. The strategies outlined in this section detail the high degree of likelihood that success with underachieving students will be more common than rare if the bottom-line variable is student success through practices that respect the individual dignity of all parties involved.

Conclusion

Metaphorically speaking, underachievement can be compared to a number of things:

- *A skin rash*: although the symptoms may look the same (i.e., low grades, dispirited attitude towards school), the underlying causes of the rash, or the underachievement, may vary considerably.
- *An onion:* no matter how many layers get peeled off, there is another layer underneath the one you just removed. Such is the case with underachievement, a complex entity that has multiple academic, social, and emotional components.
- *A labyrinth*: although there are many paths that can be chosen, most of them lead to dead ends while only a few result in success.

As evidenced throughout this chapter, the complexity of the topic of underachievement and the varying definitions of this phenomenon have resulted in a hodgepodge of theories and strategies to reverse low achievement among gifted students. As best we could, we attempted to distil some of the research and practices that, from our biased yet experienced perspectives, hold the most promise for addressing this confounding issue in positive- and goal-focused ways.

However, even with the best theory and research evidence as our North Star, our guiding beacon, the ultimate determinant of success rests with a multiplicity of individuals, including the caring educators and counsellors who wish to assist the underachieving student; the parents, whose frustrations with their teen's low academic performance must be counterbalanced with a willingness to listen and respond to their teen's concerns in a respectful manner; and the underachieving student him or herself, whose openness to dialogue and suggestions that their caregivers are providing may not always be the easiest of tasks to accept or perform. But it is essential to remember what should be obvious: that educators, parents, and students are aiming towards the same goal of academic relevance for our most capable young people.

The Pleistocene Era, a long-ago period of human history, was filled with those capable hunters and gatherers who made a choice as to how rigorously to display their talents. Indeed, life and death may have been held in the balance if too many 'Pleistocene slackers' chose to underperform. Some might argue that the stakes are not quite so high today, in the twenty-first century, and that whether gifted individuals achieve at levels commensurate with their abilities is an inconsequential choice when compared to the choices of our ancient forebears. We would beg to differ, for now, as then our world is neither rich enough nor complete enough to forego the talents of our brightest young people—gifted students—without trying multiple strategies that convey respect and dignity to them as they forge ahead towards achieving personal success and satisfaction.

Cross-References

▶ A Model for Growing Teacher Talent Scouts: Decreasing Underrepresentation of Gifted Students
▶ Attuned Pedagogy: The Artistry of Differentiated Instruction from a Taiwanese Cultural Perspective
▶ Being of Like-Mind: Giftedness in the New Zealand Context
▶ Bricolage and the Evolution of Giftedness and Talent in Taiwan
▶ Fostering Resilience in 'At-Risk' Gifted and Talented Young People
▶ Gifted Education in the Asia-Pacific: From the Past for the Future – An Introduction
▶ Identifying and Nurturing Diversely Gifted and Talented Students: Part III Introduction
▶ Identifying Underrepresented Gifted Students: A Developmental Process
▶ Motivational Issues in Gifted Education: Understanding the Role of Students' Attribution and Control Beliefs, Self-Worth Protection and Growth Orientation
▶ Some Implications for the Future of Gifted Education in the Asia-Pacific
▶ The Development of Mana: Five Optimal Conditions for Gifted Māori Student Success

Analytic chart of article data set (2007–2017)

Publication year	Author(s)	Title and journal	Coherence (3 = +)	Bias (0 = +)	Developing self (3 = +)	Narrative analysis State of becoming [+ disintegration]	0 to 9 (+)
	3902 raw found (sweep 1); (winnowed/refined) UAG=39 2007–2017						
2007	Phillipson and Ka-on Tse	Discovering patterns of achievement in Hong Kong students: An application of the Rasch measurement model. *High Ability Studies*, 18(2), 173–190.	0	2	0	No look at complexity of the developing self of individuals. Variables based and emphasising modeling rather than students.	2
2007	Alvermann, Hagood, heron-Hruby, Hughes, Williams, and Yoon	Telling themselves who they are: What one out-of-school time study revealed about underachieving readers. *Reading Psychology*, 28, 31–50.	1	0	3	Lack of coherence or focus on developing self. Heavy preconceived notion about underachievement (bias) as being students' fault.	4
2008	Kim	Underachievement and creativity: Are gifted underachievers highly creative? *Creativity Research Journal*, 20(2), 234–242.	2	2	1	No emphasis on complexity or developing self.	5
2008	Stojnov, Dzinivic, and Pavlovic	Kelly meets Foucault: Understanding school underachievement. *Journal of Constructivist Psychology*, 21, 43–59.	2	2	2	Tries to mix two theories together to bring a new perspective on UAG that is more student centric and allows for student decision-making and Choice.	6
2008	Clark, flower, Walton, and Oakley	Tackling male underachievement: Enhancing a strengths-based learning environment for middle school boys. *Professional School Counseling Journal*, 12(2), 127–132.	1	1	2	Low incidence of coherence. Bias based on historical record. Did provide emphasis on interaction and complexities of the individual.	4
2009	Timmermans, van Lier, and Koot	Pathways of behavior problems from childhood to late adolescence leading to delinquency and academic underachievement. *Journal of Clinical Child & Adolescent Psychology*, 38(5), 630–638.	1	0	0	Biased to continuance of behavioural, learned at home. No exploration of complexity or developing self.	1
2010	Kim and VanTassel-Baska	The relationship between creativity and behavior problems among underachieving elementary and high school students. *Creativity Research Journal*, 22(2), 185–193.	2	2	1	Variables emphasis, not on complexity of interactions or conflict development. Behavioural focus.	5
2010	Hebert and Schreiber	An examination of selective achievement in males. *Journal for the Education of the Gifted*, 33 (4), 570–605.	3	2	3	Honours complexity of lived developing self. Balanced emphasis on coherence.	8
2010	Morisano and Shore	Can personal goal setting tap the potential of the gifted underachiever? *Roeper Review*, 32, 249–258.	2	2	1	Goal-setting as intervention. Does not honour complexity of interactions or developing self.	5
2011	Bergner and Neubauer	Sex and training differences in mental rotation: a behavioral and neurophysiological comparison of gifted achievers, gifted underachievers and average intelligent achievers. *High Ability Studies*, 22(2), 155–177.	1	2	0	Neuropsych emphasis on brain activity. Lacks emphasis on complexity, interrelations or the developing self.	3
2011	Grantham	New directions for gifted black males suffering from bystander effects: A call for upstanders. *Roeper Review*, 33, 263–272.	0	0	0	Very biased agenda with no focus on youth other than as victims.	0
2011	Crumpton and Gregory	'I'm not learning': The role of academic relevancy for low-achieving students. *The Journal of Educational Research*, 104, 42–53.	2	2	3	Strong focus on individuals and developing self. Less nuance on coherence.	7
2012	Gaynor	Different students: How typical schools are built to fail and need to change: A structural analysis. *Journal of Education*, 192(2–3), 13–27.	0	1	0	No recognition of coherence; no awareness of student as thinking decision-makers. Exploration of external impositions of environment.	1
2012	Rubenstein, Siegle, Reis, McCoach, and Burton	A complex quest: The development and research of underachievement interventions for gifted students. *Psychology in the Schools*, 49(7), 678–694.	1	1	2	Emphasis on variables—Not complexity of developing self.	4
2012	Gibbons, Pelchar and Cochran	Gifted students from low-education backgrounds. *Roeper Review*, 34 , 114–122.	3	2	3	Personal and individual issues clearly addressed as complex factors.	8
2012	Ziegler, Ziegler, and Stoeger	Shortcomings of the IQ-based construct of underachievement. *Roeper Review*, 34, 123–132.	2	2	2	Theoretical piece pushing for new or more theory.	6
2013	Hartley and Sutton	A stereotype threat account of boys' academic underachievement. *Child Development*, 84(5), 1716–1733.	1	1	1	Does not treat individuals as complex interactional beings. Bases broad context on controlling for one factor.	3
2013	Snyder and Linnenbrink-Garcia	A developmental, person-centered approach to exploring multiple motivational pathways in gifted underachievement. *Educational Psychologist*, 48 (4), 209–228.	2	3	3	Looks at intermingling, but limited complexity focus of coherence.	8
2013	Stoeger and Ziegler	Deficits in fine motor skills and their influence on persistence among gifted elementary pupils. *Gifted Education International*, 29(1), 28–42.	0	2	1	Structural emphasis, but lacks the affective component. Focuses on variables and measurement.	3
2013	DeCorte	Giftedness considered from the perspective of research on learning and instruction. *High Ability Studies*, 24(1), 3–19.	2	2	1	Reasonable coherence but does not honour the individual and complexities of the developing self.	5
2013	Landis and Reschly	Reexamining gifted underachievement and dropout through the lens of student engagement. *Journal for the Education of the Gifted*, 36(2), 220–249.	3	2	2	Focus on complexity and interactions–Coherence. Bias towards achievement as outcome for schooling.	7

Year	Authors	Title/Source				Notes	
2013	Berger	Bring out the brilliance: A counseling intervention for underachieving students. *Professional School Counseling Journal, 17*(1), 86–96.	1	1	0	Very little—skills-based approach to fixing underachievement.	2
2013	Ford and Moore	Understanding and reversing underachievement, low achievement, and achievement gaps among high-ability African American males in urban school contexts. *Urban Review, 45*, 399–415.	1	0	1	Very biased. No emphasis on complexity of individual or developing self.	2
2014	Patall, Awad, and Cestone	Academic potential beliefs and feelings: Conceptual development and relations with academic outcomes. *Self and Identity, 13*(1), 58–80.	2	2	0	Reasonable coherence but lack of individual lived experience or developing self.	4
2015	Mowbray, Jacobs, and Boyle	Validity of the german test anxiety inventory (TAI-G) in an Australian sample. *Australian Journal of Psychology, 67*, 121–129.	1	0	1	Variables and measurement focused and controlling mechanisms for variable isolation.	2
2015	Preckel and Brunner	Academic self-concept, achievement goals, and achievement: Is there relation the same for academic achievers and underachievers? *Gifted and Talented International, 30*(1–2), 68–84.	1	1	1	Variables and measurement based.	3
2015	Garn and Jolly	A model of parental achievement-oriented psychological control in academically gifted students. *High Ability Studies, 26*(1), 105–116.	1	1	0	No emphasis on developing self. Bias noted about preconceived parenting style impact.	2
2015	Obergriesser and Stoeger	The role of emotions, motivation, and learning behavior in underachievement and results of an intervention. *High Ability Studies, 26*(1), 167–190.	1	1	0	Variable and intervention focused. No focus on complexity and developing self.	2
2015	Peterson	School counselors and gifted kids: Respecting both cognitive and affective. *Journal of Counseling & Development, 93*, 153–162.	2	3	2	Holistic exploration of topics with emphasis on giving guidance for school counsellors relating to GT field and student needs.	7
2015	Paunesku, Walton, Romero, Smith, Yeager, and Dweck	Mind-set interventions are a scalable treatment for academic underachievement. *Psychological Science, 26*(6), 784–793.	1	1	1	Variable and intervention focused. Little recognition of complexity and developing self.	3
2016	Tze, Daniels, and Klassen	Evaluating the relationship between boredom and academic outcomes: A meta-analysis. *Educational Psychology Review, 28*, 119–144.	1	2	1	Meta-analysis. Broad overview of mostly measurement pieces.	4
2016	Hofer and Stern	Underachievement in physics: When intelligent girls fail. *Learning and Individual Differences, 51*, 119–131.	2	2	0	No individual lived experiences focus or on the developing self.	4
2016	Thompson, McNicholl, and Menter	Student teachers' perceptions of poverty and educational achievement. *Oxford Review of Education, 42*(2), 214–229.	2	2	1	Heavy emphasis on nature/nurture associated with poverty. Little emphasis on complexity and the developing self.	5
2017	Heyder, Kessels, and Steinmayr	Explaining academic-track boys' underachievement in language grades: Not a lack of aptitude but students' motivational beliefs and parents' perceptions? *British Journal of Educational Psychology, 87*, 205–223.	3	3	1	Recognised coherence—But weak awareness of complexities of the self. Based most data on measurement rather than the developing self.	7
2017	Henfield, Woo and Bang	Gifted ethnic minority students and academic achievement: A meta-analysis. *Gifted Child Quarterly, 61*(1), 3–19.	1	0	1	Meta-analysis. Variable and measurement focused.	2
2017	Ritchotte and Graefe	An alternate path: The experience of high-potential individuals who left high school. *Gifted Child Quarterly, 61*(4), 275–289.	3	3	3	Although doesn't use Dabrowskian terms or focus—Much is evident in the effort. Lived experience and complexity are key and good discussion of the developing self.	9
2017	Cavilla	Observation and analysis of three gifted underachievers in an underserved, urban high school setting. *Gifted Education International, 33*(1), 62–75.	2	2	3	Honours complexity, not to the developing self-level.	7
2017	Seibert, Bauer, May, and Fincham	Emotion regulation and academic underperformance: The role of school burnout. *Learning and Individual Differences, 60*, 1–9.	1	2	2	Variable and measurement focused.	5
2017	Snyder and Adelson	The development and validation of the perceived academic underachievement scale. *The Journal of Experimental Education, 85*(4), 614–628.	1	0	1	Instrument validation based on theory about perceived underachievement versus observed underachievement.	2

References

Asbury, C. (1974). Selected factors influencing over and underachievement in young school-age children. *Review of Educational Research, 44*(4), 409–428. https://doi.org/10.3102/00346543044004409

Banerjee, P. A. (2016). A systematic review of factors linked to poor academic performance of disadvantaged students in science and maths in schools. *Cogent Education, 3*(1), 20–32. https://doi.org/10.1080/2331186X.2016.1178441

Bennett-Rappell, H., & Northcote, M. (2016). Underachieving gifted students: Two case studies. *Educational Research, 26*(3), 407–430. Retrieved from http://www.iier.org.au/iier26/bennett-rappell.pdf

Berger, C. (2013). Bring out the brilliance: A counseling intervention for underachieving students. *Professional School Counseling Journal, 17*(1), 86–96. https://doi.org/10.1177/2156759X0001700102

Betts, G. T. & Neihart, M. (1988). Profiles of the gifted and talented. *Gifted Child Quarterly, 32*(2), 248–253. Retrieved from https://doi.org/10.1177/001698628803200202

Brinckerhoff, L. (1994). Developing effective self-advocacy skills in college-bound students with learning disabilities. *Intervention in School and Clinic, 29*(4), 229–238. https://doi.org/10.1177/105345129402900407

Bronfenbrenner, U. (1943). A constant frame of reference for sociometric research. *Sociometry, 6*, 363–397. https://doi.org/10.2307/2785218

Bronfenbrenner, U. (1977). Toward an experimental ecology of human development. *American Psychologist, 32*(7), 513–531. https://doi.org/10.1037/0003-066X.32.7.513

Bronfenbrenner, U. (1979). *The ecology of human development: Experiments by nature and design.* Cambridge, MA: Harvard University Press.

Bronfenbrenner, U. (1986a). Recent advances in research on the ecology of human development. In R. K. Silbereisen, K. Eyferth, & G. Rudinger (Eds.), *Development as action in context: Problem behavior and normal youth development* (pp. 287–309). New York, NY: Springer.

Bronfenbrenner, U. (1986b). Ecology of the family as a context for human development: Research perspectives. *Developmental Psychology, 22*(6), 723–742. https://doi.org/10.1037/0012-1649.22.6.723

Bronfenbrenner, U., & Crouter, A. C. (1983). The evolution of environmental models in developmental research. In W. Kessen (Ed.), *History, theory, and methods.* Volume 1 of P. H. Mussen (Ed.), *Handbook of child psychology* (4th ed., pp. 357–414). New York, NY: Wiley.

Cavilla, D. (2017). Observation and analysis of three gifted underachievers in an underserved, urban high school setting. *Gifted Education International, 33*(1), 62–75. https://doi.org/10.1177/0261429414568181

Dabrowski, K. (1964). *Positive disintegration.* Boston, MA: Little Brown & Co.

Dabrowski, K. (1967). *Personality-shaping through positive disintegration.* Boston, MA: Little Brown & Co.

Dabrowski, K. (1976). On the philosophy of development through positive disintegration and secondary integration. *Dialectics and Humanism, 3–4*, 131–144. https://doi.org/10.5840/dialecticshumanism197633/413

Dabrowski, K., Kawczak, A., & Piechowski, M. M. (1970). *Mental growth through positive disintegration.* London, England: Gryf Publications LTD.

Dabrowski, K., & Piechowski, M. M. (1977a). *Theory of levels of emotional development: Volume 1—Multilevelness and positive disintegration.* Oceanside, NY: Dabor Science Publications.

Dabrowski, K., & Piechowski, M. M. (1977b). *Theory of levels of emotional development: Volume II—From primary integration to self-actualization.* Oceanside, NY: Dabor Science Publications.

Delisle, J. R. (2018). *Doing poorly on purpose: Strategies to reverse underachievement and respect student dignity.* Alexandria, VA: ASCD.

Dixon, R. M., Craven, R., & Martin, A. (2006). Underachievement in a whole city cohort of academically gifted children: What does it look like? *Australasian Journal of Gifted Education, 15*(2), 9–15. Retrieved from https://ro.uow.edu.au/cgi/viewcontent.cgi?referer=https://www.google.com/&httpsredir=1&article=1260&context=edupapers

Douglas, D. (2018). *The power of self-advocacy for gifted learners.* Minneapolis, MN: Free Spirit Publishing.

Dowdall, C. B., & Colangelo, N. (1982). Underachieving gifted students: Reviews and implications. *Gifted Child Quarterly, 26*(4), 179–184. https://doi.org/10.1177/001698628202600406

Fine, R. (1967). *Underachievers: How they can be helped.* New York, NY: Dutton.

Gibbons, M. M., Pelchar, T. K., & Cochran, J. L. (2012). Gifted students from low-education backgrounds. *Roeper Review, 34*(1), 114–122. https://doi.org/10.1080/02783193.2012.660685

Hebert, T. P., & Schreiber, C. A. (2010). An examination of selective achievement in gifted males. *Journal for the Education of the Gifted, 33*(4), 570–605. https://doi.org/10.1177/016235321003300406

Hildreth, G. (1966). *Introduction to the gifted child*. New York, NY: McGraw-Hill.

Kim, K. H. (2008). Underachievement and creativity: Are gifted underachievers highly creative? *Creativity Research Journal, 20*(2), 234–242. https://doi.org/10.1080/10400410802060232

Morisano, D., & Shore, B. M. (2010). Can personal goal setting tap the potential of the gifted underachiever? *Roeper Review, 32*, 249–258. https://doi.org/10.1080/02783193.2010.508156

New Zealand Principals' Federation. (n.d.). What to do about underachieving gifted children. Retrieved from NZPfcnz2.digiwebhosting.com//?q=list//What%20to%20do%20about%20New%20Zealand's%20nderachieving%20children

Obergriesser, S., & Stoeger, H. (2015). The role of emotions, motivation, and learning behavior in underachievement and results of an intervention. *High Ability Studies, 26*(1), 167–190. https://doi.org/10.1080/13598139.2015.1043003

Paunesku, D., Walton, G. M., Romero, C., Smith, E. N., Yeager, D. S., & Dweck, C. S. (2015). Mind-set interventions are a scalable treatment for academic underachievement. *Psychological Science, 26*(6), 784–793. https://doi.org/10.1177/0956797615571017

Peterson, J. S. (1993). *Talk with teens about self and stress*. Minneapolis, MN: Free Spirit Publishing.

Peterson, J. S. (2008). *The essential guide to talking with gifted teens: Ready-to-use discussions about identity, stress, relationships and more*. Minneapolis, MN: Free Spirit Publishing.

Phillips, R. (2017). Identification of gifted students at risk of underachievement using ROC curve analysis; using an understanding of the relationships and patterns of social coping, attitude toward school, and self-efficacy to underachieving gifted students: An Australian sample. Doctoral thesis, University of Wollongong, Wollongong, NSW. Retrieved from https://ro.uow.edu.au/theses1/96/

Phillipson, N. S., Shi, J., Zhang, G., Tsai, D., Quak, C. G., Matsumurn, N., & Cho, S. (2009). Recent developments in gifted education in East Asia. In L. Shavinina (Ed.), *International handbook on giftedness* (pp. 1427–1461). Berlin: Springer Science.

Phillipson, N. S., & Tse, K.-o. (2007). Discovering patterns of achievement in Hong Kong students: An application of the Rasch measurement model. *High Ability Studies, 18*(2), 173–190. https://doi.org/10.1080/13598130701709640

Plowman, P. (1971). What can be done for rural gifted children and youth? In J. P. Gowan & E. P. Torrance (Eds.), *Educating the ablest: A book of readings on the education of gifted children* (pp. 54–60). Itasca, IL: F. E. Peacock.

Preckel, F., & Brunner, M. (2015). Academic self-concept, achievement goals, and achievement: Is there relation the same for academic achievers and underachievers? *Gifted and Talented International, 30*(1–2), 68–84. https://doi.org/10.1080/15332276.2015.1137458

Pringle, M. L. (1970). *Able misfits: A study of educational and behavior difficulties of 103 very intelligent children (IQs 120–200)*. London, England: Longman.

Raph, J. B., & Tannenbaum, A. J. (1961). *Underachievement: Review of literature*. New York, NY: Teachers College Press.

Reis, S. M., & McCoach, D. B. (2000). The underachievement of gifted students: What do we know and where do we go? *Gifted Child Quarterly, 44*(3), 152–170. https://doi.org/10.1177/001698620004400302

Ritchotte, J. A., & Graefe, A. K. (2017). An alternate path: The experience of high-potential individuals who left school. *Gifted Child Quarterly, 61*(4), 275–289. https://doi.org/10.1177/0016986217722615

Rubenstein, L. D., Siegle, D., Reis, S. M., McCoach, D. B., & Burton, M. G. (2012). A complex quest: The development and research of underachievement interventions for gifted students. *Psychology in the Schools, 49*(7), 678–694. https://doi.org/10.1002/pits.21620

Schultz, R. A. (2002). Understanding giftedness and underachievement: At the edge of possibility. *Gifted Child Quarterly, 46*(3), 193–208. https://doi.org/10.1177/001698620204600304

Snyder, K. E., & Adelson, J. L. (2017). The development and validation of the perceived academic underachievement scale. *The Journal of Experimental Education, 85*(4), 614–628. https://doi.org/10.1080/00220973.2016.1268087

Snyder, K. E., & Linnenbrink-Garcia, L. (2013). A developmental, person-cantered approach to exploring multiple motivational pathways in gifted underachievement. *Educational Psychologist, 48*(4), 209–228. https://doi.org/10.1080/00461520.2013.835597

Stojnov, D., Dzinivic, V., & Pavlovic, J. (2008). Kelly meets Foucault: Understanding school underachievement. *Journal of Constructivist Psychology, 21*(1), 43–59. https://doi.org/10.1080/10720530701503876

Strang, R. (1960). *Helping your gifted child*. New York, NY: Dutton.

Tillier, W. (1998). The basic concepts of Dabrowski's theory of positive disintegration. *The Dabrowski Newsletter, 5*, 1–10.

Tsai, K.-F., & Fu, G. (2016). Underachievement in gifted students: A case study of three college physics students in Taiwan. *Universal Journal of Educational Research, 4*(4), 688–695. https://doi.org/10.13189/ujer.2016.040405

Whitmore, J. R. (1980). *Giftedness, conflict and underachievement*. Boston, MA: Allyn and Bacon.

Ziegler, A., Ziegler, A., & Stoeger, H. (2012). Shortcomings of the IQ-based construct of underachievement. *Roeper Review, 34*(2), 123–132. https://doi.org/10.1080/02783193.2012.660726

Ziv, A. (1977). *Counseling the intellectually gifted child*. Toronto, ON: The Governing Council of the University of Toronto.

James R. Delisle, PhD, has taught gifted children and those who work on their behalf for 40 years. A distinguished professor of Education at Kent State University for 25 years, Dr. Delisle retired from his professorship in 2008. Throughout his career, Dr. Delisle has taken time away from university teaching to return to his classroom roots, teaching middle school-level gifted students one day a week for 17 years. Currently, Dr. Delisle is a part-time teacher of highly gifted high school students at Scholars' Academy in Conway, South Carolina. The author of 20 books and more than 275 articles and book chapters, Dr. Delisle travels the world extensively as a consultant for school districts, government agencies and private institutions.

Robert Arthur Schultz, PhD, is a professor of Gifted Education and Curriculum Studies and serves as department chair for Early Childhood, Higher Education and Special Education at the University of Toledo. His areas of expertise in gifted education include highly/profoundly gifted, curriculum theory and development, assessment/evaluation, social and emotional needs, teacher training, parenting issues, and adolescence (since he hasn't ever outgrown this life stage!). Bob serves as a board member for the Roeper Institute as well as contributing editor to *Roeper Review, Gifted Child Quarterly* and *Journal of Educational Research*. Bob co-authored (with James R. Delisle) three books and has published over 100 articles in the field of gifted child education.

Exploring Diverse Perceptions of Wise Persons: Wisdom in Gifted Education

29

Kyungbin Park and Eunhyang Kim

Contents

Introduction	632
Conceptualising Wisdom	634
Defining the Concept of Wisdom	634
Contemporary Studies on Wisdom	634
Instruments to Measure Wisdom	636
Conceptions of Wisdom Between Populations	636
A Two-Phase Study on Wise Persons in Korea	637
Procedure of the Study	637
Conceptions of a Wise Person	638
The Four Types of a Wise Person	638
Conceptions of a Wise Person Between Different Age Groups	639
Differences in Conceptions of a Wise Man and a Wise Woman	641
Implications and Future Directions for Research and Practice	643
Conclusion	644
Cross-References	645
References	645

Abstract

Throughout history, there have been many definitions of wisdom, but the concept remains abstract and ephemeral throughout the ages and from different parts of the world. *What does it really mean to be a wise person?* Although not stated explicitly, one of the implicit expectations in gifted education would be to foster wise citizens, and not merely smart people. Therefore, agreement on the concept of a wise person is a much-needed process especially in this fast-changing world. In this chapter, various definitions of wisdom will be explored, along with

---

K. Park · E. Kim (✉)
Gachon University, Seongnam-si, Gyeonggi-do, South Korea
e-mail: sfb1132@gmail.com; mr12827@gmail.com; mac0509@gmail.com

© Springer Nature Singapore Pte Ltd. 2021
S. R. Smith (ed.), *Handbook of Giftedness and Talent Development in the Asia-Pacific*,
Springer International Handbooks of Education,
https://doi.org/10.1007/978-981-13-3041-4_29

examining some contemporary studies and instruments for measuring wisdom to shed some light on the concept of a wise person. Through an empirical study in Korea, we explored some concrete descriptors of the conception of a wise person. Then we proceeded to look at differences between age groups. Next, conceptions of a wise man and a wise woman are reported. Korea offers an interesting point of view in that it has a long history as an exemplary Asian country with Asian values and also has integrated Western values through its rapid economic development and globalisation. Hence, Korea holds a mixture of traditional Asian values and contemporary Western conceptions at the same time. Therefore, looking into the concept of a wise person in the Korean population will offer insights into the evolving conceptions of wisdom and wise persons. Additionally, implications of the study are explored.

Keywords

Wise person · Wisdom · Gifted education · Conception · Generation · Gender

The aims in this chapter are to:
1. Address the issue of wisdom in gifted education.
2. Provide a brief theoretical framework for the concept of wisdom.
3. Present research findings on the conception of a wise person.
4. Provide some implications for gifted education research and practice.

Introduction

Gifted educators aim to discover and develop students' giftedness and talents in order to find and educate gifted persons and to support them to achieve excellent performance in their fields. This is because the talents of gifted students can have a tremendous impact on society at large (De Haan & Havighurst, 1961; Marland, 1972; Passow, 1981).

Historically, as an example, Marie Curie (1867–1934), despite the difficulty of being a poor immigrant woman, accomplished a remarkable achievement in winning two Nobel Prizes (Physics, 1903; Chemistry, 1911). Her true achievement, however, is not winning the two awards, but her positive influence on the world. Marie Curie, who was the first to discover radium, did not apply for any patents, saying "scientific discoveries should be made available at no charge, for the good of the general public" (Borzendowski, 2009, p. 74). She also said that:

> we cannot hope to build a better world without improving the individual. Toward this end, each of us must work for his own highest development, accepting at the same time his share of responsibility in the general life of humanity—our particular duty being to aid those to whom we think we can be most useful. (Curie, 1923, p. 168)

This is in contrast to the case of a contemporary entrepreneur who has taken the AIDS drug patents and raised the price of the drug 55 times which pushed patients in need of treatment into despair (Shefali, 2018). Along with her academic achievements, Marie Curie formed a childcare cooperation together with other professors of Sorbonne University in France where she was working and cared for her daughter, Irène Joliot-Curie (1897–1956), as well as about ten other children. Marie Curie and her colleagues took turns in nurturing and instructing the children, sharing their knowledge and enthusiasm in science, literature, and history. The children of Marie Curie and her fellow professors were able to grow into excellent scholars, thanks to their parents' various teaching methods and extensive and profound knowledge. Marie Curie's daughter, Irène, continued on with her mother's research and won the Nobel Prize for Chemistry together with her husband for the study of artificial radiation (Gilmer, 2011). Irène Joliot–Curie was the first woman to be appointed as the Undersecretary of State for Scientific Research by the French government, in which capacity she helped in founding the Centre National de la Recherche Scientifique (Gilmer, 2011). All this began with Marie Curie, one person's talent and firm belief, which served as a driving force for the advancement of human welfare and scientific development.

As can be seen from the above examples, the directionality or how the talent is used is as important as the manifestation and the level of the talent itself. In the era of the Fourth Industrial Revolution, where the spread and influence of knowledge are becoming faster and greater, the influence of the gifted will increase even more. Therefore, it is time to look closely at the goals and directions of gifted education.

Education for the gifted should focus both on developing talent and nurturing the right values. The ultimate goal of gifted education should be to help the gifted person grow up with a high level of achievement and use their talent positively (De Haan & Havighurst, 1961; Marland, 1972; Passow, 1981). Deciding which choice is in a positive direction involves wisdom. So far, thanks to the contributions of many researchers and educators, meaningful advancements have been accumulated in how to nurture talent through education (Clark, 2013; Feldman & Goldsmith, 1986; Kanevsky, 2011; Lubinski & Benbow, 2006). Now it is time to turn our attention to how wisely talents can be used. Wise choices spring from beliefs and values (Sternberg, 2004). Therefore, we need to investigate what makes a wise person. This leads to the question, 'What does it mean to be a wise person?'

Wisdom can be distinguished from intelligence. Wisdom may include domains such as the practical application of knowledge, use of knowledge for the common social good, and integration of affect and knowledge (Jeste et al., 2010). There have been philosophical, and psychological interests in wisdom throughout human history, which attests to the aspiration of scholars to understand wise persons as well as wisdom itself. However, despite efforts to uncover the components of wisdom, researchers still have not reached a consensus on what a wise person is (Jeste et al., 2010).

Is wisdom an absolute construct that defies changes through the ages, or does it change with the rapid flow of history? Do factors such as gender, age, or culture wield any influence on the concept of wisdom? In the next section, we will examine what is meant by the term a wise person. To do this, we first look at the concepts and components of wisdom and explore the perception of a wise person among laypersons.

Conceptualising Wisdom

Defining the Concept of Wisdom

In the age where society is becoming more complex and changing rapidly, people are drawn to more fundamental and encompassing values that can be seen as unique to *Homo sapiens*. One of these values or characteristics that has aided in the survival of the human race has evolved in recent years, and this is the concept of 'wisdom'. With the emergence of Artificial Intelligence and the Fourth Industrial Revolution, people are drawn to questions such as 'What is human?', 'What defines good human existence?' and 'How can we co-exist with the incoming technology?' Wisdom has been considered the epitome of human development, a hallmark of human virtue, and a fundamental psychosocial strength from the perspectives of philosophers and psychologists in both Eastern and Western societies (Taylor, Bates, & Webster, 2011; Webster, 2010).

Explicit theories of wisdom may differ from the philosophical wisdom traditions of Eastern and Western cultures and between the East and West (Takahashi, 2000). The wisdom traditions of the West tend to emphasise the cognitive dimension of wisdom, whereas the Eastern wisdom traditions tend to integrate the cognitive and affective elements of wisdom (Ardelt, 2003). There has been a steady flow of reflections concerning wisdom, but it is only in the last few decades that wisdom has been viewed as a psychological construct entitled to a systematic and scientific investigation (Blanchard-Fields, Brannan, & Camp, 1987; Marchand, 2003). Studies that look into wisdom are gaining significant weight because wise persons are considered to be not only competent and fulfilled individually, but also disseminators of valuable insights to others, hence improving the quality of life for the society in general (Sternberg, 2004; Thomas et al., 2017). The ultimate goal of education in general and more so in gifted education is the endeavour to raise wise persons (Hollingworth, Sánchez-Escobedo, Graudina, Misiuniene, & Park, 2013). According to Sternberg (2003), the principal goal of wisdom is to maximise both self-interest and the public-interest. Without wisdom, successful academic achievement or talent development alone cannot guarantee the satisfaction or happiness of the person.

Contemporary Studies on Wisdom

Until recently, most of the work on wisdom was limited to conceptualisations and discussions, rather than concrete testing of hypotheses. As such, contemporary perceptions of wisdom are limited in number and scope (e.g., Baltes & Smith, 2008; Hershey & Farrell, 1997; Sánchez-Escobedo, Park, Hollingworth, Misiuniene, & Ivanova, 2014; Staudinger & Pasupathi, 2003; Sternberg, 2003). Psychologists have investigated individuals' perceptions of wisdom using different methodological techniques, one of which is having subjects generate lists of characteristics typical of wise people (Brent & Watson, 1980; Clayton & Birren, 1980) and having subjects rate whether different descriptors (e.g., experienced, intelligent, careless) are characteristic of wise individuals (Clayton & Birren, 1980; Heckhausen, Dixon, & Baltes, 1989; Holliday & Chandler, 1986). Clayton and Birren (1980) asked subjects to generate a list of descriptors of a wise person, which resulted in the identification of a set of 12 commonly mentioned descriptors: experienced, intuitive, introspective, pragmatic, understanding, gentle, empathetic, intelligent, peaceful, knowledgeable, and observant and have a sense of humour. In the next step, young, middle-aged, and older subjects rated paired combinations of descriptors, and these ratings were then analysed using multi-dimensional scaling techniques. Although the results of this analysis identified developmental differences in subjects' conceptions of wisdom, the more general findings were that regardless of age, individuals perceived wisdom to include cognitive, affective, and reflective characteristics (Clayton & Birren, 1980).

In another study, Holliday and Chandler (1986) tried to identify the underlying dimensions of wisdom and found that the wisdom construct was characterised by five dimensions, which are exceptional understanding, judgement and communication skills, general competencies, interpersonal skills, and social unobtrusiveness. Yet in a different study, using multidimensional scaling techniques, Sternberg (1985) tried to identify the structural basis of wisdom. He concluded that the wisdom construct contains six basic components, which are: reasoning ability, sagacity, learning from ideas and from the environment, judgement, expeditious use of information, and perspicacity. According to Sternberg, these six components can be organised into either, a reasoning polarity or a sagacity polarity that are equal in nature to Clayton and Birren's (1980) reflective and affective dimensions, respectively. Other researchers have also suggested that wisdom is best characterised as a multidimensional construct (Baltes & Staudinger, 2000; Jeste et al., 2010; Webster, 2003). Depending on the researchers, the underlying number of constructs differs, as can be seen below.

Brent and Watson (1980) revealed that a wise person can be characterised into four clusters of attributes namely: person-cognitive, practical experimental, interpersonal, and moral/ethical. Farrell and Hershey (1996) also found four clusters describing wise persons, cognitive and intellectual abilities, perceptive and intuitive skills, knowledge acquired through life experience and problem-solving, and decision-making abilities.

As described in the above literature, a subcomponent of wisdom that was cited by nearly all definitions relates to prosocial values and behaviour, suggesting that wisdom is a useful construct and serves a common good (e.g., Baltes & Staudinger, 2000; Sánchez-Escobedo et al., 2014; Sternberg, 1990).

Instruments to Measure Wisdom

As can be seen above, empirical wisdom research can be divided into studies that: (a) assess the implicit theories or the meaning of wisdom among people and (b) measure people's degree of wisdom or their wisdom-related performance based on either explicit or implicit theories of wisdom.

From a different perspective, some instruments measuring characteristics of a wise person have been developed (Ardelt, 2003; Brown & Greene, 2006; Takahashi & Overton, 2002; Webster, 2003; Wink & Helson, 1997). One of them is the *3-Dimensional Wisdom Scale* (3D-WS; Ardelt, 2003) with the purpose to assess the cognitive, reflective, and affective dimensions of the latent variable wisdom. For example, a statement related to the cognitive dimension includes, 'Ignorance is bliss' (reversed); to the reflective dimension an item such as, 'I always try to look at all sides of a problem'; and the affective dimension includes, 'Sometimes I feel a real compassion for everyone'. This scale has been used and validated in several studies (Ardelt, 2003; Ardelt, Pridgen, & Nutter-Pridgen, 2018; Bruya & Ardelt, 2018). Findings using this scale suggest that wise people tend to show characteristics including higher life satisfaction, general well-being and purpose of life, while displaying negative correlations with depressive symptoms, feelings of economic pressure, and fear of death (Ardelt, 2003).

Another previously validated measure that can be used to assess wisdom is the *Self-Assessed Wisdom Scale* (SAWS; Webster, 2003, 2007), which attempts to assess the non-cognitive aspects of wisdom. The SAWS measures five interrelated dimensions of wisdom namely: emotional regulation, critical life experiences, reminiscence and life reflection, openness to experience, and humour. For example, 'I am good at identifying subtle emotions within myself' (emotional regulation), 'I have experienced many moral dilemmas' (critical life experiences), 'Remembering my earlier days helps me gain insight into important life matters' (reminiscence and life reflection), 'I like to read books which challenge me to think differently about issues' (openness to experience) and 'There is nothing amusing about difficult situations' (humour; Webster, 2003). Results from studies using SAWS show that wise persons tend to show generativity, ego integrity, and positive attachment (e.g., Webster, 2003, 2007). The findings in these studies also showed that there is a negative association with foolishness and that wisdom is unrelated to educational level or age.

Conceptions of Wisdom Between Populations

There seem to be conceptual differences between Eastern and Western women and men, young and old persons, and past and present. For example, in Finland, wise people are perceived as collaborative, persuasive, sophisticated, and prudent (Räty & Snellman, 1992). In Latvia, wise people are associated with high social skills and intrapersonal abilities, comprehensive knowledge, and having adaptation and forecasting abilities (Ivanova & Rascevska, 2010). In the United States and Australia, a wise person is associated with experience, knowledge, and age, whereas in India and Japan, wise people are depicted as discreet, aged, and experienced (Takahashi & Bordia, 2000). A study of Taiwanese conceptions of wisdom reported four main components of wisdom as competencies and knowledge, benevolence and compassion, openness and profundity, and modesty and unobtrusiveness (Yang, 2001). In Korea, intelligent people are associated with high social skills, ability to deal with new situations, problem-solving ability, self-control, and practicality (Lim, Plucker, & Im, 2002).

In another extensive study looking into the 'wise person', Hollingworth et al. (2013) studied more than 800 adolescents from five different countries. They compared the participants' conceptions of a wise man and a wise woman by country and gender. The results showed that 'warm', 'creative', and 'cooperative' characteristics seem to be important for Mexican, Latvians, and Lithuanians and less important for Koreans and Americans. 'Individually oriented' seems to be less important for Americans than for the rest of the participants, and social respect was the most salient for Lithuanians.

A review of the results in the aforementioned studies shows diversity and commonality among different conditions. It may seem that cognitive dimensions are important in Western cultures, whereas both emotional and cognitive dimensions are emphasised in Eastern cultures. However, there is still much to explore about how wisdom is perceived in different cultures and different circumstances.

A Two-Phase Study on Wise Persons in Korea

Procedure of the Study

For the purpose of investigating the conception of a wise person, we conducted an original two-phase research study. The procedure was as follows. We used a survey measure to explore concepts of a wise person. The measure used in the study had 50 adjectives in Korean which were previously used in the study by Hollingworth et al. (2013). The measure with the adjectives was a 5-point Likert scale (do not agree = 1 to strongly agree = 5). The subjects were asked to indicate the point where they considered each adjective was appropriate in describing their conceptions for a wise man or woman. Cronbach's alpha reliability coefficient was 0.89~0.93. The *Kaiser–Meyer–Olkin* (KMO) and *Bartlett Sphericity* test results indicated that the data came from multivariable normal distribution and thus the factor analysis could be continued. The KMO value was 0.812, and Bartlett test results were significant (X^2: 12248.276, p <0.01). In the exploratory factor analysis, all items had a factor load value over 0.43; thus the validity was satisfied.

For this exploratory study, we analysed the data using the IBM SPSS 23.0 program. First, we looked at descriptive statistics (means, standard deviations). Next, we conducted factor analysis and delineated the main factors. Then, we compared the mean and ranking of the items to see if there were any differences between groups. Finally, independent t-tests and paired t-tests were done to see if differences among groups were significant.

Table 1 High-scoring adjectives about a wise person

Rank	Adjective	M	SD	Rank	Adjective	M	SD
1	Respected	3.44	1.18	11	Optimistic	2.34	1.23
2	Influential	3.03	1.24	12	Generous	2.30	1.07
3	Witty	2.91	1.12	13	Strong	2.29	1.12
4	Flexible	2.87	1.25	14	Famous	2.14	1.06
5	Humble	2.85	1.45	15	Direct	2.13	1.10
6	Cooperative	2.72	1.21	16	Joyful	2.10	1.21
7	Creative	2.70	1.26	17	Extrovert	2.08	1.09
8	Kind	2.60	1.23	18	Rational	2.05	1.08
9	Warm	2.43	1.29	19	Concrete	2.03	1.06
10	Group oriented	2.39	1.06				

Conceptions of a Wise Person

The focus of the first step of the study was to establish the conception of a wise person, so we looked at descriptive statistics (means, standard deviations) using the data from the total of 576 subjects. As a result, 19 items with a mean score above average were selected.

The 19 adjectives that ranked higher than average are shown below in Table 1. The high-ranking adjectives were 'respected', 'influential', 'witty', 'creative', 'flexible', 'humble', 'kind', 'cooperative' and so on. Among these, 'respected' and 'flexible' were consistent with the top five adjectives reported by Hollingworth et al. (2013). Also, the results were in concordance to Hershey and Farrell's (1997) findings of the adjectives classified as high in wise characteristics (i.e., 'modest', 'enlightened', 'friendly', 'confident', 'charitable', 'cheerful', 'logical', 'reasonable').

The Four Types of a Wise Person

To explore the characteristics of the wise person, we conducted a factor analysis on the 19 adjectives. As a result, the following four factors were derived (see Table 2).

In naming the four factors, we tried to think of the person who typically showed these characteristics and discussed the most appropriate title. For example, if there was someone who is 'influential', 'famous', 'creative', and 'direct', such as Curie and Einstein, what label would categorise this person? We decided to call these people *competent achievers*. After similar processes, the four types were finally named as *competent achiever, considerate leader, concordant balancer* and *confident visionary*. Below are the associated characteristics for each of the four categories of wise people:

(a) *Competent achiever*: influential, famous, creative, direct.
(b) *Considerate leader*: respected, flexible, humble, kind, warm, joyful, witty.

Table 2 The results of exploratory factor analysis

Adjectives	Factor 1	Factor 2	Factor 3	Factor 4
Influential	0.719			
Famous	0.717			
Creative	0.566			
Direct	0.495			
Humble		0.807		
Warm		0.790		
Flexible		0.731		
Kind		0.695		
Respected		0.644		
Joyful		0.607		
Witty		0.410		
Optimistic			0.720	
Group oriented			0.642	
Generous			0.412	
Cooperative			0.403	
Rational				0.687
Concrete				0.639
Strong				0.565
Extrovert				0.492

Kaiser–Meyer–Olkin (KMO) = 0.895
Bartlett's test of sphericity ($X^2 = 3833.654, p < 0.001$)

(c) *Concordant balancer*: optimistic, generous, group oriented, cooperative.
(d) *Confident visionary*: rational, concrete, strong, extrovert.

Upon deeper examination, the adjectives can be distinguished between affective and cognitive characteristics. The conceptual illustration of these four factors is shown in Figure 1.

Next, we looked at the conceptions of a wise person according to the participants' age group.

Conceptions of a Wise Person Between Different Age Groups

We checked to see if there were any differences in the conception of a wise person between different age groups, specifically subjects under age 30 and those over 30 years old. The results from independent t-test showed commonalities and differences between the two age groups (see Table 3). Whereas the ranking of the adjectives was similar, the response level was significantly higher for the over-30 age group. Similar results have been reported in other studies regarding differences between generations (Hu, Ferrari, Liu, Gao, & Weare, 2016).

In this chapter, and for the sake of convenience, we looked at the top ten items. Comparing the top ten adjectives in each group in this study, eight characteristics

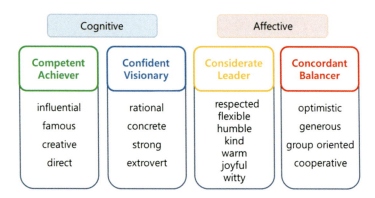

Fig. 1 Four types of adjectives related to a wise person

Table 3 The results of independent t-tests between age groups

	Adjectives	Under 30 group M	SD	Over-30 group M	SD	T
1	Respected	3.25	1.12	3.82	1.18	−5.71***
2	Influential	2.88	1.21	3.32	1.26	−4.08***
3	Witty	2.70	1.06	3.31	1.12	−6.33***
4	Flexible	2.65	1.20	3.30	1.23	−6.09***
5	Humble	2.55	1.44	3.47	1.30	−7.73***
6	Cooperative	2.53	1.17	3.14	1.21	−5.93***
7	Creative	2.68	1.25	2.72	1.28	−0.34
8	Kind	2.30	1.08	3.19	1.29	−8.22***
9	Warm	2.12	1.20	3.05	1.22	−8.75***
10	Group-oriented	2.42	1.03	2.33	1.11	0.89
11	Optimistic	2.27	1.20	2.46	1.28	−1.75
12	Generous	2.11	0.95	2.67	1.20	−5.68***
13	Strong	2.30	1.12	2.27	1.13	0.32
14	Famous	2.11	1.00	2.18	1.17	−0.67
15	Direct	2.27	1.07	1.86	1.12	4.32***
16	Joyful	1.93	1.14	2.44	1.25	−4.75***
17	Extrovert	2.13	1.06	1.98	1.13	1.63
18	Rational	1.96	1.02	2.23	1.17	−2.70**
19	Concrete	1.86	0.99	2.37	1.13	−5.34***

**p < 0.005; ***p < 0.001

(respected, influential, witty, creative, flexible, humble, cooperative, kind) concurred for the two age groups (see Fig. 3). Although there were differences in ranking, this correspondence shows that the general conceptions of a wise person may transcend generations. At closer examination, we were able to decipher some differences between the age groups, namely, in the response level and the ranking, and some adjectives that were different for the two groups. Young adults under 30 years of age

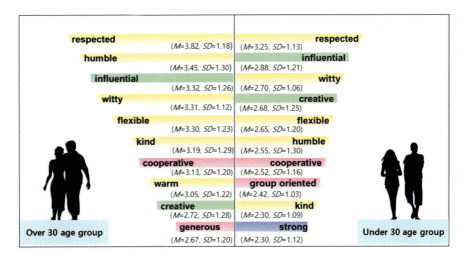

Fig. 2 Conceptions of a wise person for the two age groups

included 'group oriented' and 'strong' in the top ten characteristics, while adults over 30 included 'generous' and 'warm'. 'Generous' and 'group oriented' are related to the *concordant balancer* type, 'warm' is related to the *considerate leader* type and 'strong' is related to the *confident visionary* type. Referring to the conceptual illustration on the four types of wise persons (Fig. 1), the group of adults over 30 tended to put more weight on the affective characteristics, especially in the *considerate leader* type, whereas the conception of a wise person is more diverse for young people under 30. Young adults showed relatively higher levels of conceptions for cognitive characteristics, which are *competent achiever* and *confident visionary* type (see Fig. 2). Also, the adult group over 30 responded with a higher score compared to the under 30 group, leading to the suggestion that the older group seems to have a clearer or stronger concept of a wise person.

Differences in Conceptions of a Wise Man and a Wise Woman

As can be seen from Table 4, the ranking for the main 19 adjectives were similar for a wise man and a wise woman. The overall average score was higher for men. However, four items, creative, famous, joyful, and warm, were higher for women.

Specifically, we found an interesting tendency on the conceptions of a wise woman for subjects under age 30 group. As we believe that young adults are the most sensitive to the social characteristics of the present age, we decided to explore the results for this younger age group in more detail.

Comparing the top ten adjectives, seven (i.e., respected, influential, witty, humble, cooperative, creative, and group oriented) were the same. This result is in line

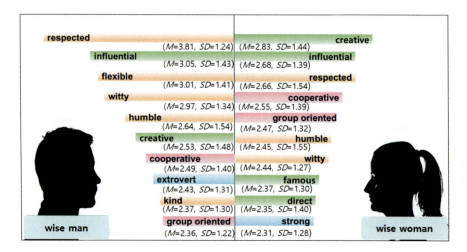

Fig. 3 Conceptions of a wise man and a wise woman

Table 4 The results of paired t-tests between the conception of a wise man and a wise woman

	Adjectives	Wise man		Wise woman		T
		M	SD	M	SD	
1	Respected	3.89	1.25	2.97	1.55	14.21***
2	Influential	3.18	1.43	2.86	1.40	5.39***
3	Witty	3.12	1.34	2.68	1.33	7.26***
4	Flexible	3.13	1.40	2.57	1.47	8.99***
5	Humble	2.92	1.56	2.77	1.57	3.14**
6	Cooperative	2.67	1.44	2.78	1.40	−1.73
7	Creative	2.57	1.49	2.82	1.44	−3.93***
8	Kind	2.65	1.39	2.55	1.37	1.84
9	Warm	2.32	1.41	2.55	1.48	−4.29***
10	Group-oriented	2.40	1.26	2.38	1.31	0.23
11	Optimistic	2.33	1.46	2.34	1.37	−0.26
12	Generous	2.29	1.32	2.31	1.33	−0.27
13	Strong	2.31	1.33	2.26	1.28	0.85
14	Famous	1.96	1.24	2.30	1.30	−5.76***
15	Direct	2.10	1.29	2.18	1.38	−1.24
16	Joyful	1.94	1.30	2.26	1.40	−6.13***
17	Extrovert	2.29	1.29	1.85	1.26	7.65***
18	Rational	2.27	1.34	1.82	1.23	7.50***
19	Concrete	2.14	1.24	1.92	1.22	4.19***

$**p < 0.005$; $***p < 0.001$

with Glück, Strasser, and Bluck (2009) research. The other three adjectives implied a diverging view of the conceptions for a wise man (flexible, extrovert, kind) and a wise woman (famous, direct, strong; see Fig. 3).

The most striking difference between the conceptions for a wise man and woman was the image of a 'soft man' and a 'strong woman'. In other words, a wise man was expected to have more emotional characteristics, such as being 'respected', 'flexible', 'witty', 'humble', and 'kind'. These five adjectives or characteristics are all included in the *considerate leader* type. On the other hand, for a wise woman, four out of the top 10 characteristics were 'creativity', 'influence', 'famous', and 'direct' which are associated with the *competent achiever* type. In addition, 'strong', ranked 10th, while 'kind' was not even included. In general, a wise woman was perceived as quite different from gender stereotypes (Belk & Snell, 1986; Räty & Snellman, 1992).

Another interesting difference can be seen from the rankings. For a wise man, 'respected' was a very special adjective. Not only was it ranked as the number one characteristic, but the response level was also significantly stronger than that shown for other adjectives or for a wise woman. We believe that at least in Korea, it seems important for a wise man to be respected. What about other cultures? It would be worthwhile to examine whether this phenomenon is confirmed in other cultures as well, considering the differences between Eastern and Western views, values, philosophies, and psychologies.

Implications and Future Directions for Research and Practice

Early gifted education focused mainly on using high IQ scores to identify gifted students, but limitations of this approach led to the need for a broader, multifaceted approach to identifying giftedness and the associated characteristics of gifted children (Borland, 2009; Park & Kim, 2018). Wisdom in gifted education is an extension of this discussion because of the relationship between the characteristics of wise persons, giftedness, and gifted education. We have stated in the beginning of this chapter, that the ultimate goal of gifted education should be to educate our students to become wise persons who have talent and use it in the right direction. For example, the discovery of gunpowder is important, but how it is used is even more important, whether it is used for detrimental means, such as for war or for the joy of fireworks in celebrations. Hence, the decision can result in saving or harming people. The decision requires a wise person to make a wise judgment. We must be deeply concerned about the direction of education related with wisdom and the future direction of gifted education in particular. In gifted education, it is always essential to develop potential (Horowitz, Subotnik, & Matthews, 2009; Robinson, Shore, & Enersen, 2006).

Although this is only a small attempt in the research about the concept and characteristics of a wise person, it provides a starting point in provoking thoughts about designing the curriculum and content for education to help develop students' potential. Can education foster students to become wiser persons? Bruya and Ardelt's study (2018) showed evidence that wisdom can be conceived as a strength to be cultivated. For example, the curriculum for gifted education could include some important values—as highlighted by the characteristics of wise persons illustrated in this chapter—so our gifted students may grow up as a *competent achiever, considerate leader, concordant balancer,* or *confident visionary.*

In addition, we need to consider the educational environment. Does the learning environment promote wisdom and respect for our gifted students? For instance, a boy, named Louis Braille (1809–1852), was blind, but he had an inquisitive mind, so at the age of only 15, he developed the Braille system for the blind (1824), which enabled blind people to read and share the wonders of the world. He wanted to change the lives of those who could not see, so he used his talent and did what no other expert thought to do. However, Braille's wonderful creation that revolutionised the lives of the blind was not acknowledged by the world for 30 years, even in the schools for the blind. Surprisingly, the reason given for the long abandonment was that it is difficult for the non-disabled to understand, and it was difficult for people to comprehend why the blind should want to read a book (Mellor, 2006). This was due mainly to the social conventions shared by the majority of the social groups in that era. If the talent and direction of this 15-year-old boy had been respected and nurtured, would the outcome have been different?

How will the wise person lead the world to be a better place? How can we educate our young gifted minds to make a difference in a positive way in the forthcoming ages? These are some questions that need to be addressed in our global educational settings. We can welcome more Braille's into our world by helping our students become wiser through the education that we provide (Sánchez-Escobedo et al., 2014; Smith & Baltes, 1993).

More research should be done to explore the conceptions of wise persons within gifted education. Commonalities and differences in conceptions between gender, generation, and culture should be investigated through international cooperation to design a broader framework for gifted education. Through future studies, investigations could address the question of whether the concept and characteristics of wise persons remain constant or whether there are some parts which may change depending on gender, culture, generation, or education.

Conclusion

We have discussed conceptions of wise people in order to shed some light on gifted education. Through the two-phase study exampled here, we proposed four types of wise persons who are *competent achievers, considerate leaders, concordant balancers,* and *confident visionaries.*

There were some interesting differences in conceptions of a wise man and a wise woman. The prominent difference is the image of soft man and strong woman. In general, a wise man and a wise woman were perceived as quite different from traditional gender stereotypes. There were also some differences between younger and older age groups. The older age group seemed to have a clearer or stronger concept of a wise person. They also put more weight on the affective aspect compared to the younger age group. Differences of conceptions can occur according to one's environment and experiences. Some initial though meaningful results were delineated in this chapter that can be used to contribute to the direction of gifted education and education in general. Further studies on the link between the diverse conceptions of wise persons and gifted education should be undertaken to explore how wisdom can be recognised and cultivated in gifted students.

Cross-References

▶ Attuned Pedagogy: The Artistry of Differentiated Instruction from a Taiwanese Cultural Perspective
▶ Bricolage and the Evolution of Giftedness and Talent in Taiwan
▶ Fostering Resilience in 'At-Risk' Gifted and Talented Young People
▶ Gifted Education in the Asia-Pacific: From the Past for the Future – An Introduction
▶ Identifying and Nurturing Diversely Gifted and Talented Students: Part III Introduction
▶ Motivational Issues in Gifted Education: Understanding the Role of Students' Attribution and Control Beliefs, Self-Worth Protection and Growth Orientation
▶ Some Implications for the Future of Gifted Education in the Asia-Pacific
▶ Spirituality and Giftedness: Threading the Path of Identity
▶ The Lives and Achievements of Four Extraordinary Australians: A Master, a Maker, an Introspector, and an Influencer
▶ Underachievement and the Quest for Dignity: Contemporary Perspectives on a Timeless Issue

References

Ardelt, M. (2003). Empirical assessment of a three-dimensional wisdom scale. *Research on Aging, 25*(3), 275–324. https://doi.org/10.1177/0164027503251764
Ardelt, M., Pridgen, S., & Nutter-Pridgen, K. L. (2018). The relation between age and three-dimensional wisdom: Variations by wisdom dimensions and education. *The Journals of Gerontology: Series B, 73*(8), 1339–1349. https://doi.org/10.1093/geronb/gbx182
Baltes, P. B., & Smith, J. (2008). The fascination of wisdom: Its nature, ontogeny, and function. *Perspectives on Psychological Science, 3*(1), 56–64. https://doi.org/10.1111/j.1745-6916.2008.00062.x
Baltes, P. B., & Staudinger, U. M. (2000). Wisdom: A metaheuristic (pragmatic) to orchestrate mind and virtues toward excellence. *American Psychologist, 55*(1), 122–136. https://doi.org/10.1037/0003-066X.55.1.122
Belk, S. S., & Snell, W. E., Jr. (1986). Beliefs about women: Components and correlates. *Personality and Social Psychology Bulletin, 12*(4), 403–413. https://doi.org/10.1177/0146167286124003
Blanchard-Fields, F., Brannan, J. R., & Camp, C. J. (1987). Alternative conceptions of wisdom: An onion-peeling exercise. *Educational Gerontology: An International Quarterly, 13*(6), 497–503. https://doi.org/10.1080/0360127870130605
Borland, J. H. (2009). Myth 2: The gifted constitute 3% to 5% of the population. Moreover, giftedness equals high IQ, which is a stable measure of aptitude: Spinal tap psychometrics in

gifted education. *Gifted Child Quarterly,* 53(4), 236–238. https://doi.org/10.1177/0016986209346825

Borzendowski, J. (2009). *Marie Curie: Mother of modern Physics.* New York, NY: Sterling Publishing Company.

Brent, S. B., & Watson, D. (1980). *Aging and wisdom: Individual and collective aspects.* Paper presented at the third annual meeting of the Gerontological Society of America, San Diego, CA.

Brown, S. C., & Greene, J. A. (2006). The wisdom development scale: Translating the conceptual to the concrete. *Journal of College Student Development, 47*(1), 1–19. https://doi.org/10.1353/csd.2006.0002

Bruya, B., & Ardelt, M. (2018). Wisdom can be taught: A proof-of-concept study for fostering wisdom in the classroom. *Learning and Instruction, 58,* 106–114. https://doi.org/10.1016/j.learninstruc.2018.05.001

Clark, B. (2013). *Growing up gifted: Developing the potential of gifted children at school and at home.* Singapore, Singapore: Pearson Education South Asia.

Clayton, V. P., & Birren, J. E. (1980). The development of wisdom across the life span: A reexamination of an ancient topic. In *Life-span development and behavior* (Vol. 3, pp. 103–135). New York, NY: Academic.

Curie, M. (1923). *Pierre Curie* (C. Kellogg & V. Kellogg, Trans.). New York, NY: Macmillan.

De Haan, R. F., & Havighurst, R. J. (1961). *Educating gifted children.* Chicago, IL: University of Chicago Press.

Farrell, A., & Hershey, D. A. (1996, November). *Descriptive dimensions underlying perceptions of wisdom.* Poster presented at the annual meeting of the Gerontological Society of America, Washington, DC.

Feldman, D. H., & Goldsmith, L. T. (1986). *Nature's gambit: Child prodigies and the development of human potential.* New York, NY: Basic Books (AZ).

Gilmer, P. J. (2011). Irène Joliot-Curie, a Nobel laureate in artificial radioactivity. In M.-H. Chiu, P. J. Gilmer, & D. F. Treagust (Eds.), *Celebrating the 100th anniversary of Madame Marie Sklodowska Curie's Nobel Prize in Chemistry* (pp. 41–57). Rotterdam, The Netherlands: Sense Publishers. Retrieved from https://www.sensepublishers.com/media/141-celebrating-the-100th-anniversary-of-madame-marie-sklodowska-curies-nobel-prize-in-chemistry.pdf

Glück, J., Strasser, I., & Bluck, S. (2009). Gender differences in implicit theories of wisdom. *Research in Human Development, 6*(1), 27–44. https://doi.org/10.1080/15427600902779370

Heckhausen, J., Dixon, R. A., & Baltes, P. B. (1989). Gains and losses in development throughout adulthood as perceived by different adult age groups. *Developmental Psychology, 25*(1), 109. https://doi.org/10.1037/0012-1649.25.1.109

Hershey, D. A., & Farrell, A. H. (1997). Perceptions of wisdom associated with selected occupations and personality characteristics. *Current Psychology, 16*(2), 115–130. https://doi.org/10.1007/s12144-997-1019-7

Holliday, S. G., & Chandler, M. J. (1986). Wisdom: Explorations in adult competence. In *Contributions to human development* (Vol. 17, pp. 100–113). Basel, Switzerland: Karger.

Hollingworth, L., Sánchez-Escobedo, P., Graudina, L., Misiuniene, J., & Park, K. (2013). Gender differences on the concept of wisdom: An international comparison. *Gifted and Talented International, 28*(1–2), 219–225. https://doi.org/10.1080/15332276.2013.11678416

Horowitz, F. D. E., Subotnik, R. F., & Matthews, D. J. (2009). The development of giftedness and talent across the life span. In *American Psychological Foundation Invitational Conference, 2005; The present volume evolved from the aforementioned conference.* Washington, DC: American Psychological Association.

Hu, C. S., Ferrari, M., Liu, R. D., Gao, Q., & Weare, E. (2016). Mainland Chinese implicit theory of wisdom: Generational and cultural differences. *The Journals of Gerontology: Series B, 73*(8), 1416–1424. https://doi.org/10.1093/geronb/gbw157

Ivanova, L., & Rascevska, M. (2010). Conceptions about wise persons in Latvia. In *Selected papers of the 2nd international conference. Gifted children: Challenges and possibilities* (pp. 16–19). Kaunas, Lithuania: Tehnologija.

Jeste, D. V., Ardelt, M., Blazer, D., Kraemer, H. C., Vaillant, G., & Meeks, T. W. (2010). Expert consensus on characteristics of wisdom: A Delphi method study. *The Gerontologist, 50*(5), 668–680. https://doi.org/10.1093/geront/gnq022

Kanevsky, L. (2011). Deferential differentiation: What types of differentiation do students want? *Gifted Child Quarterly, 55*(4), 279–299. https://doi.org/10.1177/0016986211422098

Lim, W., Plucker, J. A., & Im, K. (2002). We are more alike than we think we are: Implicit theories of intelligence with a Korean sample. *Intelligence, 30*(2), 185–208. https://doi.org/10.1016/S0160-2896(01)00097-6

Lubinski, D., & Benbow, C. P. (2006). Study of mathematically precocious youth after 35 years: Uncovering antecedents for the development of math-science expertise. *Perspectives on Psychological Science, 1*(4), 316–345. https://doi.org/10.1111/j.1745-6916.2006.00019.x

Marchand, H. (2003). An overview of the psychology of wisdom. Prometheus Research Group. Retrieved from http://www.wisdompage.com/AnOverviewOfThePsychologyOfWisdom.html

Marland, S. P. (1972). *Education of the gifted and talented (report to the Subcommittee on Education, Committee on Labor and Public Welfare, US Senate)*. Washington, DC: Government Printing Office.

Mellor, C. M. (2006). *Louis Braille: A touch of genius*. Boston, MA: National Braille Press.

Park, K., & Kim, E. (2018). The intellectual characteristics of Korean gifted elementary students through the use of Aurora-a test. *The Journal of Learner-Centered Curriculum and Instruction, 18*(3), 509–526.

Passow, A. H. (1981). The nature of giftedness and talent. *Gifted Child Quarterly, 25*(1), 5–10. https://doi.org/10.1177/001698628102500102

Räty, H., & Snellman, L. (1992). Does gender make any difference? Common-sense conceptions of intelligence. *Social Behavior and Personality: An International Journal, 20*(1), 23–34. https://doi.org/10.2224/sbp.1992.20.1.23

Robinson, A., Shore, B. M., & Enersen, D. L. (2006). *Best practices in gifted education: An evidence-based guide*. Naperville, IL: Sourcebooks.

Sánchez-Escobedo, P., Park, K., Hollingworth, L., Misiuniene, J., & Ivanova, L. (2014). A cross-comparative international study on the concept of wisdom. *Gifted Education International, 30*(3), 228–236. https://doi.org/10.1177/0261429413486575

Shefali, L. (2018). For shame: 'Pharma bro' Shkreli is in prison, but Daraprim's price is still high. *The Washington Post*. Retrieved from https://wapo.st/2rkFyh8?tid=ssn

Smith, J., & Baltes, P. B. (1993). Differential psychological ageing: Profiles of the old and very old. *Ageing & Society, 13*(4), 551–587. https://doi.org/10.1017/S0144686X00001367

Staudinger, U. M., & Pasupathi, M. (2003). Correlates of wisdom-related performance in adolescence and adulthood: Age-graded differences in 'paths' toward desirable development. *Journal of Research on Adolescence, 13*(3), 239–268. https://doi.org/10.1111/1532-7795.1303001

Sternberg, R. J. (1985). Implicit theories of intelligence, creativity, and wisdom. *Journal of Personality and Social Psychology, 49*(3), 607–627. https://doi.org/10.1037/0022-3514.49.3.607

Sternberg, R. J. (Ed.). (1990). *Wisdom: Its nature, origins, and development*. New York, NY: Cambridge University Press.

Sternberg, R. J. (2003). *Wisdom, intelligence, and creativity synthesized*. New York, NY: Cambridge University Press.

Sternberg, R. J. (2004). What is wisdom and how can we develop it? *The Annals of the American Academy of Political and Social Science, 591*(1), 164–174. https://doi.org/10.1177/0002716203260097

Takahashi, M. (2000). Toward a culturally inclusive understanding of wisdom: Historical roots in the East and West. *The International Journal of Aging and Human Development, 51*(3), 217–230. https://doi.org/10.2190/H45U-M17W-3AG5-TA49

Takahashi, M., & Bordia, P. (2000). The concept of wisdom: A cross-cultural comparison. *International Journal of Psychology, 35*(1), 1–9. https://doi.org/10.1080/002075900399475

Takahashi, M., & Overton, W. F. (2002). Wisdom: A culturally inclusive developmental perspective. *International Journal of Behavioral Development, 26*(3), 269–277. https://doi.org/10.1080/01650250143000139

Taylor, M., Bates, G., & Webster, J. D. (2011). Comparing the psychometric properties of two measures of wisdom: Predicting forgiveness and psychological well-being with the Self-Assessed Wisdom Scale (SAWS) and the Three-Dimensional Wisdom Scale (3D-WS). *Experimental Aging Research, 37*(2), 129–141. https://doi.org/10.1080/0361073X.2011.554508

Thomas, M. L., Bangen, K. J., Palmer, B. W., Martin, A. S., Avanzino, J. A., Depp, C. A., … Jeste, D. V. (2017). A new scale for assessing wisdom based on common domains and a neurobiological model: The San Diego Wisdom Scale (SD-WISE). *Journal of Psychiatric Research, 108*, 40–47. https://doi.org/10.1016/j.jpsychires.2017.09.005

Webster, J. D. (2003). An exploratory analysis of a self-assessed wisdom scale. *Journal of Adult Development, 10*(1), 13–22. https://doi.org/10.1023/A:1020782619051

Webster, J. D. (2007). Measuring the character strength of wisdom. *The International Journal of Aging and Human Development, 65*(2), 163–183. https://doi.org/10.2190/AG.65.2.d

Webster, J. D. (2010). Wisdom and positive psychosocial values in young adulthood. *Journal of Adult Development, 17*(2), 70–80. https://doi.org/10.1007/s10804-009-9081-z

Wink, P., & Helson, R. (1997). Practical and transcendent wisdom: Their nature and some longitudinal findings. *Journal of Adult Development, 4*(1), 1–15. https://doi.org/10.1007/BF02511845

Yang, S. Y. (2001). Conceptions of wisdom among Taiwanese Chinese. *Journal of Cross-Cultural Psychology, 32*(6), 662–680. https://doi.org/10.1177/0022022101032006002

Kyungbin Park is a full professor at Gachon University. She was the President of The *Asia–Pacific Federation for Giftedness* (APFG). She also served as the President for Korean Society for the Gifted (2012–2015). She has worked to implement the law for gifted education in Korea and is a member in the advisory committee of several national organisations in Korea on gifted education. Her main interest areas are in creativity, intelligence, socio-emotional development, and gifted education in early childhood. She has written articles and books on identification, evaluation, trends of research, assessment tools, characteristics, and intercultural comparisons in gifted education.

Eunhyang Kim is an assistant professor in counselling at Gachon University. She is a member of the *Korean Child and Adolescent Counseling Association* (KCACA) and the *Korean Society for the Gifted* (KSG). She has been engaged in teaching a wide range of courses to students in areas of counselling, psychology, and education. Her research interests include personality, character strengths, and counselling of the gifted. She has written several articles and books on counselling, and special education.

The Lives and Achievements of Four Extraordinary Australians: A Master, a Maker, an Introspector, and an Influencer

30

Carmel Diezmann

Contents

Introduction	651
Exemplary Creators	652
Exemplars of Extraordinary Australians: The Master, the Maker, the Introspector, and the Influencer	653
Australian Stories of Extraordinary Individuals	655
Discussion	663
Research and/or Practice: Implications and Future Directions	664
Conclusion	665
Cross-References	666
References	667

Abstract

The focus in this chapter is on the societal contributions of gifted individuals and the implications for education. This discussion is underpinned by Gardner's (1997) notion of an *Exemplary Creator* (EC) and the roles that these individuals assume as a Maker, a Master, an Introspector, or an Influencer. Following an overview of Gardner's theory of ECs and the associated societal roles, four Australians representative of these roles were selected for investigation: Victor Chang (Master), Elizabeth Blackburn (Maker), Richard Flanagan (Introspector), and May Gibbs (Influencer). Using a bibliographic approach, the lives of these individuals were explored. The investigations revealed that the ECs' childhoods:

C. Diezmann (✉)
Faculty of Education, Queensland University of Technology, Brisbane, QLD, Australia
e-mail: c.diezmann@qut.edu.au

© Springer Nature Singapore Pte Ltd. 2021
S. R. Smith (ed.), *Handbook of Giftedness and Talent Development in the Asia-Pacific*, Springer International Handbooks of Education,
https://doi.org/10.1007/978-981-13-3041-4_30

(a) created environments for their interests to flourish; (b) provided reference points for their work; (c) inspired a career direction; or (d) provided the foundations for intercultural competence. Further, each of these ECs actively pursued advanced knowledge studying or working at the forefront of knowledge in their discipline. Further, resiliency was also a strong characteristic of each of these ECs. This investigation has four implications for gifted education. First, potential ECs may be found anywhere because achievement of EC status transcends a time period, location, discipline, socio-economic status, and culture. Second, becoming an EC requires concerted long-term effort and support. Hence, gifted individuals need opportunities to pursue knowledge in their passion area beyond what is required for school. Third, resilience needs to be promoted because learning how to deal with and overcome failure is just as important as learning content. Finally, an EC can undertake vastly different roles within society as a Master, a Maker, an Introspector, or an Influencer. Hence, education should provide opportunities to foster these roles within individuals. To provide a foundation for such education, research is needed about these societal roles and how they manifest in ECs across the lifespan.

Keywords

Extraordinariness · Creativity · Gifted education · Society · Roles · Characteristics

The aims in this chapter are to:
1. Provide an overview of Gardner's (1997) theory of exemplary creators including the societal roles they assume.
2. Identify four extraordinary Australians who represent each of the four roles of exemplary creators.
3. Raise awareness of the achievements of extraordinary Australians across diverse fields.
4. Provide examples of how exemplary creators have drawn on their childhoods in their careers and pursued knowledge to an advanced level.
5. Highlight the role that resiliency played in the success of the extraordinary Australians.
6. Draw attention to the need to educate gifted individuals about the societal roles that they can assume.
7. Suggest that research using gifted individuals as the population from aligned fields to the societal roles, such as mastery learning, entrepreneurship, diary writing, and communication can inform education.
8. Propose lifespan research to provide insight into how the societal roles manifest over time.

Introduction

In 2013, Howard Gardner was honoured with the presentation of *Mind, Work, and Life: A Festschrift on the Occasion of Howard Gardner's 70th Birthday* (Kornhaber & Winner, 2014). Gardner's two-volume Festschrift comprises 116 contributions of over 1000 pages. Amongst the contributors are highly acclaimed educators and theorists, such as Jerome Bruner, Mihaly Csikszentmihalyi, Linda Darling-Hammond, David Perkins, Oliver Sacks, Lee Shulman, and Robert J. Sternberg. However, other contributors are from diverse fields such as dance (Jacques D'Amboise) and palliative care (Elizabeth McCormack). Ellen Winner, Gardner's wife, reported that she and the other Festschrift co-editor "were moved by the contributions we received. To see the powerful effect Howard has had on the lives of his students, his assistants, his colleagues, and on the field was truly overwhelming" (Kornhaber & Winner, 2014, p. xi). In Gardner's (2014) own words, he has been (and continues to be) an *Influencer*: "I don't really care whether people know my name or my face. I'd much rather that they be *influenced* by my ideas and the practices I value and attempt to encourage" (emphasis added; p. 69).

This pivotal role of an Influencer was identified by Gardner (1997) as one of four key roles that individuals with extraordinary minds assume in contributing to society. The other roles are Master, Maker, and Introspector. The *Master* "is an individual who gains complete mastery over one or more domains of accomplishment; his or her innovation occurs within established practice" (Gardner, 1997, p. 11). For example, Mozart was a master of the domain of music. The *Maker* "may have mastered existing domains, but he or she devotes energies to the creation of a new domain" (Gardner, 1997, p. 12). For example, Freud created the new domain of psychoanalysis. The *Introspector* undertakes "an exploration of his or her inner life: daily experiences, potent needs, and fears, the operation of consciousness (both that of the particular individual and that of individuals more generally)" (Gardner, 1997, p. 12). For example, Virginia Woolf's writing provided traces of her personal introspections. The *Influencer* "has a primary goal, the influencing of other individuals" (Gardner, 1997, p. 12). For example, Mahatma Ghandi influenced others through his leadership of movements and through his writings. Though the roles of Master, Maker, Introspector, and Influencer are distinct, they can be interrelated (Gardner, 1997). For example, Sigmund Freud assumed the dual roles of a *Maker* by founding psychoanalysis and an *Introspector* through the exploration of his inner self. Collectively, outstanding individuals assuming these roles are considered to be exemplary creators (EC) through their societal contributions (Gardner, 1997). Thus, the education of gifted individuals should be just as concerned about fostering their potential as exemplary creators, as it is about developing their specific intelligence or domain knowledge.

In this chapter the relationship between education and the societal roles of ECs is explored. It commences with an overview of Gardner's (1997) notion of an EC. It then explores the lives of a group of extraordinary Australians, who have assumed one or more societal roles as Influencer, Master, Maker, or Introspector to consider if, and how, their education supported these roles. The chapter concludes with recommendations for how education can support the development of each of the roles of ECs in gifted individuals.

Exemplary Creators

The identification of ECs is determined by the value of their work as judged by those in the field and the broader society (Gardner, 1997). For some creators, the value of their work is identified quickly, such as the case of J. K. Rowling (Bloomsbury Publishing, 2017):

> J.K. Rowling is the author of the record-breaking, multi-award-winning Harry Potter novels. Loved by fans around the world, the series has sold over 450 million copies, been translated into 78 languages, and made into 8 blockbuster films ... As well as receiving an OBE for services to children's literature, she has received many awards and honours, including France's Légion d'honneur and the Hans Christian Andersen Award. (para. 1)

However, for other ECs considerable time can elapse between the creation of the work and the acknowledgement of its value. For example, the mathematician John Nash was awarded the Nobel Prize for economics over four decades after writing a paper on game theory for his PhD at Princeton (Kuhn, Nirenberg, Sarnak, & Nash, 1996). Further, the value of an EC's work can continue to appreciate beyond his or her lifetime. For example, a 500-year-old painting by Leonardo da Vinci recently sold for a record US $450 million (Christie's, 2017).

ECs share two common characteristics. First, these individuals are able to leverage key elements from their childhoods and apply them later in life (Gardner, 1994): (An EC) "makes some kind of raid upon their childhood, preserving certain aspects of their own earlier life" (p. 156). For example, an individual who reflects on his or her childhood and subsequent experiences may be preparing for the role of an Introspector. Second, ECs display a high level of independence in learning about their chosen domain (Gardner, 1994):

> (An EC has) a tendency to question every assumption and to attempt to strike out on one's own as much as possible and a countervailing tendency to exhaust a domain, to probe more systematically, deeply, and comprehensively than anyone has every probed before. (p. 156)

This intensive quest for domain knowledge supports an individual to assume the role of Master of an existing domain or provides the foundational knowledge for him or her to become the Maker of a new domain. Thus, an individual's childhood experiences and his or her processes of knowledge building will be of particular interest in reviewing the lives of extraordinary individuals.

Complementing the two common characteristics of an EC (Gardner, 1994) are three metacognitive processes that extraordinary individuals employ in their lives, namely, their ability to reflect on, leverage, and frame their experiences

(Gardner, 1997). First, extraordinary individuals engage in self-monitoring behaviour (Gardner, 2002): "Extraordinary individuals stand out in the extent to which they *reflect*—often explicitly—on the events of their lives, large as well as small" (emphasis added; p. 14). These reflections can include their childhood experiences. As a result of these reflections they take action (Gardner, 2002): "Extraordinary individuals devote a great deal of time to reflecting. They think about what they want to achieve, how they are doing, when to persevere, when to shift course, when to return, freshly armed, to an earlier course" (p. 16). Second, extraordinary individuals are able to *leverage* situations to their advantage (Gardner, 2002): "Extraordinary individuals are distinguished less by their impressive 'raw powers' than by their ability to identify their strengths and then to exploit them" (p. 15) ... "They identify their strengths—in intelligence, personality, temperament, resources—and they push these hard" (p. 16). Thus, ECs see and capitalise on opportunities that others may not appreciate. Third, extraordinary individuals *frame* their experiences in such a way to lead to future success (Gardner, 2002). However, success and failure co-exist. Although failure can be substantial, it is not a deterrent (Gardner, 2002):

> Extraordinary individuals fail often and sometimes dramatically. Rather than giving up, however, they are challenged to learn from their setbacks and to convert defeats into opportunities" (p. 15) ... (Extraordinary) individuals fail, and being extremely ambitious, extraordinary individuals fail with surprising frequency. But unlike many others, their failures are neither repressed, nor do they cause the creators or leaders to give up or go fishing. (pp. 16–17)

Thus, extraordinary individuals display considerable resilience even in the face of adversity. According to Luthar et al. (2000), resilience is "*a dynamic process encompassing positive adaptation within the context of significant adversity*" (emphasis in the original; p. 543). Such adaptations by individuals might include learning from experiences, exploiting their strengths, and using situations or events to create opportunities.

Exemplars of Extraordinary Australians: The Master, the Maker, the Introspector, and the Influencer

The exemplars selected by Gardner (1997) to illustrate the roles of Master (Mozart), Maker (Freud), Introspector (Woolf), and Influencer (Ghandi) appear to be far removed from life in contemporary Australia. Hence, to examine these roles within the Australian context, the lives of four extraordinary Australians representative of each of these roles were selected: Victor Chang, Elizabeth Blackburn, Richard Flanagan, and May Gibbs (Fig. 1). The identification of these particular individuals was based on three criteria, (a) being Australian-born or growing up and being schooled in Australia or spending the majority of their career in Australia; (b) recognition of their achievements by their professional domain or society more

A Master:	A Maker:	An Introspector:	An Influencer:
Victor Chang	Elizabeth Blackburn	Richard Flanagan	May Gibbs

Photograph of Victor Chang Statue by Agesworth available at https://commons.wikimedia.org/wiki/File:Victor_Chang_bronze_statue_Klarfeld.JPG under a Creative Commons Attribution-Share Alike 3.0 Unported license	Photograph of Elizabeth Blackburn by Conrad Erb with permission from the Chemical Heritage Foundation available at https://commons.wikimedia.org/wiki/File:Elizabeth_Blackburn_CHF_Heritage_Day_2012_Rush_001.JPG under a Creative Commons Attribution-Share Alike 3.0 Unported license	Photograph of Richard Flanagan by AUrandomhouse available at https://commons.wikimedia.org/wiki/File:RichardFlanagan_300w.jpg under a Creative Commons Attribution-Share Alike 3.0 Unported license	Portrait of May Gibbs, 1916 available at https://commons.wikimedia.org/wiki/File:May_Gibbs.jpg. Public domain.

Fig. 1 Four extraordinary Australians (Agesworth 2009; AUrandomhouse 2014; Erb 2012; [May Gibbs Portrait] 1916)

broadly (Gardner, 1997); and (c) collectively, representing a diversity of disciplines. Chang was selected as a *Master* of heart surgery winning the People's Choice Awards in 1999 for 'Australian of the Century' (Time, 2016). Blackburn is a *Maker* discovering new knowledge in molecular biology (Nobel Media, 2017a). Flanagan is an *Introspector* giving personal meaning to stories that he has heard or created (Flanagan, 2014). Gibbs continues to be an *Influencer* sharing her insights into the Australian bush and the environment through children's literature (Walsh, 2007).

The investigation of the four extraordinary Australians was undertaken using impact assessment (Williams, Eiseman, Landree, & Adamson, 2009). This process commenced with the creation of outcome narratives (aka case stories) describing how and why these individuals contributed to society (i.e., outcomes) through their various roles. This retrospective account of the achievements of the selected individuals was created using a biographical approach (Smith, 1994) drawing on various electronic and print sources. Within this backward tracing approach, key elements (inputs) are likely to have influenced the

Table 1 Examples of eminent individuals and their societal roles

Roles	Gardner's exemplars	Australian exemplars	Other Australians
Masters	Amadeus Mozart	Victor Chang (decd.)	Cathy Freeman (sprinter, Olympic gold medallist).
Makers	Sigmund Freud	Elizabeth Blackburn	Terry Tao (mathematician, Field's medallist).
Introspectors	Virginia Woolf	Richard Flanagan	Peter Allen (songwriter, 'I Still Call Australia Home').
Influencers	Mahatma Gandhi	May Gibbs (decd.)	Germaine Greer (author, 'The Female Eunuch').

achievements (outputs) of the extraordinary Australians who were identified. These elements were then used to create a logic model or template for the types of inputs that are likely to support individuals with similar characteristics to achieve highly within particular roles. For pragmatic reasons, the discussion is confined to these four individuals. However, many other eminent individuals may have been selected for investigation. Table 1 shows Gardner's exemplars, the selected Australian exemplars, and other Australians who could also be exemplars for these roles.

Australian Stories of Extraordinary Individuals

This section provides an overview of the lives of the four selected extraordinary Australians focusing on the characteristics of ECs and the associated metacognitive skills.

The Master: Dr Victor Chang (1936–1991). Victor Chang was a cardiac and transplantation surgeon who pioneered modern heart transplantation (Coleman, 2014): "A gifted technician with sound clinical judgement, he inspired confidence with his engaging smile and obvious compassion" (para. 5). Chang led the National Heart Transplant Unit at St Vincent's Hospital that was established in 1984 (Harris, 1991). In 1986, Chang was recognised with the "Companion of the Order of Australia" (AC), which "is awarded for eminent achievement and merit of the highest degree in service to Australia or humanity at large" (Department of the Prime Minister and Cabinet, n.d.). Subsequently, in 1999, Chang was named 'Australian of the Century' in the People's Choice Awards (Victor Chang Cardiac Research Institute, 2015). The influence of Chang's work extended internationally (Victor Chang Cardiac Research Institute, 2019):

> A national hero, Victor Chang was hailed as "the most prominent doctor in the southern hemisphere", and his revolutionary work in the field of heart transplantation had implications for cardiac patients, not only in Australia and Southeast Asia but around the globe, (para. 2)

Chang was born in Shanghai to Australian-born parents (Victor Chang Cardiac Research Institute, 2015). However, his early life was disrupted due to the Second World War. His family lived in Shanghai, Hong Kong, Burma, Sichuan province in China, and then returned to Hong Kong in 1945 (Coleman, 2014). Chang finished his high school years in Australia living with relatives, subsequently completing his initial medical training at the University of Sydney.

Chang's life, study, and work experiences highlight the two characteristics of an EC related to childhood experiences and extensive knowledge of a particular domain. Chang drew upon his *childhood* in two ways. First, Chang's choice of medicine as a career was inspired by the early death of his mother from breast cancer in 1948 (Victor Chang Cardiac Research Institute, 2015). In addition, Chang's ability to work and collaborate across cultures reflected his early years living in multiple Asian locations as well as Australia. This cross-cultural dimension of Chang's work facilitated the spread of knowledge amongst medical personnel in Southeast Asia (Victor Chang Cardiac Research Institute, 2011):

> Dr Chang lectured extensively in China, Hong Kong, Indonesia, Singapore, and Malaysia. He also founded the Australasian-China Medical Education and Scientific Research Foundation, which sponsored South-East Asian doctors, nurses and students to work in Australia ... He also helped teams from St Vincent's travel to China, Singapore and Indonesia where they shared their medical, surgical, nursing, hospital administration and audio-visual expertise. (p. 7)

Chang's work in building medical relationships in the Asia-Pacific was one of the reasons for the award of his AC (Coleman, 2014): "His medical diplomacy favourably influenced relations between Australia and Asian countries; for this work and for his contributions to medical science he was appointed AC in 1986" (para. 4).

Second, Chang was proactive in building his extensive knowledge of heart diseases and surgery. He graduated from the University of Sydney with a Bachelor of Medical Science with first-class honours followed by a Bachelor of Medicine and a Bachelor of Surgery (Coleman, 2014). Following his university studies, Chang worked and trained in Australia, the UK, and the USA (Coleman, 2014). He interned and was a cardiothoracic surgical registrar at St Vincent's Hospital Sydney. He worked at St Anthony's and St Helier's Hospitals and the Royal Brompton Hospital specialising in heart and lung diseases. He then moved to the USA trained in cardiothoracic surgery at the Mayo Clinic, Rochester, subsequently becoming Chief Resident there. Chang returned to Australia in 1972 to work at St Vincent's Hospital as a cardiothoracic surgeon (Coleman, 2014). Chang's colleagues there included Harry Windsor, a pioneer of Australia's first heart transplant in 1968, and Mark Shanahan, who would later become his surgical partner. The trio of Windsor, Shanahan, and Chang pioneered medical advances in cardiac surgery "including valve replacement, coronary artery surgery, early valve replacement for endocarditis, positive pressure ventilation for crushed chest injury, mechanical heart assistance and repair of defects following myocardial infarction" (Farnsworth, 2008, p. 519).

Chang was awarded fellowships of the Royal Australasian College of Surgeons and the American College of Surgeons in 1973 and 1974, respectively (Coleman, 2014).

Throughout his life, Chang also demonstrated the three metacognitive skills of an EC. For example, he *framed* the passing of his mother as an inspiration to study medicine. By using antirejection drugs in transplantation surgery (Mellor, 2008) and developing a low-cost heart valve (Coleman, 2014), he demonstrated that he *reflected on* the impediments to successful and affordable heart surgery. However, most notable was his ability to *leverage* a situation. Initially, the national cardiac unit was awarded to the Royal Prince Alfred Hospital. However, Chang was persuasive in having the decision overturned (Harris, 1991): "He demonstrated that St Vincent's had enough funds—from a grateful South-east Asian donor—to go ahead with their own cardiac transplantation program and would do so" (para. 18). The decision to make St Vincent's Hospital the national cardiac unit has been validated by its record of internationally comparable transplant survival rates of 92 per cent and 85 per cent for one and five years, respectively, when Chang was Director in 1991 (Coleman, 2014). One of the best-known heart recipients of this unit is Fiona Coote. She received an initial heart transplant in 1984 as a 14-year-old, followed by a second transplant in 1986, and is alive over 30 years later (Harris, 1991; Victor Chang Cardiac Research Institute, 2015).

In the later years of Chang's life, he was recognised widely as a Master of cardiac surgery with honorary professorships and official advisory positions across Beijing, Shanghai Medical School, Indonesia, and Japan. In Australia, in 1998, Chang was awarded an honorary doctorate by the University of New South Wales "for his academic and humanitarian achievement" (Coleman, 2014). Thus, Chang was held in high esteem internationally.

The Maker: Professor Elizabeth Blackburn (1948–present). Elizabeth Blackburn is a renowned Australian-born molecular biologist now residing in the USA and is Professor of Biology and Physiology in the Department of Biochemistry and Biophysics at the University of California, San Francisco. With her colleagues, Carol Greider and Jack Szostak, Blackburn was awarded the 2009 Nobel Prize in Medicine for her co-discovery of the enzyme telomerase and its role in the development of cancer and the ageing process (Nobel Media, 2017a). Blackburn was awarded the Companion of the Order of Australia in 2010 for her contributions to science in biomedical research (ABC Science, 2010).

Blackburn displays the two characteristics of an EC (Gardner, 1997). First, she drew on her childhood experiences in her career. Blackburn was born in Hobart, Tasmania and grew up as the second of seven siblings. Elizabeth's father and mother were physicians receiving medical degrees from the Universities of Adelaide and Melbourne, respectively (Brady, 2007). As a young child, Blackburn lived near the sea and was interested in animals (Nobel Media, 2017b): "Curious about animals, I would pick up ants in our backyard and jellyfish on the beach" (n.p). *Reflecting* on her achievements, Blackburn attributes her interest in science to her experiences with animals and to science books (Nobel Media, 2017b):

> Perhaps arising from a fascination with animals, biology seemed the most interesting of sciences to me as a child. I was captivated by both the visual impact of science through science books written for young people, and an idea of romance and nobility of the scientific quest. This latter was especially engendered by the biography of Marie Curie, written by her daughter, which I read and reread as a child. By the time I was in my late teens it was clear to me that I wanted to do science. (para. 4)

However, although her schooling nurtured her interest in science, notably she did not share this interest with her classmates (Brady, 2007):

> Blackburn received warm encouragement from teachers, but she did not discuss with her friends her interest in biochemistry, an intellectual fascination grounded in her aesthetic attraction to those illustrations of amino acids and in a feeling that because biochemistry was about molecules and the workings of cells, it offered a doorway into the mystery of how life worked. I felt you had to go to that level of detail to understand life (pp. 11–12).

Second, Blackburn pursued deep knowledge in her chosen domain with her interest in science extending beyond what was required for school (Brady, 2007):

> ... she was thrilled by her recent discovery of a biology text complete with detailed illustrations of amino acids, strung together in long chains and then folded up into complex three-dimensional shapes to form enzymes and other proteins. For Liz, these elegant structures had a teasing beauty, promising tantalizing clues to the processes of life and yet also enfolding that mystery. Even the names of the amino acids—phenylalanine, leucine—struck her as poetic. Though she confessed her fascination to no one, she traced drawings of amino acids, on thin sheets of white paper and then tacked them up on her bedroom wall. (p. 1)

Despite disruption to her family life in her final year of schooling, Blackburn achieved outstanding results (Brady, 2007):

> Complete concentration enabled Liz to do exceptionally well in the end of year final statewide matriculation exams; in three of the subjects, she earned the highest scores in the state of Victoria, an achievement known as "winning the exhibitions". (p. 12)

Thus, Blackburn demonstrated the ability to *frame* her family situation as distinct from her studies.

Following Bachelor's and Master's studies in biology at the University of Melbourne, Blackburn completed her PhD at Cambridge in 1975 and did postdoctoral training at Yale University with Dr. Joseph Gall. In 1978, she co-published, with Gall, her discovery of "the molecular structure of the telomere, the region at the end of the chromosome that prevents it from disintegrating as the cell reproduces" (American Academy of Achievement, 2017, para. 3). That year, she also commenced in a faculty position at the University of California at Berkley in 1978 (American Academy of Achievement, 2017). Later Blackburn was joined at her lab by Carol Greider with their partnership ultimately leading to a Nobel Prize. Thus, Blackburn had opportunities to *leverage* her experiences with the more junior Greider and her early mentor Gall. The scientific discoveries emanating from both these partnerships highlight her status as a Maker.

The Introspector: Richard Flanagan (1961–present). Richard Flanagan is an acclaimed international novelist and winner of the 2014 Man Booker Prize for *The Narrow Road to the Deep North*. The book combines two wartime stories, his father's time as a prisoner of war and a story he had heard about a neighbour who returned home to find his village destroyed and his wife missing (Singh, 2014). Thus, Flanagan was able to *leverage* these stories and create a new story. However, the novel did not come easily with Flanagan recalling "(I) spent almost 12 years writing the book, deleting five previous novels from his (sic) laptop in despair" (Singh, 2014, para. 6).

In his Booker acceptance speech, Flanagan shared his view of novels: "Novels are not content. Nor are they a mirror to life or an explanation of life or a guide to life. Novels *are* life, or they are nothing" (emphasis in the original) (Flanagan, 2014, para. 5). Flanagan's ability to create a new life through his writing explains how he assumes the societal role of an Introspector. Gardner (1997) argues that the Introspector possesses a unique ability to create knowledge from his (or her) own human experience: "But his primary challenge is to peer deeply into his own psyche, to understand himself in a way that others do not routinely understand themselves, as individuals, as members of a group, or as human beings" (p. 96). Flanagan acknowledges the role of his experiences in his writing (Waldren, 1997):

> ... the history of literature is of writing from the edges: unless you understand your own part of the world, you can't offer anything to anyone. Tasmania is all I know, all I've got, and it's the paddock I plough, for better or worse... (para. 17)

However, coupled with Flanagan's use of experience is his ability to inhabit an alternative world according to his wife, Majda (Knox, 2017):

> When writing a novel, Flanagan's body may be seen in his house in Hobart or his shack on Bruny Island. He might be with Majda, but it's not him. "He is not a dreamy person normally, but when he's writing... he's not always there," she says. "Sometimes I have to say, 'Richard, stop writing.' Because he's back in the book and not with us" (para. 37) ... He is in another world, I can see this just by looking at him—so I try not to take him away from his dreaming. (para. 38)

Like other ECs, Flanagan draws heavily on his childhood. He credits his father with embedding in him the love of and power of language (Knox, 2017):

> "[My father] had a very strong sense of the beauty and magic of written words. He saw how oppressive it was when you didn't have access to the written word, and how liberating and transcendent if you did" ... "People who come from generations of literacy might have lost that sense of its transcendent and liberating power, but I got it from my father. Words have been like a magic carpet for me that have taken me far away from this island [Tasmania]." (para. 16)

At home, Flanagan was exposed to a broad genre of literature and discourse about language (ABC, 2008):

> There was nothing held in greater regard than writers and writing, although we had very few books, we only had a tiny little bookcase, we were library people. (para. 28) ... [However] they were without snobbery; comics, westerns, love ... those penny-dreadful westerns, anything, but the family was always reading. And they would argue about words terribly. There was a big old dictionary they'd get out and they were endlessly interested in the history and meaning of words. (para. 30)

Hence, Flannigan was raised in an environment that valued reading and provided access to books. His mother fostered his writing by making small books out of pages that he had produced for his sister who was away from home and writing the words to accompany his efforts (ABC, 2008):

> That's all I ever wanted to do, was to write books ... what she [his sister] had were these little books that I'd actually written for her when I was about three and there's sentences and words and yet I can't write words, so they're all scrawls in the shapes of sentences and paragraphs, there's some little pictures, and then my mother has written the story out. And yet it's entirely incomprehensible. Then Mum would staple them and bind them with black electrical tape. (para. 36)

Despite these early auspicious beginnings, Flanagan recognised that his aspiration to be a writer was counter to the cultural climate of Tasmania (ABC, 2008).

Flanagan achieved success as a writer by building his knowledge of writing and through perseverance. He left school at 16 and worked in the bush, and then he began his tertiary education, *leveraging* the available opportunities to build his knowledge (Waldren, 1997):

> I decided, as you could then, to go to university (University of Tasmania) and from there ended up with a Rhodes scholarship, went to Oxford for a couple of years and returned wanting to write. I didn't know how and I didn't know anyone who had done it so I worked in various menial jobs, as a laborer (sic), as a river guide, by day and wrote at night. (para. 12)

Flanagan was not an overnight success and experienced setbacks from reviewers and publishers (ABC, 2008). However, he *framed* his experiences by arguing that the views of his readership were more important than the views of other critics:

> My first novel came out and it couldn't even get a review, and it sold out within a fortnight ... and the publisher said, 'Well, you were exceptionally lucky, that's it, and we're not reprinting.' ... And the publishers refused to reprint again, they said, 'This is really unusual,' and on and on it went. After about 12 months, reviews started to appear. (para. 53) ...
> But I realised the real judgement on books isn't made by critics, it's made by countless thousands of readers over many thousands of readings ... if you have readers your books will live. (para 54)

The voices of Flanagan's readers are echoed in the acknowledgement of his contributions to literature (Holocomb, 2005): "Richard Flanagan has single-handedly given voice to Tasmania, still most widely known in the popular imagination as the former Van Diemen's Land, a penal colony and one of the furthermost outposts of the British Empire" (para. 4).

His novels are notable for their imaginative range, their risk taking and their insistence upon the foregrounding of love at the heart of human experience.

In his Booker acceptance speech, Flanagan *reflected* that he was an unlikely author (Flanagan, 2014):

> I do not come out of a literary tradition. I come from a tiny mining town in the rainforest in an island at the end of the world. My grandparents were illiterate. And I never expected to stand here before you in this grand hall in London as a writer being so honoured. (para. 3)

Though Flanagan achieved a prestigious Booker Prize—an international award for publishing outstanding fiction in the UK and Ireland—he had five unsuccessful attempts to win the Australian Miles Franklin Award, hitherto removing himself from contention (Romei, 2017):

> Look, being a writer is a journey into endless disappointments and failures, and that [the Miles] has been one of many," he said, "But I have been lucky enough, too—the Booker was a catastrophe of good luck—and I am still able to write, so I am grateful. (para. 34)

His nonparticipation in the Miles Franklin competition may be Flanagan's way of avoiding further disappointment or may signal a lack of confidence in the competition. The latter stance is one way that an Introspector can communicate his or her views about an issue. Flanagan has previously removed himself from the 2003 Tasmania Pacific Literary Prize to protest cosponsorship by the State's Forestry Commission, which he argued "promotes the cutting of old-growth forests" (Bonner, 2003, para. 4). Flanagan also used an invited lecture to strongly express his opinion about the government stance on copyright and its impact on authors' livelihoods (Thomsen, 2016). Thus, while Flanagan embodies the role of an Introspector by communicating about matters that are beyond the scope of others' experiences or imaginations, he also displays some characteristics associated with the Influencer.

The Influencer: (Cecilia) May Gibbs (1877–1969). May Gibbs was known as 'a retiring personality who shunned publicity' and 'became a virtual recluse' following the deaths of her parents in 1941 and a close friend Rene in the early 1950s (Australian National Herbarium, 2016). Nevertheless, her characters and stories have inspired an enduring love of the Australian bush (State Library New South Wales, 2017a):

> (May Gibbs) iconic children's literature and folklore is still popular, holding a special place in the Australian consciousness. Best known for *The Complete Adventures of Snugglepot and Cuddlepie*, Gibbs also wrote and illustrated many other children's books, produced long-running cartoon strips, and a variety of commercial work. A fiercely determined woman, she was Australia's first full-time, professionally trained children's book author and illustrator, developing a uniquely Australian vernacular. In 1955, May Gibbs was appointed Member of the British Empire (MBE, part of the British honours system) in acknowledgement of her important contribution to children's literature. (para. 1)

Gibbs is regarded as the 'Mother of the Gumnuts' (Walsh, 2007). The characters in her books include a variety of bush creatures, such as Snugglepot, Cuddlepie, and the Gumnut Babies. Later in her life, Gibbs *reflected on* the emergence of the bush babies (The Northcott Society and Cerebral Palsy Alliance, 2016): "It's hard to tell, hard to say, I don't know if the bush babies found me or I found the little creatures" (para. 1). Gibbs' other bush creatures included Wicked Mrs. Snake and the Big Bad Banksia Men. The influence of Gibbs' characters extended to the renaming of banksia cones as banksia men in the 1920s (Robinson, 2013).

Gibbs' rise to fame as an author and illustrator highlights the two characteristics of an EC. First, Gibbs' stories are closely related to her aspects of her childhood. As a child, Gibbs lived in rural areas exploring the bush on a pony and painting and writing about the bush (Walsh, 2007). Her stories drew on these bush experiences portraying conflicts between bush creatures and humans (Gibbs, 1918): "'I wish', said Cuddlepie, 'that all Humans were kind to Bush creatures like that' (a human rescuing a possum from a leg trap)" (p. 40). These environmentally oriented stories offered a stark contrast to English children's stories of the same era, such as *Peter Pan* (J. M. Barrie) and *Winnie-the-Pooh* (A. A. Milne), and are regarded as quintessentially Australian. In 1919, Gibbs' efforts to raise awareness for bush animals were recognised with the award of a life membership of the Royal Society for the Prevention of Cruelty to Animals (The Northcott Society and Cerebral Palsy Alliance, 2016).

Second, Gibbs sought to develop her artistic and authorial skills to an exceptionally high level. Gibbs recalled that her interest in drawing commenced at a young age (The Northcott Society and Cerebral Palsy Alliance, 2016): "I could draw before I could walk" (para. 1). The recognition of Gibbs' talent commenced in her teens when, at 15 years of age, she won her first prize for drawing at the Perth Wildflower Show (The Northcott Society and Cerebral Palsy Alliance, 2016). Gibbs' father, Herbert William Gibbs, was an artist and cartoonist (Walsh, 1981). She would later become Australia's first women cartoonist (The Northcott Society and Cerebral Palsy Alliance, 2016) suggesting that she was able to *leverage* her father's knowledge of cartooning to break through into this hitherto male-dominated field. Gibbs' artistic training included participating in an artists' camp in Western Australia with her father. She also made multiple trips to London to take art and writing classes feeding her thirst for learning by taking both day and night classes. One of these trips occurred after a fellow illustrator, Ida S. Rentoul (Outhwaite), was commissioned to do the 1908 Christmas cover for the Western Mail (The Northcott Society and Cerebral Palsy Alliance, 2016). Despite substantial previous training in London, in 1909, Gibbs returned for further training "to make a last attempt to succeed as a professional artist and writer" (The Northcott Society & Cerebral Palsy Alliance, 2016, para. 1). Thus, Gibbs *framed* her disappointment in not being selected as the illustrator of the Christmas cover as a need for additional training.

Gibbs' legacy lives on. First editions of her books are recognised as highly collectable. Her most popular book, *The Complete Adventures of Snugglepot and Cuddlepie*, was published in 1918, sold 17,000 books in its first release and has never been out of print (State Library New South Wales, 2017b). In 2005, the then

Table 2 Lives of eminent individuals and their societal roles

ECs and role	Key elements in their lives
Victor Chang (decd.) Master	Built an extensive knowledge of heart disease studying at and worked in prestigious institutions internationally. Successfully lobbied for the national heart transplant unit to be at his hospital.
Elizabeth Blackburn Maker	Studied and works in prestigious institutions internationally Partnerships with international colleagues.
Richard Flanagan Introspector	Grew up and works in relatively isolated locations. Family interest in language and books. Drew inspirations for a novel from his father's and neighbour's wartime stories.
May Gibbs (decd.) Influencer	Spent her childhood exploring and drawing the Australian bush. First Australian professionally trained book author and illustrator. Produced work for children and adults creating an Australian perspective of the bush environment.

Australian Prime Minister, John Howard, gave a first edition of *Snugglepot and Cuddlepie* to Crown Prince Frederik and Crown Princess Mary to celebrate the birth of their first child (The Sydney Morning Herald, 2005). Gibbs' characters and stories have inspired a ballet, musicals, plays, a novel, coins, and stamps and other products including children's toys, jewellery, and homewares. Upon Gibbs' passing, she received the following tribute (The Northcott Society and Cerebral Palsy Alliance, 2016): "No one will be quite as good. No one will touch such a multitude. *May Gibbs is alone in her creative genius*. For this reason, May Gibbs has gained lasting fame in her own land" (emphasis in original; para. 26). This enduring legacy marks Gibbs as an Influencer.

Discussion

The four Australian ECs were selected for investigation due to their distinctive societal roles of Master, Maker, Influencer, and/or Introspector. This investigation revealed unique aspects of their lives that appear to be integral to the ECs societal roles (Table 2): Victor Chang's (Master) knowledge of heart disease, Elizabeth Blackburn's (Maker) collaboration with international scholars, Richard Flanagan's (Introspector) immersion in language and stories in an isolated location and the dissemination of May Gibbs' (Influencer) perspective of the Australian bush.

The ECs were also similar in four ways. First, the ECs' childhoods affected their lives and careers. Their childhoods: (a) created environments for their interests to flourish (Blackburn, Flanagan, Gibbs); (b) provided reference points for their work (Flanagan, Gibbs); (c) inspired him or her to enter a career (Blackburn, Chang, Gibbs); or (d) provided the foundations for intercultural competence (Chang, Gibbs). Thus, the ways in which ECs may draw on their childhoods (Gardner, 1997) are variable and influential rather than positive or negative. Furthermore, it seems that negative experiences such as losing a parent (Chang) or living in an isolated location (Flanagan) can be overcome if framed appropriately.

Second, each of the four ECs demonstrated the characteristic to strike out on their own and develop deep discipline knowledge. They did this by pursuing education to an elite level in their discipline for their initial qualifications and subsequent training and work. For example, Blackburn did her PhD at Cambridge, completed postdoctoral training at Yale, and worked at the University of California at Berkley. These experiences went beyond developing content knowledge to knowledge of how to achieve highly in their discipline and, for some, opportunities to work successfully with collaborators (Blackburn, Chang).

Third, the three metacognitive skills of ECs, namely, reflecting, framing and leveraging, were evident to various extents throughout their lives. Collectively, these skills appeared to enable the ECs to progress in their lives and careers and ultimately overcome any setbacks that they encountered. Thus, these skills seem to work as markers of resiliency, that is, the capacity to recover quickly from difficulties and to move forward. According to Coutu (2002) resilient people:

> ...possess three characteristics: a staunch acceptance of reality; a deep belief, often buttressed by strongly held values, that life is meaningful; and an uncanny ability to improvise. You can bounce back from hardship with just one or two of these qualities, but you will only be truly resilient with all three. (p. 48)

The selected ECs each experienced substantial setbacks but worked to overcome these. Thus, to Gardner's (1994) two characteristics of an EC, I add resiliency, which is actioned by reflecting on, framing and leveraging various situations.

Research and/or Practice: Implications and Future Directions

While there is considerable research on the appropriate curriculum for gifted learners, typically this curriculum relates to content. This chapter highlights the diverse and substantial contributions of ECs in their four societal roles (Gardner, 1997). Hence, the curriculum should also provide for the identification and development of these roles that provide a valuable contribution to society. There are three avenues for research to inform practice.

First, research related to the societal roles should be undertaken using gifted individuals as the participant pool. For example, research on mastery learning and entrepreneurship, may provide a useful base for research on potential Masters and Makers, respectively. Similarly, research on diary writing and communication can provide insight into gifted individuals with a proclivity towards becoming Introspectors or Influencers. The knowledge gleaned from this research may provide the foundation for an intervention with gifted students that fosters the four roles of the EC.

Second, there is also a need for lifespan research of highly gifted individuals documenting their contributions to society from childhood to adulthood across diverse disciplines. This chapter employed backward tracing to discern the inputs that contributed to the ECs' success. Forward tracing (Williams et al., 2009) provides the particular benefits of tracking gifted individuals' achievements over time and identifying related supports. For example, in mathematics education, the documentation of the educational provisions for the mathematical prodigy Terry Tao, the Australian-born Fields Medallist (Clements, 1984; Muratori et al., 2006), can inform educational decision making for other highly gifted mathematics students.

Further, there is a need to study individuals whose potential seems to be unfulfilled to identify insurmountable obstacles to becoming an EC. For example, in a study of four musical prodigies with unfulfilled potential, Jung (2015) suggested that the following factors might have supported the achievement of distinguished careers:

> (a) access to the best music instructors; (b) strong and sustained family support for a career in music; (c) membership of a society or culture that is supportive of the translation of one's musical abilities into talents; (d) the possession of personal qualities such as perseverance, discipline, and a focus on music; (e) the possession of sound interpersonal skills; (f) access to and an ability to take advantage of, career-related and career-promoting opportunities; and (g) freedom from issues, such as health, that may detract from a full commitment to a career in music. (p. 10)

This work can be complemented by research on self-control and grit, which co-exist with talent and opportunity as determinants of success (Duckworth & Gross, 2014) and should be undertaken with gifted individuals.

Building the knowledge base on the societal roles of ECs, discipline-specific supports for high achievement and what makes some highly gifted individuals succeed as ECs while others do not (Jung, 2015) is important for evidence-based practice. Highly gifted students deserve, as do all students, educational provisions to support them fulfil their potential as individuals and members of society.

Conclusion

Four key points have emerged from this chapter. First, the biographies of these ECs showed that they were all gifted individuals with their giftedness becoming apparent variously throughout their lives. As giftedness can transcend cultures, disciplines, socio-economic status, or location (Heller, Mönks, Sternberg, & Subotnik, 2000), potentially, any gifted students may be future ECs. However, while some students might have family circumstances that are able to nurture areas of passion and build expertise, others might not, and hence, be more reliant on teachers to provide this support and guidance.

Second, an EC can undertake vastly different roles within society as a Master, a Maker, an Introspector, or an Influencer. Each of these roles differs substantively and requires the individual to develop and hone certain skills. For example, a Master needs to work at the cutting edge of a discipline, while a Maker needs to identify and seek solutions to disciplinary or interdisciplinary problems. Hence, it may be possible to identify some students as gifted based on their strengths as or orientation towards being a Master, a Maker, an Introspector, or an Influencer. Third, resilience and its associated skills need to be promoted because success and failure go hand in hand. Thus, gifted individuals can be at risk if they work only in situations where they can succeed with ease. Learning how to deal with and overcome failure is just as important as learning content.

Finally, becoming an EC requires a concerted long-term effort. All of the ECs discussed investing heavily in their education in their chosen discipline. Hence, gifted individuals should be encouraged to pursue knowledge in their passion area beyond what is required for school. This may also involve seeking out opportunities for the development of advanced knowledge through mentorships, competitions, or courses above those typical for the age group.

In this chapter, the focus was on exemplary creators—those gifted individuals who achieve eminence from their contributions to society. According to Gardner (1997), the proportion of individuals contributing at a high level is very low; "In every age a tiny percentage of individuals stand out by virtue of creative achievements" (p. 1). However, it is unhelpful to consider whether the reason for the low proportion of ECs is 'rare by nature (biology)' or 'rare by nurture (education)'. Instead, it is more productive to consider how education can be used as a mechanism to identify and develop capabilities that characterise ECs. In this chapter the emergence of ECs within the Australian context was explored. It will require outreach by all of us to determine whether individuals within our spheres of influence—who are potential ECs or their educators—join the ranks of Victor Chang, Elizabeth Blackburn, Richard Flanagan, and May Gibbs in the future.

Cross-References

- ▶ Australian Teachers Who Made a Difference: Secondary Gifted Student Perceptions of Teaching and Teacher Effectiveness
- ▶ Exploring Diverse Perceptions of Wise Persons: Wisdom in Gifted Education
- ▶ Fostering and Developing Talent in Mentorship Programs: The Mentor's Perspectives
- ▶ Fostering Resilience in 'At-Risk' Gifted and Talented Young People
- ▶ Gifted Education in the Asia-Pacific: From the Past for the Future – An Introduction
- ▶ How Do Teachers Meet the Academic Needs of High-Ability Students in Science?
- ▶ Identifying and Nurturing Diversely Gifted and Talented Students: Part III Introduction
- ▶ Motivational Issues in Gifted Education: Understanding the Role of Students' Attribution and Control Beliefs, Self-Worth Protection and Growth Orientation
- ▶ Nurturing Mathematical Talents of Young Mathematically Gifted English Language Learners
- ▶ Of Grit and Gumption, Sass and Verve: What Gifted Students Can Learn from Multicultural Picture Book Biographies
- ▶ Some Implications for the Future of Gifted Education in the Asia-Pacific

▶ The Career Decisions of Gifted Students: An Asian-Pacific Perspective
▶ Transitioning to Career: Talented Musicians' Identity Development
▶ Why Is It So? Interest and Curiosity in Supporting Students Gifted in Science

References

ABC. (2008). The Book Show: Richard Flanagan's the unknown terrorist. (R. Koval, Interviewer). Retrieved from http://www.abc.net.au/radionational/programs/archived/bookshow/richard-flanagans-the-unknown-terrorist/3289520

ABC Science. (2010). Nobel prize winner tops Australia Day honours. Retrieved from http://www.abc.net.au/science/articles/2010/01/26/2801245.htm

Agesworth. (2009). [Photograph of Victor Chang Statue]. Retrieved from https://commons.wikimedia.org/wiki/File:Victor_Chang_bronze_statue_Klarfeld.JPG

American Academy of Achievement. (2017). *Elizabeth Blackburn, PhD: Noble Prize in medicine.* Retrieved from http://www.achievement.org/achiever/elizabeth-blackburn/

AUrandomhouse. (2014). [Photograph of Richard Flanagan]. Retrieved from https://commons.wikimedia.org/wiki/File:RichardFlanagan_300w.jpg

Australian National Herbarium. (2016). *Gibbs, Cecelia May (1877–1969).* Retrieved from https://www.anbg.gov.au/biography/gibbs.may.html

Bloomsbury Publishing. (2017). *J. K. Rowling.* Retrieved from https://www.bloomsbury.com/author/jk-rowling

Bonner, R. (2003, April 22). Tasmanian literary prize shunned by its originator. *The New York Times*. Retrieved from http://www.nytimes.com/2003/04/22/books/tasmanian-literary-prize-shunned-by-its-originator.html

Brady, C. (2007). *Elizabeth Blackburn and the story of telomeres: Deciphering the ends of DNA.* Cambridge, MA: MIT Press.

Christie's. (2017). Leonardo da Vinci (1452–1519) Salvator Mundi. Retrieved from http://www.christies.com/lotfinder/paintings/leonardo-da-vinci-salvator-mundi-6110563-details.aspx?from=salesummery&intobjectid=6110563&sid=5e8f1b92-9c81-41ba-b905-e4feb350929f

Clements, K. (1984). Terence Tao. *Educational Studies in Mathematics, 15*(3), 213–238.

Coleman, M. J. (2014). Chang, Victor Peter (1936–1991). Retrieved from http://adb.anu.edu.au/biography/chang-victor-peter-14816

Coutu, D. (2002). How resilience works. *Harvard Business Review, 80*(5), 46–55.

Department of the Prime Minister and Cabinet. (n.d.). *Companion of the Order of Australia.* Retrieved from https://www.pmc.gov.au/government/its-honour/companion-order-australia#

Duckworth, A., & Gross, J. (2014). Self-control and grit: Related but separable determinants of success. *Current Directions in Psychological Science, 23*(5), 319–325. https://doi.org/10.1177/0963721414541462

Erb, C. (2012). [Photograph of Elizabeth Blackburn]. Chemical Heritage Foundation. Retrieved from https://commons.wikimedia.org/wiki/File:Elizabeth_Blackburn_CHF_Heritage_Day_2012_Rush_001.JPG

Farnsworth, A. (2008). Mark Xavier Shanahan (10/12/1932-7/8/2008). *Heart, lung and circulation, 17*(6), 519. https://doi.org/10.1016/j.hlc.2008.09.001

Flanagan, R. (2014). The man booker prizes: Richard Flanagan's acceptance speech. Retrieved from http://themanbookerprize.com/news/richard-flanagans-acceptance-speech

Gardner, H. (1994). The creators' patterns. In M. A. Boden (Ed.), *Dimensions of creativity* (pp. 143–158). Cambridge, MA: Massachusetts Institute of Technology.

Gardner, H. (1997). *Extraordinary minds: Portraits of four exceptional individuals and an examination of our own extraordinariness.* New York, NY: Basic Books.

Gardner, H. (2002). Learning from extraordinary minds. In M. Ferrari (Ed.), *The pursuit of excellence through education* (pp. 3–20). Mahwah, NJ: Lawrence Erlbaum.

Gardner, H. (2014). Howard's response to Lynn Barendsen. In M. Kornhaber & E. Winner (Eds.), *Mind, work, and life: A festschrift on the occasion of Howard Gardner's 70th birthday, with responses by Howard Gardner* (Vol. 1, pp. 67–69). Retrieved from https://howardgardner01.files.wordpress.com/2012/06/festschrift-_-volumes-1-2-_-final.pdf

Gibbs, M. (1918). *The complete adventures of Snugglepot and Cuddlepie*. Sydney, Australia: Angus and Robertson.

Harris, M. (1991). Chang, Victor Peter (1936–1991). Retrieved from http://oa.anu.edu.au/obituary/chang-victor-peter-14816

Heller, K. A., Mönks, F. J., Sternberg, R. J., & Subotnik, R. (Eds.). (2000). *The international handbook of giftedness and talent* (2nd ed.). Oxford, UK: Elsevier Science.

Holocomb, G. (2005). British Council literature: Richard Flanagan. Retrieved from https://literature.britishcouncil.org/writer/richard-flanagan

Jung, J. Y. (2015). Unfulfilled potential: The adult careers of former musical prodigies Ervin Nyiregyhazi, Fanny Mendelssohn Hensel, and David Helfgott. *Australasian Journal of Gifted Education, 24*(1), 6–12.

Knox, M. (2017, September 12). After the booker: Why Richard Flanagan isn't playing safe. Sydney Morning Herald. Retrieved from http://www.smh.com.au/entertainment/books/after-the-booker-why-richard-flanagan-isnt-playing-safe-20170908-gydcs9.html

Kornhaber, M., & Winner, E. (Eds.). (2014) *Mind, work, and life: A festschrift on the occasion of Howard Gardner's 70th birthday, with responses by Howard Gardner* (Vols. 1–2). Retrieved from https://howardgardner01.files.wordpress.com/2012/06/festschrift-_-volumes-1-2-_-final.pdf

Kuhn, H. W., Nirenberg, L., Sarnak, P., & Nash, J. (1996). *A celebration of John F. Nash, Jr.* Durham, NC: Duke University Press.

Luthar, S. S., Cicchetti, D., & Becker, B. (2000). The construct of resilience: A critical evaluation and guidelines for future work. *Child Development, 71*, 543–562.

[May Gibbs Portrait]. (1916). Australia. Retrieved from https://commons.wikimedia.org/wiki/File:May_Gibbs.jpg

Mellor, L. (2008). *Chang, Victor P.* Retrieved from https://sydney.edu.au/medicine/museum/mwmuseum/index.php/Chang,_Victor_P

Muratori, M. C., Stanley, J. C., Ng, L., Ng, J., Gross, M. U. M., Tao, T., & Tao, B. (2006). Insights from SMPY's greatest former child prodigies: Drs. Terence ('Terry') Tao and Lenhard ('Lenny') Ng reflect on their talent development. *Gifted Child Quarterly, 50*(4), 307–324.

Nobel Media. (2017a). *Elizabeth H. Blackburn: Facts*. Retrieved from https://www.nobelprize.org/nobel_prizes/medicine/laureates/2009/blackburn-facts.html

Nobel Media. (2017b). *Elizabeth H. Blackburn: Biographical*. Retrieved from https://www.nobelprize.org/nobel_prizes/medicine/laureates/2009/blackburn-bio.html

Robinson, J. (2013). A hundred years of gumnut babies. Retrieved from http://ozwords.org/?p=3574

Romei, S. (2017, December 11). Booker prize-winning author Richard Flanagan to boycott miles Franklin award. The Australian. Retrieved from http://www.theaustralian.com.au/arts/booker-prizewinning-author-richard-flanagan-to-boycott-miles-franklin-award/news-story/8ba0a410f0ad69e4869aa34c2b2ad7be

Royal Australasian College of Surgeons. (n.d.). *Mark Shanahan*. Retrieved from https://www.surgeons.org/member-services/in-memoriam/mark-shanahan/

Singh, A. (2014, October 14). Richard Flanagan wins man booker prize for the narrow road to the deep north. *The Telegraph*. Retrieved from http://www.telegraph.co.uk/culture/books/11162268/Richard-Flanagan-wins-Booker-Prize-for-The-Narrow-Road-to-the-Deep-North.html

Smith, L. M. (1994). Biographical method. In N. K. Denzin & Y. S. Lincoln (Eds.), *Handbook of qualitative research* (pp. 286–305). Thousand Oaks, CA: Sage.

State Library New South Wales. (2017a). *May Gibbs: An Australian classic*. Retrieved from http://www.sl.nsw.gov.au/node/43141/share

State Library New South Wales. (2017b). *May Gibbs*. Retrieved from http://www.sl.nsw.gov.au/stories/may-gibbs/published-author

The Northcott Society and Cerebral Palsy Alliance. (2016). *About May Gibbs*. Retrieved from https://www.maygibbs.org/about-may-gibbs/

The Sydney Morning Herald. (2005). *Australia's iconic gift*. Retrieved from http://www.smh.com.au/news/national/australias-iconic-gift/2005/10/16/1129401139822.html

Thomsen, S. (2016, May 20). Australia's 'greatest author' went berserk, saying Malcolm Turnbull wants to destroy the book industry. Business Insider Australia. Retrieved from https://www.businessinsider.com.au/australias-greatest-author-went-berserk-over-copyright-changes-saying-malcolm-turnbull-wants-to-destroy-the-book-industry-2016-5

Time. (2016). *1979–1989 Victor Chang*. Retrieved from http://content.time.com/time/specials/packages/article/0,28804,1930464_1930466_1931703,00.html

Victor Chang Cardiac Research Institute. (2011). Annual Report 2011. Retrieved from https://www.victorchang.edu.au/uploads/Victor-Chang-Annual-Report-2011.pdf

Victor Chang Cardiac Research Institute. (2015). *Victor Chang*. Retrieved from https://www.victorchang.edu.au/about-us/victor-chang

Victor Chang Cardiac Research Institute. (2019). *About us*. Retrieved from https://www.victorchang.edu.au/about-us

Waldren, M. (1997). Many hands clapping: An interview with Richard Flanagan. Retrieved from http://users.tpg.com.au/waldrenm/flanagan.html

Walsh, M. (1981). Gibbs, Cecilia May (1877–1969). Australian Dictionary of Biography, 8, 1891–1939. Volume 8, (MUP). Retrieved from http://adb.anu.edu.au/biography/gibbs-cecilia-may-6373

Walsh, M. (2007). *May Gibbs: Mother of the Gumnuts*. Sydney, Australia: Sydney University Press.

Williams, V. L., Eiseman, E., Landree, E., & Adamson, D. M. (2009). Demonstrating and communicating research impact: Preparing NIOSH programs for external review. RAND Corporation Retrieved from http://www.rand.org/pubs/monographs/2009/RAND_MG809.pdf

Carmel Diezmann, PhD, is an Adjunct Professor in the Faculty of Education at Queensland University of Technology. She is particularly interested in the cognition and creativity of gifted individuals from childhood to adulthood and has researched and published widely on giftedness and educational provisions. Carmel has taught gifted students in schools and in pullout enrichment programs, provided professional development supporting teachers to identify and cater for gifted students in their classes, worked in universities identifying academics with the capacity for excellence, and designed support programs to foster their capabilities.

The Development of Mana: Five Optimal Conditions for Gifted Māori Student Success

31

Melinda Webber

Contents

Introduction	672
The Affective and Psychosocial Needs of Gifted Māori Students	673
Ka Awatea: An Iwi Case Study of Māori Student Success	676
Mana: The Five Optimal Conditions Required for Gifted Māori Student Success	680
Conclusion	686
Cross-References	687
References	688

Abstract

There are a growing number of gifted Māori students not just attaining educational success, but thriving in the schooling context. Educational psychology has much to learn from these students, and it is incumbent upon researchers to empirically analyse the drivers of their success. While it has been acknowledged that self-concept, self-esteem, and self-efficacy affect the academic engagement of Māori students (Meissel & Rubie-Davies, 2016; Webber, 2015), few studies have examined the affective and psychosocial drivers of success, or the role of cultural factors, in the academic performance of gifted Māori students. In this chapter, the author contributes to this discussion by focusing on how self-perceptions about the value of their racial-ethnic identity and family support affect the motivation and academic engagement of gifted Māori students in New Zealand. It will be argued that little will be done to improve gifted Māori students' academic engagement and social-emotional well-being, until educators focus specifically on the development of students' connectedness to their racial-ethnic identity and their sense of *mana* (pride, status, and esteem). The

M. Webber (✉)
Faculty of Education and Social Work, The University of Auckland, Auckland, New Zealand
e-mail: m.webber@auckland.ac.nz

© Springer Nature Singapore Pte Ltd. 2021
S. R. Smith (ed.), *Handbook of Giftedness and Talent Development in the Asia-Pacific*,
Springer International Handbooks of Education,
https://doi.org/10.1007/978-981-13-3041-4_31

importance and manifestation of mana in gifted Māori students' lives and other psychosocial issues facing them will be highlighted. Solutions for change will be offered using a mana model developed as part of the Ka Awatea study (Macfarlane, Webber, McRae, & Cookson-Cox, 2014).

Keywords

Gifted Māori · Cultural efficacy · Mana · Connectedness · Racial-ethnic identity · Educational success

The aims in this chapter are to:
1. Provide an overview of the affective and psychosocial needs of gifted Māori students.
2. Outline the findings of Ka Awatea: An Iwi Case Study of Māori Student Success.
3. Reiterate five key components concerning the optimal personal, familial, school and community conditions for gifted Māori students' success that are discussed in context of the mana model: Mana Whānau (familial pride), Mana Motuhake (personal pride and a sense of embedded achievement), Mana Tū (tenacity and self-esteem), Mana Ūkaipo (belonging and connectedness), and Mana Tangatarua (broad knowledge and skills).
4. Provide an unapologetically Māori-centric model of gifted students thriving.
5. Present a strength-based model that utilises indigenous positive psychology principles (see Craven et al., 2016) and Māori worldview to reveal how gifted Māori students can thrive and flourish when a broad range of academic, cultural, and social opportunities are afforded to them.
6. Use this model to broaden the research theorising of those researchers, educators and other stakeholders who desire to see Māori gifted students attain their full potential.

Introduction

Gifted student engagement in school contexts is dependent on a number of factors: (a) the skills, background knowledge, and resources available to students; (b) the students' psychosocial attributes including self-efficacy, motivation, mindset, and task commitment, how they are identified and identify as belonging to, or in, educational settings; and (c) how the educational setting makes space and provides support and opportunities for gifted students to engage and persist. This sense of belonging and invitation to an educational space shapes gifted students' engagement with, and willingness to, persist in a particular educational setting. In this sense, educational engagement can be said to be a function of developing both a school-based social identity and academic identity. And yet, other important social identities such as racial-ethnic identity do not vanish when students enter schools. Therefore, an important question is how academic or school identities, necessary for educational engagement, intersect with racial-ethnic identities to support or constrain gifted student educational engagement, persistence and achievement? In light of this important educational question, Subotnik, Olszewski-Kubilius, and Worrell's (2011) definition of giftedness is useful in terms of thinking about the multiple influences on giftedness and talent development. According to Subotnik et al. (2011):

> Giftedness: a) reflects the values of society; b) is typically manifested in actual outcomes, especially in adulthood; c) is specific to domains of endeavor; d) is the result of the coalescing of biological, pedagogical, psychological, and psychosocial factors; and e) is relative not just to the ordinary (e.g., a child with exceptional art ability compared to peers), but to the extraordinary (e.g., an artist who revolutionises a field of art). (p. 3)

As such, in this chapter the author seeks to advance the knowledge of Māori student giftedness as a culturally located and developmental process whereby the deliberate cultivation of psychosocial variables, most notably the development of mana, plays an essential role in the manifestation of Māori student giftedness.

The Affective and Psychosocial Needs of Gifted Māori Students

Although New Zealand schools strive to create equitable learning environments, the unfortunate reality is that gifted Māori students remain under-identified and underserved. It is evident that the existing approach to gifted identification and provision works less well for them. One of the core principles of gifted education in Aotearoa/New Zealand is that "Māori perspectives and values must be embodied in all aspects of definition, identification and provision for gifted and talented learners" (Ministry of Education, 2002, p. 3). However, research has shown that this principle is not put into practice in many schools (Riley, Bevan-Brown, Bicknell, Carroll-Lind, & Kearney, 2004). Other research suggests that the enduring problem of Māori educational underperformance more generally may also be attributed to factors including: low teacher expectations of Māori (Rubie-Davies, 2015; Turner, Rubie-Davies, & Webber, 2015); deficit theorising about Māori student potential (Bishop, Berryman, Cavanagh, & Teddy, 2009); a paucity of Māori parent/family involvement in education (Berryman, Ford, & Egan, 2015; Rubie-Davies, Webber, & Turner, 2018); culturally irrelevant content and contexts for learning (Bevan-Brown, 2009; Webber & Macfarlane, 2018); and loss of cultural efficacy and pride (Webber, 2012). This author insists that including Māori identity, language, and culture in curriculum is an integral part of catering to the academic and social-cultural development of mana in gifted Māori students.

Indigenous scholars in the field of gifted education have provided useful insights in terms of understanding how giftedness is defined and identified in their communities (Christie, 2011; Faaea-Semeatu, 2011; Webber, 2011). In general, across the majority of the research, it is argued that gifted indigenous students must be encouraged to value their culture and see it as a meaningful and relevant part of their academic learning. Bevan-Brown (2005) and Macfarlane and Moltzen (2005) have found that those children whose Māori assets were utilised and developed in learning, appeared to thrive in the educational context. The New Zealand research suggests that culturally responsive learning activities increase self-esteem and confidence, resulting in gifted Māori students being more likely to develop their gifted potential (Bevan-Brown, 2005; Webber, 2011). The overarching argument is that to engage gifted Māori learners, teaching and learning strategies need to be culturally appropriate, and the focus should be on a curriculum that is culturally meaningful and relevant.

In a study of indigenous Australian conceptions of giftedness, Christie (2011) argued that giftedness is associated with leadership. The indigenous Australian elders who participated in his study stated that gifted indigenous Australian students:

> are the ones who help the other kids when the teacher is not watching. They are not competitive. They already know that they are people with destiny. They know the authority of their elders (each in a specific and significant kin relationship with them). They also know how to pay attention to significant people, and also places, things and moments. (p. 6)

Similarly, in work undertaken by Faaea-Semeatu (2011), ten Pasifika—indigenous peoples of the Pacific Islands—cultural identifiers were developed to illuminate Pasifika understandings of giftedness. Faaea-Semeatu concluded that gifted Pasifika students: are culturally flexible in both Pasifika and non-Pasifika contexts as needed; can formally recite customs, protocols, family/ancestral history, and links to honorific addresses for village genealogy; and transfer their skills, and experiences from church to the school context, for example, public speaking, showing respect, behaving in accordance to social norms, and questioning for understanding or clarification. In addition, gifted Pasifika students seek opportunities to excel and pursue excellence for family pride and also personal achievement; actively use their talents in music, sport, academic achievement and social experience, and create events for themselves to showcase their abilities; see setbacks as opportunities to aim even higher and achieve their personal best so that they are able to react more positively in any given situation; and, endeavour to excel and maintain cultural connections that will advance the status of their families, village links and community. Finally, Faaea-Semeatu (2011) states that gifted Pasifika students speak, understand or write in their mother tongue, serve faithfully in church and family contexts, and work to raise the status and prestige of their parents by virtue of success in job pathways, and career opportunities. Faaea-Semeatu (2011) concludes by stating that Pasifika giftedness will manifest when students can "utilize their innate sense of selves to master and navigate through their conflicting worlds" (p. 121).

As such, gifted education providers must work harder to cultivate a climate in which family, tribal, and wider cultural community organisations can feel comfortable to initiate involvement in education and should provide them with the appropriate opportunities to do so. Research has shown that genuine school/family/community partnership is critical because "students learn more and succeed at higher levels when home, school, and community work together to support students' learning and development" (Epstein & Sanders, 2006, p. 87). The educative process for indigenous students must include family participation in terms of designing culturally responsive curriculum material that simultaneously strengthens gifted students' cultural connections, increases their cultural competence and connection to their communities of interest, and improves their academic motivation to learn and succeed.

Many scholars and researchers have asserted that a number of psychological characteristics such as drive, grit, and motivation are as or more important to gifted student achievement than ability, particularly at the later stages of talent development (Duckworth, Kirby, Tsukayama, Berstein, & Ericsson, 2011; Subotnik et al., 2011). Other characteristics that have been suggested as having a significant role include intellectual risk taking, self-confidence, academic self-concept, self-discipline, a growth mindset, self-efficacy, and resiliency in the face of failure or disappointment (Subotnik et al., 2011). These characteristics, and the beliefs that underlie them, impact the willingness of Māori students to participate in gifted programs of learning and put forth the effort to succeed in them.

An important variable affecting the achievement of gifted Māori students is their belief about intelligence and ability—or their mindset (Dweck, 2006; Webber, 2015). Gifted Māori students who believe that their ability is flexible rather than fixed are more likely to be focused on learning, growth, and improvement and embrace academic challenge because of the opportunity to grow intellectually and gain competence. They are more likely to persist in the face of adversity and believe determination and study can positively impact their academic performance (Good, 2012). Aronson and Juarez (2012) found that culturally diverse gifted adolescents' vulnerability to stereotype threat is lessened if they hold a growth mindset about intelligence, a view that can be actively promoted by teachers and parents. Schools that place more emphasis on a growth mindset, and accentuate effort rather than innate intelligence, are more likely to create a sense of belonging for culturally diverse gifted adolescents, which is critical to retaining them in education.

Embedded achievement, racial-ethnic identity, and Māori students. The extant research suggests that gifted Māori students need to develop and maintain particular affective and psychosocial strengths in order to reconcile their gifted selves with their Māori selves (Webber & Macfarlane, 2018; Rata, 2012). This is particularly important for gifted Māori students because most educational settings do not make sufficient use of Māori language or culture. Many do not include Māori scientific knowledge in the curriculum, and nor do they celebrate Māori role models of academic excellence (Webber & Macfarlane, 2018). It is therefore unsurprising that many gifted Māori students feel that school success has nothing to do with their racial-ethnic selves.

Other researchers have suggested that there are two critical questions affecting the academic choices that students make, that are, 'can I do it' and 'do I want to do it?' (Eccles, 2006; Graham, 2009). If gifted Māori students believe that doing well in school is important to their future selves and will reap the same rewards for them as for other cultural groups in society, they are more likely to work hard and excel. Similarly, if gifted Māori students believe that they can succeed in programs for gifted students, despite negative racial-ethnic stereotypes, they are more likely to have a strong sense of embedded achievement (Altschul, Oyserman, & Bybee, 2006) and put forth the effort needed to thrive academically.

Embedded achievement refers to believing that racial-ethnic group membership involves valuing and achieving in academics (Oyserman & Lewis, 2017). A gifted Māori student with a sense of embedded achievement would believe that succeeding academically is a key part of being Māori and a way to enact their Māori identity. They would also believe that their success helps other Māori to succeed. Because negative stereotypes about Māori students include low academic achievement, disengagement from school and lack of academic ability (Webber, 2011), Māori students may be less able to recruit sufficient motivational attention to override these messages and stay focused on school success. By viewing achievement as part of being Māori, identification with this goal may be more easily facilitated. If gifted Māori students have a sense of embedded achievement and believe that their teachers expect them to do well, they are more likely to persevere with challenging learning activities with increased effort and tenacity (Macfarlane, Webber, McRae, & Cookson-Cox, 2014). When gifted Māori students experience success, they simultaneously develop and enhance their self-confidence, self-efficacy and growth mindset, and increase the perceived value of academic tasks and opportunities. In this way, the psychosocial characteristics supportive of embedded achievement can be cultivated (Macfarlane et al., 2014).

Ka Awatea: An Iwi Case Study of Māori Student Success

Te Arawa people are a confederation of Māori tribes that occupy the Rotorua Lakes district and part of the central Bay of Plenty coastline in New Zealand. In 2014, the Ka Awatea project examined the connection between Māori identity and the perceived characteristics of educational success among a selection of nominated gifted Māori high school students from Rotorua, New Zealand (Macfarlane et al., 2014). In a time when "Māori enjoying and achieving education success as Māori" was the catch phrase of New Zealand educational practice and policy (Ministry of Education, 2013, p. 5), the Ka Awatea study researchers sought to understand the role that various academic, social, interpersonal, and cultural influences have on educational engagement of gifted Māori students. In the Ka Awatea study, a social-psychological perspective on questions of gifted Māori student success was undertaken to articulate gifted Māori student achievement as a concept which is always situated in, and mediated by, social contexts, cultural settings and social group memberships (Macfarlane, Macfarlane, & Webber, 2015).

Using a Māori-centric case study approach, researchers in the Ka Awatea project conducted interview/focus groups and a qualitative questionnaire to examine the conditions for success, and the perceptions of success, from gifted Māori secondary students ($n = 132$) aged between 15 and 18 years, their family members ($n = 48$), their teachers and principals ($n = 93$) and tribal elders ($n = 10$). The gifted Māori students were nominated by their school principals for a number of reasons, most notably, high achievement, leadership, and cultural expertise. All but one student could identify their tribal affiliations, and 47% of the student participants identified as members of the local iwi—Te Arawa. All students in the Ka Awatea project attended schools in the Rotorua district. The Ka Awatea project consequently uncovered five optimal individual, family, school, and community conditions that enable gifted Māori students to mobilise their sense of efficacy and pride (a cultural construct called 'mana' in the Māori language) to achieve their educational, social and cultural goals.

The Ka Awatea study was informed by Kaupapa Māori methodology. See Smith (1997, 2005) for elaborations on the method. Kaupapa Māori theory, which underpins Kaupapa Māori research methodology, has been summarised by Graham Hingangaroa Smith (1997) as a local theoretical positioning related to being Māori, which presupposes that:

- The validity and legitimacy of Māori is taken for granted.
- The survival and revival of Māori language and culture is imperative.
- The struggle for autonomy over our own cultural well-being and over our own lives is vital to Māori survival.

These features align with the positive psychology approach taken in the Ka Awatea study in that they speak to Māori aspirations, transformation, philosophies, processes, and values. While Kaupapa Māori-informed research can be viewed as having underlying principles or philosophies that are based on a Māori worldview, methods may be drawn from a wide range of approaches (Moewaka Barnes, 2000). An important feature of Kaupapa Māori research is that one must undertake research that will have positive outcomes for Māori (Cram, 1997). As such, Kaupapa Māori research methodology provided a clearly defined cultural approach for the strength-based Ka Awatea work. The research capitalised on and prioritised Māori ways of knowing, being, and doing to explicate, measure and augment the drivers of thriving that result in gifted Māori student success.

The Ka Awatea research team were all of Te Arawa descent, based their research activities on Te Arawa tikanga (local tribal protocols), and ensured that tribal expertise was included in decision-making at all stages of the project. All data collection took place in Rotorua, New Zealand, which is the Te Arawa tribe's homeland. In the project answers to the following three research questions were elicited:

1. How do Te Arawa define giftedness?
2. In what ways do gifted Māori students, their families, teachers, and the wider Te Arawa community foster conditions that enable students' gifts to manifest?
3. How is giftedness enacted by gifted Te Arawa students? To what effect?

Selection of participants for the Ka Awatea study. Eight high schools, including one Māori-medium high school, from the Rotorua area agreed to participate in

Table 1 Study participants

Participants	Questionnaire (n)	Individual interviews (n)	Focus group interviews (n)	Total
Māori students	66	5	61	132
Teachers	38	10	32	80
School leaders	5	7	1	13
Parents/family	29	2	17	48
Elders	–	10	–	10
Total	138	35	110	283

the Ka Awatea study. To answer our research questions, the main methods of data collection were student, teacher, principal, and parent questionnaires and, student, teacher, tribal elder, and family semi-structured interviews and focus group interviews. The questions used in all data collection approaches were designed to elicit information related to the three main research questions. An outline of the study participants can be seen in Table 1.

Data collection procedure for the Ka Awatea study. All of the gifted Māori students who completed the questionnaire were Year 11–13 students (aged 15–18 years) who were given consent from their parents/caregivers to participate and who themselves agreed to participate. All students were informed that their participation was voluntary and any information they provided would be confidential. The entire questionnaire took about 25 minutes to complete, and most interviews and/or focus group discussions took between 30 and 90 minutes. Most of the data were collected within an 8-month period between mid-2012 and early 2013.

Students were nominated by school leaders by way of a relatively basic criterion: they identified as Māori and were senior students (in the final three years of high school), gifted and preferably, but not necessarily of Te Arawa tribal affiliation. The school leaders then provided the names of the students' parents, other family members, and elders who were subsequently invited to participate. Principals responded to the questionnaire or the one-to-one interview, and teachers likewise contributed by either completing the questionnaire or participating in an individual interview or focus group. Teachers from the schools were recruited on the basis of their proximity to the students, nomination from participating students, and/or their enthusiasm for Māori pedagogies.

Ka Awatea study data analysis techniques. The two techniques used were NVivo, and thematic analysis. NVivo is a qualitative data analysis (QDA) computer software package that has been designed for qualitative researchers working with very rich text-based and/or multimedia information, where deep levels of analysis on small or large volumes of data are required. NVivo was used in the Ka Awatea study to organise and descriptively analyse the unstructured data. The software was used to classify, sort, and arrange information; examine relationships in the data; and combine analysis with linking, shaping, searching, and modelling. This process enabled the research team to identify trends and cross-examine information in a multitude of ways using its search engine and query functions. NVivo was used to analyse both the study questionnaire and interview/focus group data. Through this process a body of evidence was built up to inform the research findings.

Thematic analysis was also used in this project. Thematic analysis is a widely used qualitative data analysis method. It is one of a cluster of methods that focus on identifying patterned meaning across a data set. The six-step method has been widely used across the social, behavioural, and more applied sciences (Braun & Clarke, 2006). The main purpose of thematic analysis is to identify trends and patterns across a data set that inform the research question being addressed. Patterns were identified in the Ka Awatea data set through a rigorous process of data familiarisation, data coding and theme development and revision. Thematic analysis was undertaken after the data had been organised and categorised using NVivo.

Mana: Māori students' sense of being, motivation to achieve and identity. Māori scholar Te Ahukaramū Charles Royal (2006) has argued that it is *mana* (honour, pride, and esteem) that lies at the heart of Māori positive self-image and the degree to which we feel empowered and good about ourselves. As such, the concept of mana is important for understanding gifted Māori students' participation, engagement, and achievement at school because it relates to their motivation to achieve personal and collective identity and sense of mattering (Elliott, 2009). Mattering is associated with the belief that we matter to others, "to know that in some way we are a significant part of the lives of those around us is essential to the way we value ourselves and understand our place in the social order" (Elliott, Colangelo, & Gelles, 2005, p. 224). Mana tangata, or a secure sense of mana, can be likened to a sense of mattering, in that it influences gifted Māori students' thoughts and behaviours, enabling them to act purposefully in the world to achieve their goals and aspirations (Webber & Macfarlane, 2018). In this way, the development of mana is crucial for gifted Māori students because it is a profoundly powerful psychosocial construct that affirms and advances their connectedness and mattering in the school context, undoing the potentially ruinous impact of negative societal stereotypes and academic underperformance (Macfarlane et al., 2014).

Many philosophers, academics, and educators have tried to offer succinct definitions of mana. Dell (2017) has described mana as "an elusive concept, difficult to define concisely" (p. 93), and Royal (2006), redefining mana for a modern context, described it as a "quality, energy or consciousness in the world which can be harnessed and expressed in human activities through acts of generosity and wisdom" (p. 8). Based on these explanations, and in line with Dell (2017), in the Ka Awatea study, mana was perceived as "a person's influence and profound ability to impact upon, affect and positively transform the lives of others" (p. 93).

Mana, as an achievement-orientated concept (Bowden, 1979), can only be attained through the enactment of dignified behaviour, extraordinary achievement, and generous actions. Dell (2017) has argued that people who demonstrate mana add dignity to others and positively transform communities and people. In discussing the role of mana, Royal (2005) argued that a key purpose of education is to "facilitate the flow and experience of mana in the individual and in his/her community" adding that the "outward expression of mana in the life of the individual is evidenced not only in their skills, attributes and talents … but in their 'spiritual authority', their intuitive and wisdom filled knowledge and insight of knowing what, when, how, and why to do something" (p. 68).

Royal (2005) has also argued that the purpose of education is not so much the acquisition of knowledge, but the growth of mana in the student. He suggests a number of attributes or qualities are essential for the development of mana in the individual, including that he/she does not boast about his/her own prowess or abilities; when faced with an issue or problem, they understand traditional lore and extended discussions as a process, a way of addressing an issue/problem in order to seek an answer, outcome or direction; they are gentle and humble; they listen to what the spirit is telling him/her; he/she is supported by his/her people, is a quick thinker and has an alert mind; they adhere to their thoughts and beliefs; they are industrious, knowledgeable, and have a repository of knowledge.

Mana: The Five Optimal Conditions Required for Gifted Māori Student Success

In the Ka Awatea study, five key components concerning the personal, familial, school, and community conditions for gifted student success emerged. The five conditions, described below, are Mana Whānau, Mana Motuhake, Mana Tū, Mana Ūkaipo, and Mana Tangatarua (see Fig. 1). The first condition, Mana Whānau, was central—it appeared with incredible regularity throughout the course of the study rendering it the most important condition of gifted Māori student success.

Mana Whānau: Child-centric family environments. Scholars have emphasised the critical role of family (including extended family members) in enhancing positive outcomes for children in the face of stress and difficulty (Masten

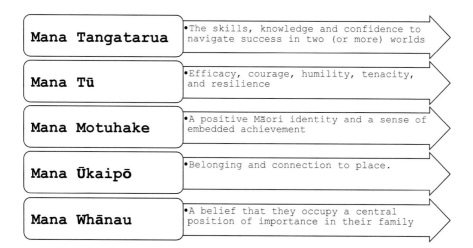

Fig. 1 The five optimal conditions for Māori student success

& Monn, 2015). The quality of parenting is related to the development of competence in children, including academic achievement, racial-ethnic connectedness, and social adaptability (Masten & Coatsworth, 1998; Priest et al., 2014). As such, family well-being and engagement in education and supportive parenting practices are important to the social-psychological and educational development of gifted Māori students.

The gifted students in the Ka Awatea study occupied a central position of importance within their family, including their school and community 'family'. The students were nurtured and encouraged by their family, teachers, and peers and were consequently socially capable and had a sense of connectedness and efficacy across a number of contexts. The students knew that their families valued education and that their school success was important because it had the potential to be a driver of success for others within their family.

The gifted students were held in high regard by their family, their peers, teachers, and members of the wider school community. Most of these students were placed at the heart of the family and were nurtured, protected, and guided towards success from an early age. Family members perceived that their role was integral to the formation of healthy lifelong attitudes and learning behaviours and viewed this as a serious undertaking if their children were to realise their potential as gifted students and emerging adults.

This child-centred positioning of the students was evident from the comments made by both the students and parents/family members. Many students were quick to praise their parents for providing them with a safe and nurturing environment where encouragement and support for all their endeavours never wavered. This constant presence of care and concern in their lives encouraged them to persist at school and strive to achieve their academic potential. Students saw educational success as a means of repaying their parents for their steadfast support and making them proud. Parents on the other hand were forthcoming about placing their children's needs first and their own second. They recognised the vulnerability of transitioning from childhood to young adulthood and were committed to ensuring their children were advantaged by having their physical, emotional, spiritual, and cultural needs met. Parents saw this task as their primary responsibility, and many sought educational opportunities themselves to ensure that they were equipped to support their children in learning. Gifted Māori students who were raised in child-centric home contexts reported that they felt compelled to respond in kind and reciprocate parental behaviours like respect, humility, thoughtfulness, and compassion. These qualities were viewed as crucial in order to become a socially capable and identity-secure individual across a range of contexts. They were also considered essential in terms of the students achieving their gifted potential.

In line with the extant research, researchers in the Ka Awatea study found that a secure home environment, valuing education, and familial support can have a positive influence on the long-term educational, social, and cultural outcomes of Māori students (Olszewski-Kubilius, 2008; Winner, 2000). Despite the parents of these students facing many of the very same parenting challenges that all parents have to face (Pfeiffer, 2013), the parents in the Ka Awatea study also had to deal with additional concerns associated with their gifted Māori child's social-psychological, cultural and academic development. Furthermore, to reconcile these challenges, many of the families tended to be remarkably child-centred and family-focused. They engaged in many learning-centric practices 'as a family' and many parents attended learning activities alongside their children as a means of 'keeping them on track'.

Mana Motuhake: A positive sense of Māori identity. Mana Motuhake (positive identity) was experienced by the gifted Māori students in the Ka Awatea study by way of their developing sense of cultural efficacy, positive connection, and belonging. This included their ability and knowledge of how to engage meaningfully with Māori culture. The students purported to have a keen sense of belonging and connectedness to others in their family, tribe, school and community. All participants also agreed that knowledge of one's genealogy, and descent lines were critical to their sense of self. Kāretu (1990) has described whakapapa (genealogical knowledge and belonging) as the glue that connects individuals to a certain place, or space, locating them within the broader network of kin relations. According to the participants in the Ka Awatea study, whakapapa was not simply about self-identifying as Māori, but also knowing about that descent and having a meaningful relationship with it. Knowledge of whakapapa had a major part to play in the academic resilience of the gifted Māori students, their developing cultural efficacy, and their ability to stay focused, as well as being committed to achieving their aspirations at school for the collective benefit of their family, iwi and community.

Family played the most important role in terms of socialising their children into the Māori world and helping them to develop cultural efficacy. In the Ka Awatea study, cultural efficacy was conceptualised as the extent to which Māori students felt they had the personal resources to engage appropriately as Māori' across a range of contexts (Houkamau & Sibley, 2011). The findings of the Ka Awatea study suggest that the most important developmental asset a parent can instil in their gifted children is to ensure that they are aware of their collective belonging, cultural connectedness, and responsibilities to others as a tribal and community member. Many of the students in the Ka Awatea study asserted that any decisions about themselves were made while simultaneously recognising their responsibilities to others. Therefore, healthy and supportive family contexts are fundamental to positive gifted Māori student identity development and for promoting, modelling, and supporting educational advancement.

The shaping of student attitudes towards Māori identity and the associated languages, values, and cultural worldviews needs to be a fundamental function of family (Webber & Macfarlane, 2018). Constructive and supportive relationships between members of family, including (importantly) extended family, are important determinants of gifted Māori students thriving and lay the foundations for positive relationships in later life (Macfarlane & Moltzen, 2005). Modelling the establishment and maintenance of supportive relationships is also a critical family function that contributes to overall student success at school.

Mana Tū: A sense of courage and resilience. Many gifted Māori students stated that they had positive self-efficacy, positive self-concept, resilience, and academic motivation to thrive in the school context and, eventually, beyond it. They tended to be aspirational, have high expectations of themselves, and enjoy overall physical, emotional, and spiritual well-being. Family members insisted that they needed to ensure their children had a healthy home environment that nurtured their physical, emotional and spiritual well-being. Family members also stated that they needed to model practical resilience strategies—for example, work ethic, perseverance, determination, and discipline—because many students looked to family as their 'first teachers' and ultimate motivation for academic persistence.

In contemporary times, many Māori students are exposed to increasingly difficult home, neighbourhood and/or school environments that can significantly obstruct their path to academic success (Borell, 2005). The gifted Māori students in the Ka Awatea study thrived at school despite having to overcome adverse personal and contextual factors and were often labelled as resilient by their teachers and parents. According to Masten and Coatsworth (1998), resilience consists largely of two components: the presence of significant adversity and the achievement of a positive outcome despite the threat or risk. However, resilience can also be thought of as a continuous interaction between the individual and characteristics of his or her environment (Ungar, 2011). In this sense, resilience is both context dependent and a collective action. Gifted Māori students who self-identify as resilient and are seen by their communities as resilient are those who successfully navigate their way through adversity, each in his or her own way and according to the strengths and resources available to the student as well as his or her family, community, and/or culture (Webber, 2017). The findings from the Ka Awatea project suggested that gifted Māori students' resilience is developed when they are afforded opportunities to work alongside their families, teachers, and learned others in coordinated, continuously negotiated, and culturally congruent ways.

Many of the students in the Ka Awatea study stood out because of their desire to learn, their generally positive attitude towards school and their motivation to pursue a career that would improve the well-being of their family. More specifically the majority of the students:

- were intrinsically motivated and did homework regularly.
- were described as being resolute and tenacious and said they were confident or were able to encourage and push themselves towards success.
- were goal-oriented and future-focused.
- saw a strong relationship between school and work and had chosen a possible career.
- had received consistent support and guidance from their family.
- appreciated extra academic support, both in the classroom and outside it, and valued parents and teachers who took a personal interest in them as individuals.
- saw choosing 'like-minded' friends as critical to their ability to stay focused at school (Macfarlane et al., 2014).

The gifted Māori students in the Ka Awatea study also had individual characteristics that they associated with academic success such as cognitive abilities, motivation, and self-efficacy. Although many students may possess these individual characteristics, the students in the Ka Awatea study seemed to rely on these capabilities to help them overcome adverse circumstances at school, home, and in the community. The development of embedded achievement (Webber & Macfarlane, 2018) was evident in most of the students and manifested as a well-developed understanding about who they were, what they wanted to achieve in life, and the direction they needed to take to realise their goals. Common personal characteristics demonstrated by the students, in addition to resilience, included tenacity, motivation, and inner will, independence, realistic aspirations, and an appreciation of Māori language, culture and identity as cultural assets. Other protective factors included support networks that existed within and outside of the school to develop their achievement, including peers, family, supportive teachers, and other encouraging adults which was essential to their academic success and persistence (Macfarlane et al., 2014). The gifted Māori students who expressed a strong connection with their culture also tended to utilise Māori identity as a support structure, calling on family and their cultural beliefs/traditions when facing difficulties in their lives. Positive Māori identity, and the associated sense of connection and embedded achievement, served as a buffer to protect them from deficit stereotypes and negative school and/or home difficulties.

In line with the extant literature, the development of students' self-esteem, positive sense of racial-ethnic identity, and educational resilience was notably linked to positive familial, cultural, and social supports. Like Priest et al. (2014), researchers in the Ka Awatea study found that parental attitudes and beliefs are clearly strong predictors of positive prosocial behaviours and cultural efficacy, in that not only do family members and other significant adults act as influential ethnic-racial socialisation agents, but connectedness with family members has also been associated with a student's ability to cope with adversity and develop cultural pride (Stevenson, Reed, & Bodison, 1996; Webber, 2017). Family socialisation also played a vital role in empowering the gifted Māori students to function successfully in the milieu of the school culture while remaining grounded in their Māori identity and culture.

The findings in the Ka Awatea study showed that families need to ensure their child strengthens their resilience by providing a healthy home environment that supports the gifted student's emotional, cultural, physical, and spiritual well-being. Many of the participants in the Ka Awatea study believed that a sense of accomplishment and interconnectedness led to a state of overall well-being.

Mana Ūkaipo: A sense of place and belonging. The gifted Māori students sought a synergy between their school-based learning and the unique Rotorua context. They wanted to see tribal role models of success made visible and utilised in schools to inspire cultural pride and aspiration. The students explicitly stated that they wanted Māori knowledge to have some resonance with their educational activities and expected Māori knowledge and history to occupy a position of importance in their school curriculum. They perceived traditional Māori scientific knowledge in particular to be a viable platform for their future aspirations and achievement. Other participants in the study were also keen to see tribal knowledge underpin relevant educational and recreational activities. Information about Te Arawa icons and special features of the area, such as the many lakes, geothermal landmarks, forests, and mountains were considered by the majority of students and family members as crucial to anchoring a person to their homelands and genealogy.

Penetito (2009) has described this as place-based learning (PBL) and argued that this educational model focuses on two essential questions: what is this place, and what is our relationship to it? PBL essentially draws on the significant features, characteristics, history, and personalities of the land or place where students are born, raised, and educated, thereby creating a synergy between learning and the unique context of the surrounding ecology. It teaches 'through' rather than 'about' culture and encompasses ecological studies, biodiversity, community education, and community relations, local history, and sustainable development (Barnhardt, 2005).

Family were especially keen to ensure that their children were steeped in tribal knowledge and were informed about their environment as well as the people who have and continue to influence the changing natural and social landscape of the area. Being familiar with their ancestors and understanding the history over time was perceived to anchor students and enable them to develop a sensitive awareness of who they descend from and the potential they hold for the future (Webber & Macfarlane, 2018). The development of a strong cultural identity and affiliation to a place was described as a protective factor.

Family strongly believed that having knowledge of their lands, people, and language was a strong foundation upon which to acquire other knowledge, other languages, and other ideologies. Advocates of PBL, such as Kawagley and Barnhardt (1999), Penetito (2009, 2010) and Kidman, Abrams, and McRae (2011) believe such a model can help alleviate the tension that currently exists between Western educational pedagogies and holistic indigenous education models. These authors also assert that PBL should provide new meanings to enquiry and knowledge that draws upon local examples. Many Ka Awatea participants asserted that PBL was the key to strengthening the relationship between gifted Māori students and their local area.

Many participants in the Ka Awatea study supported the view that tribal role models of success, either living or dead, should be promoted in schools as a strategy to stimulate aspiration, cultural pride, and achievement. Gifted Māori students with a strong identity and historical link to iconic features and people of the land are best placed to draw on this relationship and to emulate the successes of those icons (Webber & Macfarlane, 2018).

Mana Tangatarua: Navigating success in many worlds. Academic success should never come at the expense of Māori identity. All Ka Awatea participants saw both identities as vital to overall success. However, students need the appropriate 'navigational skills' and 'role models' and a strong sense of emotional and spiritual well-being to retain the dual identities successfully (Webber & Macfarlane, 2018). Ka Awatea participants indicated that supportive relationships were essential to success. Families were primarily responsible for "success as Māori" and often modelled what this should look like. Schools contributed largely to gifted Māori students' "success in the non-Māori or academic world" because they offered students additional opportunities to be innovative and courageous, to take risks in their learning, and to go to new places (which many Māori families could not afford).

Schools were seen to offer students new experiences that "unleashed their potential" to bridge multiple worlds and increase their "range of opportunities" in terms of "possible futures" (Macfarlane et al., 2014, p. 175).

While academic achievement was considered a crucial indicator of success, it was considered to be only one feature of a gifted Māori student's evolving suite of skills. Many of the gifted Māori students in the Ka Awatea study asserted their Māori identity lay at the heart of all things important and their educational attainment was considered complimentary to this. Together these two constructs, Māori identity and gifted identity, were viewed as fundamental to their personal growth, transformation, and journey from one developmental stage to the next—and from one world to the other. Academic success and cultural efficacy were viewed by all participants as requiring a nurturing family, a responsive school community, and a learning environment which includes the provision of educational, and cultural experiences beyond the classroom. As seemingly different as two (or more) worlds can be, the ability to successfully traverse them was dependent on the acquisition of navigational skills such as determination and motivation, a broad knowledge base, diligence, and forbearance, a healthy self-esteem, resilience, a strong moral compass, and a sense of embedded achievement (Webber & Macfarlane, 2018). The expression of these skills is articulated in the Māori world as one's 'mana'.

Conclusion

A secure sense of mana can influence Māori students' thoughts and behaviours, enabling them to act purposefully in the world to achieve their goals and aspirations. In this way, the development of mana is crucial because it is a profoundly powerful psychosocial construct that affirms and advances gifted Māori students' sense of purpose, drive, and belonging in the school context. It has the potential to undo the impact of negative societal stereotypes in New Zealand that speak of Māori underperformance in education as a problem located with Māori themselves (Torrance et al., 2015).

The five optimal conditions that emerged from Ka Awatea propose a hopeful stance on gifted Māori success and illustrate a clear correlation between the recognition of and support for gifted Māori students' cultural identity and their subsequent ability to translate that into the attainment of knowledge and skills and overall academic motivation. The Ka Awatea study illustrates that gifted Māori students can improve their chances of educational success if the five optimal mana imperatives are nurtured and developed. Durie (2001) has emphasised the role of schools in affirming Māori students' identities by asserting that if formal education does little to help prepare Māori students to interact within their own communities, then no matter what has been learned their education would have been incomplete. Like Penetito (2010), the Ka Awatea study proposes that there are two main ways that schools can help gifted Māori students to thrive: "firstly if it holds up a mirror to them and they can see themselves growing and developing in a way that is personally meaningful for them; and secondly, if it helps them to project themselves into the immediate world around them as well as into the world at large" (p. 35). Gifted Māori students require opportunities and encouragement to develop their talents in responsive family and school environments, which simultaneously nurture their cultural identities alongside their gifts and talents. When gifted Māori students are strong in their cultural identity and learn in contexts where their culture is valued, they are less likely to succumb to negative peer pressure and negative academic stereotypes, which undermine academic attainment and talent development.

The Ka Awatea study evidences findings which support the idea that gifted education programs should link gifted Māori students' learning to the physical and cultural environment in which students and schools are situated. Place-based educational practices and programs should integrate scientific, historical, and cultural knowledge associated with local environments as a critical ingredient for developing what Cajete (2000) has termed an interdisciplinary pedagogy of place. The ways of constructing, organising, using, and communicating knowledge that has been practised by Māori for centuries must be recognised as a form of science with its own integrity and validity and utilised in schools to ensure gifted Māori students learn in a manner that validates their language, culture, and identity.

The outcome of the Ka Awatea project indicated that when families, iwi, and the wider community are invested in education, positive school behaviours, gifted Māori student commitment to school completion, and success improve. The most important developmental asset a Māori parent can teach their gifted child is to ensure that they are aware of their mana tangata—their unique leadership potential, collective belonging, cultural connectedness, embedded achievement, and responsibilities to others.

Finally, the mana model proposed in this chapter differs from mainstream psychology approaches in that the focus of research is grounded in Māori realities, knowledge, and epistemologies even as it applies the most current psychological models of motivation, academic achievement, racial-ethnic identity development, and self-concept. It focuses and esteems what gifted Māori students, and their families, communities, and teachers are already doing to keep these students engaged in an education system not designed with them in mind.

Cross-References

- ▶ Being of Like-Mind: Giftedness in the New Zealand Context
- ▶ Fostering Resilience in 'At-Risk' Gifted and Talented Young People
- ▶ Gifted and Talented Aboriginal Students in Australia
- ▶ Gifted Education in the Asia-Pacific: From the Past for the Future – An Introduction
- ▶ Identifying and Nurturing Diversely Gifted and Talented Students: Part III Introduction
- ▶ Motivational Issues in Gifted Education: Understanding the Role of Students' Attribution and Control Beliefs, Self-Worth Protection and Growth Orientation
- ▶ Place-Based Gifted Education in Rural Schools
- ▶ Sociocultural Perspectives on the Talent Development Megamodel

- Some Implications for the Future of Gifted Education in the Asia-Pacific
- Supporting Australian Gifted Indigenous Students' Academic Potential in Rural Settings
- Underachievement and the Quest for Dignity: Contemporary Perspectives on a Timeless Issue

References

Altschul, I., Oyserman, D., & Bybee, D. (2006). Racial-ethnic identity in mid- adolescence: Content and change as predictors of academic achievement. *Child Development, 77*(5), 1155–1169. https://doi.org/10.1111/j.1467-8624.2006.00926.x

Aronson, J., & Juarez, L. (2012). Growth mindsets in the laboratory and the real world. In R. Subotnik & L. Miller (Eds.), *Malleable minds: Translating insights from psychology and neuroscience to gifted education* (pp. 19–36). Washington, DC: Department of Education.

Barnhardt, R. (2005). Indigenous knowledge systems and Alaska native ways of knowing. *Anthropology & Education Quarterly, 36*(1), 8–23. Retrieved from https://www.fws.gov/nativeamerican/pdf/tek-barnhardt-kawagley.pdf

Berryman, M., Ford, T., & Egan, M. (2015). Developing collaborative connections between schools and Māori communities. *SET: Research Information for Teachers, 3*, 18–25. https://doi.org/10.18296/set.0023

Bevan-Brown, J. (2005). Providing a culturally responsive environment for gifted Māori learners. *International Education Journal, 6*(2), 150–155. Retrieved from https://files.eric.ed.gov/fulltext/EJ854964.pdf

Bevan-Brown, J. (2009). Identifying and providing for gifted and talented Māori students. *Apex, 15*(4), 6–20. Retrieved from http://www.giftedchildren.org.nz/apex/

Bishop, R., Berryman, M., Cavanagh, T., & Teddy, L. (2009). Te Kotahitanga: Addressing educational disparities facing Māori students in New Zealand. *Teaching and Teacher Education, 25*(5), 734–742. https://doi.org/10.1016/j.tate.2009.01.009

Borell, B. (2005). Living in the city ain't so bad: Cultural identity for Māori young people in South Auckland. In J. Liu, T. McCreanor, T. McIntosh, & T. Teaiwa (Eds.), *New Zealand identities: Departures and destinations* (pp. 191–206). Wellington, New Zealand: Victoria University Press.

Bowden, R. (1979). Tapu and mana: Ritual authority and political power in traditional Māori society. *Journal of Pacific History, 14*(1), 50–61. http://doi.org/czvd9q

Braun, V., & Clarke, V. (2006). Using thematic analysis in psychology. *Qualitative Research in Psychology, 3*(2), 77–101. https://doi.org/10.1191/1478088706qp063oa

Cajete, G. (2000). *Native science: Natural laws of interdependence*. Santa Fe, NM: Clear Light Publishers.

Christie, M. (2011). Some Aboriginal perspectives on gifted and talented children and their schooling. In W. Vialle (Ed.), *Giftedness from an indigenous perspective* (pp. 36–42). Unanderra, NSW: University of Wollongong Printery.

Cram, F. (1997). Developing partnerships in research: Pākehā researchers and Māori research. *Sites, 35*(Spring), 44–63.

Craven, R. G., Ryan, R. M., Mooney, J., Vallerand, R. J., Dillon, A., Blacklock, F., & Magson, N. (2016). Toward a positive psychology of indigenous thriving and reciprocal research partnership model. *Contemporary Educational Psychology, 47*, 32–43. https://doi.org/10.1016/j.cedpsych.2016.04.003

Dell, K. M. (2017). *Disrupted Māori management theory harmonising Whānau conflict in the Māori Land Trust* (Doctoral thesis, University of Auckland, Auckland, New Zealand).

Duckworth, A. L., Kirby, T. A., Tsukayama, E., Berstein, H., & Ericsson, K. A. (2011). Deliberate practice spells success: Why grittier competitors triumph at the National Spelling Bee. *Social Psychological and Personality Science, 2*(2), 174–181. https://doi.org/10.1177/1948550610385872

Durie, M. (2001). *A framework for considering Māori educational achievement.* Paper presented to Ministry of Education staff on 9 August 2001, Wellington, New Zealand.

Dweck, C. (2006). *Mindset: The new psychology of success.* New York, NY: Random House.

Eccles, J. S. (2006). A motivational perspective on school achievement: Taking responsibility for learning, teaching, and supporting. In R. J. Sternberg & R. F. Subotnik (Eds.), *Optimizing student success with the other three Rs: Reasoning, resilience and responsibility* (pp. 199–224). Greenwich, CT: Information Age.

Elliott, G. C. (2009). *Family matters: The importance of mattering to family in adolescence.* Oxford, UK: Wiley-Blackwell.

Elliott, G. C., Colangelo, M. F., & Gelles, R. J. (2005). Mattering and suicide ideation: Establishing and elaborating a relationship. *Social Psychology Quarterly, 68*(3), 223–238. https://doi.org/10.1177/019027250506800303

Epstein, J., & Sanders, M. (2006). Prospects for change: Preparing educators for school, family, and community partnerships. *Peabody Journal of Education, 81*, 81–120. https://doi.org/10.1207/S15327930pje8102_5

Faaea-Semeatu, T. (2011). Celebrating gifted indigenous roots: Gifted and talented Pacific Island (Pasifika) students. In W. Vialle (Ed.), *Giftedness from an indigenous perspective* (pp. 116–122). Unanderra, NSW: University of Wollongong Printery.

Good, C. (2012). Reformulation the talent equation: Implications for gifted students' sense of belonging and achievement. In R. F. Subotnik, A. Robinson, C. M. Callahan, & E. J. Gubbins (Eds.), *Malleable minds: Translating insights from psychology and neuroscience to gifted education* (pp. 37–54). Storrs, CT: University of Connecticut National Research Center on the Gifted and Talented.

Graham, S. (2009). Giftedness in adolescence: African American gifted youth and their challenges from a motivational perspective. In F. D. Horowitz, R. F. Subotnik, & D. J. Matthews (Eds.), *The development of giftedness and talent across the life span* (pp. 109–129). Washington, DC: American Psychological Association.

Houkamau, C. A., & Sibley, C. G. (2011). Māori cultural efficacy and subjective wellbeing: A psychological model and research agenda. *Social Indicators Research, 103*(3), 379–398. https://doi.org/10.1007/s11205-010-9705-5

Kāretu, T. (1990). The clue to identity. *New Zealand Geographic, 5*, 112.

Kawagley, O., & Barnhardt, R. (1999). Education indigenous to place: Western science meets native reality. In G. A. Smith & D. R. Williams (Eds.), *Ecological education in action* (pp. 117–140). Albany, NY: SUNY Press.

Kidman, J., Abrams, E., & McRae, H. (2011). Imaginary subjects: School science, indigenous students, and knowledge–power relations. *British Journal of Sociology of Education, 32*(2), 203–220. https://ir.lib.uwo.ca/aprci/188

Macfarlane, A., Macfarlane, S., & Webber, M. (2015). *Sociocultural realities: Exploring new horizons.* Christchurch, New Zealand: Canterbury University Press.

Macfarlane, A., & Moltzen, R. (2005). Whiti Ki Runga! Gifted and talented Māori learners. *Kairaranga, 6*(2), 7–9. Retrieved from https://files.eric.ed.gov/fulltext/EJ914568.pdf

Macfarlane, A., Webber, M., McRae, H., & Cookson-Cox, C. (2014). *Ka Awatea: An iwi case study of Māori students' success.* [Manuscript]. Auckland, New Zealand: University of Auckland. Retrieved from http://www.maramatanga.co.nz/projects_publications

Masten, A. S., & Coatsworth, J. D. (1998). The development of competence in favourable and unfavourable environments: Lessons from research on successful children. *American Psychologist, 53*(2), 205–220. https://doi.org/10.1037/0003-066X.53.2.205

Masten, A. S., & Monn, A. R. (2015). Child and family resilience: A call for integrated science, practice, and professional training. *Family Relations, 64*(1), 5–21. https://doi.org/10.1111/fare.12103

Ministry of Education. (2002). *Initiatives in gifted and talented education.* Wellington, New Zealand: Ministry of Education.

Ministry of Education. (2013). *Ka Hikitia – Accelerating success: The Māori education strategy 2013–2017.* Wellington, New Zealand: Ministry of Education.

Moewaka Barnes, H. (2000). Kaupapa Māori: Explaining the ordinary. *Pacific Health Dialog, 7*(1), 13–16. Retrieved from http://citeseerx.ist.psu.edu/viewdoc/download?doi=10.1.1.554.9881&rep=rep1&type=pdf

Olszewski-Kubilius, P. (2008). The role of the family in talent development. In S. I. Pfeiffer (Ed.), *Handbook of giftedness in children. Psycho-educational theory, research, and best practice* (pp. 53–70). New York, NY: Springer.

Oyserman, D., & Lewis, N. A. (2017). Seeing the destination AND the path: Using identity-based motivation to understand and reduce racial disparities in academic achievement. *Social Issues and Policy Review, 11*(1), 159–194. https://doi.org/10.1111/sipr.12030

Penetito, W. (2009). Place-based education: Catering for curriculum, culture and community. *New Zealand Annual Review of Education, 18,* 5–29. https://doi.org/10.26686/nzaroe.v0i18.1544

Penetito, W. (2010). *What's Māori about Māori education?* Wellington, New Zealand: Victoria University Press.

Pfeiffer, S. I. (2013). Lessons learned from working with high-ability students. *Gifted Education International, 29*(1), 86–97. https://doi.org/10.1177/0261429412440653

Priest, N., Walton, J., White, F., Kowal, E., Baker, A., & Paradies, Y. (2014). Understanding the complexities of ethnic-racial socialization processes for both minority and majority groups: A 30-year systematic review. *International Journal of Intercultural Relations, 43,* 139–155. https://doi.org/10.1016/j.ijintrel.2014.08.003

Rata, A. (2012). *Te Pītau o te Tuakiri: Affirming Māori identities and promoting well-being in state secondary schools* (Doctoral thesis, Victoria University of Wellington, Wellington, New Zealand). Retrieved from https://core.ac.uk/download/pdf/41337843.pdf

Riley, T., Bevan-Brown, J., Bicknell, B., Carroll-Lind, J., & Kearney, A. (2004). *The extent, nature and effectiveness of planned approaches in New Zealand schools for providing for gifted and talented students. Report to the Ministry of Education.* Wellington, New Zealand: Ministry of Education.

Royal, T. (2005). *The purpose of education: Perspectives arising from Mātauranga Māori.* Wellington, New Zealand: Ministry of Education.

Royal, T. (2006, September). A modern view of mana. Keynote address at the *Joint conference of the Australian Psychological Society and the New Zealand Psychological Society*, Auckland, New Zealand.

Rubie-Davies, C. (2015). *Becoming a high expectation teacher: Raising the bar.* London, England: Routledge.

Rubie-Davies, C. M., Webber, M., & Turner, H. (2018). Māori students flourishing in education: Teacher expectations, motivation and sociocultural factors. In G. Lief & D. McInerney (Eds.), *Big theories revisited* (Research on sociocultural influences on motivation and learning series, Vol. 2). Charlotte, NC: Information Age Publishing.

Smith, G. H. (1997). *Kaupapa Māori: Theory and praxis* (Doctoral thesis, Education Department, The University of Auckland, Auckland, New Zealand).

Smith, L. T. (2005). *Decolonizing methodologies: Research and indigenous peoples.* London, England: Zed Books.

Stevenson, H. C., Reed, J., & Bodison, P. (1996). Kinship social support and adolescent racial socialization beliefs: Extending the self to family. *Journal of Black Psychology, 22*(4), 498–508.

Subotnik, R. F., Olszewski-Kubilius, P., & Worrell, F. C. (2011). Rethinking giftedness and gifted education: A proposed direction forward based on psychological science. *Psychological Science in the Public Interest, 12*(1), 3–54. https://doi.org/10.1177/1529100611418056

Torrance, D., Forde, C., Potter, I., Morrison, M., Crawford, M., & Shanks, R. (2015). What role leaders in socially just school systems? Paper presented at *BELMAS 2015*, Berkshire, UK, 10–12 July 2015.

Turner, H., Rubie-Davies, C. M., & Webber, M. (2015). Teacher expectations, ethnicity and the achievement gap. *New Zealand Journal of Educational Studies, 50*(1), 55–69. https://doi.org/10.1007/s40841-015-0004-1

Ungar, M. (2011). Community resilience for youth and families: Facilitative physical and social capital in contexts of adversity. *Children and Youth Services Review, 33*(9), 1742–1748. https://doi.org/10.1016/j.childyouth.2011.04.027

Webber, M. (2011). Look to the past, stand tall in the present: The integral nature of positive racial-ethnic identity for the academic success of Māori students. In W. Vialle (Ed.), *Giftedness from an indigenous perspective* (pp. 100–110). Unanderra, NSW: University of Wollongong Printery.

Webber, M. (2012). Identity matters: Racial-ethnic identity and Māori students. *SET: Research Information for Teachers, 2*, 20–25. https://researchspace.auckland.ac.nz/docs/uoa-docs/rights.htm

Webber, M. (2015). Diversity and the secondary years: Nga pūmanawa e waru: Identifying the characteristics of successful intelligence from a Māori perspective. In A. Macfarlane, S. Macfarlane, & M. Webber (Eds.), *Sociocultural realities: Exploring new horizons* (pp. 135–154). Christchurch, New Zealand: Canterbury University Press.

Webber, M. (2017). The role of racial-ethnic identity to the educational engagement of culturally-diverse gifted New Zealand adolescents. In N. Ballam & R. Moltzen (Eds.), *Gifted and talented education: Australasian perspectives* (pp. 253–275). Melbourne, Australia: Springer.

Webber, M., & Macfarlane, A. (2018). The transformative role of tribal knowledge and genealogy in indigenous student success. In L. Smith & E. McKinley (Eds.), *Indigenous handbook of education* (pp. 1–25). Melbourne, Australia: Springer.

Winner, E. (2000). The origins and ends of giftedness. *American Psychologist, 55*(1), 159–169. https://doi.org/10.1037/0003-066X.55.1.159

Melinda Webber, PhD, is an Associate Professor and former Research Director of the Starpath Project in the Faculty of Education at the University of Auckland, New Zealand. She is a former Fulbright/Nga Pae o te Maramatanga Indigenous Scholar who has published widely on the nature of ethnic identity development, examining the ways race, ethnicity, culture, and identity impact the lives of young people—particularly gifted Māori students. In 2016, Melinda was awarded a prestigious Marsden Fast-Start grant to undertake a research project examining the distinctive identity traits of Ngāpuhi, New Zealand's largest tribal group. In 2017, Melinda was awarded a Rutherford Discovery Fellowship to examine the role of cultural pride to academic motivation and engagement among New Zealand students.

Gifted and Talented Aboriginal Students in Australia

32

Susanne Garvis, Sally Windsor, and Donna Pendergast

Contents

Introduction	694
Understanding Different Ways of Gifted and Talented	696
Previous Research About Aboriginal Gifted and Talented Students	697
Importance of Community Ways of Working	699
Policy, Provision, and Programs Inclusive of Aboriginal and Torres Strait Islander Students	700
Implications for Research and Practice: Recommendations for Supporting Indigenous Gifted and Talented Students	703
Conclusion	704
Cross-References	705
References	705

Abstract

In Australia, gifted and talented Aboriginal students have been identified as the most educationally disadvantaged group in the education system. Suitable provision and the accommodation for inclusion of gifted Aboriginal students are needed across all states and territories in Australia, with appropriate identification and gifted programs. In this chapter we provide an overview of Australian research and critique policies and practices from states and territories across Australia. We start with the assumption that giftedness in aboriginal people "is realised and must be supported in the contexts of collective action in which

---

S. Garvis (✉) · S. Windsor
University of Gothenburg, Gothenburg, Sweden
e-mail: susanne.garvis@gu.se; sally.windsor@gu.se

D. Pendergast
Griffith University, Brisbane, QLD, Australia
e-mail: d.pendergast@griffith.edu.au

© Springer Nature Singapore Pte Ltd. 2021
S. R. Smith (ed.), *Handbook of Giftedness and Talent Development in the Asia-Pacific*,
Springer International Handbooks of Education,
https://doi.org/10.1007/978-981-13-3041-4_74

it emerges" (Christie, 2012, p. 40). These contexts integrate critical thinking and cultural values in decision-making and are based on a whole-system view of knowledge. We also acknowledge the importance of working with Aboriginal communities in local contexts to create understandings of knowledge specific to cultures. We conclude that authorities and government agencies work to ensure that the practices around Australian schooling enhance rather than undermine the always ongoing traditional collective practices of remaking strong Aboriginal culture. This starts with a long overdue and fundamental change to the provision of education for gifted and talented Aboriginal students. In our final thoughts, we suggest five steps forward for authorities and agencies to support gifted and talented Aboriginal students.

Keywords

Gifted and talented · Aboriginal people · Critical thinking · Cultural values · Local contexts · Provision

The aims in this chapter are to:
1. Provide a summary of provision and programs around gifted education for Aboriginal and Torres Strait Islander students in Australia.
2. Provide a summary of current research around gifted education for Aboriginal and Torres Strait Islander students in Australia.
3. Explain the importance of cultural values and knowledge.
4. Provide suggestions for educators, teachers, authorities, and agencies for moving forward to enhance provision for gifted education for Aboriginal and Torres Strait Islander students in Australia.

Introduction

While giftedness occurs across all cultures, regardless of socio-economic status, location, or religion, gifted Aboriginal and Torres Strait Islander students in Australia are acknowledged as an under-represented group in Australian schools (Chaffey, 2011; Thraves & Bannister-Tyrrell, 2017; Vialle, 2011). In this chapter we recognise the multitude of different language groups, communities, cultures, and histories Aboriginal and Torres Strait Islander people identify with under this broad term. Paul Chandler (2011), an Aboriginal Professor of Education, summarises the problem of under-representation of gifted Aboriginal students as:

> The biggest challenge of all is that not all cultural groups or racial groups have the same opportunities to fulfil their real potential. The oldest living civilisations on this planet are Aboriginal people, and Aboriginal people lie behind non-Aboriginal people in this country by a massive amount. With all the good work and all good intentions that

have been put in the space of Aboriginal education, we are no better than we were decades ago. (p. 2)

What emerges from the limited literature is the need for flexibility, sensitivity, and understanding when identifying and working with gifted and talented Aboriginal students in Australia. This includes understanding different notions of talent and giftedness, the development of new methods and frameworks to identify gifted and talented Aboriginal and Torres Strait Islander students and the designing of talent programs that respond to the particular learning needs of gifted Aboriginal and Torres Strait Islander learners. Ignoring Indigenous culture in any of these steps has significant implications. Kostenko and Merrotsy (2009) suggest that "if high learning ability goes unrecognised, educational opportunities and experiences necessary for optimal development will probably not be provided. This, for many students, may result in underachievement, boredom, frustration, and psychological distress" (p. 48).

Schools in Australia have a moral and legal obligation to support the learning of all students and to provide positive learning environments. There have been countless instances portrayed in both the media and in research literature on Indigenous education of schools that show a shirking of the responsibilities to provide a safe positive and fruitful learning environment for Aboriginal and Torres Strait Islander school children (cf., Christie, 2010, 2012; Goodyear, 2019). What these stories have in common is a demonstration that the starting point needs to be one of cultural understanding, as Chandler (2011) notes that "what is valued as giftedness in Aboriginal culture is a little different to what is known as giftedness in Australian non-Aboriginal culture" (p. 3). Yet while greater cultural understanding is needed, it is also important that giftedness in Indigenous young people is not narrowly conceived as something that people equate only "with exceptional ability in various cultural arts, crafts, music, traditions and ethnic languages" (Bevan-Brown, 2005, p. 150). Giftedness for Aboriginal and Torres Strait Islander children must be understood as holistic and inclusive of all knowledge.

In this chapter, a summary of the current literature in Australia will be provided, with a specific focus on state and territory provision of school-level gifted and talented programs for Aboriginal and Torres Strait Islander children across Australia. Particular attention is applied to the urgency for schools to value funds of knowledge of gifted and talented Aboriginal students and their communities and the importance of cultural understanding. Chandler (2011) explains that "from the Aboriginal perspective, giftedness is a measure of your knowledge of your ancestry, your land, your kind, and your respect as a leader or a gifted person of any kind [and] comes [with] an enormous responsibility" (p. 3). We suggest that educators and teachers must engage with "culturally responsive pedagogy" (Hogg, 2011, p. 673) and understand giftedness through various lenses. The chapter concludes with five key steps for moving forward, directed towards educators, teachers, authorities, and agencies to support gifted and talented Aboriginal and Torres Strait Islander students in Australia.

Understanding Different Ways of Gifted and Talented

Giftedness is a social construct (Bevan-Brown, 2011) dependent on cultural perspectives and worldviews (Thraves & Bannister-Tyrrell, 2017). Because "cultures differ in how they construct intelligence" (Munro, 2011, p. 25), there is also cultural variance in recognising giftedness. As such, Munro (2011) highlights that giftedness is culturally embedded and dependent on sociocultural contexts. This means that consideration is needed for different ways of knowing and thinking.

Callahan and McIntire (1994) suggest that definitions of giftedness should be developed with and in local communities to reflect cultural philosophy and norms. In the case of gifted and talented Aboriginal children, they are often overlooked as their talents cannot be displayed and nurtured by mainstream school practices. One example of this—described as a "grave error" that is common in Western education systems—is "of believing giftedness is something that happens inside a child's head... [it is rather] neither a head thing (mulkurr) or a guts thing (ŋayaŋu) but an effect of the two coming together" (Christie, 2010, pp. 5–6).

When referring to Aboriginal gifted and talented students, sociocultural contexts need to be acknowledged, including resisting the tendency to apply a generalised version of an Australian Aboriginal peoples' viewpoint (Christie, 2010). Martin and Mirraboopa (2003, p. 205) highlight this imperative and argue for a series of principles that underpin indigenist research:

- Recognition of our worldviews, our knowledges, and our realities as distinctive and vital to our existence and survival.
- Honouring our social mores as essential processes through which we live, learn and situate ourselves as Aboriginal people in our own lands and when in the lands of other Aboriginal people.
- Emphasis of social, historical, and political contexts which shape our experiences, lives, positions, and futures.
- Privileging the voices, experiences, and lives of Aboriginal people and Aboriginal lands.

As Chandler reminds us, "there is no such thing as an Aboriginal perspective because of the numerous nations and language groups" (2011, p. 3). However, he notes differences from Western knowledge systems can be acknowledged:

> What is regarded as giftedness from a western knowledge system and an Aboriginal knowledge system are quite different. The reality is, we are working in one Australia, and the best way to work together is to respect each other's knowledge systems and schooling systems... Indigenous knowledges are part of respecting and acknowledging what Aboriginal kids bring to the classroom, their knowledge of their natural environment, their knowledge of their family, their knowledge of their culture, their knowledge of language, their approaches to learning. These all need to be valued if we want to really, seriously narrow the gap. (Chandler, 2011, p. 4)

The national curriculum in Australia references Gagné's *Differentiated Model of Giftedness and Talent* (DMGT; Australian Curriculum and Reporting Authority,

2015). The model provides a national definition of giftedness that is implemented by state and territory governments. Gagné (2008) acknowledges that cultural influences can impact high achievement in the milieu part of the model. The diversity of the physical environmental influences (such as location) in addition to social and cultural influences are further recognised in Gagné's DMGT. Thus, it is possible that through:

> conscious blurring of the distinction between culture and provision ... the [DMGT] model could potentially be used to design more effective provision for talent development, specifically targeting access, activities, and format, for gifted Aboriginal students. (Thraves & Bannister-Tyrrell, 2017, p. 26)

Hence, promoting and understanding Indigenous culture is key to improved access and provisions for gifted Aboriginal students.

Finally, the increased emphasis on standardised testing such as NAPLAN as the 'only' indicators of academic achievement, similar to other neoliberal accountability measures in education (Lingard, Martino, & Rezai-Rashti, 2013), has had a detrimental effect on the education of all Indigenous students, especially those considered to be gifted and talented. While results in standardised tests paint a grim picture of Indigenous education as a whole, they are far from the full picture (Sarra, 2011).

Previous Research About Aboriginal Gifted and Talented Students

Australia's first peoples (National Congress of Australia's First Peoples, 2016) are a varied group that identify themselves as descending from "over 500 different clan groups or 'nations' around the continent, many with distinctive cultures, beliefs, and languages" (Australian Government, 2015, para. 2). Within these cultural groups, giftedness can be perceived differently with unique (and different) cultural lenses (Christie, 2010; Harslett, 1996). Today there are around 60 Indigenous languages and dialects across Australia that reflect different bodies of cultural knowledge based on interactions with the environment (Australian Government, 2015). Variation occurs not only across cultural groups, but also generationally with differences between older and younger people within cultural groups (Harslett, 1996). Given this great variation, there is strong caution that the concept of giftedness "should be considered at a local level", in order to respect the "diversity of Aboriginal peoples and communities" (Thraves & Bannister-Tyrrell, 2017, p. 3).

As already noted, there are only a small number of studies that have focused research on Aboriginal gifted and talented students. Of the research that has been conducted, most agree that conceptions of giftedness are unique to the cultural (and geographical) context. Harslett (1996) in Western Australia studied the beliefs of 177 Aboriginal participants and found that the concept of giftedness was a "consequence of some form of interaction with, or force within, the environment" (p. 102). In Christie's 2010 study of Yolŋu elders, children were considered gifted if they were:

> retiring and given to quiet respectfulness (rum'rummirr 5127), sit quietly with their role models (14), listening to the old people (4028), listening with a peaceful spirit (3529), be quietly spoken (3576) 'taking part in his own future' (4028). It's not only what he does, but 'how he sits' (1441). They are helpful (räl-wandirri 3529), and work hard (murruy'murruyyun 1558), learning as they go without questioning the old people (5156), for fear of interrupting the attainment of gakal (5127). (Christie, 2010, para. 6)

The elders in Christie's study recognised that these traits often contradicted the expectations of giftedness in Western culture, where children would be expected to be inquisitive by asking questions and thinking critically. Alternatively, Merrotsy's (2007) study in Groote Eylandt and Bickerton Island showed that when trust is established, Aboriginal children will become inquisitive and ask questions, enjoying individual autonomy that is encouraged and supported. Thus, the construct of a single view of giftedness within the diversity of Aboriginal cultures is difficult, where given the different perspectives, it is important to be culturally understanding.

There are recent publications from the 'Aboriginal voices' project which brings together a consortium of researchers committed to seeking long-term solutions to the issues identified as factors contributing to the underachievement of Indigenous students in education across Australia (Lowe et al., 2019), including those who are gifted. Within this consortium, studies from 2006 to 2017 have been analysed to determine what teaching methods are effective for Indigenous learners. According to this project team, pedagogies that were identified as effective and innovative featured:

- *Pedagogies of wonder*—described as adults listening to the wonder of the children about their own history, culture, and context and trusting children to research this rich resource.
- *Generative pedagogies*—described as culturally safe spaces created for Indigenous girls to engage with their everyday experiences of oppression, through writing.
- *Place-based pedagogies*—described as taking students out of the classroom and onto 'country' and involving rangers, educators, teachers, and community members in a collaborative approach to teaching and learning.
- *Pedagogies prioritising local Aboriginal voices*—described as involving listening to voices in the community and understanding the values and cultural elements that inform students engaging with their formal education context.

Taken together, these pedagogical approaches contribute to providing approaches that are culturally relevant and hence more likely to engage Indigenous learners.

Importance of Community Ways of Working

Over the past few decades, there has been a shift away from localised forms of "educational development that acknowledge and include Indigenous wants and needs" (Fogarty, Lovell, & Dodson, 2015, p. 2). High dependence on standardised data as a tool for policymaking means that current educational policy is "unable to recognise and respond to the complex sociocultural determinant of education performance or to incorporate local education aspirations" (Fogarty et al., 2015, p. 7). For Indigenous students, it has been found that the separation from and continued undermining of local knowledge and the mores of their communities further distances them from both the educational system as a whole and their communities (Christie, 2010; Sarra, 2011). One major study conducted by Miller in 2005 found that positive outcomes for Indigenous education relied on a range of factors including "community ownership and involvement, the incorporation of Indigenous identities, cultures, knowledge and values, and the establishment of strong partnerships with communities", among other things (Miller, 2005, p. 18).

This understanding of the importance of community is confirmed by Christie (2010) who conducted extensive consultation with Yolŋu communities from North-East Arnhem land in a project titled 'Gifted and talented: Perspectives on gifted and talented children' that aimed to identify gifted and talented children in communities and sought an understanding of how such children are identified by the communities themselves. The project recognised the disconnection of Yolŋu ways of knowing and identifying such children and the school system as it was being experienced in communities. Christie found that giftedness and talent in Yolŋu culture are most often associated with leadership and are opposed to a conception of children holding special gifts by or for themselves—"it belongs to everybody" (quote from elder Dhäŋgal in Christie, 2010, p. 2). Perhaps more importantly, Yolŋu elders explained that young people are born with their gifts and talents, derived from their embodiment of ancestral connections. The word for this embodiment is *gakal* (Christie, 2010). Gakal, an essential embodiment of giftedness, transcends temporality, space, and individual achievement in education as it is currently conceived.

It is not just in Yolŋu communities that calls for sensitivity to and collaboration between community elders and schools are heard. The Wilson (2014) review of Indigenous Education in the Northern Territory, though critiqued as paying little more than lip-service to community-based education (cf. White, 2014), consistently highlighted the need for community consultation, representation, and understanding in the education of Indigenous Territorians. In Western Australia Cooper (2005) found that "positive collaboration between non-Indigenous and Indigenous educators and community members" (p. 114) ensured the successful implementation of a gifted Indigenous program. She further explained that "fundamentally, Indigenous gifted programs are unlikely to be successful until the Indigenous community believes that a culturally sensitive caring attitude is embedded in the program and its delivery" (Cooper, 2005, p. 115).

Policy, Provision, and Programs Inclusive of Aboriginal and Torres Strait Islander Students

In attempting to review education policies relating to gifted and talented Aboriginal students, it was quickly revealed that little current policy in this area exists in any Australian state or territory. Searches of each state and territory department of education website for relevant and updated policy found nothing that mentioned Aboriginal students and very little by the way of gifted and talented policy (e.g., Queensland Department of Education, 2019; New South Wales [NSW] Department of Education, 2016). It appears the peak of policy provision was in the late 1990s and early 2000s specifically targeting gifted and talented Indigenous students, which has since been succeeded by an emphasis on policy addressing the inclusion of all Indigenous students in more general ways. An example of this was in the NSW Department of Education archives where it was found that the most recent available gifted and talented policy for the state implemented in 2006 only mentions Indigenous students in this way: "In the case of Indigenous students, schools must foster collaborative relationships with their communities" (NSW, Department of Education and Training, 2004, p. 7), whereas the Northern Territory provision for gifted Aboriginal students is limited to the checklists made available by the Northern Territory government to identify gifted Aboriginal students.

The Wilson Review of Indigenous Education in the Northern Territory (Wilson, 2014) claimed it was nearly impossible to identify "programs for high achieving Indigenous students" (p. 137). Many universities throughout Australia hold holiday programs for Aboriginal and Torres Strait Islander school-age students through their respective Indigenous research centres. Examples of such programs include:

- Murrup Barak University of Melbourne: the Indigenous Academic Enrichment Program for Aboriginal students in the state of Victoria.
- University of New South Wales (UNSW) Nura Gili Centre for Indigenous Program's Indigenous Winter School and Sydney University's summer and winter camp designed to prepare Aboriginal students for life in tertiary study.
- Edith Cowan University Kurongkurl Katitjin Centre Old Ways New Ways which aims to improve the participation of Aboriginal and Torres Strait Islander students in science subjects.

Most Australian universities, have, at some point, provided funded programs for Aboriginal young people, especially specific programs for gifted and talented students. The commonality across these programs is that they were conducted in conjunction with local leaders and elders and have a specific focus on cultural learning. Identification measures were also culturally specific to provide new ways of identifying Indigenous students (Thraves & Bannister-Tyrrell, 2017). Such programs include the *Myimbarr Learning Centre* where children were bussed to universities for extension programs guided by mentors and Aboriginal language and knowledge instruction by indigenous elders that resulted in subsequent identification of gifted Aboriginal students. Additionally, the Wii Gaay project used identification measures from Chaffey's *Coolibah Dynamic Assessment* protocols (Chaffey, Bailey, & Vine, 2003).

Another specific program developed for high-achieving indigenous students in Australia is the ASSETS program delivered by the *Commonwealth Scientific and Industrial Research Organisation* (CSIRO, 2019). The CSIRO is an independent Australian federal government agency responsible for scientific research. It also delivers a range of educational programs for students including one known as ASSETS—*Aboriginal Summer School for Excellence in Technology and Science*. ASSETS is a nine-day residential program for high-achieving Indigenous Year 10 students with an ongoing leadership and support program to nurture students through Years 11 and 12. After completing the ASSETS program, the leadership and support program nurtures students through Years 11 and 12 with opportunities to develop their leadership skills and access to information about careers and further study, with a focus on Science, Technology, Engineering, and Mathematics fields.

A key success of the programs that have been made available is that they have been specific to the local community and been able to identify students who would have previously been unidentified. The programs have also had strong community engagement from Indigenous communities to value cultural perspectives to become the drivers for change around identification, programming, and planning. This also means that programs cannot be a 'one-size-fits-all' approach to Aboriginal gifted education across Australia.

One of the major problems in Australia is that while there are individual programs that have been successful at the local level, there is currently no federal funding allocated to gifted education, meaning limited funding for gifted Aboriginal education (Walsh & Jolly, 2018). However, there are some scholarships specifically available for Indigenous students as part of educational outreach programs available from universities. For example, UNSW GERRIC gifted student enrichment programs provide scholarships for gifted Aboriginal students. Another example is Monash University that offers the *Experience Monash Indigenous Winter Camp* and the UNSW Nura Gili Indigenous Winter School Program that provide insight into university life with a focus on building motivation and confidence. These programs are either free or have reduced fees to allow access. However, these programs are not government funded. The lack of government funding across Australia may provide an explanation for the lack of programs found in the literature as well as the sustainability of programs in the long term.

In the 1990s, some states and territories had specific departments; however this has subsided with no state having a dedicated gifted unit. While there have also been two federal senate inquiries into gifted education (Parliament of Australia, 1988, 2001), very few of the recommendations have brought change in legislative measures or support. There is no consistent approach to gifted education or even provision for Aboriginal gifted and talented students across Australia (Walsh & Jolly, 2018).

The decentralisation of responsibility to individual schools for gifted education has also meant priority for funding and programs is decided by principals. "Too often school principals will argue that gifted education is not a priority in their school because the gifted students have been 'skimmed off' to attend a select entry school" (Walsh & Jolly, 2018, p. 87). This has meant that gifted education programs are fragmented and inconsistent. Alternatively, in some private schools, gifted and talented programs have become more dominant in an attempt to attract parents who can afford private education in Australia.

Furthermore, there are also problems with the education and professional learning of registered teachers around provision of gifted education. As Walsh and Jolly (2018, p. 84) point out:

> The Australian Professional Standards for Teachers (Australian Institute for Teaching and School Leadership, 2014) makes no specific reference to the needs of gifted students, despite referencing students with disabilities and students from Indigenous backgrounds. Rather, the teaching of the gifted falls under 'Standard 1: Know students and how they learn' (p. 1), which includes the focus area: 'Differentiate teaching to meet the specific learning needs of students across the full range of abilities' (p. 2). To obtain full registration as a teacher, proficiency in each of the standards must be demonstrated. It would, therefore, be possible to be a fully registered teacher and have no understanding of the needs of gifted students.

This suggests that while there is not a focus on learning how to support gifted and talented learners, there appears to be no focus at all on Aboriginal gifted and talented students. The lack of focus could also be based on Australian culture, where there is a belief that gifted children will do all right, regardless of intervention and support (Porter, 2005).

Australian research suggests one of the barriers for gifted education is negative teacher attitudes; however this can be changed following pre-service or in-service training (Hudson, Hudson, Lewis, & Watters, 2010; Kronborg & Plunkett, 2012; Pedersen & Kronborg, 2014; Plunkett & Kronborg, 2011). In one study that did, Thraves (2018) reported that teachers held diverse views about cultural minorities and lacked the cultural competence to respond to the gifted needs of these learners. The study also found that the teachers viewed the under-representation of Indigenous students in gifted education as linked to issues relating to the students and their culture, as well as school-based factors. Thraves (2018, p. 27) advocates ways forward as:

> These perceptions need to be challenged and cultural competence amongst teachers improved in this context, to assist Indigenous learners and other minorities to gain equitable and effective access to gifted provision. Additionally, participants perceive there to be a range of school-based processes that need to be addressed and refined in the problem under study is to be redressed.

From the research around teacher attitudes, the starting point seems to be a recognition of possible deficit thinking around cultural minorities and gifted education, especially within pre-service and in-service training.

Implications for Research and Practice: Recommendations for Supporting Indigenous Gifted and Talented Students

While the context of gifted education in Australia lacks support from a systematic approach and dedicated funding, there is even less provision and support for Aboriginal gifted and talented students. From reviewing the literature, we have developed five key areas that require change in order to provide provision for Aboriginal gifted and talented students.

Recommendation 1. Federal government commitment to funding to support gifted education in Australia with a specific focus on the support of Aboriginal and Torres Strait Islander gifted and talented students. A federal mandate and dedicated funding would provide states and territories with a legal requirement to support gifted and talented learners in Australian classrooms. This would also require further oversight from states and territories at the local school level and ensure adequate provision for gifted and talented programs in all schools.

Recommendation 2. Research funding is required to support the development of individual programs that are contextually and culturally specific for Indigenous gifted and talented students. Given the lack of research literature in the area, the problem could be summarised as a lack of emphasis and funding to support the development of this important research area. Funding needs to be available to support disadvantaged groups. Inclusive funding is needed to support the development of gifted and talented students from all groups in society.

Recommendation 3. Teacher education programs and in-service learning programs must enable qualified educators and teachers to focus on and reflect on their attitudes towards giftedness and then address these attitudes to bring about change. This includes developing understanding of "culturally responsive pedagogy" (Hogg, 2011, p. 673) for building awareness that giftedness can be seen through different lenses. In particular, a different lens is needed for understanding culture and context with Aboriginal gifted students. Such an awareness also acknowledges that some gifted programs are currently limited in their identification, programming and provision for gifted Aboriginal students.

Programs should include the development of new knowledge and understanding around Australian Aboriginal gifted and talented students to allow educators and teachers to become aware of how they can support the learning needs of all students in the classroom. Effective pedagogies can be:

- Pedagogies of wonder.
- Generative pedagogies.
- Place-based pedagogies.
- Play-based pedagogies.
- Pedagogies prioritising local Aboriginal voices.

Using these pedagogies together can help create culturally relevant ways of working to engage Aboriginal gifted students. Thus, there is the need for educators and teachers to develop an understanding of varied pedagogical approaches so they can be implemented to support gifted Aboriginal and Torres Strait Islander students' needs.

Recommendation 4. The Australian Professional Standards for educators and teachers should include the need for developing capabilities that focus on gifted education and especially Aboriginal gifted and talented students. While students with a disability or from an Indigenous background are mentioned, the statement requires revision to also include provision for gifted education. This would also mean that all educators and teachers are then required to have knowledge in the area, leading to change in teacher education programs. Closely aligned to this work is the recommendation that the development of new methods and frameworks to identify gifted and talented Indigenous students and the designing of talent programs that respond to the particular learning needs of gifted Aboriginal learners.

Recommendation 5. Collaborations between schools and Indigenous communities and their elders should be further encouraged, supported, and valued. Continuing professional development of teachers from both within communities and outside them should include learning from community elders about culturally specific notions of giftedness. These collaborative efforts should establish school-based outreach programs that are based on working together to provide access to all gifted Aboriginal and Torres Strait Islander students. Some universities are already providing excellent opportunities for Aboriginal gifted students to participate. Such programs should be supported by state and federal governments to increase the participation and access for Aboriginal gifted students to participate.

Conclusion

The underrepresentation of Aboriginal students in programs for the gifted and talented suggests there are significant problems with support and identification in Australian schools. Furthermore, the limited research in the area highlights the limited understanding, support, and interventions occurring in Australian schools with teachers, school administrators, and policymakers. Chaffey (2011, p. 98) warns that:

> Gifted education has the potential to contribute greatly to the emergence of equitable educational outcomes for all Indigenous students. However, I suggest it will be difficult to shift the current lamentable position if a gifted cohort does not emerge. The expectations of schools, teachers, Indigenous communities and the students themselves toward educational outcomes can be positively influenced. Without this the best of plans may be in vain.

Although giftedness from an Aboriginal perspective comes with "an enormous responsibility" (Chandler, 2011, p. 3), the literature has shown that it is critical for schools to value the kinds of knowledge that gifted and talented Aboriginal and Torres Strait Islander students and their communities hold. There are many instances that confirm Kostenko and Merrotsy's (2009) suggestion that when different learning abilities are not recognised and developed students will underachieve, squander further educational opportunities, become bored and frustrated, and become psychologically distressed from the experience of schooling. To ensure this does not continue, we suggest that teachers engage with 'culturally responsive pedagogy' (Hogg, 2011). A starting point could be the various pedagogies suggested by the Aboriginal voices' project (Lowe et al., 2019). Pedagogies of wonder, generative pedagogies, place-based pedagogies, and pedagogies that prioritise local Aboriginal voices will (re)engage gifted Indigenous learners with school-level education.

When teachers, schools, and Australian state governments appreciate and value cultural funds of knowledge that Aboriginal children bring to the classroom, educational opportunities for all Australian students can be realised. Until then, we urge lobbying for greater support and provision for Aboriginal gifted and talented students.

Cross-References

- ▶ A Model for Growing Teacher Talent Scouts: Decreasing Underrepresentation of Gifted Students
- ▶ Being of Like-Mind: Giftedness in the New Zealand Context
- ▶ Gifted Education in the Asia-Pacific: From the Past for the Future – An Introduction
- ▶ Identifying and Nurturing Diversely Gifted and Talented Students: Part III Introduction
- ▶ Identifying Gifted Learning in the Regular Classroom: Seeking Intuitive Theories
- ▶ Identifying Underrepresented Gifted Students: A Developmental Process
- ▶ Implementing the DMGT's Constructs of Giftedness and Talent: What, Why, and How?
- ▶ Place-Based Gifted Education in Rural Schools
- ▶ Some Implications for the Future of Gifted Education in the Asia-Pacific
- ▶ Supporting Australian Gifted Indigenous Students' Academic Potential in Rural Settings
- ▶ The Career Decisions of Gifted Students: An Asian-Pacific Perspective
- ▶ The Development of Mana: Five Optimal Conditions for Gifted Māori Student Success
- ▶ The Predictors of the Decisions by Gifted Students to Pursue STEM Careers: The Case of Brazilian International Students in Australia
- ▶ Underachievement and the Quest for Dignity: Contemporary Perspectives on a Timeless Issue

References

Aldous, C. R., Barnes, A., & Clark, J. A. (2008). Engaging excellent Aboriginal students in science: An innovation in culturally inclusive schooling. *Teaching Science, 54*(4), 35–39.
Australian Curriculum and Reporting Authority. (2015). *The Australian Curriculum v8.1: Student diversity – Gifted and talented students.* Retrieved from http://www.australiancurriculum.edu.au/studentdiversity/gifted-and-talented-students
Australian Government. (2015). *Indigenous peoples and culture.* Retrieved from https://www.australia.gov.au/about-australia/our-country/our-people

Australian Institute for Teaching and School Leadership. (2014). *Australian professional standards for teachers*. Retrieved from https://www.aitsl.edu.au/teach/standards

Baker, J. (2019). Oozing confidence: The new program identifying gifted students. *The Sydney Morning Herald*, np, June 9. Retrieved from https://www.smh.com.au/education/oozing-confidence-the-new-program-identifying-gifted-students-20190607-p51voe.html

Bevan-Brown, J. (2005). Providing a culturally responsive environment for gifted Māori Learners. *International Education Journal, 6*(2), 150–155. Retrieved from https://ehlt.flinders.edu.au/education/iej/articles/V6n2/Bevan/paper.pdf

Bevan-Brown, J. M. (2011). Indigenous conceptions of giftedness. In W. Vialle (Ed.), *Giftedness from an Indigenous perspective* (pp. 10–23). Wollongong, NSW: AAEGT.

Callahan, C. M., & McIntire, J. A. (1994). *Identifying outstanding talent in American Indian and Alaska Native students*. Washington, DC: US Department of Education, Office of Educational Research and Improvement.

Chaffey, G., Bailey, S., & Vine, K. (2003). Identifying high academic potential in Australian Aboriginal children using dynamic testing. *Australasian Journal of Gifted Education, 24*(2), 24–32. https://doi.org/10.21505/ajge.2015.0014

Chaffey, G. W. (2011). Is gifted education a necessary ingredient in creating a level playing field for Indigenous children in education? In W. Vialle (Ed.), *Giftedness from an Indigenous perspective* (pp. 96–99). Wollongong, NSW: AAEGT.

Chandler, P. (2011). Prodigy or problem child? Challenges with identifying Aboriginal giftedness. In W. Vialle (Ed.), *Giftedness from an Indigenous perspective* (pp. 1–9). Wollongong, NSW: AAEGT. Retrieved from http://www.aaegt.net.au/DEEWR%20Books/01%20Indig.pdf

Christie, M. (2010). *Some Aboriginal perspectives on gifted and talented children and their schooling*. Retrieved from http://www.cdu.edu.au/centres/yaci/projects_gifted_talented.html

Christie, M. (2012). A postcolonial perspective on the systemic theory of gifted education. *High Ability Studies, 23*(1), 39–41. https://doi.org/10.1080/13598139.2012.679088

Cooper, S. (2005). Gifted Indigenous programs: Unmasking potential to minority cultures. *Gifted Education International, 19*, 114–125. https://doi.org/10.1177/026142940501900205

CSIRO. (2019). *Aboriginal summer school for excellence in technology and science (ASSETS)*. Retrieved from https://www.csiro.au/en/Education/Programs/Indigenous-STEM/Programs/ASSETS

Fogarty, W., Lovell, M., & Dodson, M. (2015). A view beyond review: Challenging assumptions in Indigenous education development. In M. O'Bryan & M. Rose (Eds.), *Indigenous education in Australia: Place. Pedagogy and Epistemic assumptions. UNESCO Observatory Multi-Disciplinary Journal in the Arts 4*(2), 2–23. Retrieved from https://education.unimelb.edu.au/__data/assets/pdf_file/0009/2889612/EDITORIAL_ISSUE_2.pdf

Gagné, F. (2008). Building gifts into talents: Overview of the DMGT. Keynote address, *10th Asia-Pacific conference for giftedness, nurturing talents for the global community*. Singapore, 14–17 July. Retrieved from http://www.templetonfellows.org/program/FrancoysGagne.pdf

Goodyear, S. (2019, April 25). Why this bright Indigenous boy who speaks 3 languages almost failed out of school in Australia. Transcript of Interview with Maya Newell Director of Documentary 'In My Blood It Runs'. *CBC Radio One Newsletter*.

Harslett, M. (1996). The concept of giftedness from an Aboriginal cultural perspective. *Gifted Education International, 11*(2), 100–106. https://doi.org/10.1177/026142949601100207

Hogg, L. (2011). Funds of knowledge: An investigation of coherence within the literature. *Teaching and Teacher Education, 27*, 666–677. https://doi.org/10.1016/j.tate.2010.11.005

Hudson, P., Hudson, S., Lewis, K., & Watters, J. J. (2010). Embedding gifted education in preservice teacher education: A collaborative school-university approach. *Australian Journal of Gifted Education, 19*(2), 5–15.

Kostenko, K., & Merrotsy, P. (2009). Cultural and social capital and talent development: A study of a high ability Aboriginal student in a remote community. *Gifted and Talented International, 24*, 39–50. https://doi.org/10.1080/15332276.2009.11673528

Kronborg, L., & Plunkett, M. (2012). Examining teacher attitudes and perceptions of teacher competencies required in a new selected high school. *Australian Journal of Gifted Education, 21*, 33–47.

Lingard, B., Martino, W., & Rezai-Rashti, G. (2013). Testing regimes, accountabilities and education policy: Commensurate global and national developments. *Journal of Education Policy, 28*(5), 539–556. https://doi.org/10.1080/02680939.2013.820042

Lowe, K., Tennent, C., Guenther, J., Harrison, N., Burgess, C., Moodie, V., & Vass, G. (2019). 'Aboriginal Voices': An overview of the methodology applied in the systematic review of recent research across ten key areas of Australian Indigenous education. *The Australian Educational Researcher, 46*(2), 213–229. https://doi.org/10.1007/s13384-019-00323-5

Martin, K., & Mirraboopa, B. (2003). Ways of knowing, being and doing: A theoretical framework and methods for indigenous and indigenist research. *Journal of Australian Studies, 27*(76), 203–214. https://doi.org/10.1080/14443050309387838

Merrotsy, P. (2007). *Identifying gifted and talented Indigenous students*. Retrieved from http://simerr.une.edu.au/pages/projects/38grooteeylandt.php

Merrotsy, P. (2011). Teaching gifted Aboriginal children. In N. Harrison (Ed.), *Teaching and learning in Aboriginal education* (pp. 77–86). Melbourne, VIC: Oxford University Press.

Miller, C. (2005). *Aspects of training that meet Indigenous Australians' aspirations: A systematic review of research*. Adelaide, SA: National Centre for Vocational Education Research (NCVER).

Munro, J. (2011). Identifying gifted knowledge and learning in Indigenous cultures: Africa and Australia. In W. Vialle (Ed.), *Giftedness from an Indigenous perspective* (pp. 24–35). Wollongong, NSW: AAEGT.

National Congress of Australia's First Peoples (NCoAFP). (2016). *A national voice*. Retrieved from http://nationalcongress.com.au

New South Wales, State of Department of Education and Training. (2004). *Policy for the education of gifted and talented students*. Curriculum K–12 Directorate, Sydney, NSW.

New South Wales, State of Department of Education and Training. (2016). *Gifted and talented policy*. Retrieved 19 June 2019 from https://education.nsw.gov.au/policy-library/policies/gifted-and-talented-policy

Parliament of Australia. (1988). *Report: The education of gifted and talented children*. Senate Inquiry, Commonwealth of Australia. Retrieved from https://www.aph.gov.au/~/media/wopapub/senate/...inquiries/.../gifted/.../c01_pdf.ashx

Parliament of Australia. (2001). *The education of gifted and talented children*. Senate Inquiry, Commonwealth of Australia. Retrieved from https://www.aph.gov.au/Parliamentary_Business/Committees/Senate/Education_Employment_and_Workplace_Relations/Completed_inquiries/1999-02/gifted/report/contents

Pedersen, F., & Kronborg, L. (2014). Challenging secondary teachers to examine beliefs and pedagogy when teaching highly able students in mixed-ability health education classes. *Australasian Journal of Gifted Education, 23*, 15–27.

Plunkett, M., & Kronborg, L. (2011). Learning to be a teacher of the gifted: The importance of examining opinions and challenging misconceptions. *Gifted and Talented International, 26*, 31–46. https://doi.org/10.1080/15332276.2011.11673587

Porter, L. (2005). *Young gifted children: Meeting their needs*. Canberra, Australia: Early Childhood Association.

Queensland Department of Education. (2019). *Gifted and Talented Education*. Retrieved from https://education.qld.gov.au/parents-and-carers/school-information/life-at-school/gifted-and-talented-education

Sarra, C. (2011). *Strong and smart: Towards a pedagogy for emancipation: Education for first peoples*. Oxford/London, UK: Routledge.

Thraves, G. (2018). Teacher perceptions of gifted cultural minorities: An Australian study. *TalentEd, 30*, 17–31.

Thraves, G., & Bannister-Tyrrell, M. (2017). Australian Aboriginal peoples and giftedness: A diverse issue in need of a diverse response. *TalentEd, 29*, 18–31.

Vialle, W. J. (2011). *Giftedness from an Indigenous perspective*. Wollongong, NSW: AAEGT.

Walsh, R., & Jolly, J. (2018). Gifted education in the Australian context. *Gifted Child Today, 41*(2), 81–88. https://doi.org/10.1177/1076217517750702

White, L. (2014). *Responding to the 2014 Review of Indigenous Education in the Northern Territory: Questioning the competencies – The reviewed or the reviewers?* Northern Territory, Australia.

Wilson, B. (2014). *A Share in the Future: Review of Indigenous education in the Northern Territory: Report*. Northern Territory Department of Education. https://education.nt.gov.au/__data/assets/pdf_file/0020/229016/A-Share-in-the-Future-The-Review-of-Indigenous-Education-in-the-Northern-Territory.pdf

Susanne Garvis is a professor of child and youth studies (early childhood) at the University of Gothenburg and a guest professor at Stockholm University, Sweden. She has previously worked at Australian universities before moving to Sweden. She is known as a mixed-methods researcher with a specific focus on representing the voices of children and parents with preschool education. In Australia she was involved with gifted education programs as a teacher.

Sally Windsor is a senior lecturer at Gothenburg University's Department of Pedagogical, Curricular and Professional Studies. She is a course leader in the Education for Sustainable Development Masters' Program, the Global Teacher and Teaching Sustainability in a Global Perspective. Before moving to Sweden, she organised the Indigenous Academic Enrichment Program in 2013–2015: a camp for Aboriginal youth from around the state of Victoria, Australia. She has also spent time in schools in the Northern Territory, learning from and with communities that have long and proud histories of bilingual and 'both-ways' education.

Donna Pendergast is professor, dean and head of the School of Education and Professional Studies at Griffith University, Australia. She has an international profile in the field of teacher education and school reform and is an expert in young adolescent engagement and learning. She has been awarded the Australian Council for Educational Leadership award for leadership in education.

Supporting Australian Gifted Indigenous Students' Academic Potential in Rural Settings

33

Geraldine Townend, Peta K. Hay, Jae Yup Jung, and Susen R. Smith

Contents

Introduction	710
Potential Challenges for Gifted Indigenous Students in Rural Locations	711
Considerations Around the Identification of Academically Gifted Australian Indigenous Students in Rural Contexts	712
Programming for Australian Rural Academically Gifted Indigenous Students	715
Conclusions and Further Implications	720
Cross-References	721
References	721

Abstract

It has been consistently highlighted in Australian research that Indigenous gifted students face many challenges in rural schools. Rurality presents its own advantages and challenges, while Indigeneity also accords additional challenges that non-Indigenous peoples would not encounter during their educational journey towards excellence. It appears that gifted Indigenous students in rural contexts often face misconceptions, inequitable identification practices, and inappropriate or non-existent programming for giftedness. This chapter will draw together research that focuses on the needs of gifted Indigenous students in rural settings, highlighting the potential problems and promising practices in identification and educational programming. We will also provide culturally sensitive recommendations for educators to support the academic potential of rural-based Indigenous gifted students.

G. Townend (✉) · P. K. Hay · J. Y. Jung · S. R. Smith
GERRIC/School of Education, The University of New South Wales, Sydney, NSW, Australia
e-mail: g.townend@unsw.edu.au; p.hay@unsw.edu.au; jae.jung@unsw.edu.au; susen.smith@unsw.edu.au

© Crown 2021
S. R. Smith (ed.), *Handbook of Giftedness and Talent Development in the Asia-Pacific*, Springer International Handbooks of Education,
https://doi.org/10.1007/978-981-13-3041-4_73

Keywords

Gifted · Indigenous · Australian · Rural · Identification · Programming

The aims in this chapter are to:
1. Examine the possible difficulties and academic potential of gifted Indigenous students in rural schools.
2. Appraise the identification practices that are inclusive of gifted Indigenous students in rural settings.
3. Explore culturally responsive programming for academically gifted Indigenous students in rural settings.
4. Highlight some implications for future research and practice.

Introduction

Since the 2008 Australian Prime Minister's apology to the 'Stolen Generations' of Australian Aboriginal and Torres Strait Islander children who were taken from their families by federal and state governments (1900s to the 1970s), Australia has witnessed the rapid implementation of a policy framework focused on closing the gap in educational outcomes around the "undeniable Indigenous disadvantage" (Altman and Fogarty, 2010, p. 109). However, despite this important focus, Aboriginal and Torres Strait Islander students continue to be underrepresented in educational reform (Thraves & Bannister-Tyrrell, 2017). Though Indigenous Australian students often fail to meet national minimum standards, they were the focus of less than 0.1% of the 2018 Gonski 2.0 report on recommended educational reforms to Australian schools (Hogarth, 2018). Indigenous students and gifted students have been described as the most educationally disadvantaged groups in the Australian education system and, *ergo*, gifted Indigenous students would be the most disadvantaged (Cronin & Diezmann, 2002). Chaffey (2008) has opined that gifted education has the potential to contribute greatly to the emergence of equitable educational outcomes for all Indigenous students. He suggested that the emergence of an academically achieving gifted Indigenous cohort can positively influence other Indigenous students in schools. Supporting these students can help to address the inequity prevalent in education in rural settings and has the potential to improve educational outcomes for all students. Hence, integrating the diverse needs of Indigenous students into gifted educational practices and programs is required (Dobia, & Roffey, 2017; Lyons, Cooksey, Panizzon, Parnell, & Pegg, 2006; Smith, 2017; Thraves & Bannister-Tyrrell, 2017). Specifically, in this chapter the focus will be on the educational needs of academically gifted Indigenous students in rural settings and the need for culturally sensitive identification and programming.

Potential Challenges for Gifted Indigenous Students in Rural Locations

Education is more successful for some populations than for others; some populations are deemed 'at risk' of underachievement (Cronin & Diezmann, 2002; Smith, 2017). This disadvantage may stem from cultural attitudes towards people who are different, which can also be known as the tall poppy syndrome in the Australian context; such students need acceptance and support, or they might mask their giftedness (Lehmann, 2014). Gifted Indigenous students may be particularly at risk because their cultural and intellectual characteristics are generally not well accommodated in our school system. Furthermore, rural gifted students in general may be more likely to face challenges to work at their potential when compared to their urban counterparts (Lyons et al., 2006). The challenges of rural schooling include the nature of rural communities with regard to isolation, small class sizes, relative remoteness, and lower socio-economics. The highly transient nature of staff can impact the continuation of programming. Additionally, due to a lack of teacher training, inhibited resources due to distance, and perceptions of local community members, misconceptions and negative attitudes can further minimise the opportunities that are available to urban students (Allen, 1992; Lyons et al., 2006). Technology, although useful, may not be used to respond to learner needs with culturally contextualised activities (Forlin & Lock, 2006). Many of the Australian studies around gifted rural students have focused on the needs of Indigenous students, as a significant number of Aboriginal and Torres Strait Islander students live beyond the major metropolitan areas (Baxter, Gray, & Hayes, 2013; Plunkett, 2018).

Indigenous students living in rural Australia experience inequity both educationally and socially when compared with both non-Indigenous and non-rural students (Lyons et al., 2006). They appear to be under-identified as being gifted and, hence, underrepresented in gifted programs (Plunkett, 2018; Thraves & Bannister-Tyrrell, 2017; Wood & Vialle, 2015), and face a double-edge sword with both recognition and outcomes within education. The research suggests that such underrepresentation in gifted programs may be as a result of: possible *dissensio* between Indigenous and mainstream culture (Cronin & Diezmann, 2002; Garvis, 2006; Thraves & Bannister-Tyrrell, 2017); the cultural insensitivity of traditional methods in use to identify gifted Indigenous students (Chaffey & Bailey, 2008; Cronin & Diezmann, 2002; Plunkett, 2018); the inadequacy of culturally sensitive and responsive curriculum in gifted programs (Lyons et al., 2006); and, global misunderstandings of Indigeneity in the mainstream curriculum. Furthermore, the suggestion exists that mainstream educators may, at times, have incorrect beliefs and attitudes about the academic capabilities of Australian Indigenous students (Dobia, & Roffey, 2017; Garvis, 2006; Lyons et al., 2006; Plunkett, 2018).

Moving forward, it will be most useful to develop strategies for gifted Indigenous students in rural contexts that:

(a) Dispel the misconception that these students cannot be gifted.
(b) Encourage the development and implementation of other culturally sensitive identification instruments.
(c) Provide a framework for the development of relationships with families and the communities.
(d) Provide enhancement of teacher professional development.
(e) Increase educational expectations of Indigenous students through culturally sensitive curriculum and pedagogy (Cronin & Diezmann, 2002; Garvis, 2006; Lyons et al., 2006).

Considerations Around the Identification of Academically Gifted Australian Indigenous Students in Rural Contexts

What is excellence? In Australia, excellence is typically defined as a level of ability or performance in areas that are considered culturally or societally valuable (Cross & Burney, 2005). Unlike excellence in performance, recognition of giftedness in an individual is the recognition of an attribute or ability that is superior (Dai, 2013). Equity underpins the notion that all school students have opportunities to be both recognised and to optimise their achievements in life. However, dominant cultural constructs can limit the notion of 'valuable' which, in turn, places little or no recognition of giftedness in minority cultures.

The challenges and barriers that have been identified may play a major role in the under-identification and the underserving of the educational needs of gifted students living in rural areas. These challenges and barriers may be broadly divided into a number of categories: teacher transience and quality of teaching (Forlin & Lock, 2006; Lyons et al., 2006; Wood, 2009); professional isolation (Azano et al., 2014; Colangelo, Assouline, & New, 1999; Ellzey & Karnes, 1991; Gagnon & Mattingly, 2016; Gentry et al., 2001; Lyons et al., 2006; Mattingly & Schaefer, 2015; Plucker, 2013; Plucker & Puryear, 2018); teacher attitudes towards gifted programming (Fardell & Geake, 2005); a sense of isolation from intellectual peers (Mattingly & Schaefer, 2015); and economic disadvantage and poverty within rural and Indigenous communities (which is substantially higher than in urban areas, with some estimates putting the rate of poverty among rural children at greater than 40%; Croft, 2015; Cross & Burney, 2005; Howley, Rhodes, & Beall, 2009; Mattingly & Schaefer, 2015).

There is a notion that Indigenous communities have different conceptions of giftedness than that used by the Australian national curriculum (Plunkett, 2018). In Australia, educators commonly use Gagné's (2009, 2018) *Differentiating Model for Giftedness and Talent* (DMGT), as various versions of the DMGT feature in state and territory gifted education documents (Bannister-Tyrrell, 2017). However, whether the DMGT does, in fact, align with the values and conceptions of giftedness in rural Indigenous communities is debated. Of note, Thraves and Bannister-Tyrrell suggest that:

> ... a better understanding of Aboriginal conceptions of giftedness, and a conscious blurring of the distinction between culture and provision in Gagné's model, could potentially be used to design more effective provision for talent development, specifically targeting access, activities and format, for gifted Aboriginal students. (p. 26)

Alternative to the DMGT, gifted Indigenous children may be recognised by some Indigenous communities as:

> the ones who help the other kids when the teacher is not watching. They are not competitive. They already know that they are people with destiny. They know the authority of their elders (each in a specific and significant kin relationship with them). They also know how to pay attention to significant people, and also places, things and moments. (Christie, 2011, p. 41)

In addition, some Indigenous cultures may also emphasise the non-intellectual aspects of giftedness such as artistic creativity and the sensorimotor domains, when compared to the intellectual domains (Harslett, 1996). Moreover, attributes such as independence, helpfulness, bush skills, and sporting ability may be more highly valued than cognitive abilities (Kearins, 1982; Vasilevska, 2005). Indeed, Gibson and Vialle (2007) have suggested additional characteristics of giftedness in the domains of linguistic, spatial, interpersonal, and naturalist/spiritual intelligence among Australian Indigenous communities.

Interestingly, research on gifted Native American students living in rural areas of the United States has suggested that it may be problematic to find one identification process that works for all students. Native American students are acknowledged as a diverse group (Callahan & McIntire, 1994; Gentry & Fugate, 2012; Omdal, Rude, Betts, & Toy, 2011), and therefore there has been a lack of generalisability in research findings around characteristics (such as soft/slow speech, persuasion, quietness and an emphasis on nonverbal communication), or learning preferences (such as for co-operative learning) for these students (Christensen, 1991; Gentry, Fugate, Wu, & Castellano , 2014). By contrast, Indigenous Australians have been defined in policy documents as being a homogenous group despite the "diversity and difference that is a feature of Indigenous societies, especially in remote Australia" (Altman & Fogarty, 2010, p. 109).

Contrary to the observations around mainstream under-identification, it is interesting to consider the suggestion that it may be culturally inappropriate to be striving for certain achievement, such as in academia, as this might be perceived as a threat to Indigenous group ideology (Garvis, 2006), and hence, the possibility of alienation from cultural peers (Chaffey & Bailey, 2008). Fear around alienation from peers may be associated with the 'forced choice dilemma' (Gross, 1989, 1998; Jung, Barnett, Gross, & McCormick, 2011; Jung, McCormick, & Gross, 2012), wherein a student feels they must choose between acceptance within their peer group *or* academic success. Bradley (1989), when considering the social emotional needs of gifted Indigenous American students, highlighted their struggle to live in two different worlds—the Anglo-American and the American-Indian worlds, and hence the experience of frustration, anxiety, confusion, and low self-worth due to a conflict between two value systems. It is generally recognised that Indigenous students require guidance to help clarify their pathways, define their own personal values and determine how effectively they can live in two worlds. As Thraves and Bannister-Tyrrell (2017) state:

Appreciating cultural understandings such as how a community envisages giftedness can allow educators to build appropriate support for gifted Aboriginal students in their schools. These understandings can illuminate and possibly alter implicit deficit theories [or misconceptions] that may be unconsciously held by educators. (p. 24)

Recognition of this cultural tension is critical for educators identifying and programming for Indigenous students in Australia, as it is elsewhere (Dobia, & Roffey, 2017). Thus, when identifying giftedness in Indigenous students, optimal identification methods must seek, first, to reverse underachievement from both the social-emotional and cognitive perspectives (Chaffey, 2008). The academic underachievement and 'invisible' underachiever status of many academically gifted Indigenous children means successful inclusion in traditional gifted education provision is unlikely.

Another challenge experienced by gifted Indigenous students in rural Australia is the excessive reliance on identification procedures based on standardised tests designed for urban students that are both culturally inappropriate and contextually irrelevant to rural settings. In the main, research relating to the identification of gifted students in rural contexts have recommended the use of multiple identification instruments including: nonverbal ability instruments (e.g., the Cultural Fair Intelligence Test, Ravens Progressive Matrices and the Universal Nonverbal Intelligence Test; Pendarvis & Wood, 2009; Spicker, Southern, & Davis, 1987; Stambaugh, 2010); non-traditional identification instruments such as portfolios of student work (Montgomery, 2001); and nominations from teachers, parents, and the gifted students themselves (Clark & Zimmerman, 2001; De Leon et al., 2010; De Leon & Argus-Calvo, 1997).

Also recommended is the appropriate modification of current identification procedures, such as using one subscale score on an instrument to identify high performance or giftedness to inform the identification process (Pendarvis & Wood, 2009; Spicker, 1993). Relatedly, some researchers have proposed that identification tools for gifted students should be locally generated so that they are sensitive to the unique cultural, linguistic, ethnic, economic, and particular Indigeneity characteristics of rural students to enable success (Clark & Zimmerman, 2001; De Leon et al., 2010; Pendarvis & Wood, 2009; Montgomery, 2001). For example, other identification tools have been recommended to be adapted from other cultures for the Aboriginal gifted student population due to their provision for linguistically diverse students (e.g., Munro, 2011). Even where the identification tools or processes are effective, implementation of identification protocols requires the appropriate training of teachers (Pendarvis & Wood, 2009; Spicker et al., 1987; Stambaugh, 2010).

International researchers recommend that the identification process include assessments that identify many different aspects of giftedness to support success, rather than the narrow construct around intellectual domains alone, including the use of visual-spatial assessments, the need to use psychometrically rigorous assessments, and a need to use a multiple criteria identification process (Callahan & McIntire, 1994; Omdal et al., 2011). Research indicates that using one test may not allow for an inclusive process. Indigenous American participants scored significantly higher than European American participants in Simultaneous Processing, and European American participants scored significantly higher than Indigenous American participants in Sequential Processing. Indigenous American participants also achieved significantly higher scores in three of five Simultaneous Processing subtests (Davidson, 1992). When Shaunessy, Karnes, and Cobb (2004) compared the usefulness of three nonverbal measures of ability in the identification of culturally diverse rural gifted students of low socio-economic backgrounds in the United States, they found that the *Culture-Fair Intelligence Test* and the *Raven's Standard Progressive Matrices* identified more students as being gifted than the *Naglieri Nonverbal Abilities Test*. It is clear no single test will capture the diversity of giftedness across cultures and demographics. Multiple criteria allow for these diverse gifts to be captured. Furthermore, it may be more useful for economically disadvantaged rural areas to generate local identification instruments.

More equitable strategies and processes have been suggested by researchers to better support the identification of gifted Indigenous Australian students living in rural contexts. Dynamic testing was found to be particularly useful for the identification of Indigenous students (Chaffey & Bailey, 2008; Chaffey, Bailey, & Vine, 2003; Matthews & Farmer, 2017). Although dynamic testing can be conducted through a variety of methods, Chaffey and colleagues endorsed a 'test-intervention-retest' form of dynamic testing. Such a format of dynamic testing: assesses a student's current level of ability through an initial test; provides objective data to develop educational, social-emotional, and metacognitive interventions which are formulated to support any areas of weakness; and finally assesses the 'growth' of the student with the administration of a second test. In Chaffey and Bailey's study (2008), Indigenous Australian students, aged 8–11 years, also had one-off screening using nonverbal standardised tests. Chaffey and Bailey (2008) defend the use of the 'test-intervention-retest' form of dynamic testing as the focus is on the overarching growth that is achieved by students rather than a measure of achievement in one test at any single point in time. The focus on growth can support optimal opportunities for individual students to eventually achieve at their ability. In addition, the one-off screening using nonverbal standardised tests did not produce valid measures of potential for Indigenous Australians and those Australians from low SES backgrounds. Such students can remain 'invisible' on achievement tests as such tests do not allow for cultural diversity.

Although more studies are desirable to support the aforementioned identification processes, the existing research provides promising insights into the identification of gifted Indigenous students in rural contexts.

Programming for Australian Rural Academically Gifted Indigenous Students

Obstacles are evident in programming for gifted students in rural contexts. These challenges are experienced by all rural Australian students and include teacher transience, teacher quality, professional isolation, and teacher attitudes towards gifted programming. Forlin and Lock (2006) noted the transient nature of the staff and students in every school community, with talk during school visits reflecting on who had left and who had joined the schools. The turnover of staff at the end of each school year in rural communities was generally high, in some instances up to 90%, but there was no evidence that staff were disengaged from the schools while they were there. The highly transient nature of the staff also affected the smooth continuation of newly introduced programs and the understanding or sensitivity of new staff in selecting materials that considered the cultural needs of local school communities.

Teacher professional isolation was highlighted by Lyons et al. (2006), who emphasised that teachers in remote schools that had high numbers of Indigenous students perceived that they needed more access to teacher professional learning for giftedness in the context of both rural and Indigenous students. Science and mathematics teachers reported the need for more professional learning on using alternate teaching strategies to address rural students' special needs, diverse learning capacities and student management (Lyons et al., 2006). However, teacher professional learning is difficult to access for teachers working in rural and remote contexts.

There are further disadvantages that appear more weighted for Indigenous students in rural settings, such as a student's sense of isolation from intellectual peers. Economic disadvantage and poverty within rural and Indigenous communities is substantially higher than in urban areas, with some estimates putting the rate of poverty among rural children at greater than 40% (Croft, 2015; Cross & Burney, 2005; Howley, Rhodes, & Beall, 2009; Mattingly & Schaefer, 2015). A New Zealand study showed that socio-economic adversity can contribute significantly to adaptive outcomes for Indigenous students, including limitations in relation to aspects of identity (Ballam, 2011). There is inadequate government funding to support the needs of gifted students to compensate for the economic circumstances of rural communities (Abel, 1993; Azano et al., 2014). Therefore, the provision of appropriate educational interventions, curriculum, and pedagogy required to address the needs of gifted students, including the promotion of advanced courses of study, are unlikely to be prioritised.

Another hindrance to supporting gifted students is community attitudes, both in the general rural community and rural Indigenous community. Prominent misconceptions may be: a low valuation of education due to a low level of parental educational attainment; a scepticism of formal education that may not be considered necessary for life outcomes; or the understanding that outmigration to pursue tertiary study or professional careers will erode rural communities (Cross & Burney, 2005; Donnison & Marshman, 2018; Howley, Showalter, Klein, Sturgill, & Smith, 2013; Mattingly & Schaefer, 2015; Plunkett, 2012). Each of these misconceptions may undermine a school's attempt to develop appropriate gifted education programs.

Access to technology and appropriate technological programs is also considered a challenge in rural communities (Housand & Housand, 2015; Irvin, Hannum, Farmer, de la Varre, & Keane, 2009) despite the educational benefits for gifted students (Missett, Reed, Scot, Callahan & Slade, 2010; Swan, Coulombe-Quach, Huang, Godek, Becker, & Zhou, 2015). Even when teachers were aware of their students' additional needs, awareness of possible supportive technology was difficult for rural teachers due to their limited access to mainstream stores (Forlin & Lock, 2006).

Significant challenges to the appropriate provisions of gifted education in rural schools are the vast distances in rural and remote Australia and the harsh climate. In some schools, a proportion of students enrolled only during the wet season as their families moved to places less likely to be isolated by flooding (Forlin & Lock, 2006). Sometimes students went with their families to visit relatives for extended periods of time. There were also extremely high levels of truancy among some students. It is clear in these communities that issues of isolation significantly impact school access.

There are research publications that reveal that rural communities might, in fact, present some advantages for gifted students in general. Whether or not these advantages might also be so for Indigenous students in rural settings is not clear but are worthy of mention. Improved teacher to student ratios as a result of small classes can lead to more individualised attention (Abel, 1993; Colangelo, Assouline, Baldus, & New, 2003; Croft, 2015; Ellzey & Karnes, 1991). However, rural teachers also reported needing additional teaching materials and varied resource support (Lyons et al., 2006). For example, increasing paraprofessionals to support teachers teaching gifted students and Indigenous students in rural and remote contexts has also been recommended in a nation-wide report on Science, Technology, Engineering, and Mathematics (STEM; Lyons et al., 2006). Conversely, more opportunities for enhanced relationships with teachers (Abel, 1993) can lead to, or be the result of, more involvement in school and extracurricular activities (Colangelo et al., 2003; Jones & Southern, 1992), strong community cohesion (Plucker & Puryear, 2018) and greater access to community resources (Colangelo et al., 2003), as well as stronger relationships with friends and family (Peltier, Foldesey, Holman, & Mantranga, 1989). Other advantages include the increased opportunities for leadership roles (Colangelo et al., 2003; Jones & Southern, 1992), an enhanced sense of safety and stability (Plucker & Puryear, 2018) and greater potential for teachers to exercise autonomy in their practice (Croft, 2015; Gentry et al., 2001). These advantages should be maximised to benefit the provision of appropriate programming for diverse student needs.

Prior to considering individual school programs, it is important to regard the use of technology to support gifted students in rural contexts. Technology can respond to learner needs but can also be responsive to cultural inclusivity, include community-based learning and incorporate culturally contextualised learning activities (McLoughlin & Oliver, 2000). Technology can address the issues of isolation (both geographically and socially) when providing for diverse student needs, including gifted programs, in rural areas (Forlin & Lock, 2006). A range of ICT is being used across Australia to support the engagement of students by catering for their individual needs. Classes appear to reflect a very inclusive philosophy, with teachers employing ICT among other options to enable their diverse student clientele to access the curriculum. It is also clear that pre-service and in-service teachers must be encouraged and supported continuously in their use of technologies if they are to enable their students to be kept up to date in a rapidly changing and increasingly technological world (Forlin & Lock, 2006). Bannister, Cornish, Bannister-Tyrrell, and Gregory (2015) suggest that in-school programs should allow for the development of a way to deliver a high-quality curriculum to gifted students while they attend their local public high school. Using technology can support appropriate curriculum in local secondary schools. One of the biggest challenges encountered was the lack of information available upon which to base this type of schooling provision. Although gifted and academically capable, the provision works best with students who have inherent volition and self-motivation (Bannister et al., 2015), and clearly, needs to extend through Years 11 and 12.

In studies investigating gifted programs in rural settings, not exclusively around but inclusive of Indigenous students, a variety of educational approaches were observed. For example, Wood and Zundans-Fraser (2013) compared three program offerings in rural areas of the state of New South Wales—a gifted class (a full-time composite class of Grade 5 and 6 students called an 'Opportunity Class' operating in a comprehensive school), a withdrawal program (a one-day-a-week program that drew gifted students from multiple schools in a region), and a virtual class (that was accessed for two hours per week by the participating gifted students across a wide geographic area). The observed similar characteristics with all three programs were: positive opportunities for students to interact and develop friendships with intellectual peers; inadequacies in the process of identification of gifted students (due to an over-reliance on standardised instruments and a lack of teacher training in identification or recognition of underachievement among gifted students); issues with communication among stakeholders; irregular support due to a possible lack of understanding of giftedness; and the need for gifted students to receive an appropriate education.

Thompson (1997) investigated the introduction of a gifted program in a rural Australian school using an action research cycle of planning, acting, and reflecting on how to cater for gifted students at the school. A planning team (comprising administrators, teachers, and an external expert in gifted programming) gathered data on current provisions for gifted students, and after reflecting on the data, planned appropriate action, then reflected on the action. The process resulted in positive and consequential attitudinal and structural changes at the school including: the adoption of a local definition of giftedness; the formalised process for the identification of gifted students at the school; the commencement of a mentor program; and the offering of subject acceleration as an educational intervention. Although less formalised, Allen (1992) observed a successful process used to develop a withdrawal program from 10 schools in rural Western Australia, also with the aid of an external expert in gifted programming, that successfully focused on developing student interests, and incorporated programs in writing, anthropology, and culture.

Specific research on programming strategies to address the needs of gifted Indigenous Australian students, though sparse, highlight the need for programming opportunities that are equitable and relevant, take advantage of strengths within the communities, and provide access to advanced courses and gifted programs. Such programming in Australia includes 'selective' opportunities to join Opportunity Classes in Stage 3 or academically selective high schools in stages 4–6 alongside other in-school programming. However, the availability of these programs does not necessarily mean access for Indigenous gifted students. Craven and colleagues (2014) undertook a thematic analysis including over 80 interviews with gifted Indigenous Australian students, their parents, and educators regarding their educational experiences. It was found that more information about the application process and the advantages of attending Opportunity Classes and academically selective high schools could be provided to teachers, and Aboriginal Community Liaison Officers who then would be in a better position to effectively communicate this information to Aboriginal students and their parents. Ensuring Indigenous students are both identified and encouraged to apply for gifted programming and streaming is a necessity to changing inequity. Another finding was that professional learning for educators could focus on ensuring that pre-service teachers, and in-service teachers, are knowledgeable about Aboriginal culture and Aboriginal giftedness, and how to identify gifted Aboriginal students.

Another program, the *Moorditj Kulungar* program, is an example of a specifically designed gifted program for Indigenous students that had challenging content with a focus on Indigenous identity, Dreamtime stories, and bush food. The program also addressed components such as: sensitively supporting students to develop questioning attitudes; addressing conflicts between Indigenous and mainstream cultures; and dealing with peer pressure not to succeed (Cooper, 2005). However, Lyons et al. (2006) reported that rural Aboriginal and gifted students had less enrichment or extension opportunities than their urban peers. For example, the remoteness of rurality inhibits access to enrichment programs, venues such as museums and galleries, cultural sites or other educational sites that are more readily available in urban areas. Enrichment opportunities, such as excursions, Aboriginal culture camps, and university outreach programs support in-school initiatives and provide additional opportunities for Aboriginal students to develop their potential (Baker, 2019; Nura Gili, 2019; Thraves & Bannister-Tyrrell, 2017).

Looking to our overseas colleagues, in the United States, a program named 'Project LEAP' provided previously unidentified gifted students in rural contexts with individualised instruction and specially developed study units that responded to students' assessed strengths and interests and emphasised the language and culture of Native American participants. Project students demonstrated an overall increase in performance on the standardised achievement test scores. Schools using the program showed statistically significant increases in the number of students applying for college, and no student who applied was denied acceptance into college. Factors influencing the success of the project included the authenticity in identification of participants (using portfolio assessment), linkages between schools and community, superior qualifications of project personnel, and project administration at a higher, district level (Barber, Bledsoe, Pequin, & Montgomery, 1999).

Further research into specific programming interventions for gifted Indigenous students in rural settings could offer educators a broader set of optional interventions that are evidence based. Nevertheless, the review here suggests that there are promising directions for educators to pursue including culturally responsive curriculum that values cultural expertise, beliefs, and practices.

Conclusions and Further Implications

Research and discourse points towards the need for educational authorities and governing bodies to provide more rural and culturally relevant and equitable resources, and increased funding, to better identify and cater for the educational needs of Aboriginal and Torres Strait Islander students (Lyons et al., 2006; Thraves & Bannister-Tyrrell, 2017). Such teacher resourcing and support should allow for more flexibility in provisions and programming and help to support currently unaddressed diverse learning needs to enhance the potential and educational aspirations of rural gifted Indigenous students (Thraves & Bannister-Tyrrell, 2017).

While there is a paucity of research around what really works for gifted Indigenous Australian students, Departments of Education around the country (e.g., NSW Department of Education, 2019) could consider strategies to promote and communicate selective opportunities to principals, teachers, and the families of Indigenous students. Advocacy for Indigenous students is paramount and includes active nomination for appropriate programs. Using more appropriate, culturally sensitive, and multifaceted identification processes in proactive and ease-inducing environments may assist in dispelling the misconception that Indigenous students cannot be gifted, as well as providing a pathway to relevant schooling and programming (Cronin & Diezmann, 2002).

It is believed that Indigenous Australian students fail to realise their gifted potential because they are unable to align it to their identity (Gibson & Vialle, 2007). These students need to be actively monitored around performance and supported. Indigenous students have declining offers of Opportunity Class and academically selective high school placement which could reflect educator bias or ineffective identification processes, but could also reflect cultural values of family, connection to land and the avoidance of long commutes. Courses incorporating Indigenous Studies into the curriculum are also of importance to Indigenous stakeholders, including those that allow for participation in a broad range of activities and subjects that expose them to a variety of role models and mentors. However, to do this, these students require challenging curriculum with an equitable share of resources and attention.

More equitable selective school or class entry processes, such as those evident since the NSW Government's review of selective education access (2018), include increasing rural Aboriginal applications by providing additional support materials, improving communications about the relevancy of selective education and test preparation and collaborating with rural schools and families for more access. A selective setting or opportunity class (albeit, at times, online), alongside a balanced, culturally sensitive curriculum, would support gifted Indigenous students in rural settings. The development of 'virtual' selective settings could be beneficial for all stakeholders (Bannister et al., 2015). This would allow Indigenous students, especially those in remote areas, to remain in their own home schools with their friends, but still glean the benefits of a selective setting. As noted by Gibson and Vialle (2007):

The challenge for educators, then, is to help Aboriginal children in negotiating the process of developing self-confidence and a strong sense of identity. Educators have an important responsibility to nurture those gifted students and hopefully build a future Australia that allows Aboriginal people to embrace the contemporary world while respecting their traditional values and beliefs. We all have a lot to learn in taking these reconciliatory steps forward. (p. 196)

Cross-References

- ▶ Attuned Pedagogy: The Artistry of Differentiated Instruction from a Taiwanese Cultural Perspective
- ▶ Being of Like-Mind: Giftedness in the New Zealand Context
- ▶ Fostering Resilience in 'At-Risk' Gifted and Talented Young People
- ▶ Gifted and Talented Aboriginal Students in Australia
- ▶ Gifted Education in the Asia-Pacific: From the Past for the Future – An Introduction
- ▶ Identifying and Nurturing Diversely Gifted and Talented Students: Part III Introduction
- ▶ Identifying Underrepresented Gifted Students: A Developmental Process
- ▶ In Search of an Explanation for an Approach-Avoidance Pattern in East Asia: The Role of Cultural Values in Gifted Education
- ▶ Place-Based Gifted Education in Rural Schools
- ▶ Rural Voices: Identifying the Perceptions, Practices, and Experiences of Gifted Pedagogy in Australian Rural and Regional Schools
- ▶ Some Implications for the Future of Gifted Education in the Asia-Pacific
- ▶ Spirituality and Giftedness: Threading the Path of Identity
- ▶ The Development of Mana: Five Optimal Conditions for Gifted Māori Student Success
- ▶ Underachievement and the Quest for Dignity: Contemporary Perspectives on a Timeless Issue

References

Abel, T. H. (1993). Self-perceived strengths in leadership abilities between suburban and rural gifted students using the Leadership Strengths Indicator. *Psychological Reports, 73*, 687–690. https://doi.org/10.2466/pr0.1993.73.2.687

Allen, J. (1992). Meeting the needs of Australian rural gifted children: The use of a Curriculum Enrichment Project (CEPPS) for primary schools in Western Australia. *Gifted Education International, 8*, 23–31. https://doi.org/10.1177/026142949200800106

Altman, J., & Fogarty, W. (2010). Indigenous Australians as 'No Gaps' subjects: Education and development in remote Indigenous Australia. In I. Snyder & J. Nieuwenhuysen (Eds.), *Closing the gap in education: Improving outcomes in southern world societies* (pp. 112–132). Melbourne, VIC: Monash University Publishing.

Azano, A. P., Callahan, C. M., Missett, T. C., & Brunner, M. (2014). Understanding the experiences of gifted education teachers and fidelity of implementation in rural schools. *Journal of Advanced Academics, 25*, 88–100. https://doi.org/10.1177/1932202X14524405

Baker, J. (2019). 'Oozing confidence': The new program identifying gifted students. The Sydney Morning Herald. Retrieved from https://www.smh.com.au/education/oozing-confidence-the-new-program-identifying-gifted-students-20190607-p51voe.html

Ballam, N. (2011). Talented and living on the wrong side of the tracks. In W. Vialle (Ed.), *Giftedness from an Indigenous perspective* (pp. 123–139). Wollongong, NSW: Australian Association for the Education of the Gifted and Talented.

Bannister, B., Cornish, L., Bannister-Tyrrell, M., & Gregory, S. (2015). Creative use of digital technologies: Keeping the best and brightest in the bush. *Australian and International Journal of Rural Education, 25*(1), 52–64.

Bannister-Tyrrell, M. (2017). Gagné's DMGT 2.0: A possible model of unification and shared understandings. *Australasian Journal of Gifted Education, 26*(2), 43–50. https://doi.org/10.21505/ajge.2017.0015

Barber, C., Bledsoe, T., Pequin, L., & Montgomery, D. (1999). Increasing Native American involvement in gifted programs through authentic discovery and rural linkages. In Conference proceedings of the 19th American Council on Rural Special Education (ACRES). Retrieved from http://files.eric.ed.gov/fulltext/ED429749

Baxter, J., Gray, M., & Hayes, A. (2013). *Families in regional, rural and remote Australia: Australian Institute for Family Studies fact sheet*. Retrieved from https://aifs.gov.au/publications/families-regional-rural-and-remote-australia

Bradley, C. (1989). Give me the bow, I've got the arrow. In C. J. Maker & S. W. Schiever (Eds.), *Critical issues in gifted education* (Defensible programs for cultural and ethnic minorities) (Vol. 2, pp. 133–137). Austin, TX: Pro-Ed.

Callahan, C. M., & McIntire, J. A. (1994). *Identifying outstanding talent in American Indian and Alaska Native students*. Washington, DC: Office of Educational Research and Improvement.

Chaffey, G. (2008). Is gifted education a necessary ingredient in creating a level playing field for Indigenous children in education? *Australasian Journal of Gifted Education, 17*, 38–39.

Chaffey, G. W., & Bailey, S. B. (2008). The use of dynamic testing to reveal high academic potential and under-achievement in a culturally different population. *Gifted Education International, 24*(1), 67–81. https://doi.org/10.1177/026142940802400109

Chaffey, G., Bailey, S., & Vine, K. (2003). Identifying high academic potential in Australian Aboriginal children using dynamic testing. *Australasian Journal of Gifted Education, 12*, 42–55.

Craven, R., Yeung, A., Seaton, M., Dillon, A., McCloughan, G., Pollak, M., & Barclay, L. (2014). Cultivating capability: Explicating what works for gifted Aboriginal primary and secondary students. Final Report from the *Centre for Positive Psychology and Education, University of Western Sydney*, (p. 1–37). Retrieved from https://www.acu.edu.au/-/media/feature/pagecontent/richtext/research-at-acu/research-institutes/ippe/files/gat-final-report.pdf?la=en&hash=69C660F3ECFAF295382B73326BB85107

Christensen, R. A. (1991). A personal perspective on tribal-Alaska Native gifted and talented education. *Journal of American Indian Education, 31*, 10–14. Retrieved from https://www.jstor.org/stable/24398073

Christie, M. (2011). Some Aboriginal perspectives on gifted and talented children and their schooling. In W. Vialle (Ed.), *Giftedness from an Indigenous perspective* (pp. 36–42). Wollongong, NSW: Australian Association for the Education of the Gifted and Talented. Retrieved from http://www.aaegt.net.au/DEEWR%20Books/04%20Indig.pdf

Clark, G., & Zimmerman, E. (2001). Identifying artistically talented students in four rural communities in the united states. *The Gifted Child Quarterly, 45*, 104–114. https://doi.org/10.1177/001698620104500204

Colangelo, N., Assouline, S. G., Baldus, C. M., & New, J. K. (2003). Gifted education in rural schools. In N. Colangelo & G. Davis (Eds.), *Handbook of gifted education* (3rd ed., pp. 572–581). New York, NY: Pearson.

Colangelo, N., Assouline, S. G., & New, J. K. (1999). *Gifted education in rural schools: A national assessment*. Iowa City, IA: University of Iowa Press.

Cooper, S. (2005). Gifted Indigenous programs: Unmasking potential in minority cultures. *Gifted Education International, 19*, 114–125. https://doi.org/10.1177/026142940501900205

Croft, L. (2015). Rural teachers of the gifted: The importance of professional development. In T. Stambaugh & S. M. Wood (Eds.), *Serving gifted students in rural settings* (pp. 341–362). Waco, TX: Prufrock Press.

Cronin, R. P., & Diezmann, C. M. (2002). Jane and Gemma go to school: Supporting young gifted Aboriginal students. *Australian Journal of Early Childhood, 27*, 12–17. https://doi.org/10.1177/183693910202700404

Cross, T. L., & Burney, V. H. (2005). High ability, rural, and poor: Lessons from project aspire and implications for school counselors. *The Journal of Secondary Gifted Education, 16*, 148–156. https://doi.org/10.4219/jsge-2005-483

Dai, D. Y. (2013). Excellence at the cost of social justice? Negotiating and balancing priorities in gifted education. *Roeper Review, 35*, 93–101. https://doi.org/10.1080/02783193.2013.766961

Davidson, K. L. (1992). A comparison of Native American and White students' cognitive strengths as measured by the Kaufman Assessment Battery for Children. *Roeper Review, 14*, 111–115. https://doi.org/10.1080/02783199209553403

De Leon, J., & Argus-Calvo, B. (1997). *A model program for identifying culturally and linguistically diverse rural and gifted talented students*. (ERIC document reproductions service no. ED 406125).

De Leon, J., Argus-Calvo, B., & Medina, C. (2010). A model project for identifying rural gifted and talented students in the visual arts. *Rural Special Education Quarterly, 29*, 16–22. https://doi.org/10.1177/875687051002900304

Dobia, B., & Roffey, S. (2017). Respect for culture: Social and emotional learning with Aboriginal and Torres Strait Islander youth. In E. Frydenberg, A. Martin, & R. Collie (Eds.), *Social and emotional learning in Australia and the Asia-Pacific: Perspectives, programmes, and approaches* (pp. 313–334). Singapore, Singapore: Springer.

Donnison, S., & Marshman, M. (2018). Empowering gifted and talented youth: The "N" youth activity precinct. *Australasian Journal of Gifted Education, 27*, 47–58. https://doi.org/10.21505/ajge.2018.0005

Ellzey, J. T., & Karnes, F. A. (1991). Gifted education and rural youths: What parents and educators should know. *Gifted Child Today, 14*, 56–57. https://doi.org/10.1177/107621759101400319

Fardell, R., & Geake, J. G. (2005). Vertical semester organisation in a rural secondary school: The views of gifted students. *Australasian Journal of Gifted Education, 14*, 15–29. https://hdl.handle.net/1959.11/5601

Forlin, C., & Lock, G. (2006). Employing technologies to engage students with diverse needs in rural school communities. *Australian Journal of Teacher Education, 31*(1). Retrieved from http://ro.ecu.edu.au/ajte/vol31/iss1/4

Gagné, F. (2009). Debating giftedness: Pronat vs. antinat. In International handbook on giftedness (pp. 155–204). Springer, Dordrecht.

Gagné, F. (2018). Academic talent development: Theory and best practices. In S. Pfeiffer, E. Shaunessy-Dedrick, & M. Foley-Nicpon (Eds.), *APA handbook of giftedness and talent* (APA handbooks in psychology) (pp. 163–183). Washington, DC: American Psychological Association.

Gagnon, D. J., & Mattingly, M. J. (2016). Advanced placement and rural schools. *Journal of Advanced Academics, 27*, 266–284. https://doi.org/10.1177/1932202X16656390

Garvis, S. (2006). Optimising the learning of gifted Aboriginal students. *International Journal of Pedagogies and Learning, 2*, 42–51. https://doi.org/10.5172/ijpl.2.3.42

Gentry, M., & Fugate, C. M. (2012). Gifted Native American students: Underperforming, under-identified, and overlooked. *Psychology in the Schools, 49*, 631–646. https://doi.org/10.1002/pits.21624

Gentry, M., Fugate, C. M., Wu, J., & Castellano, J. A. (2014). Gifted Native American students: Literature, lessons, and future directions. *The Gifted Child Quarterly, 58*, 98–110. https://doi.org/10.1177/0016986214521660

Gentry, M., Rizza, M. G., & Gable, R. K. (2001). Gifted students' perceptions of their class activities: Differences among rural, urban, and suburban student attitudes. *The Gifted Child Quarterly, 45*, 115–129. https://doi.org/10.1177/001698620104500205

Gibson, K., & Vialle, W. (2007). The Australian Aboriginal view of giftedness. In S. N. Phillipson & M. McCann (Eds.), *Conceptions of giftedness: Socio-cultural perspectives* (pp. 169–196). Mahwah, NJ: Lawrence Erlbaum Associates.

Gross, M. U. M. (1989). The pursuit of excellence or the search for intimacy? The forced choice dilemma of gifted youth. *Roeper Review, 11*, 189–194. https://doi.org/10.1080/02783198909553207

Gross, M. U. M. (1998). The "me" behind the mask: Intellectually gifted students and the search for identity. *Roeper Review, 20*, 167–174. https://doi.org/10.1080/02783199809553885

Harslett, M. G. (1996). The concept of giftedness from an Aboriginal cultural perspective. *Gifted Education International, 11*(2), 100–106. https://doi.org/10.1177/026142949601100207

Hogarth, M. (2018). Words matter: How the latest school funding report (Gonski 2.0) gets it so wrong [Blog post]. *EduResearch Matters: A Voice for Australian Educational Researchers, 1*, 8.

Housand, B. C., & Housand, A. M. (2015). Best of both worlds: Technology as a pathway for meaningful choice. In T. Stambaugh & S. M. Wood (Eds.), *Serving gifted students in rural settings* (pp. 219–238). Waco, TX: Prufrock Press.

Howley, A., Rhodes, M., & Beall, J. (2009). Challenges facing rural schools: Implications for gifted students. *Journal for the Education of the Gifted, 32*, 515–536. https://doi.org/10.1177/016235320903200404

Howley, C. B., Showalter, D., Klein, R., Sturgill, D. J., & Smith, M. A. (2013). Rural math talent, now and then. *Roeper Review, 35*, 102–114. Retrieved from https://eric.ed.gov/?id=EJ1012520

Irvin, M. J., Hannum, W. H., Farmer, T. W., de la Varre, C., & Keane, J. (2009). Supporting online learning for advanced placement students in small rural schools: Conceptual foundations and intervention components of the facilitator preparation program. *Rural Educator, 31*, 29–37. https://doi.org/10.35608/ruraled.v31i1.440

Jones, E. D., & Southern, W. T. (1992). Programming, grouping, and acceleration in rural school districts: A survey of attitudes and practices. *The Gifted Child Quarterly, 36*, 112–117. https://doi.org/10.1177/001698629203600210

Jung, J. Y., Barnett, K., Gross, M. U. M., & McCormick, J. (2011). Levels of intellectual giftedness, culture, and the forced-choice dilemma. *Roeper Review, 33*, 182–197. https://doi.org/10.1080/02783193.2011.580501

Jung, J. Y., McCormick, J., & Gross, M. U. M. (2012). The forced choice dilemma: A model incorporating idiocentric/allocentric cultural orientation. *The Gifted Child Quarterly, 56*, 15–24. https://doi.org/10.1177/0016986211429169

Kearins, J. M. (1982). Cognitive strengths of Australian Aboriginal children. *Wikaru, 11*, 2–22.

Lehmann, J. (2014). Editorial. *Children Australia, 39*, 1–4. https://doi.org/10.1017/cha.2013.34

Lyons, T., Cooksey, R., Panizzon, D., Parnell, A., & Pegg, J. (2006). *Science, ICT, and mathematics education in rural and regional Australia: SiMERR National Survey*. Abridged report: vii. Retrieved from https://simerr.une.edu.au/pages/projects/1nationalsurvey/Abridged%20report/Abridged_Full.pdf

Matthews, M. S., & Farmer, J. (2017). Predicting academic achievement growth among low-income Mexican American learners using dynamic and static assessments. *Australasian Journal of Gifted Education, 26*, 5–21. https://doi.org/10.21505/ajge.2017.0002

Mattingly, M. J., & Schaefer, A. (2015). Education in rural America: Challenges and opportunities. In T. Stambaugh & S. M. Wood (Eds.), *Serving gifted students in rural settings* (pp. 53–70). Waco, TX: Prufrock Press.

McLoughlin, C., & Oliver, R. (2000). Designing learning environments for cultural inclusivity: A case study of indigenous online learning at tertiary level. *Australasian Journal of Educational Technology, 16*(1). https://doi.org/10.14742/ajet.1822

Missett, T. C., Reed, C. B., Scot, T. P., Callahan, C. M., & Slade, M. (2010). Describing learning in an advanced online case-based course in environmental science. *Journal of Advanced Academics, 22*, 10–49. https://doi.org/10.1177/1932202X1002200102

Montgomery, D. (2001). Increasing Native American Indian involvement in gifted programs in rural schools. *Psychology in the Schools, 38*, 467–475. https://doi.org/10.1002/pits.1035

Munro, J. (2011). Identifying gifted knowledge and learning in Indigenous cultures: Africa and Australia. In W. Vialle (Ed.), *Giftedness from an Indigenous perspective* (pp. 24–35).

Wollongong, NSW: AAEGT. Retrieved from http://www.aaegt.net.au/DEEWR%20Books/03%20Indig.pdf

NSW Department of Education (DoE). (2019). *Aboriginal education and communities*. NSW Government. Retrieved from https://education.nsw.gov.au/teaching-and-learning/aec

NSW Government. (2018). *Review of selective education access*. Retrieved from https://education.nsw.gov.au/about-us/strategies-and-reports/our-reports-and-reviews/review-of-selective-education-access

Nura Gili. (2019). *Indigenous winter school*. Nura Gili Centre for Indigenous Programs, UNSW, Australia. Retrieved from https://www.nuragili.unsw.edu.au/opportunities/indigenous-winter-school

Omdal, S., Rude, H., Betts, G., & Toy, R. (2011). American Indian students: Balancing western and native giftedness. In J. A. Castellano & A. D. Frazier (Eds.), *Special populations in gifted education: Understanding our most able students from diverse backgrounds* (pp. 73–98). Waco, TX: Prufrock Press.

Peltier, G., Foldesey, G., Holman, D., & Mantranga, M. (1989). *Characteristics of National Merit Scholars from small rural schools*. (ERIC document reproduction service no. ED 317343).

Pendarvis, E., & Wood, E. W. (2009). Eligibility of historically underrepresented students referred for gifted education in a rural school district: A case study. *Journal for the Education of the Gifted, 32*, 495–514. Retrieved from. https://doi.org/10.1177/016235320903200403

Plucker, J. (2013). Students from rural environments. In C. Callahan & H. L. Hertberg-Davis (Eds.), *Fundamentals of gifted education: Considering multiple perspectives* (pp. 424–434). New York, NY: Routledge.

Plucker, J. A., & Puryear, J. (2018). Students from rural environments. In C. M. Callahan & H. L. Hertberg-Davis (Eds.), *Fundamentals of gifted education: Considering multiple perspectives* (2nd ed., pp. 418–428). New York, NY: Routledge.

Plunkett, M. (2012). Justice for rural gifted students. In S. Nikakis (Ed.), *Let the tall poppies flourish: Advocating to achieve educational justice for all gifted students* (pp. 37–49). Heidelberg, Australia: Heidelberg Press.

Plunkett, M. (2018). Gifted students in rural and remote settings. In J. L. Jolly & J. M. Jarvis (Eds.), *Exploring gifted education: Australian and New Zealand perspectives* (pp. 171–192). New York, NY: Routledge.

Puryear, J. S., & Kettler, T. (2017). Rural gifted education and the effect of proximity. *The Gifted Child Quarterly, 61*, 143–152. https://doi.org/10.1177/0016986217690229

Shaunessy, E., Karnes, F. A., & Cobb, Y. (2004). Assessing potentially gifted students from lower socioeconomic status with nonverbal measures of intelligence. *Perceptual and Motor Skills, 98*, 1129–1138. https://doi.org/10.2466/pms.98.3c.1129-1138

Smith, S. R. (2017). Responding to the unique social and emotional learning needs of gifted Australian students. In E. Frydenberg, A. Martin, & R. Collie (Eds.), *Social and emotional learning in Australia and the Asia-Pacific: Perspectives, programmes, and approaches* (pp. 147–166). Singapore, Singapore: Springer.

Spicker, H. (1993). Rural Gifted Education in a Multicultural Society

Spicker, H. H., Southern, W. T., & Davis, B. I. (1987). The rural gifted child. *The Gifted Child Quarterly, 31*, 155–157. https://doi.org/10.1177/001698628703100404

Stambaugh, T. (2010). The education of students in rural areas: What do we know and what can we do? In J. VanTassel-Baska (Ed.), *Patterns and profiles from promising learners in poverty* (pp. 59–83). Waco, TX: Prufrock Press.

Swan, B., Coulombe-Quach, X., Huang, A., Godek, J., Becker, D., & Zhou, Y. (2015). Meeting the needs of gifted and talented students: Case study of a virtual learning lab in a rural middle school. *Journal of Advanced Academics, 26*, 294–319. https://doi.org/10.1177/1932202X15603366

Thompson, H. E. C. (1997). *Introducing a gifted program in a rural secondary school* (Unpublished masters thesis). University of Melbourne, Melbourne, Australia.

Thraves, G., & Bannister-Tyrrell, M. (2017). Australian Aboriginal peoples and giftedness: A diverse issue in need of a diverse response. *TalentEd, 29*, 18–31. https://hdl.handle.net/1959.11/21301

Vasilevska, S. (2005). Cultural conceptions of giftedness: Australian research on Aboriginal perceptions. *Gifted Education International, 19*, 126–131. https://doi.org/10.1177/026142940501900206

Wood, D. (2009). Project gifted: Using a project-based approach to developing teacher understanding of gifted education. *Australasian Journal of Gifted Education, 18*, 48–55.

Wood, D., & Vialle, W. (2015). Popular culture: A support or a disruption to talent development in the lives of rural adolescent gifted girls? *Australasian Journal of Gifted Education, 24*, 13–22. Retrieved from https://ro.uow.edu.au/cgi/viewcontent.cgi?article=3280&context=sspapers

Wood, D., & Zundans-Fraser, L. (2013). Reaching out: Overcoming distance and supporting rural gifted students through educational opportunities. *Australasian Journal of Gifted Education, 22*, 42–50.

Geraldine Townend, PhD, who is a Lecturer in GERRIC and the School of Education at the University of New South Wales, Australia, and was a Research Fellow and Lecturer at Griffith University, Australia, seeks to extend understanding of giftedness, twice-exceptionality, and underachievement, and to empower students, and their educators to achieve the best educational outcomes. She researches and publishes within the sociocultural paradigm. Her research has focused on the link between students' academic self-concept and their educational outcomes, particularly the importance of social comparison theory, and she is interested in the importance of the interaction between teachers and students. She lectures in gifted education and provides professional learning and support to teachers and schools across Australia to enable optimal educational outcomes within the inclusive classroom.

Peta K. Hay, PhD, is a Lecturer in the School of Education and GERRIC at The University of NSW, Australia. She lectures in gifted education in undergraduate and postgraduate capacities and provides professional learning and support to teachers and schools across Australia in the very popular Mini-COGE and Advanced Mini-COGE courses. Her research interests include the socio-affective areas of giftedness and the efficacy of school programming options for gifted students.

Jae Yup Jung, PhD, is Associate Professor in the School of Education and Director of GERRIC at The University of New South Wales, Australia. His research program incorporates various topics relating to gifted adolescents, with a particular focus on their career-related decisions. His research has been recognised with awards from the American Educational Research Association, the Mensa Education and Research Foundation/Mensa International and the Society for Vocational Psychology, and grants from the Australian Research Council and the Australian Department of Foreign Affairs and Trade. He is the editor of the *Australasian Journal of Gifted Education*, a member of the Executive Committee of the *Asia-Pacific Federation on Giftedness* (APFG) and a member of the *Council of the Australian Association for the Education of the Gifted and Talented* (AAEGT).

Susen R. Smith, PhD, is GERRIC Senior Research Fellow and Senior Lecturer in Gifted and Special Education at the School of Education and GERRIC, University of New South Wales, Australia. She has extensive experience as a teacher, curriculum consultant, and educational leader from early childhood to tertiary education and adult education. She has been an invited visiting scholar at Columbia University, City University New York, Hong Kong Institute of Education, National Taipei University of Education and Imperial College London. Her specific research interests include ecological systems theory underpinning dynamically differentiating curriculum and pedagogy models and matrices for students with giftedness, indigeneity, underachievement, multi-exceptionalities and learning difficulties. She is widely published in international journals and has keynoted at national and international conferences and serves on editorial boards, such as the *Gifted Child Quarterly, Reoper Review, and* the *Australasian Journal of Gifted Education*.